UNDERSTANDING INTERNATIONAL RELATIONS

FIFTH EDITION

The Value of Alternative Lenses

Daniel J. Kaufman

Jay M. Parker

Patrick V. Howell

Grant R. Doty

UNITED STATES MILITARY ACADEMY

McGraw Hill Learning Solutions

Boston Burr Ridge, IL Dubuque, IA New York
San Francisco St. Louis Bangkok Bogotá Caracas Kuala Lumpur
Lisbon London Madrid Mexico City Milan Montreal New Delhi
Santiago Seoul Singapore Sydney Taipei Toronto

The McGraw·Hill Companies

UNDERSTANDING INTERNATIONAL RELATIONS
The Value of Alternative Lenses

16 17 18 19 20 QVS QVS 18 17 16 15 14

ISBN-13: 978-0-07-305266-3
ISBN-10: 0-07-305266-3

Editor: Ann Jenson
Production Editor: Nina Meyer
Cover Design: Maggie Lytle
Printer/Binder: Quad/Graphics

DEDICATED TO

JAMES R. GOLDEN

For his inspirational and creative leadership in the Department of Social Sciences, United States Military Academy, West Point, New York, from 1971-1996.

His selfless commitment to excellence and untiring devotion to faculty and cadet development made an extraordinary and lasting impact on a generation of future leaders.

"The engraving on monuments . . . does not mark achievement. Only the engraving on the character and competence of our cadets and our young officers counts toward fulfillment of our mission."

-- Brigadier General George A. Lincoln
Professor of Social Sciences
U.S. Military Academy, 1947–1969

Summary of Contents

Contents

Preface to the Fifth Edition

Recognizing, as the contributors to this edition who have served in America's hot and cold wars over the past 30 years have done, that the complex challenges of our world must be met by our students, this text is written for them. Since the publication of the first edition, our students have gone from the last day of standing watch on the Berlin Wall, to the deserts of Iraq and the chaos of Mogadishu. They have served with honor in Haiti, Rwanda, Cambodia, Korea, Bosnia and Kosovo. They are currently serving in Afghanistan, Iraq and around the world as the leading edge of the United States Global War on Terror (GWOT). With each new edition, we have incorporated their feedback. We are proud of their service and humbled to know that this text has contributed to their preparation for leadership in a high risk and ambiguous world.

This book remains firmly grounded in theory, and it continues to emphasize the value of intellectual pluralism. We also renewed our emphasis on providing students of international relations with a structured way of studying a subject that has become increasingly difficult to approach in an organized, efficient manner.

We acknowledge the efforts of those architects and editors of the previous editions of Understanding International Relations, including Dennis Lowrey, Asa A. Clark IV, Joseph J. Collins, Thomas F. Lynch III, Rick Waddell, Thomas R. Schneider, Harry L. Cohen and Kimberly Field. We have remained true to the foundation they set by structuring this book on three distinct conceptual lenses.

We purposely designed the main textbook of Understanding International Relations (UIR) to be used with an accompanying reader: Through Alternative Lenses (UIR-R). The UIR is designed to be updated every five or six years and to contain the theoretical basis of the student's studies. We try to provide an introduction for every theory and block of readings to provide students the context in which the piece was written.

We update the UIR-R yearly to reflect current debates and issues in the field of international relations and foreign policy. The articles in the UIR-R are intended for one or more of the following purposes: 1) to provide additional informational material on a subject; 2) provide supplemental readings to complement or augment a point from the UIR; 3) provide supplemental readings that contradict a point from a reading in the UIR; or 4) to provide two opposing articles on a current event, providing the basis of an intellectual debate grounded in the theories the students have studied in the UIR.

In addition to our colleagues in the Department of Social Sciences at the U.S. Military Academy at West Point, we would like to once again thank the staff at McGraw-Hill for their help and patience, especially Ann Jenson, Rose Arlia, and Reuben Kantor.

The Editors, Fifth Edition

Daniel J. Kaufman
Jay M. Parker
Grant R. Doty
Patrick V. Howell

About the Editors

Daniel J. Kaufman, Brigadier General, United States Army—Dean of the Academic Board and Professor of Social Sciences, United States Military Academy. B.S., USMA; M.P.A., Harvard University; Ph.D., Massachusetts Institute of Technology

Jay M. Parker, Colonel, United States Army—Director of International Relations and National Security Studies, Professor of Political and International Affairs, Department of Social Sciences, United States Military Academy. B.A., University of Arizona; M.A., M.P.A., Arizona State University; M.A.I.R., University of Southern California; M.A., Naval War College; Ph.D., Columbia University

Patrick Howell, Major, United States Army—Course Director: International Relations, Assistant Professor, Department of Social Sciences, United States Military Academy. B.S., USMA; M.A.L.D., Fletcher School of Law and Diplomacy—Tufts University

Grant R. Doty, Major, United States Army—Former Assistant Professor, Department of Social Sciences, United States Military Academy. B.S., USMA; M.A. Yale University

About the Contributors

Matthew Abbruzzese, B.A. College of William & Mary; M.A. School of Advanced International Studies at Johns Hopkins University

Jason Amerine, B.S. USMA; M.A. Bush School of Government at Texas A&M University

Ruth Beitler, B.A. Cornell; M.A.L.D., and Ph.D., The Fletcher School of Law and Diplomacy

Asa A. Clark IV, B.S., USMA; M.A., Ph.D., University of Denver

Susan F. Bryant, B.S.F.S., Georgetown University; M.A., Yale University

Bob Cassidy, B.A. Fitchburg State College; M.A. Boston University; M.A.L.D., Ph.D., Fletcher School of Law and Diplomacy—Tufts University

Harry Cohen, B.S., USMA; M.P.A., Harvard

Joseph J. Collins, B.A. Fordham University; M.I.A., M.Phil., and Ph.D., Columbia University

Jeffrey C. Denius, B.A., Bowling Green State University; M.P.A., Harvard University

Kimberly C. Field, B.S., USMA; M.A.L.D., Fletcher School of Law and Diplomacy—Tufts University

Dr. James Forest, PhD Boston College is an assistant dean and assistant professor at the U.S. Military Academy

Mike George, B.S. USMA; M.A., Oxford University; M.A., Massachusetts Institute of Technology

Cindy R. Jebb, B.S., USMA; M.A., Ph.D. Duke University

Thomas F. Lynch, III, B.S., USMA; M.P.A.,M.A., Ph.D., Princeton University

Tony M. Martin, B.A., Campbell University; M.A. & PhD candidate, Duke University

Charles R. Miller, B.S., USMA; M.I.A., MPhil., Ph.D., Columbia University

John A. Nagl, B.S. USMA; MPhil, DPhil, Oxford Univesity

Suzanne C. Nielsen, B.S., USMA; M.A., Ph.D., Harvard University

Jin H. Pak, B.S., United States Military Academy; MPP, Kennedy School of Government.

Scott Rhind, B.A., U.S. Military Academy; M.A., University of Oxford

Scott A. Silverstone, B.A. University of New Hampshire; M.A. George Washington University; Ph.D. University of Pennsylvania

Thomas Sherlock, B.A., M.A., Farleigh Dickinson University; M.A., MPhil, Ph.D., Columbia University

Bruce Terry, BS CSU Sacramento; M.P.P. Center for European Studies, University of Maastricht, The Netherlands

Rick L. Waddell, B.S., USMA; B.A. and M.A., Oxford University; M.P.A., Webster; M.A., M.Phil., and Ph.D., Columbia University

Wally Z. Walters, B.S., USMA; M.A., George Washington University; M.Phil., Columbia University

Paul L. Yingling, B.A., Duquesne University; M.A., University of Chicago

Introduction

THE STUDY OF INTERNATIONAL RELATIONS AND THIS BOOK

"A single moon
Bright and clear
In an unclouded sky;
Yet still we stumble
In the world's darkness."
—*Zen Master Ikkyu (1394-1481)*

There are those who argue that the elements of international relations are too complex, too broad, and too dynamic to be captured by any systematic method of study. Theories, paradigms, and models are all hopeless houses of straw. The best one can hope for is the combination of intuition, timing, and luck that allows a nation to thrive or at least survive to fight another day. The sweep of history and the ever-increasing mountains of contemporary data are—at best—random sustenance for intellectual hunter-gatherers.

Others contend that the study of international relations, like the study of any other field, is governed by clear laws and well-marked boundaries of thought. Given the right model and sufficient data, one can—like Archimedes—"move the earth." As political science becomes more science than politics, the argument continues, theory will be the essential tool for ushering in the Peaceable Kingdom.

This text is premised on the assertion that to meet the challenges of international relations we must study but not fully embrace both extremes in this dichotomy. Whether struggling to make sense of the tragedies of September 11, 2001 or reaching back in time to ponder the conflicts between ancient city-states, the process is the same. Accepting the complex and dynamic nature of the international environment, students should first study in general terms how international relations theory is defined, developed, debated, and applied. They should evaluate critical cases from history with the lessons drawn from the study of international relations theory, and evaluate both the reach and the limits of theory. Next, students should practice intellectual pluralism, simultaneously using the multiple lenses provided by multiple theories to view the high risk policy challenges presented by the contemporary international environment. Finally, keeping their minds open to new ideas, they should be able to look to the future and assess how international relations theory might evolve to meet unforeseen challenges.

The editors contend that international relations theory has utility for both the scholar and the policy maker. Through its four primary functions, international relations theory gives us a series of tools to measure against events. Theory *describes* and *explains* post hoc those things that we have done. This helps us learn where we have been but does not necessarily tell us where we need to go. Theory also can, in certain circumstances, *predict*, and by extension, it can *prescribe*. What we need to understand is that no single theory does all four things and no single theory does any of those things perfectly.

Given the high risk, ambiguous, and changing nature of the world, the study of theory is often difficult. Its application is sometimes fraught with unintended consequences, occasionally successful for reasons that no one anticipated. It is not a process easily mastered or controlled. However, it is not a vague, random process that cannot be grasped or directed. It is possible for those with intellect, insight, vision, and selfless courage to learn the dynamic intricacies of international relations theory and lead others in its application.

Despite what some scholars claim, undergraduates can learn theory in a way that demonstrates its utility. To do so they must learn a broad range of theories and approaches. Where do these theories come from and how do they evolve? What do the terms "realist" and "liberal" really mean and how do these definitions differ from their current, clichéd usage? What exactly does constructivism actually construct? Why do some scholars seek to broaden the debate on the definition of power? How do scholars account for the successes or failures of international relations theories?

It is difficult to help undergraduates and policy students understand theory's utility if the teaching of international relations theory to those students is narrowly defined, presented in absolute terms, and not adequately contrasted with theory development and theory utility in other fields. If the study of international relations theory is to have any utility, theories and approaches must be placed in their proper historic and social context. Students must be shown the interaction between theory and events.

Why, for example, did realism reemerge as the dominant thinking after the Second World War? Why was realism, by contrast, so discounted and so undervalued in the period between the World Wars? Why was deterrence theory the important foundation for much of our thought in the Nuclear Age, and why did it seem suddenly so useless when the Soviet Union fell? What was the synergy between democratic peace theory and post-Cold War policy? Why did Thucydides view the world through the prism that he did; why did Machiavelli, why Napoleon, why Jefferson, why Stalin, why Hitler, and why Reagan...? What did scholars of earlier generations teach their students about international relations?

The purpose of this text is not to answer all these questions in exhaustive detail. It will, however, provide many of the tools students need to address these questions now and in the years to come. We have designed this volume to provide these tools for a specific reason. The editors of this text operate in and prepare students for the policy world. While some of our students will later study international relations at the graduate level and become professional academics, few will ever formally study international relations again. But like all undergraduates, they live in a world shaped by the challenges and opportunities of international politics. They will take on the obligations of all citizens who must contribute to democratic decision making.

We contend that for these students—regardless of where they study or what academic major they select—a narrow approach to international relations is not only impractical, it is dysfunctional. It excludes important alternatives. It places a deceptive level of confidence in the utility of limited options. It encourages a rush to judgment without critical thought. Finally, it promotes a cynical view of intellect and scholarship among students who recognize the gap between the world they study and the world they live in.

For more than a decade, the guiding philosophy of our Introduction to International Relations course has been that students must study a broad range of international relations theories. Not all theories are created equal, but each deserves an audience until fully discredited. It is impossible to learn all of the aspects of all international relations theories in a single semester. Furthermore, neither the world nor the theories of international relations are static. While there are many enduring principles and trends, the changing nature of the international environment is reflected in changing arguments of international relations literature.

However, it is possible to study a wide range of competing views, a wide array of competing theories, and their application to common and often recurring problems. Through this study, students can better understand how and why different international actors believe in, develop, and act on different theories. As different theories emerge and as existing theories are revised and advanced, students will have the fundamental tools required to address new situations and apply new theories. Furthermore, they can better define, examine, evaluate, and challenge their own views. Whether engaged in a general exercise in critical thinking, a focused course in professional training, a first step toward an academic career, or all three, the student will find great value in the study of international relations theories through the reading and discussion of a wide range of original texts.

For policy students in particular there are additional values to this process. In their professional lives, they will have to navigate complex and dangerous situations in a way that reflects a broad understanding of the issues at hand and the choices and options that can be taken. They must be mindful of alternative approaches they will inevitably confront in the course of making real decisions. Also, while the vast majority of the curriculum at most policy schools has a common basis, there are important variances at the margins, and the majority view at any given time can fall from favor as the world changes. Today's students will eventually be policy makers sitting across the table from other policy makers in the interagency arena. They will have to do so in a way that reflects an understanding and appreciation for the diverse views of others.

This embrace of intellectual pluralism and the deliberate use of multiple lenses are consistent with how this book was edited. Readers may assume that the listed contributors share common views, common experiences, and common education. Such a stereotype is understandable but incorrect. The contents of this volume were selected after long and often heated debate, reflective of a wide range of graduate programs and professional experiences. Furthermore, this volume has been significantly revised several times in the past decade to better represent the range of contemporary international relations scholarship. We fully anticipate that this process of assessment and revision will continue in the years ahead. Finally, we have prepared a companion text titled *Through Alternative Lenses: Current Debates in International Relations*. It presents contemporary issues approached from differing points of view, and when combined with this book provides students the opportunity to integrate and apply a range of theories to real world challenges.

Ultimately, our objective is to ensure that students grasp the value of multiple alternative lenses. We do not accept "either/or" approaches. We reject the premise that one size fits all. Life is about recipes, not multiple choice exams. There are no simple answers to questions such as *"Why do actors in the international arena do what they do?"* and *"What causes conflict and cooperation in the international environment?"* Arguments over the nuances of theoretical heresy are for scholars doing the necessary work of tenured academics, pursuing the perfection and advancement of theory. Undergraduate students at the introductory level must embrace the broader range of theory's utility and possibilities.

THEORY, POLICY, AND MULTIPLE LENSES

> *"A battle is something that happens at the intersection of four badly drawn maps."*
>
> *—Old British Military Cliché*

Those involved in the formulation of policy must make choices. Public policy—whether international or domestic—is about choice. Scholars can criticize the decision makers. However, unlike most scholars, decision makers (as their job title implies) must decide. They must decide based on imperfect information at moments of the highest risk on issues that generate the greatest emotions. They must decide based on the illusion of calm and perfection when dangers are great because they are unseen and generate no visible turmoil. They must decide even when the optimal solution to one particular crisis directly negates the optimal solution to several, simultaneous, seemingly unrelated, but equally pressing crises. They must decide knowing that their actions will be harshly judged by future students, scholars, and political leaders using 20/20 hindsight. Theory can provide tools to assist with these challenges, but not if we oversimplify how it is defined and how it can be applied.

Students (and even a few professors) sometimes fall into a common trap. This is the view that international relations theory is monolithic, unitary, and linear. In other words, there is one dominant theory. That theory is the one that works best at a given time. Other theories are ultimately derived from and consistent with the dominant theory or are just plain wrong. As a new theory is developed it replaces the old in a logical progression until the coming of a paradigm shift...and there are theories for that eventuality.

This view ignores the pragmatic, applied utility of multiple theories as multiple lenses operating across multiple levels of analysis. At any point in history, these multiple lenses can be applied to a given event and provide an understanding rich in explanatory and descriptive power. Depending on the specific questions you ask from the outset, you can do this at multiple levels of analysis ranging from the individual actor through the nature of the individual state and up to the level of the anarchic international system. Ultimately, however, it is a balanced combination of many theories that most fully illuminates a case. It is this balanced combination that must inform the calculated risks taken when confronted with the inevitable frightening, imperfect array of policy choices and options.

Policy making and theory application are not mutually exclusive, though some think they are. They still adhere to enduring myths, such as the one that claims that Structural Realism believes that foreign policy or—at the extreme—what happens within the state is not important. Or the myth that Complex Interdependence and "soft power" completely discount force and eliminate the need for militaries. As you will learn from carefully reading this text, neither of these myths is true. Structural Realists do not advocate shutting down the State Department, nor have Complex Interdependence theorists beat their swords into ploughshares.

At the same time, we must remember that theories can inform—but never eliminate—risk. Just as they can integrate and illuminate, competing theories clash. They do not fit perfectly. The "leftovers" unexplained by one theory are not random points outside the realm of all theory. They are covered by other theories, even if these theories have not yet been fully researched, tested, or even discovered. Individual theories may intersect at multiple points, but at multiple points they also contradict. Debates within certain paradigms are often far more contentious than those between paradigms. The student's mission, much like that of the policy maker, is to realize when one has moved beyond the generalities of a given theory and into the specifics of a real-world case, then to figure the values and risks of applying combinations of complex, ill defined, poorly taught, painfully written, and frequently contradictory theories.

To deal with this, we must honestly assess and, wherever possible, restructure our thinking to better contend with an ambiguous, high-risk world. Inevitably, one's initial views—like the views of the theorists we apply—are heavily value laden and driven by pre-desired outcomes. That is to be expected. Politics involves those issues people care deeply and passionately about—so deeply and passionately they are willing to risk their "...lives...fortunes...and sacred honor." The challenge for decision makers—and for students who aspire to someday take on that role—is to fully recognize the constraints of those emotions and beliefs and to temper their negative effects through the rigorous and informed use of multiple theories.

SCIENCE VS. SCIENCE

"Politics is more difficult than physics."
—Albert Einstein

Any discussion of the utility of international relations theory eventually must address how the social sciences and the physical sciences sharply differ. It is often assumed that hard sciences are precise, rigid, fixed with a lasting utility, and based on universal truths. Social sciences by contrast are mushy, imprecise, general to the point of being almost meaningless, with no recurring utility, and based on ideas with mass, popular appeal. Neither generalization is entirely true.

First, no science is fixed and rigid, nor is it always absolutely precise. Even when narrowly defined at the most micro of levels, scientific rules are conditioned by "givens," "excepts," and "ifs." Part of the scientific method is the rigorous definition of assumptions and the measurement of variances and setting of acceptable levels of tolerance. Furthermore, sciences evolve over time. What we know is conditioned by what we can see, and what we have experienced and, far more than we are willing to admit, what we are conditioned to expect. This is as true with the laws of physics as it is with international relations theory.

Science has also always been conditioned by what we believe. Our concepts of the physical universe—whether mythical and spiritual or secular and scientific—shape what we expect to see or not see. Like international relations theory, science provides windows for us to see beyond what we already believe. However, we are never completely free of our core beliefs.

In the past century, we have been able to "see" and "experience" much through great advancements in science and technology. The explanatory and descriptive power of science has increased dramatically. We are not, however, at "The End of Science" anymore than we are at "The End of History." Thucydides' observations of international relations still prove as valuable in our understanding of international relations as they did more than 2500 years ago. Can the same be said for our understanding of the physical universe over that same period of time?

When Thucydides was outlining the nature of the anarchic international environment and Plato was pronouncing the deep and profound principles of what would underline the political and social order for thousands of years, "scientists" of the day calculated the presence of a total of four elements, all controlled by fickle and mischievous gods living atop the nearest big mountain illuminated by a sun carried across the sky each day by a fiery chariot.

When Machiavelli was foreshadowing Allison's analysis of bureaucratic politics, and while other great Renaissance political philosophers and international relations thinkers were shaping the Westphalian order, alchemy was still the rage, medicine still pursued "bad humors" in the body through bleeding therapy, and Galileo was being threatened with torture and death for challenging the established scientific paradigms.

"Hard science" and "social science" share similarities as much as they differ. Both deal with varying degrees of macro and micro phenomena. Both are conditioned by assumptions and cognitive constraints. Both confidently predict, but with the fine print of footnotes and a blur of Greek Alphabet formulas that condition, limit, and may even eliminate key variables. Both require the choice and integration of multiple theories and models, the balancing of "best" options with "practical" options. Both require the conscious acceptance of risks in order to apply science to the "real" world of engineering and international relations theory to the "real" world of policy making.

Even with thousands of years of validation, there are those who question the utility of theory. Despite these protests, ultimately everyone uses theory. It may be a sophisticated, well-considered world view based on the best contemporary scholarship. It may be childishly naïve epistemology based on personal observation with an *N* of 1. The theory may be grounded in the arrogance of power that posits your ego as the alpha et omega. Whatever the foundation, everyone has a theory.

An interesting exercise, for example, is to take the statements of foreign policy makers who argue that there is no value in international relations theory. Take their speeches and actions, weigh them against the writings on international relations theories that were the dominant paradigm of their era, and you will find correlation. Again and again, we have seen (and scholars have empirically demonstrated) that there are frameworks and paradigms on which decision makers rely to guide their decisions. One clearly sees elements of Thucydides, Machiavelli, Morganthau, or Allison when one reflects on the choices that different decision makers have made and the consistency with which they have approached thorny problems of international politics.

In fairness, just as engineering students must learn to contend with the strengths and the weaknesses in the research of those in the hard sciences, international relations policy makers must learn to contend with the strengths and weaknesses of international relations theories. Political science, as a discipline, began in part to help integrate and reconcile the growing literature in a wide range of fields and to take us beyond the rigid world of institutions and laws and into the murky array of policy choices, anarchic systems, and human behavior. In recent years, political science has sometimes become an echo of old paradigms of hard sciences and has done so at a time when those same sciences have moved far beyond Newtonian views of causality. We focus on action-reaction while physicists are pondering the dilemma of Schrödinger's cat and the elements of chaos theory. In a *Hitchhiker's Guide to the Galaxy* universe, we are still highlighting crumbling copies of *Philosophiae Naturalis Principia Mathematica.*

There has always been and there continues to be research, adaptation, and change in the hard sciences. To argue that there are fixed, immutable points in the hard sciences that have always been recognized, that are always accepted, and that always will be is to ignore the history of those sciences. Yes, it is true; there was always gravity. However, Newton had to sit under the tree and get hit by the apple to be able to fully articulate the theory and its nuances. Yes, one could argue that the basic principles of Newtonian physics that gave way to Einstein's arguments were always there. Still, it took a patent clerk in Switzerland, one working outside the mainstream of most accepted science (and outside the normal academic research jobs), to come up with the laws of relativity. Furthermore, the contentious nature of science, when placed in the context of religious beliefs or secular politics, has caused many physical scientists to pull their punches. One needs look no further than the story of Galileo and his reversal on his speculations about the nature of the physical universe to demonstrate that point.

If we were to take the teachings of Copernicus, of Galileo, of other scientists past, we can and should justifiably give them credit for laying the foundations for modern physics and for our understandings of motion and space and time. However, if we were to stop with the teachings that they presented and the principles that they derived and attempt to replicate the moon landing with only that data, we would miss the moon by far more than a matter of miles.

International relations theory is no less and no more imperfect than the hard sciences. And in fact, it is important to note that hard sciences must then be, as international relations theory must be, adapted and formatted so it can be applied to practical situations. There is a difference between a scientist in the laboratory and an engineer building and developing and maintaining real world answers to real world problems. The basic principles are the same, but the ways in which they are used, the ways in which they are balanced, and the ways in which they are adapted, differ.

THEORIES AND REAL WORLD MELOS

> *"It will be enough for me if these words of mine are judged useful by those who want to understand clearly the events that happened in the past and which (human nature being what it is) will, at some time or other and in much the same ways, be repeated in the future."*
>
> —*Thucydides*

Ultimately, no one theory can work perfectly in combination with others. There are trade-offs and choices that must be made. If we forget these real world trade-offs in the interest of perfect, scholarly, linear causality, then we dangerously blur the line between "necessary" and "sufficient." In the study of international relations, we must remind ourselves of this crucial distinction every single day. One lens, one theory, one case, one variable may be necessary, but it is almost certainly never sufficient.

The readings in this book are meant to provide many examples. They are deliberately included in their original text rather than through the interpretations of others. Introductions are provided as a start point for discussion, not as a final conclusion or as an all-inclusive interpretation. Even with the original text, we can still miss the distinction between "necessary" and "sufficient" and opt for the overly simplistic, commonly accepted conclusion. Consider the *Melian Dialogue,* included in this book.

Thucydides' account of this event is often used to clearly and convincingly demonstrate the sharp divide between Realism and Idealism and the inevitable triumph of the former over the latter.

Except that it is not. Why would Idealists ally with a power like Sparta if all they desired was neutrality and peace? Why consider Athens the ultimate Realist and then, in the same intellectual breath, hail them for the birth and nurturing of the democratic ideal—a democratic ideal that supposedly ensures peace and non-aggression? Why put this all on the shoulders of systemic variables when individual human behavior weighed heavily on both sides and clearly drove actions? Would a Realist power, trusting that "Might Makes Right," turn back at key points as Athens did, because the goat entrails from the ritual sacrifice foretold bad fortune? Why claim the poor, helpless Melians were quickly crushed when, in fact, they resisted, thwarted, and almost turned back the Athenians? Defeat came not quickly because of the power of Athenian Might, but "...as there was also some treachery from inside" Melos; the gates of the city were opened by Melian treason when Athenian Might did not suffice. There are countless cases from Thucydides' era forward to the present warning us that if we focus on "sufficient causality" and Realism instead of the "necessary' multiple lenses that apply, we have missed the true lessons to be learned.

INTERNATIONAL RELATIONS THEORY—THE INADEQUATE IMPERATIVE

> *"Theory ... should show how one thing is related to another, and keep the important and the unimportant separate.... Theory cannot equip the mind with formulas for solving problems, nor can it mark the narrow path on which the sole solution is supposed to lie by planting a hedge of principles on either side. But it can give the mind insight into the great mass of phenomena and of their relationships, then leave it free to rise into the higher realms of action."*
>
> *—Carl von Clausewitz*

This brings us back to what international relations theory ultimately can and cannot do. International relations theory cannot provide, in and of itself, as one singular theory, an absolute, perfect guide to every action that a decision maker must make. It is not meant to do so. Those who point to particular scholarship or to debates among international relations scholars as evidence of the weakness of international relations theory completely miss the point. This is particularly important for skeptical undergraduates and for those students whose principal interest is in policy applications. Anyone who believes that by memorizing the tenets of Waltz (or Nye, or Tickner, or Allison, or Wendt) they can always and without fail make the proper foreign policy choice has not only failed to read all the nuances of Ken Waltz. They have also missed the broader questions of international relations theory.

So what is it that international relations theory can do, how do we study it, and how do we incorporate it into our decision making? It is important to remember, first and foremost, that even if you claim you do not use international relations theory, you do. Everyone has a theory. It is the way in which we organize our thoughts, it is the way in which we determine what choices and actions we will take, and it is the way in which we make sense of a confusing and chaotic universe. We structure and order what we see; we measure it against broader templates that we have derived from our experience and from the teachings of others.

Students need to remember that when making choices, it is important to understand the principles articulated in a wide range of formal theories. It is important to know the strengths and limits of these theories. It is important to recognize and accept the trade-offs and risks involved in applying these theories. Finally, it is particularly important to apply all these theories in the richest possible historic, social, and cultural context.

As we hope the use of this text will demonstrate, it is far worse, on many levels, to choose one and only one theory and rigidly adhere to it than it is to believe that there is no utility in theory and to bounce somewhat meaninglessly and recklessly from one event to another. If we narrow the study of international relations to one specific theory or even one dominant level of analysis, we have deceived ourselves about the nature of the world and the utility of international relations theory. We must use multiple lenses and ensure intellectual pluralism. It is, in our view, the key to understanding international relations.

D.J.K.
J.M.P.
P.V.H.
G.R.D.

Chapter One

Foundations of International Relations

Introduction to the Foundations Lens

This chapter is dedicated to laying the foundation for the study of international relations. Certain key concepts, definitions and traditions must be grasped before further progress can be made. Stephen Walt in *International Relations: One World Many Theories,* discusses the value of theory for foreign policy practitioners and in particular the need for a "diverse array of competing" perspectives. Subsequently he describes the various theoretical approaches that currently dominate the field of international relations and their impact on policy.

It is also important to realize that this theoretical study of international relations has, like all other sciences, been established through the use of the scientific method. Bruce Russett & Harvey Starr's *A Scientific Study of World Politics* argues the importance of continuing this practice despite the increased suffusion of international relations with political philosophies and values. The scientific approach requires research into the general trends and patterns of international behavior. The accumulation of evidence from these techniques eventually leads to probability statements, theories, or laws that accurately describe and explain the actions of humankind beyond the boundaries of the nation-state.

Having established the necessity for theory in explaining inter-state relations and the mode through which the theory has evolved, this chapter then delves into the more practical matters of defining terms and concepts. Russett & Starr in *International Actors: States and Other Players,* systematically describe the different types of actors in the international system. They begin by discussing the differences between the nation, state, and nation-state and conclude by addressing non-state actors in the contemporary system.

After determining which actors are interested in the accumulation and use of power, it becomes important to ensure that the term "power" has been defined as clearly as is possible; and this is no easy task. We have turned to Hans Morgenthau, the father of modern political realism, to discuss a concept absolutely central to the study of international relations. In his *What is Political Power,* Morgenthau defines and offers four distinctions of the term power. Following his discussion of differences between power and influence, power and force, usable and unusable power, and legitimate and illegitimate power, Morgenthau briefly addresses the issue of the depreciation of the role power in the study of international politics.

Having discussed power, we can then discuss a related, but certainly not synonymous term—"force." Force is defined as military power and although the use of force has changed since the end of the Cold War, certain tenets continue to help us in our understanding of it. In *The Four Functions of Force,* Robert J. Art describes the basic uses of military power in the international system. He then discusses how states use these techniques in pursuit of their national goals.

The use of force often comes about as a result of the Security Dilemma. In his seminal essay, *Cooperation Under the Security Dilemma*, Robert Jervis explains the theoretical underpinnings of why cooperation is difficult to achieve in the international environment. He highlights the problems created by the anarchic nature of the world, yet suggests that there are several ways that these problems can be overcome and that cooperation can be made more likely. The idea that the effects of anarchy can be mitigated has generally belonged to the idealist tradition. This is an appropriate segue to the next two sets of works on the idealist and realist traditions.

As previously stated, this book has been divided into "lenses" with the systemic lenses (Security and IPE) further divided into traditions. The systemic theories in this book, with the exception of the Marxist perspective theories, all come from the realist or idealist perspective. We realize that today, in using these theories, the distinction might not be so clear. Regardless, it is extremely helpful for students of international relations to understand the very foundations of the theory they are studying before they go on to explore the less definitive implications of it. They are then better able to wield the tool (the theory) with more effectiveness.

In *Realism and Idealisms*, Barry Hughes provides an overview of the idealist-realist tension in international relations. Specifically, he describes the two perspectives and discusses their ability to answer the "most pressing questions facing humanity" (e.g., what causes war). Hughes concludes by contrasting and briefly addressing the impact of the long-term tension between these two ideologies.

Having received an overview of the idealist-realist tension, the student will then delve into specific readings from each tradition, beginning with Niccolo Machiavelli,

from *The Prince.* Machiavelli, a Florentine bureaucrat living in the late 15th and early 16th centuries, was an analyst of power politics and the first truly to recognize the central role of power in the relations between ruler and ruled. These selections from *The Prince* are representative of a body of literature and the realist approach to politics: realism. Thomas Hobbes (1588-1679), an English philosopher, attempted to develop a scientifically-based and civic-minded political philosophy in the same tradition. Although some of the observations in these excerpts from the *Leviathan* (1651) are focused on domestic societies, they serve as intellectual roots for realism in international relations as well.

With Hans J. Morgenthau and his *A Realist Theory of International Relations,* the introduction to his classic work, *Politics Among Nations,* we see the making of modern day political realism. The influence of Machiavelli can be seen quite readily in Morgenthau's six principles. Morgenthau seeks to inform and educate policy makers in their craft and thereby help them to avoid mistakes such as the ones made at Munich in 1938.

The last section in this chapter contains works from the opposing tradition—idealism. The first is from *To Perpetual Peace: A Philosophical Sketch (1795)* by Immanuel Kant. Kant (1724-1804), a German philosopher, developed a political doctrine of the state based upon law (Rechtstaat) and the notion of *eternal* peace. His political teaching can be clearly classified as "idealist." In this essay, he rejects the realist notion that "might makes right" or that one must compromise ethics. He suggests that politics is compatible with moral principle both within a state and among states. The second work is Woodrow Wilson's *The Fourteen Points.* This selection is an excerpt from President Woodrow Wilson's address to Congress on Jan 8, 1918, which became the "signpost" of post-World War I idealism in international relations.

The chapter concludes with a case study, in the form of two works on the Peloponnesian War by Thucydides. Thucydides (c. 460-400 B.C) wrote this collection of essays to chronicle the Peloponnesian War between Athens and Sparta during the fifth century B.C. Thucydides claims that "[m]y work is not a piece of writing designed to meet the taste of an immediate public, but was done to last forever." His *Melian Dialogue* chronicling the exchange between Athenian generals and the Melians in 416 B.C., portrays the eternal "idealist vs. realist" debate in international relations. This tension, as well as other notions such as self-interest, balance of power, alliances, neutrality, evaluation of power, and the importance of the nature of the governing political regime—makes *The Melian Dialogue* a classic reading in international relations.

The Basics

The Science of International Relations

Bruce Russett and Harvey Starr
How Do We Think About World Politics?

Steven M. Walt
International Relations:
One World, Many Theories

Jack S. Levy
Theories of Interstate and Intrastate War

Actors

Bruce Russett and Harvey Starr
International Actors:
States and Other Players on the World Stage

Power

Hans J. Morgenthau
Political Power

Robert J. Art
The Four Functions of Force

Robert Jervis
Cooperation Under the Security Dilemma

How Do We Think About World Politics?

Bruce Russett & Harvey Starr

Despite the fact that international relations is a subject suffused with political philosophies and values, Russett and Starr argue for approaching the topic in a scientific manner. The scientific approach requires research into the general trends and patterns of international behavior. The accumulation of evidence from these techniques eventually leads to probability statements, theories, or laws that accurately describe and explain the actions of humankind beyond the boundaries of the nation-state.

A SCIENTIFIC STUDY OF WORLD POLITICS

Just as there have always been different philosophical views about the current or desired nature of world politics, there have also been different views about how world politics should be studied. Some people, especially the realists with their insistence on the overwhelming importance of nation-states as actors, stressed the study of diplomatic history—the study of actions by national governments. Others, especially transnationalists, attended primarily to the study and development of international law. Both approaches were highly descriptive, providing a detailed record of how states *actually* behave. They were also often prescriptive, setting forth ways in which states *should* behave, sometimes with legalistic or moral/ethical arguments.

Another approach—one not primarily associated with any of these philosophical perspectives—was to use relevant results and methods from the behavioral sciences, such as anthropology, economics, psychology, and sociology. This approach was reinforced by the rise of analytical and quantitative research concepts, models, and methods. It made greater use of the comparative study of quantitative data, and in using systematic evidence remedied the excesses of both the diplomatic-historical (realist) approach and the international law (transnationalist) approach that had dominated earlier studies.[1]

Given the crucial world problems that appeared after 1945, many scholars and analysts felt that only a more systematic understanding would lead to solutions. Problems of war and peace took on new meanings with the advent of nuclear weapons. The interdependence and complexity of the world became greater as the Western colonial empires broke up, scores of new states were created, and political and economic hierarchies around the world were reordered. Older philosophical explanations seemed inadequate.

Historical and legal approaches stressed the description of unique events and sought to explain them. The post-World War II intellectual reaction to these approaches sought

1. For treatments contrasting realism (and its variants) with idealism, transnationalism, and radical approaches (as well as their variants), see Richard W. Mansbach and John Vasquez, *In Search of Theory: A New Paradigm for Global Politics* (New York: Columbia University Press, 1981); K. J. Holsti, *The Dividing Discipline* (Boston: Allen & Unwin, 1985); and Paul R. Viotti and Mark V. Kauppi, *International Relations Theory Realism, Pluralism, Globalism* (New York: Macmillan, 1987). For a recent overview of the scientific study of international politics, see Michael Nicholson, *Formal Theories in International Relations* (Cambridge: Cambridge University Press, 1989).

instead to try to study international relations in a scientific manner, using the procedures and methods of science (as other social sciences, such as economics and psychology, had done previously). Thus, the preference was to stress *comparability* rather than uniqueness—to look for patterns of behavior and for probabilities that certain behavior would occur. A social scientific approach assumes that knowledge is possible by investigating patterns of behavior, regularities of actions, and recurring responses in political behavior. These patterns may be investigated cross-nationally (that is, by comparisons of several states at a particular time) or longitudinally (that is, by comparisons of conditions in one or more states at several points in time). Science is concerned with generalizations about classes or types of phenomena. It assumes that over the long run many historic parallels will transcend the specific times, places, and people involved.

In approaching the study of international relations in this way, stress was placed on finding and developing tools for organizing the intellectual complexity of the field the development of concepts, frameworks, and theories. These tools represent the most basic elements of science and help us avoid naive or simplistic scientism. We have already noted that events, situations, or social phenomena *can* be compared. Although in many respects events and people have unique aspects that will never occur again, all of them bear similarities to broader concepts or classes of events. As James Rosenau has noted, to "think theoretically" we must always be ready to look at some phenomenon and ask: "Of what is this an instance?"[2]

Thus, in a very basic way the scientific comparative method distinguishes the study of international relations or politics from the study of international history. Some traditionalists and historians believe that humanity—and international relations especially—is the least promising area for scientific study because events are too complex and singular. Denying the existence of regularities would leave us to study only singular cases or to produce detailed descriptions, with no cumulation of knowledge for the scholar or policymaker. If every historical event is truly unique and thus noncomparable, the gulf between the traditionalist and the scientist is indeed unbridgeable. Some scholars appear to hold this position; however, we don't believe it (and probably neither do they). Everyone has compared two events at some time. By comparing things, we admit the possibility of certain similarities across events. Using a case study to illustrate some concept or phenomenon reveals the same agreement with the principle of comparison and the possibility of patterns. The most basic rationale for the study of social relations and structures—that the past can be used as some sort of guide to the future—must also rest on the similarities of events and the existence of regularities.

Models and concepts also point us to a second basic element of science: a *probabilistic* explanation of human affairs. While science believes that things are comparable and that we should search for explanations that cover many cases, it is a false characterization of science (even the "hard" or physical sciences) to believe that science promises general laws that explain everything and will predict exactly what will happen. *All* science is based on models, propositions, or laws that are contingent—that will hold only under certain conditions. As the world approximates such conditions the probabilities that the events proposed by a model or theory will occur will vary. That the study of international relations does not now and may never look like physics with its apparent "universal laws"

---

2. James N. Rosenau, "Thinking Theory Thoroughly," in Rosenau, ed., *The Scientific Study of Foreign Policy*, rev. ed. (London: Frances Pinter, 1980), pp. 25-26.

does not mean that international relations cannot be scientific. As Rosenau warns us, "To think theoretically one must be tolerant of ambiguity, concerned with probabilities, and distrustful of absolutes." Using probabilistic explanation is what Jacob Bronowski called the "revolution" of thought in modern science, "replacing the concept of the inevitable effect with that of the probable trend. . . . History is neither determined nor random. At any moment it moves forward into an area whose general shape is known, but whose boundaries are uncertain in a calculable way".[3]

To understand world politics we need to have a high tolerance for uncertainty, the imperfect state of human knowledge, and the whys of human society and politics. The phenomena are extraordinarily complex, and we know far less than we would like. You will doubtless yearn at times for more certainty, more conviction, than the authors of this book can give about the causes and possible solutions of various problems. But knowing what it is that you don't know, why you don't know it, and what you might do to remedy your ignorance, is a part of wisdom and maturity.

THEORY AND EVIDENCE

We have noted that theory, models, and concepts lead to the basic elements of science involving comparison, contingency, and probability. Comparison also implies measurement; to compare two things means we must measure them in some way. How do we measure things? How do we measure things in such a way as to evaluate the relevance and utility of our theories? These two questions identify further basic elements of science.

We must first return to *theory*. A key element in science is the painstaking development of theory. Theory is an intellectual tool that provides us with a way to organize the complexity of the world and order facts into data and that helps us to see how phenomena are interrelated.

> More specifically, a theory is a set of interconnected statements. This set of statements comprises (1) sentences introducing terms that refer to the basic concepts of the theory (theoretical terms); (2) sentences that relate the basic concepts to each other; and (3) sentences that relate some theoretical statements to a set of possible observations.[4]

Theory organizes and simplifies reality, thus helping to separate the important from the trivial by pointing out what we really wish to look at and what is unimportant enough to ignore. This is why theory is so important—it affects not only which answers we come up with, but also what questions we ask in the first place! In what ways would a realist, transnational, or radical theory of the end of the cold war differ? We'll see below.

Theories are used to define, label, and classify the phenomena of world politics carefully. This is part of the *precision* that is basic to science. Scientific theories must be stated in a clear and precise way, so that one knows how to make, and evaluate, the measurements necessary for comparison. Science is thus about how to test, evaluate, and compare theories. Again, it is false to think of science as the only way to generate theories. Theories come from all aspects of human experience, and many of the most successful scientists, such as Louis Pasteur or Thomas Edison, had a creative knack by which they could look at things differently, draw analogies where others could not, or just pull great ideas out of the air.

---

3. Jacob Bronowski, *The Common Sense of Science* (London Heinemann, 1951), pp. 86-87. See Benjamin A. Most and Harvey Starr, *Inquiry, Logic and International Politics* (Columbia, S.C.: University of South Carolina Press, 1989), chaps. 1 and 5.

4. Garvin McCain and Erwin M. Segal, *The Game of Science*, 2nd ed. (Monterey, Calif. Brooks/Cole, 1978), p. 99. This book is a clear and helpful introduction to scientific method.

Theories tell us what to look at and how the things we look at relate to each other. In so doing, theories provide the basis for *systematic,* or scientific, evidence for our explanations of the world. Because we can argue an opposite and plausible reason or hypothesis for almost every aspect of human interaction (for example, "absence makes the heart grow fonder" and "out of sight, out of mind"), we need systematic evidence to test theory. A good theory is one that can be supported or rejected through explicit analysis and the systematic use of data. A theory that cannot be tested—and cannot be disproved in any conceivable way—cannot get us very far. Think, for example, of the proposition, "People always act to advance their own self-interest, no matter how much they delude themselves or others into thinking they are acting in someone else's interest." Since the proponent of such an argument can always support the argument ("The person in question is deluding himself about his motives"), and since that statement cannot be checked with evidence (we cannot get inside the person's mind to look), the self-interest proposition cannot be disproved, or "falsified." It is not a scientific statement because any evidence can be interpreted to agree. It also is a useless statement, because it does not tell us what the person's specific behavior will be.

We now have two more important observations about science. Despite some current questions about the nature of knowledge and our ability to communicate our understanding about the world (raised by the "post-modern" or "postpositivist" school of thought), science assumes only that at some point we must be able to match up some aspect of our theories or their predictions against data from the real world. Science assumes that at least some of the patterns we have mentioned can be measured and described. The data that we use to accomplish these purposes must be collected in very specific ways.

Another false characterization of science is that it is "value free," or in some way totally objective. This is not the case. Science is *explicit* in its procedures so that people can judge it, to see if the investigator's values or ideology have slanted the analysis. The evidence used must be objective—the procedures by which it has been collected must be made open to outside observers. Evidence must be collected in such ways as to be relevant to the question at hand. It must be collected in such ways as not to bias the results. Much of scientific endeavor, therefore, requires systematic observation and precise measurement. A careful analyst will insist on a combination of logical deduction and accurate observation—empirical evidence—in evaluating the propositions put forth. Science thus is a systematic way of obtaining information and making generalizations.

> Scientific observation is deliberate search, carried out with care and forethought, as contrasted with the casual and largely passive perceptions of everyday life. It is this deliberateness and control of the process of observation that is distinctive of science, not merely the use of special instruments.[5]

As some experienced social scientists point out, much of what we know about social phenomena is "ordinary knowledge," not derived from systematic scientific endeavors. Ordinary knowledge, or common sense, as it is sometimes called, is "that on which people can agree at a particular time and place."[6] It might include the fact that there are many countries in the world, that there is a war going on somewhere at virtually all times, and

---

5. Abraham Kaplan, *The Language of Inquiry* (San Francisco: Chandler, 1964), p. 126. Quoted, with further discussion, in Charles E. Lindblom and David K. Cohen, *Usable Knowledge: Social Science and Social Problem Solving* (New Haven, Conn.: Yale University Press, 1979), pp. 15-16.

6. See Karl W. Deutsch, "The Limits of Common Sense," in Nelson W. Polsby, et al., eds., *Politics* and *Social Life* (Boston: Houghton Mifflin, 1963), pp. 51-58.

that very big states usually have larger armies than do very small states. Yet we must also know when to doubt what passes as ordinary knowledge, when to question it, and how to supplant or supplement it by scientific knowledge when needed. Karl Deutsch has pointed out that common sense can be untrue, as were the formerly held beliefs that the world is flat or that light is white. Common sense may be simply the result of changing intellectual fashions, as in the relationship between Isaac Newton's physics and previous knowledge, or Einstein's physics and the earlier Newtonian beliefs. Most important, as pointed out above, common sense is often contradictory. Social science should be directed at key points of inquiry where ordinary knowledge is thus suspect.

Hypotheses, Laws, and Probability Statements

Theoretical statements that relate to possible observations are called *hypotheses*. The testing of hypotheses—checking their predictions against observation—is a central activity of science. Hypotheses that are confirmed in virtually all the classes of phenomena to which they are applied are often known as laws. In the social sciences, interesting laws are quite rare. The phenomena of social science are so complex, with many different influences or causes acting on a particular event, and our knowledge of these complex phenomena is still so imperfect, that few laws have been established. As stressed above, even with much more theory and research, we are likely to have only *probability statements*, statements that most phenomena of a given class will behave in a certain way most of the time. This is why social scientists find it hard to predict how particular events will develop; for example, which Soviet leader, at what specific point in time, would be willing to let the East European states go their independent ways. At best, the social scientist can give no more than a probability that a particular action (a threat, a promise, or a concession) will be followed by a specific result.

When we say we are hoping to make general statements about phenomena in international relations, we do not necessarily mean generalizations that apply to all countries at all times. Such generalizations may be approximated in physics, but they are hard to make in political science. All states, for instance, may have to react in some way to a shift in the international balance of power. But how they will react depends on other circumstances. They may react by making war, forming new alliances, building up their national power bases, or making concessions to their opponents. A state's choices depend on its opportunities (whether powerful allies are available and whether in alliance they can conceivably win a war) and on their disposition or willingness to act on various possibilities (whether their domestic ideology permits them to ally with a potential partner state, whether their government is strong enough to survive concessions to a foreign enemy).

Such factors create the contingencies useful for "nice laws," statements that cover a group of cases under a specific set of conditions. In different contexts, therefore, the same cause will have different effects. Context adds new variables that affect the relationship under study, and these variables often operate at different levels of analysis. In our discussion above, a generalization about the international system is modified by societal or governmental characteristics. The complex and changing nature of relationships in world politics makes them hard to analyze.[7]

In reviewing ideas or theories about world politics, we shall be considering propositions whose degree of truth varies greatly. Some statements of fact about *empirical reality* will be made with confidence, sometimes because they have been systematically and thor-

---

7. See Most and Starr, *Inquiry, Logic and International Politics*, especially chap. 5.

oughly tested by the standard procedures of social science. They represent, in other words, hypotheses that have been widely confirmed. In other cases statements may be made with confidence simply because they are a part of accepted "wisdom." Even though they may not rest on an elaborate basis of scientific examination, they are thought by most observers to be more or less self-evident. Perhaps they can be logically deduced from other statements that are widely accepted or that rest on solid scientific procedure.

If statements have been supported by empirical study, it is also important that they be derived by careful logic from clearly stated assumptions to show us why the statement should be correct and how it identifies a *process* or a *causal* relationship. For example, the statement "Fat people eat too much" is usually an empirically correct statement of fact—a correlation—but it tells us little of interest about causality why some people are fat, that is, why they eat too much. Often it is very difficult to uncover the process of causation that underlies a correlation we observe. Using our example, what is the cause of overeating and therefore of fatness?

We also have to be very careful about the assumptions we make. It would not be helpful to construct an elaborate logical theory about why people are overweight if one of our initial assumptions (for example, "They start out with larger stomachs to fill") was empirically incorrect. Of course, we sometimes make simplifying assumptions that we know may not be correct or are not fully correct. Such assumptions can be treated as a theory or model, to be judged against their fit to real world data. Like theories, assumptions must be relevant to enough cases to make them useful. For example, we can assume that people are rational, that competition in an industry is perfect, or that the speed of a falling body is not slowed by friction with the air. Sometimes these assumptions are close enough to reality that they do not affect our conclusions. Competition among thousands of grain farmers may be nearly perfect; the difference between the weights of iron and lead balls may not produce a significant difference in their speeds when they are dropped from the Leaning Tower of Pisa. In these cases it would take very careful observation to see any difference, and the differences would be so small that in most circumstances we would not care. But if the assumptions were wildly incorrect for a particular set of problems, the results would be irrelevant at best, disastrous at worst. What if we assumed that competition in the international sale of petroleum was perfect? Or that air resistance would make no difference in the speeds of a feather and a lead ball dropped from the tower? By following the precepts of scientific inquiry, a careful analyst will always be alert to the nature of his or her assumptions, to ways in which they may differ from reality, and to the conditions under which the difference may be significant. A careful analyst will want to know what has been simplified and to have some sense of how that simplification may lead his or her predictions to depart from observable reality.

Specifying and Testing Hypotheses

Social scientists often proceed in the following way:

1. Start with some observations or some facts that need explaining.
2. Offer some tentative hypotheses.
3. Evaluate the hypotheses in light of available facts.
4. If these facts do support the hypotheses, look for some implications—general propositions that can be deduced from the first hypotheses and facts.
5. Test such propositions on the first case or on new cases.[8]

Sometimes an analysis along these lines is referred to as a "thinking experiment." It is a purely analytical exercise, unlike clinical or laboratory experiments, in which one varies actual conditions to see what effect the changes have. With citizens and nations, we simply cannot conduct a real-life experiment. Nor are we able for this chapter to gather and document systematically a substantial body of rigorous empirical data on the case we will discuss. Instead, we shall proceed with a very tentative analysis, proposing hypotheses that would require much more theory and research but that meanwhile may produce some intriguing suggestions. Still, this exercise highlights another hallmark of science, that propositions must confront evidence and should then be revised or abandoned on that basis. As Rosenau notes, "To think theoretically one must be constantly ready to be proven wrong."

Our example is Gorbachev's decision not to use Soviet troops to suppress the dissidents of East Germany in 1989 and thus save its communist government. This was one of the most dramatic and important decisions that permitted an end to the cold war. Discussion shows some approaches to the great guessing game about the sources and stability of Soviet policy. Different hypotheses can be derived from realist, transnationalist, and radical perspectives.

Hypothesis 1

Gorbachev did not use force to support the East German government because he feared a NATO military response, perhaps culminating in World War III. A realist might say that the NATO allies could not have resisted the opportunity to gain a critical power advantage; in this case, to bring all East Germany under their control. A radical might say much the same thing but give as the reason the capitalist world's continuing wish to expand the realm of capitalism and to bring down the competing system of economic and political organization.

Evaluation

One problem with either version of this hypothesis is that the NATO countries had passed up similar opportunities in the past. When the Soviet Union crushed the Hungarian revolution in 1956 and the liberalization of Czechoslovakia known as the Prague spring in 1968, the West did virtually nothing. NATO countries implicitly acknowledged a right of the Soviet Union to do as it wished within Eastern Europe, its own sphere of influence, and that the risks involved in any NATO military response were much too great. There is little reason to think they would have judged differently for East Germany in 1989.

Hypothesis 2

Gorbachev did not use force because he secretly held goals different from those of other Soviet leaders. Perhaps he really was a "closet democrat" who wanted to see noncommunist governments in East Germany and the rest of Eastern Europe (a possible transnationalist explanation), or because he really was an agent of the CIA whose aim was to betray communism (a possible radical explanation).

Evaluation

There are virtually no facts to support either version of this hypothesis. Gorbachev has acted much more like a reformer of communism, with no fully formed goal in mind, than like someone who wanted to do away with the communist system entirely.

8. This procedure is nicely presented and illustrated in Charles A. Lave and James G. March, *An Introduction to Models in the Social Sciences* (New York: Harper & Row, 1975), chap. 1.

He came out of much the same set of party and government experiences as did other Soviet leaders, giving no hint of a desire to make a complete break with the past. As for deliberately betraying the system as a Western agent, that belief requires very great faith in the CIA. We find both versions of this hypothesis implausible.

Hypothesis 3

Gorbachev feared he could no longer make repression effective and that the effort to do so would only hasten the spread of revolution across Eastern Europe (a transnationalist hypothesis).

Evaluation
This hypothesis draws its strength from the increasing growth of transnational communications links that carry new information and ideas into and out of Eastern Europe. It implies that the people would rise in support of those ideas, and in support of one another, even in the face of terrible costs. Perhaps the Soviet people, and Soviet troops, would also have rebelled rather than permit wholesale repression. It is true that transnational linkages had grown substantially. Yet comparatively recently, in Czechoslovakia in 1968, they had little effect. While one cannot completely dismiss this hypothesis, it is implausible as a primary explanation.

Hypothesis 4

Gorbachev knew that the use of force would alienate the Western countries on whom he was relying for technological and military assistance to rebuild the Soviet economy. No Soviet leader with such a goal could afford to do something that would cut off the possibility of trade with the West (another transnational hypothesis).

Evaluation
This hypothesis also has some plausibility, but it does not fit all the facts well. Western responses to previous Soviet crackdowns on dissent had not been very strong. When in December 1981 the communist government of Poland violently repressed the Solidarity movement with Soviet approval and encouragement (but with no Soviet troops), there was only a partial and ineffective Western trade embargo; the same was true in response to the Soviet military intervention in Afghanistan. Gorbachev might have thought that once again the West would accept the Soviet sphere of influence and not enforce severe economic sanctions.

Hypothesis 5

Gorbachev did not intervene because Eastern Europe had become not an asset but a serious drain on Soviet resources; he thought that the national interest of the Soviet Union would be better served economically and politically by letting the satellites go (a realist hypothesis).

Evaluation
There is a lot of evidence that Eastern Europe had long been an economic drain, receiving many hidden subsidies such as cheap Soviet oil for barter rather than having to purchase it at world market prices for dollars. But again, such considerations had earlier had little effect. Also, national-interest explanations can too easily be created after an event—almost anything can be described as in the national interest—but the national interest is not something self-evident that all objective observers would agree on.

Hypothesis 6

Gorbachev did not intervene because the Soviet Union no longer needed the political and military buffer that Eastern Europe had provided. Gorbachev no longer, if he had ever, feared a NATO attack (another realist hypothesis).

Evaluation

Gorbachev might finally have decided the West did not wish to attack. But it is not clear why Western intentions should have so recently—in the years of tough rhetoric from the Reagan administration about the Soviet "evil empire"—seemed more benign, or why Gorbachev in particular should have reached that conclusion. Evidence for the realist view may be found in the growing Soviet and American realization that in a world of nuclear parity, nuclear weapons could not be used credibly for anything but the defense of one's homeland, and certainly not to coerce another superpower. Thus, as long as the Soviet Union retained a rough nuclear parity with the United States it could protect itself without allies or the kind of defense in depth that a shield of sullen East European satellites might provide. After 1986 Gorbachev abandoned most of his previous rhetoric in favor of totally eliminating nuclear weapons from the world, and he may have come to see them as even more necessary than the satellites.

New Propositions and Possible Tests

We did not totally reject any of the hypotheses, although the first two seemed least compelling. Even the last two, probably the strongest, are expressed in ambiguous terms and cannot be either accepted or rejected confidently. The important part of the exercise, however, is not to make a definitive choice among them, but to confront various hypotheses and consider the kind of logic and evidence that would make one more plausible than another. Each stresses different variables and even different levels of analysis. For example, as we stated Hypothesis 2, the individuality of Gorbachev is stressed (a micro explanation based on understanding how a particular individual views the world). Hypothesis 5 emphasizes economic conditions within the communist-ruled areas, and Hypothesis 6 focuses on the military relations between superpowers in an international system with bipolar nuclear capabilities (these are both macro explanations based on factors from the global political environment). Making the hypotheses more precise, with sharper definitions of economic burdens or the nuclear balance, would make it clearer how—and whether—they could be tested, confronting systematic evidence from the real world.

They might be tested in several ways. One would be to look more systematically at the several times during the cold war era in which Soviet leaders had to decide whether to use military force to suppress a rebellion. This would have to include not only instances when the Soviet government did use force, but instances when it did not (for example, when Yugoslav president Tito took his country out of the Soviet orbit in 1948). One could compare the different objective conditions and also the different public statements and reasons given for Soviet actions. Public statements may not, however, give real reasons; ultimately scholars may get access to Soviet government archives that would give us a better, but still imperfect, measure of what the real reasons were. Better still would be to treat the hypotheses as general statements about all major military powers and alliance leaders, not just the Soviet Union, to see how widely they may apply. Finally, one might test the hypothesis by predicting what would happen if a Soviet leader had to decide whether to use large-scale military force against a breakaway republic of the Soviet Union. For example, we could propose that he or she would not do so if a strong Western military response were possible (Hypothesis 1) or if the Soviet Union became much more dependent upon Western markets and capital (Hypothesis 4).

FACTS AND VALUES

Science can help us in understanding the world. Makers of political decisions take actions every day that determine the happiness and the lives of millions of people, but they do not always know what the effects of their acts will be, nor do their advisers. While recognizing that action is necessary, we must retain a sense of humility about the knowledge base of our actions. Similar self-consciousness is needed for statements of *value*. We make such statements all the time one painting is more beautiful than another; one act is morally right and another wrong. We all make these judgments, with varying degrees of confidence, and we often disagree about them. The systems of thought by which we deduce statements about goodness and beauty may start from very different premises. A Buddhist, a Sunni Moslem, an evangelical Christian, and an atheist Marxist may well agree that certain elements of life, decent living conditions, and liberties constitute, in some sense, "basic human rights." But they will differ in how they arrive at that common conclusion, about the specific forms those rights should take, and about the relative importance of each.

Rosenau warns us, "To think theoretically one has to be clear as to whether one aspires to empirical theory or value theory." We need to be concerned with values, because the values held by scholars affect what they study—what questions they ask, using what theories. One of the sources of theory thus may be the questions raised by an analyst's values or ethics. The methods of science cannot establish or compare the validity of different sets of values; these are normative questions. Some cultures value political liberty more highly than do others; poor people may rate decent living conditions as more important than political rights. Religion, ethical systems, other elements of culture, and economic conditions influence people's values and ethical judgments. Science can, however, help us clarify our thinking about values. It can help us understand the consequences of pursuing certain values and help us see to what degree policies or strategies will help us achieve our values. That is, science can help us understand the relationship between our ends and our means.

International Relations: One World, Many Theories

Stephen M. Walt

Walt discusses the value of theory for foreign policy practitioners and in particular the need for a "diverse array of competing" perspectives. Subsequently he describes the various theoretical approaches which currently dominate the field of international relations and their impact on policy.

Why should policymakers and practitioners care about the scholarly study of international affairs? Those who conduct foreign policy often dismiss academic theorists (frequently, one must admit, with good reason), but there is an inescapable link between the abstract world of theory and the real world of policy. We need theories to make sense of the blizzard of information that bombards us daily. Even policymakers who are contemptuous of "theory" must rely on their own (often unstated) ideas about how the world works in order to decide what to do. It is hard to make good policy if one's basic organizing principles are flawed, just as it is hard to construct good theories without knowing a lot about the real world. Everyone uses theories—whether he or she knows it or not—and disagreements about policy usually rest on more fundamental disagreements about the basic forces that shape international outcomes.

Take, for example, the current debate on how to respond to China. From one perspective, China's ascent is the latest example of the tendency for rising powers to alter the global balance of power in potentially dangerous ways, especially as their growing influence makes them more ambitious. From another perspective, the key to China's future conduct is whether its behavior will be modified by its integration into world markets and by the (inevitable?) spread of democratic principles. From yet another viewpoint, relations between China and the rest of the world will be shaped by issues of culture and identity: Will China see itself (and be seen by others) as a normal member of the world community or a singular society that deserves special treatment?

In the same way, the debate over NATO expansion looks different depending on which theory one employs. From a "realist" perspective, NATO expansion is an effort to extend Western influence—well beyond the traditional sphere of U.S. vital interests—during a period of Russian weakness and is likely to provoke a harsh response from Moscow. From a liberal perspective, however, expansion will reinforce the nascent democracies of Central Europe and extend NATO's conflict management mechanisms to a potentially turbulent region. A third view might stress the value of incorporating the Czech Republic, Hungary, and Poland within the Western security community, whose members share a common identity that has made war largely unthinkable.

No single approach can capture all the complexity of contemporary world politics. Therefore, we are better off with a diverse array of competing ideas rather than a single theoretical orthodoxy. Competition between theories helps reveal their strengths and weaknesses and spurs subsequent refinements, while revealing flaws in conventional wisdom. Although we should take care to emphasize inventiveness over invective, we should welcome and encourage the heterogeneity of contemporary scholarship.

"International Relations: One World, Many Theories" by Stephen M. Walt, *Foreign Policy* (Spring 1998), pp. 29-44. Reprinted with permission of the publisher.

WHERE ARE WE COMING FROM?

The study of international affairs is best understood as a protracted competition between the realist, liberal, and radical traditions. Realism emphasizes the enduring propensity for conflict between states; liberalism identifies several ways to mitigate these conflictive tendencies; and the radical tradition describes how the entire system of state relations might be formed. The boundaries between these traditions are somewhat fuzzy and a number of important works do not fit neatly into any of them, but debates within and among them have largely defined the discipline.

Realism

Realism was the dominant theoretical tradition throughout the Cold War. It depicts international affairs as a struggle for power among self-interested states and is generally pessimistic about the prospects for eliminating conflict and war. Realism dominated in the Cold War years because it provided simple but powerful explanations for war, alliances, imperialism, obstacles to cooperation, and other international phenomena, and because its emphasis on competition was consistent with the central features of the American-Soviet rivalry.

Realism is not a single theory, of course, and realist thought evolved considerably throughout the Cold War. "Classical" realists such as Hans Morgenthau and Reinhold Niebuhr believed that states, like human beings, had an innate desire to dominate others, which led them to fight wars. Morgenthau also stressed the virtues of the classical, multipolar, balance-of-power system and saw the bipolar rivalry between the United States and the Soviet Union as especially dangerous.

By contrast, the "neorealist" theory advanced by Kenneth Waltz ignored human nature and focused on the effects of the international system. For Waltz, the international system consisted of a number of great powers, each seeking to survive. Because the system is anarchic (i.e., there is no central authority to protect states from one another), each state has to survive on its own. Waltz argued that this condition would lead weaker states to balance against, rather than bandwagon with, more powerful rivals. And contrary to Morgenthau, he claimed that bipolarity was more stable than multipolarity.

An important refinement to realism was the addition of offense-defense theory, as laid out by Robert Jervis, George Quester, and Stephen Van Evera. These scholars argued that war was more likely when states could conquer each other easily. When defense was easier than offense, however, security was more plentiful, incentives to expand declined, and cooperation could blossom. And if defense had the advantage, and states could distinguish between offensive and defensive weapons, then states could acquire the means to defend themselves without threatening others, thereby dampening the effects of anarchy.

For these "defensive" realists, states merely sought to survive and great powers could guarantee their security by forming balancing alliances and choosing defensive military postures (such as retaliatory nuclear forces). Not surprisingly, Waltz and most other neorealists believed that the United States was extremely secure for most of the Cold War. Their principle fear was that it might squander its favorable position by adopting an overly aggressive foreign policy. Thus, by the end of the Cold War, realism had moved away from Morgenthau's dark brooding about human nature and taken on a slightly more optimistic tone.

Liberalism

The principal challenge to realism came from a broad family of liberal theories. One strand of liberal thought argued that economic interdependence would discourage states from using force against each other because warfare would threaten each side's prosperity. A second strand, often associated with President Woodrow Wilson, saw the spread of democracy as the key to world peace, based on the claim that democratic states were inherently more peaceful than authoritarian states. A third, more recent theory argued that international institutions such as the International Energy Agency and the International Monetary Fund could help overcome selfish state behavior, mainly by encouraging states to forego immediate gains for the greater benefits of enduring cooperation.

Although some liberals flirted with the idea that new transnational actors, especially the multinational corporation, were gradually encroaching on the power of states, liberalism generally saw states as the central players in international affairs. All liberal theories implied that cooperation was more pervasive than even the defensive version of realism allowed, but each view offered a different recipe for promoting it.

Radical Approaches

Until the 1980s, marxism was the main alternative to the mainstream realist and liberal traditions. Where realism and liberalism took the state system for granted, marxism offered both a different explanation for international conflict and a blueprint for fundamentally transforming the existing international order.

Orthodox marxist theory saw capitalism as the central cause of international conflict. Capitalist states battled each other as a consequence of their incessant struggle for profits and battled socialist states because they saw in them the seeds of their own destruction. Neomarxist "dependency" theory, by contrast, focused on relations between advanced capitalist powers and less developed states and argued that the former—aided by an unholy alliance with the ruling classes of the developing world—had grown rich by exploiting the latter. The solution was to overthrow these parasitic elites and install a revolutionary government committed to autonomous development.

Both of these theories were largely discredited before the Cold War even ended. The extensive history of economic and military cooperation among the advanced industrial powers showed that capitalism did not inevitably lead to conflict. The bitter schisms that divided the communist world showed that socialism did not always promote harmony. Dependency theory suffered similar empirical setbacks as it became increasingly clear that, first, active participation in the world economy was a better route to prosperity than autonomous socialist development; and, second, many developing countries proved themselves quite capable of bargaining successfully with multinational corporations and other capitalist institutions.

As marxism succumbed to its various failings, its mantle was assumed by a group of theorists who borrowed heavily from the wave of postmodern writings in literary criticism and social theory. This "deconstructionist" approach was openly skeptical of the effort to devise general or universal theories such as realism or liberalism. Indeed, its proponents emphasized the importance of language and discourse in shaping social outcomes. However, because these scholars focused initially on criticizing the mainstream paradigms but did not offer positive alternatives to them, they remained a self-consciously dissident minority for most of the 1980s.

Domestic Politics

Not all Cold War scholarship on international affairs fit neatly into the realist, liberal, or marxist paradigms. In particular, a number of important works focused on the characteristics of states, governmental organizations, or individual leaders. The democratic strand of liberal theory fits under this heading, as do the efforts of scholars such as Graham Allison and John Steinbruner to use organization theory and bureaucratic politics to explain foreign policy behavior, and those of Jervis, Irving Janis, and others, which applied social and cognitive psychology. For the most part, these efforts did not seek to provide a general theory of international behavior but to identify other factors that might lead states to behave contrary to the predictions of the realist or liberal approaches. Thus, much of this literature should he regarded as a complement to the three main paradigms rather than as a rival approach for analysis of the international system as a whole.

NEW WRINKLES IN OLD PARADIGMS

Scholarship on international affairs has diversified significantly since the end of the Cold War. Non-American voices are more prominent, a wider range of methods and theories are seen as legitimate, and new issues such as ethnic conflict, the environment, and the future of the state have been placed on the agenda of scholars everywhere.

Yet the sense of déjà vu is equally striking. Instead of resolving the struggle between competing theoretical traditions, the end of the Cold War has merely launched a new series of debates. Ironically, even as many societies embrace similar ideals of democracy, free markets, and human rights, the scholars who study these developments are more divided than ever.

Realism Redux

Although the end of the Cold War led a few writers to declare that realism was destined for the academic scrap heap, rumors of its demise have been largely exaggerated.

A recent contribution of realist theory is its attention to the problem of relative and absolute gains. Responding to the institutionalists' claim that international institutions would enable states to forego short-term advantages for the sake of greater long-term gains, realists such as Joseph Grieco and Stephen Krasner point out that anarchy forces states to worry about both the absolute gains from cooperation and the way that gains are distributed among participants. The logic is straightforward: If one state reaps larger gains than its partners, it will gradually become stronger, and its partners will eventually become more vulnerable.

Realists have also been quick to explore a variety of new issues. Barry Posen offers a realist explanation for ethnic conflict, noting that the breakup of multiethnic states could place rival ethnic groups in an anarchic setting, thereby triggering intense fears and tempting each group to use force to improve its relative position. This problem would be particularly severe when each group's territory contained enclaves inhabited by their ethnic rivals—as in the former Yugoslavia—because each side would be tempted to "cleanse" (preemptively) these alien minorities and expand to incorporate any others from their ethnic group that lay outside their borders. Realists have also cautioned that NATO, absent a clear enemy, would likely face increasing strains that expanding its presence eastward would jeopardize relations with Russia. Finally, scholars such as Michael Mastanduno have argued that U.S. foreign policy is generally consistent with realist principles, insofar as its actions are still designed to preserve U.S. predominance and to shape a postwar order that advances American interests.

The most interesting conceptual development within the realist paradigm has been the emerging split between the "defensive" and "offensive" strands of thought. Defensive realists such as Waltz, Van Evera, and Jack Snyder assumed that states had little intrinsic interest in military conquest and argued that the costs of expansion generally outweighed the benefits. Accordingly, they maintained that great power wars occurred largely because domestic groups fostered exaggerated perceptions of threat and an excessive faith in the efficacy of military force.

This view is now being challenged along several fronts. First, as Randall Schweller notes, the neorealist assumption that states merely seek to survive "stacked the deck" in favor of the status quo because it precluded the threat of predatory revisionist states—nations such as Adolf Hitler's Germany or Napoleon Bonaparte's France that "value what they covet far more than what they possess" and are willing to risk annihilation to achieve their aims. Second, Peter Liberman, in his book *Does Conquest Pay?*, uses a number of historical cases—such as the Nazi occupation of Western Europe and Soviet hegemony over Eastern Europe—to show that the benefits of conquest often exceed the costs, thereby casting doubt on the claim that military expansion is no longer cost-effective. Third, offensive realists such as Eric Labs, John Mearsheimer, and Fareed Zakaria argue that anarchy encourages all states to try to maximize their relative strength simply because no state can ever be sure when a truly revisionist power might emerge.

These differences help explain why realists disagree over issues such as the future of Europe. For defensive realists such as Van Evera, war is rarely profitable and usually results from militarism, hypernationalism, or some other distorting domestic factor. Because Van Evera believes such forces are largely absent in post-Cold War Europe, he concludes that the region is "primed for peace." By contrast, Mearsheimer and other offensive realists believe that anarchy forces great powers to compete irrespective of their internal characteristics and that security competition will return to Europe as soon as the U.S. pacifier is withdrawn.

New Life for Liberalism

The defeat of communism sparked a round of self-congratulation in the West, best exemplified by Francis Fukuyama's infamous claim that humankind had now reached the "end of history." History has paid little attention to this boast, but the triumph of the West did give a notable boost to all three strands of liberal thought.

By far the most interesting and important development has been the lively debate on the "democratic peace." Although the most recent phase of this debate had begun even before the Soviet Union collapsed, it became more influential as the number of democracies began to increase and as evidence of this relationship began to accumulate.

Democratic peace theory is a refinement of the earlier claim that democracies were inherently more peaceful than autocratic states. It rests on the belief that although democracies seem to fight wars as often as other states, they rarely, if ever, fight one another. Scholars such as Michael Doyle, James Lee Ray, and Bruce Russett have offered a number of explanations for this tendency, the most popular being that democracies embrace norms of compromise that bar the use of force against groups espousing similar principles. It is hard to think of a more influential, recent academic debate, insofar as the belief that "democracies don't fight each other" has been an important justification for the Clinton administration's efforts to enlarge the sphere of democratic rule.

It is therefore ironic that faith in the "democratic peace" became the basis for U.S. policy just as additional research was beginning to identify several qualifiers to this theory. First, Snyder and Edward Mansfield pointed out that states may be more prone to war when they are in the midst of a democratic transition, which implies that efforts to export democracy might actu-

Table 1: Competing Paradigms

Characteristics	Competing Paradigms: Realism	Liberalism	Constructivism
Main Theoretical Proposition	Self-interested states compete constantly for power or security	Concern for power overridden by economic/ political considerations (desire for prosperity, coommitment to liberal values	State behavior shaped by elite beliefs, collective norms, and social identiies
Main Units of Analysis	States	States	Individuals (especially elites)
Main Instruments	Economic and especially miilitary power	Varies (international institutions, ecomonic exchange, promo- tion of democracy)	Ideas and discourse
Modern theorists	Hans Morgenthau Kenneth Waltz	Michael Doyle Robert Keohane	Alexander Wendt, John Ruggie
Representative Modern Works	Waltz, *Theory of International Politics* Mearsheimer, "Back to the Future: Instability in Europe after the Cole War" (*International Security* 1990)	Keohane, *After Hegemony* Fukuyama, "The End of History?" (*National Interest*, 1989)	Wendt, "Anarchy Is What States Make of It" (*International Organization*, 1992); Koslowski & Kratochwiil, "Under- standing Changes in International Politics" (*International Organization*, 1994)
Post-Cold War Prediction	Resurgence of overt great power competition	Increased cooperation as liberal values, free markets, and international institutions spread	Agnostic because it cannot predict the content of ideas
Main Limitation	Does not account for international change	Tends to ignore the role of power	Better at describing the past then anticipating the future

ally make things worse. Second, critics such as Joanne Gowa and David Spiro have argued that the apparent absence of war between democracies is due to the way that democracy has been defined and to the relative dearth of democratic states (especially before 1945). In addition, Christopher Layne has pointed out that when democracies have come close to war in the past their decision to remain at peace ultimately had little do with their shared democratic character. Third, clearcut evidence that democracies do not fight each other is confined to the post-1945 era, and, as Gowa has emphasized, the absence of conflict in this period may be due more to their common interest in containing the Soviet Union than to shared democratic principles.

Liberal institutionalists likewise have continued to adapt their own theories. On the one hand, the core claims of institutionalist theory become more modest over time. Institutions are now said to facilitate cooperation when it is in each state's interest to do so, but it is widely agreed that they cannot force states to behave in ways that are contrary to the states' own selfish interests. On the other hand, institutionalists such as John Duffield and Robert McCalla have extended the theory into new substantive areas, most notably the study of NATO. For these scholars, NATO's highly institutionalized character helps explain why it has been able to survive and adapt, despite the disappearance of its main adversary.

The economic strand of liberal theory is still influential as well. In particular, a number of scholars have recently suggested that the "globalization" of world markets, the rise of transnational networks and nongovernmental organizations, and the rapid spread of global communications \technology are undermining the power of states and shifting attention away from military security toward economics and social welfare. The details are novel but the basic logic is familiar. As societies around the globe become enmeshed in a web of economic and social connections, the costs of disrupting these ties will effectively preclude unilateral state actions, especially the use of force.

This perspective implies that war will remain a remote possibility among the advanced industrial democracies. It also suggests that bringing China and Russia into the relentless embrace of world capitalism is the best way to promote both prosperity and peace, particularly if this process creates a strong middle class in these states and reinforces pressures to democratize. Get these societies hooked on prosperity and competition will be confined to the economic realm.

This view has been challenged by scholars who argue that the actual scope of "globalization" is modest and that these various transactions still take place in environments that are shaped and regulated by states. Nonetheless, the belief that economic forces are superseding traditional great power politics enjoys widespread acceptance among scholars, pundits, and policymakers, and the role of the state is likely to be an important topic for future academic inquiry.

Constructivist Theories

Whereas realism and liberalism tend to focus on material factors such as power or trade, constructivist approaches emphasize the impact of ideas. Instead of taking the state for granted and assuming that it simply seeks to survive, constructivists regard the interests and identities of states as a highly malleable product of specific historical processes. They pay close attention to the prevailing discourse(s) in society because discourse reflects and shapes beliefs and interests, and establishes accepted norms of behavior. Consequently, constructivism is especially attentive to the sources of change, and this approach has largely replaced marxism as the preeminent radical perspective on international affairs.

The end of the Cold War played an important role in legitimating constructivist theories because realism and liberalism both failed to anticipate this event and had some trouble explaining it. Constructivists had an explanation: Specifically, former president

Mikhail Gorbachev revolutionized Soviet foreign policy because he embraced new ideas such as "common security."

Moreover, given that we live in an era where old norms are being challenged, once clear boundaries are dissolving, and issues of identity are becoming more salient, it is hardly surprising that scholars have been drawn to approaches that place these issues front and center. From a constructivist perspective, in fact, the central issue in the post-Cold War world is how different groups conceive their identities and interests. Although power is not irrelevant, constructivism emphasizes how ideas and identities are created, how they evolve, and how they shape the way states understand and respond to their situation. Therefore, it matters whether Europeans define themselves primarily in national or continental terms; whether Germany and Japan redefine their pasts in ways that encourage their adopting more active international roles; and whether the United States embraces or rejects its identity as "global policeman."

Constructivist theories are quite diverse and do not offer a unified set of predictions on any of these issues. At a purely conceptual level, Alexander Wendt has argued that the realist conception of anarchy does not adequately explain why conflict occurs between states. The real issue is how anarchy is understood—in Wendt's words, "Anarchy is what states make of it." Another strand of constructivist theory has focused on the future of the territorial state, suggesting that transnational communication and shared civic values are undermining traditional national loyalties and creating radically new forms of political association. Other constructivists focus on the role of norms, arguing that international law and other normative principles have eroded earlier notions of sovereignty and altered the legitimate purposes for which state power may be employed. The common theme in each of these strands is the capacity of discourse to shape how political actors define themselves and their interests, and thus modify their behavior.

Domestic Politics Reconsidered

As in the Cold War, scholars continue to explore the impact of domestic politics on the behavior of states. Domestic politics are obviously central to the debate on the democratic peace, and scholars such as Snyder, Jeffrey Frieden, and Helen Milner have examined how domestic interest groups can distort the formation of state preferences and lead to suboptimal international behavior. George Downs, David Rocke, and others have also explored how domestic institutions can help states deal with the perennial problem of uncertainty, while students of psychology have applied prospect theory and other new tools to explain why decision makers fail to act in a rational fashion.

The past decade has also witnessed an explosion of interest in the concept of culture, a development that overlaps with the constructivist emphasis on the importance of ideas and norms. Thus, Thomas Berger and Peter Katzenstein have used cultural variables to explain why Germany and Japan have thus far eschewed more self-reliant military policies; Elizabeth Kier has offered a cultural interpretation of British and French military doctrines in the interwar period; and Iain Johnston has traced continuities in Chinese foreign policy to a deeply rooted form of "cultural realism." Samuel Huntington's dire warnings about an imminent "clash of civilizations" are symptomatic of this trend as well, insofar as his argument rests on the claim that broad cultural affinities are now supplanting national loyalties. Though these and other works define culture in widely varying ways and have yet to provide a full explanation of how it works or how enduring its effects might be, cultural perspectives have been very much in vogue during the past five years.

This trend is partly a reflection of the broader interest in cultural issues in the academic world (and within the public debate as well) and partly a response to the upsurge in ethnic, nationalist, and cultural conflicts since the demise of the Soviet Union.

TOMORROW'S CONCEPTUAL TOOLBOX

While these debates reflect the diversity of contemporary scholarship on international affairs, there are also obvious signs of convergence. Most realists recognize that nationalism, militarism, ethnicity, and other domestic factors are important; liberals acknowledge that power is central to international behavior; and some constructivists admit that ideas will have greater impact when backed by powerful states and reinforced by enduring material forces. The boundaries of each paradigm are somewhat permeable, and there is ample opportunity for intellectual arbitrage.

Which of these broad perspectives sheds the most light on contemporary international affairs, and which should policymakers keep most firmly in mind when charting our course into the next century? Although many academics (and more than a few policymakers) are loathe to admit it, realism remains the most compelling general framework for understanding international relations. States continue to pay close attention to the balance of power and to worry about the possibility of major conflict. Among other things, this enduring preoccupation with power and security explains why many Asians and Europeans are now eager to preserve—and possibly expand—the U.S. military presence in their regions. As Czech president Vaclav Havel has warned, if NATO fails to expand, "we might be heading for a new global catastrophe . . . [which] could cost us all much more than the two world wars." These are not the words of a man who believes that great power rivalry has been banished forever.

As for the United States, the past decade has shown how much it likes being "number one" and how determined it is to remain in a predominant position. The United States has taken advantage of its current superiority to impose its preferences wherever possible, even at the risk of irritating many of its long-standing allies. It has forced a series of one-sided arms control agreements on Russia, dominated the problematic peace effort in Bosnia, taken steps to expand NATO into Russia's backyard, and become increasingly concerned about the rising power of China. It has called repeatedly for greater reliance on multilateralism and a larger role for international institutions, but has treated agencies such as the United Nations and the World Trade Organization with disdain whenever their actions did not conform to US interests. It refused to join the rest of the world in outlawing the production of landmines and was politely uncooperative at the Kyoto environmental summit. Although U.S. leaders are adept at cloaking their actions in the lofty rhetoric of "world order," naked self-interest lies behind most of them. Thus, the end of the Cold War did not bring the end of power politics, and realism is likely to remain the single most useful instrument in our intellectual toolbox.

Yet realism does not explain everything, and a wise leader would also keep insights from the rival paradigms in mind. Liberal theories identify the instruments that states can use to achieve shared interests, highlight the powerful economic forces with which states and societies must now contend, and help us understand why states may differ in their basic preferences. Paradoxically, because U.S. protection reduces the danger of regional rivalries and reinforces the "liberal peace" that emerged after 1945, these factors may become relatively more important, as long as the United States continues to provide security and stability in many parts of the world.

Meanwhile, constructivist theories are best suited to the analysis of how identities and interests can change over time, thereby producing subtle shifts in the behavior of states and occasionally triggering far-reaching but unexpected shifts in international affairs. It matters if political identity in Europe continues to shift from the nation-state to more local regions or to a broader sense of European identity, just as it matters if nationalism is gradually supplanted by the sort of "civilizational" affinities emphasized by Huntington. Realism has little to say about these prospects, and policy makers could be blind-sided by change if they ignore these possibilities entirely.

In short, each of these competing perspectives captures important aspects of world politics. Our understanding would be impoverished were our thinking confined to only one of them. The "compleat diplomat" of the future should remain cognizant of realism's emphasis on the inescapable role of power, keep liberalism's awareness of domestic forces in mind, and occasionally reflect on constructivism's vision of change.

Theories of Interstate and Intrastate War: A Levels-of-Analysis Approach

Jack S. Levy

. . . Although some argue that the end of the Cold War has changed "all the answers and all the questions,"[1] the theme of change must be tempered by that of continuity. The world has changed in profound ways over the millennia, but many of the factors that play a central role in contemporary international conflicts would have been familiar to Thucydides, who wrote his history of the Peloponnesian War over twenty-four hundred years ago.[2] Thucydides' argument that "the strong do what they can and the weak suffer what they must" is as relevant for contemporary ethnonational conflicts as it was for the Peloponnesian War . .

I organize this theoretical review around a "levels-of-analysis framework," which was first systematized by Kenneth Waltz and then widely used by scholars in the analysis of the causes of interstate wars. I show that, with some modifications, this framework can also be useful for analyzing the intrastate wars of the contemporary era.[3]

THE LEVELS-OF-ANALYSIS FRAMEWORK

The levels-of-analysis framework suggests that the causes of war can be analyzed at the level of the individual, the nation-state, and the international system. The individual level focuses primarily on human nature and predispositions toward aggression and on individual political leaders and their belief systems, personalities, and psychological processes. The nation-state (or national) level includes both governmental variables, such as the structure of the political system and the nature of the policymaking process, and societal factors, such as the structure of the economic system, the role of public opinion, economic and noneconomic interest groups, ethnicity and nationalism, and political culture and ideology. International system- (or systemic-) level causes include the anarchic structure of the global system, the number of major powers in the system, the distribution of military and economic power among them, patterns of military alliances and international trade, and other factors that constitute the external environment common to all states . . .

Scholars generally use the levels of analysis as a framework for classifying independent variables that explain state foreign policy behaviors and international outcomes. This

1. Charles W. Kegley Jr., "The Neoidealist Moment in International Studies: Realist Myths and the New International Studies," *International Studies Quarterly* 37, no. 2 (June 1993): 141.

2. Thucydides, History of the Peloponnesian War, in *The Landmark Thucydides*, ed. Robert B. Strassler (New York: Free Press, 1996), 5.89, 352.

3. Kenneth N. Waltz, *Man, the State, and War* (New York: Columbia University Press, 1959). Waltz spoke of three "images" of war, but it is now common to speak in terms of "levels of analysis." See J. David Singer, "The Levels of Analysis Problem in International Relations," in *International Politics and Foreign Policy*, rev. ed., ed. James N. Rosenau (New York: Free Press, 1969), 20-29. This survey builds on Jack S. Levy, "The Causes of War and the Conditions of Peace," *Annual Review of Political Science* 1 (June 1998): 139-166.

JACK S. LEVY is a professor of political science at Rutgers University.

Chester A. Crocker, Fen Osler Hampson, and Panela Aall, ed. Turbulent Peace: The Challenges of Managing International Conflict Washington D.C.: United States Institute of Peace, 2001, pp. 3-27. Reprinted with Permission.

leads us to ask such questions as whether the causes of war are to be found primarily at the level of the individual, the nation-state, or international system, and how variables from different levels interact in the foreign policy process . . .

It is logically possible and in fact usually desirable for explanations to combine causal variables from different levels of analysis, because whether war or peace occurs is usually determined by multiple variables operating at more than one level of analysis. Among the factors contributing to Iraq's invasion of Kuwait in 1990, for example, were the poor condition of Iraq's economy (a domestic or societal-level variable), Iraq's need for higher oil prices and the refusal of Arab oil-producing states to lower production levels and thus allow prices to rise (a systemic variable), and Saddam Hussein's propensities for risk taking (an individual-level variable). Similarly, a unipolar system, global political economy, and democracy work together to reinforce peace . . . Michael Brown's classification . . . of the sources of internal war in terms of bad leaders, bad domestic problems, bad neighborhoods, and bad neighbors can be framed in terms of levels of analysis: the first is an individual-level factor, the second a domestic-level factor, and the third a regional system factor, and the fourth refers to the external environment of a particular state.

The preceding examples illustrate the use of independent causal variables from various levels to explain state decisions for war. We can also use causal variables from different levels to explain the foreign policy preferences of individual leaders. We have to be careful whenever we use causal variables at one level to explain behavior or outcomes at a "higher" level. Individual- or domestic-level variables, for example, do not provide a logically complete explanation of aggressive state policies unless they are combined with a "theory of foreign policy" that explains how the preferences of individual actors or domestic publics are translated into a foreign policy decision for the state. Saddam Hussein's beliefs and personality may help explain the origins of the 1990-91 Persian Gulf War, but only in conjunction with the highly centralized structure of the Iraqi regime, which allowed Saddam to make policy in the absence of any significant internal constraints. Political leaders cannot always implement their preferred policies. U.S. president William McKinley preferred to avoid war with Spain in 1898, but because of domestic pressures for war McKinley "led his country unhesitatingly toward a war which he did not want for a cause in which he did not believe."[4]

Similarly, explanations of state foreign policy preferences or behaviors do not generally provide a logically complete explanation for war or peace. Because war and peace are both dyadic or systemic outcomes resulting from the interactions of two or more states, an explanation for war and peace requires the inclusion of dyadic- or systemic-level causal variables.[5] While attempts to secure peace through a policy based on the idea of *si vis pacem, para bellum* (if you want peace, prepare for war) are sometimes effective, they can also backfire, provoke the adversary rather than deter him, and lead to war through a conflict spiral. Alternatively, a strategy of advancing peace by adopting a conciliatory policy toward the adversary often works, but it might also fail by undermining a state's credibility, leading the adversary to increase its demands in the expectation that further concessions will be forthcoming, and result in war by miscalculation.[6] A theory of war is technically

---

4. Ernest May, *Imperial Democracy* (New York: Harper and Row, 1961).

5. This does not necessarily mean that dyadic-level and systemic-level variables have a greater causal influence than do individual or domestic variables, only that they cannot be logically excluded from the analysis.

incomplete without a theory of bargaining or strategic interaction that explains how states respond to each other's actions and how they act in anticipation of each other's responses.

Although the levels-of-analysis framework has traditionally been applied to states and to interstate relations, with some modifications it can also be applied to a wide range of nonstate actors, from international organizations like the United Nations to nonstate entities like the Kosovar Albanians or transnational criminal enterprises . . . We could ask whether decisions for UN intervention are driven more by the imperatives of the situation, by politics within the United Nations, or by the leadership of the secretary-general; whether the behavior of a particular nonstate communal group is influenced primarily by the external threats and opportunities it faces, by pressures from subgroups within it (including its military arm), or by the particular beliefs and charisma of an individual leader; or whether the behavior of an international drug ring is driven by rational calculations of profit and loss given the political economy of the international drug traffic, by political infighting within the organization, or by the risk-taking propensities of individual leaders. Although the levels-of-analysis framework can be applied to any actor, the framework assumes that the actor in question is sufficiently organized that it has a decision-making body with the authority to act on behalf of the group. If the group is more amorphous, so that we cannot speak of a single group policy with inputs from different levels, it is harder to apply the levels-of-analysis framework.

Although the levels-of-analysis framework is very useful, it is not perfect. It is better for classifying the sources of a particular state's foreign policy (or the policies of any organization) than for explaining wars or other outcomes that are the product of the strategic interaction of two or more actors, though if we are cognizant of the need to explain dyadic-level outcomes the limitations of the framework can be minimized. The levels-of-analysis framework is also more useful in classifying variables than in classifying theories. Although Waltz applied his different "images" of conflict to theories,[7] most of the theories he focused on (human nature and aggressive-instinct theories, Marxist-Leninist theories of imperialism or Kantian theories of republican states, and Rousseau's systems theory based on anarchy) were "monocausal," or single-factor, theories, or at least theories for which the key variables all derived from a single level of analysis.

Although we still have some single-level theories (systemic-level realist theories, including balance-of-power theory and power transition theory, for example), most of our theories of war and peace have become more complex and involve variables from two or more levels of analysis. Liberal theories of economic interdependence and peace, for example, include both political leaders' fears of the economic costs of war and their deterrent effect on conflict (a dyadic-level factor) and the influence of domestic economic groups that have a vested interest in the continuation of peace (a societal-level factor). Contemporary theories of both globalization and conflict incorporate the structure of the global economy, internal economic sources of economic expansion and contraction, domestic pressure groups, and economic ideologies . . . Theories of environmental scarcities include both systemic-level sources of resource scarcities and environmental refugees along with their societal-level impact, including changing demographic balances and incentives for scapegoating . . . Rational choice theories emphasize the maximization of

---

6. For hypotheses on the conditions under which threats of force tend to work to induce concessions, see Jervis, *Perception and Misperception*, chap. 3.

7. Waltz, *Man, the State, and War.*

interests under constraints, but interests include both state interests and external constraints (systemic level) and the interests of elites in maintaining their own political power in the face of domestic constraints (societal level). We can often use the levels-of-analysis framework to classify the individual components of these theories, which is very useful, but not the theories themselves.

In addition, some important variables are themselves difficult to classify because they cut across the different levels of analysis. The impact of oil on the U.S. decision to intervene against Iraq in the Persian Gulf War had both systemic and societal components; the Bush administration's wish to maintain access to oil at reasonable prices involved concerns about the impact of higher oil prices on the economies of the United States, its key allies, and newly democratizing states of the former Soviet bloc, and perhaps about the economic interests of U.S.-based oil companies.[8] Oil companies are both domestic actors in the U.S. political system and transnational actors in the global political economy, and it is not always clear how best to classify them. Economic variables in general often have an international and domestic component and are difficult to classify in terms of a single level. Nevertheless, by leading us to recognize the various components of a complex concept or factor (such as the implications of oil for national economic interests and for private economic interests, or the importance of credibility for states and for individual leaders), the levels-of-analysis framework serves a useful role.

Despite its limitations, the levels-of-analysis framework is still more useful than most other frameworks for classifying alternative explanations of the causes of war and peace . . .

CONCLUSION

. . . It is difficult to reach definitive conclusions regarding the causal importance of different levels of explanatory variables for international conflict in the recent past or in coming decades. First, an assessment of the relative impact of different variables at different levels is an empirical as well as a theoretical question, and space constraints have precluded me from assessing the weight of the empirical evidence in any detail. More important, theories of international conflict have increasingly begun to incorporate variables from several different levels of analysis. This means that an evaluation of the validity of a particular theory is not necessarily congruent with the evaluation of the importance of a particular level of analysis. A focus on the relative importance of different levels of analysis distracts attention from the more important task of understanding how variables at different levels of analysis interact and the contextual conditions that affect those interactions.

In addition, theories serve multiple purposes, and the utility of variables at different levels of analysis may be more useful for some theoretical purposes than for others. The trade-off between the analytic power and predictive utility of parsimonious theories and the descriptive richness of more complex theories is particularly salient. If we want a general theory that can provide maximum explanatory power across different temporal and spatial contexts and generate predictions, then theories based on international or domestic structures are likely to be particularly useful, whereas theories based on individual-level beliefs and psychological processes are less likely to be helpful because they are so

8. The maximization of state interests is treated as a systemic-level or dyadic-level variable because it involves calculations of opportunities and constraints in the international system or in a particular relationship.

demanding in terms of the detailed data required to apply them. But if we want a theory that can guide a more nuanced interpretation of a single historical case, or perhaps small number of cases, the additional descriptive accuracy provided by theories that incorporate individual and decision-making variables can be very useful.[9]

With these caveats in mind, let me offer some tentative comments about the relative importance of variables from different levels of analysis. This will vary depending on the "level" of the actors in question. Let us first consider the great powers. The decline in the frequency of great power war over time and the low likelihood of a great power war in the future is primarily the product of systemic-level developments in military technology that make the expected costs of war between nuclear powers far greater than any conceivable benefits from war.[10] Systemic-level unipolarity also reinforces the low probability of great power war, at least for the time being, but the eventual erosion of U.S. hegemony and the rise of new economic and military powers (China in particular) may create a source of great power crises and confrontations in the future.

Globalization, which increases economic interdependence and the economic benefits of the status quo, deters militarized conflict that might upset that status quo, and spreads a liberal ideology that reinforces the existing system, is an important but secondary factor reducing the likelihood of militarized conflict between the strongest states in the system. The same can be said for democracy, which independently reinforces peace between like-minded states. The declining utility of military force may increase the salience of economic competition among leading states in the system, but . . . this is unlikely to lead to wars between the advanced industrial states. Individual-level variables play a relatively minor role at the great power level, though decisions regarding "humanitarian intervention" by the United States are likely to be influenced by the belief systems of particular presidents and key advisers but constrained by public attitudes.

At the regional level, global distributions of power will continue to be important in structuring the permissive conditions for war, at least in those areas in which the leading global powers have significant stakes. U.S. interventions in the wars over Kuwait and Kosovo would have been nearly impossible under Cold War bipolarity and Soviet objections, and continuing U.S. hegemony reduces the likelihood of certain kinds of regional wars because of U.S. interests in stability. Likely aggressors lack a great power ally who can provide ample quantities of modern armaments and who can minimize the downside risks of war by using its influence to stop a war before the costs become too great. In addition, regional states are increasingly interested in reaping the benefits of globalization through close ties with the West, a goal that would be seriously undermined by the initiation of an aggressive war. Among regional states themselves, balancing against primary threats and adjusting to changing power differentials through alliances and armaments will continue to be central themes in international relations.

---

9. On trade-offs between the generalizability of parsimonious models and the descriptive accuracy of more contextualized models, see Jack Snyder, "Richness, Rigor, and Relevance in the Study of Soviet Foreign Policy," *International Security* 9, no. 3 (winter 1984-85): 89-108; and Jack S. Levy, "Explaining Events and Testing Theories: History, Political Science, and the Analysis of International Relations," in *Bridges and Boundaries: Historians, Political Scientists, and the Study of International Relations*, ed. Colin Elman and Miriam Fendius Elman (Cambridge, Mass.: MIT Press, 2000), 39-83.

10. On the pacifying effects of nuclear weapons, see John Lewis Gaddis, *The Long Peace* (New York: Oxford University Press, 1987); and Robert Jervis, *The Meaning of the Nuclear Revolution* (Ithaca, N.Y.: Cornell University Press, 1989).

The primary sources of interstate and internal conflicts in the Third World, however, are more likely to derive from internal rather than external variables. Systemic realist theories are too limited theoretically and too tied to the great power experience of the past to provide an adequate explanation of international conflict over the next several decades. The realist assumption that states have a hierarchy of goals and that external security needs dominate, while perhaps plausible for the great powers of the past, is more questionable in the contemporary Third World, which is characterized by constant resource shortages, threats to economic subsistence and social welfare, and political regimes of only tenuous legitimacy.

Third World political leaders not only give primacy to domestic interests over external security interests, but even conceive of security primarily in domestic terms, so that maintaining domestic political stability and their own positions of power often take precedence over all other interests.[11] Political leaders may prefer to achieve their goals by promoting economic development and perhaps democratization, but they have alternative strategies at their disposal. These include domestic repression, which sometimes increases the risks of civil war, and external scapegoating and predation.

Individual-level variables generally play a greater role in determining peace or war for regional and Third World states than for the great powers, at least for the period since World War II. The end of the Cold War, by destroying the relative simplicity of the bipolar order and increasing the complexity of world politics, has probably increased the importance of leaders' perceptions of their external environment and thereby increased the relative importance of individual-level variables. At the same time, the recent decline of authoritarian regimes has decreased somewhat the importance of the beliefs or psychology of any single decision maker by bringing more people into the decision-making process.

Much of this is speculation, of course. In the years leading up to 1914 many observers believed that war was impossible because its economic impact would be so devastating.[12] They were right about the premise but not about their hypothesized conclusion. In the 1980s few scholars predicted the end of the Cold War.[13] Forecasting the future in a more complex and chaotic world is an even more daunting task. But this makes it all the more important that our attempts to understand world politics be guided by well-developed theoretical frameworks that help to structure this complexity. I hope that this elaboration of the levels-of-analysis framework and survey of some of the leading theories of war has sensitized the reader to some of the critical factors influencing interstate and intrastate conflict and provided a framework for making sense of how they fit together.

I thank Lori Gronich and Carmela Lutmar for helpful comments on this paper.

11. Holsti, The State, War, and the State of War; Ayoob, chap. 9 in this volume; and Michael N. Barnett and Jack S. Levy, "Domestic Sources of Alliances and Alignments: The Case of Egypt, 1962-1973," International Organization 9, no. 3 (summer 1991): 369-395.

12. Norman Angell, The Great Illusion, 4th ed. (New York. G. P. Putnam's Sons, 1913).

13. John Gaddis, "International Relations Theory and the End of the Cold War," International Security 17, no. 3 (winter 1992-93): 5-58.

International Actors: States and Other Players on the World Stage

Bruce Russett & Harvey Starr

Russett and Starr systematically describe the different types of actors in the international system. They begin by discussing the differences between the nation, state, and nation-state and conclude by addressing nonstate actors in the contemporary system.

HUMANS IN GROUPS: NATIONALISM AND THE NATION

In discussing the nation-state, we start with the idea of a *nation,* a people who feel themselves part of some large identity group. The nation results from a complex and lengthy process by which *nationalism* develops. The development of the concept and reality of the state is similarly complex. Historically, as we shall see, state-building occurred in Europe over a period of several hundred years before 1648, when the Treaty of Westphalia was signed, ending the Thirty Years' War. Kings and princes extended their central authority over territories that had been a disconnected hodgepodge of feudal fiefdoms. Centralization and consolidation continued throughout Europe until World War I. Each group that identified itself as a people sought to govern and represent itself through the medium of the legal and sovereign entity known as the state—that is, people who identified themselves as a nation sought their own state. State-building could take the form of unification; for example, neither Italy nor Germany was finally united into a nation-state until the latter half of the nineteenth century, when war and diplomatic maneuver were used to forge single units out of many smaller states.

Other European nationalities sought to establish their own states by separating themselves from the larger empires that dominated much of Europe until World War I. These imperial entities included the Turkish Ottoman Empire, which had begun its spread westward into eastern and central Europe in the early 1300s and then retreated only slowly after its defeat before the gates of Vienna in 1683. The Austro-Hungarian Empire was the descendant of the Austrian Empire, and before that the Holy Roman Empire of the Hapsburgs. Under Charles V, Holy Roman Emperor from 1519 to 1558, the Hapsburg territories dominated the Continent. When his Hapsburg inheritances were combined with the areas under nominal control of the Empire, Charles's dominions included what is now Spain (and its New World possessions at that time), the Netherlands, Belgium, most of Italy, Austria, and the German states of central Europe (including areas that now form Czechoslovakia and parts of Poland). A third multiethnic, or multinational, grouping was the Russian Empire. Turkish rule in Europe was ended with the two Balkan wars of 1912-13. The process by which nations separated from larger entities to form their own states culminated in the aftermath of World War I, with the final dissolution of all three of the empires noted above, as well as of Imperial Germany.

The desire of national groups to separate from larger empires and form their own states was the dominant process reflecting nationalism until the end of World War II, although there remain nations that still do not have their own states. Nationalistic separatism has vigorously reemerged over the past decade or so as a crucial issue in world politics. The Kurds and the Palestinians, for example, and their quest for states, have important effects on world politics. Thus, we shall first discuss nationalism and the nation, then the concept of the state and the meaning of the "Westphalian state system."

It should be pointed out that this process may work in reverse. As we have seen in the post-World War II period, it is possible to have governments or states that exist without a nation. In the contemporary system, most such states exist in the Third World, especially in Africa, where states have been artificially created out of the Western colonial empires. Thus in states such as Nigeria or India, the process then becomes one of creating a nation—a *we-feeling*—to match the already existing state.

So far nationalism has been discussed primarily in terms of we-ness—a condition of mind, a feeling of identification or loyalty to some group of people. This is probably the crucial factor, that people *feel* themselves to be American or German or Canadian or Romanian or Cuban. What produces the we-feeling? A number of factors have been identified. One is regionalism, sharing a common territory. People living and interacting in the same area, facing similar problems and challenges, often develop a common feeling and identity. Closely related to regionalism is the effect of common economic activities, of relying on the same resources, engaging in the same types of activities, and having common sets of economic interactions. All these provide people with a similar view of the world and common interests.

A second set of factors is related to cultural similarity. A common language is an extremely important aspect of nationalism. Indeed, in attempting to increase national cohesion, political leaders have reinstituted languages that were dead or had been used only infrequently. The resurrection of the Welsh language by nationalists in Wales is at best only a partially successful attempt to use a language to reinforce or create nationalistic feelings, whereas the use of Hebrew in Israel has been quite successful in drawing together a diverse people. Other cultural factors include a common religion, a common culture, a common set of social rules, and a common ethnic background. Finally, and maybe most importantly, is the existence of a set of historical experiences and backgrounds perceived as a common history. John Stoessinger defines nationalism as "a people's sense of collective destiny through a common past and the vision of a common future."[1]

There is a psychological element that leads a people to desire the territorial and legal aspects of the state. Without this psychological element, any government would have difficulty in ruling a group of people occupying its territory. Many conflicts in contemporary international politics arise from threats (or perceived threats) to group identification and loyalty. Many would explain the Soviet reaction to American pressure in the early 1970s for increased Jewish emigration from the USSR as reaction to a perceived threat to the national identity of Soviet peoples. The critical reaction to Vietnam War resisters in the United States during that conflict stemmed largely from the psychological threat of challenging the solidarity of the national group and appearing disloyal. The swift and often vicious reaction of governments all around the world to regional, tribal, and other movements for autonomy is based on the fear of such disloyalty spreading to other parts of their populations. Even the reform and promise of Gorbachev's perestroika and glasnost were temporarily curtailed when Gorbachev was faced with the growing desire for independence in parts of the Soviet Union, particularly the Baltic republics.

---

1. John Stoessinger, *The Might of Nations* (New York: Random House, 1979), p. 10.

States have fought intense civil wars over unity or separation. The Ibo rebellion and the attempt to establish Biafra was defeated by the Nigerian government in a war that lasted from May 1967 to January 1970. In contrast, the Bengali secession from Pakistan was successful. The Bengali population of East Pakistan rose in riots and maintained a general strike in March 1971 after being denied victory at the polls. Though sharing a common religion, East and West Pakistan differed in ethnicity, language, and economic factors and were separated by approximately 1,000 miles of Indian territory. West Pakistani armed attacks on the East Pakistanis led to the December 1971 war between India and Pakistan. The Indian victory permitted the Bengalis to declare their own independent state, Bangladesh. India, a large and diverse country, has itself been wracked by conflict among different linguistic, regional, racial, and religious groups. Violence involving the Sikh religious minority in the Punjab was responsible for the assassination of Prime Minister Indira Gandhi in 1984 and for increasing separatist violence into the 1990s. The early 1990s also saw the intensification of a Muslim drive for an independent Kashmir and insurgent separatism in the northeast state of Assam. Such communal conflict was intensified by a revival of Hindu fundamentalism, itself a reaction to the long series of challenges to the Hindu domination of India.

Fears of a breakdown in nationalism, however, are not confined to the less developed states or only to those states formed since World War II. Loyalty is based on group interaction. If some part of a group feels it is being exploited or not treated fairly, or that there *no longer exists mutual benefit* from association with the larger group, the loyalty and we-feeling will disintegrate. The *process* of national integration is a continuous one and, unless tended to, is always susceptible to disintegration. So, while many new Third World countries must worry about diverse ethnic groups that lack strong feelings of national unity, even the older states of Europe must continually work to make ethnic minorities *feel* a nationalist connection to the nation-state as a whole. There are more or less well organized nationalist movements among the Bretons and Corsicans who are governed by France, the Basques in Spain, and the Welsh and Scots in Britain. The continuing struggles in the [former] Soviet Union and [former] Yugoslavia to deal with the forces of nationalist separatism are the strongest examples of divisive nationalism. In Canada, French-speakers in the province of Quebec have a long tradition of separatist politics. Canada's handling of this problem is a good example of how an established and developed state risks being broken apart, and of the dilemmas that a democracy faces in such a situation. Attempts at nation-building included the institutionalization of bilingualism, special constitutional arrangements, and the creation of specifically Canadian images for the national flag and national anthem (the previous flag incorporated the British Union Jack and the anthem had been "God Save the Queen"). That political crises continue to occur in Canada over the proper constitutional arrangements required to deal with the separatist movement in Quebec and yet satisfy the Western provinces indicates the difficulties of building and maintaining a state. . . .

One problem in discussing nationalism is that no single factor seems sufficient by itself to create and maintain the psychological element of we-ness and the individual's supreme loyalty to the national group. Although language is important, several viable nation-states exist with multiple languages. Switzerland has four (French, German, Italian, and Romansch), and India has 14 major language groups and over 1,600 regional languages (in addition to English). Germany, Nigeria, and the United States have several major religions. Other nations have many regional differences, cultures, and ethnicities.

Perhaps the closest to a sufficient condition for a we-feeling is the existence of a common history, though it is not always clear why some experiences are perceived as shared by all and others as limited to a subgroup. The sharing of common historical experiences, particularly the anticolonial experience, receives great emphasis in many of the new states that have gained independence since World War II. In the post-World War II system, states with no logic beyond the arbitrary lines drawn on maps by colonial powers are split by diverse tribal, religious, ethnic, and racial groups and are struggling to forge group loyalty from this diversity. Data from 1986 on 166 countries show only a third of these states to be ethnically homogeneous (one group constituting at least 90 percent of the population). In almost half the countries the largest ethnic group accounted for less than 75 percent of the population, and in a quarter of them, less than 50 percent. Over a third of the countries had major religious cleavages as well. One study notes, "Most of the 168 states in the modern world are mosaics of distinct peoples whose identities and aspirations may or may not be accepted and protected by those who hold state power." While noting one estimate by a geographer that perhaps as many as 5,000 distinct communities (communal minorities, or "ethnies") exist with a claim to being a national people, this study by political scientists identifies over 260 nonsovereign peoples who could qualify as nations. They note that 50 communal groups in the Third World had active separatist or autonomy movements during the 1980s, and they identify 22 separatist rebellions around the globe during that decade.[2]

Nationalism is about loyalty to a group, and the current system is witnessing a growth of loyalties to groups other than the state. These other loyalties are based on communal ties of various kinds. The rise of religious fundamentalism is one example of the forces of fragmentation that face the nation-state today. For example, an individual may feel first a Shiite, then a Moslem, and then an Iraqi, in a loyalty chain that finds the state last on the list. One observer sees fragmentation as a major force in world politics, which will increase the number of independent actors and shrink the size of many existing states.[3] An example: Having expanded from a small area around Kiev in the ninth century, "Russia" became first the Russian Empire and then expanded further into the USSR; will it now again be Russia, and, if so, a Russia of what size?

THE STATE AS INTERNATIONAL ACTOR

Despite a number of trends to the contrary, the state (or the nation-state) has been and remains the primary actor in the global system. The number of states in the system has risen steadily since the end of World War II. One indicator is the growth in the membership of the United Nations: in 1945 there were 51 charter members of the UN; in 1991 the admission of seven states increased the membership to 166. The addition of 115 new members exemplifies the continuing desire of groups to achieve statehood in the contemporary system. [As of November 1993, there were 182 members of the United Nations].

---

2. The first set of figures was assembled from John Clements, *Clements' Encyclopedia of World Governments*, vol. 7 (Dallas: Political Research, Inc., 1986); the second set of findings was reported by Ted Robert Gurr and James R. Scarritt, "Minorities at Risk: A Global Survey," *Human Rights Quarterly* 11 *(1989), 375-405.* See also Gurr, "Ethnic Warfare and the Changing Priorities of Global Security," *Mediterranean Quarterly I* (1990),82-98, for a fuller discussion of the impact of communal separatism on world conflict.

3. See James N. Rosenau, *Turbulence in World Politics* (Princeton, N.J).: Princeton University Press, 1990).

The Development of the Westphalian State System

There have been large-scale political organizations for 7,000 years, starting with the city-states and empires of the Tigris and Euphrates and the Nile. But the state or nation-state in its present form is relatively new. While many scholars date the modern nation-state from 1648 and the Treaty of Westphalia, the state as it existed in the seventeenth century was the result of a convergence of processes that had been occurring for over 500 years before Westphalia. The 200 years from about 1450 to 1650 mark the transition from one historical epoch to another, when the combination and interaction of political, economic, technological, and religious factors were decisive in bringing about the shift to the modern Westphalian state system.[4]

For hundreds of years before this transition period, Europe consisted of a complex system of feudal entities. With the disintegration of the Roman Empire during the fifth century, the Germanic tribes that overran Roman settlements in western Europe remained organized on only the most local level, cutting their political or economic ties to the Mediterranean region. The Frankish empire of Charlemagne, established in 800, began to create the outlines of what we know now as Europe, but it too was overrun by barbarians from the east. However, after the fall of Rome the Church maintained a presence and spiritual authority across Europe, and both waves of invaders were assimilated into Christianity. By 1000 a system composed of large numbers of local political entities was in place, based on the feudal relationships between lord and vassal, an agricultural economy, and lack of trade with other parts of the world.

The leaders of these various feudal entities, and their subjects, were enmeshed in a web of multiple loyalties. The various levels and ranks of nobility were both vassals and lords, receiving fealty (loyalty or obedience) from those below them and giving fealty to those above them. In principle such loyalty culminated in two figures: the Holy Roman Emperor, in regard to secular authority and leadership, and the Pope, in regard to spiritual authority and leadership. In stark distinction from the sovereign state that was to develop, no ruler (or people under him) had a monopoly of political authority over any territory.

European history before the rise of states reflected the politics and interactions of cultures, religion, and individual nobles or princes more than of states. As noted, a convergence of political, economic, technological, and religious factors helped to create the state, replacing personal and societal bonds with international relations. All the factors were related in complex feedback loops; that is, each affected every other and was in turn affected by the results of earlier processes.[5] Scholars studying the rise of the Western national state focus on two central elements: capital and coercion. As monarchs attempted to expand, centralize, and consolidate their control over territory and people in their struggles against the feudal nobility, they needed wealth and resources (capital) and the means

---

4. See Geoffrey Barraclough, *An Introduction to Contemporary History* (New York: Penguin, 1964), for an introduction to these ideas of transition and interaction. Barraclough also reminds us to look for the differences and discontinuities in history.

5. This discussion draws upon Hedley Bull, *The Anarchical Society* (London: Macmillan, 1977); Charles Tilly, "Reflections on the History of European State-Making," in Tilly, ed., *The Formation of National States in Western Europe* (Princeton, N.J.: Princeton University Press, 1975), pp. 3-83; William H. McNeill, *The Pursuit of Power* (Chicago: University of Chicago Press, 1982); Hedley Bull and Adam Watson, eds., *The Expansion of International Society* (Oxford: Clarendon Press, 1984); Tilly, *Coercion, Capital and European States, A.D. 990-1990* (Oxford: Basil Blackwell, 1990); and Michael Mann, *States, War, and Capitalism* (Oxford: Basil Blackwell, 1988).

to prosecute war (coercion). These factors provided the opportunities that enabled kings to engage in this process and ultimately to succeed against the nobles.

One key factor was economic: the growth of towns and cities, which starting around A.D. 1000 became centers of trade, manufacturing, and communication. The processes involved in the creation of cities created *wealth.* These included the development of a money economy (to replace the localized barter system that characterized feudalism) and a commercial class—the incipient bourgeoisie, or capitalists. Each town or city came to represent a larger regional economy, including surrounding areas of agriculture and trade with those areas. Commercial interests desired continued growth and expansion, including greater trade with the agricultural areas and other towns and cities. This expansion required security and order: an authority to provide for roads and communication and a centralized bureaucracy to reduce barriers to economic expansion.

At the same time new political and technological developments concerned with coercion helped rulers to create larger, more centralized entities. Kings challenged the theoretical authority of the Holy Roman Emperor and the real military power of the nobles. To engage in such conflict the kings needed to extract ever more resources—men, arms, and particularly *money.* They thus needed to draw resources from the towns and the commercial class and form political coalitions with them. Technological factors were also crucial; military technology, especially gunpowder and cannon, made it possible for an entity with enough wealth to overcome the castle strongholds of knights and other nobility.

The kings thus required the economic surplus being produced in Europe by the commercial class in order to gain control of the technology and weapons needed to centralize large areas of territory over the opposition of the nobles. Economic surplus was also needed to help create the bureaucracy essential for collecting taxes and to raise and administer armies. And, as victory brought more territory under control, that territory in turn needed to be administered. As Charles Tilly notes, "In one way or another, conquest entailed administration." Thus, there was an important interaction between commerce and bureaucracy. And although they might have taxes imposed upon them by kings, the commercial classes of the cities saw the growing (and potential) power of kings as necessary for the conditions of security and order needed for continued commercial expansion. In an excellent analysis contrasting the experiences of Europe during this period and those of China in earlier times, William Hardy McNeill demonstrates how China lost the advantages of its earlier developments in technology and organization. The Chinese bureaucracy opposed the interactions of commerce and industry with political centralization and with the military applications of technology; these interactions were supported in Europe and eventually transformed it.[6]

Thus, one way to begin to define the state is to see it, as does Tilly, as an entity that expanded to control and govern multiple contiguous regions and their cities. It was the result of activities related to coercion and to the control of goods and services. Coercion included war, to defeat external rivals, and statemaking, to defeat internal rivals—the two elements of sovereignty, discussed below.

The interrelationships among commerce, kings, and bureaucracy in Europe promoted the rapid development and use of the military technology that also made possible European expansion to the rest of the globe. In fact, Paul Kennedy attributes the "European miracle,"

---

6. McNeill, *Pursuit of Power,* chap.3. Such comparative analyses are important in order to follow Barraclough's advice to move beyond a simple Eurocentric view of history.

or the rise of Europe rather than areas seemingly more advanced, to the interaction of all these factors. The continual wars and rivalries between kings and nobles, and then among kings, pushed each to find some advantage in arms or wealth and led to rapid technological and scientific innovations (in areas such as weaponry, transportation, navigation, and cartography), as well as innovations in commerce, finance, administration, and bureaucratic structure. The upward spiral occurred not only in arms, wealth, and power, but also and perhaps more importantly in scientific knowledge. All these factors promoted a European expansion that in turn provided another source of wealth for the European states. Tilly has stressed a key relationship: states are war-makers and wars are state-makers.[7]

Sovereignty and the Nature of the State

A final element that created the opportunity for the rise of the state system was religion, which connected all these interrelated elements. Along with the kings' challenge to secular authority, there came, in 1517, Martin Luther's challenge to the spiritual authority of the Pope and the Church of Rome. Luther's challenge was taken up by a number of German princes; Lutheranism spread across much of central Europe and resulted in a series of increasingly destructive religious wars among the newly forming states and lesser principalities. These wars dominated the history of the sixteenth century and the early seventeenth, culminating in the Thirty Years' War, which ended with the Treaty of Westphalia in 1648. They were the last factor in the creation of the sovereign state.

The central principle of the Treaty of Westphalia was apparently simple: the ruler of a territory would determine the religion of that territory. This principle had been articulated as early as the Peace of Augsburg in 1555. Despite its simplicity, this principle had enormous consequences: the major internal issue of the day—religion—was to be determined by the ruler, *not* by an external authority, whether the Holy Roman Emperor or the Pope. No longer was there even the pretense of religious or political unity in Europe. Authority was dispersed to the various kings and princes, and the basis for the sovereign state was established. On each territory there were no longer multiple loyalties and authorities; there was only one: loyalty to the authority of the king or prince. The territory and the people on that territory belonged to the ruler, who did not have to answer to an external authority. Thus the Westphalian state system distinguished itself not only from the feudal principle, but also from the basic imperial or hegemonic principle of the suzerainty of a higher authority that existed elsewhere at that time—in India, China, the Arab Islamic world, and the Mongol-Tatar system.

The key elements of the modern nation-state were now all available: a people, a territory on which they lived, a government with the authority to rule over the people and territory. But this government was also seen as the agent of the *state,* which was a *legal* entity having the special status of *sovereignty.* The very term "state," which arose in the sixteenth century, derived from the Latin *status,* which meant the "position" or "standing" of a ruler.

We can now begin to answer the question of why the state was and is the main international actor. The myth of separate secular and spiritual entities disappeared, and the authority that had been vested in both was assumed exclusively by the state. Consequently, the international norms and laws that developed provided the state with a status enjoyed by no other actor. Perhaps the operative word here is *law.* The state is a legal entity; it has been invested with a legal status and a legal equality with all other states that have been

---

7. Paul Kennedy, *The Rise and Fall of the Great Powers* (New York: Random House, 1987), chap. 1; Tilly, *Coercion, Capital and European States,* chap. 1.

denied other actors on the international or global scene. Like a corporation, the state has no concrete existence; it is a legal abstraction. Through its government and the representatives of that government, the state undertakes legal commitments, both rights and responsibilities: signing treaties, joining organizations, and the like. We should understand, then, that sovereignty can thus act to constrain states as well as give them special status (in Rosenau's terms they are "sovereignty-bound" and in some situations they may have less freedom of action than some "sovereignty-free" nonstate actors).

Sovereignty should be seen as indicating a special, theoretical relationship between each state and all other states. Hedley Bull noted that sovereignty includes "internal sovereignty, which means supremacy over all other authorities within that territory and population," and "external sovereignty, by which is meant not supremacy but independence of outside authorities. The sovereignty of states, both internal and external, may be said to exist both at a normative level and at a factual level."[8] Thus sovereignty has an ideal meaning that in principle gives states an equal legal status. That meaning is that a state has complete control over the people and territory represented by its government. Ideally, it also means that there is external autonomy: *no authority exists to order the state how to act; there is no actor with the legitimate authority to tell a state what to do.* Note that this is the essence of the "anarchic" international system.

In principle, this means there is a monopoly over the control of the means of force within the state. No other authority has a right to exercise force or maintain order within the territory of the state. Similarly, through international law, the state has been given a legal monopoly on the use of force in the global arena. Piracy and nonstate terrorism are considered illegal because they entail the use of force and violence by actors other than a state. When implemented by a state, force can be pinpointed, responsibility can be assigned, and other rules of conduct can be invoked. For example, until the creation of the League of Nations, international law was concerned with how states behaved during a special legal condition called war. This condition could exist only between two equal units—equal in the legal sense of being sovereign states. Once this condition existed, belligerents were designated by a declaration of war and neutrals by declarations of their neutrality. Each category had rights and responsibilities of behavior to other states, according to the status they had declared. The various structures of international law were rarely seen to apply to peoples who were outside the system of states, such as aboriginal populations and non-European areas, which were to be conquered, colonized, and dominated by the European nation-states.

In addition to its special legal status, the state has another important characteristic basic to its dominance of the international system territory. The government of the state represents a group of people who inhabit a piece of territory. Commentators who argue that the state is no longer dominant in the world system must confront the fact that every person lives on territory controlled (at least nominally) by a state. No other form of international actor controls territory. Governments consider territory to be of overriding importance, and the stakes involved in the loss of territory are intimately related to the onset of war.[9]

In his discussion of the territorial state, political scientist John Herz noted: "Throughout history that unit which affords protection and security to human beings has tended to

---

8. Bull, *Anarchical Society,* p. 8.

9. See Gary Goertz and Paul F. Diehl, "Territorial Changes and Recurring Conflict," in Charles S. Gochman and Alan Ned Sabrosky, eds., *Prisoners of War? Nation-States in the Modern Era* (Lexington, Mass.: D. C. Heath, 1990), pp. 57-72.

become the basic political unit."[10] This proposition can be applied to the feudal knight and the protection his castle provided to his villagers. This changed with the advent of gunpowder and the larger military forces developed by kings. The basis of the state, argued Herz, was its ability to protect people through its size—its physical territory, which created a "hard shell" around the population in an era of gunpowder and the professional armies of centralized monarchs. Although nuclear weapons and modem delivery systems make the hard shell of the state obsolete, the territoriality of the state still protects the citizens of most states from most conflicts with other states.

As we have seen, a key element of world politics is that different states or nations may not coincide *on the same territory.* The separate nationalisms of different ethnic groups may threaten to tear a state apart, as in the case of Nigeria during its civil war. Different national identities within a state may tempt another state to intervene on behalf of a minority. States may therefore suppress minority rights (Bulgaria long prohibited public use of the Turkish language by its Turkish minority); they may force minorities to emigrate (as Vietnam forced the ethnic Chinese boat people to flee) or may even kill them (as Nazi Germany systematically killed Jews). Sometimes a feeling of nationality may spill over many states, calling into question the legitimacy of separate states (as in the case of pan-Arab nationalism, or Pan-Arabism). Often people feel multiple loyalties to units both smaller and larger than their states (for example, a Scot's to Scotland, the United Kingdom, and the European Community).

While the question of the exact meaning of the state is complex and subject to debate, we can summarize the core of the concept of the nation-state as developed here: the state is a legal abstraction with institutions (the government) to control a territorial area and the people who reside in that territory.[11] In the fully integrated nation-state this control is aided by and dependent on the cement that holds the people together and gives them a loyalty to that government and state: nationalism. The state's growing control over its people and territory, its freedom from having to answer to any higher external authority, culminated in the development of the concept of sovereignty.

All of these features, but especially sovereignty and territoriality, provide the state with major advantages over nonstate actors in the global arena. The European version of the state expanded throughout the world because it had first won out in the European competition. To survive in Europe, a country needed large amounts of capital, large populations, and significant military forces. European states controlled about 7 percent of the world's territory in 1500, and by 1914 they controlled 84 percent. Tilly summarizes our arguments:

> Because of their advantages in translating national resources into success in international war, large national states superseded tribute-taking empires, federations, city-states, and all their other competitors as the predominant European entities, and as the models for state formation. Those states finally defined the character of the European state system and spearheaded its extension to the entire world.[12]

---

10. See John Herz, "Rise and Demise of the Territorial State," *World Politics 9* (1957), 473-493, as well as Herz's rethinking of the subject, "The Territorial State Revisited—Reflections on the Future of the Nation-State," *Polity* 1 (1968), 11-34.

11. For a review of the debate on the meaning of the state and sovereignty, see Yale H. Ferguson and Richard W. Mansbach, *The State, Conceptual Chaos, and the Future of International Relations Theory* (Boulder, Colo.: Lynne Rienner Publishers, 1989) and Alan James, *Sovereign Statehood* (London: Allen & Unwin, 1986).

The Security Dilemma

The system of sovereign states has other consequences for state behavior that will become clear when we discuss such topics as the world system, power and influence, deterrence and arms control, and a number of global economic and environmental problems. Sovereignty means that states exist in a formally anarchic environment. No legitimate or legal authority is empowered to control, direct, or watch over the behavior of sovereign states (as, for example, the federal government of the United States does over the 50 states of the Union). One consequence of such a system of sovereign states is that each state must in the end look out for its own security, protection, and survival. Remembering that the state in its present form was forged during continual military competition within Europe, we can better understand the origins of a realist perspective.

If there is no legitimate, legal authority to enforce order and punish rule-breakers, then there is no legal or formal recourse if allies or friends fail to assist a state—you cannot sue them to fulfill their alliance contracts! Thus, self-help in the international system means that each state must take measures to provide for its own defense. A tragic flaw of the formally anarchic state system is that the requirement for self-help often leads to the "security dilemma:" the secure environments of the various states may be mutually exclusive. The initial discussion of this phenomenon was presented by Herz:

> Wherever such anarchic society has existed—and it has existed in most periods of known history on some level—there has arisen what may be called the "security dilemma" of men, or groups, or their leaders. Groups or individuals living in such a constellation must be, and usually are, concerned about their security from being attacked, subjected, dominated or annihilated by other groups and individuals. Striving to attain security from such attack, they are driven to acquire more and more power in order to escape the power of others. This, in turn, renders the others more insecure and compels them to prepare for the worst. Since none can ever feel entirely secure in such a world of competing units, power competition ensues, and the vicious circle of security and power accumulation is on.[13]

Thus, one state's security may be seen and defined as another state's *insecurity*. The means by which one state prepares to defend its territory and people may be threatening to others—and is thus perceived as offensive, rather than defensive, behavior (what does Israeli activity look like to the Arab countries?). States may never feel secure, because they never know how much is "enough" for their security. This is particularly so when their own efforts at security spur on the efforts of others.

The formally anarchic system of sovereign states promotes a realist vision of struggle in world politics, through the security dilemma and the concomitant stress on threat, military power, and self-help. The need for military power, and for constant alertness as to its accumulation and use by others, stems directly from the structure of a system of sovereign states (and the realist assumption that human nature is flawed, sinful, and power seeking). The security dilemma is central to many other aspects of interstate relations and will reappear in several different forms later on; for example, in the discussion of deterrence. How states

---

12. Tilly, *Coercion, Capital and European States*, pp. 188; 160.

13. John Herz, "Idealist Internationalism and the Security Dilemma," *World Politics* 2 (1950), 157. See also Robert Jervis, "Cooperation Under the Security Dilemma," *World Politics* 30 (1978), 167-214; and Oran Young, "Anarchy and Social Choice: Reflections on the International Polity," *World Politics* 30 (1978), 241-263.

cope with this condition and create some degree of order out of anarchy will also be addressed throughout this book.

ALL STATES ARE LEGALLY EQUAL (BUT SOME ARE MORE EQUAL THAN OTHERS)

By the principles of sovereignty and international law all states are juridically equal. But one of the truisms in world politics is that nothing is distributed equally on the face of the globe—not people or their talents, not resources, not climate or geographic features, not technology, not air quality. In fact, many things are distributed in a highly unequal manner. Nation-states are so different from each other in resources, capabilities, available menus, and their ability to exploit and choose from those menus that some observers find it difficult to call all of these units states. Later we shall discuss in detail the concepts of power and influence, the whole range of state capabilities, and the ways in which states attempt to exert their power and influence on others. But here we may simply point out that states range widely in size, from [former states of] the Soviet Union, with over 8.6 million square miles (or 17 percent of the total global land area), to Nauru, with its 8 square miles; the smallest member of the United Nations is St. Kitts-Nevis at 101 square miles. Similarly, the People's Republic of China had a 1990 population of well over 1 *billion* people, whereas in that year microstates like Nauru and Tuvalu had populations of between 8,600 and 9,000; St. Kitts-Nevis, the smallest in the UN in population as well as size, had about 40,000 people.

Sovereignty carries with it only the *principle* of independence from outside authority; it does not ensure equality in capabilities or independence from the outside interference of others. No official authority controls states in the contemporary world system, but many are subject to powerful unofficial forces, pressures, and influences that penetrate the supposed hard shell of the state.

As international law has evolved through the years, and as a corollary of self-help, sovereignty has come to imply that the government of a state has the capacity and ability to carry out the responsibilities of a sovereign state. That is, internally, the government can impose order on its own territory and maintain the government's monopoly over the use of force. Externally, the state can defend its rights under sovereignty and carry out its responsibilities (for example, enforcing its neutrality during a war in which it is not a belligerent). All states are formally sovereign; they have achieved independent state status. Most have sought UN membership as a ticket into world society; even the smallest units have resisted pressures to continue as clients, colonies, or satellites of a larger state. As students of the international arena, we are faced with the continued resurgence of nationalism and the nation-state in a world where the hard shell is eroding for many states and can hardly be seen to exist for the smaller members.

The question of the relationship between small and large states has been perennial. Although there are any number of ways to divide states, to categorize and classify them, one division has always existed and been used in the interactions between states: a status hierarchy of size and power. We may always find large and small units, the strong and the weak, the influential and the ineffectual. The largest states of today are *proportionately* neither larger nor smaller than they were 2,000 years ago.[14] Like the debates at the Constitutional Convention in Philadelphia over the representation of states in the U.S.

---

[14] Bruce Russett, *Power and Community in World Politics* (New York: W. H. Freeman and Company, 1974), chap. 7.

Congress, the major conflicts in setting up the United Nations were over size: "The basic argument in 1944-45 was not between the Russians and the Western Allies, although there were crises in that field too. It was between the big powers and the rest. "The small countries "contested very strongly any departure from the principle of one country one vote."[15]

Yet analysts have divided countries into many different categories. For years we simply had the first world (the industrialized Western democracies), the second world (the Communist bloc of Eastern Europe), and the third world (everyone else). People also came to talk of the fourth and fifth worlds, labels based on levels of gross national product (GNP) per capita and the oil-producing capacities of states formerly classified as Third World members. Currently the World Bank uses three categories of country groups, based on economic development: low income economies (developing countries with a 1989 GNP per capita of $580 or less), middle-income economies (countries with a 1989 GNP per capita over $580 but less than $6,000), and high-income economies (with GNP per capita over $6,000). Three analytical groups of countries are also used in the World Bank analyses: "oil exporters," 10 countries whose energy exports account for at least half their GNP (the USSR is not among them); "severely indebted middle income countries," 20 countries with severe debt-servicing problems (including Argentina, Brazil, Chile, Mexico, Egypt, Morocco, the Philippines, and Poland); "OECD members," the 24 developed industrial states of the Organization for Economic Cooperation and Development, known as "the rich man's club." Some of the characteristics of these groups are presented in Table 1.

Table 1. World Bank's Categories of States

Countries	1989 population (millions)	Average annual growth in GNP per capita, 1980–1989 (percent)	1989 GNP per capita (dollars)
Low-income	2,948	4.1	330
Middle-income	1,105	0.5	2,040
High-income	831	2.3	18,330
Severely indebted middle-income	554	−0.3	1,720
OECD members	773	2.4	19,090
Oil exporters	553	−2.5	NA

Source: World Bank, *World Development Report 1991* (New York: Oxford University Press, 1991).

15. Paul Gore-Booth, *With Great Truth and Respect* (London: Constable, 1974), pp. 133-134.

NONSTATE ACTORS IN THE CONTEMPORARY SYSTEM

A variety of other, nonstate, actors are increasingly involved in the crucial issues of world politics. These intergovernmental and nongovernmental (or transnational) actors form an important part of the global environment. We noted earlier that the simplest division of levels of analysis is between the world system and the state: influences on foreign policy that originate outside the state and influences that originate within the state. Nonstate or transnational actors are considered here to be at the world-system level of analysis, because they are part of the external environment of states and thus affect the possibilities and probabilities of state actions.

In viewing world politics, the global system can be seen as a chessboard and the actors as the pieces that move about on it. Or, as did Shakespeare, we can consider the world as a stage; those groups, organizations, and individuals who interact on it are the actors. This is a useful image for several reasons. First, the word actor conveys a broad spectrum of interacting entities; it is large enough to encompass all the entities we wish to study. Second, our emphasis is on behavior, and the word helps convey the idea of an entity that is behaving or performing an action. In relation to nonstate actors, the term also helps to convey the idea that different actors have different roles, that some occupy center stage and are stars while others are bit players in the chorus. Yet they all interact in creating the finished production.

While a whole variety of nonstate actors exist in the interdependent global system (as part of what James Rosenau calls the "multi-centric" system existing outside state relations), the state is still the dominant international actor on most issues. Thus, an entity may be seen as an international actor if it is taken into account in the calculations and strategies of the leaders of states, and if its continuing functions have an impact on other actors on the world stage.

Any organized unit that commands the identification, interests, and loyalty of individuals and that affects interstate relations becomes a major competitor of nation-states. As we survey the types of nonstate actors, think of the various recent conflicts between international organizations and states: between the United Nations and South Africa; between OPEC and the industrialized West; between nonstate groups like the Palestine Liberation Organization (PLO) and Israel, or the Irish Republican Army (IRA) and the United Kingdom; or between a multinational corporation and a state, as in the case of the toxic gas accident at Union Carbide's plant in Bhopal, India. In almost every case the conflict arises when the nonstate actor challenges or tries to reduce the scope of the sovereignty of a nation-state in terms of territory, population, or control over its internal or external politics. The dramatic rise in international terrorism by a wide variety of nonstate groups is another example of this competition groups other than states employ force and violence in the global system, directly challenging the monopoly of force that international law has always granted to states.

Intergovernmental Organizations

Other international actors in the contemporary global system include *international organizations* or *intergovernmental organizations* (IGOs). This label stresses the fact that such organizations—for example, the United Nations—are composed of states, and that the individuals who are sent as representatives to such organizations represent the interests and policies of their own states. Quite often these organizations have permanent staffs at a permanent home base, so there are also individuals whose primary loyalty is to the IGO and not to their state of origin. Thus, the Secretariat of the United Nations is an international civil service of individuals who put the organization ahead of their states. This structure may cause an atmosphere of competition between the IGO and the state over the loyalty of individuals. The case of Arkady Shevchenko is illustrative. In April,1978, Shevchenko, the under secretary-general for political and Security Council affairs (a post traditionally filled by a Soviet citizen), resigned from the United Nations and chose to stay in the United States because of "serious differences of political philosophy and conviction with the present Soviet system." At one point he refused instructions to return to Moscow on the grounds that the Soviet government had "no right to give such instructions to an official of the [UN] Secretariat."

IGOs may be usefully categorized according to the scope of their memberships and the scope of their purposes. On the one hand, we have universal political organizations such as the old League of Nations and the United Nations, which aim to include as wide an international membership as possible. Such organizations are also general purpose in that they perform political, economic, developmental, military, sociocultural, and other functions for member states. Other general-purpose organizations have more limited memberships: the North Atlantic Treaty Organization, (NATO), the Organization of American States (OAS), the Organization of African Unity (OAU), and several others. The Commonwealth is not regional—its membership is not grouped in any one geographical area—but it is limited to countries with former colonial ties to the British Empire. These organizations too perform a variety of functions.

A significantly greater number of organizations, called *functional IGOs* or *limited-purpose IGOs,* perform more specific functions. The number of these more than tripled from 1945 to 1986, and their growth is shown graphically in Figure 1. Many of these IGOs are affiliated with the UN or are related to the European Community. Those connected to the UN often have or aim for universal membership. Many more have limited regional membership. Some—the Arab League, NATO, and the Warsaw Pact—stressed military functions in their early days. Others are concerned primarily with economic matters; among them are the various organs of the European Community and organizations like the Central American Common Market and the Association of Southeast Asian Nations (ASEAN). Still others provide various social services—for example, the World Health Organization (WHO) or the International Labor Organization (ILO)—and others, like the IMF and the World Bank, are involved in monetary matters and economic development. The list becomes almost endless if we include groups with even more specific functional activities: the International Statistical Institute, the International Bureau of Weights and Measures, the International Wool Study Group, or the Desert Locust Control Organization for East Africa.

Without going into great detail on the workings of the individual IGOs, let us review them as international actors.[16] First, they have a significant and continuing impact on interstate relations. The international role of many IGOs is clearly institutionalized in that states expect them to act in certain areas. They expect the UN, say, to act in areas of conflict, as it did in 1988 to bring a halt to the fighting between Iran and Iraq, and in 1990 to come to the aid of Kuwait after the Iraqi invasion. Regionally, both the European Community and the Conference on Security and Cooperation in Europe (CSCE) attempted to resolve the violence in Yugoslavia in1991. When a state finds itself in serious economic

---

16. See Harold K. Jacobson, William M. Reisinger, and Todd Mathers, "National Entanglements in International Governmental Organizations," *American Political Science Review* 80, 1(March 1986), pp.141-159.

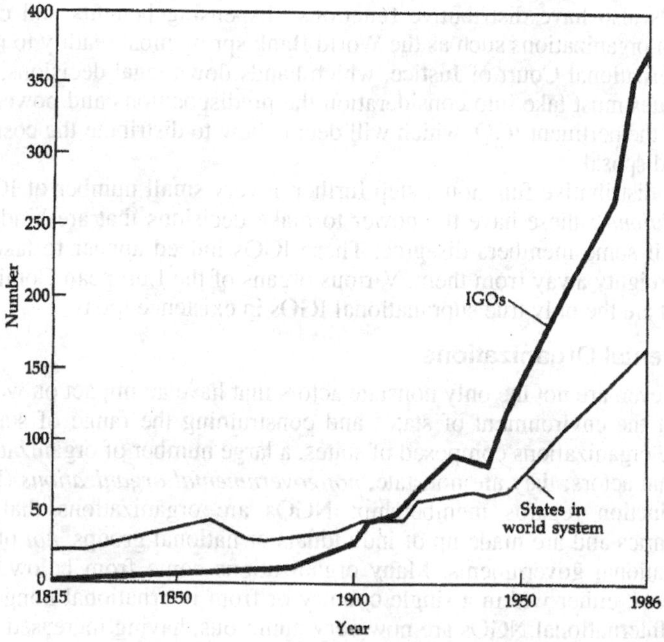

Figure 1. Growth in IGOs and States in the World System, 1815-1986.

Source: Adapted from Michael Wallace and J. D. Singer, "Intergovernmental Organization in the Global System, 1816-1964: A Quantitative Description," *International Organization* 24, 2 (Spring 1970), and Union of International Associations, *Yearbook of International Organizations,* 1986/87 (Brussels: U.I.A., 1987).

trouble, it almost automatically looks to the World Bank or the IMF for various kinds of aid. Third World states increasingly find that association with IGOs will help their economic performance. In addition, IGOs are actors in the sense that they continually affect the foreign policy behavior of their members, to the extent that member states join the organization and value the continuation of membership. Merely sending representatives to an organization, employing resources to maintain IGOs, or interacting with others through IGOs has an impact on the state. Perhaps most importantly, the IGOs may be considered actors because states and leaders *believe* that IGOs are behaving as international actors and must be taken into account in foreign policy deliberations.

IGOs have this effect in several ways. Most clearly seen in workings of the United Nations, but common to many other IGOs, is the function of acting as a forum for the member states to meet and communicate. The IGO may act passively, serving only as a line of communication or a meeting place, or actively, as a mediator. IGOs perform a number of regulative functions across such areas as economics, health, communication, and transportation; examples range from the African Postal Union to the International Atomic Energy Agency. Here IGOs, with the consent of member states, regulate how members should interact to function smoothly, efficiently, and beneficially in an area of concern. This management or coordination function is essential to the orderly functioning of day-to-day global relations.

Some IGOs also have distributive functions, dispensing benefits and costs among states. Although organizations such as the World Bank spring most readily to mind, others such as the International Court of Justice, which hands down legal decisions, are equally distributive. States must take into consideration the predispositions and power of the permanent staff of the pertinent IGO, which will decide how to distribute the costs and benefits it has at its disposal.

Taking the distributive function a step further, a very small number of IGOs may be termed *supranational;* these have the power to make decisions that are binding on their members even if some members disagree. These IGOs indeed appear to take aspects of members' sovereignty away from them. Various organs of the European Community have such power and are the only true supranational IGOs in existence today.

Nongovernmental Organizations

IGOs, however, are not the only nonstate actors that have an impact on world politics, forming part of the environment of states and constraining the range of state behavior. While IGOs are organizations composed of states, a large number of organizations are private international actors; they are nonstate, *nongovernmental organizations* (NGOs). The important distinction regards membership: NGOs are organizations that cut across national boundaries and are made up of individuals or national groups, *not* official representatives of national governments. Many organizations come from below the level of state governments, either within a single country or from international nongovernmental organizations. International NGOs are now very numerous, having increased from 134 in 1905 to 2,470 in 1972 to around 4,700 by 1986.[17] Like the IGOs, they deal with a great variety of matters. There are religious bodies, professional organizations, sports organizations, trade union groups, and political parties. Their membership may be composed either directly of individuals (the International Political Science Association) or of various national societies that themselves are composed of individuals (as the International Red Cross is composed of the various national Red Cross organizations).

Most often these organizations perform rather low-level, specifically functional tasks, promoting contact across state boundaries on matters of common interest and providing nongovernmental means of communication between individuals of many nations. NGOs help knit the global society together in much the same way that private groups do within a state, although their total membership as a portion of the world's population is only a fraction of the comparable proportion of interest group members within an economically developed democracy. Sometimes an NGO can function as a pressure group affecting national governments or international organizations. An example is the role of the International Red Cross and the World Council of Churches in mobilizing world concern and aid for African populations facing starvation. A great many NGOs are formally consulted by the international organizations concerned with their problems (health and medical organizations are consulted by the World Health Organization). Some NGOs, such as Amnesty International or the Roman Catholic Church, can exert significant influence on the policies of various states. The political focus of NGOs is usually on national governments, and they are effective through changing government policy rather than through direct action.

17. Data for NGOS and IGOS from Union of International Associations, *Yearbook of International Organizations,* 1986/87, vol. I (Brussels: U.I.A., l987). Growth in both IGOs and NGOs has slowed in recent years, with even some evidence of a decline in IGOs from the mid-1980s to the early 1990s.

Much the same is true for purely *subnational* (as contrasted to international) organizations. The role of interest or pressure groups in foreign policy formation hardly needs emphasis, but only in rare instances (the PLO is one) do NGOs act directly, without the intermediary instrument of a national government.

At the most micro level are individuals. While individuals are important to the operation and impact of transnational organizations and transnational linkages between and among states (in tourism, student exchange, and business and commercial links), individuals are most often powerless in international politics except when they can, through an official or unofficial role, affect the policy of a government. One analyst, however, claims that this is changing and that private individuals are having an ever greater impact on world affairs. Through the growing interdependence of the world system and the growing awareness of individuals of their place in the world through the "microelectronic revolution," individual acts produce significant impacts. Mathias Rust, a West German teenager acting "on behalf of world peace" landed his light plane in Red Square in 1987, exposing the vulnerabilities of Soviet air defenses and leading to the dismissal of the defense minister.[18]

Multinational Corporations

One consistent exception to the relative powerlessness of nonstate actors is the *multinational corporation* (MNC). There are at least 7,000 business corporations with subsidiaries in other countries; the number of subsidiaries runs to more than 26,000. The number and importance of MNCs have grown enormously in recent years. A selected group of 187 U.S. corporations owned a total of 107 foreign subsidiaries in 1901; by 1967 those same 187 firms owned nearly 8,000 subsidiaries. By 1980 the 350 largest MNCs had 25,000 foreign subsidiaries and combined gross sales of $2.6 trillion, and they employed 25 million people. In 1960 the value of direct foreign investment by U.S. firms was $32 billion, rising to $251 billion in 1985 (during the same period Japanese investment rose from half a billion to $84 billion, and West German investment from less than a billion to $60 billion). By the mid-1980s eight of the Western industrialized countries served as the home base for 90 percent of the large MNCs, the United States accounting for over half.

Clearly, giant corporations like these cannot help but affect the policies of many governments and the welfare of many people.[19] The oil companies, for instance, would still have tremendous impact with their pricing and marketing policies even if they did not try to change the policy or personnel of national governments. The MNC has emerged in many ways as one of the major competitors to the nation-state. Whereas nonstate liberation groups (the PLO and IRA) and separatist groups (the Basques, the Quebecois) have challenged the military and political authority of specific nation-states, the MNC is a much more broadly based and subtle competitor. This is partly because MNCs may become deeply involved in the domestic political processes of host countries, by outright bribery, by support of specific political parties or candidates, or by financing coups. Examples are the actions of the United Fruit Company in the overthrow of the Arbenz government in

---

18. See Rosenau, *Turbulence in World Politics* for these arguments; p. 288 for a discussion of the Rust incident.

19. See George Modelski, "International Content and Performance Among the World's Largest Corporations," in George Modelski, ed., *Transnational Corporations and World Order* (New York: W. H. Freeman and Company, 1979), pp. 45-65; and *Transnational Corporations in World Development: Trends and Prospects* (New York: United Nations Centre on Transnational Corporations, 1988).

Guatemala in 1954, of British Petroleum in the removal of the Mossadegh government in Iran in 1953, and the role played by ITT in the coup against the Marxist regime of Salvador Allende of Chile in 1973.

Many multinationals predate the states that have been created since the end of World War II. MNCs also have their own spheres of influence through the division of world markets. They often engage in diplomacy and espionage, traditional tools of state interaction. Most important, MNCs have very large economic resources at their disposal, which gives them an advantage over not only many of the newer and smaller states but also some of the older ones. For example, in 1984 Exxon Corporation had gross sales larger than the GNP of Switzerland and only slightly less than the GNP of Sweden. The fiftieth largest MNC, Procter and Gamble, had gross sales exceeding the GNP of Bangladesh. Of course, GNP and gross sales are not directly comparable accounting terms; the most accurate comparison would be between GNP and "value added" by the corporation. Nevertheless, the comparison suggests how very large some modern multinational corporations are compared with the often small, underdeveloped states with which they deal.

Nation-State Versus Nonstate Loyalty

Although there are competitors to the nation-state, some very formidable in special ways, the state continues to enjoy great advantages over most other international actors. In addition to the legal status of formal sovereignty, the state generally also possesses demographic, economic, military, and geographic capabilities unmatched by other actors. Some IGOs or MNCs command the loyalty of some individuals, but the nation-state commands the loyalty of very large numbers of individuals through nationalism. One clear ramification of the combination of the nation with the state (which is what nonstate actors like the PLO attempt) is that the state comes to embody the nation and all it stands for through nationalism. That is, the government of the state is seen by the people as representing and protecting cultural values as well as history and tradition. Combined with the ideas of sovereignty, this relationship is a powerful force indeed—a force that can rarely be matched by nonstate actors. Before the outbreak of World War I, the socialist parties of Europe, meeting together under the aegis of the Second International, called for loyalty to the proletariat and a refusal by workers anywhere in Europe to take up arms against other workers in the event of war. Here was a direct clash between an NGO and the states of Europe: competition for the loyalty of the workers within the various European countries, especially Germany, France, and Britain. When the war came and choices had to be made, for a variety of reasons the workers rallied to the nationalist standards of their respective states and not to the Red Flag.

Two concluding, if somewhat contradictory, comments are in order. The first is that states possess, in general, a far wider range of capabilities than do nonstate actors and thus have a much larger and more varied menu. Although there has been a tremendous growth in both IGOs and NGOs and the transnational interactions among them (and between them and states), nonstate interactions clearly reflect the structure and distribution of the power of the states in the global system, and the growth of nonstate activity has both mirrored and derived from the expansion of the state system itself in the postwar period. The second point, however, is simply that IGOs and NGOs do exist. They are given attention by states, are components of the international or global environment that influences world politics, and thus indeed affect the menu of constraints, possibilities, and probabilities of nation-states and the other international actors.

Political Power

Hans J. Morgenthau

Morgenthau defines and offers four distinctions of the term power, a fundamental concept in international relations. Following his discussion of differences between power and influence, power and force, usable and unusable power, and legitimate and illegitimate power, Morgenthau briefly addresses the issue of the depreciation of power in the study of international politics.

WHAT IS POLITICAL POWER?[1]

As Means to the Nation's Ends

International politics, like all politics, is a struggle for power. Whatever the ultimate aims of international politics, power is always the immediate aim. Statesmen and peoples may ultimately seek freedom, security, prosperity, or power itself. They may define their goals in terms of a religious, philosophic, economic, or social ideal. They may hope that this ideal will materialize through its own inner force, through divine intervention, or through the natural development of human affairs. They may also try to further its realization through nonpolitical means, such as technical cooperation with other nations or international organizations. But whenever they strive to realize their goal by means of international politics, they do so by striving for power. The Crusaders wanted to free the holy places from domination by the Infidels; Woodrow Wilson wanted to make the world safe for democracy; the Nazis wanted to open Eastern Europe to German colonization, to dominate Europe, and to conquer the world. Since they all chose power to achieve these ends, they were actors on the scene of international politics.[2]

Two conclusions follow from this concept of international politics. First, not every action that a nation performs with respect to another nation is of a political nature. Many such activities are normally undertaken without any consideration of power, nor do they normally affect the power of the nation undertaking them. Many legal, economic, humanitarian, and cultural activities are of this kind. Thus a nation is not normally engaged in international politics when it concludes an extradition treaty with another nation, when it exchanges goods and services with other nations, when it cooperates with other nations in providing relief from natural catastrophes, and when it promotes the distribution of cultural achievements throughout the world. In other words, the involvement of a nation in international politics is but one among many types of activities in which a nation can participate on the international scene.

---

1. The concept of political power poses one of the most difficult and controversial problems of political science. The value of any concept used in political science is determined by its ability to explain a maximum of the phenomena that are conventionally considered to belong to a certain sphere of political activity. Thus the coverage of a concept of political power, to be useful for the understanding of international politics, must be broader than the coverage of one adopted to operate in the field of municipal politics. The political means employed in the latter are much more narrowly circumscribed than are those employed in international politics.

2. For some significant remarks on power in relation to international politics, see Lionel Robins, *The Economic Causes of War* (London: Jonathan Cape, 1939), pp. 63 ff.

From Hans J. Morgenthau: *Politics Among Nations: The Struggle for Power and Peace*, Sixth Edition, revised by Kenneth W. Thompson, pp.31-51. Originally published in 1948. Italics added.

Second, not all nations are at all times to the same extent involved in international politics. The degree of their involvement may run all the way from the maximum at present attained by the United States and the Soviet Union, through the minimum involvement of such countries as Switzerland, Luxembourg, or Venezuela, to the complete noninvolvement of Liechtenstein and Monaco. Similar extremes can be noticed in the history of particular countries. Spain in the sixteenth and seventeenth centuries was one of the main active participants in the struggle for power on the international scene, but plays today only a marginal role in it. The same is true of such countries as Austria, Sweden, and Switzerland. On the other hand, nations like the United States, the Soviet Union, and China are today much more deeply involved in international politics than they were fifty or even twenty years ago. In short, the relation of nations to international politics has a dynamic quality. It changes with the vicissitudes of power, which may push a nation into the forefront of the power struggle, or may deprive a nation of the ability to participate actively in it. It may also change under the impact of cultural transformations, which may make a nation prefer other pursuits, for instance commerce, to those of power. The tendency of countries to be involved to a greater or lesser extent in the struggle for power prompted Arnold Wolfers to observe that they occupied positions at opposite extremes of a spectrum extending from what he called the pole of power to the pole of indifference.

Its Nature: Four Distinctions

When we speak of power in the context of this book, [*Politics Among Nations*] we have in mind not man's power over nature, or over an artistic medium, such as language, speech, sound, or color, or over the means of production or consumption, or over himself in the sense of self-control. *When we speak of power, we mean man's control over the minds and actions of other men.* By political power we refer to the mutual relations of control among the holders of public authority and between the latter and the people at large.

Political power is a psychological relation between those who exercise it and those over whom it is exercised. It gives the former control over certain actions of the latter through the impact which the former exert on the latter's minds. That impact derives from three sources: the expectation of benefits, the fear of disadvantages, the respect or love for men or institutions. It may be exerted through orders, threats, the authority or charisma of a man or of an office, or a combination of any of these.

In view of this definition, four distinctions must be made: between *power and influence*, between *power and force*, between *usable and unusable power*, between *legitimate and illegitimate power*.

The Secretary of State who advises the President of the United States on the conduct of American foreign policy has influence if the President follows his advice. But he has no power over the President; for he has none of the means at his disposal with which to impose his will upon that of the President. He can persuade but he cannot compel. The President, on the other hand, has power over the Secretary of State; for he can impose his will upon the latter by virtue of the authority of his office, the promise of benefits, and the threat of disadvantages.

Political power must be distinguished from force in the sense of the actual exercise of physical violence. The threat of physical violence in the form of police action, imprisonment, capital punishment, or war is an intrinsic element of politics. When violence becomes an actuality, it signifies the abdication of political power in favor of military or pseudo-military power. In international politics in particular, armed strength as a threat or a potentiality is the most important material factor making for the political power of a nation. If it becomes an actuality in war, it signifies the substitution of military for political power. The actual exercise of physical violence substitutes for the psychological relation between two minds, which is of the essence of political power, the physical relation between two bodies, one of which is strong enough to dominate the other's movements. It is for this reason that in the exercise of physical violence the psychological element of the political relationship is lost, and that we must distinguish between military and political power.

The availability of nuclear weapons makes it necessary to distinguish between usable and unusable power. It is one of the paradoxes of the nuclear age that, in contrast to the experience of all of prenuclear history, an increase in military power is no longer necessarily conducive to an increase in political power. The threat of all-out nuclear violence implies the threat of total destruction. As such, it can still be a suitable instrument of foreign policy when addressed to a nation which cannot reply in kind. The nation armed with nuclear weapons can assert power over the other nation by saying: Either you do as I say, or I will destroy you. The situation is different if the nation so threatened can respond by saying: If you destroy me with nuclear weapons, you will be destroyed in turn. Here the mutual threats cancel each other out. Since the nuclear destruction of one nation would call forth the nuclear destruction of the other, both nations can afford to disregard the threat on the assumption that both will act rationally.

It is only on the assumption that the nations concerned might act irrationally by destroying each other in an all-out nuclear war that the threat of nuclear war is credible and has indeed been used by the United States and the Soviet Union against each other, for instance by the Soviet Union during the Suez Crisis of 1956, by the United States during the Berlin Crisis of 1961, and by both during the Arab-Israeli War of 1973. Yet while here the threat of force can be used as a rational instrument of foreign policy, the actual use of that force remains irrational; for the threatened force would be used not for the political purpose of influencing the will of the other side but for the irrational purpose of destroying the other side with the attendant assurance of one own destruction.

Thus the magnitude of its destructiveness, as compared with the limited character of the political purposes which are the proper object of foreign policy, renders nuclear force unusable as an instrument of foreign policy. It can be rational under certain conditions to threaten the other side with destruction through the use of nuclear force in order to change the other side's will; it would be irrational to actually destroy the other side, thereby inviting one's own destruction. In contrast, conventional force is usable as an instrument of foreign policy; for by inflicting limited damage with commensurate risks to oneself, one can use it indeed as a suitable instrument for changing the other side's will.

Finally, legitimate power, that is, power whose exercise is morally or legally justified, must be distinguished from illegitimate power. Power exercised with moral or legal authority must be distinguished from naked power. The power of the police officer who searches me by virtue of a search warrant is qualitatively different from the power of a robber who performs the same action by virtue of his holding a gun. The distinction is not only philosophically valid but also relevant for the conduct of foreign policy. Legitimate power, which can invoke a moral or legal justification for its exercise, is likely to be more effective than equivalent illegitimate power, which cannot be so justified. That is to say, legitimate power has a better chance to influence the will of its objects than equivalent illegitimate power. Power exercised in self-defense or in the name of the United Nations has a better chance to succeed than equivalent power exercised by an "aggressor" nation or in violation of international law. Political ideologies, as we shall see, serve the purpose of endowing foreign policies with the appearance of legitimacy.

While it is generally recognized that the interplay of the expectation of benefits, the fear of disadvantages, and the respect or love for men or institutions, in ever changing combinations, forms the basis of all domestic politics, the importance of these factors for international politics is less obvious, but no less real. There has been a tendency to reduce political power to the actual application of force or at least to equate it with successful threats of force and with persuasion, to the neglect of charisma. That neglect, as we shall see,[3] accounts in good measure for the neglect of prestige as an independent element in international politics. Yet without taking into account the charisma of a man, such as Napoleon or Hitler, or of an institution, such as the Government or United States Constitution, evoking trust and love through which the wills of men submit themselves to the will of such a man or institution, it is impossible to understand certain phenomena of international politics which have been particularly prominent in modern times.

The importance which charismatic leadership and the response to it as love of the subject for the leader has for international politics is clearly revealed in a letter which John Durie, Scotch Presbyterian and worker for Protestant unity, wrote in 1632 to the British Ambassador Thomas Roe, explaining the decline of the power of Gustavus Adolphus of Sweden, then fighting for the Protestant cause in Germany:

> The increase of his authority is the ground of his abode; and love is the ground of his authority; it must he through love; for it cannot be through power; for his power is not in his own subjects but in strangers; not in his money, but in theirs; not in their good will, but in mere necessity as things stand now betwixt him and them; therefore if the necessity be not so urgent as it is; or if any other means be shown by God (who is able to do as much by another man as by him) to avoid this necessity; the money and the power and the assistance which it yieldeth unto him will fall from him and so his authority is lost, and his abode will be no longer: for the Love which was at first is gone. . .[4]

The President of the United States exerts political power over the executive branch of the government so long as his orders are obeyed by the members of that branch. The leader of the party has political power so long as he is able to mold the actions of the members of the party according to his will. We refer to the political power of an industrialist, labor leader, or lobbyist in so far as his preferences influence the actions of public officials. The United States exerts political power over Puerto Rico so long as the laws of the United States are observed by the citizens of that island. When we speak of the political power of the United States in Central America, we have in mind the conformity of the actions of Central American governments with the wishes of the government of the United States.[5] Thus the statement that A has or wants political power over B signifies always that A is able, or wants to be able, to control certain actions of B through influencing B's mind.

Whatever the material objectives of a foreign policy, such as the acquisition of sources of raw materials, the control of sea lanes, or territorial changes, they always entail control of the actions of others through influence over their minds. The Rhine frontier as a century-old objective of French foreign policy points to the political objective to destroy the desire of Germany to attack France by making it physically difficult or impossible for Germany to do so. Great Britain owed its predominant position in world politics throughout the nineteenth century to the calculated policy of making it either too dangerous

---

3. See Morgenthau: *The Struggle for Power: Policy of Prestige.*

4. Gunnar Westin, *Negotiations About Church Unity,* 1628–1634 (Upsala: Almquist and Wiksells, 1932), p. 208. The spelling has been modernized.

5. The examples in the text illustrate also the distinction between political power as mere social fact, as in the case of the lobbyist, and political power in the sense of legitimate authority; i.e., of the President of the United States. Both the President of the United States and the lobbyist exercise political power, however different its source and nature may be.

(because Great Britain was too strong) or unnecessary (because it strength was used with moderation) for other nations to oppose it.

The political objective of military preparations of any kind is to deter other nations from using military force by making it too risky for them to do so. The political aim of military preparations is, in other words, to make the actual application of military force unnecessary by inducing the prospective enemy to desist from the use of military force. The political objective of war itself is not per se the conquest of territory and the annihilation of enemy armies, but a change in the mind of the enemy which will make him yield to the will of the victor.

Therefore, whenever economic, financial, territorial, or military policies are under discussion in international affairs, it is necessary to distinguish between, say, economic policies that are undertaken for their own sake and economic policies that are the instruments of a political policy—a policy, that is, whose economic purpose is but the means to the end of controlling the policies of another nation. The export policy of Switzerland with regard to the United States falls into the first category. The economic policies of the Soviet Union with regard to the nations of Eastern Europe fall into the latter category. So do many economic policies of the United States in Latin America, Asia, and Europe. The distinction is of great practical importance, and the failure to make it has led to much confusion in policy and public opinion.

An economic, financial, territorial, or military policy undertaken for its own sake is subject to evaluation in its own terms. Is it economically or financially advantageous? What effects has acquisition of territory upon the population and economy of the nation acquiring it? What are the consequences of a change in a military policy for education, population, and the domestic political system? The decisions with respect to these policies are made exclusively in terms of such intrinsic considerations.

When, however, the objectives of these policies serve to increase the power of the nation pursuing them with regard to other nations, these policies and their objectives must be judged primarily from the point of view of their contribution to national power. An economic policy that cannot be justified in purely economic terms might nevertheless be undertaken in view of the political policy pursued. The insecure and unprofitable character of a loan to a foreign nation may be a valid argument against it on purely financial grounds. But the argument is irrelevant if the loan, however unwise it may be from a banker's point of view, serves the political policies of the nation. It may of course be that the economic or financial losses involved in such policies will weaken the nation in its international position to such an extent as to outweigh the political advantages to be expected. On these grounds such policies might be rejected. In such a case, what decides the issue is not purely economic and financial considerations but a comparison of the political chances and risks involved; that is, the probable effect of these policies upon the power of the nation.

When the United States provides loans or assistance to countries such as Poland which lie in the shadow of the Red Army, the purpose is not primarily economic or financial. It is rather to enable such countries to move towards a degree of independence of the influence and power of the Soviet Union. If the repayment of loans to American agencies or financial institutions is postponed with U.S. government approval, this is not for humanitarian or charitable reasons alone. Rather, it is American policy to keep open certain options for the government of Poland, options which prevent its total dependence on the Soviet Union. Such actions in the economic sphere are based on political objectives which in the long run may assure the survival of Poland as a sovereign state—however much its geographic and political position may force it to accept the position of a satellite within the sphere of the Soviet Union at least in the short run. In a word, the aim of American economic policy toward Poland is to limit Soviet influence and power in Central and Eastern Europe while increasing the leverage of the United States in the area.

THE DEPRECIATION OF POLITICAL POWER

The aspiration for power being the distinguishing element of international politics, as of all politics, *international politics is of necessity power politics*. While this fact is generally recognized in the practice of international affairs, it is frequently denied in the pronouncements of scholars, publicists, and even statesmen. Since the end of the Napoleonic Wars, ever larger groups in the Western world have been persuaded that the struggle for power on the international scene is a temporary phenomenon, a historical accident that is bound to disappear once the peculiar historic conditions that have given rise to it have been eliminated. Thus Jeremy Bentham believed that the competition for colonies was at the root of all international conflicts. "Emancipate your colonies!" was his advice to the governments, and international conflict and war would of necessity disappear.[6] Adherents of free trade, such as Cobden[7] and Proudhon[8] were convinced that the removal of trade barriers was the only condition for the establishment of permanent harmony among nations, and might even lead to the disappearance of international politics altogether. "At some future election," said Cobden, "we may probably see the test 'no foreign politics' applied to those who offer to become the representatives of free constituencies."[9] For Marx and his followers, capitalism is at the root of international discord and war. They maintain that international socialism will do away with the struggle for power on the international scene and will bring about permanent peace. During the nineteenth century, liberals everywhere shared the conviction that power politics and war were residues of an obsolete system of government, and that the victory of democracy and constitutional government over absolutism and autocracy would assure the victory of international harmony and permanent peace over power politics and war. Of this liberal school of thought, Woodrow Wilson was the most eloquent and most influential spokesman.

In recent times, the conviction that the struggle for power can be eliminated from the international scene has been connected with the great attempts at organizing the world, such as the League of Nations and the United Nations. Thus Cordell Hull, then U.S. Secretary of State, declared in 1943 on his return from the Moscow Conference, which laid the groundwork for the United Nations, that the new international organization would mean the end of power politics and usher in a new era of international collaboration.[10] Mr. Philip Noel-Baker, then British Minister of State, declared in 1946 in the House of Commons that the British government was "determined to use the institutions of the United Nations to kill power politics, in order that, by the methods of democracy, the will of the people shall prevail."[11]

---

6. *Emancipate Your Colonies* (London: Robert Heward, 1830).

7. "Free Trade! What is it? Why, breaking down the barriers that separate nations; those barriers, behind which nestle the feelings of pride, revenge, hatred, and jealousy, which every now and then burst their bounds, and deluge whole countries with blood." "Free trade is the international law of the Almighty," and free trade and peace seem to be "one and the same cause." See *Speeches by Richard Cobden* (London: Macmillan & Company, 1870), Vol. I, p. 79; *Political Writings* (New York: D. Appleton and Company, 1867), Vol. II, p. 110; letter of April 12, 1842, to Henry Ashworth, quoted in John Morley, *Life of Richard Cobden* (Boston: Roberts Brothers, 1881), p. 154.

8. "Let us suppress the tariffs, and the alliance of the peoples will thus be declared, their solidarity recognized, their equality proclaimed." *Oeuvres complètes* (Paris, 1867), Vol. I, p. 248.

9. Quoted in A.C.F. Beales, *A Short History of English Liberalism*, p. 195.

10. *New York Times*. November 19, 1943, p. 1.

While we shall have more to say later about these theories and the expectations derived from them, it is sufficient to state that the struggle for power is universal in time and space and is an undeniable fact of experience. It cannot be denied that throughout historic time, regardless of social, economic, and political conditions, states have met each other in contests for power. Even though anthropologists have shown that certain primitive peoples seem to be free from the desire for power, nobody has yet shown how their state of mind and the conditions under which they live can be recreated on a worldwide scale so as to eliminate the struggle for power from the international scene.[12] It would be useless and even self-destructive to free one or the other of the peoples of the earth from the desire for power while leaving it extant in others. If the desire for power cannot be abolished everywhere in the world, those who might be cured would simply fall victims to the power of others.

The position taken here might be criticized on the ground that conclusions drawn from the past are unconvincing, and that to draw such conclusions has always been the main stock in trade of the enemies of progress and reform. Though it is true that certain social arrangements and institutions have always existed in the past, it does not necessarily follow that they must always exist in the future. The situation is, however, different when we deal not with social arrangements and institutions created by man, but with those elemental bio-psychological drives by which in turn society is created. The drives to live, to propagate, and to dominate are common to all men.[13] Their relative strength is dependent upon social conditions that may favor one drive and tend to repress another, or that may withhold social approval from certain manifestations of these drives while they encourage others. Thus, to take examples only from the sphere of power, most societies condemn killing as a means of attaining power within society, but all societies encourage the killing of enemies in that struggle for power which is called war. Dictators look askance at the aspirations for political power among their fellow citizens, but democracies consider active participation in the competition for political power a civic duty. Where a monopolistic organization of economic activities exists, competition for economic power is absent, and in competitive economic systems certain manifestations of the struggle for economic power are outlawed, while others are encouraged. Ostrogorsky, invoking the authority of Tocqueville, states that "the passions of the American people are not of a political, but of a commercial, nature. In that world awaiting cultivation, the love of power aims less at men than at things."[14]

Regardless of particular social conditions, the decisive argument against the opinion that the struggle for power on the international scene is a mere historic accident must be derived from the nature of domestic politics. The essence of international politics is identical with its domestic counterpart. Both domestic and international politics are a struggle for power, modified only by the different conditions under which this struggle takes place in the domestic and in the international spheres.

---

11. *House of Commons Debates* (Fifth Series, 1946), Vol. 419, p. 1262.

12. For an illuminating discussion of this problem, see Malcolm Sharp, "Aggression: A Study of Values and Law," *Ethics*, Vol. 57, No. 4, Part II (July 1947).

13. Zoologists have tried to show that the drive to dominate is found even in animals, such as chickens and monkeys, who create social hierarchies on the basis of will and the ability to dominate. See e.g., Warder Allee, *Animal Life and Social Growth* (Baltimore: The Williams and Wilkens Company, 1932), and *The Social Life of Animals* (New York: W.W. Norton and Company, Inc. 1938). Cf. also the theories of Konrad Lorenz and the controversies concerning them.

14. M. Ostrogorsky, *Democracy and the Organization of Political Parties* (New York: The Macmillan Company, 1902), Vol. II, p. 592.

The tendency to dominate, in particular, is an element of all human associations, from the family through fraternal and professional associations and local political organizations, to the state. On the family level, the typical conflict between the mother-in-law and her child's spouse is in its essence a struggle for power, the defense of an established power position against the attempt to establish a new one. As such it foreshadows the conflict on the international scene between the policies of the status quo and the policies of imperialism. Social clubs, fraternities, faculties, and business organizations are scenes of continuous struggles for power between groups that either want to keep what power they already have or seek to attain greater power. Competitive contests between business enterprises as well as labor disputes between employers and employees are frequently fought not only, and sometimes not even primarily, for economic advantages, but for control over each other and over others; that is, for power. Finally, the whole political life of a nation, particularly of a democratic nation, from the local to the national level, is a continuous struggle for power. In periodic elections, in voting in legislative assemblies, in lawsuits before courts, in administrative decisions and executive measures—in all these activities men try to maintain or to establish their power over other men. The processes by which legislative, judicial, executive, and administrative decisions are reached are subject to pressures and counterpressures by "pressure groups" trying to defend and expand their positions of power. As one of the Dead Sea scrolls puts it:

> What nation likes to be oppressed by a stronger power? Or who wants his property plundered unjustly? Yet, is there a single nation that has not oppressed its neighbour? Or where in the world will you find a people that has not plundered the property of another? Where indeed?

"Of the gods we know," to quote Thucydides, "and of men we believe, that it is a necessary law of their nature that they rule wherever they can."[15] Or, as Tolstoy put it: ". . . the very process of dominating another's will was in itself a pleasure, a habit, and a necessity to Dólokhov."[16]

And in the words of John of Salisbury:

> Though it is not given to all men to seize princely or royal power, yet the man who is wholly untainted by tyranny is rare or nonexistent. In common speech the tyrant is one who oppresses a whole people by a rulership based on force; and yet it is not over a people as a whole that a man can play the tyrant, but he can do so if he will even in the meanest station. For if not over the whole body of the people, still each man will lord it as far as his power extends.[17]

In view of this ubiquity of the struggle for power in all social relations and on all levels of social organization, is it surprising that international politics is of necessity power politics? And would it not be rather surprising if the struggle for power were but an accidental and ephemeral attribute of international politics when it is a permanent and necessary element of all branches of domestic politics?

TWO ROOTS OF THE DEPRECIATION OF POLITICAL POWER

The depreciation of the role power plays on the international scene grows from two roots. One is the philosophy of international relations which dominated the better part of the nineteenth century and still holds sway over much of our thinking on international

---

15. Thucydides, Book V, 105.

16. Leo Tolstoy, *War and Peace*, Book Eight, Chapter XI.

17. John of Salisbury, *Policraticus*, translated by John Dickinson (New York: Alfred A. Knopf, 1927), Vol. VII, p. 17.

affairs. The other is the particular political and intellectual circumstances that have determined the relations of the United States of America to the rest of the world.

Nineteenth Century Philosophy

The nineteenth century was led to its depreciation of power politics by its domestic experience. The distinctive characteristic of this experience was the domination of the middle classes by the aristocracy. By identifying this domination with political domination of any kind, the political philosophy of the nineteenth century came to identify the opposition to aristocratic politics with hostility to any kind of politics. After the defeat of aristocratic government, the middle classes developed a system of indirect domination. They replaced the traditional division into the governing and governed classes, and the military method of open violence, characteristic of aristocratic rule, with the invisible chains of economic dependence. This economic system operated through a network of seemingly equalitarian legal rules which concealed the very existence of power relations. The nineteenth century was unable to see the political nature of these legalized relations. They seemed to be essentially different from what had gone, so far, under the name of politics. Therefore, politics in its aristocratic—that is, open and violent—form was identified with politics as such. The struggle, then, for political power—in domestic as well as in international affairs—appeared to be only a historic accident, coincident with autocratic government and bound to disappear with the disappearance of autocratic government.

The American Experience

This identification of power politics with aristocratic government found support in the American experience. It can be traced to three elements in that experience: the uniqueness of the American experiment, the actual isolation of the American continent from centers of the world conflict during the nineteenth century, and the humanitarian pacifism and anti-imperialism of American political ideology.

That the severance of constitutional ties with the British Crown was meant to signify the initiation of an American foreign policy distinct from what went under the name of foreign policy in Europe is clearly stated in Washington's Farewell Address. "Europe has a set of primary interests, which to us have none, or a very remote relation. Hence she must be engaged in frequent controversies, the causes of which are essentially foreign to our concerns. Hence, therefore, it must be unwise in us to implicate ourselves, by artificial ties, in the ordinary vicissitudes of her politics, or the ordinary combinations and collisions of her friendships or enmities." In 1796, European politics and power politics were identical; there was no other power politics but the one engaged in by the princes of Europe. "The toils of European ambition, rivalship, interest, humor or caprice" were the only manifestations of the international struggle for power before the eyes of America. The retreat from European politics, as proclaimed by Washington, could, therefore, be taken to mean retreat from power politics as such.

Yet American aloofness from the European tradition of power politics was more than a political program. Certain sporadic exceptions notwithstanding, it was an established political fact until the end of the nineteenth century. This fact was a result of deliberate choice as well as of the objective conditions of geography. Popular writers might see in the uniqueness of America's geographic position the hand of God which had unalterably prescribed the course of American expansion as well as isolation. But more responsible observers, from Washington on, have been careful to emphasize the conjunction of geographic conditions and a foreign policy choosing its ends in the light of geography, using geographic conditions to attain those ends. Washington referred to "our detached and distant situation" and asked:

"Why forego the advantages of so peculiar a situation?" When this period of American foreign policy drew to a close, John Bright wrote to Alfred Love: "On your continent we may hope your growing millions may henceforth know nothing of war. None can assail you; and you are anxious to abstain from mingling with the quarrels of other nations."[18]

From the shores of the North American continent, the citizens of the new world watched the strange spectacle of the international struggle for power unfolding on the distant shores of Europe, Africa, and Asia. Since for the better part of the nineteenth century their foreign policy enabled them to retain the role of spectators, what was actually the result of a passing historic constellation appeared to Americans as a permanent condition, self-chosen as well as naturally ordained. At worst they would continue to watch the game of power politics played by others. At best the time was close at hand when, with democracy established everywhere, the final curtain would fall and the game of power politics would no longer be played.

To aid in the achievement of this goal was conceived to be part of America's mission. Throughout the nation's history, the national destiny of the United States has been understood in antimilitaristic, libertarian terms. Where that national mission find, a nonaggressive, abstentionist formulation, as in the political philosophy of John C. Calhoun, it is conceived as the promotion of domestic liberty. Thus we may "do more to extend liberty by our example over this continent and the world generally, than would be done by a thousand victories." When the United States, in the wake of the Spanish-American War, seemed to desert this anti-imperialist and democratic ideal, William Graham Sumner restated its essence: "Expansion and imperialism are a grand onslaught on democracy expansion and imperialism are at war with the best traditions, principles, and interests of the American people."[19] Comparing the tendencies of European power politics with the ideals of the American tradition, Sumner thought with George Washington that they were incompatible. Yet, as a prophet of things to come, he saw that the settlement of the Spanish-American War irrevocably committed America to the same course that was engulfing Europe in revolution and war.

Thus the general conception the nineteenth century had formed of the nature of foreign affairs combined with specific elements in the American experience to create the belief that involvement in power politics is not inevitable, but only a historic accident, and that nations have a choice between power politics and other kinds of foreign policy not tainted by the desire for power.

THE SCIENCE OF PEACE: CONTEMPORARY UTOPIANISM

A word should be said about a school of thought—still influential in political and intellectual circles today—which proffers a "scientific" alternative to the "perennial wisdom" of a rationalist approach to international politics. This school of thought we may call "scientific utopianism" for lack of a better term; like the sources of self-deception as to the persistence of political power discussed above, the scientific interpretation has strong roots in nineteenth-century experience, both in Europe and in America. In this case, however, neither the relations of class domination nor geographical accident gave rise to utopian

18. Quoted in Merle Curti, *Peace and War: The American Struggle 1636–1936* (New York: W.W. Norton and Company, 1936), p. 122.

19. "The Conquest of the United States by Spain," *Essays of William Graham Sumner* (New Haven: Yale University Press, 1940), Vol. II, p. 295.

hopes for a "science of peace." Instead, the fantastic progress of the natural sciences led various thinkers to assume that the same kinds of methods, applied to individual and collective human behavior, could yield progress toward what Herbert Marcuse and others have called "the pacification of human existence."

The modern science of peace starts from the assumption that the world is thoroughly accessible to science and reason and that it contains in itself all the elements necessary for the harmonious cooperation of all mankind. It is for science to detect those elements, variously defined as harmony of interests, laws of economics, free trade, and modern communications; it is for law to apply them where they do not prevail spontaneously; and it is for negotiation and compromise to discover them under the surface of apparent conflict.

For such rationalism, it is the atavism of power politics that conceals and distorts the harmony of interests which is the true nature of international relations. Adam Smith, a founding father of classical liberalism as well as of classical economics, discovered such a fundamental harmony of interests lying beneath the surface manifestations of self-regarding, competitive economic behavior. Selfish pursuits led to greater wealth for all through the workings of an "invisible hand." Governed by an inner logic, the free market operates to dispose all for the best. Nineteenth-century liberalism had no use for even such residual traces of the miraculous in its search for a means to establish harmonious relations among states. Only strictly rational principles would do: all international conflicts were considered capable of satisfactory solutions, either through compromise or arbitration. Since all men partake of reason, they must sooner or later meet on that common ground, discovering that their conflicts are apparent rather than real and can all be solved by a rational formula acceptable to all. Were all nations at all times fully aware of their real interests, they would realize that apparently opposing interests are actually identical, that what is good for one country is of necessity good for all other countries, and that conflict is merely the product of ignorance and error.

Conflicts among nations are due, then, to maladjustments arising from lack of understanding and to the influence of political passions. Except for ignorance and emotion, reason would solve international conflicts as easily and as rationally as it has solved so many problems in the natural sciences. Proudhon was among the first to glorify the blessings of science in the international field.

> Truth is everywhere identical with itself: science represents the unity of mankind. If therefore science, instead of religion or authority, is taken in each country as social norm, the sovereign arbiter of interests, with the government amounting to nothing, all the laws of the universe will be in harmony. Nationality or fatherland will no longer exist in the political meaning of the term; there will only be birthplaces. Man, of whatever race or colour he may be, will actually be a native of the Universe; the right of citizenship he will acquire everywhere. In the same way in which in a certain district of the national territory the municipality represents the nation and exercises its authority, each nation of the globe will represent humanity and in its natural boundaries act for it. Harmony will reign among the nations, without diplomacy nor council; nothing shall from now on disturb it.[20]

"The duty of the pacifist," according to C.E.M. Joad, "is above all things to be reasonable. He should, that is to say, rely on the use of his own reason in making his appeal and he should assume that other men may be brought to use theirs. . . . Truth, in fact, will win

---

20. "Idée générale de la révolution au dix-neuvième siècle," *Oeuvres complètes*, IX (1868), p. 300; see also Proudhon, *La Guerre et la paix* (Paris: E. Dentu, 1861).

out, if people are only given a sufficient chance to find it."[21] It was with the same confidence in the power of reason that Clarence Streit asserted in 1941 that "the really big men in the United States Senate and British Parliament will champion the Union [of the two countries], once they understand it."[22]

Political history, then, becomes a succession of scientific problems capable of scientific solution—but most unreasonably handled by an ignorant and impassioned humanity. Even for so realistic an observer as Homer Lea, the problem of international affairs resolved itself into a problem of knowledge; if the "valour of ignorance" is replaced by the knowledge of the pertinent facts, man will be able to act successfully on the international scene. "The time can and will come," wrote the famous pacifist Bertha von Suttner, "when the science of politics will have replaced present day statecraft, when only those will have legislative and political power who sincerely seek only the truth and through the truth strive to attain only the good—the universal good comprehending all civilized nations."

The time Suttner spoke of has already arrived as far as the mere possession of knowledge is concerned, according to Robert S. Lynd. "The diagnosis," he wrote,

> is already fairly complete, thanks to a long list of competent studies of nationalism, imperialism, international finance and trade, and other factors within our culture that encourage war. The problem of war, more than most others, has engaged the attention of scientists from several disciplines, and the dissection has proceeded to the point where fairly unequivocal knowledge exists. The causes of war are known and accepted by a wide group of thoughtful students. But the statement of what is to be done languishes because social science shrinks from resolving the austere findings of scholarly monographs into a bold programme for action. . . . In the case of an issue like this, where the problem does not arise from lack of knowledge, what social science appears to need is the will to mass its findings so that the truth they hold will not continue to trickle away as disparate bits of scholarship. We know enough about war and its causes to present these findings, point their meanings, and propose action in a way that will hold this damaging evidence steadily and authoritatively before the eyes of the humblest citizen.[23]

It was for this age of reason to replace the old methods of power politics, secret diplomacy and war by a new, scientific approach. Territorial claims, sovereignty over national minorities, thc distribution of raw materials, the struggle for markets, disarmament, the relation between the "haves" and the "have-nots," peaceful change, and the peaceful organization of the world in general—these are not "political" problems, to be solved temporarily and always precariously according to the distribution of power among quarreling nations and its possible balance. They are "technical" problems for which reason will find the one correct solution in each case.

Thus the nineteenth century developed a "science of peace" as a separate branch of scientific knowledge. Scores of books were published bearing this title. One even received first prize in a scholarly competition.[24] The concept of a "natural frontier—which had had a strategical and political, but not a scientific, connotation in the sixteenth and seventeenth centuries—was construed by the French revolutionaries and Napoleon in the sense of a

---

21. "Pacifism: Its Personal and Social Implications," in G.P. Gooch, *In Pursuit of Peace* (London: Methuen & Company, Ltd., 1933), pp. 61, 63.

22. *Union Now With Britain* (New York: Harper & Brothers, 1941), p. 197.

23. *Knowledge for What?* (Princeton: Princeton University Press, 1939), p. 241.

24. Louis Bara, *La Science de la paix* (1872).

geographically "correct" frontier. In the seventies and eighties of the nineteenth century, public opinion in Great Britain discussed seriously the problem of the "scientific frontier," that is, a frontier which corresponds to reason, and which, consequently, makes all other frontiers in this geographical region scientifically incorrect. In his speech at Mansion House on November 9, 1878, Disraeli justified the Second Afghan War, by saying that the frontier of India was "a haphazard and not a scientific one."

The search for such a "scientific" frontier started in the second half of the eighteenth century when, on the occasion of partitions and annexations of territory, the relative value of the pieces of territory to be distributed was determined on the basis of certain "objective" standards, such as fertility, number and quality of population, and the like. Following this trend, the Congress of Vienna, upon the suggestion of Metternich, appointed a special statistical commission; it was charged with evaluating the territories under discussion by the "objective" standard of number, quality, and type of populations.[25] The delimitation of territory thus became a kind of mathematical exercise. The idea of the "good frontier," developed in the last decades of the nineteenth century in Germany with regard to Russia's territorial aspirations, had a somewhat similar connotation. The idea of the "scientific tariff" attempted to introduce science into foreign trade, building in part upon ideas put forth in the early nineteenth century by Friedrich List. The theory and practice of international plebiscites are also typical manifestations of the rationalist approach to international problems; here the will of the majority is the scientific test according to which sovereignty over territory is to be determined. In the thirties, Major Lefebure advanced his theories on "scientific disarmament." "Geopolitics" endeavoured to put foreign policy as a whole on a scientific basis.

It was only after the First World War that this tendency to reduce political problems to scientific propositions won general acceptance. "Reason is at last becoming an independent agency," wrote Lord Allen of Hartwood, "influencing the conduct of men. This is due to the coming of science. . . . Feeling himself now to be the master of nature, his mind is beginning to work rationally instead of superstitiously. When forming an opinion he observes the phenomena around him and draws his conclusions. From that moment mind begins to be an independent agency of influence. It can now therefore be considered as a political force, whereas that has never previously been possible in the history of civilization. During the last thirty years this has begun to influence public opinion."[26]

Thus began what can properly be called the age of the scientific approach to international affairs, and the end is not yet in sight. Preceded by the Hague Conferences and hundreds of smaller peace congresses, governments themselves embarked on a program of feverish activity unprecedented in recorded history, with the purpose of solving all international problems through scientific methods. The governments, the League of Nations, and private groups vied with each other in organizing international conferences, in encouraging teaching and research, and in publishing hundreds of volumes to cure the ills of humanity in a scientific way. We have recently witnessed widespread efforts to find a scientific solution for the problems of the postwar world. These are the latest, but probably not the last, manifestation of this modem intellectual trend.[27]

Our age is forever searching for the philosophers' stone, the magic formula, which, mechanically applied, will produce the desired result and thus substitute for the uncertainties

25. For details see Charles Dupuis, *Le Principe d'équilibre et le Concert Européen* (Paris: Perrin et Cie, 1909), pp. 38ff, 60 ff.

26. "Pacifism: Its Meaning and Its Task," in Gooch, *op. cit.*, pp. 22, 23.

and risks of political action the certitude of rational calculation. However, what the seekers after the magic formula want is simple, rational, mechanical; what they have to deal with is complicated, irrational, incalculable. As a consequence they are compelled, in order to present at least the semblance of scientific solutions, to simplify the reality of international politics and to rely upon what one might call the "method of the single cause."

The abolition of war is obviously the fundamental problem confronting international thought. To solve the problem one must clearly first determine its cause or causes. What makes a solution appear so difficult for the non-rationalist mind is the *variety* of causes involved—causes which have their roots in the innermost recesses of the human heart. Were it possible to reduce all those multiple, complex factors to a single cause—one capable of rational formulation—the solution of the problem of war would no longer seem impossible. This is what liberal foreign policy has been trying to do since its very inception; and since the heyday of the League of Nations most people would take it for lack of creative thought if a statesman or political thinker did not have a "constructive" plan as a remedy for the "single cause."

Are not the remnants of feudalism the great single cause making for war in this world? Let us do away with aristocratic government everywhere, the classical liberals would say, and we will have peace. In practical politics this general proposition was frequently narrowed down to more special remedies intended to meet particular situations. Thus, as we have seen, Bentham and the Benthamites pointed to the struggle for colonies as the main cause for war; they advocated abstention from colonial policy as a remedy for war. For others, tariffs were the source of all evils in the international sphere; to them, free trade was the source of all good. Others would abolish secret treaties and secret diplomacy in general and, through popular control of international policies, secure peace. Is not modern war an outgrowth of imperialism which, in turn, is a result of the contradictions of monopoly capitalism? Hence, let us do away with capitalism, the Marxists would say, and we will no longer have war: socialism is peace.

The same one-track mode of thought is found also in domestic politics. All social evils stem from our ignorance of the laws of economics: the "single tax" takes account of those laws and will solve all social problems. Our economic system is out of joint because the government spends more than it collects: balance the budget and our economic problems will be solved. Bad linguistic habits are at the root of our social evils: with the acquisition of good linguistic habits our social problems will be solved. Emerson, in "New England Reformers," thus described this kind of thinking:

> One apostle thought all men should go to farming; and another, that no man should buy or sell; that the use of money was the cardinal evil; another, that the mischief was in our diet, that we eat and drink damnation. These made unleavened bread, and were foes to the death

---

27. Cf. Charles A. Beard, *A Foreign Policy for America* (New York: Alfred A. Knopf, 1940), pp. 98–99: "In line with the new interests, the study of international law and diplomacy was encouraged in institutions of learning. Old-fashioned courses on diplomacy—cold, scholarly performances—were supplemented by courses on international relations, in which emphasis was laid of world peace and the means of promoting it. Books, pamphlets, and articles on pacification were written, published and widely circulated, often with the aid of subventions from peace funds. International peace conferences were organized and provided opportunities for travel and extended discourses. Seldom had college presidents, professors, clergymen, and leaders among women enjoyed such privileges and received such marked consideration at the hands of the general public. It looked as if a new era of usefulness and distinction had been opened for them in the field of great affairs, and they made the most of its opportunities."

> to fermentation. . . . Others attacked the system of agriculture; the use of animal manures in farming; and the tyranny of man over brute nature; these abuses polluted his food. . . . Even the insect world was to be defended—that had been too long neglected, and a society for the protection of ground worms, slugs, and mosquitoes was to be incorporated without delay. With these appeared the adepts of homeopathy; of hydropathy, of mesmerism, of phrenology, and their wonderful theories of the Christian miracles! Others assailed particular vocations, as that of the lawyer, that of the merchant, of the manufacturer, of the clergyman, of the scholar. Others attacked the institution of marriage as the fountain of social evils. Others devoted themselves to the worrying of churches and meetings for public worship; and the fertile forms of antinomianism among the elder puritans, seemed to have their match in the plenty of the new harvest of reform.[28]

In the domestic field, however, the "method of the single cause" has been of rather limited theoretical and practical importance; for here, except in periods of collective insanity, immediate personal experience reveals the absurdity of the approach; and the pressure of the affected interests prevents the quack from being mistaken for the saviour.

The utopian internationalist, on the other hand, has no direct contact with the international scene. His thought, if it is sufficiently general, can roam over the globe without ever risking collision with the stark facts of politics. He who would proclaim the Four Freedoms for the United States itself would soon learn from personal experience the enormity of the social and political problems entailed by any attempt at realizing those great principles. By contrast, proclamation of the Four Freedoms "everywhere in the world" is sufficiently general to avoid contact with historic realities and political facts.

The reformer without responsibility finds in the armory of modern international thought what he is looking for. That one panacea is frequently inconsistent with another need not trouble him. For since the "single cause" is an arbitrary abstraction from a multitude of actual causes, one abstraction and, hence, one "single cause" is as good as the next one. Since, furthermore, the hunt for the "single cause" derives from a vague desire to contribute something to the betterment of human affairs rather than from a fixed resolve to intervene in a definite political situation in a definite way, virtually any general explanation of the ills of the world and any general plan to remedy them will satisfy the psychic need involved.

Hence, the great hunting ground for the "single cause" and the "scientific formula" to remedy it has been the international scene, while their great season was the two decades between the world wars.[29] International society is not organized; thus "international organization"—in its abstract rationality a kind of legal counterpart to the utopian systems of eighteenth- and nineteenth-century philosophy—became the scientific formula which, since the leading pacifist and Nobel Prize winner, A. H. Fried, propounded it at the beginning of the century, has been the credo of a whole school of thought. Others would look to material remedies. Are not wars being fought with arms? Let us prohibit or at least reduce armaments, and war will no longer be possible or at least will be less likely. Others, again, would combine different remedies, defending the combination—"on scientific grounds"—as the only appropriate one. Thus the French Radical-Socialist party advocated "security, arbitration, disarmament" as logical successive steps

---

28. Ralph Waldo Emerson, *Essays: Second Series* (Boston: Houghton Mifflin, 1899), pp. 204–205.

29. See Kenneth W. Thompson, *Ethics, Functionalism and Power in International Politics: The Crisis in Values* (Baton Rouge, Louisiana: Louisiana University Press, 1979), pp. 35–45.

for the establishment of permanent peace; whereas the French Socialists reversed the sequence and swore to the exclusive scientific value of the formula "security through arbitration and disarmament." French foreign policy has been especially productive in abstract schemes which, like the "plan Briand," the "plan Laval," the "plan Tardieux," the "plan Herriot," or the "plan Paul-Boncour," pretended to give in one legal formula a scientific solution to the problems of European security.

In other quarters, especially since the crisis of 1929, the "single cause" of international unrest has been found in the economic field. Restrictions on international trade, the lack of raw materials, and insufficient international purchasing power drive nations to war, so the argument ran. Then let us find a scientific formula for reciprocal trade agreements, for the redistribution of raw materials, and for the floating of international loans—and there will be peace. Faced by the imperialistic aspirations of the thirties, it was reasoned that whenever nations cannot change the status quo peacefully, they will try to change it by war; thus peaceful change, scientifically defined, would make war unnecessary. Since bankers' fears for their investments was responsible for our involvement in the First World War, let us outlaw loans to belligerents: we shall thus escape participation in the next one. More recently, it has been "discovered" that national sovereignty is responsible for war; it follows that the pooling of national sovereignties in a world federation or at least in a federation of the democracies is a scientific solution to the problem of war and peace. Thus our era is always in search of the scientific formula, but an obstinate reality again and again makes the solution of today the fallacy of tomorrow.

The "scientific" era of international relations resulted in the substitution of supposedly scientific standards for genuine political evaluations; in some cases this went so far as to impede, if not entirely destroy, the ability to make any intelligent political decisions at all. Power, however limited and qualified, is the value which international politics recognizes as supreme. The test to which international political decisions must be subject refers, therefore, to the measure in which those decisions affect the distribution of power. The question which Richelieu, Hamilton (no less than Jefferson, for that matter), or Disraeli would ask before they acted on the international scene was: Does this decision increase or decrease the power of this and other nations? The question of the international "scientist" is different. Since for him the history of international affairs amounts to a succession of scientific problems, correctly or incorrectly handled by informed or misinformed officials, the supreme value is not power but truth. The quest for and the defense of power then become aberrations from the scientific attitude, which looks for causes and remedies. If we do not like the way things are, let us look for its cause and change things by changing the cause. There is essentially nothing to fight for; there is always something to analyze, to understand, and to reform.

How was it possible for the modern mind to make the belief in the all-embracing powers of science the *controlling force* of its foreign policy? Here again, the answer is to be found in the general premises of rationalistic philosophy, seemingly verified in its universal assumptions by domestic experience. The victory of liberalism in the domestic field led to a peculiar narrowing of the political, and a corresponding widening of the nonpolitical, sphere; and thus the latter was open to detached rational examination. Objectives which formerly had been seen as the prize in the struggle for political power were now approached in a dispassionate, matter-of-fact way and mastered in accordance with the specific techniques of economics, administration, or law. First the natural sciences and religion had freed themselves from political domination and had established their autonomy. Then liberalism, by conquering the state, freed an ever increasing domain from direct political domination; finally, liberalism seemed to expel even politics from the realm of the state and to make statecraft itself a science. Commerce and industry were the first to win their autonomy under reason. That which for the physiocrats was still a political program, unsuccessfully suggested to the political powers of the day, was for Adam Smith already a system of scientific truths verified by experience, the practical implications of which no reasonable man could escape. Political tribunals were replaced by independent courts composed of judges trained to render justice according to the principles of legal science. Antiquated and arbitrary election systems favoring certain political groups made way for scientific devices which would secure full and equal representation for all citizens. The civil service system put the selection of government personnel on an objective, nonpolitical basis. Today, legislative reforms are increasingly prepared by committees of experts who seem to be influenced largely by scientific instead of political considerations. Taxation, administration, and insurance become "scientific" in approach; and, finally, there is no field of governmental activity which would not be regarded as a proper area for the application of "political science."

The use of the scientific method in politics, to which the modern mind was led by its perception of the liberal experience, was and is a political fallacy in domestic affairs. There, however, the refined mechanism of political pressure and self-interest serves as an automatic check on doctrinaire excess. In the international field such a mechanism, acting directly upon the individual, does not exist. It is here, therefore, that the belief in the limitless power of the scientific formula has become particularly prolific—and particularly ineffective. For it is here that the panaceas engendered by this belief have no connection whatsoever with the forces which determine the actual course of events. Events will, therefore, either follow their course as though all those proposals by international commissions of experts and other rationalist-utopian devices had never been invented. Or those devices will be applied in an exceptional instance and will then produce effects unforeseen by their promoters and frequently disastrous to them—such as the sanctions against Italy during the Italo-Ethiopian war. Yet, as a supreme irony, this school of thought attempts to monopolize for itself the virtue of being "practical"; it treats with disdain the rare attempts to base international action on a genuine understanding of the forces determining political reality rather than on the ideal postulates of abstract reason.[30]

---

30. As far back as 1877 James Lorimer could write in "Le problème final du droit international," *Revue du droit international et de legislation comparèe*, IX (1877), p. 184: "Strangely enough, however, these speculations of English utilitarianism, taken as a whole, are of all the dissertations on the subject I know the least useful from the practical point of view." Cf. also Beard, *op. cit.*, p. 129: "Nearly every evil that was inconceivable in internationalist ideology in 1919 came to pass within the span of twenty years. It would seem then that this scheme of thought had been based upon some misconceptions respecting the nature and propensities of men and nations or, if this explanation is invalid, that internationalists had not adopted the corect 'approach' to the goal they had set before themselves. Their image of the world had not corresponded with sufficient exactness to its realities or their methods had been deficient in points of technique. They could, and some of them did, ascribe their defeats to the madness of men and nations but this was a confession that their former premises and actions had been founded upon errors of calculation. In any event the verdict was the same, unless all the blame was to be laid on Americans as the world's greatest scapegoats."

The Four Functions of Force

Robert J. Art

Art describes and distinguishes between what he sees as the four basic uses of military power in the international system and how states utilize these techniques in pursuit of their goals.

In view of what is likely to be before us, it is vital to think carefully and precisely about the uses and limits of military power. That is the purpose of this essay. It is intended as a backdrop for policy debates, not a prescription of specific policies. It consciously eschews elaborate detail on the requisite military forces for scenarios *a . . . n* and focuses instead on what military power has and has not done, can and cannot do. Every model of how the world works has policy implications. But not every policy is based on a clear view of how the world works. What, then, are the uses to which military power can be put? How have nuclear weapons affected these uses? And what is the future of force in a world of nuclear parity and increasing economic interdependence?

WHAT ARE THE USES OF FORCE?

The goals that states pursue range widely and vary considerably from case to case. Military power is more useful for realizing some goals than others, though it is generally considered of some use by most states for all of the goals that they hold. If we attempt, however, to be descriptively accurate, to enumerate all of the purposes for which states use force, we shall simply end up with a bewildering list. Descriptive accuracy is not a virtue *per se* for analysis. In fact, descriptive accuracy is generally bought at the cost of analytical utility. (A concept that is descriptively accurate is usually analytically useless.) Therefore, rather than compile an exhaustive list of such purposes, I have selected four categories that themselves analytically exhaust the functions that force can serve: defense, deterrence, compellence, and "swaggering".[1]

Not all four functions are necessarily well or equally served by a given military posture. In fact, usually only the great powers have the wherewithall to develop military forces that can serve more than two functions at once. Even then, this is achieved only vis à vis smaller powers, not vis à vis the other great ones. The measure of the capabilities of a state's military forces must be made relative to those of another state, not with reference to some absolute scale. A state that can compel another state can also defend against it and usually deter it. A state that can defend against another state cannot thereby automatically deter or compel it. A state can deter another state without having the ability to either defend against or compel it. A state that can swagger vis à vis another may or may not be able to perform any of the other three functions relative to it.

[1] The term "compellence" was coined by Thomas C. Schelling in his *Arms and Influence* (New Haven Yale University Press, 1966). Part of my discussion of compellence and deterrence draws upon his as it appears in Chapter 2 (pp. 69-86), but, as will be made clear below, I disagree with some of his conclusions.

From *International Politics Enduring Concepts and Contemporary Issues* by Robert J. Art and Robert Jervis, 1992 by HarperCollins Publishers, pp. 132-145. Reprinted by permission of HarperCollins. Italics added.

Where feasible, defense is the goal that all states aim for first. If defense is not possible, deterrence is generally the next priority. Swaggering is the function most difficult to pin down analytically; deterrence, the one whose achievement is the most difficult to demonstrate; compellence, the easiest to demonstrate but among the hardest to achieve. The following discussion develops these points more fully.

The ***defensive*** use of force is the deployment of military power so as to be able to do two things—to ward off an attack and to minimize damage to oneself if attacked. For defensive purposes, a state will direct its forces against those of a potential or actual attacker, but not against his unarmed population. For defensive purposes, a state can deploy its forces in place prior to an attack, use them after an attack has occurred to repel it, or strike first if it believes that an attack upon it is imminent or inevitable. The defensive use of force can thus involve both peaceful and physical employment and both repellent (second) strikes and offensive (first) strikes.[2] If a state strikes first when it believes an attack upon it is imminent, it is launching a preemptive blow. If it strikes first when it believes an attack is inevitable but not momentary, it is launching a preventive blow. Preemptive and preventive blows are undertaken when a state calculates, first, that others plan to attack it and, second, that to delay in striking offensively is against its interests. A state preempts in order to wrest the advantage of the first strike from an opponent. A state launches a preventive attack because it believes that others will attack it when the balance of forces turns in their favor and therefore attacks while the balance of forces is in its favor. In both cases it is better to strike first than to be struck first. The major distinction between preemption and prevention is the calculation about when an opponent's attack will occur. For preemption, it is a matter of hours, days, or even a few weeks at the most; for prevention, months or even a few years. In the case of preemption, the state has almost no control over the timing of its attack; in the case of prevention, the state can in a more leisurely way contemplate the timing of its attack. For both cases, it is the belief in the certainty of war that governs the offensive, defensive attack. For both cases, the maxim, "the best defense is a good offense," makes good sense.

The ***deterrent*** use of force is the deployment of military power so as to be able to prevent an adversary from doing something that one does not want him to do and that he might otherwise be tempted to do by threatening him with unacceptable punishment if he does it. Deterrence is thus the threat of retaliation. Its purpose is to prevent something undesirable from happening. The threat of punishment is directed at the adversary's population and/or industrial infrastructure. The effectiveness of the threat depends upon a state's ability to convince a potential adversary that it has both the will and power to punish him severely if he undertakes the undesirable action in question. Deterrence

---

2. Military power can be used in one of two modes—"physically" and "peacefully." The physical use of force refers to its actual employment against all adversary, usually but not always in a mutual exchange of blows. The peaceful use of force refers either to an explicit threat to resort to force, or to the implicit threat to use it that is communicated simply by a state's having it available for use. The physical use of force means that one nation is literally engaged in harming, destroying, or crippling those possessions which another nation holds dear, including its military forces. The peaceful use of force is referred to as such because, while force is "used" in the sense that it is employed explicitly or implicitly for the assistance it is thought to render in achieving a given goal, it does not result in any physical destruction to another nation's valued possessions. There is obviously a gray area between these two modes of use—the one in which a nation prepares (that is, gears up or mobilizes or moves about) its military forces for use against another nation but has not yet committed them such that they are inflicting damage.

therefore employs force peacefully. It is the threat to resort to force in order to punish that is the essence of deterrence. If the threat has to be carried out, deterrence by definition has failed. A deterrent threat is made precisely with the intent that it will not have to be carried out. Threats are made to prevent actions from being undertaken. If the threat has to be implemented, the action has already been undertaken. Hence deterrence can be judged successful only if the retaliatory threats have not been implemented.

Deterrence and defense are alike in that both are intended to protect the state or its closest allies from physical attacks. The purpose of both is dissuasion—persuading others *not* to undertake actions harmful to oneself. The defensive use of force dissuades by convincing an adversary that he cannot conquer one's military forces. The deterrent use of force dissuades by convincing the adversary that his population and territory will suffer terrible damage if he initiates the undesirable action. Defense dissuades by presenting an unvanquishable military force. Deterrence dissuades by presenting the certainty of retaliatory devastation.

Defense is possible without deterrence, and deterrence is possible without defense. A state can have the military wherewithall to repel an invasion without also being able to threaten devastation to the invader's population or territory. Similarly, a state can have the wherewithall credibly to threaten an adversary with such devastation and yet be unable to repel his invading force. Defense, therefore, does not necessarily buy deterrence, nor deterrence defense. A state that can defend itself from attack, moreover, will have little need to develop the wherewithall to deter. If physical attacks can be repelled or if the damage from them drastically minimized, the incentive to develop a retaliatory capability is low. A state that cannot defend itself, however, will try to develop an effective deterrent if that be possible. No state will leave its population and territory open to attack if it has the means to redress the situation. Whether a given state can defend or deter or do both vis a vis another depends upon two factors: (1) the quantitative balance of forces between it and its adversary; and (2) the qualitative balance of forces, that is, whether the extant military technology favors the offense or the defense. These two factors are situation-specific and therefore require careful analysis of the case at hand.

The ***compellent*** use of force is the deployment of military power so as to be able either to stop an adversary from doing something that he has already undertaken or to get him to do something that he has not yet undertaken. Compellence, in Schelling's words, "involves initiating an action . . . that can cease, or become harmless, only if the opponent responds."[3] Compellence can employ force either physically or peacefully. A state can start actually harming another with physical destruction until the latter abides by the former's wishes. Or, a state can take actions against another that do not cause physical harm but that require the latter to pay some type of significant price until it changes its behavior. America's bombing of North Vietnam in early 1965 was an example of physical compellence; Tirpitz's building of a German fleet aimed against England's in the two decades before World War I, an example of peaceful compellence. In the first case, the United States started bombing North Vietnam in order to compel it to stop assisting the Vietcong forces in South Vietnam. In the latter case, Germany built a battlefleet that in an engagement threatened to cripple England's in order to compel her to make a general political settlement advantageous to Germany. In both cases, one

3. Schelling, *Arms and Influence*, 72.

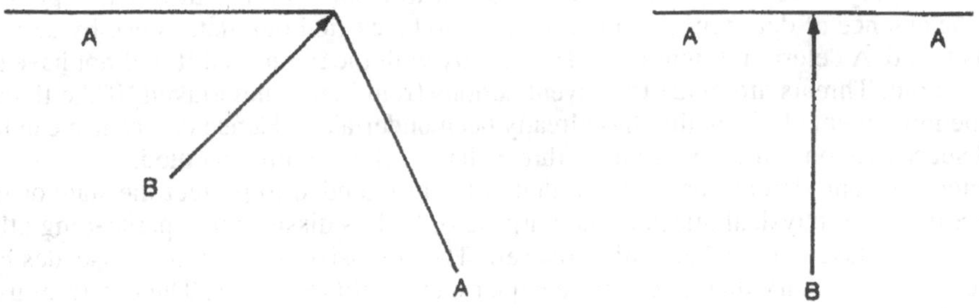

Compellence

(1) A is doing something that B cannot tolerate.
(2) B initiates action against A in order to get him to stop his intolerable actions.
(3) A stops his intolerable actions and B stops his (or both cease simultaneously).

Deterrence

(1) A is presently not doing anything that B finds intolerable.
(2) B tells A that if A changes his behavior and does something intolerable, B will punish him.
(3) A continues not to do anything B finds intolerable.

Figure 1.

state initiated some type of action against another precisely so as to be able to stop it, to bargain it away for the appropriate response from the "put upon" state.

The distinction between compellence and deterrence is one between the active and passive use of force. The success of a deterrent threat is measured by its not having to be used. The success of a compellent action is measured by how closely and quickly the adversary conforms to one's stipulated wishes. In the case of successful deterrence, one is trying to demonstrate a negative, to show why something did not happen. It can never be clear whether one's actions were crucial to, or irrelevant to, why another state chose *not* to do something. In the case of successful compellence, the clear sequence of actions and reactions lends a compelling plausibility to the centrality of one's actions. Figure 1 illustrates the distinction. In successful compellence, state B can claim that its pressure deflected state A from its course of action. In successful deterrence, state B has no change in state A's behavior to point to, but instead must resort to claiming that its threats were responsible for the continuity in A's behavior. State A may have changed its behavior for reasons other than state B's compellent action. State A may have continued with its same behavior for reasons other than state B's deterrent threat. "Proving" the importance of B's influence on A for either case is not easy, but it is more plausible to claim that B influenced A when there is a change in A's behavior than when there is not. Explaining why something did not happen is more difficult than explaining why something did.

Compellence may be easier to demonstrate than deterrence, but it is harder to achieve. Schelling argues that compellent actions tend to be vaguer in their objectives than deterrent threats and for that reason more difficult to attain.[4] If an adversary has a hard time understanding what it is that one wished him to do, his compliance with one's wishes is made more difficult. There is, however, no inherent reason why a compellent action must be vaguer than a deterrent threat with regard to how clearly the adversary understands what is wanted from him. "Do not attack me" is not any clearer in its ultimate meaning that "stop attacking my friend." A state can be as confused or as clear about what it wishes to prevent as it can be about what it wishes to stop. The clarity, or lack of it, of the objectives of compellent actions and deterrent threats does not vary according to whether the given action is compellent or deterrent in nature, but rather according to a welter of particularities associated with the given action. Some objectives, for example, are inherently clearer and hence easier to perceive than others. Some statesmen communicate more clearly than others. Some states have more power to bring to bear for a given objective than others. It is the specifics of a given situation, not any intrinsic difference between compellence and deterrence, that determines the clarity with which an objective is perceived.

We must, therefore, look elsewhere for the reason as to why compellence is comparatively harder to achieve than deterrence. It lies, not in what one asks another to do, but in *how* one asks. With deterrence, state B asks something of state A in this fashion: "Do not take action X; for if you do, I will bash you over the head with this club." With compellence, state B asks something of state A in this fashion: "I am now going to bash you over the head with this club and will continue to do so until you do what I want." In the former case, state A can easily deny with great plausibility any intention of having planned to take action X. In the latter case, state A cannot deny either that it is engaged in a given course of action or that it is being subjected to pressure by state B. If they are to be successful, compellent actions require a state to alter its behavior in a manner quite visible to all in response to an equally visible forceful initiative taken by another state. In contrast to compellent actions, deterrent threats are both easier to appear to have ignored or easier to acquiesce to without great loss of face. In contrast to deterrent threats, compellent actions more directly engage the prestige and the passions of the put-upon state. Less prestige is lost in not doing something than in clearly altering behavior due to pressure from another. In the case of compellence, a state has publicly committed its prestige and resources to a given line of conduct that it is now asked to give up. This is not so for deterrence. Thus, compellence is intrinsically harder to attain than deterrence, not because its objectives are vaguer, but because it demands more humiliation from the compelled state.

The fourth purpose to which military power can be put is the most difficult to be precise about. ***Swaggering*** is in part a residual category, the deployment of military power for purposes other than defense, deterrence, or compellence. Force is not aimed directly at dissuading another state from attacking, at repelling attacks, nor at compelling it to do something specific. The objectives for swaggering are more diffuse, ill-defined, and problematic than that. Swaggering almost always involves only the peaceful use of force and is expressed usually in one of two ways: displaying one's military might at military exercises and national demonstrations and buying or building the era's most prestigious weapons. The swagger use of force is the most egoistic: It aims to enhance the national pride of a people or to satisfy the personal ambitions of its ruler. A state or statesman swaggers in order to look and feel more powerful and important, to be taken seriously by others in the councils of international decision making, to enhance the nation's image in the eyes of

---

4. Ibid., 72-73.

others. If its image is enhanced, the nation's defense, deterrent, and compellent capabilities may also be enhanced; but swaggering is not undertaken solely or even primarily for these specific purposes. Swaggering is pursued because it offers to bring prestige "on the cheap." Swaggering is pursued because of the fundamental yearning of states and statesmen for respect and prestige. Swaggering is more something to be enjoyed for itself than to be employed for a specific, consciously thought-out end.

And yet, the instrumental role of swaggering cannot be totally discounted because of the fundamental relation between force and foreign policy that obtains in an anarchic environment. Because there is a connection between the military might that a nation is thought to possess and the success that it achieves in attaining its objectives, the enhancement of a state's stature in the eyes of others can always be justified on *realpolitik* lines. If swaggering causes other states to take one's interests more seriously into account, then the general interests of the state will benefit. Even in its instrumental role, however, swaggering is undertaken less for any given end than for all ends. The swaggering function of military power is thus at one and the same time the most comprehensive and the most diffuse, the most versatile in its effects and the least focused in its immediate aims, the most instrumental in the long run and the least instrumental in the short run, easy to justify on hardheaded grounds and often undertaken on emotional grounds. Swaggering mixes the rational and irrational more than the other three functions of military power and, for that reason, remains both pervasive in international relations and elusive to describe.

Defense, deterrence, compellence, and swaggering—these are the four general purposes for which force can be employed. Discriminating among them analytically, however, is easier than applying them in practice. This is due to two factors. First, we need to know the motives behind an act in order to judge its purpose; but the problem is that motives cannot be readily inferred from actions because several motives can be served by the same action. But neither can one readily infer the motives of a state from what it publicly or officially proclaims them to be. Such statements should not necessarily be taken at face value because of the role that bluff and dissimulation play in statecraft. Such statements are also often concocted with domestic political, not foreign audiences in mind, or else are deliberate exercises in studied ambiguity. Motives are important in order to interpret actions, but neither actions nor words always clearly delineate motives.

It is, moreover, especially difficult to distinguish defensive from compellent actions and deterrent from swaggering ones unless we know the reasons for which they were undertaken. Peaceful defensive preparations often look largely the same as peaceful compellent ones. Defensive attacks are nearly indistinguishable from compellent ones. Is he who attacks first the defender or the compeller? Deterrence and swaggering both involve the acquisition and display of an era's prestigious weapons. Are such weapons acquired to enhance prestige or to dissuade an attack? . . .

Where does all of this leave us? Our four categories tell us what are the four possible purposes for which states can employ military power. The attributes of each alert us to the types of evidence for which to search. But because the context of an action is crucial in order to judge its ultimate purpose, these four categories cannot be applied mindlessly and historically. Each state's purpose in using force in a given instance must fall into one of these four categories. We know *a priori* what the possibilities are. Which one it is, is an exercise in judgment, an exercise that depends as much upon the particulars of the given case as it does upon the general features of the given category. . . .

Table 2: The Purposes of Force

Type	Purpose	Mode	Targets	Characteristics
Defensive	Fend off attacks and/or reduce damage of an attack	Peaceful and physical	Primarily military Secondarily industrial	Defensive preparations can have dissuasion value; Defensive prep can look aggressive; first strikes can be taken for defense.
Deterrent	Prevent adversary from initiating an action	Peaceful	Primarily civilian Secondarily industrial Tertiarily military	Threats of retaliation made so as not to have to be carried out; Second strike preparations can be viewed as first strike preparations.
Compellent	Get adversary to stop doing something or start doing something	Peaceful and physical	All three with no clear ranking	Easy to recognize but hard to achieve; Compellent actions can be justified on defensive grounds.
Swaggering	Enhance prestige	Peaceful	None	Difficult to describe because of instrumental and irrational nature; swaggering can be threatening.

Cooperation Under the Security Dilemma

Robert Jervis

In this seminal essay, Jervis explains the theoretical underpinnings of why cooperation is difficult to achieve in the international environment. He highlights the problems created by the anarchic nature of the world, yet suggests that there are several ways that these problems can be overcome and cooperation can be made more likely.

I. ANARCHY AND THE SECURITY DILEMMA

The lack of an international sovereign not only permits wars to occur, but also makes it difficult for states that are satisfied with the status quo to arrive at goals that they recognize as being in their common interest. Because there are no institutions or authorities that can make and enforce international laws, the policies of cooperation that will bring mutual rewards if others cooperate may bring disaster if they do not. Because states are aware of this, anarchy encourages behavior that leaves all concerned worse off than they could be, even in the extreme case in which all states would like to freeze the status quo. This is true of the men in Rousseau's "Stag Hunt." If they cooperate to trap the stag, they will all eat well. But if one person defects to chase a rabbit—which he likes less than stag—none of the others will get anything. Thus, all actors have the same preference order, and there is a solution that gives each his first choice: (1) cooperate and trap the stag (the international analogue being cooperation and disarmament); (2) chase a rabbit while others remain at their posts (maintain a high level of arms while others are disarmed); (3) all chase rabbits (arms competition and high risk of war); and (4) stay at the original position while another chases a rabbit (being disarmed while others are armed).[1] Unless each person thinks that the others will cooperate, he himself will not. And why might he fear that any other person would do something that would sacrifice his own first choice? The other might not understand the situation, or might not be

---

1. This kind of rank-ordering is not entirely an analyst's invention, as is shown by the following section of a British army memo of 1903 dealing with British and Russian railroad construction near the Persia-Afghanistan border:

The conditions of the problem may . . . be briefly summarized as follows: a) If we make a railway to Seistan while Russia remains inactive, we gain a considerable defensive advantage at considerable financial cost;

b) If Russia makes a railway to Seistan, while we remain inactive, she gains a considerable offensive advantage at considerable financial cost;

c) If both we and Russia make railways to Seistan, the defensive and offensive advantages may be held to neutralize each other; in other words, we shall have spent a good deal of money and be no better off than we are at present. On the other hand, we shall be no worse off, whereas under alternative (b) we shall be much worse off. Consequently, the theoretical balance of advantage lies with the proposed railway extension from Quetta to Seistan.

W. G. Nicholson. "Memorandum on Seistan and Other Points Raised in the Discussion on the Defence of India." (Committee of Imperial Defence, March 20, 1903). It should be noted that the possibility of neither side building railways was not mentioned, thus strongly biasing the analysis.

able to control his impulses if he saw a rabbit, or might fear that some other member of the group is unreliable. If the person voices any of these suspicions, others are more likely to fear that he will defect, thus making them more likely to defect, thus making it more rational for him to defect. Of course in this simple case and in many that are more realistic—there are a number of arrangements that could permit cooperation. But the main point remains: although actors may know that they seek a common goal, they may not be able to reach it.

Even when there is a solution that is everyone's first choice, the international case is characterized by three difficulties not present in the Stag Hunt. First, to the incentives to defect given above must be added the potent fear that even if the other state now supports the status quo, it may become dissatisfied later. No matter how much decision makers are committed to the status quo, they cannot bind themselves and their successors to the same path. Minds can be changed, new leaders can come to power, values can shift, new opportunities and dangers can arise.

The second problem arises from a possible solution. In order to protect their possessions, states often seek to control resources or land outside their own territory. Countries that are not self-sufficient must try to assure that the necessary supplies will continue to flow in wartime. This was part of the explanation for Japan's drive into China and Southeast Asia before World War II. If there were an international authority that could guarantee access, this motive for control would disappear. But since there is not, even a state that would prefer the status quo to increasing its area of control may pursue the latter policy.

When there are believed to be tight linkages between domestic and foreign policy or between the domestic politics of two states, the quest for security may drive states to interfere pre-emptively in the domestic politics of others in order to provide an ideological buffer zone. Thus, Metternich's justification for supervising the politics of the Italian states has been summarized as follows:

> Every state is absolutely sovereign in its internal affairs. But this implies that every state must do nothing to interfere in the internal affairs of another. However, any false or pernicious step taken by any state in its internal affairs may disturb the repose of another state, and this consequent disturbance of another state's repose constitutes an interference in that state's internal affairs. Therefore, every state—or rather, every sovereign of a great power—has the duty, in the name of the sacred right of independence of every state, to supervise the governments of smaller states and to prevent them from taking false and pernicious steps in their internal affairs.[2]

More frequently, the concern is with direct attack. In order to protect themselves, states seek to control, or at least to neutralize, areas on their borders. But attempts to establish buffer zones can alarm others who have stakes there, who fear that undesirable precedents will be set, or who believe that their own vulnerability will be increased. When buffers are sought in areas empty of great powers, expansion tends to feed on itself in order to protect what is acquired, as was often noted by those who opposed colonial expansion. Balfour's complaint was typical: "Every time I come to a discussion—at intervals of, say, five years—I find there is a new sphere which we have got to guard, which is supposed to protect the gateways of India. Those gateways are getting

---

2. Paul Schroeder, *Metternich's Diplomacy at Its Zenith, 1820-1823* (Westport, Conn.: Greenwood Press 1969), 126.

further and further away from India, and I do not know how far west they are going to be brought by the General Staff."[3]

Though this process is most clearly visible when it involves territorial expansion, it often operates with the increase of less tangible power and influence. The expansion of power usually brings with it an expansion of responsibilities and commitments; to meet them, still greater power is required. The state will take many positions that are subject to challenge. It will be involved with a wide range of controversial issues unrelated to its core values. And retreats that would be seen as normal if made by a small power would be taken as an index of weakness inviting predation if made by a large one.

The third problem present in international politics but not in the Stag Hunt is the security dilemma: many of the means by which a state tries to increase its security decrease the security of others. In domestic society, there are several ways to increase the safety of one's person and property without endangering others. One can move to a safer neighborhood, put bars on the windows, avoid dark streets, and keep a distance from suspicious-looking characters. Of course these measures are not convenient, cheap, or certain of success. But no one save criminals need be alarmed if a person takes them. In international politics, however, one state's gain in security often inadvertently threatens others. In explaining British policy on naval disarmament in the interwar period to the Japanese, Ramsey MacDonald said that "Nobody wanted Japan to be insecure."[4] But the problem was not with British desires, but with the consequences of her policy. In earlier periods, too, Britain had needed a navy large enough to keep the shipping lanes open. But such a navy could not avoid being a menace to any other state with a coast that could be raided, trade that could be interdicted, or colonies that could be isolated. When Germany started building a powerful navy before World War I, Britain objected that it could only be an offensive weapon aimed at her. As Sir Edward Grey, the Foreign Secretary, put it to King Edward VII: "If the German Fleet ever becomes superior to ours, the German Army can conquer this country. There is no corresponding risk of this kind to Germany; for however superior our Fleet was, no naval victory could bring us any nearer to Berlin." The English position was half correct: Germany's navy was an anti-British instrument. But the British often overlooked what the Germans knew full well: "in every quarrel with England, German colonies and trade were . . . hostages for England to take." Thus, whether she intended it or not, the British Navy constituted an important instrument of coercion.[5]

II. WHAT MAKES COOPERATION MORE LIKELY?

Given this gloomy picture, the obvious question is, why are we not all dead? Or, to put it less starkly, what kinds of variables ameliorate the impact of anarchy and the security

---

3. Quoted in Michael Howard, *The Continental Commitment* (Harmondsworth, England: Penguin 1974), 67.

4. Quoted in Gerald Wheeler, *Prelude to Pearl Harbor* (Columbia: University of Missouri Press 1963), 167.

5. Quoted in Leonard Wainstein, "The Dreadnought Gap," in Robert Art and Kenneth Waltz, eds., *The Use of Force* (Boston: Little, Brown 1971), 155; Raymond Sontag, *European Diplomatic History, 1871-1932* (New York: Appleton-Century-Crofts 1933), 147. The French had made a similar argument 50 years earlier; see James Phinney Baxter III, *The Introduction of the Ironclad Warship* (Cambridge: Harvard University Press 1933), 149. For a more detailed discussion of the security dilemma, see Jervis, *Perception and Misperception in International Politics* (Princeton: Princeton University Press 1976), 62-76.

dilemma? The workings of several can be seen in terms of the Stag Hunt or repeated plays of the Prisoner's Dilemma. The Prisoner's Dilemma differs from the Stag Hunt in that there is no solution that is in the best interests of all the participants; there are offensive as well as defensive incentives to defect from the coalition with the others; and, if the game is to be played only once, the only rational response is to defect. But if the game is repeated indefinitely, the latter characteristic no longer holds and we can analyze the game in terms similar to those applied to the Stag Hunt. It would be in the interest of each actor to have others deprived of the power to defect; each would be willing to sacrifice this ability if others were similarly restrained. But if the others are not, then it is in the actor's interest to retain the power to defect.[6] The game theory matrices for these two situations are given below (Figure 1), with the numbers in the boxes being the order of the actors' preferences.

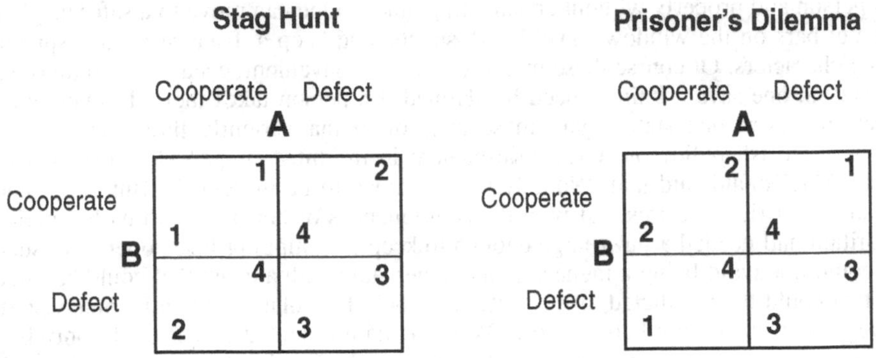

Figure 1.

We can see the logical possibilities by rephrasing our question: "Given either of the above situations, what makes it more or less likely that the players will cooperate and arrive at CC?" The chances of achieving this outcome will be increased by: (1) anything that increases incentives to cooperate by increasing the gains of mutual cooperation (CC) and/or decreasing the costs the actor will pay if he cooperates and the other does not (CD); (2) anything that decreases the incentives for defecting by decreasing the gains of taking advantage of the other (DC) and/or increasing the costs of mutual non cooperation (DD); (3) anything that increases each side's expectation that the other will cooperate.[7]

The Costs of Being Exploited (CD)

The fear of being exploited (that is, the cost of CD) most strongly drives the security dilemma; one of the main reasons why international life is not more nasty, brutish, and short is that states are not as vulnerable as men are in a state of nature. People are easy to kill, but as Adam Smith replied to a friend who feared that the Napoleonic Wars

6. Experimental evidence for this proposition is summarized in James Tedeschi, Barry Schlenker, and Thomas Bonoma, *Conflict, Power, and Games* (Chicago: Aldine 1973), 135-41.

7. The results of Prisoner's Dilemma games played in the laboratory support this argument. See Anatol Rapoport and Albert Chammah, *Prisoner's Dilemma* (Ann Arbor: University of Michigan Press 1965), 33-50. Also see Robert Axelrod, *Conflict of Interest* (Chicago: Markham 1970), 60-70.

would ruin England, "Sir, there is a great deal of ruin in a nation."[8] The easier it is to destroy a state, the greater the reason for it either to join a larger and more secure unit, or else to be especially suspicious of others, to require a large army, and, if conditions are favorable, to attack at the slightest provocation rather than wait to be attacked. If the failure to eat that day be it venison or rabbit—means that he will starve, a person is likely to defect in the Stag Hunt even if he really likes venison and has a high level of trust in his colleagues. (Defection is especially likely if the others are also starving or if they know that he is.) By contrast, if the costs of CD are lower, if people are well-fed or states are resilient, they can afford to take a more relaxed view of threats.

A relatively low cost of CD has the effect of transforming the game from one in which both players make their choices simultaneously to one in which an actor can make his choice after the other has moved. He will not have to defect out of fear that the other will, but can wait to see what the other will do. States that can afford to be cheated in a bargain or that cannot be destroyed by a surprise attack can more easily trust others and need not act at the first, and ambiguous, sign of menace. Because they have a margin of time and error, they need not match, or more than match, any others' arms in peacetime. They can mobilize in the prewar period or even at the start of the war itself, and still survive. For example, those who opposed a crash program to develop the H-bomb felt that the U.S. margin of safety was large enough so that even if Russia managed to gain a lead in the race, America would not be endangered. The program's advocates disagreed: "If we let the Russians get the super first, catastrophe becomes all but certain."[9]

When the costs of CD are tolerable, not only is security easier to attain but, what is even more important here, the relatively low level of arms and relatively passive foreign policy that a status-quo power will be able to adopt are less likely to threaten others. Thus it is easier for status quo states to act on their common interests if they are hard to conquer. All other things being equal, a world of small states will feel the effects of anarchy much more than a world of large ones. Defensible borders, large size, and protection against sudden attack not only aid the state, but facilitate cooperation that can benefit all states.

Of course, if one state gains invulnerability by being more powerful than most others, the problem will remain because its security provides a base from which it can exploit others. When the price a state will pay for DD is low, it leaves others with few hostages for its good behavior. Others who are more vulnerable will grow apprehensive, which will lead them to acquire more arms and will reduce the chances of cooperation. The best situation is one in which a state will not suffer greatly if others exploit it, for example, by cheating on an arms control agreement (that is, the costs of CD are low); but it will pay a high long-run price if cooperation with the others breaks down—for example, if agreements cease functioning or if there is a long war (that is, the costs of DD are high). The state's invulnerability is then mostly passive; it provides some protection, but it cannot be used to menace others. As we will discuss below, this situation is approximated when it is easier for states to defend themselves than to attack others, or when mutual deterrence obtains because neither side can protect itself.

The differences between highly vulnerable and less vulnerable states are illustrated by the contrasting policies of Britain and Austria after the Napoleonic Wars. Britain's geographic isolation and political stability allowed her to take a fairly relaxed view of distur-

8. Quoted in Bernard Brodie, *Strategy in the Missile Age* (Princeton: Princeton University Press 1959), 6.

9. Herbert York, *The Advisors: Oppenheimer, Teller, and the Superbomb* (San Francisco: Freeman 1976), 56-60.

bances on the Continent. Minor wars and small changes in territory or in the distribution of power did not affect her vital interests. An adversary who was out to overthrow the system could be stopped after he had made his intentions clear. And revolutions within other states were no menace, since they would not set off unrest within England. Austria, surrounded by strong powers, was not so fortunate; her policy had to be more closely attuned to all conflicts. By the time an aggressor-state had clearly shown its colors, Austria would be gravely threatened. And foreign revolutions be they democratic or nationalistic, would encourage groups in Austria to upset the existing order. So it is not surprising that Metternich propounded the doctrine summarized earlier, which defended Austria's right to interfere in the internal affairs of others, and that British leaders rejected this view. Similarly, Austria wanted the Congress system to be a relatively tight one, regulating most disputes. The British favored a less centralized system. In other words, in order to protect herself, Austria had either to threaten or to harm others, whereas Britain did not. For Austria and her neighbors the security dilemma was acute; for Britain it was not.

The ultimate cost of CD is of course loss of sovereignty. This cost can vary from situation to situation. The lower it is (for instance, because the two states have compatible ideologies, are similar ethnically, have a common culture, or because the citizens of the losing state expect economic benefits), the less the impact of the security dilemma; the greater the costs, the greater the impact of the dilemma. Here is another reason why extreme differences in values and ideologies exascerbate international conflict.

It is through the lowering of the costs of CD that the proposed Rhodesian "safety net"—guaranteeing that whites who leave the country will receive fair payment for their property—would have the paradoxical effect of making it more likely that the whites will stay. This is less puzzling when we see that the whites are in a multi-person Prisoner's Dilemma with each other. Assume that all whites are willing to stay if most of the others stay; but, in the absence of guarantees, if there is going to be a mass exodus, all want to be among the first to leave (because late-leavers will get less for their property and will have more trouble finding a country to take them in).Then the problem is to avoid a self-fulfilling prophecy in which each person rushes to defect because he fears others are going to. In narrowing the gap between the payoff for leaving first (DC) and leaving last (CD) by reducing the cost of the latter, the guarantees make it easier for the whites to cooperate among themselves and stay.

Subjective Security Demands

Decision makers act in terms of the vulnerability they feel, which can differ from the actual situation; we must therefore examine the decision makers' subjective security requirements.[10] Two dimensions are involved. First, even if they agree about the objective situation, people can differ about how much security they desire—or, to put it more precisely, about the price they are willing to pay to gain increments of security. The more states value their security above all else (that is, see a prohibitively high cost in CD), the more they are likely to be sensitive to even minimal threats, and to demand high levels of arms. And if arms are positively valued because of pressures from a military-industrial

[10] For the development of the concept of subjective security, see Arnold Wolfers, *Discord and Collaboration* (Baltimore: Johns Hopkins Press 1962), chap. 10. In the present section we assume that the state believes that its security can be best served by increasing its arms; later we will discuss some of the conditions under which this assumption does not hold.

complex, it will be especially hard for status quo powers to cooperate. By contrast, the security dilemma will not operate as strongly when pressing domestic concerns increase the opportunity costs of armaments. In this case, the net advantage of exploiting the other (DC) will be less, and the costs of arms races (that is, one aspect of DD) will be greater; therefore the state will behave as though it were relatively invulnerable.

The second aspect of subjective security is the perception of threat (that is, the estimate of whether the other will cooperate).[11] A state that is predisposed to see either a specific other state as an adversary, or others in general as a menace, will react more strongly and more quickly than a state that sees its environment as benign. Indeed, when a state believes that another not only is not likely to be an adversary, but has sufficient interests in common with it to be an ally, then it will actually welcome an increase in the other's power.

British and French foreign policies in the interwar years illustrate these points. After the rise of Hitler, Britain and France felt that increases in each other's arms increased rather than decreased their own security. The differing policies that these states followed toward Germany can be explained by their differences on both dimensions of the variable of subjective security.[12] Throughout the period, France perceived Germany as more of a threat than England did. The British were more optimistic and argued that conciliation could turn Germany into a supporter of the status quo. Furthermore, in the years immediately following World War I, France had been more willing to forego other values in order to increase her security and had therefore followed a more belligerent policy than England, maintaining a larger army and moving quickly to counter German assertiveness. As this example shows, one cannot easily say how much subjective security a state should seek. High security requirements make it very difficult to capitalize on a common interest and run the danger of setting off spirals of arms races and hostility. The French may have paid this price in the 1920's. Low security requirements avoid this trap, but run the risk of having too few arms and of trying to conciliate an aggressor.

One aspect of subjective security related to the predisposition to perceive threat is the state's view of how many enemies it must be prepared to fight. A state can be relaxed about increases in another's arms if it believes that there is a functioning collective security system. The chances of peace are increased in a world in which the prevailing international system is valued in its own right, not only because most states restrain their ambitions and those who do not are deterred (these are the usual claims for a Concert system), but also because of the decreased chances that the status quo states will engage in unnecessary conflict out of the quest for security. Indeed, if there were complete faith in collective security, no state would want an army. By contrast, the security dilemma is insoluble when each state fears that many others, far from coming to its aid, are likely to join in any attack. Winston Churchill, as First Lord of the Admiralty, was setting a high security requirement when he noted:

---

11. The question of when an actor will see another as a threat is important and understudied. For a valuable treatment (although one marred by serious methodological flaws), see Raymond Cohen, "Threat Perception in International Relations," Ph. D. diss. (Hebrew University, 1974). Among the important factors, touched on below, are the lessons from the previous war.

12. Still the best treatment is Arnold Wolfers, *Britain and France Between Two Wars* (New York: Harcourt, Brace 1940).

> Besides the Great Powers, there are many small states who are buying or building great ships of war and whose vessels may by purchase, by some diplomatic combination, or by duress, be brought into the line against us. None of these powers need, like us, navies to defend their actual safety *of* independence. They build them so as to play a part in world affairs. It is sport to them. It is death to us.[13]

It takes great effort for any one state to be able to protect itself alone against an attack by several neighbors. More importantly, it is next to impossible for all states in the system to have this capability; Thus, a state's expectation that allies will be available and that only a few others will be able to join against it is almost a necessary condition for security requirements to be compatible.

Gains from Cooperation and Costs of a Breakdown (CC and DD)

The main costs of a policy of reacting quickly and severely to increases in the other's arms are not the price of one's own arms, but rather the sacrifice of the potential gains from cooperation (CC) and the increase in the dangers of needless arms races and wars (DD). The greater these costs, the greater the incentives to try cooperation and wait for fairly unambiguous evidence before assuming that the other must be checked by force. Wars would be much more frequent even if the first choice of all states was the status quo if they were less risky and costly, and if peaceful intercourse did not provide rich benefits. Ethiopia recently asked for guarantees that the Territory of Afars and Issas would not join a hostile alliance against it when it gained independence. A spokesman for the Territory replied that this was not necessary: Ethiopia "already had the best possible guarantee in the railroad" that links the two countries and provides indispensable revenue for the Territory.[14]

The basic points are well known and so we can move to elaboration. First, most statesmen know that to enter a war is to set off a chain of unpredictable and uncontrollable events. Even if everything they see points to a quick victory, they are likely to hesitate before all the uncertainties. And if the battlefield often produces startling results, so do the council chambers. The state may be deserted by allies or attacked by neutrals. Or the postwar alignment may rob it of the fruits of victory, as happened to Japan in 1895. Second, the domestic costs of wars must be weighed. Even strong states can be undermined by dissatisfaction with the way the war is run and by the necessary mobilization of men and ideas. Memories of such disruptions were one of the main reasons for the era of relative peace that followed the Napoleonic Wars. Liberal statesmen feared that large armies would lead to despotism; conservative leaders feared that wars would lead to revolution. (The other side of this coin is that when there are domestic consequences of foreign conflict that are positively valued, the net cost of conflict is lowered and cooperation becomes more difficult.) Third—turning to the advantages of cooperation—for states with large and diverse economies the gains from economic exchange are rarely if ever sufficient to prevent war. Norman Angell was wrong about World War I being impossible because of economic ties among the powers; and before World War II, the U.S. was Japan's most important trading partner. Fourth, the gains from cooperation can be increased, not only if each side gets more of the traditional values such as wealth, but also if each comes to value the other's well-being positively. Mutual cooperation will then have a double payoff: in addition to the direct gains, there will be the satisfaction of seeing the other prosper.[15]

---

13. Quoted in Peter Gretton, *Former Naval Person* (London: Casssell 1968), 151.

14. Michael Kaufman, "Tension Increases in French Colony," *New York Times,* July 11,1976.

While high costs of war and gains from cooperation will ameliorate the impact of the security dilemma, they can create a different problem. If the costs are high enough so that DD is the last choice for both sides, the game will shift to "Chicken." This game differs from the Stag Hunt in that each actor seeks to exploit the other; it differs from Prisoner's Dilemma in that both actors share an interest in avoiding mutual non-cooperation. In Chicken, if you think the other side is going to defect, you have to cooperate because, although being exploited (CD) is bad, it is not as bad as a total breakdown (DD). As the familiar logic of deterrence shows, the actor must then try to convince his adversary that he is going to stand firm (defect) and that the only way the other can avoid disaster is to back down (cooperate). Commitment, the rationality of irrationality, manipulating the communications system, and pretending not to understand the situation, are among the tactics used to reach this goal. The same logic applies when both sides are enjoying great benefits from cooperation. The side that can credibly threaten to disrupt the relationship unless its demands are met can exploit the other. This situation may not be stable, since the frequent use of threats may be incompatible with the maintenance of a cooperative relationship. Still, de Gaulle's successful threats to break up the Common Market unless his partners acceded to his wishes remind us that the shared benefits of cooperation as well as the shared costs of defection can provide the basis for exploitation. Similarly, one reason for the collapse of the Franco-British entente more than a hundred years earlier was that decision makers on both sides felt confident that their own country could safely pursue a policy that was against the other's interest because the other could not afford to destroy the highly valued relationship.[16] Because statesmen realize that the growth of positive interdependence can provide others with new levers of influence over them, they may resist such developments more than would be expected from the theories that stress the advantages of cooperation.

Gains from Exploitation (DC)

Defecting not only avoids the danger that a state will be exploited (CD), but brings positive advantages by exploiting the other (DC). The lower these possible gains, the greater the chances of cooperation. Even a relatively satisfied state can be tempted to expand by the hope of gaining major values. The temptation will be less when the state sees other ways of reaching its goals, and/or places a low value on what exploitation could bring. The gains may be low either because the immediate advantage provided by DC (for example, having more arms than the other side) cannot be translated into a political advantage (for example, gains in territory), or because the political advantage itself is not highly valued. For instance, a state may not seek to annex additional territory because the latter lacks raw materials, is inhabited by people of a different ethnic group, would be costly to garrison, or would be hard to assimilate without disturbing domestic politics and values. A state can reduce the incentives that another state has to attack it, by not being a threat to the latter and by providing goods and services that would be lost were the other to attempt exploitation.

Even where the direct advantages of DC are great, other considerations can reduce the net gain. Victory as well as defeat can set off undesired domestic changes within the state.

---

15. Experimental support for this argument is summarized in Morton Deutsch, *The Resolution of Conflict* (New Haven: Yale University Press 1973), 181-95.

16. Roger Bullen, *Palmerston, Guizot, and the Collapse of the Entente Cordiale* (London: Athlone Press 1974), 81, 88, 93, 212. For a different view of this case, see Stanley Mellon, "Entente, Diplomacy, and Fantasy," *Reviews in European History,* II, (September 1976), 376-80.

Exploitation has at times been frowned upon by the international community, thus reducing the prestige of a state that engages in it. Or others might in the future be quicker to see the state as a menace to them, making them more likely to arm, and to oppose it later. Thus, Bismarck's attempts to get other powers to cooperate with him in maintaining the status quo after 1871 were made more difficult by the widely-held mistrust of him that grew out of his earlier aggressions.[17]

The Probability That the Other Will Cooperate

The variables discussed so far influence the payoffs for each of the four possible outcomes. To decide what to do, the state has to go further and calculate the expected value of cooperating or defecting. Because such calculations involve estimating the probability that the other will cooperate, the state will have to judge how the variables discussed so far act on the other. To encourage the other to cooperate, a state may try to manipulate these variables. It can lower the other's incentives to defect by decreasing what it could gain by exploiting the state (DC)—the details would be similar to those discussed in the previous paragraph—and it can raise the costs of deadlock (DD). But if the state cannot make DD the worst outcome for the other, coercion is likely to be ineffective in the short run because the other can respond by refusing to cooperate, and dangerous in the long run because the other is likely to become convinced that the state is aggressive. So the state will have to concentrate on making cooperation more attractive. One way to do this is to decrease the costs the other will pay if it cooperates and the state defects (CD). Thus, the state could try to make the other less vulnerable. It was for this reason that in the late 1950's and early 1960's some American defense analysts argued that it would be good for both sides if the Russians developed hardened missiles. Of course, decreasing the other's vulnerability also decreases the state's ability to coerce it, and opens the possibility that the other will use this protection as a shield behind which to engage in actions inimical to the state. But by sacrificing some ability to harm the other, the state can increase the chances of mutually beneficial cooperation.

The state can also try to increase the gains that will accrue to the other from mutual cooperation (CC). Although the state will of course gain if it receives a share of any new benefits, even an increment that accrues entirely to the other will aid the state by increasing the likelihood that the other will cooperate.[18]

This line of argument can be continued through the infinite regressions that game theory has made familiar. If the other is ready to cooperate when it thinks the state will, the state can increase the chances of CC by showing that it *is* planning to cooperate. Thus the state should understate the gains it would make if it exploited the other (DC) and the costs it would pay if the other exploited it (CD), and stress or exaggerate the gains it would make under mutual cooperation (CC) and the costs it would pay if there is deadlock (DD). The state will also want to convince the other that it thinks that the other is likely to cooperate. If the other believes these things, it will see that the state has strong incentives to cooperate, and so it will cooperate in turn. One point should be emphasized. Because the other, like the state, may be driven to defect by the fear that it will be exploited if it does not, the state should try to reassure it that this will not happen. Thus, when Khrushchev

---

17. Similarly, a French diplomat has argued that "the worst result of Louis XIV's abandonment of our traditional policy was the distrust it aroused towards us abroad." Jules Cambon, "The Permanent Bases of French Foreign Policy," *Foreign Affairs*, viii (January 1930), 179.

18. This assumes, however. that these benefits to the other will not *so* improve the other's power position that it will be more able to menace the state in the future.

indicated his willingness to withdraw his missiles from Cuba, he simultaneously stressed to Kennedy that "we are of sound mind and understand perfectly well" that Russia could not launch a successful attack against the U.S., and therefore that there was no reason for the U.S. to contemplate a defensive, pre-emptive strike of its own.[19]

There is, however, a danger. If the other thinks that the state has little choice but to cooperate, it can credibly threaten to defect unless the state provides it with additional benefits. Great advantages of mutual cooperation, like high costs of war, provide a lever for competitive bargaining. Furthermore, for a state to stress how much it gains from cooperation may be to imply that it is gaining much more than the other and to suggest that the benefits should be distributed more equitably.

When each side is ready to cooperate if it expects the other to, inspection devices can ameliorate the security dilemma. Of course, even a perfect inspection system cannot guarantee that the other will not later develop aggressive intentions and the military means to act on them. But by relieving immediate worries and providing warning of coming dangers, inspection can meet a significant part of the felt need to protect oneself against future threats, and so make current cooperation more feasible. Similar functions are served by breaking up one large transaction into a series of smaller ones.[20] At each transaction each can see whether the other has cooperated; and its losses, if the other defects, will be small. And since what either side would gain by one defection is slight compared to the benefits of continued cooperation, the prospects of cooperation are high. Conflicts and wars among status quo powers would be much more common were it not for the fact that international politics is usually a series of small transactions.

How a statesman interprets the other's past behavior and how he projects it into the future is influenced by his understanding of the security dilemma and his ability to place himself in the other's shoes. The dilemma will operate much more strongly if statesmen do not understand it, and do not see that their arms—sought only to secure the status quo may alarm others and that others may arm, not because they are contemplating aggression, but because they fear attack from the first state. These two failures of empathy are linked. A state which thinks that the other knows that it wants only to preserve the status quo and that its arms are meant only for self-preservation will conclude that the other side will react to its arms by increasing its own capability only if it is aggressive itself. Since the other side is not menaced, there is no legitimate reason for it to object to the first state's arms; therefore, objection proves that the other is aggressive. Thus, the following exchange between Senator Tom Connally and Secretary of State Acheson concerning the ratification of the NATO treaty:

> Secretary Acheson: [The treaty] is aimed solely at armed aggression.
>
> Senator Connally: In other words, unless a nation . . . contemplates, meditates, or makes plans looking toward aggression or armed attack on another nation, it has no cause to fear this treaty.
>
> Secretary Acheson: That is correct, Senator Connally, and it seems to me that any nation which claims that this treaty is directed against it should be reminded of the Biblical admonition that 'The guilty flee when no man pursueth.'

19. Walter LaFeber, ed., *The Dynamics of World Power; A Documentary History of United States Foreign Policy 1945-1973, II: Eastern Europe and the Soviet Union* (New York: Chelsea House in association with McGraw-Hill 1973), 700.

20. Thomas Schelling, *The Strategy of Conflict* (New York: Oxford University Press 63), 134-35.

Senator Connally: That is a very apt illustration.

What I had in mind was, when a State or Nation passes a criminal act, for instance, against burglary, nobody but those who are burglars or getting ready to be burglars need have any fear of the Burglary Act. Is that not true?

Secretary Acheson: The only effect [the law] would have [on an innocent person] would be for his protection, perhaps, by deterring someone else. He wouldn't worry about the imposition of the penalties on himself.[21]

The other side of this coin is that part of the explanation for détente is that most American decision makers now realize that it is at least possible that Russia may fear American aggression; many think that this fear accounts for a range of Soviet actions previously seen as indicating Russian aggressiveness. Indeed, even 36 percent of military officers consider the Soviet Union's motivations to be primarily defensive. Less than twenty years earlier, officers had been divided over whether Russia sought world conquest or only expansion.[22]

Statesmen who do not understand the security dilemma will think that the money spent is the only cost of building up their arms. This belief removes one important restraint on arms spending. Furthermore, it is also likely to lead states to set their security requirements too high. Since they do not understand that trying to increase one's security can actually decrease it, they will overestimate the amount of security that is attainable; they will think that when in doubt they can "play it safe" by increasing their arms. Thus it is very likely that two states which support the status quo but do not understand the security dilemma will end up, if not in a war, then at least in a relationship of higher conflict than is required by the objective situation.

The belief that an increase in military strength always leads to an increase in security is often linked to the belief that the only route to security is through military strength. As a consequence, a whole range of meliorative policies will be downgraded. Decision makers who do not believe that adopting a more conciliatory posture, meeting the other's legitimate grievances, or developing mutual gains from cooperation can increase their state's security, will not devote much attention or effort to these possibilities.

On the other hand, a heightened sensitivity to the security dilemma makes it more likely that the state will treat an aggressor as though it were an insecure defender of the status quo. Partly because of their views about the causes of World War I, the British were predisposed to believe that Hitler sought only the rectification of legitimate and limited grievances and that security could best be gained by constructing an equitable international system. As a result they pursued a policy which, although well designed to avoid the danger of creating unnecessary conflict with a status quo Germany, helped destroy Europe.

Geography, Commitments, Beliefs, and Security through Expansion

A final consideration does not easily fit in the matrix we have been using, although it can be seen as an aspect of vulnerability and of the costs of CD. Situations vary in the ease or difficulty with which all states can simultaneously achieve a high degree of security. The influence of military technology on this variable is the subject of the next section. Here we want to treat the impact of beliefs, geography, and commitments (many of which

---

21. U.S.Congress, Senate. Committee on Foreign Relations, *Hearings, North .Atlantic Treaty,* 8lst Cong., 1st. sess. (1949), 17.

22. Bruce Russett and Elizabeth Hanson, *Interest and Ideology* (San Francisco.: Freeman 1975), 260; Morris Janowitz, *The Professional Soldier* (New York: Free Press l960), chap. 13.

can be considered to be modifications of geography, since they bind states to defend areas outside their homelands). In the crowded continent of Europe, security requirements were hard to mesh. Being surrounded by powerful states, Germany's problem—or the problem created by Germany—was always great and was even worse when her relations with both France and Russia were bad, such as before World War I. In that case, even a status quo Germany, if she could not change the political situation, would almost have been forced to adopt something like the Schlieffen Plan. Because she could not hold off both of her enemies, she had to be prepared to defeat one quickly and then deal with the other in a more leisurely fashion. If France or Russia stayed out of a war between the other state and Germany, they would allow Germany to dominate the Continent (even if that was not Germany's aim). They therefore had to deny Germany this ability, thus making Germany less secure. Although Germany's arrogant and erratic behavior, coupled with the desire for an unreasonably high level of security (which amounted to the desire to escape from her geographic plight), compounded the problem, even wise German statesmen would have been hard put to gain a high degree of security without alarming their neighbors.

A similar situation arose for France after World War I. She was committed to protecting her allies in Eastern Europe, a commitment she could meet only by taking the offensive against Germany. But since there was no way to guarantee that France might not later seek expansion, a France that could successfully launch an attack in response to a German move into Eastern Europe would constitute a potential danger to German core values. Similarly, a United States credibly able to threaten retaliation with strategic nuclear weapons if the Soviet Union attacks Western Europe also constitutes a menace, albeit a reduced one, to the Soviet ability to maintain the status quo. The incompatibility of these security requirements is not complete. Herman Kahn is correct in arguing that the United States could have Type II deterrence (the ability to deter a major Soviet provocation) without gaining first-strike capability because the expected Soviet retaliation following an American strike could be great enough to deter the U.S. from attacking unless the U.S. believed it would suffer enormous deprivation (for instance, the loss of Europe) if it did not strike[23] Similarly, the Franco-German military balance could have been such that France could successfully attack Germany if the latter's armies were embroiled in Eastern Europe, but could not defeat a Germany that was free to devote all her resources to defending herself. But this delicate balance is very hard to achieve, especially because states usually calculate conservatively. Therefore, such a solution is not likely to be available.

For the United States, the problem posed by the need to protect Europe is an exception. Throughout most of its history, this country has been in a much more favorable position: relatively self-sufficient and secure from invasion, it has not only been able to get security relatively cheaply, but by doing so, did not menace others.[24] But ambitions and commitments have changed this situation. After the American conquest of the Philippines, "neither the United States nor Japan could assure protection for their territories by military and naval means without compromising the defenses of the other. This problem would plague American and Japanese statesmen down to 1941."[25] Furthermore, to the extent that

---

23. Kahn. *On Thermonuclear War* (Princeton: Princeton University Press 1960), 138-60. It should be noted that the French example is largely hypothetical because France had no intention of fulfilling her obligations once Germany became strong.

24. Wolfers (fn. 9), chap. 15; C. Vann Woodward, "The Age of Reinterpretation," *American Historical Review, Vol.* 67 (October I960), 1-19.

Japan could protect herself, she could resist American threats to go to war if Japan did not respect China's independence. These complications were minor compared to those that followed World War II. A world power cannot help but have the ability to harm many others that is out of proportion to the others' ability to harm it.

Britain had been able to gain security without menacing others to a greater degree than the Continental powers, though to a lesser one than the United States. But the acquisition of colonies and a dependence on foreign trade sacrificed her relative invulnerability of being an island. Once she took India, she had to consider Russia as a neighbor; the latter was expanding in Central Asia, thus making it much more difficult for both countries to feel secure. The need to maintain reliable sea lanes to India meant that no state could be allowed to menace South Africa and, later, Egypt. But the need to protect these two areas brought new fears, new obligations, and new security requirements that conflicted with those of other European nations. Furthermore, once Britain needed a flow of imports during both peace and wartime, she required a navy that could prevent a blockade. A navy sufficient for that task could not help but be a threat to any other state that had valuable trade.

A related problem is raised by the fact that defending the status quo often means protecting more than territory. Nonterritorial interests, norms, and the structure of the international system must be maintained. If all status-quo powers agree on these values and interpret them in compatible ways, problems will be minimized. But the potential for conflict is great, and the policies followed are likely to exacerbate the security dilemma. The greater the range of interests that have to be protected, the more likely it is that national efforts to maintain the status quo will clash. As a French spokesman put it in 1930: "Security! The term signifies more indeed than the maintenance of a people's homeland, or even of their territories beyond the seas. It also means the maintenance of the world's respect for them, the maintenance of their economic interests, everything in a word, which goes to make up the grandeur, the life itself, of the nation."[26] When security is thought of in this sense, it almost automatically has a competitive connotation. It involves asserting one state's will over others, showing a high degree of leadership if not dominance, and displaying a prickly demeanor. The resulting behavior will almost surely clash with that of others who define their security in the same way.

The problem will be almost insoluble if statesmen believe that their security requires the threatening or attacking of others. "That which stops growing begins to rot," declared a minister to Catherine the Great.[27] More common is the belief that if the other is secure, it will be emboldened to act against one's own state's interests, and the belief that in a war it will not be enough for the state to protect itself: it must be able to take the war to the other's homeland. These convictions make it very difficult for status quo states to develop compatible security policies, for they lead the state to conclude that its security requires that others be rendered insecure.

---

25. William Braisted, *The United States Navy in the Pacific, 1897-1909* (Austin: University of Texas Press 1958), 240.

26. Cambon (fn. 17), 185.

27. Quoted in Adam Ulam, *Expansion and Co-Existence* (New York: Praeger 1968), 5. In 1920 the U.S. Navy's General Board similarly declared "A nation must advance or retrocede in world position." Quoted in William Braisted, *The United States Navy in the Pacific, 1909-1922* (Austin: University of Texas Press 1971), 488.

In other cases, "A country engaged in a war of defense might be obliged for strategic reasons to assume the offensive," as a French delegate to an interwar disarmament conference put it.[28] That was the case for France in 1799:

> The Directory's political objectives were essentially defensive, for the French wanted only to protect the Republic from invasion and preserve the security and territory of the satellite regimes in Holland, Switzerland, and Italy. French leaders sought no new conquests; they wanted only to preserve the earlier gains of the Revolution. The Directory believed, however, that only a military offensive could enable the nation to achieve its defensive political objective. By inflicting rapid and decisive defeats upon one or more members of the coalition, the directors hoped to rupture allied unity and force individual powers to seek a separate peace.[29]

It did not matter to the surrounding states that France was not attacking because she was greedy, but because she wanted to be left in peace. Unless there was some way her neighbors could provide France with an alternate route to her goal, France had to go to war.

Offense, Defense, and the Security Dilemma

Another approach starts with the central point of the security dilemma—that an increase in one state's security decreases the security of others—and examines the conditions under which this proposition holds. Two crucial variables are involved: whether defensive weapons and policies can be distinguished from offensive ones, and whether the defense or the offense has the advantage. The definitions are not always clear, and many cases are difficult to judge, but these two variables shed a great deal of light on the question of whether status-quo powers will adopt compatible security policies. All the variables discussed so far leave the heart of the problem untouched. But when defensive weapons differ from offensive ones, it is possible for a state to make itself more secure without making others less secure. And when the defense has the advantage over the offense, a large increase in one state's security only slightly decreases the security of the others, and status-quo powers can all enjoy a high level of security and largely escape from the state of nature.

Offense-Defense Balance

When we say that the offense has the advantage, we simply mean that it is easier to destroy the other's army and take its territory than it is to defends one's own. When the defense has the advantage, it is easier to protect and to hold than it is to move forward, destroy, and take. If effective defenses can be erected quickly, an attacker may be able to keep territory he has taken in an initial victory. Thus, the dominance of the defense made it very hard for Britain and France to push Germany out of France in World War I. But when superior defenses are difficult for an aggressor to improvise on the battlefield and must be constructed during peacetime, they provide no direct assistance to him.

The security dilemma is at its most vicious when commitments, strategy, or technology dictate that the only route to security lies through expansion. Status-quo powers must then act like aggressors; the fact that they would gladly agree to forego the opportunity for expansion in return for guarantees for their security has no implications for their behavior.

---

28. Quoted in Marion Boggs, *Attempts to Define and Limit "Aggressive" Armament in Diplomacy and Strategy* (Columbia: University of Missouri Studies, XVI, No. 1, 1941), 41.

29. Steven Ross, *European Diplomatic History, 1789-1815* (Garden City, N.Y.: Doubleday 1969), 194.

Even if expansion is not sought as a goal in itself, there will be quick and drastic changes in the distribution of territory and influence. Conversely, when the defense has the advantage, status-quo states can make themselves more secure without gravely endangering others.[30] Indeed, if the defense has enough of an advantage and if the states are of roughly equal size, not only will the security dilemma cease to inhibit status-quo states from cooperating, but aggression will be next to impossible, thus rendering international anarchy relatively unimportant. If states cannot conquer each other, then the lack of sovereignty, although it presents problems of collective goods in a number of areas, no longer forces states to devote their primary attention to self-preservation. Although, if force were not usable, there would be fewer restraints on the use of nonmilitary instruments, these are rarely powerful enough to threaten the vital interests of a major state.

Two questions of the offense-defense balance can be separated. First, does the state have to spend more or less than one dollar on defensive forces to offset each dollar spent by the other side on forces that could be used to attack? If the state has one dollar to spend on increasing its security, should it put it into offensive or defensive forces? Second, with a given inventory of forces, is it better to attack or to defend? Is there an incentive to strike first or to absorb the other's blow? These two aspects are often linked: if each dollar spent on offense can overcome each dollar spent on defense, and if both sides have the same defense budgets, then both are likely to build offensive forces and find it attractive to attack rather than to wait for the adversary to strike.

These aspects affect the security dilemma in different ways. The first has its greatest impact on arms races. If the defense has the advantage, and if the status-quo powers have reasonable subjective security requirements, they can probably avoid an arms race. Although an increase in one side's arms and security will still decrease the other's security, the former's increase will be larger than the latter's decrease. So if one side increases its arms, the other can bring its security back up to its previous level by adding a smaller amount to its forces. And if the first side reacts to this change, its increase will also be smaller than the stimulus that produced it. Thus a stable equilibrium will be reached. Shifting from dynamics to statics, each side can be quite secure with forces roughly equal to those of the other. Indeed, if the defense is much more potent than the offense, each side can be willing to have forces much smaller than the other's, and can be indifferent to a wide range of the other's defense policies.

The second aspect—whether it is better to attack or to defend—influences short-run stability. When the offense has the advantage, a state's reaction to international tension will increase the chances of war. The incentives for pre-emption and the "reciprocal fear of surprise attack" in this situation have been made clear by analyses of the dangers that exist when two countries have first-strike capabilities.[31] There is no way for the state to increase its security without menacing, or even attacking, the other. Even Bismarck, who once called preventive war "committing suicide from fear of death," said that "no government, if it regards war as inevitable even if it does not want it, would be so foolish as to leave to the enemy the choice of time and occasion and to wait for the moment which is most con-

30. Thus, when Wolfers argues that a status-quo state that settles for rough equality of power with its adversary, rather than seeking preponderance, may be able to convince the other to reciprocate by showing that it wants only to protect itself, not menace the other, he assumes that the defense has an advantage. See Arnold Wolfers, *Discord and Collaboration* (Baltimore: Johns Hopkins Press, 1962), p. 126.

31. Thomas Schelling, *The Strategy of Conflict* (New York: Oxford University Press, 1963), chap. 9.

venient for the enemy."[32] In another arena, the same dilemma applies to the policeman in a dark alley confronting a suspected criminal who appears to be holding a weapon. Though racism may indeed be present, the security dilemma can account for many of the tragic shootings of innocent people in the ghettos.

Beliefs about the course of a war in which the offense has the advantage further deepen the security dilemma. When there are incentives to strike first, a successful attack will usually so weaken the other side that victory will be relatively quick, bloodless, and decisive. It is in these periods when conquest is possible and attractive that states consolidate power internally—for instance, by destroying the feudal barons—and expand externally. There are several consequences that decrease the chance of cooperation among status-quo states. First, war will be profitable for the winner. The costs will be low and the benefits high. Of course, losers will suffer; the fear of losing could induce states to try to form stable cooperative arrangements, but the temptation of victory will make this particularly difficult. Second, because wars are expected to be both frequent and short, there will be incentives for high levels of arms, and quick and strong reaction to the other's increases in arms. The state cannot afford to wait until there is unambiguous evidence that the other is building new weapons. Even large states that have faith in their economic strength cannot wait, because the war will be over before their products can reach the army. Third, when wars are quick, states will have to recruit allies in advance.[33] Without the opportunity for bargaining and re-alignments during the opening stages of hostilities, peacetime diplomacy loses a degree of the fluidity that facilitates balance-of-power policies.

Because alliances must be secured during peacetime, the international system is more likely to become bipolar. It is hard to say whether war therefore becomes more or less likely, but this bipolarity increases tension between the two camps and makes it harder for status-quo states to gain the benefits of cooperation. Fourth, if wars are frequent, statesmen's perceptual thresholds will be adjusted accordingly and they will be quick to perceive ambiguous evidence as indicating that others are aggressive. Thus, there will be more cases of status-quo powers arming against each other in the incorrect belief that the other is hostile.

When the defense has the advantage, all the foregoing is reversed. The state that fears attack does not pre-empt—since that would be a wasteful use of its military resources but rather prepares to receive an attack. Doing so does not decrease the security of others, and several states can do it simultaneously; the situation will therefore be stable, and status-quo powers will be able to cooperate. When Herman Kahn argues that ultimatums "are vastly too dangerous to give because . . . they are quite likely to touch off a pre-emptive strike,"[34] he incorrectly assumes that it is always advantageous to strike first.

More is involved than short-run dynamics. When the defense is dominant, wars are likely to become stalemates and can be won only at enormous cost. Relatively small and weak states can hold off larger and stronger ones, or can deter attack by raising the costs of conquest to an unacceptable level. States then approach equality in what they can do to each other. Like the .45-caliber pistol in the American West, fortifications were the "great equalizer" in some periods. Changes in the status quo are less frequent and cooperation is more common wherever the security dilemma is thereby reduced.

---

32. Quoted in Fritz Fischer, *War of Illusions* (New York: Norton, 1975), 377, 461.

33. George Quester, *Offense and Defense in the International System* (New York: John Wiley, 1977), 105–06.

34. Herman Kahn, *On Thermonuclear War* (Princeton: Princeton University Press, 1960), p.211 (also see p. 144).

Many of these arguments can be illustrated by the major powers' policies in the periods preceding the two world wars. Bismarck's wars surprised statesmen by showing that the offense had the advantage, and by being quick, relatively cheap, and quite decisive. Falling into a common error, observers projected this pattern into the future.[35] The resulting expectations had several effects. First, states sought semipermanent allies. In the early stages of the Franco-Prussian War, Napoleon III had thought that there would be plenty of time to recruit Austria to his side. Now, others were not going to repeat this mistake. Second, defense budgets were high and reacted quite sharply to increases on the other side. It is not surprising that Richardson's theory of arms races fits this period well. Third, most decision makers thought that the next European war would not cost much blood and treasure.[36] That is one reason why war was generally seen as inevitable and why mass opinion was so bellicose. Fourth, once war seemed likely, there were strong pressures to pre-empt. Both sides believed that whoever moved first could penetrate the other deep enough to disrupt mobilization and thus gain an insurmountable advantage. (There was no such belief about the use of naval forces. Although Churchill made an ill-advised speech saying that if German ships "do not come out and fight in time of war they will be dug out like rats in a hole,"[37] everyone knew that submarines, mines, and coastal fortifications made this impossible. So at the start of the war each navy prepared to defend itself rather than attack, and the short-run destabilizing forces that launched the armies toward each other did not operate.)[38] Furthermore, each side knew that the other saw the situation the same way, thus increasing the perceived danger that the other would attack, and giving each added reasons to precipitate a war if conditions seemed favorable. In the long and the short run, there were thus both offensive and defensive incentives to strike. This situation casts light on the common question about German motives in 1914: "Did Germany unleash the war deliberately to become a world power or did she support Austria merely to defend a weakening ally," thereby protecting her own position?[39] To some extent, this question is misleading. Because of the perceived advantage of the offense, war was seen as the best route both to gaining expansion and to avoiding drastic loss of influence. There seemed to be no way for Germany merely to retain and safeguard her existing position.

Of course the war showed these beliefs to have been wrong on all points. Trenches and machine guns gave the defense an overwhelming advantage. The fighting became

---

35. For a general discussion of such mistaken learning from the past, see Jervis, *Perception and Misperception in International Relations* (Princeton: Princeton University Press,1976), chap.6. The important and still not completely understood question of why this belief formed and was maintained throughout the war is examined in Bernard Brodie, *War and Politics* (New York: Macmillan,1973), 262–70; Brodie, "Technological Change, Strategic Doctrine, and Political Outcomes," in Klaus Knorr, ed., *Historical Dimensions of National Security Problems* (Lawrence: University Press of Kansas, 1976), 290–92: and Douglas Porch, "The French Army and the Spirit of the Offensive,1900–14," in Brian Bond and Ian Roy, eds., *War and Society* (New York: Holmes & Meier, 1975), 117–43.

36. Some were not so optimistic. Grey's remark is well-known: "The lamps are going out all over Europe; we shall not see them lit again in our life-time." The German Prime Minister, Bethmann Hollweg, also feared the consequences of the war. But the controlling view was that it would certainly pay for the winner.

37. Quoted in Martin Gilbert, *Winston* S. *Churchill,* III, *The Challenge of War,* 1914–1916 (Boston: Houghton Mifflin, 1971), 84.

38. Quester (fn. 4), 98–99. Robert Art, *The Influence of Foreign Policy on Seapower,* II (Beverly Hills: Sage Professional Papers in International Studies Series. 1973), 14–18, 26–28.

39. Konrad Jarausch, The Illusion of Limited War: Chancellor Bethmann Hollweg's Calculated Risk, July 1914," *Central European History,* II (March 1969), 50.

deadlocked and produced horrendous casualties. It made no sense for the combatants to bleed themselves to death. If they had known the power of the defense beforehand, they would have rushed for their own trenches rather than for the enemy's territory. Each side could have done this without increasing the other's incentives to strike. War might have broken out anyway: but at least the pressures of time and the fear of allowing the other to get the first blow would not have contributed to this end. And, had both sides known the costs of the war, they would have negotiated much more seriously. The obvious question is why the states did not seek a negotiated settlement as soon as the shape of the war became clear. Schlieffen had said that if his plan failed, peace should be sought.[40] The answer is complex, uncertain, and largely outside of the scope of our concerns. But part of the reason was the hope and sometimes the expectation that breakthroughs could be made and the dominance of the offensive restored. Without that hope, the political and psychological pressures to fight to a decisive victory might have been overcome.

The politics of the interwar period were shaped by the memories of the previous conflict and the belief that any future war would resemble it. Political and military lessons reinforced each other in ameliorating the security dilemma. Because it was believed that the First World War had been a mistake that could have been avoided by skillful conciliation, both Britain and, to a lesser extent, France were highly sensitive to the possibility that interwar Germany was not a real threat to peace, and alert to the danger that reacting quickly and strongly to her arms could create unnecessary conflict. And because Britain and France expected the defense to continue to dominate, they concluded that it was safe to adopt a more relaxed and nonthreatening military posture.[41] Britain also felt less need to maintain tight alliance bonds. The Allies' military posture then constituted only a slight danger to Germany; had the latter been content with the status quo, it would have been easy for both sides to have felt secure behind their lines of fortifications. Of course the Germans were not content, so it is not surprising that they devoted their money and attention to finding ways out of a defense-dominated stalemate. *Blitzkrieg* tactics were necessary if they were to use force to change the status quo.

The initial stages of the war on the Western Front also contrasted with the First World War. Only with the new air arm were there any incentives to strike first, and these forces were too weak to carry out the grandiose plans that had been both dreamed and feared. The armies, still the main instrument, rushed to defensive positions. Perhaps the allies could have successfully attacked while the Germans were occupied in Poland.[42] But belief in the defense was so great that this was never seriously contemplated. Three months after the start of the war, the French Prime Minister summed up the view held by almost everyone but Hitler: on the Western Front there is "deadlock. Two Forces of equal strength and the one that attacks seeing such enormous casualties that it cannot move without endan-

40. Brodie, *War and Politics* (New York: Macmillan, 1973), 58.

41. President Roosevelt and the American delegates to the League of Nations Disarmament Conference maintained that the tank and mobile heavy artillery had reestablished the dominance of the offensive, thus making disarmament more urgent (Marion Boggs, *Attempts to Define and Limit "Aggressive"" Armament in Diplomacy and Strategy* [Columbia: University of Missouri Studies, XVI, No. 1, 1941], pp. 31, 108), but this was a minority position and may not even have been believed by the Americans. The reduced prestige and influence of the military, and the high pressures to cut government spending throughout this period also contributed to the lowering of defense budgets.

42. Jon Kimche, *The Unfought Battle* (New York: Stein, 1968); Nicholas William Bethell, *The War Hitler Won: The Fall of Poland, September* 1939 (New York: Holt, 1972); Alan Alexandroff and Richard Rosecrance, "Deterrence in 1939," *World Politics, XXIX* (April 1977), 404–24.

gering the continuation of the war or of the aftermath."[43] The Allies were caught in a dilemma they never fully recognized, let alone solved. On the one hand, they had very high war aims; although unconditional surrender had not yet been adopted, the British had decided from the start that the removal of Hitler was a necessary condition for peace.[44] On the other hand, there were no realistic plans or instruments for allowing the Allies to impose their will on the other side. The British Chief of the Imperial General Staff noted, "The French have no intention of carrying out an offensive for years, if at all"; the British were only slightly bolder.[45] So the Allies looked to a long war that would wear the Germans down, cause civilian suffering through shortages, and eventually undermine Hitler. There was little analysis to support this view—and indeed it probably was not supportable—but as long as the defense was dominant and the numbers on each side relatively equal, what else could the Allies do?

To summarize, the security dilemma was much less powerful after World War I than it had been before. In the later period, the expected power of the defense allowed status-quo states to pursue compatible security policies and avoid arms races. Furthermore, high tension and fear of war did not set off short-run dynamics by which each state, trying to increase its security, inadvertently acted to make war more likely. The expected high costs of war, however, led the Allies to believe that no sane German leader would run the risks entailed in an attempt to dominate the Continent, and discouraged them from risking war themselves.

Technology and Geography.

Technology and geography are the two main factors that determine whether the offense or the defense has the advantage. As Brodie notes, "On the tactical level, as a rule, few physical factors favor the attacker but many favor the defender. The defender usually has the advantage of cover. He characteristically fires from behind some form of shelter while his opponent crosses open ground."[46] Anything that increases the amount of ground the attacker has to cross, or impedes his progress across it, or makes him more vulnerable while crossing, increases the advantage accruing to the defense. When states are separated by barriers that produce these effects, the security dilemma is eased, since both can have forces adequate for defense without being ablc to attack. Impenetrable barriers would actually prevent war; in reality, decision makers have to settle for a good deal less. Buffer zones slow the attacker's progress; they thereby give the defender time to prepare, increase problems of logistics, and reduce the number of soldiers available for the final assault. At the end of the 19th century, Arthur Balfour noted Afghanistan's "non-conducting" qualities. "So long as it possesses few roads, and no railroads, it will be impossible for Russia to make effective use of her great numerical superiority at any point immediately vital to the Empire." The Russians valued buffers for the same reasons; it is not surprising that when Persia was being divided into Rus-

---

43. Roderick Macleod and Denis Kelly, eds., *Time Unguarded: The Ironside Diaries, 1937–1940* (New York: McKay, 1962), 173.

44. For a short time, as France was falling, the British Cabinet did discuss reaching a negotiated peace with Hitler. The official history downplays this, but it is covered in P.M.H. Bell, *A Cerain Eventuality* (Farnborough, England: Saxon House, 1974), 40–48.

45. Macleod and Kelly (fn. 14), 174. In flat contradiction to common sense and almost everything they believed about modern warfare, the Allies planned an expedition to Scandinavia to cut the supply of iron ore to Germany and to aid Finland against the Russians. But the dominant mood was the one described above.

46. Brodie (fn. 11), 179.

sian and British spheres of influence some years later, the Russians sought assurances that the British would refrain from building potentially menacing railroads in their sphere. Indeed, since railroad construction radically altered the abilities of countries to defend themselves and to attack others, many diplomatic notes and much intelligence activity in the late 19th century centered on this subject.[47]

Oceans, large rivers, and mountain ranges serve the same function as buffer zones. Being hard to cross, they allow defense against superior numbers. The defender has merely to stay on his side of the barrier and so can utilize all the men he can bring up to it. The attacker's men, however, can cross only a few at a time, and they are very vulnerable when doing so. If all states were self-sufficient islands, anarchy would be much less of a problem. A small investment in shore defenses and a small army would be sufficient to repel invasion. Only very weak states would be vulnerable, and only very large ones could menace others. As noted above, the United States, and to a lesser extent Great Britain, have partly been able to escape from the state of nature because their geographical positions approximated this ideal.

Although geography cannot be changed to conform to borders, borders can and do change to conform to geography. Borders across which an attack is easy tend to be unstable. States living within them are likely to expand or be absorbed. Frequent wars are almost inevitable since attacking will often seem the best way to protect what one has. This process will stop, or at least slow down, when the state's borders reach—by expansion or contraction—a line of natural obstacles. Security without attack will then be possible. Furthermore, these lines constitute salient solutions to bargaining problems and, to the extent that they are barriers to migration, are likely to divide ethnic groups, thereby raising the costs and lowering the incentives for conquest.

Attachment to one's state and its land reinforce one quasi-geographical aid to the defense. Conquest usually becomes more difficult the deeper the attacker pushes into the other's territory. Nationalism spurs the defenders to fight harder; advancing not only lengthens the attacker's supply lines, but takes him through unfamiliar and often devastated lands that require troops for garrison duty. These stabilizing dynamics will not operate, however, if the defender's war materiel is situated near its borders, or if the people do not care about their state, but only about being on the winning side. In such cases, positive feedback will be at work and initial defeats will be insurmountable.[48]

Imitating geography, men have tried to create barriers. Treaties may provide for demilitarized zones on both sides of the border, although such zones will rarely be deep enough to provide more than warning. Even this was not possible in Europe, but the Russians adopted a gauge for their railroads that was broader than that of the neighboring states, thereby complicating the logistics problems of any attacker—including Russia.

Perhaps the most ambitious and at least temporarily successful attempts to construct a system that would aid the defenses of both sides were the interwar naval treaties, as they affected Japanese-American relations. As mentioned earlier, the problem was that the United States could not defend the Philippines without denying Japan the ability to protect

---

47. Arthur Balfour, "Memorandum, Committee on Imperial Defence, April 30, 1903, pp. 2–3; see the telegrams by Sir Arthur Nicolson, in G. P. Gooch and Harold Temperley, eds., *British Documents on the Origins of the War,* Vol.4 (London: H.M.S.0.,1929),429,524.These barriers do not prevent the passage of long-range aircraft; but even in the air, distance usually aids the defender.

48. See,for example, the discussion of warfare among Chinese warlords in Hsi-Sheng Chi, "The Chinese Warlord System as an International System," in Morton Kaplan, ed., *New Approaches to International Relations* (New York: St. Martin's, 1968), 405–25.

her home islands.[49] (In 1941 this dilemma became insoluble when Japan sought to extend her control to Malaya and the Dutch East Indies. If the Philippines had been invulnerable, they could have provided a secure base from which the U.S. could interdict Japanese shipping between the homeland and the areas she was trying to conquer.) In the 1920s and early 1930s each side would have been willing to grant the other security for its possessions in return for a reciprocal grant, and the Washington Naval Conference agreements we designed to approach this goal. As a Japanese diplomat later put it, their country's "fundamental principle" was to have a "strength insufficient for attack and adequate for defense."[50] Thus, Japan agreed in 1922 to accept a navy only three-fifths as large as that of the United States, and the U.S. agreed not to fortify its Pacific islands.[51] (Japan had earlier been forced to agree not to fortify the islands she had taken from Germany in World War I.) Japan's navy would not be large enough to defeat America's anywhere other than close to the home islands. Although the Japanese could still take the Philippines, not only would they be unable to move farther, but they might be weakened enough by their efforts to be vulnerable to counterattack. Japan, however, gained security. An American attack was rendered more difficult because the American bases were unprotected and because, until 1930, Japan was allowed unlimited numbers of cruisers, destroyers, and submarines that could weaken the American fleet as it made its way across the ocean.[52]

The other major determinant of the offense-defense balance is technology. When weapons are highly vulnerable, they must be employed before they are attacked. Others can remain quite invulnerable in their bases. The former characteristics are embodied in unprotected missiles and many kinds of bombers. (It should be noted that it is not vulnerability *per se* that is crucial, but the location of the vulnerability. Bombers and missiles that are easy to destroy only after having been launched toward their targets do not create destabilizing dynamics.) Incentives to strike first are usually absent for naval forces that are threatened by a naval attack. Like missiles in hardened silos, they are usually well protected when in their bases. Both sides can then simultaneously be prepared to defend themselves successfully.

In ground warfare under some conditions, forts, trenches, and small groups of men in prepared positions can hold off large numbers of attackers. Less frequently, a few attackers can storm the defenses. By and large, it is a contest between fortifications and supporting light weapons on the one hand, and mobility and heavier weapons that clear the way for the attack on the other. As the erroneous views held before the two world wars show, there is no simple way to determine which is dominant. "[T]hese oscillations are not smooth and predictable like those of a swinging pendulum. They are uneven in both extent and time. Some occur in the course of a single battle or campaign, others in the course of a war, still others during a series of wars." Longer-term oscillations can also be detected:

---

49. Some American decision makers, including military officers, thought that the best way out of the dilemma was to abandon the Philippines.

50. Quoted in Elting Morrison, *Turmoil and Tradition:* A *Study of he Life and Times of Henry L. Stimson* (Boston: Houghton Mifflin, 1960), 326.

51. The U.S. "refused to consider limitations on Hawaiian defenses, since these works posed no threat to Japan." William Braisted, *The United States Navy in the Pacific, 1909–1922* (Austin: University of Texas Press, 1971), 612.

52. That is part of the reason why the Japanese admirals strongly objected when the civilian leaders decided to accept a seven-to-ten ratio in lighter craft in 1930. Stephen Pelz, *Race to Pearl Harbor* (Cambridge: Harvard University Press, 1974), 3.

> The early Gothic age, from the twelfth to the late thirteenth century, with its wonderful cathedrals and fortified places, was a period during which the attackers in Europe generally met serious and increasing difficulties, because the improvement in the strength of fortresses outran the advance in the power of destruction. Later, with the spread of firearms at the end of the fifteenth century, old fortresses lost their power to resist. An age ensued during which the offense possessed, apart from short-term setbacks, new advantages. Then, during the seventeenth century, especially after about 1660, and until at least the outbreak of the War of the Austrian Succession in 1740, the defense regained much of the ground it had lost since the great medieval fortresses had proved unable to meet the bombardment of the new and more numerous artillery.[53]

Another scholar has continued the argument: "The offensive gained an advantage with new forms of heavy mobile artillery in the nineteenth century, but the stalemate of World War I created the impression that the defense again had an advantage; the German invasion in World War II, however, indicated the offensive superiority of highly mechanized armies in the field."[54]

The situation today with respect to conventional weapons is unclear. Until recently it was believed that tanks and tactical air power gave the attacker an advantage. The initial analyses of the 1973 Arab-Israeli war indicated that new anti-tank and anti-aircraft weapons have restored the primacy of the defense. These weapons are cheap, easy to use, and can destroy a high proportion of the attacking vehicles and planes that are sighted. It then would make sense for a status-quo power to buy lots of $20,000 missiles rather than buy a few half-million dollar fighter-bombers. Defense would be possible even against a large and well-equipped force; states that care primarily about self-protection would not need to engage in arms races. But further examinations of the new technologies and the history of the October War cast doubt on these optimistic conclusions and leave us unable to render any firm judgment.[55]

Concerning nuclear weapons, it is generally agreed that defense is impossible—a triumph not of the offense, but of deterrence. Attack makes no sense, not because it can be beaten off, but because the attacker will be destroyed in turn. In terms of the questions under consideration here, the result is the equivalent of the primacy of the defense. First, security is relatively cheap. Less than one percent of the G.N.P. is devoted to deterring a direct attack on the United States; most of it is spent on acquiring redundant systems to provide a lot of insurance against the worst conceivable contingencies. Second, both sides can simultaneously gain security in the form of second-strike capability. Third, and related to the foregoing, second-strike capability can be maintained in the face of wide variations in the other side's military posture. There is no purely military reason why each side has to react quickly and strongly to the other's increases in arms. Any spending that the other devotes to trying to achieve first-strike capability can be neutralized by the state's spending much smaller sums on protecting its second-strike capability. Fourth, there are no incentives to strike first in a crisis.

---

53. John Nef, *War and Human Progress* (New York: Norton,1963),185. Also see *ibid*, 237,242–43, and 323; C.W.Oman, *The Art of War in the Middle Ages* (Ithaca, N.Y.: Cornell University Press,1953), 70–72; John Beeler, *Warfare in Feudal Europe*, 730–1200 (Ithaca, N.Y.: Cornell University Press, 1971), 212–14; Michael Howard, *War in European History* (London: Oxford University Press l976), 33–37.

54. Quincy Wright, *A Sudy of War* (abridged ed.; Chicago: University of Chicago Press, 1964), 142. Also see 63–70,74–75. There are important exceptions to these generalizations—the American Civil War, for instance, falls in the middle of the period Wright says is dominated by the offense.

55. Geoffrey Kemp, Robert Pfaltzgraff, and Uri Ra'anan, eds., *The Other Arms Race* (Lexington, Mass.: D.C. Heath,1975); James Foster, "The Future of Conventional Arms Control," *Policy Sciences*, No. 8 (Spring 1977), 1–19.

Important problems remain, of course. Both sides have interests that go well beyond defense of the homeland. The protection of these interests creates conflicts even if neither side desires expansion. Furthermore, the shift from defense to deterrence has greatly increased the importance and perceptions of resolve. Security now rests on each side's belief that the other would prefer to run high risks of total destruction rather than sacrifice its vital interests. Aspects of the security dilemma thus appear in a new form. Are weapons procurements used as an index of resolve? Must they be so used? If one side fails to respond to the other's buildup, will it appear weak and thereby invite predation? Can both sides simultaneously have images of high resolve or is there a zero-sum element involved? Although these problems are real, they are not as severe as those in the prenuclear era: there are many indices of resolve, and states do not so much judge images of resolve in the abstract as ask how likely it is that the other will stand firm in a particular dispute. Since states are most likely to stand firm on matters which concern them most, it is quite possible for both to demonstrate their resolve to protect their own security simultaneously.

Offense-Defense Differentiation

The other major variable that affects how strongly the security dilemma operates is whether weapons and policies that protect the state also provide the capability for attack. If they do not, the basic postulate of the security dilemma no longer applies. A state can increase its own security without decreasing that of others. The advantage of the defense can only ameliorate the security dilemma. A differentiation between offensive and defensive stances comes close to abolishing it. Such differentiation does not mean, however, that all security problems will be abolished. If the offense has the advantage, conquest and aggression will still be possible. And if the offense's advantage is great enough, status-quo powers may find it too expensive to protect themselves by defensive forces and decide to procure offensive weapons even though this will menace others. Furthermore, states will still have to worry that even if the other's military posture shows that it is peaceful now, it may develop aggressive intentions in the future.

Assuming that the defense is at least as potent as the offense, the differentiation between them allows status-quo states to behave in ways that are clearly different from those of aggressors. Three beneficial consequences follow. First, status-quo powers can identify each other, thus laying the foundations for cooperation. Conflicts growing out of the mistaken belief that the other side is expansionist will be less frequent. Second, status-quo states will obtain advance warning when others plan aggression. Before a state can attack, it has to develop and deploy offensive weapons. If procurement of these weapons cannot be disguised and takes a fair amount of time, as it almost always does, a status-quo state will have the time to take countermeasures. It need not maintain a high level of defensive arms as long as its potential adversaries are adopting a peaceful posture. (Although being so armed should not, with the one important exception noted below, alarm other status-quo powers.) States do, in fact, pay special attention to actions that they believe would not be taken by a status-quo state because they feel that states exhibiting such behavior are aggressive. Thus the seizure or development of transportation facilities will alarm others more if these facilities have no commercial value, and therefore can only be wanted for military reasons. In 1906, the British rejected a Russian protest about their activities in a district of Persia by claiming that this area was "only of [strategic] importance [to the Russians] if they wished to attack the Indian frontier, or to put pressure upon us by making us think that they intend to attack it."[56]

---

56. Richard Challener, *Admirals, Generals, and American Foreign Policy, 1898–1914* (Princeton: Princeton University Press, 1973), 273; Grey to Nicolson, in Gooch and Temperley (fn. 18), 414.

The same inferences are drawn when a state acquires more weapons than observers feel are needed for defense. Thus, the Japanese spokesman at the 1930 London naval conference said that his country was alarmed by the American refusal to give Japan a 70 percent ratio (in place of a 60 percent ratio) in heavy cruisers: "As long as America held that ten percent advantage, it was possible for her to attack. So when America insisted on sixty percent instead of seventy percent, the idea would exist that they were trying to keep that possibility, and the Japanese people could not accept that.[57] Similarly, when Mussolini told Chamberlain in January 1939 that Hitler's arms program was motivated by defensive considerations, the Prime Minister replied that "German military forces were now so strong as to make it impossible for any Power or combination of Powers to attack her successfully. She could not want any further armaments for defensive purposes; what then did she want them for?"[58]

Of course these inferences can be wrong—as they are especially likely to be because states underestimate the degree to which they menace others.[59] And when they are wrong, the security dilemma is deepened. Because the state thinks it has received notice that the other is aggressive, its own arms building will be less restrained and the chances of cooperation will be decreased. But the dangers of incorrect inferences should not obscure the main point: when offensive and defensive postures are different, much of the uncertainty about the other's intentions that contributes to the security dilemma is removed.

The third beneficial consequence of a difference between offensive and defensive weapons is that if all states support the status-quo, an obvious arms control agreement is a ban on weapons that are useful for attacking. As President Roosevelt put it in his message to the Geneva Disarmament Conference in 1933: "If all nations will agree wholly to eliminate from possession and use the weapons which make possible a successful attack, defenses automatically will become impregnable, and the frontiers and independence of every nation will become secure."[60] The fact that such treaties have been rare—the Washington naval agreements discussed above and the anti-ABM treaty can be cited as examples—shows either that states are not always willing to guarantee the security of others, or that it is hard to distinguish offensive from defensive weapons.

Is such a distinction possible? Salvador de Madariaga, the Spanish statesman active in the disarmament negotiations of the interwar years, thought not: "A weapon is either offensive or defensive according to which end of it you are looking at." The French Foreign Minister agreed (although French policy did not always follow this view): "Every arm can be employed offensively or defensively in turn. . . . The only way to discover whether arms are intended for purely defensive purposes or are held in a spirit of aggression is in all cases to enquire into the intentions of the country concerned." Some evidence for the validity of this argument is provided by the fact that much time in these unsuccessful negotiations was devoted to separating offensive from defensive weapons. Indeed, no simple and unambiguous definition is possible and in many cases no judgment can be reached. Before the American entry into World War I, Woodrow Wilson wanted to arm

---

57. Quoted in James Crowley, *Japan's Quest for Autonomy* (Princeton: Princeton University Press 1966), 49. American naval officers agreed with the Japanese that a ten-to-six ratio would endanger Japan's supremacy in her home waters.

58. E.L. Woodward and R. Butler, ed., *Documents on British Foreign Policy, 1919–1939.* Third series, III (London: H.M.S.O., 1950), 526.

59. Jervis (fn. 6), 69–72, 352–55.

60. Quoted in Merze Tate, *The United States and Armaments* (Cambridge: Harvard University Press, 1948), 108.

merchantmen only with guns in the back of the ship so they could not initiate a fight, but this expedient cannot be applied to more common forms of armaments.[61]

There are several problems. Even when a differentiation is possible, a status-quo power will want offensive arms under any of three conditions. (1) If the offense has a great advantage over the defense, protection through defensive forces will be too expensive. (2) Status-quo states may need offensive weapons to regain territory lost in the opening stages of war. It might be possible, however, for a state to wait to procure these weapons until war seems likely, and they might be needed only in relatively small numbers, unless the aggressor was able to construct strong defenses quickly in the occupied areas. (3) The state may feel that it must be prepared to take the offensive either because the other side will make peace only if it loses territory or because the state has commitments to attack if the other makes war on a third party. As noted above, status-quo states with extensive commitments are often forced to behave like aggressors. Even when they lack such commitments, status-quo states must worry about the possibility that if they are able to hold off an attack, they will still not be able to end the war unless they move into the other's territory to damage its military forces and inflict pain. Many American naval officers after the Civil War, for example, believed that "only by destroying the commerce of the opponent could the United States bring him to terms."[62]

A further complication is introduced by the fact that aggressors as well as status-quo powers require defensive forces as a prelude to acquiring offensive ones, to protect one frontier while attacking another, or for insurance in case the war goes badly. Criminals as well as policemen can use bulletproof vests. Hitler as well as Maginot built a line of forts. Indeed, Churchill reports that in 1936 the German Foreign Minister said: "As soon as our fortifications are constructed [on our western borders] and the countries in Central Europe realize that France cannot enter German territory, all these countries will begin to feel very differently about their foreign policies, and a new constellation will develop."[63] So a state may not necessarily be reassured if its neighbor constructs strong defenses.

More central difficulties are created by the fact that whether a weapon is offensive or defensive often depends on the particular situation—for instance, the geographical setting and the way in which the weapon is used. "Tanks . . . spearheaded the fateful German thrust through the Ardennes in 1940, but if the French had disposed of a properly concentrated armored reserve, it would have provided the best means for their cutting off the penetration and turning into a disaster for the Germans what became instead an overwhelming victory."[64] Anti-aircraft weapons seem obviously defensive—to be used, they must wait for the other side to come to them. But the Egyptian attack on Israel in 1973 would have been impossible without effective air defenses that covered the battlefield. Nevertheless, some distinctions are possible. Sir John Simon, then the British Foreign Secretary, in response to the views cited earlier, stated that just because a fine line could not be drawn, "that was no reason for saying that there were not stretches of territory on either side which all practical men and women knew to be well on this or that side of the line." Although there are almost no weapons and strategies that are useful only for attacking, there are some that are almost exclusively defensive. Aggressors could want them for pro-

---

61. Boggs (fn. 12), 15, 40.

62. Kenneth Hagan, *American Gunboat Diplomacy and the Old* Navy, *1877–1889* (Westport, Conn.: Greenwood Press 1973), 20.

63. Winston Churchill, *The Gathering Storm* (Boston: Houghton, 1948), 206.

64. Brodie, *War and Politics* (fn. 6), 325.

tection, but a state that relied mostly on them could not menace others. More frequently, we cannot "determine the absolute character of a weapon, but [we can] make a comparison . . . [and] discover whether or not the offensive potentialities predominate, whether a weapon is more useful in attack or in defense."[65]

The essence of defense is keeping the other side out of your territory. A purely defensive weapon is one that can do this without being able to penetrate the enemy's land. Thus a committee of military experts in an interwar disarmament conference declared that armaments "incapable of mobility by means of self-contained power," or movable only after long delay, were "only capable of being used for the defense of a State's territory."[66] The most obvious examples are fortifications. They can shelter attacking forces, especially when they are built right along the frontier,[67] but they cannot occupy enemy territory. A state with only a strong line of forts, fixed guns, and a small army to man them would not be much of a menace. Anything else that can serve only as a barrier against attacking troops is similarly defensive. In this category are systems that provide warning of an attack, the Russian's adoption of a different railroad gauge, and nuclear land mines that can seal off invasion routes.

If total immobility clearly defines a system that is defensive only, limited mobility is unfortunately ambiguous. As noted above, short-range fighter aircraft and antiaircraft missiles can be used to cover an attack. And, unlike forts, they can advance with the troops. Still, their inability to reach deep into enemy territory does make them more useful for the defense than for the offense. Thus, the United States and Israel would have been more alarmed in the early 1970s had the Russians provided the Egyptians with long-range instead of short-range aircraft. Naval forces are particularly difficult to classify in these terms, but those that are very short-legged can be used only for coastal defense.

Any forces that for various reasons fight well only when on their own soil in effect lack mobility and therefore are defensive. The most extreme example would be passive resistance. Noncooperation can thwart an aggressor, but it is very hard for large numbers of people to cross the border and stage a sit-in on another's territory. Morocco's recent march on the Spanish Sahara approached this tactic, but its success depended on special circumstances. Similarly, guerrilla warfare is defensive to the extent to which it requires civilian support that is likely to be forthcoming only in opposition to a foreign invasion. Indeed, if guerrilla warfare were easily exportable and if it took ten defenders to destroy each guerrilla, then this weapon would not only be one which could be used as easily to attack the other's territory as to defend one's own, but one in which the offense had the advantage: so the security dilemma would operate especially strongly.

If guerrillas are unable to fight on foreign soil, other kinds of armies may be unwilling to do so. An army imbued with the idea that only defensive wars were just would fight less effectively, if at all, if the goal were conquest. Citizen militias may lack both the ability and the will for aggression. The weapons employed, the short term of service, the time required for mobilization, and the spirit of repelling attacks on the homeland, all lend themselves much more to defense than to attacks on foreign territory.[68]

---

65. Boggs (fn. 12), 42, 83. For a good argument about the possible differentiation between offensive and defensive weapons in the 1930s, see Basil Liddell Hart, "Aggression and the Problem of Weapons," *English Review, Vol* 55 (July 1932), 71–78.

66. Quoted in Boggs (fn. 12), 39.

67. On these grounds, the Germans claimed in 1932 that the French forts were offensive (*ibid*, 49). Similarly, fortified forward naval bases can be necessary for launching an attack; see Braisted (fn. 22), 643.

Less idealistic motives can produce the same result. A leading student of medieval warfare has described the armies of that period as follows: "Assembled with difficulty, insubordinate, unable to maneuver, ready to melt away from its standard the moment that its short period of service was over, a feudal force presented an assemblage of unsoldier-like qualities such as have seldom been known to coexist. Primarily intended to defend its own borders from the Magyar, the Northman, or the Saracen . . . , the institution was utterly unadapted to take the offensive."[69] Some political groupings can be similarly described. International coalitions are more readily held together by fear than by hope of gain. Thus Castlereagh was not being entirely self-serving when in 1816 he argued that the Quadruple Alliance "could only have owed its origin to a sense of common danger; in its very nature it must be conservative; it cannot threaten either the security or the liberties of other States."[70] It is no accident that most of the major campaigns of expansion have been waged by one dominant nation (for example, Napoleon's France and Hitler's Germany), and that coalitions among relative equals are usually found defending the status quo. Most gains from conquest are too uncertain and raise too many questions of future squabbles among the victors to hold an alliance together for long. Although defensive coalitions are by no means easy to maintain—conflicting national objectives and the free-rider problem partly explain why three of them dissolved before Napoleon was defeated—the common interest of seeing that no state dominates provides a strong incentive for solidarity.

Weapons that are particularly effective in reducing fortifications and barriers are of great value to the offense. This is not to deny that a defensive power will want some of those weapons if the other side has them: Brodie is certainly correct to argue that while their tanks allowed the Germans to conquer France, properly used French tanks could have halted the attack. But France would not have needed these weapons if Germany had not acquired them, whereas even if France had no tanks, Germany could not have foregone them since they provided the only chance of breaking through the French lines. Mobile heavy artillery is, similarly, especially useful in destroying fortifications. The defender, while needing artillery to fight off attacking troops or to counterattack, can usually use lighter guns since they do not need to penetrate such massive obstacles. So it is not surprising that one of the few things that most nations at the interwar disarmament conferences were able to agree on was that heavy tanks and mobile heavy guns were particularly valuable to a state planning an attack.[71]

Weapons and strategies that depend for their effectiveness on surprise are almost always offensive. That fact was recognized by some of the delegates to the interwar disarmament conferences and is the principle behind the common national ban on concealed weapons. An earlier representative of this widespread view was the mid-19th-century Philadelphia newspaper that argued: "As a measure of defense, knives, dirks, and sword canes are entirely useless. They are fit only for attack, and all such attacks are of murderous character. Whoever carries such a weapon has prepared himself for homicide."[72]

---

68. The French made this argument in the interwar period; see Richard Challener, *The French Theory of the Nation in Arms* (NewYork: Columbia University Press, 1955),181–82.The Germans disagreed; see Boggs (fn.12), 44–45.

69. Oman (fn.24), 57–58.

70. Quoted in Charles Webster, *The Foreign Policy of Castlereagh, II, 1815–1822* (London: G. Belland Sons, 1963), 510.

71. Boggs (fn.12), 14–15, 47–48, 60.

It is, of course, not always possible to distinguish between forces that are most effective for holding territory and forces optimally designed for taking it. Such a distinction could not have been made for the strategies and weapons in Europe during most of the period between the Franco-Prussian War and World War I. Neither naval forces nor tactical air forces can be readily classified in these terms. But the point here is that when such a distinction is possible, the central characteristic of the security dilemma no longer holds, and one of the most troublesome consequences of anarchy is removed.

Offense-Defense Differentiation and Strategic Nuclear Weapons.

In the interwar period, most statesmen held the reasonable position that weapons that threatened civilians were offensive.[73] But when neither side can protect its civilians, a counter-city posture is defensive because the state can credibly threaten to retaliate only in response to an attack on itself or its closest allies. The costs of this strike are so high that the state could not threaten to use it for the less-than-vital interest of compelling the other to abandon an established position.

In the context of deterrence, offensive weapons are those that provide defense. In the now familiar reversal of common sense, the state that could take its population out of hostage, either by active or passive defense or by destroying the other's strategic weapons on the ground, would be able to alter the status quo. The desire to prevent such a situation was one of the rationales for the anti-ABM agreements; it explains why some arms controllers opposed building ABMs to protect cities, but favored sites that covered ICBM fields. Similarly, many analysts want to limit warhead accuracy and favor multiple re-entry vehicles (MRVs), but oppose multiple independently targetable re-entry vehicles (MIRVs). The former are more useful than single warheads for penetrating city defenses, and ensure that the state has a second-strike capability. MIRVs enhance counterforce capabilities. Some arms controllers argue that this is also true of cruise missiles, and therefore do not want them to be deployed either. There is some evidence that the Russians are not satisfied with deterrence and are seeking to regain the capability for defense. Such an effort, even if not inspired by aggressive designs, would create a severe security dilemma.

What is most important for the argument here is that land-based ICBMs are both offensive and defensive, but when both sides rely on Polaris-type systems (SLBMs), offense and defense use different weapons. ICBMs can be used either to destroy the other's cities in retaliation or to initiate hostilities by attacking the other's strategic missiles. Some measures—for instance, hardening of missile sites and warning systems—are purely defensive, since they do not make a first strike easier. Others are predominantly offensive—for instance, passive or active city defenses, and highly accurate warheads. But ICBMs themselves are useful for both purposes. And because states seek a high level of insurance, the desire for protection as well as the contemplation of a counterforce strike can explain the acquisition of extremely large numbers of missiles. So it is very difficult to infer the other's intentions from its military posture. Each side's efforts to increase its own security by procuring more missiles decreases, to an extent determined by the relative efficacy of the offense and the defense, the other side's security. That is not the case when both sides use SLBMs. The point is not that sea-based systems are less vulnerable than

72. Quoted in Philip Jordan, *Frontier Law ancl Order* (Lincoln: University of Nebraska Press, 1970), 7; also see 16–17.

73. Boggs (fn.12), 20, 28.

land-based ones (this bears on the offense-defense ratio) but that SLBMs are defensive, retaliatory weapons. First, they are probably not accurate enough to destroy many military targets.[74] Second, and more important, SLBMs are not the main instrument of attack against other SLBMs. The hardest problem confronting a state that wants to take its cities out of hostage is to locate the other's SLBMs, a job that requires not SLBMs but anti-submarine weapons. A state might use SLBMs to attack the other's submarines (although other weapons would probably be more efficient), but without antisubmarine warfare (ASW) capability the task cannot be performed. A status-quo state that wanted to forego offensive capability could simply forego ASW research and procurement.

There are two difficulties with this argument, however. First, since the state's SLBMs are potentially threatened by the other's ASW capabilities, the state may want to pursue ASW research in order to know what the other might be able to do and to design defenses. Unless it does this, it cannot be confident that its submarines are safe. Second, because some submarines are designed to attack surface ships, not launch missiles, ASW forces have missions other than taking cities out of hostage. Some U.S. officials plan for a long war in Europe which would require keeping the sea lanes open against Russian submarines. Designing an ASW force and strategy that would meet this threat without endangering Soviet SLBMs would be difficult but not impossible, since the two missions are somewhat different.[75] Furthermore, the Russians do not need ASW forces to combat submarines carrying out conventional missions; it might be in America's interest to sacrifice the ability to meet a threat that is not likely to materialize in order to reassure the Russians that we are not menacing their retaliatory capability.

When both sides rely on ICBMs, one side's missiles can attack the other's, and so the state cannot be indifferent to the other's building program. But because one side's SLBMs do not menace the other's, each side can build as many as it wants and the other need not respond. Each side's decision on the size of its force depends on technical questions, its judgment about how much destruction is enough to deter, and the amount of insurance it is willing to pay for—and these considerations are independent of the size of the other's strategic force. Thus the crucial nexus in the arms race is severed.

Here two objections not only can be raised but have been, by those who feel that even if American second-strike capability is in no danger, the United States must respond to a Soviet buildup. First, the relative numbers of missiles and warheads may be used as an index of each side's power and will. Even if there is no military need to increase American arms as the Russians increase theirs, a failure to respond may lead third parties to think that the U.S. has abandoned the competition with the U.S.S.R. and is no longer willing to pay the price of world leadership. Furthermore, if either side believes that nuclear "superiority" matters, then, through the bargaining logic, it will matter. The side with "superiority" will be more likely to stand firm in a confrontation if it thinks its "stronger" military position helps it, or if it thinks that the other thinks its own "weaker" military position is a handicap. To allow the other side to have more SLBMs—even if one's own second-strike capability is unimpaired—will give the other an advantage that can be translated into political gains.

---

74. See, however, Desmond Ball, "The Counterforce Potential of American SLBM Systems," *Journal of Peace Research,* XIV (No. 1, 1977), 23–40.

75. Richard Garwin, "Anti-Submarine Warfare and National Security," *Scientirc American* Vol. 227 (July 1972), 14–25.

The second objection is that superiority *does* matter, and not only because of mistaken beliefs. If nuclear weapons are used in an all-or-none fashion, then all that is needed is second-strike capability. But limited, gradual, and controlled strikes are possible. If the other side has superiority, it can reduce the state's forces by a slow-motion war of attrition. For the state to strike at the other's cities would invite retaliation; for it to reply with a limited counterforce attack would further deplete its supply of missiles. Alternatively, the other could employ demonstration attacks—such as taking out an isolated military base or exploding a warhead high over a city—in order to demonstrate its resolve. In either of these scenarios, the state will suffer unless it matches the other's arms posture.[76]

These two objections, if valid, mean that even with SLBMs one cannot distinguish offensive from defensive strategic nuclear weapons. Compellence may be more difficult than deterrence.[77] But if decision makers believe that numbers of missiles or of warheads influence outcomes, or if these weapons can be used in limited manner, then the posture and policy that would be needed for self-protection is similar to that useful for aggression. If the second objection has merit, security would require the ability to hit selected targets on the other side, enough ammunition to wage a controlled counterforce war, and the willingness to absorb limited countervalue strikes. Secretary Schlesinger was correct in arguing that this capability would not constitute a first-strike capability. But because the "Schlesinger Doctrine" could be used not only to cope with a parallel Russian policy, but also to support an American attempt to change the status quo, the new American stance would decrease Russian security. Even if the U.S.S.R. were reassured that the present U.S. Government lacked the desire or courage to do this, there could be no guarantee that future governments would not use the new instruments for expansion. Once we move away from the simple idea that nuclear weapons can only be used for all-out strikes, half the advantage of having both sides rely on a sea-based force would disappear because of the lack of an offensive-defensive differentiation. To the extent that military policy affects political relations, it would be harder for the United States and the Soviet Union to cooperate even if both supported the status quo.

Although a full exploration of these questions is beyond the scope of this paper, it should be noted that the objections rest on decision makers' beliefs—beliefs, furthermore, that can be strongly influenced by American policy and American statements. The perceptions of third nations of whether the details of the nuclear balance affect political conflicts—and, to a lesser extent, Russian beliefs about whether superiority is meaningful—are largely derived from the American strategic debate. If most American spokesmen were to take the position that a secure second-strike capability was sufficient and the increments over that (short of a first-strike capability) would only be a waste of money, it is doubtful whether America's allies or the neutrals would judge the superpowers' useful military might or political will by the size of their stockpiles. Although the Russians stress war-fighting ability, they have not contended that marginal increases in strategic forces bring political gains; any attempt to do so could be rendered less effective by an American assertion that this is nonsense. The bargaining advantages of possessing nuclear "superiority" work best when both

---

76. The latter scenario, however, does not require that the state closely match the number of missiles the other deploys.

77. Thomas Schelling, Arms and Influence (New Haven: Yale University Press,1966), 69–75. Schelling's arguments are not entirely convincing, however. For further discussion, see Jervis, "Deterrence Theory Re-Visited," Working Paper No. 14, UCLA Program in Arms Control and International Security.

sides acknowledge them. If the "weaker" side convinces the other that it does not believe there is any meaningful difference in strength, then the "stronger" side cannot safely stand firm because there is no increased chance that the other will back down.

This kind of argument applies at least as strongly to the second objection. Neither side can employ limited nuclear options unless it is quite confident that the other accepts the rules of the game. For if the other believes that nuclear war cannot be controlled, it will either refrain from responding—which would be fine—or launch all-out retaliation. Although a state might be ready to engage in limited nuclear war without acknowledging this possibility—and indeed, that would be a reasonable policy for the United States—it is not likely that the other would have sufficient faith in that prospect to initiate limited strikes unless the state had openly avowed its willingness to fight this kind of war. So the United States, by patiently and consistently explaining that it considers such ideas to be mad and that any nuclear wars will inevitably get out of control, could gain a large measure of protection against the danger that the Soviet Union might seek to employ a "Schlesinger Doctrine" against an America that lacked the military ability or political will to respond in kind. Such a position is made more convincing by the inherent implausibility of the arguments for the possibility of a limited nuclear war.

In summary, as long as states believe that all that is needed is second-strike capability, then the differentiation between offensive and defensive forces that is provided by reliance on SLBMs allows each side to increase its security without menacing the other, permits some inferences about intentions to be drawn from military posture, and removes the main incentive for status-quo powers to engage in arms races.

Four Worlds

The two variables we have been discussing—whether the offense or the defense has the advantage, and whether offensive postures can be distinguished from defensive ones—can be combined to yield four possible worlds (see Figure 2).

	Offense has the Advantage	Defense has the Advantage
Offensive posture not distinguishable from Defensive one	1 Doubly Dangerous	2 Security Dilemma, but security requirements may be compatible
Offensive posture distinguishable from Defensive one	3 No security dilemma, but aggression possible. Status-quo states can follow different policy than aggressors. Warning given.	4 Doubly Stable

Figure 2.

The first world is the worst for status-quo states. There is no way to get security without menacing others, and security through defense is terribly difficult to obtain. Because offensive and defensive postures are the same, status-quo states acquire the same kind of arms that are sought by aggressors. And because the offense has the advantage over the defense, attacking is the best route to protecting what you have; status-quo states will therefore behave like aggressors. The situation will be unstable. Arms races are likely. Incentives to strike first will turn crises into wars. Decisive victories and conquests will be common. States will grow and shrink rapidly, and it will be hard for any state to maintain its size and influence without trying to increase them. Cooperation among status-quo powers will be extremely hard to achieve.

There are no cases that totally fit this picture, but it bears more than a passing resemblance to Europe before World War I. Britain and Germany, although in many respects natural allies, ended up as enemies. Of course much of the explanation lies in Germany's ill-chosen policy. And from the perspective of our theory, the powers' ability to avoid war in a series of earlier crises cannot be easily explained. Nevertheless, much of the behavior in this period was the product of technology and beliefs that magnified the security dilemma. Decision makers thought that the offense had a big advantage and saw little difference between offensive and defensive military postures. The era was characterized by arms races. And once war seemed likely, mobilization races created powerful incentives to strike first. In the nuclear era, the first world would be one in which each side relied on vulnerable weapons that were aimed at similar forces and each side understood the situation. In this case, the incentives to strike first would be very high—so high that status-quo powers as well as aggressors would be sorely tempted to pre-empt. And since the forces could be used to change the status quo as well as to preserve it, there would be no way for both sides to increase their security simultaneously. Now the familiar logic of deterrence leads both sides to see the dangers in this world. Indeed, the new understanding of this situation was one reason why vulnerable bombers and missiles were replaced. Ironically, the 1950s would have been more hazardous if the decision makers had been aware of the dangers of their posture and had therefore felt greater pressure to strike first. This situation could be recreated if both sides were to rely on MIRVed ICBMs.

In the second world, the security dilemma operates because offensive and defensive postures cannot be distinguished; but it does not operate as strongly as in the first world because the defense has the advantage, and so an increment in one side's strength increases its security more than it decreases the other's. So, if both sides have reasonable subjective security requirements, are of roughly equal power, and the variables discussed earlier are favorable, it is quite likely that status-quo states can adopt compatible security policies. Although a state will not be able to judge the other's intentions from the kinds of weapons it procures, the level of arms spending will give important evidence. Of course a state that seeks a high level of arms might be not an aggressor but merely an insecure state, which if conciliated will reduce its arms, and if confronted will reply in kind. To assume that the apparently excessive level of arms indicates aggressiveness could therefore lead to a response that would deepen the dilemma and create needless conflict. But empathy and skillful statesmanship can reduce this danger. Furthermore, the advantageous position of the defense means that a status-quo state can often maintain a high degree of security with a level of arms lower than that of its expected adversary. Such a state demonstrates that it lacks the ability or desire to alter the status quo, at least at the present time. The strength of the defense also allows states to react slowly and with restraint when they fear that others are menacing them. So, although status-quo powers will to some extent be threatening to others, that extent will be limited.

This world is the one that comes closest to matching most periods in history. Attacking is usually harder than defending because of the strength of fortifications and obstacles. But purely defensive postures are rarely possible because fortifications are usually supplemented by armies and mobile guns which can support an attack. In the nuclear era, this world would be one in which both sides relied on relatively invulnerable ICBMs and believed that limited nuclear war was impossible. Assuming no MIRVs, it would take more than one attacking missile to destroy one of the adversary's. Pre-emption is therefore unattractive. If both sides have large inventories, they can ignore all but drastic increases on the other side. A world of either ICBMs or SLBMs in which both sides adopted the "Schlesinger Doctrine"would probably fit in this category too. The means of preserving the status quo would also be the means of changing it, as we discussed earlier. And the defense usually would have the advantage, because compellence is more difficult than deterrence. Although a state might succeed in changing the status quo on issues that matter much more to it than to others, status-quo powers could deter major provocations under most circumstances.

In the third world there may be no security dilemma, but there are security problems. Because states can procure defensive systems that do not threaten others, the dilemma need not operate. But because the offense has the advantage, aggression is possible, and perhaps easy. If the offense has less of an advantage, stability and cooperation are likely because the status-quo states will procure defensive forces. They need not react to others who are similarly armed, but can wait for the warning they would receive if others started to deploy offensive weapons. But each state will have to watch the others carefully, and there is room for false suspicions. The costliness of the defense and the allure of the offense can lead to unnecessary mistrust, hostility, and war, unless some of the variables discussed earlier are operating to restrain defection.

A hypothetical nuclear world that would fit this description would be one in which both sides relied on SLBMs, but in which ASW techniques were very effective. Offense and defense would be different, but the former would have the advantage. This situation is not likely to occur; but if it did, a status-quo state could show its lack of desire to exploit the other by refraining from threatening its submarines. The desire to have more protecting you than merely the other side's fear of retaliation is a strong one, however, and a state that knows that it would not expand even if its cities were safe is likely to believe that the other would not feel threatened by its ASW program. It is easy to see how such a world could become unstable, and how spirals of tensions and conflict could develop.

The fourth world is doubly safe. The differentiation between offensive and defensive systems permits a way out of the security dilemma; the advantage of the defense disposes of the problems discussed in the previous paragraphs. There is no reason for a status-quo power to be tempted to procure offensive forces, and aggressors give notice of their intentions by the posture they adopt. Indeed, if the advantage of the defense is great enough, there are no security problems. The loss of the ultimate form of the power to alter the status quo would allow greater scope for the exercise of nonmilitary means and probably would tend to freeze the distribution of values.

This world would have existed in the first decade of the 20th century if the decision makers had understood the available technology. In that case, the European powers would have followed different policies both in the long run and in the summer of 1914. Even Germany, facing powerful enemies on both sides, could have made herself secure by developing strong defenses. France could also have made her frontier almost impregnable. Furthermore, when crises arose, no one would have had incentives to strike first. There would have been no competitive mobilization races reducing the time available for negotiations.

In the nuclear era, this world would be one in which the superpowers relied on SLBMs, ASW technology was not up to its task, and limited nuclear options were not taken seriously. We have discussed this situation earlier; here we need only add that, even if our analysis is correct and even if the policies and postures of both sides were to move in this direction, the problem of violence below the nuclear threshold would remain. On issues other than defense of the homeland, there would still be security dilemmas and security problems. But the world would nevertheless be safer than it has usually been.

The Realist-Liberal Tension

Realist Tradition

Liberal Tradition

The Realist-Liberal Tension

Realist Tradition

Thucydides
Introduction to The History of the Peloponnesian War

Thucydides
The Melian Dialogue

Niccolò Machiavelli
From The Prince

Thomas Hobbes
Of the Natural Condition of Mankind

Hans J. Morgenthau
Six Principles of Political Realism

Liberal Tradition

Scott Silverstone
The Liberal Tradition and International Relations

Immanuel Kant
Perpetual Peace

Woodrow Wilson
The Fourteen Points

Michael Doyle
Liberalism and World Politics

Introduction to the Realist Tradition

The realist tradition examines the relationships among men dating back to the beginning of recorded history. Distrust and cynicism dominate this view of human relations. This text focuses on authors whose writings form the roots of the realist tradition. From the 4th Century B.C. to the 20th century, their emphases range from the first great western empire, to the rivalry of the Italian city states of the 15th century, England during the formation of sovereign states foreign affairs following the Second World War, and the madness of Hitlerian Germany. The passage of time and the development of the nation state and international governing organizations have failed to moderate their view of human nature, which is basically "bad." As a result, there is little to no belief in the possibility of relationships built on trust. Only a limited role for morality, if any, exists in this dark view of the world where life is seen as "solitary, poor, nasty, brutish, and short."[1] The realist tradition espouses that survival and security are or should be the most important factors considered in enacting state policy, and that the primary consideration in accomplishing those goals is the relative power of nations and states in the international arena.

In *The History of the Peloponnesian War*, the disgraced Athenian General, Thucydides, described his beloved Athens' efforts to secure its empire. Athens, a democracy, operated a naval empire that dominated many of the cities along the Adriatic and Aegean Seas. That empire, which has been compared to the present day American Empire, sought to secure its preeminence by ensuring allegiance of tributary cities and acquiring more colonies. Those actions led Athens to the overextension of its power and resources and eventually its downfall. In order to secure themselves in a global environment of anarchy, empires must recognize that "the strong do what they can and the weak suffer what they must."[2] The leaders of these states have an obligation to secure their "self-preservation."

Thucydides' depiction of the Melian dialogue, contrasts the individual's desire to see righteousness rule in international relations with the wicked reality that justice is defined by the powerful. In this dialogue the Melians' appeal to the Athenians', democratic sense of justice and argue their own right to neutrality. The Athenians educate the Melian's on the state of nature, where "right, as the world goes, is only in question between equals in power… [and] of the gods we believe, and of men we know, that by a necessary law of nature they rule wherever they can."[3] For the Athenians to permit the Melians their desired independence would have been interpreted as weakness and a sign of fear by Athens' allies and enemies alike. Thucydides' history focuses on Athens' search for power, the only thing that guaranteed its success, freedom, and its privileged position.

Thomas Hobbes' 17th century discourse on the Leviathan relates the rise of the sovereign nation state. Published three years after the Treaty of Westphalia and as the English Civil Wars were concluding, the Leviathan argues for a strong central state. In order to accrue the gains from industry, a strong state provides the policing powers required to maintain order; "where there is no common power, there is no law: where no law, no injustice…The notions of right and wrong, justice and injustice have no

1. From Thomas Hobbes, Leviathan, first published in 1651.

2. Strassler, Robert B, ed, *The History of the Peloponnesian War*, by Thucydides (New York, NY, Touchstone, 1998) p. 352.

3. Ibid.

place."[4] Hobbes describes the world as chaotic and in a state of anarchy. In a world where all men are equal, there is no individual security, anything gained by industry or perseverance is vulnerable to the whims of others. Hobbes aimed to provide a guide for achieving security based on the concept of a strong central state as the key actor.

Niccolo Machiavelli's *The Prince* was also a guide book. *The Prince* was written for the Duke of Urbino, a member of one of the dominant families of early 16th century Italy. A leadership manual for the Italian City-States, these principalities competed for dominance over each other for hundreds of years before the unification of Italy in the 19th Century. This dominance would help secure their survival in a country without a central authority to mediate conflict. Machiavelli's suggested path for successful rule included not just relations among City-States, but relations within City-States as well. Machiavelli was a former soldier and political consultant to one of the leading City-States of his day. He is probably the author most often linked to realism. His name has become synonymous with politics that emphasize underhanded, amoral, self-serving, calculating actions. This common misperception fails to recognize Machiavelli's intent, which was not to facilitate principalities being led by the "ungrateful, fickle, hypocrites and dissemblers , evaders of dangers, [and] lovers of gain," but to inform the princes who operated in this environment.[5] His goal was to promote the effective rule of these City-States in a world where morality had little place except as a tool to engender the support of the people, and it is "much safer to be feared than loved."[6]

Most recently, Hans Morgenthau, a refugee from Hitler's Germany, described international relations as "governed by objective laws that have their roots in human nature."[7] His writings are partly a continuation of each of the previous writers. There is no room for morality in his depiction of the world. Politicians, who chose to develop foreign policy based on some noble concept of morality and justice, have often "ended by making it [the world] worse."[8] His writings reflect the Munich Agreement of 1938, in which the leaders of Germany and France responded to Adolf Hitler's naked aggression with a policy of appeasement. Their opportunity to turn Hitler back was foregone in order to pursue a policy they felt would bring "Peace in Our Time." Unfortunately, World War II followed less than twelve months later. This experience illustrates that just and moral intentions "do not guarantee the moral goodness and political success of the policies they inspire."[9]

Realism is not a program for pessimism and hopelessness. Its authors have drawn on history's lessons to explain certain themes in the behavior of men. They have applied these recurrent themes to a world-view or school of thought that promotes the basic need of humans, survival. This search for survival continues today, as asymmetric warfare and terrorism have made the world less secure and the possibility of cooperation between society's extremes seems to have diminished with globalization and the ability of radical fundamentalists to reach all perceived enemies. This raises the question: what are the implications of these views in today's world in which the sovereignty of state is challenged by trans-national & sub-national actors as well as multi-national corporations?

---

4. Hobbes.

5. Leo Paul S. de Alvarez ed., *The Prince*, by Niccolo Machiavelli, (Waveland Press, Illlinois) p101.

6. Ibid.

7. Hans Morgenthau, *Politics Among Nations: The Struggle for Power and Peace*, 6th edition, revised by K. Thompson, McGraw-Hill Inc., p. 4.

8. Ibid, p. 5.

9. Ibid p. 6

Introduction to *The History of the Peloponnesian War*

Thucydides

Thucydides the Athenian wrote the history of the war fought between Athens and Sparta, beginning the account at the very outbreak of the war, in the belief that it was going to be a great war and more worth writing about than any of those which had taken place in the past. My belief was based on the fact that the two sides were at the very height of their power and preparedness, and I saw, too, that the rest of the Hellenic world was committed to one side or the other; even those who were not immediately engaged were deliberating on the courses which they were to take later. This was the greatest disturbance in the history of the Hellenes, affecting also a large part of the non-Hellenic world, and indeed, I might almost say, the whole of mankind. For though I have found it impossible, because of its remoteness in time, to acquire a really precise knowledge of the distant past or even of the history preceding our own period, yet, after looking back into it as far as I can, all the evidence leads me to conclude that these periods were not great periods either in warfare or in anything else. . . .

Not many years after the end of tyrannies in Hellas the battle of Marathon was fought between the Persians and the Athenians. Ten years later the foreign enemy returned with his vast armada for the conquest of Hellas, and at this moment of peril the Spartans, since they were the leading power, were in command of the allied Hellenic forces. In face of the invasion the Athenians decided to abandon their city; they broke up their homes, took to their ships, and became a people of sailors. It was by a common effort that the foreign invasion was repelled; but not long afterwards the Hellenes—both those who had fought in the war together and those who later revolted from the King of Persia—split into two divisions, one group following Athens and the other Sparta. These were clearly the two most powerful states, one being supreme on land, the other on the sea. For a short time the war-time alliance held together, but it was not long before quarrels took place and Athens and Sparta, each with her own allies, were at war with each other, while among the rest of the Hellenes states that had their own differences now joined one or other of the two sides. So from the end of the Persian War till the beginning of the Peloponnesian War, though there were some intervals of peace, on the whole these two Powers were either fighting with each other or putting down revolts among their allies. They were consequently in a high state of military preparedness and had gained their military experience in the hard school of danger.

The Spartans did not make their allies pay tribute, but saw to it that they were governed by oligarchies who would work in the Spartan interest. Athens, on the other hand, had in the course of time taken over the fleets of her allies (except for those of Chios and Lesbos) and had made them pay contributions of money instead. Thus the forces available to Athens alone for this war were greater than the combined forces had ever been when the alliance was still intact.

In investigating past history, and in forming the conclusions which I have formed, it must be admitted that one cannot rely on every detail which has come down to us by way of tradition. People are inclined to accept all stories of ancient times in an uncritical way– even when these stories concern their own native countries . . .

However, I do not think that one will be far wrong in accepting the conclusions I have reached from the evidence which I have put forward. It is better evidence than that of the poets, who exaggerate the importance of their themes, or of the prose chroniclers, who are less interested in telling the truth than in catching the attention of their public, whose authorities cannot be checked, and whose subject-matter, owing to the passage of time, is mostly lost in the unreliable streams of mythology. We may claim instead to have used only the plainest evidence and to have reached conclusions which are reasonably accurate, considering that we have been dealing with ancient history. As for this present war, even though people are apt to think that the war in which they are fighting is the greatest of all wars and, when it is over, to relapse again into their admiration of the past, nevertheless, if one looks at the facts themselves, one will see that this was the greatest war of all.

In this history I have made use of set speeches some of which were delivered just before and others during the war. I have found it difficult to remember the precise words used in the speeches which I listened to myself and my various informants have experienced the same difficulty; so my method has been, while keeping as closely as possible to the general sense of the words that were actually used, to make the speakers say what, in my opinion, was called for by each situation.

And with regard to my factual reporting of the events of the war I have made it a principle not to write down the first story that came my way, and not even to be guided by my own general impressions; either I was present myself at the the events which I have described or else I heard of them from eye-witnesses whose reports I have checked with as much thoroughness as possible. Not that even so the truth was easy to discover: different eye-witnesses give different accounts of the same events, speaking out of partiality for one side or the other or else from imperfect memories. And it may well be that my history will seem less easy to read because of the absence in it of a romantic element. It will be enough for me, however, if these words of mine are judged useful by those who want to understand clearly the events which happened in the past and which (human nature being what it is) will, at some timc or other and in much the same ways, be repeated in the future. *My work is not a piece of, writing designed to meet the taste of an immediate public, but was done to last for ever.*

The greatest war in the past was the Persian War; yet in this war the decision was reached quickly as a result of two naval battles and two battles on land. The Peloponnesian War, on the other hand, not only lasted for a long time, but throughout its course brought with it unprecedented suffering for Hellas. Never before had so many cities been captured and then devastated, whether by foreign armies or by the Hellenic powers themselves (some of these cities, after capture, were resettled with new inhabitants); never had there been so many exiles; never such loss of life—both in the actual warfare and in internal revolutions. Old stories of past prodigies, which had not found much confirmation in recent experience, now became credible. Wide areas, for instance, were affected by violent earthquakes; there were more frequent eclipses of the sun than had ever been recorded before; in various parts of the country there were extensive droughts followed by famine; and there was the plague which did more harm and destroyed more life than almost any other single factor. All these calamities fell together upon the Hellenes after the outbreak of war.

War began when the Athenians and the Peloponnesians broke the Thirty Years Truce which had been made after the capture of Euboea.[1] As to the reasons why they broke the truce, I propose first to give an account of the causes of complaint which they had against each other and of the specific instances where their interests clashed: this is in order that there should be no doubt in anyone's mind about what led to this great war falling upon the Hellenes. But the real reason for the war is, in my opinion, most likely to be disguised by such an argument. *What made war inevitable was the the growth of Athenian power and the fear which this caused in Sparta.*

1. In 446-5 B.C.

The Melian Dialogue

Thucydides

Next summer Alcibiades sailed to Argos with twenty ships and seized 300 Argive citizens who were still suspected of being pro-Spartan. These were put by the Athenians into the nearby islands under Athenian control.

The Athenians also made an expedition against the island of Melos. They had thirty of their own ships, six from Chios, and two from Lesbos; 1,200 hoplites, 300 archers, and twenty mounted archers, all from Athens; and about 1,500 hoplites from the allies and the islanders.

The Melians are a colony from Sparta. They had refused to join the Athenian empire like the other islanders, and at first had remained neutral without helping either side; but afterwards, when the Athenians had brought force to bear on them by laying waste their land, they had become open enemies of Athens.

Now the generals Cleomedes, the son of Lycomedes, and Tisias, the son of Tisimachus, encamped with the above force in Melian territory and, before doing any harm to the land, first of all sent representatives to negotiate. The Melians did not invite these representatives to speak before the people, but asked them to make the statement for which they had come in front of the governing body and the few. The Athenian representatives then spoke as follows:

"So we are not to speak before the people, no doubt in case the mass of the people should hear once and for all and without interruption an argument from us which is both persuasive and incontrovertible, and should so be led astray. This, we realize, is your motive in bringing us here to speak before the few. Now suppose that you who sit here should make assurance doubly sure. Suppose that you, too, should refrain from dealing with every point in detail in a set speech, and should instead interrupt us whenever we say something controversial and deal with that before going on to the next point? Tell us first whether you approve of this suggestion of ours."

The Council of the Melian replied as follows:

"No one can object to each of us putting forward our own views in a calm atmosphere. That is perfectly reasonable. What is scarcely consistent with such a proposal is the present threat, indeed the certainty, of your making war on us. We see that you have come prepared to judge the argument yourselves, and that the likely end of it all will be either war, if we prove that we are in the right, and so refuse to surrender, or else slavery."

Athenians: If you are going to spend the time in enumerating your suspicions about the future, or if you have met here for any other reason except to look the fact in the face and on the basis of these facts to consider how you can save your city from destruction, there is no point in our going on with this discussion. If, however, you will do as we suggest, then we will speak on.

Melians: It is natural and understandable that people who are placed as we are should have recourse to all kinds of arguments and different points of view. However, you are right in saying that we are met together here to discuss the safety of our country and, if you will have it so, the discussion shall proceed on the lines that you have laid down.

Athenians: Then we on our side will use no fine phrases saying, for example, that we have a right to our empire because we defeated the Persians, or that we have come against you now because of the injuries you have done us—a great mass of words that nobody would believe. And we ask you on your side not to imagine that you will influence us by saying that you, though a colony of Sparta, have not joined Sparta in the war, or that you have never done us any harm. Instead we recommend that you should try to get what it is possible for you to get, taking into consideration what we both really do think; since you know as well as we do that, when these matters are discussed by practical people, *the standard of justice depends on the equality of power to compel and that in fact the strong do what they have the power to do and the weak accept what they have to accept.*

Melians: Then in our view (since you force us to leave justice out of account and to confine ourselves to self-interest)—in our view it is at any rate useful that you should not destroy a principle that is to the general good of all men—namely, that in the case of all who fall into danger there should be such a thing as fair play and just dealing, and that such people should be allowed to use and to profit by arguments that fall short of a mathematical accuracy. And this is a principle which affects you as much as anybody, since your own fall would be visited by the most terrible vengeance and would be an example to the world.

Athenians: As for us, even assuming that our empire does come to an end, we are not despondent about what would happen next. One is not so much frightened of being conquered by a power which rules over others, as Sparta does (not that we are concerned with Sparta now), as of what would happen if a ruling power is attacked and defeated by its own subjects. So far as this point is concerned, you can leave it to us to face the risks involved. What we shall do now is to show you that it is for the good of our own empire that we are here and that it is for the preservation of your city that we shall say what we are going to say. We do not want any trouble in bringing you into our empire, and we want you to be spare for the good both of yourselves and of ourselves.

Melians: And how could it be just as good for us to be the slaves as for you to be the masters?

Athenians: You, by giving in, would save yourselves from disaster; we, by not destroying you, would be able to profit from you.

Melians: So you would not agree to our being neutral, friends instead of enemies, but allies of neither side?

Athenians: No, because it is not so much your hostility that injures us; it is rather the case that, if we were on friendly terms with you, our subjects would regard that as a sigh of weakness in us, whereas your hatred is evidence of our power.

Melians: Is that your subjects' idea of fair play—that no distinction should be made between people who are quite unconnected with you and people who are mostly your own colonists or else rebels whom you have conquered?

Athenians: So far as right and wrong are concerned they think that there is no difference between the two, that those who still preserve their independence do so because they are strong, and that if we fail to attack them it is because we are afraid. So that by conquering you we shall increase not only the size but the security of our empire. We rule the sea and you are islanders, and weaker islanders too than the others; it is therefore particularly important that you should not escape.

Melians: But do you think there is no security for you in what we suggest? For here again, since you will not let us mention justice, but tell us to give in to your interests, we, too, must tell you what our interests are and, if yours and ours happen to coincide, we must try to persuade you of the fact. It is not certain that you will make enemies of all states who are at present neutral, when they see what is happening here and naturally conclude that in course of time you will attack them too? Does not this mean that you are strengthening the enemies you have already and are forcing others to become your enemies even against their intentions and their inclinations?

Athenians: As a matter of fact we are not so much frightened of states on the continent. They have their liberty, and this means that it will be a long time before they begin to take precautions against us. We are more concerned about islanders like yourselves, who are still unsubdued, or subjects who have already become embittered by the constraint which our empire imposes on them. These are the people who are most likely to act in a reckless manner and to bring themselves and us, too, into the most obvious danger.

Melians: Then surely, if such hazards are taken by you to keep your empire and by your subjects to escape from it, we who are still free would show ourselves great cowards and weaklings if we failed to face everything that comes rather than submit to slavery.

Athenians: No, not if you are sensible. This is no fair fight, with honour on one side and shame on the other. It is rather a question of saving your lives and not resisting those who are far too strong for you.

Melians: Yet we know that in war fortune sometimes makes the odds more level than could be expected from the difference in numbers of the two sides. And if we surrender, then all our hope is lost at once, whereas, so long as we remain in action, there is still a hope that we may yet stand upright.

Athenians: Hope, that comforter in danger! If one already has solid advantages to fall back upon, one can indulge in hope. It may do harm, but will not destroy one. *But hope is by nature an expensive commodity*, and those who are risking their all on one cast find out what it means only when they are already ruined; it never fails them in the period when such a knowledge would enable them to take precautions. Do not let this happen to you, you who are weak and whose fate depends on a single movement of the scale. And do not be like those people who, as so commonly happens, miss the chance of saving themselves in a human and practical way, and, when every clear and distinct hope has left them in their adversity, turn to what is blind and vague, to prophecies and oracles and such things which by encouraging hope lead men to ruin.

Melians: It is difficult, and you may be sure that we know it, for us to oppose your power and fortune, unless the terms be equal. Nevertheless we trust that the gods will give us fortune as good as yours, because we are standing for what is right against what is wrong; and as for what we lack in power, we trust that it will be made up for by our alliance with the Spartans, who are bound, if for no other reason, then for honour's sake, and because we are their kinsmen, to come to our help. Our confidence, therefore, is not so entirely irrational as you think.

Athenians: So far as the favour of the gods is concerned, we think we have as much right to that as you have. Our aims and our actions are perfectly consistent with the beliefs men hold about the gods and with the principles which govern their own conduct. Our opinion of the gods and our knowledge of men lead us to conclude that it is a general and necessary law of nature to rule whatever one can. This is not a law that we made ourselves, nor were we the first to act upon it when it was made. We found it already in existence, and we shall leave it to exist for ever among those who come after us. We are merely acting in accordance with it, and we know that you or anybody else with the same power as ours would be acting in precisely the same way. And therefore, so far as the gods are concerned, we see no good reason why we should fear to be at a disadvantage. But with regard to your views about Sparta and your confidence that she, out of a sense of honour, will come to your aid, we must say that we congratulate you on your simplicity but do not envy you your folly. In matters that concern themselves or their own constitution the Spartans are quite remarkably good; as for their relations with others, that is a long story, but it can be expressed shortly and clearly by saying that of all people we know the Spartans are most conspicuous for believing that what they like doing is honourable and what suits their interests is just. And this kind of attitude is not going to be of much help to you in your absurd quest for safety at the moment.

Melians: But this is the very point where we can feel most sure. Their own self-interest will make them refuse to betray their own colonists, the Melians, for that would mean losing the confidence of their friends among the Hellenes and doing good to their enemies.

Athenians: You seem to forget that if one follows one's self-interest one wants to be safe, whereas the path of justice and honour involves one in danger. And, where danger is concerned, the Spartans are not, as a rule, very venturesome.

Melians: But we think that they would even endanger themselves for our sake and count the risk more worth taking than in the case of others, because we are so close to the Peloponnese that they could operate more easily, and because they can depend on us more than on others, since we are of the same race and share the same feelings.

Athenians: Goodwill shown by the party that is asking for help does not mean security for the prospective ally. What is looked for is a positive preponderance of power in action. And the Spartans pay attention to this point even more than others do. Certainly they distrust their own native resources so much that when they attack a neighbour they bring a great army of allies with them. It is hardly likely therefore that, while we are in control of the sea, they will cross over to an island.

Melians: But they still might send others. The Cretan sea is a wide one, and it is harder for those who control it to intercept others than for those who want to slip through to do so safely. And even if they were to fail in this, they would turn against your own land and against those of your allies left unvisited by Brasidas. So, instead of troubling about a country which has nothing to do with you, you will find trouble nearer home, among your allies, and in your own country.

Athenians: It is a possibility, something that has in fact happened before. It may happen in your case, but you are well aware that the Athenians have never yet relinquished a single siege operation through fear of others. But we are somewhat shocked to find that, though you announced your intention of discussing how you could preserve yourselves, in all this talk you have said absolutely nothing which could justify a man in thinking that he could be preserved. Your chief points are concerned with what you hope may happen in the future, while your actual resources are too scanty to give you a chance of survival against the forces that are opposed to you at this moment. You will therefore be showing an extraordinary lack of common sense if, after you have asked us to retire from this meeting, you still fail to reach a conclusion wiser than anything you have mentioned so far. Do not be led astray by a false sense of honour—a thing which often brings men to ruin when they are faced with an obvious danger that somehow affects their pride. For in many cases men have still been able to see the dangers ahead of them, but this thing called dishonour, this word, by its own force of seduction, has drawn them into a state where they have surrendered to an idea, while in fact they have fallen voluntarily into irrevocable disaster, in dishonour that is all the more dishonourable because it has come to them from their own folly rather than their misfortune. You, if you take the right view, will be careful to avoid this. You will see that there is nothing disgraceful in giving way to the greatest city in Hellas when she is offering you such reasonable terms—alliance on a tribute-paying basis and liberty to enjoy your own property. And, when you are allowed to choose between war and safety, you will not be so insensitively arrogant as to make the wrong choice. This is the safe rule—to stand up to one's equals, to behave with deference towards one's superiors, and to treat one's inferiors with moderation. Think it over again, then, when we have withdrawn from the meeting, and let this be a point that constantly recurs to your minds—that you are discussing the fate of your country, that you have only one country, and that its future for good or ill depends on this one single decision which you are going to make.

The Athenians then withdrew from the discussion. The Melians, left to themselves, reached a conclusion which was much the same as they had indicated in their previous replies. Their answer was as follows:

"Our decision, Athenians, is just the same as it was at first. We are not prepared to give up in a short moment the liberty which our city has enjoyed from its foundation for 700 years. We put our trust in the fortune that the gods will send and which has saved us up to now, and in the help of men—that is, of the Spartans; and so we shall try to save ourselves. But we invite you to allow us to be friends of yours and enemies to neither side, to make a treaty which shall be agreeable to both you and us, and so to leave our country."

The Melians made this reply, and the Athenian, just as they were breaking off the discussion, said:

"Well, at any rate, judging from this decision of yours, you seem to us quite unique in your ability to consider the future as something more certain than what is before your eyes, and to see uncertainties as realities, simply because you would like them to be so. As you have staked most on and trusted most in Spartans, luck, and hopes, so in all these you will find yourselves most completely deluded."

The Athenian representatives then went back to the army, and the Athenian generals, finding that the Melians would not submit, immediately commenced hostilities and built a wall completely round the city of Melos, dividing the work out among the various states. Later they left behind a garrison of some of their own and some allied troops to blockade the place by land and sea, and with the greater part of their army returned home. The force left behind stayed on and continued with the siege.

About the same time the Argives invaded Phliasia and were ambushed by the Phliasians and the exiles from Argos, losing about eighty men.

Then, too, the Athenians at Pylos captured a great quantity of plunder from Spartan territory. Not even after this did the Spartans renounce the treaty and make war, but they issued a proclamation saying that any of their people who wished to do so were free to make raids on the Athenians. The Corinthians also made some attacks on the Athenians because of private quarrels of their own, but the rest of the Peloponnesians stayed quiet.

Meanwhile the Melians made a night attack and captured the part of the Athenian lines opposite the market-place. They killed some of the troops, and then, after bringing in corn and everything else useful that they could lay their hands on, retired again and made no further move, while the Athenians took measures to make their blockade more efficient in [the] future. So the summer came to an end.

In the following winter the Spartans planned to invade the territory of Argos, but when the sacrifice for crossing the frontier turned out unfavourably, they gave up the expedition. The fact that they had intended to invade made the Argives suspect certain people in their city, some of whom they arrested, though others succeeded in escaping.

About this same time the Melians again captured another part of the Athenian lines where there were only a few of the garrison on guard. As a result of this, another force came out afterwards from Athens under the command of Philocrates, the son of Demeas. Siege operations were now carried on vigorously and, as there was also some treachery from inside, the Melians surrendered unconditionally to the Athenians, who put to death all the men of military age whom they took, and sold the women and children as slaves. Melos itself then took over for themselves, sending out later a colony of 500 men.[1]

---

1. That there were Melian survivors, who were restored by Lysander at the end of the war, is stated by Xenophon (*Hellenica*, II, 2,9).

From *The Prince*

Niccoló Machiavelli

CHAPTER 5: HOW CITIES OR PRINCIPALITIES ARE TO BE GOVERNED THAT PREVIOUS TO BEING CONQUERED HAD LIVED UNDER THEIR OWN LAWS

Conquered states that have been accustomed to liberty and the government of their own laws can be held by the conqueror in three different ways. The first is to ruin them, the second, for the conqueror to go and reside there in person; and the third is to allow them to continue to live under their own laws, subject to a regular tribute, and to create in them a government of a few, who will keep the country friendly to the conqueror. Such a government, having been established by the new prince, knows that it cannot maintain itself without the support of his power and friendship, and it becomes its interest therefore to sustain him. A city that has been accustomed to free institutions is much easier held by its own citizens than in any other way, if the conqueror desires to preserve it. The Spartans and the Romans will serve as examples of these different ways of holding a conquered state.

The Spartans held Athens and Thebes, creating there a government of a few; and yet they lost both these states again. The Romans, for the purpose of retaining Capua, Carthage, and Numantia, destroyed them, but did not lose them. They wished to preserve Greece in somewhat the same way that the Spartans had held it, by making her free and leaving her in the enjoyment of her own laws, but did not succeed; so that they were obliged to destroy many cities in that country for the purpose of holding it. In truth there was no other safe way of keeping possession of that country but to ruin it. And whoever becomes master of a city that has been accustomed to liberty, and does not destroy it, must himself expect to be ruined by it. For they will always resort to rebellion in the name of liberty and their ancient institutions, which will never be effaced from their memory, either by the lapse of time, or by benefits bestowed by the new master. No matter what he may do, or what precautions he may take, if he does not separate and disperse the inhabitants, they will on the first occasion invoke the name of liberty and the memory of their ancient institutions, as was done by Pisa after having been held over a hundred years in subjection by the Florentines.

But it is very different with states that have been accustomed to live under a prince. When the line of the prince is once extinguished, the inhabitants, being on the one hand accustomed to obey, and on the other having lost their ancient sovereign, can neither agree to create a new one from amongst themselves, nor do they know how to live in liberty; and thus they will be less prompt to take up arms, and the new prince will readily be able to gain their good will and to assure himself of them. But republics have more vitality, a greater spirit of resentment and desire of revenge, for the memory of their ancient liberty neither can nor will permit them to remain quiet, and therefore the surest way of holding them is either to destroy them, or for the conqueror to go and live there. . . .

Translated by Christian E. Detmold; first published in the United States in 1882. Italics added.

CHAPTER 17: OF CRUELTY AND CLEMENCY, AND WHETHER IT IS BETTER TO BE LOVED THAN FEARED

Coming down now to the other aforementioned qualities, I say that every prince ought to desire the reputation of being merciful, and not cruel; at the same time, he should be careful not to misuse that mercy. Cesar Borgia was reputed cruel, yet by his cruelty he reunited the Romagna to his states, and restored that province to order, peace, and loyalty; and if we carefully examine his course, we shall find it to have been really much more merciful than the course of the people of Florence, who to escape the reputation of cruelty, allowed Pistoja to be destroyed. A prince, therefore, should not mind the ill repute of cruelty, when he can thereby keep his subjects united and loyal; for a few displays of severity will really be more merciful than to allow, by an excess of clemency, disorders to occur, which are apt to result in rapine and murder; for these injure a whole community whilst the executions ordered by the prince fall only upon a few individuals. And, above all others, the new prince will find it almost impossible to avoid the reputation of cruelty, because new states are generally exposed to many dangers. . . .

A prince, however, should be slow to believe and to act; nor should he be too easily alarmed by his own fears, and should proceed moderately and with prudence and humanity, so that an excess of confidence may not make him incautious, nor too much mistrust make him intolerant. This, then, gives rise to the question "whether it be better to be beloved than feared," or "to be feared than beloved." It will naturally be answered that it would be desirable to be both the one and the other; but as it is difficult to be both at the same time, *it is much more safe to be feared than to be loved, when you have to choose between the two.* For it may be said of men in general that they are ungrateful and fickle dissemblers, avoiders of danger, and greedy of gain. So long as you shower benefits upon them, they are all yours; they offer you their blood, their substance, their lives, and their children, provided the necessity for it is far off; but when it is near at hand, then they revolt. And the prince who relies upon their words, without having otherwise provided for his security, is ruined; for friendships that are won by rewards, and not by greatness and nobility of soul, although deserved, yet are not real, and cannot be depended upon in time of adversity.

Besides, men have less hesitation in offending one who makes himself beloved than one who makes himself feared; for love holds by a bond of obligation which, as mankind is bad, is broken on every occasion whenever it is for the interest of the obliged party to break it. But fear holds by the apprehension of punishment, which never leaves men. A prince however, should make himself feared in such a manner that, if he has not won the affections of his people, he shall at least not incur their hatred; for the being feared, and not hated, can go very well together, if the prince abstains from taking the substance of his subjects, and leaves them their women. And if you should be obliged to inflict capital punishment upon any one, then be sure to do so only when there is manifest cause and proper justification for it; and, above all things, abstain from taking people's property, for men will sooner forget the death of their fathers than the loss of their patrimony. Besides, there will never be any lack of reasons for taking people's property; and a prince who once begins to live by rapine will ever find excuses for seizing other people's property. On the other hand, reasons for taking life are not so easily found, and are more readily exhausted. But when a prince is at the head of his army, with a multitude of soldiers under his command, then it is above all things necessary for him to disregard the reputation of cruelty; for without such severity an army cannot be kept together, nor disposed for any successful feat of arms. . . .

To come back now to the question whether it be better to be beloved than feared, I conclude that, as men love of their own free will, but are inspired with fear by the will of the prince, a wise prince should always rely upon himself, and not upon the will of others; but, above all, should he always strive to avoid being hated, as I have already said above.

CHAPTER 18: IN WHAT MANNER PRINCES SHOULD KEEP THEIR FAITH

It must be evident to every one that it is more praiseworthy for a prince always to maintain good faith, and practise integrity rather than craft and deceit. And yet the experience of our own times has shown that those princes have achieved great things who made small account of good faith, and who understood by cunning to circumvent the intelligence of others; and that in the end they got the better of those whose actions were dictated by loyalty and good faith. . . .

A sagacious prince then cannot and should not fulfil his pledges when their observance is contrary to his interest, and when the causes that induced him to pledge his faith no longer exist. If men were all good, then indeed this precept would be bad; but as men are naturally bad, and will not observe their faith towards you, you must, in the same way not observe yours to them; and no prince ever yet lacked legitimate reasons with which to color his want of good faith. Innumerable modern examples could be given of this, and it could easily be shown how many treaties of peace, and how many engagements, have been made null and void by the faithlessness of princes; and he who has best known how to play the fox has ever been the most successful.

But it is necessary that the prince should know how to color this nature well, and how to be a great hypocrite and dissembler. For men are so simple, and yield so much to immediate necessity, that the deceiver will never lack dupes. . . .

It is not necessary, however, for a prince to possess all the above-mentioned qualities; but it is essential that he should at least seem to have them. I will even venture to say, that to have and to practise them constantly is pernicious, but to seem to have them is useful. For instance, a prince should seem to be merciful, faithful, humane, religious, and upright, and should even be so in reality, but he should have his mind so trained that, when occasion requires it, he may know how to change to the opposite. And it must be understood that a prince, and especially one who has but recently acquired his state, cannot perform all those things which cause men to be esteemed as good; he being often obliged, for the sake of maintaining his state, to act contrary to humanity, charity, and religion. And therefore is it necessary that he should have a versatile mind, capable of changing readily, according as the winds and changes of fortune bid him; and, as has been said above, not to swerve from the good if possible, but to know how to resort to evil if necessity demands it.

A prince then should be very careful never to allow anything to escape his lips that does not abound in the above-named five qualities, so that to see and to hear him he may seem all charity, integrity, and humanity, all uprightness, and all piety. And more than all else it is necessary for a prince to seem to possess the last quality; for mankind in general judge more by what they see and hear than by what they feel, every one being capable of the former, and but few of the latter. Everybody sees what you seem to be, but few really feel what you are; and these few dare not oppose the opinion of the many, who are protected by the majesty of the state; for the actions of all men, and especially those of princes, are judged by the result, where there is no other judge to whom to appeal.

A prince then should look mainly to the successful maintenance of his state. The means which he employs for this will always be accounted honorable, and will be praised by everybody; for the common people are always taken by appearances and by results, and it is the vulgar mass that constitutes the world. But a very few have rank and station, whilst the many have nothing to sustain them. A certain prince of our time, whom it is well not to name, never preached anything but peace and good faith; but if he had always observed either the one or the other, it would in most instances have cost him his reputation or his state. . . .

CHAPTER 21: HOW PRINCES SHOULD CONDUCT THEMSELVES TO ACQUIRE A REPUTATION

. . . It is also important for a prince to give striking examples of his interior administration, (similar to those that are related of Messer Bernabo di Milano), when an occasion presents itself to reward or punish any one who has in civil affairs either rendered great service to the state, or committed some crime, so that it may be much talked about. But, above all, a prince should endeavor to invest all his actions with a character of grandeur and excellence. A prince, furthermore, becomes esteemed when he shows himself either a true friend or a real enemy; that is, when, regardless of consequences, he declares himself openly for or against another, which will always be more creditable to him than to remain neutral. For if two of your neighboring potentates should come to war amongst themselves, they are either of such character that, when either of them has been defeated, you will have cause to fear the conqueror, or not. In either case, it will always be better for you to declare yourself openly and make fair war; for if you fail to do so, you will be very apt to fall a prey to the victor, to the delight and satisfaction of the defeated party, and you will have no claim for protection or assistance from either the one or the other. For the conqueror will want no doubtful friends, who did not stand by him in time of trial; and the defeated party will not forgive you for having refused, with arms in hand, to take the chance of his fortunes. . . .

And it will always be the case that he who is not your friend will claim neutrality at your hands, whilst your friend will ask your armed intervention in his favor. Irresolute princes, for the sake of avoiding immediate danger, adopt most frequently the course of neutrality, and are generally ruined in consequence. But when a prince declares himself boldly in favor of one party, and that party proves victorious, even though the victor be powerful, and you are at his discretion, yet is he bound to you in love and obligation; and men are never so base as to repay these by such flagrant ingratitude as the oppressing you under these circumstances would be.

Moreover, victories are never so complete as to dispense the victor from all regard for justice. But when the party whom you have supported loses, then he will ever after receive you as a friend, and, when able, will assist you in turn; and thus you will have become the sharer of a fortune which in time may be retrieved.

In the second case, when the contending parties are such that you need not fear the victor, then it is the more prudent to give him your support; for you thereby aid one to ruin the other, whom he should save if he were wise; for although he has defeated his adversary, yet he remains at your discretion, inasmuch as without your assistance victory would have been impossible for him. And here it should be noted, that a prince ought carefully to avoid making common cause with any one more powerful than himself, for the purpose of attacking another power, unless he should be compelled to do so by necessity. For if the former is victorious, then you are at his mercy; and princes should, if possible, avoid placing themselves in such a position.

The Venetians allied themselves with France against the Duke of Milan, an alliance which they could easily have avoided, and which proved their ruin. But when it is unavoidable, as was the case with the Florentines when Spain and the Pope united their forces to attack Lombardy, then a prince ought to join the stronger party, for the reasons above given. Nor is it to be supposed that a state can ever adopt a course that is entirely safe; on the contrary, a prince must make up his mind to take the chance of all the doubts and uncertainties; for such is the order of things that one inconvenience cannot be avoided except at the risk of being exposed to another. And it is the province of prudence to discriminate amongst these inconveniences, and to accept the least evil for good.

A prince should also show himself a lover of virtue, and should honor all who excel in any one of the arts, and should encourage his citizens quietly to pursue their vocations, whether of commerce, agriculture, or any other human industry; so that the one may not abstain from embellishing his possessions for fear of their being taken from him, nor the other from opening new sources of commerce for fear of taxes. But the prince should provide rewards for those who are willing to do these things, and for all who strive to enlarge his city or state. And besides this, he should at suitable periods amuse his people with festivities and spectacles. And as cities are generally divided into guilds and classes, he should keep account of these bodies, and occasionally be present at their assemblies, and should set an example of his affability and magnificence; preserving, however, always the majesty of his dignity, which should never be wanting on any occasion or under any circumstances.

Of the Natural Condition of Mankind

Thomas Hobbes

MEN BY NATURE EQUAL

. . . Nature hath made men so equal, in the faculties of the body, and mind; as that though there be found one man sometimes manifestly stronger in body, or of quicker mind than another, yet when all is reckoned together, the difference between man and man is not so considerable as that one man can thereupon claim to himself any benefit, to which another may not pretend, as well as he. For as to the strength of body, the weakest has strength enough to kill the strongest, either by secret machination, or by confederacy with others that are in the same danger with himself.

And as to the faculties of the mind, setting aside the arts grounded upon words, and especially that skill of proceeding upon general, and infallible rules, called science; which very few have, and but in few things; as being not a native faculty, born with us; nor attained, as prudence, while we look after somewhat else, I find yet a greater equality amongst men than that of strength. For prudence is but experience; which equal time, equally bestows on all men, in those things they equally apply themselves unto. That which may perhaps make such equality incredible is but a vain conceit of one's own wisdom, which almost all men think they have in a greater degree, than the vulgar; that is, than all men but themselves, and a few others, whom by fame, or for concurring with themselves, they approve. For such is the nature of men, that howsoever they may acknowledge many others to be more witty, or more eloquent, or more learned; yet they will hardly believe there be many so wise as themselves; for they see their own wit at hand, and other men's at a distance. But this proveth rather that men are in that point equal, than unequal. For there is not ordinarily a greater sign of the equal distribution of any thing, than that every man is contented with his share. . . .

FROM EQUALITY PROCEEDS DIFFIDENCE

From this equality of ability, ariseth equality of hope in the attaining of our ends. And therefore if any two men desire the same thing, which nevertheless they cannot both enjoy, they become enemies; and in the way to their end, which is principally their own conservation, and sometimes their delectation only, endeavour to destroy or subdue one another. And from hence it comes to pass, that where an invader hath no more to fear than another man's single power; if one plant, sow, build, or possess a convenient seat, others may probably be expected to come prepared with forces united, to dispossess, and deprive him, not only of the fruit of his labour, but also of his life or liberty. And the invader again is in the like danger of another.

FROM DIFFIDENCE WAR

And from this diffidence of one another, there is no way for any man to secure himself, so reasonable, as anticipation; that is, by force or wiles, to master the persons of all men he can, so long, till he see no other power great enough to endanger him: and this is no more than his own conservation requireth, and is generally allowed. Also because there

From Thomas Hobbes, *Leviathan*, first published 1651. Italics added.

be some, that taking pleasure in contemplating their own power in the acts of conquest, which they pursue farther than their security requires; if others, that otherwise would be glad to be at ease within modest bounds, should not by invasion increase their power, they would not be able, long time, by standing only on their defence, to subsist. And by consequence, such augmentation of dominion over men being necessary to a man's conservation, it ought to be allowed him.

Again, men have no pleasure, but on the contrary a great deal of grief, in keeping company, where there is no power able to overawe them all. For every man looketh that his companion should value him at the same rate he sets upon himself: and upon all signs of contempt, or undervaluing, naturally endeavours, as far as he dares, (which amongst them that have no common power to keep them in quiet, is far enough to make them destroy each other), to extort a greater value from his contemners, by damage; and from others, by the example.

So that in the nature of man, we find three principal causes of quarrel. First, competition; secondly, diffidence; thirdly, glory.

The first, maketh men invade for gain; the second, for safety; and the third, for reputation. The first use violence, to make themselves masters of other men's persons, wives, children, and cattle; the second, to defend them; the third, for trifles, as a word, a smile, a different opinion, and any other sign of undervalue, either direct in their persons, or by reflection in their kindred, their friends, their nation, their profession, or their name.

OUT OF CIVIL STATES, THERE IS ALWAYS WAR OF EVERY ONE AGAINST EVERY ONE

Hereby it is manifest, that during the time men live without a common power to keep them all in awe, they are in that condition which is called war; and such a war, as is of every man, against every man. For WAR, consisteth not in battle only, or the act of fighting; but in a tract of time, wherein the will to contend by battle is sufficiently known: and therefore the notion of *time* is to be considered in the nature of war; as it is in the nature of weather. For as the nature of foul weather lieth not in a shower or two of rain; but in an inclination thereto of many days together: so the nature of war, consisteth not in actual fighting; but in the known disposition thereto, during all the time there is no assurance to the contrary. All other time is PEACE.

THE INCOMMODITIES OF SUCH A WAR

Whatsoever therefore is consequent to a time of war, where every man is enemy to every man; the same is consequent to the time, wherein men live without other security, than what their own strength, and their own invention shall furnish them withal. In such condition, there is no place for industry; because the fruit thereof is uncertain: and consequently no culture of the earth; no navigation, nor use of the commodities that may be imported by sea; no commodious building; no instruments of moving, and removing, such things as require much force; no knowledge of the face of the earth; no account of time; no arts; no letters; no society; and which is worst of all, continual fear and danger of violent death; *and the life of man, solitary, poor, nasty, brutish, and short.*

It may seem strange to some man that has not well weighed these things; that nature should thus dissociate and render men apt to invade, and destroy one another: and he may therefore, not trusting to this inference, made from the passions, desire perhaps to have the same confirmed by experience. Let him therefore consider with himself, when taking a journey, he arms himself, and seeks to go well accompanied; when going to sleep, he locks his doors; when even in his house he locks his chests; and this when he knows there be laws, and public officers, armed, to revenge all injuries shall be done him; what opinion he has of his fellow-subjects, when he rides armed; of his fellow citizens, when he locks his doors; and of his children, and servants, when he locks his chests. Does he not there as much accuse mankind by his actions, as I do by my words? But neither of us accuse man's nature in it. The desires and other passions of man are in themselves no sin. No more are the actions that proceed from those passions, till they know a law that forbids them: which till laws be made they cannot know: nor can any law be made, till they have agreed upon the person that shall make it.

It may peradventure be thought there was never such a time nor condition of war as this; and I believe it was never generally so over all the world: but there are many places, where they live so now. For the savage people in many places of America, except the government of small families, the concord whereof dependeth on natural lust, have no government at all; and live at this day in the brutish manner, as I said before. Howsoever, it may be perceived what manner of life there would be, where there were no common power to fear, by the manner of life, which men that have formerly lived under a peaceful government, use to degenerate into, in a civil war.

But though there had never been any time wherein particular men were in a condition of war one against another, yet in all times, kings, and persons of sovereign authority, because of their independency, are in continual jealousies, and in the state and posture of gladiators; having their weapons pointing, and their eyes fixed on one another; that is, their forts, garrisons, and guns upon the frontiers of their kingdoms; and continual spies upon their neighbours; which is a posture of war. But because they uphold thereby, the industry of their subjects; there does not follow from it that misery which accompanies the liberty of particular men.

IN SUCH A WAR NOTHING IS UNJUST

To this war of every man, against every man, this also is consequent; that nothing can be unjust. The notions of right and wrong, justice and injustice have there no place. Where there is no common power, there is no law: where no law, no injustice. Force and fraud are in war the two cardinal virtues. Justice and injustice are none of the faculties neither of the body, nor mind. If they were, they might be in a man that were alone in the world, as well as his senses and passions. They are qualities that relate to men in society, not in solitude. It is consequent also to the same condition, there there be no propriety, no dominion, no *mine* and *thine* distinct; but only that to be every man's, that he can get: and for so long, as he can keep it. And thus much for the ill condition, which man by mere nature is actually placed in; though with a possibility to come out of it, consisting partly in the passions, partly in his reason. . . .

THE PASSIONS THAT INCLINE MEN TO PEACE

The passions that incline men to peace, are fear of death; desire of such things as are necessary to commodious living; and a hope by their industry to obtain them. And reason suggesteth convenient articles of peace, upon which men may be drawn to agreement. . . .

Six Principles of Political Realism

Hans J. Morgenthau

This selection is the introduction to Morgenthau's classic work Politics Among Nations, *considered by many to be the foundation of modern realist thought. The influence of Machiavelli can be seen quite readily in Morgenthau's six principles. Like Machiavelli, Morgenthau seeks to inform and educate policy makers in their craft and thereby avoid mistakes such as the ones made at Munich in 1938.*

1. *Political realism believes that politics, like society in general, is governed by objective laws that have their roots in human nature.* In order to improve society it is first necessary to understand the laws by which society lives. The operation of these laws being impervious to our preferences, men will challenge them only at the risk of failure.

Realism, believing as it does in the objectivity of the laws of politics, must also believe in the possibility of developing a rational theory that reflects, however imperfectly and one-sidedly, these objective laws. It believes also, then, in the possibility of distinguishing in politics between truth and opinion—between what is true objectively and rationally, supported by evidence and illuminated by reason, and what is only a subjective judgment, divorced from the facts as they are and informed by prejudice and wishful thinking.

Human nature, in which the laws of politics have their roots, has not changed since the classical philosophies of China, India, and Greece endeavored to discover these laws. Hence, novelty is not necessarily a virtue in political theory, nor is old age a defect. The fact that a theory of politics, if there be such a theory, has never been heard of before tends to create a presumption against, rather than in favor of, its soundness. Conversely, the fact that a theory of politics was developed hundreds or even thousands of years ago—as was the theory of the balance of power—does not create a presumption that it must be outmoded and obsolete. A theory of politics must be subjected to the dual test of reason and experience. To dismiss such a theory because it had its flowering in centuries past is to present not a rational argument but a modernistic prejudice that takes for granted the superiority of the present over the past. To dispose of the revival of such a theory as a "fashion" or "fad" is tantamount to assuming that in matters political we can have opinions but no truths.

For realism, theory consists in ascertaining facts and giving them meaning through reason. It assumes that the character of a foreign policy can be ascertained only through the examination of the political acts performed and of the foreseeable consequences of these acts. Thus we can find out what statesmen have actually done, and from the foreseeable consequences of their acts we can surmise what their objectives might have been.

Yet examination of the facts is not enough. To give meaning to the factual raw material of foreign policy, we must approach political reality with a kind of rational outline, a map that suggests to us the possible meanings of foreign policy. In other words, we put ourselves in the position of a statesman who must meet a certain problem of foreign policy under certain circumstances, and we ask ourselves what the rational alternatives are from which a statesman may choose who must meet this problem under these circumstances (presuming always that he acts in a rational manner), and which of these rational alterna-

From Hans J. Morgenthau: *Politics Among Nations: The Struggle for Power and Peace*, Sixth Edition, revised by Kenneth W. Thompson, pp. 4–17. Originally published in 1948. Italics added.

tives this particular statesman, acting under these circumstances, is likely to choose. It is the testing of this rational hypothesis against the actual facts and their consequences that gives theoretical meaning to the facts of international politics.

2. *The main signpost that helps political realism to find its way through the landscape of international politics is the concept of interest defined in terms of power.* This concept provides the link between reason trying to understand international politics and the facts to be understood. It sets politics as an autonomous sphere of action and understanding apart from other spheres, such as economics (understood in terms of interest defined as wealth), ethics, aesthetics, or religion. Without such a concept a theory of politics, international or domestic, would be altogether impossible, for without it we could not distinguish between political and nonpolitical facts, nor could we bring at least a measure of systemic order to the political sphere.

We assume that statesmen think and act in terms of interest defined as power, and the evidence of history bears that assumption out. That assumption allows us to retrace and anticipate, as it were, the steps a statesman—past, present, or future—has taken or will take on the political scene. We look over his shoulder when he writes his dispatches; we listen in on his conversation with other statesmen; we read and anticipate his very thoughts. Thinking in terms of interest defined as power, we think as he does, and as disinterested observers we understand his thoughts and actions perhaps better than he, the actor on the political scene, does himself.

The concept of interest defined as power imposes intellectual discipline upon the observer, infuses rational order into the subject matter of politics, and thus makes the theoretical understanding of politics possible. On the side of the actor, it provides for rational discipline in action and creates that astounding continuity in foreign policy which makes American, British, or Russian foreign policy appear as in intelligible, rational continuum, by and large consistent within itself regardless of the different motives, preferences, and intellectual and moral qualities of successive statesmen. A realist theory of international politics, then, will guard against two popular fallacies; the concern with motives and the concern with ideological preferences.

To search for the clue to foreign policy exclusively in the motives of statesmen is both futile and deceptive. It is futile because motives are the most illusive of psychological data, distorted as they are, frequently beyond recognition, by the interests and emotions of actor and observer alike. Do we really know what our own motives are? And what do we know of the motives of others?

Yet even if we had access to the real motives of statesmen, that knowledge would help us little in understanding foreign policies, and might well lead us astray. It is true that the knowledge of the statesman's motives may give us one among many clues as to what the direction of his foreign policy might be. It cannot give us, however, the one clue by which to predict his foreign policies. History shows no exact and necessary correlation between the quality of motives and the quality of foreign policy. This is true in both moral and political terms.

We cannot conclude from the good intentions of a statesman that his foreign policies will be either morally praiseworthy or politically successful. Judging his motives, we can say that he will not intentionally pursue policies that are morally wrong, but we can say nothing about the probability of their success. If we want to know the moral and political qualities of his actions, we must know them, not his motives. How often have statesmen been motivated by the desire to improve the world, and ended by making it worse? And how often have they sought one goal, and ended by achieving something they neither expected nor desired?

Neville Chamberlain's politics of appeasement were, as far as we can judge, inspired by good motives; he was probably less motivated by considerations of personal power than were many other British prime ministers, and he sought to preserve peace and to assure the happiness of all concerned. Yet his policies helped to make the Second World War inevitable, and to bring untold miseries to millions of people. Sir Winston Churchill's motives, on the other hand, were much less universal in scope and much more narrowly directed toward personal and national power, yet the foreign policies that sprang from these inferior motives were certainly superior in moral and political quality to those pursued by his predecessor. Judged by his motives, Robespierre was one of the most virtuous men who ever lived. Yet it was the utopian radicalism of that very virtue that made him kill those less virtuous than himself, brought him to the scaffold, and destroyed the revolution of which he was a leader.

Good motives give assurance against deliberately bad policies; they do not guarantee the moral goodness and political success of the policies they inspire. What is important to know, if one wants to understand foreign policy, is not primarily the motives of a statesman, but his intellectual ability to comprehend the essentials of foreign policy, as well as his political ability to translate what he has comprehended into successful political action. It follows that while ethics in the abstract judges the moral qualities of motives, political theory must judge the political qualities of intellect, will, and action.

A realist theory of international politics will also avoid the other popular fallacy of equating the foreign policies of a statesman with his philosophic or political sympathies, and of deducing the former from the latter. Statesmen, especially under contemporary conditions, may well make a habit of presenting their foreign policies in terms of their philosophic and political sympathies in order to gain popular support for them. Yet they will distinguish with Lincoln between their "*official* duty," which is to think and act in terms of the national interest, and their "*personal* wish," which is to see their own moral values and political principles realized throughout the world. Political realism does not require, nor does it condone, indifference to political ideals and moral principles, but it requires indeed a sharp distinction between the desirable and the possible—between what is desirable everywhere and at all times and what is possible under the concrete circumstances of time and place.

It stands to reason that not all foreign policies have always followed so rational, objective, and unemotional a course. The contingent elements of personality, prejudice, and subjective preference, and of all the weaknesses of intellect and will which flesh is heir to, are bound to deflect foreign policies from their rational course. Especially where foreign policy is conducted under the conditions of democratic control, the need to marshal popular emotions to the support of foreign policy cannot fail to impair the rationality of foreign policy itself. Yet a theory of foreign policy which aims at rationality must for the time being, as it were, abstract from these irrational elements and seek to paint a picture of foreign policy which presents the rational essence to be found in experience, without the contingent deviations from rationality which are also found in experience.

Deviations from rationality which are not the result of the personal whim or the personal psychopathology of the policy maker may appear contingent only from the vantage point of rationality, but may themselves be elements in a coherent system of irrationality. The possibility of constructing, as it were, a counter-theory of irrational politics is worth exploring.

When one reflects upon the development of American thinking on foreign policy, one is struck by the persistence of mistaken attitudes that have survived—under whatever guises—both intellectual argument and political experience. Once that wonder, in true

Aristotelian fashion, has been transformed into the quest for rational understanding, the quest yields a conclusion both comforting and disturbing: we are here in the presence of intellectual defects shared by all of us in different ways and degrees. Together they provide the outline of a kind of pathology of international politics. When the human mind approaches reality with the purpose of taking action, of which the political encounter is one of the outstanding instances, it is often led astray by any of four common mental phenomena; residues of formerly adequate modes of thought and action now rendered obsolete by a new social reality; demonological interpretations of reality which substitute a fictitious reality—peopled by evil persons rather than seemingly intractable issues—for the actual one; refusal to come to terms with a threatening state of affairs by denying it through illusory verbalization; reliance upon the infinite malleability of a seemingly obstreperous reality.

Man responds to social situations with repetitive patterns. The same situation, recognized in its identity with previous situations, evokes the same response. The mind, as it were, holds in readiness a number of patterns appropriate for different situations; it then requires only the identification of a particular case to apply to it the preformed pattern appropriate to it. Thus the human mind follows the principle of economy of effort, obviating an examination *de novo* of each individual situation and the pattern of thought and action appropriate to it. Yet when matters are subject to dynamic change, traditional patterns are no longer appropriate: they must be replaced by new ones reflecting such change. Otherwise a gap will open between traditional patterns and new realities, and thought and action will be misguided.

On the international plane it is no exaggeration to say that the very structure of international relations—as reflected in political institutions, diplomatic procedures, and legal arrangements—has tended to become at variance with, and in large measure irrelevant to, the reality of international politics. While the former assumes the "sovereign equality" of all nations, the latter is dominated by an extreme inequality of nations, two of which are called superpowers because they hold in their hands the unprecedented power of total destruction, and many of which are called "ministates" because their power is minuscule even compared with that of the traditional nation states. It is this contrast and incompatibility between the reality of international politics and the concepts, institutions, and procedures designed to make intelligible and control the former, which has caused, at least below the great-power level, the unmanageability of international relations which borders on anarchy. International terrorism and the different government reactions to it, the involvement of foreign governments in the Lebanese civil war, the military operations of the United States in Southeast Asia, and the military intervention of the Soviet Union in Eastern Europe cannot be explained or justified by reference to traditional concepts, institutions, and procedures.

All these situations have one characteristic in common. The modern fact of interdependence requires a political order which takes that fact into account, while in reality the legal and institutional superstructure, harking back to the nineteenth century, assumes the existence of a multiplicity of self-sufficient, impenetrable, sovereign nation states. These residues of an obsolescent legal and institutional order not only stand in the way of a rational transformation of international relations in light of the inequality of power and the interdependence of interests, but they also render precarious, if not impossible, more rational policies within the defective framework of such a system.

It is a characteristic of primitive thinking to personalize social problems. That tendency is particularly strong when the problem appears not to be susceptible to rational understanding and successful manipulation. When a particular person or group of persons is identified with the recalcitrant difficulty, that may seem to render the problem both intellectually accessible and susceptible of solution. Thus belief in Satan as the source of evil makes us "understand" the nature of evil by focusing the search for its origin and control upon a particular person whose physical existence we assume. The complexity of political conflict precludes such simple solutions. Natural catastrophes will not be prevented by burning witches; the threat of a powerful Germany to establish hegemony over Europe will not be averted by getting rid of a succession of German leaders. But by identifying the issue with certain persons over whom we have—or hope to have—control we reduce the problem, both intellectually and pragmatically, to manageable proportions. Once we have identified certain individuals and groups of individuals as the source of evil, we appear to have understood the causal nexus that leads from the individuals to the social problem; that apparent understanding suggests the apparent solution: Eliminate the individuals "responsible" for it, and you have solved the problem.

Superstition still holds sway over our relations within society. The demonological pattern of thought and action has now been transferred to other fields of human action closed to the kind of rational enquiry and action that have driven superstition from our relations with nature. As William Graham Sumner put it, "The amount of superstition is not much changed, but it now attaches to politics, not to religion."[1] The numerous failures of the United States to recognize and respond to the polycentric nature of Communism is a prime example of this defect. The corollary of this indiscriminate opposition to Communism is the indiscriminate support of governments and movements that profess and practice anti-Communism. American policies in Asia and Latin America have derived from this simplistic position. The Vietnam War and our inability to come to terms with mainland China find here their rationale. So do the theory and practice of counterinsurgency, including large-scale assassinations under the Phoenix program in Vietnam and the actual or attempted assassinations of individual statesmen. Signs of a similar approach have been evident more recently in Central America.

The demonological approach to foreign policy strengthens another pathological tendency, which is the refusal to acknowledge and cope effectively with a threatening reality. The demonological approach has shifted our attention and concern towards the adherents of communism—individuals at home and abroad, political movements, foreign governments—and away from the real threat: the power of states, Communist or not. McCarthyism not only provided the most pervasive American example of the demonological approach but was also one of the most extreme examples of this kind of misjudgment: it substituted the largely illusory threat of domestic subversion for the real threat of Russian power.

Finally, it is part of this approach to politics to believe that no problems—however hopeless they may appear—are really insoluble, given well-meaning, well-financed, and competent efforts. I have tried elsewhere to lay bare the intellectual and historical roots of this belief;[2] here I limit myself to pointing out its persistent strength despite much experience to the contrary, such as the Vietnam War and the general decline of American power. This preference for economic solutions to political and military problems is powerfully reinforced by the interests of potential recipients of economic support, who prefer the obviously profitable transfer of economic advantages to painful and risky diplomatic bargaining.

---

1. "Mores of the Present and Future," in *War and Other Essays* (New Haven: Yale University Press, 1911), p. 159.

2. *Scientific Man versus Power Politics* (Chicago: University of Chicago Press, 1946).

The difference between international politics as it actually is and a rational theory derived from it is like the difference between a photograph and a painted portrait. The photograph shows everything that can be seen by the naked eye; the painted portrait does not show everything that can be seen by the naked eye, but it shows, or at least seeks to show, one thing that the naked eye cannot see: the human essence of the person portrayed.

Political realism contains not only a theoretical but also a normative element. It knows that political reality is replete with contingencies and systemic irrationalities and points to the typical influences they exert upon foreign policy. Yet it shares with all social theory the need, for the sake of theoretical understanding, to stress the rational elements of political reality; for it is these rational elements that make reality intelligible for theory. Political realism presents the theoretical construct of a rational foreign policy which experience can never completely achieve.

At the same time political realism considers a rational foreign policy to be good foreign policy; for only a rational foreign policy minimizes risks and maximizes benefits and, hence, complies both with the moral precept of prudence and the political requirement of success. Political realism wants the photographic picture of the political world to resemble as much as possible its painted portrait. Aware of the inevitable gap between good—that is, rational—foreign policy and foreign policy as it actually is, political realism maintains not only that theory must focus upon the rational elements of political reality, but also that foreign policy ought to be rational in view of its own moral and practical purposes.

Hence, it is no argument against the theory here presented that actual foreign policy does not or cannot live up to it. That argument misunderstands the intention of this book, which is to present not an indiscriminate description of political reality, but a rational theory of international politics. Far from being invalidated by the fact that, for instance, a perfect balance of power policy will scarcely be found in reality, it assumes that reality, being deficient in this respect, must be understood and evaluated as an approximation to an ideal system of balance of power.

3. *Realism assumes that its key concept of interest defined as power is an objective category which is universally valid, but it does not endow that concept with a meaning that is fixed once and for all.* The idea of interest is indeed of the essence of politics and is unaffected by the circumstances of time and place. Thucydides' statement, born of the experiences of ancient Greece, that "identity of interests is the surest of bonds whether between states or individuals" was taken up in the nineteenth century by Lord Salisbury's remark that "the only bond of union that endures" among nations is "the absence of all clashing interests." It was erected into a general principle of government by George Washington:

> A small knowledge of human nature will convince us, that, with far the greatest part of mankind, interest is the governing principle; and that almost every man is more or less, under its influence. Motives of public virtue may for a time, or in particular instances, actuate men to the observance of a conduct purely disinterested; but they are not of themselves sufficient to produce persevering conformity to the refined dictates and obligations of social duty. Few men are capable of making a continual sacrifice of all views of private interest, or advantage, to the common good. It is vain to exclaim against the depravity of human nature on this account; the fact is so, the experience of every age and nation has proved it and we must in a

> great measure, change the constitution of man, before we can make it otherwise. No institution, not built on the presumptive truth of these maxims can succeed.[3]

It was echoed and enlarged upon in our century by Max Weber's observation:

> Interests (material and ideal), not ideas, dominate directly the actions of men. Yet the "images of the world" created by these ideas have very often served as switches determining the tracks on which the dynamism of interests kept actions moving.[4]

Yet the kind of interest determining political action in a particular period of history depends upon the political and cultural context within which foreign policy is formulated. The goals that might be pursued by nations in their foreign policy can run the whole gamut of objectives any nation has ever pursued or might possibly pursue.

The same observations apply to the concept of power. Its content and the manner of its use are determined by the political and cultural environment. Power may comprise anything that establishes and maintains the control of man over man. Thus power covers all social relationships which serve that end, from physical violence to the most subtle psychological ties by which one mind controls another. Power covers the domination of man by man, both when it is disciplined by moral ends and controlled by constitutional safeguards, as in Western democracies, and when it is that untamed and barbaric force which finds its laws in nothing but its own strength and its sole justification in its aggrandizement.

Political realism does not assume that the contemporary conditions under which foreign policy operates, with their extreme instability and the ever present threat of large-scale violence, cannot be changed. The balance of power, for instance, is indeed a perennial element of all pluralistic societies, as the authors of *The Federalist* papers well knew; yet it is capable of operating, as it does in the United States, under the conditions of relative stability and peaceful conflict. If the factors that have given rise to these conditions can be duplicated on the international scene, similar conditions of stability and peace will then prevail there, as they have over long stretches of history among certain nations.

What is true of the general character of international relations is also true of the nation state as the ultimate point of reference of contemporary foreign policy. While the realist indeed believes that interest is the perennial standard by which political action must be judged and directed, the contemporary connection between interest and the nation state is a product of history, and is therefore bound to disappear in the course of history. Nothing in the realist position militates against the assumption that the present division of the political world into nation states will be replaced by larger units of a quite different character, more in keeping with the technical potentialities and the moral requirements of the contemporary world.

The realist parts company with other schools of thought before the all-important question of how the contemporary world is to be transformed. The realist is persuaded that this transformation can be achieved only through the workmanlike manipulation of the perennial forces that have shaped the past as they will the future. The realist cannot be persuaded that we can bring about that transformation by confronting a political reality that has its own laws with an abstract ideal that refuses to take those laws into account.

---

3. *The Writings of George Washington*, edited by John C. Fitzpatrick (Washington: United States Printing Office, 1931–44), Vol. X, p. 363.

4. Marianne Weber, Max Weber (Tuebingen: J.C.B. Mohr, 1926), pp. 347–8. See also Max Weber, *Gesammelte Aufsätze zur Religions-soziologie* (Tuebingen: J.C.B. Mohr, 1920), p. 252.

4. *Political realism is aware of the moral significance of political action.* It is also aware of the ineluctable tension between the moral command and the requirements of successful political action. And it is unwilling to gloss over and obliterate that tension and thus to obfuscate both the moral and the political issue by making it appear as though the stark facts of politics were morally more satisfying than they actually are, and the moral law less exacting that it actually is.

Realism maintains that universal moral principles cannot be applied to the actions of states in their abstract universal formulation, but that they must be filtered through the concrete circumstances of time and place. The individual may say for himself: "*Fiat justitia, pereat mundus* (Let justice be done, even if the world perish)," but the state has no right to say so in the name of those who are in its care. Both individual and state must judge political action by universal moral principles, such as that of liberty. Yet while the individual has a moral right to sacrifice himself in defense of such a moral principle, the state has no right to let its moral disapprobation of the infringement of liberty get in the way of successful political action, itself inspired by the moral principle of national survival. There can be no political morality without prudence; that is, without consideration of the political consequences of seemingly moral action. Realism, then, considers prudence—the weighing of the consequences of alternative political actions—to be the supreme virtue in politics. Ethics in the abstract judges action by its conformity with the moral law; political ethics judges action by its political consequences. Classical and medieval philosophy knew this, and so did Lincoln when he said:

> I do the very best I know how, the very best I can, and I mean to keep doing so until the end. If the end brings me out all right, what is said against me won't amount to anything. If the end brings me out wrong, ten angels swearing I was right would make no difference.

5. *Political realism refuses to identify the moral aspirations of a particular nation with the moral laws that govern the universe.* As it distinguishes between truth and opinion, so it distinguishes between truth and idolatry. All nations are tempted—and few have been able to resist the temptation for long—to clothe their own particular aspirations and actions in the moral purposes of the universe. To know that nations are subject to the moral law is one thing, while to pretend to know with certainty what is good and evil in the relations among nations is quite another. There is a world of difference between the belief that all nations stand under the judgment of God, inscrutable to the human mind, and the blasphemous conviction that God is always on one's side and that what one wills oneself cannot fail to be willed by God also.

The lighthearted equation between a particular nationalism and the counsels of Providence is morally indefensible, for it is that very sin of pride against which the Greek tragedians and the Biblical prophets have warned rulers and ruled. That equation is also politically pernicious, for it is liable to engender the distortion in judgment which, in the blindness of crusading frenzy, destroys nations and civilizations—in the name of moral principle, ideal, or God himself.

On the other hand, it is exactly the concept of interest defined in terms of power that saves us from both that moral excess and that political folly. For if we look at all nations, our own included, as political entities pursuing their respective interests defined in terms of power, we are able to do justice to all of them. And we are able to do justice to all of them in a dual sense: We are able to judge other nations as we judge our own and, having judged them in this fashion, we are then capable of pursuing policies that respect the interests of other nations, while protecting and promoting those of our own. Moderation in policy cannot fail to reflect the moderation of moral judgment.

6. *The difference, then, between political realism and other schools of thought is real, and it is profound.* However much of the theory of political realism may have been misunderstood and misinterpreted, there is no gainsaying its distinctive intellectual and moral attitude to matters political.

Intellectually, *the political realist maintains the autonomy of the political sphere*, as the economist, the lawyer, the moralist maintain theirs. He thinks in terms of interest defined as power, as the economist thinks in terms of interest defined as wealth; the lawyer, of the conformity of action with legal rules; the moralist, of the conformity of action with moral principles. The economist asks: "How does this policy affect the wealth of society, or a segment of it?" The lawyer asks: "Is this policy in accord with the rules of law?" The moralist asks: "Is this policy in accord with moral principles?" And the political realist asks: "How does this policy affect the power of the nation?" (Or of the federal government, of Congress, of the party, of agriculture, as the case may be.)

The political realist is not unaware of the existence and relevance of standards of thought other than political ones. As political realist, he cannot but subordinate these other standards to those of politics. And he parts company with other schools when they impose standards of thought appropriate to other spheres upon the political sphere. It is here that political realism takes issue with the "legalistic-moralistic approach" to international politics. That this issue is not, as has been contended, a mere figment of the imagination, but goes to the very core of the controversy, can be shown from many historical examples. Three will suffice to make the point.[5]

In 1939 the Soviet Union attacked Finland. This action confronted France and Great Britain with two issues, one legal, the other political. Did that action violate the Covenant of the League of Nations and, if it did, what countermeasures should France and Great Britain take? The legal question could easily be answered in the affirmative, for obviously the Soviet Union had done what was prohibited by the Covenant. The answer to the political question depends, first, upon the manner in which the Russian action affected the interests of France and Great Britain; second upon the existing distribution of power between France and Great Britain, on the one hand, and the Soviet Union and other potentially hostile nations, especially Germany, on the other; and, third, upon the influence that the countermeasures were likely to have upon the interests of France and Great Britain and the future distribution of power. France and Great Britain, as the leading members of the League of Nations, saw to it that the Soviet Union was expelled from the League, and they were prevented from joining Finland in the war against the Soviet Union only by Sweden's refusal to allow their troops to pass through Swedish territory on their way to Finland. If this refusal by Sweden had not saved them, France and Great Britain would shortly have found themselves at war with the Soviet Union and Germany at the same time.

---

[5] See the other examples discussed in Hans J. Morgenthau, "Another 'Great Debate': The National Interest of the United States," *The American Political Science Review*, Vol. XLVI (December 1952), pp. 979 ff. See also Hans J. Morgenthau, *Politics in the 20th Century*, Vol. I, *The Decline of Democratic Politics* (Chicago: University of Chicago Press, 1962), pp. 79 ff; and abridged edition (Chicago: University of Chicago Press, 1971), pp. 204 ff.

The policy of France and Great Britain was a classic example of legalism in that they allowed the answer to the legal question, legitimate within its sphere, to determine their political actions. Instead of asking both questions, that of law and that of power, they asked only the question of law; and the answer they received could have no bearing on the issue that their very existence might have depended upon.

The second example illustrates the "moralistic approach" to international politics. It concerns the international status of the Communist government of China. The rise of that government confronted the Western world with two issues, one moral, the other political. Were the nature and policies of that government in accord with the moral principles of the Western world? Should the Western world deal with such a government? The answer to the first question could not fail to be in the negative. Yet it did not follow with necessity that the answer to the second question should also be in the negative. The standard of thought applied to the first—the moral—question was simply to test the nature and the policies of the Communist government of China by the principles of Western morality. On the other hand, the second—the political—question had to be subjected to the complicated test of the interests involved and the power available on either side, and of the bearing of one or the other course of action upon these interests and power. The application of this test could well have led to the conclusion that it would be wiser not to deal with the Communist government of China. To arrive at this conclusion by neglecting this test altogether and answering the political question in terms of the moral issue was indeed a classic example of the "moralistic approach" to international politics.

The third case illustrates strikingly the contrast between realism and the legalistic-moralistic approach to foreign policy. Great Britain, as one of the guarantors of the neutrality of Belgium, went to war with Germany in August 1914 because Germany had violated the neutrality of Belgium. The British action could be justified either in realistic or legalistic-moralistic terms. That is to say, one could argue realistically that for centuries it had been axiomatic for British foreign policy to prevent the control of the Low Countries by a hostile power. It was then not so much the violation of Belgium's neutrality per se as the hostile intentions of the violator which provided the rationale for British intervention. If the violator had been another nation but Germany, Great Britain might well have refrained from intervening. This is the position taken by Sir Edward Grey, British Foreign Secretary during that period. Under Secretary for Foreign Affairs Hardinge remarked to him in 1908: "If France violated Belgian neutrality in a war against Germany, it is doubtful whether England or Russia would move a finger to maintain Belgian neutrality, while if the neutrality of Belgium was violated by Germany, it is probable that the converse would be the case." Whereupon Sir Edward Grey replied: "This is to the point." Yet one could also take the legalistic and moralistic position that the violation of Belgium's neutrality per se, because of its legal and moral defects and regardless of the interests at stake and of the identity of the violator, justified British and, for that matter, American intervention. This was the position which Theodore Roosevelt took in his letter to Sir Edward Grey of January 22, 1915:

> To me the crux of the situation has been Belgium. If England or France had acted toward Belgium as Germany has acted I should have opposed them, exactly as I now oppose Germany. I have emphatically approved your action as a model for what should be done by those who believe that treaties should be observed in good faith and that there is such a thing as international morality. I take this position as an American who is no more an Englishman than he is a German, who endeavors loyally to serve the interests of his own country, but who also endeav-

ors to do what he can for justice and decency as regards mankind at large, and who therefore feels obliged to judge all other nations by their conduct on any given occasion.

This realist defense of the autonomy of the political sphere against its subversion by other modes of thought does not imply disregard for the existence and importance of these other modes of thought. It rather implies that each should be assigned its proper sphere and function. Political realism is based upon a pluralistic conception of human nature. Real man is a composite of "economic man," "political man," "moral man," "religious man," etc. A man who was nothing but "political man" would be a beast, for he would be completely lacking in moral restraints. A man who was nothing but "moral man" would be a fool, for he would be completely lacking in prudence. A man who was nothing but "religious man" would be a saint, for he would be completely lacking in worldly desires.

Recognizing that these different facets of human nature exist, political realism also recognizes that in order to understand one of them one has to deal with it on its own terms. That is to say, if, I want to understand "religious man," I must for the time being abstract from the other aspects of human nature and deal with its religious aspect as if it were the only one. Furthermore, I must apply to the religious sphere the standards of thought appropriate to it, always remaining aware of the existence of other standards and their actual influence upon the religious qualities of man. What is true of this facet of human nature is true of all the others. No modern economist, for instance, would conceive of his science and its relations to other sciences of man in any other way. It is exactly through such a process of emancipation from other standards of thought, and the development of one appropriate to its subject matter, that economics has developed as an autonomous theory of the economic activities of man. To contribute to a similar development in the field of politics is indeed the purpose of political realism.

It is in the nature of things that a theory of politics which is based upon such principles will not meet with unanimous approval—nor does, for that matter, such a foreign policy. For theory and policy alike run counter to two trends in our culture which are not able to reconcile themselves to the assumptions and results of a rational, objective theory of politics. One of these trends disparages the role of power in society on grounds that stem from the experience and philosophy of the nineteenth century; we shall address ourselves to this tendency later in greater detail.[6] The other trend, opposed to the realist theory and practice of politics, stems from the very relationship that exists, and must exist, between the human mind and the political sphere. For reasons that we shall discuss later[7] the human mind in its day-by-day operations cannot bear to look the truth of politics straight in the face. It must disguise, distort, belittle, and embellish the truth—the more so, the more the individual is actively involved in the processes of politics, and particularly in those of international politics. For only by deceiving himself about the nature of politics and the role he plays on the political scene is man able to live contentedly as a political animal with himself and his fellow men.

Thus it is inevitable that a theory which tries to understand international politics as it actually is and as it ought to be in view of its intrinsic nature, rather than as people would like to see it, must overcome a psychological resistance that most other branches of learning need not face. A book devoted to the theoretical understanding of international politics therefore requires a special explanation and justification.

6. Morgenthau: *Political Power.*

7. Morgenthau: *The Ideological Elements in International Politics.*

The Liberal Tradition and International Relations

Scott A. Silverstone

In the field of international relations, most scholars acknowledge that the realist tradition, with its pessimistic claims about human nature, the relentless and often violent struggle for security and power, and the inherently competitive character of international anarchy, remains the dominant approach in the study of state behavior. Realists claim a heritage reaching back to the venerable Greek historian Thucydides and his chronicle of the Peloponnesian War in the fifth century B.C., as well as such great political philosophers as Machiavelli and Hobbes. Despite the fact that much of the study and practice of international relations is anchored in this centuries old tradition, another western philosophical tradition, liberalism, has made important contributions to the field as well. While liberalism can also claim a heritage that reaches back at least to the Enlightenment period of the eighteenth century, liberal scholars, as well as liberal ideas at work in actual world politics, have enjoyed increasing prominence in recent decades.

In many ways, liberalism can be considered a challenge to the dark vision presented by realists, an alternative way to conceive of human nature and the possibilities for overcoming the most competitive and destructive aspects of state behavior. In fact, Enlightenment beliefs about the rationality of individuals and the potential for progress in human affairs have been a primary motivation behind liberalism for centuries, as successive generations struggled with the problems of repressive government, poverty, and the increasingly destructive character of warfare. This was particularly true after World War I and World War II, which showcased the immense scale of violence now possible in the industrial and nuclear age. Most liberals did not deny that humans were often driven by insecurity, distrust or the quest for power, nor could they deny the fact that states seemed locked in cycles of competition and warfare. Liberals simply denied that this was inevitable, and have since sought ways to understand how states can, and do, break the cycle of competition and violence realists seem resigned to.

Interestingly, one of the greatest critics of liberal international relations theory of the twentieth century, the British historian E. H. Carr (who derisively referred to it as "utopianism"), ultimately argued that realism alone was "barren," that it led to the "sterilization of thought." It forces humans, he argued, to simply adapt to the realities of seemingly irresistible forces at work in the world, while providing no plan of action or larger purpose to change the worst traits of human behavior. Carr asserted, however, that "such a conclusion is plainly repugnant to the most deep-seated belief of man about himself. That human affairs can be directed and modified by human action and human thought...The human will," he believed, "will continue to seek an escape from the logical consequences of realism."[1] It is this effort to direct and modify human action and thought that liberal scholars and policy practitioners have taken most seriously, and which distinguishes them most clearly from realists.

---

1. Edward Hallett Carr, *The Twenty Years' Crisis: 1919-1939* (New York: Harper and Row, 1964), 10, 92-93.

Like realism, liberalism is based on a set of logically connected assumptions that can form the basis of specific liberal theories. Most importantly, liberals contend that humans are rational and self-interested actors. This is obviously an assumption shared by realists. Unlike realists, however, liberals contend that individuals and the states they lead can achieve these self-interests, to include security and prosperity, through cooperation with other states. While realists argue that states exist in a zero-sum world – in which a gain for one state must come at the expense of another – liberals argue that states can seek *mutual interests* with other states. That is, states can discover ways to better achieve their own security and prosperity by coordinating their behavior rather than perpetually competing against one another. An important supporting assumption is that humans are capable of learning from mistakes and successes, humans have choice in how they pursue their interests, and can adjust their behavior if they discover that competition only leads to greater dangers and less prosperity. Learning and change in behavior are the root of human progress.

It is important to emphasize that liberals do not ignore the security imperative that realists focus on. This is clearly evident in the writings of such prominent early liberal philosophers as John Lock and James Madison, who argue that security from violent death must be the first priority of any political actor. Without physical security, no other human aspirations are possible. What liberals stress, however, is that it is possible to maximize security, not by accumulating more power than others, but through alternative means. President Woodrow Wilson made this point at the end of World War I. What form of security did the balance of power system provide, he asked, when reviewing the tragic loss of 8.5 million lives and the ruin spread across much of Europe? The balance of power, Wilson argued, was bankrupt as a means to achieve security, it only magnified insecurity and could not prevent this horrible war.[2] While many realists would throw up their hands believing that a balance of power system was the best states were capable of to achieve security, President Wilson argued that humans could be enlightened enough to create a new cooperative system to achieve a more stable and lasting peace without great power war.

While liberals over the past centuries would all tend to share these assumptions about human behavior and international relations, Michael Doyle points out that there is "no canonical description of liberalism."[3] In other words, there is no single, definitive version of the liberal worldview. Robert Keohane notes that there are three basic types of liberal theories: republican, commercial, and regulatory.[4] The oldest version is republican, which has its roots in both ancient Greek and Roman political philosophy. The main claim here is that the way in which a state's government is organized will have an effect on how it behaves internationally. Specifically, republican institutions, such as popular representation and political checks and balances among different parts of the government, are said to constrain the use of military force. In the Enlightenment period this argument was advanced first by the American founders, who believed that the federal character of the

---

2. Woodrow Wilson, *Woodrow Wilson's Case for the League of Nations*, ed. Hamilton Foley (London: Oxford University Press, 1923).

3. Michael W. Doyle, "Liberalism and World Politics," *American Political Science Review*, vol. 80, no. 4 (December 1986), 1152.

4. Robert O. Keohane, "International Liberalism Reconsidered," in ed. John Dunn, *The Economic Limitations of Modern Politics* (Cambridge: Cambridge University Press, 1990), 176-82.

American republic would make it less war prone,[5] and by the German philosopher Immanuel Kant, who argued that the cause of "perpetual peace" would be best served by a "pacific union" among republican states.[6] In recent decades international relations scholars have argued over the proposition that democracies will not fight wars with other democracies, and that an international system with more democracies will produce a more peaceful world.[7] While republican, or democratic peace, versions of liberalism have been prominent in international relations theory recently, they are the most restrictive because they only apply to the behavior of democratic states.

The second form of liberal theory in Keohane's typology is commercial liberalism. As the name implies, this form of liberalism looks to trade as a potent form of cooperation that makes war less likely. Among the Enlightenment liberal philosophers, Montesquieu is the first to make this claim, arguing that "the natural effect of commerce is to lead to peace. Two nations that trade together become mutually dependent if one has an interest in buying, the other has an interest in selling; and all unions are based on mutual needs."[8] In a way, commercial liberalism can be considered one form of the third type of liberal theory: regulatory liberalism. Regulatory liberalism is based on the simple claim that states can best pursue their mutual interests in many different areas of international life – such as security, economic growth, environmental protection, health and social welfare – by creating rules to guide their behavior, rules that facilitate cooperation and increase trust, that help in the sharing of information and resources and the adjudication of disputes. Another term used to describe this type of liberal approach is "institutionalism," which captures the important fact that states can create sets of rules that define appropriate behavior, that set out rights actors should enjoy and the obligations they should assume. This is the essence of what social institutions are.

Keohane makes two important points about states' efforts to regulate their interaction through rules. First, authoritarian as well as democratic states can take part in this effort. Authoritarian states of various kinds are capable of recognizing that their interests can best be met through "mutually beneficial agreements" with other states, just as well as democracies can.[9] Second, the effort to discover mutual interests and develop rules to regulate cooperative interaction is not an easy task.[10] While liberals do not accept the realist notion that anarchy necessarily produces competitive state behavior, they do accept that the lack of enforcement of agreements in world politics makes states wary of being cheated. Also, cooperation through rules means that states must voluntarily accept limits on their behavior, which might be difficult to do. Despite these incentives not to cooperate, if states calculate that their interests are still better met through cooperation than through rejection of cooperation, the basis for regulated behavior exists.

5. Scott A. Silverstone, *Divided Union: The Politics of War in the Early American Republic* (Ithaca: Cornell University Press, 2004).

6. Immanuel Kant, *Perpetual Peace: a Philosophical Sketch* [1795], ed. Hans Reiss, trans. H. B. Nisbet (Cambridge: Cambridge University Press, 1970), 100-101.

7. Michael E. Brown, Sean M. Lynn-Jones and Steven E. Miller, *Debating the Democratic Peace* (Cambridge: MIT Press, 1996).

8. Quoted in Albert O. Hirschman, *The Passions and the Interests: Political Arguments for Capitalism Before its Triumph* (Princeton: Princeton University Press, 1977), 80.

9. Keohane, "International Liberalism Reconsidered," 180.

10. Ibid., 181-82.

In the twentieth century, while liberal theory met with serious setbacks between the world wars, since World War II liberal ideas have inspired several important developments in world politics. At the end of WWI, President Wilson became the most passionate voice arguing for the rejection of the balance of power system, which had been the basis of the international order since the emergence of the modern state system. In its place he proposed a new liberal order based on several key features: 1) democratic governance within states to give voice to what he believed would be the natural interests of citizens of all countries in peace; 2) a system of arbitration of state conflicts to prevent the inevitable disputes from turning violent; and 3) a League of Nations embodying a system of collective security, in which all members would pledge to aid any other member that became the victim of aggression from those states that did not abide by the principle of peaceful conflict resolution. Wilson's vision never materialized, however, with America's rejection of membership in the League of Nations, the Great Depression that produced a collapse in free trade among states, and the rise of militancy from Italy, Japan and Germany that could not be contained by any notion of collective security. The coming of the second great power war in twenty years, and the emergence of the Cold War between the U.S. and the USSR after that war, led many in the field of international relations to decry the "utopianism," the "idealism," of early twentieth century liberal thought.

Despite the dominance of realism that accompanied WWII and the coming of the Cold War, it is essential to recognize that several of the most important developments in world politics from mid-century on were the result of liberal ideas. The creation of the UN system, of course, is among them. Despite the failure of the League of Nations after WWI, the devastation of WWII motivated a strong demand for an international organization to facilitate coordinated efforts to prevent war and pursue a range of social and economic goals. The UN has clearly fallen short of its founders' visions. In fact, realists point to the UN as an example of the continuing dominance of power politics that impede international cooperation. Better examples of liberal theory at work come in the form of the post-war international economic system and the European integration movement.

Even before WWII was won, American and British government officials were looking ahead to the post-war order. In 1944 economic planners met in Bretton Woods, New Hampshire, to create a set of institutions that would foster free trade, economic development, and the stability of currencies. One of the most important lessons of the inter-war period was that depression and the collapse of international trade not only produced intense competition among states as they were forced to be economically self-sufficient (which Japan concluded required empire for survival), it produced the domestic conditions in Germany for the rise of Nazism and German aggression. A cooperative trade system, they concluded, was essential to prevent a repeat of this devastating history. What emerged from the Bretton Woods conference was the General Agreement on Tariffs and Trade (GATT), the forerunner to the current World Trade Organization (WTO), which established the basis for the increasingly open trade system that is such an important part of contemporary world politics. Bretton Woods also created the European Bank for Reconstruction and Development, which became the World Bank, a central institution for supporting economic development, and the International Monetary Fund, which helps control destabilizing fluctuations of states' currency values.

The European integration movement, embodied now in the European Union, began in 1952 with the creation of the European Coal and Steel Community (ECSC). The ECSC integrated the French and German coal and steel industries as a way to prevent these historic adversaries from independently producing military armaments. While integration developed in fits and starts over the decades, this movement was the vehicle for solving the security dilemma among European states, who now regard war among themselves as unthinkable. Considering the history of Europe, which has been called the "cockpit" of great power wars for centuries, this accomplishment is nothing short of revolutionary in world politics. In addition to liberal theory as the source of cooperation in the international economic system and European integration, the last several decades have seen an explosion of state efforts to coordinate their policies on such diverse mutual interests as arms control, human rights and environmental protection, the control of narcotics trafficking and organized crime, and health crises such as AIDS, just to name a few.

State behavior is too complicated to be captured in its entirety by either realism or liberalism. Each has made major contributions to our efforts as students of international relations to explain state behavior in systematic ways, and each can offer guidance as we wrestle with policy options to confront the challenges of security and prosperity today and in the future. The challenge is to be nimble enough to draw from each tradition to make sense of the complexity of international politics.

Scott Silverstone is <info TK> Department of Social Sciences, United States Military Academy.

To Perpetual Peace: A Philosophical Sketch (1795)

Immanuel Kant

Kant (1724–1804), a German philosopher, developed a political doctrine of the state based upon law (Rechtstaat) and the notion of eternal peace. His political teaching can be clearly classified as "idealist." In this essay, he rejects the realist notion that "might makes right" or that one must compromise ethics. He suggests that politics is compatible with moral principle both within a state and among states.

FIRST SECTION: WHICH CONTAINS THE PRELIMINARY ARTICLES FOR PERPETUAL PEACE AMONG NATIONS

1. No treaty of peace that tacitly reserves issues for a future war shall be held valid.[1]

For if this were the case, it would be a mere truce, a suspension of hostilities, not *peace*, which means the end of all hostilities, so much so that even to modify it by "perpetual" smacks of pleonasm. A peace treaty nullifies all existing causes for war, even if they are unknown to the contracting parties, and even if they are assiduously ferreted out from archival documents. When one or both parties to a peace treaty, being too exhausted to continue the war, has a mental reservation (*reservatio mentalis*) concerning some presently unmentioned pretension that will be revived at the first opportune moment, since ill will between the warring parties still remains, that reservation is a bit of mere Jesuitical casuistry. If we judge such actions in their true character, they are beneath the dignity of a ruler, just as a willingness to indulge in reasoning of this sort is beneath his minister's dignity.

If, however, enlightened concepts of political prudence lead us to believe that the true honor of a nation lies in its continual increase of power by whatever means necessary, this judgment will appear academic and pedantic.

2. No independent nation, be it large or small, may be acquired by another nation by inheritance, exchange, purchase, or gift.

A nation is not (like the ground on which it is located) a possession *(partrimonium)*. It is a society of men whom no one other than the nation itself can command or dispose of. Since, like a tree, each nation has its own roots, to incorporate it into another nation as a graft, denies its existence as a moral person, turns it into a thing, and thus contradicts the concept of the original contract, without which a people *[Volk]* has no rights.[2] Everyone is aware of the danger that this purported right of acquisition by the marriage of nations to

---

[1] See *Theory and Practice*, 298, 303 and *Perpetual Peace*, 384-86. Footnotes hereafter refer to Immanuel Kant, *Perpetual Peace and Other Essays*, trans. Ted Humphrey (Indianapolis, In. Hackett Publishing, Inc., 1988).

[2] A hereditary monarchy is not a nation that can be inherited by another nation; only the right to rule it can be inherited by another physical person. Consequently, the nation acquires a ruler, but the ruler as such (i.e., as one who already has another kingdom) does not acquire the nation. (See *Universal History*, p. 26)

one another—a custom unknown in other parts of the world—has brought to Europe, even in the most recent times. It is a new form of industry, in which influence is increased without expending energy, and territorial possessions are extended merely by establishing family alliances. The hiring out of the troops of one nation to another for use against an enemy not common to both of them falls under this principle, for by this practice subjects are used and wasted as mere objects to be manipulated at will.

3. Standing armies (miles perpetuus) shall be gradually abolished.

For they constantly threaten other nations with war by giving the appearance that they are prepared for it, which goads nations into competing with one another in the number of men under arms, and this practice knows no bounds. And since the costs related to maintaining peace will in this way finally become greater than those of a short war, standing armies are the cause of wars of aggression that are intended to end burdensome expenditures.[3] Moreover, paying men to kill or be killed appears to use them as mere machines and tools in the hands of another (the nation), which is inconsistent with the rights of humanity *[Menschheit]*. The voluntary, periodic military training of citizens so that they can secure their homeland against external aggression is an entirely different matter. The same could be said about the hoarding of treasure (for of the three sorts of power, the *power of an army,* the *power of alliance,* and the *power of money,* the third is the most reliable instrument of war). Thus, except for the difficulty in discovering the amount of wealth another nation possesses, the hoarding of treasure could be regarded as preparation for war that necessitates aggression.

4. No national debt shall be contracted in connection with the foreign affairs of the nation.

Seeking either internal or external help for the national economy (e.g., for improvement of roads, new settlements, storage of food against years of bad harvest, and so on) is above suspicion. However, as an instrument in the struggle among powers, the credit system—the ingenious invention of a commercial people [England] during this century—of endlessly growing debts that remain safe against immediate demand (since the demand for payment is not made by all creditors at the same time) is a dangerous financial power. It is a war chest exceeding the treasure of all other nations taken together, and it can be exhausted only by an inevitable default in taxes (although it can also be forestalled indefinitely by the economic stimulus that derives from credit's influence on industry and commerce). This ease in making war, combined with the inclination of those in power to do so—an inclination that seems innate in human nature—is a great obstacle to perpetual peace. Thus, forbidding foreign debt must be a preliminary article for perpetual peace, for eventual yet unavoidable national bankruptcy must entangle many innocent nations, and that would clearly injure them. Consequently, other nations are justified in allying themselves against such a nation and its pretensions.[4]

---

3. See *Theory and Practice,* 290-96.

4. Kant's conception of the state of nature is clearly similar to, perhaps influenced by, Hobbes's. Kant would have been able to read either Hobbes's *De Cive,* where the state of nature is discussed in chapter 1, section 12, or the Latin translation of Leviathan, where the relevant discussion is chapter 13, as it is in the original English version.

5. No nation shall forcibly interfere with the constitution and government of another.

For what can justify its doing so? Perhaps some offense that one nation's subjects give to those of another? Instead, this should serve as a warning by providing an example of the great evil that a people falls into through its lawlessness. Generally, the bad example that one free person furnishes for another (as a *scandalum acceptum)* does not injure the latter. But it would be different if, as a result of internal discord, a nation were divided in two and each part, regarding itself as separate nation, lay claim to the whole; for (since they are in a condition of anarchy) the aid of a foreign nation to one of the parties could not be regarded as interference by the other in its constitution. So long, however, as this internal conflict remains undecided, a foreign power's interference would violate the rights of an independent people struggling with its internal ills. Doing this would be an obvious offense and would render the autonomy of every nation insecure.

6. No nation at war with another shall permit such acts of war as shall make mutual trust impossible during some future time of peace: Such acts include the use of Assassins (percussores), Poisoners (venefici), breach of surrender, instigation of treason (perduellio) in the opposing nation, etc.

These are dishonorable stratagems. Some level of trust in the enemy's way of thinking *[Denkungsart]* must be preserved even in the midst of war, for otherwise no peace can ever be concluded and the hostilities would become a war of extermination *(bellum internecinum).* Yet war is but a sad necessity in the state of nature (where no tribunal empowered to make judgments supported by the power of law exists), one that maintains the rights of a nation by mere might, where neither party can be declared an unjust enemy (since this already presupposes a judgment of right) and the outcome of the conflict (as if it were a so-called "judgment of God") determines the side on which justice lies. A war of punishment *(bellum punitivum)* between nations is inconceivable (for there is no relation of superior and inferior between them). From this it follows that a war of extermination—where the destruction of both parties along with all rights is the result—would permit perpetual peace to occur only in the vast graveyard of humanity as a whole. Thus, such a war, including all means used to wage it, must be absolutely prohibited. But that the means named above inexorably lead to such war becomes clear from the following: Once they come into use, these intrinsically despicable, infernal acts cannot long be confined to war alone. This applies to the use of spies (uti *exploratoribus),* where only the dishonorableness *of others* (which can never be entirely eliminated) is exploited; but such activities will also carry over to peacetime and will thus undermine it. . . .

SECOND SECTION: WHICH CONTAINS THE DEFINITIVE ARTICLES FOR PERPETUAL PEACE AMONG NATIONS

The state of peace among men living in close proximity is not the natural state *(status naturalis);* instead, the natural state is one of war, which does not just consist in open hostilities, but also in the constant and enduring threat of them. The state of peace must therefore be *established,* for the suspension of hostilities does not provide the security of peace, and unless this security is pledged by one neighbor to another (which can happen only in a state of *lawfulness*), the latter, from whom such security has been requested, can treat the former as an enemy.[5]

First Definitive Article of Perpetual Peace

The civil constitution of every nation should be republican.

The sole established constitution that follows from the idea *[Idee]* of an original contract, the one on which all of a nation's just *[rechtliche]*[6] legislation must be based, is republican. For, first, it accords with the principles of *the freedom* of the members of a society (as men), second, it accords with the principles of the *dependence* of everyone on a single, common [source of] legislation (as subjects), and third, it accords with the law of the equality of them all (as citizens). Thus, so far as [the matter of] right is concerned, republicanism is the original foundation of all forms of civil constitution. Thus, the only question remaining is this, does it also provide the only foundation for perpetual peace? . .

Second Definitive Article for a Perpetual Peace

The right of nations shall be based on a federation of free states.

As nations, peoples can be regarded as single individuals who injure one another through their close proximity while living in the state of nature (i.e., independently of external laws). For the sake of its own security, each nation can and should demand that the others enter into a contract resembling the civil one and guaranteeing the rights of each. This would be a federation *of nations,* but it must not be a nation consisting of nations. The latter would be contradictory, for in every nation there exists the relation of *ruler* (legislator) to *subject* (those who obey, the people); however, many nations in a single nation would constitute only a single nation, which contradicts our assumption (since we are here weighing the rights of *nations* in relation to one another, rather than fusing them into a single nation). . .

---

5. It is commonly assumed that one ought not to take hostile action against another unless one has already been actively *injured* by that person and that is entirely correct if both parties live in a state [governed by] *civil law.* For by entering into civil society, each person gives every other (by virtue of the sovereignty that has power over them both) the requisite security. However, a man (or a people) who is merely in a state of nature denies me this security and injures me merely by being in this state. For although he does not actively *(facto)* injure me, he does so by virtue of the lawlessness of his state *(statu iniusto),* by which he constantly threatens me, and I can require him either to enter with me into a state of civil law or to remove himself from my surroundings. Thus, the postulate on which all the following articles rest is: "All men who can mutually influence one another must accept some civil constitution."

Every just constitution, as far as the persons who accept it are concerned, will be one of the three following:

1. one conforming to the civil rights of men in a nation (*ius civitatis);*
2. one conforming to the *rights of nations* in relation to one another;
3. one conforming to the *rights of world citizenship,* so far as men and nations stand in mutually influential relations as citizens of a universal nation of men *(ius cosmopoliticum).* These are not arbitrary divisions, but ones that are necessary in relationship to the idea *[Idee]* of perpetual peace. Because if even only one of these [nations] had only physical influence on another, they would be in a state of nature, and consequently they would be bound together in a state of war. Our intention here is to free them from this.

6. See Note on the Text, p. 26. See *Theory and Practice,* 290 ff.

Third Definitive Article for a Perpetual Peace

Cosmopolitan right shall be limited to conditions of universal hospitality.

As in the preceding articles, our concern here is not with philanthropy, but with *right,* and in this context *hospitality* (hospitableness) means the right of an alien not to be treated as an enemy upon his arrival in another's country. If it can be done without destroying him, he can be turned away; but as long as he behaves peaceably he cannot be treated as an enemy. He may request the *right* to be a *permanent visitor* (which would require a special, charitable agreement to make him a fellow inhabitant for a certain period), but the *right to visit,* to associate, belongs to all men by virtue of their common ownership of the earth's surface; for since the earth is a globe, they cannot scatter themselves infinitely, but must, finally, tolerate living in close proximity, because originally no one had a greater right to any region of the earth than anyone else. Uninhabitable parts of this surface—the sea and deserts—separate these communities, and yet ships and camels (the *ship* of the desert) make it possible to approach one another across these unowned regions, and the right to the *earth's surface* that belongs in common to the totality of men makes commerce possible. The inhospitableness that coastal dwellers (e.g., on the Barbary Coast) show by robbing ships in neighboring seas and by making slaves of stranded seafarers, or of desert dwellers (the Arabic Bedouins), who regard their proximity to nomadic peoples as giving them a right to plunder, is contrary to natural right, even though the latter extends the right to hospitality, i.e., the privilege of aliens to enter, only so far as makes attempts at commerce with native inhabitants possible. In this way distant parts of the world can establish with one another peaceful relations that will eventually become matters of public law, and the human race can gradually be brought closer and closer to a cosmopolitan constitution.[7]

ON THE DISAGREEMENT BETWEEN MORALS AND POLITICS IN RELATION TO PERPETUAL PEACE

Taken objectively morality is in itself practical, for it is the totality of unconditionally binding laws according to which we *ought* to act, and once one has acknowledged the authority of its concept of duty, it would be utterly absurd to continue wanting to say that one *cannot* do his duty. For if that were so, then this concept would disappear from morality *(ultra posse nemo obligatur);* consequently, there can be no conflict between politics as an applied doctrine of right and morals as a theoretical doctrine of right (thus no conflict between practice and theory). [If such a conflict were to occur], one would have to understand morality as a universal *doctrine of prudence,* i.e., a theory of maxims by which to choose the most efficient means of furthering one's own interests, which is to deny that morality exists at all.

Politics says, *"Be ye wise as serpents," to which morality adds (as a limiting condition), "and innocent as doves."*[8] Where both of these maxims cannot coexist in a command, there one finds an actual conflict between politics and morality; but if the two are completely united the concept of opposition is absurd, and the question as to how the conflict is to be resolved cannot even be posed as a problem. However, the proposition, *"Honesty is the best policy,"* is beyond all refutation, and is the indispensable condition of all

[7] Many of the themes in this Article are also covered in *Spec. Beg. Human History.*

[8] Matt. 10:16; compare also Hume, *Enquiry Concerning Morals*, 271.

policy. The divinity who protects the boundaries of morality does not yield to Jupiter (the protector of power), for the latter is still subject to fate. That is, reason is not yet sufficiently enlightened that it can survey the series of predetermining causes and predict with certainty what the happy or unhappy consequences that follow in accord with nature's mechanism from men's activities will be (though one can hope that they come out as one wishes). But with respect to everything we have to do in order to remain on the path of duty (according to rules of wisdom), reason does provide us with enlightenment sufficient to pursue our ultimate goals.

Now even if the practical man *[Praktiker]* (for whom morality is mere theory) admits that we can do what we ought to do, he bases his disconsolate rejection of our fond hope on the following consideration: he asserts that, human nature being what it is, we can predict that man will never want to do what is required to achieve the goal *[Zweck]* of perpetual peace. Certainly, the will of all *individual* men (the *distributive* unity of the wills of *all)* to live under a lawful constitution that accords with principles of freedom is not sufficient to attain this goal; only the will of *all together* (the *collective* unity of combined wills) is. The solution to so difficult a task requires that civil society become a whole. Implementing this state of right (in practice) can begin only *with force,* and this coercion will subsequently provide a basis for public right, because an additional unifying cause must be superimposed on the differences among each person's particular desires in order to transform them into a common will—and this is something no single person can do. Furthermore, in actual experience we can certainly anticipate great deviations from that (theoretical) idea of right (for we can hardly expect the legislator to have such moral sensibilities that having united the wild mass into a people, he will then allow them to create a legal constitution through their general will).

For this reason it is said that he who once has power in hand will not have laws prescribed to him by the people. And once a nation is no longer subject to external laws it will not allow itself to be subjected to the judgment of other nations regarding the way in which it should seek to uphold its rights against them. Even a continent that feels itself to be superior to another, regardless of whether or not the latter stands in the way of the former, will not fail to exercise the means of increasing its power, plundering and conquering. Thus, all theoretical plans for civil, international, and cosmopolitan rights dissolve into empty, impractical ideals; by contrast, a practice that is based on empirical principles of human nature and that does not regard it demeaning to formulate its maxims in accord with the way of the world can alone hope to find a secure foundation for its structure of political prudence.

To be sure, if neither freedom nor the moral law that is based on it exist, and if everything that happens or can happen is mere mechanism of nature, then politics (as the art of using that mechanism to govern men) would be the whole of practical wisdom, and the concept of right would be a contentless thought. But if we find it absolutely necessary to couple politics with the concept of right, and even to make the latter a limiting condition of politics, the compatibility of the two must be conceded, I can actually think of a *moral politician,* i.e., one who so interprets the principles of political prudence that they can be coherent with morality, but I cannot think of *a political moralist,* i.e., one who forges a morality to suit the statesman's advantage.

The moral politician will make it a principle that once a fault that could not have been anticipated is found in a nation's constitution or in its relations with other nations, it becomes a duty, particularly for the rulers of nations, to consider how it can be corrected as soon as possible and in such a way as to conform with natural right, which stands in our eyes as a model presented by an idea of reason; and this ought to be done even at the cost of self-sacrifice. Since it is contrary to all political prudence consistent with morality to sever a bond of political or cosmopolitan union before a better constitution is prepared to put in its place, it would also be truly absurd that such a fault be immediately and violently repaired. However, it can be required of those in power that they at least take to heart the maxim that such changes are necessary so as continuously to approach the goal (of the constitution most in accord with laws of right). A nation may already possess republican rule, even if under its present constitution it has a despotic *ruling power,* until gradually the people are capable of being influenced by the mere idea of the law's authority (just as if it possessed physical power) and thus is found able to be its own legislator which [ability] is originally based on [natural] right). If—through a violent *revolution* caused by a bad constitution—a constitution conforming to law were introduced by illegal means, it must not be permissible to lead the people back to the old one, even though everyone who violently or covertly participated in the revolution would rightly have been subject to the punishment due rebels. But as to the external relations among nations, it cannot be expected that a nation will give up its constitution, even if despotic (which is the stronger in relation to foreign enemies), so long as it risks the danger of being overrun by other nations; consequently, it is permissible to delay the intention to implement improvements until a better opportunity arises.[9]

It may be that despotic moralists (those who fail in practice) violate rules of political prudence in many ways (by adopting or proposing premature measures); still, experience will gradually bring them to give up their opposition to nature and to follow a better course. By contrast with this, the moralizing politician attempts, on the pretext that human nature is not *capable* of attaining the good as prescribed in the idea of reason, to extenuate political principles that are contrary to it, and thus these principles make progress *impossible* and perpetuate the violation of right.

Instead of employing the practical science [*Praxis*] that these politically prudent [*staatskluge*] men make so much of, they use devious practices [*Praktiken*] to influence the current ruling power (so as to insure their own private advantage), even at the expense of the people and, where possible, the entire world, acting just like lawyers (for whom law is a trade, not a matter of legislation) when they go into politics. For since it is not their business to be overly concerned with legislation, but rather to carry out momentary commands under the law of the land, they must always regard every existing legal constitution as best—and when it is amended in higher places, they regard these amendments as for the best, too; in that way, everything follows in its proper mechanical order. But, granted that this deftness at being all things to all men gives the politically prudent the illusion of being able to judge a *national constitution* in general against concepts of right (consequently, *a priori,* not empirically); and granted that they make a great to do of knowing *men* (which is certainly to be expected, since they deal with so many of them), though without knowing *man* and what can be made of him (for which a high standpoint of anthropological observation is required);

---

9. These are permissive laws of reason: to allow a condition of public right afflicted with injustice to continue until everything is either of itself or through peaceful means ripe for a complete transformation, for any legal constitution, even if it conforms with right only to a small degree, is better than none, and the latter fate (anarchy) would result from premature reform. Political wisdom, therefore, will make it a duty, given the present state of things, to evaluate reforms against the ideal of public right. Revolutions brought about by nature itself will not find excuses for still greater oppression, but will use revolution as a call of nature to create a lawful constitution based on principles of freedom, for only this fundamental reform is enduring.

nonetheless, if, as reason prescribes, they attempt to use these concepts in civil and international law, they cannot make the transition except in a spirit of charlatanism. For they will continue to follow their customary procedure (of mechanically applying despotically imposed laws of coercion) in an area where the concepts of reason only permit lawful compulsion that accords with principles of freedom, and it is under such principles alone that a rightful and enduring constitution is possible. The supposed practical man *[Praktiker]* believes he can ignore the idea of right and solve this problem empirically, the solution being based on his experience of the national constitutions that have heretofore been most lasting, though oftentimes contrary to right. The maxims that he uses to this end (though he does not make them public) consist, roughly speaking, of the following sophistries.

1. Fac et excusa.[10] Seize every favorable opportunity for arbitrary usurpation (of a right of a nation either over its own people or over another neighboring people); the justification can be presented far more easily and elegantly *after the fact,* and the violence more easily glossed over (especially in the first case, where the supreme internal power is also the legislative authority, which one must obey without argument), than if one first thinks out convincing reasons and waits for objections to them. This audacity itself gives a certain appearance of an inner conviction that the act is right, and after the fact the god of success, *bonus eventus,* is the best advocate.

2. Si fecisti, nega.[11] Whatever crime you have committed—e.g., that you have reduced your people to despair and hence brought them to rebellion—deny that the guilt is *yours;* instead, maintain that it is the obstinacy of the subjects, or, if you have conquered a neighboring people, that the guilt belongs to human nature, for if one does not forestall others by using force, one can surely count on their anticipating it and becoming one's conqueror.

3. Divide et impera.[12] That is, if there are certain privileged persons among your people who have merely chosen you to be their leader *(primus inter pares),*[13] destroy their unity and separate them from the people; and if, in turn, the people have delusions of greater freedom, everyone will depend on your unchecked will. Or if you are concerned with foreign nations, then sowing discord among them is a relatively certain method of subjecting them one after another to your will, all the while appearing to defend the weaker.

Certainly no one will be taken in by these political maxims, for all of them are widely known; nor are men ashamed of them, as if their injustice were altogether too apparent. For great powers never heed the judgment of the masses, feeling shame only in the face of others like them; and as regards the foregoing principles, not their becoming public knowledge, but only their *failure* can make those powers feel ashamed (for among themselves they agree on the morality of the maxims). And in this way their *political* honor, on which they can always count, is retained, namely, by the expansion of their power by whatever means they choose.

. . . .

From all these twistings and turnings of an immoral doctrine of prudence regarding how men are to be brought out of the warlike state of nature into the state of peace, we receive at least this much illumination: Men can no more escape the concept of right in

10. Act first, then justify.

11. If you are the perpetrator, deny it.

12. Divide and conquer.

13. First among equals.

their private relations than in their public ones; nor can they openly risk basing their politics on the handiwork of prudence alone, and, consequently, they cannot altogether refuse obedience to the concept of public right.(which is particulrly important in the case of international right). Instead, they give this concept all due honor, even if they also invent a hundred excuses and evasions to avoid observing it in practice, attributing to cunning force the authority that is the original source and bond of right. In order to end this sophistry (if not the injustice that it glosses over) and to force the false representatives of those in earthly power to confess that rather than right it is might that they advocate—a fact that is clear from the tone they adopt, as if they were entitled to give orders—it will do well to expose the fraud to which they subject themselves and others and to reveal the highest principle from which perpetual peace as an end proceeds. We will show that all the evil that stands in the way of perpetual peace derives from the fact that the political moralist begins where the moral politician rightly stops; and, since the former subordinates his principles to his ends (i.e., puts the cart before the horse), he defeats his own purpose of effecting an agreement between politics and morals.

In order to bring practical philosophy into harmony with itself, it is first necessary to resolve this question: In problems of practical reason, must we begin from *material principles,* the end *[Zweck]* (as object of the will *[Willkur]),* or from its *formal* one, i.e., the one (which rests only on freedom in external relations) that is expressed thus: "Act so that you can will that your maxim ought to become a universal law (no matter what the end *[Zweck]* may be)"?

Without doubt the latter principle must take precedence, because as a principle of right it has unconditioned necessity, whereas the former is necessary only if one assumes the existence of those empirical conditions through which the proposed end can be realized. And if this end (e.g., perpetual peace) were also a duty, it must itself be derived from the formal principle of external action. Now the first principle, that of the *political moralists* (concerning the problem of civil, international and cosmopolitan right), proposes a mere *technical task (problema technicum);* by contrast, the second is the principle of the *moral politician,* for whom it is a *moral task (problema morale),* and its method of pursuing perpetual peace—which one now desires not merely as a physical good, but also as a condition that arises from acknowledging one's duty—is completely distinct.

Solving the first problem, namely, the problem that political prudence proposes, requires considerable natural knowledge so that one can use nature's mechanism to attain the desired end; yet it is uncertain how this mechanism will function as far as its consequences for perpetual peace are concerned; and this is so in all three areas of public right. Whether the people's obedience and prosperity will be better preserved over a long period of time by harshness or by appeals to vanity, by granting supreme power to a single ruler or to several united ones, or, perhaps, merely by a devoted aristocracy or by the power of the people is uncertain. History furnishes examples of the opposite effects being produced by all forms of government (with the singular exception of true republicanism, which alone can appeal to the sensibility of a moral politician). Still more uncertainty arises in the area of *international right*—a form of right purportedly based on statutes worked out by ministers—for in fact it is a term without content, and it rests on contracts whose very act of conclusion contains the secret reservation for their violation. By contrast, the solution to the second problem, the problem of *political wisdom,* impresses itself on us, as it were, for it obviously puts all artificiality to shame, and leads directly to the end [*Zweck*]. Yet prudence cautions us not to employ power in direct pursuit of it, but rather to approach it indirectly through those conditions presented by favorable circumstances.

Thus, it may be said: "Seek first the kingdom of pure practical reason and its *righteousness,* and your end *[Zweck]* (the blessing of perpetual peace) will come to you of itself." For this characteristic is inherent in morals—especially as regards its fundamental principle of public right (consequently, in relation to a politics that is *a priori* knowable)—that the less it makes conduct depend on the proposed end, be it a physical or moral advantage, the more conduct will in general harmonize with morality. And this is because such conduct derives directly from the general will that is given *a priori* (in a single people or in the relations of different peoples to one another), which alone determines what is right among men. If only it is acted on in a consistent way, this unity of the will of all can, along with the mechanism of nature, be the cause of the desired result and can make the concept of right effective. So, for example, it is a fundamental principle of moral politics that in uniting itself into a nation a people ought to subscribe to freedom and equality as the sole constituents of its concept of right, and this is not a principle of prudence, but is founded on duty. By contrast, political moralists do not even deserve a hearing, no matter how much they argue that the natural mechanism of a group of people who enter into society invalidates that fundamental principle and vitiates its intention, or seek to substantiate their contentions by use of ancient and modern examples of badly organized constitutions (e.g., of democracies without systems of representation). This is especially so since such a damaging theory may bring about the evil that it prophesies, for in it man is thrown into the same class as other living machines, which need only to become conscious that they are not free in order to become in their own eyes the most wretched of all the earth's creatures.

The true, albeit somewhat boastful proverb, *Fiat iustia, pereat mundus*—"Let justice reign, even if all the rogues in the world should perish"—is a sound principle of right that cuts across the sinuous paths of deceit and power. But it must not be misunderstood nor, perhaps, taken as permission simply to press with the utmost vigour for one's own right (for that would conflict with moral duty); instead, those in power should understand it to pose an obligation not to deny or diminish anyone's rights through either dislike or sympathy. Above all, this requires that the nation have an internal constitution founded on principles of right and that it also unite itself (analogously to a universal nation) with other neighboring and distant nations so they can settle their differences legally. This proposition means only that adherence to political maxims must not be based on the benefit or happiness that each nation anticipates from so doing—thus, not on the end [Zweck] that each nation makes an object (of its desire) and its supreme (though empirical) principle of political wisdom; instead, adherence must derive from the pure concept of the duty of right (from the *ought,* whose principle is given *a priori* through pure reason), let the physical consequences be what they may. The world will certainly not cease to exist if there are fewer bad men. The intrinsic characteristic of moral evil is that its aims (especially in relation to other like-minded persons) are self-contradictory and self-destructive, and it thus makes way for the (moral) principle of goodness, even if progress in doing so is slow.

. . . .

Objectively (i.e., in theory) there is utterly no conflict between morality and politics. But subjectively (in the self-seeking inclinations of men, which, because they are not based on maxims of reason, must not be called the [sphere of] practice *[Praxis])* this conflict will always remain, as well it should; for it serves as the whetstone of virtue, whose true courage (according to the principle, "*tu ne cede malis, sed contra audentior ito*")[14] in the present case consists not so much in resolutely standing up to the evils and sacrifices that must be taken on; rather, it consists in detecting, squarely facing, and conquering the deceit of the evil principle in ourselves, which is the more dangerously devious and treacherous because it excuses all our transgressions with an appeal to human nature's frailty.

In fact, the political moralist can say that the ruler and the people, or the people and the people, do not treat *one another* wrong *[unrecht]* if, through violence and fraud they war against one another, although they do in general act wrong *[unrecht]* when they deny respect to the concept of right, on which alone peace can be perpetually based. When one person violates the rights of another who is just as lawlessly disposed towards him, then whatever *happens* to them as they destroy themselves is entirely right; enough of their race will always survive so that this game will not cease, even into the remotest age, and they can serve as a warning to later generations. In this manner, the course of world events justifies providence. For the moral principle in man never dies out, and with the continuous progress of culture, reason, which is able pragmatically to apply the ideas of right in accordance with the moral principle, grows through its persistence in doing so, and guilt for transgressions grows concomitantly. (Given that the human race never can and never will be in a better condition) it seems impossible to be able to use a theodicy to provide any justification whatsoever for creation, namely, that such a race of generally corrupt beings should have been put on earth. We will be unavoidably driven to such skeptical conclusions, if we do not assume that pure principles of right have objective reality, i.e., that they permit themselves to be applied and that peoples in nations and even nations in their relations with one another must for their parts behave in conformity with them, no matter how objectionable empirical politics may find them. Thus, true politics cannot progress without paying homage to morality; and although politics by itself is a difficult art, its union with morality is not art at all, for this union cuts through the [Gordian] knot that politics cannot solve when politics and morality come into conflict. The rights of men must be held sacred, however great the cost of sacrifice may be to those in power. Here one cannot go halfway, cooking up hybrid, pragmatically-conditioned rights (which are somewhere between the right and the expedient); instead, all politics must bend its knee before morality, and by so doing it can hope to reach, though but gradually, the stage where it will shine in light perpetual.

---

14. "do not yield to missfortune, but press on more boldly/Than your fortune allows you." Vergil, *Aeneid*, VI, 95. (Lind translation).

The Fourteen Points

Woodrow Wilson

This is an excerpt from President Woodrow Wilson's address to Congress on January 8, 1918, which became the "signpost" of post-World War I idealism in international relations.

Gentlemen of the Congress:

. . . It will be our wish and purpose that the processes of peace, when they are begun, shall be absolutely open and that they shall involve and permit henceforth no secret understandings of any kind. The day of conquest and aggrandizement is gone by, so is also the day of secret covenants entered into in the interest of particular governments and likely at some unlooked-for moment to upset the peace of the world. It is this happy fact, now clear to the view of every public man whose thoughts do not still linger in an age that is dead and gone, which makes it possible for every nation whose purposes are consistent with justice and the peace of the world to avow now or at any other time the objects it has in view.

We entered this war because violations of right had occurred which touched us to the quick and made the life of our own people impossible unless they were corrected and the world secured once for all against their recurrence. What we demand in this war, therefore, is nothing peculiar to ourselves. It is that the world be made fit and safe to live in; and particularly that it be made safe for every peace-loving nation which, like our own, wishes to live its own life, determine its own institutions, be assured of justice and fair dealing by the other peoples of the world as against force and selfish aggression. All the peoples of the world are in effect partners in this interest, and for our own part we see very clearly that unless justice be done to others it will not be done to us. The program of the world's peace, therefore, is our program: and that program, the only possible program, as we see it, is this:

I. Open covenants of peace, openly arrived at, after which there shall be no private international understandings of any kind but diplomacy shall proceed always frankly and in the public view.

II. Absolute freedom of navigation upon the seas, outside territorial waters, alike in peace and in war, except as the seas may be closed in whole or in part by international action for the enforcement of international covenants.

III. The removal, so far as possible, of all economic barriers and the establishment of an equality of trade conditions among all the nations consenting to the peace and associating themselves for its maintenance.

IV. Adequate guarantees given and taken that national armaments will be reduced to the lowest point consistent with domestic safety.

V. A free, open-minded, and absolutely impartial adjustment of all colonial claims, based upon a strict observance of the principle that in determining all such questions of sovereignty the interests of the populations concerned must have equal weight with the equitable claims of the government where title is to be determined.

VI. The evacuation of all Russian territory and such a settlement of all questions affecting Russia as will secure the best and freest cooperation of the other nations of the world in

From *The Fourteen Points*, Wilson's Address to Congress, Woodrow Wilson, January 8, 1918.

obtaining for her an unhampered and unembarrassed opportunity for the independent determination of her own political development and national policy and assure her of a sincere welcome into the society of free nations under institutions of her own choosing; and, more than a welcome, assistance also of every kind that she may need and may herself desire. The treatment accorded Russia by her sister nations in the months to come will be the acid test of their good will, of their comprehension of her needs as distinguished from their own interests, and of their intelligent and unselfish sympathy.

VII. Belgium, the whole world will agree, must be evacuated and restored, without any attempt to limit the sovereignty which she enjoys in common with all other free nations. No other single act will serve as this will serve to restore confidence among the nations in the laws which they have themselves set and determined for the government of their relations with one another. Without this healing act the whole structure and validity of international law is forever impaired.

VIII. All French territory should be freed and the invaded portions restored, and the wrong done to France by Prussia in 1871 in the matter of Alsace-Lorraine, which has unsettled the peace of the world for nearly fifty years, should be righted, in order that peace may once more be made secure in the interest of all.

IX. A readjustment of the frontiers of Italy should be effected along clearly recognizable lines of nationality.

X. The people of Austria-Hungary, whose place among the nations we wish to see safeguarded and assured, should be accorded the freest opportunity of autonomous development.

XI. Rumania, Serbia, and Montenegro should be evacuated: occupied territories restored; Serbia accorded free and secure access to the sea; and the relations of the several Balkan states to one another determined by friendly counsel along historically established lines of allegiance and nationality; and international guarantees of the political and economic independence and territorial integrity of the several Balkan states should be entered into.

XII. The Turkish portions of the present Ottoman Empire should be assured a secure sovereignty, but the other nationalities which are now under Turkish rule should be assured an undoubted security of life and an absolutely unmolested opportunity of autonomous development, and the Dardanelles should be permanently opened as a free passage to the ships and commerce of all nations under international guarantees.

XIII. An independent Polish state should be erected which should include the territories inhabited by indisputably Polish populations, which should be assured a free and secure access to the sea, and whose political and economic independence and territorial integrity should be guaranteed by international covenant.

XIV. A general association of nations must be formed under specific covenants for the purpose of affording mutual guarantees of political independence and territorial integrity to great and small states alike.

In regard to these essential rectifications of wrong and assertions of right we feel ourselves to be intimate partners of all the governments and peoples associated together against the Imperialists. We cannot be separated in interest or divided in purpose. We stand together until the end.

For such arrangements and covenants we are willing to fight and to continue to fight until they are achieved; but only because we wish the right to prevail and desire a just and stable peace such as can be secured only by removing the chief provocations to war, which this program does not remove. We have no jealousy of German greatness, and there is nothing in this program that impairs it. We grudge her no achievement or distinction of learning or of pacific enterprise such as have made her record very bright and very enviable. We do not wish to injure her or to block in any way her legitimate influence or power. We do not wish to fight her either with arms or with hostile arrangements of trade if she is willing to associate herself with us and the other peace-loving nations of the world in covenants of justice and law and fair dealing. We wish her only to accept a place of equality among the peoples of the world,—the new world in which we now live,—instead of a place of mastery.

Neither do we presume to suggest to her any alteration or modification of her institutions. But it is necessary, we must frankly say, and necessary as a preliminary to any intelligent dealings with her on our part, that we should know whom her spokesmen speak for when they speak to us, whether for the Reichstag majority or for the military party and the men whose creed is imperial domination.

We have spoken now, surely, in terms too concrete to admit of any further doubt or question. An evident principle runs through the whole program I have outlined. It is the principle of justice to all peoples and nationalities, and their right to live on equal terms of liberty and safety with one another, whether they be strong or weak. Unless this principle be made its foundation no part of the structure of international justice can stand. The people of the United States could act upon no other principle; and to the vindication of this principle they are ready to devote their lives, their honor, and everything that they possess. The moral climax of this the culminating and final war for human liberty has come, and they are ready to put their own strength, their own highest purpose, their own integrity and devotion to the test.

Liberalism and World Politics

Michael W. Doyle

Michael Doyle explores the connections and differences inherent in the liberal or idealist traditions as they descended from the writings of Schumpeter, Machiavelli, and Kant. He specifically addresses the traditions of liberal pacifism and liberal imperialism.

Promoting freedom will produce peace, we have often been told. In a speech before the British Parliament in June of 1982, President Reagan proclaimed that governments founded on a respect for individual liberty exercise "restraint" and "peaceful intentions" in their foreign policy. He then announced a "crusade for freedom" and a "campaign for democratic development".[1]

In making these claims the president joined a long list of liberal theorists (and propagandists) and echoed an old argument: the aggressive instincts of authoritarian leaders and totalitarian ruling parties make for war. Liberal states, founded on such individual rights as equality before the law, free speech and other civil liberties, private property, and elected representation are fundamentally against war this argument asserts. When the citizens who bear the burdens of war elect their governments, wars become impossible. Furthermore, citizens appreciate that the benefits of trade can be enjoyed only under conditions of peace. Thus the very existence of liberal states, such as the U.S., Japan, and our European allies, makes for peace.

Building on a growing literature in international political science, I reexamine the liberal claim President Reagan reiterated for us. I look at three distinct theoretical traditions of liberalism, attributable to three theorists: Schumpeter, a brilliant explicator of the liberal pacifism the president invoked; Machiavelli, a classical republican whose glory is an imperialism we often practice; and Kant.

Despite the contradictions of liberal pacifism and liberal imperialism, I find, with Kant and other liberal republicans, that liberalism does leave a coherent legacy on foreign affairs. *Liberal states are different.* They are indeed peaceful, yet they are also prone to make war, as the U.S. and our "freedom fighters" are now doing, not so covertly, against Nicaragua. Liberal states have created a separate peace, as Kant argued they would, and have also discovered liberal reasons for aggression, as he feared they might. I conclude by arguing that the differences among liberal pacifism, liberal imperialism, and Kant's liberal internationalism are not arbitrary but rooted in differing conceptions of the citizen and the state.

LIBERAL PACIFISM

There is no canonical description of liberalism. What we tend to call *liberal* resembles a family portrait of principles and institutions, recognizable by certain characteristics—for example, individual freedom, political participation, private property, and equality of opportunity—that most liberal states share, although none has perfected them all. Joseph Schumpeter clearly fits within this family when he considers the international effects of capitalism and democracy.

---

1. See Ronald Reagan, "Address to Parliament," *The New York Times*, June 9, 1982.

From *American Political Science Review*, Vol. 80, No. 4, December 1986. Reprinted with permission. Italics added.

Schumpeter's "Sociology of Imperialisms," published in 1919, made a coherent and sustained argument concerning the pacifying (in the sense of nonaggressive) effects of liberal institutions and principles.[2] Unlike some of the earlier liberal theorists who focused on a single feature such as trade[3] or failed to examine critically the arguments they were advancing, Schumpeter saw the interaction of capitalism and democracy as the foundation of liberal pacifism, and he tested his arguments in a sociology of historical imperialisms.

He defines *imperialism* as "an objectless disposition on the part of a state to unlimited forcible expansion".[4] Excluding imperialisms that were mere "catchwords" and those that were "object-ful" (e.g., defensive imperialism), he traces the roots of objectless imperialism to three sources, each an atavism. Modern imperialism, according to Schumpeter, resulted from the combined impact of a "war machine," warlike instincts, and export monopolism.

Once necessary, the war machine later developed a life of its own and took control of a state's foreign policy: "Created by the wars that required it, the machine now created the wars it required".[5] Thus, Schumpeter tells us that the army of ancient Egypt, created to drive the Hyksos out of Egypt, took over the state and pursued militaristic imperialism. Like the later armies of the courts of absolutist Europe, it fought wars for the sake of glory and booty, for the sake of warriors and monarchs—wars *gratia* warriors.

A warlike disposition, elsewhere called "instinctual elements of bloody primitivism," is the natural ideology of a war machine. It also exists independently; the Persians, says Schumpeter,[6] were a warrior nation from the outset.

Under modern capitalism, export monopolists, the third source of modern imperialism, push for imperialist expansion as a way to expand their dosed markets. The absolute monarchies were the last clear-cut imperialisms. Nineteenth-century imperialisms merely represent the vestiges of the imperialisms created by Louis XIV and Catherine the Great. Thus, the export monopolists are an atavism of the absolute monarchies, for they depend completely on the tariffs imposed by the monarchs and their militaristic successors for revenue.[7] Without tariffs, monopolies would be eliminated by foreign competition.

Modern (nineteenth century) imperialism, therefore, rests on an atavistic war machine, militaristic attitudes left over from the days of monarchical wars, and export monopolism, which is nothing more than the economic residue of monarchical finance. In the modern era, imperialists gratify their private interests. From the national perspective, their imperialistic wars are objectless.

Schumpeter's theme now emerges. Capitalism and democracy are forces for peace. Indeed, they are antithetical to imperialism. For Schumpeter, the further development of capitalism and democracy means that imperialism will inevitably disappear. He maintains

---

2. See Joseph Schumpeter, *Capitalism, Socialism, and Democracy* (New York: Harper Torchbooks, 1950) and Michael W. Doyle, *Empires* (Ithaca: Cornell University Press, 1986), pp. 155-59.

3. See Charles de Montesquieu, *Spirit of Laws* (New York: Hafner, 1949), vol. 1, bk. 20, chap. 1.

4. See Joseph Schumpeter, "The Sociology of Imperialism," in *Imperialism and Social Classes* (Cleveland: World Publishing Company, 1955), p. 6.

5. Ibid., p. 25.

6. Ibid., pp. 25-32.

7. Ibid., pp. 82-83.

that capitalism produces an unwarlike disposition; its populace is "democratized, individualized, rationalized".[8] The people's energies are daily absorbed in production. The disciplines of industry and the market train people in "economic rationalism"; the instability of industrial life necessitates calculation. Capitalism also "individualizes"; "subjective opportunities" replace the "immutable factors" of traditional, hierarchical society. Rational individuals demand democratic governance.

Democratic capitalism leads to peace. As evidence, Schumpeter claims that throughout the capitalist world an opposition has arisen to "war, expansion, cabinet diplomacy"; that contemporary capitalism is associated with peace parties; and that the industrial worker of capitalism is "vigorously anti-imperialist." In addition, he points out that the capitalist world has developed means of preventing war, such as the Hague Court and that the least feudal, most capitalist society—the United States—has demonstrated the least imperialistic tendencies.[9] An example of the lack of imperialistic tendencies in the U.S., Schumpeter thought, was our leaving over half of Mexico unconquered in the war of 1846-48.

Schumpeter's explanation for liberal pacifism is quite simple: Only war profiteers and military aristocrats gain from wars. No democracy would pursue a minority interest and tolerate the high costs of imperialism. When free trade prevails, "no class" gains from forcible expansion because

> foreign raw materials and food stuffs are as accessible to each nation as though they were in its own territory. Where the cultural backwardness of a region makes normal economic intercourse dependent on colonization it does not matter, assuming free trade, which of the "civilized" nations undertakes the task of colonization.[10]

Schumpeter's arguments are difficult to evaluate. In partial tests of quasiSchumpeterian propositions, Michael Haas[11] discovered a cluster that associates democracy, development, and sustained modernization with peaceful conditions. However, M. Small and J. D. Singer[12] have discovered that there is no clearly negative correlation between democracy and war in the period 1816-1965—the period that would be central to Schumpeter's argument.[13]

Later in his career, in *Capitalism, Socialism, and Democracy,* Schumpeter,[14] acknowledged that "almost purely bourgeois commonwealths were often aggressive when it seemed to pay—like the Athenian or the Venetian commonwealths." Yet he stuck to his pacifistic guns, restating the view that capitalist democracy "steadily tells . . . against the use of military force and for peaceful arrangements, even when the balance of pecuniary advantage is clearly on the side of war which, under modern circumstances, is not in general very likely."[15] A recent study by R. J. Rummel (1983) of "libertarianism" and inter-

---

8. Ibid, p. 68.

9. Ibid, pp. 95-96.

10. Ibid., pp. 75-76.

11. See Michael Haas, *International Conflict* (New York: Bobbs-Merrill, 1974), pp. 464-65.

12. See Melvin Small and J. David Singer, "The War-Proneness of Democratic Regimes," *The Jerusalem Journal of International Relations*, 1(4):50-69.

13. See Johathan Wilkenfeld, "Domestic and Foreign Conflict Behavior of Nations," *Journal of Peace Research*, 5:56-69 and Quincy Wright, *A Study of History* (Princeton: Princeton University Press, 1980), p. 841.

14. See Schumpeter, 1950, pp. 127-28.

15. Ibid., p. 128.

national violence is the closest test Schumpeterian pacifism has received.[16] "Free" states (those enjoying political and economic freedom) were shown to have considerably less conflict at or above the level of economic sanctions than "nonfree" states. The free states, the partly free states (including the democratic socialist countries such as Sweden), and the nonfree states accounted for 24%, 26%, and 61%, respectively, of the international violence during the period examined.

These effects are impressive but not conclusive for the Schumpeterian thesis. The data are limited, in this test, to the period 1976 to 1980. It includes, for example, the Russo-Afghan War, the Vietnamese invasion of Cambodia, China's invasion of Vietnam, and Tanzania's invasion of Uganda but just misses the U.S., quasi-covert intervention in Angola (1975) and our not so covert war against Nicaragua (1981-). More importantly, it excludes the cold war period, with its numerous interventions, and the long history of colonial wars (the Boer War, the Spanish-American War, the Mexican Intervention, etc.) that marked the history of liberal, including democratic capitalist, states.

The discrepancy between the warlike history of liberal states and Schumpeter's pacifistic expectations highlights three extreme assumptions. First, his "materialistic monism" leaves little room for noneconomic objectives, whether espoused by states or individuals. Neither glory, nor prestige, nor ideological justification, nor the pure power of ruling shapes policy. These nonmaterial goals leave little room for positive-sum gains, such as the comparative advantages of trade. Second, and relatedly, the same is true for his states. The political life of individuals seems to have been homogenized at the same time as the individuals were "rationalized, individualized, and democratized." Citizens—capitalists and workers, rural and urban—seek material welfare. Schumpeter seems to presume that ruling makes no difference. He also presumes that no one is prepared to take those measures (such as stirring up foreign quarrels to preserve a domestic ruling coalition) that enhance one's political power, despite detrimental effects on mass welfare. Third, like domestic politics, world politics are homogenized. Materially monistic and democratically capitalist, all states evolve toward free trade and liberty together. Countries differently constituted seem to disappear from Schumpeter's analysis. "Civilized" nations govern "culturally backward" *regions.* These assumptions are not shared by Machiavelli's theory of liberalism.

LIBERAL IMPERIALISM

Machiavelli argues, not only that republics are not pacifistic, but that they are the best form of state for imperial expansion. Establishing a republic fit for imperial expansion is, moreover, the best way to guarantee the survival of a state.

Machiavelli's republic is a classical mixed republic. It is not a democracy—which he thought would quickly degenerate into a tyranny—but is characterized by social equality, popular liberty, and political participation.[17] The consuls serve as "kings," the senate as an aristocracy managing the state, and the people in the assembly as the source of strength.

---

16. See Rudolf J. Rummel, "Libertarianism and International Violence," *Journal of Conflict Resolution,* 27 (1983):27-71.

17. See Niccolo Machiavelli, *The Prince and the Discourses,* Max Lerner, ed., Luigi Ricci and Christian Detmold, trans. (New York: Modern Library, 1950), bk. 1, chap. 2, p. 112. See also Mark Huilung, *Citizen Machiavelli* (Princeton: Princeton University Press, 1983), chap. 2; Harvey C. Mansfield, "Machiavelli's New Regime," *Italian Quarterly,* 13:63-95; J. G. A. Popcock, *The Machiavellian Moment* (Princeton: Princeton University Press, 1975), pp. 198-99; and Quentin Skinner, Machiavelli (New York: Hill and Wang, 1981), chap. 3.

Liberty results from "disunion"—the competition and necessity for compromise required by the division of powers among senate, consuls, and tribunes (the last representing the common people). Liberty also results from the popular veto. The powerful few threaten the rest with tyranny, Machiavelli says, because they seek to dominate. The mass demands not to be dominated, and their veto thus preserves the liberties of the state.[18] However, since the people and the rulers have different social characters, the people need to be "managed" by the few to avoid having their recklessness overturn or their fecklessness undermine the ability of the state to expand.[19] Thus the senate and the consuls plan expansion, consult oracles, and employ religion to manage the resources that the energy of the people supplies.

Strength, and then imperial expansion, results from the way liberty encourages increased population and property, which grow when the citizens know their lives and goods are secure from arbitrary seizure. Free citizens equip large armies and provide soldiers who fight for public glory and the common good because these are, in fact, their own.[20] If you seek the honor of having your state expand, Machiavelli advises, you should organize it as a free and popular republic like Rome, rather than as an aristocratic Republic like Sparta or Venice. Expansion thus calls for a free republic.

"Necessity"—political survival—calls for expansion. If a stable aristocratic republic is forced by foreign conflict "to extend her territory, in such a case we shall see her foundations give way and herself quickly brought to ruin"; if, on the other hand, domestic security prevails, "the continued tranquility would enervate her, or provoke internal dissensions, which together, or either of them separately, will apt to prove her ruin".[21] Machiavelli therefore believes it is necessary to take the constitution of Rome, rather than that of Sparta or Venice, as our model.

Hence, this belief leads to liberal imperialism. We are lovers of glory, Machiavelli announces. We seek to rule or, at least, to avoid being oppressed. In either case, we want more for ourselves and our states than just material-welfare (materialistic monism). Because other states with similar aims thereby threaten us, we prepare ourselves for expansion. Because our fellow citizens threaten us if we do not allow them either to satisfy their ambition or to release their political energies through imperial expansion, we expand.

There is considerable historical evidence for liberal imperialism. Machiavelli's (Polybius's) Rome and Thucydides' Athens both were imperial republics in the Machiavellian sense.[22] The historical record of numerous U.S. interventions in the postwar period supports Machiavelli's argument,[23] but the current record of liberal pacifism, weak as it is, calls some of his insights into question. To the extent that the modern populace actually controls (and thus unbalances) the mixed republic, its diffidence may outweigh elite ("senatorial") aggressiveness.

18. See Machiavelli, bk. 1, chap. 5, p. 122.

19. Ibid., bk. 1, chap. 53, pp. 249-250.

20. Ibid., bk. 2, chap. 2, pp. 287-90.

21. Ibid., bk. 1, chap. 6, p. 129.

22. See Thucydides, *The Peloponnesian War*, Rex Warner, ed. and trans. (Baltimore: Penguin, 1954), bk. 6.

23. See Raymond Aron, *Peace and War: A Theory of International Relations*, Richard Howard and Annette Baker Fox, trans. (Garden City, NY: Doubleday, 1966), chaps. 3-4 and Richard Barnet, *Intervention and Revolution* (Cleveland: World Publishing Co., 1968), chap. 11.

We can conclude either that (1) liberal pacifism has at least taken over with the further development of capitalist democracy, as Schumpeter predicted it would or that (2) the mixed record of liberalism—pacifism and imperialism—indicates that some liberal states are Schumpeterian democracies while others are Machiavellian republics. Before we accept either conclusion, however, we must consider a third apparent regularity of modern world politics.

LIBERAL INTERNATIONALISM

Modern liberalism carries with it two legacies. They do not affect liberal states separately, according to whether they are pacifistic or imperialistic, but simultaneously.

The first of these legacies is the pacification of foreign relations among liberal states.[24] During the nineteenth century, the United States and Great Britain engaged in nearly continual strife; however, after the Reform Act of 1832 defined actual representation as the formal source of the sovereignty of the British parliament, Britain and the United States negotiated their disputes. They negotiated despite, for example, British grievances during the Civil War against the North's blockade of the South, with which Britain had close economic ties. Despite severe Anglo-French colonial rivalry, liberal France and liberal Britain formed an entente against illiberal Germany before World War I. And from 1914 to 1915, Italy, the liberal member of the Triple Alliance with Germany and Austria, chose not to fulfill its obligations under that treaty to support its allies. Instead, Italy joined in an alliance with Britain and France, which prevented it from having to fight other liberal states and then declared war on Germany and Austria. Despite generations of Anglo-American tension and Britain's wartime restrictions on American trade with Germany, the United States leaned toward Britain and France from 1914 to 1917 before entering World War I on their side.Beginning in the eighteenth century and slowly growing since then, a zone of peace, which Kant called the "pacific federation" or "pacific union," has begun to be established among liberal societies. More than 40 liberal states currently make up the union. Most are in Europe and North America, but they can be found on every continent as Table 1 indicates.

Here the predictions of liberal pacifists (and President Reagan) are borne out: liberal states do exercise peaceful restraint, and a separate peace exists among them. This separate peace provides a solid foundation for the United States' crucial alliances with the liberal powers, e.g., the North Atlantic Treaty Organization and our Japanese alliance. This foundation appears to be impervious to the quarrels with our allies that bedeviled the Carter and Reagan administrations. It also offers the promise of a continuing peace among liberal states, and as the number of liberal states increases, it announces the possibility of global peace this side of the grave or world conquest.

---

24. Clarence Streit, *Union Now: A Proposal for a Federal Union of the Leading Democracies* (New York: Harpers, 1938), pp. 88, 90-92 seems to have been the first to point out (in contemporary foreign relations) the empirical tendency of democracies to maintain peace among themselves, and he made this the foundation of his proposal for a (nonKantian) federal union of the 15 leading democracies of the 1930s. In a very interesting book, Ferdinand A. Hermens, *The Tyrants' War and the People's Peace* (Chicago: University of Chicago Press, 1944) explored some of the policy implications of Streit's analysis. Dean V. Babst, "A Force for Peace," *Industrial Research*, 14 (April 1972):55-58 performed a quantitative study of this phenomenon of "democratic peace," and Rudolf J. Rummel (1983) did a similar study of "libertarianism" (in the sense of laissez faire) focusing on the postwar period that drew on an unpublished study (Project No. 48) noted in Appendix 1 of his *Understanding Conflict and War*, 5 vols. (Beverly Hills: Sage Publications, 1979), p. 386. I use the term *liberal* in a wider, Kantian sense in my discussion of this issue (see Michael W. Doyle, "Kant, Liberal Legaxies, and Foreign Affairs: Part I," *Philosophy and Public Affairs*, 12 (1983):205-35). In that essay I survey the period from 1790 to the present and find no war among liberal states.

Of course, the probability of the outbreak of war in any given year between any two given states is low. The occurrence of a war between any two adjacent states, considered over a long period of time, would be more probable. The apparent absence of war between liberal states, whether adjacent or not, for almost 200 years thus may have significance. Similar claims cannot be made for feudal, fascist, communist, authoritarian, or totalitarian forms of rule,[25] nor for pluralistic or merely similar societies. More significant perhaps is that when states are forced to decide on which side of an impending world war they will fight, liberal states all wind up on the same side despite the complexity of the paths that take them there. These characteristics do not prove that the peace among liberals is statistically significant nor that liberalism is the sole valid explanation for the peace.[26] They do suggest that we consider the possibility that liberals have indeed established a separate peace—but only among themselves.

Liberalism also carries with it a second legacy: international "imprudence".[27] Peaceful restraint only seems to work in liberals' relations with other liberals. Liberal states have fought numerous wars with nonliberal states. (For a list of international wars since 1816 see Table 2.)

Many of these wars have been defensive and thus prudent by necessity. Liberal states have been attacked and threatened by nonliberal states that do not exercise any special restraint in their dealings with the liberal states. Authoritarian rulers both stimulate and respond to an international political environment in which conflicts of prestige, interest, and pure fear of what other states might do all lead states toward war. War and conquest have thus characterized the careers of many authoritarian rulers and ruling parties, from Louis XIV and Napoleon to Mussolini's fascists, Hitler's Nazis, and Stalin's communists.

Yet we cannot simply blame warfare on the authoritarians or totalitarians, as many of our more enthusiastic politicians would have us do.[28] Most wars arise out of calculations and miscalculations of interest, misunderstandings, and mutual suspicions, such as those that characterized the origins of World War I. However, aggression by the liberal state has also characterized a large number of wars. Both France and Britain fought expansionist colonial wars throughout the nineteenth century. The United States fought a similar war with Mexico from 1846 to 1848, waged a war of annihilation against the American Indians, and intervened militarily against sovereign states many times before and after World War II. Liberal states invade weak nonliberal states and display striking distrust in dealings with powerful nonliberal states.[29]

Neither realist (statist) nor Marxist theory accounts well for these two legacies. While they can account for aspects of certain periods of international stability,[30] neither the logic of the balance of power nor the logic of international hegemony explains the separate peace maintained for more than 150 years among states sharing one particular form of governance—liberal principles and institutions. Balance of power theory expects—indeed is premised upon—flexible arrangements of geostrategic rivalry that include preventive war.

---

25. See Doyle, 1983: 222.

26. Dean V. Babst, "A Force for Peace," *Industrial Research*, 14 (April 1972):56 did make a preliminary test of the significance of the distribution of alliance partners in World War I. He found that the possibility that the actual distribution of alliance partners could have occurred by chance was less than 1%. However, this assumes that there was an equal possibility that any two nations could have gone to war with each other, and this is a strong assumption. Rummel (1983) has a further discussion of the issue of statistical significance as it applies to his libertarian thesis.

27. See David Hume, "Of the Balance of Power," in *Essays: Moral, Political, and Literary* (Oxford: Oxford University Press, 1963), pp. 346-47.

Table 2. International Wars Listed Chronologically

British-Maharattan (1817-1818)	Franco-Prussian (1870-1871)	Chaco (1932-1935)
Greek (1821-1828)	Dutch-Achinese (1873-1878)	Italo-Ethiopian (1935-1936)
Franco-Spanish (1823)	Balkan (1875-1877)	Sino-Japanese (1937-1941)
First Anglo-Burmese(1823-1826)	Russo-Turkish (1877-1878)	Changkufeng (1938)
Javanese (1825-1830)	Bosnian (1878)	Nomohan (1939)
Russo-Persian (1826-1828)	Second British-Afghan (1878-1880)	World War II (1939-1945)
Russo-Turkish (1828-1829)	Pacific (1879-1883)	Russo-Finnish (1939-1940)
First Polish (1831)	British-Zulu (1879)	Franco-Thai (1940-1941)
First Syrian (1831-1832)	Franco-Indochinese (1882-1884)	Indonesian (1945-1946)
Texas (1835-1836)	Mahdist (1882-1885)	Indochinese (1945-1954)
First British-Afghan (1838-1842)	Sino-French (1884-1885)	Madagascan (1947-1948)
Second Syrian (1839-1840)	Central American (1885)	First Kashmir (1947-1949)
Franco-Algerian (1839-1847)	Serbo-Bulgarian (1885)	Palestine (1948-1949)
Peruvian-Bolivian (1841)	Sino-Japanese (1894-1895)	Hyderabad (1948)
First British-Sikh (1845-1846)	Franco-Madagascan (1894-1895)	Korean (1950-1953)
Mexican-American (1846-1848)	Cuban (1895-1898)	Algerian (1954-1962)
Austro-Sardinian (1848-1849)	Italo-Ethiopian (1895-1896)	Russo-Hungarian (1956)
First Schleswig-Holstein (1848-1849)	First Philippine (1896-1898)	Sinai (1956)
Hungarian (1848-1849)	Greco-Turkish (1897)	Tibetan (1956-1959)
Second British-Sikh (1848-1849)	Spanish-American (1898)	Sino-Indian (1962)
Roman Republic (1849)	Second Philippine (1899-1902)	Vietnamese (1965-1975)
La Plata (1851-1852)	Boer (1899-1902)	Second Kashmir (1965)
First Turco-Montenegran (1852-1853)	Boxer Rebellion (1900)	Six Day (1967)
Crimean (1853-1856)	Ilinden (1903)	Israeli-Egyptian (1969-1970)
Anglo-Persian (1856-1857)	Russo-Japanese (1904-1905)	Football (1969)
Sepoy (1857-1859)	Central American (1906)	Bangladesh (1971)
Second Turco-Montenegran (1858-1859)	Central American (1907)	Philippine-MNLF (1972-)
Italian Unification (1859)	Spanish-Moroccan (1909-1910)	Yom Kippur (1973)
Spanish-Moroccan (1859-1860)	Italo-Turkish (1911-1912)	Turco-Cypriot (1974)
Italo-Roman (1860)	First Balkan (1912-1913)	Ethiopian-Eritrean (1974-)
Italo-Sicilian (1860-1861)	Second Balkan (1913)	Vietnamese-Cambodian (1975-)
Franco-Mexican (1862-1867)	World War I (1914-1918)	Timor (1975-)
Ecuadorian-Colombian (1863)	Russian Nationalities (1917-1921)	Saharan (1975-)
Second Polish (1863-1864)	Russo-Polish (1919-1920)	Ogaden (1976-)
Spanish-Santo Dominican (1863-1865)	Hungarian-Allies (1919)	Ugandan-Tanzanian (1978-1979)
Second Schleswig-Holstein (1864)	Greco-Turkish (1919-1922)	Sino-Vietnamese (1979)
Lopez (1864-1870)	Riffian (1921-1926)	Russo-Afghan (1979-)
Spanish-Chilean (1865-1866)	Druze (1925-1927)	Iran-Iraqui (1980-)
Seven Weeks (1866)	Sino-Soviet (1929)	
Ten Years (1868-1878)	Manchurian (1931-1933)	

Note: This table is taken from Melvin Small and J. David Singer: *Resort to Arms* (Beverly Hills: Sage Publications, 1982, pp. 79–80. This is a partial list of international wars fought between 1816 and 1980. In Appendices A and B, Small and Singer identify a total of 575 wars during this period, but approximately 159 of them appear to be largely domestic, or civil wars.

This list excludes covert interventions, some of which have been directed by liberal regimes against other liberal regimes—for example, the United States' effort to destabilize the Chilean elections and Allende's government. Nonetheless, it is significant that such interventions are not pursued publicly as acknowledged policy. The covert destabilization campaign against Chile is recounted by the Senate Select Committee to Study Governmental Operations with Respect to Intelligence Activities (1975, Covert Action in Chile, 1963–73)

Following the argument of this article, this list also excludes civil wars. Civil wars differ from international wars, not in the ferocity of combat, but in the issues that engender them. Two nations that could abide one another as independent neighbors separated by a border might well be the fiercest enemies if forced to live together in one state, jointly deciding how to raise and spend taxes, choose leaders, and legislate fundamental questions of value. Notwithstanding these differences, no civil wars that I recall upset the argument of liberal pacification.

Hegemonies wax and wane, but the liberal peace holds. Marxist "ultra-imperialists" expect a form of peaceful rivalry among capitalists, but only liberal capitalists maintain peace. Leninists expect liberal capitalists to be aggressive toward nonliberal states, but they also (and especially) expect them to be imperialistic toward fellow liberal capitalists.

Kant's theory of liberal internationalism helps us understand these two legacies. The importance of Immanuel Kant as a theorist of international ethics has been well appreciated,[31] but Kant also has an important analytical theory of international politics. *Perpetual Peace,* written in 1795,[32] helps us understand the interactive nature of international relations. Kant tries to teach us methodologically that we can study neither the systemic relations of states nor the varieties of state behavior in isolation from each other. Substantively, he anticipates for us the ever-widening pacification of a liberal pacific union, explains this pacification, and at the same time suggest why liberal states are not pacific in their relations with nonliberal states. Kant argues that perpetual peace will be guaranteed by the ever-widening acceptance of three "definitive articles" of peace. When

---

28. There are serious studies showing that Marxist regimes have higher military spending per capita than non-Marxist regimes (see James Payne, "Marxism and Militarism," *Polity,* forthcoming, but this should not be interpreted as a sign of the inherent agressiveness of authoritarian or totalitarian governments or of the inherent and global peacefulness of liberal regimes. Marxist regimes, in particular, represent a minority in the current international system; they are strategically encircles, and due to their lack of domestic legitimacy, they might be said to "suffer" the twin burden of needing defenses against both external and internal enemies. Stanislav Andreski, "On the Peaceful Disposition of Military Dictatorships," *Journal of Strategic Studies,* 3 (1980):3-10, moreover, argues that (purely) military dictatorships, due to their domestic fragility, have little incentive to engage in foreign military adventures. According to Walter C. Clemens, "The Superpowers and the Third World," in Charles Kegley and Pat McGowan, eds., *Foreign Policy: USA/USSR* (Beverly Hills: Sage Publications, 1982): 117-18, the United States intervened in the Third World more than twice as often during the period 1946-1976 as the Soviet Union did in 1946-79. Relatedly, Barry Posen and Stephen VanEvera in "Overarming and Underwhelming," *Foreign Policy,* 40 (1980):105 and in "Reagan Administration Defense Policy," in Kenneth Oye, Robert Lieber, and Donald Rothchild, eds., *Eagle Defiant* (Boston: Little Brown, 1983): pp. 86-89, found that the United States devoted one quarter and the Soviet Union one tenth of their defense budgets to forces designed for Third World interventions (where responding to perceived threats would presumably have a less than purely defensive character).

29. See Michael W. Doyle, "Kant, Liberal Legacies, and Foreign Affairs: Part 2," *Philosophy and Public Affairs,* 12 (1983):323-35.

30. See Aron, 1966, pp. 151-54 and Bruce Russett, "The Mysterious Case of Vanishing Hegemony," *International Organization,* 39 (1985):207-31.

31. See A. C. Armstrong, "Kant's Philosophy of Peace and War," *The Journal of Philosophy,* 28 (1931):197-204; Karl Friedrich, *Inevitable Peace* (Cambridge, MA: Harvard University Press, 1948); W. B. Gallie, *Philosophers of Peace and War* (Cambridge: Cambridge University Press, 1978), chap. 1; William Galston, *Kant and the Problem of History* (Chicago: Chicago University Press, 1975); Pierre Hassner, "Immanuel Kant," in Leo Strauss and Joseph Cropsey, eds., *History of Political Philosophy* (Chicago: Rand McNally, 1972); F. H. Hinsley, "Power and the Pursuit of Peace," in Stanley Hoffmann, ed., *The State of War* (New York: Praeger, 1967), chap. 4; Stanley Hoffmann, "Rousseau on War and Peace," in Hoffmann, pp. 45-87; Kenneth Waltz, "Kant, Liberalism, and War," *American Political Science Review,* 56 (1962):331-40; and Howard Williams, *Kant's Political Philosophy* (Oxford: Basil Blackwell, 1983).

32. See Immanuel Kant, *Kant's Political Writings,* Hans Reiss, ed. H. B. Nisbet, trans. (Cambridge: Cambridge University Press, 1970), pp. 93-130. All citations from Kant are from *Kant's Political Writings.* The works discussed and the abbreviations by which they are identified in the text are as follows: *PP Perpetual Peace* (1795); *UH The Idea for a Universal History with a Cosmopolitan Purpose* (1784); *CF The Contest of Faculties* (1798); *MM The Metaphysics of Morals* (1797).

all nations have accepted the definitive articles in a metaphorical "treaty" of perpetual peace he asks them to sign, perpetual peace will have been established.

The First Definitive Article requires the civil constitution of the state to be republican. By *republican* Kant means a political society that has solved the problem of combining moral autonomy, individualism, and social order. A private property and market-oriented economy partially addressed that dilemma in the private sphere. The public, or political, sphere was more troubling. His answer was a republic that preserved juridical freedom—the legal equality of citizens as subjects—on the basis of a representative government with a separation of powers. Juridical freedom is preserved because the morally autonomous individual is by means of representation a self-legislator making laws that apply to all citizens equally, including himself or herself. Tyranny is avoided because the individual is subject to laws he or she does not also administer.[33]

Liberal republics will progressively establish peace among themselves by means of the pacific federation, or union *(foedus pacificum),* described in Kant's Second Definitive Article. The pacific union will establish peace within a federation of free states and securely maintain the rights of each state. The world will not have achieved the "perpetual peace" that provides the ultimate guarantor of republican freedom until "a late stage and after many unsuccessful attempts". [34] At that time, all nations will have learned the lessons of peace through right conceptions of the appropriate constitution, great and sad experience, and good will. Only then will individuals enjoy perfect republican rights or the full guarantee of a global and just peace. In the meantime, the "pacific federation" of liberal republics—"an enduring and gradually expanding federation likely to prevent war"—brings within it more and more republics—despite republican collapses, backsliding, and disastrous wars—creating an ever-expanding separate peace .[35] Kant emphasizes that

> it can be shown that this idea of federalism, extending gradually to encompass all states and thus leading to perpetual peace, is practicable and has objective reality. For if by good fortune one powerful and enlightened nation can form a republic (which is by nature inclined to seek peace), this will provide a focal point for federal association among other states. These will join up with the first one, thus securing the freedom of each state in accordance with the idea of international right, and the whole will gradually spread further and further by a series of alliances of this kind.[36]

The pacific union is not a single peace treaty ending one war, a world state, nor a state of nations. Kant finds the first insufficient. The second and third are impossible or potentially tyrannical. National sovereignty precludes reliable subservience to a state of nations; a world state destroys the civic freedom on which the development of human capacities rests.[37] Although Kant obliquely refers to various classical interstate confederations and modern diplomatic congresses, he develops no systematic organizational embodiment of this treaty and presumably does not find institutionalization necessary.[38]

---

33. Kant, *PP,* pp. 99-102 and Patrick Riley, *Kant's Political Philosophy* (Totowa, NJ: Rowman and Littlefield, 1983), chap. 5.

34. Kant, *UH,* p. 47.

35. Kant, *PP,* p. 105.

36. Ibid, p. 104.

37. Kant, *UH,* p. 50.

He appears to have in mind a mutual nonaggression pact, perhaps a collective security agreement, and the cosmopolitan law set forth in the Third Definitive Article.[39]

The Third Definitive Article establishes a cosmopolitan law to operate in conjunction with the pacific union. The cosmopolitan law "shall be limited to conditions of universal hospitality." In this Kant calls for the recognition of the "right of a foreigner not to be treated with hostility when he arrives on someone else's territory." This "does not extend beyond those conditions which make it possible for them [foreigners] to attempt to enter into relations [commerce] with the native inhabitants".[40] Hospitality does not require extending to foreigners either the right to citizenship or the right to settlement, unless the foreign visitor would perish if they were expelled. Foreign conquest and plunder also find no justification under this right. Hospitality does appear to include the right of access and the obligation of maintaining the opportunity for citizens to exchange goods and ideas without imposing the obligation to trade (a voluntary act in all cases under liberal constitutions).

Perpetual peace, for Kant, is an epistemology, a condition for ethical action, and, most importantly, an explanation of how the "mechanical process of nature visibly exhibits the purposive plan of producing concord among men, even against their will and indeed by means of their very discord".[41] Understanding history requires an epistemological foundation, for without a teleology, such as the promise of perpetual peace, the complexity of history would overwhelm human understanding.[42] Perpetual peace, however, is not merely a heuristic device with which to interpret history. It is guaranteed, Kant explains in the "First Addition" to *Perpetual Peace* ("On the Guarantee of Perpetual Peace"), to result from men fulfilling their ethical duty or, failing that, from a hidden plan.[43] Peace is an ethical duty because it is only under conditions of peace that all men can treat each other as ends, rather than means to an end.[44] In order for this duty to be practical, Kant needs, of course,

---

38. See Riley, chap. 5 and Wolfgang Schwarz, "Kant's Philosophy of Law and International Peace," *Philosophy and Phenomenonological Research*, 23(1962):71-80.

39. Kant's *foedus pacificum* is thus neither a *pactum pacis* (a single peace treaty) nor a *civitas gentium* (a world state). He appears to have anticipated something like a less formally institutionalized League of Nations or United Nations. One could argue that in practice, these two institutions worked for liberal states and only for liberal states, but no specifically liberal "pacific union" was institutionalized. Instead, liberal states have behaved for the past 180 years as if such a Kantian pacific union and treaty of perpetual peace had been signed.

40. Kant, *PP*, p. 106.

41. Ibid, p. 108 and Kant, *UH*, pp. 44-45.

42. Kant, *UH*, pp. 51-53.

43. In the *Metaphysics of Morals (the Rechtslehre)* Kant seems to write as if perpetual peace is only an epistemological device and, while an ethical duty, is empirically merely a "pious hope" (*MM*, pp. 164-75)—though even here he finds that the pacific union is not "impracticable (*MM*, p. 171). In the *Universal History (UH)*, Kant writes as if the brute force of physical nature drives men toward inevitable peace. Yirmiahu Yovel, *Kant and the Philsophy of History* (Princeton: Princeton University Press, 1980), pp. 168 ff. argues that from a post-critical (post-*Critique of Judgment*) perspective, *Perpetual Peace* reconciles the two views of history. "Nature" is human-created nature (culture or civilization). Perpetual peace is the "*a priori* of the *a posteriori*"—a critical perspective that then enables us to discern causal, probabilistic patterns in history. Law and the "political technology" of republican constitutionalism are separate from ethical development, but both interdependently lead to perpetual peace—the first through force, fear, and self-interest; the second through progressive enlightenment—and both together lead to perpetual peace through the widening of the circumstances in which engaging in right conduct poses smaller and smaller burdens.

to show that peace is in fact possible. The widespread sentiment of approbation that he saw aroused by the early success of the French revolutionaries showed him that we can indeed be moved by ethical sentiments with a cosmopolitan reach.[45] This does not mean, however, that perpetual peace is certain ("prophesiable"). Even the scientifically regular course of the planets could be changed by a wayward comet striking them out of orbit. Human freedom requires that we allow for much greater reversals in the course of history. We must, in fact, anticipate the possibility of backsliding and destructive wars—though these will serve to educate nations to the importance of peace.[46]

In the end, however, our guarantee of perpetual peace does not rest on ethical conduct. As Kant emphasizes,

> we now come to the essential question regarding the prospect of perpetual peace. What does nature do in relation to the end which man's own reason prescribes to him as a duty, i.e. how does nature help to promote his *moral purpose?* And how does nature guarantee that what man ought to do by the laws of his freedom (but does not do) will in fact be done through nature's compulsion, without prejudice to the free agency of man? . . . This does not mean that nature imposes on us a duty to do it, for duties can only be imposed by practical reason. On the contrary, nature does it herself, whether we are willing or not: *facta volentem ducunt. nolentem tradunt.* [47]

The guarantee thus rests, Kant argues, not on the probable behavior of moral angels, but on that of "devils, so long as they possess understanding".[48] In explaining the sources of each of the three definitive articles of the perpetual peace, Kant then tells us how we (as free and intelligent devils) could be motivated by fear, force, and calculated advantage to undertake a course of action whose outcome we could reasonably anticipate to be perpetual peace. Yet while it is possible to conceive of the Kantian road to peace in these terms, Kant himself recognizes and argues that social evolution also makes the conditions of moral behavior less onerous and hence more likely.[49] In tracing the effects of both political and moral development, he builds an account of why liberal states do maintain peace among themselves and of how it will (by implication, has) come about that the pacific union will expand. He also explains how these republics would engage in wars with nonrepublics and therefore suffer the "sad experience" of wars that an ethical policy might have avoided.

The first source of the three definitive articles derives from a political evolution—from a constitutional law. Nature (providence) has seen to it that human beings can live in all the regions where they have been driven to settle by wars. (Kant, who once taught geography, reports on the Lapps, the Samoyeds, the Pescheras.) "Asocial sociability" draws men together to fulfill needs for security and material welfare as it drives them into conflicts over the distribution and control of social products.[50] This violent natural evolu-

---

44. Kant, *UH*, p. 50 and Jeffrie Murphy, *Kant: The Philosophy of Right* (New York: St. Martins, 1970), chap. 3.

45. Kant, *CF*, pp. 181-82 and Yovel, pp. 153-54.

46. Kant, *UH*, pp. 47-48.

47. Kant, *PP*, p. 112.

48. Ibid.

49. Kant, *CF*, pp. 187-89 and George A. Kelley, *Idealism, Politics, and History* (Cambridge: Cambridge University Press, 1969), pp. 106-13.

50. Kant, *UH*, pp. 44-45; PP, pp. 110-11.

tion tends towards the liberal peace because "asocial sociability" inevitably leads toward republican governments, and republican governments are a source of the liberal peace.

Republican representation and separation of powers are produced because they are the means by which the state is "organized well" to prepare for and meet foreign threats (by unity) and to tame the ambitions of selfish and aggressive individuals (by authority derived from representation, by general laws, and by nondespotic administration).[51] States that are not organized in this fashion fail. Monarchs thus encourage commerce and private property in order to increase national wealth. They cede rights of representation to their subjects in order to strengthen their political support or to obtain willing grants of tax revenue.[52]

Kant shows how republics, once established, lead to peaceful relations. he argues that once the aggressive interests of absolutist monarchies are tamed and the habit of respect for individual rights engrained by republican government, wars would appear as the disaster to the people's welfare that he and the other liberals thought them to be. The fundamental reason is this:

> If, as is inevitability the case under this constitution, the consent of the citizens is required to decide whether or not war should be declared, it is very natural that they will have a great hesitation in embarking on so dangerous an enterprise. For this would mean calling down on themselves all the miseries of war, such as doing the fighting themselves, supplying the costs of the war from their own resources, painfully making good the ensuing devastation, and, as the crowning evil, having to take upon themselves a burden of debts which will embitter peace itself and which can never be paid off on account of the constant threat of new wars. But under a constitution where the subject is not a citizen, and which is therefore not republican, it is the simplest thing in the world to go to war. For the head of state is not a fellow citizen, but the owner of the state and war will not force him to make the slightest sacrifice so far as his banquets, hunts, pleasure palaces and court festivals are concerned. He can thus decide on war, without any significant reason, as a kind of amusement, and unconcernedly leave it to the diplomatic corps (who are always ready for such purposes) to justify the war for the sake of propriety.[53]

Yet these domestic republican restraints do not end war. If they did, liberal states would not be warlike, which is far from the case. They do introduce republican caution—Kant's "hesitation"—in place of monarchical caprice. Liberal wars are only fought for popular, liberal purposes, The historical liberal legacy is laden with popular wars fought to promote freedom, to protect private property, or to support liberal allies against nonliberal enemies. Kant's position is ambiguous. He regards these wars as unjust and warns liberals of their susceptibility to them.[54] At the same time, Kant argues that each nation "can and ought to" demand that its neighboring nations enter into the pacific union of liberal states.[55] Thus to see how the pacific union removes the occasion of wars among liberal states and not wars between liberal and nonliberal states, we need to shift our attention from constitutional law to international law, Kant's second source.

Complementing the constitutional guarantee of caution, international law adds a second source for the definitive articles: a guarantee of respect. The separation of nations that

---

51. Kant, *PP*, pp. 112-13.

52. Hassner, pp. 583-86.

53. Kant, *PP*, p. 100.

54. Ibid., p. 106.

55. Ibid, p. 102.

asocial sociability encourages is reinforced by the development of separate languages and religions. These further guarantee a world of separate states—an essential condition needed to avoid a "global, soul-less despotism." Yet, at the same time, they also morally integrate liberal states: "as culture grows and men gradually move towards greater agreement over their principles, they lead to mutual understanding and peace".[56] As republics emerge (the first source) and culture progresses, an understanding of the legitimate rights of all citizens and of all republics comes into play; and this, now that caution characterizes policy, sets up the moral foundations for the liberal peace. Correspondingly, international law highlights the importance of Kantian publicity. Domestically, publicity helps ensure that the officials of republics act according to the principles they profess to hold just and according to the interests of the electors they claim to represent. Internationally, free speech and the effective communication of accurate conceptions of the political life of foreign peoples is essential to establishing and preserving the understanding on which the guarantee of respect depends. Domestically just republics, which rest on consent, then presume foreign republics also to be consensual, just, and therefore deserving of accommodation. The experience of cooperation helps engender further cooperative behavior when the consequences of state policy are unclear but (potentially) mutually beneficial. At the same time, liberal states assume that nonliberal states, which do not rest on free consent, are not just. Because nonliberal governments are in a state of aggression with their own people, their foreign relations become for liberal governments deeply suspect. In short, fellow liberals benefit from a presumption of amity; nonliberals suffer from a presumption of enmity. Both presumptions may be accurate; each, however, may also be self-confirming.

Lastly, cosmopolitan law adds material incentives to moral commitments. The cosmopolitan right to hospitality permits the "spirit of commerce" sooner or later to take hold of every nation, thus impelling states to promote peace and to try to avert war. Liberal economic theory holds that these cosmopolitan ties derive from a cooperative international division of labor and free trade according to comparative advantage. Each economy is said to be better off than it would have been under autarky; each thus acquires an incentive to avoid policies that would lead the other to break these economic ties. Because keeping open markets rests upon the assumption that the next set of transactions will also be determined by prices rather than coercion, a sense of mutual security is vital to avoid security-motivated searches for economic autarky. Thus, avoiding a challenge to another liberal state's security or even enhancing each other's security by means of alliance naturally follows economic interdependence.

A further cosmopolitan source of liberal peace is the international market's removal of difficult decisions of production and distribution from the direct sphere of state policy. A foreign state thus does not appear directly responsible for these outcomes, and states can stand aside from, and to some degree above, these contentious market rivalries and be ready to step in to resolve crises. The interdependence of commerce and the international contacts of state officials help create crosscutting transnational ties that serve as lobbies for mutual accommodation. According to modern liberal scholars international financiers and transnational and transgovernmental organizations create interests in favor of accommodation. Moreover, their variety has ensured that no single conflict sours an entire relationship by setting off a spiral of reciprocated retaliation.[57] Conversely, a sense of suspicion, such as that characterizing relations between liberal and nonliberal governments, can lead to restrictions on the range of

56. Ibid., p. 104.

contacts between societies, and this can increase the prospect that a single conflict will determine an entire relationship.

No single constitutional, international, or cosmopolitan source is alone sufficient, but together (and only together) they plausibly connect the characteristics of liberal polities and economies with sustained liberal peace. Alliances founded on mutual strategic interest among liberal and nonliberal states have been broken; economic ties between liberal and nonliberal states have proven fragile; but the political bonds of liberal rights and interests have proven a remarkably firm foundation for mutual nonaggression. A separate peace exists among liberal states.

In their relations with nonliberal states, however, liberal states have not escaped from the insecurity caused by anarchy in the world political system considered as a whole. Moreover, the very constitutional restraint, international respect for individual rights, and shared commercial interests that establish grounds for peace among liberal states establish grounds for additional conflict in relations between liberal and nonliberal societies.

CONCLUSION

Kant's liberal internationalism, Machiavelli's liberal imperialism, and Schumpeter's liberal pacifism rest on fundamentally different views of the nature of the human being, the state, and international relations.[58] Schumpeter's humans are rationalized, individualized, and democratized. They are also homogenized, pursuing material interests "monistically." Because their material interests lie in peaceful trade, they and the democratic state that these fellow citizens control are pacifistic. Machiavelli's citizens are splendidly diverse in their goals but fundamentally unequal in them as well, seeking to rule or fearing being dominated. Extending the rule of the dominant elite or avoiding the political collapse of their state, each calls for imperial expansion.

Kant's citizens, too, are diverse in their goals and individualized and rationalized, but most importantly, they are capable of appreciating the moral equality of all individuals and of treating other individuals as ends rather than as means. The Kantian state thus is governed publicly according to law, as a republic. Kant's is the state that solves the problem of governing individualized equals, whether they are the "rational devils" he says we often find ourselves to be or the ethical agents we can and should become. Republics tell us that

> in order to organize a group of rational beings who together require universal laws for their survival, but of whom each separate individual is secretly inclined to exempt himself from them, the constitution must be so designed so that although the citizens are opposed to one another in their private attitudes, these opposing views may inhibit one another in such a way that the public conduct of the citizens will be the same, as if they did not have such evil attitudes.[59]

Unlike Machiavelli's republics, Kant's republics are capable of achieving peace among themselves because they exercise democratic caution and are capable of appreciating the international rights of foreign republics. These international rights of republics

---

57. See Zbigniew Brzezinzki and Samuel Huntington, *Political Power: USA/USSR* (New York: Viking Press, 1963), chap. 9; Robert Keohane and Joseph Nye, *Power and Interdependence* (Boston: Little Brown, 1977), chap. 7; Richard Neustadt, *Alliance Politics* (New York: Columbia University Press, 1970); and Karl Polanyi, *The Great Transformation* (Boston: Beacon Press, 1944), chaps. 1-2.

58. For a comparative discussion of the political foundations of Kant's ideas, see Shklar (1984, pp. 232-38).

59. Kant, pp, p. 113.

derive from the representation of foreign individuals, who are our moral equals. Unlike Schumpeter's capitalist democracies, Kant's republics—including our own—remain in a state of war with nonrepublics. Liberal republics see themselves as threatened by aggression from nonrepublics that are not constrained by representation. Even though wars often cost more than the economic return they generate, liberal republics also are prepared to protect and promote—sometimes forcibly—democracy, private property, and the rights of individuals overseas against nonrepublics, which, because they do not authentically represent the rights of individuals, have no rights to noninterference. These wars may liberate oppressed individuals overseas; they also can generate enormous suffering.

Preserving the legacy of the liberal peace without succumbing to the legacy of liberal imprudence is both a moral and a strategic challenge. The bipolar stability of the international system, and the near certainty of mutual devastation resulting from a nuclear war between the superpowers, have created a "crystal ball effect" that has helped to constrain the tendency toward miscalculation present at the outbreak of so many wars in the past.[60] However, this "nuclear peace" appears to be limited to the superpowers. It has not curbed military interventions in the Third World. Moreover, it is subject to a desperate technological race designed to overcome its constraints and to crises that have pushed even the superpowers to the brink of war. We must still reckon with the war fevers and moods of appeasement that have almost alternately swept liberal democracies.

Yet restraining liberal imprudence, whether aggressive or passive, may not be possible without threatening liberal pacification. Improving the strategic acumen of our foreign policy calls for introducing steadier strategic calculations of the national interest in the long run and more flexible responses to changes in the international political environment. Constraining the indiscriminate meddling of our foreign interventions calls for a deeper appreciation of the "particularism of history, culture, and membership,"[61] but both the improvement in strategy and the constraint on intervention seem, in turn, to require an executive freed from the restraints of a representative legislature in the management of foreign policy and a political culture indifferent to the universal rights of individuals. These conditions, in their turn, could break the chain of constitutional guarantees, the respect for representative government, and the web of transnational contact that have sustained the pacific union of liberal states.

Perpetual peace, Kant says, is the end point of the hard journey his republics will take. The promise of perpetual peace, the violent lessons of war, and the experience of a partial peace are proof of the need for and the possibility of world peace. They are also the grounds for moral citizens and statesmen to assume the duty of striving for peace.

---

60. See Albert Carnesale, et. al., *Living With Nuclear Weapons* (New York: Bantam, 1983), p. 43 and Kenneth Waltz, "The Stability of a Bipolar World," *Daedalus*, 93 (1964):881-90.

61. Michael Walzer. *Spheres of Justice* (New York: Basic Books, 1983). p.5.

Chapter Two

Security Lens

Introduction to Security Lens

"The Security Lens"

SECURITY AS A LENS FOR VIEWING INTERNATIONAL RELATIONS

Looking through the Security Lens, we view international relations as a system. A systems approach presumes that the causes of state behavior are external to the state; for example, other states, alliances, or the international economic system. The ***Security Lens*** (like the ***International Political Economy Lens*** you will study later) is a systems-level approach for studying international relations. This approach assumes that actors in the international system are unitary and rational. Conversely, and as the name suggests, the ***Sub-systemic Lens*** assumes that internal factors are the principal cause of state behavior. In some scholarly writings this delineation is not always readily apparent. While scholars generally subscribe to specific conceptual lenses (e.g., Hans Morgenthau and realism), their writings do not always limit themselves entirely to either a systemic or a sub-systemic analysis. Kenneth Waltz, for example, is best known for the developments of Structural Realism. He is often incorrectly cited for ignoring or discounting altogether any sub-systemic analysis. The best scholars in any discipline seldom deal in absolutes. But while he and other realists address sub-systemic phenomena in their explorations of recurring questions of international politics, they ultimately ascribe the greatest explanatory power to systemic level variables.

What is the security lens? What are the intellectual origins and premises of classical and structural realism? Of Collective Security and Democratic Peace Theory? What are the limitations of this lens for providing insights into international relations?

As with all theories in political science, those in the ***Security*** lens helps us to understand and focus our attention on important aspects of international relations. This lens serves as a powerful tool for understanding the two central questions of international relations—***"Why do states do what they do"?*** and ***"What causes cooperation and conflict among states?"*** Theory here seeks to explain state behavior as a search for security, showing that the motivation for policy is the accumulation and use of power in order to ensure survival at all levels. We understand international relations more fully by using the Security Lens as a *first cut* at the larger context of international relations. By supplementing our initial understanding with explanations gained through the other lenses presented in this book, we gain a much more comprehensive understanding of interstate relations.

The theories in the Security Lens generally can be categorized according to the two foundational traditions of political thought - realist and idealist. Starting with the realist tradition, the study of realism includes two theories: *classical* and *Structural* (or *neo-*) *Realism.* Relying on certain assumptions about the character of humankind, classical realism is the earliest manifestation of this lens. In later realist writings, Structural Realism or neo-realism, the focus shifts to explain how states behave in terms of their position relative to one another. Three central concepts underlie both these strands of realist thought: *anarchy (complete lack of any kind of central authority), power (located and wielded by sovereign states only),* and the *security dilemma (gains in one state's security by definition reduce the security of other states.)* In the realist view, these three concepts affect relations between sovereign states and explain the political importance of force. To explore the

Security Lens, the text presents several representative realist studies, dividing them into Balance of Power, Balance of Threat, and Structural Realism.

The idealist tradition section of the Security Lens concludes the chapter with two works reflective of the idealist approach to international relations. The differences between realists and idealists lie in beliefs about the ability to overcome the conditions of anarchy, the role of morality and international law, and the efficacy of international institutions. Specifically, *Collective Security* argues that values and universalisms can indeed bind all states, thereby ensuring cooperation and hence security for all. Likewise, *Democratic Peace Theory* posits that the way to maintain a relatively peaceful international arena is through states' adherence to democratic norms.

Based on these concepts, Security Lens theories pose several crucial questions. Is humankind doomed to repeat cycles of cataclysmic war and regenerative peace endlessly, or can other worldwide cooperative forces transcend the conflictual nature of humankind? Have the changes wrought by the vastly increased number of states and the proliferation of technologies of mass destruction affected the state's search for security? Has the political role of force changed? What effects will shifts in the locus of political power have on the prospects for international peace and cooperation? The readings in the Security Lens illuminate these and other significant aspects of international relations.

CONCLUSION

The ***Security*** Lens helps define and illuminate the consequences of international anarchy. It explains that states do what they do in order to ensure their own security and survival. The Security Lens explains how states attempt to escape from the effects of anarchy by seeking international stability through a balance of power or through collective security arrangements..

As the first, and for centuries, the dominant approach to international relations, the realist tradition is often sharply criticized for what it omits or fails to foresee. Indeed, the shortcomings of realism are sometimes stretched unfairly to paint the entire discipline of political science. For example, realism's "failure" to explain the outcome of the Vietnam War or its inability to predict the precise circumstances leading to the end of the Cold War are seen as clear evidence of the folly of any systematic approach to international politics. Some of these criticisms reflect a failure to grasp the dynamic and evolutionary nature of theory in any disciplines. Indeed some of the most effective criticism of realism comes from other realists. It is sometimes forgotten that one of the harshest evaluations of the conduct of the Vietnam War was Hans Morgenthau's 1967 *Vietnam and the United States*.

The idealist tradition theories have been a response to realism. Criticism of theories such as Democratic Peace and Collective Security are mainly founded on the idea that to assume that the conditions of anarchy and the security dilemma may be overcome is a dangerous, even foolhardy notion, certain to result in the ultimate demise of a subscribing state.

The weakness of some critics neither eliminates the valid criticisms nor alters the need for the continued critical study of this lens. For example the Security Lens does not illuminate all the other concerns of a state—especially issues of economics and domestic politics. It does not help us understand how states decide what their specific national interests are, or how they should promote those interests. The international system bounds the range of choices without specifying which of the optional choices a state will make. As a result, theories in this lens sometimes fail to explain adequately state behavior. The language of the Security Lens is also a barrier to some students. Terms such as "anarchy", "rational", and even "realism" carry a range of biases and pejorative semantic baggage. There are assumptions of agreed upon meaning that upon closer examination represent anything but consensus. "Power", for example, is one term most people think they can easily define. However, on closer examination one finds volumes of complex literature by respected scholars and practitioners who try to define the key concept clearly. To help understand these and other important issues, we will examine other lenses in the remaining two sections of this volume.

Suggestions for Further Readings

Art, Robert and Robert Jervis. *International Politics: Enduring Concepts and Contemporary Issues, 4th Ed.* New York: HarperCollins, 1996.

Art, Robert and Kenneth Waltz, ed. *The Use of Force.* New York: University Press of America, 1993.

Baldwin, David, ed. *Neorealism and NeoLiberalsim..* New York: Columbia University Press, 1993.

Brodie, Bernard. *War and Politics.* New York: Macmillan, 1973.

Brown, Michael E., Sean M. Lynn -Jones and Steven Miller, eds. *Debating the Democratic Peace.* Cambridge, MA: MIT Press, 1996.

Bull, Hedley. *The Anarchical Society: A Study of Order in World Politics.* New York: Columbia University Press, 1977.

Carr, E. H.. *The Twenty Years' Crisis, 1919-1939: An Introduction to the Study of International Relations.* New York: Harper and Row, 1964.

Claude, Inis L., Jr. *Power and International Politics.* New York: Random House, 1962.

Craig, Gordon A. and Alexander George. *Force and Statecraft.* 2nd Ed. New York: Oxford University Press, 1990.

Diesing, Paul and Glenn H. Snyder. *Conflict Among Nations.* Princeton: Princeton University Press, 1977.

Dougherty, James E. and Robert L. Pfaltzgraff, Jr. *Contending Theories of International Relations*, 4th Ed. New York: Addison-Wesley, 1996.

Doyle, Michael W. *Ways of War and Peace.* New York: W.W. Norton , 1997.

Ferguson, Yale H. and Richard Mansbach. *The Elusive Quest: Theory and International Politics.* Columbia: University of South Carolina Press, 1993.

Herz, John. *Political Realism and Political Idealism.* Chicago: University of Chicago Press, 1951.

Jervis, Robert. *System Effects.* Princeton, NJ: Princeton University Press, 1997.

Keohane, Robert O., ed. *Neo-Realism and Its Critics.* New York: Columbia University Press, 1986.

Kissinger, Henry. *Diplomacy.* New York : Simon & Schuster, 1994.

Levy, Jack S.. *War in the Modern Great Power System, 1495-1975.* Lexington, KY: University of Kentucky Press, 1983.

Machiavelli, Niccolo'. *The Prince.* Ed. Quentin Skinner. Trans. Russell Price. New York: Cambridge University Press, 1988.

MacKinder, Halford J. "The Geographical Pivot of History." *The Geographic Journal* XXXIII (April 1904).

Mahan, Alfred Thayer. *The Influence of Sea Power Upon History, 1660-1783.* Boston: Little, Brown and Co., 1890.

Morgenthau, Hans J. *Politics Among Nations: the Struggle for Power and Peace*, 6th Ed, Rev. Kenneth W. Thompson. New York: Alfred A. Knopf, 1985.
Niebuhr, Reinhold. *Moral Man and Immoral Society*. New York: Charles Scribner's Sons, 1959.
Nye, Joseph S., Jr. *Understanding International Conflict: An Introduction to Theory and History*. New York: HarperCollins, 1993.
Paul, T.V. *Asymmetric Conflicts: War Initiation by Weaker Powers*. New York: Cambridge University Press, 1994.
Poundstone, William. *Prisoner's Dilemma: John von Neuman, Game Theory, and the Puzzle of the Bomb*. New York: Doubleday, 1992.
Ray, James Lee, "Does Democracy Cause Peace?" *Annual Review of Political Science* 1 (1998): 27-46.
Schelling, Thomas C. *Arms and Influence*. New Haven: Yale University Press, 1966.
Snyder, Glenn. *Alliance Politics*. Ithaca, NY: Cornell University Press, 1997.
Spykman, Nicholas J. *The Geography of Peace*. New York: Harcourt, Brace, and Co., 1942.
Thucydides, *The Peloponnesian War*. New York: Penguin, 1982.
Van Evera, Stephen. *The Causes of War*. Ithaca, NY: Cornell University Press, 1999.
Walt, Stephen. *The Origins of Alliances*. Ithaca, NY: Cornell University Press, 1987.
Waltz, Kenneth. *Theory of International Politics*. New York: Random House, 1979.
Waltz, Kenneth. *Man, The State and War: A Theoretical Analysis*. New York: Columbia University Press, 1969.

Realist Tradition Theories

Balance of Power Theory

Hans J. Morgenthau
Elements of National Power

Hans J. Morgenthau
The Balance of Power

Balance of Threat Theory

Steven M. Walt
Explaining Alliance Formation

Steven M. Walt
Alliance Formation and the Balance of World Power

Structural Realism

Kenneth N. Waltz
Political Structures

Kenneth N. Waltz
Structural Causes and Military Effects

Kenneth Waltz
Anarchic Orders and Balance of Power

Kenneth N. Waltz
Structural Realism After the Cold War

Introduction to Balance of Power

Hans J. Morgenthau's *Politics Among Nations: The Struggle for Power* serves as the basis for what has been called "classical realism." The readings reproduced here describe his "Balance of Power" theory.

Morgenthau, who has been called the "founding father"[1] of International Relations, published this book in the wake of World War Two and there can be little doubt that his experience as a refugee who fled Hitlerite Germany greatly affected his view of the world. Perhaps it is not surprising that his outlook was largely pessimistic and his view of human nature was quite Hobbesian. As Stanley Hoffman notes, *Politics Among Nations* was largely a "[revolt] against utopian thinking, past and present."[2]

You have already read two chapters out of *Politics Among Nations* and as such should have no problem identifying Balance of Power's lens and its location on the realist-idealist continuum. Furthermore, having read the "Six Principles of Political Realism" [chapter one] one can clearly see that this theory is in the "realist tradition."

In chapter two, which you don't read, Morgenthau expresses that his "book has two purposes." First it strives "to detect and understand the forces that determine political relations among nations [more accurately states or nation-states] and to comprehend the ways in which those forces act upon each other and upon the international political relations and institutions."[3] In effect, Morgenthau wanted to explain "why states do what they do" and "what causes cooperation and conflict among states" (i.e., this textbook's two central questions).

The method he utilized to detect and understand those international forces is simply the inductive process. Specifically, he sought to survey history to ascertain patterns in behavior which he could codify in the form of a theory. While a teacher of international law, not history, Morgenthau "quite deliberately couched his work in the terms of general propositions and grounded them in history . . . and derived [his hypotheses] from the view of nineteenth-century and early twentieth-century historians of statecraft (such as Treitschke, and also Weber)."[4]

The readings from *Politics Among Nations* that follow will allow you to ascertain his hypotheses. In addition to the previous readings from Morgenthau in the "Foundations" block (i.e., "Political Power" and the "Six Principles of Political Realism") the subsequent reading, "Elements of National Power" [chapter 9] gives us his independent variables. Also related to the independent variable, but not included here, is Morgenthau's more nuanced description of why states seek power. While in general, states seek security, he claims that states "struggle for" and pursue power for three specific reasons: maintenance of the status quo [chapter 4]; imperialistic gains [chapter 5]; and prestige [chapter 6].

---

1. Stanley Hoffmann, "International Relations: An American Social Science," in *Janus and Minerva: Essays in the Theory and Practice of International Relations*, (1987), 3-23.

2. Ibid.

3. Hans J. Morgenthau, *Politics Among Nations: The Struggle for Power and Peace*, 6th ed., ed. Kenneth Thompson (New York: Alfred A. Knopf, 1985), 18.

4. Hoffman.

The final reading, "The Balance of Power" [chapter 11], describes his dependent variables (i.e., the resulting change in state behavior or international cooperation or conflict given a change in the independent variable).

The secondary purpose of his book remains important today. Having realized that "no study of . . . international politics . . . is able to divorce knowledge from action and pursue knowledge for its own sake," he writes:

> Since in this [post-World War Two] world situation the United States holds a position of predominant power, and hence of foremost responsibility, the understanding of the forces that mold international politics and of the factors that determine its course has become for the United States more than an interesting intellectual preoccupation. It has become a vital necessity.[5]

As Stanley Hoffmann writes, he had a "missionary impulse to teach the new world power all the lessons that it had [previously failed to learn regarding power politics]."[6] Therefore, Morgenthau sought to have Balance of Power serve as a policy which would help the leaders of a post-World War Two United States maintain "international peace." Specifically, he believed that America's reversion to isolationism following the "Great War" contributed significantly to an environment that resulted in a second world war. Unless the United States could resist its atavistic tendency towards isolationism, Morgenthau felt that the world risked yet another war.

America's "containment" policy, which predominated during the Cold War, has undeniable and significant parallels with Morgenthau's Balance of Power, and the tenets and prescriptions of Balance of Power are applicable today, particularly when considering the rise of a peer competitor, such as China. Further, Morgenthau talks of the importance of regional balances of power. In fact, he writes that in addition to the world-wide balance of power, there are frequently "a number of subsystems that . . . maintain within themselves a balance of power of their own." The US has recognized that often a regional balance of power is the key to regional stability. It becomes clear then that classical realism, or Balance of Power Theory, maintains its position as a vital link in a complete understanding of why states do what they do and the causes of conflict and cooperation among states.

The question in today's world is: how does a state balance against a non-state actor—Inter-governmental organizations (IGO) and Non-governmental organizations (NGO)?

5. Morgenthau, 25.

6. Hoffman.

Elements of National Power

Hans J. Morgenthau

What are the factors that make for the power of a nation vis-à-vis other nations? What are the components of what we call national power? If we want to determine the power of a nation, what factors are we to take into consideration? Two groups of elements have to be distinguished: those which are relatively stable, and those which are subject to constant change.

GEOGRAPHY

The most stable factor upon which the power of a nation depends is obviously geography. For instance, the fact that the continental territory, of the United States is separated from other continents by bodies of water three thousand miles wide to the east and more than six thousand miles wide to the west is a permanent factor that determines the position of the United States in the world. It is a truism to say that the importance of this factor today is not what it was in the times of George Washington or President McKinley. But it is fallacious to assume, as is frequently done, that the technical development of transportation, communications, and warfare has eliminated altogether the isolating factor of the oceans. This factor is certainly much less important today than it was fifty or a hundred years ago, but from the point of view of the power position of the United States it still makes a great deal of difference that the United States is separated from the continents of Europe and Asia by wide expanses of water instead of bordering directly on, let us say, France, China, or Russia. In other words, the geographical location of the United States remains a fundamental factor of permanent importance which the foreign policies of all nations must take into account, however different its bearing upon political decisions might be today from what it was in other periods of history.

Similarly, the separation of Great Britain from the European continent by a small body of water, the English Channel, is a factor that Julius Caesar could no more afford to overlook than could William the Conqueror, Philip II, Napoleon, or Hitler. However much other factors may have altered its importance throughout the course of history, what was important two thousand years ago is still important today, and all those concerned with the conduct of foreign affairs must take it into account. . . .

Conquest of a considerable portion of a country without prospects for speedy recovery usually breaks the will to resist of the conquered people. This is, as we have seen, the political purpose of military conquests. Similar conquests—especially if as under Napoleon and Hitler, they did not have a limited objective, but aimed at the very existence of Russia as a nation—had a rather stimulating effect upon Russian resistance. For not only were the conquered parts of Russia small in comparison with those which were left in Russian hands, but the task of the invader became more difficult with every step he advanced. He had to keep an ever greater number of troops supplied over ever lengthening lines of communication deep in a hostile country. Thus geography has made the conquest of Russian territory, as soon as the objectives of such conquest became ill defined and tended to become unlimited, a liability for the conqueror rather than an asset. Instead of the conqueror's swallowing the territory and gaining strength from it, it is rather the territory that swallows the conqueror, sapping his strength.

The possibility of nuclear war has enhanced the importance of the size of territory as a source of national power. In order to make a nuclear threat credible, a nation requires a territory large enough to disperse its industrial and population centers as well as its nuclear installations. The conjunction between the large radius of nuclear destruction and the relatively small size of their territories imposes a severe handicap upon the ability of the traditional nation states, such as Great Britain and France, to make a nuclear threat credible. Thus it is the quasi-continental size of their territory which allows nations, such as the United States, the Soviet Union, and China, to play the role of major nuclear powers.

Another geographical factor, however, constitutes at the same time a weakness and an asset for the international position of the Soviet Union. We are referring to the fact that neither high mountains nor broad streams separate the Soviet Union from its western neighbors and that the plains of Poland and Eastern Germany form a natural continuation of the Russian plain. There exists, then, no natural obstacle to invasion on the western frontier of Russia, either on the part of the Soviet Union or on the part of the Soviet Union's western neighbors. Thus, from the fourteenth century to the present, White Russia and the westernmost part of Russia proper have been the scene of continuous thrusts and counterthrusts and a field of battle where Russia and its western neighbors met. The lack of a natural frontier—that is, of a frontier predetermined, like the Italian or the Spanish, by geographical factors—has been a permanent source of conflict between Russia and the West. Similarly, yet for the opposite reason, the possibility of such a frontier between France and Germany in the form of the Rhine, to which France always aspired and which it had rarely the strength to attain, has been a permanent source of conflict between those two countries since the times of the Romans. As concerns Russia, the bolshevist foreign minister Vishinsky summed up the transcendent importance of geography when he said, upon being reproached for following a Czarist policy on the Dardanelles: "If a warship has to sail from the Mediterranean to the Black Sea, it must pass through the Dardanelles whether the government in Moscow is Czarist or Communist."[1]

NATURAL RESOURCES

Another relatively stable factor that exerts an important influence upon the power of a nation with respect to other nations is natural resources.

Food

To start with the most elemental of these resources, food: a country that is self-sufficient, or nearly self-sufficient, has a great advantage over a nation that is not and must be able to import the foodstuffs it does not grow, or else starve. It is for this reason that the power and, in times of war, the very existence of Great Britain, which before the Second World War grew only 30 percent of the food consumed in the British Isles, has always been dependent upon its ability to keep the sea lanes open over which the vital food supplies had to be shipped in. Whenever its ability to import food was challenged, as in the two world wars through submarine warfare and air attacks, the very power of Great Britain was challenged, and its survival as a nation put in jeopardy.

For the same reason, Germany, though to a much smaller extent deficient in foodstuffs than Great Britain, in order to survive a war was bound to pursue three principal goals, either severally or in combination: first, the avoidance of a long war through a speedy victory

1. Quoted after Denis Healey, *Neutrality* (London: Ampersand Ltd., 1955), p. 36.

before its food reserves were exhausted; second, the conquest of the great food-producing areas of eastern Europe; and third, the destruction of British seapower, which cut Germany off from access to overseas sources of food. In both world wars, Germany was unable to attain the first and third objectives. It reached the second goal in the First World War too late to be of decisive effect. Thus the Allied blockade, by imposing upon the German people privations that sapped their will to resist, was one of the essential factors in the victory of the Allies. In the Second World War, Germany became virtually self-sufficient with regard to food, not primarily through conquest, but through the deliberate starvation and the outright killing of millions of people in conquered territories.

A deficiency in home-grown food has thus been a permanent source of weakness for Great Britain and Germany which they must somehow overcome, or face the loss of their status as great powers. A country enjoying self-sufficiency, such as the United States, need not divert its national energies and foreign policies from its primary objectives in order to make sure that its populations will not starve in war. Since such countries are reasonably free from worry on that count, they have been able to pursue much more forceful and single-minded policies than otherwise would have been possible. Self-sufficiency in food has thus always been a source of great strength.

Conversely, permanent scarcity of food is a source of permanent weakness in international politics. Of the truth of this observation, India was the prime example before the so-called green revolution drastically increased its food supply. The scarcity of food from which India suffered was the result of two factors: the increase in population, outstripping the supply of food, and the insufficiency of exports to pay for the import of the food necessary to make up the deficit. This dual imbalance, which made the ever present threat of mass starvation one of the main concerns of government, put an insuperable handicap upon any active foreign policy India might have wanted to pursue. Regardless of the other assets of national power which were at its disposal, the deficiencies in food compelled it to act in its foreign policy from weakness rather than from strength. The same observation applies with particular force to the nations of the Third World that continuously live under the threat of famine and the actuality of undernourishment without most of any of the other assets which go into the making of national power. These are the so-called "basket cases" that are limited to hoping that international generosity will help them to survive the next famine.

Self-sufficiency in food, or lack of it, is a relatively stable factor in national power, but it is sometimes, as the example of contemporary India shows, subject to decisive changes. There may be changes in the consumption of food brought about by changing conceptions of nutrition. There may be changes in the technique of agriculture which may increase or decrease the output of agricultural products. The outstanding examples of the influence of changes in the agricultural output upon national power are, however, to be found in the disappearance of the Near East and of North Africa as power centers and in the descent of Spain from a world power to a third-rate power. . . .

Raw Materials

What holds true of food is of course also true of those natural resources which are important for industrial production and, more particularly, for the waging of war. The absolute and relative importance natural resources in the form of raw materials have for the power of a nation depends necessarily upon the technology of the warfare practiced in a particular period of history. Before the large-scale mechanization of warfare, when hand-to-hand fighting was the prevalent military technique, other factors, such as the personal qualities of the individual soldier, were more important than the availability of the raw materials with which his weapons were made. In that period of history which extends from the beginning of historic time well into the nineteenth century, natural resources played a subordinate role in determining the power of a nation. With the increasing mechanization of warfare, which since the industrial revolution has proceeded at a faster pace than in all preceding history, national power has become more and more dependent upon the control of raw materials in peace and war. It is not by accident that the two most powerful nations today, the United States and the Soviet Union, come closest to being self-sufficient in the raw materials necessary for modern industrial production, and control at least the access to the sources of those raw materials which they do not themselves produce.

As the absolute importance of the control of raw materials for national power has increased in proportion to the mechanization of warfare, so certain raw materials have gained in importance over others. This has happened whenever fundamental changes in technology have called for the use of new materials or the increased use of old ones. In 1936, a statistician rated the share of a number of basic minerals in industrial production for military purposes and assigned them the following values: coal, 40; oil, 20; iron, 15; copper, lead, manganese, sulfur, 4 each; zinc, aluminum, nickel, 2 each.[2] Half a century before, the share of coal would certainly have been considerably greater, since as a source of energy it had at that time only small competition from water and wood and none from oil. The same would have been true of iron which then had no competition from light metals and such substitutes as plastics. Great Britain, which was self-sufficient in coal and iron, was the one great world power of the nineteenth century.

The influence the control of raw materials can exert upon national power and the shifts in the distribution of power which it can bring about are demonstrated in our own day most strikingly by the case of uranium. Only a few years ago the control or lack of control of uranium deposits was entirely irrelevant for the power of a nation. The author we have quoted above,[3] writing in 1936, did not even mention this mineral in his evaluation of the relative military importance of minerals. The release of atomic energy from the uranium atom and the use of that energy for warfare have at once modified the actual and potential hierarchy of nations in view of their relative power. Nations that control deposits of uranium, such as Canada, Czechoslovakia, the Soviet Union, the Union of South Africa, and the United States, have risen in the power calculations. Others that neither possess nor have access to deposits of that mineral have fallen in terms of relative power.

The Power of Oil

Since the First World War, oil as a source of energy has become more and more important for industry and war. Most mechanized weapons and vehicles are driven by oil; consequently, countries that possess considerable deposits of oil have acquired an influence in international affairs which in some cases can be attributed primarily, if not exclusively, to that possession. "One drop of oil," said Clemenceau during the First World War, "is worth one drop of blood of our soldiers." The emergence of oil as an indispensable raw material has brought about a shift in the relative power of the politically leading nations.

---

2. Ferdinand Friedensburg, *Die mineralischen Bodenschätze als weltpolitische und militärische Machtfaktoren* (Stuttgart: F. Enke, 1936), p. 175.

3. See preceding note

The Soviet Union has become more powerful since it is self sufficient in this respect, while Japan has grown considerably weaker, since it is completely lacking in oil deposits.

Aside from its location as the land bridge of three continents, the Near East is strategically important because of the oil deposits of the Arabian peninsula. Control over them traditionally has been an important factor in the distribution of power, in the sense that whoever is able to add them to his other sources of raw materials adds that much strength to his own resources and deprives his competitors proportionately. It is for this reason that Great Britain, the United States and, for a time, France embarked in the Near East upon what has aptly been called "oil diplomacy": that is, the establishment of spheres of influence giving them exclusive access to the oil deposits in certain regions.

Yet oil is no longer one of many raw materials important in the measurement of a nation's power. It is now a material factor whose very possession threatens to overturn centuries-old patterns of international politics. The embargo on oil by the oil-producing states in the winter of 1973–74, together with the drastic rise in the price of oil, suddenly clarified certain basic aspects of world politics which we might have understood theoretically, but which were brought home in earnest by the drastic change in power relations brought on by the new politics of oil.

Traditionally a functional relationship has existed between political, military, and economic power. That is to say, political power has been throughout history a function of military and—in recent times more particularly—of economic power. Take for instance the expansion of Europe into what later became the colonial areas of the Western Hemisphere, Africa, and Asia. That expansion was primarily due to a technological gap between the colonial powers and the colonized nations. In other words, the conquest of India by Great Britain (much inferior in manpower and in many other aspects of national power) was largely made possible by Great Britain's possession of a higher technology which, when transformed into military power, the Indian states could not resist.

Those relationships of a functional nature between technology and economic power, on the one hand, and political and military power, on the other, have been disturbed—one might even say destroyed—by the recent use of oil as a political weapon. Many of those oil-producing states are states only by way of what might be called semantic courtesy. Measured in terms of natural resources, they have nothing but sand and oil. But it is the oil which seemingly overnight has made those small plots on the map which we call states important and even powerful factors in world politics. In other words, a state which has nothing to go on by way of power, which is lacking in all the elements which traditionally have gone into the making of national power, suddenly becomes a powerful factor in world politics because it has one important asset—oil. This is indeed an event which is of revolutionary importance for world politics.

Two basic factors in our period of history have made possible this divorce of political power from military and industrial-technological power. (1) Free trade between the private producers and consumers of certain raw materials and monopolistically controlled trade through colonial and semicolonial arrangements by the consumer governments has been replaced by monopolistic or quasi-monopolistic controls on the part of the producer governments acting in concert. Formerly the consumers could keep the price low through colonial arrangements and the control of consumption; now the producers can keep the price high by controlling production. (2) Formerly producers and consumers of raw materials were tied together by complementary interests, the balance of which favored the consumer. The latter's needs were limited as compared with the number of potential producers and the quantity of raw materials available. The consumer had, accordingly, a choice among several producers to buy from, and also of the quantity to buy from the several producers chosen. Today, what was once a buyer's market has become a seller's market. The consumption of raw materials has enormously increased, not only in absolute terms—between 1760 and 1913 imports of food and raw materials to Great Britain increased seventy-fold—but also relative to available resources. Thus oil has become the lifeblood of industrially advanced nations, many of which are completely (*e.g.* Japan) or in considerable measure (*e.g.* the nations of Western Europe) dependent upon imports from other nations.

The power which oil bestows is, first of all, the result of the technological development of modern industrial nations. Twenty or fifty years ago oil did not bestow such power upon producing nations because the use of oil as the lifeblood of modem industry was limited. When nations which have large deposits of oil are able to co-operate and coordinate policies, as the oil- exporting states were during the fall of 1973, they can apply a stranglehold to the consuming nations; they can impose political conditions which the consuming nations can refuse to meet only at the risk of enormous political, economic, and social dislocations.

A state which is powerless in all other respects, which is not a major force in terms of traditional power, can exert enormous—and under certain conditions even decisive—power over nations which have all the implements of power at their disposal except one—deposits of oil. Thus a nation like Japan, one of the foremost industrial nations of the world and potentially a great power, is completely dependent upon the supply of oil from abroad. If for some reason the oil-producing nations were to impose a total embargo upon Japan, they could destroy her political, economic, and social fabric, and if they were to connect that threat of a total embargo with political conditions, they could impose their will upon Japan. They could reduce Japan to the status of satellite, a dependency of the oil-producing nations. To a certain extent those nations have already tasted that power. During the Middle Eastern war of October, 1973, they forced Japan and the nations of Western Europe (which are only partially dependent on the import of oil) to take certain political steps which they would not have taken on their own initiative, but which they felt they had to take under the circumstances because otherwise they would have risked political, social, and economic ruin.

It is not only the quasi-monopoly which the oil-producing nations acting in concert have on the supply of oil which has caused such dislocation. It is particularly, and in the long run more importantly, the control (whether actual or potential) they exert over the price of oil that has become one of the main factors of instability in the world economy and one of the main sources of inflation. The inflationary tendencies which were already at work in the industrial nations of the world were greatly aggravated by the fourfold increase in the price of oil in 1973 and the further doubling of the wellhead price in 1978.

It is important to note that this situation is potentially of a permanent nature. As long as the oil-producing nations cooperate against the consuming nations, as long as there is no competition among them for markets or for economic or political advantages, they will be able to impose virtually any conditions on the oil-consuming nations, just as they did in the wake of the 1973 war. In the case of a country like Japan it would be suicide to refuse such conditions. In the case of other nations, such as the United States, whose main sources of energy are domestic, it would mean severe discomfort of the kind already experienced in 1973. The nations of Western Europe, for example West Germany, whose main sources of petroleum come from abroad, would face catastrophe if they attempted to defy those nations upon whom they depend for oil.

While there is no way of destroying this stranglehold short of war, there is a way of mitigating its results. It lies in weakening the monopolistic or quasi-monopolistic position of the oil-producing nations by strengthening the position of the oil-consuming ones. The latter fall into two categories: those like Japan, who are utterly dependent upon the importation of oil, and for whom therefore the access to foreign oil is a matter of life and death; and those like the United States, who, by virtue of domestic sources of energy, can be inconvenienced and harmed, but not mortally wounded, by the political manipulation of oil. The latter are able to protect themselves from the more severe consequences of such manipulation by limiting the importation of oil, by restricting its domestic use, by stockpiling reserves, and by embarking upon a crash program, after the model of the Manhattan Project for the discovery of nuclear fission, to develop alternative sources of energy. The very existence of such a four-pronged policy would have a salutary effect upon all concerned. It would strengthen the morale of the oil consumers and give pause to the producers.

Such a policy would also lay the psychological and material groundwork for a policy of sharing between those consumers who possess considerable domestic sources of energy and those who lack them. For the oil producers are able to strike at a consumer, such as the United States, not only directly by cutting off its supply, but also indirectly by bringing its principal allies, such as the Federal Republic of Germany and Japan, to their knees. Thus the United States is doubly vulnerable to the political manipulation of oil, and it must meet that dual threat by making itself as quickly and as much as possible independent of foreign oil supplies and by making a fraction of its domestic resources available to its most endangered allies.

Finally, if one looks at this situation created by the political use of oil from an over-all point of view, one realizes that it is the specific result of what we identified earlier as the main characteristic of contemporary world politics: the disjunction between the organizational structures and political processes through which we act on the world scene, on the one hand, and the objective conditions under which humanity lives, on the other. Thus one is struck by the utter irrationality of leaving the control of nuclear power which can destroy mankind to sovereign nation states. The same applies to entrusting the control of oil—which can destroy in a different way (less dramatically but almost as thoroughly) the civilization of the highly developed industrial nations—to so-called nation states which are sovereign only in a very limited sense. The states belonging to the "nuclear club" are no longer, and the oil-producing states have never been capable of performing the functions for which government is established in the first place, that is, to protect and promote the life, liberty, and happiness of its citizens. Their power is essentially destructive.

INDUSTRIAL CAPACITY

The example of uranium illustrates, however, the importance of another factor for the power of a nation—industrial capacity. The Congo has vast deposits of high-grade uranium. Yet, while this fact has increased the value of that country as a prize of war and, therefore, its importance from the point of view of military' strategy, it has not affected the power of the Congo in relation to other nations. For the Congo does not have the industrial plant to put the uranium deposits to industrial and military use. On the other hand, for Great Britain, Canada, and the United States, as for Czechoslovakia and the Soviet Union, the possession of uranium signifies an enormous increase in power. In these countries the industrial plants exist or can be built, or they can easily be used in a neighboring country, where uranium can be transformed into energy to be employed in peace and war.

The same situation can be exemplified by coal and iron. The United States and the Soviet Union have drawn a good deal of their national strength from the possession of vast amounts of these two raw materials because they possess also industrial plants that can transform them into industrial products. The Soviet Union has built its plant, and is still in the process of building it, at enormous human and material sacrifices. It is willing to make the sacrifices because it recognizes that without the industrial plant it cannot build and maintain a military establishment commensurate with its foreign policy. Without this plant the Soviet Union cannot play the important part in international politics which it intends to play.

India follows the United States and the Soviet Union closely as a depository of coal and iron. Its reserves of iron ore in the two provinces of Bihar and Orissa alone are estimated at 2.7 billion tons. Furthermore, India's output of manganese, which is indispensable for the production of steel, was a million tons as early as 1939, topped only by the output of the Soviet Union. But despite these riches in raw materials, without which no nation can attain first rank in modern times, India cannot be classified today as a first-rate power even faintly comparable to the United States and the Soviet Union. The reason for this lag between the potentialities and actualities of power, which concerns us in the context of this discussion (others will be mentioned later), is the lack of an industrial establishment commensurate with the abundance of raw materials. While India can boast of a number of steel mills, such as the Tata Iron Works, which are among the most modern in existence, it has no per capita productive capacity, especially for finished products, that can be compared with even one of the second-rate industrial nations. In 1980 fewer than six million Indians—less than one per cent of the total population—were employed in industry. So we see that India possesses, in the abundance of some of the key raw materials, one of the elements that go into the making of national power, and to that extent it may be regarded as a potentially great power. Actually, however, it will not become a great power so long as it is lacking in other factors without which no nation in modern times can attain the status of a great power. Of these factors industrial capacity is one of the most important.

The technology of modern warfare transportation and communications has made the over-all development of heavy industries an indispensable element of national power. Since victory in modern war depends upon the number and quality of highways, railroads, trucks, ships, airplanes, tanks, and equipment and weapons of all kinds, from mosquito nets and automatic rifles to oxygen masks and guided missiles, the competition among nations for power transforms itself largely into competition for the production of bigger, better, and more implements of war. The quality and productive capacity of the industrial plant, the know-how of the working man, the skill of the engineer, the inventive genius of the scientist, the managerial organization—all these are factors upon which the industrial capacity of a nation and, hence, its power depend.

Thus it is inevitable that the leading industrial nations should be identical with the great powers, and a change in industrial rank, for better or for worse, should be accompanied or followed by a corresponding change in the hierarchy of power. So long as Great Britain as an industrial nation had no equal, it was the most, powerful nation on earth, the only one that deserved to be called a world power. The decline of France as a power in comparison with Germany, which was unmistakable after 1870 and was only seemingly and temporarily arrested during the decade following the First World War, was in part but the political and military manifestation of the industrial backwardness of France and of the industrial predominance of Germany on the European continent.

The Soviet Union, while having been potentially always a great power, became one in fact only when it entered the ranks of the foremost industrial powers in the thirties, and it became the rival of the United States as the other superpower only when it acquired in the fifties the industrial capacity for waging nuclear war. Similarly, the potential of China as a great power will only be realized if and when it acquires a similar industrial capacity. When the United States was at the height of Its power in the forties, the *Economist* of London related that power to American economic strength by saying:

> In any comparison of potential resources of the Great Powers the United States, even before Hitler's war, far outstripped every other nation in the world in material strength, in scale of industrialization, in weight of resources, in standards of living, by every index of output and consumption. And the war, which all but doubled the American national income while it either ruined or severely weakened every other Great Power, has enormously increased the scale upon which the United States now towers above its fellows. Like mice in the cage of an elephant, they follow with apprehension the movements of the mammoth. What chance would they stand if it were to begin to throw its weight about, they who are in some danger even if it only decides to sit down?[4]

This drastic increase in the importance of industrial capacity for national power has also accentuated the traditional distinction between great and small powers. The very term "superpower" points to an unprecedented accumulation of power in the hands of a few nations, which sets these nations apart not only from the small ones but from the traditional great powers as well. What distinguishes the superpowers from all other nations, aside from their ability to wage all-out nuclear war and absorb a less than all-out nuclear attack, is their virtual industrial self-sufficiency and their technological capacity to stay abreast of the other nations. By the same token, the dependence of the nations of the third and fourth rank upon the nations of the first rank, which we can call superpowers, has also drastically increased. The military power of the former depends to a sometimes decisive extent upon the willingness of the latter to supply them with modern weapons and the implements of modem communications and transportation. Without this supply many of them would be helpless in confrontation with an enemy thus supplied.

MILITARY PREPAREDNESS

What gives the factors of geography, natural resources, and industrial capacity their actual importance for the power of a nation is military preparedness. The dependence of national power upon military preparedness is too obvious to need much elaboration. Military preparedness requires a military establishment capable of supporting the foreign policies pursued. Such ability derives from a number of factors of which the most significant, from the point of view of our discussion, are technological innovations, leadership, and the quantity and quality of the armed forces.

Technology

The fate of nations and of civilizations has often been determined by a differential in the technology of warfare for which the inferior side was unable to compensate in other ways. Europe, in the period of its expansion from the fifteenth through the nineteenth century, carried its power on the vehicle of a technology of warfare superior to that of the Western Hemisphere, Africa, and the Near and Far East. The addition of infantry, firearms,

---

4. *Economist*, May 24, 1947, p. 785.

and artillery to the traditional weapons in the fourteenth and fifteenth centuries spelled a momentous shift in the distribution of power in favor of those who used those weapons before their enemies did. The feudal lords and independent cities, who in the face of these new weapons continued to rely upon cavalry and the castles which until then had been practically immune against direct attack, now found themselves suddenly dislodged from their position of preponderance.

Two events illustrate dramatically this shift in power which politically and militarily marks the end of the Middle Ages and the beginning of the modem era of history. First, in the battles of Morgarten in 1315 and of Laupen in 1339, armies composed of Swiss infantry inflicted disastrous defeats upon feudal cavalry, demonstrating that foot soldiers recruited from the common people were superior to an aristocratic and expensive army of equestrians. The second is the invasion of Italy in 1494 by Charles VIII of France. With infantry and artillery, Charles VIII broke the power of the proud Italian city-states, until then secure behind their walls. The seemingly irresistible destructiveness of these new techniques of warfare made an indelible impression upon contemporaries, some of which is reflected in the writings of Machiavelli and other Florentine writers of the time.[5]

The twentieth century has thus far witnessed four major innovations in the technique of warfare. They gave at least a temporary advantage to the side that used them before the opponent did, or before he was able to protect himself against them. First, the submarine was used in the First World War by Germany primarily against British shipping and seemed to be capable of deciding the war in favor of Germany until Great Britain found in the convoy an answer to that menace. Second, the tank was used in considerable and concentrated numbers by the British, but not by the Germans, in the closing phase of the First World War, giving the Allies one of their assets for victory. Third, strategic and tactical co-ordination of the air force with the land and naval forces contributed greatly to the German and Japanese superiority in the initial stages of the Second World War. Pearl Harbor and the disastrous defeats that the British and the Dutch suffered at the hands of the Japanese on land and at sea in 1941 and 1942 were the penalties to be paid for technological backwardness in the face of a more progressive enemy. If one reads the somber review of British defeats which Churchill gave in the secret session of Parliament on April 23, 1942,[6] one is struck by the fact that all these defeats on land, on the sea, and in the air have one common denominator: the disregard or misunderstanding of the change in the technology of warfare brought about by air power. Finally, nations which possess nuclear weapons and the means to deliver them have an enormous technological advantage over their competitors.

However, the availability of nuclear weapons also results in two extraordinary paradoxes, referred to above, as concerns its bearing upon national power. Both paradoxes stem from the enormous destructiveness of nuclear weapons. It is by virtue of that destructiveness that a quantitative increase in nuclear weapons, in contrast to conventional ones, does not of necessity signify a corresponding increase in national power. Once a nation possesses all the nuclear weapons necessary to destroy all the enemy targets it has chosen for destruction, taking all possible contingencies, such as a first strike by the enemy, into consideration, additional nuclear weapons will not increase that nation's power.

---

5. See the account by Felix Gilbert, "Machiavelli: The Renaissance of the Art of War," in *Makers of Modern Strategy,* edited by Edward Mead Earle (Princeton: Princeton University Press, 1944), pp. 8, 9.

6. *Winston Churchill's Secret Session Speeches* (New York: Simon and Schuster, 1946), pp. 53 ff.

The other paradox lies in the inverse relationship between the degree of destructiveness of nuclear weapons and their rational usability. High-yield nuclear weapons are instruments of indiscriminate mass destruction and can therefore not be used for rational military purposes. They can be used to deter a war by threatening total destruction; but they cannot be used to fight a war in a rational manner. A nation armed with nothing but high-yield nuclear weapons could draw very little political power from its military posture; for it would have no military means by which to impose its will upon another nation, aside from threatening it with total destruction.

If such a nation has a second-strike nuclear capability, it will threaten total destruction in return and then the two threats either will cancel each other out or will lead to the mutual destruction of the belligerents. If the threatened nation has no nuclear means of retaliation, it will either suffer total destruction or surrender unconditionally as did Japan in 1945 after Hiroshima and Nagasaki had been destroyed by nuclear bombs. In other words, the threatening nation could wipe the nonnuclear nation off the face of the earth, either piecemeal, city by city, or in one devastating blow, but it could not subtly adapt the degree of military pressure to be used to the degree of psychological resistance to be overcome. The absence of conventional weapons, susceptible to such subtle adaptations, and the sole reliance upon high-yield nuclear weapons would make a nation less powerful than it would be if it possessed a combination of high-yield nuclear weapons for the purpose of deterrence and an armory of conventional weapons usable for the ordinary purposes of warfare. Hence the paradox that in order to make nuclear weapons usable one must reduce their yield to approximate that of conventional weapons.

Leadership

Aside from the timely use of technological innovations, the quality of military leadership has always exerted a decisive influence upon national power. The power of Prussia in the eighteenth century was primarily a reflection of the military genius of Frederick the Great and of the strategic and tactical innovations introduced by him. The art of warfare had changed between the death of Frederick the Great in 1786 and the battle of Jena in 1806 when Napoleon destroyed the Prussian army, which in itself was then as good and strong as it had been twenty years before. But, what was more important, military genius was lacking in its leaders who were fighting the battles of Frederick the Great all over again. On the other side military genius was in command, employing new ideas in strategy and tactics. This factor decided the issue in favor of France.

The Maginot Line psychology of the French general staff in the period between the two world wars has become a byword for faulty strategic thinking. While the tendencies of modern technology, especially its trend toward mechanization of transportation and of communications, pointed toward the probability of a war of movement, the French general staff continued to think in terms of the trench warfare of the First World War. The German general staff on the other hand, fully alive to the strategic potentialities of mechanized warfare, planned its campaigns in terms of unprecedented mobility. The conflagration of these two conceptions, not only in France but also in Poland and the Soviet Union, produced in the "blitzkrieg" a superiority of German power which brought Germany close to final victory. The intellectual shock and the military and political devastation caused by the onslaught of Hitler's panzers and dive bombers upon the Polish cavalry in 1939 and upon the immobile French army in 1940 ushered in a new period of military history, similar to the one initiated by Charles VIII's invasion of Italy in 1494.

But, while the Italian states had nobody to fall back on in order to recover their strength, in the Second World War the superior technology of the United States and the superior manpower of the Soviet Union turned Hitler's innovations to his destruction.

Quantity and Quality of Armed Forces

The power of a nation in military terms is also dependent upon the quantity of men and arms and their distribution among the different branches of the military' establishment. A nation may have a good grasp of technological innovations in warfare. Its military leaders may excel in the strategy and tactics appropriate to the new techniques of war. Yet such a nation may be militarily and, in consequence, also politically weak if it does not possess a military establishment that in its over-all strength and in the strength of its component parts is neither too large nor too small in view of the tasks it may be called upon to perform. Must a nation, in order to be strong, possess a large army or is its power not impaired by having, at least in peacetime, only small land forces, composed of highly trained, heavily armed specialized units? Have battle-ready forces-in-being become more important than trained reserves? Have large surface navies become obsolete, or do aircraft carriers still fulfill a useful purpose? How large a military establishment can a nation afford in view of its resources and commitments? Does concern for national power require large-scale peacetime production of aircraft and other mechanized weapons, or should a nation, in view of rapid changes in technology, spend its resources on research and on the production of limited quantities of improved types of weapons?

Whether a nation gives the right or the wrong answer to such questions of a quantitative character has obviously a direct bearing upon national power. Can decision in war be forced by one new weapon, such as artillery, as was thought at the turn of the fifteenth century, or the submarine, as the Germans thought in the First World War, or the airplane, as was widely believed in the period between the two world wars, or the inter-continental guided missiles, as many believe today? The wrong answers given to some of these questions by Great Britain and France in the period between the two world wars preserved for them the semblance of power in terms of the traditional military conceptions. But those errors brought them to the brink of final defeat in the course of the Second World War, whose military technique required different answers to these questions. Upon the quality of the answers we give to these and similar questions today will depend the future power of the United States in relation to other nations.

POPULATION

When we turn from material factors and those compounded of material and human elements to the purely human factors that determine the power of a nation, we have to distinguish quantitative and qualitative components. While among the latter we count national character, national morale, and the quality of diplomacy and of government in general, the former needs to be discussed in terms of size of population.

Distribution

It would, of course, not be correct to say that the larger the population of a country the greater the power of that country. For if such an unqualified correlation existed between size of population and national power, China, whose population is estimated as being over 1 billion people,[7] would be the most powerful nation on earth, followed by India with about 730 million. The Soviet Union with about 272 million and the United States with 234 million would run third and fourth, respectively. Though one is not justified in considering a country to be very powerful because its population is greater than that of most other countries, it is still true that no country can remain or become a first-rate power which does not belong to the more populous nations of the earth. Without a large population it is impossible to establish and keep going the industrial plant necessary for the successful conduct of modern war; to put into the field the large number of combat groups to fight on land, on the sea, and in the air; and, finally, to fill the cadres of the troops, considerably more numerous than the combat troops, which must supply the latter with food, means of transportation and communication, ammunition, and weapons. It is for this reason that imperialistic countries stimulate population growth with all kinds of incentives, as did Nazi Germany and Fascist Italy, and then use that growth as an ideological pretext for imperialistic expansion. . . .

Since size of population is one of the factors upon which national power rests, and since the power of one nation is always relative to the power of others, the relative size of the population of countries competing for power and, especially, the relative rate of their growth deserve careful attention. A country inferior in size of population to its competitor will view with alarm a declining rate of growth if the population of its competitor tends to increase more rapidly. Such has been the situation of France with regard to Germany between 1870 and 1940. During that period, the population of France increased by four million, whereas Germany registered a gain of twenty-seven million. While in 1800 every seventh European was a Frenchman, in 1930 only every thirteenth was a Frenchman. In 1940, Germany had at its disposal about fifteen million men fit for military service, whereas France had only five million.

On the other hand, ever since the unification in 1870, Germany has viewed sometimes with alarm, and always with respect, the Russian population figures, which show a greater rate of increase than Germany's. Looking at the situation as it existed at the outbreak of the First World War solely from the point of view of population trends, Germany could feel that time was on Russia's side, and France could feel that time was on the side of Germany, while both Austria and Russia, for other reasons already alluded to,[8] could believe that postponement of the conflict would favor the opponent. Thus all the protagonists, with the exception of Great Britain, had reasons of their own to prefer a war in 1914 to a peaceful settlement which they could not regard as definite, but only as a breathing spell before the unavoidable settling of accounts.

As the shifts in the distribution of power within Europe in recent history have been roughly duplicated by the changes in population trends, so the emergence of the United States as the great power center of the West, taking the place of Western and Central Europe, can be read in the population figures of the respective countries. In 1870, the population of France as well as of Germany exceeded that of the United States. Yet, in 1940, the population of the United States had increased by 100 million while the combined increase in the populations of France and Germany in the same period amounted to only thirty-one million.

---

7. All Population figures, unless indicated otherwise, are derived from the information reported in the U.S. Census Bureau Report for mid-June 1983, *New York Times*, September 4, 1983, p. A9.

8. See page 63.

It is thus obvious that a nation cannot be the first rank without a population sufficiently large to create and apply the material implements of national power. On the other hand, it has become obvious only in recent times that a large population can also exert a drastically negative influence upon national power. This has happened in so-called underdeveloped nations, such as India and Egypt, whose populations have greatly increased, by virtue of a decrease in the mortality rates, while their food supply did not keep pace with the increase in population. These countries were continually faced with the threat of famine and with the need to take care of large masses of undernourished and diseased people. They had to divert scarce resources from the development of their national power to the feeding and care of their populations. The largeness of their population, far from being an asset for their national power, is an obstacle to its development. For such nations, to bring the number of their population into harmony with their resources is a necessity, and if resources cannot be increased, population control is a precondition of national power.[9]

Trends

It is obvious from what has been said thus far that in trying to assess the future distribution of power the prediction of population trends plays an important role. All other factors remaining approximately equal, a considerable decline in the manpower of a nation in comparison with its competitors on the international scene spells a decline in national power, and a considerable increase, under similar conditions, amounts to a gain in national strength. When, toward the end of the nineteenth century, the British Empire was the only world power in existence, its population amounted to about 400 million; that is, approximately one fourth of the total population of the world. In 1946, it came close to 550 million. Since India's population was then estimated at 400 million, these figures illustrate the enormous loss in national power, in terms of size of population alone, which Great Britain suffered in the loss of India.

From the point of view of population, the position of the United States will continue to show considerable strength in comparison with Western Europe because of the latter's anticipated small increases. But compared with the population trend in Latin America, the position of the United States is well on its way to deterioration. Latin America shows the greatest rate of increase of any major region in the world. In 1900, Latin America had an estimated sixty-three million inhabitants to seventy-five million for the United States. The population of Argentina alone more than doubled between 1914 and 1965 and is now almost twenty-eight million. In the same period the population of the United States has only risen from 99 to 234 million.

It is, however, not sufficient to know the over-all population figures of different countries in order to assess correctly the influence of the population factor upon national power. The age distribution within a given population is an important element in power calculations. All other things being equal, a nation with a relatively large population of maximum potential usefulness for military' and productive purposes (roughly between twenty and forty years of age) will have an edge in power over a nation in whose population the older age groups predominate.

It must be pointed out, however, that the projection of population trends is hazardous even without the interference of war or natural catastrophes. The estimates of population

---

9. Cf. above page 88.

trends which were made in the forties painted a rather pessimistic picture of the increase of the American population as compared with that of the Soviet Union. Yet today the population of the United States exceeds by a wide margin the number that some population experts of great repute expected it to reach by 1975. Even in a field whose scientific accuracy appears to be relatively high, the prediction of national power is beset with uncertainties. But these uncertainties do not affect the importance of population trends for the development of national power. Nor can they diminish the active concern of statesmen with the population trends of their own nations.

Echoing Augustus and his successors on the throne of the Roman Empire, Sir Winston Churchill, as British Prime Minister, expressed this concern when he said in his radio address of March 22, 1943:

> One of the most somber anxieties which beset those who look thirty, or forty, or fifty years ahead, and in this field one can see ahead only too clearly, is the dwindling birth-rate. In thirty years, unless present trends alter, a smaller working and fighting population will have to support and protect nearly twice as many old people; in fifty years the position will be worse still. If this country is to keep its high place in the leadership of the world, and to survive as a great power that can hold its own against external pressures, our people must be encouraged by every means to have larger families.

NATIONAL CHARACTER

Its Existence

Of the three human factors of a qualitative nature which have a bearing on national power, national character and national morale stand out both for their elusiveness from the point of view of rational prognosis and for their permanent and often decisive influence upon the weight a nation is able to put into the scales of international politics. We are not concerned here with the question of what factors are responsible for the development of a national character. We are only interested in the fact—contested but (it seems to us) incontestable, especially in view of the anthropological concept of the "culture pattern"—that certain qualities of intellect and character occur more frequently and are more highly valued in one nation than in another. To quote Coleridge:

> . . . But that there is an invisible spirit that breathes through a whole people, and is participated by all, though not by all alike; a spirit which gives a color and character both to their virtues and vices, so that the same action, such I mean as are expressed by the same words, are yet not the same in a Spaniard as they would be in a Frenchman, I hold for an undeniable truth, without the admission of which all history would be a riddle. I hold likewise that the difference of nations, their relative grandeur and meanness, all, in short, which they are or do, (not indeed at one particular time, under the accidental influence of a single great man, as the Carthaginians under the great Xantippus, and afterwards under their own Hannibal,) but all in which they persevere, as a nation, through successions of changing individuals, are the result of this spirit; . . .[10]

These qualities set one nation apart from others, and they show a high degree of resiliency to change. A few examples, taken at random, will illustrate the point.

---

10. Samuel Taylor Coleridge, *Essays on his own Times* (London: William Pickering, 1850), Vol. II, pp. 668–9.

Is it not an incontestable fact that, as John Dewey[11] and many others have pointed out, Kant and Hegel are as typical of the philosophic tradition of Germany as Descartes and Voltaire are of the French mind, as Locke and Burke are of the political thought of Great Britain, as William James and John Dewey are of the American approach to intellectual problems? And can it be denied that these philosophic differences are but expressions, on the highest level of abstraction and systematization, of fundamental intellectual and moral traits that reveal themselves on all levels of thought and action and that give each nation its unmistakable distinctiveness? The mechanistic rationality and the systematic perfection of Descartes' philosophy reappear in the tragedies of Corneille and Racine no less than in the rationalistic fury of Jacobin reform. They reappear in the sterility of the academic formalism that characterizes much of the contemporary intellectual life of France. They reappear in the scores of peace plans, logically perfect but impracticable, in which French statecraft excelled in the period between the two world wars. On the other hand, the trait of intellectual curiosity which Julius Caesar detected in the Gauls has remained throughout the ages a distinctive characteristic of the French mind.

Locke's philosophy is as much a manifestation of British individualism as Magna Carta, due process of law, or Protestant sectarianism. In Edmund Burke, with his undogmatic combination of moral principle and political expediency, the political genius of the British people reveals itself as much as in the Reform Acts of the nineteenth century or the balance-of-power policies of Cardinal Wolsey and Canning. What Tacitus said of the destructive political and military propensities of the Germanic tribes fitted the armies of Frederick Barbarossa no less than those of William II and of Hitler. It fits, too, the traditional rudeness and clumsy deviousness of German diplomacy. The authoritarianism, collectivism, and state worship of German philosophy have their counterpart in the tradition of autocratic government, in servile acceptance of any authority so long as it seems to have the will and force to prevail, and, concomitant with it, the lack of civil courage, the disregard of individual rights, and the absence of a tradition of political liberty. The description of the American national character, as it emerges from Tocqueville's *Democracy in America*, has not been deprived of its timeliness by the intervention of more than a century. The indecision of American pragmatism between an implicit dogmatic idealism and reliance upon success as a measure of truth is reflected in the vacillations of American diplomacy between the Four Freedoms and the Atlantic Charter, on the one hand, and "dollar diplomacy," on the other. . . .

National Character and National Power

National character cannot fail to influence national power; for those who act for the nation in peace and war, formulate, execute, and support its policies, elect and are elected, mold public opinion, produce and consume—all bear to a greater or lesser degree the imprint of those intellectual and moral qualities which make up the national character. The "elementary force and persistence" of the Russians, the individual initiative and inventiveness of the Americans, the undogmatic common sense of the British, the discipline and thoroughness of the Germans are some of the qualities which will manifest themselves, for better or for worse, in all the individual and collective activities in which the members of a nation may engage. In consequence of the differences in national character, the German and Russian governments, for instance, have been able to embark upon foreign policies

11. *German Philosophy and Politics* (New York: G.P. Putnam's Sons, 1942), *passim*.

that the American and British governments would have been incapable of pursuing, and vice versa. Antimilitarism, aversion to standing armies and to compulsory military service are permanent traits of the American and British national character. Yet the same institutions and activities have for centuries stood high in the hierarchy of values of Prussia, from where their prestige spread over all of Germany. In Russia the tradition of obedience to the authority of the government and the traditional fear of the foreigner have made large permanent military establishments acceptable to the population.

Thus the national character has given Germany and Russia an initial advantage in the struggle for power, since they could transform in peacetime a greater portion of their national resources into instruments of war. On the other hand, the reluctance of the American and British peoples to consider such a transformation, especially on a large scale and with respect to manpower, except in an obvious national emergency, has imposed a severe handicap upon American and British foreign policy. Governments of militaristic nations are able to plan, prepare, and wage war at the moment of their choosing. They can, more particularly, start a preventive war whenever it seems to be most propitious for their cause. Governments of pacifist nations, of which the United States was the outstanding example until the end of the Second World War, are in this respect in a much more difficult situation and have much less freedom of action. Restrained as they are by the innate antimilitarism of their peoples, they must pursue a more cautious course in foreign affairs. Frequently the military strength actually at their disposal will not be commensurate with the political commitments that their concern for the national interest imposes upon them. In other words, they will not have the armed might sufficient to back up their policies. When they go to war, they may well do so on the terms of their enemies. In the past they have had to rely upon other traits in the national character and upon other compensating factors, such as geographical location and industrial potential, to carry them over the initial period of weakness and inferiority to ultimate victory. Such can be the effects, for good or evil, of the character of a nation.

The observer of the international scene who attempts to assess the relative strength of different nations must take national character into account, however difficult it may be to assess correctly so elusive and intangible a factor. Failure to do so will lead to errors in judgment and policies, such as the depreciation of the recuperative force of Germany after the First World War and the underestimation of Russian staying power in 1941–42. The Treaty of Versailles could restrict Germany in all the other implements of national power, such as territory, sources of raw materials, industrial capacity, and military establishment. But it could not deprive Germany of all those qualities of intellect and character which enabled it within a period of two decades to rebuild what it had lost and to emerge as the strongest single military power in the world. The virtually unanimous opinion of the military experts who in 1942 gave the Russian army only a few more months of resistance may have been correct in purely military terms, such as military strategy, mobility, industrial resources, and the like. Yet this expert opinion was obviously mistaken in underrating that factor of "elementary force and persistence" which better judgment has recognized as the great source of Russian strength in its dealings with Europe. The pessimism that in 1940 denied Great Britain a chance for survival had its roots in a similar neglect or misreading of the national character of the British people.

We have already mentioned in another context the contempt in which American power was held by the German leaders before the Second World War.[12] It is interesting to

12. See Morgenthau: *The Struggle for Power: Policy of Prestige.*

note that exactly the same mistake, and for the same reason, was made by the German leaders during the First World War. Thus, in October 1916, the German Secretary of the Navy estimated the significance of the United States joining the Allies to be "zero," and another German minister of that period declared in a parliamentary speech, after the United States had actually entered the war on the side of the Allies: "The Americans cannot swim and they cannot fly, the Americans will never come." In both cases, the German leaders underestimated American power by paying attention exclusively to the quality of the military establishment at a particular moment, to the antimilitarism of the American character, and to the factor of geographical distance. They disregarded completely the qualities of the American character, such as individual initiative, gift for improvisation, and technical skill, which, together with the other material factor and under favorable conditions, might more than outweigh the disadvantages of geographical remoteness and of a dilapidated military establishment.

On the other hand, the belief of many experts, at least until the battle of Stalingrad in 1943, in the invincibility of Germany drew its strength from the material factors as well as from certain aspects of the German national character which seemed to favor total victory. These experts neglected other aspects of the national character of the German people, in particular their lack of moderation. From the emperors of the Middle Ages and the princes fighting the Thirty Years' War to William II and Hitler, this lack of moderation has proved to be the one fatal weakness of the German national character. Unable to restrain goal and action within the limits of the possible, the Germans have time and again squandered and ultimately destroyed the national power of Germany built upon other material and human factors.

NATIONAL MORALE

More elusive and less stable, but no less important than all the other factors in its bearing upon national power, is what we propose to call national morale. National morale is the degree of determination with which a nation supports the foreign policies of its government in peace or war. It permeates all activities of a nation, its agricultural and industrial production as well as its military establishment and diplomatic service. In the form of public opinion, it provides an intangible factor without whose support no government, democratic or autocratic, is able to pursue its policies with full effectiveness, if it is able to pursue them at all. Its presence or absence and its qualities reveal themselves particularly in times of national crisis, when either the existence of the nation is at stake or else a decision of fundamental importance must be taken upon which the survival of the nation might well depend.

Its Instability

While certain traits of the national character may easily manifest themselves in the national morale of the people at a certain moment of history, such as the common sense of the British, the individualism of the French, the tenacity of the Russians, no conclusion can be drawn from the character of a nation as to what the morale of that nation might be under certain contingencies. Their national character seems to qualify the American people to a particular degree for playing the role of a first-rate power under the conditions of the twentieth century. Yet nobody can foresee with any degree of certainty what the national morale of the American people would be like under the conditions of hardship and disintegration which prevailed in the different belligerent countries of Europe and

Asia during certain phases of the Second World War and of the postwar years. Nor is there a way of anticipating the reactions of the British people to a repetition of the experiences of the Second World War. They stood up under the "blitz" and V-weapons once. Could they stand up under them a second time? And what about nuclear weapons? Similar questions can be asked of all nations, and no rational answers are forthcoming.

American national morale, in particular, has been in recent years the object of searching speculation at home and abroad; for American foreign policy and, through it, the weight of American power in international affairs is to a peculiar degree dependent upon the moods of American public opinion, as they express themselves in the votes of Congress, election results, polls, and the like. Would the United States join the United Nations and stay with it despite disappointments? Would Congress support the economic and military assistance program for Europe, and for how long would it vote billions for foreign aid throughout the world? How far were the American people willing to go in supporting South Korea, and under what conditions would they continue to do so? Would they be willing to cope indefinitely with the liabilities, risks, and frustrations attributed to the Soviet Union, without either relaxing their efforts or trying to end it all by drastic action? The main factor upon which the answers to these questions depended or depend is the state of national morale at the decisive moment.

The national morale of any people will obviously break at a certain point. The breaking point is different for different peoples and under different circumstances. Some peoples will be brought close to the breaking point by tremendous and useless losses in war, such as the French after the Nivelle offensive in 1917 in the Champagne. One great defeat will suffice to under- mine the national morale of others, such as the defeat the Italians suffered in 1917 at Caporetto, which cost them three hundred thousand men in prisoners and the same number in deserters. The morale of others, such as the Russians in 1917, will break under the impact of a combination of tremendous war losses in men and territory and the mismanagement of an autocratic government. The morale of others will only slowly decline and, as it were, corrode at the edges—not break at all in one sudden collapse, even when exposed to a rare combination of governmental mismanagement, devastation, invasion, and a hopeless war situation. Such was the case of the Germans in the last stage of the Second World War, when a number of military leaders and former high officials gave up the lost cause while the masses of the people fought on until practically the moment of Hitler's suicide. The persistence of German morale in 1945 under most unfavorable circumstances illustrates dramatically the unpredictability of such collective reactions. Under much less severe circumstances the national morale of Germany collapsed in November 1918, a precedent that should have presaged a similar collapse of German morale some time in the summer of 1944, after the Allied invasion of France. Tolstoy gives in *War and Peace* a vivid analysis of the independent importance of morale for military success:

> Military science assumes that the relative strength of forces is identical with their numerical proportions. Military science maintains that the greater the number of soldiers, the greater their strength. *Les gros bataillons ont toujours raison.*
>
> To say this is as though one were in mechanics to say that forces were equal or unequal simply because the masses of the moving bodies were equal or unequal.
>
> Force (the volume of motion) is the product of the mass into the velocity.
>
> In warefare the force of armies is the product of the mass multiplied by something else, an unknown x.

> Military science, seeing in history an immense number of examples in which the mass of an army does not correspond with its force, and in which small numbers conquer large ones, vaguely recognizes the existence of this unknown factor, and tries to find it sometimes in some geometrical disposition of the troops, sometimes in the superiority of the weapons, and most often in the genius of the leaders. But none of those factors yield results that agree with the historical facts.
>
> One has but to renounce the false view that glorifies the effect of the activity of the heroes of history in warfare in order to discover this unknown quantity, X.
>
> X is the spirit of the army, the greater or less desire to fight and to face dangers on the part of all men composing the army, which is quite apart from the question whether they are fighting under leaders of genius or not, with cudgels or with guns that fire thirty times a minute. The men who have the greater desire to fight always put themselves, too, in the more advantageous position for fighting. The spirit of the army is the factor which multiplied by the mass gives the product of the force. To define and express the significance of this unknown factor, the spirit of the army, is the problem of science.
>
> This problem can only be solved when we cease arbitrarily substituting for that unknown factor x the conditions under which the force is manifested, such as the plans of the general, the arming of the men and so on, and recognize this unknown factor in its entirety as the greater or less desire to fight and face danger. Then only by expressing known historical facts in equations can one hope from comparison of the relative value of this unknown factor to approach its definition. Ten men, or battalions or divisions are victorious fighting with fifteen men or battalions or divisions, that is, they kill or take prisoner all of them while losing four of their own side, so that the loss has been four on one side and fifteen on the other. Consequently, four on one side have been equivalent to fifteen on the other, and consequently $4x = 15y$. Consequently $\frac{x}{y} = \frac{15}{4}$.
>
> This equation does not give us the value of the unknown factors, but it does give us the ratio between their values. And from the reduction to such equations of various historical units (battles, campaigns, periods of warfare) a series of numbers are obtained, in which there must be and may be discovered historical laws.[13]

The Quality of Society and Government as Decisive Factors

While national morale is subjected to its ultimate test in war, it is important whenever a nation's power is brought to bear on an international problem. It is important partly because of the anticipated effects of national morale upon military strength, partly because national morale influences the determination with which the government pursues its foreign policies. Any segment of the population which feels itself permanently deprived of its rights and of full participation in the life of the nation will tend to have a lower national morale, to be less "patriotic" than those who do not suffer from such disabilities. The same is likely to be true of those whose vital aspirations diverge from the permanent policies pursued by the majority or by the government. Whenever deep dissensions tear a people apart, the popular support that can be mustered for a foreign policy will always be precarious and will be actually small if the success or failure of the foreign policy has a direct bearing upon the issue of the domestic struggle.

Autocratic governments, which in the formulation of their policies do not take the wishes of the people into account, cannot rely upon much popular support for their foreign policies. Such was the case in countries like Czarist Russia and the Austrian monarchy.

---

13. Leo Tolstoy, *War and Peace*, Part XIV, Chapter II.

The example of Austria is particularly instructive. Many of the foreign policies of that country, especially with respect to the Slavic nations, aimed at weakening the latter in order better to be able to keep in check the Slavic nationalities living under Austrian rule. In consequence, these Slavic nationalities tended to be at best indifferent to the foreign policies of their own government and at worst to support actively the policies of Slavic governments directed against their own. Thus it is not surprising that during the First World War whole Slavic units of the Austro-Hungarian army went over to the Russians. The government dared to use other such units only against non-Slavic enemies, such as the Italians. For similar reasons, during the First World War the German army used Alsatian units against the Russians, and Polish units against the French.

The Soviet Union had a similar experience of lack of morale during the Second World War when large contingents composed in the main of Ukrainians and Tartars deserted to the Germans. Great Britain had the same experience with India, whose national energies supported but unwillingly and with reservations the foreign policies of its alien master—if they did not, like Bose and his followers during the Second World War, come to the assistance of the alien master's enemy. Napoleon and Hitler had to learn to their dismay that among the spoils of foreign conquest popular support of the conqueror's policies is not necessarily to be found. The amount and strength of the support Hitler, for instance, found among the conquered peoples of Europe was in inverse ratio to the quality of the national morale of the particular people.

Any country with deep and unbridgeable class divisions will find its national morale in a precarious state. French power ever since the thirties has suffered from this weakness. From the time of Hitler's ascent to power, the vacillating foreign policies of the French governments, following each other in rapid succession and concealing their impotence behind the ideologies of a status quo they were unwilling and incapable of defending, has already weakened the national morale of the French people as a whole. The crises of 1938–39, with the ever renewed threat of war and general mobilizations to meet it, followed by Hitler's successes, demobilizations, and an increasingly precarious peace, had contributed powerfully to the general decay of French morale. While there was decay everywhere, there was actual collapse only in two important sectors of French society. On the one hand, faced with social legislation limiting their powers, considerable groups of the French upper classes rallied to the cry: "Rather Hitler (the enemy dictator) then Blum (the French Socialist)!" Although Hitler threatened the position of France in Europe and its very existence as a nation, these groups were unable to give wholehearted support to the French foreign policy opposing Hitler. Alter the conquest of France they favored the domination of France by Hitler rather than its liberation from the foreign dictator. On the other hand, the Communists, for different reasons, undermined the national morale of France so long as Hitler fought only the capitalists of the West. It was only after he had attacked the Soviet Union that they contributed new strength to French national morale by fighting in the forefront of the resistance against the invader.

However unpredictable the quality of national morale, especially at a moment of great crisis, there are obvious situations where national morale is likely to be high, while under certain different conditions the odds are in favor of a low state of national morale. One can say, in general, that the more closely identified a people are with the actions and objectives of their government—especially, of course, in foreign affairs—the better are the chances for national morale to be high, and vice versa. Thus it can surprise only those who mistakenly think of the modern totalitarian state in terms of the autocracies of the eighteenth and nineteenth centuries that in Nazi Germany national morale was high almost to the last. It declined slowly rather than breaking in one sudden collapse as it did in November 1918. The great bulk of the Russian people, despite the greatest hardships in war and peace, have consistently shown a high degree of national morale.

The modern totalitarian state has been able to fill the gap between government and people, a gap that was typical of the monarchies of the eighteenth and nineteenth centuries, through the use of democratic symbols, totalitarian control of public opinion, and policies actually or seemingly benefiting the people. Practically all national energies flow into the channels chosen by the government, and the identification of the individual with the state, which we have recognized as one of the characteristics of modern politics,[14] reaches under the stimulation of totalitarianism the intensity of religious fervor. Therefore, so long as totalitarian governments are or seem to be successful, or can at least hold out hope for success, they can count upon the determined support of their peoples for the foreign policies they pursue.

What totalitarianism can achieve only by force, fraud, and deification of the state, democracy must try to accomplish through the free interplay of popular forces, guided by a wise and responsible government. Where the government is unable to prevent the degeneration of this interplay into class, racial, or religious conflicts, tending to split the national community into warring groups, national morale is likely to be low, at least among the victimized groups if not among the people as a whole. The policies of France before and during the Second World War illustrate this point. So does the weakness of the foreign policies in peace and war of countries where feudal aristocracies or autocratic dictators control the government and oppress the people. The governments of such nations can never choose and pursue their foreign objectives with any degree of determination, even at the risk of war, because they can never be sure of the support of their peoples. They constantly fear lest the domestic opposition exploit difficulties and reverses in the international field for the purpose of overthrowing the regime. Where, however, a government speaks as the mouthpiece, and acts as the executor, of the popular will, national morale is likely to reflect the real identity between popular aspirations and governmental actions. The national morale of Denmark under the German occupation from 1940 to the end of the Second World War illustrates this point no less strikingly than did the national morale of Germany until the defeat at Stalingrad.

In the last analysis, then, the power of a nation, in view of its national morale, resides in the quality of its government. A government that is truly representative, not only in the sense of parliamentary' majorities, but above all in the sense of being able to translate the inarticulate convictions and aspirations of the people into international objectives and policies, has the best chance to marshal the national energies in support of those objectives and policies. The adage that free men fight better than slaves can be amplified into the proposition that nations well governed are likely to have a higher national morale than nations poorly governed. The quality of government is patently a source of strength or weakness with respect to most of the factors upon which national power depends, especially in view of the influence the government exerts upon natural resources, industrial capacity, and military' preparedness. For the quality of national morale, the quality of government takes on a special importance. Whereas it operates upon the other elements of national power as one among several influences, all more or less manageable by human

---

14. See Morgenthau: *The Essence of National Power.*

action, it is the only tangible factor among intangibles which accounts for the quality of national morale. Without national morale, national power is either nothing but material force or else a potentiality that awaits its realization in vain. Yet the only means of deliberately improving national morale lies in the improvement of the quality of government. All else is a matter of chance.

THE QUALITY OF DIPLOMACY[15]

Of all the factors that make for the power of a nation, the most important, however unstable, is the quality of diplomacy. All the other factors that determine national power are, as it were, the raw material out of which the power of a nation is fashioned. The quality of a nation's diplomacy combines those different factors into an integrated whole, gives them direction and weight, and awakens their slumbering potentialities by giving them the breath of actual power. The conduct of a nation's foreign affairs by its diplomats is for national power in peace what military strategy and tactics by its military leaders are for national power in war. It is the art of bringing the different elements of the national power to bear with maximum effect upon those points in the international situation which concern the national interest most directly.

Diplomacy, one might say, is the brains of national power, as national morale is its soul. If its vision is blurred, its judgment defective, and its determination feeble, all the advantages of geographical location, of self sufficiency in food, raw materials, and industrial production, of military' preparedness, of size and quality of population will in the long run avail a nation little. A nation that can boast of all these advantages, but not of a diplomacy commensurate with them, may achieve temporary successes through the sheer weight of its natural assets. In the long run, it is likely to squander the natural assets by activating them incompletely, haltingly, and wastefully for the nation's international objectives.

In the long run, such a nation must yield to one whose diplomacy is prepared to make the most of whatever other elements of power are at its disposal, thus making up through its own excellence for deficiencies in other fields. By using the power potentialities of a nation to best advantage, a competent diplomacy can increase the power of a nation beyond what one would expect it to be in view of all the other factors combined. Often in history the Goliath without brains or soul has been smitten and slain by the David who had both. Diplomacy of high quality will bring the ends and means of foreign policy into harmony with the available resources of national power. It will tap the hidden sources of national strength and transform them fully and securely into political realities. By giving direction to the national effort, it will in turn increase the independent weight of certain factors, such as industrial potential, military preparedness, national character, and morale. It is for this reason that national power is apt to rise to its height fulfilling all its potentialities, particularly in times of war, when ends and means of policy are clearly laid out.

The United States, in the period between the two world wars, furnishes a striking example of a potentially powerful nation playing a minor role in world affairs because its foreign policy refused to bring the full weight of its potential strength to bear upon international problems. As far as the power of the United States on the international scene was concerned, the advantages of geography, natural resources, industrial potential, and size

15. By the term "diplomacy," as used in the following pages, we refer to the formation and execution of foreign policy on all levels, the highest as well as the subordinate.

and quality of population might as well have not existed at all, for American diplomacy proceeded as though they did not exist.

The transformation American foreign policy has undergone since the end of the Second World War seemed to have answered definitively the question whether, and to what extent, American diplomacy is willing and able to transform the potentialities of national power into political actualities. Yet at the beginning of that period, in an article significantly entitled, "Imperialism or Indifference," the London *Economist* still doubted the answer. After enumerating the factors that, taken by themselves, would make the United States the most powerful nation on earth, the *Economist* continued:

> But though these things are essential ingredients, they are not all that it takes to make a Great Power. There must also be the willingness, and the ability, to use economic resources in support of national policy. The rulers of Soviet Russia . . . are not likely, at least for a generation to come, to have nearly as good cards in their hands as the Americans. But the nature of their system of concentrated power and iron censorship enables them to play a forcing game. The Americans' hand is all trumps; but will any of them ever be played? And for what purpose?[16]

The classic example of a country that, while in other respects hopelessly outclassed, returned to the heights of power chiefly by virtue of its brilliant diplomacy is France in the period from 1890 to 1914. After is defeat in 1870 at the hands of Germany, France was a second-rate power, and Bismarck's statecraft, by isolating it, kept it in that position. With Bismarck's dismissal in 1890, Germany's foreign policy turned away from Russia and was unwilling to alleviate Great Britain's suspicion. French diplomacy took full advantage of those mistakes of German foreign policy. In 1894, France added a military alliance to the political understanding reached with Russia in 1891; in 1904 and 1912, it entered into informal agreements with Great Britain. The configuration of 1914, which found France aided by potent allies and Germany deserted by one (Italy) and burdened with the weakness of the others (Austria-Hungary, Bulgaria, Turkey) was in the main the work of a galaxy of brilliant French diplomatists: Camille Barrère, Ambassador to Italy, Jules Cambon, Ambassador to Germany, Paul Cambon, Ambassador to Great Britain, Maurice Paléologue, Ambassador to Russia. . . .

Nations must rely upon the quality of their diplomacy to act as a catalyst for the different factors that constitute their power. In other words, these different factors, as they are brought to bear upon an international problem by diplomacy, are what is called a nation's power. Therefore it is of the utmost importance that the good quality of the diplomatic service be constant. And constant quality is best assured by dependence upon tradition and institutions rather than upon the sporadic appearance of outstanding individuals. . . .

THE QUALITY OF GOVERNMENT

The best conceived and most expertly executed foreign policy, drawing upon an abundance of material and human resources, must come to naught if it cannot draw also upon good government. Good government, viewed as an independent requirement of national power,[17] means three things: balance between, on the one hand, the material and human resources that

---

16. *Economist*, May 24, 1947, p. 785.

17. We have already spoken of the quality of government as a requirement of national morale; earlier in this chapter.

go into the making of national power and, on the other, the foreign policy to be pursued; balance among those resources; and popular support for the foreign policies to be pursued.

The Problem of Balance Between Resources and Policy

Good government, then, must start by performing two different intellectual operations. First, it must choose the objectives and methods of its foreign policy in view of the power available to support them with a maximum chance of success. A nation that sets its sights too low, forgoing foreign policies well within the reach of its power, abdicates its rightful role in the council of nations; the United States fell into that error in the interwar period. A nation may also set its sights too high and pursue policies that cannot be successfully executed with the available power; this was the error which the United States committed during the peace negotiations in 1919. As Lloyd George put it: "The Americans appeared to assume responsibility for the sole guardianship of the Ten Commandments and for the Sermon on the Mount; yet, when it came to a practical question of assistance and responsibility, they absolutely refused to accept it." A nation may try to play the role of a great power without having the prerequisites for doing so, and will court disaster, as Poland did in the interwar period. Or, being a great power, it may embark upon a policy of unlimited conquest, overtaxing its strength; the unsuccessful world-conquerors, from Alexander to Hitler, illustrate that point.

Thus the national power available determines the limits of foreign policy. There is only one exception to that rule, and that is when the very existence of the nation is at stake. Then the policy of national survival overrides the rational considerations of national power, and the emergency reverses the normal relationship between policy and considerations of power, establishing the primacy of the former. A nation is then called upon to subordinate all other interests to that of survival and to make a national effort that rationally could not have been expected of it. This is what Great Britain did in the fall and winter of 1940–41.

The Problem of Balance Among Resources

Once a government has brought its foreign policy into balance with the power available to it, it must bring the different elements of national power into balance with each other. A nation does not necessarily attain the maximum of national power because it is very rich in natural resources, possesses a very large population, or has built an enormous industrial and military establishment. It attains that maximum when it has at its disposal a sufficient quantity and quality, in the right mixture, of those resources of power which will allow it to pursue a given foreign policy with a maximum chance of success. Great Britain, when it was at the summit of its power, was deficient in many of the elements of national power, such as natural resources, size of population, and ground troops. Yet it had developed to unchallengeable supremacy that one element of national power, the navy, which was a perfect instrument for the British policy of overseas expansion, and at the same time assured the uninterrupted flow from abroad of those raw materials and foodstuffs without which Great Britain could not have survived. In view of this policy, of the available natural resources, and of the geographic location, a large population and a standing army would have been for Great Britain a handicap rather than an asset. On the other hand, had Great Britain continued to pursue a policy of continental expansion, as it did during the better part of the Middle Ages, it would have been in need of both.

A large population is a source of weakness rather than of strength, as the example of India has shown us,[18] if it cannot be adequately fed with the available resources. The hasty building of great industrial and military establishments by totalitarian methods creates certain elements of national power, but in its very process destroys others, such as national morale and the physical resilience of the population; the developments in the Soviet satellites of Eastern Europe are a case in point. To plan for a military establishment that is too big to be supported by the available industrial capacity, and hence can be built and maintained only at the price of galloping inflation, economic crisis, and deterioration of morale, is to plan for national weakness rather than for power. In a national emergency, when the very existence of the nation is at stake, the American government, for instance, can and must offer the people guns instead of butter; if it cannot make a case for such an emergency, it must strike a balance between military and civilian requirements by allocating a fair share of the economic product for civilian consumption. Another government, such as the Chinese or Korean, might not need to take such considerations of civilian welfare into account. In other words, a government in its building of national power cannot be oblivious to the character of the nation it governs. One nation will revolt against hardships that another nation will take patiently in its stride, and sometimes a nation will surprise the world and itself by the sacrifices it willingly makes for the defense of its interests and its existence.

The Problem of Popular Support

A contemporary government, especially one subject to democratic control, has only performed part of its task when it has established the two types of balances which we have discussed above. Another task, perhaps the most difficult of all, still lies ahead of it. It must secure the approval of its own people for its foreign policies and the domestic ones designed to mobilize the elements of national power in support of them. That task is difficult because the conditions under which popular support can be obtained for a foreign policy are not necessarily identical with the conditions under which a foreign policy can be successfully pursued. As Tocqueville put it, with special reference to the United States:

> Foreign politics demand scarcely any of those qualities which are peculiar to a democracy; they require, on the contra, the perfect use of almost all those in which it is deficient. Democracy is favorable to the increase of the internal resources of a state; it diffuses wealth and comfort, promotes public spirit, and fortifies the respect for law in all classes of society: all these are advantages which have only an indirect influence over the relations which one people bears to another. But a democracy can only with great difficulty regulate the details of an important undertaking, persevere in a fixed design, and work out its execution in spite of serious obstacles. It cannot combine its measures with secrecy or await their consequences with patience. . . .
>
> The propensity that induces democracies to obey impulse rather than prudence, and to abandon mature design for the gratification of a momentary passion, was clearly seen in America on the breaking out of the French Revolution. It was then as evident to the simplest capacity as it is at the present time that the interest of the Americans forbade them to take any part in the contest which was about to deluge Europe with blood, but which could not injure their own country. But the sympathies of the people declared themselves with so much violence in favor of France that nothing but the inflexible character of Washington and the immense popularity which he enjoyed could have prevented the Americans from declaring war against England. And even then, the exertions which the austere reason of that great man made to

---

18. See the section on National Resources earlier in *this chapter*.

> repress the generous but imprudent passions of his fellow citizens nearly deprived him of the sole recompense which he ever claimed, that of his country's love. The majority reprobated his policy, but it was afterwards approved by the whole nation.[19]

Thinking required for the successful conduct of foreign policy can be diametrically opposed to the rhetoric and action by which the masses and their representatives are likely to be moved. The peculiar qualities of the statesman's mind are not always likely to find a favorable response in the popular mind. The statesman must think in terms of the national interest, conceived as power among other powers. The popular mind, unaware of the fine distinctions of the statesman's thinking, reasons more often than not in the simple moralistic and legalistic terms of absolute good and absolute evil. The statesman must take the long view, proceeding slowly and by detours, paying with small losses for great advantage; he must be able to temporize, to compromise, to bide his time. The popular mind wants quick results; it will sacrifice tomorrow's real benefit for today's apparent advantage.

If Tocqueville's point is well taken, the kind of thinking required for the successful conduct of foreign policy will at times be opposed to considerations by which people are moved. A foreign policy that is passionately and overwhelmingly supported by public opinion cannot be assumed for that reason alone to be good foreign policy. On the contrary, the harmony between foreign policy and public opinion may well have been achieved at the price of surrendering the principles of good foreign policy to the unsound preferences of public opinion.

In the American case these inherent difficulties are aggravated by the fact that the United States is almost continuously recovering from the last elections or preparing for the next one. Especially in the latter case, the temptation is overwhelming for an administration to seek to gain electoral advantage by catering to the preferences of public opinion, regardless of foreign policy. Thus one requirement of the statesman's art is to steer a middle course between respect for the perennial principles of sound foreign policy and the fickle preferences of public opinion.

These considerations shed an illuminating light upon the apparent paradox of President Jimmy Carter, who emerged from the Democratic primaries in 1980 as virtually unbeatable in his appeal to the electorate, yet under his leadership the United States had suffered a string of humiliating defeats in its relations with other nations. The most spectacular of these defeats was the continuing captivity of fifty hostages in Iran. By foreswearing from the outset any form of violence in response to this outrage, Carter deprived himself of any leverage against Iran. The disadvantages he was able to threaten Iran with, primarily economic sanctions, were bound to be ineffective. The advantages he could offer (such as economic and military aid) did not outweigh, in the eyes of the Iranians, the risks and liabilities American largesse would entail. Thus the United States stood helpless—in a situation which in most other periods of American history would have called forth swift action to settle the issue, even at the risk of some American lives.

But the President, by putting the emphasis on saving American lives by peaceful means, hit upon a sympathetic chord in American public opinion. Carter did what Wilson had allegedly done before: "He kept us out of war." He did so without abandoning the most visible and sentimental American objective: saving those fifty American lives. It apparently did not occur to public opinion or to the President that the leader responsible for American foreign policy has a duty not only to preserve lives, but also to preserve the long-term interests of the nation.

---

19. Alexis de Tocqueville, *Democracy in America* (New York: Alfred A. Knopf, 1945), Vol. I, pp. 234–5.

The same mixture of rhetorical commitment and political inaction has secured public support for our policies toward the Soviet Union and assured their ineffectiveness at the same time. Regardless of one's interpretation of the significance of the Soviet military takeover of Afghanistan, the belligerent verbal reaction of the President was out of all proportion to the actual measures taken in response to that takeover.

Yet while that belligerence may have surprised the Russians, the absence of action commensurate with that rhetoric did nothing to induce a change in their policies. The Russians will go as far as they can without provoking the United States into a nuclear confrontation. Positive cases in point are the Cuban missile crisis and the successive Berlin crises; a negative confirmation of this thesis is the continuing military occupation of Afghanistan.

However, the President's belligerent stance appeared to be a great success in domestic politics. The President who had declared his intention to make the protection and promotion of human rights the cornerstone of his foreign policy spoke to the Soviet Union in the language of John Foster Dulles. Public-opinion polls registered overwhelming popular approval: once again, a futile foreign policy was compensated for by domestic triumph. Here, however, Mr. Carter encountered another dilemma, superimposed upon the one between foreign policy and domestic politics. It evolved from the rational unacceptability of nuclear confrontation.

The need of great powers to defend and promote their interests by the use of force as a last resort implies in the case of the United States and the Soviet Union the possibility of using nuclear weapons as an instrument of force. Yet the use of nuclear weapons not as a single, isolated demonstration, as at Hiroshima and Nagasaki, but as normal instruments of warfare would mean the destruction of all the belligerents as viable societies. Nuclear weapons thus used—in contrast to conventional weapons—would not be a rational means to the rational ends of foreign policy, but instruments of desperation denoting suicide and genocide. This was the second fundamental dilemma Carter faced.

The anarchic character of the international system forced him, following a convention coterminous with history, to contemplate resort to physical violence as the ultimate factor in the settlement of international issues. Yet the irrationality of the all-out use of such violence made him shrink from the use even of conventional violence lest it might escalate into nuclear war. Thus in an international crisis today the President acts with utmost caution, if he acts at all, and he compensates for the lack of effective action with belligerent talk. In this tendency, President Carter did not stand alone.

Popular support is the precondition of the President's stewardship of foreign policy. The creation of a public opinion supporting him, even at the sacrifice of some elements of foreign policy, is a task which a President can only shun at the risk of losing office and, with it, his ability to pursue any foreign policy at all. The question to which Carter's conduct gave rise concerned not the need of a compromise between the requirements of a sound foreign policy and the demands of public opinion, but the point at which the compromise was to be made. Aside from faulting him for ignorance and incompetence, the critics maintained that he surrendered too many principles of a sound foreign policy to the demands of public opinion. The issue was not whether the President ought to pursue the national interest regardless of the possibility of nuclear war, but where to draw the line between concern for the national interest and fear of nuclear war. The question was whether Carter, in his anxiety to stay as far away as possible from nuclear war, had not needlessly sacrificed important national interests.

Confronted with this dilemma between a good foreign policy and a bad one that public opinion demands, a government must avoid two pitfalls. It must resist the temptation to sacrifice what it considers good policy upon the altar of public opinion, abdicating leadership and exchanging short-lived political advantage for the permanent interests of the country. It must also avoid widening the unavoidable gap between the requirements of good foreign policy and the preferences of public opinion. It widens that gap if, shunning tolerable compromise with the preferences of public opinion, it sticks in every detail to a foreign policy it considers to be right, and sacrifices public support to the stubborn pursuit of that policy.

Instead, the government, to be successful in its foreign and domestic policies alike, must comply with three basic requirements. It must recognize that the conflict between the requirements of good foreign policy and the preferences of public opinion is in the nature of things and, hence, unavoidable, and that it can perhaps be narrowed, but it can never be bridged, by concessions to the domestic opposition. Second, the government must realize that it is the leader and not the slave of public opinion; that public opinion is not a static thing to be discovered and classified by public-opinion polls as plants are by botanists, but that it is a dynamic, ever changing entity to be continuously created and recreated by informed and responsible leadership; that it is the historic mission of the government to assert that leadership lest it be the demagogue who asserts it.[20] Third, it must distinguish between what is desirable in its foreign policy and what is essential, and while it may be willing to compromise with public opinion on nonessentials, it must fight, even at the risk of its own fortunes, for what it regards to be the irreducible minimum of good foreign policy.

A government may have a correct understanding of the requirements of foreign policy and of the domestic politics to support them, but if it fails in marshaling public opinion behind these policies, its labors will be in vain, and all the other assets of national power of which the nation can boast will not be used to best advantage. Of this truth the policies of contemporary democratic governments, including those of the United States, offer abundant proof.[21]

Domestic Government and Foreign Policy

It is not enough, however, for a government to marshal national public opinion behind its foreign policies. It must also gain the support of the public opinion of other nations for its foreign and domestic policies. This requirement is a reflection of the changes that have occurred in recent times in the character of foreign policy. . . . Foreign policy is being pursued in our time not only with the traditional weapons of diplomacy and military might, but also with the novel weapon of propaganda. For the struggle for power on the interna-

---

20. Lord Norwich, who as Mr. Duff Cooper occupied in the interwar period important cabinet posts and other government positions, puts his finger on the common misunderstanding of public opinion and the government's relation to it when he says in his memoirs (*Old Men Forget* [London: Hart-Davis, 1953]) of Neville Chamberlain: "The Prime Minister's main mistake seems to me to be two. He believes public opinion is what the "Times" tells him it is—and he believes Conservative opinion is what the Chief Whip says it is." Unfortunately, this passive acceptance of what somebody says public opinion wants has become—and not only in the England of the interwar period—one of the main obstacles to good foreign policy.

21. This theme has been elaborated in Hans J. Morgenthau, "The Conduct of Foreign Policy," *Aspects of American Government*, Sydney Bailey, editor (London: The Hansard Society, 1950), pp. 99 ff.; and *In Defense of the National Interest* (New York: Alfred A. Knopf, 1951; Washington, D.C.: University Press of America, 1982), pp. 221 ff.

tional scene is today not only a struggle for military supremacy and political domination, but in a specific sense a struggle for the minds of men. The power of a nation, then, depends not only upon the skill of its diplomacy and the strength of its armed forces but also upon the attractiveness for other nations of its political philosophy, political institutions, and political policies. This is true in particular of the United States and the Soviet Union, who compete with each other not only as the two political and military superpowers but also as the foremost representatives of two different political philosophies, systems of government, and ways of life.

Thus whatever these superpowers—and this is true also, in a lesser degree, of other nations—do or do not do, achieve or fail to achieve, in their domestic and foreign policies has a direct bearing upon their standing as these representatives and, hence, upon their power. A nation, for instance, that embarked upon a policy of racial discrimination could not help losing the struggle for the minds of the colored nations of the earth. An underdeveloped nation that could increase in a spectacular fashion the health, literacy, and standard of living of its people would thereby have achieved a considerable increase in its power in other underdeveloped regions of the world.

At this point, then, as at others to be mentioned later, the traditional distinction between foreign and domestic policies tends to break down. One might almost be tempted to say that there are no longer any purely domestic affairs, for whatever a nation does or does not do is held for or against it as a reflection of its political philosophy, system of government, and way of life. A domestic achievement that is intelligible to other nations in terms of their aspirations cannot fail to increase the power of the nation; a domestic failure, equally intelligible, is bound to decrease it.

The Balance of Power

Hans J. Morgenthau

The aspiration for power on the part of several nations, each trying either to maintain or overthrow the status quo, leads of necessity to a configuration that is called the balance of power[1] and to policies that aim at preserving it. We say "of necessity" advisedly. For here again we are confronted with the basic misconception that has impeded the understanding of international politics and has made us the prey of illusions. This misconception asserts that men have a choice between power politics and its necessary outgrowth, the balance of power, on the one hand, and a different, better kind of international relations on the other. It insists that a foreign policy based on the balance of power is one among several possible foreign policies and that only stupid and evil men will choose the former and reject the latter.

It will be shown in the following pages that the international balance of power is only a particular manifestation of a general social principle to which all societies composed of a number of autonomous units owe the autonomy of their component parts; that the balance of power and policies aiming at its preservation are not only inevitable but are an essential stabilizing factor in a society of sovereign nations; and that the instability of the international balance of power is due not to the faultiness of the principle but to the particular conditions under which the principle must operate in a society of sovereign nations.

BALANCE OF POWER AS UNIVERSAL CONCEPT

The concept of "equilibrium" as a synonym for "balance" is commonly employed in many sciences—physics, biology, economics, sociology, and political science. It signifies stability within a system composed of a number of autonomous forces. Whenever the equilibrium is disturbed either by an outside force or by a change in one or the other elements composing the system, the system shows a tendency to re-establish either the original or a new equilibrium. Thus equilibrium exists in the human body. While the human body changes in the process of growth, the equilibrium persists as long as the changes occurring in the different organs of the body do not disturb the body's stability. This is especially so if the quantitative and qualitative changes in the different organs are proportionate to each other. When, however, the body suffers a wound or loss of one of its organs through outside interference, or experiences a malignant growth or a pathological transformation of one of its organs, the equilibrium is disturbed, and the body tries to overcome the disturbance by re-establishing the equilibrium either on the same or a different level from the one that obtained before the disturbance occurred.[2]

The same concept of equilibrium is used in a social science, such as economics, with reference to the relations between the different elements of the economic system, e.g., between savings and investments, exports and imports, supply and demand, costs and prices. Contemporary capitalism itself has been described as a system of "countervailing

---

1. The term "balance of power" is used in the text with four different meanings: (1) as a policy aimed at a certain state of affairs, (2) as an actual state of affairs, (3) as an approximately equal distribution of power, (4) as any distribution of power. Whenever the term is used without qualification, it refers to the actual state of affairs in which power is distributed among several nations with approximate equality.

power."[3] It also applies to society as a whole. Thus we search for a proper balance between different geographical regions, such as the East and the West, the North and the South; between different kinds of activities, such as agriculture and industry, heavy and light industries, big and small businesses, producers and consumers, management and labor; between different functional groups, such as city and country, the old, the middle-aged, and the young, the economic and the political sphere, the middle classes and the upper and lower classes.

Two assumptions are at the foundation of all such equilibriums: first, that the elements to be balanced are necessary for society or are entitled to exist and, second, that without a state of equilibrium among them one element will gain ascendancy over the others, encroach upon their interests and rights, and may ultimately destroy them. Consequently, it is the purpose of all such equilibriums to maintain the stability of the system without destroying the multiplicity of the elements composing it. If the goal were stability alone, it could be achieved by allowing one element to destroy or overwhelm the others and take their place. Since the goal is stability plus the preservation of all the elements of the system, the equilibrium must aim at preventing any element from gaining ascendancy over the others. The means employed to maintain the equilibrium consist in allowing the different elements to pursue their opposing tendencies up to the point where the tendency of one is not so strong as to overcome the tendency of the others, but strong enough to prevent the others from overcoming its own. In the words of Robert Bridges:

> Our stability is but balance: and wisdom lies
> In masterful administration of the unforeseen.

Nowhere have the mechanics of social equilibrium been described more brilliantly and at the same time more simply than in *The Federalist*. Concerning the system of checks and balances of the American government, No. 51 of *The Federalist* says:

> This policy of supplying, by opposite and rival interests, the defect of better motives, might be traced to the whole system of human affairs, private as well as public. We see it particularly dis-

---

2. Cf., for instance, the impressive analogy between the equilibrium in the human body and in society in Walter B. Cannon. *The Wisdom of the Body* (New York: W. W. Norton and Company, 1932), pp. 393, 294: "At the outset it is noteworthy that the body politic itself exhibits some indications of crude automatic stabilizing processes. In the previous chapter I expressed the postulate that a certain degree of constancy in a complex system is itself evidence that agencies are acting or are ready to act to maintain that constancy. And moreover, that when a system remains steady it does so because any tendency towards change is met by increased effectiveness of the factor or factors which resist the change. Many familiar facts prove that these statements are to some degree true for society even in its present unstabilized condition. A display of conservatism excites a radical revolt and that in turn is followed by a return to conservatism. Loose government and its consequences bring the reformers into power, but their tight reins soon provoke restiveness and the desire for release. The noble enthusiasms and sacrifices of war are succeeded by moral apathy and orgies of self-indulgence. Hardly any strong tendency in a nation continues to the stage of disaster; before that extreme is reached corrective forces arise which check the tendency and they commonly prevail to such an excessive degree as themselves to cause a reaction. A study of the nature of these social swings and their reversal might lead to valuable understanding and possibly to means of more narrowly limiting the disturbances. At this point, however. we merely note that the disturbances are roughly limited, and that this limitation suggests, perhaps, the early stages of social homeostasis." (Reprinted by permission of the publisher. Copyright 1932, 1939. by Walter B. Cannon.)

3. John K. Galbraith, *American Capitalism, the Concept of Countervailing Power,* (Boston: Houghton Mifflin, 1952).

> played in all the subordinate distributions of power, where the constant aim is to divide and arrange the several offices in such a manner as that each may be a check on the other—that the private interests of every individual may be a sentinel over the public rights. These inventions of prudence cannot be less requisite in the distribution of the supreme powers of the state.

In the words of John Randolph, "You may cover whole skins of parchment with limitations, but power alone can limit power . . ."[4]

TWO MAIN PATTERNS OF THE BALANCE OF POWER

Two factors are at the basis of international society: one is the multiplicity, the other is the antagonism of its elements, the individual nations. The aspirations for power of the individual nations can come into conflict with each other—and some, if not most of them, do at any particular moment in history—in two different ways. In other words, the struggle for power on the international scene can be carried on in two typical patterns.

The Pattern of Direct Opposition

Nation A may embark upon an imperialistic policy with regard to Nation B, and Nation B may counter that policy with a policy of the status quo or with an imperialistic policy of its own. France and its allies opposing Russia in 1812, Japan opposing China from 1931 to 1941, the United Nations vs. the Axis from 1941 on, correspond to that pattern. The pattern is one of direct opposition between the nation that wants to establish its power over another nation and the latter, which refuses to yield.

Nation A may also pursue an imperialistic policy toward Nation C, which may either resist or acquiesce in that policy, while Nation B follows with regard to Nation C either a policy of imperialism or one of the status quo. In this case, the domination of C is a goal of A's policy. B, on the other hand, is opposed to A's policy because it either wants to preserve the status quo with respect to C or wants the domination of C for itself. The pattern of the struggle for power between A and B is here not one of direct opposition, but of competition, the object of which is the domination of C, and it is only through the intermediary of that competition that the contest for power between A and B takes place. This pattern is visible, for instance, in the competition between Great Britain and Russia for the domination of Iran, in which the struggle for power between the two countries has repeatedly manifested itself during the last hundred years. It is also clear in the competition for dominant influence in Germany which in the aftermath of the Second World War has marked the relations between France, Great Britain, the Soviet Union, and the United States. The competition between the United States and China or between the Soviet Union and China for control of the countries of Southeast Asia offers another example of the same pattern.

It is in situations such as these that the balance of power operates and fulfills its typical functions. In the pattern of direct opposition, the balance of power results directly from the desire of either nation to see its policies prevail over the policies of the other. A tries to increase its power in relation to B to such an extent that it can control the decisions of B and thus lead its imperialistic policy to success. B, on the other hand, will try to increase its power to such an extent that it can resist A's pressure and thus frustrate A's policy, or else embark upon an imperialistic policy of its own with a chance for success. In the latter case, A must, in turn, increase its power in order to be able to resist B's imperialistic pol-

[4] Quoted after William Cabel Bruce, *John Randolph of Roanoke* (New York and London: G.P. Putnam, (1922), Vol. II, p. 211.

icy and to pursue its own with a chance for success. This balancing of opposing forces will go on, the increase in the power of one nation calling forth an at least proportionate increase in the power of the other, until the nations concerned change the objectives of their imperialistic policies—if they do not give them up altogether—or until one nation gains or believes it has gained a decisive advantage over the other. Then either the weaker yields to the stronger or war decides the issue.

So long as the balance of power operates successfully in such a situation, it fulfills two functions. It creates a precarious stability in the relations between the respective nations, a stability that is always in danger of being disturbed and, therefore, is always in need of being restored. This is, however, the only stability obtainable under the assumed conditions of the power pattern. For we are here in the presence of an inevitable inner contradiction of the balance of power. One of the two functions the balance of power is supposed to fulfill is stability in the power relations among nations; yet these relations are, as we have seen, by their very nature subject to continuous change. They are essentially unstable. Since the weights that determine the relative position of the scales have a tendency to change continuously by growing either heavier or lighter, whatever stability the balance of power may achieve must be precarious and subject to perpetual adjustments in conformity with intervening changes. The other function that a successful balance of power fulfills under these conditions is to insure the freedom of one nation from domination by the other.

Owing to the essentially unstable and dynamic character of the balance, which is not unstable and dynamic by accident or only part of the time, but by nature and always, the independence of the nations concerned is also essentially precarious and in danger. Here again, however, it must be said that, given the conditions of the power pattern, the independence of the respective nations can rest on no other foundation than the power of each individual nation to prevent the power of the other nations from encroaching upon its freedom. The following diagram illustrates this situation:

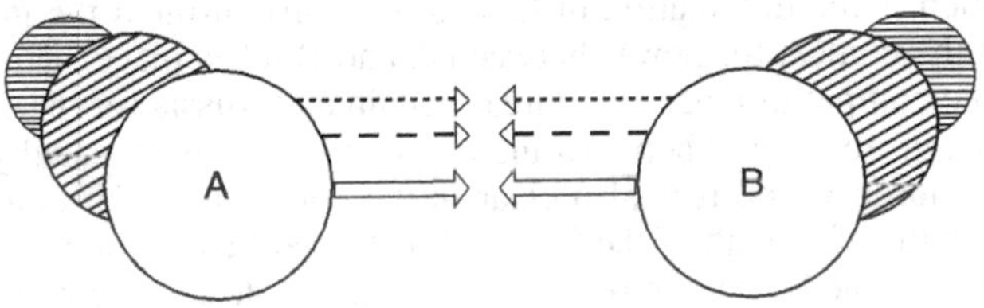

The Pattern of Competition

In the other pattern, the pattern of competition, the mechanics of the balance of power are identical with those discussed. The power of A necessary to dominate C in the face of B's opposition is balanced, if not outweighed, by B's power, while, in turn, B's power to gain dominion over C is balanced, if not outweighed, by the power of A. The additional function, however, that the balance fulfills here, aside from creating a precarious stability and security in the relations between A and B, consists in safeguarding the independence of C against encroachments by A or B. The independence of C is a mere function of the power relations existing between A and B.

If these relations take a decisive turn in favor of the imperialistic nation—that is, A—the independence of C will at once be in jeopardy:

If the status quo nation—that is, B—should gain a decisive and permanent advantage, C's freedom will be more secure in the measure of that advantage:

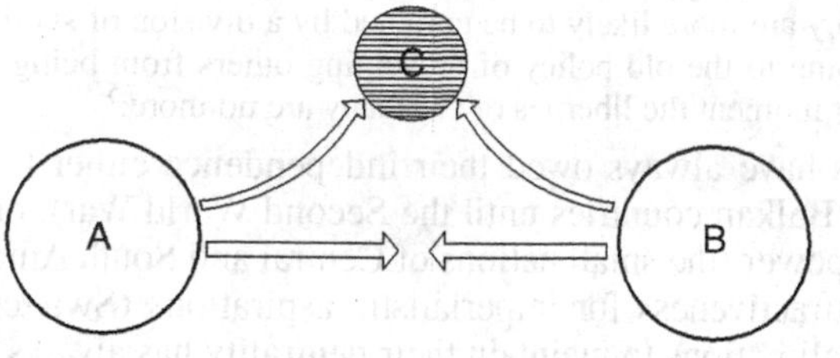

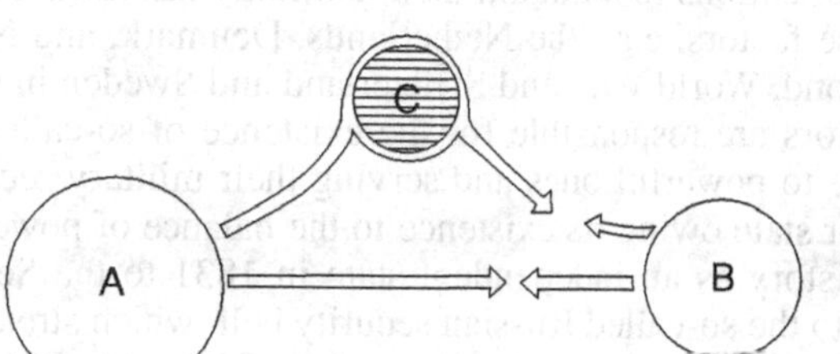

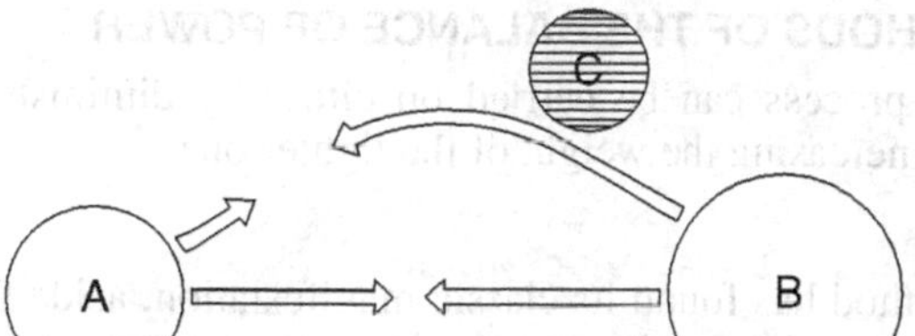

If finally, the imperialistic nation—A—should give up its imperialistic policies altogether or shift them permanently from C to another objective—that is, D—the freedom of C would be permanently secured:

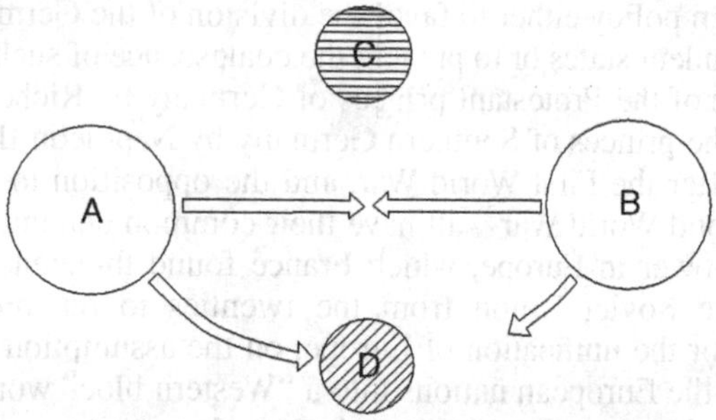

No one has recognized this function of the balance of power to preserve the independence of weak nations more clearly than Edmund Burke. He said in 1791 in his "Thoughts on French Affairs":

> As long as those two princes [the King of Prussia and the German Emperor], are at variance, so long the liberties of Germany are safe. But if ever they should so far understand one another as to be persuaded that they have a more direct and more certainly defined interest in

> a proportioned mutual aggrandizement than in a reciprocal reduction, that is, if they come to think that they are more likely to be enriched by a division of spoil than to be rendered secure by keeping to the old policy of preventing others from being spoiled by either of them, from that moment the liberties of Germany are no more.[5]

Small nations have always owed their independence either to the balance of power (Belgium and the Balkan countries until the Second World War), or to the preponderance of one protecting power (the small nations of Central and South America, and Portugal), or to their lack of attractiveness for imperialistic aspirations (Switzerland and Spain). The ability of such small nations to maintain their neutrality has always been due to one or the other or all of these factors, e.g., the Netherlands, Denmark, and Norway in the First, in contrast to the Second, World War, and Switzerland and Sweden in both world wars.

The same factors are responsible for the existence of so-called buffer states—weak states located close to powerful ones and serving their military security. The outstanding example of a buffer state owing its existence to the balance of power is Belgium from the beginning of its history as an independent state in 1831 to the Second World War. The nations belonging to the so-called Russian security belt, which stretches along the western and southwestern frontiers of the Soviet Union from Finland to Bulgaria, exist by leave of their preponderant neighbor, whose military and economic interests they serve. . . .

DIFFERENT METHODS OF THE BALANCE OF POWER

The balancing process can be carried on either by diminishing the weight of the heavier scale or by increasing the weight of the lighter one.

Divide and Rule

The former method has found its classic manifestation, aside from the imposition of onerous conditions in peace treaties and the incitement to treason and revolution, in the maxim "divide and rule." It has been resorted to by nations who tried to make or keep their competitors weak by dividing them or keeping them divided. The most consistent and important policies of this kind in modern times are the policy of France with respect to Germany and the policy of the Soviet Union with respect to the rest of Europe. From the seventeenth century to the end of the Second World War, it has been an unvarying principle of French foreign policy either to favor the division of the German Empire into a number of small independent states or to prevent the coalescence of such states into one unified nation. The support of the Protestant princes of Germany by Richelieu, of the Rhinebund by Napoleon I, of the princes of Southern Germany by Napoleon III, of the abortive separatist movements after the First World War, and the opposition to the unification of Germany after the Second World War—all have their common denominator in considerations of the balance of power in Europe, which France found threatened by a strong German state. Similarly, the Soviet Union from the twenties to the present has consistently opposed all plans for the unification of Europe, on the assumption that the pooling of the divided strength of the European nations into a "Western bloc" would give the enemies of the Soviet Union such power as to threaten the latter's security.

The other method of balancing the power of several nations consists in adding to the strength of the weaker nation. This method can be carried out by two different means: Either B can increase its power sufficiently to offset, if not surpass, the power of A, and

---

5. *Works*, Vol. IV (Boston: Little, Brown, and Company, 1889), p. 331.

vice versa; or B can pool its power with the power of all the other nations that pursue identical policies with regard to A, in which case A will pool its power with all the nations pursuing identical policies with respect to B. The former alternative is exemplified by the policy of compensations and the armament race as well as by disarmament; the latter, by the policy of alliances.

Compensations

Compensations of a territorial nature were a common device in the eighteenth and nineteenth centuries for maintaining a balance of power which had been, or was to be, disturbed by the territorial acquisitions of one nation. The Treaty of Utrecht of 1713, which terminated the War of the Spanish Succession, recognized for the first time expressly the principle of the balance of power by way of territorial compensations. It provided for the division of most of the Spanish possessions, European and colonial, between the Hapsburgs and the Bourbons "*ad conservandum in Europa equilibrium*" as the treaty put it.

The three partitions of Poland in 1772, 1793, and 1795, which in a sense mark the end of the classic period of the balance of power, . . . reaffirm its essence by proceeding under the guidance of the principle of compensations. Since territorial acquisitions at the expense of Poland by any one of the interested nations—Austria, Prussia, and Russia—to the exclusion of the others would have upset the balance of power, the three nations agreed to divide Polish territory in such a way that the distribution of power among themselves would be approximately the same after the partitions as it had been before. In the treaty of 1772 between Austria and Russia, it was even stipulated that "the acquisitions. . . shall be completely equal, the portion of one cannot exceed the portion of the other."

Fertility of the soil and number and quality of the populations concerned were used as objective standards by which to determine the increase in power which the individual nations received through the acquisition of territory. While in the eighteenth century this standard was rather crudely applied, the Congress of Vienna refined the policy of compensations by appointing in 1815 a statistical commission charged with evaluating territories by the standard of number, quality, and type of population.

In the latter part of the nineteenth and the beginning of the twentieth century, the principle of compensations was again deliberately applied to the distribution of colonial territories and the delimitation of colonial or semicolonial spheres of influence. Africa, in particular, was during that period the object of numerous treaties delimiting spheres of influence for the major colonial powers. Thus the competition between France, Great Britain, and Italy for the domination of Ethiopia was provisionally resolved, after the model of the partitions of Poland, by the treaty of 1906, which divided the country into three spheres of influence for the purpose of establishing in that region a balance of power among the nations concerned. Similarly, the rivalry between Great Britain and Russia with respect to Iran led to the Anglo-Russian treaty of 1907, which established spheres of influence for the contracting parties and a neutral sphere under the exclusive domination of Iran. The compensation consists here not in the outright cession of territorial sovereignty, but rather in the reservation, to the exclusive benefit of a particular nation, of certain territories for commercial exploitation, political and military penetration, and eventual establishment of sovereignty. In other words, the particular nation has the right, without having full title to the territory concerned, to operate within its sphere of influence without competition or opposition from another nation. The other nation, in turn, has the right to claim for its own sphere of influence the same abstinence on the part of the former.

Even where the principle of compensations is not deliberately applied, however, as it was in the aforementioned treaties, it is nowhere absent from political arrangements, territorial or other, made within a balance-of-power system. For, given such a system, no nation will agree to concede political advantages to another nation without the expectation, which may or may not be well founded, of receiving proportionate advantages in return. The bargaining of diplomatic negotiations, issuing in political compromise, is but the principle of compensations in its most general form, and as such it is organically connected with the balance of power.

Armaments

The principal means, however, by which a nation endeavors with the power at its disposal to maintain or re-establish the balance of power are armaments. The armaments race in which Nation A tries to keep up with, and then to outdo, the armaments of Nation B, and vice versa, is the typical instrumentality of an unstable, dynamic balance of power. The necessary corollary of the armaments race is a constantly increasing burden of military preparations devouring an ever greater portion of the national budget and making for ever deepening fears, suspicions, and insecurity. The situation preceding the First World War, with the naval competition between Germany and Great Britain and the rivalry of the French and German armies, illustrates this point.

It is in recognition of situations such as these that, since the end of the Napoleonic Wars, repeated attempts have been made to create a stable balance of power, if not to establish permanent peace, by means of the proportionate disarmament of competing nations. The technique of stabilizing the balance of power by means of a proportionate reduction of armaments is somewhat similar to the technique of territorial compensations. For both techniques require a quantitative evaluation of the influence that the arrangement is likely to exert on the respective power of the individual nations. The difficulties in making such a quantitative evaluation—in correlating, for instance, the military strength of the French army of 1932 with the military power represented by the industrial potential of Germany—have greatly contributed to the failure of most attempts at creating a stable balance of power by means of disarmament. The only outstanding success of this kind was the Washington Naval Treaty of 1922, in which Great Britain, the United States, Japan, France, and Italy agreed to a proportionate reduction and limitation of naval armaments. Yet it must be noted that this treaty was part of an over-all political and territorial settlement in the Pacific which sought to stabilize the power relations in that region on the foundation of Anglo-American predominance.

Alliances

The historically most important manifestation of the balance of power, however, is to be found not in the equilibrium of two isolated nations but in the relations between one nation or alliance of nations and another alliance.

The General Nature of Alliances: Alliances are a necessary function of the balance of power operating within a multiple-state system. Nations A and B, competing with each other, have three choices in order to maintain and improve their relative power positions. They can increase their own power, they can add to their own power the power of other nations, or they can withhold the power of other nations from the adversary. When they make the first choice, they embark upon an armaments race. When they choose the second and third alternatives, they pursue a policy of alliances.

Whether or not a nation shall pursue a policy of alliances is, then, a matter not of principle but of expediency. A nation will shun alliances if it believes that it is strong enough to hold its own unaided or that the burden of the commitments resulting from the alliance is likely to outweigh the advantages to be expected. It is for one or the other or both of these reasons that, throughout the better part of their history, Great Britain and the United States have refrained from entering into peacetime alliances with other nations.

Yet Great Britain and the United States have also refrained from concluding an alliance with each other even though, from the proclamation of the Monroe Doctrine in 1823 to the attack on Pearl Harbor in 1941, they have acted, at least in relation to the other European nations, as if they were allied. Their relationship during that period provides another instance of a situation in which nations dispense with an alliance. It occurs when their interests so obviously call for concerted policies and actions that an explicit formulation of these interests, policies, and actions in the form of a treaty of alliance appears to be redundant.

With regard to the continent of Europe, the United States and Great Britain have had one interest in common: the preservation of the European balance of power. In consequence of this identity of interests, they have found themselves by virtual necessity in the camp opposed to a nation which happened to threaten that balance. And when Great Britain went to war in 1914 and 1939 in order to protect the European balance of power, the United States first supported Great Britain with a conspicuous lack of that impartiality befitting a neutral and then joined her on the battlefield. Had in 1914 and 1939 the United States been tied to Great Britain by a formal treaty of alliance, it might have declared war earlier, but its general policies and concrete actions would not have been materially different than they actually were.

Not every community of interests, calling for common policies and actions, also calls for legal codification in an explicit alliance. Yet, on the other hand, an alliance requires of necessity a community of interests for its foundation.[6] Under what conditions, then, does an existing community of interests require the explicit formulation of an alliance? What is it that an alliance adds to the existing community of interests?

An alliance adds precision, especially in the form of limitation, to an existing community of interests and to the general policies and concrete measures serving them. The interests nations have in common are not typically so precise and limited as to geographic region, objective, and appropriate policies as has been the American and British interest in the preservation of the European balance of power. Nor are they so incapable of precision and limitation as concerns the prospective common enemy. For, while a typical alliance is directed against a specific nation or group of nations, the enemy of the Anglo-American community of interests could in the nature of things not be specified beforehand, since whoever threatens the European balance of power is the enemy. As Jefferson shifted his sympathies back and forth between Napoleon and Great Britain according to who seemed to threaten the balance of power at the time, so during the century following the Napoleonic Wars, Great Britain and the United States had to decide in the light of circumstances ever liable to change who posed at the moment the greatest threat to the balance of power. This blanket character of the enemy, determined not individually but by the function he performs, brings to mind a similar characteristic of collective security, which is directed against the abstractly designed aggressor, whoever he may be.

---

6. Glancing through the treaties of alliance of the seventeenth and eighteenth centuries, one is struck by the meticulous precision with which obligations to furnish troops, equipment, logistic support, food, money, and the like, were defined.

The typical interests which unite two nations against a third are both more definite as concerns the determination of the enemy and less precise as concerns the objectives to be sought and the policies to be pursued. In the last decades of the nineteenth century, France was opposed to Germany, and Russia was opposed to Austria, while Austria was allied with Germany against France and Russia. How could the interests of France and Russia be brought upon a common denominator, determining policy and guiding action? How could, in other words, the *casus foederis* be defined so that both friend and foe would know what to expect in certain contingencies affecting their respective interest? It was for the treaty of alliance of 1894 to perform these functions. Had the objectives and policies of the Franco-Russian alliance of 1894 been as clear as were the objectives and policies of Anglo-American cooperation in Europe, no alliance treaty would have been necessary. Had the enemy been as indeterminate, no alliance treaty would have been feasible.

Not every community of interests calling for co-operation between two or more nations, then, requires that the terms of this co-operation be specified through the legal stipulations of a treaty of alliance. It is only when the common interests are inchoate in terms of policy and action that a treaty of alliance is required to make them explicit and operative. These interests, as well as the alliances expressing them and the policies serving them, can be distinguished in five different ways according to: their intrinsic nature and relationship, the distribution of benefits and power, their coverage in relation to the total interests of the nations concerned, their coverage in terms of time, and their effectiveness in terms of common policies and actions. In consequence, we can distinguish alliances serving identical, complementary, and ideological interests and policies. We can further distinguish mutual and one-sided, general and limited, temporary and permanent, operative and inoperative alliances. . . .

Alliances vs. World Domination: While the balance of power as a natural and inevitable outgrowth of the struggle for power is as old as political history itself, systematic theoretic reflections, starting in the sixteenth century and reaching their culmination in the eighteenth and nineteenth centuries, have conceived the balance of power generally as a protective device of an alliance of nations, anxious for their independence, against another nation's designs for world domination, then called universal monarchy. B, directly threatened by A, joins with C, D, and E, potentially threatened by A, to foil A's designs. Polybius has pointed to the essence of this configuration in his analysis of the relations between the Romans, the Carthaginians, and Hiero of Syracuse:

> The Carthaginians, being shut in on all sides, were obliged to resort to an appeal to the states in alliance with them. Hiero during the whole of the present war had been most prompt in meeting their requests, and was now more complaisant than ever, being convinced that it was in his own interest for securing both its Sicilian dominions and his friendship with the Romans, that Carthage should be preserved, and that the stronger Power should not be able to attain its ultimate object entirely without effort. In this he reasoned very wisely and sensibly, for such matters should never be neglected, and we should never contribute to the attainment by one state of a power so preponderant, that none dare dispute with it even for their acknowledged rights.[7]

. . . The wars against the France of 1789 and against Napoleon show the same configuration of one preponderant nation aiming at world domination and being opposed by a coalition of nations for the sake of preserving their independence. The manifesto with

---

7. Polybius I, 83.

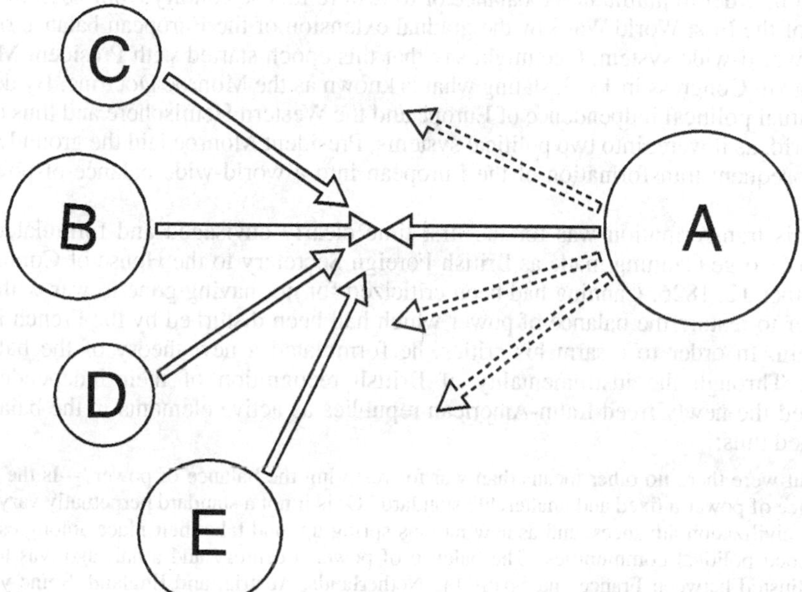

which the first coalition initiated these wars in 1792 declared that "no power interested in the maintenance of the balance of power in Europe could see with indifference the Kingdom of France, which at one time formed so important a weight in this great balance, delivered any longer to domestic agitations and to the horrors of disorder and anarchy which, so to speak, have destroyed her political existence." And when these wars approached their conclusion, it was still the purpose of the Allied powers, in the words of the Convention of Paris of April 23, 1814, "to put an end to the miseries of Europe, and to found her repose upon a just redistribution of forces among the nations of which she is composed"; that is, upon a new balance of power. The coalitions that fought the Second World War against Germany and Japan owed their existence to the same fear, common to all their members, of the latter nations' imperialism, and they pursued the same goal of preserving their independence in a new balance of power. Similarly, the Western bi- and multilateral alliances have since the late forties pursued the objective of putting a halt to the imperialistic expansion of the Soviet Union through the creation of a new world balance of power.

Alliances vs. Counteralliances: The struggle between an alliance of nations defending their independence against one potential conqueror is the most spectacular of the configurations to which the balance of power gives rise. The opposition of two alliances, one or both pursuing imperialistic goals and defending the independence of their members against the imperialistic aspirations of the other coalition, is the most frequent configuration within a balance-of-power system. . . .

From the beginning of the modern state system at the turn of the fifteenth century to the end of the Napoleonic Wars in 1815, European nations were the active elements in the balance of power. Turkey was the one notable exception. Alliances and counteralliances were formed in order to maintain the balance or to restore it. The century from 1815 to the outbreak of the First World War saw the gradual extension of the European balance of power into a world-wide system. One might say that this epoch started with President Monroe's message to Congress in 1823, stating what is known as the Monroe Doctrine. By declaring the mutual political indpendence of Europe and the Western Hemisphere and thus dividing the world, as it were, into two political systems, President Monroe laid the groundwork for the subsequent transformation of the European into a world-wide balance-of-power system.

This transformation was for the first time clearly envisaged and formulated in the speech George Canning made as British Foreign Secretary to the House of Commons on December 12, 1826. Canning had been criticized for not having gone to war with France in order to restore the balance of power which had been disturbed by the French invasion of Spain. In order to disarm his critics, he formulated a new theory of the balance of power. Through the instrumentality of British recognition of their independence, he included the newly freed Latin-American republics as active elements in the balance. He reasoned thus:

> But were there no other means than war for restoring the balance of power?—Is the balance of power a fixed and unalterable standard? Or is it not a standard perpetually varying, as civilization advances, and as new nations spring up, and take their place among established political communities? The balance of power a century and a half ago was to be adjusted between France and Spain, the Netherlands, Austria, and England. Some years after, Russia assumed her high station in European politics. Some years after that again, Prussia became not only a substantive, but a preponderating monarchy.—Thus, while the balance of power continued in principle the same, the means of adjusting it became more varied and enlarged. They became enlarged, in proportion to the increased number of considerable states—in proportion, I may say, to the number of weights which might be shifted into the one or the other scale. . . . Was there no other mode of resistance, than by a direct attack upon France—or by a war to be undertaken on the soil of Spain? What, if the possession of Spain might be rendered harmless in rival hands—harmless as regarded us—and valueless to the possessors? Might not compensation for disparagement be obtained . . . by means better adapted to the present time? If France occupied Spain, was it necessary, in order to avoid the consequences of that occupation—that we should blockade Cadiz? No. I looked another way—I saw materials for compensation in another hemisphere. Contemplating Spain, such as our ancestors had known her, I resolved that if France had Spain, it should not be Spain "with the Indies." I called the New World into existence, to redress the balance of the Old. [8]

This development toward a world-wide balance of power operating by means of alliances and counteralliances was consummated in the course of the First World War, in which practically all nations of the world participated actively on one or the other side. The very designation of that war as a "world" war points to the consummation of the development. . . .

In the years immediately preceding the First World War, the balance of power in the Balkans increased in importance; for, since the Triple Alliance between Austria, Germany, and Italy seemed approximately to balance the Triple Entente between France, Russia, and Great Britain, the power combination that gained a decisive advantage in the Balkans might easily gain a decisive advantage in the over-all European balance of power. It was

---

8. *Speeches of the Right Honourable George Canning (London, 1836), Vol. VI, pp. 109-11.*

this fear that motivated Austria in July 1914 to try to settle its accounts with Serbia once and for all, and that induced Germany to support Austria unconditionally. It was the same fear that brought Russia to the support of Serbia, and France to the support of Russia. In his telegraphic message of August 2, 1914, to George V of England, the Russian Czar summed the situation up well when he said that the effect of the predominance of Austria over Serbia "would have been to upset balance of power in Balkans, which is of such vital interest to my Empire as well as to those Powers who desire maintenance of balance of power in Europe.... I trust your country will not fail to support France and Russia in fighting to maintain balance of power in Europe."[9]

After the First World War, France maintained permanent alliances with Poland, Czechoslovakia, Yugoslavia, and Romania and, in 1935, concluded an alliance—which was, however, not implemented—with the Soviet Union. This policy can be understood as a kind of preventive balance-of-power policy which anticipated Germany's comeback and attempted to maintain the status quo of Versailles in the face of such an eventuality. On the other hand, the formation in 1936 of an alliance between Germany, Italy, and Japan, called the Axis, was intended as a counterweight against the alliance between France and the Eastern European nations, which would at the same time neutralize the Soviet Union.

Thus the period between the two world wars stands in fact under the sign of the balance of power by alliances and counteralliances, although in theory the principle of the balance of power was supposed to have been superseded by the League of Nations principle of collective security. Yet, actually, collective security . . . did not abolish the balance of power. Rather, it reaffirmed it in the form of a universal alliance against any potential aggressor, the presumption being that such an alliance would always outweigh the aggressor. Collective security differs however, from the balance of power in the principle of association by virtue of which the alliance is formed. Balance-of-power alliances are formed by certain individual nations against other individual nations or an alliance of them on the basis of what those individual nations regard as their separate national interests. The organizing principle of collective security is the respect for the moral and legal obligation to consider an attack by any nation upon any member of the alliance as an attack upon all members of the alliance. Consequently, collective security is supposed to operate automatically; that is, aggression calls the counteralliance into operation at once and, therefore, protects peace and security with the greatest possible efficiency. Alliances within a balance-of-power system, on the other hand, are frequently uncertain in actual operation, since they are dependent upon political considerations of the individual nations. The defection of Italy from the Triple Alliance in 1915 and the disintegration of the French system of alliances between 1935 and 1939 illustrate this weakness of the balance of power.

THE "HOLDER" OF THE BALANCE

Whenever the balance of power is to be realized by means of an alliance—and this has been generally so throughout the history of the Western world—two possible variations of this pattern have to be distinguished. To use the metaphor of the balance, the system may consist of two scales, in each of which are to be found the nation or nations identified with the same policy of the status quo or of imperialism. The continental nations of Europe have generally operated the balance of power in this way.

---

9. *British Documents on the Origins of the War, 1898-1914* (London: His Majesty's Stationery Office, 1926), Vol. XI, p. 276.

The system may, however, consist of two scales plus a third element, the "holder" of the balance or the "balancer." The balancer is not permanently identified with the policies of either nation or group of nations. Its only objective within the system is the maintenance of the balance, regardless of the concrete policies the balance will serve. In consequence, the holder of the balance will throw its weight at one time in this scale, at another time in the other scale, guided only by one consideration—the relative position of the scales. Thus it will put its weight always in the scale that seems to be higher than the other because it is lighter. The balancer may become in a relatively short span of history consecutively the friend and foe of all major powers provided they all consecutively threaten the balance by approaching predominance over the others and are in turn threatened by others about to gain such predominance. To paraphrase a statement of Palmerston: While holder of the balance has no permanent friends, it has no permanent enemies either; it has only the permanent interest of maintaining the balance of power itself.

The balancer is in a position of "splendid isolation." It is isolated by its own choice; for, while the two scales of the balance must vie with each, to add its weight to theirs in order to gain the overweight necessary for success, it must refuse to enter into permanent ties with either side. The holder of the balance waits in the middle in watchful detachment to see which is likely to sink. Its isolation is "splendid"; for, since its support or lack of support is the decisive factor in the struggle for power, its foreign policy, if cleverly managed, is able to extract the highest price from those whom it supports. But since this support, regardless of the price paid for it, is always uncertain and shifts from one side to the other in accordance with the movements of the balance, its policies are resented and subject to condemnation on moral grounds. Thus it has been said of the outstanding balancer in modern times, Great Britain, that it lets others fight its wars, that it keeps Europe divided in order to dominate the continent, and that the fickleness of its policies is such as to make alliances with Great Britain impossible. "*Perfidious Albion*" has become a byword in the mouths of those who either were unable to gain Great Britain's support, however hard they tried, or else lost it after they had paid what seemed to them too high a price.

The holder of the balance occupies the key position in the balance-of-power system, since its position determines the outcome of the struggle for power. It has, therefore, been called the "arbiter" of the system, deciding who will win and who will lose. By making it impossible for any nation or combination of nations to gain predominance over the others, it preserves its own independence as well as the independence of all the other nations, and is thus a most powerful factor in international politics.

The holder of the balance can use this power in three different ways. It can make its joining one or the other nation or alliance dependent upon certain conditions favorable to the maintenance or restoration of the balance. It can make its support of the peace settlement dependent upon similar conditions. It can, finally, in either situation see to it that the objectives of its own national policy, apart from the maintenance of the balance of power, are realized in the process of balancing the power of others. . . .

The classic example of the balancer has, however, been provided by Great Britain. To Henry VIII is attributed the maxim: *cui adhaero praeest* (he whom I support will prevail). He is reported to have had himself painted holding in his right hand a pair of scales in perfect balance, one of them occupied by France, the other by Austria, and holding in his left hand a weight ready to be dropped in either scale. Of England under Elizabeth I it was said "that France and Spain are as it were the Scales in the Balance of Europe and England the

Tongue or the Holder of the Balance."[10] In 1624, a French pamphlet invited King Jacob to follow the glorious example of Elizabeth and Henry VIII, "who played his role so well between the Emperor Charles V and King Francis by making himself feared and flattered by both and by holding, as it were, the balance between them . . ."

DOMINANT AND DEPENDENT SYSTEMS

We have spoken thus far of the balance of power as if it were one single system comprehending all nations actively engaged in international politics. Closer observation, however, reveals that such a system is frequently composed of a number of subsystems that are interrelated with each other, but that maintain within themselves a balance of power of their own. The interrelationship between the different systems is generally one of subordination, in the sense that one dominates because of the relatively great weight accumulated in its scales, while the others are, as it were, attached to the scales of that dominant system.

Thus, in the sixteenth century, the dominant balance of power operated between France and the Hapsburgs, while at the same time an autonomous system kept the Italian states in equilibrium. In the latter part of the seventeenth century a separate balance of power developed in Northern Europe out of the challenge with which the rise of Swedish power confronted the nations adjacent to the Baltic Sea. The transformation of Prussia into a first rate power in the eighteenth century brought about a particular German balance of power, the other scale of which had Austria as its main weight. This autonomous system, "a little Europe within the great," was dissolved only in 1866 with the expulsion of Austria from the Germanic Confederation as a consequence of the Prusso-Austrian War of the same year. The eighteenth century saw also the development of an Eastern balance of power occasioned by the ascendancy of Russia. The partitions of Poland, by virtue of the principle of compensations, between Russia, Prussia, and Austria are the first spectacular manifestations of that new system.

Throughout the nineteenth century until the present day, the balance of power in the Balkans has been of concern to the nations of Europe. As early as 1790 Turkey concluded a treaty with Prussia in which the latter promised to go to war with Austria and Russia "because of the prejudice which the enemies, in crossing the Danube, have brought to the desirable and necessary balance of power." In the latter part of the nineteenth century one began to speak of an African balance of power with reference to a certain equilibrium among the colonial acquisitions of the great powers. Later on, the balance of power in the Western Hemisphere, in the Pacific, in the Far and Near East were added to the diplomatic vocabulary. One even spoke of an "Austrian equilibrium" and of the Austrian monarchy with its antagonistic nationalities it was said that it "is constrained to apply to itself the rules of conduct which the powers of Europe with their perpetual rivalries follow with regard to each other."[11]

It is not by accident that the autonomy of such local balance-of-power systems is the greater and their subordination to a dominant system the less noticeable, the more removed they are physically from the center of the struggle for power—the more they operate at the periphery of the dominant system, out of reach of the dominant nations. Thus an Italian bal-

---

10. William Camden, *Annales of the History of the Most Renowned and Victorious Princess Elizabeth, Late Queen of England* (London, 1635), p. 196.

11. Albert Sorel, *L'Europe et la révolution français* (Paris: E. Plon, 1885) Vol. I, p.443.

ance of power could develop during the fifteenth century in relative autonomy, while the great nations of Europe were occupied in other regions. For the better part of the history of Western civilization the different balance-of-power systems of Asia, Africa, and America were entirely independent of the configurations of the European nations, to the point of being hardly known to them.

The balance of power in the Western Hemisphere up to the Second World War and in Eastern Europe until the end of the eighteenth century owe their relative autonomous development to their location at the periphery of the power centers of the time. The partitions of Poland which were intended to preserve the balance of power in Eastern Europe were executed by the directly interested nations without interference of any other nation. The alliance concluded in 1851 between Brazil and Uruguay against Argentina for the purpose of maintaining the balance of power in South America had only a very remote connection with the European balance of power. On the other hand, it has now become possible to speak of an autonomous African balance of power. Since the indigenous peoples of Africa have started to compete for power with each other and with non-African nations, Africa is no longer solely an object of the struggle for power centered elsewhere.

The more intimately a local balance of power is connected with the dominant one, the less opportunity it has to operate autonomously and the more it tends to become merely a localized manifestation of the dominant balance of power. The balance of power within the German Confederation from Frederick the Great to the War of 1866 presents an intermediate situation between full autonomy and complete integration. It combines a certain degree of autonomy with integration into the dominant system. While the equilibrium between Prussia and Austria was, as we have seen, a precondition for the preservation of the liberties of the members of the Germanic Confederation, this equilibrium was also indispensable for the maintenance of the European balance of power as a whole.

The German balance thus fulfilled a dual function: one within its own framework, another for the general system of which it was a part. Conversely, the fusion of Prussia and Austria or the domination of one by the other would not only have been destructive of the independence of the individual German states but would as well have threatened the freedom of the other European nations. "If Europe," as Edmund Burke put it, "does not conceive the independence and the equilibrium of the empire to be in the very essence of the system of balance of power in Europe . . . all the politics of Europe for more than two centuries have been miserably erroneous."[12] The perpetuation of the balance between Prussia and Austria was, therefore, in the interest not only of the other members of the Germanic Confederation but of all European nations.

When, as a consequence of the War of 1866, Prussia and later Germany gained a permanent advantage over Austria which destroyed the balance between the two nations and made Germany predominant in Europe, it became one of the functions of the European balance of power to preserve at least the independence of Austria against infringement by its stronger neighbor. It was in consequence of that permanent European interest that after the First World War the victorious Allies sought by legal, economic, and political measures to prevent the fusion of Austria with Germany. Moreover, it was within the logic of

---

12. *Works,* Vol. IV (Boston: Little, Brown and Company, 1889), p. 330.

this situation that Hitler regarded the annexation of Austria as a necessary stepping stone on the road toward the overthrow of the European balance of power.

The balance of power in the Balkans has fulfilled a similar function since the last decades of the nineteenth century. Here, too, the maintenance of a balance of power among the Balkan nations has been regarded as a prerequisite for the maintenance of the European balance. Whenever the local balance was threatened, the great nations of Europe intervened in order to restore it. The statement of the Russian Czar at the beginning of the First World War, quoted above, clearly illustrates that connection.

STRUCTURAL CHANGES IN THE BALANCE OF POWER

In recent times the relations between the dominant balance of power and the local systems have shown an ever increasing tendency to change to the detriment of the autonomy of the local systems. The reasons for this development lie in the structural changes that the dominant balance of power has under gone since the First World War and that became manifest in the Second. We have already indicated the gradual expansion of the dominant balance-of-power system from Western and Central Europe to the rest of the continent, and from there to other continents, until finally the First World War saw all the nations of the earth actively participating in a world-wide balance of power.

Hand in hand with the consummation of this expansion went a shift of the main weights of the balance from Europe to other continents. At the outbreak of the First World War in 1914, the main weights in the balance were predominantly European: Great Britain, France, and Russia in one scale, Germany and Austria in the other. At the end of the Second World War, the principal weights in each scale were either entirely non-European, as in the case of the United States, or predominantly non-European, as in the case of the Soviet Union. In consequence, the whole structure of the world balance of power has changed. At the end of the First World War and even at the beginning of the Second, the two scales of the balance, so to speak, were still in Europe: only the weights of the scales came from all over the earth. The main protagonists of the power contest and the principal stakes for which it was fought were still predominantly European. To paraphrase the words of George Canning, already quoted, non-European powers were called in only for the purpose of redressing the balance of power of Europe. In Churchill's words of 1940, "The New World, with all its power and might, steps forth to the rescue and the liberation of the Old."

Today the balance of power of Europe is no longer the center of world politics around which local balances would group themselves, either in intimate connection or in lesser or greater autonomy. Today the European balance of power has become a mere function of the world-wide balance of which the United States and the Soviet Union are the main weights, placed on opposite scales. The distribution of power in Europe is only one of the concrete issues over which the power contests between the United States and the Soviet Union is being waged.

What is true of the formerly dominant system is true of all the traditional local systems as well. The balance of power in the Balkans, no less than the balances in the Near and Far East, have shared the fate of the general European system. They have become mere functions of the new world-wide balance, mere "theaters" where the power contest between the two great protagonists is fought out. One might say that of all the local balance-of-power systems only the South American system has retained a certain measure of autonomy, protected as it is by the predominance of the United States.

EVALUATION OF THE BALANCE OF POWER

Considering especially its changed structure, how are we to evaluate the balance of power and to assess its future usefulness for the preservation of peace and security in the modern world?

In explaining its nature and operation, we have stressed its inevitable connection with, and protective function for, a multiple-state system. Throughout its history of more than four hundred years the policy of the balance of power succeeded in preventing any one state from gaining universal dominion. It also succeeded in preserving the existence of all members of the modern state system from the conclusion of the Thirty Years' War in 1648 to the partitions of Poland at the end of the eighteenth century. Yet universal dominion by any one state was prevented only at the price of warfare, which from 1648 to 1815 was virtually continuous and in the twentieth century has twice engulfed practically the whole world. And the two periods of stability, one starting in 1648, the other in 1815, were preceded by the wholesale elimination of small states and were interspersed, starting with the destruction of Poland, by a great number of isolated acts of a similar nature.

What is important for our discussion is the fact that these acts were accomplished in the name of the very principle of the balance of power whose chief claim to serve as the fundamental principle of the modern state system had been that it was indispensable for the preservation of the independence of the individual states. Not only did the balance of power fail to protect the independence of Poland, but the very principle of territorial compensation each member for the territorial aggrandizement of any other member brought about the destruction of the Polish state. The destruction of Poland in the name of the balance of power was but the first and most spectacular instance of a series of partitions, annexations, and destructions of independent states which, from 1815 to the present, have all been accomplished in application of that same principle. Failure to fulfill its function for individual states and failure to fulfill it for the state system as a whole by any means other than actual or potential warfare points up the three main weaknesses of the balance of power as the guiding principle of international politics: its uncertainty, its unreality, and its inadequacy.

The Uncertainty of the Balance of Power

The idea of a balance among a number of nations for the purpose of preventing any one of them from becoming strong enough to threaten the independence of the others is a metaphor taken from the field of mechanics. It was appropriate to the way of thinking of the sixteenth, seventeenth, and eighteenth centuries, which liked to picture society and the whole universe as a gigantic mechanism, a machine or a clockwork, created and kept in motion by the divine watchmaker. Within that mechanism, and within the smaller mechanisms composing it, the mutual relations of the individual parts could be, it was believed, exactly determined by means of mechanical calculations, and their actions and reactions accurately foreseen. The metaphor of two scales kept in balance by an equal distribution of weights on either side, providing the mechanism for the maintenance of stability and order on the international scene, has its origin in this mechanistic philosophy. It was applied to the practical affairs of international politics in the spirit of that philosophy.

The balance of power, mechanically conceived, is in need of an easily recognizable quantitative criterion by which the relative power of a number of nations can be measured and compared. For it is only by means of such a criterion, comparable to the pounds and ounces of a real pair of scales, that one can say with any degree of assurance that a certain nation tends to become more powerful than another or that they tend to maintain a balance of power between them. Furthermore, it is only by means of such a criterion that variations in power can be converted into quantitative units to be transferred from one scale to the other in order to restore the balance. The theory and practice of the balance of power found such a criterion, as we have seen, in territory, population, and armaments. The policies of compensations and of competitive armaments have served throughout the history of the modern state system as the practical application of that criterion.

But does the power of a nation actually repose in the extension of its territory? Is a nation the more powerful the more territory it possesses? Our examination of the factors that make for the power of a nation has shown that the answer can be in the affirmative only with qualifications so far-reaching as almost to nullify the affirmative character of the answer. . .

National character and, above all, national morale and the quality of government, especially in the conduct of foreign affairs, are the most important, but also the most elusive, components of national power. It is impossible for the observer of the contemporary scene or the explorer of future trends to assess even with approximate accuracy the relative contributions these elements may make to the power of different nations. Furthermore, the quality of these contributions is subject to incessant change, unnoticeable at the moment the change actually takes place and revealed only in the actual test of crisis and war. Rational calculation of the relative strength of several nations, which is the very lifeblood of the balance of power, becomes a series of guesses the correctness of which can be ascertained only in retrospect. . . .

An eighteenth-century opponent of the balance of power tried to demonstrate the absurdity of the calculations common at the time by asking which of two princes was more powerful: one who possessed three pounds of military strength, four pounds of statesmanship, five pounds of zeal, and two pounds of ambition, or one who had twelve pounds of military strength, but only one pound of all the other qualities? The author gives the advantage to the former prince, but whether his answer will be correct under all circumstances is certainly open to question, even under the assumption—patently hypothetical—that the quantitative determination of the relative weight of these different qualities were possible.

This uncertainty of power calculations is inherent in the nature of national power itself. It will therefore come into play even in the most simple pattern of the balance of power; that is, when one nation opposes another. This uncertainty is, however, immeasurably magnified when the weights in one or the other or in both scales are composed not of single units but of alliances. Then it becomes necessary to compute not only one's own and the opponent's national power and to correlate one with the other, but to perform the same operation on the national power of one's allies and those of the opponent. The risk of guessing is greatly aggravated when one must assess the power of nations belonging to a different civilization from one's own. It is difficult enough to evaluate the power of Great Britain or of France. It is much more difficult to make a correct assessment of the power of China, Japan, or even the Soviet Union. The crowning uncertainty, however, lies in the fact that one cannot always be sure who are one's own allies and who are the opponent's. Alignments by virtue of alliance treaties are not always identical with the alliances that oppose each other in the actual contest of war. . . .

The Unreality of the Balance of Power

This uncertainty of all power calculations not only makes the balance of power incapable of practical application but leads also to its very negation in practice. Since no nation can be sure that its calculation of the distribution of power at any particular moment in history is correct, it must at least make sure that its errors, whatever they may be, will not put the nation at a disadvantage in the contest for power. In other words, the nation must try to have at least a margin of safety which will allow it to make erroneous calculations and still maintain the balance of power. To that effect, all nations actively engaged in the struggle for power must actually aim not at a balance—that is, equality—of power, but at superiority of power in their own behalf. And since no nation can foresee how large its miscalculations will turn out to be, all nations must ultimately seek the maximum of power obtainable under the circumstances. Only thus can they hope to attain the maximum margin of safety commensurate with the maximum of errors they might commit. The limitless aspiration for power, potentially always present, as we have seen, in the power drives of nations, finds in the balance of power a mighty incentive to transform itself into an actuality.

Since the desire to attain a maximum of power is universal, all nations must always be afraid that their own miscalculations and the power increases of other nations might add up to an inferiority for themselves which they must at all costs try to avoid. Hence all nations who have gained an apparent edge over their competitors tend to consolidate that advantage and use it for changing the distribution of power permanently in their favor. This can be done through diplomatic pressure by bringing the full weight of that advantage to bear upon the other nations, compelling them to make the concessions that will consolidate the temporary advantage into a permanent superiority. It can also be done by war. Since in a balance-of-power system all nations live in constant fear lest their rivals deprive them, at the first opportune moment, of their power position, all nations have a vital interest in anticipating such a development and doing unto the others what they do not want the others to do unto them. . . .

It will forever be impossible to prove or disprove the claim that by its stabilizing influence the balance of power has aided in avoiding many wars. One cannot retrace the course of history, taking a hypothetical situation as one's point of departure. But, while nobody can tell how many wars there would have been without the balance of power, it is not hard to see that most of the wars that have been fought since the beginning of the modern state system have their origin in the balance of power. Three types of wars are intimately connected with the mechanics of the balance of power: preventive war, already referred to, where normally both sides pursue imperialistic aims, anti-imperialistic war, and imperialistic war itself. . . .

The dynamics of international politics as they play between status quo and imperialistic nations, lead of necessity to such a disturbance of the balance of power that war appears as the only policy that offers the status quo nations at least a chance to redress the balance of power in their favor.

Yet the very act of redressing the balance carries within itself the elements of a new disturbance. The dynamics of power politics as outlined previously make this development inevitable. Yesterday's defender of the status quo is transformed by victory into the imperialist of today, against whom yesterday's vanquished will seek revenge tomorrow. The ambition of the victor who took up arms in order to restore the balance, as well as the resentment of the loser who could not overthrow it, tend to make the new balance a virtually invisible point of transition from one disturbance to the next. Thus the balancing process has frequently led to the substitution of one predominant power, disturbing the balance, for another one. . . .

The Balance of Power as Ideology

Our discussion has thus far proceeded on the assumption that the balance of power is a device for the self-defense of nations whose independence and existence are threatened by a disproportionate increase in the power of other nations. What we have said of the balance of power is true only under the assumption that the balance of power is used genuinely for its avowed purposes of self-protection. Yet we have already seen how the power drives of nations take hold of ideal principles and transform them into ideologies in order to disguise, rationalize, and justify themselves. They have done this with the balance of power. What we have said above about the popularity of anti-imperialistic ideologies in general applies to the balance of power.

A nation seeking empire has often claimed that all it wanted was equilibrium A nation seeking only to maintain the status quo has often tried to give a change in the status quo the appearance of an attack upon the balance of power. . . .

The difficulties in assessing correctly the relative power positions of nations have made the invocation of the balance of power one of the favored ideologies of international politics. Thus it has come about that the term is being used in a very loose and unprecise manner. When a nation would like to justify one of its steps on the international scene, it is likely to refer to it as serving the maintenance or restoration of the balance of power. When a nation would like to discredit certain policies pursued by another nation, it is likely to condemn them as a threat to, or a disturbance of, the balance of power. Since it is the inherent tendency of the balance of power in the proper meaning of the term to preserve the status quo, the term has, in the vocabulary of status quo nations, become a synonym for the status quo and for any distribution of power existing at any particular moment. Any change in the existing distribution of power is therefore opposed as disturbing the balance of power. In this way a nation interested in the preservation of a certain distribution of power tries to make its interest appear to be the outgrowth of the fundamental, universally accepted principle of the modern state system and, hence, to be identical with an interest common to all nations. The nation itself, far from defending a selfish, particular concern, poses as the guardian of that general principle; that is, as the agent of the international community.

In this sense one speaks, for instance, of the balance of power in the Western Hemisphere which might be disturbed by the policies of non-American nations, or of the balance of power in the Mediterranean which must be defended against Russian intrusion. Yet what one means to defend in either case is not the balance of power but a particular distribution of power regarded as favorable to a particular nation or group of nations. The New York Times wrote in one of its reports on the Foreign Ministers' Conference in Moscow in 1947: "The new unity of France, Britain and the United States . . . may be only temporary but it does alter the balance of power perceptibly."[13] What was actually meant was not that the balance of power in the proper meaning of the term had been altered, but that the distribution of power which existed after the conference was more favorable to the Western powers than the one that existed before.

The use of the balance of power as an ideology accentuates difficulties inherent in the mechanics of the balance of power. Yet it must be noted that the ready use as an ideology to which the balance of power lends itself is not an accident. It is a potentiality inherent in its very essence. The contrast between pretended precision and the actual lack of it, between the pretended aspiration for balance and the actual aim of predominance—this contrast, which, as we have seen, is of the very essence of the balance of power, makes the latter in a certain measure an ideology to begin with. The balance of power thus assumes a reality and a function that it actually does not have, and therefore tends to disguise, rationalize, and justify international politics as it actually is . . .

13. April 27, 1947, p. E3.

Introduction to Balance of Threat

While in graduate school at Berkeley (where he studied under Kenneth Waltz) Stephen M. Walt began research which culminated in the publication of *The Origins of Alliances* in 1987. Walt, who is currently at Harvard University, was interested in addressing a number of "puzzles" including what he saw as "several anomalies" with Balance of Power theory.[1] Specifically, if states responded to, as Morgenthau and others assert, imbalances in power, then Walt wondered "why some alliances grow both larger and stronger over time (often dwarfing their opponents)?"[2] The two readings from Walt's book reprinted here provide the basics necessary to develop hypotheses for what is often called "Balance of Threat" theory.

In the first reading, "Explaining Alliance Formation" [chapter two of his book], Walt begins by briefly identifying and describing two possible state responses to a "significant external threat."[3] As becomes clear later in the reading, Walt is not asserting that these responses represent reality. On the contrary, at this point in his book, he is merely positing two "competing" hypotheses. Subsequent to this discussion of possible state behavior (i.e., dependent variable), Walt introduces his independent variables when he describes his sources of threat. These so-called elements of threat serve as the basis of his theory and make it distinctive from Balance of Power.

While some interpret his explicit "hypotheses" at the end of this reading as the Balance of Threat theory's definitive hypotheses, this assessment is incorrect. They are in fact "competing" hypotheses. As he notes in his concluding paragraph of this reading, "because the implications of each hypothesis are different, it is important to determine which of the hypotheses presented here offers the best guide to state behavior. The next task, therefore, is to assemble a body of evidence that will enable use to perform this assessment."

In the middle chapters of his book which you do not read, Walt uses the Middle East as a laboratory in which to test the "competing hypotheses" that he advanced in chapter two. In chapters three and four, he investigates "the principle alliances in [this region] from 1955-1979" to identify "the most important causes for the various alliances."[4] Using this historical background, Walt then proceeds in chapters five, six and seven, to "examine the competing hypotheses" regarding state behavior in response to an imbalance of threat. He does this to ascertain which of the two posited actions in fact reflect reality.

Finally, in his concluding chapter, largely reproduced here as the second reading ("Alliance Formation"), Walt declares which behavior he found in his research to be most common for states facing an imbalance of threat. He then summarizes the findings from

1. Steven M. Walt, *The Origins of Alliances* (Ithaca, NY: Cornell University Press, 1990), ix.
2. Ibid., x.
3. Ibid., 17.
4. Ibid., 50.

the earlier chapters and concludes that states are most likely to balance rather than bandwagon with a threatening state.

While written during the Cold War, Walt's theory is arguably just as applicable for all states facing an imbalance of threat regardless of the systemic polarity. In fact, during the Gulf War, difficult question was raises, a question that Balance of Threat theory may have helped address. Specifically, why were we fighting with, rather than against, soldiers from Syria, a traditional and ideological enemy of the United States? This apparently strange (and admittedly temporary) "alliance," which some argue ran contrary to Balance of Power predictions, was logical given Walt's theory.

Because the United States will continue to support existing alliances and form others, and because it is a near certainty that the US will participate in multilateral operations with allies, is important that we know the reasons that these alliances came to be.

Explaining Alliance Formation

Stephen M. Walt

ALLIANCES AS A RESPONSE TO THREAT: BALANCING AND BANDWAGONING

When confronted by a significant external threat, states may either balance or bandwagon. *Balancing* is defined as allying with others against the prevailing threat; *bandwagoning* refers to alignment with the source of danger. Thus two distinct hypotheses about how states will select their alliance partners can be identified on the basis of whether the states ally against or with the principal external threat.[1]

These two hypotheses depict very different worlds. If balancing is more common than bandwagoning, then states are more secure, because aggressors will face combined opposition. But if bandwagoning is the dominant tendency, then security is scarce, because successful aggressors will attract additional allies, enhancing their power while reducing that of their opponents. . . .

Both scholars and statesmen have repeatedly embraced one or the other of these hypotheses, but they have generally failed either to frame their beliefs carefully or to evaluate their accuracy. Accordingly, I present each hypothesis in its simplest form and then consider several variations. I then consider which type of behavior—balancing or bandwagoning—is more common and suggest when each response is likely to occur.

Balancing Behavior

The belief that states form alliances in order to prevent stronger powers from dominating them lies at the heart of traditional balance-of-power theory. According to this view, states join alliances to protect themselves from states or coalitions whose superior resources could pose a threat. States choose to balance for two main reasons.

First, they place their survival at risk if they fail to curb a potential hegemon before it becomes too strong. To ally with the dominant power means placing ones trust in its continued benevolence. The safer strategy is to join with those who cannot readily dominate their allies, in order to avoid being dominated by those who can. As Winston Churchill explained Britain's traditional alliance policy; "For four hundred years the foreign policy of England has been to oppose the strongest, most aggressive, most dominating power on the Continent. . . . [I]t would have been easy . . . and tempting to join with the stronger and share the fruits of his conquest. However, we always took the harder course, joined with the less strong powers, . . . and thus defeated the Continental military tyrant whoever he was."[2] More recently, Henry Kissinger advocated a rapprochement with China, because he believed that in a triangular relationship it was better to align with the weaker side.

Second, joining the weaker side increases the new member's influence within the alliance, because the weaker side has greater need for assistance. Allying with the strong side, by contrast,

---

1. My use of the terms *balancing* and *bandwagoning* follows that of Kenneth Waltz (who credits it to Stephen Van Evera) in his *Theory of International Politics* (Reading, Mass., 1979). Arnold Wolfers uses a similar terminology in his essay "The Balance of Power in Theory and Practice," in *Discord and Collaboration: Essays on International Politics* (Baltimore, Md., 1962), pp. 122–24.

2. Winston S. Churchill, *The Second World War*, vol. 1: *The Gathering Storm* (Boston, 1948), pp. 207–8.

gives the new member little influence (because it adds relatively less to the coalition) and leaves it vulnerable to the whims of its partners. Joining the weaker side should be the preferred choice.

Bandwagoning Behavior

The belief that states will balance is unsurprising, given the many familiar examples of states joining together to resist a threatening state or coalition. Yet, despite the powerful evidence that history provides in support of the balancing hypothesis, the belief that the opposite response is more likely is widespread. According to one scholar: "In international politics, nothing succeeds like success. Momentum accrues to the gainer and accelerates his movement. The appearance of irreversibility in his gains enfeebles one side and stimulates the other all the more. The bandwagon collects those on the sidelines."[3]

The bandwagoning hypothesis is especially popular with statesmen seeking to justify overseas involvements or increased military budgets. For example, German admiral Alfred von Tirpitz's famous risk theory rested on this type of logic. By building a great battle fleet, Tirpitz argued, Germany could force England into neutrality or alliance with her by posing a threat to England's vital maritime supremacy.

Bandwagoning beliefs have also been a recurring theme throughout the Cold War. Soviet efforts to intimidate both Norway and Turkey into not joining NATO reveal the Soviet conviction that states will accommodate readily to threats, although these moves merely encouraged Norway and Turkey to align more closely with the West.[4] Soviet officials made a similar error in believing that the growth of Soviet military power in the 1960s and 1970s would lead to a permanent shift in the correlation of forces against the West. Instead, it contributed to a Sino-American rapprochement in the 1970s and the largest peacetime increase in U.S. military power in the 1980s.

American officials have been equally fond of bandwagoning notions. According to NSC-68, the classified study that helped justify a major U.S. military buildup in the 1950s; "In the absence of an affirmative decision [to increase U.S. military capabilities] . . . our friends will become more than a liability to us, they will become a positive increment to Soviet power."[5] President John F. Kennedy once claimed that "if the United States were to falter, the whole world . . . would inevitably begin to move toward the Communist bloc."[6] And though Henry Kissinger often argued that the United States should form balancing alliances to contain the Soviet Union, he apparently believed that U.S. allies were likely to bandwagon. As he put it, "If leaders around the world . . . assume that the U.S. lacked either the forces or the will . . . they will accommodate themselves to what they will regard as the dominant trend."[7] Ronald Reagan's claim, "If we cannot defend ourselves [in Central America] . . . then we cannot expect

---

3. W. Scott Thompson, "The Communist International System," *Orbis 20,* no. 4 (1977).

4. For the effects of the Soviet pressure on Turkey, see George Lenczowski, *The Middle East in World Affairs,* 4th ed. (Ithaca, 1980), pp. 134–38; and Bruce R. Kuniholm, *The Origins of the Cold War in the Near East* (Princeton, N.J., 1980), pp. 355–78. For the Norwegian response to Soviet pressure, see Herbert Feis, *From Trust to Terror: The Onset of the Cold War, 1945–50* (New York, 1970), p. 381; and Geir Lundestad, *America, Scandinavia, and the Cold War: 1945–1949* (New York, 1980), pp. 308–9.

5. NSC–68 ("United States Objectives and Programs for National Security"), reprinted in Gaddis and Etzold, *Containment, p.* 404. Similar passages can be found on pp. 389, 414, and 434.

6. Quoted in Seyom Brown, *The Faces of Power: Constancy and Change in United States Foreign Policy from Truman to Johnson* (New York, 1968), p. 217.

7. Quoted in U.S. House Committee on Foreign Affairs, *The Soviet Union and the Third World: Watershed in Great Power Policy?* 97th Cong., 1st sess., 1977, pp. 157–58.

to prevail elsewhere. . . . [O]ur credibility will collapse and our alliances will crumble," reveals the same logic in a familiar role—that of justifying overseas intervention. . . . [8]

Different Sources of Threat

Balancing and bandwagoning are usually framed solely in terms of capabilities. Balancing is alignment with the weaker side, bandwagoning with the stronger. This conception should be revised, however, to account for the other factors that statesmen consider when deciding with whom to ally. Although power is an important part of the equation, it is not the only one. It is more accurate to say that states tend to ally with or against the foreign power that poses the greatest threat. For example, states may balance by allying with other strong states if a weaker power is more dangerous for other reasons. Thus the coalitions that defeated Germany in World War I and World War II were vastly superior in total resources, but they came together when it became clear that the aggressive aims of the Wilhelmines and Nazis posed the greater danger. Because balancing and bandwagoning are more accurately viewed as a response to threats, it is important to consider other factors that will affect the level of threat that states may pose: aggregate power, geographic proximity, offensive power, and aggressive intentions.

Aggregate Power

All else being equal, the greater a state's total resources (e.g., population, industrial and military capability, and technological prowess), the greater a potential threat it can pose to others. Recognizing this fact, Walter Lippmann and George Kennan defined the aim of U.S. grand strategy as that of preventing any single state from controlling more industrial resources than the United States did. In practical terms, it means allying against any state that appears powerful enough to dominate the combined resources of industrial Eurasia.[9] Similarly, Sir Edward Grey, British foreign secretary in 1914, justified British intervention against the Dual Alliance by saying: "To stand aside would mean the domina-tion of Germany; the subordination of France and Russia; the isolation of Britain . . . and ultimately Germany would wield the whole power of the continent."[10] In the same way, Castlereagh's efforts to create a "just distribution of the forces in Europe" revealed his own concern for the distribution of aggregate power.[11] The total power that states can wield is thus an important component of the threat that they pose to others.

Although power can pose a threat, it can also be prized. States with great power have the capacity to either punish enemies or reward friends. By itself, therefore, a state's aggregate power may provide a motive for balancing or bandwagoning.

8. *New York Times,* April 28, 1983, p. A12. In the same speech, Reagan also said: "If Central America were to fall, what would the consequences be for our position in Asia and Europe and for alliances such as NATO? . . . Which ally, which friend would trust us then?"

9. For a summary of these ideas, see Gaddis, *Strategies of Containment,* pp. 25-88. Kennan's ideas are found in *Realities of American Foreign Policy* (Princeton, N.J., 1954), pp. 63-65. Lippmann's still compelling analysis is found in Walter Lippmann, *The Cold War: A Study of U.S. Foreign Policy* (New York, 1947).

10. Quoted in Bernadotte C. Schmitt, *The Coming of the War in 1914* (New York, 1968), 2: 115.

11. Castlereagh's policy is described in Harold Nicolson, *The Congress of Vienna* (New York, 1946), pp. 205-6.

Geographic Proximity

Because the ability to project power declines with distance, states that are nearby pose a greater threat than those that are far away.[12] Other things being equal, therefore, states are more likely to make their alliance choices in response to nearby powers than in response to those that are distant. For example, the British Foreign Office responded to German complaints about the attention paid to Germany's naval expansion by saying: "If the British press pays more attention to the increase of Germany's naval power than to a similar movement in Brazil . . . this is no doubt due to the proximity of the German coasts and the remoteness of Brazil."[13] More recently, President Reagan justified U.S. intervention in Central America in much the same way: "Central America is much closer to the United States than many of the world's trouble spots that concern us. . . . El Salvador is nearer to Texas than Texas is to Massachusetts. Nicaragua is just as close to Miami, San Antonio, and Tucson as those cities are to Washington."[14]

As with aggregate power, proximate threats can lead to balancing or bandwagoning. When proximate threats trigger a balancing response, alliance networks that resemble checkerboards are the likely result. Students of diplomatic history have long been taught that neighbors of neighbors are friends, and the tendency for encircling states to align against a central power was first described in Kautilya's writings in the fourth century.[15] Examples include France and Russia against Wilhelmine Germany, France, and the Little Entente in the 1930s; the Soviet Union and Vietnam against China and Cambodia in the 1970s; and the tacit alignment between Iran and Syria against Iraq and its various Arab supporters.

Alternatively, when a threat from a proximate power leads to bandwagoning, the familiar phenomenon of a sphere of influence is created. Small states bordering a great power may be so vulnerable that they choose to bandwagon rather than balance, especially if a powerful neighbor has demonstrated its ability to compel obedience. Thus Finland, whose name has undeservedly become synonymous with bandwagoning, chose to do so only after being defeated by the Soviet Union twice within a five-year period.

---

12. See Harvey Starr and Benjamin A. Most, "The Substance and Study of Borders in International Relations Research," *International Studies Quarterly, 20,* no. 4 (1976). For a discussion of the relationship between power and distance, see Kenneth A. Boulding, Conflict *and Defense: A General Theory* (New York, 1962), pp. 229-30, 245-47. For an interesting practical critique, see Albert Wohlstetter, "Illusions of Distance," *Foreign Affairs,* 46, no. 2 (1968).

13. Quoted in Paul M. Kennedy, *The Rise of the Anglo-German Antagonism, 1860-1914* (London, 1980), p. 421.

14. *New York Times,* April 28, 1983, p. A12.

15. Kautilya's analysis ran as follows: "The king who is situated anywhere immediately on the circumference of the conqueror's territory is termed the enemy. The king who is likewise situated close to the enemy, but separated from the conqueror only by the enemy, is termed the friend (of the conqueror). . . . In front of the conqueror and close to the enemy, there happen to be situated kings such as the conqueror's friend, next to him the enemy^s friend, and next to the last, the conqueror's friend, and next, the enemy's friend's friend." See Kautilya, "Arthasastra," in *Balance of Power,* ed. Paul A. Seabury (San Francisco, 1965), p. 8.

Offensive Power

All else being equal, states with large offensive capabilities are more likely to provoke an alliance than are those that are incapable of attacking because of geography, military posture, or something else.[16] Although offensive capability and geographic proximity are clearly related—states that are close to one another can threaten one another more readily—they are not identical.[17]

Offensive power is also closely related but not identical to aggregate power. Specifically, offensive power is the ability to threaten the sovereignty or territorial integrity of another state at an acceptable cost. The ease with which aggregate power can be converted into offensive power (i.e., by amassing large, mobile military capabilities) is affected by the various factors that determine the relative advantage to the offense or defense at any particular period.

Once again, the effects of offensive power may vary. The immediate threat that offensive capabilities pose may create a strong incentive for others to balance.[18] Tirpitz's risk strategy backfired for precisely this reason. England viewed the German battle fleet as a potent offensive threat and redoubled its own naval efforts while reinforcing ties with France and Russia.[19] However, when offensive power permits rapid conquest vulnerable states may see little hope in resisting. Balancing may seem unwise because one's allies may not be able to provide assistance quickly enough. This tendency may be one reason that spheres of influence emerge: states that close to a country with large offensive capabilities (and that are far from potential allies) may be forced to bandwagon because balancing alliances are simply not viable.[20]

Aggressive Intensions

Finally, states that are viewed as aggressive are likely to provoke others to balance against them. As noted earlier, Nazi Germany faced an overwhelming countervailing coalition because it combined substantial power with extremely dangerous ambitions. Indeed, even states with rather

---

16. The best discussions of the implications of offense and defense are in Robert Jervis, "Cooperation under the Security Dilemma," *World Politics*, 30, no. 3 (1978); Stephen W. Van Evera, "Causes of War" (diss., University of California, Berkeley, 1984); and George Quester, *Offense and Defense in the International System* (New York, 1977). For an analysis and critique of these theories, see Jack S. Levy, "The Offensive/Defensive Balance of Military Technology: A Theoretical and Historical Analysis," *International Studies Quarterly*, 28, no. 2 (1984).

17. The distinction lies in the fact that there are a variety of factors unrelated to geographic proximity that alter the offense/defense balance. Proximity also tends to produce greater conflicts of interest, such as border disputes, between the states involved. These conflicts of interest are the result of proximity but can be distinct from the issue of offensive or defensive advantages.

18. See William L. Langer, *European Alliances and Alignments* (New York, 1950), pp. 35; Raymond J. Sontag, *European Diplomatic History, 1871-1932* (New York, 1933), pp. 4-5; Jervis, "Cooperation under the Security Dilemma," p. 189; and Quester, *Offense and Defense in the International System*, pp. 105-6.

19. As Imanuel Geiss notes: "Finding an agreement with Britain along German lines without a substantial naval agreement thus amounted to squaring the circle." See his *German Foreign Policy, p.* 131. See also Kennedy, *Rise of Anglo-German Antagonism*, pp. 416-423.

20. Thus alliance formation becomes more frenetic when the offense is believed to have the advantage: great powers will balance more vigorously, and weak states will bandwagon more frequently. A world of tight alliances and few neutral states is the likely result.

modest capabilities may prompt others to balance if they are perceived as especially aggressive. Thus Libyan conduct has prompted Egypt, Israel, France, the United States, Chad, and the Sudan to coordinate political and military responses against Colonel Qadhafi's activities.[21]

Perceptions of intent are likely to play an especially crucial role in alliance choices. For example, changing perceptions of German aims helped create the Triple Entente. Whereas Bismarck had carefully defended the status quo after 1870, the expansionist ambitions of his successors alarmed the other European powers.[22] Although the growth of German power played a major role, the importance of German intentions should not be overlooked. The impact of perceptions is nicely revealed in Eyre Crowe's famous 1907 memorandum defining British policy toward Germany. Crowe's analysis is all the more striking because he had few objections to the growth of German power per se:

> The mere existence and healthy activity of a powerful Germany is an undoubted blessing to this world. . . . So long, then, as Germany competes for an intellectual and moral leadership of the world in reliance on its own natural advantages and energies England cannot but admire. . . . [S]o long as Germany's action does not overstep the line of legitimate protection of existing rights it can always count upon the sympathy and good will, and even the moral support of England. . . . It would be of real advantage if the determination not to bar Germany's legitimate and peaceful expansion were . . . pronounced as authoritatively as possible, provided that care was taken . . . to make it quite clear that this benevolent attitude will give way to determined opposition at the first sign of British or allied interests being adversely affected.[23]

In short, Britain will oppose Germany only if Germany is aggressive and seeks to expand through conquest. Intention, not power, is crucial.

When a state is believed to be unalterably aggressive, other states are unlikely to bandwagon. After all, if an aggressor's intentions cannot be changed by an alliance with it, a vulnerable state, even if allied, is likely to become a victim. Balancing with others may be the only way to avoid this fate. Thus Prime Minister de Broqueville of Belgium rejected the German ultimatum of August 2, 1914, saying: "If die we must, better death with honor. We have no other choice. Our submission would serve no end. . . . Let us make no mistake about it, if Germany is victorious, Belgium, whatever her attitude, will be annexed to the

---

21. For a discussion of Libya's international position, see Claudia Wright, "Libya and the West: Headlong into Confrontation?" *International Affairs*, 58, no. 1 (1981-1982). More recently, both the United Stated and France have taken direct military action against Libya and a number of other countries have imposed economic sanctions against Qadhafi's regime.

22. See Craig, *Germany 1866-1945*, pp. 101, 242-47, and chap. 10; Geiss, *German Foreign Policy*, pp. 66-68; and Kennedy, *Rise of Anglo-German Antagonism*, chaps. 14 and 20.

23. "Memorandum by Sir Eyre Crowe on the Present State of British Relations with France and Germany, January 1, 1907," in *British Documents on the Origins of the War, 1898–1914*, ed. G. P. Gooch and Harold Temperley (London, 1928), 3: 397-420. See also G. W. Monger, *The End of Isolation: British Foreign Policy, 1900–1907* (London, 1963), pp. 313-15. Sir Edward Grey drew a similar conclusion about Britain's alliance policy: "Great Britain has not in theory been opposed to the predominance of a strong group in Europe when it seemed to make for stability and peace. . . . [I]t is only when the dominant power becomes aggressive that she, by an instinct of self-defence, if not by deliberate policy, gravitates to anything that can be fairly described as a Balance of Power." See Edward Grey, Viscount of Fallodon, K.G., *Twenty-Five Years, 1892–1916* (New York, 1925), 1: 8 and passim. See also Kennedy, *Rise of Anglo-German Antagonism, p.* 431.

Reich."[24] Thus the more aggressive or expansionist a state appears to be, the more likely it is to trigger an opposing coalition.

By defining the basic hypotheses in terms of threats rather than power alone, we gain a more complete picture of the factors that statesmen will consider when making alliance choices. One cannot determine a priori, however, which sources of threat will be most important in any given case; one can say only that all of them are likely to play a role. And the greater the threat, the greater the probability that the vulnerable state will seek an alliance.

The Implications of Balancing and Bandwagoning

The two general hypotheses of balancing and bandwagoning paint starkly contrasting pictures of international politics. Resolving the question of which hypothesis is more accurate is especially important, because each implies very different policy prescriptions. *What sort of world does each depict, and what policies are implied?*

If balancing is the dominant tendency, then threatening states will provoke others to align against them. Because those who seek to dominate others will attract widespread opposition, status quo states can take a relatively sanguine view of threats. Credibility is less important in a balancing world, because one's allies will resist threatening states out of their own, self-interest, not because they expect others to do it for them. Thus the fear of allies defecting will decline. Moreover, if balancing is the norm and if statesmen understand this tendency, aggression will be discouraged because those who contemplate it will anticipate resistance.

In a balancing world, policies that convey restraint and benevolence are best. Strong states may be valued as allies because they have much to offer their partners, but they must take particular care to avoid appearing aggressive. Foreign and defense policies that minimize the threat one poses to others make the most sense in such a world.

A bandwagoning world, by contrast, is much more competitive. If states tend to ally with those who seem most dangerous, then great powers will be rewarded if they appear both strong and potentially aggressive. International rivalries will be more intense, because a single defeat may signal the decline of one side and the ascendancy of the other. This situation is especially alarming in a bandwagoning world, because additional defections and a further decline in position are to be expected. Moreover, if statesmen believe that bandwagoning is widespread, they will be more inclined to use force. This tendency is true for both aggressors and status quo powers. The former will use force because they will assume that others will be unlikely to balance against them and because they can attract more allies through belligerence or brinkmanship. The latter will follow suit because they will fear the gains their opponents will make by appearing powerful and resolute.[25]

Finally, misperceiving the relative propensity to balance or bandwagon is dangerous, because the policies that are appropriate for one situation will backfire in the other. If statesmen follow the balancing prescription in a bandwagoning world, their moderate

---

24. Quoted in Luigi Albertini, *The Origins of the War of 1914* (London, 1952), 3: 458.

25. It is worth noting that Napoleon and Hitler underestimated the costs of aggression by assuming that their potential enemies would bandwagon. After Munich, for example, Hitler dismissed the possibility of opposition by claiming that British and French statesmen were "little worms." Napoleon apparently believed that England could not "reasonably make war on us unaided" and assumed that the Peace of Amiens guaranteed that England had abandoned its opposition to France. On these points, see Fest, *Hitler*, pp. 594–95; Liska, *Nations in Alliance, p.* 45; and Geoffrey Bruun, *Europe and the French Imperium: 1799–1814* (New York, 1938), p. 118. Because Hitler and Napoleon believed in a bandwagoning world, they were excessively eager to go to war.

responses and relaxed view of threats will encourage their allies to defect, leaving them isolated against an overwhelming coalition. Conversely, following the bandwagoning prescription in a world of balancers (employing power and threats frequently) will lead others to oppose you more and more vigorously.[26]

These concerns are not merely theoretical. In the 1930s, France failed to recognize that her allies in the Little Entente were prone to bandwagon, a tendency that French military and diplomatic policies reinforced. As noted earlier, Soviet attempts to intimidate Turkey and Norway after World War II reveal the opposite error; they merely provoked a greater U.S. commitment to these regions and cemented their entry into NATO. Likewise, the self-encircling bellicosity of Wilhelmine Germany and Imperial Japan reflected the assumption, prevalent in both states, that bandwagoning was the dominant tendency in international affairs.

When Do States Balance? When Do They Bandwagon?

These examples highlight the importance of identifying whether states are more likely to balance or bandwagon and which sources of threat have the greatest impact on the decision. . . . In general, *we should expect balancing behavior to be much more common than bandwagoning*, and we should expect bandwagoning to occur only under certain identifiable conditions.

Although many statesmen fear that potential allies will align with the strongest side, this fear receives little support from most of international history. For example, every attempt to achieve hegemony in Europe since the Thirty Years War has been thwarted by a defensive coalition formed precisely for the purpose of defeating the potential hegemon. Other examples are equally telling. Although isolated cases of bandwagoning do occur, the great powers have shown a remarkable tendency to ignore other temptations and follow the balancing prescription when necessary.

This tendency should not surprise us. Balancing should be preferred for the simple reason that no statesman can be completely sure of what another will do. Bandwagoning is dangerous because it increases the resources available to a threatening power and requires placing trust in its continued forbearance. Because perceptions are unreliable and intentions can change, it is safer to balance against potential threats than to rely on the hope that a state will remain benevolently disposed.

But if balancing is to be expected, bandwagoning remains a possibility. Several factors may affect the relative propensity for states to select this course.

Strong versus Weak States

In general, *the weaker the state, the more likely it is to bandwagon rather than balance*. This situation occurs because weak states add little to the strength of a defensive coalition but incur the wrath of the more threatening states nonetheless. Because weak states can do little to affect the outcome (and may suffer grievously in the process), they must choose the winning side. Only when their decision can affect the outcome is it rational for them to join the weaker alliance. By contrast, strong states can turn a losing coali-

---

26. This situation is analogous to Robert Jervis's distinction between the deterrence model and the spiral model. The former calls for opposition to a suspected aggressor, the latter for appeasement. Balancing and bandwagoning are the alliance equivalents of deterring and appeasing. See Robert Jervis, *Perception and Misperception in International Politics* (Princeton, N.J., 1976), chap. 3.

tion into a winning one. And because their decision may mean the difference between victory and defeat, they are likely to be amply rewarded for their contribution.

Weak states are also likely to be especially sensitive to proximate power. Where great powers have both global interests and global capabilities, weak states will be concerned primarily with events in their immediate vicinity. Moreover, weak states can be expected to balance when threatened by states with roughly equal capabilities but they will be tempted to bandwagon when threatened by a great power. Obviously, when the great power is capable of rapid and effective action (i. e., when its offensive capabilities are especially strong), this temptation will be even greater.

The Availability of Allies

States will also be tempted to bandwagon when allies are simply unavailable. This statement is not simply tautological, because states may balance by mobilizing their own resources instead of relying on allied support. They are more likely to do so, however, when they are confident that allied assistance will be available. Thus a further prerequisite for balancing behavior is an effective system of diplomatic communication. The ability to communicate enables potential allies to recognize their shared interests and coordinate their responses. If weak states see no possibility of outside assistance, however, they may be forced to accommodate the most imminent threat. Thus the first Shah of Iran saw the British withdrawal from Kandahar in 1881 as a signal to bandwagon with Russia. As he told the British representative, all he had received from Great Britain was "good advice and honeyed words—nothing else."[27] Finland's policy of partial alignment with the Soviet Union suggests the same lesson. When Finland joined forces with Nazi Germany during World War II, it alienated the potential allies (the United States and Great Britain) that might otherwise have helped protect it from Soviet pressure after the war.

Of course, excessive confidence in allied support will encourage weak states to free-ride, relying on the efforts of others to provide security. Free-riding is the optimal policy for a weak state, because its efforts will contribute little in any case. Among the great powers, the belief that allies are readily available encourages buck-passing; states that are threatened strive to pass to others the burdens of standing up to the aggressor. Neither response is a form of bandwagoning, but both suggest that effective balancing behavior is more likely to occur when members of an alliance are not convinced that their partners are unconditionally loyal.

Taken together, these factors help explain the formation of spheres of influence surrounding the great powers. Although strong neighbors of strong states are likely to balance, small and weak neighbors of the great powers may be more inclined to bandwagon. Because they will be the first victims of expansion, because they lack the capabilities to stand alone, and because a defensive alliance may operate too slowly to do them much good, accommodating a threatening great power may be tempting.

Peace and War

Finally, the context in which alliance choices are made will affect decisions to balance or bandwagon. States are more likely to balance in peacetime or in the early stages of a war, as they seek to deter or defeat the powers posing the greatest threat. But once the outcome appears certain, some will be tempted to defect from the losing side at an opportune moment. Thus

---

27. Quoted in C. J. Lowe, *The Reluctant Imperialists* (New York, 1967), p. 85.

both Rumania and Bulgaria allied with Nazi Germany initially and then abandoned Germany for the Allies, as the tides of war ebbed and flowed across Europe in World War II.

The restoration of peace, however, restores the incentive to balance. As many observers have noted, victorious coalitions are likely to disintegrate with the conclusion of peace. Prominent examples include Austria and Prussia after their war with Denmark in 1864, Britain and France after World War I, the Soviet Union and the United States after World War II, and China and Vietnam after the U.S. withdrawal from Vietnam. This recurring pattern provides further support for the proposition that balancing is the dominant tendency in international politics and that bandwagoning is the opportunistic exception.

Summary of Hypotheses on Balancing and Bandwagoning

Hypotheses on Balancing

1. *General form*: States facing an external threat will align with others to oppose the states posing the threat.
2. The greater the threatening state's aggregate power, the greater the tendency for others to align against it.
3. The nearer a powerful state, the greater the tendency for those nearby to align against it. Therefore, neighboring states are less likely to be allies than are states separated by at least one other power.
4. The greater a state's offensive capabilities, the greater the tendency for others to align against it. Therefore, states with offensively oriented military capabilities are likely to provoke other states to form defensive coalitions.
5. The more aggressive a state's perceived intentions, the more likely others are to align against that state.
6. Alliances formed during wartime will disintegrate when the enemy is defeated.

Hypotheses on Bandwagoning

The hypotheses on bandwagoning are the opposite of those on balancing.

1. *General form*: States facing an external threat will ally with the most threatening power.
2. The greater a state's aggregate capabilities, the greater the tendency for others to align with it.
3. The nearer a powerful state, the greater the tendency for those nearby to align with it.
4. The greater a state's offensive capabilities, the greater the tendency for others to align with it.
5. The more aggressive a state's perceived intentions, the less likely other states are to align against it.
6. Alliances formed to oppose a threat will disintegrate when the threat becomes serious.

Hypotheses on the Conditions Favoring Balancing or Bandwagoning

1. Balancing is more common than bandwagoning.
2. The stronger the state, the greater its tendency to balance. Weak states will balance against other weak states but may bandwagon when threatened by great powers.
3. The greater the probability of allied support, the greater the tendency to balance. When adequate allied support is certain, however, the tendency for free-riding or buck-passing increases.
4. The more unalterably aggressive a state is perceived to be, the greater the tendency for others to balance against it.

5. In wartime, the closer one side is to victory, the greater the tendency for others to bandwagon with it.

CONCLUSION

The hypotheses examined in this chapter imply very different worlds. If balancing is the norm, if ideology exerts little effect or is often divisive, and if foreign aid and penetration are rather weak causes, then hegemony over the international system will be extremely difficult to achieve. Most states will find security plentiful. But if the bandwagoning hypothesis is more accurate, if ideology is a powerful force for alignment, and if foreign aid and penetration can readily bring reliable control over others, then hegemony will be much easier (although it will also be rather fragile).[28] Even great powers will view their security as precarious.

Because the implications of each hypothesis are different, it is important to determine which of the hypotheses presented here offers the best guide to state behavior. The next task, therefore, is to assemble a body of evidence [presented in Chapters 3 and 4—and not included in this text] that will enable us to perform this assessment.

---

28. If bandwagoning is common, a dominant position may be fragile because a few small defeats may cause a flood of defections. Once allies have concluded that the dominant power's fortunes are waning, the bandwagoning hypothesis predicts that they will quickly realign. The fortunes of the great powers are thus highly elastic in a bandwagoning world, because small events anywhere will have major consequences.

Alliance Formation and the Balance of World Power

Stephen M. Walt

I began . . . by arguing that the forces that shape international alliances are among the most important in international politics. In particular, I suggested that many debates over foreign policy and grand strategy are based primarily on conflicting beliefs about the origins of international alliances. These beliefs have been especially important in postwar U.S. foreign policy, but the United States is hardly unique in this regard.[1] By examining existing theory, European diplomatic history, and the contemporary debate on U.S. foreign policy, I identified several popular hypotheses that are often used to explain how states choose their friends. After surveying changing alliance commitments in the Middle East—a region that seemed especially appropriate for testing these different hypotheses—I compared the evolution of Middle East alliances with the predictions offered by each one. Balance of threat and ideological explanations each contributed useful insights; the other hypotheses fared less well.

Three tasks remain. The first is to summarize the analysis . . . and compare the explanatory power of these competing hypotheses directly. The second is to extend the analysis beyond the Middle East. Because my aim has been to evaluate a set of propositions applicable to the broader realm of international politics, it is important that I consider whether these propositions can account for other patterns of alliance formation. To show that they can, I will use the ideas developed here to explain the current array of superpower commitments, what one might call the fundamental division of world power. Finally, because alliance theory continues to play a crucial (if largely unrecognized) role in contemporary debates on grand strategy, the third task is to outline the lessons that policy-makers in the United States should draw from these results.

ANALYZING ALLIANCE FORMATION: AN ASSESSMENT

Balancing and Bandwagoning

Compared with the other hypotheses examined in this book, the general hypothesis that states choose allies in order to balance against the most serious threat was the clear winner. Its merits were shown in two important ways. First, balancing was far more common than bandwagoning, and bandwagoning was almost always confined to especially weak and isolated states. Second, the importance of ideological distinctions declined as the level of threat increased; ideological solidarity was most powerful when security was high or when ideological factors and security considerations reinforced each other.[2]

---

[1] On the role of hidden assumptions about alliances in postwar US. grand strategy, see Larson, "The Bandwagon Metaphor."

[2] Saudi Arabia, Syria, and Egypt joined forces after 1967; Jordan and Israel(!) collaborated to thwart Syrian intervention In 1970; and Syria and Jordan staged a dramatic rapprochement after Sinai II. One could recite examples ad infinitum, but the point should be clear: the need to balance an external threat was usually more important than the desire to support states espousing similar ideologies.

Balance of Power versus Balance of Threat

The evidence presented in this book demonstrates the value of balance of threat theory, which should be viewed as a refinement of traditional balance of power theory. As discussed [earlier] . . . , states balance against the states that pose the greatest threat, and the latter need not be the most powerful states in the system. Just as national power is produced by several different components (e.g., military and economic capability, natural resources, and population), the level of threat that a state poses to others is the product of several interrelated components. Whereas balance of power theory predicts that states will react to imbalances of power, balance of threat theory predicts that when there is an imbalance of threat (i.e., when one state or coalition appears especially dangerous), states will form alliances or increase their internal efforts in order to reduce their vulnerability.

The distinction is subtle but important. Balance of threat theory improves on balance of power theory by providing greater explanatory power with equal parsimony.[3] By using balance of threat theory, we can understand a number of events that we cannot explain by focusing solely on the distribution of aggregate capabilities. For example, balance of threat theory explains why the coalitions that defeated Germany and its allies in World War I and World War II grew to be far more powerful than their opponents, in contrast to the predictions of balance of power theory. The answer is simple: Germany and its allies combined power, proximity, offensive capabilities, and extremely aggressive intentions. As a result, they were more threatening (though weaker) and caused others to form a more powerful coalition in response.[4] In the same way, balance of threat theory helps explain why states in the Middle East form alliances primarily to deal with threats from their neighbors, not in response to shifts in the global balance of power. They do so because their neighbors are usually more dangerous than either superpower, partly because of geographic proximity. Similarly, Nasser's turbulent relations with the other Arabs are explained as much by shifts in Egyptian intentions as by changes in Egypt's relative power. The same is true for Syria; its isolation during much of the 1960s was based in part on the extremism of the Ba'th, not on Syria's rather modest capabilities during this period.

Finally, balance of threat theory can also explain alliance choices when a state's potential allies are roughly equal in power. In such a circumstance, a state will ally with the side it believes is least dangerous. Thus balance of threat theory can also predict how states will

3. Balance of threat theory may appear to be less parsimonious than traditional balance of power theory, because threats are the product of several different components, including the distribution of aggregate power. In fact, the two theories are equally parsimonious; balance of threat theory, however, is more general and abstract. Whenever one moves to a more general or abstract level of analysis, one inevitably includes more variables. More general theories by definition incorporate a broader range of phenomena. But a more general theory is not less parsimonious, as long as the principal ideas that organize its relevant variables are as few in number as the principal ideas of the less general theory it replaces The principal concept that informs balance of power theory is power, which consists of components such as military and economic capability and population. The principal concept that informs balance of threat theory is threat, which consists of aggregate power, proximity, offensive capability, and perceived intentions. Balance of threat theory is a more general explanation of state conduct but not a more complicated one.

4. Moreover, the alliances against Germany remained united until Germany was totally defeated, largely because of the widespread recognition of German bellicosity. Thus the two most important alliances in the twentieth century are inconsistent with balance of power theory but are readily explained by balance of threat theory.

choose between the United States and the Soviet Union, something that balance of power theory cannot do.[5]

In short, as shown in Figure 1, balance of threat theory subsumes balance of power theory. Aggregate power is an important component of threat, but not the only one. By conceiving of alliances as responses to imbalances of threat (not just imbalances of power), we gain a more complete and accurate picture of behavior in the international political realm.

Focusing on threats rather than power alone also helps account for several apparent anomalies in the evidence. The first is the unwillingness of Arab states to ally with Israel, even when such an alliance would have been an obvious military asset. This failure is readily understood when we recall that such an alliance would have posed a potentially lethal threat to the legitimacy of the Arab states involved because of the importance attached to Arab solidarity.[6]

An even more intriguing anomaly is the difficulty the Arab states have faced when seeking to form alliances together to balance against Israel.[7] Although Israel has grown steadily larger and stronger since 1948, its neighbors have been surprisingly incapable of joining forces effectively in response. Israel's Arab opponents have balanced by allying with either the United States or the Soviet Union, but not with one another. With the exception of the alliances during the October War in 1973, Arab alliances against Israel were largely symbolic, in contrast to what the balancing hypothesis would predict.[8]

This anomaly can be explained in two different ways. First, it illustrates the natural tendency for states to pass the buck, in the hope that other similarly situated states will accept the "honor" of opposing the common enemy.[9] This tendency was apparent during the War of Attrition. Why should Syria, Iraq, and Jordan risk war with Israel when Egypt was willing to do their fighting for them? The tendency was even stronger before 1967, because none of the states had a strong material interest in challenging Israel.

This type of behavior is especially pronounced in multipolar, regional subsystems embedded within a bipolar global system. In this circumstance, the regional states need not cooperate with one another because they can rely upon superpower support instead. Thus balancing behavior predominates, but regional powers prefer the support of a distant superpower to cooperation with another regional actor. The reason is obvious: the superpowers can do more to help, and helping a neighbor may be dangerous if it becomes too strong as a result. This situation is due, of course, to geographic proximity. Thus the Arabs balanced by seeking Soviet or U.S. support rather than by aiding one another.

5. As Glenn Snyder has written: "It might be argued that the alignment . . . [of lesser powers in a bipolar world] is not affected by the logic of system structure [i. e, the distribution of power] at all. If left to their own devices, they will align with the superpower that appears least threatening to their own security or that is most congenial ideologically." See Snyder and Diesing, *Conflict among Nations*, p. 421.

6. The exception is Jordan, which relied on implicit Israeli military guarantees during its brief war against the PLO and Syria in 1970.

7. The most obvious example is Nasser's inability to obtain significant support from the Eastern Command during the War of Attrition.

8. The Arab coalition in the Six Day War was as much a product of inter-Arab rivalries as it was a response to a perceived threat to the Arabs from Israel.

9. On the concept of buck-passing, see Posen, *Sources of Military Doctrine*, pp. 63, 232.

Balance of Power Theory

Imbalances of power ——— cause ———> alliances against the strongest state

An imbalance of power occurs when the strongest state or coalition in the system possesses significantly greater power than the second strongest. Power is the product of several different components, including population, economic and military capability, technological skill, and political cohesion.

Balance of Threat Theory

Imbalances of threat ——— cause———> alliances against the most threatening state

An imbalance of threat occurs when the most threatening state or coalition is significantly more dangerous than the second most threatening state or coalition. The degree to which a state threatens others is the product of its aggregate power, its geographic proximity, its offensive capability, and the aggressiveness of its intentions.

Figure 1. Balance of Power versus Balance of Threat Theory

A second reason the Arab states often failed to balance effectively against Nasser is the fact that they posed greater threats to one another than Nasser did. As shown [earlier] . . . , the ideology of pan-Arabism contributed to this problem, by making each Arab state an enemy of Nasser and a potential threat to all the other Arab states. Nasser's ambitions and charisma simply made it worse. And as noted, alignment with a superpower was just as effective and far less dangerous than helping an Arab rival challenge Nasser successfully. Thus, until the Six Day War made Nasser a real enemy (instead of a largely symbolic one), effective balancing behavior among Arab states was confined primarily to thwarting the ambitions of Arab rivals.

In short, these anomalies are readily explained in light of the theory. All things considered, balance of threat theory is strongly endorsed by the evidence examined here. As we will see, evidence from a global perspective is equally compelling.

Ideological Solidarity

This study also showed that ideological solidarity is less important than external threats as a cause of alliances. The states examined here did show a slight preference for alignment with other similar states, but the preference was readily abandoned in the face of significant threats or discredited by the rivalries that emerged between ideologically kindred regimes.

This hypothesis was most useful in explaining alliance decisions when the prevailing array of threats was either modest or indeterminate. Thus ideology was a more important factor in explaining superpower commitments largely because the two superpowers are roughly equal in terms of their other characteristics. Ideological considerations become crucial by default.

Another important conclusion was that many apparently ideological alliances were a particular form of balancing behavior. Thus balance of threat theory also subsumes the hypotheses about ideological solidarity. For the fragile regimes of the Arab world, a challenge to the ruler's legitimacy could easily be a more potent threat than any enemy army. The various pacts among Jordan, Saudi Arabia, and monarchical Iraq, for example, were alliances among similar regimes, intended to counter the threat from the aggressive revolutionary nationalism espoused by leaders such as Nasser. The failed attempts to unite the Ba'th regimes of Syria and Iraq (and thus isolate Egypt) sprang from essentially the same desire (i.e., to balance an ideological threat).

In the same way, the apparently strong effect of ideology on alliances between the superpowers and the regional states may in part reflect balancing behavior as well, in the form of a self-fulfilling prophecy. Because both superpowers have behaved as if ideology were important, they have reinforced any innate tendency for regional powers to favor one superpower over the other for ideological reasons. We should be cautious, therefore, in interpreting the tendency for superpower-client relations to exhibit ideological solidarity; the role of ideology alone in such alliances is probably less than it would appear.

Finally, the impact of ideological factors was most evident in the case of pan-Arabism, but its effects were almost entirely negative. As long as the goal of Arab unity was a touchstone of Arab legitimacy, each Arab regime posed a potential threat to all the others. But the more fiercely any single state sought the objective professed by all, the more likely it was to experience conflicts with the rest. As noted earlier, the divisive character of pan-Arab ideology was one important reason the Arab world did not balance effectively against Israel. Among other things, this example shows that ideological factors can in some circumstances override other incentives for alignment. To repeat, however, this ideology tended to discourage alignment rather than promote it.

The history of inter-Arab relations reveals a final paradox, one with several important implications. The greater the devotion to Arab solidarity, the greater the conviction that Israel is a foreign invader that all Arab states should oppose. At the same time, however, this belief makes it more difficult to pursue that goal effectively. Paradoxically, therefore, as pan-Arab sentiment declines (and is replaced by a more limited, state-centered nationalism) the need to fight for the "sacred" cause of the Palestinian Arabs declines, but the ideological barriers to coordinated action are reduced. Inter-Arab cooperation becomes easier as it becomes less important, and vice versa.

This paradox has obvious implications for Israeli security, which is threatened by Arab military cooperation. The analysis suggests that the likelihood of a grand Arab coalition is slight, unless it is based on tangible objectives such as recovering the occupied territories. An ideological alliance against the Jewish state will be either extremely unstable (because each member fears its partners) or extremely unlikely (because the power of pan-Arab ideology has evaporated). Among other things, this situation means that territorial concessions are very much in Israel's interest, because they remove the most significant incentives for the formation of an effective Arab alliance. Returning the Sinai to Egypt was an obvious example of this approach, and one that greatly enhanced Israel's security.

Foreign Aid and Penetration

Neither foreign aid nor penetration has proven to be of much use as an explanation of alliance formation. Both hypotheses ignore the prior motives that encourage the provision of foreign assistance or the establishment of extensive elite contacts—and both can be subsumed within the more general hypotheses already considered. Foreign aid is merely one form of balancing behavior, and the establishment of extensive contacts between separate national elites is often an indicator of a close alignment.

Even more important, the modest independent impact of aid and penetration is revealed by the fact that even extremely vulnerable and dependent clients have retained considerable freedom of action. Efforts to use foreign aid to control an ally usually have led to considerable resentment, and attempts to manipulate an ally's foreign or domestic policies through covert penetration usually have backfired badly. In short, both of these instruments have been found to be a predictable result of political alignment, but neither has been a very powerful cause.

The principal exception to both these conclusions is the U.S. relationship with Israel. By manipulating its level of foreign assistance, the United States has been able to extract significant concessions from Israel on a number of occasions. Although U.S. leverage is not absolute, the lack of ready alternatives to U.S. support has made Israel especially vulnerable to this type of pressure.

At the same time, however, the success of pro-Israeli forces in penetrating the U.S. political system in recent years has greatly reduced the impact of Israel's substantial overall dependence. Their success in this regard is an obvious exception to the conclusion that penetration is not an effective instrument of alliance diplomacy. However, this success is the result of a unique array of circumstances. The extreme openness of the U.S. political system, the unusual cohesion of U.S. Jewry as a political interest group, and the limited goals that pro-Israeli forces seek have all contributed to the considerable political impact of pro-Israeli forces in the United States.

As a result, although this exception has a significant impact on U.S. foreign policy in the Middle East, its theoretical importance is limited. In most cases, penetration remains at most a minor cause of alliance formation. What this case does suggest is that the usual U.S. concerns about foreign penetration are often misplaced. This study suggests that Soviet penetration of the relatively impermeable regimes of the Third World is not a significant danger, because such efforts almost always fail when other incentives for alignment are lacking. A greater problem may well be the manipulation of U.S. foreign policy by elites whose interests may not always be identical with those of the nation as a whole. . . .[10]

ALLIANCE FORMATION AND THE BALANCE OF WORLD POWER?

The propositions developed in this book tell us a great deal about the current balance of world power. I make two claims in particular. First, contrary to the usual pessimism, I believe the present distribution of world power greatly favors the United States and its allies. Second, this favorable imbalance of power can be explained by the central propositions I have advanced and tested in this book. To support these claims, I offer a rough assessment of the current distribution of capabilities and then show how this situation is the direct result of the general tendencies identified earlier.

The Fundamental (Im)Balance of World Power

Measuring the effective power of states or coalitions is complicated and difficult. Fortunately, a detailed net assessment is not necessary here. A rough but reliable comparison of the Soviet and U.S. alliance systems can be obtained by considering the following items: population, GNP, size of armed forces, and defense expenditures.[11] Members of the respective alliance networks have been identified either by the existence

---

10. As noted elsewhere in this book, how one evaluates the impact of pro-Israeli forces (or other ethnic lobbies, for that matter) will be governed by whether or not one feels that the allegiances such groups advocate are harmful or beneficial to the overall national interest. Resolving that question—if it is possible at all—is obviously beyond the scope of this book.

11. On the problems of estimating national power, see Knorr, *Power of Nations,* chaps. 3 and 4; Harold Sprout and Margaret Sprout, *Foundations of International Politics* (Princeton, N.J., 1962); Morgenthau, *Politics among Nations,* pt. 3; and Ray S. Cline, *World Power Assessment 1977: A Calculus of Strategic Drift* (Washington, D.C., 1978).

of a formal security treaty or by the presence of a significant level of security cooperation between the ally and the superpower in question.[12] The Soviet system includes the Warsaw Pact and Moscow's various regional clients; the U.S. alliance network includes NATO, Japan, and the regional powers with substantial security ties to the United States.

The current distribution of capabilities between these two alliances is shown in Table 1. The results are striking. The United States and its allies surpass the Soviet alliance network by a considerable margin in the primary indicators of national power. This statement is true if one looks solely at the core alliances of NATO and the Warsaw Pact, if China and India are included or excluded, and if each superpower's array of allies within the developing world is considered. Significantly, the worst case for the Soviet Union—China tacitly allied with the West and India neutral—is probably the most likely case as well. The Soviet Union faces a gap of more than 3 to 1 in population and GNP, to say nothing of its technological disadvantages.[13] The disparity is smaller in terms of mobilized power (defense spending, size of armed forces), because the Soviets and their allies have sought to compensate for their relative weakness by devoting a larger percentage of their national resources to defense. Despite these efforts, however, the Soviet alliance system still trails that of the United States in these categories as well.

These results highlight the explanatory power of balance of threat theory. If states were concerned solely with balancing power, we would expect to see many of the current allies of the United States align with the Soviet Union instead.[14] This anomaly is even more striking when we recall that the United States was overwhelmingly the world's most powerful country immediately after World War II, yet was able to bring most of the other industrial powers into an alliance against the Soviet Union.[15] The explanation of the anomaly lies in the fact

---

12. In addition to formal treaty relationships, these calculations include states with permanent military training missions from either superpower. States that accept security assistance from both superpowers at the same time are considered neutral and are not included. See the information presented in U.S. Joint Chiefs of Staff, *U.S. Military Posture for FY1987,* overleaf to p. 1; and U.S. Department of Defense, *Soviet Military Power 1986,* pp. 126-27 and passim. Of course, one might argue that many of the states that are included in these calculations are not really allied with either superpower, because the presence of military advisers or the provision of military equipment does not by itself constitute a significant commitment. If so, this problem affects both superpowers. As a result, these figures should not be biased. To minimize any possibility of distortion, however, Table 1 reports results reflecting several different assumptions about each superpower's allies. Moreover, the sources used to identify each superpower's military commitments are more likely to exaggerate Soviet strength than to minimize it. These calculations thus provide a strong test of the proposition that the United States enjoys a considerable advantage.

13. According to the U.S. undersecretary of defense, research and engineering, in 1986 the United States led the Soviet Union in fourteen out of twenty areas of basic technology. The two states were tied in the other six areas (the Soviets led in none) In terms of deployed military systems, U.S. technology was superior in sixteen out of thirty-one, even in nine, and behind in only four. See "The Statement by the Undersecretary of Defense, Research and Engineering to the 99th Congress," in U.S. Department of Defense, *The FY1987 Department of Defense Program for Research and Development* (Washington, D.C., 86), pp. II-1I, II-12.

14. This result contradicts the size principle that William Riker and others have derived from the postulates of n-person game theory. Riker predicts that coalitions will be just large enough to win (but no larger) in order to maximize each player's share of the spoils. But as Table 1 shows, the margin of aggregate power amassed by the United States and its allies far exceeds the minimum necessary to oppose the Soviet Union. For Riker's argument, see his *Theory of Political Coalitions.*

15. In 1950, the United States produced approximately 40 percent of gross world product; the Soviet Union managed only 13.5 percent. U.S. naval and air power were far superior, and the United States had a clear advantage in deliverable atomic weaponry.

Table 3: Comparison of capabilities of U.S. and Soviet alliance syste

Coalitions	Population	GNP	Number in armed forces	Defense spending
U.S. + NATO[a] / USSR + WTO[b]	1.95:1	2.93:1	1.06:1	1.14:1
U.S. + NATO + PRC[c] / USSR + WTO	4.61:1	3.08:1	1.77:1	1.25:1
U S + NATO + Other[d] / USSR + WTO + Other	2.64:1	3.25:1	1.15:1	1.25:1
U.S + NATO + Other + PRC / USSR + WTO + Other	4.19:1	3.39:1	1.58:1	1.36:1
U.S. + NATO + Other / USSR + WTO + Other + India	1.25:1	3.04	1.03:1	1.23:1

a. NATO is the North Atlantic Treaty Organization plus Japan.
b. WTO is the Warsaw Treaty Organization.
c. PRC is People's Republic of China.
d. "Other" refers to allies outside of NATO and the WTO.
Source: See Appendix 2 in Steven Walt, *The Origins of Alliances* (Ithaca, NY: Cornell University Press, 1987).

that although the United States has been more powerful, the Soviet Union has appeared to be more dangerous.

Explaining the Imbalance

What explains this striking imbalance of power? Why is the Soviet Union at such a disadvantage? Recall the main themes developed in the previous three chapters. First, states tend to balance against threats, and the level of threat is determined by several factors. Second, ideology is usually a less important cause of alignment, and certain ideologies may promote conflict more than they encourage cooperation. Third, attempts to induce alignment through bribery or penetration will face a host of obstacles and are unlikely to succeed in the absence of other incentives for alignment. Taken together, these propositions provide a persuasive explanation of the durable imbalance of power between East and West.

Aggregate Power

In a bipolar world, competition between the two greatest powers is virtually guaranteed. Thus the current rivalry between the United States and the Soviet Union is itself an example of balancing against power. For the Soviets, this prospect is especially daunting. The rigid logic of bipolarity has locked them in competition with history's wealthiest and most technologically advanced society. Even before we consider the allies that each superpower has attracted, therefore, we see that the Soviet Union begins from a relatively weaker position.

Proximity

As the events examined in earlier chapters showed, states are more sensitive to threats that are nearby than to dangers from far away. This tendency contributes directly to Soviet isolation. Because the Soviet Union is the largest and most powerful country on the Eurasian landmass, it poses a significant threat to the numerous countries that lie on or near its borders. Soviet relations with neighbors tend to be either imperial or hostile; the neighbors are either under de facto Soviet control or aligned with the United States.

The United States, by contrast, has only two countries on its borders. Neither is especially powerful. Because U.S. policy toward both has been benevolent in recent decades, both have chosen to ally with the united States.[16] Even more important, the United States is separated by two oceans from the other vital centers of world power. For the middle-level powers of Western Europe and Asia, the United States is the perfect ally. Its aggregate power ensures that its voice will be heard and its actions will be felt, and it is driven by its own concern for Soviet expansion to contribute substantially to its allies' defense. At the same time, the United States is far enough away so as not to pose a significant threat to these allies. Thus the United States is geographically isolated but politically popular, whereas the Soviet Union is politically isolated as a consequence of its geographic proximity to other states.[17] The distribution of aggregate power places the Soviet Union against the United States; geography places the Soviet Union against virtually all the other important and powerful countries in the world. If a Soviet strategic planner could be granted one wish, it should be to move his country somewhere else.[18]

Offensive Power

The Soviet response to this unfavorable situation is both predictable and selfdefeating. Faced by an encircling coalition of vastly superior latent resources, the Soviet Union devotes a large share of its national income to amassing military power. The Soviet Union leads the world in total defense expenditures, and it spends a far greater percentage of GNP on defense than the United States and its principal allies spend. This response is itself a form of balancing behavior; the Soviets compensate for their lack of powerful allies through greater internal effort.[19]

At the same time, the Soviet Union spends its rubles primarily on offensive capabilities. Soviet conventional forces are tailored for offensive warfare, and Soviet military doctrine

16. Significantly, the two most anti-U.S. countries in the Western hemisphere—Cuba and Nicaragua—have both been the targets of considerable U.S. interference in recent decades.

17. This observation stands Halford Mackinder's notion of the heartland on its head. He suggested that Russia gained great advantages from its central position, because "who rules Eastern Europe commands the Heartland, who rules the Heartland commands the World Island: who rules the World Island commands the World." By this logic the outcome of World War II should have established Soviet rather than U.S. hegemony. Mackinder's analysis may be true in a purely military sense, but it neglects the implications of balance of threat theory. In particular, occupation of the heartland greatly increases the number of potential enemies one must face. For Mackinder's analysis, see "The Geographical Pivot of History," *Geographical Journal*, 23, no. 4 (1904): 421-44. For recent analyses, see Robert E. Harkavy, *Great Power Competition for Overseas Bases: The Geopolitics of Access Diplomacy* (New York, 1982), chap. 6; and Paul M. Kennedy, "Mahan vs. Mackinder: Two Views on Naval Strategy," *Strategy and Diplomacy: Collected Essays* (London, 1983).

18. The aim of the U.S. strategy of containment, of course, is to prevent them from doing just that.

19. Thus Soviet emphasis on military power, which is usually attributed either to the political clout of the Soviet military or to the expansionist aims of the CPSU, may in fact be largely the result of the Soviet Union's unfavorable geopolitical position.

places great emphasis on preemption and the virtues of the offensive.[20] This emphasis may be due in part to its unfavorable geographic position; like Wilhelmine Germany and contemporary Israel, the Soviet Union may view an offensive capability as desirable if it must fight on several fronts.[21] Whatever the motive, this response merely increases Soviet isolation. Because it also increases the potential threat to others, the Soviet Union's large offensive capability reinforces the cohesion of the alliance that is already arrayed against it.[22]

Aggressive Intentions

The final source of threat—perceived intentions—also works against the Soviet Union. Soviet statements suggest that the nation sees bandwagoning as the normal behavior of states, a view consistent with its emphasis on offensive military forces.[23] The result has been a counterproductive reliance on threats and intimidation, ranging from Stalin's pressure on Turkey, Iran, and Norway to the more recent attempts to browbeat NATO into halting deployment of intermediate-range nuclear missiles. The invasion of Afghanistan and the periodic interventions in Eastern Europe, Soviet support for terrorist organizations, and events such as the downing of a Korean airliner in 1983 also reinforce suspicions about Soviet intentions.

Finally, the Soviet leaders have never abandoned their public commitment to promoting world revolution. Although this policy may increase their popularity with radical groups, it reinforces the already strong tendency for the world's most capable and powerful states to ally against them. To make matters worse, the radical allies of the Soviet Union are neither powerful nor popular, especially with their neighbors. Soviet support for world revolution, in short, may cost the Soviet Union more friends than it gains.

---

20. On the offensive character of Soviet military doctrine, see Phillip A. Peterson and John G. Hines, "The Conventional Offensive in Soviet Theater Strategy," *Orbis*, 27, no. 3 (1983); Stephen M. Meyer, "Soviet Theatre Nuclear Forces, Part 1; Development of Doctrine and Objectives," *Adelphi Paper No. 187* (London, 1984); Benjamin Lambeth, "How to Think about Soviet Military Doctrine," *RAND Paper P-5939* (Santa Monica, Calif., 1978); and Jack L. Snyder, "Civil-Military Relations and the Cult of the Offensive," *International Security*, 9, no. 1 (1984).

21. If encircled states have offensive capabilities, they can try to deal with their enemies sequentially, as Germany's Schlieffon Plan attempted in World War I and as Israel accomplished during the Six Day War. As Germany found out, there are serious problems with this approach, in part because the scale of operations and quality of opposition was far greater than that faced by Israel. On this point, see Richard Ned Lebow, "The Soviet Offensive in Europe: The Schlieffen Plan Revisited?" *International Security, 9, no. 4* (1985); and Snyder, "Civil-Military Relations." The Soviet preference for an offensive doctrine may also reveal a lack of effective civilian influence, given that most modern militaries prefer offensive doctrines. On this point, see Posen, *Sources of Military Doctrine,* pp. 42-51.

22. Recent examples of balancing behavior by the West are the sustained U.S. defense buildup begun by the Carter administration and accelerated under Reagan; the rapprochement with China in the 19705; the modernization of Norwegian coastal and air defenses and the pre-positioning of equipment for a U.S. marine battalion in Norway itself; NATO's decision to deploy 572 intermediate-range nuclear missiles to balance Soviet deployment of the SS-20; and the 1976 agreement for an annual 3 percent real increase in alliance defense spending. Allied responses still fall short of U.S. preferences, a phenomenon best explained by the theory of collective goods. See Olson and Zeckhauser, "Economic Theory of Alliances."

23. The Soviet concept of the correlation of forces, for example, is reminiscent of bandwagoning logic. Soviet commentators maintain that as the correlation of forces shifts towards socialism, the result is a progressive acceleration of favorable world trends. The idea that countervailing tendencies might balance a temporary advantage is notably absent. On this point, see William Zimmerman, *Soviet Perspectives on International Relations* (Princeton, N.J., 1969), pp. 159-64 and passim; and Simes, "Soviet Policy towards the United States," pp. 310-11.

So on virtually every dimension of threat, the Soviet Union ends up the loser. Given the general tendency for states to balance, this situation is good news for the United States. Although the United States has failed to play its hand perfectly, it has retained the friendship of the world's most important countries. By comparison, the Soviet Union has succeeded in drawing into its orbit a set of regimes that combine serious internal problems with widespread regional unpopularity. Given the Soviet Union's geographic position, past Soviet policies, and the tendencies analyzed in this book, that is precisely what one would expect.

Further confirmation can be found by comparing each superpower's experience in the Third World. These different sources of threat have been partly reversed in the developing world, which explains why the Soviet Union has done relatively better there. The Soviet Union's ability to project military power on a global scale has been and remains distinctly inferior to that of the United States, and the Soviets have adopted a more sympathetic attitude toward Third World nationalism and the nonaligned movement.[24] By contrast, the United States denounced neutralism as immoral, was hostile to leftist nationalist movements, and repeatedly used its considerable military capabilities against a variety of developing countries.[25] Thus where Soviet power and perceived intentions threatened the developed world but not the former colonies, U.S. power and U.S. actions did just the opposite. The same factors that explain the close ties of the United States with the industrial states of Eurasia therefore also account for its relatively poorer standing throughout much of the rest of the world.

The Impact of Ideology

In light of the analysis [previously] presented, the Soviet situation looks even worse. As noted, Marxism-Leninism threatens many of the world's most powerful countries. Less widely recognized is the fact that, like pan-Arabism, Leninism is a divisive ideology that inadvertently promotes conflict among its adherents. Soviet Marxism-Leninism calls for leadership to be wielded by an infallible vanguard party, the CPSU. Any Marxist states that follow their own interests rather than Soviet directives thus pose a direct challenge to the authority of the ruling ideology. Ideological disagreements can escalate quickly into fratricidal quarrels, because the legitimacy of each member's position is at stake.[26] It is hardly an accident that every Communist state that has been physically able to establish a position independent from Moscow has done so and that conflicts between Communist regimes have been among the world's most virulent quarrels. Ideological disagreements are not the only source of intra-Communist conflicts, but they have clearly exacerbated relations between Communist states. In short, the alleged unity of leftist forces in contemporary international politics is probably more apparent than real.

The U.S. democratic system provides an advantage here as well. Democratic regimes enjoy unusually good relations because they do not engage in intense ideological disputes with

---

24. See Andrew Marshall, "Sources of Soviet Power: The Military Potential in the 1980s," in *Prospects of Soviet Power in the 1980s*, ed. Christoph Bertram (Hamden, Conn., 1980), pp. 65-66; and Stephen S. Kaplan, *Diplomacy of Power: Soviet Armed Forces as a Political Instrument* (Washington, D.C., 1981), chap. 5.

25. See Barnet, *Intervention and Revolution*; and Blechman and Kaplan, *Force without War.*

26. See Lowenthal, "Factors of Unity and Factors of Conflict"; and Brzezinski, *Soviet Bloc*, chap. 19, especially pp. 494-96.

one another. And because the world's democracies are wealthy and technologically advanced (whereas most Marxist countries are not), the U.S. alliance system is both impressive in its capabilities and unusually cohesive, by both historical and contemporary standards.[27]

Foreign Aid and Penetration

Neither foreign aid nor penetration is likely to help the Soviet Union overcome these serious liabilities. There is little the Soviets can offer the industrial economies of Western Europe and Japan (save for raw materials, whose importance is declining), and they have already demonstrated their inability to provide competitive economic benefits to the Third World.[28] The superiority of the Western economic system helps explain why even Marxist states such as Angola have sought close economic ties with the West.[29] Similarly, Soviet efforts to penetrate the Western alliance via propaganda and subversion have failed completely, and Soviet attempts to foster loyal Third World allies through subversion and educational assistance have yielded few rewards save in a small number of backward and weak countries. In any case, the United States and its allies retain the dominant position in educating most Third World elites.[30]

Finally, as chapter 7 showed, these instruments do not ensure that clients will be either obedient or loyal, and efforts to use them to enforce compliance are more likely to produce suspicion and hostility. In short, the powerful role of nationalism in most countries will limit the impact of these instruments as independent causes of alignment, for the reasons noted earlier.

The global position of the United States is thus doubly reassuring. Not only is the United States the leading member of a coalition possessing superior latent and mobilized capabilities, but this alliance is bound together by a host of powerful and durable forces. And the effects of the controllable causes of alignment place the Soviets in a vicious circle. Surrounded by a powerful coalition led by their principal rival, they respond by devoting a disproportionate effort to amassing military power. But the more they seek to balance this geopolitical dilemma by mobilizing greater resources, the more they reinforce their own encirclement. The current balance of world power, in short, is likely to remain extremely stable.[31] The question thus becomes: What should U.S. policy-makers do to exploit these advantages to the fullest? What does balance of threat theory imply for U.S. grand strategy?

---

27. Despite the perennial predictions of NATO's impending collapse, it is still remarkable that a coalition of fifteen (with the inclusion of Spain, sixteen) nations has endured for more than thirty years. For a pessimistic view, see Eliot A. Cohen, "The Long-Term Crisis in the Alliance," *Foreign Affairs,* 61, no. 2 (1982-1983). For more optimistic assessments, consult Bruce Russett and Donald R. Deluca, "Theatre Nuclear Forces: Public Opinion in Western Europe," *Political Science Quarterly,* 98, no. 2 (1983); and Richard C. Eichenberg, "The Myth of Hollanditis," *International Security,* 8, no. 2 (1983): 143-59. As events in Hungary, Czechoslovakia, and Poland reveal, the Warsaw Pact is hardly a model of cohesion, assuming one is concerned with voluntary adherence to an alliance.

28. For example, less than 1 percent of all global development assistance comes from the Soviet Union. On the limitations of the Soviet Union as a source of economic aid, see Henry Bienen, "Soviet Political Relations with Africa," *International Security,* 6, no. 4 (1982); U.S. House Committee on Foreign Affairs, *The Soviet Union and the Third World,* p. 170 and passim; and CIA, *Communist Aid to Non-Communist LDCs, 1979 and 1954-1979,* p. 8. On the declining importance of raw materials, see Peter Drucker, "A Changed World Economy," *Foreign Affairs,* 64, no. 4 (1986).

29. See Feinberg and Oye, "After the Fall."

30. See CIA, *Cormmunist Aid to Non-Communist LDCs, 1979 and 1954-1979,* p. 9; and U.S. House Committee on Foreign Affairs, *The Soviet Union and the Third World,* p. 82.

MAINTAINING CONTAINMENT: ALLIANCE FORMATION AND U.S. GRAND STRATEGY

Since the onset of the Cold War, U.S. grand strategy has sought to prevent any single power from controlling the war-making potential of industrial Eurasia. In practice, this goal means containing Soviet expansion.[32] More recently, the United States has added the goal of preserving Western access to oil from the Middle East. In light of the results derived in this study, what steps will best achieve these objectives?

First, because balancing is the dominant tendency in international politics, the world's most important countries are strongly disposed to ally with the United States. AS a result, the United States can afford to take a relaxed view of most international developments. Not only is it relatively immune from most adverse events (especially relative to other countries), but it can count on widespread support from a set of valuable allies when truly serious threats emerge.

Second, the precise level of U.S. power is probably less important than the way in which it is used. Because lesser powers are usually insensitive to the state of the superpower balance, only a truly massive shift in the relative power of the United States and the Soviet Union is likely to alter their alliance preferences. A military buildup will not win the United States new friends, and a marginal decline will not cause its current allies to defect. Indeed, given the propensity for states to balance, U.S. allies would be likely to do more if the United States did not insist on trying to do everything.

Third, the United States should worry far less about its allies defecting and worry more about how it provokes opposition through misplaced belligerence. The fear that U.S. allies will bandwagon if U.S. credibility weakens has been pervasive since World War II, and it is responsible for the most counterproductive excesses in postwar U.S. foreign policy.[33] This fear is exacerbated by the allies themselves, which have an obvious interest in voicing their doubts so as to persuade the United States to do more on their behalf. Their doubts should not be taken too seriously; it will rarely be in their interest to abandon U.S. protection.[34] This [chapter] has suggested, I hope, how fanciful the fear of bandwagoning really is. Among other things, the predominance of balancing behavior means that intervention in peripheral areas for the sake of credibility can be greatly reduced. Indeed, efforts to demonstrate U.S. credibility through the frequent use of force are more likely to cause others to fear U.S. ambitions or to question U.S. judgment.[35] Because balancing is more common than bandwagoning, the less threatening the United States appears, the more popular it is likely to be.

---

31. As it has been throughout the Cold War. The U.S. alliance network has controlled over 60 percent of gross world product since 1950; the Soviets and their allies have controlled about 15 percent. There have been minor fluctuations, and the distribution within the Western alliance has shifted as U.S. allies have recovered from World War II, but the stability of this overall distribution is striking.

32. See Gaddis, *Strategies of Containment,* especially chap. 2; Kennan, *Realities of American Foreign Policy;* Lippmann, *The Cold War;* and Nicholas Spykman, *America's Strategy in World Politics* (New York, 1942).

33. See Larson, "The Bandwagon Metaphor"; and Hoffman, "Detente," in Nye, *Making of America's Soviet Policy,* p. 242.

34. Indeed, the United States might well be better off were its credibility slightly less reliable. By allowing incompetent clients to founder on occasion, the United States would provide its other allies with additional incentives to perform well both at home and in relations with the United States. The belated decisions to encourage the ouster of Ferdinand Marcos of the Philippines and Baby Doc Duvalier of Haiti suggest that it is possible to abandon corrupt and unpopular allies without endangering commitments elsewhere. Indeed, the effects on similarly situated allies may be salutory.

Fourth, the United States should not overestimate the consensus that unites it with many of its allies in the developing world. Regional powers are far more concerned with local threats than with superpower rivalry. As a result, attempts to enlist them in an anti-Soviet crusade will continue to be counterproductive. Those countries that are directly threatened by Soviet power are natural U.S. allies. To seek a "strategic consensus" against the Soviet Union in other areas, as John Foster Dulles and Alexander Haig sought to do, ignores the regional issues that are of greater importance to these erstwhile partners. And efforts to forge a global alliance against Moscow make it much easier for clients of the United States to exploit its assistance for their own reasons. At best, these grand designs will be stillborn. At worst, they will exacerbate regional rivalries and increase the likelihood of substantial Soviet involvement.[36]

Fifth, knee-jerk opposition to leftist forces in the Third World should be abandoned. Not only is ideology a relatively weak cause of alignment, but the Marxist doctrines that the United States is so fearful of are as likely to lead to intra-Communist conflict as they are to produce unity. The examples of Mao, Tito, Togliatti, Mugabe, Berlinguer, Carillo, and Pol Pot all demolish the myth of Marxist solidarity, a fact that has escaped many of those responsible for postwar U.S. foreign policy.[37] As George Kennan's original formulation of containment prescribed, the United States should seek to exploit these natural divisions, rather than working to reinforce the fragile unity of leftist regimes through its own actions.[38]

Sixth, the United States should also reject the simplistic belief that Soviet arms recipients are reliable agents of the Kremlin. As shown repeatedly in this study, neither superpower has gained much leverage through the use of military or economic assistance in the Middle East. The provision of arms did not give the Soviet Union reliable influence in Yugoslavia, China, Somalia, Indonesia, or Zimbabwe either. At the same time, U.S. statesmen should recognize that U.S. aid programs will rarely enable the United States to control its clients. To cite the most obvious case, Israel is both dependent on U.S. support and independent of U.S. control. By exaggerating the effectiveness of aid programs, the United States exaggerates the size of the Soviet bloc and overlooks the possibility of weaning clients away from Moscow by providing appropriate political incentives. It is also likely to

---

35. The widespread condemnation the United States received after the bombing of Libya in April 1986 is an obvious example of this problem, as is current U.S. support for the contras in Central America.

36. Secretary of State Alexander Haig's green light for Israel's invasion of Lebanon was undoubtedly part of the U.S. effort to increase strategic cooperation with Israel in 19811982 in order to counter the Soviet Union. In retrospect, this decision led to a setback for the United States and a disaster for Israel. On Haig's role in Israel's decision to attack, see Ze'ev Schiff, "Green Light, Lebanon," *Foreign Policy,* no. 50 (1983).

37. To mention but one example, Henry Kissinger repeatedly warned of the dangers that revolutionary Marxist regimes posed to world order. This fear underlay U.S. intervention in Chile and Angola and prolonged the futile search for "peace with honor" in Vietnam. Yet Kissinger's memoirs reveal his awareness that Marxist ideology is ultimately divisive. As he wrote there: "One of the great ironies of relations among Communist countries is that Communist ideology, which always claimed that it would end conflict, has in fact made it intractable. In systems based on infallible truth there can be only one authorized interpretation; a rival claim to represent true orthodoxy is a mortal challenge." See Kissinger, *Years of Upheaval,* p. 47. On Kissinger's suspicion of revolutionary forces, see Gaddis, *Strategies of Containment,* pp. 337-39; Hoffmann, "Detente," pp. 241-42; and especially Henry A. Kissinger, "Domestic Structure and Foreign Policy," in Kissinger, *American Foreign Policy* (New York, 1974), especially pp. 12, 34-43.

38. On this point, see Gaddis, *Strategies of Containment,* pp. 42-48.

provide its allies with too much, in the mistaken belief that such aid will cement their allegiance and enhance its control.

A final implication is that the domestic situation of the United States may be more important than anything else. External events impinge on U.S. power; internal conditions generate it. Losses abroad will add up slowly (if at all) and will be compensated by balancing behavior by allies and by the United States itself. Thus a final prescription is to avoid policies that jeopardize the overall health of the U.S. economy. It is far more important to maintain a robust and productive economic system than it is to correct minor weaknesses in defense capability or to control the outcome of some insignificant clash in the developing world.

A FINAL WORD

In international politics, no agency or institution guarantees security and prosperity. The United States should find it heartening, however, that its position in the world and the most important causes of security cooperation among states combine to favor it. These conclusions do not mean that U.S. alliances are indestructible, that isolationism is preferable, or that Western defense capabilities could not be improved.[39] What they do mean is that the United States could hardly ask for much more. The principal causes of alliances work to its advantage and isolate the Soviet Union from virtually all of the world's strategically significant states. If this fact is recognized, the task of formulating a grand strategy that would reinforce these advantages should be greatly simplified. In the preceding pages, I have tried to sketch what such a strategy would be.[40]

My argument thus comes full circle. By clarifying and testing a number of hypotheses about the causes of alliances, I have sought to resolve several important debates about U.S. foreign and military policy. This approach is appropriate, because the realm of international politics remains one in which states must base their choices on predictions of how other states will respond. Armed with a better understanding of how states choose their friends, the goal of maximizing international support (and minimizing opposition) should be greatly simplified. These insights do not ensure success, of course, but they certainly improve the odds.

---

39. For analyses of the security problems facing the United States and its allies, along with various solutions, see Barry R. Posen and Stephen W. Van Evera, "Reagan Administrahon Defense Policy: Departure from Containment," *International Security,* 8, no. 1 (1983); Carnegie Endowment for International Peace, *Challenges for U.S. National Security: Assessing the Balance: Defense Spending and Conventional Forces* (Washington, D.C., 1981), pt. 2; William W. Kaufmann, "NonNuclear Deterrence," in *Alliance Security: NATO and the No-First-Use Question,* ed. John Steinbruner and Leon V. Sigal (Washington, D.C., 1984); Asa Clark et al., *The Defense Reform Debate* (Baltimore, Md., 1984); *Report of the European Security Study, Strengthening Conventional Deterrence in Europe: Proposals for the 1980s* (New York, 1983); Barry R. Posen, "Measuring the European Conventional Balance: Coping with Complexity in Threat Assessment," *International Security,* 9, no. 3 (1984-1985); and Jeffrey Record, *Revising American Military Strategy: Tailoring Means to Ends* (Washington, D.C., 1984)

40. Of course, should the Soviet Union reduce its military forces significantly, or should Mikhail Gorbachev succeed in convincing the West that Soviet intentions are essentially benevolent, then the cohesion of the Western alliance would almost certainly decline. Under these conditions, however, the alliance might also be less necessary.

Introduction to Structural Realism

Kenneth N. Waltz presented his theory of international relations, often called structural or neo-realism, in a 1979 book titled *Theory of International Politics.* While written during the Cold War, and despite fresh post-Cold War critiques, it remains a classic of international relations.

In a previous, work entitled *Man, the State and War,*[1] Waltz describes the three levels of analysis that social scientists use to explain state behavior and the causes of war: the individual, the state and the system as a whole. He, in company with others such as Gottfried-Karl Kindermann and Hedley Bull,[2] arrived at the conclusion that it was in fact the latter, the system of states, which is the most important. *Theory of International Politics* was Waltz's attempt to construct such a systemic theory which "remedies the defects of present theories"[3] such as Morgenthau's Balance of Power theory. You will read excerpts from three chapters of this important work.

This reformulation of Balance of Power theory as espoused by Morgenthau contains many of the key ideas of the realist tradition. In particular, as you read excerpts of Waltz's *Theory of International Politics*, it is clear that he believes that the international system is anarchic and is populated by self-serving states which pursue security. He parts company with classical realists, however, in two significant ways. First, Waltz does not believe that states seek power as an end but rather only as a means to ensuring security. Second, the balancing of power is not something calculatedly done by statesmen; rather, the tendency of the system toward equilibrium is almost automatic.[4]

The first reading, primarily from chapter five of *Theory of International Politics* and titled "Political Structures," addresses what Waltz sees as Structural Realism's independent variables. As you read the passage regarding "domestic political structures," do not be misled. Just as one may use a familial example of two siblings to describe Morgenthau's Balance of Power theory, Waltz simply describes the elements of domestic political system to serve as an analogy thereby making the elusive international-political structure easier to "catch on" to later. While Waltz would not deny that individuals, institutions, and agencies within a state do matter in the development of foreign policy, he contends in his introduction that "a theory indicates that some factors are more important than others and specifies relations among them."[5] For Waltz, the factor that matters most is structure. He therefore, "isolates" structure and ignores all other sub-systemic variables. In fact, by definition systemic theories are not concerned with factors inside the state. Here we see his major causal relationship between structure and state behavior.

---

1. Kenneth Waltz, *Man, the State, and War: A Theoretical Analysis,* (New York: Columbia University Press, 1954).

2. James E. Dougherty and Robert L. Pfaltzgraff Jr., *Contending Theories of International Relations: A Comprehensive Survey,* (New York : Harper & Row, 1997), 80, 547.

3. Kenneth Waltz, *Theory of International Politics,* (New York: McGraw-Hill, 1979), p. 1.

4. Dougherty and Pfaltzgraff, 41.

5. Waltz, *Theory of International Politics*, 8.

The title of the second reading, "Structural Causes and Military Effects" (chapter eight in *Theory of International Politics*), candidly signals one of neo-realism's "cause" (independent variable)–"effect" (dependent variable) relationships. As his famous quote notes, "units differently juxtaposed and combined behave differently and in interacting produce different outcomes."[6] Specifically, having used the inductive process to look at various historical examples of differently structured systems (i.e., independent variable), Waltz hypothesizes about what "outcomes" (i.e., systemic "cooperation or conflict") we should expect in bi-polar versus multi-polar systems. Waltz's conclusion regarding which of the two systems (i.e., bi-polar or multi-polar) is most stable stands in stark contrast to what other realists such as Morgenthau would have conjectured.

In the final Structural Realism reading, an excerpt from Waltz's *Structural Realism After the Cold War,* Waltz answers the question so many wanted to ask him following the conclusion of the Cold War, "How can we use Structural Realism to explain state behavior in a uni-polar system?" While acknowledging an increased role of influences other than structure, he first explains why the system is indeed uni-polar and then goes on to answer this question.[7]

While neo-realism has been both praised and critiqued since the publication of *Theory of International Politics*, it is clear that the change in structure occasioned by the end of the Cold War provides social scientists with an additional data point with which to assess its utility and validity. For example, consider how Waltz's hypotheses regarding system stability and state behavior holds up against your understanding of the role of the United States in the post-Cold War world.

Neo-realism remains significant because in addition to the changes in state behavior resulting from changes in polarity, Waltz expects pole states act differently than non-pole states. While the United States is unlikely to decline as a pole in the near future, structural realists would likely advise the military to carefully watch those states which may become "peer competitors" such as China and India and to watch that other non-pole states do not balance against us.

6. Ibid., 81.

7. Ibid.

Political Structures

Kenneth N. Waltz

Only through some sort of systems theory can international politics be understood. To be a success, such a theory has to show how international politics can be conceived of as a domain distinct from the economic, social, and other international domains that one may conceive of. To mark international-political systems off from other international systems, and to distinguish systems-level from unit-level forces, requires showing how political structures are generated and how they affect, and are affected by, the units of the system. How can we conceive of international politics as a distinct system? What is it that intervenes between interacting units and the results that their acts and interactions produce? To answer these questions, this chapter first examines the concept of social structure and then defines structure as a concept appropriate for national and for international politics.

I

A system is composed of a structure and of interacting units. The structure is the system-wide component that makes it possible to think of the system as a whole. The problem is. . . to contrive a definition of structure free of the attributes and the interactions of units. Definitions of structure must leave aside, or abstract from, the characteristics of units, their behavior, and their interactions. Why must those obviously important matters be omitted? They must be omitted so that we can distinguish between variables at the level of the units and variables at the level of the system. *The problem is to develop theoretically useful concepts to replace the vague and varying systemic notions that are customarily employed—notions such as environment, situation, context, and milieu.* Structure is a useful concept if it gives clear and fixed meaning to such vague and varying terms.

We know what we have to omit from any definition of structure if the definition is to be useful theoretically. Abstracting from the attributes of units means leaving aside questions about the kinds of political leaders, social and economic institutions, and ideological commitments states may have. Abstracting from relations means leaving aside questions about the cultural, economic, political, and military interactions of states. To say what is to be left out does not indicate what is to be put in. The negative point is important nevertheless because the instruction to omit attributes is often violated and the instruction to omit interactions almost always goes unobserved. But if attributes and interactions are omitted, what is left? The question is answered by considering the double meaning of the term "relation." As S. F. Nadel points out, ordinary language obscures a distinction that is important in theory. "Relation" is used to mean both the interaction of units and the positions they occupy vis-a-vis each other.[1] To define a structure requires ignoring how units relate with one another (how they interact) and concentrating on how they stand in relation to one another (how they are arranged or positioned). Interactions, as I have insisted, take place at the level of the units. How units stand in relation to one another, the way they are arranged or positioned, is not a property of the units. The arrangement of units is a property of the system.

---

[1] S. F. Nadel, *The Theory of Social Structure* (Glencoe, Ill.: Free Press, 1957), pp. 8–11.

By leaving aside the personality of actors, their behavior, and their interactions, one arrives at a purely positional picture of society. Three propositions follow from this. First, structures may endure while personality, behavior, and interactions vary widely. Structure is sharply distinguished from actions and interactions. Second, a structural definition applies to realms of widely different substance so long as the arrangement of parts is similar.[2] Third, because this is so, theories developed for one realm may with some modification be applicable to other realms as well. . . .

II

The concept of structure is based on the fact that units differently juxtaposed and combined behave differently and in interacting produce different outcomes. I first want to show how internal political structure can be defined. In a book on international-political theory, domestic political structure has to be examined in order to draw a distinction between expectations about behavior and outcomes in the internal and external realms. Moreover, considering domestic political structure now will make the elusive international-political structure easier to catch later on.

Structure defines the arrangement, or the ordering, of the parts of a system. Structure is not a collection of political institutions but rather the arrangement of them. How is the arrangement defined? The constitution of a state describes some parts of the arrangement, but political structures as they develop are not identical with formal constitutions. In defining structures, the first question to answer is this: What is the principle by which the parts are arranged?

Domestic politics is hierarchically ordered. The units—institutions and agencies—stand vis-à-vis each other in relations of super- and subordination. The ordering principle of a system gives the first, and basic, bit of information about how the parts of a realm are related to each other. In a polity the hierarchy of offices is by no means completely articulated, nor are all ambiguities about relations of super- and subordination removed. Nevertheless, political actors are formally differentiated according to the degrees of their authority, and their distinct functions are specified. By "specified" I do not mean that the law of the land fully describes the duties that different agencies perform, but only that broad agreement prevails on the tasks that various parts of a government are to undertake and on the extent of the power they legitimately wield. Thus Congress supplies the military forces; the President commands them. Congress makes the laws; the executive branch enforces them; agencies administer laws; judges interpret them. Such specification of roles and differentiation of functions is found in any state, the more fully so as the state is more highly developed. The specification of functions of formally differentiated parts gives the second bit of structural information. This second part of the definition adds some content to the structure, but only enough to say more fully how the units stand in relation to one another. The roles and the functions of the British Prime Minister and Parliament, for example, differ from those of the American President and Congress. When offices are juxtaposed and functions are combined in different ways, different behaviors and outcomes result, as I shall shortly show.

The placement of units in relation to one another is not fully defined by a system's ordering principle and by the formal differentiation of its parts. The standing of the units also changes with changes in their relative capabilities. In the performance of their functions, agencies may gain capabilities or lose them. The relation of Prime Minister to Parliament and of President to Congress depends on, and varies with, their relative

---

2. *Ibid.*, pp. 104–9.

capabilities. The third part of the definition of structure acknowledges that even while specified functions remain unchanged, units come to stand in different relation to each other through changes in relative capability.

A domestic political structure is thus defined: first, according to the principle by which it is ordered; second, by specification of the functions of formally differentiated units; and third, by the distribution of capabilities across those units. Structure is a highly abstract notion, but the definition of structure does not abstract from everything. To do so would be to leave everything aside and to include nothing at all. The three-part definition of structure includes only what is required to show how the units of the system are positioned or arranged. Everything else is omitted. Concern for tradition and culture, analysis of the character and personality of political actors, consideration of the conflictive and accommodative processes of politics, description of the making and execution of policy—all such matters are left aside. Their omission does not imply their unimportance. They are omitted because we want to figure out the expected effects of structure on process and of process on structure. That can be done only if structure and process are distinctly defined. . . .

III

I defined domestic political structures first by the principle according to which they are organized or ordered, second by the differentiation of units and the specification of their functions, and third by the distribution of capabilities across units. Let us see how the three terms of the definition apply to international politics.

1. Ordering Principles

Structural questions are questions about the arrangement of the parts of a system. The parts of domestic political systems stand in relations of super- and subordination. Some are entitled to command; others are required to obey. Domestic systems are centralized and hierarchic. The parts of international-political systems stand in relations of coordination. Formally, each is the equal of all the others. None is entitled to command; none is required to obey. International systems are decentralized and anarchic. The ordering principles of the two structures are distinctly different, indeed, contrary to each other. Domestic political structures have governmental institutions and offices as their concrete counterparts. International politics, in contrast, has been called "politics in the absence of government."[3] International organizations do exist, and in ever-growing numbers. Supranational agents able to act effectively, however, either themselves acquire some of the attributes and capabilities of states, as did the medieval papacy in the era of Innocent III, or they soon reveal their inability to act in important ways except with the support, or at least the acquiescence, of the principal states concerned with the matters at hand. Whatever elements of authority emerge internationally are barely once removed from the capability that provides the foundation for the appearance of those elements. Authority quickly reduces to a particular expression of capability. In the absence of agents with system-wide authority, formal relations of super- and subordination fail to develop.

The first term of a structural definition states the principle by which the system is ordered. Structure is an organizational concept. The prominent characteristic of international politics, however, seems to be the lack of order and of organization. How can one think of

---

3. William T. R. Fox, "The Uses of International Relations Theory," in William T. R. Fox, ed., *Theoretical Aspects of International Relations* (Notre Dame, Ind.: University of Notre Dame Press, 1959), p. 35.

international politics as being any kind of an order at all? The anarchy of politics internationally is often referred to. If structure is an organizational concept, the terms "structure" and "anarchy" seem to be in contradiction. If international politics is "politics in the absence of government," what are we in the presence of? In looking for international structure, one is brought face to face with the invisible, an uncomfortable position to be in.

The problem is this: how to conceive of an order without an orderer and of organizational effects where formal organization is lacking. . . .

Beyond the survival motive, the aims of states may be endlessly varied; they may range from the ambition to conquer the world to the desire merely to be left alone. Survival is a prerequisite to achieving any goals that states may have, other than the goal of promoting their own disappearance as political entities. The survival motive is taken as the ground of action in a world where the security of states is not assured, rather than as a realistic description of the impulse that lies behind every act of state. The assumption allows for the fact that no state always acts exclusively to ensure its survival. It allows for the fact that some states may persistently seek goals that they value more highly than survival; they may, for example, prefer amalgamation with other states to their own survival in form. It allows for the fact that in pursuit of its security no state will act with perfect knowledge and wisdom—if indeed we could know what those terms might mean. . . .

Actors may perceive the structure that constrains them and understand how it serves to reward some kinds of behavior and to penalize others. But then again they either may not see it or, seeing it, may for any of many reasons fail to conform their actions to the patterns that are most often rewarded and least often punished. To say that "the structure selects" means simply that those who conform to accepted and successful practices more often rise to the top and are likelier to stay there. The game one has to win is defined by the structure that determines the kind of player who is likely to prosper. . . .

2. The Character of the Units

The second term in the definition of structure specifies the functions performed by differentiated units. Hierarchy entails relations of super- and subordination among a system's parts, and that implies their differentiation. In defining domestic political structure the second term, like the first and third, is needed because each term points to a possible source of structural variation. The states that are the units of international-political systems are not formally differentiated by the functions they perform. Anarchy entails relations of coordination among a system's units, and that implies their sameness. The second term is not needed in defining international-political structure, because, so long as anarchy endures, states remain like units. International structures vary only through a change of organizing principle or, failing that, through variations in the capabilities of units. Nevertheless I shall discuss these like units here, because it is by their interactions that international-politics structures are generated.

Two questions arise: Why should states be taken as the units of the system? Given a wide variety of states, how can one call them "like units"? Questioning the choice of states as the primary units of international-political systems became popular in the 1960s and 1970s as it was at the turn of the century. Once one understands what is logically involved, the issue is easily resolved. Those who question the state-centric view do so for two main reasons. First, states are not the only actors of importance on the international scene. Second, states are declining in importance, and other actors are gaining, or so it is said. Neither reason is cogent, as the following discussion shows.

States are not and never have been the only international actors. But then structures are defined not by all of the actors that flourish within them but by the major ones. In defining a system's structure one chooses one or some of the infinitely many objects comprising the system and defines its structure in terms of them. For international-political systems, as for any system, one must first decide which units to take as being the parts of the system. . . .

States are the units whose interactions form the structure of international-political systems. They will long remain so. The death rate among states is remarkably low. Few states die; many firms do. . . . To call states "like units" is to say that each state is like all other states in being an autonomous political unit. It is another way of saying that states are sovereign. But sovereignty is also a bothersome concept. Many believe, as the anthropologist M. G. Smith has said, that "in a system of sovereign states no state is sovereign."[4] The error lies in identifying the sovereignty of states with their ability to do as they wish. To say that states are sovereign is not to say that they can do as they please, that they are free of others' influence, that they are able to get what they want. Sovereign states may be hardpressed all around, constrained to act in ways they would like to avoid, and able to do hardly anything just as they would like to. The sovereignty of states has never entailed their insulation from the effects of other states' actions. To be sovereign and to be dependent are not contradictory conditions. Sovereign states have seldom led free and easy lives. What then is sovereignty? To say that a state is sovereign means that it decides for itself how it will cope with its internal and external problems, including whether or not to seek assistance from others and in doing so to limit its freedom by making commitments to them. States develop their own strategies, chart their own courses, make their own decisions about how to meet whatever needs they experience and whatever desires they develop. It is no more contradictory to say that sovereign states are always constrained and often tightly so than it is to say that free individuals often make decisions under the heavy pressure of events.

Each state, like every other state, is a sovereign political entity. And yet the differences across states, from Costa Rica to the Soviet Union, from Gambia to the United States, are immense. States are alike, and they are also different. So are corporations, apples, universities, and people. Whenever we put two or more objects in the same category, we are saying that they are alike not in all respects but in some. No two objects in this world are identical, yet they can often be usefully compared and combined. "You can't add apples and oranges" is an old saying that seems to be especially popular among salesmen who do not want you to compare their wares with others. But we all know that the trick of adding dissimilar objects is to express the result in terms of a category that comprises them. Three apples plus four oranges equals seven pieces of fruit. The only interesting question is whether the category that classifies objects according to their common qualities is useful. One can add up a large number of widely varied objects and say that one has eight million things, but seldom need one do that.

States vary widely in size, wealth, power, and form. And yet variations in these and in other respects are variations among like units. In what way are they like units? How can they be placed in a single category? States are alike in the tasks that they face, though not in their abilities to perform them. The differences are of capability, not of function. States

[4] Smith should know better. Translated into terms that he has himself so effectively used, to say that states are sovereign is to say that they are segments of a plural society. See his "A Structural Approach to Comparative Politics" in David Easton, ed., *Varieties of Politics Theories* (Englewood Cliffs, N.J.: Prentice-Hall, 1966), p. 122; cf. his "On Segmentary Lineage Systems," *Journal of the Royal Anthropological Society of Great Britain and Ireland* 86 (July–December 1956).

perform or try to perform tasks, most of which are common to all of them; the ends they aspire to are similar. Each state duplicates the activities of other states at least to a considerable extent. Each state has its agencies for making, executing, and interpreting laws and regulations, for raising revenues, and for defending itself. Each state supplies out of its own resources and by its own means most of the food, clothing, housing, transportation, and amenities consumed and used by its citizens. All states, except the smallest ones, do much more of their business at home than abroad. One has to be impressed with the functional similarity of states and, now more than ever before, with the similar lines their development follows. From the rich to the poor states, from the old to the new ones, nearly all of them take a larger hand in matters of economic regulation, of education, health, and housing, of culture and the arts, and so on almost endlessly. The increase of the activities of states is a strong and strikingly uniform international trend. The functions of states are similar, and distinctions among them arise principally from their varied capabilities. International politics consists of like units duplicating one another's activities.

3. The Distribution of Capabilities

The parts of a hierarchic system are related to one another in ways that are determined both by their functional differentiation and by the extent of their capabilities. The units of an anarchic system are functionally undifferentiated. The units of such an order are then distinguished primarily by their greater or lesser capabilities for performing similar tasks. This states formally what students of international politics have long noticed. The great powers of an era have always been marked off from others by practitioners and theorists alike. Students of national government make such distinctions as that between parliamentary and presidential systems; governmental systems differ in form. Students of international politics make distinctions between international-political systems only according to the number of their great powers. The structure of a system changes with changes in the distribution of capabilities across the system's units. And changes in structure change expectations about how the units of the system will behave and about the outcomes their interactions will produce. . . . Internationally, like units sometimes perform different tasks. . . but two problems should be considered.

The first problem is this: Capability tells us something about units. Defining structure partly in terms of the distribution of capabilities seems to violate my instruction to keep unit attributes out of structural definitions. As I remarked earlier, structure is a highly but not entirely abstract concept. The maximum of abstraction allows a minimum of content, and that minimum is what is needed to enable one to say how the units stand in relation to one another. States are differently placed by their power. And yet one may wonder why only *capability is* included in the third part of the definition, and not such characteristics as ideology, form of government, peacefulness, bellicosity, or whatever. The answer is this: Power is estimated by comparing the capabilities of a number of units. Although capabilities are attributes of units, the distribution of capabilities across units is not. The distribution of capabilities is not a unit attribute, but rather a system-wide concept. . . .

The second problem is this: Though relations defined in terms of interactions must be excluded from structural definitions, relations defined in terms of grouping of states do seem to tell us something about how states are placed in the system. Why not specify how states stand in relation to one another by considering the alliances they form? Would doing so not be comparable to defining national political structures partly in terms of how presidents and prime ministers are related to other political agents? It would not be. Nationally as internationally, structural definitions deal with the relation of agents and agencies in terms of the organization of realms and not in terms of the accommodations and conflicts that may occur within them or the groupings that may now and then form. Parts of a government may draw together or pull apart, may oppose each other or cooperate in greater or lesser degree. These are the relations that form and dissolve within a system rather than structural alterations that mark a change from one system to another. This is made clear by the example that runs nicely parallel to the case of alliances. Distinguishing systems of political parties according to their number is common. A multiparty system changes if, say, eight parties become two, but not if two groupings of the eight form merely for the occasion of fighting an election. By the same logic, an international-political system in which three or more great powers have split into two alliances remains a multipolar system—structurally distinct from a bipolar system, a system in which no third power is able to challenge the top two. . . .

In defining international-political structures we take states with whatever traditions, habits, objectives, desires, and forms of government they may have. We do not ask whether states are revolutionary or legitimate, authoritarian or democratic, ideological or pragmatic. We abstract from every attribute of states except their capabilities. Nor in thinking about structure do we ask about the relations of states—their feelings of friendship and hostility, their diplomatic exchanges, the alliances they form, and the extent of the contacts and exchanges among them. We ask what range of expectations arises merely from looking at the type of order that prevails among them and at the distribution of capabilities within that order. We abstract from any particular qualities of states and from all of their concrete connections. What emerges is a positional picture, a general description of the ordered overall arrangement of a society written in terms of the placement of units rather than in terms of their qualities.

IV

I have now defined the two essential elements of a systems theory of international politics—the structure of the system and its interacting units. In doing so I have broken sharply away from common approaches. As we have seen, some scholars who attempt systems approaches to international politics conceive of a system as being the product of its interacting parts, but they fail to consider whether anything at the systems level affects those parts. Other systems theorists, like students of international politics in general, mention at times that the effects of the international environment must be allowed for; but they pass over the question of how this is to be done and quickly return their attention to the level of interacting units. Most students, whether or not they claim to follow a systems approach, think of international politics in the way Fig. 1 suggests. $N_{1,2,3}$ are states internally generating their external effects. $X_{1,2,3}$ are states acting externally and interacting with each other. No systemic force or factor shows up in the picture.

Because systemic effects are evident, international politics should be seen as in Fig. 2. The circle represents the structure of an international-political system. As the arrows indicate, it affects both the interactions of states and their attributes.[5] Although structure as an organizational concept has proved elusive, its meaning can be explained simply. While states retain their autonomy, each stands in a specifiable relation to the others. They form some sort of an order. We can use the term "organization" to cover this preinstitutional condition if we think of an organization as simply a constraint, in the manner of W. Ross Ashby (1956, p. 131). Because states constrain and limit each other, international politics

5. No essentials are omitted from Fig. 2, but some complications are. A full picture would include, for example, coalitions possibly forming on the right-hand side.

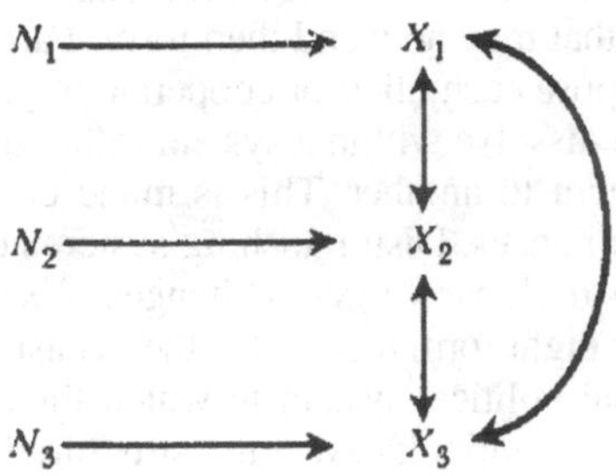

Figure 1.

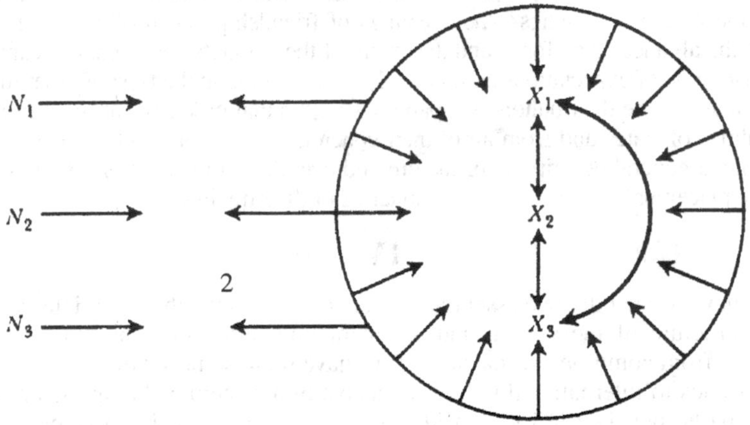

Figure 2.

can be viewed in rudimentary organizational terms. Structure is the concept that makes it possible to say what the expected organizational effects are and how structures and units interact and affect each other.

Thinking of structure as I have defined it solves the problem of separating changes at the level of the units from changes at the level of the system. If one is concerned with the different expected effects of different systems, one must be able to distinguish changes of systems from changes within them, something that would-be systems theorists have found exceedingly difficult to do. A three-part definition of structure enables one to discriminate between those types of changes:

- Structures are defined, first, according to the principle by which a system is ordered. Systems are transformed if one ordering principle replaces another. To move from an anarchic to a hierarchic realm is to move from one system to another.
- Structures are defined, second, by the specification of functions of differentiated units. Hierarchic systems change if functions are differently defined and allotted.

For anarchic systems, the criterion of systems change derived from the second part of the definition drops out since the system is composed of like units.

- Structures are defined, third, by the distribution of capabilities across units. Changes in this distribution are changes of system whether the system be an anarchic or a hierarchic one . . .

V

Counting Poles And Measuring Power

How should we count poles, and how can we measure power? These questions must be answered in order to identify variations of structure. Almost everyone agrees that at some time since the war the world was bipolar. Few seem to believe that it remains so. For years Walter Lippmann wrote of the bipolar world as being perpetually in the process of rapidly passing away (e.g., 1950 and 1963). Many others now carry on the tradition he so firmly established. To reach the conclusion that bipolarity is passing, or past, requires some odd counting. The inclination to count in funny ways is rooted in the desire to arrive at a particular answer. Scholars feel a strong affection for the balance-of-power world of Metternich and Bismarck, on which many of their theoretical notions rest. That was a world in which five or so great powers manipulated their neighbors and maneuvered for advantage. Great powers were once defined according to their capabilities. Students of international politics now seem to look at other conditions. The ability or inability of states to solve problems is said to raise or lower their rankings. The relations of states may be examined instead of their capabilities, and since the former are always multilateral, the world is said to be multipolar. Thus the dissolution of blocs was said to signal the end of bipolarity even though to infer bipolarity from the existence of blocs in itself confuses the relations with the capabilities of states. The world was never bipolar because two blocs opposed each other, but because of the preeminence of bloc leaders.

In addition to confusion about what to count, one often finds that those who try to identify great powers by gauging their capabilities make their measurements strangely. Of all the ways of playing the numbers game the favorite is probably this: to separate the economic, military, and political capabilities of nations in gauging their ability to act. Henry Kissinger, for example, while Secretary of State, observed that although militarily "there are two superpowers," economically "there are at least five major groupings." Power is no longer "homogeneous." Throughout history, he added, "military, economic, and political potential were closely related. To be powerful a nation had to be strong in all categories." This is no longer so. "Military muscle does not guarantee political influence. Economic giants can be militarily weak, and military strength may not be able to obscure economic weakness. Countries can exert political influence even when they have neither military nor economic strength" (October 10, 1973, p. 7). If the different capabilities of a nation no longer reinforce each other, one can focus on a nation's strengths and overlook its weaknesses. Nations are then said to be superpowers even though they have only some of the previously required characteristics. China has more than 800 million people; Japan has a strong economy; Western Europe has the population and the resources and lacks only political existence. As commonly, the wanted number of great powers is reached by projecting the future into the present. When Europe unites . . .; if Japan's economy continues to grow . . .; once China's industrious people have developed their resources. . . . And then, although the imagined future lies some decades ahead, we hear that the world is no longer bipolar. A further variant is to infer another country's status from our policy toward it. Thus Nixon, when he was President, slipped easily from talking of China's becoming a superpower to conferring superpower status on her. In one of the statements that smoothed the route to Peking, he accomplished this in two paragraphs (August 5, 1971, p. 16). And the headlines of various news stories before, during, and after his visit confirmed China's new rank. This was the greatest act of creation since Adam and Eve, and a true illustration of the superpower status of the United States. A country becomes a superpower if we treat it like one. We create other states in our image.

Many of those who have recently hailed the world's return to multipolarity have not unexpectedly done so because they confuse structure and process. How are capabilities distributed? What are the likely results of a given distribution? These are distinct questions. The difficulty of counting poles is rooted in the failure to observe the distinction. A systems theory requires one to define structures partly by the distribution of capabilities across units. States, because they are in a self-help system, have to use their combined capabilities in order to serve their interests. The economic, military, and other capabilities of nations cannot be sectored and separately weighed. States are not placed in the top rank because they excel in one way or another. Their rank depends on how they score on *all* of the following items: size of population and territory, resource endowment, economic capability, military strength, political stability and competence. States spend a lot of time estimating one another's capabilities, especially their abilities to do harm. States have different combinations of capabilities which are difficult to measure and compare, the more so since the weight to be assigned to different items changes with time. We should not be surprised if wrong answers are sometimes arrived at. Prussia startled most foreigners, and most Prussians, by the speed and extent of her victories over Austria in 1866 and over France in 1870. Ranking states, however, does not require predicting their success in war or in other endeavors. We need only rank them roughly by capability. Any ranking at times involves difficulties of comparison and uncertainties about where to draw lines. Historically, despite the difficulties, one finds general agreement about who the great powers of a period are, with occasional doubt about marginal cases. The recent inordinate difficulty of counting great powers arose not from problems of measurement but from confusion about how polarities should be defined.

Counting the great powers of an era is about as difficult, or as easy, as saying how many major firms populate an oligopolistic sector of an economy. The question is an empirical one, and common sense can answer it. Economists agree that, even when the total number of firms in a sector is large, their interactions can be understood, though not fully predicted, through theories about oligopoly if the number of consequential firms reduces to a small number by virtue of the preeminence of a few of them. International politics can be viewed in the same way. The 150-odd states in the world appear to form a system of fairly large numbers. Given the inequality of nations, however, the number of consequential states is small. From the Treaty of Westphalia to the present, eight major states at most have sought to coexist peacefully or have contended for mastery. Viewed as the politics of the powerful, international politics can be studied in terms of the logic of small-number systems.

Structural Causes and Military Effects

Kenneth N. Waltz

To say that few [poles] are better than many is not to say that two is best of all. The stability of pairs—of corporations, of political parties, of marriage partners—has often been appreciated. Although most students of international politics probably believe that systems of many great powers would be unstable, they resist the widespread notion that two is the best of small numbers. Are they right to do so? For the sake of stability, peace, or whatever, should we prefer a world of two great powers or a world of several or more? [We] will show why *two* is the best of small numbers. We reached some conclusions, but not that one, by considering economic interdependence. Problems of national security in multi- and bipolar worlds do clearly show the advantages of having two great powers, and only two, in the system.

I

To establish the virtues of two-party systems requires comparing systems of different number. Because the previous chapter was concerned only with systems of small and of still smaller numbers, we did not have to consider differences made by having two, three, four, or more principal parties in a system. We must do so now. By what criteria do we determine that an international-political system changes, and conversely, by what criteria do we say that a system is stable? Political scientists often lump different effects under the heading of stability. I did this in 1964 and 1967 essays, using stability to include also peacefulness and the effective management of international affairs, which are the respective concerns of this chapter and the next one. It is important, I now believe, to keep different effects separate so that we can accurately locate their causes.

Anarchic systems are transformed only by changes in organizing principle and by consequential changes in the number of their principal parties. To say that an international-political system is stable means two things: *first*, that it remains anarchic; *second*, that no consequential variation takes place in the number of principal parties that constitute the system. "Consequential" variations in number are changes of number that lead to different expectations about the effect of structure on units. The stability of the system, so long as it remains anarchic, is then closely linked with the fate of its principal members. The close link is established by the relation of changes in number of great powers to transformation of the system. The link does not bind absolutely, however, because the number of great powers may remain the same or fail to vary consequentially even while some powers fall from the ranks of the great ones only to be replaced by others. International-political systems are remarkably stable, as Table 1 graphically shows. The multipolar system lasted three centuries because as some states fell from the top rank others rose to it through the relative increase of their capabilities. The system endured even as the identity of its members changed. The bipolar system has lasted three decades because no third state has been able to develop capabilities comparable to those of the United States and the

Table 1. Great Powers 1700–1979

	1700	1800	1875	1910	1935	194
Turkey	X					
Sweden	X					
Netherlands	X					
Spain	X					
Austria (Austria-Hungary)	X	X	X	X		
France	X	X	X	X	X	
England (Great Britain)	X	X	X	X	X	
Prussia (Germany)		X	X	X	X	
Russia (Soviet Union)		X	X	X	X	X
Italy			X	X	X	
Japan				X	X	
United States				X	X	X

Soviet Union. The system appears robust, although unlikely to last as long as its predecessor—a matter to be considered in the fourth part of this chapter.

The link between the survival of particular great powers and the stability of systems is also weakened by the fact that not all changes of number are changes of system. That bipolar and multipolar systems are distinct is widely accepted. Systems of two have qualities distinct from systems of three or more. What is the defining difference? The answer is found in the behavior required of parties in self-help systems: namely, balancing. *Balancing is differently done in multi- and bipolar systems.* Though many students of international politics believe that the balance-of-power game requires at least three or four players, two will do. Where two powers contend, imbalances can be righted only by their internal efforts. With more than two, shifts in alignment provide an additional means of adjustment, adding flexibility to the system. This is a crucial difference between multi- and bipolar systems. Beyond two, what variations of number are consequential? Three and four are threshold numbers. They mark the transition from one system to another because the opportunities offered for balancing through combining with others vary in ways that change expected outcomes. Systems of three have distinctive and unfortunate characteristics. Two of the powers can easily gang up on the third, divide the spoils, and drive the system back to bipolarity. In multipolar systems four is then the lowest acceptable number, for it permits external alignment and promises considerable stability. Five is thought of as another threshold number, being the lowest number that promises stability while providing a role for a balancer; and I shall examine that claim. Beyond five no threshold appears. We know that complications accelerate as numbers grow because of the difficulty everyone has in coping with the uncertain behavior of many others and because of the ever larger number and variety of coalitions that can be made, but we have no grounds for saying that complications pass a threshold as we move, say, from seven to eight. Luckily, as a practical matter, no increase in the number of great powers is in prospect.

Until 1945 the nation-state system was multipolar, and always with five or more powers. In all of modern history the structure of international politics has changed but once. We have only two systems to observe. By inference and analogy, however, some conclusions can be drawn about international systems with smaller or larger numbers of great powers. The next part of this chapter shows that five parties do not constitute a distinct system and considers the different implications of systems of two and of four or more.

II

With only two great powers, a balance-of-power system is unstable; four powers are required for its proper functioning. For ease and nicety of adjustment a fifth power, serving as balancer, adds a further refinement. This is the conventional wisdom. Should we accept it? Is five a nice compromise between the simplest possible system of two and numbers so large as to make anarchic systems hopelessly complex?

The notion of a balancer is more a historical generalization than a theoretical concept. The generalization is drawn from the position and behavior of Britain in the eighteenth and nineteenth centuries. British experience shows what conditions have to prevail if the role of balancer is to be effectively played. The first of these was that the margin of power on the side of the aggressor not be so large that British strength added to the weaker side would be insufficient to redress the balance. When the states of the continent were nearly in balance, Britain could act with effect. The second condition was that Britain's ends on the continent remain negative, for positive ends help to determine alignments. A state that wishes to secure a piece of territory ordinarily has to ally with states that do not already have it. The goals of the state then lessen the scope of its diplomatic maneuver. Finally, to be effective in the role of balancer, Britain required a status in power at least equal to that of the mightiest. British weakness vis-à-vis European countries has to the present day meant entanglement with them. Only when continental powers were nearly in balance or when Britain was impressively strong was she able to remain aloof until the moment arrived when her commitment could be diplomatically decisive. These are highly special conditions, made more so by the fact that political preferences must not lead the balancer to identify with any actual or potential grouping of states. Balance-of-power theory cannot incorporate the role of balancer because the playing of the role depends on such narrowly defined and historically unlikely conditions. The number five has no special charm, for there is no reason to believe that the odd party will be able and willing to serve as balancer.

Such considerations lead to more general doubts about the vaunted advantages of flexible alliances. To be helpful, flexibility has to mean that, where one or more states threaten others, some state will join one side or defect from the other in order to tilt the balance against the would-be aggressors. The old balance-of-power system here looks suspiciously like the new collective-security system of the League and the United Nations. Either system depends for its maintenance and functioning on neutrality of alignment at the moment of serious threat. To preserve the system, at least one powerful state must overcome the pressure of ideological preference, the pull of previous ties, and the conflict of present interests in order to add its weight to the side of the peaceful. It must do what the moment requires.

Since one of the interests of each state is to avoid domination by other states, why should it be difficult for one or a few states to swing to the side of the threatened? After all, they experience a common danger. But A may instead say to *B:* "Since the threat is to you as well as to me, I'll stand aside and let you deal with the matter." If *B* acts effectively, A gains free benefits. If *B*, having become resentful, does not, A and *B* both lose. Contemplation of a common fate may not lead to a fair division of labor—or to any labor at all. Whether or not it does depends on the size of the group and the inequalities within it, as well as on the character of its members.[1]

One sees the difficulties in any multipolar system where some states threaten others while alignments are uncertain. French Foreign Minister Flandin told British Prime Minister Baldwin that Hitler's military occupation of the Rhineland in 1936 provided the occasion for Britain to take the lead in opposing Germany. As the German threat grew, some British and French leaders could hope that if their countries remained aloof, Russia and Germany would balance each other off or fight each other to the finish.[2] Uncertainties about who threatens whom, about who will oppose whom, and about who will gain or lose from the actions of other states accelerate as the number of states increases. Even if one assumes that the goals of most states are worthy, the timing and content of the actions required to reach them become more and more difficult to calculate. Rather than making the matter simpler, prescribing general rules for states to follow simply illustrates the impossibility of believing that states can reconcile two conflicting imperatives—to act for their own sakes, as required by their situations, and to act for the system's stability or survival, as some scholars advise them to do. Political scientists who favor flexibility of national alignment have to accept that flexibility comes only as numbers increase and thus also as complexities and uncertainties multiply.

With more than two states, the politics of power turn on the diplomacy by which alliances are made, maintained, and disrupted. Flexibility of alignment means both that the country one is wooing may prefer another suitor and that one's present alliance partner may defect. Flexibility of alignment narrows one's choice of policies. A state's strategy must please a potential or satisfy a present partner. A comparable situation is found where political parties compete for votes by forming and re-forming electoral coalitions of different economic, ethnic, religious, and regional groups. The strategy, or policy, of a party is made for the sake of attracting and holding voters. If a party is to be an electoral success, its policy cannot simply be the one that its leaders believe to be best for the country. Policy must at least partly be made for the sake of winning elections. Similarly, with a number of approximately equal states, strategy is at least partly made for the sake of attracting and holding allies. If alliances may form, states will want to look like attractive partners. Suitors alter their appearance and adapt their behavior to increase their eligibility. Those who remain unattractive, finding that they compete poorly, are likely to try all the harder to change their appearance and behavior. One has to become attractive enough in personality

---

1. Olson, Mancur, Jr. (1965). *The Logic of Collective Action.* Cambridge: Harvard University Press. pp. 36, 45.

2. Nicolson, Nigel (ed.) (1966). *Harold Nicolson: Diaries and Letters, 1930-1939.* London: Collins. pp. 247-49; Young, C. Kenneth (1976). *Stanley Baldwin.* London: Weidenfeld and Nicolson. pp. 128-130.

and policy to be considered a possible choice. The alliance diplomacy of Europe in the years before World War I is rich in examples of this. Ever since the Napoleonic Wars, many had believed that the "Republican" and the "Cossack" could never become engaged, let alone contract a marriage. The wooing of France and Russia, with each adapting somewhat to the other, was nevertheless consummated in the alliance of 1894 and duly produced the Triple Entente as its progeny when first France and England and then Russia and England overcame their long-standing animosities in 1904 and 1907, respectively.

If pressures are strong enough, a state will deal with almost anyone. Litvinov remarked in the 1930s that to promote its security in a hostile world the Soviet Union would work with any state, even with Hitler's Germany.[3] It is important to notice that states will ally with the devil to avoid the hell of military defeat. It is still more important to remember that the question of who will ally with which devil may be the decisive one. In the end Hitler's acts determined that all of the great powers save Italy and Japan would unite against him.[4]

In the quest for security, alliances may have to be made. Once made, they have to be managed. European alliances beginning in the 1890s hardened as two blocs formed. The rigidity of blocs, it is thought, contributed strongly to the outbreak of the First World War. The view is a superficial one. Alliances are made by states that have some but not all of their interests in common. The common interest is ordinarily a negative one: fear of other states. Divergence comes when positive interests are at issue. Consider two examples. Russia would have preferred to plan and prepare for the occasion of war against Austria-Hungary. She could hope to defeat her, but not Germany, and Austria-Hungary stood in the way of Russia's gaining control of the Straits linking the Mediterranean and the Black Seas. France, however, could regain Alsace-Lorraine only by defeating Germany. Perception of a common threat brought Russia and France together. Alliance diplomacy, and a large flow of funds from France to Russia, helped to hold them together and to shape an alliance strategy more to the taste of France than of Russia. Alliance strategies are always the product of compromise since the interests of allies and their notions of how to secure them are never identical. In a multipolar system, moreover, despite the formation of blocs, one's allies may edge toward the opposing camp. If a member of one alliance tries to settle differences, or to cooperate in some ways, with a member of another alliance, its own allies become uneasy. Thus British-German cooperation in 1912 and 1913 to dampen Balkan crises, and the settling of some colonial questions between them, may have been harmful. The reactions of their allies dissuaded Britain and Germany from playing similar roles in Southeastern Europe in 1914, yet gave each of them some hope that the other's alliance would not hold firm.[5] Greater cohesion of blocs would have permitted greater flexibility of policy. But then the cohesion of blocs, like the discipline of parties, is achieved through expert and careful management; and the management of blocs is exceedingly difficult among near-equals since it must be cooperatively contrived.

---

3. Moore, Barrington, Jr. (1950). *Soviet Politics: the Dilemma of Power.* Cambridge: Harvard University Press. pp. 350-55.

4. As Winston Churchill said to his private secretary the night before Germany"s invasion of Russia, "If Hitler invaded Hell I would make at least a favourable reference to the Devil in the House of Commons." Churchill, Winston S. (1950) *The Grand Alliance* Boston: Houghton Mifflin, p.370.

5. Jervis, Robert (1976). *Perception and Misperception in International Politics.* Princeton: Princeton University Press. p. 110.

If competing blocs are seen to be closely balanced, and if competition turns on important matters, then to let one's side down risks one's own destruction. In a moment of crisis the weaker or the more adventurous party is likely to determine its side's policy. Its partners can afford neither to let the weaker member go to the wall nor to advertise their disunity by failing to back a venture even while deploring its risks. The prelude to World War I provides striking examples. The approximate equality of alliance partners made them closely interdependent. The interdependence of allies, plus the keenness of competition between the two camps, meant that while any country could commit its associates, no one country on either side could exercise control. If Austria-Hungary marched, Germany had to follow; the dissolution of the Austro-Hungarian Empire would have left Germany alone in the middle of Europe. If France marched, Russia had to follow; a German victory over France would be a defeat for Russia. And so it was all around the vicious circle. Because the defeat or the defection of a major ally would have shaken the balance, each state was constrained to adjust its strategy and the use of its forces to the aims and fears of its partners. In one sense the unstable politics of the Balkans carried the world into war. But that statement rather misses the point. Internationally, destabilizing events and conditions abound. The important questions to ask are whether they are likely to be managed better, and whether their effects are absorbed more readily, in one system than in another.

The game of power politics, if really played hard, presses the players into two rival camps, though so complicated is the business of making and maintaining alliances that the game may be played hard enough to produce that result only under the pressure of war. Thus the six or seven great powers of the interwar period did not move into a two-bloc formation until more than two years after World War II began. The forming of two blocs, moreover, did not make the multipolar system into a bipolar one any more than the forming of opposing coalitions for the purpose of fighting an election turns a multiparty into a two-party system. Even with the greatest of external pressure, the unity of alliances is far from complete. States or parties in wartime or in electoral alliance, even as they adjust to one another, continue to jockey for advantage and to worry about the constellation of forces that will form once the contest is over.

In multipolar systems there are too many powers to permit any of them to draw clear and fixed lines between allies and adversaries and too few to keep the effects of defection low. With three or more powers flexibility of alliances keeps relations of friendship and enmity fluid and makes everyone's estimate of the present and future relation of forces uncertain. So long as the system is one of fairly small numbers, the actions of any of them may threaten the security of others. There are too many to enable anyone to see for sure what is happening, and too few to make what is happening a matter of indifference. Traditionally students of international politics have thought that the uncertainty that results from flexibility of alignment generates a healthy caution in everyone's foreign policy.[6] Conversely they have believed that bipolar worlds are doubly unstable—that they easily erode or explode. This conclusion is based on false reasoning and scant evidence. Military interdependence varies with the extent to which, and the equality with which, great powers rely on others for their security. In a bipolar world, military interdependence declines even more sharply than economic interdependence. Russia and America depend militarily mainly on themselves. They balance each other by "internal" instead of "external" means, relying on their own capabili-

---

6. Kaplan, Morton A. (1957). *System and Process in International Politics*. New York: Wiley, 1964. pp. 22-36; Morgenthau, Hans J. (1961). *Purpose of American Politics*. New York: Knopf. Part 4.

ties rather than on the capabilities of allies. Internal balancing is more reliable and precise than external balancing. States are less likely to misjudge their relative strengths than they are to misjudge the strength and reliability of opposing coalitions. Rather than making states properly cautious and forwarding the chances of peace, uncertainty and miscalculation cause wars.[7] In a bipolar world uncertainty lessens and calculations are easier to make.

Much of the skepticism about the virtues of bipolarity arises from thinking of a system as being bipolar if two blocs form within a multipolar world. A bloc unskillfully managed may indeed fall apart. In a multipolar world the leaders of both blocs must be concerned at once with alliance management, since the defection of an ally may be fatal to its partners, and with the aims and capabilities of the opposing bloc. The prehistory of two world wars dramatically displays the dangers. The fair amount of effort that now goes into alliance management may obscure the profound difference between old-style and new-style alliances. In alliances among equals, the defection of one party threatens the security of the others. In alliances among unequals, the contributions of the lesser members are at once wanted and of relatively small importance. Where the contributions of a number of parties are highly important to all of them, each has strong incentive both to persuade others to its views about strategy and tactics and to make concessions when persuasion fails. The unity of major partners is likely to endure because they all understand how much they depend on it. Before World War I, Germany's acceptance of Italy's probable defection from the Triple Alliance signaled her relative unimportance. In alliances among unequals, alliance leaders need worry little about the faithfulness of their followers, who usually have little choice anyway. Contrast the situation in 1914 with that of the United States and Britain and France in 1956. The United States could dissociate itself from the Suez adventure of its two principal allies and subject them to heavy financial pressure. Like Austria-Hungary in 1914, they tried to commit or at least immobilize their alliance partner by presenting a *fait accompli*. Enjoying a position of predominance, the United States could continue to focus its attention on the major adversary while disciplining its allies. The ability of the United States, and the inability of Germany, to pay a price measured in intra-alliance terms is striking. It is important, then, to distinguish sharply between the formation of two blocs in a multipolar world and the structural bipolarity of the present system.

In bipolar as in multipolar worlds, alliance leaders may try to elicit maximum contributions from their associates. The contributions are useful even in a bipolar world, but they are not indispensable. Because they are not, the policies and strategies of alliance leaders are ultimately made according to their own calculations and interests. Disregarding the views of an ally makes sense only if military cooperation is fairly unimportant. This is the case both in the Warsaw Treaty Organization and in the North Atlantic Treaty Organization. In 1976, for example, the Soviet Union's military expenditures were well over 90 percent of the WTO total, and those of the United States were about 75 percent of the NATO total. In fact if not in form, NATO consists of guarantees given by the United States to its European allies and to Canada. The United States, with a preponderance of nuclear weapons and as many men in uniform as the West European states combined, may be able to protect them; they cannot protect her. Because of the vast differences in the capabilities of member states, the roughly equal sharing of burdens found in earlier alliance systems is no longer possible.

---

7. Blainey, Geoffrey (1970). *The Causes of War.* London: Macmillan. pp. 108-119.

Militarily, interdependence is low in a bipolar world and high in a multipolar one. Great powers in a multipolar world depend on one another for political and military support in crises and war. To assure oneself of steadfast support is vital. This cannot be the case in a bipolar world, for third parties are not able to tilt the balance of power by withdrawing from one alliance or by joining the other. Thus two "losses" of China in the postwar world—first by the United States and then by the Soviet Union—were accommodated without disastrously distorting, or even much affecting, the balance between America and Russia. Nor did France, in withdrawing her forces from NATO, noticeably change the bipolar balance. That American policy need not be made for the sake of France helps to explain her partial defection. The gross inequality between the two superpowers and the members of their respective alliances makes any realignment of the latter fairly insignificant. The leader's strategy can therefore be flexible. In balance-of-power politics old style, flexibility of alignment made for rigidity of strategy or the limitation of freedom of decision. In balance-of-power politics new style, the obverse is true: Rigidity of alignment in a two-power world makes for flexibility of strategy and the enlargement of freedom of decision. Although concessions to allies are sometimes made, neither the United States nor the Soviet Union alters its strategy or changes its military dispositions simply to accommodate associated states. Both superpowers can make long-range plans and carry out their policies as best they see fit, for they need not accede to the demands of third parties.

In a multipolar world, states often pool their resources in order to serve their interests. Roughly equal parties engaged in cooperative endeavors must look for a common denominator of their policies. They risk finding the lowest one and easily end up in the worst of all possible worlds. In a bipolar world, alliance leaders make their strategies mainly according to their own calculations of interests. Strategies can be designed more to cope with the main adversary and less to satisfy one's allies. Alliance leaders are free to follow their own line, which may of course reflect their bad as well as their good judgment, their imaginary as well as their realistic fears, their ignoble as well as their worthy ends. Alliance leaders are not free of constraints. The major constraints, however, arise from the main adversary and not from one's own associates.

III

Neither the United States nor the Soviet Union has to make itself acceptable to other states; they do have to cope with each other. In the great-power politics of multipolar worlds, who is a danger to whom, and who can be expected to deal with threats and problems, are matters of uncertainty. In the great-power politics of bipolar worlds, who is a danger to whom is never in doubt. This is the first big difference between the politics of power in the two systems. The United States is the obsessing danger for the Soviet Union, and the Soviet Union for the United States, since each can damage the other to an extent no other state can match. Any event in the world that involves the fortunes of either automatically elicits the interest of the other. President Truman, at the time of the Korean invasion, could not very well echo Neville Chamberlain's words in the Czechoslovakian crisis by claiming that the Koreans were a people far away in the East of Asia of whom Americans knew nothing. We had to know about them or quickly find out. In the 1930s France lay between England and Germany. The British could believe, and we could too, that their frontier and ours lay on the Rhine. After World War II no third great power could lie between the United States and the Soviet Union, for none existed. The statement that peace is indivisible was controversial, indeed untrue, when it was made by Litvinov in the 1930s. Political slogans express wishes better than realities. In a bipolar world the wish becomes reality. A war or threat of war anywhere is a concern to both of the superpowers if it may lead to significant gains or losses for either of them. In a two-power competition a loss for one appears as a gain for the other. Because this is so, the powers in a bipolar world promptly respond to unsettling events. In a multipolar world dangers are diffused, responsibilities unclear, and definitions of vital interests easily obscured. Where a number of states are in balance, the skillful foreign policy of a forward power is designed to gain an advantage over one state without antagonizing others and frightening them into united action. At times in modern Europe, possible gains seemed greater than likely losses. Statesmen could hope to push an issue to the limit without causing all of the potential opponents to unite. When possible enemies are several in number, unity of action among them is difficult to arrange. National leaders could therefore think—or desperately hope as did Bethmann Hollweg and Adolf Hitler before two World Wars—that no united opposition would form. Interdependence of parties, diffusion of dangers, confusion of responses: These are the characteristics of great-power politics in multipolar worlds.

If interests and ambitions conflict, the absence of crises is more worrisome than their recurrence. Crises are produced by the determination of a state to resist a change that another state tries to make. The situation of the United States and of the Soviet Union disposes them to do the resisting, for in important matters they cannot hope that others will do it for them. Political action in the postwar world has reflected this condition. Communist guerrillas operating in Greece prompted the Truman Doctrine. The tightening of the Soviet Union's control over the states of Eastern Europe led to the Marshall Plan and the Atlantic Defense Treaty, and these in turn gave rise to the Cominform and the Warsaw Pact. The plan to form a West German government produced the Berlin Blockade. And so on through the 1950s, '60s, and '70s. Our responses are geared to the Soviet Union's actions, and theirs to ours, which has produced an increasingly solid bipolar balance.

In a bipolar world there are no peripheries. With only two powers capable of acting on a world scale, anything that happens anywhere is potentially of concern to both of them. Bipolarity extends the geographic scope of both powers' concern. It also broadens the range of factors included in the competition between them. Because allies add relatively little to the superpowers' capabilities, they concentrate their attention on their own dispositions. In a multipolar world, who is a danger to whom is often unclear; the incentive to regard all disequilibrating changes with concern and respond to them with whatever effort may be required is consequently weakened. In a bipolar world changes may affect each of the two powers differently, and this means all the more that few changes in the world at large or within each other's national realm are likely to be thought irrelevant. Competition becomes more comprehensive as well as more widely extended. Not just military preparation but also economic growth and technological development become matters of intense and constant concern. Self-dependence of parties, clarity of dangers, certainty about who has to face them: These are the characteristics of great-power politics in a bipolar world.

Miscalculation by some or all of the great powers is the source of danger in a multipolar world; overreaction by either or both of the great powers is the source of danger in a bipolar world. Bipolarity encourages the United States and the Soviet Union to turn unwanted events into crises, while rendering most of them relatively inconsequential. Each can lose heavily only in war with the other; in power and in wealth, both gain more by the peaceful development of internal resources than by wooing and winning—or by fighting and subduing—

other states in the world. A five-percent growth rate sustained for three years increases the American gross national product by an amount exceeding one-half of West Germany's GNP, and all of Great Britain's (base year 1976). For the Soviet Union, with one-half of our GNP, imaginable gains double in weight. They would still be of minor importance. Only Japan, Western Europe, and the Middle East are prizes that if won by the Soviet Union would alter the balance of GNPs and the distribution of resources enough to be a danger.

Yet since World War II the United States has responded expensively in distant places to wayward events that could hardly affect anyone's fate outside of the region. Which is worse: miscalculation or overreaction? Miscalculation is more likely to permit the unfolding of a series of events that finally threatens a change in the balance and brings the powers to war. Overreaction is the lesser evil because it costs only money and the fighting of limited wars.

The dynamics of a bipolar system, moreover, provide a measure of correction. In a hot war or a cold war—as in any close competition—the external situation dominates. In the middle 1950s John Foster Dulles inveighed against the immoral neutralists. Russian leaders, in like spirit, described neutralists as either fools themselves or dupes of capitalist countries. But ideology did not long prevail over interest. Both Russia and America quickly came to accept neutralist states and even to lend them encouragement. The Soviet Union aided Egypt and Iraq, countries that kept their communists in jail. In the late 1950s and throughout the '60s, the United States, having already given economic and military assistance to communist Yugoslavia, made neutralist India the most favored recipient of economic aid.[8] According to the rhetoric of the Cold War, the root cleavage in the world was between capitalist democracy and godless communism. But by the size of the stakes and the force of the struggle, ideology was subordinated to interest in the policies of America and Russia, who behaved more like traditional great powers than like leaders of messianic movements. In a world in which two states united in their mutual antagonism far overshadow any other, the incentives to a calculated response stand out most clearly, and the sanctions against irresponsible behavior achieve their greatest force. Thus two states, isolationist by tradition, untutored in the ways of international politics, and famed for impulsive behavior, soon showed themselves—not always and everywhere, but always in crucial cases—to be wary, alert, cautious, flexible, and forbearing.

Some have believed that a new world began with the explosion of an atomic bomb over Hiroshima. In shaping the behavior of nations, the perennial forces of politics are more important than the new military technology. States remain the primary vehicles of ideology. The international brotherhood of autocrats after 1815, the cosmopolitan liberalism of the middle nineteenth century, international socialism before World War I, international communism in the decades following the Bolshevik revolution: In all of these cases international movements were captured by individual nations, adherents of the creed were harnessed to the nation's interest, international programs were manipulated by national governments, and ideology became a prop to national policy. So the Soviet Union in crisis became Russian, and American policy, liberal rhetoric aside, came to be realistically and cautiously constructed. By the force of events, they and we were impelled to behave in ways belied both by their words and by ours. Political scientists, drawing their inferences from the characteristics of states, were slow to appreciate the process. Inferences drawn from the characteristics of small-number systems are bet-

8. From 1960 to 1967 our economic aid to India exceeded our combined economic and military aid to any other country (US Agency for International Development, various years).

ter borne out politically. Economists have long known that the passage of time makes peaceful coexistence among major competitors easier. They become accustomed to one another; they learn how to interpret one another's moves and how to accommodate or counter them. "Unambiguously," as Oliver Williamson puts it, "experience leads to a higher level of adherence" to agreements made and to commonly accepted practices.[9] Life becomes more predictable.

Theories of perfect competition tell us about the market and not about the competitors. Theories of oligopolistic competition tell us quite a bit about both. In important ways, competitors become like one another as their competition continues. This applies to states as to firms. Thus William Zimmerman found not only that the Soviet Union in the 1960s had abandoned its Bolshevik views of international relations but also that its views had become much like ours.[10] The increasing similarity of competitors' attitudes, as well as their experience with one another, eases the adjustment of their relations.

These advantages are found in all small-number systems. What additional advantages do pairs enjoy in dealing with each other? As a group shrinks, its members face fewer choices when considering whom to deal with. Partly because they eliminate the difficult business of choosing, the smallest of groups manages its affairs most easily. With more than two parties, the solidarity of a group is always at risk because the parties can try to improve their lots by combining. Interdependence breeds hostility and fear. With more than two parties, hostility and fear may lead *A* and *B* to seek the support of *C*. If they both court *C*, their hostility and fear increase. When a group narrows to just two members, choice disappears. On matters of ultimate importance each can deal only with the other. No appeal can be made to third parties. A system of two has unique properties. Tension in the system is high because each can do so much for and to the other. But because no appeal can be made to third parties, pressure to moderate behavior is heavy.[11] Bargaining among more than two parties is difficult. Bargainers worry about the points at issue. With more than two parties, each also worries about how the strength of his position will be affected by combinations he and others may make. If two of several parties strike an agreement, moreover, they must wonder if the agreement will be disrupted or negated by the actions of others.

Consider the problem of disarmament. To find even limited solutions, at least one of the following two conditions must be met. First, if the would-be winner of an arms race is willing to curtail its program, agreement is made possible. In the 1920s the United States—the country that could have won a naval arms race—took the lead in negotiating limitations. The self-interest of the would-be losers carried them along. Such was the necessary, though not the only, condition making the Washington Naval Arms Limitation Treaty possible. Second, if two powers can consider their mutual interests and fears without giving much thought to how the military capabilities of others affect them, agreement is made possible. The 1972 treaty limiting the deployment of antiballistic missiles is a dramatic example of this. Ballistic missile defenses, because they promise to be effective

---

9. Williamson, Oliver E. (1965). "A dynamic theory of inter-firm behavior." In Bruce M. Russet (ed.), *Economic Theories of International Politics*. Chicago: Markham, 1968. p. 227.

10. Zimmerman, William (1969). *Soviet Perspectives on International Relations, 1956-1967*. Princeton: Princeton University Press. pp. 135, 282.

11. Simmel, Georg (July, 1906). "The Number of members as determining the social form of the group." *Journal of Sociology*, vol. 8.

against missiles fired in small numbers, are useful against the nuclear forces of third parties. Because of their vast superiority, the United States and the Soviet Union were nevertheless able to limit their defensive weaponry. To the extent that the United States and the Soviet Union have to worry about the military strength of others, their ability to reach bilateral agreements lessens. So far those worries have been small.[12]

The simplicity of relations in a bipolar world and the strong pressures that are generated make the two great powers conservative. Structure, however, does not by any means explain everything. I say this again because the charge of structural determinism is easy to make. To explain outcomes one must look at the capabilities, the actions, and the interactions of states, as well as at the structure of their systems. States armed with nuclear weapons may have stronger incentives to avoid war than states armed conventionally. The United States and the Soviet Union may have found it harder to learn to live with each other in the 1940s and '50s than more experienced and less ideological nations would have. Causes at both the national and the international level make the world more or less peaceful and stable. I concentrate attention at the international level because the effects of structure are usually overlooked or misunderstood and because I am writing a theory of international politics, not of foreign policy.

In saying that the United States and the Soviet Union, like duopolists in other fields, are learning gradually how to cope with each other, I do not imply that they will interact without crises or find cooperation easy. The quality of their relations did, however, perceptibly change in the 1960s and '70s. Worries in the 1940s and '50s that tensions would rise to intolerable levels were balanced in the 1960s and '70s by fears that America and Russia would make agreements for their mutual benefit at others' expense. West Europeans—especially in Germany and France—have fretted. Chinese leaders have sometimes accused the Soviet Union of seeking world domination through collaboration with the United States. Worries and fears on any such grounds are exaggerated. The Soviet Union and the United States influence each other more than any of the states living in their penumbra can hope to do. In the world of the present, as of the recent past, a condition of mutual opposition may require rather than preclude the adjustment of differences. Yet first steps toward agreement do not lead to second and third steps. Instead they mingle with other acts and events that keep the level of tension quite high. This is the pattern set by the first major success enjoyed by the Soviet Union and the United States in jointly regulating their military affairs—the Test Ban Treaty of 1963. The test ban was described in the United States as possibly a first big step toward wider agreements that would increase the chances of maintaining peace. In the same breath it was said that we cannot lower our guard, for the Soviet Union's aims have not changed.[13] Because they must rely for their security on their own devices, both countries are wary of joint ventures. Since they cannot know that benefits will be equal, since they cannot be certain that arrangements made will reliably bind both of them, each shies away from running a future risk for the sake of a present benefit. Between parties in a self-help system, rules of reciprocity and caution prevail. Their concern for peace and stability draws them together; their fears drive them apart. They are rightly called *frère ennemi* and adversary partners.

---

12. Richard Burt has carefully considered some of the ways in which the worries are growing. Burt, Richard (1976). *New Weapons Technologies: Debate and Directions.* London: Adelphi Papers, no. 126

13. Rusk, Dean (August 13, 1963). "Text of Rusk's statement to Senators about Test Ban Treaty." *New York Times.*

But may not the enmity obliterate the brotherhood and the sense of opposition obscure mutual interests? A small-number system can always be disrupted by the actions of a Hitler and the reactions of a Chamberlain. Since this is true, it may seem that we are in the uncomfortable position of relying on the moderation, courage, and good sense of those holding positions of power. Given human vagaries and the unpredictability of the individual's reaction to events, one may feel that the only recourse is to lapse into prayer. We can nonetheless take comfort from the thought that, like others, those who direct the activities of great states are by no means free agents. Beyond the residuum of necessary hope that leaders will respond sensibly, lies the possibility of estimating the pressures that encourage them to do so. In a world in which two states united in their mutual antagonism far overshadow any other, the incentives to a calculated response stand out most clearly, and the sanctions against irresponsible behavior achieve their greatest force. The identity as well as the behavior of leaders is affected by the presence of pressures and the clarity of challenges. One may lament Churchill's failure to gain control of the British government in the 1930s, for he knew what actions were required to maintain a balance of power. Churchill was not brought to power by the diffused threat of war in the '30s but only by the stark danger of defeat after war began. If a people representing one pole of the world now tolerates inept rulers, it runs clearly discernible risks. Leaders of the United States and the Soviet Union are presumably chosen with an eye to the tasks they will have to perform. Other countries, if they wish to, can enjoy the luxury of selecting leaders who will most please their peoples by the way in which internal affairs are managed. The United States and the Soviet Union cannot.

It is not that one entertains the utopian hope that all future American and Russian rulers will combine in their persons a complicated set of nearly perfect virtues, but rather that the pressures of a bipolar world strongly encourage them to act internationally in ways better than their characters may lead one to expect. I made this proposition in 1964; Nixon as president confirmed it. It is not that one is serenely confident about the peacefulness, or even about the survival, of the world, but rather that cautious optimism is justified so long as the dangers to which each must respond are so clearly present. Either country may go berserk or succumb to inanation and debility. That necessities are clear increases the chances that they will be met, but gives no guarantees. Dangers from abroad may unify a state and spur its people to heroic action. Or, as with France facing Hitler's Germany, external pressures may divide the leaders, confuse the public, and increase their willingness to give way. It may also happen that the difficulties of adjustment and the necessity for calculated action simply become too great. The clarity with which the necessities of action can now be seen may be blotted out by the blinding flash of nuclear explosions. The fear that this may happen strengthens the forces and processes I have described.

IV

A system of two has many virtues. Before explaining any more of them, the question of the durability of today's bipolar world should be examined. The system is dynamically stable, as I have shown. I have not, however, examined the many assertions that America and Russia are losing, or have lost, their effective edge over other states, as has happened to previous great powers and surely may happen again. Let us first ask whether the margin of American and Russian superiority *is* seriously eroding, and then examine the relation between military power and political control.

Surveying the rise and fall of nations over the centuries, one can only conclude that national rankings change slowly. War aside, the economic and other bases of power change little more rapidly in one major nation than they do in another. Differences in economic growth rates are neither large enough nor steady enough to alter standings except in the long run. France and her major opponents in the Napoleonic Wars were also the major initial participants in World War I, with Prussia having become Germany and with the later addition of the United States. Even such thorough defeats as those suffered by Napoleonic France and Wilhelmine Germany did not remove those countries from the ranks of the great powers. World War II did change the cast of great-power characters; no longer could others compete with the United States and the Soviet Union, for only they combine great scale in geography and population with economic and technological development. Entering the club was easier when great powers were larger in number and smaller in size. With fewer and bigger ones, barriers to entry have risen. Over time, however, even they can be surmounted. How long a running start is needed before some third or fourth state will be able to jump over the barriers? Just how high are they?

Although not as high as they once were, they are higher than many would have us believe. One of the themes of recent American discourse is that we are a "declining industrial power." C.L. Sulzberger, for example, announced in November of 1972 that "the U.S. finds itself no longer the global giant of twenty years ago." Our share of global production, he claimed, "has slipped from 50 to 30 percent".[14] Such a misuse of numbers would be startling had we not become accustomed to hearing about America's steady decline. In the summer of 1971 President Nixon remarked that 25 years ago "we were number one in the world militarily" and "number one economically" as well. The United States, he added, "was producing more than 50 percent of all the world's goods." But no longer. By 1971, "instead of just America being number one in the world from an economic standpoint, the preeminent world power, and instead of there being just two superpowers, when we think in economic terms and economic potentialities, there are five great power centers in the world today" (July 6, 1971).

The trick that Sulzberger and Nixon played on us, and no doubt on themselves, should be apparent. In 1946, Nixon's year of comparison, most of the industrial world outside of the United States lay in ruins. By 1952, Sulzberger's year of comparison, Britain, France, and Russia had regained their prewar levels of production but the German and Japanese economic miracles had not been performed. In the years just after the war, the United States naturally produced an unusually large percentage of the world's goods.[15] Now again, as before the war, we produce about one quarter of the world's goods, which is two and three times as much as the two next-largest economies namely, the Soviet Union's and Japan's. And that somehow means that rather than being number one, we have become merely one of five?

A recovery growth rate is faster than a growth rate from a normal base. The recovery rates of other economies reduced the huge gap between America and other industrial countries to one still huge, but less so. No evidence suggests further significant erosion of America's present position. Much evidence suggests that we became sufficiently accustomed to

---

14. Sulzberger, C. L. (November 15, 1972). "New balance of peace." *New York Times*. p. 47.

15. Nixon and Sulzberger do, however, overestimate American postwar economic dominance. W. S.and E. S. Woytinsky credit the United States with 40.7 percent of world income in 1948, compared to 26 percent in 1938. Theirs seems to be the better estimate.Woytinsky, W.S., and E. S. Woytinsky (1953). *World Population and Production*. New York: Twentieth Century Fund, pp. 389, 393–395

our abnormal postwar dominance to lead us now to an unbecoming sensitivity to others' advances, whether or not they equal our own. In the economic/technological game, the United States holds the high cards. Economic growth and competitiveness depend heavily on technological excellence. The United States has the lead, which it maintains by spending more than other countries on research and development. Here again recent statements mislead. The *International Economic Report of the President,* submitted in March of 1976, warned the Congress that "the United States has not been keeping pace with the growth and relative importance of R&D efforts of some of its major foreign competitors, especially Germany and Japan".[16] This should be translated to read as follows: Germany's and Japan's increases in R&D expenditures brought them roughly to the American level of spending by 1973 (see Appendix Table II). Much of America's decline in expenditure over the decade reflects reduced spending on space and defense-related research and development, which have little to do with economic standing anyway. Since expenditure is measured as a percentage of GNP, moreover, America's national expenditure is still disproportionately large. The expenditure is reflected in results, as several examples suggest. In 29 years following the 1943 resumption of Nobel Prize awards in science Americans won 86 of the 178 given.[17] In 1976 we became the first country ever to sweep the Nobel Prizes. (This of course led to articles in the press warning of an approaching decline in America's scientific and cultural eminence, partly because other countries are catching up in research expenditures in ways that I have just summarized. One suspects the warning is merited; we can scarcely do better.) Between 1953 and 1973 the United States produced 65 percent of 492 major technological innovations. Britain was second with 17 percent.[18] In 1971, of every ten thousand employees in the American labor force, 61.9 were scientists and engineers. The comparable figures for the next ranking noncommunist countries were 38.4 for Japan, 32.0 for West Germany, and 26.2 for France. Finally, our advantage in the export of manufactured goods has depended heavily on the export of high technology products. In the three years from 1973 through 1975 those exports grew at an annual average rate of 28.3 percent.

However one measures, the United States is the leading country. One may wonder whether the position of leader is not a costly one to maintain. Developing countries, Russia and Japan for example, have gained by adopting technology expensively created in countries with more advanced economies. For four reasons this is no longer easily possible. First, the complexity of today's technology means that competence in some matters can seldom be separated from competence in others. How can a country be in the forefront of any complicated technology without full access to the most sophisticated computers? Countries as advanced as the Soviet Union and France have felt the difficulties that the question suggests. Second, the pace of technological change means that lags lengthen and multiply. "The countries only a little behind," as Victor Basiuk has said, "frequently find themselves manufacturing products already on the threshold of obsolescence." Third, even though the United States does not have an internal market big enough to permit the full and efficient exploitation of some possible technologies, it nevertheless approaches the required scale more closely than anyone else does. The advantage is a big one since most projects will continue to be national

16. CIEP: Council on International Economic Policy (March 1976). *International Economic Report of the President.* Washington, D.C.: GPO. p. 119.

17. Smith, Bruce L. R., and Joseph J. Karlesky (1977). *The State of Academic Science,* vol. 1. New Rochelle, N.Y.: Change Magazine Press. p. 4.

18. ibid.

rather than international ones. Fourth, economic and technological leads are likely to become more important in international politics. This is partly because of the military stalemate. It is also because in today's world, and more so in tomorrow's, adequate supplies of basic materials are not easily and cheaply available. To mine the seabeds, to develop substitutes for scarce resources, to replace them with synthetics made from readily available materials: These are the abilities that will become increasingly important in determining the prosperity, if not the viability, of national economies.

I have mentioned a number of items that have to be entered on the credit side of the American ledger. Have I not overlooked items that should appear as debit entries? Have I not drawn a lopsided picture? Yes, I have; but then, it's a lopsided world. It is hard to think of disadvantages we suffer that are not more severe disadvantages for other major countries. The Soviet Union enjoys many of the advantages that the United States has and some that we lack, especially in natural resource endowments. With half of our GNP, she nevertheless has to run hard to stay in the race. One may think that the question to ask is not whether a third or fourth country will enter the circle of great powers in the foreseeable future but rather whether the Soviet Union can keep up.

The Soviet Union, since the war, has been able to challenge the United States in some parts of the world by spending a disproportionately large share of her smaller income on military means. Already disadvantaged by having to sustain a larger population than America's on one-half the product, she also spends from that product proportionately more than the United States does on defense—perhaps 11 to 13 percent as compared to roughly 6 percent of GNP that the United States spent in the years 1973 through 1975.[19] The burden of such high military spending is heavy. Only Iran and the confrontation states of the Middle East spend proportionately more. Some have worried that the People's Republic of China may follow such a path, that it may mobilize the nation in order to increase production rapidly while simultaneously acquiring a large and modern military capability. It is doubtful that she can do either, and surely not both, and surely not the second without the first. As a future superpower, the People's Republic of China is dimly discernible on a horizon too distant to make speculation worthwhile.

Western Europe is the only candidate for the short run—say, by the end of the millennium. Its prospects may not be bright, but at least the potential is present and needs only to be politically unfolded. Summed, the nine states of Western Europe have a population slightly larger than the Soviet Union's and a GNP that exceeds hers by 25 percent. Unity will not come tomorrow, and if it did, Europe would not instantly achieve stardom. A united Europe that developed political competence and military power over the years would one day emerge as the third superpower, ranking probably between the United States and the Soviet Union.

Unless Europe unites, the United States and the Soviet Union will remain economically well ahead of other states. But does that in itself set them apart? In international affairs, force remains the final arbiter. Thus some have thought that by acquiring nuclear weapons third countries reduce their distance from the great powers. "For, like gunpowder in another age," so one argument goes, "nuclear weapons must have the ultimate result of making the small the equal of the great".[20] Gunpowder did not blur the distinction between the great powers

---

19. Some estimates of the Soviet Union' spending are higher. Cf. Brennan, Donald G. (Spring 1977). "The Soviet military build-up and its implications for the negotiations on strategic arms limitations." *Orbis*, vol. 21.

and the others, however, nor have nuclear weapons done so. Nuclear weapons are not the great equalizers they were sometimes thought to be. The world was bipolar in the late 1940s, when the United States had few atomic bombs and the Soviet Union had none. Nuclear weapons did not cause the condition of bipolarity; other states by acquiring them cannot change the condition. Nuclear weapons do not equalize the power of nations because they do not change the economic bases of a nation's power. Nuclear capabilities reinforce a condition that would exist in their absence: Even without nuclear technology the United States and the Soviet Union would have developed weapons of immense destructive power. They are set apart from the others not by particular weapons systems but by their ability to exploit military technology on a large scale and at the scientific frontiers. Had the atom never been split, each would far surpass others in military strength, and each would remain the greatest threat and source of potential damage to the other.

Because it is so research-intensive, modern weaponry has raised the barriers that states must jump over if they are to become members of the superpower club. Unable to spend on anywhere near the American or Russian level for research, development, and production, middle powers who try to compete find themselves constantly falling behind.[21] They are in the second-ranking powers' customary position of imitating the more advanced weaponry of their wealthier competitors, but their problems are now much bigger. The pace of the competition has quickened. If weaponry changes little and slowly, smaller countries can hope over time to accumulate weapons that will not become obsolete. In building a nuclear force, Britain became more dependent on the United States. Contemplating the example, dc Gaulle nevertheless decided to go ahead with France's nuclear program. He may have done so believing that missile-firing submarines were the world's first permanently invulnerable force, that for them military obsolescence had ended. The French are fond of invulnerability. Given the small number of submarines France has planned, however, only one or two will be at sea at any given time. Continuous trailing makes their detection and destruction increasingly easy. And France's 18 land-based missiles can be blanketed by Russia's intermediate-range ballistic missiles, which she has in abundant supply. French officials continue to proclaim the invulnerability of their forces, as I would do if I were they. But I would not find my words credible. With the United States and thc Soviet Union, each worries that the other may achieve a first-strike capability, and each works to prevent that. The worries of lesser nuclear powers are incomparably greater, and they cannot do much to allay them.

In the old days weaker powers could improve their positions through alliance, by adding the strength of foreign armies to their own. Cannot some of the middle states do together what they are unable to do alone? For two decisive reasons, the answer is no. Nuclear forces do not add up. The technology of warheads, of delivery vehicles, of detection and surveillance devices, of command and control systems, counts more than the size of forces. Combining separate national forces is not much help. To reach top technological levels would require complete collaboration by, say, several European states. To achieve this has proved

20. Stillman, Edmund O., and William Pfaff (1961). *The New Politics: America and the End of the Post-war World.* New York: McCann. p. 135.

21. Between 1955 and 1965, Britain, France, and Germany spent 10 percent of the American total on military R&D; between 1970 and 1974, 27 percent. As Richard Burt concludes, unless European countries collaborate on producing and procuring military systems and the United Staes buys European, exploitation of new technology will widen the gap in the capabilities of allies (1976, pp.20–21; and see Appendix Table VI).

politically impossible. As de Gaulle often said, nuclear weapons make alliances obsolete. At the strategic level he was right. That is another reason for calling NATO a treaty of guarantee rather than an old-fashioned alliance. To concert their power in order to raise their capabilities to the level of the superpowers, states would have to achieve the oligopolists' unachievable "collusive handling of all relevant variables." Recalling Fellner, we know that this they cannot do. States fear dividing their strategic labors fullyfrom research and development through production, planning and deployment. This is less because one of them might in the future be at war with another, and more because anyone's decision to use the weapons against third parties might be fatal to all of them. Decisions to use nuclear weapons may be decisions to commit suicide. Only a national authority can be entrusted with the decision, again as de Gaulle always claimed. The reasons Europeans fear American unwillingness to retaliate on their behalf are the reasons middle states cannot enhance their power to act at the global and strategic levels through alliances compounded among themselves.[22] I leave aside the many other impediments to nuclear cooperation. These are impediments enough. Only by merging and losing their political identities can middle states become superpowers. The nonadditivity of nuclear forces shows again that in our bipolar world efforts of lesser states cannot tilt the strategic balance.

Saying that the spread of nuclear weapons leaves bipolarity intact does not imply indifference to proliferation. It will not make the world multipolar; it may have other good or bad effects. The bad ones are easier to imagine. Bipolarity has been proof against war between the great powers, but enough wars of lesser scale have been fought. The prospect of a number of states having nuclear weapons that may be ill-controlled and vulnerable is a scary one, not because proliferation would change the system, but because of what lesser powers might do to one another. In an influential 1958 article, Albert Wohlstetter warned of the dangers of a "delicate balance of terror." Those dangers may plague countries having small nuclear forces, with one country tempted to fire its weapons preemptively against an adversary thought to be momentarily vulnerable. One must add that these dangers have not in fact appeared. Reconsideration of nuclear proliferation is called for, but not here since I want only to make the point that an increase in the number of nuclear states does not threaten the world's bipolar structure.

Limitations of technology and scale work decisively against middle states competing with the great powers at the nuclear level. The same limitations put them ever further behind in conventional weaponry. Increasingly, conventional weaponry has become unconventional. Weapons systems of high technology may come to dominate the battlefield. One American officer describes an escort plane, under development for tactical strike missions, that "will throw an electronic blanket over their air defenses that will allow our aircraft to attack without danger from anything more than lucky shots." Another describes electronic-warfare capability as "an absolute requirement for survival in any future conflicts".[23] Though the requirement may be an absolute one, it is a requirement that only the United States and, belatedly, the Soviet Union will be able to meet. From rifles to tanks, from aircraft to missiles, weapons have multiplied in cost. To buy them in numbers and variety sufficient for military effectiveness exceeds the economic capability of most states.

22. For the same reasons, a lagging superpower cannot combine with lesser states to compensate for strategic weakness.

23. Middleton, Drew (September 13, 1976). "Growing use of electronic warfare is becoming a source of major concern for world's military powers." *New York Times*. p. 7.

From about 1900 onward, only great powers, enjoying economies of scale, could deploy modern fleets. Other states limited their ships to older and cheaper models, while their armies continued to be miniatures of the armies of great powers. Now armies, air forces, and navies alike can be mounted at advanced levels of technology only by great powers. Countries of German or British size enjoy economies of scale in manufacturing steel and refrigerators, in providing schools, health services, and transportation systems. They no longer do so militarily. Short of the electronic extreme, the cost and complication of conventional warfare exclude middle states from developing the full range of weapons for land, air, and sea warfare.[24]

Great powers are strong not simply because they have nuclear weapons but also because their immense resources enable them to generate and maintain power of all types, military and other, at strategic and tactical levels. The barriers to entering the superpower club have never been higher and more numerous. The club will long remain the world's most exclusive one.

V

No one doubts that capabilities are now more narrowly concentrated than ever before in modern history. But many argue that the concentration of capabilities does not generate effective power. Military power no longer brings political control. Despite its vast capability, is the United States "a tied Gulliver, not a master with free hands"?[25] And does the Soviet Union also fit the description? The two superpowers, each stalemated by the other's nuclear force, are for important political purposes effectively reduced to the power of lesser states. That is a common belief. The effective equality of states emerges from the very condition of their gross inequality. We read, for example, that the "change in the nature of the mobilizable potential has made its actual use in emergencies by its unhappy owners quite difficult and self-defeating. As a result, nations endowed with infinitely less can behave in a whole range of issues as if the difference in power did not matter." The conclusion is driven home by adding that the United States thinks in "cataclysmic terms," lives in dread of all-out war, and bases its military calculations on the forces needed for the ultimate but unlikely crisis rather than on what might be needed in the less spectacular cases that are in fact more likely to occur.[26]

In the widely echoed words of John Herz, absolute power equals absolute impotence, at least at the highest levels of force represented by the American and Russian nuclear armories.[27] At lesser levels of violence many states can compete as though they were substantially equal. The best weapons of the United States and the Soviet Union are useless, and the distinct advantage of those two states is thus negated. But what about American or Russian nuclear weapons used against minor nuclear states or against states having no nuclear weap-

---

24. Vital has made these points nicely for small states. They apply to middle states as well Vital, David, 1967. *The Inequality of States.* Oxford: Oxford University Press, pp. 63–77.

25. Hoffmann, Stanley (January 11, 1976). "Groping toward a new world order." *New York Times.* sec. iv, p.1

26. Hoffmann, Stanley (Fall 1964). "Europe's identity crisis: between the past and America." *Daedalus,* vol. 93. pp. 1279, 1287-88; Knorr, Klaus (1966). *On the Uses of Military Power in the Nuclear Age.* Princeton: Princeton University Press.

27. Herz, John H. (1959). *International Politics in the Atomic Age.* New York: Columbia University. pp. 22, 167.

ons? Here again the "best" weapon of the most powerful states turns out to be the least usable. The nation that is equipped to "retaliate massively" is not likely to find the occasion to use its capability. If amputation of an arm were the only remedy available for an infected finger, one would be tempted to hope for the best and leave the ailment untreated. The state that can move effectively only by committing the full power of its military arsenal is likely to forget the threats it has made and acquiesce in a situation formerly described as intolerable. Instruments that cannot be used to deal with small cases—those that are moderately dangerous and damaging—remain idle until the big case arises. But then the use of major force to defend a vital interest would run the grave risk of retaliation. Under such circumstances the powerful are frustrated by their strength; and although the weak do not thereby become strong, they are, it is said, able to behave as though they were.

Such arguments are repeatedly made and have to be taken seriously. In an obvious sense, part of the contention is valid. When great powers are in a stalemate, lesser states acquire an increased freedom of movement. That this phenomenon is now noticeable tells us nothing new about the strength of the weak or the weakness of the strong. Weak states have often found opportunities for maneuver in the interstices of a balance of power. In a bipolar world, leaders are free to set policy without acceding to the wishes of lesser alliance members. By the same logic, the latter are free not to follow the policy that has been set. As we once did, they enjoy the freedom of the irresponsible since their security is mainly provided by the efforts that others make. To maintain both the balance and its by-product requires the continuing efforts of America and Russia. Their instincts for self-preservation call forth such efforts. The objective of both states must be to perpetuate an international stalemate as a minimum basis for the security of each of them—even if this should mean that the two big states do the work while the small ones have the fun.

Strategic nuclear weapons deter strategic nuclear weapons (though they may also do more than that). Where each state must tend to its own security as best it can, the means adopted by one state must be geared to the efforts of others. The cost of the American nuclear establishment, maintained in peaceful readiness, is functionally comparable to the cost incurred by a government in order to maintain domestic order and provide internal security. Such expenditure is not productive in the sense that spending to build roads is, but it is not unproductive either. Its utility is obvious, and should anyone successfully argue otherwise, the consequences of accepting the argument would quickly demonstrate its falsity. Force is least visible where power is most fully and most adequately present.[28] Power maintains an order; the use of force signals a possible breakdown. The better ordered a society and the more competent and respected its government, the less force its policemen are required to employ. Less shooting occurs in present-day Sandusky than did on the western frontier. Similarly, in international politics states supreme in their power have to use force less often. "Non-recourse to force"—as both Eisenhower and Khrushchev seem to have realized—is the doctrine of powerful states. Powerful states need to use force less often than their weaker neighbors because the strong can more often protect their interests or work their wills in other ways—by persuasion and cajolery, by economic bargaining and bribery, by the extension of aid, and finally by posing deterrent threats. Since states with large nuclear armories do not actually "use" them, force is said to be discounted. Such reasoning is fallacious. Possession of power should not be identified with the use of force, and the usefulness

28. Carr, Edward Hallet (1946). *The Twenty Years' Crisis: 1919-1939*, 2nd. ed. New York: Harper and Row, 1964. pp. 103, 129-32.

of force should not be confused with its usability. To introduce such confusions into the analysis of power is comparable to saying that the police force that seldom if ever employs violence is weak or that a police force is strong only when policemen are shooting their guns. To vary the image, it is comparable to saying that a man with large assets is not rich if he spends little money or that a man is rich only if he spends a lot of it.

But the argument, which we should not lose sight of, is that just as the miser's money may depreciate grossly in value over the years, so the great powers' military strength has lost much of its usability. If military force is like currency that cannot be spent or money that has lost much of its worth, then is not forbearance in its use merely a way of disguising its depreciated value? Conrad von Hötzendorf, Austrian Chief of Staff prior to the First World War, looked at military power as though it were a capital sum, useless unless invested. In his view, to invest military force is to commit it to battle.[29] In the reasoning of Conrad, military force is most useful at the moment of its employment in war. Depending on a country's situation, it may make much better sense to say that military force is most useful when it dissuades other states from attacking, that is, when it need not be used in battle at all. When the strongest state militarily is also a status-quo power, nonuse of force is a sign of its strength. Force is most useful, or best serves the interests of such a state, when it need not be used in the actual conduct of warfare. Throughout a century that ended in 1914, the British navy was powerful enough to scare off all comers, while Britain carried out occasional imperial ventures in odd parts of the world. Only as Britain's power weakened were her military forces used to fight a full-scale war. In being used, her military power surely became less useful.

Force is cheap, especially for a status-quo power, if its very existence works against its use. What does it mean, then, to say that the cost of using force has increased while its utility has lessened? It is highly important, indeed useful, to think in "cataclysmic terms," to live in dread of all-out war, and to base military calculations on the forces needed for the ultimate but unlikely crisis. That the United States does so, and that the Soviet Union apparently does too, makes the cataclysm less likely to occur. The web of social and political life is spun out of inclinations and incentives, deterrent threats and punishments. Eliminate the latter two, and the ordering of society depends entirely on the former—a utopian thought impractical this side of Eden. Depend entirely on threat and punishment, and the ordering of society is based on pure coercion. International politics tends toward the latter condition. The daily presence of force and recurrent reliance on it mark the affairs of nations. Since Thucydides in Greece and Kautilya in India, the use of force and the possibility of controlling it have been the preoccupations of international-political studies.[30]

John Herz coined the term "security dilemma" to describe the condition in which states, unsure of one anothers' intentions, arm for the sake of security and in doing so set a vicious circle in motion. Having armed for the sake of security, states feel less secure and buy more arms because the means to anyone's security is a threat to someone else who in

---

29. "The sums spent for the war power is money wasted," he maintained, "if the war power remains unsed for obtaining political advantages. In some cases the mere threat will suffice and the war power thus becomes useful, but others can be obtained only through the warlike use of the war power itself, that is, by war undertaken in time; if this moment is missed, the capital is lost. In this sense, war becomes a great financial enterprise of the State" quoted in Vagts, Alfred (1956), *Defense and Diplomacy: The Soldier and the Conduct of Foreign Relations*. New York: King's Crown Press. p.361.

30. Art, Robert J. and Kenneth N. Waltz (1971). "Technology, strategy, and the uses of force." In Art and Waltz (eds.), *The Use of Force*. Boston: Little, Brown.

turn responds by arming.[31] Whatever the weaponry and however many states in the system, states have to live with their security dilemma, which is produced not by their wills but by their situations. A dilemma cannot be solved; it can more or less readily be dealt with. Force cannot be eliminated. How is peace possible when force takes its awesome nuclear form? We have seen in this chapter that two can deal with the dilemma better than three or more. Second-strike nuclear forces are the principal means used. Those means look almost entirely unusable. Is that a matter of regret? Why is "usable" force preferred—so that the United States and the Soviet Union would be able to fight a war such as great powers used to do on occasion? The whole line of reasoning implied in assertions that the United States and the Soviet Union are hobbled by the unusability of their forces omits the central point. Great powers are best off when the weapons they use to cope with the security dilemma are ones that make the waging of war among them unlikely. Nuclear forces are useful, and their usefulness is reinforced by the extent to which their use is forestalled. The military forces of great powers are most useful and least costly if they are priced only in money and not also in blood.

Odd notions about the usability and usefulness of force result from confused theory and a failure of historical recall. Great powers are never "masters with free hands." They are always "Gullivers," more or less tightly tied. They usually lead troubled lives. After all, they have to contend with one another, and because great powers have great power, that is difficult to do. In some ways their lot may be enviable; in many ways it is not. To give a sufficient example, they fight more wars than lesser states do.[32] Their involvement in wars arises from their position in the international system, not from their national characters. When they are at or near the top, they fight; as they decline, they become peaceful. Think of Spain, Holland, Sweden, and Austria. And those who have declined more recently enjoy a comparable benefit.[33] Some people seem to associate great power with great good fortune, and when fortune does not smile, they conclude that power has evaporated. One wonders why.

As before, great powers find ways to use force, although now not against each other. Where power is seen to be balanced, whether or not the balance is nuclear, it may seem that the resultant of opposing forces is zero. But this is misleading. The vectors of national force do not meet at a point, if only because the power of a state does not resolve into a single vector. Military force is divisible, especially for states that can afford a lot of it. In a nuclear world, contrary to some assertions, the dialectic of inequality does not produce the effective equality of strong and weak states. Nuclear weapons deter nuclear weapons; they also serve to limit escalation. The temptation of one country to employ increasingly larger amounts of force is lessened if its opponent has the ability to raise the ante. Force can be used with less hesitation by those states able to parry, to thrust, and to threaten at varied

---

31. Herz, John H. (January, 1950). "Idealist internationalism and the security dilemma." *World Politics*, vol. 2. p. 157.

32. Wright, Quincy (1965). *A Study of War: Second Edition, with a Commentary on War since 1942*. Chicago: University of Chicago Press. pp. 221-223, Table 22; Woods, Frederick Adams, and Alexander Baltzly (1915). *Is War Diminishing?* Boston: Houghton Mifflin. Table 46.

33. Notice how one is misled by failing to understand how a state's behavior is affected by its placement. With Thucydides, contrast this statement of A. J. P. Taylor's: "For years after the second world war, I continued to believe that there would be another German bid for European supremacy and that we must take precautions against it. Events have proved me totally wrong. I tried to learn lessons from history, which is always a mistake. The Germans have changed their national character" June 4, 1976, "London Diary". *New Statesman*, vol. 91, p. 742.

levels of military endeavor. For more than three decades, power has been narrowly concentrated; and force has been used, not orgiastically as in the world wars of this century, but in a controlled way and for conscious political purposes, albeit not always the right ones. Power may be present when force is not used, but force is also used openly. A catalogue of examples would be both complex and lengthy. On the American side of the ledger it would contain such items as the garrisoning of Berlin, its supply by airlift during the blockade, the stationing of troops in Europe, the establishment of bases in Japan and elsewhere, the waging of war in Korea and Vietnam, and the "quarantine" of Cuba. Seldom if ever has force been more variously, more persistently, and more widely applied; and seldom has it been more consciously used as an instrument of national policy. Since World War II we have seen the political organization and pervasion of power, not the cancellation of force by nuclear stalemate.

Plenty of power has been used, although at times with unhappy results. Just as the state that refrains from applying force is said to betray its weakness, so the state that has trouble in exercising control is said to display the defectiveness of its power. In such a conclusion the elementary error of identifying power with control is evident. If power is identical with control, then those who are free are strong; and their freedom has to be taken as an indication of the weakness of those who have great material strength. But the weak and disorganized are often less amenable to control than those who are wealthy and well disciplined. Here again old truths need to be brought into focus. One old truth, formulated by Georg Simmel, is this: When one "opposes a diffused crowd of enemies, one may oftener gain isolated victories, but it is very hard to arrive at decisive results which definitely fix the relationships of the contestants".[34]

A still older truth, formulated by David Hume, is that "force is always on the side of the governed." "The soldan of Egypt or the emperor of Rome," he went on to say, "might drive his harmless subjects like brute beasts against their sentiments and inclination. But he must, at least, have led his *mamalukes* or *praetorian bands,* like men, by their opinion".[35] The governors, being few in number, depend for the exercise of their rule on the more or less willing assent of their subjects. If sullen disregard is the response to every command, no government can rule. And if a country, because of internal disorder and lack of coherence, is unable to rule itself, no body of foreigners, whatever the military force at its command, can reasonably hope to do so. If insurrection is the problem, then it can hardly be hoped that an alien army will be able to pacify a country that is unable to govern itself. Foreign troops, though not irrelevant to such problems, can only be of indirect help. Military force, used internationally, is a means of establishing control over a territory, not of exercising control within it. The threat of a nation to use military force, whether nuclear or conventional, is preeminently a means of affecting another state's external behavior, of dissuading a state from launching a career of aggression and of meeting the aggression if dissuasion should fail.

Dissuasion, whether by defense or by deterrence, is easier to accomplish than "compellence," to use an apt term invented by Thomas C. Schelling.[36] *Compellence is more difficult to achieve, and its contrivance is a more intricate affair.* In Vietnam, the United States faced

---

34. Simmel, Georg (March, 1904). "The sociology of conflict, II." *American Journal of Sociology,* vol. 9. p. 675.

35. Hume, David (1741). "Of the first principles of government." In Henry D. Aiken (ed.), *Hume's Moral and Political Philosophy.* New York: Hafner, 1948. p. 307.

36. Schelling, Thomas (1966). *Arms and Influence.* New Haven: Yale University Press. p. 70–71.

not merely the task of compelling a particular action but of promoting an effective political order. Those who argue from such a case that force has depreciated in value fail in their analyses to apply their own historical and political knowledge. The master builders of imperial rule, such men as Bugeaud, Galliéni, and Lyautey, played both political and military roles. In like fashion, successful counterrevolutionary efforts have been directed by such men as Templer and Magsaysay, who combined military resources with political instruments.[37] Military forces, whether domestic or foreign, are insufficient for the task of pacification, the more so if a country is rent by faction and if its people are politically engaged and active. Some events represent change; others are mere repetition. The difficulty experienced by the United States in trying to pacify Vietnam and establish a preferred regime is mere repetition. France fought in Algeria between 1830 and 1847 in a similar cause. Britain found Boers terribly troublesome in the war waged against them from 1898 to 1903. France, when she did the fighting, was thought to have the world's best army, and Britain, an all powerful navy.[38] To say that militarily strong states are feeble because they cannot easily bring order to minor states is like saying that a pneumatic hammer is weak because it is not suitable for drilling decayed teeth. It is to confuse the purpose of instruments and to confound the means of external power with the agencies of internal governance. Inability to exercise *political* control over others does not indicate *military* weakness. Strong states cannot do everything with their military forces, as Napoleon acutely realized; but they are able to do things that militarily weak states cannot do. The People's Republic of China can no more solve the problems of governance in some Latin American country than the United States can in Southeast Asia. But the United States can intervene with great military force in far quarters of the world while wielding an effective deterrent against escalation. Such action exceeds the capabilities of all but the strongest of states.

Differences in strength do matter, although not for every conceivable purpose. To deduce the weakness of the powerful from this qualifying clause is a misleading use of words. One sees in such a case as Vietnam not the *weakness* of great military power in a nuclear world but instead a clear illustration of the *limits* of military force in the world of the present as always.

Within the repeated events, an unmentioned difference lurks. Success or failure in peripheral places now means less in material terms than it did to previous great powers. That difference derives from the change in the system. Students of international politics tend to think that wars formerly brought economic and other benefits to the victors and that in contrast the United States cannot now use its military might for positive accomplishment.[39] Such views are wrong on several counts. First, American successes are overlooked. Buttressing the security of Western Europe is a positive accomplishment; so was defending South Korea, and one can easily lengthen the list. Second, the profits of past military ventures are overestimated. Before 1789, war may have been "good business"; it has seldom paid thereafter.[40] Third, why the United States should be interested in extending military control over others when we have so many means of nonforceful leverage is left unspecified. America's internal efforts, moreover, add more to her wealth than any

---

37. Huntington, Samuel P. (1962). "Patterns of violence in world politics." In Huntington (ed.), *Changing Patterns of Military Politics.* New York: Free Press. p. 28.

38. Blainey, Geoffrey (1970). *The Causes of War.* London: Macmillan. p. 205.

39. Morgenthau, Hans J. (1970); Organski, A. F. K. (1968). *World Politics*, 2nd ed. New York: Knopf. pp. 328-29.

imaginable gains scored abroad. The United States, and the Soviet Union as well, have more reason to be satisfied with the status quo than most earlier great powers had. Why should we think of using force for positive accomplishment when we are in the happy position of needing to worry about using force only for the negative purposes of defense and deterrence? To fight is hard, as ever; to refrain from fighting is easier because so little is at stake. Leon Gambetta, French premier after France's defeat by Prussia, remarked that because the old continent is stifling, such outlets as Tunis are needed. This looks like an anticipation of Hobson. The statement was merely expediential, for as Gambetta also said, Alsace-Lorraine must always be in Frenchmen's hearts, although for a long time it could not be on their lips (June 26, 1871). Gains that France might score abroad were valued less for their own sake and more because they might strengthen France for another round in the French-German contest. Jules Ferry, a later premier, argued that France needed colonies lest she slip to the third or fourth rank in Europe.[41] Such a descent would end all hope of retaking Alsace-Lorraine. And Ferry, known as *Le Tonkinoise,* fell from power in 1885 when his southeast Asian ventures seemed to be weakening France rather than adding to the strength she could show in Europe. For the United States in the same part of the world, the big stake, as official statements described it, was internally generatedour honor and credibility, although the definition of those terms was puzzling. As some saw early in that struggle, and as most saw later on, in terms of global politics little was at stake in Vietnam.[42] The international-political insignificance of Vietnam can be understood only in terms of the world's structure. America's failure in Vietnam was tolerable because neither success nor failure mattered much internationally. Victory would not make the world one of American hegemony. Defeat would not make the world one of Russian hegemony. No matter what the outcome, the American-Russian duopoly would endure.

Military power no longer brings political control, but then it never did. Conquering and governing are different processes. Yet public officials and students alike conclude from the age-old difficulty of using force effectively that force is now obsolescent and that international structures can no longer be defined by the distribution of capabilitites across states.

How can one account for the confusion? In two ways. The first, variously argued earlier, is that the usefulness of force is mistakenly identified with its use. Because of their favored positions, the United States and the Soviet Union need to use force less than most earlier great powers did. Force is more useful than ever for upholding the status quo, though not for changing it, and maintaining the status quo is the minimum goal of any great power. Moreover, because the United States has much economic and political leverage over many other states, and because both the United States and the Soviet Union are more nearly self-sufficient than most earlier great powers were, they need hardly use force to secure ends other than their own security. Nearly all unfavorable economic and political outcomes have too little impact to call for their using force to prevent them, and strongly

40. Schumpeter, Joseph A. (1919). "The sociology of imperialism." In Joseph Schumpeter, *Imperialism and Social Classes.* Translated by Heinz Norden. New York: Meridian Books, 1955. p. 18; Sorel, Albert (1885). Europe under the Old Regime. Ch. 1, vol. 1 of *L'Europe et la Revolution Francaise.* Translated by Francis H. Herrick, 1947. New York: Harper and Row, 1964. pp. 1-70; Osgood, Robert E., and Robert W. Tucker (1967). *Force, Order, and Justice.* Baltimore: Johns Hopkins Press. p. 40.

41. Power, Thomas F. (1944). *Jules Ferry and the Renaissance of French Imperialism.* New York: Octagon Books. p. 192.

42. Stoessinger, John G. (1976). shows that this was Kissinger's view, in *Henry Kissinger: The Anguish of Power.* New York: W. W. Norton. Chapter 8.

preferred economic and political outcomes can be sufficiently secured without recourse to force. For achieving economic gains, force has seldom been an efficient means anyway. Because the United States and the Soviet Union are secure in the world, except in terms of each other, they find few international-political reasons for resorting to force. Those who believe that force is less useful reach their conclusion without asking whether there is much reason for today's great powers to use force to coerce other states.

The second source of confusion about power is found in its odd definition. We are misled by the pragmatically formed and technologically influenced American definition of power—a definition that equates power with control. Power is then measured by the ability to get people to do what one wants them to do when otherwise they would not do it.[43] That definition may serve for some purposes, but it ill fits the requirements of politics. To define "power" as "cause" confuses process with outcome. To identify power with control is to assert that only power is needed in order to get one's way. That is obviously false, else what would there be for political and military strategists to do? To use power is to apply one's capabilities in an attempt to change someone else's behavior in certain ways. Whether *A*, in applying its capabilities, gains the wanted compliance of *B* depends on *A*'s capabilities and strategy, on *B*'s capabilities and counterstrategy, and on all of these factors as they are affected by the situation at hand. Power is one cause among others, from which it cannot be isolated. The common relational definition of power omits consideration of how acts and relations are affected by the structure of action. To measure power by compliance rules unintended effects out of consideration, and that takes much of the politics out of politics.

According to the common American definition of power, a failure to get one's way is proof of weakness. In politics, however, powerful agents fail to impress their wills on others in just the ways they intend to. The intention of an act and its result will seldom be identical because the result will be affected by the person or object acted on and conditioned by the environment within which it occurs. What, then, can be substituted for the practically and logically untenable definition? I offer the old and simple notion that an agent is powerful to the extent that he affects others more than they affect him. The weak understand this; the strong may not. Prime Minister Trudeau once said that, for Canada, being America's neighbor "is in some ways like sleeping with an elephant. No matter how friendly or even tempered is the beast . . . one is affected by every twitch and grunt".[44] As the leader of a weak state, Trudeau understands the meaning of our power in ways that we overlook. Because of the weight of our capabilities, American actions have tremendous impact whether or not we fashion effective policies and consciously put our capabilities behind them in order to achieve certain ends.

How is power distributed? What are the effects of a given distribution of power? These two questions are distinct, and the answer to each of them is extremely important politically. In the definition of power just rejected, the two questions merge and become hopelessly confused. Identifying power with control leads one to see weakness wherever one's will is thwarted. Power is a means, and the outcome of its use is necessarily uncertain. To be politically pertinent, power has to be defined in terms of the distribution of capabilities; the extent of one's power cannot be inferred from the results one may or may not get. The paradox that some have found in the so-called impotence of American power disappears if power is given

43. Dahl, Robert A. (July, 1957). "The concept of power." *Behavioral Science*, vol. 2.

44. Turner, Louis (1971). *Invisible Empires*. New York: Harcourt, Brace Jovanovich. p. 166.

a politically sensible definition. Defining power sensibly, and comparing the plight of present and of previous great powers, shows that the usefulness of power has increased.

VI

International politics is necessarily a small-number system. The advantages of having a few more great powers is at best slight. We have found instead that the advantages of subtracting a few and arriving at two are decisive. The three-body problem has yet to be solved by physicists. Can political scientists or policymakers hope to do better in charting the courses of three or more interacting states? Cases that lie between the simple interaction of two entities and the statistically predictable interactions of very many are the most difficult to unravel. We have seen the complications in the military affairs of multipolar worlds. The fates of great powers are closely linked. The great powers of a multipolar world, in taking steps to make their likely fates happier, at times need help from others. Friedrich Meinecke described the condition of Europe at the time of Frederick the Great this way: "A set of isolated power-States, alone yet linked together by their mutually grasping ambitions—that was the state of affairs to which the development of the European State-organism had brought things since the close of the Middle Ages".[45] Militarily and economically, interdependence developed as the self-sufficient localities of feudal Europe were drawn together by modern states. The great powers of a bipolar world are more self-sufficient, and interdependence loosens between them. This condition distinguishes the present system from the previous one. Economically, America and Russia are markedly less interdependent and noticeably less dependent on others than earlier great powers were. Militarily, the decrease of interdependence is more striking still, for neither great power can be linked to any other great power in "their mutually grasping ambitions."

Two great powers can deal with each other better than more can. Are they also able to deal with some of the world's common problems better than more numerous great powers can? I have so far emphasized the negative side of power. *Power does not bring control.* What does it bring? [We must consider] the possibilities of, and the need for, international management and control. . . .

---

45. Meinecke, Friedrich (1924). *Machiavellism.* Translated by Douglas Scott. London: Routledge and Kegan Paul, 1957. p. 321.

Anarchic Orders and Balances of Power

Kenneth N. Waltz

How can a theory of international politics be constructed? Just as any theory must be. First, one must conceive of international politics as a bounded realm or domain; second, one must discover some law-like regularities within it; and third, one must develop a way of explaining the observed regularities. . . . [We have] shown how political structures account for some recurrent aspects of the behavior of states and for certain repeated and enduring patterns. Wherever agents and agencies are coupled by force and competition rather than by authority and law, we expect to find such behaviors and outcomes. They are closely identified with the approach to politics suggested by the rubric, Realpolitik. The elements of Realpolitik, exhaustively listed, are these: The ruler's, and later the state's, interest provides the spring of action; the necessities of policy arise from the unregulated competition of states; calculation based on these necessities can discover the policies that will best serve a state's interests; success is the ultimate test of policy, and success is defined as preserving and strengthening the state. Ever since Machiavelli, interest and necessity—and raison d'état, the phrase that comprehends them—have remained the key concepts of Realpolitik. From Machiavelli through Meinecke and Morgenthau the elements of the approach and the reasoning remain constant. Machiavelli stands so clearly as the exponent of Realpolitik that one easily slips into thinking that he developed the closely associated idea of balance of power as well. Although he did not, his conviction that politics can be explained in its own terms established the ground on which balance-of-power theory can be built.

Realpolitik indicates the methods by which foreign policy is conducted and provides a rationale for them. Structural constraints explain why the methods are repeatedly used despite differences in the persons and states who use them. Balance-of-power theory purports to explain the result that such methods produce. Rather, that is what the theory should do. If there is any distinctively political theory of international politics, balance-of-power theory is it. And yet one cannot find a statement of the theory that is generally accepted. Carefully surveying the copious balance-of-power literature, Ernst Haas discovered eight distinct meanings of the term, and Martin Wight found nine (1953, 1966). Hans Morgenthau, in his profound historical and analytic treatment of the subject, makes use of four different definitions (1973). Balance of power is seen by some as being akin to a law of nature; by others, as simply an outrage. Some view it as a guide to statesmen; others as a cloak that disguises their imperialist policies. Some believe that a balance of power is the best guarantee of the security of states and the peace of the world; others, that it has ruined states by causing most of the wars they have fought.[1]

1. Along with the explication of balance-of-power theory in the pages that follow, the reader may wish to consult a historical study of balance-of-power politics in practice. The best brief work is Wight (1973).

KENNETH WALTZ is an adjunct professor of political science at Columbia University.

To believe that one can cut through such confusion may seem quixotic. I shall nevertheless try. It will help to hark back to several basic propositions about theory. (1) A theory contains at least one theoretical assumption. Such assumptions are not factual. One therefore cannot legitimately ask if they are true, but only if they are useful. (2) Theories must be evaluated in terms of what they claim to explain. Balance-of-power theory claims to explain the results of states' actions, under given conditions, and those results may not be foreshadowed in any of the actors' motives or be contained as objectives in their policies. (3) Theory, as a general explanatory system, cannot account for particularities.

Most of the confusions in balance-of-power theory, and criticisms of it, derive from misunderstanding these three points. A balance-of-power theory, properly stated, begins with assumptions about states: They are unitary actors who, at a minimum, seek their own preservation and, at a maximum, drive for universal domination. States, or those who act for them, try in more or less sensible ways to use the means available in order to achieve the ends in view. Those means fall into two categories: internal efforts (moves to increase economic capability, to increase military strength, to develop clever strategies) and external efforts (moves to strengthen and enlarge one's own alliance or to weaken and shrink an opposing one). The external game of alignment and realignment requires three or more players, and it is usually said that balance-of-power systems require at least that number. The statement is false, for in a two-power system the politics of balance continue, but the way to compensate for an incipient external disequilibrium is primarily by intensifying one's internal efforts. To the assumptions of the theory we then add the condition for its operation: that two or more states coexist in a self-help system, one with no superior agent to come to the aid of states that may be weakening or to deny to any of them the use of whatever instruments they think will serve their purposes. The theory, then, is built up from the assumed motivations of states and the actions that correspond to them. It describes the constraints that arise from the system that those actions produce, and it indicates the expected outcome: namely, the formation of balances of power. Balance-of-power theory is microtheory precisely in the economist's sense. The system, like a market in economics, is made by the actions and interactions of its units, and the theory is based on assumptions about their behavior.

A self-help system is one in which those who do not help themselves, or who do so less effectively than others, will fail to prosper, will lay themselves open to dangers, will suffer. Fear of such unwanted consequences stimulates states to behave in ways that tend toward the creation of balances of power. Notice that the theory requires no assumptions of rationality or of constancy of will on the part of all of the actors. The theory says simply that if some do relatively well, others will emulate them or fall by the wayside. Obviously, the system won't work if all states lose interest in preserving themselves. It will, however, continue to work if some states do, while others do not, choose to lose their political identities, say, through amalgamation. Nor need it be assumed that all of the competing states are striving relentlessly to increase their power. The possibility that force may be used by some states to weaken or destroy others does, however, make it difficult for them to break out of the competitive system.

The meaning and importance of the theory are made clear by examining prevalent misconceptions of it. Recall our first proposition about theory. A theory contains assumptions that are theoretical, not factual. One of the most common misunderstandings of balance-of-power theory centers on this point. The theory is criticized because its assumptions are erroneous. The following statement can stand for a host of others:

If nations were in fact unchanging units with no permanent ties to each other, and if all were motivated primarily by a drive to maximize their power, except for a single balancer whose aim was to prevent any nation from achieving preponderant power, a balance of power might in fact result. But we have seen that these assumptions are not correct, and since the assumptions of the theory are wrong, the conclusions are also in error (Organski 1968, p. 292).

The author's incidental error is that he has compounded a sentence some parts of which are loosely stated assumptions of the theory, and other parts not. His basic error lies in misunderstanding what an assumption is. From previous discussion, we know that assumptions are neither true nor false and that they are essential for the construction of theory. We can freely admit that states are in fact not unitary, purposive actors. States pursue many goals, which are often vaguely formulated and inconsistent. They fluctuate with the changing currents of domestic politics, are prey to the vagaries of a shifting cast of political leaders, and are influenced by the outcomes of bureaucratic struggles. But all of this has always been known, and it tells us nothing about the merits of balance-of-power theory.

A further confusion relates to our second proposition about theory. Balance-of-power theory claims to explain a result (the recurrent formation of balances of power), which may not accord with the intentions of any of the units whose actions combine to produce that result. To contrive and maintain a balance may be the aim of one or more states, but then again it may not be. According to the theory, balances of power tend to form whether some or all states consciously aim to establish and maintain a balance, or whether some or all states aim for universal domination.[2] Yet many, and perhaps most, statements of balance-of-power theory attribute the maintenance of a balance to the separate states as a motive. David Hume, in his classic essay "Of the Balance of Power," offers "the maxim of preserving the balance of power" as a constant rule of prudent politics (1742, pp. 142-44). So it may be, but it has proved to be an unfortunately short step from the belief that a high regard for preserving a balance is at the heart of wise statesmanship to the belief that states must follow the maxim if a balance of power is to be maintained. This is apparent in the first of Morgenthau's four definitions of the term: namely, "a policy aimed at a certain state of affairs." The reasoning then easily becomes tautological. If a balance of power is to be maintained, the policies of states must aim to uphold it. If a balance of power is in fact maintained, we can conclude that their aim was accurate. If a balance of power is not produced, we can say that the theory's assumption is erroneous. Finally, and this completes the drift toward the reification of a concept, if the purpose of states is to uphold a balance, the purpose of the balance is "to maintain the stability of the system without destroying the multiplicity of the elements composing it." Reification has obviously occurred where one reads, for example, of the balance operating "successfully" and of the difficulty that nations have in applying it (1973, pp. 167-74, 202-207).

Reification is often merely the loose use of language or the employment of metaphor to make one's prose more pleasing. In this case, however, the theory has been drastically distorted, and not only by introducing the notion that if a balance is to be formed, somebody must want it and must work for it. The further distortion of the theory arises when rules are derived from the results of states' actions and then illogically prescribed to the

2. Looking at states over a wide span of time and space, Dowty concludes that in no case were shifts in alliances produced "by considerations of an overall balance of power" (1969, p. 95).

actors as duties. A possible effect is turned into a necessary cause in the form of a stipulated rule. Thus, it is said, "the balance of power" can "impose its restraints upon the power aspirations of nations" only if they first "restrain themselves by accepting the system of the balance of power as the common framework of their endeavors." Only if states recognize "the same rules of the game" and play "for the same limited stakes" can the balance of power fulfill "its functions for international stability and national independence" (Morgenthau 1973, pp. 219-20).

The closely related errors that fall under our second proposition about theory are, as we have seen, twin traits of the field of international politics: namely, to assume a necessary correspondence of motive and result and to infer rules for the actors from the observed results of their action. What has gone wrong can be made clear by recalling the economic analogy (Chapter 5, part III, 1). In a purely competitive economy, everyone's striving to make a profit drives the profit rate downward. Let the competition continue long enough under static conditions, and everyone's profit will be zero. To infer from that result that everyone, or anyone, is seeking to minimize profit, and that the competitors must adopt that goal as a rule in order for the system to work, would be absurd. And yet in international politics one frequently finds that rules inferred from the results of the interactions of states are prescribed to the actors and are said to be a condition of the system's maintenance. Such errors, often made, are also often pointed out, though seemingly to no avail. S. F. Nadel has put the matter simply: "an orderliness abstracted from behaviour cannot guide behaviour" (Nadel 1957, p. 148; cf. Durkheim 1893, pp. 366, 418; Shubik 1959, pp. 11, 32).

Analytic reasoning applied where a systems approach is needed leads to the laying down of all sorts of conditions as prerequisites to balances of power forming and tending toward equilibrium and as general preconditions of world stability and peace. Some require that the number of great powers exceed two; others that a major power be willing to play the role of balancer. Some require that military technology not change radically or rapidly; others that the major states abide by arbitrarily specified rules. But balances of power form in the absence of the "necessary" conditions, and since 1945 the world has been stable, and the world of major powers remarkably peaceful, even though international conditions have not conformed to theorists' stipulations. Balance-of-power politics prevail wherever two, and only two, requirements are met: that the order be anarchic and that it be populated by units wishing to survive.

For those who believe that if a result is to be produced, someone, or everyone, must want it and must work for it, it follows that explanation turns ultimately on what the separate states are like. If that is true, then theories at the national level, or lower, will sufficiently explain international politics. If, for example, the equilibrium of a balance is maintained through states abiding by rules, then one needs an explanation of how agreement on the rules is achieved and maintained. One does not need a balance-of-power theory, for balances would result from a certain kind of behavior explained perhaps by a theory about national psychology or bureaucratic politics. A balance-of-power theory could not be constructed because it would have nothing to explain. If the good or bad motives of states result in their maintaining balances or disrupting them, then the notion of a balance of power becomes merely a framework organizing one's account of what happened, and that is indeed its customary use. A construction that starts out to be a theory ends up as a set of categories. Categories then multiply rapidly to cover events that the embryo theory had not contemplated. The quest for explanatory power turns into a search for descriptive adequacy.

Finally, and related to our third proposition about theory in general, balance-of-power theory is often criticized because it does not explain the particular policies of states. True, the theory does not tell us why state X made a certain move last Tuesday. To expect it to do so would be like expecting the theory of universal gravitation to explain the wayward path of a falling leaf. A theory at one level of generality cannot answer questions about matters at a different level of generality. Failure to notice this is one error on which the criticism rests. Another is to mistake a theory of international politics for a theory of foreign policy. Confusion about the explanatory claims made by a properly stated balance-of-power theory is rooted in the uncertainty of the distinction drawn between national and international politics or in the denials that the distinction should be made. For those who deny the distinction, for those who devise explanations that are entirely in terms of interacting units, explanations of international politics are explanations of foreign policy, and explanations of foreign policy are explanations of international politics. Others mix their explanatory claims and confuse the problem of understanding international politics with the problem of understanding foreign policy. Morgenthau, for example, believes that problems of predicting foreign policy and of developing theories about it make international-political theories difficult, if not impossible, to contrive (1970b, pp. 253-58). But the difficulties of explaining foreign policy work against contriving theories of international politics only if the latter reduces to the former. Graham Allison betrays a similar confusion. His three "models" purport to offer alternative approaches to the study of international politics. Only model I, however, is an approach to the study of international politics. Models II and III are approaches to the study of foreign policy. Offering the bureaucratic politics approach as an alternative to the state-as-an-actor approach is like saying that a theory of the firm is an alternative to a theory of the market, a mistake no competent economist would make (1971; cf. Allison and Halperin 1972). If Morgenthau and Allison were economists and their thinking continued to follow the same pattern, they would have to argue that the uncertainties of corporate policy work against the development of market theory. They have confused and merged two quite different matters.[3]

Any theory covers some matters and leaves other matters aside. Balance-of-power theory is a theory about the results produced by the uncoordinated actions of states. The theory makes assumptions about the interests and motives of states, rather than explaining them. What it does explain are the constraints that confine all states. The clear perception of constraints provides many clues to the expected reactions of states, but by itself the theory cannot explain those reactions. They depend not only on international constraints but also on the characteristics of states. How will a particular state react? To answer that question we need not only a theory of the market, so to speak, but also a theory about the firms that compose it. What will a state have to react to? Balance-of-power theory can give general and useful answers to that question. The theory explains why a certain similarity of behavior is expected from similarly situated states. The expected behavior is similar, not identical. To explain the expected differences in national responses, a theory would have to show how the different internal structures of states affect their external policies and actions. A theory of foreign policy would not predict the detailed content of policy but

3. The confusion is widespread and runs both ways. Thus Herbert Simon thinks the goal of classical economic theorists is unattainable because he wrongly believes that they were trying to predict the behavior of rational man without making an empirical investigation of his psychological properties. (1957, p. 199).

instead would lead to different expectations about the tendencies and styles of different countries' policies. Because the national and the international levels are linked, theories of both types, if they are any good, tell us some things, but not the same things, about behavior and outcomes at both levels.

[Previously] I constructed a systems theory of international politics. In this chapter, I have stated balance-of-power theory as a further development of that theory. [Later] I shall refine the theory by showing how expectations vary with changes in the structure of international systems. At this point I pause to ask how good the theory so far developed is.

Before subjecting a theory to tests, one asks whether the theory is internally consistent and whether it tells us some things of interest that we would not know in its absence. That the theory meets those requirements does not mean that it can survive tests. Many people prefer tests that, if flunked, falsify a theory. Some people, following Karl Popper (1934, Chapter 1), insist that theories are tested only by attempting to falsify them. Confirmations do not count because, among other reasons, confirming cases may be offered as proof while consciously or not cases likely to confound the theory are avoided. This difficulty, I suggest later, is lessened by choosing hard cases—situations, for example, in which parties have strong reasons to behave contrary to the predictions of one's theory. Confirmations are also rejected because numerous tests that appear to confirm a theory are negated by one falsifying instance. The conception of theory. . . , however, opens the possibility of devising tests that confirm. If a theory depicts a domain, and displays its organization and the connections among its parts, then we can compare features of the observed domain with the picture the theory has limned (cf. Harris 1970). We can ask whether expected behaviors and outcomes are repeatedly found where the conditions contemplated by the theory obtain.

Structural theories, moreover, gain plausibility if similarities of behavior are observed across realms that are different in substance but similar in structure, and if differences of behavior are observed where realms are similar in substance but different in structure. This special advantage is won: international-political theory gains credibility from the confirmation of certain theories in economics, sociology, anthropology, and other such nonpolitical fields.

Testing theories, of course, always means inferring expectations, or hypotheses, from them and testing those expectations. Testing theories is a difficult and subtle task, made so by the interdependence of fact and theory, by the elusive relation between reality and theory as an instrument for its apprehension. Questions of truth and falsity are somehow involved, but so are questions of usefulness and uselessness. In the end, one sticks with the theory that reveals most, even if its validity is suspect. I shall say more about the acceptance and rejection of theories elsewhere. Here I say only enough to make the relevance of a few examples of theory testing clear. Others can then easily be thought of. Many are provided in the first part of this chapter and in all parts of the next three, although I have not always labeled them as tests or put them in testable form.

Tests are easy to think up, once one has a theory to test, but they are hard to carry through. Given the difficulty of testing any theory, and the added difficulty of testing theories in such non- experimental fields as international politics, we should exploit all of the ways of testing I have mentioned—by trying to falsify, by devising hard confirmatory tests, by comparing features of the real and the theoretical worlds, by comparing behaviors in realms of similar and of different structure. Any good theory raises many expectations.

Multiplying hypotheses and varying tests are all the more important because the results of testing theories are necessarily problematic. That a single hypothesis appears to hold true may not be very impressive. A theory becomes plausible if many hypotheses inferred from it are successfully subjected to tests.

Knowing a little bit more about testing, we can now ask whether expectations drawn from our theory can survive subjection to tests. What will some of the expectations be? Two that are closely related arise in the above discussion. According to the theory, balances of power recurrently form, and states tend to emulate the successful policies of others. Can these expectations be subjected to tests? In principle, the answer is "yes." Within a given arena and over a number of years, we should find the military power of weaker and smaller states or groupings of states growing more rapidly, or shrinking more slowly, than that of stronger and larger ones. And we should find widespread imitation among competing states. In practice, to check such expectations against historical observations is difficult.

Two problems are paramount. First, though balance-of-power theory offers some predictions, the predictions are indeterminate. Because only a loosely defined and inconstant condition of balance is predicted, it is difficult to say that any given distribution of power falsifies the theory. The theory, moreover, does not lead one to expect that emulation among states will proceed to the point where competitors become identical. What will be imitated, and how quickly and closely? Because the theory does not give precise answers, falsification again is difficult. Second, although states may be disposed to react to international constraints and incentives in accordance with the theory's expectations, the policies and actions of states are also shaped by their internal conditions. The failure of balances to form, and the failure of some states to conform to the successful practices of other states, can too easily be explained away by pointing to effects produced by forces that lie outside of the theory's purview.

In the absence of theoretical refinements that fix expectations with certainty and in detail, what can we do? As I have just suggested, and as the sixth rule for testing theories set forth in Chapter 1 urges, we should make tests ever more difficult. If we observe outcomes that the theory leads us to expect even though strong forces work against them, the theory will begin to command belief. To confirm the theory one should not look mainly to the eighteenth-century heyday of the balance of power when great powers in convenient numbers interacted and were presumably able to adjust to a shifting distribution of power by changing partners with a grace made possible by the absence of ideological and other cleavages. Instead, one should seek confirmation through observation of difficult cases. One should, for example, look for instances of states allying, in accordance with the expectations the theory gives rise to, even though they have strong reasons not to cooperate with one another. (The alliance of France and Russia, made formal in 1894, is one such instance.) One should, for example, look for instances of states making internal efforts to strengthen themselves, however distasteful or difficult such efforts might be. The United States and the Soviet Union following World War II provide such instances: the United States by rearming despite having demonstrated a strong wish not to by dismantling the most powerful military machine the world had ever known; the Soviet Union by maintaining about three million men under arms while striving to acquire a costly new military technology despite the terrible destruction she had suffered in war.

These examples tend to confirm the theory. We find states forming balances of power whether or not they wish to. They also show the difficulties of testing. Germany and Austria-Hungary formed their Dual Alliance in 1879. Since detailed inferences cannot be drawn from the theory, we cannot say just when other states are expected to counter this move. France and Russia waited until 1894. Does this show the theory false by suggesting that states may or may not be brought into balance? We should neither quickly conclude that it does nor lightly chalk the delayed response off to "friction." Instead, we should examine diplomacy and policy in the 15-year interval to see whether the theory serves to explain and broadly predict the actions and reactions of states and to see whether the delay is out of accord with the theory. Careful judgment is needed. For this, historians' accounts serve better than the historical summary I might provide.

The theory leads us to expect states to behave in ways that result in balances forming. To infer that expectation from the theory is not impressive if balancing is a universal pattern of political behavior, as is sometimes claimed. It is not. Whether political actors balance each other or climb on the bandwagon depends on the system's structure. Political parties, when choosing their presidential candidates, dramatically illustrate both points. When nomination time approaches and no one is established as the party's strong favorite, a number of would-be leaders contend. Some of them form coalitions to check the progress of others. The maneuvering and balancing of would-be leaders when the party lacks one is like the external behavior of states. But this is the pattern only during the leaderless period. As soon as someone looks like the winner, nearly all jump on the bandwagon rather than continuing to build coalitions intended to prevent anyone from winning the prize of power. Bandwagoning, not balancing, becomes the characteristic behavior.[4]

Bandwagoning and balancing behavior are in sharp contrast. Internally, losing candidates throw in their lots with the winner. Everyone wants someone to win; the members of a party want a leader established even while they disagree on who it should be. In a competition for the position of leader, bandwagoning is sensible behavior where gains are possible even for the losers and where losing does not place their security in jeopardy. Externally, states work harder to increase their own strength, or they combine with others, if they are falling behind. In a competition for the position of leader, balancing is sensible behavior where the victory of one coalition over another leaves weaker members of the winning coalition at the mercy of the stronger ones. Nobody wants anyone else to win; none of the great powers wants one of their number to emerge as the leader.

If two coalitions form and one of them weakens, perhaps because of the political disorder of a member, we expect the extent of the other coalition's military preparation to slacken or its unity to lessen. The classic example of the latter effect is the breaking apart of a war-winning coalition in or just after the moment of victory. We do not expect the strong to combine with the strong in order to increase the extent of their power over others, but rather to square off and look for allies who might help them. In anarchy, security is the highest end. Only if survival is assured can states safely seek such other goals as tranquility, profit, and power. Because power is a means and not an end, states prefer to join the weaker of two coalitions. They cannot let power, a possibly useful means, become the end they pursue. The goal the system encourages them to seek is security. Increased power may or may not serve that end. Given two coalitions, for example, the greater success of one in drawing members to it may tempt the other to risk preventive war, hoping for victory through surprise before disparities widen. If states wished to maximize power, they would join the stronger side, and we would see not balances forming but a world hegemony forged. This does not happen because balancing, not bandwagoning, is the behavior

4. Stephen Van Evera suggested using "bandwagoning" to serve as the opposite of "balancing."

induced by the system. The first concern of states is not to maximize power but to maintain their positions in the system.

Secondary states, if they are free to choose, flock to the weaker side; for it is the stronger side that threatens them. On the weaker side, they are both more appreciated and safer, provided, of course, that the coalition they join achieves enough defensive or deterrent strength to dissuade adversaries from attacking. Thus Thucydides records that in the Peloponnesian War the lesser city states of Greece cast the stronger Athens as the tyrant and the weaker Sparta as their liberator (circa 400 B.C., Book v, Chapter 17). According to Werner Jaeger, Thucydides thought this "perfectly natural in the circumstances," but saw "that the parts of tyrant and liberator did not correspond with any permanent moral quality in these states but were simply masks which would one day be interchanged to the astonishment of the beholder when the balance of power was altered" (1939, I, 397). This shows a nice sense of how the placement of states affects their behavior and even colors their characters. It also supports the proposition that states balance power rather than maximize it. States can seldom afford to make maximizing power their goal. International politics is too serious a business for that.

The theory depicts international politics as a competitive realm. Do states develop the characteristics that competitors are expected to display? The question poses another test for the theory. The fate of each state depends on its responses to what other states do. The possibility that conflict will be conducted by force leads to competition in the arts and the instruments of force. Competition produces a tendency toward the sameness of the competitors. Thus Bismarck's startling victories over Austria in 1866 and over France in 1870 quickly led the major continental powers (and Japan) to imitate the Prussian military staff system, and the failure of Britain and the United States to follow the pattern simply indicated that they were outside the immediate arena of competition. Contending states imitate the military innovations contrived by the country of greatest capability and ingenuity. And so the weapons of major contenders, and even their strategies, begin to look much the same all over the world. Thus at the turn of the century Admiral Alfred von Tirpitz argued successfully for building a battleship fleet on the grounds that Germany could challenge Britain at sea only with a naval doctrine and weapons similar to hers (Art 1973, p. 16).

The effects of competition are not confined narrowly to the military realm. Socialization to the system should also occur. Does it? Again, because we can almost always find confirming examples if we look hard, we try to find cases that are unlikely to lend credence to the theory. One should look for instances of states conforming to common international practices even though for internal reasons they would prefer not to. The behavior of the Soviet Union in its early years is one such instance. The Bolsheviks in the early years of their power preached international revolution and flouted the conventions of diplomacy. They were saying, in effect, "we will not be socialized to this system." The attitude was well expressed by Trotsky, who, when asked what he would do as foreign minister, replied, "I will issue some revolutionary proclamations to the peoples and then close up the joint" (quoted in Von Laue 1963, p. 235). In a competitive arena, however, one party may need the assistance of others. Refusal to play the political game may risk one's own destruction. The pressures of competition were rapidly felt and reflected in the Soviet Union's diplomacy. Thus Lenin, sending foreign minister Chicherin to the Genoa Conference of 1922, bade him farewell with this caution: "Avoid big words" (quoted in Moore 1950, p. 204). Chicherin, who personified the carefully tailored traditional diplomat rather than the simply uniformed revolutionary, was to refrain from inflammatory rhetoric for the sake of working deals. These he successfully completed with that other pariah power and ideological enemy, Germany.

The close juxtaposition of states promotes their sameness through the disadvantages that arise from a failure to conform to successful practices. It is this "sameness," an effect of the system, that is so often attributed to the acceptance of so-called rules of state behavior. Chiliastic rulers occasionally come to power. In power, most of them quickly change their ways. They can refuse to do so, and yet hope to survive, only if they rule countries little affected by the competition of states. The socialization of nonconformist states proceeds at a pace that is set by the extent of their involvement in the system. And that is another testable statement.

The theory leads to many expectations about behaviors and outcomes. From the theory, one predicts that states will engage in balancing behavior, whether or not balanced power is the end of their acts. From the theory, one predicts a strong tendency toward balance in the system. The expectation is not that a balance, once achieved, will be maintained, but that a balance, once disrupted, will be restored in one way or another. Balances of power recurrently form. Since the theory depicts international politics as a competitive system, one predicts more specifically that states will display characteristics common to competitors: namely, that they will imitate each other and become socialized to their system. In this chapter, I have suggested ways of making these propositions more specific and concrete so as to test them. In remaining chapters, as the theory is elaborated and refined, additional testable propositions will appear.

Structural Realism After the Cold War

Kenneth N. Waltz

BALANCING POWER

With the demise of the Soviet Union, the international political system became unipolar. In the light of structural theory, unipolarity appears as the least durable of international configurations. This is so for two main reasons. One is that dominant powers take on too many tasks beyond their own borders, thus weakening themselves in the long run. Ted Robert Gurr, after examining 336 polities, reached the same conclusion that Robert G. Wesson had reached earlier: "Imperial decay is . . . primarily a result of the misuse of power which follows inevitably from its concentration."[1] The other reason for the short duration of unipolarity is that even if a dominant power behaves with moderation, restraint, and forbearance, weaker states will worry about its future behavior. America's founding fathers warned against the perils of power in the absence of checks and balances. Is unbalanced power less of a danger in international than in national politics? Throughout the Cold War, what the United States and the Soviet Union did, and how they interacted, were dominant factors in international politics. The two countries. however, constrained each other. Now the United States is alone in the world. As nature abhors a vacuum, so international politics abhors unbalanced power. Faced by unbalanced power, some states try to increase their own strength or they ally with others to bring the international distribution of power into balance. The reactions of other states to the drive for dominance of Charles I of Spain, of Louis XIV and Napoleon I of France, of Wilhelm II and Adolph Hitler of Germany, illustrate the point.

Will the preponderant power of the United States elicit similar reactions? Unbalanced power, whoever wields it, is a potential danger to others. The powerful state may, and the United States does, think of itself as acting for the sake of peace, justice, and well-being in the world. These terms, however, are defined to the liking of the powerful, which may conflict with the preferences and interests of others. In international politics, overwhelming power repels and leads others to try to balance against it. With benign intent, the United States has behaved, and until its power is brought into balance, will continue to behave in ways that sometimes frighten others.

For almost half a century, the constancy of the Soviet threat produced a constancy of American policy. Other countries could rely on the United States for protection because protecting them seemed to serve our security interests. Even so, beginning in the 1950s, West European countries and, beginning in the 1970s, Japan had increasing doubts about the reliability of the American nuclear deterrent. As Soviet strength increased, West European countries began to wonder whether America could be counted on to use its deterrent on their behalf, thus risking its own cities. When President Carter moved to reduce Ameri-

[1] Quoted by Ted Robert Gurr. "Persistence and Change in Political Systems. l800-1971." *American Political Science Review* 68, 4 (December 1974), p 1504 Cf. Paul Kennedy. *The Rise and Fall of Great Powers: Economic Change and Military Conflict from 1500 to 2000* (New York: Random House. 1987).

Unpublished paper, April, 1999. Reprinted with permission of the author.

can troops in Korea, and later when the Soviet Union invaded Afghanistan and strengthened its forces in the Far East, Japan developed similar worries.

With the disappearance of the Soviet Union, the United States no longer faces a major threat to its security. As General Colin Powell said when he was chairman of the Joint Chiefs of Staff: "I'm running out of demons. I'm running out of enemies. I'm down to Castro and Kim II Sung."[2] Constancy of threat produces constancy of policy; absence of threat permits policy to become capricious. When few if any vital interests are endangered, a country's policy becomes sporadic and self willed.

The absence of serious threats to American security gives the United States wide latitude in making foreign-policy choices. A dominant power acts internationally only when the spirit moves it. One example is enough to show this. When Yugoslavia's collapse was followed by genocidal war in successor states, the United States failed to respond until Senator Robert Dole moved to make Bosnia's peril an issue in the forthcoming presidential election; and it acted not for the sake of its own security but to maintain its leadership position in Europe. American policy was generated not by external security interests but by internal political pressure and national ambition.

Aside from specific threats it may pose, unbalanced power leaves weaker states feeling uneasy and gives them reason to strengthen their positions. The United States has a long history of intervening in weak states, often with the intention of bringing democracy to them. American behavior over the past century in Central America provides little evidence of self-restraint in the absence of countervailing power. Contemplating our history and measuring our capabilities, other countries may well wish for ways to fend off our benign ministrations. Concentrated power invites distrust because it is so easily misused. To understand why some states want to bring power into a semblance of balance is easy, but with power so sharply skewed, what country or group of countries has the material capability and the political will to bring the "unipolar moment" to an end?

The expectation that following victory in a great war a new balance of power will form is firmly grounded in both history and theory. The last four grand coalitions (two against Napoleon and one in each of the World Wars of the twentieth century) collapsed once victory was achieved. Victories in major wars leave the balance of power badly skewed. The winning side emerges as a dominant coalition. The international equilibrium is broken; theory leads one to expect its restoration.

Clearly something has changed. Some believe that America is so nice that, despite the dangers of unbalanced power, others do not feel the fear that would spur them to action. Michael Mastanduno, among others, believes this to be so, although he ends his essay with the thought that "eventually power will check power."[3] Others believe that the leaders of states have learned that playing the game of power politics is costly and unnecessary. I shall say more about that in another essay, but in fact the explanation for sluggish balancing is a simple one. In the aftermath of earlier great wars, the materials for constructing a new balance were readily at hand. Previous wars left a sufficient number of great powers

---

2. *Communism's Collapse Poses a Challenge to America's Military,* U.S. News and World Report 3 (October 14, 1991), p. 28.

3. Michael Mastanduno. "Preserving the Unipolar Moment: Realist Theories and U.S. Grand Strategy after the Cold War." *International Security* 21 (Spring 1997), p. 488. And see Josef Joffe's interesting analysis of America's role. "'Britain' or 'Bismarck?' Toward an American Grand Strategy after Bipolarity;." *International Security* 19 (Spring 1995).

standing to permit a new balance to be rather easily constructed. Theory enables one to say that a new balance of power will form but not to say how long it will take. International conditions determine that. Those who refer to the unipolar moment are right. In our perspective, the new balance is emerging slowly; in historical perspectives, it will come in the blink of an eye.

I ended a 1993 article this way: "One may hope that America's internal preoccupations will produce not an isolationist policy, which has become impossible, but a forbearance that will give other countries at long last the chance to deal with their own problems and make their own mistakes. But I would not bet on it."[4] I should think that few would do so now. Charles Kegley has said, sensibly, that if the world becomes multipolar once again, realists will be vindicated.[5] Seldom do signs of vindication appear so promptly.

The candidates for becoming the next great powers, and thus restoring a balance, are the European Union, China, and Japan, and, in a more distant future, Russia.

The countries of the European Union have been remarkably successful in integrating their national economies. The achievement of a large measure of economic integration without a corresponding political unity is an accomplishment without historical precedent. On questions of foreign and military policy, however, the European Union can act only with the consent of its members, making bold or risky action impossible. The European Union has all the tools—population, resources, technology, and military capabilities—but lacks the organizational ability and the collective will to use them. As Jacques Delors said when he was President of the European Commission: "It will be for the European Council, consisting of heads of state and government . . . to agree on the essential interests they share and which they will agree to defend and promote together."[6] Policies that must be arrived at by consensus can be carried out only when they are fairly inconsequential. Inaction as Yugoslavia sank into chaos and war signaled that Europe will not act to stop wars even among near neighbors. Western Europe was unable to make its own foreign and military policies when it was an organization of six or nine states living in fear of the Soviet Union. With less pressure and more members, it has even less hope of doing so now. Only when the United States decides on a policy are European countries able to follow it.

One must wonder whether Europe will remain in its supine position forever. Now as earlier, European leaders express discontent with Europe's secondary position, chafe at America's making must of the important decisions, and show a desire to direct their own destiny. French leaders often vent their frustration and pine for a world, as Foreign Minister Hubert Védrine recently put it, "of several poles, not just a single one." President Jacques Chirac and Prime Minister Lionel Jospin call for a strengthening of such multilateral institutions as the IMF and the UN, although how this would diminish America's influence is not explained. More to the point, Védrine complains that since President Kennedy, Americans have talked of a European pillar for the alliance, a pillar which is never built.[7] German and British leaders now more often express similar discontent. Europe, however, will not be able to claim a louder voice in alliance affairs unless it builds

4. Waltz, "The Emerging Structure of International Politics," p. 79.

5. Charles W. Kegley, Jr. "The Neoidealist Moment in International Studies? Realist Myths and the New International Realities." *International Studies Quarterly* 37 (June. 1993). p. 149.

6. Jacques Delors. "European Integration and Security,"" *Survival* 33 (.March/April 1991), p. 106.

7. Craig R. Whitney,. NATO at 50: With Nations at Odds, Is It a Misalliance?" *New York Times*, February 15 1999, p. Al.

a platform for giving it expression. If Europeans ever mean to write a tune to go with their libretto, they will have to develop the unity in foreign and military affairs that they are achieving in economic matters. If French leaders were to propose merging their nuclear force with Britain's to form the nucleus of a European military organization, the United States and the world would begin to treat Europe as a major force.

The European Economic Community was formed in 1957 and has grown incrementally to its present proportions. But where is the incremental route to a European foreign and military policy to be found? European leaders have not been able to find it or even tried very hard to do so. In the absence of radical change, Europe will remain a cipher in international politics for as far ahead as the eye can see.

Throughout modem history, international politics centered on Europe. Two world wars ended Europe's dominance. The all-but-inevitable movement from unipolarity to multipolarity is taking place not in Europe but in Asia. Meanwhile, the internal development and the external reaction of China and Japan are steadily raising both countries to the great power level. China will emerge as a great power even without trying very hard so long as it remains politically united and competent. Strategically, China can quite easily raise its nuclear forces to a level of parity with the United States if it has not already done so.[8] China has five to seven intercontinental missiles (DF-5s) able to hit almost any American target and a dozen or more missiles able to reach its west coast (DF-4s).[9] Liquid-fueled, immobile missiles are vulnerable, but would we risk the destruction of, say, Seattle, San Francisco, and San Diego if China happens to have a few more DF-4s than we think or if we should fail to destroy all of them on the ground? Deterrence is much easier to contrive than most Americans have surmised. Economically, China's growth rate, given its present stage of economic development, can be sustained at eight or nine percent for perhaps another decade. Even during Asia's near economic collapse of the 1990s, China's growth rate remained approximately in that range. A growth rate of eight or nine percent doubles a country's economy every nine or eight years.

Unlike China, Japan is obviously reluctant to assume the mantle of a great power. Its reluctance, however, is steadily though slowly waning. Economically, Japan's power has grown and spread remarkably. The growth of a country's economic capability to the great-power level places it at the center of regional and global affairs. It widens the range of a state's interests and increases their importance. The high volume of a country's external business thrusts it ever more deeply into world affairs. In a self-help system, the possession of most but not all of the capabilities of a great power leaves a state vulnerable to others who have the instruments that the lesser state lacks. Even though one may believe that fears of nuclear blackmail are misplaced, one must wonder whether Japan will remain immune to them.

Countries have always competed for wealth and security, and the competition has often led to conflict. Historically states have been sensitive to changing relations of power among them. Japan is made uneasy now by the steady growth of China's military budget. Its nearly three-million strong army, undergoing modernization, and the gradual growth of its sea- and

---

8. Nuclear panty is reached when countries have second-strike forces. It does not require quantitative or qualitative equality of forces. See K. Waltz, "Nuclear Myths and Political Realities," *American Political Science Review* 84 (September 1990).

9. David E. Sanger and Erik Eckholm. "Will Beijing's Nuclear Arsenal Stay Small or Will it Mushroom?" *New York Times,* p. A1.

air-power projection capabilities, produce apprehension in all of China's neighbors and add to the sense of instability in a region where issues of sovereignty and territorial disputes abound. The Korean peninsula has more military forces per square kilometer than any other portion of the globe. Taiwan is an unending source of tension. Disputes exist between Japan and Russia over the Kurile Islands, and between Japan and China over the Senkaku or Diaoyu Islands. Cambodia is a troublesome problem for both Vietnam and China. Half a dozen countries lay claim to all or some of the Spratly Islands, strategically located and supposedly rich in oil. The presence of China's ample nuclear forces, combined with the drawdown of American military forces, can hardly be ignored by Japan, the less so since economic conflicts with the United States cast doubt on the reliability of American military guarantees. Reminders of Japan's dependence and vulnerability multiply in large and small ways. For example, as rumors about North Korea's developing nuclear capabilities gained credence, Japan became acutely aware of its lack of observation satellites. Uncomfortable dependencies and perceived vulnerabilities have led Japan to acquire greater military capabilities, even though many Japanese may prefer not to.

Given the expectation of conflict, and the necessity of taking care of one's interests, one may wonder how any state with the economic capability of a great power can refrain from arming itself with the weapons that have served so well as the great deterrent. For a country to choose not to become a great power is a structural anomaly. For that reason, the choice is a difficult one to sustain. Sooner or later, usually sooner, the international status of countries has risen in step with their material resources. Countries with great-power economies have become great powers, whether or not reluctantly. Some countries may strive to become great powers; others may wish to avoid doing so. The choice, however, is a constrained one. Because of the extent of their interests, larger units existing in a contentious arena tend to take on system-wide tasks. Profound change in a country's international situation produces radical change in its external behavior. After the Second World War, the United States broke with its centuries-long tradition of acting unilaterally and refusing to make long-term commitments. Japan's behavior in the past half century reflects the abrupt change in its international standing suffered because of its defeat in war. In the previous half century, after victory over China in 1894-95, Japan pressed for preeminence in Asia, if not beyond. Does Japan once again aspire to a larger role internationally? Its concerted regional activity, its seeking and gaining prominence in such bodies as the IMF and the World Bank, its obvious pride in economic and technological achievements indicate that it does. The behavior of states responds more to external conditions than to internal habit if external change is profound.

When external conditions press firmly enough, they shape the behavior of states. Increasingly, Japan will be pressed to enlarge its conventional forces and to add nuclear ones in order to protect its interests. Japanese reasons for hesitating to take the final step into the great-power arena are obvious and need not be rehearsed. Yet when a country receives less attention and respect, and gets its way less often than it feels it should, internal inhibitions about becoming a great power are likely to turn into public criticisms of the government for not taking its proper place in the world. India, Pakistan, China, and perhaps North Korea have nuclear weapons capable of deterring others from threatening their vital interests. How long can Japan live alongside other nuclear states while denying itself similar capabilities'? Conflicts and crises are certain to make Japan aware of the disadvantages of being without the military instruments that other powers command. Japanese nuclear inhibitions arising from World War II will not last indefinitely; one may expect them to expire as generational memories fade.

Japanese officials have indicated that when the protection of America's extended deterrent is no longer thought to be sufficiently reliable, Japan will equip itself with a nuclear force, whether or not openly. Like a number of other countries, Japan has put itself politically and technologically in a position to do so. Consistently since the mid-1950s, the government has defined all of its Self-Defense Forces as conforming to constitutional requirements. Nuclear weapons purely for defense would be deemed constitutional should Japan decide to make some.[10] As a secret report of the Ministry of Foreign Affairs put it in 1969: "For the time being, we will maintain the policy of not possessing nuclear weapons. However, regardless of joining the NPT or not, we will keep the economic and technical potential for the production of nuclear weapons, while seeing to it that Japan will not be interfered with in this regard."[11] In March of 1988, Prime Minister Takeshita called for a defensive capability matching Japan's economic power.[12] Only a balanced conventional-nuclear military capability would meet this requirement. In June 1994, Prime Minister Tsutumu Hata mentioned in Parliament that Japan had the ability to make nuclear weapons.[13]

Where some see Japan as a "global civilian power" and believe it likely to remain one, others see a country that has skillfully used the protection America has afforded and adroitly adopted the means of maintaining its security to its regional environment.[14] Prime Minister Shigeru Yoshida in the early 1950s suggested that Japan should rely on American protection until it had rebuilt its economy as it gradually prepared to stand on its own feet.[15] Japan has laid a firm foundation for doing so by developing much of its own weaponry instead of relying on cheaper imports. Remaining months or moments away from having a nuclear military capability is well designed to protect the country's security without unduly alarming its neighbors.

The hostility of China, of both Koreas, and of Russia combines with inevitable doubts about the extent to which Japan can rely on the United States to protect its security.[16] Whether reluctantly or not. Japan and China will follow each other on the route to becoming great powers. China has the greater long-term potential. Japan, with the world's sec-

---

10. Norman D. Levin "Japan's Defense Policy: The Internal Debate," in Harry H. Kendall and Clara Joewono. *Japan, ASEAN, and the United States* (Berkeley: Institute of East Asian Studies, 1990).

11. "The Capability to Develop Nuclear Weapons Should be Kept: Ministry of Foreign Affairs Secret Document in 1969.",Mainichi, August 1, 1994, p. 41, as quoted in Selig S. Harrison, "Japan and Nuclear Weapons," in Selig S. Harrison, ed. *Japan's Nuclear Future* (Washington DC: Carnegie Endowment for International Peace, 1996), p. 9.

12. David Arase, "U.S. and ASEAN Perceptions of Japan's Role in the Asian-Pacific Region," in Kendall and Joewono, eds. *Japan, ASEAN, and the United States*, p. 276.

13. David E. Sanger, "In Face-Saving Reverse, Japan Disavows Any Nuclear-Arms Expertise," *New York Times*, June 22, 1994, p. 10.

14. Michael J. Green, "State of the Field Report: Research on Japanese Security Policy.". *Access Asia Review* 2 (September 1998), judiciously summarized different interpretations of Japan's security policy

15. Kenneth B. Pyle, *The Japanese Question: Power and Purpose in a New Era.* (Washington, DC: AEI Press. 1992). p. 26.

16. Andrew Hanami, for example, points out that Japan wonders whether the United States would help defend Hokkaido. "Japan and the Military Balance of Power in Northeast Asia." *Journal of East Asian Affairs*. 7 (Summer/Fall 1994). p. 364.

ond or third largest defense budget and the ability to produce the most technologically advanced weaponry is closer to great-power status at the moment.

When Americans speak of preserving the balance in East Asia through our military presence,[17] Chinese understandably take this to mean that we intend to maintain the strategic hegemony we now enjoy in the *absence* of a balance of power. When China makes steady but quite modest efforts to improve the quality of its inferior forces, we see a future threat to our and others' interests.[18] Whatever worries the United States has and whatever threats it feels, Japan has them earlier and feels them more severely. Japan has gradually reacted to them. China then worries as Japan improves its airlift and sealift capabilities and as the United States raises its support level for forces in Korea.[19] The actions and reactions of China, Japan, and Korea. with or without American participation, are creating a new balance of power in East Asia. which is becoming part of the new balance of power in the world.

Historically, encounters of East and West have often ended in tragedy. Yet, as we know from happy experience, nuclear weapons moderate the behavior of their possessors and render them cautious whenever crises threaten to go out of control. Fortunately, the changing relations of East and West, and the changing relations of countries within the East and the West, are taking place in a nuclear context. The tensions and conflicts that intensify when profound changes in world politics take place will continue to mar the relations of nations while nuclear weapons keep the peace among those who enjoy their protection.

America's policy of containing China by keeping a hundred thousand troops in East Asia and by providing security guarantees to Japan and South Korea is intended to keep a new balance of power from forming in Asia. By continuing to keep a hundred thousand troops in Western Europe, where no military threat is in sight, and by extending NATO eastward, America pursues the same goal in Europe. The American aspiration to freeze historical development by working to keep the world unipolar is doomed. In the not very long run, the task will exceed America's economic, military, demographic, and political resources; and the very effort to maintain a dominant position is the surest way to undermine it. The effort to maintain dominance stimulates some countries to work to overcome it. As theory shows and history confirms, that is how balances of power are made. Multipolarity is developing before our eyes: To all but the myopic it can be seen on the horizon. Moreover, it is emerging in accordance with the balancing imperative.

American leaders seem to believe that America's preeminent position will last indefinitely. The United States would then remain the dominant power without rivals rising to challenge it—a position without precedent in modem history. Balancing, of course, is not universal and omnipresent. A dominant power may suppress balancing as the United States has done in Europe. Whether or not balancing takes place also depends on the decisions of governments. Stephanie Neuman's book, *International Relations Theory and the Third World,* abounds in examples of states that failed to mind their own security interests

---

17. Richard Bernstein and Ross H. Munro, *The Coming Conflict with China* (New York: Knopf, 1997); Andrew J. Nathan and Robert S. Ross, *The Great Wall and the Empty Fortress: China's Search for Security* (New York: W. W. Norton, 1997).

18. The IISS (ref. p. 1, above) estimates China's military spending at $31.7 billion for 1995 and Japan's at $50.2 billion. Some other estimates put China's spending around $50 billion.

19. Michael J. Green and Benjamin L. Self. "Japan's Changing China Policy: From Commercial Liberalism to Reluctant Realism." *Survival* 38 (Summer 1996), p. 43.

through internal efforts or external arrangements, and as, one would expect. suffered invasions, loss of autonomy, and dismemberment.[20]

States are free to disregard the imperatives of power, but they must expect to pay a price for doing so. Moreover, relatively weak and divided states may find it impossible to concert their efforts to counter a hegemonic state despite ample provocation. This has long been the condition of the western hemisphere.

Victory in war, however, often breeds lasting enmities. Magnanimity in victory is rare. Winners of wars, facing few impediments to the exercise of their wills, often act in ways that create future enemies. Thus Germany, by taking Alsace and most of Lorraine from France in 1871, earned its lasting enmity; and the Allies' harsh treatment of Germany after World War I produced a similar effect. In contrast, Bismarck persuaded the Kaiser not to march his armies along the road to Vienna after the great victory at Königgrätz in 1866. In the Treaty of Prague, Prussia took no Austrian territory. Thus Austria, having become Austria-Hungary, was available as an alliance partner for Germany in 1879. Rather than learning from history, the United States is repeating past errors by extending its influence over what used to be the province of the vanquished.[21]

Rather than learning from Bismarck, the United States is repeating past errors. Having bested the Soviet Union in the Cold War, the United States now pushes its winning coalition into what used to be the vanquished's front yard. This alienates Russia and nudges Russia toward China instead of drawing Russia toward Europe and America. Late in 1996, expecting a measure of indifference, I asked an official in the Indian Ministry of External Affairs whether India was concerned over our expansive NATO policy. He immediately replied that a policy seemingly designed to bring Russia and China together of course was of great concern to India. Despite much talk about the "globalization" of international politics, American political leaders to a dismaying extent think of East or West rather than of their interaction. With a history of conflict along a 9600 mile border, with ethnic minorities sprawling across it, with a mineral-rich and sparsely-populated Siberia facing China's teeming millions, Russia and China will find it difficult to cooperate effectively, but we are doing our best to help them do so. Indeed. the United States provides the key to Russian-Chinese relations over the past half century. Feeling American antagonism and fearing American power, China drew close to Russia after the war and remained so until the United States seemed less, and the Soviet Union more, of a threat to China. The relatively harmonious relations the United States and China enjoyed during the 1970s began to turn sour in the late 1980s when Russian power visibly declined and American hegemony became imminent. To alienate Russia by expanding NATO, and to alienate China by pressing it to change its policies and by lecturing its leaders on how to rule their country, are policies that only an overwhelmingly powerful country could afford to, and only a foolish one be tempted, to follow.

The United States cannot prevent a new balance of power from forming. It can hasten its coming as we have been earnestly doing.

---

20. Tellingly, John Lewis Gaddis comments that he has never known a time when there was less support among historians for an announced policy. "History, Grand Strategy and NATO Enlargement," *Survival,* 40 (Spring 1998), 147.

21. Tellingly, John Lewis Gaddis comments that he has never known a time when there was less support among historians for an announced policy. "History, Grand Strategy and NATO Enlargement," *Survival,* 40 (Spring 1998), 147.

In this section of the paper, the discussion of balancing has been more empirical and speculative than theoretical. I therefore end it with some reflections on balancing theory.

Structural theory, and the theory of balance of power that follows from it. do not lead one to expect that states will always or even usually engage in balancing behavior. Balancing is a strategy for survival, a way of attempting to maintain a state's autonomous way of life. To argue that bandwagoning represents a behavior more common to states than balancing has become a bit of a fad. Whether states bandwagon more often than they balance is an interesting question. To believe that an affirmative answer would refute balance-of-power theory is, however, to misinterpret the theory and to commit what one might call the numerical fallacy—to draw a qualitative conclusion directly from a quantitative result. States try various strategies of survival. Balancing is one of them: bandwagoning is another. The latter may sometimes seem a less demanding and more rewarding strategy than balancing, requiring less effort and extracting lower costs while promising concrete rewards. Amidst the uncertainties of international and the shifting pressures of domestic politics, states have to make perilous choices. They may hope to avoid war by appeasing adversaries, a weak form of bandwagoning, rather than by rearming and realigning in order to thwart them. Moreover, many states have insufficient resources for balancing and little room for maneuver. They may have to jump on the wagon only later to wish they could fall off.

Balancing theory does not predict uniformity of behavior but rather the strong tendency of major states in the system, or in regional subsystems, to resort to balancing when they need to. That states try different strategies of survival is hardly surprising. The recurrent emergence of balancing behavior, and the appearance of the patterns the behavior produces, should all the more be seen as impressive evidence supporting the theory.

CONCLUSION

Every time peace breaks out people pop up to proclaim that realism is dead. That is another way of saying that international politics has been transformed. The world, however, has not been transformed; the structure of international politics has simply been remade by the disappearance of the Soviet Union, and for a time, possibly quite a long time, we will live with unipolarity. Moreover, international politics was not remade by the forces and factors that some believe are creating a new world order. Those who set the Soviet Union on the path of reform were old Soviet apparatchiks trying to right the Soviet economy in order to preserve its position in the world. The revolution in Soviet affairs and the ending of the cold war, were not brought about by democracy, interdependence, or international institutions. Instead the cold war ended exactly as structural realism led one to expect. As I said some years ago, the cold war "is firmly rooted in the structure of postwar international politics and will last as long as that structure endures."[22] So it did. and the Cold War ended only when the bipolar structure of the world disappeared.

Structural change affects the behavior of states and the outcomes their interactions produce. It does not break the essential continuity of international politics. The transformation of international politics alone could do that. Transformation, however, awaits the day when the international system is no longer one populated by states that have to help themselves. If the day were here, one would be able to say who could be relied on to help

22. Waltz, "The Origins of War in Neorealist Theory," *Journal of Interdisciplinary History,* 18 (Spring 1988), p. 628.

the disadvantaged or endangered. Instead, the ominous shadow of the future continues to cast its pall over interacting states. States' perennial uncertainty about their fates presses governments to prefer relative over absolute gains. Without the shadow, the leaders of states would no longer have to ask themselves how they will get along tomorrow as well as today. States could combine their efforts cheerfully and work to maximize collective gain without worrying about how each might fare in comparison to others.

Occasionally, one finds the statement that governments in their natural, anarchic condition act myopically, that is, on calculations of immediate interest while hoping that the future will take care of itself. Realists are said to suffer from this optical defect.[23] Political leaders may be astigmatic, but responsible ones who behave realistically do not suffer from myopia. Robert Axelrod and Robert Keohane believe that World War I might have been averted if certain states had been able to see how long the future's shadow was.[24] Yet, as their discussion shows, the future was what the major states concerned were obsessively worried about. The war was prompted less by considerations of present security and more by worries about how the balance might change later. The problems of governments do not arise from their short time horizons. They see the long shadow of the future, but they have trouble reading its contours, perhaps because they try to look too far ahead and see imaginary dangers. In 1914, Germany feared Russia's rapid industrial and population growth. France and Britain suffered from the same fear about Germany, and in addition Britain worried about the rapid growth of Germany's navy. In an important sense, World War I was a preventive war all around. Future fears dominated hopes for short-term gains. States do not live in the happiest of conditions that Horace in one of his odes imagined for man:

> Happy the man, and happy he alone, who can say,
> Tomorrow do thy worst, for I have lived today.

Robert Axelrod has shown that the "tit-for-tat" tactic, and no other, maximizes collective gain over time. The one condition for success is that the game be played under the shadow of the future.[25] Because states coexist in a self-help system, they may, however, have to concern themselves not with maximizing collective gain but with lessening, preserving, or widening the gap in welfare and strength between themselves and others. The contours of the future's shadow look different in hierarchic and anarchic systems. The shadow may facilitate cooperation in the former; it works against it in the latter. Worries about the future do not make cooperation and institution building among nations impossible; they do strongly condition their operation and limit their accomplishment. Liberal institutionalists were right to start their investigations with structural realism. Until and unless a transformation occurs. it remains the basic theory of international politics.

---

23. The point is made by Keohane, *After Hegemony: Cooperation and Discord in the World Political Economy* (Princeton: Princeton University Press. 1984), pp. 99, 103, 108.

24. Robert Axelrod and Robert O. Keohane, "Achieving Cooperation Under Anarchy: Strategies and Institutions," in David Baldwin, ed. *Neorealism and Neoliberalism: The Contemporary Debate* (New York: Columbia University Press, 1993). For German leaders, they say, "the shadow of the Future seemed so small" (p 99). Robert Powell shows that "a longer shadow . . . leads to greater military allocations." See "Guns, Butter, and Anarchy." *American Political Science Review* 87 (March, 1993), p. 116; and see p. 117 on the incompatibility of liberal institutionalism and structural realism.

25. Robert Axelrod. *The Evolution of Cooperation,* (New York: Basic Books. 1984).

Liberal Tradition Theories

Collective Security

Inis L. Claude, Jr
Collective Security as an Approach to Peace

Inis L. Claude, Jr.
Collective Security versus Balance of Power

Democratic Peace Theory

Bruce Russett
Why Democratic Peace?

Edward Mansfield & Jack Snyder
Democratic Transitions & War

Introduction to Collective Security

Collective Security provides another approach for viewing international relations. Like previous theories it helps answer the enduring questions of international relations: *Why do states do what they do* and *what causes conflict and cooperation among states?*

In the preface to the first reading (not reprinted here), Inis L. Claude, Jr. notes that "the permanent features of the behavior of states . . . include the urge for order as well as the lust for power, and the desire for cooperation as well as the bent toward rivalry."[1] Although collective security is an idealist tradition theory which focuses on such things as morality, cooperation, the perfectibility of state behavior, and the importance of international institutions and law, it shares two important elements with our "realist tradition" theories (i.e., Balance of Power, Balance of Threat, and Structural Realism). In addition to being a systemic theory which is not concerned with factors inside the state, collective security holds that power can be harnessed as part of a collective good rather than as a means for state to simply get what, this places it firmly in the Realism-Security Lens.

The first reading titled "Collective Security as an Approach to Peace" looks at collective security as a theory of international relations. This is a chapter out of Claude's book *Swords into Plowshares: The Problems and Progress of International Organization*, first published in 1956. In this passage Claude eloquently lays out both the subjective and objective requirements of collective security. As with our previous theoretical readings, hypotheses for the "theory" of Collective Security can easily be developed by focusing on the course's two central questions. First, what does Claude say drives state behavior (i.e., why do states do what they do)—e.g., why would states want to join a collective security arrangement such as the UN or a collective defense organization such as NATO and what behavior is expected of states that are members of these arrangements? Second, what promotes cooperation or may lead to conflict?

The second reading is also by Claude. Specifically, the excerpts from his 1962 book *Power and International Relations* (1962) examine the differences and similarities between collective security and balance of power. A comparison of the two theories can help clarify the important role of power and deterrence for both theories despite their ideological differences.

President Woodrow Wilson was one of the earliest promoters of the idea of collective security. Specifically, Wilson believed that the balance of power was unlikely to produce a stable international order and that an alternative was required. Wilson, like Hugo Grotius (the "father of international law")[2] before him, wanted to build an international community of states. This community, based on international law and specific rules and norms of behavior, would be regulated by international institutions such as the League of Nations. It was thought that the linkages established by these international institutions would moderate or ideally even eliminate the need for power politics.

---

1. Inis L. Claude, Jr., *Swords into Plowshares: The Problems and Progress of International Organization*, (New York: McGraw-Hill, 1984), vii.

2. Paul Christopher, *The Ethics of War and Peace: An Introduction to Legal and Moral Issues* (Englewood Cliffs, NJ: Prentice Hall, 1994), 70-110.

While many students of international relations consider Wilson's conception of collective security and the role of international organizations as naïve and merely hypothetical, Claude disputes this notion. In the introduction to *Swords into Plowshares: The Problems and Progress of International Organization* (again, not reprinted here), he writes:

> Sincere and sensible men may differ as to how much and what kind of world unity is possible and desirable, how it can or should be achieved, and how quickly it is likely to be or ought to be attempted. These are important questions... However, we are not simply confronted with a debate about hypothetical possibilities for the future. The growing complexities of international relations has already produced international organizations [and a world which is already] organizing.[3]

Given the existence, albeit imperfect functioning, of such intergovernmental organizations (IGOs) as the United Nations (UN) and the North Atlantic Treaty Organization (NATO), the power and security based theory of Collective Security clearly has value beyond mere intellectual discourse, particularly for officers whom may find themselves fighting under the auspices of these organizations. As the May 1997 *National Security Strategy* notes, "After World War II . . . [the United States] remained engaged overseas and, with our allies, worked to create international structures . . . [including] the United Nations, NATO and 42 other defense arrangements . . . [that together with economic organizations have] enabled us to strengthen security and prosperity and win the Cold War."[4] Furthermore, practically all of the military missions since the end of the Cold War have been "combined" operations with our UN and NATO allies.

While the world may not perfectly mirror the "ideal" envisioned by Kant or Wilson, the fact that it has idealist elements (e.g., IGOs, international laws, cooperation, etc.) is significant. Because realist tradition theories such as Balance of Power have difficulty addressing such things, the theory of Collective Security may well provide a significant degree of illumination of the world of international relations by helping to describe, explain or predict state behavior or systemic cooperation.

Another interesting point is that though collective security organizations can be argued to be a product of Kant's "federation of free states", and from the Liberal Tradition, it appears as if the first functioning organization to meet Liberal Kant's ideal might be the world's foremost military alliance—NATO. Originally based on the Realist Tradition's basic premise of survival, since the end of the Cold War, NATO has transformed and, while making being a functioning democracy under the rule of law requirements to join NATO, enlarged to 26 countries.

This raises the question, as NATO continues to grow larger and larger, meaning more and more countries go from being outside of, to inside of, NATO, will it remain an alliance or become a collective security organization—or will it be both?

---

3. Ibid., p. 3.

4. William J. Clinton, *A National Security Strategy for a New Century* (May 1997), on the WWW at: http://www.whitehouse.gov/WH/EOP/NSC/Strategy/ (date accessed: 27 May 1998).

Collective Security as an Approach to Peace

Inis L. Claude, Jr.

The twentieth-century hope that international organizations might serve to prevent war, or, failing that, to defend states subjected to armed attack in defiance of organized efforts to maintain the peace, has been epitomized in the concept of collective security. The notion that an international agency purporting to pursue these objectives must establish and operate a collective security system has held a central place in orthodox thinking about international organization since World War I. This has not been regarded as the only means by which peace and order might be promoted; typically, a system of collective security has been conceived as operating in intimate connection with elaborate arrangements for facilitating the peaceful settlement of disputes, on the assumption that the two mechanisms will supplement and reinforce each other. Nevertheless, collective security has generally been regarded as indispensable. The idea that a peaceful and stable world order can be maintained without benefit of a collective security system has seemed to most persons concerned with international organization as far-fetched as the idea that a society can properly educate its children without operating a system of schools and colleges or care for its sick and wounded without hospitals and clinics. Thus, the failure of the League of Nations has frequently been attributed to the defectiveness of its collective security system, and the observation that the United Nations has not established and cannot be expected to establish a collective security system typically engenders the response that it must do so if it is to save the world from destruction.

Ostensible exceptions are to be found in the viewpoint of serious advocates of world government, who regard collective security as an inadequate substitute for the more fundamental transformation of the international system that they propose, and in the attitude of analysts who are committed, usually in the name of "political realism," to the position that the nature of international politics cannot effectively be altered and who therefore consider the effort to create a collective security system a useless and perhaps even a mischievous tampering with a system that reasonable men should simply accept. Even these exceptions are more apparent than real, for both sets of critics tend to share the assumption that it is normal for international organizations to be in the collective security business; in their eyes, no less than in those of devoted champions of international organization, collective security is associated with international organization as ham is with eggs.

All concerned have tended to regard collective security as a halfway house between the terminal points of international anarchy and world government. Rejecting the views that the former cannot be changed and that the latter can be attained in the foreseeable future, international organizationalists have conceived collective security as an alternative, far enough from anarchy to be useful and far enough from world government to be feasible. They have been divided among themselves as to whether it should be envisaged as a temporary expedient, contributing to the ultimate possibility of world government, or a permanent solution to the problem of world order, eliminating the ultimate necessity of world government. But, regardless of their differing expectations concerning the probability that collective security will yield ideal results, they have been united in the belief that its requirements are less revolutionary than those posed by world government, and that it is therefore within the realm of possibility in an age dominated by the basic values of a multi-state system.

The achievement of orthodox status is very often fatal to the integrity of a concept. When it becomes popular and respectable to endorse the concept, men are strongly tempted to proclaim their belief in it whether or not they genuinely understand its meaning or fully accept its implications. If the tension between their urge to *believe in* it and their disinclination to *believe that* it is valid becomes too strong, they tend to resolve the difficulty by altering its meaning, packing into the terminological box a content that they can more readily accept.

Collective security has paid this familiar price for its incorporation into the orthodoxy of twentieth-century thought about international order. It began as a specialized concept, a technical term in the vocabulary of international relations. Collective security was the name given by the planners of a new world order after World War I to the system for maintenance of international peace that they intended as a replacement for the system commonly known as the balance of power. The new system as they envisaged it involved the establishment and operation of a complex scheme of national commitments and international mechanisms designed to prevent or suppress aggression by any state against any other state, by presenting to potential aggressors the credible threat and to potential victims of aggression the reliable promise of effective collective measures, ranging from diplomatic boycott through economic pressure to military sanctions, to enforce the peace. It was conceived as a systematic arrangement that should serve, with the highest degree of predictability that human contrivance could muster, to confront would-be aggressors, whoever they might be and wherever they might venture to strike, with an overwhelming collection of restraining power assembled by the mass of states in accordance with clear and firm obligations accepted and proclaimed in advance. In short, collective security was put forward as a particular and preferred method for keeping the peace; its advocates emphasized its differentiation from other methods, giving special attention to the argument that it was different from and superior to the system of competing alliances that was associated with the balance of power concept.

In the half century that has elapsed since the concept of collective security gained prominence as the central feature of the Wilsonian scheme for reforming the international system, it has largely lost its clarity and specificity. New wine has been mixed with the old in the semantic bottle whose label has come to be prized for its own sake, diluting the flavor of the original vintage. Collective security has been appropriated as an honorific designation for virtually any and all multilateral activities that statesmen or scholars may regard, or wish to have regarded, as conducive to peace and order. In a particularly ironic twist of fate, the label has been applied to alliances, bilateral or multilateral, by their champions—in flagrant disregard of the fact that the notion of a collective security system was originally developed in reaction against and in the hope of providing a substitute for the traditional system of competing alliances. This is a case, *par excellence,* of the misappropriation of ideological funds; the Wilsonian curse is avoided and the Wilsonian blessing is invoked by the expedient of describing alliances (one's own—not those of one's rivals) as elements of a collective security arrangement. Various kinds of activity undertaken by the United Nations and by such regional agencies as the Organization of American States (OAS) for the purpose of controlling threats to the peace are treated as instances of the collective security function. In the extreme case, collective security becomes simply a synonym for world peace, and the claim that a government believes in collective security is reduced to meaning that it fears and abhors war. Thus, a term that originally connoted a particular method for preserving world order—a means whose feasibility and appropriateness to the end could be studied and evaluated—has been converted into a catchall designation for a variety of means and even for the end itself.

The damage that this development has inflicted upon the intellectual integrity and the analytical usefulness of the concept of collective security inspires regret that the original formulators and elaborators of the concept did not give it a more prosaic and ideology-proof label—let us say, method No. 5. A means so designated would have been less likely to be confused with the end that it was alleged to promote, and it would hardly have been eligible for the process of sanctification that has robbed collective security of its concrete meaning while giving it a featured place in the orthodox creed of internationalism. Method No. 5 might have remained subject to pragmatic evaluation; finding it unacceptable or inapplicable, statesmen and scholars would not have felt impelled to declare it indispensable but would have thought it sensible to consider reverting to method No. 4 or going on to method No. 6, without apologizing for the abandonment of No. 5 or attempting to convince themselves or others that No. 4 or No. 6 was really method No. 5. To have labeled the Wilsonian scheme in such a way would have been to acknowledge the variety of methods that might be conceived and adopted by international agencies in the quest for order and to discourage the ideological fixation that has tended to restrict thought about international organization to the issue of whether and how it can effectuate collective security when the issue ought to be defined in more open terms: If collective security does not seem promising, what other methods for promoting internatinal peace and security might be attempted?[1]

But this is wishful thinking. We have to live with the vagueness and confusion that have grown up around the concept of collective security. I can only inform the reader that I use the term to refer to the particular type of system for the enforcement of peace that was contemplated but never fully established by the statesmen of the League era, while warning him that it is frequently used with such looseness and imprecision that analysis of the concept and evaluation of its merits as a formula for world order are fraught with peculiar difficulty.

THE THEORY OF COLLECTIVE SECURITY

Collective security depends less heavily than pacific settlement upon the precise accuracy of a set of assumptions about the nature and causes of war. By the same token, it purports to be applicable to a wider variety of belligerent situations, assuming that not all wars arise from the same type of causation. It is at once a second line of defense against the wars which pacific settlement should but does not prevent, and a supplementary defense, on the flanks of pacific settlement, against the wars which are not within the range of the latter; thus, it adds to the protective system of world peace the benefits of both defense in depth and defense in breadth.

---

[1] I have reiterated this point more elaborately in "The Collectivist Theme in International Relations," *International Journal*, Autumn, 1969, pp. 639-656. The foregoing analysis of the dilution of collective security is drawn in part from my article, "The United Nations and Collective Security," in Richard B. Gray, ed., *International Security Systems* (Itasca, Illinois: Peacock, 1969), pp. 108-126.

The necessary assumption of collective security is simply that wars are likely to occur and that they ought to be prevented. The conflicts may be the fruit of unreflective passion or of deliberate planning; they may represent efforts to settle disputes, effects of undefinably broad situations of hostility, or calculated means to realize ambitious designs of conquest. They may be launched by the irresponsible dictate of cynical autocrats or the democratic will of a chauvinistic people—although the champions of collective security have frequently evinced the conviction that most wars are likely to stem from the former type of initiative. The point is that the theory of collective security is not invalidated by the discovery that the causes, functional purposes, and initiatory mechanisms of war are varied.

However, the basic assumption about the problem of war is more precise in certain important respects. Collective security is a specialized instrument of international policy in the sense that it is intended only to forestall the arbitrary and aggressive use of force, not to provide enforcement mechanisms for the whole body of international law; it assumes that, so far as the problem of world order is concerned, the heart of the matter is the restraint of military action rather than the guarantee of respect for all legal obligations. Moreover, it assumes that this ideal may be realized, or at least approximated, by a reformation of international policy, without the institution of a revolution in the structure of the international system.

To some degree, collective security shares with pacific settlement the belief that governments, or the peoples who may be in a position to influence their governments, are amenable to moral appeals against the misuse of force, and it may also be described as a rationalistic approach to peace. But the rational appeal directed by collective security to potential belligerents is not so much a suggestion of a decent and sensible alternative to violence, which characterizes pacific settlement, as a threat of dire consequences if the warning against violence is imprudently ignored. The stock in trade of pacific settlement is investigation, conciliation, arbitration, and the like—equipment for inducing rational decision to follow a morally respectable course; the stock in trade of collective security is diplomatic, economic, and military sanctions—equipment for inducing rational decision to avoid threatened damage to the national self-interest. Pacific settlement assumes, at least for tactical purposes, the moral ambiguity of a situation of conflict; avoiding an inital judgment on the moral merits of the positions held by disputants, it applies pressure equally to the two parties to adopt positive moral attitudes conducive to an agreed solution. Collective security, on the other hand, assumes the moral clarity ofa situation, the assignability of guilt for a threat to or breach of the peace. It focuses, in short, upon the concept of aggression, with its implication that the parties to a military encounter can be characterized aa aggressor and victim. After the identification of the culpable party, collective security discards primary concern with the factor of international morality im favor of the principle of power. Whereas pacific settlement fails if it proves impossible to make states rationally calm enough to behave morally, collective security falls down if either of two assumptions proves invalid: that blame can be confidently assessed for international crises, and that states are rationally calculating enough to behave prudently.

Collective security may be described as resting upon the proposition that war can be prevented by the deterrent effect of overwhelming power upon states which are too rational to invite certain defeat. In this respect, it is fundamentally similar to a balance of power system involving defensive alliances. However, as we shall see, collective security has other essential aspects which are its distinguishing marks, and which validate the Wilsonian claim that collective security is basically different from the system of policy which it was explicitly designed to replace.

However simple the collective security approach may seem upon superficial acquaintance, the truth is that it assumes the satisfaction of an extraordinarily complex network of requirements. The first group of prerequisites includes those of a *subjective* character, related to the general acceptability of the responsibilities of collective security; the second group may be characterized as a category of *objective* requirements, related to the suitability of the global situation to the operation of collective security.

Subjective Requirements of Collective Security

In contrast to pacific settlement, which is mainly concerned to evoke peaceful attitudes from quarreling states, collective security depends upon a positive commitment to the value of world peace by the great mass of states. Its basic requirement is that the premise of the "indivisibility of peace" should be deeply established in the thinking of governments and peoples. Collective security rests upon the assumption that it is true, and that governments and peoples can be expected to recognize and act upon the truth, that the fabric of human society has become so tightly woven that a breach any where threatens disintegration everywhere. Unchecked aggression in one direction emboldens and helps to empower its perpetrator to penetrate in other directions, or, more abstractly, successful use of lawless force in one situation contributes to the undermining of respect for the principle of order in all situations. The geographical remoteness of aggression is irrelevant; Kant's prophetic insight that "The intercourse . . . which has been everywhere steadily increasing between the nations of the earth, has now extended so enormously that a violation of right in one part of the world is felt all over it,"[2] must be universally acknowledged. The world's thinking must undergo the transformation that was exemplified by British Prime Minister Neville Chamberlain, when he switched from sighing, in the fall of 1938, "How horrible, fantastic, incredible it is that we should be digging trenches and trying on gas-masks here, because of a quarrel in a far-away country between people of whom we know nothing," to asserting, one year later, that "If, in spite of all, we find ourselves forced to embark upon a struggle . . . we shall not be fighting for the political future of a far-away city in a foreign land; we shall be fighting for the preservation of those principles, the destruction of which would involve the destruction of all possibility of peace and security for the peoples of the world."[3] Collective security requires rejection of the isolationist ideal of localizing wars, in terms of both its possibility and its desirability, and recommends to all the classic advice proffered by Alfred Nemours, the representative of Haiti, in the League debate concerning Italian aggression against Ethiopia: "Great or small, strong or weak, near or far, white or coloured, let us never forget that one day we may be somebody's Ethiopia."[4]

In requiring conviction of the indivisibility of peace, collective security demands what is essentially a factual agreement; it then imposes a related normative requirement: loyalty to the world community. The system will work only if the peoples of the world identify their particular interests so closely with the general interest of mankind that they go beyond mere recognition of interdependence to a feeling of involvement in the destiny of all nations. The responsibilities of participation in a collective security system are too onerous to be borne by any but a people actuated by genuine sympathy for any and all vic-

2. *Perpetual Peace*, p. 21.

3. Cited in Alan Bullock, *Hitler: A Study in Tyranny* (New York Harper, 1953), p. 499.

4. Cited in F.P. Walters, *A History of the League of Nations Volume II* (London: Oxford University Press, 1952), p. 653.

tims of aggression, and loyalty to the values of a global system of law and order. The operation of a collective security system must always be precarious unless the conviction that what is good for world peace is necessarily good for the nation is deeply engrained in governments and peoples.

This fundamental commitment does not require that what Arnold Wolfers characterized as milieu goals be considered superior to national interests, but that they be conceived *as* national interests of the highest order. Dedicated service to the larger international system is to be acknowledged as the indispensable means for safeguarding the most vital interests of one's own state. In this faith, the leaders of states and their constituents must be prepared to subordinate to the requirements of the collective securitv system their apparent and immediate national interests—to incur economic loss and run the risk of war, even in situations when national interests do not seem to be involved, or when this policy seems to conflict with national interests or to undermine established national policies. This means that states must renounce both pacifism and the right to use war as an instrument of national policy, while standing ready to resort to force for the fulfillment of their international obligations. As Arnold J. Toynbee has put it: "We have got to give up war for all the purposes for which sovereign communities have fought since war has been in existence, but we have still got to be willing to accept the risks and the losses of war for a purpose for which hitherto people have never thought of fighting."[5] It means that states must abandon as illusions anv convictions they may have traditionally held that they are peculiarly safe against aggression, overcome the temptation to regard any specific conflict as immaterial to or even favorable to their interests, and dedicate themselves to the performance of duties which may upset the equilibrium of their national life and disrupt relationships which they have laboriously constructed. All this theoretically takes place within a system which assumes the maintenance of the basic multi-state character of international society, and demands not that national loyalties be abandoned, but that they merely be harmonized by the enlightened conception that national interests are identifiable with the global interest. What it really requires is that a state adopt this conception once and for all, and thereafter act on the assumption that it is valid, despite contrary appearance that may arise from time to time.

Collective security is a design for providing the certainty of collective action to frustrate aggression—for giving to the potential victim the reassuring knowledge, and conveying to the potential law-breaker the deterring conviction, that the resources of the community will be mobilized against any abuse of national power. This ideal permits no *ifs* or *buts.* If it merely encourages states to hope for collective support in case they are victims of attack, it must fail to stimulate the revisions of state behavior at which it aims and upon which its ultimate success depends; if the hope which it encourages should prove illusory, it stands convicted of contributing to the downfall of states whose security it purported to safeguard. If it merely warns potential aggressors that they may encounter concerted resistance, it fails to achieve full effectiveness in its basic function, that of discouraging resort to violence, and if its warning should be revealed as a bluff, it stimulates the contempt for international order which it is intended to eradicate. The theory of collective security is replete with absolutes, of which none is more basic than the requirement of certainty.

In accordance with this essential of the collective security system, the states which constitute the system must be willing to accept commitments which involve the sacrifice

---

5. Royal Institute of International Affairs, *The Future of the League of Nations,* p. 14. Cf. Werner Levi, *Fundamentals of World Organization* (Minneapolis: University of Minnesota Press, 1950), p.77.

of their freedom of action or inaction in the most crucial of future situations. They must say in advance what they will do; they must agree to dispense with *ad hoc* national judgments, and bind themselves to a pattern of action from which they will not be at liberty to deviate. This pattern may be prescribed, at least in part, by the explicit terms of a multilateral treaty. It may, additionally or alternatively, be determined by the decision of an international agency. What is essential, in either case, is that the states upon which the operation of collective security depends should clearly renounce the right to withhold their support from a collective undertaking against whatever aggressions may arise.

Moreover, the renunciation of national decision-making capacity necessarily includes surrender of discretionary competence to resort to forcible action in the absence of international authorization. Collective security can tolerate the maintenance of a carefully restricted right of self-defense, to be exercised within the bounds of international supervision, but it is a fundamental requirement of a full-fledged system that an international authority should be the master of all situations involving the use of coercive instruments. Basically, the state must abdicate its traditional control over the elements of national power, accepting the responsibility to act or to refrain from acting in accordance with the stipulations of a multilateral agreement and the dictates of an international agency. Thus, the state exposes itself to obligations determined by the community for dealing with situations which may be created by the action and policy of other states.

It is very clear that the acceptance of this kind of commitment is a drastic if not a revolutionary act for a national state. It involves a relinquishment of sovereignty in the most crucial area of policy; "To all intents and purposes a state's right of disposal of its military potential is the most sensitive segment of national sovereignty, and that part which traditionally is impervious to foreign decision or control."[6] For constitutional democracies, it implies a transfer of power to make vital decisions which is likely to collide with established concepts of the distribution of governmental functions and powers, and a rigidification of national policy which is difficult to reconcile with the democratic principle that the people have an inalienable right to change their minds through the continuous operation of the mechanism of majority rule. It requires democratic statesmen, as democrats, to follow policies which their people may not approve in the circumstances, and, as statesmen, to abjure the exercise of the most cherished virtue of statesmanship, that of demonstrating empirical wisdom by making sound decisions in the light of the unique characteristics of a given situation. Thus, the good politician is required to betray the democratic ideal of doing what the people want, the shrewd politician is required to violate his vote-getting instincts, and the wise statesman is required to follow the rule book in a manner befitting an automaton. Finally, it means that governments and peoples must develop an unprecedented degree of confidence in the judgment and good will of foreigners, for the discretionary authority which is subtracted from the competence of the democratic majority and the national leadership is added to that of an international organization. Indeed, it is ultimately transferred to unidentifiable foreign states—those whose policy may be so obtuse that they provoke aggression against themselves, and those whose policy may be so cynical that they deliberately resort to aggression.

The essential commitments of a collective security system necessitate the willingness of nations to fight for the status quo. Collective security is not inherently an attempt to per-

---

6. Karl Loewenstein, "Sovereignty and International Co-operation," *American Journal of International Law*, April 1954, p. 235.

petuate an existing state of affairs; it is entirely compatible with a system of peaceful change, and such a system is in fact absolutely necessary for producing the kind of status quo and the kind of attitudes toward the status quo that are required if the ideal of collective security is to be realized. But at any given moment, the function of collective security is to combat assaults upon the currently legitimate pattern of national rights, and the responsibility of participating peoples is to cooperate in that enterprise without regard to any underlying sympathies they may have for claims of frustrated justice that may be enunciated by the assailants. As a general proposition, peace through justice must be the watchword of collective secutiry. However, its provisional rule of action can hardly be any other than peace *over* justice, and the member states of the system must be prepared to go to war to preserve the system which keeps the peace, even though this involves injury to innocent people and the squelching of valid objections to the moral legitimacy of the legally established state of things.

A basic requirement of collective security is that it function impartially. It is a design for preserving the integrity of the anonymous victim of attack by the anonymous aggressor; it is no respecter of states, but an instrument to be directed against any aggressor, on behalf of any violated state. This description points to one of the significant differences between a balance of power system and a collective security system: in the former, collaborative activity is directed against *undue power,* as such, while in the latter it is turned against *aggressive policy,* whether that policy be pursued by a giant which threatens to grow to earth-shaking proportions or by a pygmy which has scant prospect of becoming a major factor in world politics.[7]

The demands imposed by the principle of anonymity upon the states which form a collective security system provide further indications of the distinction between the new and the old regimes for the management of international relations. If collective security is to operate impartially, governments and peoples must exhibit a fundamental flexibility of policy and sentiment. France must be as ready to defend Germany as Belgium against aggression, and Britain must be equally willing to join in collective sanctions against the United States or the Soviet Union. In short, collective security recognizes no traditional friendships and no inveterate enmities, and permits no alliances *with* or alliances *against.* It is true that a balance of power system, in the long run, requires similar changes of partners and redefinitions of villains, but in the short run, such a system operates through the basic mechanism of alliances. For the purposes of collective security, an alliance is either superfluous—since every state is already committed to the defense of every other state—or it is incompatible with the system—since it implies that its members will defend each other but not outsiders, and raises doubt that they will join in international sanctions as readily against one of their number as against other states. The principle of alliance tends to inject into international relations a concept of the advance identification of friends and enemies that is alien to the basic proposition of collective security: whoever commits aggression is everybody's enemy; whoever resists aggression is everybody's friend. Membership in a collective security system involves alliance with nobody in particular but with everybody in general.

All of this adds up to the fundamental subjective requirement that all states be willing to entrust their destinies to collective security. Confidence is the quintessential condition of the success of the system; states must be prepared to rely upon its effectiveness and

7. Cf. Wright, *Problems of Stability and Progress in International Relations,* p. 355.

impartiality. If they are so prepared, they are likely to behave in such a way as to maximize the probability that this confidence will prove justified. If they are not, they are almost certain to resort to policies which undermine the system and make it unworthy of the confidence which they decline to bestow upon it. The familiar dilemma of circularity appears here: collective security cannot work unless the policies of states are inspired by confidence in the system, but it requires an extraordinary act of political faith for states to repose confidence in the system without previous demonstration that collective security works. States are, in effect, urged to assume the applicability of the notion of self-fulfilling prophecy, if they act as if the system will work, it will do so—otherwise it will fail. The stakes are high in the world of power politics, and states do not lightly undertake such experiments in the critical field of national security.

This analysis of the subjective requirements of collective security proves nothing if not that the realization of the ideal first institutionally espoused by the League makes singularly stringent demands upon the human beings of the twentieth century. It calls for a moral transformation of political man. It offends the most pacific and the most bellicose of men; it challenges neutralism and isolationism as well as militarism and imperialism; it clashes with the views of the most conservative supporters of national sovereignty and the most liberal proponents of democratic control of foreign policy; it demands alike the dissolution of ancient national hatreds and the willingness to abandon traditional national friendships. Indeed, the question inexorably arises whether the demands imposed upon the human mind and will by collective security are in truth less rigorous than those imposed by the ideal of world government. Is collective security really a halfway house? If human beings were fully prepared to meet the subjective requirements of collective security, would they be already prepared for world government?

Objective Requirements of Collective Security

The prerequisites thus far discussed have to do with the human situation. Collective security also depends upon the satisfaction of a number of basic conditions in the external sphere—in the power situation, the legal situation, and the organizational situation.

The ideal setting for a collective security system is a world characterized by a considerable diffusion of power. The most favorable situation would be one in which all states commanded approximately equal resources, and the least favorable, one marked by the concentration of effective power in a very few major states. The existence of several. great powers of roughly equal strength is essential to collective security.

Given a power configuration meeting this minimal requirement, a collective security system next demands substantial universality of membership. It might be argued that potential aggressors might just as well be omitted, since they presumably will dishonor both the negative obligations and the positive responsibilities incumbent upon members, or that they might better be left out, since their absence will facilitate the planning and initiation of collective measures to restrain their misbehavior. This is a plausible view, even though it ignores the value for an organized community of having lawless elements clearly subject to the legal regime—surely, criminals are the last persons who ought to be formally exempted from the bonds of the law. The basic objection to this position is that it misses the point that collective security knows no "probable aggressor" but assumes that *any* state may become an aggressor. In a sense, this is an expression of the *abstractness* which is a leading characteristic of collective security; for better or for worse, collective security is not an expedient for dealing with a concrete threat to world peace, but a design for a system of world order. In another sense, however, this is an implication of the *generality* of collective security. The system is intended to provide security for every state against the particular threat which arouses its national anxiety, and if every potential aggressor, every state which is or might become the source of the misgivings of another state, were excluded, the system would have very sparse membership indeed.

In any event, a workable system of collective security can hardly afford the exclusion or abstention of a major power. It is particularly damaging to have an important commercial and naval power on the outside, for the danger of its refusal to cooperate and to acquiesce in the infringement of its normal rights is sufficient to render improbable the effective application of economic sanctions to an aggressor. The doctrine of collective security relies heavily upon the proposition that nonmilitary measures will normally be adequate to stifle aggression—its military commitments are acceptable only because of the presumption that they will rarely be invoked—but economic sanctions are peculiarly dependent upon universal application for their efficacy.

Balance of power theory has never been able to present a satisfactory resolution of the problem of simultaneously maximizing the effectiveness and the symmetry of deterrence. If it stresses the maintenance of equilibrium between A and B, it maximizes symmetry but minimizes effectiveness; A and B are equally protected against attack by each other, but neither is well protected, for either may prove willing to attack when the odds are even. If, on the other hand, it opts for disequilibrium, it maximizes effectiveness but minimizes symmetry; the stronger A is quite secure against attack by the weaker B, but the latter is at the mercy of the former. The ideal must be to combine the superior deterrent effect of disequilibrium with the mutuality of protection afforded by equilibrium. How can A and B be simultaneously more powerful than each other? Collective security offers a theoretical solution to this problem. It opts uncompromisingly for preponderance as the more effective deterrent principle, and provides for symmetry of deterrence by promising that the preponderance of power, being at the disposal of the community rather than in the hands of a single state or coalition, will be available to any state for defensive purposes but to no state for aggressive purposes. Thus, collective security purports to establish a portable preponderance, ready to be shifted to the defense of any victim of aggression and capable of making any such victim superior to its adversary. Ideally, collective security makes preponderance safe for the world by harnessing it to the purposes of a community intent upon guaranteeing the security of all its members.

This analysis, stressing the assumption that it is possible to create such an imbalance of power in favor of the upholders of world order that aggression will be prevented by the certainty of defeat or defeated by the minimal efforts of collective forces, indicates the basic importance for a collective security system of the objective conditions of power diffusion and organizational comprehensiveness. This assumption may be invalidated by the inadequate diffusion of power. If the power configuration is such that no state commands more than, say, ten percent of the world's strength, the possibility is open for collective security to mobilize up to ninety percent against any state, a very comfortable margin of superiority. If, however, one state controls a very substantial portion of global power resources, forty-five percent, for instance, the collective matching of its strength is doubtful and the massing of overwhelming power against it is manifestly impossible. The importance of universality is also clarified by this analysis; as a collective security system approaches all inclusiveness, the possibility of its disposing of sufficient resources to outclass any aggressor grows; as it moves in the opposite direction, that possibility is correspondingly diminished.

The point is that collective security is not a design for organizing coalition warfare in the twentieth-century sense, but a plan for organizing international police action in an unprecedented sense. Its aim is not to sponsor the winning team in a free-for-all, but to eliminate international brawls by forcing aggressive states to forfeit their matches before being decisively beaten. It purports to require of participating states not that they should consent to compulsory involvement in major wars, but that they should accept obligatory service in a system for preventing major wars, and it can expect to retain their loyal support only if it succeeds in reducing, rather than increasing, their exposure to the perils of military involvement. All this is dependent upon the existence of a power situation and the achievement of an organizational situation making the massive overpowering of potential aggressors a feasible objective. The first essential of a police force is that its power should be so considerable, and that of its possible opponents so negligible, that any contest will be virtually won before it has begun; otherwise, its function will be that of conducting warfare, no matter how it may be described.

The intrinsic disadvantages of a collective security force are so great that its margin of superiority is always smaller than any purely objective standard of measurement would reveal. Since it confronts an anonymous aggressor, its capacity for formulating advance plans of action is severely limited. Since it is by definition a coalition force, its strength is very likely to be less than that of the sum of its parts. Its value depends heavily upon its ability to act quickly, so as to forestall threatened aggression, and yet its very inability to concentrate on plans for defeating a specific enemy and its complex structure militate against promptness in the effective mobilization of its potential strength. Collective security can command little confidence if it promises to become effective only after an aggressor has ravaged a country. Given the nature of modern war, a military campaign cannot be organized overnight, and the power of an aggressive state is maximized by preparatory measures. The collaborative force required for the implementation of collective security must be overwhelmingly preponderant in theory if it is to be even somewhat preponderant in practice.

The situation envisaged by collective security is marked not only by the wide distribution of power among states and the possibility of the near-monopolization of power by the community, but also by the general reduction of power, as embodied in military instruments. That is to say, collective security is based upon the assumption of partial disarmament. In strict theoretical terms, the system might work as well at a high level of armament as at a low level, but the intrusion of the subjective factor makes it virtually essential that collective security have a substantially demilitarized world to work in. This is because collective security is fundamentally an attempt to mobilize the world's antiwar forces for the prevention of war by the threat to make war; the ambiguity of the system is underlined by the fact that it relies for its initiation upon recognition that the risk of war is intolerable, and for its operation upon willingness to accept the risk of war. Its army of pacifists is tentatively willing to use force only because it abhors the use of force. Being precariously founded upon this psychological and moral paradox, collective security requires a power situation that permits it to do its job with a minimum of military exertion. If every state is reduced to military weakness, no aggressor will be strong enough to make a catastrophic war out of an encounter with the community's forces, and no member of the enforcement team will be tempted to feel that its joining up has been a jump from the military frying pan into the military fire. Just as the peaceful citizen may be less inclined to volunteer as a policeman if potential criminals are equipped with machine guns rather than mere fists, the willingness of peacefully inclined states to participate in the venture of collective security is dependent upon the magnitude of the military involvement prospectively required; they are prepared to serve as whistle-blowing and nightstick wielding policemen, but they reserve decision about becoming full-fledged soldiers.

At this point, we again encounter the troublesome problem of circularity. Collective security cannot work unless states disarm, but states will not disarm until collective security has clearly shown that it merits confidence. The maintenance of national military strength is an indication that states are unwilling to entrust their fate to a community agency, but their armament policy, born of lack of confidence in collective security, prevents the development of an effective collective security system.

Another significant objective requirement might be described as the universality of economic vulnerability. Collective security assumes that the states of the world are as interdependent for their strength as for their peace, and that its restraining function can be exercised in large part by the imposition of isolation, the organization of deprivation, without resort to collective measures of suppression. It envisages a world in which every state is not only susceptible to the impact of organized force, but also, vulnerable to the squeeze of organized boycott, and it accordingly regards economic sanctions as its first line of attack. It recognizes the vital importance of holding the military weapon in reserve, but it offers to its participating members the reassuring possibility that they may be able to discharge their responsibilities by the relatively painless and humane method of denying to aggressors the benefits of normal intercourse, rather than by running the risks involved in the resort to arms.

In summary, collective security assumes the existence of a world in which every state is so limited by the distribution of power, the reduction of military power levels by a disarmament program, and the lack of economic self-sufficiency, that any state which may develop aggressive inclinations can be held in check by methods which probably need not include the large-scale use of force. It assumes the possibility of securing the acceptance by states of theoretically formidable responsibilities for enforcing the peace, only because it assumes the improbability that it will be necessary to invoke the performance of the most drastic enforcement duties.

Finally, collective security requires the creation of a legal and structural apparatus capable of giving institutional expression to its basic principles. This involves the legal establishment of the prohibition of aggression, the commitment of states to collaborate in the suppression of aggression, and the endowment of an international organization with authority to determine when and against what state sanctions are to be initiated, to decide upon the nature of the inhibitory measures, to evoke the performance of duties to which states have committed themselves, and to plan and direct the joint action which it deems necessary for the implementation of collective security. The meaningfulness of the system is dependent upon the capacity of the organizational mechanism to exercise these vital functions without obstruction. In specific terms, this means that the decision to set the system into operation against a particular state must not be subject to the veto of an obstinate minority, and that no state can be permitted to nullify its commitment to act on behalf of the community by withholding its assent from a decision to call for the performance of that obligation. The elaboration of an adequate supervisory agency is no less important to collective security than the satisfaction of the subjective requirements and the realization of the prerequisite conditions in the global power situation . . .

Collective Security versus Balance of Power

Inis L. Claude, Jr.

THE WILSONIAN CONTRAST BETWEEN BALANCE OF POWER AND COLLECTIVE SECURITY

In this original version, which I shall call the Wilsonian doctrine in recognition of the fact that Wilson was its most ardent and articulate exponent, the concept of collective security involves the creation of an international system in which the danger of aggressive warfare by any state is to be met by the avowed determination of virtually all other states to exert pressure of every necessary variety—moral, diplomatic, economic, and military—to frustrate attack upon any state. The expectation of collective resistance to aggression is conceived as a deterrent threat to states which might be tempted to misuse their power and as a promise of security to all states which might be subject to attack. The scheme is collective in the fullest sense; it purports to provide security *for* all states, by the action of all states, *against* all states which might challenge the existing order by the arbitrary unleashing of their power.

The Wilsonian concept of collective security was presented in deliberate and emphatic contrast to the pre-existant balance of power system. In addressing the League to enforce peace, Wilson stressed the need for "a new and more wholesome diplomacy,"[1] and he pictured the new system as one in which states would cooperate in the common cause of guaranteeing security and justice to all, rather than engage in competitive alliances as in the old system, and in which coercion would serve the common peace and order, rather than function, as formerly, in the interest of political ambition and selfish hostility.[2] Henceforth, Wilson's theme was *change;* he would ring out the old and ring in the new system of international relations; he would inform the powers of Europe that American participation in world affairs depended upon their conforming to the demand that they "*take an entirely new course of action.*"[3] Advocates of collective security, from Wilson's day to the present, have tended to define and characterize it in sharp contrast to the balance of power system.

The old system was pictured as relying upon the hope that equilibrium could be maintained and would suffice to discourage militarist adventures. The collective security system was presented as a more effective scheme in that it promised to confront would-be aggressors with an overwhelming preponderance of power. Peace would henceforth be based not upon a precarious, uncertain, unstable equilibrium, with its minimal deterrent effect, but upon "a force . . . so much greater than the force of any nation . . . or any alliance hitherto formed or projected that no nation, no probable combination of nations could face or withstand it."[4] As a British military leader stated the case:

1. Scott, *President Wilson's Foreign Policy,* p. 191.
2. *Ibid.,* pp. 192-195.
3. Cited in Miller, *op. cit.,* I, 42. Italics in original.
4. Wilson, in Scott, *op. cit.,* p. 248.

> The efforts of European statesmen [under the old system] were directed to securing peace by organizing a balance of military power sufficiently exact to make the risk of attack by the group in one scale upon the group in the other prohibitive. This procedure failed... . The Covenant of the League of Nations endeavours to find a better guarantee against war by substituting for the small group of Powers a single group so large that its authority cannot be challenged with impunity. The Balance of Power is replaced by the Concert or Concentration of Power.
>
> The guarantees . . . promise to make an attempt by any one state or group of states to win by force the power to dominate its neighbours far more dangerous to its originators than it has been in the past. The war of nations which was a development arising out of the balance of power, will tend under the concentration of power to become less and less possible and may eventually become impossible.[5]

In traditional balance of power theory, the dilemma of preponderance was insoluble. Preponderance was clearly desirable, and perhaps necessary, to provide maximum inhibition against aggression, but it was itself subject to aggressive misuse; nobody could be trusted with overwhelming power. How could preponderance be made available as a deterrent without being available as an instrument of aggression? From the standpoint of the balance system, this could not be arranged. The superior deterrent effect of preponderance had to be sacrificed. Equilibrium had to be preferred because it was a safer configuration; if it had the demerit of relative ineffectiveness as an inhibitor of aggression, it nevertheless had the compensatory merit of equalizing the inability of states and groups of states to attack others with assurance of success. If nobody was very secure in an equilibrium situation, neither was anybody very insecure.

Collective security purported to solve this dilemma. It postulated a preponderance which would be available to everybody for defensive purposes, but to nobody for aggressive purposes. The community would have overwhelming force to deter any violation of the common order, but no segment of the community would be so strong as to pose a threat to the security of another segment and thus to precipitate a competitive power struggle. Collective preponderance would discourage any potential aggressor without placing a dangerous concentration of power at the disposal of any state or combination. Thus, a break was contemplated in the vicious circle in which one state's security is another state's insecurity.

An important implication of this theory was that a collective security system would emancipate small and weak states from the precarious position which they occupied in a balance system. The old system was indicted as one in which small states were treated as pawns at the disposal of the players of the game, means to the ends of the great powers. In the operation of that system, small states might be protected or they might be chopped to bits; their fate was dependent upon the convenience, the calculations of self-interest, of the major participants. In contrast, the collective security system was presented as a scheme for guaranteeing the fundamental rights and interests of the weak as well as the strong. Small states would be enveloped in a protective community, not caught in the machinations of great power rivalries.

Finally, collective security was contrasted with balance of power as an *organized* system replacing a haphazard arrangement. The balance of power system was considered so decentralized as to be no system at all in any meaningful sense; it was essentially a euphe-

---

5. Major-General Sir Frederic Maurice, in Harold Temperley, ed, *A History of the Peace Conference of Paris* (London 1924), VI, 525, 533.

mism for anarchy. States operated autonomously to affect the general power situation, and only by some happy accident could their uncoordinated maneuvers produce a satisfactory basis for order.[6] The balance of power offered an "individualistic or particularistic solution of the problem of security," whereas collective security implied "a totally different conception of the problem,"[7] stressing the requirement that the community create an institutional apparatus capable of supervising and coordinating the policies of states in the interest of maintaining the general order. There is an integral relationship between the concept of collective security and the rise of general international organizations in the twentieth century; collective security envisages a community of states organized for peace, repudiating the expectation that peace will reliably emerge as a precipitate of spontaneous interaction among competitive states.

The Wilsonian concept of collective security treats the states of the world as members of a single community, laced together by unbreakable ties of interdependence. Each state has a supreme interest in the maintenance of the common order; the security of each is involved in the safeguarding of all against aggressive assault. Since the community is regarded as all-inclusive, the system is inner-oriented. It is postulated that threats to the common peace may arise within the community, and that they must be dealt with by the combined power resources of members of the community, cooperating under the auspices of its central institutions. The world is conceived not as a *we*-group and a *they*-group of nations, engaged in competitive power relations, but as an integral *we*-group in which danger may be posed by "one of us" and must be met by "all the rest of us." The hope for successful maintenance of order rests firmly upon the theory of deterrence. It must be clearly established that aggression by any member of the community against any other will inexorably activate the combination of the general membership to meet the challenge. The promise of collective action—expressed in legal commitment prepared for effectuation by the operation of an institutional mechanism, and based upon the awareness of the involvement of national interests in the common order—is conceived as a warning to possible initiators, and a reassurance to possible victims, of aggressive attack.

THE BLURRING OF THE CONTRAST

As the terminology of collective security has made its way into the standard vocabulary of international relations, the distinctiveness of its connotation has been considerably diluted. Particularly among journalists and political leaders, there has been a growing tendency to interpret collective security in literal, common-sense fashion, applying it to any *favorably regarded* alignment of two or more states. The italicized words are important, for they indicate the attachment of ideological value to elective security which has accompanied the blurring of its meaning. Since World War II, collective security has been used with increasing frequency to mean "a good alliance" or collection of alliances. An alliance is *collective* in the sense that it binds two or more states to act together; it is a *security* arrangement if it is judged to be, or if it is presented as, a pact intended for legitimate defensive purposes rather than for aggression. Thus, in the Cold War, each side tends to appropriate the label of collective security for its pattern of alliances and to deny that label to the arrangements formulated by its rival. In one of the innumerable instances which might be cited, Secretary of Defense Neil H. McElroy, speaking in New York on April 23,

6. See Gulick, *Europe's Classical Balance of Power,* pp. 85-86.

7. Bourquin, *Collective Security, p. 444.*

1959, described the American program of building a network of alliances against Soviet expansion as the expression of a policy of collective security, and asserted that "Basically, the doctrine of collective security requires strength among our allies around the world."[8]

Obviously, this is a strange use of a term that was originally identified with the replacement of the alliance system by a fundamentally different scheme for managing international relations. Wilsonians are stood on their heads by a semantic practice which tags an alliance system as a collective security arrangement. To some degree, this practice probably reflects a simple failure to appreciate the fact that collective security was developed as a technical term to designate a system sharply differentiated from the alliance system. The misuse of the term is the penalty which theoreticians of international relations must pay for the lack of an esoteric vocabulary. It is likely, however, that some degree of deliberate misappropriation of semantic funds is also involved in the case. Whatever their failures, the Wilsonians clearly succeeded in establishing the conviction that collective security represents a brand of international morality vastly superior to that incorporated in the balance of power system. Hence, considerable ideological advantage is presumed to result from the embellishment of alliances with the morally attractive verbiage of collective security. . . .[9]

SIMILARITIES BETWEEN BALANCE OF POWER AND COLLECTIVE SECURITY

The concepts of balance of power and collective security share a fundamental preoccupation with the problem of power in international relations, and the basic purpose of providing a system within which that problem may be reduced to manageable proportions. In both theories there is a hypothetical mistrust of *any* state which appears to be so preponderantly powerful that it can trespass with impunity upon the basic interests of other states. The problem is stated somewhat differently in the two schemes; balance of power focuses mistrust upon *aggressive capacity,* while collective security focuses upon *aggressive policy;* the one asks, "Who is too strong?" while the other asks, "Who commits aggression?" Nevertheless, in the balance of power scheme states do take into account the presumed policy intentions as well as the estimated power potentials of other states; they may line up with A against B, not on the ground that A is weaker than B, but on the ground that B, being both strong and untrustworthy, poses a threat and that A, being strong and trustworthy, can give valuable aid in meeting that threat.[10] The calculations of policy intention may be difficult to make with accuracy, but the point is that they are integral elements in the operation of a balance of power system; whenever a weak state contracts an alliance with one great power against another, it is betting its life on the proposition that the former is a friend and the latter an enemy of its security. If the balance of power system involves concern with aggressive policy, so does the collective security system involve concern with aggressive capacity. Its basic strategy is the organization of such a formidable aggregation of national forces that no single state or probable combination of states can expect to attain a position of strength which would permit it to commit aggression with impunity. Collec-

---

8. *Thc New York Timcs,* Apr. 4, 1959. For further citations and discussion of the tendency to use the terrninology of collective security in this fashion, see Inis L. Claude Jr. *Swords Into Plowshares,* 2nd ed. (New York: Random House, 1959) pp. 252-254.

9. Cf. Robert E. Osgood, "Woodrow Wilson, Collective Security, and the Lessons of History," in Latham, ed., *The Philosophy and Policies of Woodrow Wilson, p.* 189.

10. See the fuller discussion of this point, see Claude, *Power and International Relations.*

tive security tolerates no preponderance save the collective superiority of the community which is mobilizable only for the defense of its members. Hence, the two schemes represent fundamental agreement on the peril represented by any state or group of states which possesses overwhelming power.

Both systems are grounded on the basic concept of *deterrence;* in their ideal operational pictures, they manage power and policy situations in the pluralistic world of independent states in such fashion that potential disturbers of the peace are kept in check by the threat that their troublemaking enterprises will be defeated. Thus, both share the assumption that statesmen will be rational enough to recognize the sufficiency of the power which confronts them, and prudent enough to refrain from challenging that power.

The deterrent strategy of collective security explicitly involves preponderance—not the preponderance of one state or one alliance, achieved in a competitive power struggle and available to serve the policy of its possessors, but the preponderance of the community, achieved through the cooperative combination of its members and available to serve the peace-keeping policy of the community. Collective security is too nervous to rely on the hope that aggressive statesmen will be inhibited by subtle calculations of equilibrium; it is comfortable only when such leaders are confronted by the obvious fact that they are grossly outclassed.

It is more difficult to find an unambiguous strategy of deterrence in the doctrine of the balance of power. The idea of equilibrium has left an indelible imprint upon this theory, supporting the impression that the balance system involves reliance upon *mere* equality of opposing power to keep aggressors in check. But the concept of equality is as troublesome, as difficult to fit into a genuinely acceptable role, in balance of power theory as in democratic theory or international legal theory; men will not discard it, but they do not quite know what to do with it. Few theorists would insist that states operating in a balance system typically aspire to sheer equality *vis à vis* their rivals, or that the architects of an alignment designed to check a predatory power are likely to be conscientious about limiting the power of their grouping to a meticulously calculated equality. One does not expect to find diplomatic notes in which statesmen advise would-be allies to join a rival grouping, saying, "It appears that our side is rather too strong already, and it could improve the equilibrium if you would add your weight to the other side." A realistic statement of the theory of the balance system would suggest that states adopt the view that the "dangerous" state or states must be held in check by the accumulation of power at *least* equal to, and preferably greater than its own. This is to say that there is no real contrast between collective security and balance of power as deterrent systems, despite the association of the term preponderance with the one and the term equilibrium with the other. In both, the confrontation of the potential attacker with equal power is regarded as the minimal requirement, and the mobilization of superior power against him is treated as the optimal achievement. Collective security is merely more explicit concerning the latter half of this proposition.

Both systems involve the paradox of "war for peace"; they indicate that the fulfillment of the urge for peace is to be achieved by the possession of capacity to fight and the assertion of will to fight. This combination of power and policy is deemed both a prerequisite to successful deterrence—since the operative inhibitory factor is not power per *se* but the evident willingness to *use* power—and an essential hedge against the possible failure of deterrence. In neither scheme is deterrence assumed to be infallibly effective; aggressive attack may occur, in which case the resistance of states committed to "maintaining the balance of power" or "upholding collective security" must be translated from threat to actuality. Balance of power and collective security join in espousing a brand of "pacifism" which requires that states be ready and willing to fight.

The two systems are similar in that they postulate participation in joint action by states even when they are not directly and immediately challenged by a given disturber of the peace. Both require that states reject the narrow and short-sighted view that their interests are implicated only in an assault aimed specifically at themselves, and recognize their stake in controlling upheavals that affect the larger context within which they function. Self-defense becomes a matter of acting with others to forestall the development of a situation in the system at large which would presumably be disadvantageous to the interests of the state in the longer run, rather than confining response to an attack in the *here* and *now*. In the balance system, A joins in the defense of B and C against D, lest D gain a position in the power configuration which might enable it later to conquer A. The collective security principle decrees the same response, rationalized in the rather different terms that peace is indivisible and that the safety of the entire community demands the treatment of an attack upon one member as an attack upon all members. As we shall see, a vital difference between the two systems arises out of the interpretation and application of this general rule of response to aggression against other states. For the moment, however, the significant point is that both systems, in principle, rely upon acceptance of this rule.

In accordance with the above position, it is evident that both systems envisage collective action in the sense of parallel and reciprocally reinforcing action by units which have and retain essentially separate and independent status. Deterrence is sought by an arrangement which brings several or many autonomous policy-making units to adopt identical policies. Repression of disorder is sought by an arrangement which brings such units to use their power in a common enterprise. Both are, in the broadest sense, systems dependent upon the coordination of the policy and action of independent states and subject to the difficulties which are inherent in such an undertaking. Again, there are differences between the systems in this connection, but they arise out of a fundamental similarity.

Since both systems seek deterrence, they share the necessity of rendering the policy of states toward potential troublemakers as predictable as possible. Neither scheme can operate effectively without the creation of a reasonably dependable expectation that certain states at least will react in forceful opposition to the challenge of an aggressor. The typical instrument of advance commitment in the balance system is the alliance, while collective security envisages a broader arrangement, usually involving obligations of common action undertaken in the constitutional document of a general international organization. In the abstract, the concept of collective security is usually taken to imply the creation of a *universal* partnership for common action, as contrasted with the limited grouping defined by an alliance. It should be noted, however, that theorists of collective security have often qualified this contrast by suggesting that, in particular cases, only a selected group of states would be required and should be called upon to carry out the obligations to which all states have bound themselves. Even with this qualification, substantial differences remain between the two systems on this point. Nevertheless, both systems, in seeking to promote the necessary degree of predictability in the behavior of states, impinge upon the sovereignty of states. In contracting alliances and in joining universal collective security organizations, states are taking fundamentally similar steps, since in either case they are renouncing in some degree the right to formulate policy on a wholly discretionary basis—

the right to be totally unpredictable—in a future situation. The retention of an absolutely free hand in national decision-making is compatible only with anarchy, or with isolation from whatever system of international relations may exist. . . .

The case for the sharp differentiation of the concepts of balance of power and collective security is shaken by the fact that analyses of the basic conditions required for the successful functioning of the systems implied by the two concepts show marked similarities. One can argue, for instance, that the balance system requires the diffusion of power among a number of major states so that no single state will control such a large fraction of the world's power resources as to make the task of counter-balancing it inordinately difficult precisely the same requirement can be cited for the collective security system, to avoid the possibility that any state will be invulnerable to the pressure of collective sanctions. A power configuration marked by bipolarity is equally unfavorable to the operation of the balance system or a collective security system. One can demonstrate that a successful balance system requires that national policies be adaptable to contingencies, not rigidly fixed, so that old friends can be resisted when they endanger the stability of the system and former enemies can be supported when the exigencies of the power system so require. A similar flexibility of policy, involving the capacity to switch the foci of friendship and enmity, is essential to collective security. Democracy with its tendency to impose the restraints of public opinion upon policy makers and thereby to restrict their capacity to do what the system requires in a given situation, is an impediment to the smooth functioning of either the balance or the collective security system. Other illustrations could be adduced to drive home the point that these two systems were designed to deal with essentially the same world; they rest upon broadly similar assumptions concerning the nature of the setting in which they are to operate. This observation tends to invalidate the claim that collective security is a logical successor to balance of power in the twentieth century; the changes in the character of international relations which impede the successful working of balance system also minimize the possibility of an effective system of collective security.

Further indications of the closeness of the two systems to each other are provided by passages in the literature relating to the balance of power which could equally well be taken as commentary on collective security. Friedrich von Gentz was elaborating his theory of the balance when he wrote that all states should rally to the defense of any state threatened by aggression, since all are endangered by an assault upon any member of the system, and concluded that "We must hear of no insulary systems, no indifference to a danger apparently foreign to their own immediate interests, no absolute neutrality."[11] Yet it is clear that this position might have been argued in the same terms by Woodrow Wilson, pleading for the acceptance of the concept of collective security. . . .

ESSENTIAL DISTINCTONS BETWEEN BALANCE OF POWER AND COLLECTIVE SECURITY

Wilson was essentially correct in thinking that the differences between the two concepts were significant enough to make the collective security system a distinctive approach to the management of power in international relations. He was at the heart of the matter when he said:

---

11. *Fragments Upon the Balance of Power in Europe*, pp.105-106.

> I shall never myself consent to an entangling alliance, but I would gladly assent to a disentangling alliance—an alliance which would disentangle the peoples of the world from those combinations ill which they seek their own separate and private interests and unite the people of the world to preserve the peace of the world upon a basis of common right and justice.[12]

Collective security implies a general alliance, a universal alliance, which is disentangling in the sense that it eliminates the pattern of competitive alignments which characterizes the balance system; it avoids the sort of entanglement in organized rivalries which Wilson frequently castigated as conducive to war. It calls for an alliance system which *unites* the nations in defense of the order of the community, instead of one which *divides* them into antagonistic groups, jockeying for position against each other. Cordell Hull had this concept of collective security in mind when he wrote of the United Nations: "It is not an alliance against a combination of other nations but against any aggressor. It is an alliance not for war but for peace."[13]

The balance of power system involves alliances which are essentially *externally-oriented* groupings, designed to organize cooperative action among their members for the purpose of dealing with conflict situations posed by states or groups of states on the outside. By contrast, the collective security system looks *inward*, seeking to provide security for all its members against any of their number who might contemplate aggression.[14] Balance of power postulates two or more worlds in jealous confrontation, while collective security postulates one world, organized for the cooperative maintenance of order within its bounds.

The schemes agree in recognizing both conflict and cooperation as basic tendencies in international relations, and in treating conflict as a danger to be met by cooperation. But balance of power stresses the possibility of achieving order through the arrangement of appropriate patterns of conflictual relations, while collective security looks instead to the development of a structure of general cooperation to hold conflict in check. The one emphasizes the manipulation of rivalry; the other, the exploitation of cooperative potential. For balance of power, competitive struggle is the general condition, to be dealt with by the realization of cooperative arrangements within limited groupings. For collective security, general cooperation looms as an ideal possibility for coping with outbreaks of sharp conflict which are ranked as occasional phenomena rather than standard expressions of the character of international relations. Balance of power treats conflict as general and cooperation as exceptional; collective security treats conflict as exceptional and cooperation as an *attainable* general circumstance to restrict conflict. The former promises competitive security, while the latter promises cooperative security.

The principle of collective security requires that states identify their national interest so completely with the preservation of the total world order that they stand ready to join in collective action to put down any aggressive threat by any state, against any other state anywhere. By assumption, peace and security are indivisible; the initiation of war anywhere is a challenge to the interest of all states, because it undermines the general order which is central to the security of every state. The balance of power concept, on the other hand, leaves much more latitude for the *ad hoc* calculation of what the national interest requires in particular circumstances. It does not postulate a seamless web of international peace and order, nor assume as self-evident the proposition that every state has a stake in preventing war or sup-

---

12. Cited in Walworth, *op. cit.*, II, 39.

13. *The Memoirs of Cordell Hull*, II, 1948.

14. Cf. Ben T. Moore, *NATO and the Future of Europe* (New York: Harper, 1958), p. 115.

pressing aggression wherever it may occur. On the contrary, states applying the balance principle may ignore some conflicts as irrelevant to their interests; they may welcome some conflicts as likely to affect their competitors in a way favorable to their own position in the general configuration of power; they may even regard aggression as a means legitimately available to themselves for improving or safeguarding their situation. Collective security decrees a set response in support of any victim of aggression; balance of power confirms the freedom of the state to pick and choose. Clearly, collective security is more thoroughly anti-war and more deeply committed in principle to supporting the victim of aggression as such.

The difference in this respect is fundamentally a difference regarding the *facts.* The balance principle says that a state should join in resistance to an aggressor *only if* its own security is affected; the collective security principle says that a state should do so always *because* its interests are affected by any aggression. The contrast is well illustrated in passages from Louis J. Halle and Lester B. Pearson. Halle asserts that "it is no part of an American policy-maker's duties to concern himself with the welfare of foreigners except as their welfare may relate to American interests. . . . Their fate is not our business except as it bears on our fate";[15] Pearson rejects a narrow continentalism as wrongly implying "that other free and friendly countries are and can be kept outside our own fate."[16] Between *only if* and *always because* lies a profound disagreement about the facts of international life. Is war anywhere a danger to all men everywhere? Do all nations have so great a stake in maintaining world order that their real interest requires them to cooperate in supporting any state which is the object of aggression? The judgment implicit in the balance system is an equivocal, pragmatic "Not necessarily—statesmen should try to evaluate each situation as it arises," while collective security expresses the clear and dogmatic affirmative, calling for advance commitment based on the conviction that this judgment is unalterably valid for all future contingencies.

This difference points to the fundamental contrast between the two concepts, which has to do with the degree of managerial centralization that they entail. Balance of power is a system only by courtesy; while the accusation that it amounts to anarchy is too strong, it is assuredly a most unsystematic system. It depends upon the autonomous, self-directed operations of a multitude of states and particularly of a smaller group of major states, and it therefore produces a continuing series of improvisations. Collective security, on the other hand, represents the urge for systematization, the institutionalization of international relations. It proposes to coordinate the policies of states in accordance with firmly established general principles and to create institutions capable of providing some degree of centralized supervision and management of the system. The two systems may lead to the same action in a given case, but the balance system leaves this result to the contingencies of diverse calculations and autonomous maneuvers, while the collective security system undertakes to make it the predictable outcome of the operation of international machinery in the application of settled principle. As Wright puts it, the collective security system differs from the balance system "as art differs from nature."[17]

> Policies of balance of power naturally lead to policies of collective security which become institutionalized through common organs, procedures, and rules of law to assure that aggres-

---

15. *Civilization and Foreign Policy,* p. 184-185.

16. *Democracy and World Politics* (Princeton: Princeton University Press,1955), p. 42.

17. *The Study of International Relations,* p. 204.

> sion will be always confronted by insuperable force. International organization to promote collective security is, therefore, only a planned development of the natural tendency of balance of power policies. It is the natural tendency of states, when faced by an emergency, to gang up against the aggressor who, if successful against his first victim, will eventually turn on the others. Collective security seeks to supplement this natural tendency by positive obligations and convenient agencies and procedures to enlist common action.[18]

Typically, the exponent of the balance of power concept is preoccupied with the problem of dealing with a concrete and immediate issue affecting the security of his state—*e.g.*, how the United States can cope with the dynamics of Soviet expansionism—and he is unwilling to be diverted by consideration of the requirements for an adequate general system of international relations. An excellent illustration of this phenomenon is provided by Arnold Wolfers in his essay, "Collective Defense versus Collective Security."[19] Wolfers evidently values the balance principle primarily because it does not significantly limit the freedom of the state to maneuver in the pursuit of its objectives, and condemns the collective security principle because it does so limit the state. He does not render a comparative judgment of the adequacy of the two systems as means for the maintenance of international order, for he is concerned with a specific problem, not with the general system. The balance of power system represents an aversion to systematic regulation of international relations; it enshrines the principle of the freedom of states to maneuver at will.

It is equally typical of champions of collective security to focus their attention upon the abstract issue of the general pattern, the broad framework, of the international community, rather than the concrete problems of foreign policy in the here and now. They are system-conscious. In this they reflect a fundamental characteristic of collective security, concern for the systematic management of relations among states.

---

18. *Ibid.*, p.163.

19. Alliance Policy in the Cold War, pp. 49-74.

Democratic Peace Theory and Its Effects

"Scholars and leaders now commonly say 'Democracies almost never fight each other.' What does that mean? Is it true? If so, what does it imply for the future of international politics?"[1] In recent international relations studies, debate surrounding Democratic Peace Theory has been very contentious. Whether the democratic peace exists, whether there is a theory that can explain it, and whether it warrants serious attention in the formulation of policy are all matters of considerable dispute.

In a field of study that has been dominated by realist world views and associated theoretical manifestations, the practical idealism of the democratic peace is a significant challenge. Democratic Peace Theory suggests that there are qualitatively different international relations within the community of liberal democracies (referred to by some as the "Zone of Peace"). This contradicts critical realist assumptions. For theories such as classic and structural realism, assumptions about the similar nature of all states heavily discount factors such as differing forms of state governance.

The observation of the relative lack of war among democracies is itself a matter of dispute. Whether or not democracies *have* ever fought one another turns on definitions of democracy at different points in history as well as the definitions of what constitutes war. However, accepting (as most analysts do) that there *is* a statistically different level of peaceful relations among established liberal democratic states still leaves us with the democratic peace merely as a data point.

Democracy + Democracy = Peace (or ≠ war) is an observation. Theory requires an explanation to account for the outcome. What is it about democracy that causes peace? This is the question that a theory of democratic peace must address.

The reading from Bruce Russett that follows is drawn from chapters 2 of his book, *Grasping the Democratic Peace: Principles for a Post-Cold War World*. In the reading, Russett provides a theoretical approach explaining *why* democratic peace exists. This is part of the book's larger effort to "document, explain, and speculate about the implications of the phenomenon of the democratic peace."[2] He builds on the concepts about the significance of liberal democracy—sometimes called republicanism—highlighted by Immanuel Kant and Michael Doyle (see previous chapters in this reader: Kant, "To Perpetual Peace" [1795] and Doyle, "Liberalism and World Politics," [1986]). Russett explores the reasons why democracy may indeed be the cause of peace among democratic states. Conversely, he also explores some alternative explanations of relative peace between democracies that may render democracy spurious. In other words, he addresses whether there is some other characteristic that democracies have in common that better accounts for relative peace among them.

Russett is a Yale University Professor and is well known within the field of international relations as a leading statistical analyst. With the publication of his book in 1993, Russett entered the debates concerning the validity of the democratic peace to provide statistically rigorous tests of the correlation between a variety of independent variables that

1. Bruce Russett, *Grasping at the Democratic Peace: Principles for a Post-Cold War World* (Princeton, NJ: Princeton University Press, 1993), 3.
2. Ibid., 4.

might account for the dependent variable of peace among democracies. Russett finds that democracy is *not* a spurious variable in explaining why democracies do not go to war with each other. While his book provides a valuable contribution to the debate about the democratic peace, it has not settled it.

The significance of the debate is all the greater in light of critical elements of American policy that explicitly accept the observation as valid and then use it to support efforts to promulgate democracy worldwide. Indeed, the promulgation of democracies is an explicit component of American *National Security Strategy.*[3] The policy relevance of the observation of democratic peace highlights all the more powerfully the need to fully understand what it is about democracy that should be transmitted to other countries.

Where Russet discusses democratic peace, Edward D. Mansfield and Jack Snyder write about the conflicts that may emerge as nations attempt to transition to democracy. Their work, entitled Democratic Transitions and War, is written in the realist tradition as the authors discuss the potential conflicts that may emerge at the domestic level. Mansfield and Snyder explain why "[s]tatistical evidence covering the past two centuries shows that in this transitional phase of democratization, countries become more aggressive and war prone, not less, and they fight wars with democratic states.'[4] The writers utilize statistical evidence correlating nations' regime changes with the probability of war. They focus on the fact that numerous parties with competing interests frequently reach polite stalemates that are overcome by the "elite mobilization of mass groups"[5] who create conflict.

Fareed Zakaria offers a counterpoint to the concept of Democratic Peace by contrasting the spectrum of liberalism embodies within the world's 118 declared democracies. "Constitutional liberalism," he states, "has led to democracy, but democracy does not seem to bring constitutional liberalism."[6] A unique aspect of Zakaria's article is that he does not question whether or not a nation that is described as a democracy may truly be considered a democracy. Instead, he focuses on the "spectrum of illiberal democracy, ranging from modest offenders like Argentina to near-tyrannies like Kazakstan and Belarus, with countries like Romania and Bangladesh in between."[7] Zakaria concludes that, "It is only with other democracies that [Democratic Peace Theory] holds. When divining the cause behind this correlation, one thing becomes clear: the democratic peace is actually the liberal peace."[8]

---

3. George W. Bush, *The National Security Strategyof the United States of America* (September 2002), on the WWW at: http://www.whitehouse.gov/nsc/nss.html (date accessed: 7 May 2004).

4. Chester A. Crocker, Fen Osler Hampson and Panela Aall, ed., *Turbulent Peace: The Challenges of Managing International Conflict* (1995), p. 113.

5. ibid., p 121.

6. Fareed Zakaria, *The Rise of Illiberal Democracy* (November/December 1997).

7. ibid.

8. ibid.

Why Democratic Peace?

Bruce Russett

When democratic states were rare, the Kantian perspective had little practical import, and power politics reigned. But if the Kantian perspective is correct, recent events replacing authoritarian regimes with democratic values and institutions in much of Asia, Eastern Europe, and Latin America[1] may have profound implications not just for governmental practices within states, but for worldwide peace among states. It may be possible in part to supersede the "realist" principles (anarchy, the security dilemma of states) that have dominated practice to the exclusion of "liberal" or "idealist" ones since at least the seventeenth century.

Politics within a democracy is seen as largely a nonzero-sum enterprise; by cooperating, all can gain something even if all do not gain equally, and the winners are restrained from crushing the losers. Indeed, today's winners may, as coalitions shift, wish tomorrow to ally with today's losers. If the conflicts degenerate to physical violence, either by those in control of the state or by insurgents, all can lose. In most international politics—the anarchy of a self-help system with no overall governing authority—these norms and practices are not the same. "Realists" remind us of the powerful norms of legitimate self-defense and the acceptability of military deterrence, norms much more extensive internationally than within democratic states. Politics among nations takes on a more zero-sum hue, with the state's sovereign existence at risk.

The principles of anarchy and self-help in a zero-sum world are most acute in "structural realist" theories of international relations. The nature of states' internal systems of government is seen as nearly irrelevant; their overall behavior is basically determined by the structure of the international system and their position in that structure. "Peace" is a fleeting condition, dependent upon deterrence and eternal vigilance. By this structural realist understanding the kind of stable peace that exists among democracies cannot last, because eventually democracies would be compelled, by the structure of the international system and their eternal security dilemma, to enter a state of war or at best of military deterrence[2]. Realism has no place for an expectation that democracies will not fight each other. To the degree we establish that peace between democracies is a fact, and are able to explain it theoretically, we build an alternative view of the world with great import for expectations and for policy. We begin with the theories.

---

1. The trend to democratic government has been documented worldwide up to 1988 by Gastil 1989 and later by Freedom House (McColm et al. 1992), and traced back to the eighteenth century by Modelski 1989 and Gurr et al. 1991 (Gastil, Raymond. 1989. *Freedom in the World: Political Rights and Civil Liberties*, 1988-1989. New York: Freedom House; McColm, R. Bruce, et al. 1992. *Freedom in the World: Political Rights and Civil Liberties 1991-92*. New York: Freedom House; Modelski, George. 1988. *Is America's Decline Inevitable*? Wassenaar: Netherlands Institute for Advanced Study; Gurr, Ted Robert. 1974. "Persistence and Change in Political Systems." *American Political Science Review* 68, 4: 1482-1504); also see Starr, Harvey. 1991. "Democratic Dominoes: Diffusion Approaches to the Speread of Democracy." Journal of Conflict Resolution 35, 2: 356-81. and Huntington, Samuel P. 1989. "No Exit: The Errors of Endism." *The National Interest* 17, 1: 3-11.

2. Waltz, Kenneth. 1979. *Theory of International Relations*. Reading, MA: Addison Wesley;Mearsheimer, John. 1990, "Back to the Future: Instability in Europe after the Cold War." *International Security* 15, 1: 5-56.

If scholars are near consensus that democratically governed states rarely go to war with each other or even fight each other at low levels of lethal violence, this does not mean there is anything like consensus on why the phenomenon occurs. Nor can the same generalization be supported for relations among other kinds of political systems (for example, military or other dictatorships). Sharing common forms of political structure and political culture in general does not prevent war between independent states.[3] If similarity of form of government in general were enough then we would have seen peace between the Soviet Union and China, between the Soviet Union and its formerly communist East European neighbors, and between China and Vietnam. Despite important differences in political values and organization among the communist countries, they were much more like one another in values and ideology than like the democracies or even like right-wing dictatorships. Yet war between these countries, and disputes that threatened to erupt in war, were commonplace.

Certainly some kinds of differences, if politically salient, can cause conflict. But that becomes virtually tautological unless one can specify what differences will be salient. For sixteenth-century Europe religious differences between Catholics and Protestants provided politically salient ideological reasons for killing each other; by the twentieth century those differences were irrelevant to violent conflict save in isolated pockets like Northern Ireland. Thus it seems likely that the reasons for "democratic peace" are either rooted somehow in the nature of democracy itself, or are correlated in the modern world with the phenomenon of democracy.

Some scholars vigorously question the causal inference that democracies are at peace with each other simply because they are democratic. They point instead to other influences that are correlated with democracy and hence create a spurious relation between democracy itself and general peace between democratic states. Without going into the vast range of hypotheses about the causes of war and peace, we need to consider some of the most important ones that might specifically account for the relationship between democratic states.

ALTERNATIVE EXPLANATIONS

Alternative hypotheses to explain the phenomenon include the following.

Transnational and international institutions make peace

The states in question are peaceful toward each other because they are bound by common ties in a network of institutions crossing national boundaries. Democracies often do share many common institutions. Analysts may emphasize the role of the European Community (EC), for example, and certainly one of the major motivations of the founders of the institutions that evolved into the EC was to bind together previously hostile states so that they would be unable to make war on each other. Some international organizations clearly have this intention. Others, not primarily addressed to war prevention, help to resolve many troublesome conflicts of interest that might feed suspicion and hostility. But states and ethnic groups typically share common institutions just because they have major interests in conflict as well as in common; institutions are supposed to provide a means to resolve those conflicts

---

3. Weart suggests that certain types of oligarchies rarely have fought each other in various historical eras (Weart, Spencer. Forthcoming. *Never at War: Why Don't Democracies Fight One Another?)*, but Bremer 1992 finds no evidence for this in the modern world (Bremer, Stuart A. 1992. "Dangerous Dyads: Conditions Affecting the Likelihood of Interstate War, 1816-1965." *Journal of Conflict Resolution* 36, 2: 309-41). Previous analyses of very broad measure of social and cultural similarity have produced mixed results.

peacefully. If the common institutions cannot do so, or if one party is coerced into unwillingly sharing common institutions with another, the institutions exacerbate conflict and may become the occasion for civil war.[4] Hence the existence of common intergovernmental or supranational institutions cannot so plausibly be invoked as a prior reason for the absence of war. Peaceful relations must in some degree precede the institutions.

An influential variant of the institutional approach focuses on transnationalism: individual autonomy and pluralism within democratic states foster the emergence of transnational linkages and institutions—among individuals, private groups, and governmental agencies. Those linkages can serve to resolve transnational conflicts peaceably and, by forming transnational alliances into other states, inhibit their national governments from acting violently toward each other. This perspective derives from classics both of international integration theory and of bureaucratic politics and foreign policy.[5] It is not, however, completely separable from the matter of democracy. Democracies foster, and are fostered by, the pluralism arising from many independent centers of power and influence; autocracies do not. Democracies are open to many private and governmental transnational linkages; autocracies rarely are. (Recall the late and unlamented Iron Curtain.) Thus transnationalism cannot easily be considered separately from the distinction between democracies and other kinds of states. Since it is substantially correlated with the "open" institutions of democratic politics, it cannot be treated analytically or empirically as an independent cause.

Distance Prevents War

Most wars are fought between physically adjacent states, thanks to their combination of capability and willingness (reasons) to fight neighbors.[6] Likewise, individuals are most likely to be murdered by friends and close relatives with whom they are in constant contact. But until after World War II democracies tended to be relatively few and far between. Hence the absence of murderous quarrels between democracies was not too surprising, and may need—at least for the pre-1945 era—little further explanation. Even for much of the post-1945 period, the rarity of contiguous democratic states outside of Western Europe might explain much of the absence of violent conflict between democracies.[7] Yet the more

---

4. Russett 1967, chap. 12, finds that, if anything, states sharing membership in international organizations are more likely to be involved in violent conflict with each other (Russett, Bruce. 1967. *International Regions and the International System: A Study in Political Ecology.* Chicago: Rand McNally).

5. See, for example, Deutsch, Karl W., et al. 1957. *Political Community and the North Atlantic Area.* Princeton, NJ: Princeton University Press and Destler, I.M., H. Sato, P. Clapp, and H. Fukui. 1976. *Managing an Alliance: The Politics of U.S.-Japanese Relations.* Washington, D.C.: Brookings Institution, esp. chap. 5. A milestone in the transnational relations literature is Keohane, Robert O., and Joseph S. Nye. 1977. *Power and Interdependence: World Politics in Transition.* Boston, MA: Little Brown, with institutions defined less as formal organizations than as "recognized patterns of practice around which expectations converge" (Young, Oran R. 1980. "Internatinal Regimes: Problems of Concept Formation." *World Politics* 32, 3: 331-56) and as facilitators of communication. An important new look at transnational relations is Risse-Knappen, Thomas. Forthcoming. *Cooperation among Democracies: Norms, Transnational Relations, and the European Influence on U.S. Foreign Policy.*

6. First established by Richardson, corroborated in reviews by Wilkinson; Singer 1981; and Diehl 1991, and confirmed as an independent influence by Bremer 1992. (See Singer, J. David. 1981. "Accounting for International War: The State of the Discipline." *Journal of Peace Research* 18, 1: 1-18; Diehl, Paul. 1991. "Geography and War: A Review and Assessment of the Empirical Literature." *International Interactions* 17, 1: 11-27; Bremer, Stuart A. 1992a. "Dangerous Dyads: Conditions Affecting the Likelihood of Interstate War, 1816-1965." *Journal of Conflict Resolution* 36, 2: 309-41.)

recent one's snapshot of the international system, with many contiguous democracies in Europe and the Western Hemisphere, the less conclusive the distance argument seems.

Alliances Make Peace

Allies may be presumed to choose each other because of their common interests, and hence to be already peacefully inclined toward each other. Moreover, their common interests are likely to concern security against a common enemy. If so, they are not likely to fight each other. Many democracies have shared common interests in presenting a unified alliance front. NATO and the Western alliance system provide the most recent example, but in both world wars the democracies found themselves ranged together (with some non-democracies alongside, to be sure) against the non-democratic Central/Axis powers.[8] So of course democracies won't fight each other.

One trouble with this hypothesis is that it begs the question. Did they not fight each other because they were allied, or did they ally because they feared a common foe (and hence did not fight each other)? And if the latter, did they fear a common foe because they were united in a desire to preserve their common democratic institutions? If the latter, then democracy, not alliance, accounts for the peace among them.

A related hypothesis accounts for peace among members of multilateral alliances not by the alliance per se, but by the active policy of a dominant major power to keep peace within the alliance. Such a hegemonic power may make it very clear to the small powers that in the interest of common security against a major power rival it simply will not tolerate violence among them. Surely in the Western Hemisphere (Rio Pact) and in NATO the United States played such a role, with threats to withhold economic and military assistance to the culprits.[9]

The trouble with this variant of the hypothesis, however, is that as a generalization it is empirically backward. Repeated systematic analyses, beginning with Bueno de Mesquita's[10], affirm that allies are in general more likely to fight each other, even while still formally allied, than are nonallies. Again, the reasons are not so mysterious: the apparently "common" interests may be enforced by a big power with the capability and will to keep straying allies in the fold. Military action by the Soviet Union against Hungary in 1956 provides an example. Consistent with this interpretation, Bremer (1992a)[11] finds allied states likely to fight each other when both states

---

7. Huntington 1989 expressed great skepticism about democratic peace on this ground, and even Small and Singer 1976 strongly implied that their pioneering results on the absence of war between democracies were only an effect of distance (Huntington, Samuel P. 1989. "No Exit: The Errors of End-ism." *The National Interest* 17, 1: 3-11; Small, Melvin, and J. David Singer. 1976. "The War-Proneness of Democratic Regimes." *Jerusalem Journal of International Relations* 1, 1: 50-69).

8. Siverson and Emmons 1991 confirm a generalization, stronger since World War II than before it, that democracies are more likely to ally with each other than with nondemocracies (Siverson, Randolph, and Juliann Emmons. 1991. "Birds of a Feather: Democratic Political Systems and Alliance Choices." *Journal of Conflict Resolution* 35, 2: 285-306). Bueno de Mesquita and Lalman 1992, chap. 5, do not confirm that over the long period they analyze (Bueno de Mesquita, Bruce, and David Lalman. 1992. *War and Reason*. New Haven, CT: Yale University Press).

9. Weede 1983 attributed peace among states of the Western alliance system to the U.S. hegemonic role. Recently (1992), however, he has acknowledged that mutual democracy provides a better explanation (Weede, Erich. 1983. "Extended Deterrence by Superpower Alliance." *Journal of Conflict Resolution* 27, 2: 231-54).

10. Bueno de Mesquita, Bruce. 1981. *The War Trap*. New Haven, CT: Yale University Press.

are militarized. But democratic allied states are different; they are not likely to have violent conflicts with each other.[12]

Wealth Makes Peace

Since democracies are often wealthy, it can be hard to separate their effects. Several variants of this argument persist. One is that for politically stable, economically advanced, and rapidly growing countries the cost/benefit ratio of any war fought on or near their home territories with another advanced state looks extraordinarily unpromising. Historically many wars have been fought to acquire territory; the value of acquiring as war booty the territory of an advanced industrial country would rarely compensate for the costs of wartime destruction and the problems of pacifying newly incorporated peoples[13]. The disincentives would be magnified for highly interdependent economies, which suffer even from damage inflicted on each other's territory that destroys investments, markets, or sources of imports. Interdependence also creates groups with vested interests in continuing economic exchange.[14]

The wealth-makes-peace argument is thus closely related to the one that transnational interests of trade and investment make peace. Writers as various as the nineteenth-century liberal Richard Cobden, the Marxist Karl Kautsky, and Joseph Schumpeter argued that the web of economic interdependence would promote international peace. Yet Lenin and other theorists of imperialism opined otherwise. Economic interdependence, for example between the United States and Japan, provides both glue and friction. Even where a relationship between trade and peace can be demonstrated, there may be a chicken-and-egg problem. Weak economic ties within the industrialized world during the Depression help explain the political tensions that produced World War II, but after that war peaceful relations were largely established before high levels of economic interdependence were reached in the 1970s.[15] Some systematic evidence indicates that trade diminishes political conflict, with the party receiving greater benefits from trade acting on greater incentives.[16] But if one party perceives the benefits as markedly asymmetrical against it, the effects are not pacific. Trade between rich and poor states may concentrate on raw materials, with the threat of military action by the rich state in the background or forefront. Other research (Pollins 1989a, b)[17] points the primary causal arrow from political relations to economic

---

11. Bremer, Stuart A. 1992a. "Dangerous Dyads: Conditions Affecting the Likelihood of Interstate War, 1816-1965." *Journal of Conflict Resolution* 36, 2: 309-41.

12. Siverson, Randolph, and Juliann Emmons. 1991. "Birds of a Feather: Democratic Political Systems and Alliance Choices." *Journal of Conflict Resolution* 35, 2: 285-306; Bueno de Mesquita, Bruce, and David Lalman. 1992. *War and Reason.* New Haven, CT: Yale University Press, 166–67.

13. Mueller, John. 1989. *Retreat from Doomsday: The Obsolescence of Major War.* New York: Basic Books; Shepherd, W. Geoffrey. 1986. *The Ultimate Deterrent.* New York: Praeger.

14. Rosecrance, Richard. 1986. *The Rise of the Trading State.* New York: Basic; Milner, Helen. 1988. *Resisting Protectionism.* Princeton, NJ: Princeton University Press.

15. Russett, Bruce, and Harvey Starr. 1992. 4th ed. *World Politics: The Menu for Choice.* New York: W.H. Freeman, 385–92.

16. Gasiorowski, Mark, and Solomon Polacheck. 1982. "Conflict and Interdependence: East-West Trade and Linkages in the Era of Detente." *Journal of Conflict Resolution* 26, 4: 709-29; Polachek, Solomon. 1980. "Conflict and Trade." *Journal of Conflict Resolution* 24, 1: 55-78.

ones ("trade follows the flag") rather than the other way. As with other generalizations, the conclusions are often context-dependent or indeterminate.[18]

Yet another variant of the wealth-makes-peace view emphasizes growth. Many democracies have experienced fairly consistent rapid economic growth during the past half-century. Rapidly growing states may generally be less inclined to initiate conflict. The reasons are similar to those regarding the connection between wealth and lack of conflict. A special case, however, may be made regarding growth he democracies. States often engage in international conflict to divert attention and anger from domestic problems.[19] Democratic governments are not immune to such temptations They often initiate international disputes during economic slowdowns or recessions, or if in economic difficulty respond more aggressively when others initiate disputes.[20] But rapidly growing democracies would not have such an incentive for conflict between them.

Political Stability Makes Peace

The diversionary effects of economic instability are related to those of political instability. States with stable and durable political systems will lack incentives to externalize domestic discontent into conflict with foreign countries. They will be even more reluctant to engage in conflict against other states that are politically stable. If they see the government of the would-be opponent as possessing substantial legitimacy, they will expect the population at large, and those sectors of society that have ensured domestic stability, to back it in international conflict.[21] Unstable governments have more to gain from scapegoating and diversion, and are more likely to do so when they confront an adversary that faces substantial domestic political problems.

If stable governments are less likely to initiate international disputes especially against other stable governments it is important to note that twentieth-century European and Anglo-American democracies were generally more stable—more durable and adaptable—than were non-democracies.[22] The more years a given type of political system lasts, the better its odds of surviving another year. Perhaps the inherent stability that characterizes many democratic political systems accounts for their low rate of conflict with other

---

17. Pollins, Brian. 1989a. "Does Trade Still Follow the Flag?" American Political Science Review 83, 2: 465-80; and ibid., 1989b. "Conflict, Cooperation, and Commerce: The Effect of International Political Interactions on Bilateral Trade Flows." *American Journal of Political Science* 33: 3: 737-61.

18. Russett, Bruce. 1967. *International Regions and the International System: A Study in Political Ecology.* Chicago: Rand McNally; Bueno de Mesquita, Bruce, and David Lalman. 1992. *War and Reason.* New Haven, CT: Yale University Press, p. 289.

19. Levy, Jack S. 1989. The Diversionary Theory of War: A Critique." In *Handbook of War Studies,* ed. Manus Midlarsky, pp. 259-88. Boston: Unwin Hyman.

20. Ostrom, Charles W., and Brian Job. 1986. "The President and the Political Use of Force." *American Political Science Review* 80, 2: 541-66; Russett, Bruce. 1990. *Controlling the Sword: the Democratic Governance of National Security.* Cambridge, MA: Harvard University Press, ch. 2; Russett, Bruce, and Gad Barzilai. 1991. "The Political Economy of Military Actions: Israel and the United States." In *The Political Economy of Military Spending in the United States,* ed. Alex Mintz. London: Unwin Hyman; Mintz, Alex, and Bruce Russett. 1992. "The Dual Economy and Israeli Use of Force." In *Defense, Welfare and Growth,* ed. Steve Chan and Alex Mintz, pp. 179-97. London: Routledge.

21. Huth, Paul, and Bruce Russett. 1993. "General Deterrence between Enduring Rivals: Testing Three Competing Models." *American Political Science Review* 87, 1: 61-73; Maoz, Zeev. 1989. "Joining the Club of Nations: Political Development and International Conflict, 1816-1976." *International Studies Quarterly* 33, 2" 199-231.

22. Gurr, Ted Robert. 1974. "Persistence and Change in Political Systems." *American Political Science Review* 68, 4: 1482-1504.

democracies. In fact, the combination of variables denoted as stable democracy becomes a component of the theory to be developed and tested in this book.

Conceptually and empirically the competing explanations overlap somewhat and reinforce each other. Some of them are quite plausible. The network of international institutions has been strongest in the past half-century among the democratic, allied, prosperous, and politically stable states of Western Europe. Yet counterexamples can be cited for each proffered explanation. There have not been wars even between poor but democratic states, yet World War II is an obvious example of a war pitting advanced capitalist states against each other. Argentina and Britain fought in 1982 despite their common alliance with the United States. The Soviet Union, after achieving apparent stability by the early 1920s, nevertheless fought four wars. Later we will analyze the incidence of wars and less violent conflicts between states in the post-1945 era, with proper statistical controls to test many of the above alternative hypotheses. Even when controls for physical distance, alliance, wealth, economic growth, and political stability are incorporated into the analysis, an independent explanatory role for democracy remains.[23] Nevertheless, no merely empirical relationship can be compelling without a powerful theoretical explanation. Nor can it be clear how widely, in different historical and cultural contexts, the relationship may apply. Two kinds of theories, one stressing norms and the other stressing political structures, offer explanations to which we now turn.

DEMOCRATIC NORMS AND CULTURE?

We should begin with the common assertion that democracies are inherently more peaceful or "dovish" internationally because of the political culture favoring the peaceful resolution of disputes, or because democratic processes produce restraint by the general populace which will have to pay the price of war in blood and money.[24] Individual examples of the operation of these factors can easily be found. Over the course of a long war democratic governments may experience seriously eroding domestic support for the war effort, and may feel constrained, if they do go to war, to pursue strategies designed to minimize their own costs, especially in casualties. (U.S. strategy against Iraq in 1991 immediately comes to mind.)

This is a strong assertion, however, and, overall, the evidence for it as a generalization is not very compelling.[25] It ignores the evidence for the familiar "rally 'round the flag effect" typically induced by the threat or use of force by democracies against other countries. Hostility especially to certain kinds of foreigners—those seen as

---

23. Also see Bremer 1992a 1993 for the effect of democracy even with other controls for relative power, great power status, hegemony, and militarization (Bremer, Stuart A. 1992a. "Dangerous Dyads: Conditions Affecting the Likelihood of Interstate War, 1816-1965." *Journal of Conflict Resolution* 36, 2: 309-41).

24. Schumpeter, Joseph. 1955. *Imperialism and Social Classes.* Cleveland, OH: World Publishing; Snyder, Jack. 1991. *Myths of Empire: Domestic Politics and International Ambition.* Ithaca, NY: Cornell University Press.

25. Bueno de Mesquita and Lalman 1992, 155, find that by their measure the mean domestic costs to democracies of using force are greater than for nondemocracies, but the difference is small (Bueno de Mesquita, Bruce, and David Lalman. 1992. *War and Reason.* New Haven, CT: Yale University Press). Bremer 1992, 1993 suggests a mixed picture; i.e., democracies are less likely to originate wars with all kinds of states, but more likely to join ongoing wars being fought by other states (Bremer, Stuart A. 1992a. "Dangerous Dyads: Conditions Affecting the Likelihood of Interstate War, 1816-1965." *Journal of Conflict Resolution* 36, 2: 309-41).

governed autocratically—can often be mobilized to support military actions by democracies.[26] Elites can even feel impelled by popular pressures to act militarily (Russett 1990, chap. 2).[27] Also, so long as this explanation focuses on the characteristics of single states, it cannot explain the consistent evidence that democracies are about as war-prone and disputatious in general (not toward other democracies) as are other kinds of states.[28] Nor can it explain the pattern of nineteenth- and twentieth-century imperialism by democracies.[29] And it would have us believe that the United States was regularly on the defensive, rarely on the offensive, during the Cold War. Though there are elements of plausibility in the argument that democracies are inherently peaceful, it contains too many holes, and is accompanied by too many exceptions to be usable as a major theoretical building block.

A more plausible theoretical strain, however yields a more limited assumption. It focuses on powerful norms within democratic states against the use of lethal force under certain conditions—namely "dovishness" in relations between democracies, though not necessarily in their relations with other kinds of states. Several authors offer a perspective emphasizing social diversity, perceptions of individual rights, overlapping group memberships, cross-pressures, shifting coalitions, expectations of limited government, and toleration of dissent by a presumably loyal opposition The basic norm of democratic theory is that disputes can be resolved without force through democratic political processes that in some balance ensure both majority rule and minority rights. A norm of equality operates both as voting equality and certain egalitarian rights to human dignity. Democratic government rests on the consent of the governed, but justice demands that consent not be abused. Resort to organized lethal violence, Or the threat of it, is considered illegitimate, and unnecessary to secure one's "legitimate" rights. Dissent within broad limits by a loyal opposition is expected and even needed for enlightened policy-making, and the opposition's basic loyalty to the system is to he assumed in the absence of evidence to the contrary.[30]

All participants in the political process are expected to share these norms. Even though all these images may be founded to a large extent on myth as well as on reality, they may operate as powerful restraints On violence between such systems. In practice the norms do sometimes break down, but the normative restraints on violent behavior—by state and citizens—are fully as important as the state's monopoly on the legitimate use of force in keeping incidents of the organized use of force rare. The norms themselves may be more important than any particular institutional structure (two-party/ multiparty, repub-

---

26. Geva, Nehemia, Karl DeRouen, and Alex Mintz. 1993. "The Political Incentive Explanation of the 'Democratic Peace' Phenomenon: Evidence from Experimental Research," *International Interactions* 18, 3: 215-29; Mintz, Alex, and Nehemia Geva. 1993. "Why Don't Democracies Fight Each Other? An Experimental Assessment of the 'Political Incentive' Explanation." *Journal of Conflict Resolution* 37, 3.

27. Russett, Bruce. 1990. *Controlling the Sword: the Democratic Governance of National Security.* Cambridge, MA: Harvard University Press, ch. 2.

28. Recently, Maoz, Zeev, and Nasrin Abdolali. 1989. "Regime Types and International Conflict." *Journal of Conflict Resolution* 33, 1: 3-35; Bremer, Stuart A. 1992a. "Dangerous Dyads: Conditions Affecting the Likelihood of Interstate War, 1816-1965." *Journal of Conflict Resolution* 36, 2: 309-41.

29. On Snyder's 1991 effort see Zakaria, Fareed. 1992. "Realism and Domestic Politics: A Review Essay." *International Security* 17, 1: 177-98.

30. Most of the authors cited earlier write predominantly from this perspective.

lican/parliamentary) or formal constitutional provision. If institutions precede the development of norms In the polity, the basis for restraint is likely to be less secure.

By this hypothesis, the *culture, perceptions,* and *practices* that permit compromise and the peaceful resolution of conflicts without the threat of violence within countries come to apply across national boundaries toward other democratic countries. In short, if people in a democracy perceive themselves as autonomous self-governing people who share norms of live-and-let-live, they will respect the rights of others to self-determination if those others are also perceived as self-governing and hence not easily led into aggressive foreign policies by a self-serving elite. The same structures and behaviors that "we" assume will limit our aggression, both internally and externally, may he expected similarly to limit similarly governed people in other polities. Those who claim the principle of self-determination for themselves are expected to extend it to others. Within a transnational democratic culture, as within a democratic nation, others are seen as possessing rights and exercising those rights in a spirit of enlightened self-interest. Acknowledgment of those rights allows us to mitigate our fears that they will try to dominate us. That acknowledgment also prevents us from wishing to dominate them; a norm that it would be wrong to do so in effect raises the "costs" to us of doing so.

By contrast, these restraints do not apply toward a country governed by very different and non-democratic principles. According to democratic norms, authoritarian states do not rest on the proper consent of the governed, and thus they cannot properly represent the will of their peoples—if they did, they would not need to rule through undemocratic, authoritarian institutions. Rulers who control their own people by such means, who do not behave in a just way that respects their own people's rights to self-determination, cannot be expected to behave better toward peoples outside their states. "Because non-liberal governments are in a state of aggression with their own people, their foreign relations become for liberal governments deeply suspect. In short, fellow liberals benefit from a presumption of amity; nonliberals suffer from a presumption of enmity".[31] The essence of America's Cold War ideology was that it had no quarrel with the Russian people, but only with the atheistic communist elites who repressed them. A vision of thc other people as not in self-governing control of their own destiny justified a hostile policy. Authoritarian states are expected to aggress against others if given the power and the opportunity. By this reasoning, democracies must be eternally vigilant and may even need to engage in defensively motivated war or preemptive action anticipating an immediate attack.

Whereas wars against other democratic states are neither expected nor considered legitimate, wars against authoritarian states may often be both. Thus an international system composed of both democratic and authoritarian states will include both zones of peace (actual and expected, among the democracies) and zones of war or at best deterrence between democratic and authoritarian states. And by this reasoning democracies may fight wars and other lethal conflicts as often as authoritarian states do—which is what most of the systematic empirical evidence indicates. They just will not fight each other.

The presumption of enmity from and toward non-democracies was exemplified by American determination to root out aggressive fascism and Nazism in Japan and Germany after World War II, and to establish the basis for democratic government there. It took more dubious forms in many Cold War interventions (including covert operations, which we shall

31. Doyle, Michael. 1986. "Liberalism and World Politics." *American Political Science Review* 80, 4: 1151-61.

consider later) and in the 1989 invasion of Panama. Elihu Root's (1917) wartime rhetoric, in his presidential address to the American Society of International Law, expressed the tradition vividly:

> So long as military autocracy continues, democracy is not safe from attacks, which are certain to come, and certain to find it unprepared. The conflict is inevitable and universal; and it is *à l'outrance.* To be safe democracy must kill its enemy when it can and where it can. The world can not be half democratic and half autocratic. It must he all democratic or all Prussian. There can be no compromise. If it is all Prussian, there can be no real international law. If it is all democratic, international law honored and observed may well be expected as a natural development of the principles which make democratic self-government possible.[32]

These assumptions lead to the following propositions about democracies' external relations. The norms of regulated political competition, compromise solutions to political conflicts, and peaceful transfer of power are externalized by democracies in their dealing with other national actors in world politics. On the other hand, non-democracies may not externalize these norms. Hence, when two democracies come into a conflict of interest, they are able to apply democratic norms in their interaction, and these norms prevent most conflicts from mounting to the threat or use of military force. If they do go that far, at least they will not go to all-out war. By contrast, when a democracy comes into conflict with a non-democracy it will not expect the non-democratic state to be restrained by those norms. It may feel obliged to adapt to the harsher norms of international conduct of the latter, lest it be exploited or eliminated by the non-democratic state that takes advantage of the inherent moderation of democracies. Similarly, conflict between non-democracies may be dominated by the norm of forceful conduct and search for decisive (noncompromise) outcome or elimination of the adversary.

Axelrod's[33] work on the evolution of cooperation and norms shows how norms of behavior depend heavily on the environment in which they are applied. When a player employing a conditionally cooperative strategy like tit-for-tat is confronted by someone playing a consistently noncooperative strategy, noncooperation dominates. Short of teaching cooperation to "meanies"—which takes a long time—noncooperative strategies typically force cooperative strategies to become noncooperative.[34]

Legal systems in democratic states seem to make distinctions between democratic and authoritarian states when deciding whether to enforce in their own courts the laws of other nations. Other democratic states are recognized as within a "zone of law," a legal community defined by various institutional and ideological similarities. Courts in democracies share enough common values to recognize and enforce each other's law in accord with pluralist principles of tolerance and reciprocity. They do not, however, recognize the legal systems of nondemocratic states as equal partners; they are seen as lacking the political autonomy of democratic legal systems, and hence not appropriate as providing norms for conflict resolution.[35]

---

32. Root, Elihu. 1917. "The Effect of Democracy on International Law." Presidential address to the annual meeting of the American Society or International Law, Washington, D.C., April 26.

33. Axelrod, Robert. 1984. *The Evolution of Cooperation.* New York: Basic Books; Behr, Roy. 1980. "Nice Guys Finish Last . . . Sometimes." *Journal of Conflict Resolution* 25, 2: 289-300; Dacey, Raymond, and Norman Pendergraft, 1988. "The Optimality of Tit-for-tat." *International Interactions* 15, 1: 45-64.

34. I owe this argument to Zeev Maoz. See Maoz, Zeev. 1989. "Joining the Club of Nations: Political Development and International Conflict, 1816-1976." *International Studies Quarterly* 33, 2" 199-231.

35. Burley, Anne-Marie. 1992. "Law Among Liberal States: Liberal Internationalism and the Act of State Doctrine." *Columbia Law Review* 92, 8: 1907-96.

Governments and political institutions can change rapidly after a revolution, but norms take time to develop. Laws can change faster than the practices in which norms are embedded. Formal norms such as one of nonrecourse to war can be written into a constitution, but become effective only with the repeated practice of bargaining and conciliation.[36] Thus if violent conflicts between democracies do occur, we would expect them to take place between democratic states that are relatively young in terms of the tenure of the democratic regime. That is, they would occur between states in at least one of which democratic norms have not matured to a degree that is expressed in moderate and dependable strategies of peaceful conflict management. Democratic governments in which democratic norms are not yet fully developed are likely to be unstable, or to be perceived by other states as unstable, so they may be unable to practice norms of democratic conflict resolution internationally. Equally important, the democratic states with whom they develop conflicts of interest may not perceive them as dependable in their practices. Newness and instability cloud others' perceptions.

Of course, democracies have not fought wars only out of motivations of self-defense, however broadly one may define self-defense to include anticipation of others' aggression or to include "extended deterrence" for the defense of allies and other interests. Many of them have also fought imperialist wars to acquire or hold colonies, or to retain control of states formally independent but within their spheres of influence. Here is another aspect of perception and misperception, of cases where democracies have fought against people who on one ground or another could be characterized as not self-governing.

The nineteenth-century objects of colonial expansion were peoples who in most instances were outside the European state system. They were in most instances not people with white skins, and whose institutions of government did not conform to the Western democratic institutional forms of their colonizers. Europeans' ethnocentric views of those peoples carried the *assumption* that they did not have institutions of self-government. Not only were they available for imperial aggrandizement, they could be considered candidates for betterment and even "liberation"—the white man's burden, or *mission civilatrice.* They could be brought the benefits not only of modern material civilization, but of Western principles of self-government. If they did not have such institutions already, then by definition they were already being exploited and repressed. Their governments or tribal leaders could not, in this ethnocentric view, be just or consensual, and thus one need have few compunctions about conquering these legitimate candidates for "liberal" imperialism.[37] Later, when Western forms of self-government did begin to take root on a local basis in many of the colonies, the extremes of pseudo-Darwinian racism lost their legitimacy. Decolonization came not only because the colonial governments lost the power to retain their colonies, but because in many cases they lost confidence in their normative right to rule.

We can now summarize all this discussion about restraints on violent conflict among democracies in a set of propositions as follows.

36. Kratochwil, Friedrich. 1991. *Rules, Norms and Decisions.* London: Cambridge University Press.

37. As we shall see later, in fact "preindustrial" peoples often had participatory forms of government that shared many democratic attributes.

The Cultural/Normative Model

1. In relations with other states, decisionmakers (whether they be few or many) will try to follow the same norms of conflict resolution as have been developed within and characterize their domestic political processes.
2. They will expect decisionmakers in other states likewise to follow the same norms of conflict resolution as have been developed within and characterize those other states' domestic political processes.

A. Violent conflicts between democracies will be rare because:

3. In democracies, the relevant decisionmakers expect to be able to resolve conflicts by compromise and nonviolence, respecting the rights and continued existence of opponents.
4. Therefore democracies will follow norms of peaceful conflict resolution with other democracies, and will expect other democracies to do so with them.
5. The more stable the democracy, the more will democratic norms govern its behavior with other democracies, and the more will other democracies expect democratic norms to govern its international behavior
6. If violent conflicts between democracies do occur, at least one of the democracies is likely to be politically unstable.

B. Violent conflicts between nondemocracies, and between democracies and nondemocracies, will be more frequent because:

7. In nondemocracies, decisionmakers use, and may expect their opponents to use, violence and the threat of violence to resolve conflict as part of their domestic political processes.
8. Therefore nondemocracies may use violence and the threat of violence in conflicts with other states, and other states may expect them to use violence and the threat of violence in such conflicts.
9. Democratic norms can be more easily exploited to force concessions than can nondemocratic ones; to avoid exploitation democracies may adopt nondemocratic norms in dealing with nondemocracies.

The numbered propositions are part of the deductive structure, and whereas it will be useful further to illustrate their application and plausibility, we will not subject most of them to rigorous empirical testing. The basic empirical statements A and B, however, will be so tested, in the form that *violent conflicts between democracies should be observed much less frequently than between democracies and nondemocracies.* Indeed, because of the susceptibility of democratic norms to exploitation, we may well find *violent conflicts between democracies and at least some kinds of nondemocracies to be more frequent than would be expected* if conflicts were distributed around the international system totally by chance. Proposition 6, that if *violent conflicts do arise between democracies at least one of the democracies is likely to be politically unstable* also is empirically testable. As such, it can provide some extra empirical content to the basic hypothesis about the relative frequency of violent conflict of democracies with other democracies and with nondemocracies.

Propositions 5 and 6 therefore incorporate into the cultural/normative theoretical structure the point about political stability that was initially treated as one of several alternative perspectives on the phenomenon of peace between democracies. They do not yet, however, indicate just why force might be used when one democracy in a pair is politically unstable.

As noted in the discussion about the possible role of economic growth or its absence, increasing evidence is accumulating that democracies are more likely to use or threaten to use military force, in general, when the economy has been doing badly. Most of the studies cited there also indicate that democracies are more likely to use or threaten to use military force in the year or months immediately preceding an election.[38] The motivation, of diverting hostility toward foreigners and of producing a "rally 'round the flag" effect for the party in power, is similar. If we expand the notion of political instability to include domestic political threats to the government because of its economic policy shortcomings, or competition in a close election, this gives us a temporal context for the possible use of military force by democracies. It suggests that the "unstable" state will initiate, or escalate, the use of force in a diplomatic dispute. But it does not tell us against whom it may direct that force.

To do that, we can elaborate the hypothesis as suggesting that the threat or use of *force will be directed against states that a democracy perceives as politically unstable.* At least two possible reasons for this come to mind: The state may see an unstable democratic regime as under these political pressures, and hence as a real danger needing to be forcibly constrained or deterred. Alternatively, an unstable democratic regime may seem a publicly more legitimate and acceptable object for diverting hostility and provoking a 'rally effect. That is, the government may truly feel itself threatened in some degree by such a regime, or, if not, it may believe that the public will at least accept perception of a threat. If the adversary is perceived as a stable democracy, by contrast, the cultural/normative argument suggests little political benefit in trying to invoke a rally against it. Thus instability may work both as encouraging the use or threat of force by the "unstable" regime, and in selecting an "unstable" object for the exercise of force.

Empirically it will be very difficult to sort out the mechanism systematically. Even in the 1946-86 period with many democracies in the international system, table 1.2 showed only fourteen militarized disputes between democracies. In their manifestation of threat or use of force all of them were extremely localized, typically an air incursion or shelling in the general direction of a boat lasting a single day. None were reciprocated uses of military force, in which the attacked party made any military reprisal, and nearly all of them were bloodless. Most could plausibly have been unauthorized acts by local commanders. In most instances it is hard to show that they were deliberate and considered governmental acts of the sort plausibly included under the rubric of politically motivated incidents just discussed. And while one can identify who actually used force or first threatened to use it, it is not so easy to say which side played the greater role in provoking the incident. Thus one should not expect to find a systematic pattern of motivation in such low-level incidents. In near-wars, however—where the level of violence may be greater, and the degree of central control and deliberate act may be stronger—we may find some such evidence.

We should also, by extension, expect such events to occur *between states where one or both states' status as a democracy leaves some basis for doubt.* Perceptions of instability may be based on the recency and immaturity of experience with democratic processes and norms: a new democracy will not yet have developed wide experience in practices of democratic conflict resolution. Perceptions of instability may also be based on a high degree of violent opposition to the democratic government: a democracy under siege of domestic terrorism, insurgency, or civil war is one in which the ostensible norms of peaceful conflict resolution simply are not working well. If a government's practice of democratic forms of government is very recent and subject to violent domestic challenge, or its practice of democracy is incom-

38. They are not, however, more likely just before elections to engage in the full-scale use of military force known as war; if anything they are more likely to go to war during the year just after the election has passed (Gaubatz, Jurt Taylor. 1991. "Election Cycles and War." *Journal of Conflict Resolution* 35, 2: 212-44).

plete or imperfect by the standards of the day, it may be imperfectly constrained by the norms of democratic government that are supposed to keep conflict nonviolent. Or uncertainty about the commitment to democratic norms by the state with which one has a conflict of interest may lead to perceptions and expectations that it will practice those norms imperfectly.

The list of numbered propositions above often implies a dichotomy between democratic and nondemocratic states. But in the real world such a dichotomy masks degrees of democratic practice. Therefore if we find militarized disputes between democracies we should typically find that one party or both is only recently democratic, is subject to violent domestic challenge, or is toward the center of a democratic to nondemocratic continuum. We should also, in a revised version of proposition 6, look for evidence that one party, correctly or not, *perceives* the other as not really democratic.

STRUCTURAL AND INSTITUTIONAL CONSTRAINTS?

As with the normative and cultural argument, it is best to avoid assuming that democracies are dovish or peaceful in all their relations. Rather, a plausible argument can be constructed on the strategic principles of rational action; that is, about how states, in interactions of threat and bargaining, behave in anticipation of how their bargaining adversaries will behave. Decision-makers develop images of the government and public opinion of other countries. They regard some governments or peoples as slow to fight, or as ready and eager to do so. In forming these images leaders look for various cues: in other leaders' and countries' past behavior in diplomatic or military disputes, and in other countries' form of government. Perhaps other governments will see a democracy as culturally (normatively) dovish on the above grounds, but Kant's own view argued that *institutional constraints*—a structure of division of powers, checks and balances—would make it difficult for democratic leaders to move their countries into war.

Democracies are constrained in going to war by the need to ensure broad popular support, manifested in various institutions of government. Leaders must mobilize public opinion to obtain legitimacy for their actions. Bureaucracies, the legislature, and private interest groups often incorporated in conceptualizations of the "state" must acquiesce. The nature and mix of institutions varies in different kinds of states (for example, "strong" states and "weak" states, parliamentary and presidential systems) but it is complex. Popular support in a democracy can be built by rhetoric and exhortation, but not readily compelled.

The complexity of the mobilization process means that leaders will not readily embark on an effort to prepare the country for war unless they are confident they can demonstrate a favorable ratio of costs and benefits to be achieved, at acceptable risk.[39] Moreover, the complexity of the process requires time for mobilization, as the leaders of various institutions are convinced and formal approval is obtained. Not only may it take longer for democracies to gear up for war, the process is immensely more public than in an authoritarian state. Democratic governments can respond to sudden attack by using emergency powers, and by the

---

39. Lake 1992 (also Brawley 1992) makes a structural argument that democracies with broad franchises are inherently less imperialistic than are autocratic states, and while democracies may fight to resist autocracies, the conjuncture of two democracies with low imperialist drive makes them unlikely to fight each other (Lake, David. 1992. "Powerful Pacifists: Democratic States and War." *American Political Science Review* 86, 1: 24-37; Brawley, Mark R. 1992. "Regime Types, Markets and War: The Importance of Pervasive Rents in Foreign Policy." Paper presented at the annual meeting of the International Studies Association, Atlanta, April.) His empirical test is indirect, however, of a derived proposition that democracies will win wars in which they engage more often than will autocracies. The latter can alternatively be attributed to democracies' greater ability to motivate their citizens and to superior information-processing capability (Russett, Bruce. 1990. *Controlling the Sword: the Democratic Governance of National Security.* Cambridge, MA: Harvard University Press).

same powers can even strike preemptively in crisis. But in normal times they are ill suited to launching surprise attacks.[40] Apparently for these reasons, major-power democracies seem never to have launched preventive war (a deliberate attack not under immediate provocation) against another major power.[41] The greater the scale, cost, and risk of using violence, the more effort must be devoted to preparations in public, and of the public.

Even if two states were totally ignorant of each other's form of government, structural delays in the process of mobilization for war in both states would provide time to elapse for negotiation and other means of peaceful conflict resolution. Yet perceptions matter here too. If another nation's leaders regard a state as democratic, they will anticipate a difficult and lengthy process before the democracy is likely to use significant military force against them. They will expect an opportunity to reach a negotiated settlement if they wish to achieve such a settlement. Perhaps most importantly, a democracy will not fear a surprise attack by another democracy, and thus need not cut short the negotiating process or launch a preemptive strike in anticipation of surprise attack.

If democratic leaders generally consider other democracies to be reluctant and slow to fight because of institutional constraints (and possibly because of a general aversion of the people to war), they will not fear being attacked by another democracy. Two democratic states—each constrained from going to war and anticipating the other to be so inhibited—likely will settle their conflicts short of war. Bueno de Mesquita and Lalman[42] provide a deductive argument that two such states, each with perfect information about the other's constraints, will always settle their conflicts by negotiation or by retaining the status quo. In the real world perfect information is lacking, but the presence of democratic institutions provides a visible and generally correct signal of "practical dovishness"—restraints on war in the form of institutional constraint if not of inherent disposition. Reading that sign, democracies will rarely if ever go to war with each other.

Leaders of nondemocratic states may also anticipate that a democratic country will be slow to go to war. But if they are themselves aggressive, they may be more likely to threaten or bully a democracy to make concessions. In turn, that would raise the threshold of provocation facing the democracy, and perhaps overcome its initial inhibition against fighting. That would explain why the overall frequency of war fighting by democracies is no different from that of nondemocratic states.[43] But leaders of two nondemocratic states,

---

40. Ben Hunt has suggested, in a personal communication, that the degree of elites' control by public opinion may be the key variable, and that, while it is highly correlated with democracy, the correlation is not perfect—some democracies' elites may be less constrained than are others by public opinion, and some autocracies more so than others.

41. Schweller, Randall L. 1992. "Domestic Structure and Preventative War: Are Democracies More Pacific?" *World Politics* 44, 2: 235-69.

42. Bueno de Mesquita, Bruce, and David Lalman. 1992. *War and Reason.* New Haven, CT: Yale University Press, ch. 4.

43. Bueno de Mesquita and Lalman 1992, chap. 5, present this hypothesis and some confirming evidence. (Similar reasoning goes back at least to Wright 1942, 842-45, and Starr 1992, extends the insight that forms of government signal a state's likely international behavior.) They reject the argument that "the political culture of democracies leads to an abhorrence of violence" in general, and build their theory on the assumption that democratic leaders "face a greater political cost for using force." In context they treat this as an institutional constraint, though in a personal communication Bueno de Mesquita suggested that democratic norms may similarly raise the costs. See Bueno de Mesquita, Bruce, and David Lalman. 1992. *War and Reason.* New Haven, CT: Yale University Press; Wright, Quincy. 1942. *A Study of War.* Chicago: University of Chicago Press; STARR TK)

neither encumbered by powerful structural constraints, are more likely than two democratic states to escalate to war.

This argument can be summarized as follows.

The Structural/Institutional Model:

A. Violent conflicts between democracies will be infrequent because:

1. In democracies, the constraints of checks and balances, division of power, and need for public debate to enlist widespread support will slow decisions to use large-scale violence and reduce the likelihood that such decisions will be made.
2. Leaders of other states will perceive leaders of democracies as so constrained.
3. Thus leaders of democracies will expect, in conflicts with other democracies, time for processes of international conflict resolution to operate, and they will not fear surprise attack.

B. Violent conflicts between nondemocracies, and between democracies and nondemocracies, will be frequent because:

4. Leaders of nondemocracies are not constrained as leaders of democracies are, so they can more easily, rapidly, and secretly initiate large-scale violence.
5. Leaders of states (democracies and nondemocracies) in conflict with nondemocracies may initiate violence rather than risk surprise attack.
6. Perceiving that leaders of democracies will be constrained, leaders of nondemocracies may press democracies to make greater concessions over issues in conflict.
7. Democracies may initiate large-scale violence with nondemocracies rather than make the greater concessions demanded.

DISTINGUISHING THE EXPLANATIONS

The cultural/normative and institutional/structural explanations are not neatly separable. Institutions depend on norms and procedures. For example, stability, which we treated as a measure of normative acceptance of democratic processes, is also an institutional constraint if political structures are not subject to overthrow. States may also consider the dominant norms in other states, as well as their institutions, as signals; thus both explanations also depend in part on perceptions. Great emphasis on reading signals of the other's intention, however, slights the importance of self-constraint. Institutions may slow or obstruct one's own ability to fight. Perhaps more importantly, a norm that it is somehow not "right" to fight another democracy raises the moral and political cost, and thus limits one's own willingness to do so. Bueno de Mesquita and Lalman[44] neglect this, as well as the opposition a democratic government might find among its own population against fighting another *democratic government.*[45] Within democracies, structural impediments to using force are less strong than within autocracies; normative restraints must bear the load. So we should not assume that normative constraints are unimportant in relations between democracies. Both norms and institutions may contribute to the phenomenon of peace

---

44. Bueno de Mesquita, Bruce, and David Lalman. 1992. *War and Reason.* New Haven, CT: Yale University Press.

45. Geva, Nehemia, Karl DeRouen, and Alex Mintz. 1993. "The Political Incentive Explanation of the 'Democratic Peace' Phenomenon: Evidence from Experimental Research," *International Interactions* 18, 3: 215-29.

between democracies; they are somewhat complementary and overlapping. But they are also in some degree distinctive and competing explanations, allowing us to look for greater impact of one or another in various contexts.

Other influences such as trade and the network of international law and organizations as suggested by Kant, likely also play a role in directly supplementing and strengthening that of democracy. Further elaboration of the theoretical arguments is probably needed. Certainly, detailed empirical work is necessary on how institutions operate, and on how perceptions toward other countries evolve, so as to make it possible to weigh the relative power of institutional and normative explanations. So too is the creation and application of systematic empirical tests to differentiate between the two kinds of explanations for violence in the modern interstate system. One such test, distinguishing between measures of democracy as stability (normative) and of democracy as the adoption of particular institutions, will he performed later in this book. The prediction about stable democracies being less likely than unstable ones to use military force against each other is embedded in the normative model, and more tenuously so in the structural one.

Another way of differentiating between the two is to look for other hypotheses that may be derived from either, and tested. One such hypothesis for the normative model is represented in work by Dixon (1993, also 1992).[46] He postulates that *democracies with norms of using third-party intervention for peaceful and non-coercive resolution of conflicts internally will carry those norms into management of their international conflicts with other democracies.* Dixon then looks at how international conflicts have been settled in the post-World War II era. Not only does he confirm our results from Table 1.2 that conflicts between democracies are much less likely to escalate to lethal violence and to be settled peacefully, but he finds that they are much more likely to be settled by some means of third-party conflict management, such as the use of good of offices, mediation, and intervention. Also, all conflicts between democracies were ended either by agreement or by stalemate; none terminated in a settlement imposed by one of them or by a third party. Such a pattern is much more readily explicable by common norms than by characteristics of internal democratic institutions acting as constraint. Leng (1993)[47] similarly infers support for the normative argument from evidence that in interstate crises democracies are much more likely to use strategies of reciprocating the escalatory or de-escalatory moves of other states than are authoritarian regimes. He argues that reciprocation is an engrained democratic norm, as contrasted with behavior like bullying, appeasing, or stonewalling.

Another test can be derived from the patterns of strategic interaction as discussed in the model of structural constraints. By that argument, two democracies engaged in a conflictual bargaining process with each other can reasonably expect each other not to escalate the dispute to the point of war or serious violence. Therefore, many bargaining models predict there would be few strategic restraints on escalating the conflict up to, but not beyond, the point of an exchange of lethal violence. In fact, each state might have strong incentives to go that far for the purpose of showing resolve; perhaps even escalating to the

46. Dixon, William. 1992. "Democracy and the Peaceful Settlement of International Conflict." Paper presented at the annual meeting of the American Political Science Association, Chicago, September; and Dixon, William,. 1993. "Democracy and the Management of International Conflict." *Journal of Conflict Resolution* 37, 1: 42-68.

47. Leng, Russell. 1993. ":Reciprocating Influence Strategies and success in Interstate Crisis Bargaining." *Journal of Conflict Resolution* 37, 1: 3-41.

first (limited) use of force in confidence that the other would be unlikely to reply in any substantial military manner. Such behavior is implicit in the bargaining "game" of chicken, which is widely applied to crisis negotiation[48]. This reasoning, therefore, leads to the prediction that disputes between democracies should commonly escalate to the display and even limited use of force, though not to war. But as Table 1.2 showed, that is not the case. Democracy/democracy pairs are less likely to enter into militarized disputes at all than are other pairs of states, and less likely to escalate them at any level up the escalation ladder—not just at the top to war.[49]

Rather, this suggests that *to use or threaten to use force is not usually normatively acceptable behavior in disputes between democracies,* even in the form of symbolic, ritualized bargaining behavior. Relations between democracies therefore fit into the category of "stable peace"[50] or a "security community"[51] in which states not only do not fight each other, they do not expect to fight each other, or significantly prepare to fight each other. In such relationships disputes are routinely settled without recourse to threat and military deterrence. Dependent as the definition of security community has been on expectations, it has been a difficult phenomenon to observe reliably; here, in the relative absence of militarized dispute and escalation, is a reasonably objective measure.

We shall continue to juxtapose the normative and structural models for their relative explanatory power throughout the book. It is also important to explore the outer limits of the empirical domain to which the proposition about lack of war between democracies may apply. All the systematic empirical work to date has employed modern and Westernized definitions of both war and democracy. Careful relaxation of these definitions, in ways appropriate to other times and contexts, may also produce insights about the relative importance of normative and institutional constraints.

---

48. Brams, Steven J., and D. Marc Kilgour. 1988. *Game theory and National Security.* Oxford: Basil Blackwell; Brams, Steven J. 1990. *Negotiation Games: Applying Game Theory to Bargaining and Arbitration.* London: Routledge; Poundstone, William. 1992. *Prisoner's Dilemma.* New York: Doubleday.

49. Fearon (1992) argues from the structural tradition that escalation represents a costly signal especially for democratic leaders, who risk being forced to back down in front of their powerful domestic audience. If so, disputes between democracies should indeed show less escalation, but the initiation of disputes between democracies would not necessarily be less frequent (Fearon, James. 1992. "Audience Costs, Learning, and the Escalation of International Disputes." Manuscript, Political Science Department, University of Chicago).

50. Boulding, Kenneth. 1979. *Stable Peace.* Austin: University of Texas Press.

51. Deutsch, Karl W., et al. 1957. *Political Community and the North Atlantic Area.* Princeton, NJ: Princeton University Press.

Democratic Transitions and War

Edward D. Mansfield and Jack Snyder

DANGERS OF TRANSITION

The idea that democracies never fight wars against each other has become an axiom for many scholars. It is, as one scholar puts it, "as close as anything we have to an empirical law in international relations."[1] This "law" is invoked by U.S. statesmen to justify a foreign policy that encourages democratization abroad. In his 1994 State of the Union address, President Bill Clinton asserted that no two democracies had ever gone to war with each other, thus explaining why promoting democracy abroad was a pillar of his foreign policy.

It is probably true that a world in which more countries were mature, stable democracies would be safer and preferable for the United States. But countries do not become mature democracies overnight. They usually go through a rocky transition in which mass politics mixes with authoritarian elite politics in a volatile way. Statistical evidence covering the past two centuries shows that in this transitional phase of democratization, countries become more aggressive and war prone, not less, and they do fight wars with democratic states. In fact, states undergoing regime change in a democratic direction are about twice as likely to fight wars soon thereafter as are states that are not undergoing a regime change. Also, democratizing states are more prone to fight wars than are states undergoing regime change in an autocratic direction.

The 1990s bore out this historical pattern of democratization, nationalism, and war. In the decade following the collapse of the Berlin Wall, armed violence was intense in a number of regions that had just begun to experiment with electoral democracy and increased pluralism of public debate, including such hotbeds of ethnic warfare as the former Yugoslavia, the post-Soviet Caucasus, and Burundi in Central Africa.[2] At the close of the millennium, this trend was still going strong. Ethiopia and Eritrea, both adopting electoral forms of government in the 1990s, fought a bloody border war in 1999-2000.[3] The nuclear-armed, elected regimes of India and Pakistan fought a war in 1999 in the mountainous borderlands of Kashmir. Prime Minister Vladimir Putin ascended to the presidency

---

1. Jack S. Levy, "Domestic Politics and War," *Journal of Interdisciplinary History* 18, no. 4 (spring 1988): 662.

2. Jack Snyder, *From Voting to Violence: Democratization and Nationalist Conflict* (New York: Norton, 2000), chaps. 5 and 6.

3. Ted Robert Gurr, *Peoples versus States: Minorities at Risk in the New Century* (Washington, D.C.: United States Institute of Peace Press, 2000), 293. Gurr considers Ethiopia as making a transition to "anocracy" (a partially democratic, mixed regime) in 1994. On Eritrea, see Ruth Iyob, "The Eritrean Experiment: A Cautious Pragmatism?" *Journal of Modern African Studies* 35, no. 4 (December 1997): 647-673.

EDWARD D. MANSFIELD is the Hum Rosen Professor of Political Science at the University of Pennsylvania.

JACK L. SNYDER is the Robert and Renee Belfer Professor of International Relations at Columbia University.

Chester A. Crocker, Fen Osler Hampson, and Panela Aall, ed. Turbulent Peace: The Challenges of Managing International Conflict Washington D.C.: United States Institute of Peace, 2001, pp. 113-126.

of Russia's shaky new democracy by riding the popularity of his war in 1999-2000 against the unruly autonomous region of Chechnya.[4] After the fall of the Suharto dictatorship in Indonesia, elections and referenda led quickly to violence and international intervention in the province of East Timor, a former Portuguese colony seeking national independence in 1999, and to ethnic mayhem elsewhere in Indonesia.

The following evidence, which has been updated from an article we published in Foreign Affairs in 1995, should raise questions about the U.S. policy of promoting peace by promoting democratization.[5] The expectation that the spread of democracy will probably contribute to peace in the long run, once new democracies mature, provides little comfort to those who may face a heightened risk of war in the short run. Pushing nuclear-armed great powers like Russia or China toward democratization is like spinning a roulette wheel: Many of the outcomes are undesirable. Of course, in most cases the initial steps on the road to democratization will not be produced by any conscious policy of the United States. The roulette wheel is already spinning for Russia and perhaps will be soon for China. Washington and the international community need to think not so much about encouraging or discouraging democratization as about helping to smooth the transition in ways that minimize its risks.

THE EVIDENCE

In earlier research we conducted some preliminary statistical tests of the relationship between democratization and war.[6] Since then, the data and measures of regime type on which we relied have been updated and extended.[7] Here, we use these more recent data and measures to reevaluate the argument that democratic transitions promote war.

Our statistical analysis relies on the classifications of regimes and wars from 1811 to 1992 used by most scholars studying the democratic peace. Starting with these standard data, we classify each state as a democracy, an autocracy, or a mixed regime—that is, a state with both democratic and autocratic features. Initially, this classification is based on a composite index developed by Keith Jaggers and Ted Robert Gurr that emphasizes the constitutional constraints on the chief executive, the competitiveness of domestic politics, the openness of the process for selecting the chief executive, and the strength of the rules governing participation in politics.[8] However, we also break down the classification of each state's regime type into three of the components that make up this index: the openness of the process for selecting the head of state, the extent of the constraints on the chief executive, and the competitiveness of political participation.[9] In the following tests we

4. Michael R. Gordon, "Russia Votes, Like It or Not: Chechnya War Fever Gives Pause in the West," *New York Times*, December 21, 1999, AI, A22.

5. Edward D. Mansfield and Jack Snyder, "Democratization and War," *Foreign Affairs* 74, no. 3 (May-June 1995): 79-97. As noted later, we have updated the statistical findings and commentary on contemporary events, but the historical and conceptual discussion here remains largely unchanged from that article.

6. See Edward D. Mansfield and Jack Snyder, "Democratization and the Danger of War," *International Security* 20, no. 1 (summer 1995): 5-38; and Mansfield and Snyder, "Democratization and War."

7. See Keith Jaggers and Ted Robert Gurr, "Tracking Democracy's Third Wave with the Polity III Data," *Journal of Peace Research* 32, no. 4 (1995): 469-482.

8. Ibid.

Figure 1. Regime Change and Probability of War: Composite Index

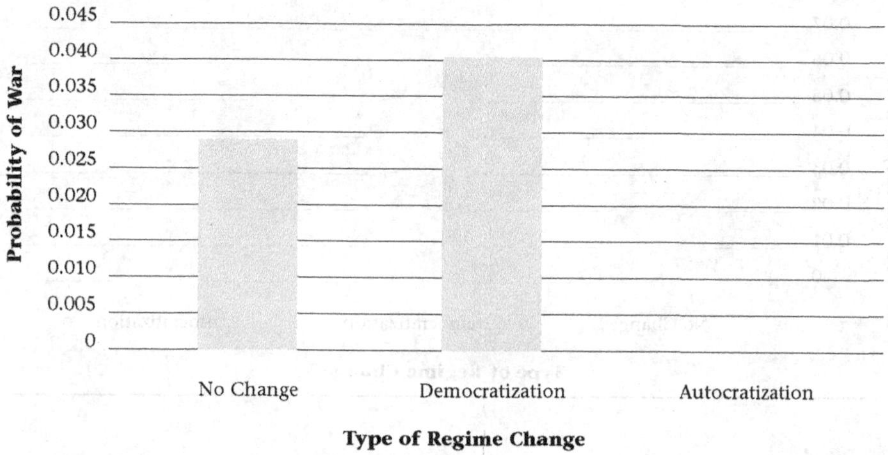

Note: The composite index measures the constitutional constraints on the chief executive, the competitiveness of domestic politics, the openness of the process for selecting the chief executive, and the strength of the rules governing political participation. See Jaggers and Gurr, "Tracking Democracy's Third Wave with the Polity III Data," *Journal of Peace Research* 32, no. 4 (1995): 469-482. Note that our analyses based on the composite index yield no case where autocratization led to the outbreak of an international war.

Figure 2. Regime Change and Probability of War: Openness of Selection of the Chief Executive

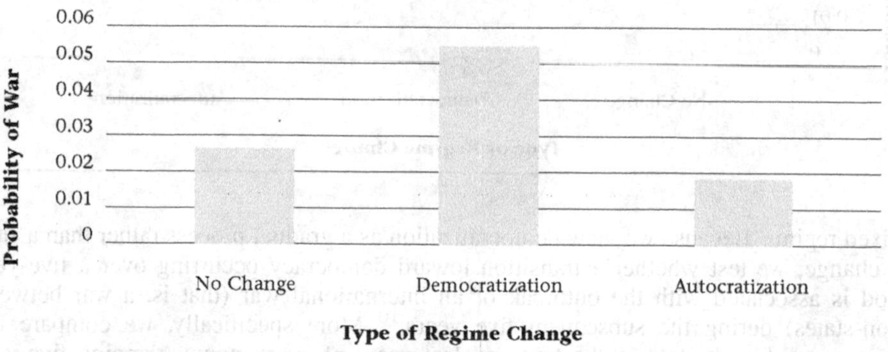

analyze separately Jaggers and Gurr's composite index and each of the three component factors just mentioned.

Democratizing states are those that made any change in a democratic direction—that is, from autocracy to democracy, from a mixed regime to democracy, or from autocracy to

9. For the procedures used to code these variables, see Mansfield and Snyder, "Democratization and the Danger of War."

Figure 3. Regime Change and Probability of War: Constraints on the Chief Executive

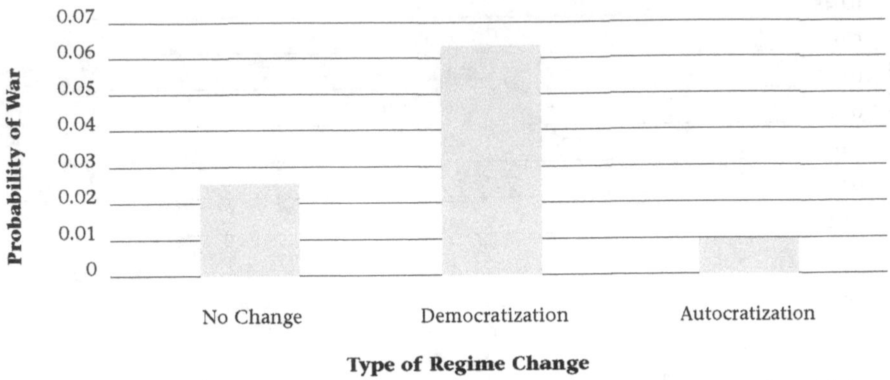

Figure 4. Regime Change and Probability of War: Competitiveness of Political Participation

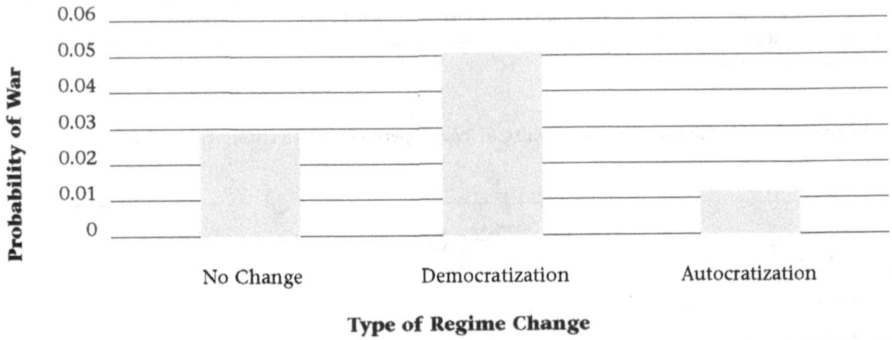

a mixed regime. Because we view democratization as a gradual process rather than a sudden change, we test whether a transition toward democracy occurring over a five-year period is associated with the outbreak of an international war (that is, a war between nation-states) during the subsequent five years.[10] More specifically, we compare the regime type of each state in the first and last years of every nonoverlapping five-year period beginning in 1811 to determine whether a democratic transition took place. We then determine whether each state became embroiled in an interstate war during the following five-year interval.

10. On the definition of and data on international wars, see Melvin Small and J. David Singer, *Resort to Arms: International and Civil Wars, 1816-1980* (Beverly Hills, Calif.: Sage Publications, 1982); and Singer and Small, "Correlates of War Project: International and Civil Wars Data, 1816-1992" (data set, stored at the Inter-University Consortium for Political and Social Research, Ann Arbor, Michigan, 1994).

While our focus is on democratization, it is also important to assess the effects of autocratization on war. It is only through such an analysis that we can determine whether the effect of democratization on war reflects a more general tendency for any regime change, whether in a democratic or an autocratic direction, to promote belligerence. We therefore code states as autocratizing if they made a change in an autocratic direction during any five-year period analyzed here—that is, a change from democracy to autocracy, from a mixed regime to autocracy, or from democracy to a mixed regime.

To assess the strength of the relationship between democratization and war, we construct a series of contingency tables. Based on these tables, we compare the probability that a democratizing state will go to war with the probabilities of war for states in transition toward autocracy and for states undergoing no regime change. The results of all of these tests—which are presented in Figures 1–4—show that democratizing states were more likely to fight wars than were states that had undergone no change in regime. Given the rarity with which wars break out, it is not surprising that the observed probabilities of war are small. Nonetheless, states experiencing a democratic transition have been about 40 percent more likely to become involved in hostilities than states experiencing no regime change, if we focus on the composite index. Democratizing countries have been roughly twice as likely to become embroiled in belligerence than stable regimes, if we code regimes using the openness of the process for selecting the head of state, the extent of the constraints on the chief executive, or the competitiveness of political participation.

Furthermore, the effects of democratization on war do not stem from a more general tendency for regime change to stimulate antagonism. As shown in figures 1–4, autocratizing countries are even less likely to engage in war than stable regimes, regardless of which variable is used to measure regime type. Thus, while the roughness of this simple statistical analysis is obvious, our results continue to indicate that democratization has precipitated war during the nineteenth and twentieth centuries.[11]

NATIONALISM AND DEMOCRATIZATION

The connection between democratization and nationalism is striking in both the historical record and today's headlines. We did not measure nationalism directly in our statistical tests. Nonetheless, historical and contemporary evidence strongly suggests that rising nationalism often goes hand in hand with rising democracy. It is no accident that the end of the Cold War brought both a wave of democratization and a revival of nationalist sentiment in the former communist states.

In eighteenth-century Britain and France, when nationalism first emerged as an explicit political doctrine, it meant self-rule by the people. It was the rallying cry of commoners and rising commercial classes against rule by aristocratic elites, who were charged with the sin of ruling in their own interests rather than those of the nation. Indeed, dynastic rulers and imperial courts had hardly been interested in promoting nationalism as a banner of solidarity in their realms. They typically ruled over a linguistically and culturally diverse conglomeration of subjects and claimed to govern by divine right, not in the interest of the nation. Often, these rulers were more closely tied by kinship, language, or culture to elites in other states than to their own subjects. The position of the communist ruling class was strikingly similar: a transnational elite that ruled over an amalgamation of

11. For additional evidence on this score, see Edward D. Mansfield and Jack Snyder, "Democratic Transitions, Institutional Strength, and War" (typescript).

peoples and claimed legitimacy from the Communist Party's role as the vanguard of history, not from the consent of the governed. Popular forces challenging either traditional dynastic rulers or communist elites naturally tended to combine demands for national self-determination and democratic rule.

This concoction of nationalism and incipient democratization has been an intoxicating brew, leading in case after case to ill-conceived wars of expansion. The earliest instance remains one of the most dramatic. During the French Revolution the radical Brissotin parliamentary faction polarized politics by harping on the king's slow response to the threat of war with other dynastic states. In the ensuing wars of the French Revolution, citizens flocked to join the revolutionary armies to defend popular self-rule and the French nation. Even after the revolution turned profoundly antidemocratic, Napoleon was able to harness this popular nationalism to the task of conquering Europe, substituting the popularity of empire for the substance of democratic rule.

After this experience, Europe's ruling elites decided to band together in 1815 in the Concert of Europe to contain the twin evils of nationalism and democratization. In this scheme, Europe's crowned heads tried to unite in squelching demands for constitutions, electoral and social democracy, and national self-determination. For a time nationalism and democratization were both held back, and Europe enjoyed a period of relative peace.

But in the long run, the strategy failed in the face of the economic changes strengthening popular forces in Western and Central Europe. British and French politicians soon saw that they would have to rule by co-opting nationalist and democratic demands rather than suppressing them. Once the specter of revolution returned to Europe in 1848, this reversal of political tactics was complete, and it led quickly to the Crimean War. British foreign secretary Lord Palmerston and French emperor Napoleon III both tried to manage the clamor for a broader political arena by giving democrats what they wanted in foreign affairs—a "liberal" war to free imprisoned nations from autocratic rule and to expand commerce.

But this was just the dress rehearsal for history's most potent combination of mass politics and rising nationalism, which occurred in Germany around the turn of the twentieth century. Chancellor Otto von Bismarck, counting on the conservative votes of a docile peasantry, granted universal suffrage in the newly unified Reich after 1870, but in foreign and military affairs, he kept the elected Reichstag subordinate to the cabinet appointed by the kaiser. Like the sorcerer's apprentice, however, Bismarck underestimated the forces he was unleashing. With the rise of an industrial society, Bismarck's successors could not control this truncated democracy, in which over 90 percent of the population voted. Everyone was highly politicized, yet no faction could achieve its aims through the limited powers of the Reichstag. As a result, people organized direct pressure groups outside electoral party politics. Some of these clamored for economic benefits, but many of them found it tactically useful to cloak their narrow interests in a broader vision of the nation's interests. This mass nationalist sentiment exerted constant pressure on German diplomacy in the Wilhelmine years before 1914 and pushed its vacillating elites toward war.

Democratization and nationalism also became linked in Japan on the eve of the Manchurian invasion in 1931. During the 1920s Japan expanded its suffrage and experimented with two-party electoral competition, though a council of elder military statesmen still made the ultimate decisions about who would govern. These semielected governments of the 1920s supported free trade, favored naval arms control, and usually tried to rein in the Japanese army's schemes to undermine the Open Door policy in China. Young Turks in the army developed a populist, nationalist doctrine featuring a centrally planned economy within an autarkic, industrialized, expanded empire while scapegoating Japan's alleged internal and external enemies, including leftist workers, rich capitalists, liberals, democrats, Americans, and Russians. After the economic crash of the late 1920s, this nationalist formula became persuasive, and the Japanese military had little trouble gaining popular support for imperial expansion and the emasculation of democracy. As in so many previous cases, nationalism proved to be a way for militarist elite groups to appear populist in a democratizing society while obstructing the advance to full democracy.

The interconnection among nationalism, democratization, and war was likewise present among some of the postcommunist states in the 1990s. Shortly after the breakup of the Soviet Union, one-quarter of Russia's voters, disgruntled by economic distress, backed the tough-talking nationalist party of the anti-Semite Vladimir Zhirinovsky in the 1993 parliamentary elections. Commentators were calling it "Weimar Russia." In this climate ostensible liberals like Russian president Boris Yeltsin and his Western-oriented foreign minister, Andrei Kozyrev, found themselves on the defensive on ethnic and foreign policy issues. Partly for this reason, Yeltsin decided to use military force to try to prevent secession from the Russian Federation by the ethnic Chechen rebels. As it turned out, Russian public opinion opposed the military intervention in Chechnya, which was characterized by Russia's relatively free press as a brutal, costly, and incompetent debacle. To help his reelection bid in 1996, Yeltsin promised to end the war. Nonetheless, a chronic undercurrent of nationalism and loathing of the Chechens in the political discourse of Russia's shaky democracy left public opinion primed and ready for manipulation on this issue. Following a series of mysterious terrorist bombings in Moscow, which were attributed to "Chechens," and Chechen bandit raids into Russian territory in the summer of 1999, Yeltsin's new prime minister, Vladimir Putin, used a popular renewal of the military intervention in Chechnya to position himself as Yeltsin's successor. Although the label "Weimar Russia" proved to be an exaggeration, warlike nationalism was nonetheless intertwined with the fundamental workings of Russia's incipient democracy in the 1990s.

In the post-Soviet Caucasus, the new country of Armenia moved quite far in the direction of electoral democracy in the early 1990s while at the same time supporting an invasion of its ethnic foes in the neighboring state of Azerbaijan. The Azeris have been less successful in sustaining momentum toward democracy. However, in Azerbaijan's one relatively free and fair presidential election, the winner, Abulfez Elchibey, attacked the incumbent for being insufficiently nationalist and populist. Elchibey's platform emphasized Turkic identity and the strengthening of the Azeri nation-state to try to mount a counteroffensive against the Armenians.

The early stages of democratization were also implicated in the violent breakup of communist Yugoslavia. Especially in Serbia the political and military elites of the old regime, facing pressure for democratization, cynically but successfully created a new basis for popular legitimacy through nationalist propaganda in the mass media they controlled. In the climate of opinion that this manipulation fostered, Serbian elections in the late 1980s and 1990s became contests among different varieties of nationalists, each trying to outbid the others to claim the mantle of the true defenders of Serbdom against its ethnic foes.

THE SORCERER'S APPRENTICE

Although democratization often leads to war, that does not mean that the average voter wants war. Public opinion in democratizing states often starts off highly averse to the costs and risks of war. In that sense the public opinion polls taken in Russia in early 1994 were typical. Respondents said, for example, that Russian policy should make sure the rights of Russians in neighboring states were not infringed, but not at the cost of military intervention. Notwithstanding the ambivalence of the Russian public's view of the Chechen problem during the 1990s, by 1999 the Russians had been primed by inflammatory media coverage and the Putin government's military faits accomplis to adopt a more belligerent stance toward the perennially troublesome Chechens.

Numerous historical and recent cases point to the effectiveness of calculated elite efforts to whip up belligerent nationalism among an initially pacific population during the earliest stages of a democratic transition. For example, Napoleon III successfully exploited the domestic prestige from France's share of the victory in the Crimean War to consolidate his rule, despite the popular reluctance and war weariness that had accompanied the war. Having learned this lesson well, Napoleon tried this tactic again in 1859. On the eve of his military intervention in the Italian struggle with Austria, he admitted to his ministers that "on the domestic front, the war will at first awaken great fears; traders and speculators of every stripe will shriek, but national sentiment will [banish] this domestic fright; the nation will be put to the test once more in a struggle that will stir many a heart, recall the memory of heroic times, and bring together under the mantle of glory the parties that are steadily drifting away from one another day after day."[12] Napoleon was trying not just to follow opinion but to make opinion bellicose, in order to stir a national feeling that would enhance the state's ability to govern a split and stalemated political arena.

Much the same has happened in contemporary Serbia. Despite the memories of Ustashe atrocities in World War II, intermarriage rates between Croats and Serbs living in Croatia were as high as one in three during the 1980s. Opinion was made bellicose by propaganda campaigns in state-controlled media that, for example, carried purely invented reports of rapes of Serbian women in Kosovo and even more so by the fait accompli of launching the war itself.

In short, democratizing states are war prone not because war is popular with the mass public, but because domestic pressures create incentives for elites to drum up nationalist sentiment.

THE CAUSES OF DEMOCRATIC WARS

Democratization typically creates a syndrome of weak central authority, unstable domestic coalitions, and high-energy mass politics. It brings new social groups and classes onto the political stage. Political leaders, finding no way to reconcile incompatible interests, resort to shortsighted bargains or reckless gambles in order to maintain their governing coalitions. Elites need to gain mass allies to defend their weakened positions. Both the newly ambitious elites and the embattled old ruling groups often use appeals to nationalism to stay astride their unmanageable political coalitions.

12. Alain Plessis, *The Rise and Fall of the Second Empire, 1852-1871* (Cambridge: Cambridge University Press, 1985), 146-147.

Needing public support, such elites rouse the masses with nationalist propaganda but find that their mass allies, once mobilized by passionate appeals, are difficult to control. So are the powerful remnants of the old order—the military, for example—which promote militarism because it strengthens them institutionally. This is particularly true because democratization weakens the central government's ability to keep policy coherent and consistent. Governing a society that is democratizing is like driving a car while throwing away the steering wheel, stepping on the gas, and fighting over which passenger will be in the driver's seat. The result, often, is war.

Political Stalemate and Imperialist Coalitions

Democratization creates a wider spectrum of politically significant groups with diverse and incompatible interests. In the period when the great powers were first democratizing, kings, aristocrats, peasants, and artisans shared the historical stage with industrialists, an urban working class, and a middle-class intelligentsia. Similarly, in the postcommunist world former party apparatchiks, atavistic heavy industrialists, and downwardly mobile military officers share the stage with populist demagogues, freemarket entrepreneurs, disgruntled workers, and newly mobilized ethnic groups. In principle, mature democratic institutions can integrate even the widest spectrum of interests through competition for the favor of the average voter. But where political parties and representative institutions are still in their infancy, the diversity of interests may make political coalitions difficult to maintain. Often the solution is a belligerent nationalist coalition.

In Britain during the period leading up to the Crimean War, neither the Whigs nor the Tories could form a lasting governing coalition because so many groups refused to enter stable political alliances. None of the old elites would coalesce with the parliamentary bloc of radicals elected by urban middle-class and Irish voters. Moreover, protectionist Tories would not unite with free-trading Whigs and Peelite Tories. The social and political mid-Victorian equipoise between traditional and modern Britain created a temporary political stalemate. Lord Palmerston's pseudoliberal imperialism turned out to be the only successful formula for creating a durable ruling coalition during this transitional period of democratization.

The stalemate in German electoral politics in the Wilhelmine era was even more serious. In principle, coalitions of the left and the right might have formed a two-party system to vie for the favor of the average voter, thus moderating policy. In fact, both left and right were too internally divided to mount effective coalitions with internally consistent policies. Progressives dreamed of a bloc extending "from Bassermann to Bebel," from the liberal-democratic middle classes through the marxist working classes, but the differences between labor and capital chronically barred this development. Conservatives had more success in forging a "marriage of iron and rye," but fundamental differences between military-feudal Junkers and Ruhr industrialists over issues ranging from the distribution of tax burdens to military strategy made their policies incoherent. Germany wound up with plans for a big army and a costly navy, and nobody willing to pay for it.

In more recent times incipient democratization has likewise caused political impasses by widening the political spectrum to include too many irreconcilable political forces. In the final days of Yugoslavia, efforts by moderates such as former prime minister Ante Markovic to promote a federalist, democratic, economic reformist platform were hindered not only by ethnic divisions but also by the cleavage between market-oriented business interests on the one hand and party bosses and military officers on the other. Similarly, in Russia the difficulty of reconciling liberal, neocommunist, and nationalist political platforms and the social interests behind them led in the early 1990s to parliamentary stalemate, attempts to break the stalemate by presidential decree, tanks in the streets, and the resort to freelancing by break-away regions, the military, and spontaneous privatizers of state property. One interpretation of Yeltsin's decision to use force in Chechnya is that he felt it necessary to show that he could act decisively to prevent the unraveling of central authority, with respect not only to ethnic separatists but also to other ungovernable groups in a democratizing society. Chechnya, it was hoped, would allow Yeltsin to demonstrate his ability to coerce Russian society while at the same time exploiting a potentially popular nationalist issue.

Inflexible Interests and Short Time Horizons

Groups threatened by social change and democratization, including still-powerful elites, are often compelled to take an inflexible view of their interests, especially when their assets cannot be readily adapted to changing political and economic conditions. In extreme cases there may be only one solution that will maintain the social position of the group. For Prussian landowners, it was agricultural protection in a nondemocratic state; for the Japanese military, it was organizational autonomy in an autarkic empire; for the Serbian military and party elites, it was a Serbian nationalist state. Since military bureaucracies and imperial interest groups occupied key positions in many authoritarian great powers, whether monarchal or communist, most interests threatened by democratization have been bound up with military programs and the state's international mission. Compromises that may lead down the slippery slope to social extinction or irrelevance have little appeal to such groups. This adds to the difficulty of finding an exit from the domestic political impasse and may make powerful domestic groups impervious to the international risks of their strategies.

Competing for Popular Support

The trouble intensifies when elites in a democratizing society try to recruit mass allies to their cause. Threatened elite groups have an overwhelming incentive to mobilize mass backers on the elites' terms, using whatever special resources they might retain. These resources have included monopolies of information (the Wilhelmine navy's unique "expertise" in making strategic assessments), propaganda assets (the Japanese army's public relations blitz justifying the invasion of Manchuria), patronage (Lord Palmerston's gifts of foreign service postings to the sons of cooperative journalists), wealth (the Krupp steel company's bankrolling of mass nationalist and militarist leagues), organizational skills and networks (the Japanese army's exploitation of rural reservist organizations to build a social base), and the ability to use the control of traditional political institutions to shape the political agenda and structure the terms of political bargains (the Wilhelmine ruling elite's agreement to eliminate anti-Catholic legislation in exchange for Catholic support in the Reichstag on the naval budget).

This elite mobilization of mass groups takes place in a highly competitive setting. Elite groups mobilize mass support to neutralize mass threats (for instance, creating patriotic leagues to counter workers' movements) and counter other elite groups' successful efforts at mass mobilization (such as the German Navy League, a political counterweight to the Junker-backed Agrarian League). The elites' resources allow them to influence the direction of mass political participation, but the imperative to compete for mass favor makes it difficult for a single elite group to control the outcome of this process. For example, mass groups that gain access to politics through elite-supported nationalist organizations often try to outbid their erstwhile sponsors. By 1911 German popular nationalist lobbies were in a position to claim that if Germany's foreign foes were really as threatening as the ruling elites had portrayed them, then the government had sold out German interests in reaching a compromise with France over the Moroccan dispute. In this way, elite mobilization of the masses adds to the ungovernability and political impasse of democratizing states.

Ideology takes on particular significance in the competition for mass support. New entrants to the political process, lacking established habits and good information, may be uncertain where their political interests lie. Ideology can yield big payoffs, particularly when there is no efficient free marketplace of ideas to counter false claims with reliable facts. Elites try out all sorts of ideological appeals depending on the social position they are defending, the nature of the mass group they want to recruit, and the kinds of appeals that seem politically plausible. A nearly universal element of these ideological appeals, however, is nationalism, which has the advantage of positing a community of interest uniting elites and masses. This distracts attention from class cleavages that divide elites from the masses they are trying to recruit.

The Weakening of Central Authority

The political impasse and recklessness of democratizing states are deepened by the weakening of the state's authority. The autocrat can no longer dictate to elite interest groups or mass groups. Meanwhile, democratic institutions lack the strength to integrate these contending interests and views. Parties are weak and lack mass loyalty. Elections are rigged or intermittent. Institutions of public political participation are distrusted because they are subject to manipulation by elites and arbitrary constraints imposed by the state, which fears the outcome of unfettered competition.

Among the great powers, the problem was not excessive authoritarian power at the center but the opposite. The Aberdeen coalition that brought Britain into the Crimean War was a makeshift cabinet headed by a weak leader with no substantial constituency. Likewise, on the eve of the Franco-Prussian War, Napoleon III's regime was in the process of caving in to its liberal opponents, who dominated the parliament elected in 1869. As Europe's armies prepared to hurtle from their starting gates in July 1914, Austrian leaders, perplexed by the contradictions between the German chancellor's policy and that of the German military, asked, "Who rules in Berlin?" Similarly, the 1931 Manchurian incident was a fait accompli by the local Japanese military; Tokyo was not even informed. The return to imperial thinking in Moscow was the result of Yeltsin's weakness, not his strength. As the well-informed Moscow analyst Sergei Karaganov recently argued, the breakdown of the Leninist state "has created an environment where elite interests influence [foreign] policy directly."[13]

In each of these cases, the weak central leadership resorts to the same strategies as do the more parochial elite interests, using nationalist ideological appeals and special-interest payoffs to maintain their short-run viability, despite the long-run risks that these strategies may unleash.

---

13. Sergei Karaganov, "Russia's Elites," in *Damage Limitation*, ed. Robert Blackwill and Sergei Karaganov (Berkeley: University of California Press, 1967), 250.

Prestige Strategies

One of the simplest but riskiest strategies for a hard-pressed regime in a democratizing country is to shore up its prestige at home by seeking victories abroad. During the Chechen intervention newspaper commentators in Moscow and the West were reminded of Russian interior minister Viacheslav Plehve's fateful remark in 1904, on the eve of the disastrous Russo-Japanese War, that what the tsar needed was "a short, victorious war" to boost his prestige. Though this strategy often backfires, it is a perennial temptation as a means for coping with the political strains of democratization. German chancellor Johannes Miquel, who revitalized the imperialist-protectionist "coalition of iron and rye" at the turn of the century, told his colleagues that "successes in foreign policy would make a good impression in the Reichstag debates, and political divisions would thus be moderated."[14] The targets of such strategies often share this analysis. Richard Cobden, for example, argued in 1854 that military victories abroad would confer enough prestige on the military-feudal landed elite to allow them to raise food tariffs and snuff out democracy: "Let John Bull have a great military triumph, and we shall have to take off our hats as we pass the Horse Guards for the rest of our lives."[15]

Prestige strategies make the country vulnerable to slights to its reputation. Napoleon III, for example, was easily goaded into a full declaration of war in 1870 by Bismarck's insulting editorial work on a leaked telegram from the kaiser. For those who want to avoid such diplomatic provocations, the lesson is to make sure that compromises forced on the leaders of democratizing states do not take away the fig leaves needed to sustain their domestic prestige.

MANAGING THE DANGERS

Though mature democratic states have virtually never fought wars against each other, promoting democracy may not promote peace because states are especially war prone during the transition toward democracy. This does not mean, however, that democratization should be squelched in the interests of peace. Many states are now democratizing or on the verge of it, and stemming that turbulent tide, even if it were desirable, may not be possible. Consequently, the task is to draw on an understanding of the process of democratization to keep its unwanted side effects to a minimum.

Of course, democratization does not always lead to extreme forms of aggressive nationalism, just as it does not always lead to war. But it makes those outcomes more likely. Cases in which states democratized without triggering a nationalist mobilization are particularly interesting, since they may hold clues about how to prevent such unwanted side effects. Among the great powers, the obvious successes were the democratization of Germany and Japan after 1945, owing to occupation by liberal democracies and the favorable international setting provided by the Marshall Plan, the Bretton Woods economic system, and the democratic military alliance against the Soviet threat. More recently, numerous Latin American states have democratized without nationalism or war. Border skirmishes between Peru and Ecuador, however, coincided with democratizing trends in both states and a nationalist turn in Ecuadoran political discourse. Moreover, all three pre-

---

14. J. C. G. Rohl, *Germany without Bismarck* (Berkeley: University of California Press, 1967), 250.

15. Richard Cobden, letter to John Bright, October 1, 1854, quoted in John Morley, *The Life of Richard Cobden*, abridged ed. (London: Thomas Nelson), 311-312.

vious wars between that pair over the past two centuries occurred in periods of partial democratization.

In such cases, however, the cure is probably more democracy, not less. In "Wilhelmine Argentina," the Falkland Islands/Malvinas War came when the military junta needed a nationalist victory to stave off pressure for the return of democracy; the arrival of full democracy has produced more pacific policies. Among the Eastern European states, nationalist politics has been unsuccessful in the most fully democratic ones—Poland, the Czech Republic, and Hungary—as protest votes have gone to former communists. Nationalism has figured more prominently in the politics of the less democratic formerly communist states that are nonetheless partially democratizing. States like Turkmenistan that remain outright autocracies have no nationalist mobilization—indeed no political mobilization of any kind. The rule seems to be: Go fully democratic, or don't go at all.

In any given case, other factors may override the relative bellicosity of democratizing states. These might include the power of the democratizing state, the strength of the potential deterrent coalition of states constraining it, the attractiveness of more peaceful options available to the democratizing state, and the nature of the groups making up its ruling coalition. What is needed is to identify the conditions that lead to relatively peaceful democratization and try to create those circumstances.

One of the major findings of scholarship on democratization in Latin America is that the process goes most smoothly when elites threatened by the transition—especially the military—are given a golden parachute. Above all, they need a guarantee that they will not wind up in jail if they relinquish power. The history of the democratizing great powers broadens this insight. Democratization was least likely to lead to war when the old elites saw a reasonably bright future for themselves in the new social order. British aristocrats, for example, had more of their wealth invested in commerce and industry than in agriculture, so they had many interests in common with the rising middle classes. They could face democratization with relative equanimity. In contrast, Prussia's capital-starved, small-scale Junker landholders had no choice but to rely on agricultural protection and military careers.

In today's context one of the most pressing threats to the elites of potentially democratizing authoritarian states stems from international efforts to prosecute them for crimes they committed under the old regime. In Rwanda and Burundi, for example, this was one of the factors that created an incentive for hard-liners to gamble on playing the ethnic conflict card as a way to hang on to power. In some transitional countries from the 1980s to the mid-1990s, such as Chile and South Africa, immunity deals encouraged old elites to relinquish their positions of power. More recently, however, international organizations, courts, and activist groups have been arguing that immunity arrangements do not apply to perpetrators of war crimes, genocide, torture, and other crimes against humanity. By indicting still-powerful figures like then Serbian president Slobodan Milosevic and by retroactively stripping immunity from former dictators like Chile's Augusto Pinochet, this new practice makes it difficult to offer credible golden parachutes to thugs who might in the future act as implacable spoilers of a democratic transition.

The transition to democracy proceeds more peacefully when the institutions needed for the functioning of a democratic society are already partially in place before mass-suffrage elections are held. South Africa, for example, experienced a relatively successful transition because of the legacy of well-developed, whites-only civic institutions that it inherited from the apartheid regime and expanded to include the whole population after the transition: a rationalized state bureaucracy, the rule of law, elections, a parliament, political parties, schools, and a professionalized media. In contrast, Burundi, which had elections abruptly pressed upon its ethnic Tutsi minority dictatorship by international donors in 1993, had none of these institutions to build upon; as a result, within months of the elections, over one hundred thousand people were killed in ethnic strife. Wherever possible, the patient building of the institutional preconditions of democracy should precede the unleashing of competitive mass electoral politics.

Another top priority must be creating a free, competitive, and responsible marketplace of ideas in the newly democratizing states. Most of the war-prone democratizing great powers had pluralistic public debates, but the debates were skewed to favor groups with money, privileged access to the media, and proprietary control over information ranging from archives to intelligence about the military balance. Pluralism is not enough. Without a level playing field, pluralism simply creates the incentive and opportunity for privileged groups to propound self-serving myths, which historically have often taken a nationalist turn. One of the rays of hope in the Chechen affair was the alacrity with which Russian journalists exposed the costs of the fighting and the lies of the government and the military. Though elites should get a golden parachute regarding their pecuniary interests, they should be given no quarter on the battlefield of ideas. Mythmaking should be held up to the utmost scrutiny by aggressive journalists who maintain their credibility by scrupulously distinguishing fact from opinion and tirelessly verifying their sources. Promoting this kind of journalistic infrastructure is probably the most highly leveraged investment the West can make in a peaceful democratic transition.

Finally, the kind of ruling coalition that emerges in the course of democratization depends a great deal on the incentives created by the international environment. Both Germany and Japan started on the path toward liberal, stable democratization in the mid-1920s, encouraged by abundant opportunities for trade with and investment by the advanced democracies and by credible security treaties that defused nationalist scaremongering in domestic politics. When the international supports for free trade and democracy were yanked out in the late 1920s, their liberal coalitions collapsed. For China, whose democratization may occur in the context of expanding economic ties with the West, a steady Western commercial partnership and security presence is likely to play a major role in shaping the incentives of proto-democratic coalition politics.

In the long run the enlargement of the zone of stable democracy will probably enhance prospects for peace. In the short run much work remains to be done to minimize the dangers of the turbulent transition.

Chapter Three

International Political Economy Lens

Introduction to International Political Economy Lens[1]

"The Lens of International Political Economy"

Although extensive, the Security Lens is not always fully satisfactory as an approach to studying international relations. While necessary, it is not always sufficient. Not every international action is undertaken in order to gain power for the express purpose of self-preservation and survival. Furthermore, non-state actors conduct significant international activity. For both of these reasons, the theory in the Security Lens is incomplete in explaining why international actors do what they do and the causes of conflict and cooperation among states.[2]

International Political Economy (IPE) provides an alternative—though often complementary—approach for explaining non-military activity and the broader sweep of international relations.[3] This lens suggests that international relations is best understood as the relationship between ***wealth*** and ***power.*** The end of the Cold War suggested a need for improved approaches for understanding the manner in which cooperation and conflict stem from non-military activity. Questions about the interplay of politics and economics became increasingly important and, in fact, as long-dominant theories of international relation often missed the historic salience of this relationship.

The post-World War II era featured such a strong tendency toward economic cooperation among the states of the West. The Security Lens' exclusive focus upon security and survival does not fully explain the development of cooperative agreements such as the World Trade Organization (WTO), or cooperative institutions such as the European Economic Community (EEC) and the International Monetary Fund (IMF).[4] As new answers to these and other questions were needed, international relations scholars looked to older, pre-World War I ideas and ideologies for answers. IPE is the product of this scholarly quest.

WHAT IS IPE?

As it has developed (see table 3.1), IPE is a web of theories that endeavor to explain what Robert Gilpin calls the "reciprocal and dynamic interaction of economics and politics witnessed in international relations."[5] IPE incorporates international issues and ideas on three distinct levels. First, IPE is a set of policy issues—including those involved with economic growth, trade, finance, development, debt and collective goods. IPE is also the conceptual nexus between international politics and economics. Here, students and practitioners of international relations struggle to discern the points of reinforcement and conflict between wealth and power, states and markets, and absolute and relative economic gains. Finally, IPE is a set of alternative theories about the conceptual relationships between politics and eco-

---

1. revised April 24, 2004: J. Forest

2. Robert Gilpin, *The Political Economy of International Relations* (Princeton: Princeton University Press, 1987).

3. Robert Gilpin, *U.S. Power and the Multinational Corporation* (New York: Basic Books, 1975).

4. Robert O. Keohane, *After Hegemony: Cooperation and Discord in the World Political Economy* (Princeton: Princeton University Press, 1984).

5. Gilpin, *U.S. Power and the Multinational Corporation* 21.

nomics in international affairs. Modern IPE incorporates assumptions and norms from older ideologies, including classical mercantilism, liberalism, and Marxism to understand the nature and consequences of these political and economic relationships. The lens of IPE—based on three alternative holistic IPE ideologies—focuses our thinking upon issues involving states and markets, wealth and power, and absolute versus relative gains.

Despite continuing evolution, each ideology has maintained a unique set of core assumptions about the manner in which politics and economics interact at the level of the individual, the society, and the international system. Each suggests an alternative view of the dominant patterns of cooperation and discord in international relations, and of the reasons for these patterns (see for example, the phases of Marxism discussed in the selection by Thomas Lynch). These ideologies establish the foundations upon which modern IPE theories have been derived: mercantilism, hegemonic stability theory, regime theory, complex interdependence, and dependency theory. We must appreciate the ideological foundation of each IPE theory in order to fully understand them fully and to use them for explaining international relations.

While dissimilar in many respects, IPE theories share many ideas. First, most recognize the existence of other actors on the international stage. Second, these systemic theories explain patterns of cooperation and conflict systemically; that is, by arguing that the international system shapes these patterns more than do the individual actors. Finally, most of these theories agree that there is no fixed hierarchy of issues in the conduct of international relations. These theories highlight the significance of political and economic interactions for international relations. Table 3-3 compares the common systemic points among IPE theories.

The Security Lens focuses narrowly on issues of international power and state security and emphasizes the primacy of state-to-state military interaction in explaining international relations. Consistent with our goal of intellectual pluralism, the IPE lens broadens our understanding significantly by incorporating political and economic interchange: focusing on the relationship between wealth and power. IPE expands the ability of an international policy maker, analyst or theorist to understand why states (and other international actors) do what they do. A careful study of the similarities and differences between these theories is critical to any complete understanding of international relations.

Suggestions for Further Readings:

Axelrod, Robert M. 1984. *The Evolution of Cooperation.* New York: Basic Books.

Baldwin, David A. 1985. *Economic Statecraft.* Princeton: Princteon University Press.

Banks, Jeffrey S. and Eric A. Hanushek. 1995. *Modern Political Economy: Old Topics, New Directions.* New York: Cambridge University Press.

Brugger, Bill and Stephen Reglar. 1994. *Politics, Economy and Society in Contemporary China.* Stanford, CA: Stanford University Press.

Cardoso, Fernando and Enzo Faletto. 1979. *Dependency and Development in Latin America.* Berkeley: University of California Press.

Crane, George T. and Abla Awami, eds. 1991. *The Theoretical Evolution of International Political Economy: A Reader.* New York: Oxford University Press.

Eichengreen, Barry. 1989. "Hegemonic Stability Theories of the International Monetary System." In *Can Nations Agree?* eds. Richard N. Cooper, et. al. Washington DC: Brookings Institution.

Eichengreen, Barry. 1996. *Globalizing Capital: A History of the International Monetary System.* Princeton: Princeton University Press.

Frieden, JeffreyA and David A. Lake. 1995. *International Political Economy: Perspectives on Global Power and Wealth.* 4th Ed. New York: St. Martin's Press.

Gilpin, Robert. 1981. *War and Change In International Politics*. Cambridge: Cambridge University Press.

Gilpin, Robert. 1987. *The Political Economy of International Relations*. Princeton: Princeton University Press.

Greico, Joseph M. 1990. *Cooperation Among Nations: Europe, America and Non-Tariff Barriers to Trade*. Ithaca: Cornell University Press.

Haas, Ernst. 1964. *Beyond The Nation-State: Functionalism and International Organization*. Stanford: Stanford University Press.

Haggard, Stephan. 1990. *Pathways from the Periphery: The Politics of Growth in the Newly Industrialized Countries*. Ithaca: Cornell University Press.

Hiscox, Michael J. 2001. "Class Versus Industry Cleavages: Inter-Industry Factor Mobility and the Politics of Trade." *International Organization* 55, p. 1-46.

Irwin, Douglas A. 1996. *Against the Tide: An Intellectual History of Free Trade*. Princeton: Princeton University Press.

Keohane, Robert O. and Helen V. Milner. eds. 1996. *Internationalization and Domestic Politics*. Cambridge: Cambridge University Press.

Keohane, Robert O. and Lia Martin. 1995. "The Promise of Institutionalist Theory." *International Security* 20, no.1 (Summer), p. 39-51.

Keohane, Robert O. and Joseph S. Nye, Jr. 1989. *Power and Interdependence, 2nd Ed.* Glenview, Illinois: Scott, Foresman, and Co.

Keohane, Robert. O. 1984. *After Hegemony: Cooperation and Discord in the World Political Economy.* Princeton: Princeton University Press.

Kindleberger, Charles. 1973. *The World in Depression: 1929-1939.* Berkeley: University of California Press.

Krasner, Stephen D, ed. 1983. *International Regimes*. Ithaca, NY: Cornell University Press.

Krugman, Paul. 1998. *The Accidental Theorist: and Other Dispatches From the Dismal Science*. New York: Norton.

Lairson, Thomas D. and David Skidmore. 1997. *International Political Economy: The Struggle for Power and Wealth.* 2nd Ed. Fort Worth: Harcourt Brace College Publishers.

Lake, David. 1993. "Leadership, Hegemony, and the International Economy: Naked Emperor or Tattered Monarch with Potentia.," *International Studies Quarterly* 37, p. 459-489.

Lewis, W. Arthur. 1978. *The Evolution of the International Economic Order*. Princeton: Princeton University Press.

Mansfield, Edward D. and Brian M. Pollins. eds. 2003. *Economic Interdependence and International Conflict: New Perspectives on an Enduring Debate*. Ann Arbor: University of Michigan Press.

Mattli, Walter. 1999. *The Logic of Regional Integration: Europe and Beyond.* Cambridge: Cambridge University Press.

Mearsheimer, John J. 1996. "The False Promise of International Institutions." *International Security* 19 (Winter), p. 5-49.

Mitrany, David. 1975. *The Functional Theory of International Politics*. London: St. Martin's Press.

Oatley, Thomas. 2003. *International Political Economy: Interests and Institutions in the Global Economy. New York: Pearson Longman.*

Oneal, John R. and Bruce M. Russett. 1997. "The Classical Liberals Were Right: Democracy, Interdependence and Conflict." *International Studies Quarterly* 41 (March), p. 267-294.

Oye, Kenneth A. 1992. *Economic Discrimination and Political Exchange*. Princeton: Princeton University Press.

Oye, Kenneth, ed. 1986. *Cooperation Under Anarchy*. Princeton: Princeton University Press.

Rosenau, James N. and Ernst-Otto Czempiel, ed. 1990. *Global Changes and Theoretical Challenges: Approaches to World Politics for the 1990s*. Lexington, MA: Lexington Books.

Simmons, Beth. 1994. *Who Adjusts? Domestic Sources of Foreign Economic Policy During the Interwar Years*. Princeton: Princeton University Press.

Spero, Joan Edelman. 1990. *The Politics of International Economic Relations*. 4th Edition. New York: St. Martin's Press.

Stein, Arthur A. 1984. "The Hegemon's Dilemma: Great Britain, the United States and the International Economic Order," *International Organization*. 38:2 (Spring).

Tucker, Robert C, ed. 1975. *The Lenin Anthology*. New York: W.W. Norton and Company.

Verdier, Daniel. 1998. "Democratic Convergence and Free Trade." *International Studies Quarterly* 42, p. 1-24.

Wagener, Hans-Jurgen, ed. 1998. *Economic Thought in Communist and Post-Communist Europe*. London: Routledge.

Waligorski, Conrad. 1997. *Liberal Economics and Democracy: Keynes, Galbraith, Thurow and Reich*. Lawrence, KA: University Press of Kansas.

Walker, Angus. 1979. *Marx: His Theory and Its Context*, 2nd Ed. London: Rivers Oram Press.

Wallerstein, Emmanuel. 1974. "Dependence in an Interdependent World." *African Studies Review*. No. 17, (April), p. 1-26.

Weidmann, Franz. 1968. *Hegel*. New York: Pegasus.

Wilbur, Charles, K. and Kenneth P. Jameson, ed. 1992. *The Political Economy of Development and Underdevelopment, 5th Edition*. New York: McGraw Hill.

Yarbrough, Beth V. and Robert M. Yarbrough. 1992. *Cooperation and Governance in International Trade: The Strategic Organizational Approach*. Princeton, NJ: Princeton University Press

Zahariadis, Nikolaos. 1999. *Contending Perspectives in International Political Economy*. Fort Worth: Harcourt Brace

TalA Comparison of Root Ideologies and Evolved Theories

These IPE Ideologies. . .			. . .provided the foundation for. . .	. . .these IPE Theories		
Classical Mercantilism	**Liberalism**	**Marxism**		**Mercantilism**	**Complex Interdependence**	**Dependency**
			Assumptions:			
state	individual	classes (of individuals)	**Main Actor?**	•	individuals in firms, MNCs	classes (of states)
maximize state power	maximize individual utility	maximize class wealth	**Goal of Actor?**	•	maximize economic efficiency & global GNP	•
power (military)	open exchange of... (goods, services & ideas	violent revolt	**Principal Means to Act?**	Power (Military & Economic)	•	•
security & power	insulate, obstruct exchange	protect upper class	**Role of State?**	•	facilitate inter-state cooperation, encourage regimes	subjugate poor states
politics **drives** economy (ambiguous effect)	economy **should drive** politics (cooperative effect)	economy **drives** politics (conflictual effect)	**Politics vs. Economics?**	•	•	•
			Policy Implications:			
*	*	*	**Goal of International Relations?**	state power & control	maximize global wealth & peace	overcome inequities
*	*	*	**Nature of Relations?**	"zero sum" (conflictual)	"positive sum" (cooperative)	"zero sum" (conflictual)
*	*	*	**Stakes of Relations?**	Relative State Gains	Absolute Global Gains	Relative Class Gains
*	*	*	**Relations: Dynamic/Stable?**	dynamic stability [See (1)]	stable dynamism [See(2)]	fundamental instability
*	*	*	**Best Possible World?**	stable balance of power, Hegemon leads coop.	states bow to international coop., one-world globalism	end of world capitalism, equal dist. of all wealth
*	*	*	**Best State Policy?**	balance, lead, use power	support Regimes & global coop., fade-out as a global actor	break world capitalism, cease to be a major actor

Notes:

* = Not fully predictive or policy oriented on this point

• = Adheres to the position of associated Ideology (see facing page)

(1) Dynamic Stability = World is constantly in flux, moving from one group of powerful states to another. This process is, nonetheless, rarely violent when all states participate cautiously and with respect to their power.

(2) Stable Dynamism = World is usually in a peaceful equilibrium state. This equilibrium is maintained as cooperative economic forces encourage states toward dynamic technological advancements in a spirit of mutual interdependence.

IPE Perspectives

Robert Gilpin

Three Ideologies of Political Economy

Three Ideologies of Political Economy

Robert Gilpin

In this non-theoretical reading, Gilpin provides a summary of the three dominant ideologies of International Political Economy—mercantilism, liberalism, and Marxism—and their critiques. Because these three perspectives fundamentally differ over many important assumptions about the relationship between states and markets, a solid grasp of this reading is necessary to comprehend fully this text's IPE theories: Mercantistist Theory, Hegemonic Stability Theory, Product Cycle Theory, Regime Theory, Complex Interdependence, Neo-Liberal Development Theory, Imperialist Theory, and Dependency Theory.

Over the past century and a half, the ideologies of liberalism, nationalism, and Marxism have divided humanity. This book uses "ideology" to refer to "systems of thought and belief by which [individuals and groups] explain. . . how their social system operates and what principles it exemplifies".[1] The conflict among these three moral and intellectual positions has revolved around the role and significance of the market in the organization of society and economic affairs.

Through an evaluation of the strengths and weaknesses of these three ideologies it is possible to illuminate the study of the field of international political economy. The strengths of each perspective set forth here will be applied to subsequent discussions of specific issues, such as those of trade, investment, and development. Although my values are those of liberalism, the world in which we live is one best described by the ideas of economic nationalism and occasionally by those of Marxism as well. *Eclecticism may not be the route to theoretical precision, but sometimes it is the only route available.*

The three ideologies differ on a broad range of questions such as: What is the significance of the market for economic growth and the distribution of wealth among groups and societies? What ought to be the role of markets in the organization of domestic and international society? What is the effect of the market system on issues of war or peace? These and similar questions are central to discussions of international political economy.

These three ideologies are fundamentally different in their conceptions of the relationships among society, state, and market, and it may not be an exaggeration to say that every controversy in the field of international political economy is ultimately reducible to differing conceptions of these relationships. The intellectual clash is not merely of historical interest. *Economic liberalism, Marxism,* and *economic nationalism* are all very much alive at the end of the twentieth century; they define the conflicting perspectives that individuals have with regard to the implications of the market system for domestic and international society. Many of the issues that were controversial in the eighteenth and nineteenth centuries are once again being intensely debated.

It is important to understand the nature and content of these contrasting "ideologies" of political economy. The term "ideology" is used rather than "theory" because each position entails a total belief system concerning the nature of human beings and society and is

1. Robert L. Heilbroner, *The Nature and Logic of Capitalism* (New York: W. W. Norton, 1985), p. 107.

Gilpin, Robert; *The Political Economy of International Relations. 1987 by Princeton University Press, pp. 25-64. Reprinted by permission of Princeton University Press. Italics added.*

thus akin to what Thomas Kuhn has called a paradigm.[2] As Kuhn demonstrates, intellectual commitments are held tenaciously and can seldom be dislodged by logic or by contrary evidence. This is due to the fact that these commitments or ideologies allege to provide scientific descriptions of how the world *does* work while they also constitute normative positions regarding how the world *should* work.

Although scholars have produced a number of "theories" to explain the relationship of economics and politics, these three stand out and have had a profound influence on scholarship and political affairs. In highly oversimplified terms, economic nationalism (or, as it was originally called, *mercantilism*), which developed from the practice of statesmen in the early modern period, assumes and advocates the primacy of politics over economics. It is essentially a doctrine of state-building and asserts that the market should be subordinate to the pursuit of state interests. It argues that political factors do, or at least should, determine economic relations. *Liberalism*, which emerged from the Enlightenment in the writings of Adam Smith and others, was a reaction to mercantilism and has become embodied in orthodox economics. It assumes that politics and economics exist, at least ideally, in separate spheres; it argues that markets—in the interest of efficiency, growth, and consumer choice—should be free from political interference. *Marxism*, which appeared in the mid-nineteenth century as a reaction against liberalism and classical economics, holds that economics drives politics. Political conflict arises from struggle among classes over the distribution of wealth. Hence, political conflict will cease with the elimination of the market and of a society of classes. Since both nationalism and Marxism in the modern era have developed largely in reaction to the tenets of liberal economics, my discussion and evaluation of these ideologies will begin with economic liberalism.

THE LIBERAL PERSPECTIVE

Some scholars assert that there is no such thing as a liberal theory of political economy because liberalism separates economics and politics from one another and assumes that each sphere operates according to particular rules and a logic of its own.[3] This view is itself, however, an ideological position and liberal theorists do in fact concern themselves with both political and economic affairs. Whether it is made explicit in their writings or is merely implicit, one can speak of a liberal theory of political economy.

There is a set of values from which liberal theories of economics and of politics arise; in the modern world these political and economic values have tended to appear together.[4] Liberal economic theory is committed to free markets and minimal state intervention, although, as will be pointed out below, the relative emphasis on one or the other may differ. Liberal political theory is committed to individual equality and liberty, although again the emphasis may differ. We are primarily concerned here with the economic component of liberal theory.

The liberal perspective on political economy is embodied in the discipline of economics as it has developed in Great Britain, the United States, and Western Europe. From Adam Smith to its contemporary proponents, liberal thinkers have shared a coherent set of

2. See Thomas S. Kuhn, *Structure of Scientific Revolutions* (Chicago: University of Chicago Press, 1962).

3. The term "liberal" is used in this book in its European connotation, that is, a commitment to individualism, free market, and private property. This is the dominant perspective of most American economists and of economics as taught in American universities. Thus, both Paul Samuelson and Milton Friedman, despite important differences between their political and theoretical views, are regarded here as representatives of the American liberal tradition.

4. See Charles E. Lindblom, *Politics and Markets: The World's Political-Economic Systems* (New York: Basic Books, 1977).

assumptions and beliefs about the nature of human beings, society, and economic activities. Liberalism has assumed many forms—classical, neo-classical, Keynesian, monetarist, Austrian, rational expectation, etc. These variants range from those giving priority to equality and tending toward social democracy and state interventionism to achieve this objective, to those stressing liberty and noninterventionism at the expense of social equality. All forms of economic liberalism, however, are committed to the market and the price mechanism as the most efficacious means for organizing domestic and international economic relations. Liberalism may, in fact, be defined as a doctrine and set of principles for organizing and managing a market economy in order to achieve maximum efficiency, economic growth, and individual welfare.

Economic liberalism assumes that a market arises spontaneously in order to satisfy human needs and that, once it is in operation, it functions in accordance with its own internal logic. Human beings are by nature economic animals, and therefore markets evolve naturally without central direction. As Adam Smith put it, it is inherent in mankind to "truck, barter and exchange." To facilitate exchange and improve their well-being, people create markets, money, and economic institutions. Thus, in his "The Economic Organization of a P.O.W. Camp," R. A. Radford[5] shows how a complex and sophisticated market arose spontaneously in order to satisfy human wants, but his tale also demonstrates how a form of government was necessary to police and maintain this primitive market system.[6]

The rationale for a market system is that it increases economic efficiency, maximizes economic growth, and thereby improves human welfare. Although liberals believe that economic activity also enhances the power and security of the state, they argue that the primary objective of economic activity is to benefit individual consumers. Their ultimate defense of free trade and open markets is that they increase the range of goods and services available to the consumer.

The fundamental premise of liberalism is that the individual consumer, firm, or household is the basis of society. Individuals behave rationally and attempt to maximize or satisfy certain values at the lowest possible cost to themselves. Rationality applies only to endeavor, not to outcome. Thus, failure to achieve an objective due to ignorance or some other cause does not, according to liberals, invalidate their premise that individuals act on the basis of a cost/benefit or means/ends calculus. Finally, liberalism argues that an individual will seek to acquire an objective until a market equilibrium is reached, that is, until the costs associated with achieving the objective are equal to the benefits. Liberal economists attempt to explain economic and, in some cases, all human behavior on the basis of these individualistic and rationalistic assumptions.[7]

Liberalism also assumes that a market exists in which individuals have complete information and are thus enabled to select the most beneficial course of action. Individual producers and consumers will be highly responsive to price signals, and this will create a flexible economy in which any change in relative prices will elicit a corresponding change in patterns of production, consumption, and economic institutions; the latter are conceived ultimately to be the product rather than the cause of economic behavior.[8] Further, in a truly

---

5. See R.A. Radford, "The Economic Organization of a P.O.W. Camp," *Economica* 12 (1945): 189-201.

6. I would like to thank Michael Doyle for bringing this interesting article to my attention.

7. See Ronald Rogowski, "Rationalist Theories of Politics: A Midterm Report," *World Politics* 30 (1978): 296-323.

8. See Lance E. Davis and Douglass C. North (with the assistance of Calla Smorodin), *Institutional Change and American Economic Growth* (Cambridge: Cambridge University Press, 1971).

competitive market, the terms of exchange are determined solely by considerations of supply and demand rather than by the exercise of power and coercion. If exchange is voluntary, both parties benefit. In colloquial terms, a "free exchange is no robbery."

Economics, or rather the economics taught in most American universities (what Marxists call orthodox or bourgeois economics), is assumed to be an empirical science of maximizing behavior. Behavior is believed to be governed by a set of economic "laws" that are impersonal and politically neutral; therefore, economics and politics should and can be separated into distinct spheres. Governments should not intervene in the market except where a "market failure" exists [9] or in order to provide a so-called public or collective good.[10]

A market economy is governed principally by the law of demand.[11] This "law" (or, if one prefers, assumption) holds that people will buy more of a good if the relative price falls and less if it rises; people will also tend to buy more of a good as their relative income rises and less as it falls. Any development that changes the relative price of a good or the relative income of an actor will create an incentive or disincentive to acquire (or produce) more or less of the good; this law in turn has profound ramifications throughout the society. Although certain exceptions to this simple concept exist, it is fundamental to the operation and success of a market system of economic exchange.

On the supply side of the economy, liberal economics assumes that individuals pursue their interests in a world of scarcity and resource constraints. This is a fundamental and inescapable condition of human existence. Every decision involves an opportunity cost, a trade-off among alternative uses of available resources.[12] The basic lesson of liberal economics is that "there is no such thing as a free lunch"; to get something one must be willing to give up something else.

Liberalism also assumes that a market economy exhibits a powerful tendency toward equilibrium and inherent stability, at least over the long term. This "concept of a self-operating and self-correcting equilibrium achieved by a balance of forces in a rational universe" is a crucial one for the economists' belief in the operation of markets and the laws that are believed to govern them.[13] If a market is thrown into a state of disequilibrium due to some external (exogenous) factor such as a change in consumer tastes or productive technology, the operation of the price mechanism will eventually return it to a new state of equilibrium. Prices and quantities will once again balance one another. Thus, a change in either the supply or the demand for a good will elicit corresponding changes in the price of the good. The principal technique of modern economic analysis, comparative statics, is based on this assumption of a tendency toward systemic equilibrium.[14]

---

9. See William J. Baumol, *Welfare Economics and the Theory of the State*, 2d. ed. (Cambridge: Harvard University Press, 1965).

10. See Mancur Olson, Jr., *The Logic of Collective Action: Public Goods and the Theory of Groups* (Cambridge: Harvard University Press, 1965).

11. See Gary S. Becker, *The Economic Approach to Human Behavior* (Chicago: University of Chicago Press, 1976), p. 6.

12. See Paul A. Samuelson, *Economics*, 11th ed., with the assistance in Statistical Updating of William Samuelson (New York: McGraw-Hill, 1980), p. 27.

13. J. B. Condliffe, *The Commerce of Nations* (New York: W. W. Norton, 1950), p. 112.

14. The method of comparative statics was invented by David Ricardo. It consists of a model of a market in a state of equilibrium, the introduction of an exogenous variable into the system, and a calculation of the new equilibrium state. Because this mode of analysis is generally unconcerned with the origins of the exogenous variable itself, it is limited as a means of examining the problem of economic change.

An additional liberal assumption is that a basic long-term harmony of interests underlies the market competition of producers and consumers, a harmony that will supercede any temporary conflict of interest. Individual pursuit of self-interest in the market increases social well-being because it leads to the maximization of efficiency, and the resulting economic growth eventually benefits all. Consequently, everyone will gain in accordance with his or her contribution to the whole, but, it should be added, not everyone will gain equally because individual productivities differ. Under free exchange, society as a whole will be more wealthy, but individuals will be rewarded in terms of their marginal productivity and relative contribution to the overall social product.

Finally, most present-day liberal economists believe in progress, defined most frequently as an increase in wealth per capita. They assert that the growth of a properly functioning economy is linear, gradual, and continuous.[15] It proceeds along what an economist colleague has called "the MIT standard equilibrium growth curve." Although political or other events—wars, revolution, or natural disasters—can dramatically disrupt this growth path, the economy will return eventually to a stable pattern of growth that is determined principally by increases in population, resources, and productivity. Moreover, liberals see no necessary connection between the process of economic growth and political developments such as war and imperialism; these political evils affect and may be affected by economic activities, but they are essentially caused by political and not by economic factors. For example, liberals do not believe that any causal relationship existed between the advance of capitalism in the late nineteenth century and the upheavals of imperialism after 1870 and the outbreak of the First World War. Liberals believe economics is progressive and politics is retrogressive. Thus they conceive of progress as divorced from politics and based on the evolution of the market.

On the basis of these assumptions and commitments, modern economists have constructed the empirical science of economics. Over the past two centuries, they have deduced the "laws" of maximizing behavior, such as those of the theory of comparative advantage, the theory of marginal utility, and the quantity theory of money. As Arthur Lewis has commented to me, economists discover new laws at the rate of about one per quarter century. These "laws" are both contingent and normative. They assume the existence of economic man—a rational, maximizing creature—a variant of the species homo sapiens that has been relatively rare in human history and has existed only during peculiar periods of favorable conditions. Further, these laws are normative in that they prescribe how a society must organize itself and how people must behave if they are to maximize the growth of wealth. Both individuals and societies may violate these laws, but they do so at the cost of productive efficiency. Today, the conditions necessary for the operation of a market economy exist, and the normative commitment to the market has spread from its birthplace in Western civilization to embrace an increasingly large portion of the globe. Despite setbacks, the modern world has moved in the direction of the market economy and of increasing global economic interdependence precisely because markets *are* more efficient than other forms of economic organization.[16]

In essence, liberals believe that trade and economic intercourse are a source of peaceful relations among nations because the mutual benefits of trade and expanding interdependence among national economies will tend to foster cooperative relations. Whereas

---

15. See Gerald M. Meier and Robert E. Baldwin, *Economic Development: Theory, History, Policy* (New York: John Wiley and Sons), p. 70.

16. See John Hicks, *A Theory of Economic History* (Oxford: Oxford University Press, 1969).

politics tends to divide, economics tends to unite peoples. A liberal international economy will have a moderating influence on international politics as it creates bonds of mutual interests and a commitment to the status quo. However, it is important to emphasize again that although everyone will, or at least can, be better off in "absolute" terms under free exchange, the "relative" gains will differ. It is precisely this issue of relative gains and the distribution of the wealth generated by the market system that has given rise to economic nationalism and Marxism as rival doctrines.

THE NATIONALIST PERSPECTIVE

Economic nationalism, like economic liberalism, has undergone several metamorphoses over the past several centuries. Its labels have also changed: mercantilism, statism, protectionism, the German Historical School, and, recently, New Protectionism. Throughout all these manifestations, however, runs a set of themes or attitudes rather than a coherent and systematic body of economic or political theory. Its central idea is that economic activities are and should be subordinate to the goal of state building and the interests of the state. All nationalists ascribe to the primacy of the state, of national security, and of military power in the organization and functioning of the international system. Within this general commitment two basic positions can be discerned. Some nationalists consider the safeguarding of national economic interests as the minimum essential to the security and survival of the state. For lack of a better term, this generally defensive position may be called "benign" mercantilism.[17] On the other hand, there are those nationalists who regard the international economy as an arena for imperialist expansion and national aggrandizement. This aggressive form may be termed "malevolent" mercantilism. The economic policies of Nazi economic minister Hjalmar Schacht toward eastern Europe in the 1930s were of this type.[18]

Although economic nationalism should be viewed as a general commitment to state building, the precise objectives pursued and the policies advocated have differed in different times and in different places. Yet, as Jacob Viner has cogently argued in an often-quoted passage, economic nationalist (or what he calls mercantilist) writers share convictions concerning the relationship of wealth and power:

> I believe that practically all mercantilists, whatever the period, country, or status of the particular individual, would have subscribed to all of the following propositions: (1) wealth is an absolutely essential means to power, whether for security or for aggression; (2) power is essential or valuable as a means to the acquisition or retention of wealth; (3) wealth and power are each proper ultimate ends of national policy; (4) there is long-run harmony between these ends, although in particular circumstances it may be necessary for a time to make economic sacrifices in the interest of military security and therefore also of long-run prosperity.[19]

Whereas liberal writers generally view the pursuit of power and wealth, that is, the choice between "guns and butter," as involving a trade-off, nationalists tend to regard the two goals as being complementary.[20]

---

17. One can identify Friedrich List with the benign mercantilist position. List believed that true cosmopolitanism could only be possible when all states had been developed. For a discussion of benign and malevolent mercantilism, see Robert Gilpin, *U.S. Power and the Multinational Corporation: The Political Economy of Foreign Direct Investment* (New York: Basic Books, 1975), pp. 234-37.

18. See Albert O. Hirschman, *National Power and the Structure of Foreign Trade* (Berkeley: University O California Press, 1945).

19. Jacob Viner, *The Long View and the Short: Studies in Economic Theory and Policy* (New York: Free Press, 1958), p. 286

Economic nationalists stress the role of economic factors in international relations and view the struggle among states—capitalist, socialist, or whatever—for economic resources as pervasive and indeed inherent in the nature of the international system itself. As one writer has put it, since economic resources are necessary for national power, every conflict is at once both economic and political.[21] *States, at least over the long run, simultaneously pursue wealth and national power.*

As it evolved in the early modern era, economic nationalism responded to and reflected the political, economic, and military developments of the sixteenth, seventeenth, and eighteenth centuries: the emergence of strong national states in constant competition, the rise of a middle class devoted at first to commerce and increasingly to manufacturing, and the quickening pace of economic activities due to changes within Europe and the discovery of the New World and its resources. The evolution of a monetarized market economy and the wide range of changes in the nature of warfare that have been characterized as the "Military Revolution" were also critically important.[22] Nationalists (or "mercantilists," as they were then called) had good cause to identify a favorable balance of trade with national security.

For several reasons, the foremost objective of nationalists is industrialization (Sen, 1984). In the first place, nationalists believe that industry has spillover effects (externalities) throughout the economy and leads to its overall development. Second, they associate the possession of industry with economic self-sufficiency and political autonomy. Third, and most important, industry is prized because it is the basis of military power and central to national security in the modern world. In almost every society, including liberal ones, governments pursue policies favorable to industrial development. As the mercantilist theorist of American economic development, Alexander Hamilton, wrote: "not only the wealth but the independence and security of a country appear to be materially connected to the prosperity of manufactures";[23] no contemporary dependency theorist has put it better. This nationalist objective of industrialization, as will be argued [later], is itself a major source of economic conflict.

Economic nationalism, both in the early modern era and today, arises in part from the tendency of markets to concentrate wealth and to establish dependency or power relations between the strong and the weak economies. In its more benign or defensive form it attempts to protect the economy against untoward external economic and political forces. Defensive economic nationalism frequently exists in less developed economies or in those advanced economies that have begun to decline; such governments pursue protectionist and related policies to protect their nascent or declining industries and to safeguard domestic interests. In its more malevolent form, economic nationalism is the conduct of economic warfare. This type is most prevalent in expanding powers. The classic example is Nazi Germany.

In a world of competing states, the nationalist considers relative gain to be more important than mutual gain. Thus nations continually try to change the rules or regimes governing international economic relations in order to benefit themselves disproportionately with respect to other economic powers. As Adam Smith shrewdly pointed out, everyone wants to be a monopolist and will attempt to be one unless prevented by competitors.

---

20. Klaus Knorr, *British Colonial Theories, 1570-1850* (Toronto: University of Toronto Press, 1944), p. 10.

21. See Ralph G. Hawtrey, *Economic Aspects of Sovereignty* (London: Longmans, 1952).

22. See Michael Roberts, *The Military Revolution* (Belfast: Boyd, 1956).

23. Quoted in W. W. Rostow, *Politics and Stages of Growth* (New York: Cambridge University Press, 1971), p. 189.

Therefore, a liberal international economy cannot develop unless it is supported by the dominant economic states whose own interests are consistent with its preservation.

Whereas liberals stress the mutual benefits of international commerce, nationalists as well as Marxists regard these relations as basically conflictual. Although this does not rule out international economic cooperation and the pursuit of liberal policies, economic interdependence is never symmetrical; indeed, it constitutes a source of continuous conflict and insecurity. Nationalist writers from Alexander Hamilton to contemporary dependency theorists thus emphasize national self-sufficiency rather than economic interdependence.

Economic nationalism has taken several different forms in the modern world. Responding to the Commercial Revolution and the expansion of international trade throughout the early period, classical or financial mercantilism emphasized the promotion of trade and a balance of payments surplus. Following the Industrial Revolution, industrial mercantilists like Hamilton and List stressed the supremacy of industry and manufacturing over agriculture. Following the First and Second World Wars these earlier concerns have been joined by a powerful commitment to the primacy of domestic welfare and the welfare state. In the last decades of this century, the increasing importance of advanced technology, the desire for national control over the "commanding heights" of the modern economy, and the advent of what might best be called "policy competitiveness" have become the distinctive features of contemporary mercantilism. In all ages, however, the desire for power and independence have been the overriding concern of economic nationalists.

Whatever its relative strengths and weaknesses as an ideology or theory of international political economy, the nationalist emphasis on the geographic location and the distribution of economic activities provide it with powerful appeal. Throughout modern history, states have pursued policies promoting the development of industry, advanced technology, and those economic activities with the highest profitability and generation of employment within their own borders. As far as they can, states try to create an international division of labor favorable to their political and economic interests. Indeed, economic nationalism is likely to be a significant influence in international relations as long as the state system exists.

THE MARXIST PERSPECTIVE

Like liberalism and nationalism, Marxism has evolved in significant ways since its basic ideas were set forth by Karl Marx and Friedrich Engels in the middle of the nineteenth century.[24] Marx's own thinking changed during his lifetime, and his theories have always been subject to conflicting interpretations. Although Marx viewed capitalism as a global economy, he did not develop a systematic set of ideas on international relations; this responsibility fell upon the succeeding generation of Marxist writers. The Soviet Union and China, furthermore, having adopted Marxism as their official ideology, have reshaped it when necessary to serve their own national interests.

As in liberalism and nationalism, two basic strands can be discerned in modern Marxism. The first is the evolutionary Marxism of social democracy associated with Eduard Bernstein and Karl Kautsky; in the contemporary world it has tapered off and is hardly distinguishable from the egalitarian form of liberalism. At the other extreme is the revolutionary Marxism of Lenin and, in theory at least, of the Soviet Union. Because of its tri-

24. Although there were important differences between the views of Engels and Marx, I shall refer to Marx throughout this discussion as standing for the combined contribution of both men.

umph as the ruling ideology in one of the world's two superpowers, this variation is the more important and will be stressed here.

As Robert Heilbroner[25] has argued, despite the existence of these different Marxisms, four essential elements can be found in the overall corpus of Marxist writings. The *first* element is the dialectical approach to knowledge and society that defines the nature of reality as dynamic and conflictual; social disequilibria and consequent change are due to the class struggle and the working out of contradictions inherent in social and political phenomena. There is, according to Marxists, no inherent social harmony or return to equilibrium as liberals believe. The *second* element is a materialist approach to history; the development of productive forces and economic activities is central to historical change and operates through the class struggle over distribution of the social product. The *third* is a general view of capitalist development; the capitalist mode of production and its destiny are governed by a set of "economic laws of motion of modern society." The *fourth* is a normative commitment to socialism; all Marxists believe that a socialist society is both the necessary and desirable end of historical development.[26] It is only the third of these beliefs that is of interest here.

Marxism characterizes capitalism as the private ownership of the means of production and the existence of wage labor. It believes that capitalism is driven by capitalists striving for profits and capital accumulation in a competitive market economy. Labor has been dispossessed and has become a commodity that is subject to the price mechanism. In Marx's view these two key characteristics of capitalism are responsible for its dynamic nature and make it the most productive economic mechanism yet. Although its historic mission is to develop and unify the globe, the very success of capitalism will hasten its passing. The origin, evolution, and eventual demise of the capitalist mode of production are, according to Marx, governed by three inevitable economic laws.

The first law, the law of disproportionality, entails a denial of Say's law, which (in oversimplified terms) holds that supply creates its own demand so that supply and demand will always be, except for brief moments, in balance.[27] Say's law maintains that an equilibrating process makes overproduction impossible in a capitalist or market economy. Marx, like John Maynard Keynes, denied that this tendency toward equilibrium existed and argued that capitalist economies tend to overproduce particular types of goods. There is, Marx argued, an inherent contradiction in capitalism between its capacity to produce goods and the capacity of consumers (wage earners) to purchase those goods, so that the constantly recurring disproportionality between production and consumption due to the "anarchy" of the market causes periodic depressions and economic fluctuations. He predicted that these recurring economic crises would become increasingly severe and in time would impel the suffering proletariat to rebel against the system.

The second law propelling the development of a capitalist system, according to Marxism, is the law of the concentration (or accumulation) of capital. The motive force of capitalism is the drive for profits and the consequent necessity for the individual capitalist to accumulate and invest. Competition forces the capitalists to increase their efficiency and capital investment or risk extinction. As a result, the evolution of capitalism is toward increasing

25. See Robert Heilbroner, *Marxism: For and Against* (New York: W. W. Norton, 1980).

26. *Ibid.*, pp. 20-21.

27. See Thomas Sowell, *Say's Law: An Historical Analysis* (Princeton: Princeton University Press, 1972).

concentrations of wealth in the hands of the efficient few and the growing impoverishment of the many. With the petite bourgeoisie being pushed down into the swelling ranks of the impoverished proletariat, the reserve army of the unemployed increases, labor's wages decline, and the capitalist society becomes ripe for social revolution.

The third law of capitalism is that of the falling rate of profit. As capital accumulates and becomes more abundant, the rate of return declines, thereby decreasing the incentive to invest. Although classical liberal economists had recognized this possibility, they believed that a solution could be found through such countervailing devices as the export of capital and manufactured goods and the import of cheap food.[28] Marx, on the other hand, believed that the tendency for profits to decline was inescapable. As the pressure of competition forces capitalists to increase efficiency and productivity through investment in new labor-saving and more productive technology, the level of unemployment will increase and the rate of profit or surplus value will decrease. Capitalists will thereby lose their incentive to invest in productive ventures and to create employment. This will result in economic stagnation, increasing unemployment, and the "immiserization" of the proletariat. In time, the ever-increasing intensity and depth of the business cycle will cause the workers to rebel and destroy the capitalist economic system.

The core of the Marxist critique of capitalism is that although the individual capitalist is rational (as liberals assume), the capitalist system itself is irrational. The competitive market necessitates that the individual capitalist must save, invest, and accumulate. If the desire for profits is the fuel of capitalism, then investment is the motor and accumulation is the result. In the aggregate, however, this accumulating capital of individual capitalists leads to the periodic overproduction of goods, surplus capital, and the disappearance of investment incentives. In time, the increasing severity of the downturns in the business cycle and the long-term trend toward economic stagnation will cause the proletariat to overthrow the system through revolutionary violence. Thus, the inherent contradiction of capitalism is that, with capital accumulation, capitalism sows the seeds of its own destruction and is replaced by the socialist economic system.[29]

Marx believed that in the mid-nineteenth century, the maturing of capitalism in Europe and the drawing of the global periphery into the market economy had set the stage for the proletarian revolution and the end of the capitalist economy. When this did not happen, Marx's followers, such as Rudolf Hilferding and Rosa Luxemburg, became concerned over the continuing vitality of capitalism and its refusal to disappear. The strength of nationalism, the economic successes of capitalism, and the advent of imperialism led to a metamorphosis of Marxist thought that culminated in Lenin's *Imperialism* (1939), first published in 1917. Written against the backdrop of the First World War and drawing heavily upon the writings of other Marxists, Imperialism was both a polemic against his ideological enemies and a synthesis of Marxist critiques of a capitalist world economy. In staking out his own position, Lenin in effect converted Marxism from

28. John Stuart Mill, *Principles of Political Economy* (Baltimore: Penguin Books, 1970 [1848]), pp. 97-104.

29. In effect, the Marxists are accusing the defenders of capitalism with employing the fallacy of composition. This is "a fallacy in which what is true of a part is, on that account alone, alleged to be also *necessarily* true of the whole" (Samuelson, ßp. 11). Similarly, Keynes argued that although individual saving is a virtue, if everyone saved it would be a calamity.

essentially a theory of domestic economy to a theory of international political relations among capitalist states.

Lenin set himself the task of accounting for the fact that nationalism had triumphed over proletarian internationalism at the outbreak of the First World War and thereby sought to provide the intellectual foundations for a reunification of the international communist movement under his leadership. He wanted to show why the socialist parties of the several European powers, especially the German Social Democrats under Karl Kautsky, had supported their respective bourgeoisies. He also tried to explain why the impoverishment of the proletariat had not taken place as Marx had predicted, and instead wages were rising and workers were becoming trade unionists.

In the years between Marx and Lenin, capitalism had experienced a profound transformation. Marx had written about a capitalism largely confined to western Europe, a closed economy in which the growth impulse would one day cease as it collided with various constraints. Between 1870 and 1914, however, capitalism had become a vibrant, technological, and increasingly global and open system. In Marx's day, the primary nexus of the slowly developing world economy was trade. After 1870, however, the massive export of capital by Great Britain and subsequently by other developed economies had significantly changed the world economy; foreign investment and international finance had profoundly altered the economic and political relations among societies. Furthermore, Marx's capitalism had been composed mainly of small, competitive, industrial firms. By the time of Lenin, however, capitalist economies were dominated by immense industrial combines that in turn, according to Lenin, were controlled by the great banking houses (*haut finance*). For Lenin, the control of capital by capital, that is, of industrial capital by financial capital, represented the pristine and highest stage of capitalist development.

Capitalism, he argued, had escaped its three laws of motion through overseas imperialism. The acquisition of colonies had enabled the capitalist economies to dispose of their unconsumed goods, to acquire cheap resources, and to vent their surplus capital. The exploitation of these colonies further provided an economic surplus with which the capitalists could buy off the leadership ("labor aristocracy") of their own proletariat. Colonial imperialism, he argued, had become a necessary feature of advanced capitalism. As its productive forces developed and matured, a capitalist economy had to expand abroad, capture colonies, or else suffer economic stagnation and internal revolution. Lenin identified this necessary expansion as the cause of the eventual destruction of the international capitalist system.

The essence of Lenin's argument is that a capitalist international economy does develop the world, but does not develop it evenly. Individual capitalist economies grow at different rates and this differential growth of national power is ultimately responsible for imperialism, war, and international political change. Responding to Kautsky's argument that capitalists were too rational to fight over colonies and would ally themselves in the joint exploitation of colonial peoples (the doctrine of "ultra-imperialism"), Lenin stated that this was impossible because of what has become known as the "law of uneven development":

> This question [of the possibility of capitalist alliances to be more than temporary and free from conflict] need only be stated clearly enough to make it impossible for any other reply to be given than that in the negative; for there can be no other conceivable basis under capitalism for the division of spheres of influence . . . than a calculation of the *strength* of the participants in the division, their general economic, financial, military strength, etc. And the strength of these participants in the division does not change to an equal degree, for under capitalism the development of different undertakings, trusts, branches of industry, or

> countries cannot be *even*. Half a century ago, Germany was a miserable, insignificant country, as far as its capitalist strength was concerned, compared with the strength of England at that time. Japan was similarly insignificant compared with Russia. Is it "conceivable" that in ten or twenty years' time the relative strength of the imperialist powers will have remained *un*changed? Absolutely inconceivable.[30]

In effect, in this passage and in his overall attempt to prove that an international capitalist system was inherently unstable, Lenin added a fourth law to the original three Marxist laws of capitalism. The law is that, as capitalist economies mature, as capital accumulates, and as profit rates fall, the capitalist economies are compelled to seize colonies and create dependencies to serve as markets, investment outlets, and sources of food and raw materials. In competition with one another, they divide up the colonial world in accordance with their relative strengths. Thus, the most advanced capitalist economy, namely Great Britain, had appropriated the largest share of colonies. As other capitalist economies advanced, however, they sought a redivision of colonies. This imperialist conflict inevitably led to armed conflict among the rising and declining imperial powers. The First World War, according to this analysis, was a war of territorial redivision between a declining Great Britain and other rising capitalist powers. Such wars of colonial division and redivision would continue, he argued, until the industrializing colonies and the proletariat of the capitalist countries revolted against the system.

In more general terms, Lenin reasoned that because capitalist economies grow and accumulate capital at differential rates, a capitalist international system can never be stable for longer than very short periods of time. In opposition to Kautsky's doctrine of ultra-imperialism, Lenin argued that all capitalist alliances were temporary and reflected momentary balances of power among the capitalist states that would inevitably be undermined by the process of uneven development. As this occurred, it would lead to intracapitalist conflicts over colonial territories.

The law of uneven development, with its fateful consequences, had become operative in his own age because the world had suddenly become finite; the globe itself had become a closed system. For decades the European capitalist powers had expanded, gobbling up overseas territory, but the imperialist powers increasingly came into contact and therefore into conflict with one another as the lands suitable for colonization diminished. He believed that the final drama would be the imperial division of China and that, with the closing of the global undeveloped frontier, imperialist clashes would intensify. In time, conflicts among the imperialist powers would produce revolts among their own colonies and weaken Western capitalism's hold on the colonialized races of the globe.

Lenin's internationalization of Marxist theory represented a subtle but significant reformulation. In Marx's critique of capitalism, the causes of its downfall were economic; capitalism would fail for economic reasons as the proletariat revolted against its impoverishment. Furthermore, Marx had defined the actors in this drama as social classes. Lenin, however, substituted a political critique of capitalism in which the principal actors in effect became competing mercantilistic nation-states driven by economic necessity. Although international capitalism was economically successful, Lenin argued that it was politically unstable and constituted a war-system. The workers or the labor aristocracy in the developed capitalist countries temporarily shared in the exploitation of colonial peoples but ulti-

---

30. See V. I. Lenin, *Imperialism: The Highest Stage of Capitalism* (New York: International Publishers, 1939 [1917]), p. 119.

mately would pay for these economic gains on the battlefield. Lenin believed that the inherent contradiction of capitalism resided in the consequent struggle of nations rather than in the class struggle. Capitalism would end due to a revolt against its inherent bellicosity and political consequences.

In summary, Lenin argued that the inherent contradiction of capitalism is that it develops the world and plants the political seeds of its own destruction as it diffuses technology, industry, and military power. It creates foreign competitors with lower wages and standards of living who can out compete the previously dominant economy on the battlefield of world markets. Intensification of economic and political competition between declining and rising capitalist powers leads to economic conflicts, imperial rivalries, and eventually war. He asserted that this had been the fate of the British-centered liberal world economy of the nineteenth century. Today he would undoubtedly argue that, as the U.S. economy declines, a similar fate threatens the twentieth-century liberal world economy, centered in the United States.

With the triumph of Bolshevism in the Soviet Union, Lenin's theory of capitalist imperialism became the orthodox Marxist theory of international political economy; yet other heirs of the Marxist tradition have continued to challenge this orthodoxy. It has also been modified by subsequent changes in the nature of capitalism and other historical developments. Welfare-state capitalism has carried out many of the reforms that Lenin believed to be impossible, the political control of colonies is no longer regarded by Marxists as a necessary feature of imperialism, the finance capitalist of Lenin's era has been partially displaced by the multinational corporation of our own, the view that capitalist imperialism develops the less developed countries has been changed to the argument that it underdevelops them, and some Marxists have been so bold as to apply Marxist theory to Lenin's own political creation, the Soviet Union. Thus modified, at the end of the twentieth century Marxism in its various manifestations continues to exercise a powerful influence as one of the three dominant perspectives on political economy.

A CRITIQUE OF THE PERSPECTIVES

As we have seen, liberalism, nationalism, and Marxism make different assumptions and reach conflicting conclusions regarding the nature and consequences of a world market economy or (as Marxists prefer) a world capitalist economy. The position of this [article] is that *these contrasting ideologies or perspectives constitute intellectual commitments or acts of faith.* Although particular ideas or theories associated with one position or another may be shown to be false or questionable, these perspectives can be neither proved nor disproved through logical argument or the presentation of contrary empirical evidence. There are several reasons for the persistence of these perspectives and their resistance to scientific testing.

In the first place, they are based on assumptions about people or society that cannot be subjected to empirical tests. For example, the liberal concept of rational individuals cannot be verified or falsified; individuals who appear to be acting in conflict with their own interest may actually be acting on incorrect information or be seeking to maximize a goal unknown to the observer and thus be fulfilling the basic assumption of liberalism. Moreover, liberals would argue that although a particular individual in a particular case might be shown to have behaved irrationally, in the aggregate the assumption of rationality is a valid one.

Second, predictive failure of a perspective can always be argued away through the introduction into the analysis of ad hoc hypotheses.[31] Marxism is replete with attempts to explain the predictive failures of Marxist theory. Lenin, for example, developed the concept of "false consciousness" to account for the fact that workers became trade unionists rather than members of a revolutionary proletariat. Lenin's theory of capitalist imperialism may also be viewed as an effort to explain the failure of Marx's predictions regarding the collapse of capitalism. More recently, as will be discussed below, Marxists have been compelled to formulate elaborate theories of the state to explain the emergence of the welfare state and its acceptance by capitalists, a development that Lenin said was impossible.

Third, and most important, the three perspectives have different purposes and to some extent exist at different levels of analysis. Both nationalists and Marxists, for example, can accept most of liberal economics as a tool of analysis while rejecting many of its assumptions and normative foundations. Thus Marx used classical economics with great skill, but his purpose was to embody it in a grand theory of the origins, dynamics, and end of capitalism. The fundamental difference, in fact, between liberalism and Marxism involves the questions asked and their sociological assumptions rather than the economic methodology that they employ.[32]

As reformulated by Lenin, Marxism has become nearly indistinguishable from the doctrine of political realism.[33] Political realism, like economic nationalism, stresses the primacy of the state and national security. Although the two are very close, realism is essentially a political position whereas economic nationalism is an economic one. Or, put another way, economic nationalism is based on the realist doctrine of international relations.

Both in Lenin's theory and in political realism, states struggle for wealth and power, and the differential growth of power is the key to international conflict and political change.[34] However, the assumptions of the two theories regarding the basis of human motivation, the theory of the state, and the nature of the international system are fundamentally different. Marxists regard human nature as malleable and as easily corrupted by capitalism and correctable by socialism; realists believe that political conflict results from an unchanging human nature.

Whereas Marxists believe that the state is ultimately the servant of the dominant economic class, realists see the state as a relatively autonomous entity pursuing national interests that cannot be reduced to the particularistic interests of any class. For Marxists, the international system and foreign policy are determined by the structure of the domestic economy; for realists, the nature of the international system is the fundamental determinant of foreign policy. In short, Marxists regard war, imperialism, and the state as evil manifestations of a capitalism that will disappear with the communist revolution; realists hold them to be inevitable features of an anarchical international political system.

The difference between the two perspectives, therefore, is considerable. For the Marxist, though the state and the struggles among states are a consequence of the capitalist mode of production, the future will bring a realm of true harmony and peace following the inevitable revolution that the evil capitalist mode of production will spawn. The realist, on the other hand, believes there will be no such nirvana because of the inherently self-centered nature of human beings and the anarchy of the international system itself. The struggle among groups and states is virtually ceaseless, although there is occasionally a temporary respite. It seems unlikely that either prediction will ever receive scientific verification.

---

31. See Mark Blaug, *Economic Theory in Retrospect*, 3d ed. (New York: Cambridge University Press, 1978), p. 717 on the use of ad hoc hypotheses to explain away predictive failures.

32. Ibid., pp. 276-77.

33. See Robert O. Keohane, *After Hegemony: Cooperation and Discord in the World Political Economy* (Princeton University Press, 1984), pp. 276-77.

34. See Robert Gilpin, *War and Change in World Politics* (New York: Cambridge University Press, 1981).

Each of the three perspectives has strengths and weaknesses, to be further explored below. Although no perspective provides a complete and satisfactory understanding of the nature and dynamism of the international political economy, together they provide useful insights. They also raise important issues that will be explored in succeeding chapters.

Critique of Economic Liberalism

Liberalism embodies a set of analytical tools and policy prescriptions that enable a society to maximize its return from scarce resources; its commitment to efficiency, and the maximization of total wealth provides much of its strength. The market constitutes the most effective means for organizing economic relations, and the price mechanism operates to ensure that mutual gain and hence aggregate social benefit tend to result from economic exchange. In effect, liberal economics says to a society, whether domestic or international, "if you wish to be wealthy, this is what you must do."

From Adam Smith to the present, liberals have tried to discover the laws governing the wealth of nations. Although most liberals consider the laws of economics to be inviolable laws of nature, these laws may best be viewed as prescriptive guides for decision makers. If the laws are violated, there will be costs; the pursuit of objectives other than efficiency will necessarily involve an opportunity cost in terms of lost efficiency. Liberalism emphasizes the fact that such trade-offs always exist in national policy. An emphasis on equity and redistribution, for example, is doomed to failure in the long run if it neglects considerations of efficiency. For a society to be efficient, as socialist economies have discovered, it cannot totally disregard the pertinent economic "laws."

The foremost defense of liberalism is perhaps a negative one. Although it may be true, as Marxists and some nationalists argue, that the alternative to a liberal system could be one in which all gain equally, it is also possible that the alternative could be one in which all lose in absolute terms. Much can be said for the liberal harmony of interest doctrine; yet, as E. H. Carr has pointed out, evidence to support this doctrine has generally been drawn from historical periods in which there was "unparalleled expansion of production, population and prosperity".[35] When sustaining conditions break down (as happened in the 1930s and threatens to occur again in the closing decades of the century), disharmony displaces harmony and, I shall argue, the consequent breakdown of liberal regimes tends to lead to economic conflict wherein everyone loses.

The major criticism leveled against economic liberalism is that its basic assumptions, such as the existence of rational economic actors, a competitive market, and the like, are unrealistic. In part, this attack is unfair in that liberals knowingly make these simplifying assumptions in order to facilitate scientific research; no science is possible without them. What is more important, as defenders correctly point out, is that they should be judged by their results and ability to predict rather than by their alleged reality.[36] From this perspective and within its own sphere, economics has proven to be a powerful analytical tool.

By the same token, however, liberal economics can be criticized in several important respects. As a means to understand society and especially its dynamics, economics is limited; it cannot serve as a comprehensive approach to political economy. Yet liberal economists have tended to forget this inherent limitation, to regard economics as the master

35. Edward Hallett Carr, *The Twenty Years' Crisis, 1919-1939*, 2d ed. (London: Macmillan, 1951 [1939]), p. 44.

36. See Richard Posner, *Economic Analysis of Law*, 2d. ed. (Boston: Little, Brown, 1977), ch. 1.

social science, and to permit economics to become imperialistic. When this occurs, the nature and basic assumptions of the discipline can lead the economist astray and limit its utility as a theory of political economy.

The first of these limitations is that economics artificially separates the economy from other aspects of society and accepts the existing sociopolitical framework as a given, including the distribution of power and property rights; the resource and other endowments of individuals, groups, and national societies; and the framework of social, political, and cultural institutions. The liberal world is viewed as one of homogeneous, rational, and equal individuals living in a world free from political boundaries and social constraints. Its "laws" prescribe a set of maximizing rules for economic actors regardless of where and with what they start; yet in real life, one's starting point most frequently determines where one finishes.[37]

Another limitation of liberal economics as a theory is a tendency to disregard the justice or equity of the outcome of economic activities. Despite heroic efforts to fashion an "objective" welfare economics, the distribution of wealth within and among societies lies outside the primary concern of liberal economics. There is some truth in the Marxist criticism that liberal economics is a tool kit for managing a capitalist or market economy. Bourgeois economics is, in the Marxist view, a discipline of engineering rather than a holistic science of society. It tells one how to achieve particular objectives at the least cost under a given set of constraints; it does not purport to answer questions regarding the future and destiny of man, questions dear to the hearts of Marxists and economic nationalists.

Liberalism is also limited by its assumption that exchange is always free and occurs in a competitive market between equals who possess full information and are thus enabled to gain mutually if they choose to exchange one value for another. Unfortunately, as Charles Lindblom has argued, exchange is seldom free and equal.[38] Instead, the terms of an exchange can be profoundly affected by coercion, differences in bargaining power (monopoly or monopsony), and other essentially political factors. In effect, because it neglects both the effects of noneconomic factors on exchange and the effects of exchange on politics, liberalism lacks a true "political economy."

A further limitation of liberal economics is that its analysis tends to be static. At least in the short run, the array of consumer demands, the institutional framework, and the technological environment are accepted as constants. They are regarded as a set of constraints and opportunities within which economic decisions and trade-offs are made. Questions about the origins of, or the directions taken by, economic institutions and the technological apparatus are, for the liberal, a secondary matter. Liberal economists are incrementalists who believe that social structures tend to change slowly in response to price signals. Although liberal economists have attempted to develop theories of economic and technological change, the crucial social, political, and technological variables affecting change are considered to be exogenous and beyond the realm of economic analysis. As Marxists charge, liberalism lacks a theory of the dynamics of international political economy and tends to assume the stability and the virtues of the economic status quo.

Liberal economics, with its laws for maximizing behavior, is based on a set of highly restrictive assumptions. No society has ever or could ever be composed of the true "economic man" of liberal theory. A functioning society requires affective ties and the subordination of individual self-interest to larger social values; if this were not the case the society

---

37. See Ralf Dahrendorf, *Life Chances* (Chicago: University of Chicago Press, 1979).

38. Lindblom, pp. 40-50.

would fly apart.[39] Yet Western society has gone far in harnessing for social and economic betterment a basic tendency in human beings toward self-aggrandizement.[40] Through release of the market mechanism from social and political constraints, Western civilization has reached a level of unprecedented affluence and has set an example that other civilizations wish to emulate. It has done so, however, at the cost of other values. As liberal economics teaches, nothing is ever achieved without a cost.

Critique of Economic Nationalism

The foremost strength of economic nationalism is its focus on the state as the predominant actor in international relations and as an instrument of economic development. Although many have argued that modern economic and technological developments have made the nation-state an anachronism, at the end of the twentieth century the system of nation-states is actually expanding; societies throughout the world are seeking to create strong states capable of organizing and managing national economies, and the number of states in the world is increasing. Even in older states, the spirit of nationalist sentiments can easily be inflamed, as happened in the Falkland War of 1982. Although other actors such as transnational and international organizations do exist and do influence international relations, the economic and military efficiency of the state makes it preeminent over all these other actors.

The second strength of nationalism is its stress on the importance of security and political interests in the organization and conduct of international economic relations. One need not accept the nationalist emphasis on the primacy of security considerations to appreciate that the security of the state is a necessary precondition for its economic and political well-being in an anarchic and competitive state system. A state that fails to provide for its own security ceases to be independent. Whatever the objectives of the society, the effects of economic activities upon political independence and domestic welfare always rank high among its concerns.[41]

The third strength of nationalism is its emphasis on the political framework of economic activities, its recognition that markets must function in a world of competitive groups and states. The political relations among these political actors affect the operation of markets just as markets affect the political relations. In fact, the international political system constitutes one of the most important constraints on and determinant of markets. Since states seek to influence markets to their own individual advantage, the role of power is crucial in the creation and sustaining of market relations; even Ricardo's classic example of the exchange of British woolens for Portuguese wine was not free from the exercise of state power.[42] Indeed, as Carr has argued, every economic system must rest on a secure political base.[43]

One weakness of nationalism is its tendency to believe that international economic relations constitute solely and at all times a zero-sum game, that is, that one state's gain must of necessity be another's loss. Trade, investment, and all other economic relations are viewed

39. See Karl Polanyi, *The Great Transformation: The Political and Economic Origins of Our Time* (Boston: Beacon Press, 1957).

40. See Jean Baechler, *Les Origines du capitalisme* (Paris: Editions Gallimard, 1971). (*The Origins of Capitalism*, trans. Barry Cooper (Oxford: Basil Blackwell, 1975)).

41. Susan Strange, "Protectionism and World Politics," *International Organization* 39 (1985): 234.

42. Nazli Choucri, "International Political Economy: A Theoretical Perspective," in Ole Holsti, et. al., *Change in the International System* (Boulder, Co.: Westview Press, 1980), p. 111.

43. See Carr.

by the nationalist primarily in conflictual and distributive terms. Yet, if cooperation occurs, markets *can* bring mutual (albeit not necessarily equal) gain, as the liberal insists. The possibility of benefit for all is the basis of the international market economy. Another weakness of nationalism is due to the fact that the pursuit of power and the pursuit of wealth usually do conflict, at least in the short run. The amassing and exercising of military and other forms of power entail costs to the society, costs that can undercut its economic efficiency. Thus, as Adam Smith argued, the mercantilist policies of eighteenth-century states that identified money with wealth were detrimental to the growth of the real wealth created by productivity increases; he demonstrated that the wealth of nations would have been better served by policies of free trade. Similarly, the tendency today to identify industry with power can weaken the economy of a state. Development of industries without regard to market considerations or comparative advantage can weaken a society economically. Although states in a situation of conflict must on occasion pursue mercantilistic goals and policies, over the long term, pursuit of these policies can be self-defeating.

In addition, nationalism lacks a satisfactory theory of domestic society, the state, and foreign policy. It tends to assume that society and state form a unitary entity and that foreign policy is determined by an objective national interest. Yet, as liberals correctly stress, society is pluralistic and consists of individuals and groups (coalitions of individuals) that try to capture the apparatus of the state and make it serve their own political and economic interests. Although states possess varying degrees of social autonomy and independence in the making of policy, foreign policy (including foreign economic policy) is in large measure the outcome of the conflicts among dominant groups within each society. Trade protectionism and most other nationalist policies result from attempts by one factor of production or another (capital, labor, or land) to acquire a monopoly position and thereby to increase its share of the economic rents. Nationalist policies are most frequently designed to redistribute income from consumers and society as a whole to producer interests.[44]

Nationalism can thus be interpreted as either a theory of state building or a cloak for the interests of particular producer groups that are in a position to influence national policy. In their failure to appreciate fully or distinguish between the two possible meanings of economic nationalism, nationalists can be faulted for not applying, both to the domestic level and to the determination of foreign policy, their assumption that the political framework influences economic outcomes. They fail to take sufficient account of the fact that domestic political groups frequently use a nationalist rationale, especially that of national security, to promote their own interests.

Whereas in the past, land and capital were the primary carriers of nationalist sentiments, in advanced economies labor has become the most nationalistic and protectionist of the three factors of production. In a world of highly mobile capital and resources, labor seeks to use the state to advance its threatened interests. The increased power of labor in the contemporary welfare state, as I shall argue below, has become a major force for economic nationalism.

The validity of nationalists' emphasis on protectionism and industrialization is more difficult to ascertain. It is true that all great industrial powers have had strong states that protected and promoted their industries in the early stages of industrialization and that without

---

44. The literature on the political economy of tariffs and other forms of trade protectionism as rent-seeking is extensive. As noted earlier, the subject of economic policy making falls outside the scope of this book. See Bruno Frey, *International Political Economics* (New York: Basil Blackwell, 1984) for an excellent discussion of this approach to tariff policy and related topics.

such protectionism, the "infant" industries of developing economies probably would not have survived the competition of powerful firms in more advanced economies. Yet it is also the case that high levels of protectionism in many countries have led to the establishment of inefficient industries and even retarded economic development.[45] In the final quarter of the twentieth century, economies like those of Taiwan and South Korea, which have limited protectionism while favoring competitive export industries, have performed better than those less developed countries that have attempted to industrialize behind high tariff walls while pursuing a strategy of import substitution.

The nationalist's bias toward industry over agriculture also must get a mixed review. It is true that industry can have certain advantages over agriculture and that the introduction of industrial [46]technology into a society has slipover effects that tend to transform and modernize all aspects of the economy as it upgrades the quality of the labor force and increases the profitability of capital.[47] Yet one must remember that few societies have developed without a prior agricultural revolution and a high level of agricultural productivity .[48] In fact, certain of the most prosperous economies of the world, for example, Denmark, the American farm belt, and western Canada, are based on efficient agriculture.[49] In all these societies, moreover, the state has promoted agricultural development.

One may conclude that the nationalists are essentially correct in their belief that the state must play an important role in economic development. A strong state is required to promote and, in some cases, to protect industry as well as to foster an efficient agriculture. Yet this active role of the state, though a necessary condition, is not a sufficient condition. A strong and interventionist state does not guarantee economic development; indeed, it might retard it. The sufficient condition for economic development is an efficient economic organization of agriculture and industry, and in most cases this is achieved through the operation of the market. Both of these political and economic conditions have characterized the developed economies and the rapidly industrializing countries of the contemporary international system.

It is important to realize that, whatever its relative merits or deficiencies, economic nationalism has a persistent appeal. Throughout modern history, the international location of economic activities has been a leading concern of states. From the seventeenth century on states have pursued conscious policies of industrial and technological development. Both to achieve stable military power and in the belief that industry provides a higher "value added"[50] than agriculture, the modern nation-state has had as one of its major objectives the establishment and protection of industrial

---

45. Charles P. Kindleberger, *Economic Response: Comparative Studies in Trade, Finance, and Growth* (Cambridge: Harvard University Press, 1978), pp. 19-38.

46.

47. John Cornwall, *Modern Capitalism: Its Growth and Transformation* (New York: St. Martin's Press, 1977) provides a representative argument of the benefits of industry over agriculture in economic development.

48. W. Arthur Lewis, *The Evolution of the International Economic Order* (Princeton: Princeton University Press, 1978).

49. Jacob Viner, *International Trade and Economic Development* (Glencoe, Ill.: Free Press, 1952).

50. See Avinash K. Dixit, "How Should the U.S. Respond to Other Countries' Trade Policies?" Unpublished, (1985), pp. 22-23 for a good discussion of the concept of "value added" or super-profit and its utility.

power. As long as a conflictual international system exists, economic nationalism will retain its strong attraction.

Critique of Marxist Theory

Marxism correctly places the economic problem—the production and distribution of material wealth—where it belongs, at or near the center of political life. Whereas liberals tend to ignore the issue of distribution and nationalists are concerned primarily with the *international* distribution of wealth, Marxists focus on both the domestic and the international effects of a market economy on the distribution of wealth. They call attention to the ways in which the rules or regimes governing trade, investment, and other international economic relations affect the distribution of wealth among groups and states.[51] However, it is not necessary to subscribe to the materialist interpretation of history or the primacy of class struggle in order to appreciate that the ways in which individuals earn their living and distribute wealth are a critical determinant of social structure and political behavior.

Another contribution of Marxism is its emphasis on the nature and structure of the division of labor at both the domestic and international levels. As Marx and Engels correctly pointed out in *The German Ideology*, every division of labor implies dependence and therefore a political relationship (Marx and Engels, 1947 [1846]). In a market economy the economic nexus among groups and states becomes of critical importance in determining their welfare and their political relations. The Marxist analysis, however, is too limited, because economic interdependence is not the only or even the most important set of interstate relations. The political and strategic relations among political actors are of equal or greater significance and cannot be reduced to merely economic considerations, at least not as Marxists define economics.

The Marxist theory of international political economy is also valuable in its focus on international political change. Whereas neither liberalism nor nationalism has a comprehensive theory of social change, Marxism emphasizes the role of economic and technological developments in explaining the dynamics of the international system. As embodied in Lenin's law of uneven development, the differential growth of power among states constitutes an underlying cause of international political change. Lenin was at least partially correct in attributing the First World War to the uneven economic growth of power among industrial states and to conflict over the division of territory. There can be little doubt that the uneven growth of the several European powers and the consequent effects on the balance of power contributed to their collective insecurity. Competition for markets and empires did aggravate interstate relations. Furthermore, the average person's growing awareness of the effects on personal welfare and security of the vicissitudes of the world market and the economic behavior of other states also became a significant element in the arousal of nationalistic antagonisms. For nations and citizens alike, the growth of economic interdependence brought with it a new sense of insecurity, vulnerability, and resentment against foreign political and economic rivals.

Marxists are no doubt also correct in attributing to capitalist economies, at least as we have known them historically, a powerful impulse to expand through trade and especially through the export of capital. The classical liberal economists themselves observed that

---

51. See Benjamin J. Cohen, *Organizing the World's Money: The Political Economy of International Monetary Relations* (New York: Basic Books, 1977).

economic growth and the accumulation of capital create a tendency for the rate of return (profit) on capital to decline. These economists, however, also noted that the decline could be arrested through international trade, foreign investment, and other means. Whereas trade absorbs surplus capital in the manufacture of exports, foreign investment siphons off capital. Thus, classical liberals join Marxists in asserting that capitalist economies have an inherent tendency to export goods and surplus capital.

This tendency has led to the conclusion that the nature of capitalism is international and that its internal dynamics encourage outward expansionism. In a closed capitalist economy and in the absence of technological advance, underconsumption, surplus capital, and the resulting decline in the rate of profit would eventually lead to what John Stuart Mill called "the stationary state".[52] Yet, in an open world economy characterized by expanding capitalism, population growth, and continuing improvement in productivity through technological advance, there is no inherent economic reason for economic stagnation to take place.

On the other hand, a communist or socialist economy has no inherent *economic* tendency to expand internationally. In a communist economy, investment and consumption are primarily determined by the national plan and, moreover, the state has a monopoly of all foreign exchange.[53] A communist economy may of course have a political or strategic motive for exporting capital, or it may need to invest abroad in order to obtain vital sources of raw materials. A Marxist regime may also find it profitable to invest abroad or to engage in other commercial transactions. Certainly the Soviet Union has been rightly credited on occasion with being a shrewd trader, and Ralph Hawtrey's point that the advent of a communist or socialist government does not eliminate the profit motive but merely transfers it to the state has some merit.[54] Nevertheless, the incentive structure of a communist society with its stress on prestige, power, and ideology is unlikely to encourage the economy's expansion abroad. The tendency is rather for economics to be subordinated to politics and the nationalistic goals of the state.[55]

Marxists are certainly correct that capitalism needs an open world economy. Capitalists desire access to foreign economies for export of goods and capital; exports have a Keynesian demand effect in stimulating economic activity in capitalist economies, and capital exports serve to raise the overall rate of profit. Closure of foreign markets and capital outlets would be detrimental to capitalism, and a closed capitalist economy would probably result in a dramatic decline in economic growth. There is reason to believe that the capitalist system (certainly as we have known it) could not survive in the absence of an open world economy. The essential character of capitalism, as Marx pointed out, is cosmopolitan; the capitalist's ideology is international. Capitalism in just one state would undoubtedly be an impossibility.

In the nineteenth and twentieth centuries the dominant capitalist states, Great Britain and the United States, employed their power to promote and maintain an open world economy. They used their influence to remove the barriers to the free flow of goods and capital. Where necessary, in the words of Simon Kuznets, "the greater power of the developed nations imposed upon the reluctant partners the opportunities of international trade and

---

52. Mill, p. 111.

53. P. J. D. Wiles, *Communist International System* (Oxford: Basil Blackwell, 1968 presents a valuable analysis of the contrasting behavior of capitalist and communist economies.

54. See Hawtrey.

55. See Jacob Viner, "International Relations Between State-Controlled National Economies," in Jacob Viner, *International Economics: Studies by Jacob Viner* (Glencoe, Ill.: Free Press, 1951.

division of labor".[56] In pursuit of their own interests, they created international law to protect the property rights of private traders and investors.[57] And when the great trading nations became unable or unwilling to enforce the rules of free trade, the liberal system began its steady retreat. Up to this point, therefore, the Marxists are correct in their identification of capitalism and modern imperialism.

The principal weakness of Marxism as a theory of international political economy results from its failure to appreciate the role of political and strategic factors in international relations. Although one can appreciate the insights of Marxism, it is not necessary to accept the Marxist theory that the dynamic of modern international relations is caused by the needs of capitalist economies to export goods and surplus capital. For example, to the extent that the uneven growth of national economies leads to war, this is due to national rivalries, which can occur regardless of the nature of domestic economies—witness the conflict between China and the Soviet Union. Although competition for markets and for capital outlets can certainly be a cause of tension and one factor causing imperialism and war, this does not provide an adequate explanation for the foreign policy behavior of capitalist states.

The historical evidence, for example, does not support Lenin's attribution of the First World War to the logic of capitalism and the market system. The most important territorial disputes among the European powers, which precipitated the war, were not those about overseas colonies, as Lenin argued, but lay within Europe itself. The principal conflict leading to the war involved redistribution of the Balkan territories of the decaying Ottoman Empire. And insofar as the source of this conflict was economic, it lay in the desire of the Russian state for access to the Mediterranean.[58] Marxism cannot explain the fact that the three major imperial rivals—Great Britain, France, and Russia—were in fact on the same side in the ensuing conflict and that they fought against a Germany that had few foreign policy interests outside Europe itself.

In addition, Lenin was wrong in tracing the basic motive force of imperialism to the internal workings of the capitalist system. As Benjamin J. Cohen has pointed out in his analysis of the Marxist theory of imperialism, the political and strategic conflicts of the European powers were more important; it was at least in part the stalemate on the Continent among the Great Powers that forced their interstate competition into the colonial world.[59] Every one of these colonial conflicts (if one excludes the Boer War) was in fact settled through diplomatic means. And, finally, the overseas colonies of the European powers were simply of little economic consequence. As Lenin's own data show, almost all European overseas investment was directed to the "lands of recent settlement" (the United States, Canada, Australia, South Africa, Argentina, etc.) rather than to the dependent colonies in what today we call the Third World.[60]9 In fact, contrary to Lenin's view that politics follows investment, international finance during this period was largely a servant of foreign policy, as was also the case with French loans to Czarist Russia.[61] Thus, despite its proper focus on political change, Marxism is seriously flawed as a theory of political economy.

---

56. Simon Kuznets, *Modern Economic Growth: Rate, Structure, and Spread* (New Haven: Yale University Press, 1966), p. 335.

57. See Charles Lipson, *Standing Guard: Protecting Foreign Capital in the Nineteenth and Twentieth Centuries* (Berkeley: University of California Press, 1985).

58. See Hawtrey, pp. 117-18.

59. See Benjamin J. Cohen, *The Question of Imperialism: The Political Economy of Dominance and Dependence* (New York: Basic Books, 1973).

60. Lenin, p. 64.

THREE CHALLENGES TO A WORLD MARKET ECONOMY

Despite its serious limitations as a theory of the market or the capitalist world economy, Marxism does raise three issues that cannot be easily dismissed and that are crucial to understanding the dynamics of international relations in the contemporary era. The first is the economic and political implications of the process of uneven growth. The second is the relationship of a market economy and foreign policy. The third is the capacity of a market economy to reform and moderate its less desirable features.

The Process of Uneven Growth

There are two fundamentally opposed explanations for the fact that uneven economic growth tends to lead to political conflict. Marxism, especially Lenin's law of uneven development, locates the sources of the conflict in the advanced capitalist economies' need to export surplus goods and capital and to engage in imperialistic conquest. Political realism holds that conflict among states over economic resources and political superiority is endemic in a system of international anarchy. From the realist perspective, the process of uneven growth generates conflict between rising and declining states as they seek to improve or maintain their relative position in the international political hierarchy.

As already argued, there appears to be no reliable method to resolve this controversy and choose one theory over the other. Both Marxism and political realism can account for the tendency of uneven growth to cause political conflict among states. Awkward facts and contrary evidence can easily be "explained away" by the use of ad hoc hypotheses. As neither of these theories appears capable of meeting the test of falsifiability, scholars of international political economy are forced to identify with one or another depending on their assumptions about the relationship of international economics and international politics.

My position on this issue is that of political realism; the process of uneven growth stimulates political conflict because it undermines the international political status quo. Shifts in the location of economic activities change the distribution of wealth and power among the states in the system. This redistribution of power and its effect on the standing and welfare of individual states accentuate the conflict between rising and declining states. If this conflict is not resolved it can lead to what I have elsewhere called a "hegemonic war" whose ultimate result is to determine which state or states will be dominant in the new international hierarchy.[62] A realist interpretation, I believe, is far superior to that of Marxism in explaining the relationship of uneven growth and political conflict.

Thus, in contrast to Lenin's use of the "law of uneven development" to explain the First World War, one can counterpose Simon Kuznets' essentially realist explanation. In his *Modern Economic Growth*, Kuznets interrupts his detailed analysis of economic growth to inquire whether a connection existed between the phenomenon of economic growth and the first great war of this century.[63]

Kuznets first emphasizes the great growth in power that preceded the outbreak of the war. "The growing productive power of developed nations, derived from the science-oriented technology that played an increasing role in modern economic growth, has meant

---

61. Herbert Feis, Europe, The World's Baker, 1870-1914 (New Haven: Yale University Press, 1964 [1930] and Eugene Staley, War and the Private Investor (Garden City, N.Y.: Doubleday, Doran, 1935) have effectively made this argument.

62. See Gilpin, 1981.

63. See Kuznets.

also greater power in armed conflict and greater capacity for protracted struggle".[64] Together, continuing capital accumulation and modern technology had enabled nations to conduct wars of unprecedented magnitude.

Second, Kuznets regards such great wars as the "ultimate tests of changes in relative power among nations, tests to resolve disagreements as to whether such shifts have indeed occurred and whether the political adjustments pressed for are really warranted".[65] In other words, the role of war is to test whether the redistribution of power in the system wrought by economic growth has operated to change the fundamental balance of power in the system, and if the balance has shifted, then consequent political and territorial adjustments reflecting the new distribution are to be expected. In an age of rapid and continuous economic growth there will be frequent and significant shifts of relative economic, and hence of military, power. "If wars are needed to confirm or deny such shifts, the rapidity and frequency with which shifts occur may be the reason for the frequent conflicts that serve as tests".[66] Thus a great war is caused by the uneven growth of state power.

And, finally, Kuznets argues that "major wars are associated with the emergence in the course of modern economic growth of several large and developed nations".[67] A century of uneasy peace had been possible because, during much of the period, there was only one large advanced country generating economic growth. The emergence of other industrialized and growing societies, especially Germany after 1870, eventually led to hegemonic war. The emergence of several large economically developed countries is the necessary, if not sufficient, condition for the occurrence of world wars. "In this sense it was a century of Pax Britannica that ended when the leading country could no longer lead and impose its peace on such a large part of the world".[68] It seems impossible to say more than this about the connection between economic growth and military conflict.

Market Economies and Foreign Policy

Another Marxist criticism of a market or capital society is that it tends to pursue an aggressive foreign policy. Liberals, of course, take the opposite position that capitalist economies are fundamentally pacific. For example, Joseph Schumpeter in his essay on imperialism argued that capitalists are antibellicose and modern wars are due to the holdover of precapitalist "vestigial" social structures.[69] In a truly capitalist society, he maintained, the foreign policy would be pacifist.[70] Marxists, liberals, and nationalists have long debated the issue of whether economic interdependence is a source of peaceful relations or a source of conflict among nation-states. Liberals believe that the mutual benefits of trade and the expanding web of interdependence among national economies tend to foster cooperative relations. They believe, as Norman Angell tried to demonstrate in his famous *The Great Illusion*[71], written four years prior to the First World War, that war has become

---

64. *Ibid.*, p. 344.

65. *Ibid.*, p. 345.

66. *Ibid.*

67. *Ibid.*

68. *Ibid.*

69. See Joseph A. Schumpeter, *Imperialism and Social Classes* (New York: Meridian, 1951).

70. Michael Doyle, "Kant, Liberal Legacies, and Foreign Affairs," Parts 1 and 2, Philosophy and Public Affairs 12 (1983): 205-23 and 323-53 has argued in an excellent two-part article that liberal economies, which he—in contrast to Schumpeter—distinguishes from capitalist ones, do in fact have a low propensity to war in comparison with other liberal societies.

unthinkable because it is antithetical to modern industrial society and does not pay. But for nationalists, trade is merely another arena for international competition, because economic interdependence increases the insecurity of states and their vulnerability to external economic and political forces.

From Montesquieu's statement that "peace is the natural effect of trade," through the writings of John Bight and Richard Cobden in the nineteenth century, to contemporary theorists of functionalism and economic interdependence, liberals have viewed international economics as separable from politics and as a force for peace. Whereas politics tends to divide, economics tends to unite peoples. Trade and economic interdependence create bonds of mutual interest and a vested interest in international peace and thus have a moderating influence on international relations.

The basic assumption of Marxists and economic nationalists, on the other hand, is that international interdependence is not only a cause of conflict and insecurity, but it creates dependency relations among states. Because interdependence is never symmetrical, trade becomes a source for increasing the political power of the strong over the weak. Therefore Marxists and economic nationalists advocate policies of economic autarky.

The historical record does not lend much support to either position; the patterns of economic and political relations are highly contradictory. Political antagonists may be major trading partners, as was the case with Great Britain and Germany in the First World War; or, as was the case with the United States and the Soviet Union after the Second World War, they may have negligible economic intercourse. What the evidence suggests is that whether trade aggravates or moderates conflicts is dependent upon the political circumstances. Attention, therefore, should be given to interrelated factors that appear to influence the ways in which trade affects international political relations.

The first factor affecting the political consequences of trade is the existence or absence of a dominant or hegemonic liberal power that can establish and manage the international trading system. The great eras of economic interdependence have been identified with the unchallenged supremacy of hegemonic trading power such as Great Britain in the nineteenth century and the United States after the Second World War. When the domination of these powers waned and they were challenged by rising powers, trade conflicts increased.

The second factor determining the political effects of trade is the rate of economic growth in the system. Although it is true that the decline of protectionism and the enlargement of world markets stimulates economic growth, the corollary is also true; a rapid rate of economic growth leads to increasing trade and economic interdependence. By the same token, a slowdown in the rate of economic growth makes adjustment difficult, intensifies international trade competition, and exacerbates international political relations.

The third factor affecting the political results of trading relations is the degree of homogeneity or heterogeneity of industrial structure, which in turn determines the composition of imports and exports.[72] Although it is true that industrial nations trade more with one another than with nonindustrial countries, when nations have highly homogeneous or even similar industrial structures and exports, competitive trading relations and commercial conflict frequently result in periods of economic stagnation.[73] By the same

71. See Norman Angell, *The Great Illusion: A Study of the Relations of Military Power in Nations to Their Economic and Social Advantage*, 3d ed., rev. and enl. (New York: Putnam, 1911).

72. See Kaname Akamatsu, "A Theory of Unbalanced Growth in the World Economy," *Weltwirtschaftliches* Archiv 86 (1961): 196-215.

73. See John Hicks, *A Theory of Economic History* (Oxford: Oxford University Press, 1969), pp. 56-59.

token, heterogeneity of industrial structure tends to produce complementary trading relations. Thus, the heterogeneity of the industrial structures of Great Britain and other nations in the early and mid-nineteenth century resulted in generally harmonious trading relations. As other nations industrialized by-the end of the century, commercial conflict became intense. The same phenomenon may be observed in the contemporary era, as rising industrial powers such as Japan and the newly industrializing countries (NICs) overtake and surpass the United States.

The major point to be made in these matters is that trade and other economic relations are not in themselves critical to the establishment of either cooperative or conflictual international relations. No generalizations on the relationship of economic interdependence and political behavior appear possible. At times economic intercourse can moderate and at others aggravate these relations. What can be said with some justification is that trade is not a guarantor of peace. On the other hand, the collapse of trade has frequently led to the outbreak of international conflict.[74] In general, the character of international relations and the question of peace or war are determined primarily by the larger configurations of power and strategic interest among both the great and small powers in the system.

The Significance of Welfare Capitalism

The third problem raised by the Marxist critique of a market or capitalist economy is its capacity to reform itself. At the heart of the debate between Lenin and Kautsky on the future of capitalism was the possibility that capitalism could eliminate its worst features. For Kautsky and the social democrats, the peaceful transition of capitalism into socialism was possible as a result of the growth of workers' strength in the Western democracies. To Lenin this seemed impossible and in fact absurd because of the very nature of a capitalist economy:

> It goes without saying that if capitalism could develop agriculture, which today lags far behind industry everywhere, if it could raise the standard of living of the masses, who are everywhere still poverty-stricken and underfed, in spite of the amazing advance in technical knowledge, there could be no talk of a superabundance of capital. This "argument" the petty-bourgeois critics of capitalism [read Kautsky] advance on every occasion. But if capitalism did these things it would not be capitalism; for uneven development and wretched conditions of the masses are fundamental and inevitable conditions and premises of this mode of production.[75]

Leaving aside the tautological nature of Lenin's argument, what he described as an impossibility under capitalism now exists in the welfare states of the mid-twentieth century. Even if one admits that the welfare state was forced on the capitalist class by the working class, the crucial point is that it has largely addressed all three of the Marxist laws of capitalism and has satisfied most of Lenin's requirements for a reformed capitalism, that is, a capitalism that guarantees full employment and the economic welfare of the masses. The productivity of agriculture has been vastly increased through government support of research programs, the progressive income tax and other programs involving transfer payments have significantly redistributed income, and the advent of Keynesian economics and demand management through fiscal and monetary policy have moderated the operation of the "law of disproportionality" and dampened cyclical fluctuations through the stimulation of consumer demand.

---

74. See Condliffe, p. 527.

75. Lenin, pp. 62-63.

Table 1. Nullification of Marxist Laws by Welfare States

Marxist Law	*Welfare State*
(1) Law of Disproportionality	Demand management through fiscal and monetary policy
(2) Law of Accumulation	Income redistribution through progressive income tax and transfer payments
	Support for trade unions
	Regional and small business policies
(3) Law of the Falling Rate of Profit	Government support of education and research to increase the efficiency of all factors of production

In addition, government regulations and antitrust policies decrease the concentration of capital while government support of mass education and industrial research and development increases the efficiency and profitability of both labor and capital. As Joseph Schumpeter has written, capitalism is the first economic system to benefit the lower rungs of society.[76] Indeed, one can argue that capitalism has done all those things that Lenin predicted it could not do and has done so even though the reforms of capitalism embodied in the welfare state were initially strongly resisted by the capitalist class.[77] (See Table 1) In fact, the expansion of capitalism following the Second World War produced the greatest era of general economic prosperity in the history of the world.

However, the Marxist critique of a capitalist or global market economy still cannot be easily dismissed; it raises an important question regarding the future of the market system. Although capitalism by itself cannot be held accountable for imperialism and war and although it has survived numerous crises and has proved that it could be highly flexible and reform itself, its continued existence is still problematic. Therefore let us turn directly to the question of the capacity of welfare capitalism to survive in the rapidly changing world of nation-states in the final years of this century.

WELFARE CAPITALISM IN A NON-WELFARE INTERNATIONALIST CAPITALIST WORLD

Despite capitalism's successes and domestic reforms, one can reasonably argue that Lenin's fourth law of uneven development remains in force, and that this will eventually doom capitalism and the liberal market economy. It is possible that, with the advent of the

76. See Joseph A. Schumpeter, *Capitalism, Socialism and Democracy*, 3d ed. (New York: Harper and Row, 1950).

77. Contemporary Marxists themselves have attempted to explain this anomaly in Marxist theory by arguing that the capitalist state is semiautonomous and can take actions that, though contrary to the interests of individual capitalists, are in the interest of the preservation of capitalism as a system. Such arguments among Marxists over the theory of the state have become highly scholastic (see Martin Carnoy, *The State and Political Theory* (Princeton: Princeton University Press, 1984). These theories are not convincing and, like Lenin's theory of imperialism, are best regarded as ad hoc hypotheses that seek to explain away the predictive failures of Marxist theory rather than as extensions of the theory.

welfare state, the inherent contradictions of capitalism have simply been transferred from the domestic level of the nation-state to the international level. At this level there is no welfare state; there is no world government to apply Keynesian policies of demand management, to coordinate conflicting national policies, or to counter tendencies toward economic disequilibrium. In contrast to domestic society, there is no state to compensate the losers, as is exemplified in the dismissal by wealthy countries of the demands of the less developed countries for a New International Economic Order (NIEO); nor is there an effective international government response to cheating and market failures.

In the anarchy of international relations, the law of uneven development and the possibility of intracapitalist clashes still applies. One could even argue that the advent of national welfare states has accentuated the economic conflicts among capitalist societies.[78] The new commitment of the capitalist welfare state to full employment and domestic economic well-being causes it to substitute interventionist policies for the free play of market forces and thereby brings it into conflict with the policies of other states pursuing a similar set of economic goals.

Welfare states are potentially highly nationalistic because governments have become accountable to their citizenry for the elimination of economic suffering; sometimes the best way to achieve this goal is to pass on economic difficulties to other societies. In times of economic crisis public pressures encourage national governments to shift the burdens of unemployment and economic adjustment to other societies; thus, economic and interstate competition through the market mechanism subtly shifts to interstate conflict for economic and political advantage. This nationalistic struggle to gain economic advantage and to shift the costs of economic distress to others again threatens the future of international capitalism.

The issue of the future of capitalist society in the era of the welfare state is central to the question of the applicability of the core of Marx's general theory of historical development to the world of the late twentieth century. One proposition of Marx's theory was that "no social order ever perishes before all the productive forces for which there is room in it have developed; and new, higher relations of production never appear before the material conditions of their existence have matured in the womb of the old society itself",[79] that is, one mode of production is not transcended by the next until it has exhausted its inherent productive potential. Each phase of human experience, according to Marxism, has its own historical mission to fulfill in elevating human productive capacities and thereby setting the stage for the phase to follow. Each mode advances until further progress is no longer possible; then historical necessity dictates that the fetters holding back society are removed by the class chosen to carry it to the next level of material achievement and human liberation.

The implications of this formulation are intriguing for the future of capitalism envisioned by Marxist theory. According to Marx, the historical function of capitalism was to develop the world and its productive potential and then to bequeath to its heir, socialism, a fully developed and industrialized world economy. Although Marx provided no timetable for this cataclysmic event to take place, he lived out his life in the expectation that the revolution was imminent.

---

78. See Melvyn B. Krauss, *The New Protectionism: The Welfare State and International Trade* (New York: New York University Press, 1978)

79. Karl Marx, *Karl Marx: Selected Writings*, ed. David McLellan (Oxford: Oxford University Press, 1977 [1859], pp. 388-91.

As Albert Hirsehman has shown, Marx failed to recognize (or more likely suppressed) the significance of these ideas for his analysis of the eventual demise of capitalism, that is, if no mode of production comes to an end until it plays out its historical role and if the assigned task of capitalism is to develop the world, then the capitalist mode of production has many decades, perhaps centuries or even millennia, yet to run.[80] If one further discounts, as Marxists do, the "limits to growth" argument, capitalism's assigned task of the economic development of the planet, including its oceans and nearby space, will require a very long time indeed.

Hirschman suggests that this must have been an uncomfortable thought for Marx, who until his dying day was so frequently disappointed in his longing to see the coming of the revolution. In Hirschman's view, this explains why Marx focused on European capitalism as a closed rather than an open economy and why he failed to develop a theory of imperialism even though one would have expected this of him as an assiduous student of Hegel. As Hirschman points out, Hegel anticipated all subsequent theories of capitalist imperialism.

Hirschman concludes that Marx, in his own writings, suppressed Hegel's theory of capitalist imperialism because of its disturbing implications for Marx's predictions concerning the survivability of capitalism. If no social system is displaced by another until it exhausts the productive potential inherent in it, then an imperialistic capitalism as it expands beyond Europe into Asia, Africa, and elsewhere will add new life to the capitalist mode of production. Through the mechanisms of overseas trade and foreign investment, the inevitable collapse of capitalism may thus be postponed for centuries. Indeed, if such a collapse must await the elevation of the developing world to the economic and technological levels of the most advanced economy, then in a world of continuing technological advance, the requisite full development of the productive capacities of capitalism may never be reached.

Rosa Luxemburg appears to have been the first major Marxist theorist to appreciate the historic significance of this reasoning; she argued that as long as capitalism remains an open system and there are underdeveloped lands into which the capitalist mode of production can expand, Marx's prediction of economic stagnation and political revolution will remain unfulfilled.[81] In response to this troubling (at least for Marxists) prospect, Lenin's *Imperialism*, as noted earlier, transformed the Marxist critique of international capitalism. He argued that although capitalism does develop the world and is an economic success, the closing-in of political space through capitalist imperialism and the territorial division of the globe among rising and declining capitalist powers leads to international conflict. Thus, Lenin argued that the masses would revolt against capitalism as a war-prone political system rather than as a failed economic system.

Whether or not one accepts these several formulations and reformulations of Marxist thought, they do raise a fundamental issue. As Marx himself pointed out, the logic of the dynamics of a market or capitalist economy is expansive and international. The forces of the market reach out and bring the whole world within their confines, and they are destructive of traditional ways. The basic anarchy of the market mechanism produces instabilities in the lives of individuals and whole societies.

---

80. See Albert O. Hirschman, *Essays in Trespassing: Economics to Politics and Beyond* (New York: Cambridge University Press, 1981), ch. 7.

81. Stephen Rousseas, *Capitalism and Catastrophe: A Critical Appraisal of the Limits to Capitalism*, Chapter 5 (New York: Cambridge University Press, 1979) is an excellent discussion of her views.

The modern welfare state and protectionism have developed to cushion these deleterious effects, and herein lies the most serious problem for the capitalist system and its survival. As Keynes appreciated, the logic of the welfare state is to close the economy, because the government must be able to isolate the economy from external restraints and disturbances in order to control and manage it. The international flow of trade, money, and finance undermines the Keynesian management of an economy by decreasing domestic policy autonomy. Goods, Keynes wrote at the height of the Great Depression, should be "homespun",[82] and capital should stay at home where it can benefit the nation and the nation's working class.

Thus, the logic of the market economy as an inherently expanding global system collides with the logic of the modern welfare state. While solving the problem of a closed economy, the welfare state has only transferred the fundamental problem of the market economy and its survivability to the international level. The problem of reconciling welfare capitalism at the domestic level with the nature of the international capitalist system has become of increasing importance.

The resolution of this basic dilemma between domestic autonomy and international norms is essential to the future viability of the market or capitalist economy. How can one reconcile these two opposed means of organizing economic affairs? Which will prevail—national economic interventionism or the rules of the international market economy? What are the conditions that promote peace and cooperation among market economies? Is a dominant or hegemonic power required to resolve the conflict? A look at the past successes and failures of international capitalism reveals that temporary resolutions of this dilemma or failures to resolve it have been crucial in recent history. In the 1980s the future of the world market economy and the continuing survival of the capitalist mode of production are dependent upon solutions developed or not developed by the United States and its major economic partners.

In another guise this was the problem posed by Richard Cooper in his influential book, *The Economics of Interdependence*.[83] An increasingly interdependent world economy requires either an international agreement to formulate and enforce the rules of an open world market economy and to facilitate the adjustment of differences or a high degree of policy coordination among capitalist states. Without one or the other, a market economy will tend to disintegrate into intense nationalist conflicts over trade, monetary arrangements, and domestic policies. With the relative decline of American power and its ability or willingness to manage the world economy, this issue has become preeminent in the world economy. If there is no increase in policy coordination or decrease in economic interdependence among the leading capitalist economies, the system could indeed break into warring states, just as Lenin predicted.

The long-term survivability of a capitalist or international market system, at least as we have known it since the end of the Second World War, continues to be problematic. Although the welfare state "solved" the problem of domestic capitalism identified by Marx, continuing conflicts among capitalist societies over trade, foreign investment, and international monetary affairs in the contemporary world remind us that the debate between Lenin and Kautsky over the international nature of capitalism is still relevant. As

---

82. John Maynard Keynes, "National Self-sufficiency." Yale Review 22:755-69.

83. Richard Cooper, *The Economics of Interdependence: Economic Policy in the Atlantic Community* (New York: McGraw-Hill).

American power and leadership decline due to the operation of the "law of uneven development," will confrontation mount and the system collapse as one nation after another pursues "beggar-my-neighbor" policies, as Lenin would expect? Or, will Kautsky prove to be correct that capitalists are too rational to permit this type of internecine economic slaughter to take place?

CONCLUSION

The foregoing analysis of economic ideologies leads to three general propositions. The *first* is that the global or territorial distribution of economic activities, especially of industry and technology, is a central concern of modern statecraft; behind the technical discussions of trade, foreign investment, and monetary affairs are conflicting national ambitions and the fundamental question of "who is to produce what and where." The *second* point is that the international division of labor is a product of both national policies and relative efficiency; although states can and do ignore the market as they seek to influence the location of economic activities, this entails economic costs; the price mechanism operates to transform national efficiencies and international economic relations over the long run. And *third*, due to these changes and the uneven growth of national economies, the inherent stability of the international market or capitalist system is highly problematic; it is the nature of the dynamics of this system that it erodes the political foundations upon which it must ultimately rest and thereby raises the crucial question of finding a new political leadership to ensure the survival of a liberal international economic order.

Realist Tradition/ Economic Nationalist Theories

Mercantilist Theory

Alexander Hamilton
Report on Manufactures

Robert Gilpin
The Nationalist Theory of International Trade

Hegemonic Stability Theory

Robert Gilpin
The Theory of Hegemonic Stability

Introduction to Mercantilist Theory[1]

The following selections of *Understanding International Relations* address the realist perspective toward the relationship between global politics and global economics. We begin with a discussion of economic nationalism, otherwise known as mercantilism. At its core, mercantilist theory addresses a key element of a state's pursuit of power: wealth. In a most basic sense, proponents of mercantilism believe that the market should be controlled by the state in order to maximize the state's wealth and power. According to Jacob Viner, mercantilists typically subscribe to all of the following propositions: (1) wealth is an absolutely essential means to power, whether for security or aggression; (2) power is essential or valuable as a means of acquisitions or retention of wealth; (3) wealth and power are each proper ultimate ends of national policy; and (4) there is a long-term harmony between these ends, although in particular circumstances it may be necessary for a time to make economic sacrifices in the interest of military security and therefore also of long-run prosperity.[2]

The father of modern-day mercantilism is also one of our country's founding fathers, Alexander Hamilton. His *Report on the Subject of Manufactures*, presented to the House of Representatives in 1791, argued in favor of economic protectionism as the sure way to promote industrialization and, by extension, national security. Selected excerpts from Hamilton's report are provided as the first selection of our intellectual journal into the realist world of global economic theory. This is followed by two selections from Robert Gilpin's 1987 book *The Political Economy of International Relations*, both of which are also identified with the realist intellectual tradition.

The first reading, "The Nationalist Theory of International Trade," provides an explanation of—and arguments for—economic nationalism. After a brief historical description of the roots of mercantilist thought, Gilpin expands on the implications of this theory for our understanding of the relationship between politics and economics in international relations. Starting with the premise that states require access to means (i.e., wealth and power) necessary for survival, Gilpin notes that they have the option to produce these items internally or pursue them through trade. Obviously, realists and liberalists differ on how this trade should be conducted. While liberalists insist that free and open trade will always maximize systemic wealth through comparative advantage, mercantilists disagree.

By describing the elements of, and motives for, various mercantilist policy prescriptions such as "economic protectionism" or "industrial policy," Gilpin's hypotheses should become clear. Specifically, by keeping in mind that the imposition of a protectionist tariff is a state action (i.e., dependent variable) which is driven by some particular motives, it becomes obvious how Gilpin contributes to our understanding of "why states do what they do" and "what causes conflict and cooperation among states." For example, using an inductive analysis of state economic policies over the past century, one may be able to conclude that a positive causal relationship exists between economic nationalism and con-

---

1. revised April 24, 2004: J. Forest

2. Jacob Viner, *The Long View and the Short: Studies in Economic Theory and Policy* (New York: Free Press, 1958), 286.

flict. This theory has implications for explaining how a state may act when its wealth is threatened, or when it seeks to maximize its *relative* wealth and power.

In today's context of increasing globalization and economic interdependence, mercantilist theory helps us understand a state's economic policies (e.g., trade barriers) including those which involve the purchase of inexpensive goods and services in the world marketplace. Further, different states have different views on protectionism versus free trade. For example, developed states need constant encouragement and attention to abide by the rules and constraints of free trade regimes. Meanwhile, developing states often cannot be encouraged to open their markets and enter into an unrestrained liberal trading order for the same mercantilist-oriented reasons that Alexander Hamilton espoused over two hundred years ago. In both situations, the realms of economics and politics intersect on regional and global levels. Thus, mercantilism offers an important perspective for understanding international relations.

SUGGESTED QUESTIONS FOR DISCUSSION AND DEBATE

- What are the implications of mercantilism for conflict or cooperation among states?
- Why would a state pursue economic nationalist/protectionist policies?
- What would be a good counter-argument to mercantilist theory?

Report on Manufactures

Alexander Hamilton

The expediency of encouraging manufactures in the United States, which was not long since deemed very questionable, appears at this time to be pretty generally admitted. The embarrassments, which have obstructed the progress of our external trade, have led to serious reflections on the necessity of enlarging the sphere of our domestic commerce: the restrictive regulations, which in foreign markets abridge the vent of the increasing surplus of our Agricultural produce, serve to beget an earnest desire, that a more extensive demand for that surplus may be created at home: And the complete success, which has rewarded manufacturing enterprise, in some valuable branches, conspiring with the promising symptoms, which attend some less mature essays, in others, justify a hope, that the obstacles to the growth of this species of industry are less formidable than they were apprehended to be, and that it is not difficult to find, in its further extension, a full indemnification for any external disadvantages, which are or may be experienced, as well as an accession of resources, favorable to national independence and safety.

There still are, nevertheless, respectable patrons of opinions, unfriendly to the encouragement of manufactures. The following are, substantially, the arguments by which these opinions are defended.

"In every country (say those who entertain them) Agriculture is the most beneficial and *productive* object of human industry. This position, generally, if not universally true, applies with peculiar emphasis to the United States, on account of their immense tracts of fertile territory, uninhabited and unimproved. . . .

"To endeavor, by the extraordinary patronage of Government, to accelerate the growth of manufactures, is, in fact, to endeavor, by force and art, to transfer the natural current of industry from a more, to a less beneficial channel. Whatever has such a tendency must necessarily be unwise. Indeed it can hardly ever be wise in a government, to attempt to give a direction to the industry of its citizens. This, under the quick-sighted guidance of private interest, will, if left to itself, infallibly find its own way to the most profitable employment: and it is by such employment, that the public prosperity will be most effectually promoted. To leave industry to itself, therefore, is, in almost every case, the soundest as well as the simplest policy.

"If contrary to the natural course of things, an unseasonable and premature spring can be given to certain fabrics, by heavy duties, prohibitions, bounties, or by other forced expedients; this will only be to sacrifice the interests of the community to those of particular classes. Besides the misdirection of labor, a virtual monopoly will be given to the persons employed on such fabrics; and an enhancement of price, the inevitable consequence of every monopoly, must be defrayed at the expense of the other parts of the society. It is far preferable, that these persons should be engaged in the cultivation of the earth, and that we should procure, in exchange for its productions, the commodities, with which foreigners are able to supply us in greater perfection, and upon better terms."

It ought readily to be conceded that the cultivation of the earth—as the primary and most certain source of national supply . . . has intrinsically a strong claim to pre-eminence over every other kind of industry.

Reprinted from Alexander Hamilton, *The Reports of Alexander Hamilton*, Jacob Cooke, ed., New York: Harper and Row, 1964.

But, that it has a title to any thing like an exclusive predilection, in any country, ought to be admitted with great caution. That it is even more productive than every other branch of industry requires more evidence than has yet been given in support of the position. That its real interests, precious and important as, without the help of exaggeration, they truly are, will be advanced, rather than injured by the due encouragement of manufactures, may, it is believed, be satisfactorily demonstrated. And it is also believed that the expediency of such encouragement in a general view may be shown to be recommended by the most cogent and persuasive motives of national policy.

The foregoing suggestions are not designed to inculcate an opinion that manufacturing industry is more productive than that of Agriculture. They are intended rather to show that the reverse of this proposition is not ascertained; that the general arguments which are brought to establish it are not satisfactory; and, consequently that a supposition of the superior productiveness of Tillage ought to be no obstacle to listening to any substantial inducements to the encouragement of manufactures, which may be otherwise perceived to exist, through an apprehension; that they may have a tendency to divert labour from a more to a less profitable employment.

. . . . But without contending for the superior productiveness of Manufacturing Industry, it may conduce to a better judgment of the policy, which ought to be pursued respecting its encouragement, to contemplate the subject, under some additional aspects, tending not only to confirm the idea, that this kind of industry has been improperly represented as unproductive in itself; but to evince in addition that the establishment and diffusion of manufactures have the effect of rendering the total mass of useful and productive labor, in a community, greater than it would otherwise be . . .

. . . . [M]anufacturing establishments not only occasion a positive augmentation of the Produce and Revenue of the Society, but . . . they contribute essentially to rendering them greater than they could possibly be, without such establishments. These circumstances are:

1) . . . . The Division Of Labour

It has justly been observed, that there is scarcely any thing of greater moment in the economy of a nation than the proper division of labour. The separation of occupations causes each to be carried to a much greater perfection, than it could possibly acquire, if they were blended . . .

. . . . [T]he mere separation of the occupation of the cultivator, from that of the Artificer, has the effect of augmenting *the productive powers* of labour, and with them, the total mass of the produce or revenue of a Country. In this single view of the subject, therefore, the utility of Artificers of Manufacturers, towards promoting an increase of productive industry, is apparent.

2) . . . . An Extension Of The Use Of Machinery, A Point Which, Though Partly Anticipated Requires To Be Placed In One Or Two Additional Lights

The employment of Machinery forms an item of great importance in the general mass of national industry . . . . It shall be taken for granted, and the truth of the position referred to observation, that manufacturing pursuits are susceptible in a greater degree of the application of machinery, than those of Agriculture. If so all the difference is lost to a community, which, instead of manufacturing for itself, procures the fabrics requisite to its supply from other Countries. The substitution of foreign for domestic manufactures is a transfer to foreign nations of the advantages accruing from the employment of Machinery, in the modes in which it is capable of being employed, with most utility and to the greatest extent.

3) . . . . The Additional Employment Of Classes Of The Community, Not Originally Engaged In The Particular Business

This is not among the least valuable of the means, by which manufacturing institutions contribute to augment the general stock of industry and production. In places where those institutions prevail, besides the persons regularly engaged in them, they afford occasional and extra employment to industrious individuals and families, who are willing to devote the leisure resulting from the intermissions of their ordinary pursuits to collateral labours, as a resource for multiplying their acquisitions or their enjoyments . . . .

. . . . It is worthy of particular remark, that, in general, women and children are rendered more useful, and the latter more early useful by manufacturing establishments than they would otherwise be . . . .

4) . . . . Promoting Of Emigration From Foreign Countries

If it be true then, that it is the interest of the United States to open every possible avenue to emigration from abroad, it affords a weighty argument for the encouragement of manufactures; which, . . . will have the strongest tendency to multiply the inducements to it.

Here is perceived an important resource, not only for extending the population, and with it the useful and productive labour of the country, but likewise for the prosecution of manufactures, without deducting from the number of hands, which might otherwise be drawn to Tillage and even for the indemnification of Agriculture for such as might happen to be diverted from it. . .

5) . . . . Furnishing Greater Scope For The Diversity Of Talents And Dispositions, Which Discriminate Men From Each Other

This is a much more powerful means of augmenting the fund of national Industry than may at first sight appear. It is a just observation, that minds of the strongest and most active powers for their proper objects fall below mediocrity and labour without effect, if confined to uncongenial pursuits. And it is thence to be inferred, that the results of human exertion may be immensely increased by diversifying its objects. When all the different kinds of industry obtain in a community, each individual can find his proper element, and can call into activity the whole vigour of his nature. And the community is benefitted by the services of its respective members, in the manner, in which each can serve it with most effect.

6) . . . . Affording A More Ample And Various Field For Enterprise

. . . . To cherish and stimulate the activity of the human mind, by multiplying the objects of enterprise, is not among the least considerable of the expedients, by which the wealth of a nation may be promoted . . . . The spirit of enterprise, useful and prolific as it is, must necessarily be contracted or expanded in proportion to the simplicity or variety of the occupations and productions, which are to be found in a Society. It must be less in a nation of mere cultivators, than in a nation of cultivators and merchants; less in a nation of cultivators and merchants, than in a nation of cultivators, artificers and merchants.

7) . . . . Creating, In Some Instances, A New, And Securing In All A More Certain And Steady Demand, For Surplus Produce Of This Soil

It is evident, that the exertions of the husbandman will be steady or fluctuating, vigorous or feeble, in proportion to the steadiness or fluctuation, adequateness or inadequateness, of the markets on which he must depend, for the vent of the surplus, which may be produced by his labor; and that such surplus in the ordinary course of things will be greater or less in the same proportion.

For the purpose of this vent, a domestic market is greatly to be preferred to a foreign one; because it is in the nature of things, far more to be relied upon.

To secure such a market, there is no other expedient, than to promote manufacturing establishments. Manufacturers who constitute the most numerous class, after the Cultivators of land, are for that reason the principal consumers of the surplus of their labour.

The foregoing considerations seem sufficient to establish, as general propositions, that it is the interest of nations to diversify the industrious pursuits of the individuals who compose them—that the establishment of manufactures is calculated not only to increase the general stock of useful and productive labour; but even to improve the state of Agriculture in particular, certainly to advance the interest of those who are engaged in it . . . .

If the system of perfect liberty to industry and commerce were the prevailing system of nations, the arguments which dissuade a country, in the predicament of the United States, from the zealous pursuit of manufactures, would doubtless have great force. It will not be affirmed, that they might not be permitted, with few exceptions, to serve as a rule of national conduct. In such a state of things, each country would have the full benefit of its peculiar advantages to compensate for its deficiencies or disadvantages. If one nation were in a condition to supply manufactured articles on better terms than another, that other might find an abundant indemnification in a superior capacity to furnish the produce of the soil. And a free exchange, mutually beneficial, of the commodities, which each was able to supply, on the best terms, might be carried on between them, supporting in full vigour the industry of each . . . .

But the system which has been mentioned, is far from characterising the general policy of Nations. The prevalent one has been regulated by an opposite spirit. The consequence of it is, that the United States are to a certain extent in the situation of a country precluded from foreign Commerce. They can indeed, without difficulty obtain from abroad the manufactured supplies, of which they are in want; but they experience numerous and very injurious impediments to the emission and vent of their own commodities. Nor is this the case in reference to a single foreign nation only. The regulations of several countries, with which we have the most extensive intercourse, throw serious obstructions in the way of the principal staples of the United States.

In such a position of things, the United States cannot exchange with Europe on equal terms; and the want of reciprocity would render them the victim of a system which should induce them to confine their views to Agriculture, and refrain from Manufactures. A constant and increasing necessity, on their part, for the commodities of Europe, and only a partial and occasional demand for their own, in return, could not but expose them to a state of impoverishment, compared with the opulence to which their political and natural advantages authorize them to aspire.

. . . . It is for the United States to consider by what means they can render themselves least dependent on the combinations, right or wrong, of foreign policy.

The remaining objections to a particular encouragement of manufacturers in the United States now require to be examined.

One of these turns on the proposition, that Industry, if left to itself, will naturally find its way to the most useful and profitable employment: whence it is inferred that manufactures without the aid of government will grow up as soon and as fast, as the natural state of things and the interest of the community may require.

Against the solidity of this hypothesis, in the full latitude of the terms, very cogent reasons may be offered. These have relations to—the strong influence of habit and the spirit of imitation—the fear of want of success in untried enterprises—the intrinsic difficulties incident to first essays towards a competition with those who have previously attained to perfection in the business to be attempted—the bounties premiums and other artificial encouragements, with which foreign nations second the exertions of their own Citizens in the branches, in which they are to be rivalled.

Experience teaches, that men are often so much governed by what they are accustomed to see and practice, that the simplest and most obvious improvements, in the most ordinary occupations, are adopted with hesitation, reluctance, and by slow gradations. The spontaneous transition to new pursuits, in a community long habituated to different ones, may be expected to be attended with proportionably greater difficulty. When former occupations ceased to yield a profit adequate to the subsistence of their followers, or when there was an absolute deficiency of employment in them, owing to the superabundance of hands, changes would ensue; but these changes would be likely to be more tardy than might consist with the interest either of individuals or of the Society. In many cases they would not happen, while a bare support could be insured by an adherence to ancient courses; though a resort to a more profitable employment might be practicable. To produce the desirable changes as early as may be expedient, may therefore require the incitement and patronage of government.

The superiority antecedently enjoyed by nations, who have preoccupied and perfected a branch of industry, constitutes a more formidable obstacle, than either of those, which have been mentioned, to the introduction of the same branch into a country in which it did not before exist. To maintain between the recent establishments of one country and the long matured establishments of another country, a competition upon equal terms, both as to quality and price, is in most cases impracticable. The disparity, in the one or in the other, or in both, must necessarily be so considerable as to forbid a successful rivalship, without the extraordinary aid and protection of government.

But the greatest obstacle of all to the successful prosecution of a new branch of industry in a country, in which it was before unknown, consists, as far as the instances apply, in the bounties premiums and other aids which are granted, in a variety of cases, by the nations, in which the establishments to be imitated are previously introduced. It is well known (and particular examples in the course of this report will be cited) that certain nations grant bounties on the exportation of particular commodities, to enable their own workmen to undersell and supplant all competitors in the countries to which those commodities are sent. Hence the undertakers of a new manufacture have to contend not only with the natural disadvantages of a new undertaking, but with the gratuities and remunerations which other governments bestow. To be enabled to contend with success, it is evident that the interference and aid of their own government are indispensable.

There remains to be noticed an objection to the encouragement of manufactures, of a nature different from those which question the probability of success. This is derived from its supposed tendency to give a monopoly of advantages to particular classes, at the expense of the rest of the community, who, it is affirmed, would be able to procure the requisite supplies of manufactured articles on better terms from foreigners, than from our own Citizens, and who, it is alleged, are reduced to the necessity of paying an enhanced price for whatever they want, by every measure, which obstructs the free competition of foreign commodities.

But though it were true, that the immediate and certain effect of regulations controlling the competition of foreign with domestic fabrics was an increase of Price, it is universally true, that the contrary is the ultimate effect with every successful manufacture. When a domestic manufacture has attained to perfection, and has engaged in the prosecution of it a competent number of Persons, it invariably becomes cheaper. Being free from the heavy charges which attend the importation of foreign commodities, it can be afforded, and accordingly seldom or never fails to be sold Cheaper, in process of time, than was the foreign Article for which it is a substitute. The internal competition which takes place, soon does away [with] every thing like Monopoly, and by degrees reduces the price of the Article to the *minimum* of a reasonable profit on the Capital employed. This accords with the reason of the thing, and with experience.

Whence it follows, that it is the interest of a community, with a view to eventual and permanent economy, to encourage the growth of manufactures. In a national view, a temporary enhancement of price must always be well compensated by permanent reduction of it.

There seems to be a moral certainty, that the trade of a country which is both manufacturing and Agricultural will be more lucrative and prosperous than that of a Country, which is merely Agricultural.

One reason for this is found in that general effort of nations . . . to produce from their own soils, the articles of prime necessity requisite to their own consumption and use, and which serves to render their demand for a foreign supply of such articles, in a great degree occasional and contingent. . . .

Another circumstance which gives a superiority of commercial advantages to states that manufacture as well as cultivate, consists in the more numerous attractions, which a more diversified market offers to foreign Customers, and in the greater scope which it affords to mercantile enterprise. . . .

From these circumstances collectively—two important inferences are to be drawn, one, that there is always a higher probability of a favorable balance of Trade, in regard to countries in which manufactures founded on the basis of a thriving Agriculture flourish, than in regard to those, which are confined wholly or almost wholly to Agriculture; the other (which is also a consequence of the first), that countries of the former description are likely to possess more pecuniary wealth, or money, than those of the latter.

. . . . [T]he uniform appearance of an abundance of specie, as the concomitant of a flourishing state of manufactures, and of the reverse, where they do not prevail, afford a strong presumption of their favorable operation upon the wealth of a Country.

Not only the wealth, but the independence and security of a country, appear to be materially connected with the prosperity of manufactures. Every nation, with a view to those great objects, ought to endeavour to possess within itself all the essentials of national supply. These comprise the means of *Subsistence, habitation, clothing,* and *defence*.

The possession of these is necessary to the perfection of the body politic; to the safety as well as to the welfare of the society; the want of either is the want of an important Organ of political life and Motion; and in the various crises which await a state, it must severely feel the effects of any such deficiency. The extreme embarrassments of the United States during the late War, from an incapacity of supplying themselves, are still matter of keen recollection: A future war might be expected again to exemplify the mischiefs and dangers of a situation to which that incapacity is still in too great a degree applicable, unless changed by timely and vigorous exertion. To effect this change, as fast as shall be prudent, merits all the attention and all the Zeal of our Public Councils; it is the next great work to be accomplished.

The want of a Navy, to protect our external commerce, as long as it shall Continue, must render it a peculiarly precarious reliance, for the supply of essential articles, and must serve to strengthen prodigiously the arguments in favour of manufactures.

In order to a better judgment of the Means proper to be resorted to by the United States, it will be of use to Advert to those which have been employed with success in other Countries. The principal of these are—

1) Protecting Duties—Or Duties On Those Foreign Articles Which Are The Rivals Of The Domestic Ones Intended To Be Encouraged

Duties of this nature evidently amount to a virtual bounty on the domestic fabrics since by enhancing the charges on foreign articles, they enable the National Manufacturers to undersell all their foreign Competitors . . . .

2) Prohibitions Of Rival Articles, Or Duties Equivalent To Prohibitions

This is another and an efficacious mean of encouraging national manufactures but in general it is only fit to be employed when a manufacture, has made such progress and is in so many hands as to insure a due competition, and an adequate supply on reasonable terms . . . .

3) Prohibitions Of The Exportation Of The Materials Of Manufactures

The desire of securing a cheap and plentiful supply for the national workmen, and where the article is either peculiar to the Country, or of peculiar quality there, the jealousy of enabling foreign workmen to rival those of the nation with its own Materials, are the leading motives to this species of regulation. It ought not to be affirmed, that it is in no instance proper, but it is, certainly one which ought to be adopted with great circumspection, and only in very plain Cases . . . .

4) Pecuniary Bounties

This has been found one of the efficacious means of encouraging manufactures, and, is in some views, the best . . . .

Bounties have not, like high protecting duties, a tendency to produce scarcity. An increase of price is not always the immediate, though, where the progress of a domestic Manufacture does not counteract a rise, it is commonly the ultimate effect of an additional duty. In the interval, between the laying of the duty and the proportional increase of price, it may discourage importation, by interfering with the profits to be expected from the sale of the article.

It cannot escape notice, that the duty upon the importation of an article can no otherwise aid the domestic production of it, than by giving the latter greater advantages in the home market. It can have no influence upon the advantageous sale of the article produced in foreign markets; no tendency, therefore, to promote its exportation.

The true way to conciliate these two interests is to lay a duty on foreign *manufactures* of the material, the growth of which is desired to be encouraged, and to apply the produce of that duty, by way of bounty, either upon the production of the material itself or upon its manufacture at home, or upon both . . . .

5) Premiums

These are of a nature allied to bounties, though distinguishable from them in some important features.

Bounties are applicable to the whole quantity of an article produced, or manufactured, or exported, and involve a correspondent expense. Premiums serve to reward some particular excellence or superiority, some extraordinary exertion or skill, and are dispensed only in a small number of cases. .

6) The Exemption Of The Materials Of Manufactures From Duty

The policy of that Exemption as a general rule particularly in reference to new Establishments is obvious. It can hardly ever be advisable to add the obstructions of fiscal burthens to the difficulties which naturally embarrass a new manufacture; and where it is matured and in condition to become an object of revenue it is generally speaking better that the fabric than the Material should be the subject of Taxation. .

7) Drawbacks Of The Duties Which Are Imposed On The Materials Of Manufactures

It has already been observed as a general rule that duties on those materials ought with certain exceptions, to be forborne. Of these exceptions, three cases occur, which may serve as examples—one, where the material is itself an object of general or extensive consumption, and a fit and productive source of revenue: Another, where a manufacture of a simpler kind, the competition of which with a like domestic article is desired to be restrained, partakes of the Nature of a raw material, from being capable, by a further process to be converted into a manufacture of a different kind, the introduction or growth of which is desired to be encouraged; a third where the Material itself is a production of the country, and in sufficient abundance to furnish a cheap and plentiful supply to the national Manufacturers.

8) The Encouragement Of New Inventions And Discoveries, At Home, And Of The Introduction Into The United States Of Such As May Have Been Made In Other Countries; Particularly Those Which Relate To Machinery

. . . . The usual means of that encouragement are pecuniary rewards, and, for a time, exclusive privileges. The first must be employed according to the occasion, and the utility of the invention, or discovery. For the last, so far as respects "authors and inventors," provision has been made by Law . . . .

It is customary with manufacturing nations to prohibit, under severe penalties, the exportation of implements and machines, which they have either invented or improved. There are already objects for a similar regulation in the United States; and others may be expected to occur from time to time. The adoption of it seems to be dictated by the principle of reciprocity. Greater liberality, in such respects, might better comport with the general spirit of the country; but a selfish exclusive policy, in other quarters, will not always permit the free indulgence of a spirit which would place us upon an unequal footing. As far as prohibitions tend to prevent foreign competitors from deriving the benefit of the improvements made at home, they tend to increase the advantages of those by whom they may have been introduced, and operate as an encouragement to exertion.

9) Judicious Regulations For The Inspection Of Manufactured Commodities

. . . . Contributing to prevent frauds upon consumers at home and exporters to foreign countries, to improve the quality & preserve the character of the national manufactures, it cannot fail to aid the expeditious and advantageous sale of them, and to serve as a guard against successful competition from other quarters . . . .

10) The Facilitating Of Pecuniary Remittances From Place To Place

—is a point of considerable moment to trade in general, and to manufactures in particular; by rendering more easy the purchase of raw materials and provisions and the payment for manufactured supplies. A general circulation of Bank paper, which is to be expected from the institution lately established will be a most valuable mean to this end. .

11) The Facilitating Of The Transportation Of Commodities

The great copiousness of the subject of this Report has insensibly led to a more lengthy preliminary discussion than was originally contemplated, or intended. It appeared proper to investigate principles, to consider objections, and to endeavour to establish the utility of the thing proposed to be encouraged, previous to a specification of the objects which might occur, as meriting or requiring encouragement, and of the measures, which might be proper, in respect to each. The first purpose having been fulfilled, it remains to pursue the second.

In the selection of objects, five circumstances seem entitled to particular attention, the capacity of the Country to furnish the raw material—the degree in which the nature of the manufacture admits of a substitute for manual labour in machinery—the facility of execution—the extensiveness of the uses, to which the article can be applied—its subserviency to other interests, particularly the great one of national defence. There are however objects, to which these circumstances are little applicable, which for some special reasons, may have a claim to encouragement.

In countries where there is great private wealth, much may be effected by the voluntary contributions of patriotic individuals; but in a community situated like that of the United States, the public purse must supply the deficiency of private resource. In what can it be so useful, as in prompting and improving the efforts of industry?

The Nationalist Theory of International Trade

Robert Gilpin

Economic nationalists emphasize the costs of trade to particular groups and states and favor economic protectionism and state control over international trade. Their criticisms of liberal trade theory may be summarized in three broad categories: (1) the implications of free trade for economic development and the international division of labor, (2) relative rather than absolute gains (the distributive effects of trade), and (3) the effect on national autonomy and impact on domestic welfare.[1]

Although the roots of economic nationalism can be found in the mercantilist writers of the seventeenth and eighteenth centuries, Alexander Hamilton's *Report on the Subject of Manufactures,* presented to the U.S. House of Representatives in 179I, contains the intellectual origins of modern economic nationalism and the classic defense of economic protectionism.[2] Hamilton modernized the eighteenth-century mercantilist thesis and developed a dynamic theory of economic development based on the superiority of manufacturing over agriculture. He set forth what we today would call an "import substitution" strategy of economic development: "Not only the wealth, but the independence and security of a country, appear to be materially connected with the prosperity of manufactures. Every nation, with a view of these great objects, ought to endeavor to possess within itself, all the essentials of national supply. These comprise the means of subsistence, habitation, clothing, and defense".[3] From Hamilton on, nationalists have argued that the location of economic activities should be a central concern of state policy.

As the economic theorist of the first colony to revolt against a European imperial system, Hamilton's ideas are worth considering in some detail. According to Hamilton and subsequent proponents of economic nationalism, governments can transform the nature of their economies and thus their position in the international economy through what are now called "industrial policies." The transfer of the factors of production from more advanced economies can be encouraged to develop particular industries. Hamilton argued, for example, that the migration, especially of skilled labor, should be encouraged to expedite industrialization. The nation should also encourage the importation of foreign capital and should establish a banking system to provide investment capital. In short, Hamilton's *Report* set forth a dynamic theory of comparative advantage based on government policies of economic development .

Like other mercantilists before him, Hamilton identified national power with the development manufactures and regarded economics as subordinate the fundamental task

---

[1] Blackhurst, Richard, Nicolas Marian and Jan Tumlir. 1977. *Trade Liberalization, Protectionism and Interdependence.* Geneva: GATT Studies in International Trade, No. 5, pp. 29-42.

[2] Hamilton, Alexander. 1928 [1791]. "Report on the subject of Manufactures." In Arthur Harrison Cole, ed., *Industrial and Commercial Correspondence of Alexander Hamilton, Anticipating his Report on Manufacturing.* Chicago: A.W. Shaw Co.

[3] Ibid., p. 284.

of state building. Although his ideas on protectionism were not to achieve full force in America until the victory of the rapidly industrializing North in the Civil War, they exerted a powerful influence at home and abroad. Developing nations that emphasize protectionism, industrialization, and state intervention owe more than they may appreciate to Hamilton's conception of economic development.

In the nineteenth century Hamilton's ideas had their greatest impact in Germany, where the intellectual ground had already been prepared by Johann Fichte and Georg Hegel. Friedrich List, after a number of years in the United States, carried Hamilton's views to Germany. With Wilhelm Roscher, Gustav Schmoller, and others, List helped establish the German Historical School of economic analysis, whose ideas found ready acceptance in a Germany whose traditional industries were under attack by a flood of low-cost British imports. This school's fierce and systematic attack on liberalism had a powerful influence on the development of Germany and on the world economy generally.

In his influential *National System of Political Economy*,[4] List argued that the free trade theories of the classical British economists were the economic policy of the strong, that there was no "natural" or immutable international division of labor based on the law of comparative advantage, and that the division of labor was merely a historical situation resulting from prior uses of economic and political power. The British, List argued, had actually used the power of the state to protect their own infant industries against foreign competition while weakening their opponents by military force, and they only became champions of free trade after having achieved technological and industrial over their rivals.[5]

List believed that the British were merely seeking to advance their own national economic interests by gaining unimpeded access to foreign markets through free trade. He regarded British promotion of what is now called an "interdependent world economy" as another expression of Britain's selfish national interests and believed that a true cosmopolitan world economy as espoused by economic liberals would be possible only when other nations became equal to Britain in industrial power. List and other German economic nationalists advocated political unification, development of railroads to unify the economy physically, and erection of high tariff barriers to foster economic unification, protect the development of German industry, and thus create a powerful German state.

Many believed that the success of protectionism in Germany and the role of the state in German industrial development vindicated the theories of economic nationalism. As Thorstein Veblen argued in his classic study, *Imperial Germany and the Industrial Revolution*.[6] Germany was the first society to pursue a systematic industrial policy and the scientific development of its economy. The rapid advance of German wealth and military power in the latter part of the nineteenth century set an example for other societies. Whereas the economic success of Great Britain initially seemed to establish the virtues of liberalism, that of Germany legitimized the doctrine of economic nationalism as a guide to trade policy and economic development.

Proponents of economic nationalism at the end of the twentieth century again challenge the liberal assumption that comparative advantage is relatively static. They argue that the law of comparative advantage is primarily rationalization for the exist-

---

4. List, Friedrich. 1904 (1841). *The National System of Political Economy.* Trans. Sampson S. Lloyd. New York: Longmans, Green.

5. Condliffe, J.B. 1950. *The Commerce of Nations.* New York: W.W. Norton, p. 71.

6. Veblen, Thorstein. 1939. *Imperial Germany and the Industrial Revolution.* New York: Viking Press.

ing international division of labor and advocate a trade policy that encourages the development of preservation of domestic industry. On the one hand, nationalist emphasis on industrialization has, in the less developed economies, focused on the adoption of an "import-substitution" development strategy. On the other hand, a number of advanced countries, responding to the stunning success of the Japanese economy in the 1970s and 1980s, have adopted industrial policies designed to develop specific industrial sectors. These nationalist tendencies will be evaluated below.

Whereas economic liberals emphasize the absolute gains in global wealth from a regime of free trade, economic nationalists the nineteenth century and their twentieth-century descendants stress the international distribution of the gains from trade. Nationalists note that in a world of free trade the terms of trade tend to favor the most industrially advanced economy. The German Historical School asserted that the British pursued protectionist policies until British industry was strong enough to outcompete every other economy and that British technical superiority in manufactured products and processes enabled Great Britain to enjoy highly favorable terms of trade relative to the exporters of lower-technology products, food, and raw materials.

Economic nationalists also believe that free trade undermines national autonomy and state control over the economy by exposing the economy to the vicissitudes and instabilities of the world market and exploitation by other, more powerful economies. They argue that specialization, especially in commodity exports, reduces flexibility, increases the vulnerability of the economy to untoward events, subordinates the domestic economy to the international economy, and threatens domestic industries on which national security, established jobs, or other values are dependent. Although these arguments are frequently used to cloak the special interests of particular groups and industries, they are important in the formulation of national economic policy in all countries.

The economic nationalists of the German Historical School called attention to the ways in which the rise of a highly interdependent world economy affected national security, while nineteenth-century liberals were accurately arguing that the world had never before enjoyed a comparable era of peace and prosperity. The expansion of trade, the flow of foreign investment, and the efficiency of the international monetary system ushered in a period of economic growth that spread from England throughout the system. Perhaps never before or since has the cosmopolitan interest been so well joined to the national interest of the dominant power as under the Pax Britannica. But although all may indeed have gained, some did gain more than others, as the nationalists emphasized. The expansion of global economic interdependence created new forms of national insecurity and novel arenas of international conflict along with economic growth.

FREE TRADE VERSUS ECONOMIC PROTECTIONISM

Numerous controversies between liberal proponents of free trade and their nationalist critics have emerged with the intensification of international trade and interdependence since the 1850s. The issues are concerned with the effects of international trade on domestic welfare and industrial development, the economic and political effect of increasing interdependence, and the role of government policies and corporate power in the distribution of benefits as well as other crucial questions. Unfortunately, relatively little research has been done on many of these issues and there are serious problems in testing trade theories. As one authority put it, there is much room for disagreement over trade and its effects because most propositions have never been tested.[7] Indeed, the issues may never be resolved because the assumptions and objectives of the two positions are so different.

The issue of free trade versus protectionism lies at the heart of the conflict between economic liberals and economic nationalists. This debate historically has appeared in differing forms: the "infant" industry argument for protection, the debate over the benefits and costs of international specialization, and (for lack of a better term) the "senile" or perhaps the "second infancy" industry problem.[8] These three controversies are interrelated, but the following discussion will attempt to keep them separate.

Liberals believe that the historical record supports the superiority of a policy of free trade over protectionism. Great Britain, they point out, surpassed its rivals after I848 precisely because it adopted a policy of free trade. France, an industrial leader in the eighteenth century, fell behind because it resorted to high levels of protectionism and its industry then became inefficient.[9] Nationalists, on the other hand, note that Britain used force against its economic rivals and adopted free trade only after its industry had developed behind the shield of protectionism. As for Germany, it too protected its nascent industries from what has been characterized as the "imperialism of free trade," that is, the British effort to direct investment abroad away from competitive industries (Semmel, 1970).[10,11] The advantages of being first, nationalists argue, are aso great that industrialization requires the protection of infant industry.

In principle, both liberals and nationalists accept the rationale for protecting infant industries.[12] Both acknowledge that an industrial economy may have particular advantages over a nonindustrialized economy that make it very difficult for the latter to establish its own industries. In the words of John Stuart Mill, "there may be no inherent advantage on one part, or disadvantage on the other, but only a present superiority of acquired skill and experience. A country which has this skill and experience yet to acquire, may in other respects be better adapted to the production than those which were earlier in the field".[13]

Liberals and nationalists disagree fundamentally, however, on the specific purpose of protectionism as it relates to infant industries. For liberals, protectionism is in the nature of an experiment to test whether a nation really does have an inherent comparative advantage in a particular industry. Mill said "it is essential that the protection should be confined to cases in which there is good ground of assurance that the industry which it fosters will after a time be able to dispense with it; nor should the domestic producers ever be allowed

---

7. Dixit, Avinash K. 1983. "Tax Policy in Open Economies." Discussion Papers in Economics, No. 51. Woodrow Wilson School, Princeton University, p.80.

8. Dixit, Avinash K. 1986. "Trade Policy: An Agenda for Research." In Krugman, Paul R., ed. 1986. *Strategic Trade Policy and the New International Economics.* Cambridge: MIT Press, Chapter 12.

9. Kindleberger, Charles P. 1978. *Economic Response: Comparative Studies in Trade, Finance, and Growth.* Cambridge: Harvard University Press, ch. 3.

10. Semmel, Bernard. 1970. *The Rise of Free Trade Imperialism: Classical Political Economy, the Empire of Free Trade, and Imperialism, 1750-1850.* Cambridge: Cambridge University Press.

11. The concept of the "imperialism of free trade," developed by Gallagher and Robinson (1953), is that free trade is but another form of economic imperialism (Gallagher, John, and Ronald Robinson. 1953. "The Imperialism of Free Trade," *Economic History Review*, 2nd ser., 6: 1-15).

12. Corden, W.M. 1974. *Trade Policy and Economic Welfare.* Oxford: Clarendon Press, ch. 9.

13. Mill, John Stuart. 1970 [1848]. *Principles of Political Economy.* Baltimore: Penguin Books, pp. 283-84.

to expect that it will be continued to them beyond the time necessary for a fair trial of what they are capable of accomplishing".[14] Liberals regard protectionism at best as a necessary but temporary expedient and as a stepping stone to a system of free trade.

Economic nationalists, on the other hand, tend to regard protectionism as an end in itself. The nationalist's foremost objectives, at least in the short run, are not free trade and wealth accumulation but state building and industrial power. In most developing countries industrialization is the primary goal of national policy, and the fundamental purpose of a tariff is to establish particular industries frequently without regard to the economic rationale for doing so.

Economic nationalists assume the superiority of industry over both agriculture and commodity production. Industry is believed to be not only valuable in itself because it contributes a high value-added to national production, but it is alleged to have powerful secondary effects, positive externalities, and "backward linkages" or spinoffs that stimulate the entire economy and speed overall economic development[15] Its effects on the quality of the work force, business entrepreneurship, and the overall options of the society make industrialization an objective in its own right.

In response to the nationalist argument for protection, liberals argue that every economy has a comparative advantage in something and therefore should not fear free trade. Through each doing what it can do best, regardless of what that is, everyone can gain. Thus, in anticipation of the nationalist contention that the advent of intra-industrial trade and the application of industrial organization theory to trade gives aid and comfort to the nationalist defense of protectionism, Krugman has defended letting the market determine international specialization and trade patterns:

> But who produces what? Can we say anything about the direction of trade? Obviously not: by ruling out comparative advantage we have made the question of who exports what indeterminate. In any case, it doesn't matter. To realize the gains from trade, all that matters is that countries specialize in producing different things. Whether Germany produces large refrigerators and France small ones, or vice versa, is not important; that they do not each produce both types is.[16]

For nationalists, however, who produces what is of the utmost importance. What concerns them is precisely the international location of those economic activities that, in their judgment, contribute most to the political position and overall development of the economy. In a world in which comparative advantage is highly arbitrary and where, again to quote Krugman,[17] "the other interesting point is that the outcome of the process of specialization may depend on initial conditions. . . . History matters. A country, having once been established as an exporter in some industry, may maintain this position simply because of the economies of scale gained—unless comparative advantage moves far enough away." The nationalist can find in this statement ample support for the protection of infant industries.

The traditional nationalist defense of infant industry protection has been joined in recent years by the prospect of strategic trade policy, to be discussed later in this chapter.

---

14. Ibid., p. 284.

15. Cornwall, John. 1977. *Modern Capitalism: Its Growth and Transformation.* New York: St. Martin's Press.

16. Krugman, Paul R. 1981. "Economies of Scale, Imperfect Competition, and Trade: An Exposition." Unpublished, p. 10.

17. Ibid., p. 19.

Whereas infant industry protection is largely defensive, strategic trade policy is essentially offensive. Its central message is "import protection for export promotion." Through the erection of entry barriers, the use of government subsidies, and the husbanding of domestic demand to give advantage to domestic firms, one's own corporations can acquire the economies of scale and other advantages that will enable them to dominate world markets. In the modern world of intra-industry trade, the line between defensive infant industry protection and strategic trade policy has become very thin indeed.

The outcome of the debate over the protection of industries is indeterminate. As List and more recent authors have noted, every country has protected its industries to some extent in the early stages of industrialization. Contemporary developments in trade theory have provided a new and additional rationale for this protectionism. Yet it does not follow that protectionism necessarily leads to the development of a viable industrial structure. Indeed, in many instances protectionism has demonstrably hindered the development of an efficient industrial base, for example, import-substitution strategies have proved bankrupt in many less developed economies. The success of strategic trade policy, as exemplified by the commercial difficulties of the European Airbus consortium, has yet to prove its worth. The whole issue of free trade versus protection does not lend itself to easy answers.

Considering only the issue of infant industry protection, one may conclude that trade can be both a destroyer and an engine of growth.[18] The superior competitiveness of industry in advanced economies can wipe out economic sectors in less developed economies, as happened to the historic Indian handicraft textile industry. But as a rapidly industrializing India and other NICs have demonstrated, trade between advanced and less developed economies can also be an important source of economic growth for the latter. The developing country's response to the opportunities provided by the international trading system is critically important.

It is worth noting that nationalists are myopic in their evaluation of trade and protectionism when they stress the inequitable international distributive effects of free trade while overlooking the domestic distributive effects of protectionism.[19] The domestic consequence of protectionism is a redistribution of income from consumers and society as a whole to the protected producers and the state. Liberals correctly note that protectionism creates economic rents that these latter interests collect.[20] Economic nationalism thus may be viewed as sacrificing the welfare of the whole society to that of particular groups. It is an alliance of the state with producer interests and, for this reason, the primary proponents of protectionist doctrine tend to be state bureaucracies and domestic producers whose economic interests lie with the protected industrial sectors.

---

18. Gould, J.D. 1972. *Economic Growth in History: Survey and Analysis.* London: Methuen, ch. 4.

19. Johnson, Harry G., ed. 1967. *Economic Nationalism in Old and New States.* Chicago: University of Chicago Press.

20. A "rent" is defined by economists as "a payment to a resource owner above the amount his resources could command in their next best alternative use. An economic rent is a receipt in excess of the opportunity cost of a resource" (Tollison, Robert D. 1982. "Rent-Seeking: A Survey." *Kyklos* 35: 575-602). They are "earned only by the owners of resources that cannot be augmented rapidly and at low cost to meet an increased demand for the goods they are used to produce" (Posner, Richard. 1977. *Economic Analysis of Law.* 2nd. ed. Boston: Little, Brown). Land and skills are good examples. In the modern world a technological monopoly can produce rent or technological profits. This fact is central to the debate over what is called strategic trade policy.

The more important consideration, however, is that liberals and nationalists have different objectives and judge the success of policies by different standards. Liberals judge trade and protectionism in terms of consumer welfare and the maximization of global efficiency. Nationalists stress what they consider be producer and state interests.

Liberals and nationalists also divide on the benefits and costs of specialization. From Adam Smith on, liberals have believed that specialization and an expanding market lead to increased efficiencies in production and hence to a more rapid rate of economic growth. They also believe that the long-term benefits of specialization and free trade outweigh any associated costs, because national specialization based on comparative advantage will maximize both domestic and international economic welfare. Economic nationalists, stressing the costs of international specialization and increasing interdependence, believe those costs to range from the loss of national sovereignty to an enhanced vulnerability of national welfare to the negative impact of foreign developments.

In this debate over the benefits and costs of specialization, the fact that the industries most vital for national security and military power are frequently the ones most involved in international trade is significant.[21] Furthermore, import-sensitive industries frequently are major providers of domestic employment. Thus, specialization and changes in specialization raise fundamental issues of national concern.

The clash between liberals and nationalists over the benefits and costs of specialization, although partially based on differing economic and political objectives, also rests on differing assumptions regarding the nature of international economic relations. Liberals consider these relations to be essentially harmonious; nationalists believe that conflict is inevitable. As will be argued below, neither assumption is valid in itself. Rather, its validity rests on the larger configuration of global economic and political conditions at a particular time. The degree of harmony or disharmony is dependent upon the extent of complementarity of trade as well as the overall political relations among trading nations. Liberal trading practices flourish best when governed by a liberal hegemonic power or agreement among dominant liberal states.

Another controversy regarding free trade and protectionism may be labeled the "senile" or declining industry argument; this assumes that there are certain advantages to backwardness or disadvantages to being first.[22] As newly industrializing countries catch up with older industrial countries, the former enjoy the benefits of lower wage rates, of being able to adopt advanced and efficient technologies, and other advantages.[23] Industry in the older industrial country therefore needs protection against the aggressive and "unfair" tactics of the newcomer. Whereas liberals reject the protection of inefficient declining industries as a wasteful diversion of scarce resources from investment in more promising growth industries, nationalists employ a variety of stratagems to defend declining industrial sectors. Arguments put forth include the need to protect industrial sectors vital to national security and emotional appeals to save jobs threatened by the unfair practices of foreign competitors. Although there may be occasions when such arguments have

---

21. Condliffe, J.B. 1950. *The Commerce of Nations.* New York: W.W. Norton, p. 799.

22. Rostow, W.W. 1980. *Why the Poor Get Richer and the Rich Slow Down: Essays in the Marshallian Long Period.* Austin: University of Texas Press.

23. Gershenkron, Alexander. 1962. *Economic Backwardness in Historical Perspective, A Book of Essays.* Cambridge: Belknap Press of Harvard University Press.

validity, in most cases the real purpose of protectionism is to safeguard particular threatened inefficient industries.

In the 1980s an effort has been made by certain economists, including some of a liberal persuasion, to develop a rationale for protecting senile industries that is complementary to the argument for protecting infant industries.[24] They argue that the usual disadvantages of being first have been enhanced by the increasingly rapid rate of global changes in comparative advantage and the intensified impact of external shocks. They note that with the quadrupling of the price of energy in 1973, the existing capital stock of all advanced countries was made obsolete and consumer preferences were suddenly transformed. Further, adjustment to these rapid and massive changes has been retarded and transition costs are aggravated by low rates of economic growth, domestic economic rigidities, and market imperfections. It is argued that the transition costs of phasing out older industries in favor of newer ones have grown so much that the costs of adjusting to rapid change may exceed its benefits. Furthermore, business investment may be discouraged if overly rapid obsolescence and intense foreign competition make it impossible for a business to capture the benefits of the investment. Under these circumstances, an industry may find itself caught 'in a process of change and adaptation so profound as to put it in a position akin to that of an infant industry," for example, American automobile manufacturing.[25] The state, therefore, should develop an industrial policy to cushion the effects on the economy of untoward external developments.

More generally, there are those who argue that both liberalization of trade and industrial specialization have reached a point of diminishing returns, causing a shift in the benefits and costs of free trade. Although traditional trade theory maintains that the benefits of trade and specialization will always be greater than its costs, it has assumed a relatively slow rate of change in comparative advantage so that displacement of workers is gradual and associated adjustment costs are low. At the end of the twentieth century, however, the liberalization of trade, the increasing number of sellers, and the dynamic nature of comparative advantage have greatly accelerated the rate of industrial change and thus raised adjustment costs.

Some liberal economists argue that specialization based on considerations of static comparative advantage has even become extremely risky in a highly uncertain world where governments constantly intervene in the market.[26] Specialization makes the welfare of the society vulnerable to the market and to political forces beyond national control. In the past this situation was applicable only to the producers of raw materials, but now it applies increasingly to industrial producers as well. Some argue that the solution to this increased uncertainty and rapid rate of change might be is for the country to develop a "portfolio" of industries and protective tariffs that will reduce the cost and risk of specialization. A major purpose of industrial policy is to ensure that the nation does not put all of its eggs in one industrial basket and does develop an optimum level of foreign trade.

To summarize, economic nationalists criticize the liberal doctrine of free trade because the doctrine is politically naive and fails to appreciate the extent to which the

---

24. Whitman sets forth the rationale for protecting "senile" or mature industries. (Whitman, Marina v. N. 1981. "International Trade and Investment: Two Perspectives." *Essays in International Finance, No. 143.* International Finance Section. Department of Economics. Princeton University).

25. Ibid., p. 22.

26. Brainard, William C., and Richard N. Cooper. 1968. "Uncertainty and Diversification in International Trade." *Studies in Agricultural Economics, Trade, and Development* 8: 257–85.

terms of trade and the rules governing trade are determined by the exercise of power, because the doctrine is static and slights the problem of adjustment costs, and because it ignores the problems of uncertainty in its stress on the benefits of specialization. Despite these serious limitations, however, liberal trade theory retains its essential validity; it cannot be dismissed simply as a rationalization of the interests of the strong. Although trade does tend to benefit the strong, at least in short-run terms, all can gain in absolute terms and some gain both relatively and absolutely, as is seen in the present-day examples of Japan and the NICs. It is important to remember that when the world has reverted to nationalist trade policies, as it did in the 1930s, everyone has lost. The ultimate defense of free trade, as Smith pointed out, is that there are benefits for all from a territorially based international division of labor.

As one would expect from economic theory itself, there are both costs and benefits to free trade, and tradeoffs always exist. These must be considered by every nation as it formulates its commercial policy; no nation has yet chosen to pursue either an exclusively free trade or an exclusively nationalistic policy. A nation's mix of these two policies is a function of its domestic economy and of world economy. The interplay of these domestic and international factors has produced swings between liberal and nationalist trade regimes over the past two hundred years. In the late twentieth century, an analysis of the postwar regime of liberalized trade reveals that the pendulum is once again swinging in the direction of economic nationalism.

Until the early 1970s, the history of the postwar trading system was one of increasing liberalization. Led by the American hegemon, the major trading nations moved in the direction of the precepts of liberal trade theory. With the relative decline of American power and the development of adverse economic conditions, this movement was reversed. By the mid-1980s, economic nationalism had become a potent force in global trading relations. To appreciate this change and its significance, one must begin with the General Agreement on Tariffs and Trade (GATT)

Introduction to Hegemonic Stability Theory[1]

In the previous selection, Gilpin provided a number of arguments in favor of economic nationalism (mercantilism), suggesting that a state will naturally seek to maximize its relative wealth and power by imposing protectionist tariffs or other such measures regulating foreign trade. After reviewing these arguments, Gilpin poses a question for consideration: given the anarchic, self-help environment framed by the realist intellectual tradition, we would expect to see a great deal of mercantilism, and yet we do not. Instead, we have economic cooperation in many forms throughout the world. Why is this? His answer to this questions leads to an exploration of Hegemonic Stability Theory, which focuses on the role of a hegemon in providing a liberal trade order.

As Gilpin observes, the expression 'theory of hegemonic stability' was coined by Robert Keohane (1980). 'Hegemony' comes from the Greek word for political leadership. In short, a hegemon is a dominant state—the largest, most powerful state in a given international system. Consequently, a hegemon will have a strong incentive to "shape" the international environment to its liking. Thus, Hegemonic Stability Theory (or HST) "interprets the rise and operation of the modern international economy in terms of successive liberal dominant powers."[2]

When Gilpin's book—*The Political Economy of International Relations*—was published in 1987, the United States appeared to be in decline as a great power, losing the economic race to Japan and Europe. The world economic order was in transition, moving away from post-World War II cooperation and liberalism, and moving toward protectionism and economic nationalism. While Gilpin's primary intent was to explore the changes occurring in the international political economy, he also wanted to explore the themes of "economic hegemony, the dynamics of the world economy, and the tendency of economic activity over the long term to transform the structure of the international political system."[3] Given that realists have difficulty explaining cooperation (and since Gilpin himself is a political realist), he wanted to discover the reasons why states would cooperate in the economic arena.

The following selection of *Understanding International Relations* is excerpted from chapter three of Gilpin's book. In that chapter, entitled "The Dynamics of the International Political Economy," he described three contemporary theories of International Political Economy: the "theory of the dual economy," derived principally from economic liberalism; the theory of the "Modern World System", (MWS), which was strongly influenced by Marxism; and the theory of "Hegemonic Stability," which closely but not completely mirrors mercantilism. While Gilpin asserts that these three theories account for "the emer-

---

1. revised April 24, 2004: J. Forest

2. Robert Gilpin, *The Political Economy of International Relations*, (Princeton, NJ: Princeton University Press, 1987), p. 66, note 1 and p.88.

3. Ibid., p. xiv.

gence, expansion, and functioning of the international political economy,"[4] only the latter theory is featured here.

As noted earlier, Gilpin is not the original author of Hegemonic Stability Theory; instead, he takes elements from the works of Charles Kindleberger (1973) and Robert Keohane (1980) and synthesizes these together with his own work. He is careful to point out that there is limited historical evidence from which to draw conclusions since there have been only two liberal hegemons in modern history, Great Britain and the United States (although he acknowledges in a footnote that some do consider 17th century Holland as a hegemon as well).[5] Despite that caveat, he concludes that the theory is quite useful for explaining and understanding the international political economy.

Through Gilpin's focus on the liberal hegemon's behavior, and given the reasonable assumption that an "open and liberal world economy" would result in greater cooperation, Hegemonic Stability Theory addresses both of our central questions: "Why do states do what they do?" and "What causes cooperation and conflict among states?" Three groups of hypotheses are easily derived from this reading. First, Gilpin begins by identifying the requirements for a "open and liberal world economy" (i.e., cooperation). Given that cooperation and/or conflict is this text's traditional dependent variable, it is logical to consider those "requirements" as independent variables.

Second, Gilpin's analysis of HST focuses primarily on the actions of one particular type of state: a liberal hegemon. Using the past cases of "cooperation," Gilpin identifies what behavior one would expect from these states in a specific environment (i.e., a liberal trading order). These roles and responsibilities will serve as dependent variables. Finally, Gilpin asks what happens to the level of cooperation or conflict (i.e., dependent variable) as a hegemon declines (i.e., independent variable).

Given the United States' position as a hegemon (or perhaps a hegemon in decline) this theory's value cannot be understated. For example, with U.S. engagements in such places as Afghanistan, Bosnia, Haiti, Indonesia, Iraq and Kosovo, several questions come to mind. For example: "Why does the U.S. always have to be the world's policeman?" and "What would happen to international cooperation if the U.S. abandoned its role as the global hegemon?" Hegemonic Stability Theory helps us formulate answers to such questions in developing our understanding of international relations.

QUESTIONS FOR DISCUSSION AND DEBATE

- What does Hegemonic Stability Theory suggest about long-term international stability or conflict?
- Why does the hegemon eventually decline?
- If a state is a liberal hegemon, what does it do to provide international stability?
- If a state is not a hegemon but is in a hegemonic system, what sort of state behavior modifications would you expect to see?
- If the international system lacks a liberal hegemon, what does this theory suggest about the potential for international conflict or cooperation?

---

4. Ibid., p. 65.

5. Ibid., 73 and note 8.

The Theory of Hegemonic Stability

Robert Gilpin

According to the theory of hegemonic stability as set forth initially by Charles Kindleberger (although he preferred the term "leadership" or "responsibility"), an open and liberal world economy requires the existence of a hegemonic or dominant power. In the words of Robert Keohane, the theory "holds that hegemonic structures of power, dominated by a single country, are most conducive to the development of strong international regimes whose rules are relatively precise and well obeyed. . . .the decline of hegemonic structures of power can be expected to presage a decline in the strength of corresponding international economic regimes"[1]. The hegemonic power is both able and willing to establish and maintain the norms and rules of a liberal economic order, and with its decline the liberal economic order is greatly weakened.

The key word in the preceding paragraph is "liberal," that is, the theory relates to the existence of an international economy based on the precepts of the free market such as openness and nondiscrimination. The theory does not argue that an international economy would be unable to exist and function in the absence of hegemony. International economies obviously have always existed in one form or another. Rather, it argues that a particular type of international economic order, a liberal one, could not flourish and reach its full development other than in the presence of such a hegemonic power.

The mere existence of a hegemonic power, however, is not sufficient to ensure the development of a liberal international economy. In addition, the hegemon itself must be committed to the values of liberalism or, to use John Ruggie's language, its *social purpose* and domestic distribution of power must be favorably disposed toward a liberal international order.[2] The domestic economic structures of the hegemon and of other societies are obviously important determinants of the disposition of states toward a liberal international economy.[3] Hegemony without a liberal commitment to the market economy is more likely to lead to imperial systems and the imposition of political and economic restrictions on lesser powers, for example, the Soviet bloc today. And, finally, "a congruence of social purpose" in support of a liberal system must exist among the major economic powers.[4] Other powerful states must also have an interest in the growth of market relations; the hegemon can encourage but cannot compel other powerful states to follow the rules of an open world economy. Thus, three prerequisites—hegemony,

---

1. Keohane, Robert O. 1980. "The Theory of Hegemonic Stability and Changes in International Economic Regimes, 1967-1977." in Holsti et al., 1980, *Change in the International System* (Westview Press) Chapter 6, p. 132.

2. Ruggie, John Gerard. 1982. "International Regimes, Transactions, and Change: Embedded Liberalism in the Postwar Economic Order." *International Organization* 36: p. 382.

3. Katzenstein, Peter J. 1976. "International Relations and Domestic Structures: Foreign Economic Policies of Advanced Industrial States." *International Organization* 30: 1-45.

4. Ruggie, 1982, p. 384.

liberal ideology, and common interests—must exist for the emergence and expansion of the liberal market system.[5]

Hegemony or leadership is based on a general belief in its legitimacy at the same time that it is constrained by the need to maintain it; other states accept the rule of the hegemon because of its prestige and status in the international political system.[6] A considerable degree of ideological consensus, or what Marxists following Antonio Gramsci would call "ideological hegemony," is required if the hegemon is to have the necessary support of other powerful states.[7] If other states begin to regard the actions of the hegemon as self-serving and contrary to their own political and economic interests, the hegemonic system will be greatly weakened. It will also deteriorate if the citizenry of the hegemonic power believes that other states are cheating, or if the costs of leadership begin to exceed the perceived benefits. In such situations, powerful groups become less and less willing to subordinate their interests to the continuation of the systems.

Historically, the conjuncture of circumstances favorable to hegemonic leadership and the emergence of a liberal world economy has occurred only twice. The first was the era of the *Pax Britannica* that extended from the end of the Napoleonic Wars to the outbreak of the First World War. With the political triumph of the middle class, committed to the ideology of liberalism, Great Britain used its influence to usher in the age of free trade. The example of British economic success, the general acceptance of liberal ideals among the major economic powers, and the recognized benefits of trade encouraged states to negotiate tariff reductions and to open their borders to the world market.[8] Similarly, the United States took the lead in promoting a liberal international economic order following the Second World War. The General Agreement on Tariffs and Trade (GATT) and the International Monetary Fund (IMF), embodying liberal principles, were established by the United States and its allies. American leadership was exercised subsequently in the reduction of trade barriers. During these eras of British and American preeminence the international market and global economic interdependence expanded.[9]

As formulated originally by Kindleberger and subsequently extended and modified by others, including this writer, the theory of hegemonic stability argues that an open market economy constitutes a collective or public good.[10] Such a good "is one the consumption of which by an individual, household, or firm does not reduce the amount available for other potential consumers."[11] A road or a sidewalk is a prime example. However, because an

---

5. These conditions are treated in greater detail in Gilpin, Robert. 1982. "Trade, Investment, and Technology Policy." in Giersch, Herbert, 1984. "The Age of Schumpeter." *American Economic Review* 74 (May): 103-109.

6. Frohlich, Norman, Joe A. Oppenheimer, and Oran R. Young. 1971. *Political Leadership and Collective Goods.* Princeton: Princeton University Press.

7. Keohane, Robert O. 1984. *After Hegemony: Cooperation and Discord in the World Political Economy.* Princeton: Princeton University Press, pp. 44-45.

8. Kindleberger, Charles P. 1978. *Economic Response: Comparative Studies in Trade, Finance, and Growth.* Cambridge: Harvard University Press, chapter 3.

9. A number of writers identify Holland in the seventeenth century as a hegemonic power, but the case is not a convincing one. Although Holland certainly was the leading economy, it did not exercise influence over the international system comparable to Great Britain in the nineteenth and the United States in the twentieth century. The seventeenth century, it should be recalled, was the height of the first mercantilist era.

10. Olson, Mancur, 1965. *The Logic of Collective Action: Public Goods and the Theory of Groups.* Cambridge: Harvard University Press.

individual can "consume" the good without paying for it, collective goods tend to be underprovided unless the interests of some actor cause it to assume a disportionate share of the costs or some agency (e.g., government) exists that can force consumers to pay for the good.

In the realm of international relations, a number of collective goods are said to exist. An open and liberal trading regime based on the Most-Favored Nation (MFN) principle of nondiscrimination and unconditional reciprocity—that is, a tariff concession made to one country must be extended to others—is an example of such a collective good.[12] Another frequently cited example is a stable international currency, because it facilitates commerce from which everyone can benefit. A third, and more debatable, collective good is the provision of international security.[13] Individual states, the argument runs, can enjoy these collective goods whether or not they contribute to the maintenance of the good.

According to the theory, *the hegemon or leader has the responsibility to guarantee provision of the collective goods of an open trading system and stable currency.* The theory assumes that a liberal economic system cannot be self-sustaining but must be maintained over the long term through the actions of the dominant economy. An open world economy is particularly threatened by the "free rider" problem, wherein cheaters benefit from the collective goods but refuse to pay their "fair" share toward providing it.[14] Also, particular states attempt to advance their interests at the expense of others, for example, by exploiting a monopolistic position. According to the theory of hegemonic stability, these temptations to cheat and exploit others too frequently overwhelm the liberal argument that a hegemon is unnecessary because trade is by definition of mutual benefit.

The hegemonic economy, according to the theory of hegemonic stability, performs several roles crucial to the operation of the world economy. It uses its influence to create international regimes defined simply as "principles, norms, rules, and decision-making procedures around which actor expectations converge in a given issue-area."[15] The regime prescribes legitimate and proscribes illegitimate behavior in order to limit conflict, ensure equity, or facilitate agreement.[16] The hegemonic power must prevent cheating and free riding, enforce the rules of a liberal economy, and encourage others to share the costs of maintaining the system. The gold standard of the nineteenth century and the postwar Bretton Woods system are notable examples of an economic regime in which the hegemon establishes and enforces the rules of a liberal market regime and suppresses the ever-present tendencies toward economic nationalism.

---

11. Kindleberger, Charles P. 1981. "Dominance and Leadership in the International Economy: Exploitation, Public Goods, and Free Rides," *International Studies Quarterly* 25: 242-54, p. 243.

12. The term "unconditional reciprocity" means that concessions made to one member of the GATT are automatically available to all other members. Thus, it is very close to the Most-Favored Nation principle. "Conditional reciprocity," on the other hand, means that concessions are made only to those other parties who specifically reciprocate.

13. Jervis, Robert. 1982. "Security Regimes." *International Organization* 36: 357-78.

14. Frey, Bruno. 1984. *International Political Economics.* New York: Basil Blackwell, chapter 7.

15. Krasner, Stephen D. 1982. "Structural Causes and Regime Consequences: Regimes as Intervening Variables." *International Organization* 36: 185-205.

16. Keohane, Robert O. 1982. "The Demand for International Regimes." *International Organization* 36: p. 354.

As Kindleberger has argued, "for the world economy to be stable, it needs a stabilizer, some country that would undertake to provide a market for distress goods, a steady if not countercyclical flow of capital, and a rediscount mechanism for providing liquidity when the monetary system is frozen in panic."[17] The hegemon must also prevent states with monopoly power from exploiting others. It must also encourage states that at least initially would lose from free trade to remove their trade barriers.[18]

Furthermore, in a world of flexible exchange rates and integrated capital markets, the hegemon "must also manage, in some degree, the structure of foreign-exchange rates and provide a degree of coordination of domestic monetary policies."[19] If there were no hegemonic power to create and manage international regimes, this theory suggests, the international economy would become unstable as liberalism and free trade gave way to the forces of economic nationalism.[20]

In addition, the growth and dynamism of the hegemonic power serve as an example of the benefits of the market system and perform as an engine of growth for the rest of the system; its imports stimulate the growth of other economies and its investments provide developing countries with the financing needed for growth. Through the process of technology transfer and knowledge diffusion, it also supplies developing economies with the technology and technical expertise required for their industrialization and economic development. This role of the hegemon in the global process of economic growth is a cement that helps hold the system together; when this growth declines, centrifugal forces increasingly manifest themselves.[21]

Although the two hegemons in the modern world have in turn been the dominant military state in the international system, they have radiated their influence largely through the exercise of economic power. The hegemon, in the words of Robert Keohane, "must have control over raw materials, control over sources of capital, control over markets, and competitive advantages in the production of highly valued goods."[22] The hegemon is provided with the means of leadership over other economies through control of financial capital, particular technologies, and natural resources.

Thus, although hegemonic leadership benefits those economies able to take advantage of liberalized exchange, an interdependent world economy also creates external vulnerabilities and a nexus of power relations. As Hirschman[23] has written, the essence of economic power, or at least one form of it, is the capacity to interrupt commercial intercourse. The actual or threatened cutoff of trade, finance, or technology can be a potent means of leverage over other states. The ability of the hegemon to

---

17. Kindleberger, 1981, p. 247.

18. Johnson, Harry G. 1976, *Trade Negotiations and the New International monetary System*. Graduate Institute of International Studies, Geneva, and the Trade Policy Research Centre, London. (Leiden: A.W. Sijthoff), pp. 17, 20.

19. Kindleberger, 1981, p. 247.

20. Keohane (1984a) provides a critique of the reasoning that a hegemonic power is necessary for the creation and preservation of a liberal international economy.

21. I am indebted to Robert Walker for this observation.

22. Keohane (1984), *op. cit.* p. 32.

23. Hirschman, Albert O. 1945. *National Power and the Structure of Foreign Trade*. Berkeley: University of California Press, p. 16.

exercise its power through the mechanisms of economic interdependence contributes to its governance and management of the international market economy, but, as will be pointed out below, it also enables the hegemon to exploit its dominant position.[24]

The relatively large size of the hegemon's market is a source of considerable power and enables it to create an economic sphere of influence.[25] The hegemon can gain influence over other states by opening its market to "friendly" states or denying access to "unfriendly ones." Although the utility of economic sanctions tends to be greatly exaggerated, they are the foremost example of this power.[26] As will be discussed later, the United States has also extended its hegemonic power considerably through the overseas expansion of its powerful multinational corporations.

The central role of the hegemon's currency in the international monetary system provides it with financial and monetary power. Both Great Britain in the nineteenth century and, to a much greater extent, the United States in the twentieth have used to their own advantage the right of seigniorage "which is the profit that comes to the seigneur, or sovereign power, from the issuance of money."[27] The United States has also employed its financial power to reward friends with access to capital markets and to punish enemies through the denial of access. Also, in the case of the United States, the financial perquisites of the hegemon have been crucial to its ability to maintain its dominant position and domestic prosperity into the 1980s.

The ultimate basis of the economic strength of the hegemon is the flexibility and mobility of its economy.[28] In the long term, economic power is neither the possession of particular monopolies and/or technologies nor economic self-sufficiency, but rather the capacity of the economy to transform itself and to respond to changes in the global economic environment, such as shifts in comparative advantage or price changes. The inflexibility of the British economy in the late nineteenth century in response to the rise of new industrial powers was an important cause of its decline.[29] Similarly, the difficulties experienced by the United States during the closing decades of the twentieth century in adjusting to profound shifts in the global location of industry and

---

24. The relationship of interdependence and power is a complex one. In part this is the case because "interdependence" has so many meanings. Cooper (1985, pp. 1196–1200) explores numerous aspects of this subject in "Economic Interdependence and Coordination of Economic Policies" in Ronald W. Jones and Peter B. Kenen, eds., *Handbook of International Economics* (Amsterdam: North-Holland, 1985), Vol. 2, chapter 23, pp. 1196–1200.

25. The concept of an economic sphere of influence is an interesting but undeveloped one. It is found, for example, in the writings of Alfred Marshall. See Nazli Chourcri, "International Political Economy: A Theoretical Perspective" in Holsti, 1980 (see footnote 1), p. 110, for a brief discussion of the subject.

26. In recent years much has been written on economic sanctions and related topics. My own view that economic sanctions are of little utility is discussed in Gilpin "Structural Constraints on Economic Leverage: Market-type Systems," in Gordon H. McCormack and Richard E. Bissell, eds., Strategic Dimensions of Economic Behavior, Chapter 6 (New York: Praeger, 1984). David Baldwin: *Economic Statecraft* (Princeton: Princeton University Press, 1985) and G. C. Hufbauer and Jeffrey J. Schott: *Economic Sanctions Reconsidered: History and Current Policy* (Washington: Institute for International Economics, 1985) are the best and most extensive recent examinations of the subject.

27. Kindleberger, 1981, p. 248.

28. Hawtrey, Ralph G. 1952. *Economic Aspects of Sovereignty.* London: Longmans.

29. Lewis, W. Arthur. 1978. *Growth and Fluctuations,* 1870-1913. London: George Allen and Unwin, p. 133.

the revolution in the price of energy have undermined its power and international position.[30]

Although a favorable political environment is required for the release and development of market forces, the international market tends to operate according to a logic of its own. As noted above, economic competition and the price mechanism drive the market economy toward ever higher levels of productive efficiency, economic growth, and the integration of national markets. In time, the market produces profound shifts in the location of economic activities and affects the international redistribution of economic and industrial power. The unleashing of market forces transforms the political framework itself, undermines the hegemonic power, and creates a new political environment to which the world must eventually adjust. With the inevitable shift in the international distribution of economic and military power from the core to rising nations in the periphery and elsewhere, the capacity of the hegemon to maintain the system decreases. Capitalism and the market system thus tend to destroy the political foundations on which they must ultimately depend.

Although both Great Britain and the United States accelerated their relative decline through their own actions, the hegemonic system is ultimately unstable.[31] For internal and external reasons, the hegemonic power loses its will and its ability to manage the system. Domestic consumption (both public and private) and the costs of defending the system militarily rise relative to national savings and productive investment, as seen in the case of the United States.[32] The hegemon grows weary and frustrated with the free riders and the fact that its economic partners are gaining more from liberalized trade than it is. More efficient, dynamic, and competitive economies rise that undercut the hegemon's international position and the economic surplus that had financed the costs of global hegemony.[33] In time, the hegemon becomes less able and willing to manage and stabilize the economic system. Thus, an inherent contradiction exists in a liberal world economy: the operation of the market system transforms the economic structure and diffuses power, thereby undermining the political foundations of that structure.

The important and interesting question of how hegemonic decline can be inevitable, given the alleged overwhelming power of the hegemon, lies beyond the scope of this book. Suffice it to say that although all dominant powers must one day decline, they display great differences in their longevity. Venice may be said to have been the hegemonic economic power of the western Mediterranean for a millennium; British hegemony lasted over a century; and American hegemony was in decline after a brief three decades.[34]

As Kindleberger suggests (in part echoing Cooper's views discussed earlier), renewed economic stability requires either a new hegemon, an agreed-upon set of rules binding all (including the weakened hegemon), or continuous policy coordination among the reigning

---

30. Kindleberger (1962), in *Foreign Trade and the National Economy* (New Haven: Yale University Press), chapter 7, analyzes the problem of economic transformation and its importance for adjustment to economic change.

31. Kindleberger, 1981, p. 251.

32. Oye, Kenneth A., Robert J. Lieber, and Donald Rothchild, eds., 1983, *Eagle Defiant: United States Foreign Policy in the 1980's,* (Boston: Little Brown), chapter 1.

33. Some speculations on these matters are presented in Gilpin, Robert 1981. War *and Change in World Politics.* New York: Cambridge University Press.

34. *Ibid.*

economic powers.[35] The declining hegemon may also seek, as did the Reagan Administration, to reassert its dominant economic and political position. If none of these options materializes, the liberal system begins to break down. Although no particular outcome is inevitable, the theory suggests that the world economy will be increasingly characterized by economic conflicts.

The extent of these conflicts depends upon the capacity of the hegemon to adjust to its decline. As the locus of economic growth and the leading sectors shift in new directions, can the hegemon develop new competitive industries? Is it able to bring its political commitments and economic power back into balance? Can the hegemon and the rising economic powers cooperate to solve the problems that inevitably attend major economic transformations? The answers to these and other questions determine whether a liberal economic order can survive hegemonic decline.

Although the liberal international regimes associated with the declining hegemon may erode, other factors such as the *force of inertia*, the *absence of an alternative*, and the residue of common interests or *social purposes* among the dominant powers operate to maintain the system.[36] As Keohane cogently argues, the norms of the regimes themselves inhibit proscribed behavior.[37] Regimes are more easily maintained than created, as states learn their benefits.[38] In Kindleberger's words, "regimes are more readily maintained than established since marginal costs are below average costs; as hegemonic periods come to an end with the waning of the leading country's economic vitality, new regimes needed to meet new problems are difficult to create. . . .it took [eighty years] to create and get functioning the World Health Organization despite the clear benefits to all countries from controlling the spread of disease. And it takes work to maintain regimes; in the absence of infusions of attention and money, they tend in the long run to decay."[39] And just as it is more costly to create than to maintain a regime, considerable costs must be incurred to bring down a regime. Thus, as has been pointed out, the nineteenth century trading and monetary regimes continued to survive long after British hegemony began its decline with the emergence of rival powers.

With the relative decline of the hegemon in international competitiveness and other measures of economic capabilities, however, the possibility increases that a financial crisis or some other calamity will occur that will cause a dramatic collapse of the system, particularly if a divergence of interests among the major powers takes place. For example, the financial panic of 1929 and the subsequent conflictual policies of the Great Powers utterly destroyed the economic regimes that had been revived after the First World War. Although a similar eventuality is highly unlikely in the contemporary world, one should not assume that the regimes created by American hegemonic leadership are somehow invulnerable.

The crucial role of the hegemon, Kindleberger points out, is that of crisis management and not simply the routine one of regime maintenance. If a liberal world economy is to

---

35. Kindleberger, 1981, *op cit.*, pp. 251-52

36. Krasner, Stephen D. 1978, *Defending the National Interest: Raw Materials Investments and U.S. Foreign Policy.* Princeton: Princeton University Press, pp. 342-43

37. Keohane, 1984.

38. Haas, Ernest B. 1980. "Why Collaborate? Issue-Linkage and International Regimes." *World Politics* 32: 357-405.

39. Kindleberger, Charles P. 1986, "International Public Goods without International Government." American *Economic Review* 76: 8

survive, the hegemon must be able and willing to respond quickly to threats to the system. For example, as Kindleberger has argued, the ability of Great Britain to be the "lender of last resort" substantially moderated the financial crises of 1825, 1836, 1847, 1866, and 1907; in contrast, its inability to play this crisis management role in 1929 and the unwillingness of the United States to take over this task of "lender of last resort" in the face of pyramiding bank failures was a major cause of the collapse of the international financial system and of the Great Depression.[40] In the final decades of the twentieth century the international economy confronts the dangers accompanying the relative decline of American hegemony. The international debt problem, the increase in trade protectionism, and other issues could trigger a crisis over which the United States and its economic partners could easily lose control. Such a failure of crisis management could once again bring down the liberal international economic order.

40. Kindleberger, *ibid.*, pp. 8-9.

Liberal Tradition/ Liberal Perspective Theories

Regime Theory

Robert O. Keohane

Cooperation and International Regimes

Complex Interdependence Theory

Robert O. Keohane and Joseph S. Nye

Complex Interdependence

Neo-Liberal Development Theory

Lawrence H. Summers and Vinod Thomas

Recent Lessons of Development

Introduction to Regime Theory

Robert Keohane is the leading exponent of what has come to be known as "Regime Theory." From his days as a graduate student at Harvard in the mid-1960s, Keohane was troubled by many of the central assumptions of the realist model. With the publication of *After Hegemony: Cooperation and Discord in World Political Economy* (which is excerpted below), Keohane emerged as one of the most thoughtful critics of the dominant paradigm in international relations theory. His writings are largely responsible for initiating and then broadening the debate over the prospects for durable cooperation among states in an international environment characterized by anarchy.

While acknowledging that "cooperation remains scarce relative to discord," he admonishes scholars not to "wait for cooperation to become the rule rather than the exception before studying it, for ignorance of how to promote cooperation can lead to discord, conflict, and economic disaster before cooperation ever has a chance to prevail."[1] It is not surprising, therefore, that in addition to developing "regime theory," Keohane is also the author for another of our more "idealist" theories: Complex Interdependence.

Publishing this book in 1984, Keohane clearly had prescriptive goals in mind. He writes, "my purpose is to . . . [improve] our ability to prescribe remedies"[2] to failed attempts at cooperation. In fact, Keohane points out that he has deliberately avoided professional jargon in the book in order to attract as broad an audience as possible and cautions against "pigeonholing his argument" into traditional ideologies of international relations.[3]

Keohane notes in chapter one that *After Hegemony* is "about how cooperation has been, and can be organized in the world political economy when common interests exist."[4] This stated objective clearly points to which of the two central questions (i.e., why states do what they do or how international relations reflect cooperation and conflict) he addresses.

Regime Theory stands in stark contraposition to Robert Gilpin's Hegemonic Stability Theory (or HST). Arguing in the orthodox realist or mercantilist tradition, Robert Gilpin, maintains that powerful states promote cooperation by constructing international political economies that favor their interests and ideologies. Regimes or institutions—which constitute the norms, values, and mechanisms which enable cooperation—are established by the hegemon to enhance its global position. As we have found in his reading on HST, Gilpin expects the decline of these institutions and cooperation (i.e., dependent variable) as the power of the hegemon recedes (i.e., independent variable).

For Keohane, the key puzzle is why cooperation often succeeds in a world in which discord still predominates. Keohane's puzzle is especially interesting in light of the decline of American hegemony beginning in the 1960s. If the United States has declined as a hegemon, Keohane asks why some regimes and the resulting cooperation persist

---

1. *After Hegemony. Cooperation and Discord in the World Political Economy* (Princeton, NJ: Princeton University Press, 1984), 5-6.

2. Ibid., 6.

3. Ibid., 11-12.

4. Ibid., 6.

longer than HST (if correct) would predict. This reading from chapter four of *After Hegemony* attempts to provide his answer.

For Keohane, the importance of his book rests on its critique and modification of realism in its egoistic variant. Realist theories which seek to explain and predict international behavior on the basis of interests and power alone provide, according to Keohane, important insights but cannot explain much of world politics. For that, they must be supplemented by theories stressing the importance of international institutions which may serve as an intervening variable. One of the tasks you face as theorists is to grasp Keohane's assessment of power and understand how his theoretical perspective differs from orthodox realist explanations for cooperation.

While many theorists immediately identify regime theory with economics (e.g., WTO, or NAFTA), it also has significance for the military and other types of organizations. The laws of land warfare which were codified at The Hague in 1899 and 1907 and in Geneva in subsequent years are also considered "regimes" and have significant implications for the making and executing of foreign policy.

Whereas the theory of Hegemonic Stability Theory (HST) is lacking in explaining why the United States receives extraordinary help from certain states in the Global War on Terror on some matters; but faces downright hostility and interference from those same countries in other areas.

Cooperation and International Regimes

Robert O. Keohane

Hegemonic leadership can help to create a pattern of order. Cooperation is not antithetical to hegemony; on the contrary, hegemony depends on a certain kind of asymmetrical cooperation, which successful hegemons support and maintain. . . . Contemporary international economic regimes were constructed under the aegis of the United States after World War II. In accounting for the creation of international regimes, hegemony often plays an important role, even a crucial one.

Yet the relevance of hegemonic cooperation for the future is questionable. . . . The United States is less preponderant in material resources now than it was in the 1950s and early 1960s. Equally important, the United States is less willing than formerly to define its interests in terms complementary to those of Europe and Japan. The Europeans, in particular, are less inclined to defer to American initiatives, nor do they believe so strongly that they must do so in order to obtain essential military protection against the Soviet Union. Thus the subjective elements of American hegemony have been eroded as much as the tangible power resources upon which hegemonic systems rest. But neither the Europeans nor the Japanese are likely to have the capacity to become hegemonic powers themselves in the foreseeable future.[1]

This prospect raises the issue of cooperation "after hegemony," which is the central theme of [*After Hegemony*]. . . . It also leads back to a crucial tension between economics and politics: international coordination of policy seems highly beneficial in an interdependent world economy, but cooperation in world politics is particularly difficult. One way to relax this tension would be to deny the premise that international economic policy coordination is valuable by assuming that international markets will automatically yield optimal results.[2] The decisive objection to this argument is that, in the absence of cooperation, governments will interfere in markets unilaterally in pursuit of what they regard as their own interests, whatever liberal economists may say. They will intervene in foreign exchange markets, impose various restrictions on imports, subsidize favored domestic industries, and set prices for commodities such as petroleum.[3] Even if one accepted coop-

[1] Historically, hegemonies have usually arisen only after major wars. The two principal modern powers that could be considered hegemonic leaders—Britain after 1815 and the United States after 1945—both emerged victorious from world conflicts. I am assuming, in regarding hegemony as unlikely in the foreseeable future, that any world war would have such disastrous consequences that no country would emerge as hegemonic over a world economy resembling that of the present. For a discussion of the cycle of hegemony, see Gilpin, Robert, 1981. *War and Change in World Politics* (Cambridge: Cambridge University Press); Modelski, George, 1978. The long cycle of global politics and the nation-state. *Comparative Studies in Society and History,* vol. 20, no. 2 (April), pp. 214-38; and Modelski, George, 1982. Long cycles and the strategy of US international economic policy. In Avery and Rapkin, 1982, *America in a Changing World Political Economy* (New York: Longman), pp. 97-118.

[2] Corden, W.M., 1981. *The Revival of Protectionism.* Occasional Papers, No. 14. New York: Group of Thirty.

[3] Strange, Susan, 1979. The management of surplus capacity: or how does theory stand up to protectionism 1970s style? *International Organization,* vol. 33, no. 3 (Summer), pp. 303-34.

eration to maintain free markets, but no other form of policy coordination, the further objection could be raised that economic market failure would be likely to occur.[4] Suboptimal outcomes of transactions could result, for a variety of reasons including problems of collective action. It would take an ideological leap of faith to believe that free markets lead necessarily to optimal results.

Rejecting the illusion that cooperation is never valuable in the world political economy, we have to cope with the fact that it is very difficult to organize. One recourse would be to lapse into fatalism—acceptance of destructive economic conflict as a result of political fragmentation. Although this is a logically tenable position for those who believe in the theory of hegemonic stability, even its most powerful theoretical advocate shies away from its bleak normative implications.[5] A fatalistic view is not taken here. Without ignoring the difficulties that beset attempts to coordinate policy in the absence of hegemony, this book contends that nonhegemonic cooperation is *pos*sible, and that it can be facilitated by international regimes.

In making this argument, I will draw a distinction between the creation of international regimes and their maintenance. . . . When shared interests are sufficiently important and other key conditions are met, cooperation can emerge and regimes can be created without hegemony. Yet this does not imply that regimes can be created easily, much less that contemporary international economic regimes actually came about in this way. . . . I [contend] that international regimes are easier to maintain than to create, and that recognition of this fact is crucial to understanding why they are valued by governments. Regimes may be maintained, and may continue to foster cooperation, even under conditions that would not be sufficiently benign to bring about their creation. Cooperation is possible after hegemony not only because shared interests can lead to the creation of regimes, but also because the conditions for maintaining existing international regimes are less demanding than those required for creating them. Although hegemony helps to explain the creation of contemporary international regimes, the decline of hegemony does not necessarily lead symmetrically to their decay.

This chapter analyzes the meaning of two key terms: *"cooperation"* and *"international regimes."* It distinguishes cooperation from harmony as well as from discord, and it argues for the value of the concept of international regimes as a way of understanding both cooperation and discord. Together the concepts of cooperation and international regimes help us clarify what we want to explain: how do patterns of rule-guided policy coordination emerge, maintain themselves, and decay in world politics?

HARMONY, COOPERATION, AND DISCORD

Cooperation must be distinguished from harmony. Harmony refers to a situation in which actors' policies (pursued in their own self-interest without regard for others) *automatically* facilitate the attainment of others' goals. The classic example of harmony is the hypothetical competitive-market world of the classical economists, in which the Invisible Hand ensures that the pursuit of self-interest by each contributes to the interest of all. In this idealized, unreal world, no one's actions damage anyone else; there are no "negative externalities," in the economists' jargon. Where harmony reigns, cooperation is unneces-

---

4. Cooper, Richard.1983, "Managing Risks to the International Economic System." In Herring, Richard J., ed.1983, *Managing International Risk.* New York: Cambridge University Press, Chapter 1, pp. 45-46.

5. Gilpin, Robert.1981. *War and Change in World Politics.* New York: Cambridge University Press.

sary. It may even be injurious, if it means that certain individuals conspire to exploit others. Adam Smith, for one, was very critical of guilds and other conspiracies against freedom of trade. Cooperation and harmony are by no means identical and ought not to be confused with one another.

Cooperation requires that the actions of separate individuals or organizations—which are not in pre-existent harmony—be brought into conformity with one another through a process of negotiation, which is often referred to as "policy coordination." Charles E. Lindblom has defined policy coordination as follows:[6]

> A set of decisions is coordinated if adjustments have been made in them, such that the adverse consequences of any one decision for other decisions are to a degree and in some frequency avoided, reduced, or counterbalanced or overweighed.

Cooperation occurs when actors adjust their behavior to the actual or anticipated preferences of others, through a process of policy coordination. To summarize more formally, *intergovernmental cooperation takes place when the policies actually followed by one government are regarded by its partners as facilitating realization of their own objectives, as the result of a process of policy coordination.*

With this definition in mind, we can differentiate among cooperation, harmony, and discord, as illustrated by Figure 1. First, we ask whether actors' policies automatically facilitate the attainment of others' goals. If so, there is harmony: no adjustments need to take place. Yet harmony is rare in world politics. Rousseau sought to account for this rarity when he declared that even two countries guided by the General Will in their internal affairs would come into conflict if they had extensive contact with one another, since the General Will of each would not be general for both. Each would have a partial, self-interested perspective on their mutual interactions. Even for Adam Smith, efforts to ensure state security took precedence over measures to increase national prosperity. In defending the Navigation Acts, Smith declared: "As defense is of much more importance than opulence, the act of navigation is, perhaps, the wisest of all the commercial regulations of England". Waltz summarizes the point by saying that "in anarchy there is no automatic harmony".[7]

Yet this insight tells us nothing definitive about the prospects for cooperation. For this we need to ask a further question about situations in which harmony does not exist. Are attempts made by actors (governmental or nongovernmental) to adjust their policies to each others' objectives? If no such attempts are made, the result is discord: a situation in which governments regard each others' policies as hindering the attainment of their goals, and hold each other responsible for these constraints .

Discord often leads to efforts to induce others to change their policies; when these attempts meet resistance, policy conflict results. Insofar as these attempts at policy adjustment succeed in making policies more compatible, however, cooperation ensues. The policy coordination that leads to cooperation need not involve bargaining or negotiation at all. What Lindblom calls "adaptive" as opposed to "manipulative" adjustment can take place: one country may shift its policy in the direction of another's preferences without regard for the effect of its action on the other state, defer to the other country, or partially shift its policy in order to avoid adverse consequences for its partner. Or nonbargained manipula-

---

6. Lindblom, Charles E. 1965. *The Intelligence of Democracy* (New York: The Free Press).

7. Waltz, Kenneth, 1959. *Man, the State, and War* (New York: Columbia University Press).

tion—such as one actor confronting another with a *fait accompli*—may occur.[8] Frequently, of course, negotiation and bargaining indeed take place, often accompanied by other actions that are designed to induce others to adjust their policies to one's own. Each government pursues what it perceives as its self-interest, but looks for bargains that can benefit all parties to the deal, though not necessarily equally.

Harmony and cooperation are not usually distinguished from one another so clearly. Yet, in the study of world politics, they should be. Harmony is apolitical. No communication is necessary, and no influence need be exercised. Cooperation, by contrast, is highly political: somehow, patterns of behavior must be altered. This change may be accomplished through negative as well as positive inducements. Indeed, studies of international crises, as well as game-theoretic experiments and simulations, have shown that under a variety of conditions strategies that involve threats and punishments as well as promises and rewards are more effective in attaining cooperative outcomes than those that rely entirely on persuasion and the force of good example.[9]

Cooperation therefore does not imply an absence of conflict. On the contrary, it is typically mixed with conflict and reflects partially successful efforts to overcome conflict, real or potential. Cooperation takes place only in situations in which actors perceive that their policies are actually or potentially in conflict, not where there is harmony. Cooperation should not be viewed as the absence of conflict, but rather as a reaction to conflict or potential conflict. Without the specter of conflict, there is no need to cooperate.

The example of trade relations among friendly countries in a liberal international political economy may help to illustrate this crucial point. A naive observer, trained only to appreciate the overall welfare benefits of trade, might assume that trade relations would be harmonious: consumers in importing countries benefit from cheap foreign goods and increased competition, and producers can increasingly take advantage of the division of labor as their export markets expand. But harmony does not normally ensue. Discord on trade issues may prevail because governments do not even seek to reduce the adverse consequences of their own policies for others, but rather strive in certain respects to increase the severity of those effects. Mercantilist governments have sought in the twentieth century as well as the seventeenth to manipulate foreign trade, in conjunction with warfare, to damage each other economically and to gain productive resources themselves.[10] Governments may desire "positional goods," such as high status,[11] and may therefore resist even mutually beneficial cooperation if it helps others more than themselves. Yet even when neither power nor positional motivations are present, and when all participants would ben-

8. Lindblom, *op. cit.* 7, pp. 33–34 and ch. 4.

9. Axelrod, Robert, 1981. The emergence of cooperation among egoists. *American Political Science Review*, vol. 75, no. 2 (June), pp. 306-18; Axelrod, Robert, 1984. *The Evolution of Cooperation* (New York: Basic Books); Lebow, Richard Ned, 1981. *Between War and Peace: the Nature of International Crisis* (Baltimore: The Johns Hopkins University Press); Snyder, Glenn H. and Paul Diesing, 1977. *Conflict Among Nations: Bargaining, Decision Making, and System Structure in International Crises* (Princeton: Princeton University Press).

10. Wilson, Charles, 1957. *Profit and Power. A Study of England and the Dutch Wars* (Cambridge: Cambridge University Press); Hirschman, Albert O.1945/1980. *National Power and the Structure of Foreign Trade.* Berkeley: University of California Press.

11. Hirsch, Seev, 1976. *Location of Industry and International Competitiveness;* Oxford: Clarendon Press.

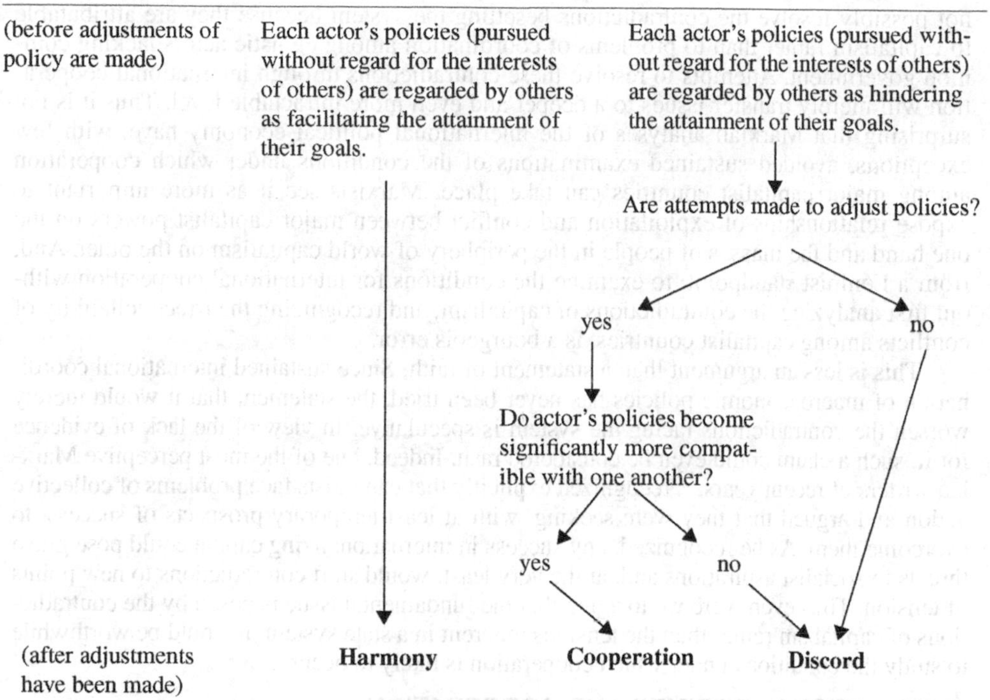
(before adjustments of policy are made)
Each actor's policies (pursued without regard for the interests of others) are regarded by others as facilitating the attainment of their goals.
Each actor's policies (pursued without regard for the interests of others) are regarded by others as hindering the attainment of their goals.
Are attempts made to adjust policies?
yes
no
Do actor's policies become significantly more compatible with one another?
yes
no
(after adjustments have been made)
Harmony
Cooperation
Discord

Figure 1. Harmony, Cooperation, and Discord

efit in the aggregate from liberal trade, discord tends to predominate over harmony as the initial result of independent governmental action.

This occurs even under otherwise benign conditions because some groups or industries are forced to incur adjustment costs as changes in comparative advantage take place. Governments often respond to the ensuing demands for protection by attempting, more or less effectively, to cushion the burdens of adjustment for groups and industries that are politically influential at home. Yet unilateral measures to this effect almost always impose adjustment costs abroad, and discord continually threatens. Governments enter into international negotiations in order to reduce the conflict that would otherwise result. Even substantial potential common benefits do not create harmony when state power can be exercised on behalf of certain interests and against others. In world politics, harmony tends to vanish: attainment of the gains from pursuing complementary policies depends on cooperation.

Observers of world politics who take power and conflict seriously should be attracted to this way of defining cooperation, since my definition does not relegate cooperation to the mythological world of relations among equals in power. Hegemonic cooperation is not a contradiction in terms. Defining cooperation in contrast to harmony should, I hope, lead readers with a Realist orientation to take cooperation in world politics seriously rather than to dismiss it out of hand. To Marxists who also believe in hegemonic power theories, however, even this definition of cooperation may not seem to make it relevant to the contemporary world political economy. From this perspective, mutual policy adjustments cannot possibly resolve the contradictions besetting the system because they are attributable to capitalism rather than to problems of coordination among egoistic actors lacking common government. Attempts to resolve these contradictions through international cooperation will merely transfer issues to a deeper and even more intractable level. Thus it is not surprising that Marxian analyses of the international political economy have, with few exceptions, avoided sustained examinations of the conditions under which cooperation among major capitalist countries can take place. Marxists see it as more important to expose relationships of exploitation and conflict between major capitalist powers on the one hand and the masses of people in the periphery of world capitalism on the other. And, from a Leninist standpoint, to examine the conditions for international cooperation without first analyzing the contradictions of capitalism, and recognizing the irreconcilability of conflicts among capitalist countries, is a bourgeois error.

This is less an argument than a statement of faith. Since sustained international coordination of macroeconomic policies has never been tried, the statement that it would merely worsen the contradictions facing the system is speculative. In view of the lack of evidence for it, such a claim could even be considered rash. Indeed, one of the most perceptive Marxian writers of recent years,[12] recognized explicitly that capitalists face problems of collective action and argued that they were seeking, with at least temporary prospects of success, to overcome them. As he recognized, any success in internationalizing capital could pose grave threats to socialist aspirations and, at the very least, would shift contradictions to new points of tension. Thus even were we to agree that the fundamental issue is posed by the contradictions of capitalism rather than the tensions inherent in a state system, it would be worthwhile to study the conditions under which cooperation is likely to occur.

INTERNATIONAL REGIMES AND COOPERATION

One way to study cooperation and discord would be to focus on particular actions as the units of analysis. This would require the systematic compilation of a data set composed of acts that could be regarded as comparable and coded according to the degree of cooperation that they reflect. Such a strategy has some attractive features. The problem with it, however, is that instances of cooperation and discord could all too easily be isolated from the context of beliefs and behavior within which they are embedded. This book does not view cooperation atomistically as a set of discrete, isolated acts, but rather seeks to understand patterns of cooperation in the world political economy. Accordingly, we need to examine actors' expectations about future patterns of interaction, their assumptions about the proper nature of economic arrangements, and the kinds of political activities they regard as legitimate. That is, we need to analyze cooperation within the context of international institutions, broadly defined, as in chapter 1, in terms of practices and expectations. Each act of cooperation or discord affects the beliefs, rules, and practices that form the context for future actions. Each act must therefore be interpreted as embedded within a chain of such acts and their successive cognitive and institutional residues.

This argument parallels Clifford Geertz's discussion of how anthropologists should use the concept of culture to interpret the societies they investigate. Geertz sees culture as the "webs of significance" that people have created for themselves. On their surface, they are enigmatical; the observer has to interpret them so that they

12. Hymer, Steven, 1972. The internationalization of capital. *Journal of Economic Issues*, vol. 6, no. 1, (March), pp. 91-111.

make sense. Culture, for Geertz, "is a context, something within which [social events] can be intelligibly described".[13] It makes little sense to describe naturalistically what goes on at a Balinese cock-fight unless one understands the meaning of the event for Balinese culture. There is not a world culture in the fullest sense, but even in world politics, human beings spin webs of significance. They develop implicit standards for behavior, some of which emphasize the principle of sovereignty and legitimize the pursuit of self-interest, while others rely on quite different principles. Any act of cooperation or apparent cooperation needs to be interpreted within the context of related actions, and of prevailing expectations and shared beliefs, before its meaning can be properly understood. Fragments of political behavior become comprehensible when viewed as part of a larger mosaic.

The concept of international regime not only enables us to describe patterns of cooperation; it also helps to account for both cooperation and discord. Although regimes themselves depend on conditions that are conducive to interstate agreements, they may also facilitate further efforts to coordinate policies. . . . To understand international cooperation, it is necessary to comprehend how institutions and rules not only reflect, but also affect, the facts of world politics.

Defining and Identifying Regimes

When John Ruggie introduced the concept of international regimes into the international politics literature in 1975, he defined a regime as "a set of mutual expectations, rules and regulations, plans, organizational energies and financial commitments, which have been accepted by a group of states" (p. 570). More recently, a collective definition, worked out at a conference on the subject, defined international regimes as "sets of implicit or explicit principles, norms, rules and decision-making procedures around which actors' expectations converge in a given area of international relations. Principles are beliefs of fact, causation, and rectitude. Norms are standards of behavior defined in terms of rights and obligations. Rules are specific prescriptions or proscriptions for action. Decision-making procedures are prevailing practices for making and implementing collective choice".[14]

This definition provides a useful starting-point for analysis, since it begins with the general conception of regimes as social institutions and explicates it further. The concept of norms, however, is ambiguous. It is important that we understand norms in this definition simply as standards of behavior defined in terms of rights and obligations. Another usage would distinguish norms from rules and principles by stipulating that participants in a social system regard norms, but not rules and principles, as morally binding regardless of considerations of narrowly defined self-interest. But to include norms, thus defined, in a definition of necessary regime characteristics would be to make the conception of regimes based strictly on self-interest a contradiction in terms. Since this book regards regimes as largely based on self-interest, I will maintain a definition of norms simply as standards of behavior, whether adopted on grounds of self-interest or otherwise. Only in chapter 7 will the possibility again be taken seriously that some regimes may contain norms and principles justified on the basis of values extending beyond self-interest, and regarded as obligatory on moral grounds by governments.

---

13. Geertz, Clifford, 1973. *The Interpretation of Cultures* (New York: Basic Books).

14. Krasner, 1983. *International Regimes*. Ithaca: Cornell University Press, p. 2

The principles of regimes define, in general, the purposes that their members are expected to pursue. For instance, the principles of the postwar trade and monetary regimes have emphasized the value of open, nondiscriminatory patterns of international economic transactions; the fundamental principle of the nonproliferation regime is that the spread of nuclear weapons is dangerous. Norms contain somewhat clearer injunctions to members about legitimate and illegitimate behavior, still defining responsibilities and obligations in relatively general terms. For instance, the norms of the General Agreement on Tariffs and Trade (GATT) do not require that members resort to free trade immediately, but incorporate injunctions to members to practice nondiscrimination and reciprocity and to move toward increased liberalization. Fundamental to the nonproliferation regime is the norm that members of the regime should not act in ways that facilitate nuclear proliferation.

The rules of a regime are difficult to distinguish from its norms; at the margin, they merge into one another. Rules are, however, more specific: they indicate in more detail the specific rights and obligations of members. Rules can be altered more easily than principles or norms, since there may be more than one set of rules that can attain a given set of purposes. Finally, at the same level of specificity as rules, but referring to procedures rather than substances, the decisionmaking procedures of regimes provide ways of implementing their principles and altering their rules.

An example from the field of international monetary relations may be helpful. The most important principle of the international balance-of-payments regime since the end of World War II has been that of liberalization of trade and payments. A key norm of the regime has been the injunction to states not to manipulate their exchange rates unilaterally for national advantage. Between 1958 and 1971 this norm was realized through pegged exchange rates and procedures for consultation in the event of change, supplemented with a variety of devices to help governments avoid exchange-rate changes through a combination of borrowing and internal adjustment. After 1973 governments have subscribed to the same norm, although it has been implemented more informally and probably less effectively under a system of floating exchange rates. Ruggie[15] has argued that the abstract principle of liberalization, subject to constraints imposed by the acceptance of the welfare state, has been maintained throughout the postwar period: "embedded liberalism" continues, reflecting a fundamental element of continuity, ill the international balance-of-payments regime. 'The norm of nonmanipulation has also been maintained, even though the specific rules of the 1958–71 system having to do with adjustment have been swept away.

The concept of international regime is complex because it is defined in terms of four distinct components: principles, norms, rules, and decision making procedures. It is tempting to select one of these levels of specificity—particularly, principles and norms or rules and procedures—as *the* defining characteristic of regimes.[16] Such an approach, however, creates a false dichotomy between principles on the one hand and rules and procedures on the other. As we have noted, at the margin norms and rules cannot be sharply distinguished from each other. It is difficult if not impossible to tell the difference between an "implicit rule" of broad significance and a well-understood, relatively specific operating principle. Both rules and principles may affect expectations and even values. In a strong international regime, the linkages between principles and rules are likely to be tight. Indeed, it is

---

15. Ruggie, John Gerard, 1983. *The Antimonies of Interdependence: National Welfare and the International Division of Labor.* New York: Columbia University Press.

16. Krasner, 1983. *op. cit.* 15; Ruggie, *ibid.*

precisely the linkages among principles, norms, and rules that give regimes their legitimacy. Since rules, norms, and principles are so closely intertwined, judgments about whether changes in rules constitute changes of regime or merely changes *within* regimes necessarily contain arbitrary elements.

Principles, norms, rules, and procedures all contain injunctions about behavior: they prescribe certain actions and proscribe others. They imply obligations, even though these obligations are not enforceable through a hierarchical legal system. It clarifies the definition of regime, therefore, to think of it in terms of injunctions of greater or lesser specificity. Some are far-reaching and extremely important. They may change only rarely. At the other extreme, injunctions may be merely technical, matters of convenience that can be altered without great political or economic impact. In-between are injunctions that are both specific enough that violations of them are in principle identifiable and that changes in them can be observed, and sufficiently significant that changes in them make a difference for the behavior of actors and the nature of the international political economy. It is these intermediate injunctions—politically consequential but specific enough that violations and changes can be identified—that I take as the essence of international regimes.[17]

A brief examination of international oil regimes, and their injunctions, may help us clarify this point. The pre–1939 international oil regime was dominated by a small number of international firms and contained explicit injunctions about where and under what conditions companies could produce oil, and where and how they should market it. The rules of the Red Line and Achnacarry or "As-Is" agreements of 1928 reflected an "anti-competitive ethos": that is, the basic principle that competition was destructive to the system and the norm that firms should not engage in it.[18] This principle and this norm both persisted after World War II, although an intergovernmental regime with explicit rules was not established, owing to the failure of the Anglo-American Petroleum Agreement. Injunctions against price-cutting were reflected more in the practices of companies than in formal rules. Yet expectations and practices of major actors were strongly affected by these injunctions, and in this sense the criteria for a regime—albeit a weak one—were met. As governments of producing countries became more assertive, however, and as formerly domestic independent companies entered international markets, these arrangements collapsed; after the mid-to-late 1960s, there was no regime for the issue-area as a whole, since no injunctions could be said to be accepted as obligatory by all influential actors. Rather, there was a "tug of war" [19]in which all sides

---

17. Some authors have defined "regime" as equivalent to the conventional concept of international system. For instance, Puchala and Hopkins claim that "a regime exists in every substantive issue-area in international relations where there is discernibly patterned behavior" (Puchala, Donald J. and Raymond F. Hopkins, 1983. International regimes: lessons from the inductive analysis. In Krasner, Steven D., ed., 1983. *International Regimes* [Ithaca: Cornell University Press], p. 63). To adopt this definition would be to make either "system" or "regime" a redundant term. At the opposite extreme, the concept of regime could be limited to situations with genuine normative content, in which governments followed regime rules *instead* of pursuing their own self-interests when the two conflicted. If this course were chosen, the concept of regime would be just another way of expressing ancient "idealist" sentiments in international relations. The category of regime would become virtually empty. This dichotomy poses a false choice between using "regime" as a new label for old patterns and defining regimes as utopias. Either strategy would make the term irrelevant.

18. Turner, Louis, 1978. *Oil Companies in the International System* (London: George Allen and Unwin for the Royal Institute of International Affairs).

19. Hirschman, Albert O., 1981. *Essays in Trespassing: Economics to Politics and Beyond;* New York: Cambridge University Press.

resorted to self-help. The Organization of Petroleum Exporting Countries (OPEC) sought to create a producers' regime based on rules for prorationing oil production, and consumers established an emergency oil-sharing system in the new International Energy Agency to counteract the threat of selective embargoes.

If we were to have paid attention only to the principle of avoiding competition, we would have seen continuity: whatever the dominant actors, they have always sought to cartelize the industry one way or another. But to do so would be to miss the main point, which is that momentous changes have occurred. At the other extreme, we could have fixed our attention on very specific particular arrangements, such as the various joint ventures of the 1950s and 1960s or the specific provisions for controlling output tried by OPEC after 1973, in which case we would have observed a pattern of continual flux. The significance of the most important events the demise of old cartel arrangements, the undermining of the international majors' positions in the 1960s, and the rise of producing governments to a position of influence in the 1970s—could have been missed. Only by focusing on the intermediate level of relatively specific but politically consequential injunctions, whether we call them rules, norms, or principles, does the concept of regime help us identify major changes that require explanation.

As our examples of money and oil suggest, we regard the scope of international regimes as corresponding, in general, to the boundaries of issue-areas, since governments establish regimes to deal with problems that they regard as so closely linked that they should be dealt with together. Issue-areas are best defined as sets of issues that are in fact dealt with in common negotiations and by the same, or closely coordinated, bureaucracies, as opposed to issues that are dealt with separately and in uncoordinated fashion. Since issue-areas depend on actors' perceptions and behavior rather than on inherent qualities of the subject-matters, their boundaries change gradually over time. Fifty years ago, for instance, there was no oceans issue-area, since particular questions now grouped under that heading were dealt with separately; but there was an international monetary issue-area even then.[20] Twenty years ago trade in cotton textiles had an international regime of its own—the Long-Term Agreement on Cotton Textiles—and was treated separately from trade in synthetic fibers.[21] Issue-areas are defined and redefined by changing patterns of human intervention; so are international regimes.

Self-Help and International Regimes

The injunctions of international regimes rarely affect economic transactions directly: state institutions, rather than international organizations, impose tariffs and quotas, intervene in foreign exchange markets, and manipulate oil prices through taxes and subsidies. If we think about the impact of the principles, norms, rules, and decision-making procedures of regimes, it becomes clear that insofar as they have any effect at all, it must be exerted on national controls, and especially on the specific interstate agreements that affect the exercise of national controls.[22] International regimes must be distinguished from these

---

20. Keohane, Robert O. and Joseph S. Nye, Jr., 1977. *Power and Interdependence: World Politics in Transition.* Boston: Little Brown, ch. 4.

21. Aggarwal, Vinod, 1981. *Hanging by a Thread: International Regime Change in the Textile/Apparel System*, 1950-1979 (Ph.D. dissertation. Stanford University).

22. *Ibid.*

specific agreements; as we will see in chapter 6, a major function of regimes is to facilitate the making of specific cooperative agreements among governments.

Superficially, it could seem that since international regimes affect national controls, the regimes are of superior importance—just as federal laws in the United States frequently override state and local legislation. Yet this would be a fundamentally misleading conclusion. In a well-ordered society, the units of action—individuals in classic liberal thought—live together within a framework of constitutional principles that define property rights, establish who may control the state, and specify the conditions under which subjects must obey governmental regulations. In the United States, these principles establish the supremacy of the federal government in a number of policy areas, though not in all. But world politics is decentralized rather than hierarchic: the prevailing principle of sovereignty means that states are subject to no superior government.[23] The resulting system is sometimes referred to as one of "self-help".[24]

Sovereignty and self-help mean that the principles and rules of international regimes will necessarily be weaker than in domestic society. In a civil society, these rules "specify terms of exchange" within the framework of constitutional principles.[25] In world politics, the principles, norms, and rules of regimes are necessarily fragile because they risk coming into conflict with the principle of sovereignty and the associated norm of self-help. They may promote cooperation, but the fundamental basis of order on which they would rest in a well-ordered society does not exist. They drift around without being tied to the solid anchor of the state.

Yet even if the principles of sovereignty and self-help limit the degree of confidence to be placed in international agreements, they do not render cooperation impossible. Orthodox theory itself relies on mutual interests to explain forms of cooperation that are used by states as instruments of competition. According to balance-of-power theory, cooperative endeavors such as political-military alliances necessarily form in self-help systems.[26] Acts of cooperation are accounted for on the grounds that mutual interests are sufficient to enable states to overcome their suspicions of one another. But since even orthodox theory relies on mutual interests, its advocates are on weak ground in objecting to interpretations of system-wide cooperation along these lines. There is no logical or empirical reason why mutual interests in world politics should be limited to interests in combining forces against adversaries. As economists emphasize, there can also be mutual interests in securing efficiency gains from voluntary exchange or oli-gopolistic rewards from the creation and division of rents resulting from the control and manipulation of markets.

International regimes should not be interpreted as elements of a new international order "beyond the nation-state." They should be comprehended chiefly as arrangements motivated by self-interest: as components of systems in which sovereignty remains a constitutive principle. This means that, as Realists emphasize, they will be shaped largely by their most powerful members, pursuing their own interests. But regimes can also affect state interests, for the notion of self-interest is itself elastic and largely subjective. Perceptions of self-interest depend both on actors' expectations of the likely consequences that

23. Ruggie, John Gerard,1983. *op cit.* 16.

24. Waltz, Kenneth N., 1979. *Theory of International Politics.* McGraw-Hill.

25. North, Dougless C., 1981. *Structure and Change in Economic History.* New York: W. W. Norton, p. 203.

26. Waltz, *op. cit.* 25, p. 23

will follow from particular actions and on their fundamental values. Regimes can certainly affect expectations and may affect values as well. Far from being contradicted by the view that international behavior is shaped largely by power and interests, the concept of international regime is consistent both with the importance of differential power and with a sophisticated view of self-interest. Theories of regimes can incorporate Realist insights about the role of power and interest, while also indicating the inadequacy of theories that define interests so narrowly that they fail to take the role of institutions into account.

Regimes not only are consistent with self-interest but may under some conditions even be necessary to its effective pursuit. They facilitate the smooth operation of decentralized international political systems and therefore perform an important function for states. In a world political economy characterized by growing interdependence, they may become increasingly useful for governments that wish to solve common problems and pursue complementary purposes without subordinating themselves to hierarchical systems of control.

CONCLUSIONS

In this chapter international cooperation has been defined as a process through which policies actually followed by governments come to be regarded by their partners as facilitating realization of their own objectives, as the result of policy coordination. Cooperation involves mutual adjustment and can only arise from conflict or potential conflict. It must therefore be distinguished from harmony. Discord, which is the opposite of harmony, stimulates demands for policy adjustments, which can either lead to cooperation or to continued, perhaps intensified, discord.

Since international regimes reflect patterns of cooperation and discord over time, focusing on them leads us to examine long-term patterns of behavior, rather than treating acts of cooperation as isolated events. Regimes consist of injunctions at various levels of generality, ranging from principles to norms to highly specific rules and decisionmaking procedures. By investigating the evolution of the norms and rules of a regime over time, we can use the concept of international regime both to explore continuity and to investigate change in the world political economy.

From a theoretical standpoint, regimes can be viewed as intermediate factors, or "intervening variables," between fundamental characteristics of world politics such as the international distribution of power on the one hand and the behavior of states and nonstate actors such as multinational corporations on the other. The concept of international regime helps us account for cooperation and discord. To understand the impact of regimes, it is not necessary to posit idealism on the part of actors in world politics. On the contrary, the norms and rules of regimes can exert an effect on behavior even if they do not embody common ideals but are used by self-interested states and corporations engaging in a process of mutual adjustment.

Introduction to Complex Interdependence

Following World War Two and throughout much of the Cold War, international relations were largely viewed through the security lens. This emphasis on security through military power while often appropriate, has recently been questioned. While Marxists, and mercantilists did consider economic factors, these theories still fell generally in the realist tradition of Hobbes and Machiavelli. Scholars continued to neglect the impact of growing economic integration coupled with the increasing role that non-state actors played in international relations. Furthermore, examples of cooperation in a world which realists would predict none was problematic.

Robert Keohane and Joseph Nye's *Power and Interdependence* published in 1977, was an attempt to address many of these shortcomings. Specifically, this book offers the theory of Complex Interdependence as an alternative to explain cooperation and state behavior.

Keohane and Nye believed that "many of the failures of American foreign policy. . . had their roots in the limitations of realist assumptions."[1] In this book they sought to explore the controversy between idealists and realists in an effort to "distill and blend the wisdom in both positions by developing a coherent theoretical framework for the political analysis of interdependence."[2] Recognizing that one model is insufficient to explain all events, Keohane and Nye assess the conditions under which each model helps predict events and provide satisfactory explanations.

The authors' primary purpose was to identify the "major features of world politics when . . . interdependence is extensive." As this statement implies, their independent variable is the level of interdependence and the dependent variable addresses both state behavior (i.e., why states do what they do) and systemic cooperation or conflict.

In the first part of the reading [from chapter one of *Power and Interdependence*] Keohane and Nye address a portion of their independent variable. Specifically, they define and provide an overview of the concept of interdependence including a discussion of how theorists can measure it. They then introduce what they call their two "ideal types" or classifications of world politics. By acknowledging that neither "type" perfectly reflects reality, Keohane and Nye might agree that they are extremes on a continuum with reality lying somewhere in between. This continuum, which is not explicitly addressed, is likewise part of their independent variable.

Subsequently [from chapter two of *Power and Interdependence*], Keohane and Nye discuss what they see as the resulting characteristics of one "ideal type." These characteristics, based as they are on more or less interdependence, result in "distinctive" political processes or state behavior (i.e., dependent variable). The linkage to a systemic outcome of cooperation or conflict (and resulting hypothesis) is not difficult to ascertain.

Complex interdependence is often mistakenly said to eliminate a role for military force. This is not so. Military force serves as a last resort, but military forces are often a

---

1. Robert O. Keohane and Joseph Nye, *Power and Interdependence* (Toronto: Little, Brown and Company, 1977), viii.
2. Ibid., 4.

major player in policies of engagement and integration. In the 1997 *National Military Strategy*,[3] the Joint Chiefs of Staff note that in order to "shape" the international environment effectively the military must execute "peacetime engagement activities." These activities include, "information sharing and contacts between our military and the armed forces of other nations, [promotion of] trust and confidence and [encouragement of] measures that increase our security and that of our allies, partners, and friends." It continues by stating that "by increasing understanding and reducing uncertainty, engagement builds constructive security relationships, helps to promote the development of democratic institutions, and helps keep some countries from becoming adversaries tomorrow." By understanding the theoretical underpinnings of this political policy of fostering integration and to a lesser degree interdependence, one can better understand why the American military is engaged in missions all over the world.

3. Joint Chiefs of Staff, *National Military Strategy: Shape, Respond, Prepare Now—A Military Strategy for a New Era* (1997) located on the WWW at: http://www.dtic.mil:80/jcs/nms.html (date accessed: 27 May 1998).

Complex Interdependence

Robert O. Keohane and Joseph S. Nye

We live in an era of interdependence. This vague phrase expresses a poorly understood but widespread feeling that the very nature of world politics is changing. The power of nations—that age-old touchstone of analysts and statesmen—has become more elusive. . . . "calculations of power are even more delicate and deceptive than in previous ages."[1] Henry Kissinger, though deeply rooted in the classical tradition, has stated that "the traditional agenda of international affairs—the balance among major powers, the security of nations—no longer defines our perils or our possibilities. . . . Now we are entering a new era. Old international patterns are crumbling; old slogans are uninstructive; old solutions are unavailing. The world has become interdependent in economics, in communications, in human aspirations."[2]

How profound are the changes? A modernist school sees telecommunications and jet travel as creating a "global village" and believes that burgeoning social and economic transactions are creating a "world without borders." To greater or lesser extent, a number of scholars see our era as one in which the territorial state, which has been dominant in world politics for the four centuries since feudal times ended, is being eclipsed by nonterritorial actors such as multinational corporations, transnational social movements, and international organizations. As one economist put it, "the state is about through as an economic unit."[3]

Traditionalists call these assertions unfounded "globaloney." They point to the continuity in world politics. Military interdependence has always existed, and military power is still important in world politics—witness nuclear deterrence; the Vietnam, Middle East, and India-Pakistan wars; and Soviet influence in Eastern Europe or American influence in the Caribbean. Moreover, as the Soviet Union has shown, authoritarian states can, to a considerable extent, control telecommunications and social transactions that they consider disruptive. Even poor and weak countries have been able to nationalize multinational corporations, and the prevalence of nationalism casts doubt on the proposition that the nation-state is fading away.

Neither the modernists nor the traditionalists have an adequate framework for understanding the politics of global interdependence. Modernists point correctly to the fundamental changes now taking place, but they often assume without sufficient analysis that advances in technology and increases in social and economic transactions will lead to a new world in which states, and their control of force, will no longer be important. Traditionalists are adept at showing flaws in the modernist vision by pointing out how military interdependence continues, but find it very difficult accurately to interpret today's multidimensional economic, social, and ecological interdependence.

Our task . . . is not to argue either the modernist or traditionalist position. Because our era is marked by both continuity and change, this would be fruitless. Rather, our task

---

1. Stanley Hoffman, "Notes on the Elusiveness of Modern Power," *InternationalJournal.*30 (Spring 1975): 184.

2. A New National Partnership," speech by Secretary of State Henry A. Kissinger at Los Angeles, January 4, 1975. News release, Department of State, Bureau of Public Affairs, Office of .Media Services,

3. Charles Kindleberger, *American Business Record* (New Haven: Yale University Press, 1969, 207.

Table 1. Political Processes Under Conditions of Realism and Complex Interdependence

	Realism	Complex Interdependence
Goals of Actors	Military security will be the dominant goal.	Goals of states will vary by issue area. Transgovernmental politics will make goals difficult to define. Transational actors will pursue their own goals.
Instruments of state policy	Military force will be most effective, although economic and other instruments will also be used.	Power resources specific to issue areas will be more relevant. Manipulation of interdependence, international organizations, and transnational actors will be major instuments.
Agenda formation	Potential shifts in the balance of power and security threats will set agenda in high politics and will strongly influence other agendas.	Agenda will be affected by changes in the distribution of power resources within issue areas; the status of international regimes; changes in the importance of trans national actors; linkages from other issues and politicization as a result of rising sensitivity interdependence.
Linkages of issues	Linkages will reduce differences in outcomes among issue areas and reinforce international hierarchy.	Linkages by strong states will be more difficult to make since force will be ineffective. Linkages by weak states through international organizations will erode rather than reinforce hierarchy.
Roles of international organizations	Roles are minor, limited by state power and the importance of military force.	Organizations will set agendas, induce coaltion-formation, and act as arenas for political action by weak states. Ability to choose the organizational forum for an issue and to mobilize votes will be an important political resource.

is to provide a means of distilling and blending the wisdom in both positions by developing a coherent theoretical framework for the political analysis of interdependence. We shall develop several different but potentially complementary models, or intellectual tools, for grasping the reality of interdependence in contemporary world politics.

Equally important, we shall attempt to explore the *conditions* under which each model will be most likely to produce accurate predictions and satisfactory explanations . . .

INTERDEPENDENCE AS AN ANALYTIC CONCEPT

In common parlance, *dependence* means a state of being determined or significantly affected by external forces. *Interdependence,* most simply defined, means *mutual* dependence. Interdependence in world politics refers to situations characterized by reciprocal effects among countries or among actors in different countries.

These effects often result from international transactions—flows of money, goods, people, and messages across international boundaries. Such transactions have increased dramatically since World War II: Yet this interconnectedness is not the same as interdependence. The effects of transactions on interdependence will depend on the constraints, or costs, associated with them. A country that imports all of its oil is likely to be more dependent on a continual flow of petroleum than a country importing furs, jewelry, and perfume (even of equivalent monetary value) will be on uninterrupted access to these luxury goods. Where there are reciprocal (although not necessarily symmetrical) costly effects of transactions, there is interdependence. Where interactions do not have significant costly effects, there is simply interconnectedness. The distinction is vital if we are to understand the *politics* of interdependence.

Costly effects may be imposed directly and intentionally by another actor—as in Soviet-American strategic interdependence, which derives from the mutual threat of nuclear destruction. But some costly effects do not come directly or intentionally from other actors. For example, collective action may be necessary to prevent disaster for an alliance (the members of which are interdependent), for an international economic system (which may face chaos because of the absence of coordination, rather than through the malevolence of any actor), or for an ecological system threatened by a gradual increase of industrial effluent.

We do not limit the term *interdependence* to situations of mutual benefit. Such a definition would assume that the concept is only useful analytically where the modernist view of the world prevails: where threats of military force are few and levels of conflict are low. It would exclude from interdependence cases of mutual dependence, such as the strategic interdependence between the United States and the Soviet Union. Furthermore, it would make it very ambiguous whether relations between industrialized countries and less developed countries should be considered interdependent or not. Their inclusion would depend on an inherently subjective judgment about whether the relationships were "mutually beneficial."

Because we wish to avoid sterile arguments about whether a given set of relationships is characterized by interdependence or not, and because we seek to use the concept of interdependence to integrate rather than further to divide modernist and traditional approaches, we choose a broader definition. Our perspective implies that interdependent relationships will always involve costs, since interdependence restricts autonomy; but it is impossible to specify *a priori* whether the benefits of a relationship will exceed the costs. This will depend on the values of the actors as well as on the nature of the relationship. Nothing guarantees that relationships that we designate as "interdependent" will be characterized by mutual benefits.

Two different perspectives can be adopted for analyzing the costs and benefits of an interdependent relationship. The first focuses on the joint gains or joint losses to the parties involved. The other stresses *relative* gains and distributional issues. Classical economists adopted the first approach in formulating their powerful insight about comparative advantage: that undistorted international trade will provide overall net benefits. Unfortunately, an exclusive focus on joint gain may obscure the second key issue: how those gains are divided. Many of the crucial political issues of interdependence revolve around the old question of politics, "who gets what?"

It is important to guard against the assumption that measures that increase joint gain from a relationship will somehow be free of distributional conflict. Governments and nongovernmental organizations will strive to increase their shares of gains from transactions, even when they both profit enormously from the relationship. Oil-exporting governments and multinational oil companies, for instance, share an interest in high prices for petroleum; but they have also been in conflict over shares of the profits involved.

We must therefore be cautious about the prospect that rising interdependence is creating a brave new world of cooperation to replace the bad old world of international conflict. As every parent of small children knows, baking a larger pie does not stop disputes over the size of the slices. An optimistic approach would overlook the uses of economic and even ecological interdependence in competitive international politics.

The difference between traditional international politics and the politics of economic and ecological interdependence is *not* the difference between a world of "zero-sum" (where one side's gain is the other side's loss) and "nonzero-sum" games. Military interdependence need not be zero-sum. Indeed, military allies actively seek interdependence to provide enhanced security for all. Even balance of power situations need not be zero-sum. If one side seeks to upset the status quo, then its gain is at the expense of the other. But if most or all participants want a stable status quo, they can jointly gain by preserving the balance of power among them. Conversely, the politics of economic and ecological interdependence involve competition even when large net benefits can be expected from cooperation. There are important continuities, as well as marked differences, between the traditional politics of military security and the politics of economic and ecological interdependence.

We must also be careful not to define interdependence entirely in terms of situations of *evenly balanced* mutual dependence. It is *asymmetries* in dependence that are most likely to provide sources of influence for actors in their dealings with one another. Less dependent actors can often use the interdependent relationship as a source of power in bargaining over an issue and perhaps to affect other issues. At the other extreme from pure symmetry is pure dependence (sometimes disguised by calling the situation interdependence); but it too is rare. Most cases lie between these two extremes. And that is where the heart of the political bargaining process of interdependence lies.

POWER AND INTERDEPENDENCE

Power has always been an elusive concept for statesmen and analysts of international politics; now it is even more slippery. The traditional view was that military power dominated other forms, and that states with the most military power controlled world affairs.

But the resources that produce power capabilities have become more complex . . . Hans Morgenthau, author of the leading realist text on international politics, went so far in his reaction to the events of the early 1970s as to announce an historically unprecedented severing of the functional relationship between political, military, and economic power shown in the possession by militarily weak countries of "monopolistic or quasi-monopolistic control of raw materials essential to the operation of advanced economies."

Power can be thought of as the ability of an actor to get others to do something they otherwise would not do (and at an acceptable cost to the actor). Power can also be conceived in terms of control over outcomes. In either case, measurement is not simple. We can look at the initial power resources that give an actor a potential ability; or we can look at that actor's actual influence over patterns of outcomes. When we say that asymmetrical interdependence can be a source of power we are thinking of power as control over resources, or the *potential* to affect outcomes. A less dependent actor in a relationship often has a significant political resource, because changes in the relationship (which the actor may be able to initiate or threaten) will be less costly to that actor than to its partners. This advantage does not guarantee, however, that the political resources provided by favorable asymmetries in interdependence will lead to similar patterns of control over outcomes. There is rarely a one-to-one relationship between power measured by any type of resources and power measured by effects on outcomes. Political bargaining is the usual means of translating potential into effects, and a lot is often lost in the translation.

To understand the role of power in interdependence, we must distinguish between two dimensions, *sensitivity* and *vulnerability.* Sensitivity involves degrees of responsiveness within a policy framework—how quickly do changes in one country bring costly changes in another, and how great are the costly effects? It is measured not merely by the volume of flows across borders but also by the costly effects of changes in transactions on the societies or governments. Sensitivity interdependence is created by interactions within a framework of policies. Sensitivity assumes that the framework remains unchanged. The fact that a set of policies remains constant may reflect the difficulty in formulating new policies within a short time, or it may reflect a commitment to a certain pattern of domestic and international rules.

An example of sensitivity dependence is the way the United States, Japan, and Western Europe were affected by increased oil prices in 1971 and again in 1973–74 and 1975. In the absence of new policies, which could take many years or decades to implement, the sensitivity of these economies was a function of the greater costs of foreign oil and the proportion of petroleum they imported. The United States was less sensitive than Japan to petroleum price rises, because a smaller proportion of its petroleum requirements was accounted for by imports, but as rapid price increases and long lines at gasoline stations showed, the United States was indeed sensitive to the outside change . . .

Sensitivity interdependence can be social or political as well as economic. For example, there are social "contagion effects," such as . . . the way in which the development of radical student movements during the late 1960s was reinforced by knowledge of each other's activities. The rapid growth of transnational communications has enhanced such sensitivity. Television, by vividly presenting starvation in South Asia to Europeans and Americans about to sit down to their dinners, is almost certain to increase attention to and concern about the issue in European and American societies. Sensitivity to such an issue may be reflected in demonstrations or other political action, even if no action is taken to alleviate the distress (and no economic sensitivity thereby results).

Using the word *interdependence,* however, to refer only to sensitivity obscures some of the most important political aspects of mutual dependence. We must also consider what the situation would be if the framework of policies could be changed. If more alternatives were available, and new and very different policies were possible, what would be the costs of adjusting to the outside change? In petroleum, for instance, what matters is not only the proportion of one's needs that is imported, but the alternatives to imported energy and the costs of pursuing those alternatives. Two countries, each importing 35 percent of their petroleum needs, may seem equally sensitive to price rises; but if one could shift to domestic sources at moderate cost, and the other had no such alternative, the second state would be more *vulnerable* than the first. The vulnerability dimension of interdependence rests on the relative availability and costliness of the alternative that various actors face.

Under the Bretton Woods monetary regime during the late 1960s, both the United States and Great Britain were sensitive to decisions by foreign speculators or central banks to shift assets out of dollars or sterling, respectively. But the United States was less vulnerable than Britain because it had the option (which it exercised in August 1971) of changing the rules of the system at what it considered tolerable costs. The underlying capabilities of the United States reduced its vulnerability, and therefore made its sensitivity less serious politically.

In terms of the costs of dependence, sensitivity means liability to costly effects imposed from outside before policies are altered to try to change the situation. Vulnerability can be defined as an actor's liability to suffer costs imposed by external events even after policies have been altered. Since it is usually difficult to change policies quickly, immediate effects of external changes generally reflect sensitivity dependence. Vulnerability dependence can be measured only by the costliness of making effective adjustments to a changed environment over a period of time.

Vulnerability is particularly important for understanding the political structure of interdependence relationships. In a sense, it focuses on which actors are "the definers of the *ceteris paribus* clause," or can set the rules of the game. Vulnerability is clearly more relevant than sensitivity, for example, in analyzing the politics of raw materials such as the supposed transformation of power after 1973. All too often, a high percentage of imports of a material is taken as an index of vulnerability, when by itself it merely suggests that sensitivity may be high. The key question for determining vulnerability is how effectively altered policies could bring into being sufficient quantities of this, or a comparable, raw material, and at what cost. The fact that the United States imports approximately 85 percent of its bauxite supply does not indicate American vulnerability to actions by bauxite exporters, until we know what it would cost (in time as well as money) to obtain substitutes.

How does this distinction help us understand the relationship between interdependence and power? Clearly, it indicates that sensitivity interdependence will be less important than vulnerability interdependence in providing power resources to actors. If one actor can reduce its costs by altering its policy, either domestically or internationally, the sensitivity patterns will not be a good guide to power resources.

Consider trade in agricultural products between the United States and the Soviet Union from 1972 to 1975. Initially, the American economy was highly sensitive to Soviet grain purchases: prices of grain rose dramatically in the United States. The Soviet Union was also sensitive to the availability of surplus American stocks, since its absence could have internal political as well as economic implications. The vulnerability asymmetries, however, ran strongly in favor of the United States, since its alternatives to selling grain to the USSR (such as government storage, lower domestic prices, and more food aid abroad) were more attractive than the basic Soviet alternative to buying grain from the United States (slaughtering livestock and reducing meat consumption). Thus, as long as the United States government could retain coherent control of the policy—that is, as long as interest groups with a stake in expanded trade did not control it—agricultural trade could be used as a tool in political bargaining with the Soviet Union.

Vulnerability interdependence includes the strategic dimension that sensitivity interdependence omits, but this does not mean that sensitivity is politically unimportant. Rapidly rising sensitivity often leads to complaints about interdependence and political efforts to alter it, particularly in countries with pluralistic political systems. Textile and steel workers and manufacturers, oil consumers, and conservatives suspicious of radical movements originating abroad are all likely to demand government policies to protect their interests. Policymakers and policy analysts, however, must examine underlying patterns of vulnerability interdependence when they decide on strategies. What can they do, at what cost? And what can other actors do, at what cost, in response? Although patterns of sensitivity interdependence may explain where the shoe pinches or the wheel squeaks, coherent policy must be based on an analysis of actual and potential vulnerabilities. An attempt to manipulate asymmetrical sensitivity interdependence without regard for underlying patterns of vulnerability is likely to fail.

Manipulating economic or sociopolitical vulnerabilities, however, also bears risks. Strategies of manipulating interdependence are likely to lead to counterstrategies. It must always be kept in mind, furthermore, that military power dominates economic power in the sense that economic means alone are likely to be ineffective against the serious use of military force. Thus, even effective manipulation of asymmetrical interdependence within a nonmilitary area can create risks of military counteraction. When the United States exploited Japanese vulnerability to economic embargo in 1940–41, Japan countered by attacking Pearl Harbor and the Philippines. Yet military actions are usually very costly; and for many types of actions, these costs have risen steeply during the last thirty years.

Table 2 shows the three types of asymmetrical interdependence that we have been discussing. The dominance ranking column indicates that the power resources provided by military interdependence dominate those provided by nonmilitary vulnerability, which in turn dominate those provided by asymmetries in sensitivity. Yet exercising more dominant forms of power brings higher costs. Thus, *relative to cost,* there is no guarantee that military means will be more effective than economic ones to achieve a given purpose. We can expect, however, that as the interests at stake become more important, actors will tend to use power resources that rank higher in both dominance and cost.

A movement from one power resource to a more effective, but more costly, resource, will be most likely where there is a substantial *incongruity* between the distribution of power resources on one dimension and those on another. In such a situation, the disadvantaged actor's power position would be improved by raising the level at which the controversy is conducted. For instance, in a concession agreement, a multinational oil company may seem to have a better bargaining position than the host government. The agreement may allow the company to set the level of output, and the price, of the petroleum produced, thus making government revenues sensitive to company decisions. Yet such a situation is inherently unstable, since the government may be stronger on the vulnerability dimension. Once the country has determined that it can afford to alter the agreement unilaterally, it may have the upper hand. Any attempt by the company to take advantage of its superior position on the sensitivity dimension, without recognizing its weakness at the vulnerability level (much less at the level of military force) is then likely to end in disaster.

We conclude that a useful beginning in the political analysis of international interdependence can be made by thinking of asymmetrical interdependencies as sources of power among actors. Such a framework can be applied to relations between transnational actors (such as multinational corporations) and governments as well as interstate relations. Different types of interdependence lead to potential political influence, but under different constraints. Sensitivity interdependence can provide the basis for significant political influence only when the rules and norms in effect can be taken for granted, or when it would be prohibitively costly for dissatisfied states to change their policies quickly. If one set of rules puts an actor in a disadvantageous position, that actor will probably try to

Table 2. Asymmetrical Interdependence and Its Uses

Source of Interdependence	Dominance ranking	Cost ranking	Contemporary use
Military (costs of using military force)	1	1	Used in extreme situations or against weak foes when costs may be slight.
Nonmilitary vulnerability (costs of pursuing alternative policies)	2	2	Used when normative constraints are low, and international rules are not considered binding (including nonmilitary relations between adversaries, and situations of extremely high conflict between close partners and allies).
Nonmilitary sensitivity (costs of change under existing policies)	3	3	A power resource in the short run or when normative constraints are high and international rules are binding. Limited, since if high costs are imposed, disadvantaged actors may formulate new policies.

change those rules if it can do so at reasonable cost. Thus influence deriving from favorable asymmetries in sensitivity is very limited when the underlying asymmetries in vulnerability are unfavorable. Likewise, if a state chafes at its economic vulnerabilities, it may use military force to attempt to redress that situation as Japan did in 1941; or, it may subtly threaten to use force, as did the United States in 1975, when facing the possibility of future oil boycotts. But in many contemporary situations, the use of force is so costly, and its threat so difficult to make credible, that a military strategy is an act of desperation.

Yet this is not the whole story of power and interdependence. Just as important as understanding the way that manipulation of interdependence can be an instrument of power is an understanding of that instrument's limits. Asymmetrical interdependence by itself cannot explain bargaining outcomes, even in traditional relations among states. As we said earlier, power measured in terms of resources or potential may look different from power measured in terms of influence over outcomes. We must also look at the "translation" in the political bargaining process. One of the most important reasons for this is that the commitment of a weaker state may be much greater than that of its stronger partner. The more dependent actor may be (or appear to be) more willing to suffer. At the politico-military level, the United States' attempt to coerce North Vietnam provides an obvious example.

Yet the point holds even in more cooperative interstate relations. In the Canadian-American relationship, for example, the use or threat of force is virtually excluded from consideration by either side. The fact that Canada has less military strength than the United States is therefore not a major factor in the bargaining process. The Canadians can take advantage of their superior position on such economic issues as oil and natural gas exports without fearing military retaliation or threat by the United States. Moreover, other conditions of contemporary international interdependence tend to limit the abilities of statesmen to manipulate asymmetrical interdependence. In particular, the smaller state may have greater internal political unity than the larger one. Even though the more powerful state may be less dependent in aggregate terms, it may be more fragmented internally and its coherence reduced by conflicts of interest and difficulties of coordination within its own government . . .

What we have said is sufficient to indicate that we do not expect a measure of potential power, such as asymmetrical interdependence, to predict perfectly actors' successes or failures at influencing outcomes. It merely provides a first approximation of initial bargaining advantages available to either side. Where predictions based on patterns of asymmetrical interdependence are incorrect, one must look closely for the reasons. They will often be found in the bargaining process that translates power resources into power over outcomes . . .

REALISM AND COMPLEX INTERDEPENDENCE

One's assumptions about world politics profoundly affect what one sees and how one constructs theories to explain events. We believe that the assumptions of political realists, whose theories dominated the postwar period, are often an inadequate basis for analyzing the politics of interdependence. The realist assumptions about world politics can be seen as defining an extreme set of conditions or *ideal type*. One could also imagine very different conditions. In this chapter, we shall construct another ideal type, the opposite of realism. We call it *complex interdependence*. After establishing the differences between realism and complex interdependence, we shall argue that complex interdependence sometimes comes closer to reality than does realism. When it does, traditional explanations of change in international regimes become questionable and the search for new explanatory models becomes more urgent.

For political realists, international politics, like all other politics, is a struggle for power but, unlike domestic politics, a struggle dominated by organized violence . . . Three assumptions are integral to the realist vision. First, states as coherent units are the dominant actors in world politics. This is a double assumption: states are predominant; and they act as coherent units. Second, realists assume that force is a usable and effective instrument of policy. Other instruments may also be employed, but using or threatening force is the most effective means of wielding power. Third, partly because of their second assumption, realists assume a hierarchy of issues in world politics, headed by questions of military security: the "high politics" of military security dominates the "low politics" of economic and social affairs.

These realist assumptions define an ideal type of world politics. They allow us to imagine a world in which politics is continually characterized by active or potential conflict among states, with the use of force possible at any time. Each state attempts to defend its territory and interests from real or perceived threats. Political integration among states is slight and lasts only as long as it serves the national interests of the most powerful states. Transnational actors either do not exist or are politically unimportant. Only the adept exercise of force or the threat of force permits states to survive, and only while statesmen succeed in adjusting their interests, as in a well-functioning balance of power, is the system stable.

Each of the realist assumptions can be challenged. If we challenge them all simultaneously, we can imagine a world in which actors other than states participate directly in world politics, in which a clear hierarchy of issues does not exist, and in which force is an ineffective instrument of policy. Under these conditions—which we call the characteristics of complex interdependence—one would expect world politics to be very different than under realist conditions . . .

We do not argue, however, that complex interdependence faithfully reflects world political reality. Quite the contrary: Both it and the realist portrait are ideal types. Moth situations will fall somewhere between these two extremes. Sometimes, realist assumptions will be accurate, or largely accurate, but frequently complex interdependence will provide a better portrayal of reality. Before one decides what explanatory model to apply to a situation or problem, one will need to understand the degree to which realist or complex interdependence assumptions correspond to the situation.

The Characteristics of Complex Interdependence

Complex interdependence has three main characteristics:

1. *Multiple channels* connect societies, including: informal ties between governmental elites as well as formal foreign office arrangements; informal ties among nongovernmental elites (face-to-face and through telecommunications); and transnational organizations (such as multinational banks or corporations). These channels can be summarized as interstate, transgovernmental, and transnational relations. *Interstate* relations are the normal channels assumed by realists. *Transgovernmental* applies when we relax the realist assumption that states act coherently as units; *transnational* applies when we relax the assumption that states are the only units.

2. The agenda of interstate relationships consists of multiple issues that are not arranged in a clear or consistent hierarchy. This *absence of hierarchy among issues* means, among other things, that military security does not consistently dominate the agenda. Many issues arise from what used to be considered domestic policy, and the distinction between domestic and foreign issues becomes blurred. These issues are considered in several government departments (not just foreign offices), and at several levels. Inadequate policy coordination on these issues involves significant costs. Different issues generate different coalitions, both within governments and across them, and involve different degrees of conflict. Politics does not stop at the waters' edge.

3. *Military force is not used by governments toward other governments within the region, or on the issues, when complex interdependence prevails.* It may, however, be important in these governments' relations with governments outside that region, or on other issues. Military force could, for instance, be irrelevant to resolving disagreements on economic issues among members of an alliance, yet at the same time be very important for that alliance's political and military relations with a rival bloc. For the former relationships this condition of complex interdependence would be met; for the latter, it would not.

Traditional theories of international politics implicitly or explicitly deny the accuracy of these three assumptions. Traditionalists are therefore tempted also to deny the relevance of criticisms based on the complex interdependence ideal type. We believe, however, that our three conditions are fairly well approximated on some global issues of economic and ecological interdependence and that they come close to characterizing the entire relationship between some countries . . .

Multiple Channels

A visit to any major airport is a dramatic way to confirm the existence of multiple channels of contact among advanced industrial countries; there is a voluminous literature to prove it.[4] Bureaucrats from different countries deal directly with one another at meetings and on the telephone as well as in writing. Similarly, nongovernmental elites frequently get together in the normal course of business, in organi-

---

4. See Edward L. Morse, "Transnational Economic Processes," in Robert O. Keohane and Joseph S. Nye, Jr., eds., *Transnational Relations and World Politics* (Cambridge, MA: Harvard University Press, 1972).

zations such as the Trilateral Commission, and in conferences sponsored by private foundations.

In addition, multinational firms and banks affect both domestic and interstate relations. The limits on private firms, or the closeness of ties between government and business, vary considerably from one society to another; but the participation of large and dynamic organizations, not controlled entirely by governments, has become a normal part of foreign as well as domestic relations. These actors are important not only because of their activities in pursuit of their own interests, but also because they act as transmission belts, making government policies in various countries more sensitive to one another. As the scope of governments' domestic activities has broadened. and as corporations. banks, and (to a lesser extent) trade unions have made decisions that transcend national boundaries, the domestic policies of different countries impinge on one another more and more. Transnational communications reinforce these effects. Thus, foreign economic policies touch more domestic economic activity than in the past, blurring the lines between domestic and foreign policy and increasing the number of issues relevant to foreign policy. Parallel developments in issues of environmental regulation and control over technology reinforce this trend.

Absence of Hierarchy Among Issues

Foreign affairs agendas—that is, sets of issues relevant to foreign policy with which governments are concerned—have become larger and more diverse. No longer can all issues be subordinated to military security. As Secretary of State Kissinger described the situation in 1975:

> progress in dealing with the traditional agenda is no longer enough. A new and unprecedented kind of issue has emerged. The problems of energy, resources, environment, population, the uses of space and the seas now rank with questions of military security, ideology and territorial rivalry which have traditionally made up the diplomatic agenda.[5]

Kissinger's list, which could be expanded. illustrates how governments' policies, even those previously considered merely domestic, impinge on one another. The extensive consultative arrangements developed by the OECD, as well as the GATT, IMF, and the European Community, indicate how characteristic the overlap of domestic and foreign policy is among developed pluralist countries. The organization within nine major departments of the United States government (Agriculture, Commerce, Defense, Health, Education and Welfare, Interior, Justice, Labor, State, and Treasury) and many other agencies reflects their extensive international commitments. The multiple, overlapping issues that result make a nightmare of governmental organization.[6]

When there are multiple issues on the agenda, many of which threaten the interests of domestic groups but do not clearly threaten the nation as a whole, the problems of formulating a coherent and consistent foreign policy increase. In 1975 energy was a foreign policy problem, but specific remedies, such as a tax on gasoline and automobiles, involved domestic legislation opposed by auto workers and companies alike. As one commentator

---

5. Henry A. Kissinger, "A New National Partnership," *Department of State Bulletin*, February 17, 1975, 199.

6. See the report of the Commission on the Organization of the Government for the Conduct of Foreign Policy (Murphy Commission) (Washington, D.C.: U.S. Government Printing Office, 1975), and the studies prepared for that report. See also Raymond Hopkins, "The International Role of 'Domestic' Bureaucracy," *International Organization* 30, no. 3 (Summer 1976).

observed. "virtually every time Congress has set a national policy that changed the way people live . . .the action came after a consensus had developed, hit by bit, over the years, that a problem existed and that there was one best way to solve it."[7] Opportunities for delay, for special protection, for inconsistency and incoherence abound when international politics requires aligning the domestic policies of pluralist democratic countries.

Minor Role of Military Force

Political scientists have traditionally emphasized the role of military force in international politics.... [F]orce dominates other means of power: if there are no constraints on one's choice of instruments (a hypothetical situation that has only been approximated in the two world wars), the state with superior military force will prevail. If the security dilemma for all states were extremely acute, military force, supported by economic and other resources, would clearly be the dominant source of power. Survival is the primary goal of all states, and in the worst situations, force is ultimately necessary to guarantee survival. Thus military force is always a central component of national power.

Yet particularly among industrialized, pluralist countries, the perceived margin of safety has widened: Fears of attack in general have declined, and fears of attacks by *one another* are virtually nonexistent. France has abandoned the *tous azimuts* (defense in all directions) strategy that President de Gaulle advocated (it was not taken entirely seriously even at the time). Canada's last war plans for fighting the United States were abandoned half a century ago. Britain and Germany no longer feel threatened by each other. Intense relationships of mutual influence exist between these countries, but in most of them force is irrelevant or unimportant as an instrument of policy.

Moreover, force is often not an appropriate way of achieving other goals (such as economic and ecological welfare) that are becoming more important. It is not impossible to imagine dramatic conflict or revolutionary change in which the use or threat of military force over an economic issue or among advanced industrial countries might become plausible. Then realist assumptions would again be a reliable guide to events. But in most situations, the effects of military force are both costly and uncertain.[8]

Even when the direct use of force is barred among a group of countries, however, military power can still be used politically. Each superpower continues to use the threat of force to deter attacks by other superpowers on itself or its allies; its deterrence ability thus serves an indirect. protective role, which it can use in bargaining on other issues with its allies. This bargaining tool is particularly important for the United States, whose allies are concerned about potential Soviet threats and which has fewer other means of influence over its allies than does the Soviet Union over its Eastern European partners. The United States has, accordingly, taken advantage of the Europeans' (particularly the Germans') desire for its protection and linked the issue of troop levels in Europe to trade and monetary negotiations. Thus, although the first-order effect of deterrent force is essentially negative—to deny effective offensive power to a superpower opponent—a state can use the force positively—to gain political influence.

Thus, even for countries whose relations approximate complex interdependence, two serious qualifications remain: (1) drastic social and political change could cause force again to become an important direct instrument of policy: and (2) even when elites' inter-

---

7. *The New York Times*, May 22, 1975.

8. For a valuable discussion, see Klaus Knorr, *The Pou;er oJ Nations: The Political Economy of International Relations* (New York: Basic Books, 1975).

ests are complementary, a country that uses military force to protect another may have significant political influence over the other country

In North-South relations, or relations among Third World countries, as well as in East-West relations, force is often important. military power helps the Soviet Union to dominate Eastern Europe economically as well as politically. The threat of open or covert American military intervention has helped to limit revolutionary changes in the Caribbean, especially in Guatemala in 1954 and in the Dominican Republic in 1965. Secretary of State Kissinger, in January 19-5. issued a veiled warning to members of the Organization of Petroleum Exporting Countries (OPEC) that the United States might use force against them "where there is some actual strangulation of the industrialized world."[9]

Even in these rather conflictual situations, however, the recourse to force seems less likely now than at most times during the century before 1945. The destructiveness of nuclear weapons makes any attack against a nuclear power dangerous. Nuclear weapons are mostly used as a deterrent. Threats of nuclear action against much weaker countries may occasionally be efficacious, but they are equally or more likely to solidify relations between one's adversaries. The limited usefulness of conventional force to control socially mobilized populations has been shown by the United States failure in Vietnam as well as by the rapid decline of colonialism in Africa. Furthermore, employing force on one issue against an independent state with which one has a variety of relationships is likely to rupture mutually profitable relations on other issues. In other words, the use of force often has costly effects on nonsecurity goals. And finally, in Western democracies, popular opposition to prolonged military conflicts is very high.[10]

It is clear that these constraints bear unequally on various countries, or on the same countries in different situations. Risks of nuclear escalation affect everyone, but domestic opinion is far less constraining for communist states, or for authoritarian regional powers, than for the United States, Europe, or Japan. Even authoritarian countries may be reluctant to use force to obtain economic objectives when such use might be ineffective and disrupt other relationships. Both the difficulty of controlling socially mobilized populations with foreign troops and the changing technology of weaponry may actually enhance the ability of certain countries, or nonstate groups, to use terrorism as a political weapon without effective fear of reprisal.

The fact that the changing role of force has uneven effects does not make the change less important, but it does make matters more complex. This complexity is compounded by differences in the usability of force among issue areas. When an issue arouses little interest or passion, force may be unthinkable. In such instances, complex interdependence may be a valuable concept for analyzing the political process. But if that issue becomes a matter of life and death—as some people thought oil might become—the use or threat of force could become decisive again. Realist assumptions would then be more relevant.

It is thus important to determine the applicability of realism or of complex interdependence to each situation. Without this determination, further analysis is likely to be confused. Our purpose in developing an alternative to the realist description of world politics is to encourage a differentiated approach that distinguishes among dimensions and areas of world politics—not (as some modernist observers do) to replace one oversimplification with another.

---

9. *Business Week*, January 13, 1975

10. Stanley Hoffmann, "The Acceptability of Military Force," and Laurence Martin, "The Utility of Military Force," in *Force in Modern Societies: Its Place in International Politics* (Adelphi Paper, International Institute for Strategic Studies. 1973). See also Knorr, The Power of Nations.

The Political Processes of Complex Interdependence

The three main characteristics of complex interdependence give rise to distinctive political processes, which translate power resources into power as control of outcomes. As we argued earlier, something is usually lost or added in the translation. Under conditions of complex interdependence the translation will be different than under realist conditions, and our predictions about outcomes will need to be adjusted accordingly.

In the realist world, military security will be the dominant goal of states. It will even affect issues that are not directly involved with military power or territorial defense. Non-military problems will not only be subordinated to military ones; they will be studied for their politico-military implications. Balance of payments issues, for instance, will be considered at least as much in the light of their implications for world power generally as for their purely financial ramifications . . .

In a world of complex interdependence, however, one expects some officials, particularly at lower levels, to emphasize the *variety* of state goals that must be pursued. In the absence of a clear hierarchy of issues, goals will vary by issue, and many not be closely related. Each bureaucracy will pursue its own concerns; and although several agencies may reach compromises on issues that affect them all, they will find that a consistent pattern of policy is difficult to maintain. Moreover, transnational actors will introduce different goals into various groups of issues.

Linkage Strategies

Goals will therefore vary by issue area under complex interdependence, but so will the distribution of power and the typical political processes. Traditional analysis focuses on *the* international system, and leads us to anticipate similar political processes on a variety of issues. Militarily and economically strong states will dominate a variety of organizations and a variety of issues, by linking their own policies on some issues to other states' policies on other issues. By using their overall dominance to prevail on their weak issues, the strongest states will, in the traditional model, ensure a congruence between the overall structure of military and economic power and the pattern of outcomes on any one issue area. Thus world politics can be treated as a seamless web.

Under complex interdependence, such congruence is less likely to occur. As military force is devalued, militarily strong states will find it more difficult to use their overall dominance to control outcomes on issues in which they are weak. And since the distribution of power resources in trade, shipping, or oil, for example, may be quite different, patterns of outcomes and distinctive political processes are likely to vary from one set of issues to another. If force were readily applicable, and military security were the highest foreign policy goal, these variations in the issue structures of power would not matter very much. The linkages drawn from them to military issues would ensure consistent dominance by the overall strongest states. But when military force is largely immobilized, strong states will find that linkage is less effective. They may still attempt such links, but in the absence of a hierarchy of issues, their success will be problematic.

Dominant states may try to secure much the same result by using overall economic power to affect results on other issues. If only economic objectives are at stake, they may succeed: money, after all, is fungible. But economic objectives have political implications, and economic linkage by the strong is limited by domestic, transnational, and transgovernmental actors who resist having their interests traded off. Furthermore, the international actors may be different on different issues, and the international organizations in which negotiations take place are often quite separate. Thus it is difficult, for example, to imagine a militarily or economically strong state linking concessions on monetary policy to reciprocal concessions in oceans policy . . .

Thus as the utility of force declines, and as issues become more equal in importance, the distribution of power within each issue will become more important. If linkages become less effective on the whole, outcomes of political bargaining will increasingly vary by issue area.

Agenda Setting

Our second assumption of complex interdependence, the lack of clear hierarchy among multiple issues, leads us to expect that the politics of agenda formation and control will become more important. Traditional analyses lead statesmen to focus on politico-military issues and to pay little attention to the broader politics of agenda formation. Statesmen assume that the agenda will be set by shifts in the balance of power, actual or anticipated, and by perceived threats to the security of states. Other issues will only be very important when they seem to affect security and military power. In these cases, agendas will be influenced strongly by considerations of the overall balance of power.

Yet, today, some nonmilitary issues are emphasized in interstate relations at one time, whereas others of seemingly equal importance are neglected or quietly handled at a technical level. International monetary politics, problems of commodity terms of trade, oil, food, and multinational corporations have all been important during the last decade; but not all have been high on interstate agendas throughout that period.

Traditional analysts of international politics have paid little attention to agenda formation: to how issues come to receive sustained attention by high officials. The traditional orientation toward military and security affairs implies that the crucial problems of foreign policy are imposed on states by the actions or threats of other states. These are high politics as opposed to the low politics of economic affairs. Yet, as the complexity of actors and issues in world politics increases, the utility of force declines and the line between domestic policy and foreign policy becomes blurred: as the conditions of complex interdependence are more closely approximated, the politics of agenda formation becomes more subtle and differentiated.

Under complex interdependence we can expect the agenda to be affected by the international and domestic problems created by economic growth and increasing sensitivity to interdependence . . . Discontented domestic groups will politicize issues and force more issues once considered domestic onto the interstate agenda. Shifts in the distribution of power resources within sets of issues will also affect agendas. During the early 1970s the increased power of oil-producing governments over the transnational corporations and the consumer countries dramatically altered the policy agenda. Moreover, agendas for one group of issues may change as a result of linkages from other groups in which power resources are changing; for example, the broader agenda of North-South trade issues changed after the OPEC price rises and the oil embargo of 1973–74. Even if capabilities among states do not change, agendas may be affected by shifts in the importance of transnational actors . . .

Transnational and Transgovernmental Relations

Our third condition of complex interdependence, multiple channels of contact among societies, further blurs the distinction between domestic and international politics. The availability of partners in political coalitions is not necessarily limited by national boundaries as traditional analysis assumes. The nearer a situation is to complex interdependence, the more we expect the outcomes of political bargaining to be affected by transnational relations. Multinational corporations may be significant both as independent actors and as instruments manipulated by governments. The attitudes and policy stands of domestic groups are likely to be affected by communications, organized or not, between them and their counterparts abroad.

The multiple channels of contact found in complex interdependence are not limited to nongovernmental actors. Contacts between governmental bureaucracies charged with similar tasks may not only alter their perspectives but lead to transgovernmental coalitions on particular policy questions. To improve their chances of success, government agencies attempt to bring actors from other governments into their own decision-making processes as allies. Agencies of powerful states such as the United States have used such coalitions to penetrate weaker governments in such countries as Turkey and Chile. They have also been used to help agencies of other governments penetrate the United States bureaucracy . . .

The existence of transgovernmental policy networks leads to a different interpretation of one of the standard propositions about international politics—that states act in their own interest. Under complex interdependence, this conventional wisdom begs two important questions: which self and which interest? A government agency may pursue its own interests under the guise of the national interest; and recurrent interactions can change official perceptions of their interests . . .

The ambiguity of the national interest raises serious problems for the top political leaders of governments. As bureaucracies contact each other directly across national borders (without going through foreign offices), centralized control becomes more difficult. There is less assurance that the state will be united when dealing with foreign governments or that its components will interpret national interests similarly when negotiating with foreigners. The state may prove to be multifaceted, even schizophrenic. National interests will be defined differently on different issues, at different times, and by different governmental units. States that are better placed to maintain their coherence (because of a centralized political tradition such as France's) will be better able to manipulate uneven interdependence than fragmented states that at first glance seem to have more resources in an issue area.

Role of International Organizations

Finally, the existence of multiple channels leads onc to predict a different and significant role for international organizations in world politics. Realists in the tradition of Hans J. Morgenthau have portrayed a world in which states, acting from self-interest, struggle for "power and peace." Security issues are dominant; war threatens. In such a world, one may assume that international institutions will have a minor role, limited by the rare congruence of such interests. International organizations are then clearly peripheral to world politics. But in a world of multiple issues, perfectly linked, in which coalitions are formed transnationally and transgovernmentally, the potential role of international institutions in political bargaining is greatly increased. In particular, they help set the international agenda, and act as catalysts for coalition-formation and as arenas for political initiatives and linkage by weak states . . .

Complex interdependence therefore yields different political patterns than does the realist conception of the world (Table 1 summarizes these differences.) Thus, one would expect traditional theories to fail to explain international regime change in situations of complex interdependence. But, for a situation that approximates realist conditions, traditional theories should be appropriate

Introduction to Neo-Liberal Development

As a new millennium dawns, the future of mankind seems intricately linked to the ability of states to address daunting economic and social challenges, both domestically and in the global arena. Competition for scarce resources, environmental threats, and relatively new issues, including the AIDS epidemic, threaten the global stability on which the prosperity of wealthier nations depends. As the populations of many countries continue to rise at an alarming and unsustainable rate, regional conflicts over such issues as land and fresh water are certain to increase. Not surprisingly, the question of economic development has captured the attention of global leaders as never before.

Neo-Liberal Development is the first of two (the other is Dependency Theory) development theories in this text. While both may be used to describe or explain state actions they are largely prescriptive in nature—that is, they provide approaches to solving the problem of underdevelopment that exists for many countries.

In contrast to approach taken by Neo-Liberal Development theorists, competition and conflict for scarce resources motivated 19th Century political thinkers like Karl Marx to describe a zero-sum economic warfare between "oppressive capitalists" and the "downtrodden masses." The Marxist mantra evolved in the early years of this century to incorporate new ideas about the relationship between "have states" and "have-not states." In the aftermath of World War II, the idealistic leaders of many countries in Asia, Africa and Latin America rejected western capitalism as a cynical tool to maintain an unequal system of economic dependency. This in turn led to the imposition and elaboration by many "Third World" leaders of a host of Marxist-based strategies for economic and social development, which will be discussed at more length in the next section of this book.

As the Cold War drew to a close, a process stimulated in part by the apparent inadequacy of Marxist-Leninist economic prescriptions, leaders throughout the world took a new look at the basic question of development and how to make it happen. The earlier view that democracy is antithetical to development and that the strongarm state with a strong leader at the helm is essential, has been discredited.[1] The progress of the World Bank, one institution focused on economic development for almost five decades, has been chronicled in their annual *World Development Reports*. The consensus is that both developed and developing countries have responsibilities in improving global economic development. (Here we find the independent variables for this prescriptive "theory".)

The Neo-Liberal Development reading, *Entering the 21st Century: World Development Report 1999/2000,* identifies the changes that have been set in motion as contributing to—and as manifestations of—two phenomena: globalization and localization. Globalization, requires national governments to reach out to international partners as the best way to manage changes affecting trade, financial flows, and the global environment. Localization, which reflects the growing desire of people for a greater say in their government, pushes national governments to reach down to regions and cities to address the root problems of development.

---

[1]. Lawrence H, Summers and Vinod Thomas, "Recent Lessons of Development", *The World Bank Research Observer* (July 1993): 1.

The report highlights the development lessons learned over the past fifty years. First, macroeconomic stability is essential. Second, development policies must address the basic human needs of the population directly. Third, no one policy will trigger development; a comprehensive approach is needed. Fourth, institutions matter; sustained development should be rooted in processes that are grounded in social inclusion and flexibility in dealing with changing circumstances.[2]

Recognizing the prescriptive nature of Neo-liberal Development Theory it should be clear that it provides a "menu" from which underdeveloped states and developed states alike "order" to help developing states modernize. Hence, it is from this menu that we find our dependent variables and indeed an explanation of aspects of our foreign policy.

The concepts and precepts of Neo-Liberal Development have seemed to have found a sympathetic ear in the President of the United States, George Bush. In March 2002, President Bush announced the creation of a new way in which the United States would give developmental aid. In his Millennium Challenge Account (MCA), President Bush declared that aid would be contingent upon "sound policies". In other words, the US would give aid only if the developing country met certain objectives—conditional aid.

---

2. World Bank, *Entering the 21st Century: World Development Report 1999/2000* (September 15, 1999).

Recent Lessons of Development

Lawrence H. Summers and Vinod Thomas

Across a wide spectrum of opinion there is agreement that governments have done too much of the things that they cannot do well—regulating markets and producing ordinary goods—and not enough of the things they must do well—maintaining macroeconomic stability and making necessary public investments. However, this agreement leaves a great deal unresolved. There are questions about implementation and concerns about external constraints of various kinds. First, the East Asian success stories remain open to differing interpretations. As their success continues, the position taken by some economists that they succeeded despite government efforts at channeling market forces is increasingly implausible. Second, the question of the best sequence and pace of reform remains open. Third, an earlier view that democracy is antithetical to development and that the strong-arm state with a strong leader at the helm is essential has been discredited. Finally, there is the ever-present danger that some new problem will arise.

Development is the most pressing challenge facing the human race. Despite the enormous opportunities created by the advances in technology, more than 1 billion people, one-fifth of the world's population, live on less than US$1 a day, a standard of living that the United States and Europe attained two centuries ago.

In the past the development effort may have mattered primarily to the citizens of poor countries. But now demographic, political, and technological trends make development an urgent priority for rich countries as well. Ninety-five percent of the growth in the world's labor force will take place in the developing world over the next quarter of a century. With the end of the cold war, economic and environmental issues will occupy the center of the diplomatic stage, and these issues will increasingly involve developing nations. As improvements in transportation and communication shrink the world, the rich and poor countries will inevitably impinge more and more on each other. International television's impact on the less-advanced nations and the sharp increase in refugee flows worldwide are harbingers of things to come.

A remarkable transformation in prevailing views about how governments can best promote economic development has occurred in recent years. Where it was once thought that government needed to occupy an economy's commanding heights by allocating credit, rationing foreign exchange, ensuring against dependence, and operating key industries, today it is widely accepted that government's responsibility for directing the production and distribution of goods and services should be much reduced and the private sector's role much enhanced. It is in those tasks for which markets prove inadequate or fail altogether—for example, investing in education, health, or physical infrastructure-that government has a central role.

For some time now, the advice of the Bretton Woods institutions (the World Bank and the International Monetary Fund) has reflected the view that economic progress is impeded by governments that seek to supplant, rather than support, markets. That view has recently been taken on board by policymakers in many parts of the world. Most publicized has been the collapse of communism in what was once the Soviet bloc. China, where one-fourth of the people in the developing world live, calls itself socialist, but the past decade has witnessed spectacular growth of the nonstate sector and very substantial price liberalization.

India, where one-fifth of the population of the developing world lives, is now undertaking a program of structural adjustment and liberalization that is mild by Eastern European standards but would have been unthinkable even two years ago. Chile and Mexico have demonstrated to other Latin American nations the benefits that liberalization can bring. And change is coming, albeit slowly, in Africa, as agricultural marketing boards are dismantled and investment licensing schemes are scaled back.

For fifteen years, the World Bank's *World Development Reports* have been distilling the lessons of the record in various aspects of economic development. In a synthesis of what has been learned to date, the 1991 report (World Bank 1991) described the emerging consensus in favor of what was labeled the "market-friendly" strategy, one in which governments sustain rather than supersede markets. That report coincided with a growing literature on thinking about development (for example, Krugman 1993; Srinivasan 1991; Ranis and Schultz 1988) and on the lessons of growth and development (for example, Journal of Economic Perspectives 1990; Barro 1989; Stern 1989; Chenery and Srinivasan 1988; WIDER various years). This article summarizes what we consider to be the main policy conclusions from the development experience of the past thirty years and then considers a number of unresolved issues and challenges for the future.

THE DEVELOPMENT RECORD

In thinking about development strategy, it is a mistake to lose sight of the enormous progress that has been made and continues to be made in the developing world. Average incomes in developing countries have doubled over the past three decades faster, that is, than in the United Kingdom during the Industrial Revolution, in the United States during its spurt to industrial maturity in the nineteenth century, or in Japan during its prewar growth spurt. Economic progress in some developing countries has been dramatic: Turkey doubled its average income in twenty years (1957-77), Brazil in eighteen years (1961-79), the Republic of Korea in eleven years (1966-77), and China in ten years (1977-87).

Tremendous social progress has also been achieved in the developing world. Infant mortality rates have been cut in half, total fertility rates have been lowered by 40 percent, and life expectancy has increased by nearly a decade, equivalent to twice the gain from eliminating both cancer and heart disease in the United States. A child born in Shanghai today has a smaller chance of dying in the first year of life, a longer life expectancy beyond one year, and a greater chance of learning to read than a child born in New York City. Social advance has been most striking in East Asia. It is estimated that the incidence of absolute poverty (that is, the percentage of the population that subsists below the poverty line) in that region has fallen dramatically in the past three decades, from a third of the population in 1970 to a tenth in 1990 (Johansen 1992).

Many people think of the 1980s as a "lost decade" for development. Indeed the economies of Latin America, the Middle East and North Africa, and Sub-Saharan Africa, where average incomes declined in real terms during the decade, did have a difficult time during the 1980s. But growth of income per capita weighted by population was slightly above the historic average during the decade. In other words, the income of the average person worldwide grew more in the 1980s than in the 1970s. This reflects the acceleration of growth in India and China, where more than 2 billion people live: average incomes in China expanded at roughly 8 percent a year in the 1980s, while those in India increased by more than 3 percent a year.

Of course, this relatively favorable record conceals enormous variations in growth rates and poverty reduction across countries. Per capita incomes in some economies have doubled twice over since 1960 and are well on the way to a third doubling. But thirty-six nations with a combined population of nearly 500 million people have seen low or declining average incomes over the past twenty-five years. Poverty remains a formidable problem, and substantial economic progress has yet to touch millions of people. Before turning to the more detailed implications of this record of divergence for national policy, three broad facts of experience are worth emphasizing.

First, peace is prerequisite to successful development. Most of the economically successful countries have been able to enjoy sociopolitical stability. By contrast, most of the thirty-six countries that have lost ground over the past twenty-five years were involved in a substantial military conflict (Sivard 1989). In Africa, where development performance has been most disappointing, 7 million lives have been lost in wars in the past thirty years.

Second, nations shape their own destinies. Poor domestic policies, more than an unfavorable external environment, are usually to blame for development failures. By any measure more foreign assistance goes to Africa, where performance has been poor, than to parts of Asia, where it has been better. Net capital inflows over the past quarter of a century to the most successful area of the developing world, East Asia, were less than one percent of the region's gross domestic product (GDP). Moreover, East Asia has not had the benefit of natural resources to export. And countries such as the Korea and Indonesia, despite debt burdens similar to those of some of the highly indebted countries, have not experienced debt crises because they used the proceeds of borrowing to make investments yielding high returns. The recognition that countries make their own histories has begun to be reflected in models of economic growth, which increasingly factor in aspects of a country's policy environment that affect performance (Easterly and others 1991; Romer 1990; Lucas 1988).

Third, the proper blend of state and market in the economy is a decisive factor. A review of the record identifies some important characteristics of successful government intervention. Most of these follow from the general principle of supporting, rather than supplanting, markets and the related idea that, as Keynes (1926) put it, "the important thing for government is not to do the things which individuals are doing already and to do them a little better or a little worse; but to do those things which at present are not done at all."

Market development itself requires government action. The socialist economies in transition, from Eastern Europe to East Asia, are finding out that the establishment of the rules of the game by the government is crucial to the success of market reforms. The need for government action goes further, its rationale resting on various notions of market failure. Investment in human capital and physical infrastructure by the government are usually justified because of externalities or spillover effects in the consumption or production of both of these categories and the inadequate incentives for markets to take them into account. In the case of primary education, for example, there are consumption related spillovers. The benefits to literacy go well beyond the gains to the individuals becoming literate. In the case of physical infrastructure such as roads, there are production related externalities based on the need to make lumpy investments or to integrate the service in large networks. Negative spillovers, too, justify government intervention: environmental pollution and congestion are inadequately accounted for by the market.

The central issue, then, is one of the state and the market, but it is not a question of intervention versus laissez faire—a popular dichotomy but a false one. As discussed below, it is rather a question of the proper division of responsibilities between the two and of efficiency in their respective functions.

LEARNING FROM EXPERIENCE

The relation between government and market can be seen under three broad headings: human and physical infrastructure, competitive climate for enterprise, and macroeconomic management. A fourth area, institutional development, cuts across all three. The areas, of course, are interrelated. A relatively undistorted and competitive domestic economy rewards the buildup of human capital more generously than one that is highly regulated and protected. At the same time, investments in education make the domestic economy more productive by speeding the adoption of new technology. To take another example, a stable macroeconomic framework allows the domestic price system to work effectively because it helps to avoid inflation. But microeconomic efficiency also makes it easier to keep inflation low: with fewer unviable enterprises, there will be less need for subsidies that swell the public sector deficit. And, reforms in all these areas work better if a country's institutional framework, embracing both market and government institutions, is improved.

Human and Physical Infrastructure

Perhaps the most important investments governments need to make are in people. The economic returns from public and private investments in education and health are often extremely high (Psacharopoulos and Woodhall 1985; Easterlin 1981). Improving peoples' health and education strengthens the demand for smaller families, which, together with better provision of family planning services, helps to tackle the population problem in many parts of the world. Markets in developing countries often cannot be relied upon to provide people—especially the poor—with adequate education (particularly primary education), health care, nutrition, and family planning services. The returns to government development of various forms of physical infrastructure are also usually very high (Jimenez forthcoming). The incentives for the private sector to develop adequate infrastructure, such as rural roads, are often lacking.

A child born in Africa today is more likely to be malnourished than to go to school at all, and is more likely to die before the age of five than to go to secondary school. And yet because basic health care services are labor-intensive, they can be effectively produced in developing countries. By one recent calculation for Pakistan, providing 1,000 girls with one extra year of schooling would raise their market productivity by between 10 and 15 percent and would avert nearly seven hundred births and close to fifty infant deaths. (Summers 1992).

Many governments are investing far too little in human development (World Bank 1991; United Nations Development Programme 1990). In Brazil and Pakistan rapid economic growth alone was insufficient to improve social indicators substantially. In Chile and Jamaica, however, these indicators improved even in periods of slow growth. Among low-income countries, Guinea and Sri Lanka have the same per capita income, but average life expectancy is some two-thirds longer in Sri Lanka. Brazil and Uruguay have similar per capita incomes, but infant mortality is two-thirds lower in Uruguay.

Governments must also make necessary tangible investments in infrastructure. However appropriate the incentive framework, firms cannot function if the water runs brown, and nothing happens when a coin is put in the phone. Too often, as in the case of electricity and water supply, failed government efforts to provide or maintain infrastructure lead to very expensive attempts at private sector substitution. For example, in India power plants operate with a capacity utilization of less than 50 percent, yet firms are forced to install their own generators because the risk of interruptions is so great.

Ensuring that governments make the necessary investments in both tangible and intangible infrastructure is partially a matter of making sure they have adequate resources. But in addition to increasing the quantity of human investment, governments must improve its quality. Too often, capital investments go forward without adequate provision for the recurrent expenditures they entail, which results in wasteful underutilization. Too often water is provided at little or no cost to industry and then is wasted, while clean water is unavailable where it is desperately needed to improve health. Targeting expenditures appropriately is crucial. Expenditures are frequently poorly targeted and involve a great deal of leakage.

The need to shift priorities in spending is wide-ranging. It will pay to reduce heavy subsidies for higher education and to spend much more on primary education, from which the returns are relatively higher. The case for a similar switch in spending on the margin, from expensive curative health care systems to primary systems, is also strong. In too many developing countries half the national health budget goes to a few hospitals that do open heart surgery in or near the nation's capital, whereas immunizations cannot be afforded in rural areas. The question of priorities goes beyond the area of human resources. In many countries there is scope for substantially reducing spending on the military in favor of increased spending on human and physical infrastructure.

Competitive Climate for Enterprise

Growth led by the private sector needs a permissive, rather than a prohibitive, environment. Almost no one disagrees that communism is the longest route from capitalism to capitalism. For all their faults, competitive markets are the most effective way yet found to get goods and services produced and distributed efficiently. External and domestic competition provides the incentives that unleash entrepreneurship and technological progress (Balassa 1977; Bhagwati 1978; Krueger 1978; Porter 1990).

Openness to trade, investment, and ideas encourages domestic producers to cut costs and improve productivity by introducing new technologies and to develop new and better products (Chenery, Robinson, and Syrquin 1986). A high level of protection for domestic industry, conversely, has held development back by decades in many places. The effect of import protection on firms in Chile and Turkey, for instance, and the effect of greater competition in export markets on firms in Brazil, Japan, and Korea confirm the decisive contribution to efficiency that the external economy can make.

Many developing countries are taking to heart the lessons from worldwide experience in trade liberalization. As a result of the various liberalization episodes of the 1970s and 1980s, the developing world is more open today than at any time in recent history. But the threat of increasing protectionism is ever present, not least from the industrial countries. In fact, as the developing countries liberalized, the industrial countries on average raised trade restrictions in the 1980s: development prospects can be substantially improved if all countries roll back trade barriers.

A permissive domestic environment is one where government seeks to reduce, rather than increase, the cost of doing business. That means doing away with licensing requirements for investment, avoiding debilitating restrictions that limit firms' ability to downsize, and reducing tariffs and quotas on capital goods whose cost is found to affect growth performance significantly (De Long and Summers 1992). One study found that the price of traded capital goods was 50 percent higher in Africa than in other parts of the developing world (World Bank 1989). Creating a competitive climate for the private sector also entails avoiding government monopsonies or punitive regulations. The success of the Nigerian government's action in abolishing agricultural marketing boards and moving toward a realistic exchange rate illustrates what deregulation can accomplish. Cocoa output has risen 50 percent since 1986, both rubber and cotton production has more than quadrupled, and soybean production and processing of soybean products have increased even more. A permissive environment is also one where market forces are able to set prices without price controls or large subsidies. The former Soviet Union, where the price of oil at any realistic exchange rate has been less than $1 a barrel for many years, is an extreme example of distortions caused by subsidies, but large subsidies to energy and energy-using products are ubiquitous in developing countries.

Governments have a history of failure in attempting to manage directly the production of private goods and services. Around the world the record of public enterprise management is one of disaster. It may be true in theory that a properly managed public enterprise can often be as productive and efficient as a private one, but the reality is that politics usually intrudes and efficiency is sacrificed (Nellis 1986; Jones 1982). Public enterprise managers are rarely permitted to shed labor in order to produce at minimum cost. And procurement is often treated as a way of enriching contractor and procurement officers rather than producing efficiently.

Nigeria provides an example of what can go wrong when government tries to operate what should be private industry. Between 1973 and 1990 the Nigerian government invested $115 billion in its public sector, or about $1,000 for every citizen. This investment, depending on what exchange rate is used, represented as much as four years' worth of gross national product. Yet there is little growth to show for it. Public sector assets are operating at a capacity utilization rate of less than 40 percent. And a $3 billion steel complex sits empty, awaiting the $1 billion of investment necessary to complete it. Mexico, by contrast, provides an example of what privatization can accomplish. Large-scale privatization has attracted substantial foreign investment and has already considerably improved efficiency. Indeed, several countries have found that the expectation that enterprises will be privatized creates an impetus for increased efficiency.

Macroeconomic Management

Sound macroeconomic policies with sustainable fiscal deficits and realistic exchange rates are a prerequisite to progress (Fischer 1986). Large government budget deficits absorb domestic saving and foreign funds that could otherwise be channeled to the private sector. Crowding out productive investments by farmers, entrepreneurs, and large businesses, government deficits place the financial system under great strain. Often they induce rapid inflation, which in turn exacerbates the deficit, creating a vicious cycle. Deficits also lead to over-valued exchange rates, which stifle exports, damage domestic producers, and create pressures for protectionism. Evidence is accumulating from country experience of widespread ill-effects of large fiscal deficits (Corden 1989; World Bank 1988; Tanzi and Blejer 1986, for example).

A distinguishing feature of the East Asian experience is that the public sector exercised discipline in its spending; such discipline is essential to ensure that rents from government interventions are kept to a minimum. Fiscal discipline was practiced in different ways. In Taiwan before 1987, a law limited the value of outstanding government bonds to no more than 40 percent of the central government's annual budget. Thailand limits its budget deficit to 20 percent of expenditures. In Indonesia the openness of the capital account has served as a check on irresponsible fiscal behavior that could precipitate currency speculation and crisis. Malaysia, however, ran a large deficit (a high of 19 percent of GDP in 1982) but cut it sharply (5 percent in 1990) when performance was threatened.

To be sure, fiscal and financial instability have sometimes been partly inflicted on governments by external events—or by internal shocks such as civil wars or natural disasters. But governments can choose how to respond to such pressures. In such countries as Cote d'Ivoire, Kenya, Mexico, and Nigeria, the response to a temporary economic upswing was an unsustainable increase in public spending. Countries such as Botswana, Chile, Colombia, Indonesia, Korea, Malaysia, Mauritius, and Thailand managed to keep their macroeconomic policies on course, and their broader economic performance has benefited accordingly.

If a persistent government budget deficit is the surest route to economic failure, an artificially overvalued exchange rate must be the runner-up. Underlying such overvaluation are expansionary fiscal and monetary policies, excessive borrowing, and inadequate trade and exchange rate policies. Overvaluation leads to the rationing of foreign exchange, which is invariably associated with its discretionary allocation and appropriation by government officials and their friends. Overvaluation also creates pressures for layer after layer of controls on imports, capital flows, and even travel. And it destroys emerging export industries, perhaps the most important foundation for growth that any developing country enjoys. The extent of exchange rate misalignment and its deleterious effects on performance are now well documented (see, for example, Edwards 1989; Williamson 1987).

Institutional Development

The better a country's institutional capabilities are, the more effective such actions will be. Similar policy reforms have produced different results across countries (Thomas and others 1991), and one of the explanations is the variation in the capacity of institutions to implement the reforms. Institutional development refers to market as well as to government institutions. In many countries market development requires less government intervention. Market institutions are often stifled by a series of harmful interventions. Governments sometimes intervene in the market to address political instability and other political constraints. But, all too often, the resulting combination of pervasive distortions and predatory states leads to development disasters. Reversing this process is a crucial part of institutional development. It requires political will and a political commitment to market reform and market development.

But it is a myth that "government is the problem, not the solution." When governments do the things they should not do, they are stretched too thin to do the things they must do. Governments need to assist in the efficient development of markets. Only governments can provide the institutional framework for exchanges. This means rules governing property rights, and it means enforcement based on preestablished principles of contracts. The establishment of a well-functioning legal system and judiciary and of secure property rights is an essential complement to economic reforms.

Reform of the public sector is a priority in many countries. In addition to market liberalization and privatization, it includes reforming the civil service, rationalizing public expenditures, and reforming some state-owned enterprises. Related economic reforms include better delivery of public goods, supervision of banks, and legislation to encourage financial development. Adopting these reforms will increase the quality of governance and the capacity of the state to implement development policy and enable society to establish checks and balances.

WHAT ARE THE UNCERTAINTIES?

Across a wide spectrum of opinion there is agreement on the basic principles we have just described. Governments have done too much of the things they cannot do well—regulating markets and producing ordinary goods—and too little of the things they must do well—maintaining macroeconomic stability and making necessary public investments. Governments, in ways that will differ from country to country, need to do less of certain things and to do them better. But the agreement on these points leaves a great deal unresolved. There are questions about implementation and concerns about external constraints of various kinds.

First, the East Asian success stories remain open to differing interpretations (Wade 1990; James, Naya, and Meier 1989). Government, at key stages in each of these countries' development, did seek to affect the allocation of resources across sectors through industrial, trade, and credit allocation policies. *World Development Report 1991* noted some key conditions under which East Asian interventions were far more effective than similar actions in other parts of the world. Government interventions were disciplined by international competition. And they were flexible enough to be changed on the basis of the evidence about their effectiveness.

As the success of Japan, Korea, and Taiwan continues, the position taken by some economists that they succeeded despite government efforts at channeling market forces is increasingly implausible. But there is still room for disagreement, and so for research on two questions: how important in explaining East Asian growth is the contribution of sectoral interventions relative to the contribution of overall macroeconomic stability, outward orientation, and investments in capital and people, and what is unique about these countries that enabled interventionist policies to succeed there when they have been so unsuccessful in the rest of the world? Answering the latter question is essential if the East Asian experience is to provide guidance to other countries.

Second, what is the best sequence and pace of reform If the role of government that we have just described is agreed to be appropriate, there remains the question of how policies should be reformed. On the sequencing question, experience suggests that it is wrong to think of reform as a series of obstacles, each of which must be surmounted. Policy changes typically occur simultaneously or nearly simultaneously on many fronts. But as a general proposition it appears that macroeconomic stabilization is essential to reform and needs to come early, and that it is usually best to delay financial liberalization until macroeconomic stability has been put in place and the viability of enterprises has been restored (Fischer and Gelb 1991). On the question of the pace of reform there is also room for disagreement. here hyperinflation is rampant or looming, the case for urgent action is clear. But where the threat is not imminent, as in much of Africa, China, or India, the case for "big bang"—style reform is much weaker. Particularly where reform will involve large displacements of workers who will not be quickly reemployed, there are legitimate grounds for favoring gradual transitions. The difficulty, of course, is that gradual transitions are often favored by those whose first choice would be no transition at all.

Third, what is the relationship between political and economic reform? An earlier view that democracy was antithetical to development and that the strong-arm state with a strong leader at the helm was essential has now been discredited. A number of studies, some summarized in World Bank (1991), have found no systematic relationship between liberties and rates of economic growth and evidence of a positive relationship between liberties and social performance. These findings are reassuring to friends of both economic and political freedom, but doubts remain. Most of the major development success stories—for example, Chile, China, Korea, or Singapore—had governments that were or are authoritarian in many respects. It is possible that democracy can foster growth by making it impossible for hopelessly incompetent and corrupt governments to remain in power, but one also has to wonder whether democracy can be inconsistent with outstanding performance. A related issue involves the sequencing of political and economic reform—-the ordering of glasnost and perestroika. It is easier to identify examples of successful economic reform that preceded political reform than that immediately followed it.

Fourth, can adjustment to the "market-friendly" approach work in very low-income countries, especially in Africa? It is hard to answer this question in the absence of a clearly specified alternative strategy. One of the hard lessons of the adjustment efforts of the past decade is that adjustment and reform take time to yield results (World Bank 1989). Government credibility, once lost, is restored only very slowly. And would-be investors, whether foreign or domestic, can always delay investment, waiting to see how things turn out before deciding whether to invest. Most of the success stories—Japan and Germany after World War II and Chile, Korea, and Mexico more recently—took time, and things often got worse before they got better. The process appears even more protracted in very low-income countries. It is no accident that programs put in place with the cooperation of the Bretton Woods institutions involve a higher ratio of adjustment to austerity than would have been the case a few years ago.

Fifth, will the external global economic conditions make export-led growth possible on a large scale over the next twenty-five years? Export-led strategies have not invariably been the most effective. Looking at the record of the period between the two world wars and of the immediate postwar period, it is not difficult to understand the appeal of import substitution notions. Brazil, with relatively closed markets, was about the fastest-growing country in the world from 1965 to 1980. The liberal advice that most developing countries receive must be based on one of two premises. One is that it will be widely ignored, so the adding-up problem—that is, the problem that increased exports from all will deny benefits to individual countries-will not arise, and those few countries that increase their export capacity will benefit. The other is that many countries will be able to increase exports greatly without depressing their terms of trade, either because industrial markets for domestic products will grow without protectionist policies being imposed, or because trade among developing countries will become more important in the future than it has been in the past (World Bank 1992a). These premises are not self-evident as reform sweeps the developing world, industrial country growth slows, and the Uruguay Round flounders. Although it has been true in the past that the external climate has been a less important barrier to development than misguided domestic policies, this may change as domestic policies improve and protectionism in the industrial world

Sixth, will natural environmental constraints hold back development or force a new paradigm based on notions of sustainability? Environmental concerns are very important and have been too little reflected for too long in policymaking in both developing and industrial countries. To a large extent environmental problems are a consequence of policies that are misguided on narrow economic grounds—subsidies to energy, failure to give farmers title to their land and adequate credit, public ownership of major industries, inefficient charging for water, and so forth. And where they are not, the difficulty is to do the right cost-benefit analysis and implement the most cost-effective policies for sustainable development (World Bank 1992b). Of particular importance are steps to eradicate the severe forms of environmental degradation, such as poor sanitation and water and air pollution, that threaten human lives and well-being. The agenda for environmental reform is a large one. Accepting the challenge to accelerate development in an environmentally responsible manner will involve substantial shifts in policies and priorities and will require substantial investments. Failing to accept it will be far more costly. Seventh, and finally, there is the ever present danger that some new problem will surface. The only real constant of experience is the unpredictability of the future.

NOTE

When this article was written, Lawrence H. Summers was the chief economist and vice president of Development Economics at the World Bank; he is now U.S. Treasury Undersecretary for International Affairs; Vinod Thomas is the chief economist in the East Asia and Pacific Region at the World Bank.

References

The word "processed" describes informally reproduced works that may not be commonly available through library systems.

Balassa, Bela. 1977. *Policy Reform in Developing Countries.* New York: Oxford University Press.

Barro, Robert. 1989. "A Cross-Country Study of Growth, Saving, and Government." *NBER Working Paper 2855.* National Bureau of Economic Research, Cambridge, Mass. Processed.

Behrman, Jere, and Nancy Birdsall. 1983. "The Quality of Schooling: Quantity Alone is Misleading." *American Economic Review* 73: 928-46.

Bhagwati, Jagdish. 1978. *Foreign Trade Regimes and Economic Development: Anatomy and Consequences of Exchange Control.* Cambridge, Mass.: Ballinger.

Chenery, Hollis, Sherman Robinson, and Moshe Syrquin. 1986. *Industrialization and Growth: A Comparative Study.* New York: Oxford University Press.

Chenery, Hollis, and T. N. Srinivasan. 1988. *Handbook of Development Economics.* 2 vols. New York: North-Holland.

Corden, Max. 1989. "Macroeconomic Adjustment in Developing Countries." *The World Bank Research Observer* 4 (1, January): 51-64.

Das Gupta, Partha. 1993. *An Inquiry into Well Being and Destitution.* Oxford, U.K.: Clarendon Press.

De Long, J. Bradford, and Lawrence H. Summers. 1992. "Equipment Investment and Economic Growth." *Quarterly Journal of Economics* 106 (May): 445-502.

Dornbusch, Rudiger, and Sebastian Edwards. 1989. "The Macroeconomics of Populism in Latin America." WPS 316. World Bank, Country Economics Department, Washington D.C. Processed.

Easterlin, Richard. 1981. "Why Isn't the Whole World Developed?" *Journal of Economic History* 44 (1, March): 1-17.

Easterly, William, Robert G. King, Ross Levine, and Sergio Rebelo. 1991. "How Do National Policies Affect Long-Run Growth? A Research Agenda." WPS 794. World Bank, Country Economics Department, Washington, D.C. Processed.

Edwards, Sebastian. 1989. "Real Exchange Rates in the Developing Countries; Concepts and Measurement." *NBER Working Paper 2950.* National Bureau of Economic Research, Cambridge, Mass. Processed.

Fischer, Stanley. 1986. "Issues in Medium-Term Macroeconomic Adjustment." *The World Bank Research Observer* 1 (2, July): 163-82. Fischer, Stanley, and Alan Gelb. 1991. "The Process of Socialist Economic Transformation." *Journal of Economic Perspectives* 5 (4): 91-106.

James, William E., Seiji Naya, and Gerald M. Meier. 1989. *Asian Development.* Madison: University of Wisconsin Press.

Jimenez, Emmanuel. Forthcoming. "Human and Physical Infrastructure: Public Investment and Pricing Policies in Developing Countries." In Jere Behrman and T. N. Srinivasan, eds., *Handbook of Development Economics,* vol. 3. Amsterdam: North Holland.

Johansen, Frida. 1992. "Poverty in East Asia." *World Bank, East Asia and Pacific Region,* Washington, D.C. Processed.

Jones, Leroy P. 1982. *Public Enterprise in Less-Developed Countries.* Cambridge, U.K.: Cambridge University Press.

Journal of Economic Perspectives. 1990. Various articles. 4 (3). Keynes, John Maynard. 1926. "The End of Laissez-Faire." In *The Collected Writings of John Maynard Keynes.* (1972). New York: St. Martin's Press.

Krueger, Anne. 1978. *Liberalization Attempts and Consequences.* Cambridge, Mass.: Ballinger. Krugman, Paul. 1993. "Toward a Counter-Counterrevolution in Development Theory." In *Proceedings of the World Bank Annual Conference on Development Economics 1992.* Washington, D.C.: World Bank.

Lucas, Robert E. 1988. "On the Mechanics of Economic Development." *Journal of Monetary Economics* 22 2-42.

Nellis, John R. 1986. *Public Enterprises in Sub-Saharan Africa. World Bank Discussion Paper 1.* Washington D.C.

Porter, Michael E. 1990. *The Competitive Advantage of Nations.* New York: Free Press.

Psacharopoulos, George, and Maureen Woodhall. 1985. *Education for Development: An Analysis of Investment Choices.* New York: Oxford University Press.

Ranis, Gustav, and T. Paul Schultz. 1988. *The State of Development Economics.* New York: Blackwell.

Romer, Paul M. 1990. "Endogenous Technological Changes." *Journal of Political Economics* 98 (5, Pt. 2): 71-102.

Sivard, Ruth Leger. 1989. *World Military and Social Expenditures 1989.* 13th ed. Washington D.C.: World Priorities.

Srinivasan, T. N. 1991. "Development Thought, Strategy and Policy: Then and Now." Background paper for *World Development Report 1991.* World Bank, Washington, D.C. Processed.

Stern, Nicholas. 1989. "The Economics of Development: A Survey." *Economic Journal* 99: 597-685.

Summers, Lawrence H. 1992. "Investing in All the People." WPS 90S. World Bank, Office of the Vice President, Development Economics, Washington, D.C. Processed.

Tanzi, Vito, and M. I. Blejer. 1986. "Public Debt and Fiscal Policy in Developing Countries." *IMF Working Paper WP/86/5.* Washington D.C. Processed.

Thomas, Vinod, Ajay Chhibber, Mansoor Dailami, and Jaime de Melo. 1991. *Restructuring Economies in Distress.* New York: Oxford University Press.

United Nations Development Programme. 1990. *Human Development Report.* New York: Oxford University Press.

Wade, Robert. 1990. *Governing the Market: Economic Theory and the Role of Government in East Asian Industrialization.* Princeton, N.J.: Princeton University Press.

Williamson, John. 1987. "Exchange Rate Policy for Developing Countries." *Journal of Foreign Exchange and International Finance* 1 (1, January): 39-46.

World Bank. 1988. *World Development Report 1988.* New York: Oxford University Press.

—.1989. *Sub-Saharan Africa: From Crisis to Sustainable Growth.* Washington D.C.

—.1991. *World Development Report 1991: The Challenge of Development.* New York: Oxford University Press.

—.1992a. *Global Economic Prospects and the Developing Countries 1992.* Washington D.C.

—.1992b. *World Development Report 1992: Development and the Environment.* New York: Oxford University Press.

World Institute for Development Economics Research (WIDER). Various years. *Research for Action.* Helsinki.

Marxist Perspective Theories

Overview

Thomas F. Lynch III

Foundations of Radicalism

Dependency Theory

Theotonio Dos Santos

The Structure of Dependence

Foundations of Radicalism

Thomas F. Lynch III

Although Marxism largely address domestic relations between "classes" of people within states (i.e., a theory of internal politics), it does serve as the basis for Imperialist and Dependency theories which describe relations between states. Therefore, Lynch's description of Marxist thought and its evolution is essential to grasp subsequent Marxist-based theoretical readings.

Radicalism is an approach to understanding international relations which breaks from standard analytical norms and conventions while simultaneously demanding sweeping and often violent change in the global political system. There are many variants of radicalism. Some of these, like *anarchism* and *nihilism*, have had a significant sway in certain regions of the world only to pass from the scene as victims of their own failures or (in some cases) successes.[1] Other variants of radicalism, including *terrorism* and *religious fundamentalism*, remain contemporary international forces for violent upheaval in international politics; yet they lack the unitary political ideology and the shared agenda for political action required for analysis as a systemic lens for understanding international relations.[2]

One variant of radicalism, nonetheless, lives on as a powerful critique of traditional international relations theory, while simultaneously offering a comprehensive approach toward reforming the international economic system. This variant, known as *Dependency Theory*, has a rich intellectual pedigree, incorporating key notions of *Marxism* and *Marxist-Leninism* with a contemporary revolutionary credo of considerable resonance in the less developed nations of the world. To understand Dependency's radical vision of international relations, the student of international politics must become familiar with the basics of *Marxist* ideology.

1. Nineteenth century Europe featured many groups of *anarchists*. All shared a general disdain for political action through elections and parliaments. *Anarchists*, however, could never agree on the reasons they abhorred "legitimate" political action nor upon the appropriate alternative courses for political action. Prominent anarchists spanned a wide gulf from trade union heads working for general worker strikes to the ultra-radicals who led a shocking wave of assassinations throughout Europe in the 1890s. Basically, anarchists were individualistic radicals incapable of categorization into any one single creed. Consequently, anarchism defies analytical assessment in this essay.

Nineteenth century Russia underwent siege by a set of domestic radical groups collectively known as *nihilists*. Unified by their hatred for the Tsarist monarchy, nihilists shared a belief that all morality was baseless, and that all existing political and social institutions must be violently destroyed for future improvement. Nihilists staged a string of successful assassinations in the Russian royal family during the period from 1868-1885. These successes led to premature forecasts that nihilism would lead to a world-wide movement for violent political upheaval. Instead, nihilists were victims of their own successes and their loose, unintegrated organization in Russia. Before any internationalization of nihilism took place, the Cheka (Russian Secret Police) tracked-down and butchered the leaders of the nihilist movement in reprisal for the nihilist assassination of Tsar Alexander II in 1881. *Nihilism*, therefore, never became a international force for radicalism.

A richly detailed description of the origins and subsequent demise of these earlier forms of radicalism can be found in Roland N. Stromberg, *An Intellectual History of Modern Europe*. 2nd Edition. (Englewood Cliffs, New Jersey: Prentice-Hall, 1975).

FROM MARXISM TO DEPENDENCY—IDEOLOGY TO THEORY

Marxism is an ideology purporting to identify the motivations and instincts of all humans in their natural environment. It is not, however, an autonomous theory of international relations. *Marxist* ideology does, nonetheless, set the stage for the evolution of a distinct theory in the "lens" of International Political Economy (IPE) known as *Dependency Theory*. Dependency theory builds upon the fundamental Marxist notions of economically-divergent classes. Dependency theory then expands this understanding into propositions concerning the fundamental inequality of states based upon the international economic requirements of capitalism.

THE RADICAL TENETS OF MARXISM—THE BASIS OF DEPENDENCY

The writings of Karl Marx and his partner, Friedrich Engels, set the stage for dependency by outlining a coherent view of how societies organize, how economic production evolves through history, and how each state in the world political economy is "predetermined" in the path of economic development it must take. In *Marxism*, man's fundamental nature is viewed as pre-disposed toward conflict. This conflict stems from the aggressive pursuit of economic well-being in the various modes of historic economic organization. In this fashion, *Marxism* presumes that economics determines politics.

The intellectual "Grandfather" of modern radicalism is the renowned and often misunderstood Karl Marx. Marx was born in 1818 to wealthy Jewish parents in Trier, Germany. Marx's father, Heinrich, was a legal advocate (lawyer) who converted to Christianity while Marx was still young. Heinrich undertook this conversion in order to legitimize his law firm and to expand his business contacts. Heinrich Marx hoped that young Karl would become a lawyer like his father. Heinrich sent Karl to the finest Prussian universities in the hopes that a father-and-son legal team would ensue. While at universities in Bonn and Berlin, however, Karl's interests turned from law toward studies into the forces of change and progress in societal organization. Marx's growing intellectual obsession with the subject of the rise and fall of societies was influenced greatly by "German mysticism" and the philosophy of *the dialectic*, developed by Prussian philosopher Georg Hegel.[3]

Marx's studies of Hegel taught him that human societies organized around simple, immutable principles of life; and that there existed a logical and progressive path of societal organization toward a more "perfect" world. Marx broke with Hegel, however, over the issue

---

2. For an explanation (or theory) of international relations to be "systemic" it must exhibit global import and be broadly generalizable to the universal human condition. Those strains of radical thought which do not represent a global ideology or transnational call to revolutionary political action may, therefore, be of local or regional interest (like the IRA in Northern Ireland, or the rise of revolutionary Islamic fundamentalism in the Middle East), but cannot be considered truly systemic international relations theory. As this essay concentrates on broadly generalizable strains of radicalism, localized and regional variants of radicalism, as well as those lacking an organized philosophy of understanding and action, will be omitted. For a more detailed discussion of systemic international relations theory, see Kenneth Waltz, *Man, The State, and War: A Theoretical Essay* (New York: Columbia University Press, 1959); and Bruce Bueno de Mesquita, "Toward a Scientific Understanding of International Conflict: A Personal View." *International Studies Quarterly.* Vol. 29 (1985): 121-135. For a summary of the view that revolutionary Islam is less a transnational political force and more an umbrella for a diverse and disorganized group of nationalistic political ideologies, see Leon T. Hadar, "What Green Peril?" *Foreign Affairs*, 72:2 (Spring 1993): 27-42.

3. Robert L. Heilbroner, *The Worldly Philosophers*, 6th Edition (New York: Simon and Schuster, 1986) 136-170.

of the dominant principle guiding human existence. Hegel believed that the main organizing principle of life was imbedded in political organization. Marx believed that the essence of humanity was much more materialistic—anchored in human economics. For Marx, it was the productive forces of life that determined how humans organized society into political units and, in turn, the ensuing social relations between humans.[4]

The notion of Class—the economically-driven division of society between "haves" and "have nots"—is central to Marx's basic understanding of "how and why" societies organize in the manner they do.[5] In explaining the pervasive influence of economic class in human relations, Marx retained Hegel's deterministic notion of the dialectic.[6] Specifically, he agreed with the Hegelian notion that human progress is driven by the recurring process of a thesis (the present) clashing with an antithesis (the exact opposite of the present) until the two produce a compromise synthesis (a place somewhere in between, which becomes the future). Once the synthesis is achieved, a good Hegelian believed that this synthesis became the new operating thesis, which would spontaneously generate a new antithesis, whereupon the dialectic struggle between thesis and antithesis would automatically begin again.[7]

Yet Hegel and his followers believed that the *thesis* of human existence at any given time was based upon an individual society's integration of the role of the individual and the role of the state—*Politics*. Marx, on the other hand, was convinced that the human condition was actually materialistic—that is, based upon the physical, not the ideological nature of human existence. For Marx, the essence of the human "physical condition" was associated with the production and consumption of material goods—*Economics*. For this reason, Marxism has as its central focus the creative and destructive societal processes necessary to advance human wealth. Society, therefore, must be assessed on its wealth-generating ability and the characteristics of human inter-relations that flow from this productive processes.[8] Marx felt that human *economic classes* evolved through a *dialectic (thesis-antithesis-synthesis)* process. (see Figure 1)

Marx's focus upon the material and the pre-determined manner in which economic production establishes the social relations possible between humans is known as the concept of dialectic materialism. In dialectic materialism, new economic classes come into existence through the relatively peaceful process of class conflict and accommodation. This process, Marx argued, was necessary to spawn each new, improved iteration of human economic history. For Marx, societies evolved through the logical, successive and progressive periods of economic organization.[9] Combining the notions of class divisions (the spark plug of human conflict) and dialectic materialism (the guarantor of progressive economic evolution), Marx crafted an explanation of human economic history known as historical materialism. Historical materialism is the key to Marxism. It

---

4. For a deeper discussion of the life and times of Karl Marx, placed in the context of his writings and philosophies, see Angus Walker, *Marx: His Theory and Its Context*, 2nd Edition (London: Rivers Oram Press, 1979).

5. Anthony Brewer, *Marxist Theories of Imperialism*, (London: Routledge, 1980).

6. The dialectic viewed the process of mankind's historical evolution as logical, patterned, based upon tension and constructive conflict, and necessarily good. See, Franz Wiedmann, *Hegel*, (New York: Pegasus, 1968).

7. Heilbroner, op. cit.

8. Walker, op. cit.

9. *Karl Marx: The Essential Writings*, ed. Frederic L. Bender, (Boulder: Westview Press, 1972).

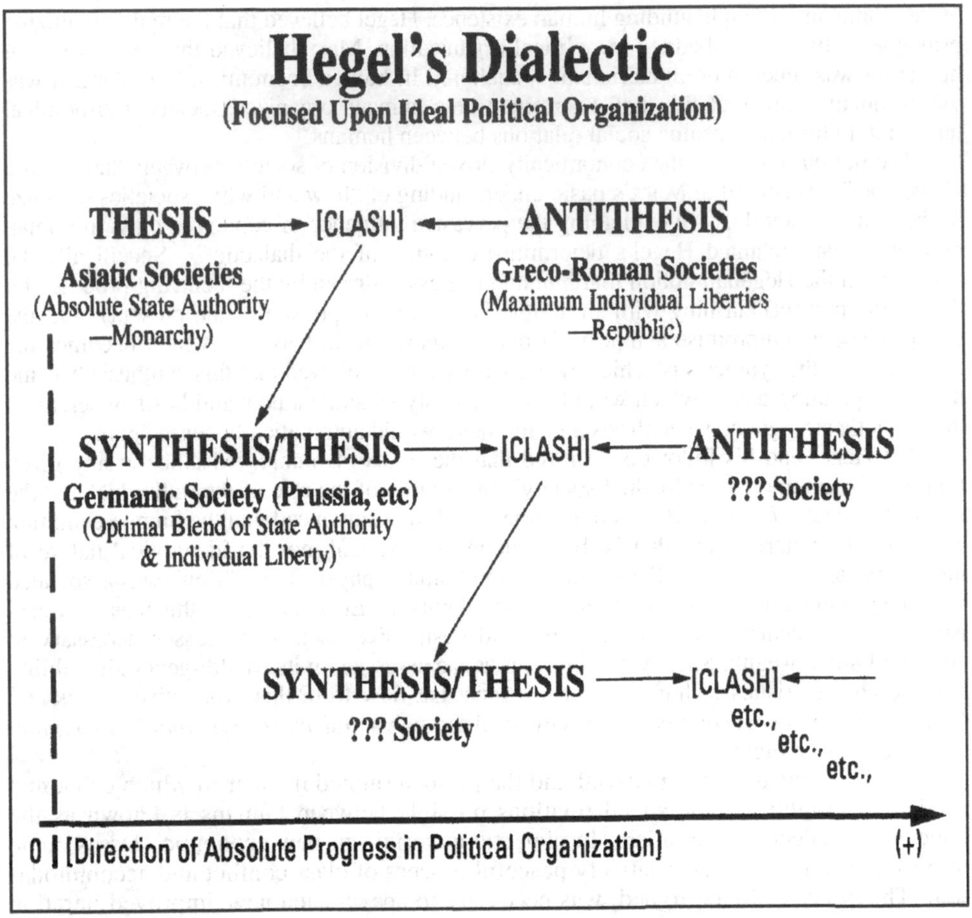

Figure 1.

features six distinct periods of human economic history: primitive communism, the slave system, the feudal system, capitalism, socialism, and, eventually, communism. (See Figure 2.)

In the first three stages of human development, Marx argued that mankind went through a logical process of economic specialization vital to advance economic standards of living. For Marx, *primitive communism* was a period of ideal social relations between humans, but this human harmony was doomed by the appalling poverty and economic misery endemic at the time. In primitive communism, social harmony was the norm because no human or group of humans felt themselves superior to others. According to Marx, this harmony accrued because all humans were involved in essentially the same economic activities—crude, seasonally-driven periods of hunting, gathering and hibernation. Human-kind's basic harmony notwithstanding, this undifferentiated economic organization of society was incapable of generating higher wealth, longer life spans, or specialized services in medicine and science. As a result, Marx concluded that economic

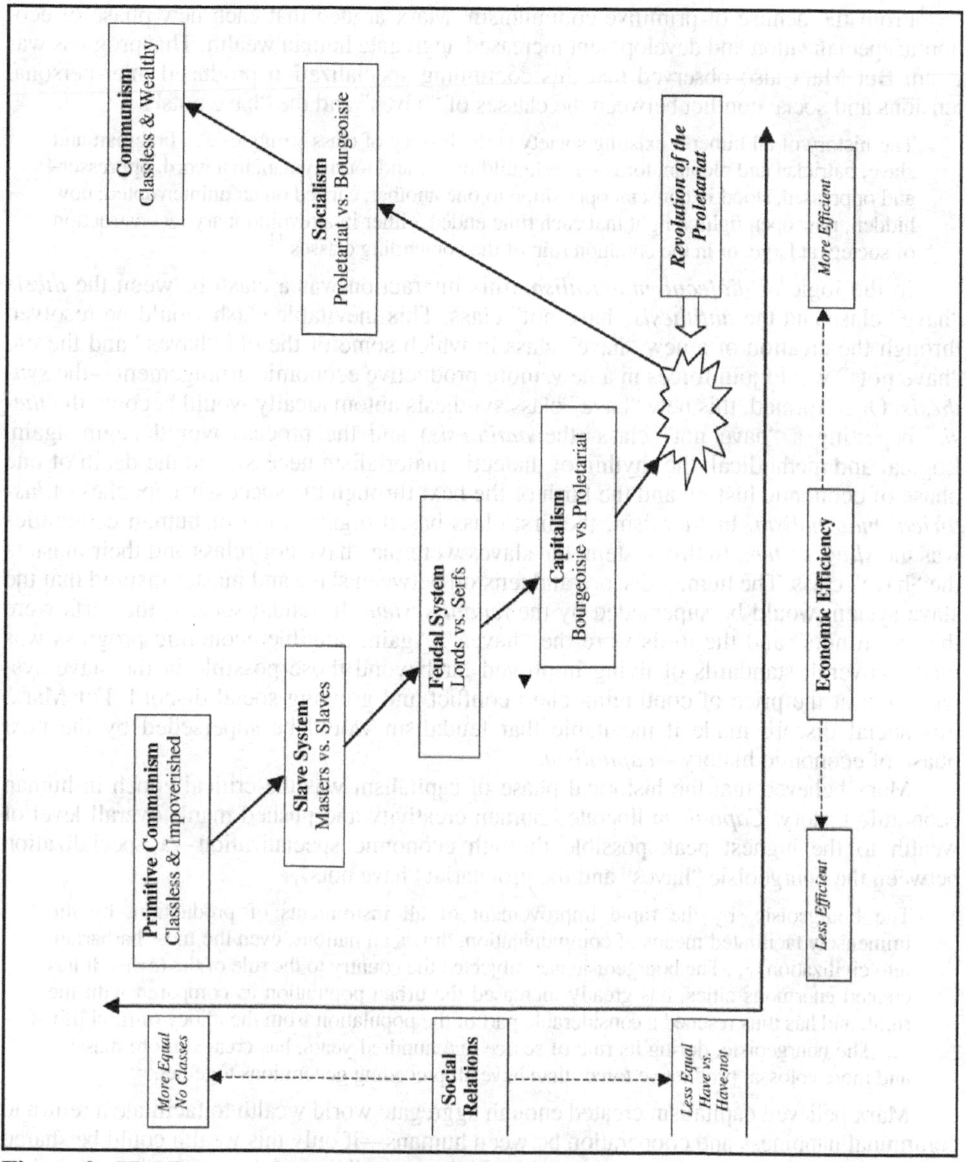

Figure 2. The Process of Marx's Dialectic Materialism

efficiency mandated that humans group into specialized productive *classes*—one class to own the means of economic production and the other class to work for those who owned the means of production. The byproduct of this economic specialization would free the "owners" of the means of production to think, dream, and invent, thereby modernizing the overall economy and producing greater aggregate net wealth.[10]

From the demise of primitive communism, Marx argued that each new phase of economic specialization and development increased aggregate human wealth. This progress was good. But Marx also observed that this continuing specialization produced inter-personal tensions and social conflict between the classes of "haves" and the "have nots".

> The history of all hitherto existing society is the history of class struggles . . . Freeman and slave, patrician and plebian, lord and serf,guildmaster and journeyman, in a word, oppressor-and oppressed, stood in constant opposition to one another, carried on an uninterrupted, now hidden, now open fight, a fight that each time ended, either in a revolutionary reconstruction of society at large, or in the common ruin of the contending classes.[11]

In the logic of *dialectic materialism*, this interaction was a clash between the *thesis* "have" class and the *antithesis* "have not" class. This inevitable clash would be resolved through the creation of a new "have" class in which some of the old "haves" and the old "have nots" would join forces in a new, more productive economic arrangement—the *synthesis*. Once formed, this new "have" class synthesis automatically would become the *thesis*, begetting a "have not" class (the *antithesis*) and the process would begin again. Logical and methodical, the rhythm of dialectic materialism necessitated the death of one phase of economic history and the birth of the next through the successive epoches of *historical materialism*. In Marxism, the first class-based organization of human economics was the *slave system*. In this system, the slaves were the "have not" class and their masters the "have" class. The human discord and tension between slave and master insured that the slave system would be superseded by the *feudal system*. In feudal society, the serfs were the "have nots" and the lords were the "haves". Again, tangible economic progress was made—overall standards of living improved far beyond those possible in the slave system—but at the price of continuing class conflict and growing social discord. For Marx, this social discord made it inevitable that feudalism would be superseded by the next phase of economic history—*capitalism*.[12]

Marx believed that the historical phase of capitalism was the critical epoch in human economic history. *Capitalism* liberated human creativity and pushed man's overall level of wealth to the highest peak possible through economic specialization—a specialization between the bourgeoisie "haves" and the proletariat "have nots".

> The bourgeoisie, by the rapid improvement of all instruments of production, by the immensely facilitated means of communication, draws all nations, even the most barbarian, into civilization. . . . The bourgeoisie has subjected the country to the rule of the towns. It has created enormous cities, has greatly increased the urban population as compared with the rural, and has thus rescued a considerable part of the population from the idiocy of rural life. . . . The bourgeoisie, during its rule of scarce one hundred years, has created more massive and more colossal productive forces than have all preceding generations together.[13]

Marx believed capitalism created enough aggregate world wealth to facilitate a return to communal happiness and cooperation between humans—if only this wealth could be shared equally amongst all. Yet, Marx argued that the longstanding social stratification of society

10. Walker, op. cit.

11. Karl Marx and Friedrich Engels, *The Communist Manifesto*, ed. Friedrich Engels (New York: International Publishers, 1948) 9.

12. *Marx and Engels: Basic Writings on Politics and Philosophy*, ed. Lewis S. Feuer, (Garden City, New York: Doubleday Company, 1959).

13. Marx and Engels, *The Communist Manifesto*, ed. Friedrich Engels, op. cit., 14-15.

into an intensely greedy bourgeoisie and impoverished, growing proletariat created a schism that precluded any peaceful accommodation between the two.

For this reason, Marx asserted that *dialectic materialism* must terminate with the *capitalist* phase. History could no longer evolve from one mode of production to another by that relatively docile process of struggle and accommodation between one period's "haves" and "have nots". Marx argued that *capitalism* was so ossified in its class divisions that only a violent revolution by the lower economic class against the bourgeoisie upper class could fulfill the logic of economic history's pre-determined plan—the return of peaceful and harmonious social relations between all humans at a sustainable level of economic growth and an egalitarian distribution of individual wealth.

> The social conditions of the old society no longer exist for the proletariat. The proletarian is without property; his relation to his wife and children has no longer anything in common with bourgeois family relations; . . . Law, morality, religion, are to [the proletarian] so many bourgeois prejudices, behind which lurk in ambush just as many bourgeois interests. . . .The proletarian cannot become masters . . . except by abolishing their own previous mode of appropriation, and thereby also every other previous mode of appropriation. All previous movements were movements of minorities . . . [t]he proletarian movement is the. . . movement of the immense majority, in the interest of the immense majority. The proletariat. . . . cannot raise itself up, without the whole incumbent strata of official society being sprung into the air. . . . into open revolution.[14]

Marx predicted, therefore, that a "revolution of the proletariat" was both inevitable and vital to unseat the bourgeoisie class. Only such a violent undertaking could unseat the bourgeoisie from its throne of power and elevate the proletariat to temporary political control of the wealth-abundant capitalist state. Once it possessed political control of the apparatus of the state, Marx argued, the proletariat "haves" could undertake a temporary period of *socialism.* During this period of socialism, the proletariat would brutally "re-educate" the bourgeoisie "have nots" against further exploitation of fellow humans, while simultaneously reallocating bourgeoisie wealth to all in the society.

> If the proletariat during its contest with the bourgeoisie is compelled, by the force of circumstances, to organize itself as a class; if, by means of a revolution, it makes itself the ruling class, and, as such sweeps away by force the old conditions of production, then it will, along with these conditions, have swept away the conditions for the existence of class antagonisms, and will thereby have abolished its own supremacy as a class.[15]

At the end of this brief period of socialism, Marx envisioned a final, *communist* phase of historical materialism.[16] The communist phase would feature a return to the classless world of primitive communism. "In place of the old bourgeoisie society, . . . shall [be] an association in which the free development of each is the condition for the free development of all."[17] This time, however, social harmony and justice would be sustainable due to the sound productive base developed by capitalism for future, non-exploitative economic growth. Indeed, in the ultimate economic state of *communism*, mankind's social interactions would revert to a fundamentally harmonious nature. The social chaos and conflict

14. Ibid. 20-21.

15. Ibid. 31.

16. *Marx and Engels: Basic Writings on Politics and Philosophy,* op. cit.

17. Marx and Engels, *The Communist Manifesto,* ed. Friedrich Engels, op. cit., 31.

bred by economic class conflict would be purged from the planet, and all humans would become healthy, wealthy and fulfilled.

Both Marx and his prolific colleague, Friedrich Engels, felt that a cogent exposition of the logic of historical materialism would encourage a "class consciousness" on the part of the proletariat. Both were hopeful that the proletariat could be inspired to band together and take its case "to the streets" through a violent overthrow of the bourgeoisie. Marx and Engels each fully expected their forecast revolution to occur by the mid-1800s. Each of them spent their family savings and life-blood in numerous efforts to spur revolt by the workers of such cities as Paris, London and New York. Both died in the late 1800s as impoverished, unfulfilled and frustrated prophets.[18]

LENIN'S REVISION OF THE MARXIST LEGACY

After the deaths of Marx and Engels, Marxism remained a powerful intellectual force for radical change within the various states of Europe. Its prescriptive failings were the subject of the ongoing meetings of the *Second Communist International* (1871-1914), a broad coalition of international Marxist groups committed to facilitating the revolution and to "keeping faith" with the international proletariat.[19] Yet, before the *Second Communist International* could devise a workable plan for the "revolution of the proletariat", an even greater frustration befell the surviving disciples of Marxism—the "Crisis of 1914". In the wake of the first battles of World War I, Marx's critical "revolution of the proletariat" seemed total folly. Not only had the proletariat of capitalist western Europe failed to take up arms against its tyrannical bourgeoisie oppressors, it had instead gone to war *on behalf* of the bourgeoisie of its state *and against* the fellow proletariat from adjoining countries! A Marxist crisis of faith was at hand, and it took the fertile imagination and international speculations of Vladimir Illich Lenin to rescue Marxism from the "junk pile of historical irrelevance".[20]

Lenin revitalized Marxism while writing in exile at a Swiss hideaway in late 1916. Lenin adapted Marx to the realities of the 20th century while borrowing liberally from the non-Marxist writings of J. A. Hobson and others on the topic of "underconsumption" in mature capitalist states.[21] Lenin's writings asserted that Marx remained fundamentally correct about the corrosive nature of capitalism, but had failed to identify a critical seventh phase of economic evolution. In "*Imperialism, The Highest Stage of Capitalism*" [1917], Lenin writes a section entitled "Imperialism as a Special State of Capitalism", which refines Marxist "historical materialism" in a significant way. Lenin contends that Marx died before he recognized that the terrified bourgeoisie of Europe had devised a way to co-opt the proletariat and to stave off, albeit temporarily, the inevitable revolution. This time-buying technique, Lenin argued, was the hallmark of a new, post-capitalist phase of historical materialism: The "Imperialist Phase" of human economic development. [See Figure 3]

The *Imperialist Phase* was one in which the bourgeoisie exported finance capital and finished products to colonies overseas, while in turn extracting cheap resources and material wealth from these poor colonies. With their imperialist booty, the bourgeoisie of the capital-

---

18. Heilbroner, op. cit.

19. Stromberg, op. cit.

20. Ibid.

21. Brewer, *Marxist Theories of Imperialism*, op. cit.

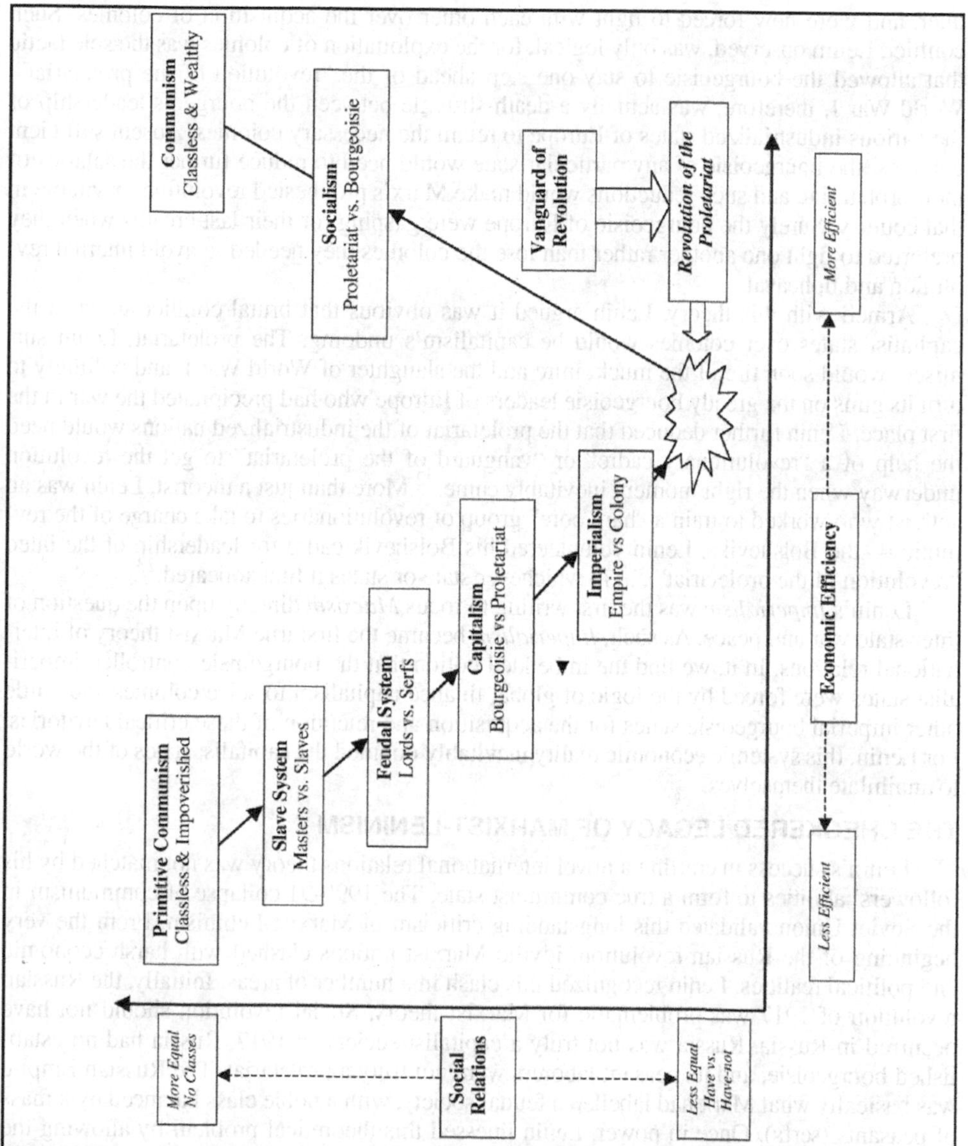

Figure 3. Imperialism as a Special State of Capitalism

ist world bought-off the naive proletariat of Europe for a pittance of that to which the proletariat was entitled.

The capitalists, Lenin reasoned, were clever; yet not quite clever enough. In the process of gobbling-up colonies the capitalist states of Europe had run out of new real estate to conquer, and were now forced to fight with each other over the acquisition of colonies. Such conflict, Lenin observed, was only logical, for the exploitation of colonies was the sole tactic that allowed the bourgeoisie to stay one step ahead of the "revolution of the proletariat". World War I, therefore, was actually a death-struggle between the bourgeois leadership of the various industrialized states of Europe to retain the necessary colonies. Absent sufficient colonies, the bourgeoisie of any particular state would need to reduce further the salaries of their proletariat, and such reductions would make Marx's prophesied revolution inevitable in that country. Surely the bourgeoisie of Europe were gasping for their last breaths when they preferred to fight one another rather than lose the colonies they needed to avoid internal revolution and upheaval.

Armed with this theory, Lenin argued it was obvious that brutal conflict amongst the capitalist states over colonies would be capitalism's undoing. The proletariat, Lenin surmised, would soon tire of the muck, mire and the slaughter of World War I, and willingly to turn its guns on the greedy bourgeoisie leaders of Europe who had precipitated the war in the first place. Lenin further deduced that the proletariat of the industrialized nations would need the help of a "revolutionary cadre" or "vanguard of the proletariat" to get the revolution underway when the right moment inevitably came.[22] More than just a theorist, Lenin was an activist who worked to train a "hard core" group of revolutionaries to take charge of the revolution—the Bolsheviks. Lenin volunteered his Bolshevik cadre for leadership of the fated "revolution of the proletariat" . . . in whichever state or states it first appeared.[23]

Lenin's *Imperialism* was the first writing to focus *Marxism* directly upon the question of inter-state war and peace. As such, *Imperialism* became the first true Marxist theory of international relations. In it, we find the imbedded notion that the bourgeoisie-controlled imperialist states were forced by the logic of global finance capitalism to seize colonies and battle other imperial bourgeoisie states for the acquisition and retention of these critical territories. For Lenin, this systemic economic reality inevitably doomed the capitalist states of the world to annihilate themselves.

THE CHECKERED LEGACY OF MARXIST-LENINISM

Lenin's success in crafting a novel international relations theory was not matched by his followers' abilities to form a true communist state. The 1990-91 collapse of communism in the Soviet Union validated this longstanding criticism of Marxist-Leninism. From the very beginning of the Russian revolution, idyllic Marxist notions clashed with harsh economic and political realities. Lenin recognized this clash in a number of areas. Initially, the Russian revolution of 1917 was problematic for Marxist theory. Social revolution should not have occurred in Russia. Russia was not truly a capitalist society in 1917. Russia had no established bourgeoisie, and its peasant laborers were not truly a proletariat. The Russian Empire was basically what Marx had labelled a feudal society, with a noble class balanced by a mass of peasants (serfs). Once in power, Lenin finessed this theoretical problem by allowing the USSR a brief fling with capitalism—the "New Economic Program" (NEP), which ran from 1921-1927. Novel at best, NEP never did create a flourishing capitalist state before it was swept aside by Josef Stalin's forced waves of agricultural and industrial collectivization (from 1927-37).

---

22. *The Lenin Anthology*, ed. Robert C. Tucker, (New York: W.W. Norton and Company, 1975).

23. Stromberg, op. cit.; and Vladimir Lenin, "What Is To Be Done?" in *The Lenin Anthology*, op. cit.

Revolutionary Marxism also was challenged by the failure of the Russian revolution to serve as the catalyst for a wave of "proletarian revolutions" all across war-weary Europe. As he wrote in *"What Is To Be Done?"*, Lenin firmly believed that a successful revolution of the proletariat in one European state would precipitate a wave of revolutions across all others.[24] This faith in the international power of Marxism began to wane for Lenin and his Bolshevik faithful as peace "broke out" across Europe without any attendant collapse of the old capitalist regimes.

Frustrated, yet unbowed, the Bolsheviks formally broke ties with the *Second Communist International* in March 1919 and created a Soviet-dominated *Third Communist International* (or Comintern). Here again, pragmatism overshadowed pure Marxist theory. The Comintern abandoned a previous Marxist-Leninist belief in the international force of a "bottoms-up" revolution in individual capitalist states in favor of a "copy-us" approach to social revolution where the Soviet model was the only acceptable path to revolution and post-revolutionary socialism. The Comintern became a major vehicle for Bolshevik leaders to carry on Soviet foreign policy. Stalin effectively used the Comintern to legitimize Soviet assistance to a wide array of communist organizations in countries ranging from Argentina to China. By the time Stalin disbanded the Comintern in 1943, it had sewn the seeds for post-World War II communist expansion. Indeed, the Comintern's failure in whipping up inter-war revolution in western Europe was balanced by the successes it enjoyed in nurturing communist organizations led by Josef Broz Tito in Yugoslavia, Mao Tse Tung in China, Kim Il Sung in Korea and Ho Chi Minh in Vietnam. Given popular legitimacy by their heroic resistance to Japanese and German aggression during World War II, these Comintern-inspired communist leaders would come to political power in the decade from 1945-54.

The successes enjoyed by Comintern-inspired communist parties after World War II rapidly internationalized the potency and (to the western world) the threat of world-wide communist revolution. The reality of international communism, we now know, was much different.

The post-World War II appeal of communism had much less to do with a heartfelt allegiance to Moscow's rules for organizing a successful communist society, and much more to do with the power of the Marxist social critique and its call for violent revolutionary action to break the oppressive shackles of capitalist imperialism. Thus, the nationalist organizations in the newly liberated states of the world did willingly accept Moscow's military and financial help in overthrowing occupying capitalist powers, yet Moscow did not often gain undying fealty in return for this help. As Tito demonstrated in 1947, and Mao showed again in 1969, reciprocal allegiance to Moscow extended only so far. Each of these communist statesmen interpreted Marxist ideology in accordance with their own needs, chafing at Moscow's insistence that all communist states follow Soviet policy. Willing to exploit Moscow for aid and arms, but not to be tied to Moscow's policy demands, many newly liberated states turned to their own interpretation of the essence of Marxism in international relations.

As the 1950s gave way to the 1960s, newly emerging states on the continents of Africa, Asia, and Latin America began to reformulate Marxist and Marxist-Leninist notions about the fundamental unfairness of capitalism in a fashion more in concert with their interests rather than with those emanating from Moscow. Indeed, even as the power of Moscow to control international communism waned, the power of Marxist concepts highlighting the fundamental unfairness of capitalism and calling for the revolution of the "have nots" over the "haves" gained new life in the form of *dependency theory.*

24. Lenin, "What Is To Be Done?" in *The Lenin Anthology*, op. cit.

THE MARXIST-LENINIST LEGACY AND DEPENDENCY THEORY

As a theory of international relations and international political economy, Marxist-Leninism is both a *social critique* of international affairs and *a call to action.* Each of these aspects resonate in the writings of dependency theorists. Specifically, the social critique of Marxism is captured in dependency theory beliefs that the industrialized countries of the capitalist world need to exploit impoverished colonies to survive economically. *Dependency theory* thus derives from an imbedded Marxist-Leninist notion: The inequality of economic status exhibited between states in the international political economy is a permanent feature of the capitalist world economy that causes tension and armed conflict, and it will continue to do so until the capitalist mode of production passes onto the 'ash-heap of economic history'.

Dependency also echoes the Marxist revolutionary *call to action.* It does so in two ways. Initially, dependency theory agrees that world capitalism only can be altered by violent overthrow, and through any means possible. It also contends that capitalist elites from well developed "have" states will remain parasitic on lesser developed countries unless the fundamental principles of the capitalist economic order are forcibly altered. Lenin's theory of Imperialism, therefore, extended the Marxist notion of "class" into a form appealing to modern Third World international relations theorists; yet, it did so in a fashion that neither Marx or Lenin could have fully anticipated.

DEPENDENCY'S WORLD VIEW

Born in the Third World, dependency theory is a variant of Marxism that must be evaluated independently from the Marxist-Leninist communist experiments in the USSR, Eastern Europe and China. As Professor Richard Sklar of UCLA wrote in 1988, ". . . [s]ocialism in Africa persists with vigor as a political movement and a philosophy of social protest."[25] The same can be said of socialism and communism in significant portions of Asia, Latin America and the Middle East. Indeed, dependency theory remains a pervasive force in Third World notions of the international political economy even as the Marxist experiments in Russia and Eastern Europe have collapsed.

Dependency theory developed over the period from the late 1950s to the early 1970s. This period featured a rapid growth in the number of states in the world, as the former colonies of Britain, France, the Netherlands and other "imperialist powers" obtained their independence. As these countries entered the world economy as newly sovereign states, many found themselves tormented by grave economic difficulties. Most of these states suffered from persistent unemployment and poverty and faced serious problems when trying to produce industrial products for sale in the international market place. These states began to perceive that the world capitalist economy was "stacked" against them.[26]

Many international relations theorists recognized the economic challenges faced by the newly-liberated colonies and empathized with their difficulties. A wave of international relations theorists born or residing in these ex-colonial states (Fernando Enrique Cardoso, Theotonio Dos Santos, Arghiri Emmanuel, Andre' Gunder Frank and Immanuel Wallerstein) were joined by their colleagues from industrialized states, including Paul Baran and Gunnar Myrdal, in asserting that the world economy was inherently biased against "late developing"

---

25. Richard L. Sklar, "Beyond Capitalism and Socialism in Africa," *The Journal of Modern African Studies*, Vol. 26 (March 1, 1988): 1-21.

26. Robert Gilpin, *The Political Economy of International Relations* (Princeton: Princeton University Press, 1987).

economies.[27] These theorists helped explain the difficulties faced by the "new states" by updating the Marxist notion of "haves" and "have nots", arguing that Lenin had described yet never fully explored the permanently debilitating economic consequences to the colonies created during western imperialism.

In the dependency analysis of world history, imperialism created an entire class of "have not" states in the international economy. Ex-colonies were poor and exploited precisely because of their long history as subordinate elements of the world capitalist system. The attainment of political independence was not enough to break this web of economic exploitation and poverty. The operation of trade and finance markets in the international capitalist system perpetuated dependence by the ex-colonies on the ex-colonists. Any future development of ex-colonies under the international capitalist system must remain uneven, distorted, and, at the very best, partial. In this view, formally labeled dependency theory by Brazilian scholar Theotonio Dos Santos, there can be no development in the "have not states" without revolution. Here, however, the revolution is no longer that of the proletariat over the bourgeoisie, but one bent on the total destruction of the international capitalist system and its replacement with an international socialist system.[28]

As originally conceived, *dependency theory* incorporates three fundamental notions of Marxist thought: 1) A Marxist-based ideology detailing the need for the impoverished economic class to seize power; 2) A blueprint for the brutal and often repressive political and economic actions required immediately after the revolution to prevent reversal of the revolution by the old bourgeoisie apparatus of the state; 3) An appealing view of the future to help placate the people of the nation during the turbulent and violent period necessary to consolidate the anti-capitalist revolution.

Dependency theory, however, grafts a Marxist-Leninist revolutionary credo and the Marxist notion of "class" onto a very different understanding of the fundamental unfairness of the international capitalist economic order. Dependency adherents argue that Lenin captured a fundamental truth of world capitalism when he noted that developed capitalist states require underdeveloped colonies to sustain their economic growth and prosperity. They disagree with Lenin when he asserts that developed capitalist states would fight to the death over the amalgamation and retention of colonies.[29]

Dependency theory instead contends that developed capitalist states are a unified group of "haves". Thus, these "haves" will cooperate with each other in order to keep the lesser developed, "have not" colonies impoverished. In this theoretical conception, class is divided into the economic "have" states of the North, and the economic "have not" states of the South; and the North can only prosper if the South remains destitute. This view, in turn, forms the basis for the concept of *dependent development* central to dependency theory: late-

---

27. Brewer, *Marxist Theories of Imperialism*, op. cit.

28. Dependency theory has a sibling, known as *structural theory.* While structural theory shares all of Marxist-Leninist-inspired dependency theory critiques of the world capitalist system (also referred to as the "dual economy"), it argues that the natural processes of this system can be reformed without resort of all-out revolution. For purposes of this essay, I will treat these theories as Siamese twins, and refer to the development strategies of each under the broad rubric of *"dependency theory".* Those readers desiring a deeper understanding of the reform processes proposed under structuralism should consult, Joan Spero, *The Politics of International Relations*, 4th Ed. (New York: St. Martin's Press, 1990), 147-59; Gilpin, *The Political Economy of International Relations*, op. cit., 263-90; and Theotonio Dos Santos, "The Structure of Dependence", *American Economic Review* No. 60 (1970): 231-36.

29. Brewer, *Marxist Theories of Imperialism*, op. cit.

industrializing states of the Third World depend upon the technology, money and know-how of the early developing states of the First World to such a degree that their growth is totally dependent upon the vicissitudes of a world capitalist economy that is stacked against them. In the language pioneered by Theotonio Dos Santos and extended by the writings of Johan Galtung, the First World "Core" states must economically exploit and impoverish the Third World "Periphery" states in order to prosper in the world political economy.[30]

Dependency theorists highlight the continuing economic trials and tribulations of the Periphery states—famine, an extremely skewed pattern of wealth distribution between rich and poor, enormous international debt, and a continuous outflow of wealth from the Periphery to the Core through multinational industries and banks—as evidence of the systemic impoverishment of the South imposed by the North. Theotonio Dos Santos and others cite the multinational corporation (MNC) as the chief agent of evil in the domination of Core over Periphery in the 20th century. MNCs are seen as agents for Core interests.[31] They operate with success in the Periphery by co-opting and rewarding "special agents" who run the huge businesses and maintain the repressive governments that keep the population working for scant wages on inhumane factory assembly lines or on backward, run-down farms.[32]

Dependency theory further argues that authoritarian political structures must exist in the Periphery, further harming its citizens. Authoritarian governments are the norm in the Periphery because democracy would fundamentally challenge the powerful position of those agents of the Core states who must maintain control of the Periphery bureaucracy to continue systematic economic exploitation. For this reason, representative, democratic governments are atypical in Third World countries. Those few Periphery states with voting rights usually practice politics of fear and intimidation at the polls, so free choice and unbiased voting is merely fiction.[33]

DEPENDENCY'S CALL TO ACTION

In keeping with Marxist revolutionary credo, dependency theory argues that the only way to break the vicious cycle of dependent development is for the citizens of the Periphery to overthrow their corrupt, "Core-puppet" governments violently, and then to use the structures of their state government to break the Periphery state from the shackles of the world capitalist economy. While agreeing on the need to unseat violently the manipulative agents of the Core in the positions of political power in the Periphery, dependency theorists differ on the best technique to be used then in decoupling the Periphery state from the international capitalist economy.

Some *dependentsias* argue for policy approaches featuring extreme *economic self-reliance* by the Periphery state—in some cases approaching total self-reliance (or autarky). Others contend that a "*Basic Needs Approach*"—encouraging very limited association with the world capitalist economy on projects designed to enhance domestic literacy, health care, nutritional deficiencies, and population control efforts, while avoiding all other contacts—might prove the best way for the Periphery to break from the ties binding them unfairly to the Core states. Still other dependency theorists argue for a *New Interna-*

---

30. Dos Santos, "The Structure of Dependence", op. cit.; and Johan Galtung, "A Structural Theory of Imperialism, *Journal of Peace Research*, No. 2 (1971): 81-117.

31. Osvaldo Sunkel, "Big Business and 'Dependencia'," *Foreign Affairs*, (1972): 517-31.

32. Brewer, *Marxist Theories of Imperialism*, op. cit.

33. Tony Smith, *The Patterns of Imperialism* (Cambridge: Cambridge University Press, 1981).

tional Economic Order (NIEO) designed to restructure the worst features of the capitalist economic system, thereby enabling continued Periphery participation in a "fairer" world capitalist economic order. The chief demands of these NIEO proponents are: 1) reform of commodity markets in favor of Third World exports, 2) promotion of favorable incentives for increased industrialization of the Third World, 3) relief of most of the international debt held in the Third World as acknowledgement that unfair treatment by the Core led to the accrual of most Third World debt.[34]

DEPENDENCY THEORY, ITS CRITICS AND ITS CONTEMPORARY CRISIS

Although it remains a powerful and appealing force in many parts of the Third World, dependency theory faces stern challenges from *liberals* and *mercantilists*. In the late 1980s and early 1990s, these challenges to dependency have made great inroads in the Third World. These inroads grew from both the failure of dependency-based efforts to sustain viable development, and from the highly publicized successes enjoyed by those Periphery states following a more standard model of interaction with the world capitalist economy.

Many Periphery experiments with economic self-reliance and Basic Needs approaches in the 1960s and 1970s fell flat. States like Brazil experienced brief, initial successes while striving to be economically "self sufficient", but then went through agonizing economic collapse when buffeted by a surge in world oil prices and a collapse in the value of the Brazilian currency.[35] A collective Periphery effort to force NIEO upon the industrialized states through the UN, conducted most fiercely during the mid-1970s, produced a severe backlash from the "have states". Core states first blocked all NIEO demands, and then withdrew financial support for many of the aid and developmental programs they had started in the 1950s and 1960s. As a result, Third World "solidarity" seemingly produced a worse-off Periphery rather than an improved international economic order.[36]

In the meantime, *liberals* continued to argue against the basic underpinnings of dependency theory. For *liberals*, the failure of economic development in the "have not" states was less the fault of the world capitalist system than of the ignorant (and often greedy) economic policies promulgated by the leaders of Periphery states. W. Arthur Lewis articulates this liberal critique of dependency theory in many of his writings during the 1960s and 1970s. Lewis champions the liberal assertion that Periphery colonies have precipitated their own economic downfall by trying to industrialize before establishing a proper agricultural base.[37]

In the late 1980s, liberals were aided in their counter-attack by the economic development achieved in some key Periphery states—collectively known as the NICs (Newly Industrialized Countries). Miraculous economic growth in the most prominent of the NICs—the "Four Tigers" of Taiwan, Singapore, Hong Kong, and South Korea—is held up by liberals as evidence that prudent adherence to basic capitalist economic principles can elevate Periph-

---

[34] Andre Gunder Frank, *Dependent Accumulation and Underdevelopment*, (London: MacMillan, 1978); and Fernando Cardoso and Enzo Faletto, *Dependency and Development in Latin America*, (Berkeley: University of California Press, 1979).

[35] Peter Evans, *Dependent Development: The Alliance of Multinational, State, and Local Capital in Brazil* (Princeton: Princeton University Press, 1979).

[36] Michael Doyle, "Ideologies and the New International Economic Order," *World Politics* (April 1983): 426-64.

[37] W. Arthur Lewis, *The Evolution of the International Economic Order*, (Princeton: Princeton University Press, 1978).

ery states into the club of wealthy Core states. These four states, liberals argue, refused to play the "dependency game" of economic isolation or NIEO and instead developed robust free markets while taking advantage of unfettered international free trade. This approach enabled them to become high technology export giants over the brief span of some 20-25 years from 1960 to 1985. Swayed by the success of the "Four Tigers" many Third World states have opted to play copy-cat in the hopes of becoming NICs themselves. Since 1975, dozens of Periphery states have "liberalized" their economies away from failed dependency experiments in the hopes that they too will become economic "miracles".[38] These experiments have a long way to go; yet the fact that they are underway indicates the degree to which the liberal critique of dependency has fragmented once-uniform Third World efforts toward radical international economic reform.[39]

For *mercantilists* like Stephen Krasner, Periphery claims of economic impoverishment by the global economic system are merely a cover for Periphery desires to restructure the international political hierarchy. Krasner observes that power is the source of wealth, but this power is autonomous and dominant, not beholden to inter-state camaraderie based upon an economic "have club" and "have not club".[40] Mercantilists, therefore, view the whole dependency argument as an economic smoke-screen designed to mask a more basic desire in the Third World to wrest greater international political power.[41] As detailed by Krasner, NIEO was a clarion call for many "have" states: "resist or be mugged".[42] Growing Third World demands for radical adjustment of the rules of the global capitalist economy frightened developed states and hardened their approach toward the Periphery. In the 1980s, many developed states withdrew their support for development projects in the Periphery as the Third World began to default on massive 1960s state-to-state loans and 1970s commercial-bank loans, while at the same time screaming for greater debt relief. By the early 1990s, developed states became increasingly reluctant to support Third World development projects without first "auditing" these states and putting them on a rigid budgetary diet, monitored by the International Monetary Fund (IMF). Moreover, industrial states have taken a dim view of recent Third World demands for heavy economic compensation for environmental clean-up and preservation projects. Refusing to legitimize any Third World claims for further wealth transfer, developed states stand arm-in-arm while refusing Periphery linkage of wealth transfer to greater environmentalism.[43] This rise in Core state solidarity has complicated greatly Third World strategies toward "leveling" the international economic "playing field". In turn, the solidarity has left Periphery states very fragmented over which of a potpourri of alternative development approaches to pursue in the 1990s.

---

38. For a pessimistic viewpoint on the prospects for other Third World states to emulate the success of the "Four Tigers", see, Robin Broad and John Cavanaugh, "No More NICs," *Foreign Policy* No. 72, (Fall 1988): 81-103.

39. Gilpin, *The Political Economy of International Relations*, op. cit.

40. Stephen Krasner, *Structural Conflict: The Third World Against Global Liberalism*, (Berkeley, CA: University of California Press, 1985).

41. Benjamin Cohen, *The Question of Imperialism: The Political Economy of Dominance and Dependency*, (New York: Basic Books, 1973).

42. Krasner, *Structural Conflict: The Third World Against Global Liberalism*, op. cit.

43. Kendall W. Stiles, "IMF Conditionality: Coercion or Compromise?" *World Development*, Vol 18. No. 7, (1990): 959-974.

THE LEGACY OF RADICALISM IN INTERNATIONAL RELATIONS

While acknowledging dependency's critics, enumerating its recent prescriptive failings, and indicating the degree to which the Third World has become fragmented in its approach to pursuing development, students of international political economy must continue to consider carefully its imbedded social critique of international capitalism.[44]

Dependency theory argues that the international capitalist system has inherent distributional failures which prevent it from ever developing the whole world evenly. In this failing, capitalism breeds a class-division of states into "haves" and "have-nots". From this division, international conflict and violence naturally follow.

Dependency theory remains skeptical that many more states can follow the model of the "Four Tigers". The theory forecasts failure for most of those Periphery states currently attempting similar liberal reforms.[45] If few of these reforms succeed, dependency theory likely will get its second wind.[46]

Dependency also preaches "strength in numbers" to the states of the underdeveloped world. The ongoing fragmentation in Third World approaches to development is thus frustrating for dependency, but not terminal. As individual Third World efforts toward development are tried and fail, dependency theory stands ready to remind prodigal Periphery states that organized revolution against the Core states remains the viable, logical remedy for Third World suffering. The forecast of continuing impoverishment and the inevitable necessity of violent revolution to overthrow the international capitalist system, therefore, remain the lasting legacies of radicalism and *Marxism* which live on, albeit just beneath the surface, in the Third World.

---

44. This assessment is based upon the rationale summarized in this conclusion in addition to the reasons outlined in the final chapter of Gilpin, *The Political Economy of International Relations*, op. cit.

45. Broad and Cavanaugh, op. cit.

46. G. K. Helleiner, "Conventional Foolishness and Overall Ignorance: Current Approaches to Global Transformation and Development," *The Political Economy of Development and Under-development*," ed. Charles K. Wilber and Kenneth P. Jameson, 5th Ed. (New York: McGraw-Hill, Inc., 1992): 36-54.

Introduction to Dependency Theory

Like Imperialist Theory, Dependency Theory is Marxist in nature. Class (i.e., "haves" vs. "have-nots") is therefore essential to both. Unlike Marxism which addresses "classes of people" and Imperialist Theory, which focused primarily on relations between great powers (i.e., "have" states vs. other "have" states), however, Dependency Theory focuses on relations between "classes of states" – "have" states vs. "have-not" states.

Dependency Theory does two things: It provides one approach to solving the problem of underdevelopment that exists for many states often simplistically labeled "the South," the "Third World," the "Periphery, or "Less Developed Countries" (LDCs). Dependency Theory also expands upon Hobson and Lenin's treatment of how and why capitalist states behave the way they do towards underdeveloped states.

Dependency Theory's independent variable is simply the existence of the two economic classes: the "haves" and the "have-nots".

As Hobson and Lenin noted, industrializing states, in a never-ending search for markets and resources, extended their reach into many undeveloped countries over a century ago. The trade relationship between the industrializing states and the undeveloped states became one favorable only to the developed state while the undeveloped state was forced into a subordinate position of resource supplier and finished good purchaser. Exploitation of undeveloped states by industrialized states became endemic by the end of the 19th century.

Modernization Theory dominated the thinking on development in the 1950s. The foundation of Modernization Theory is the concept of the superiority of industrialized society over all others, even to the point of industrialization being considered the only correct way for undeveloped societies to tap into the growth being experienced in the North. Inherent in Modernization Theory is the placement of the blame for underdevelopment on the underdeveloped states themselves. Dependency Theory was a reaction to this perspective that holds instead that the condition of underdeveloped states was based more upon the relationship of the underdeveloped states with the colonizers, than upon any internal development strategy. Marxists quickly pointed out the connection between exploitive imperialists and Marxist-Leninist ideology. Furthermore, as Lynch notes in "Foundations of Radicalism," they called for extreme measures (i.e., two-step call to action) to be taken to break the cycle of poverty and dependence.

Theotonio Dos Santos was one of the first to attempt to flesh out a theory of dependency. In his article "The Structure of Dependence," Dos Santos further describes the "problem" of dependency and then discusses the state action (i.e., the dependent variable) required to break it. Dependency Theory is therefore largely prescriptive.

As with Imperialist Theory, a word of caution is necessary regarding Dependency Theory's connection to Marxism. Do not let the end of the Cold War and the debunking of Marxist ideology in its Soviet Communist manifestation allow Dependency Theory to be swept into the dustbin of history as well. Marxism looks at the impact of imperialism on the historical dialectic, while Dependency Theory looks at the impact of imperialism on underdeveloped states.

The Cold War promulgated an illusion of the global importance of undeveloped and underdeveloped states as the two superpowers fought over fence states. The non-aligned movement was a reaction to this all-or-nothing, East or West attitude. The end of the Cold War brought an end to the non-aligned movement and its corresponding regime. However, post-Cold War expectations about the development that would accompany the New World Order have gone largely unmet. Therefore, unsatisfied underdeveloped states, although not publicly espousing Marxist doctrine, may lean more toward radical approaches.

Recognizing the prescriptive nature of both Dependency Theory and Neo-liberal Development Theory it should be clear that they serve as the "menu" from which underdeveloped states order. Regardless of the "facts" (often provided by the developed world) proving that the neo-liberal approach is best, it is unwise to assume that developing states will automatically recognize these facts and select the so-called rational choice. On the contrary, the promise of quick and radical changes may result in the pursuit of the less than logical policy.

The Structure of Dependence

Theotonio Dos Santos

This paper attempts to demonstrate that the dependence of Latin American countries on other countries cannot be overcome without a qualitative change in their internal structures and external relations. We shall attempt to show that the relations of dependence to which these countries are subjected conform to a type of international and internal structure which leads them to underdevelopment or more precisely to a dependent structure that deepens and aggravates the fundamental problems of their peoples.

1. WHAT IS DEPENDENCE?

> By dependence we mean a situation in which the economy of certain countries is conditioned by the development and expansion of another economy to which the former is subjected. The relation of interdependence between two or more economies, and between these and world trade, assumes the form of dependence when some countries (the dominant ones) can expand and can be self-sustaining, while other countries (the dependent ones) can do this only as a reflection of that expansion, which can have either a positive or a negative effect on their immediate development.[1]

The concept of dependence permits us to see the internal situation of these countries as part of world economy. In the Marxian tradition, the theory of imperialism has been developed as a study of the process of expansion of the imperialist centers and of their world domination. In the epoch of the revolutionary movement of the Third World, we have to develop the theory of laws of internal development in those countries that are the object of such expansion and are governed by them. This theoretical step transcends the theory of development which seeks to explain the situation of the underdeveloped countries as a product of their slowness or failure to adopt the patterns of efficiency characteristic of developed countries (or to "modernize" or "develop" themselves). Although capitalist development theory admits the existence of an "external" dependence, it is unable to perceive underdevelopment in the way our present theory perceives it, as a consequence and part of the process of the world expansion of capitalism—a part that is necessary to and integrally linked with it.

In analyzing the process of constituting a world economy that integrates the so-called "national economies" in a world market of commodities, capital, and even of labor power, we see that the relations produced by this market are unequal and combined—unequal because development of parts of the system occurs at the expense of other parts. Trade relations are based on monopolistic control of the market, which leads to the transfer of surplus generated in the dependent countries to the dominant countries; financial relations are, from the viewpoint of the dominant powers, based on loans and the export of capital, which permit them to receive interest and profits; thus increasing their domestic surplus and strengthening their control over the economies of the other countries. For the dependent countries these relations represent an export of profits and interest which carries off part of the surplus generated domestically and leads to a loss of control over their productive resources. In order to permit these disadvantageous relations, the dependent countries

1. Theotonio Dos Santos, *La crisis de la teoria del desarrollo y las relaciones de dependencia en América Latina*, Boletin del CESO, 3 (Santiago, Chile, 1968).

From *American Economic review*, Vol. 60, 1970, pp. 231-236. Reprinted with permission of the American Economic Association. Portions of the text and some footnotes have been omitted.

must generate large surpluses, not in such a way as to create higher levels of technology but rather superexploited manpower. The result is to limit the development of their internal market and their technical and cultural capacity, as well as the moral and physical health of their people. We call this combined development because it is the combination of these inequalities and the transfer of resources from the most backward and dependent sectors to the most advanced and dominant ones which explains the inequality, deepens it, and transforms it into a necessary and structural element of the world economy.

2. HISTORIC FORMS OF DEPENDENCE

Historic forms of dependence are conditioned by: (1) the basic forms of this world economy which has its own laws of development; (2) the type of economic relations dominant in the capitalist centers and the ways in which the latter expand outward; and (3) the types of economic relations existing inside the peripheral countries which are incorporated into the situation of dependence within the network of international economic relations generated by capitalist expansion. It is not within the purview of this paper to study these forms in detail but only to distinguish broad characteristics of development.

Drawing on an earlier study, we may distinguish: (1) Colonial dependence, trade export in nature, in which commercial and financial capital in alliance with the colonialist state dominated the economic relations of the Europeans and the colonies, by means of a trade monopoly complemented by a colonial monopoly of land, mines, and manpower (serf or slave) in the colonized countries. (2) Financial-industrial dependence which consolidated itself at the end of the nineteenth century, characterized by the domination of big capital in the hegemonic centers, and its expansion abroad through investment in the production of raw materials and agricultural products for consumption in the hegemonic centers. A productive structure grew up in the dependent countries devoted to the export of these products (which Levin labeled export economies;[2] other analysis in other regions[3,4]), producing what ECLA has called "foreign-oriented development" *(desarrollo hacia afuera)* [5]. (3) In the postwar period a new type of dependence has been consolidated, based on multinational corporations which began to invest in industries geared to the internal market of underdeveloped countries. This form of dependence is basically technological-industrial dependence [6].

Each of these forms of dependence corresponds to a situation which conditioned not only the international relations of these countries but also their internal structures: the orientation of production, the forms of capital accumulation, the reproduction of the economy, and, simultaneously, their social and political structure.

3. THE EXPORT ECONOMIES

In forms (1) and (2) of dependence, production is geared to those products destined for export (gold, silver, and tropical products in the colonial epoch; raw materials and agricultural products in the epoch of industrial-financial dependence); i. e., production is determined by demand from the hegemonic centers. The internal productive structure is characterized by rigid specialization and monoculture in entire regions (the Caribbean, the

---

2. I. V. Levin, *The Export Economies* (Harvard Univ. Press, 1964).

3. Gunnar Myrdal, *Asian Drama* (Pantheon, 1968).

4. K. Nkrumah, *Neocolonialismo, última etapa del imperialismo*, Siglo XXI (Mexico, 1966).

5. Cepal, *La CEPAL y el Análisis del Desarrollo Latinoamericano* (1968, Santiago, Chile)

6. Theotonio Dos Santos, *El nuevo caracter de la dependencia*, CESO (Santiago de Chile, 1968).

Brazilian Northeast, etc.). Alongside these export sectors there grew up certain complementary economic activities (cattle-raising and some manufacturing, for example) which were dependent, in general, on the export sector to which they sell their products. There was a third, subsistence economy which provided manpower for the export sector under favorable conditions and toward which excess population shifted during periods unfavorable to international trade.

Under these conditions, the existing internal market was restricted by four factors: (I) Most of the national income was derived from export, which was used to purchase the inputs required by export production (slaves, for example) or luxury goods consumed by the hacienda- and mine-owners, and by the more prosperous employees. (2) The available manpower was subject to very arduous forms of superexploitation, which limited its consumption. (3) Part of the consumption of these workers was provided by the subsistence economy, which served as a complement to their income and as a refuge during periods of depression. (4) A fourth factor was to be found in those countries in which land and mines were in the hands of foreigners (cases of an enclave economy): a great part of the accumulated surplus was destined to be sent abroad in the form of profits, limiting not only internal consumption but also possibilities of reinvestment.[7] In the case of enclave economies the relations of the foreign companies with the hegemonic center were even more exploitative and were complemented by the fact that purchases by the enclave were made directly abroad.

4. THE NEW DEPENDENCE

The new form of dependence, (3) above, is in process of developing and is conditioned by the exigencies of the international commodity and capital markets. The possibility of generating new investments depends on the existence of financial resources in foreign currency for the purchase of machinery and processed raw materials not produced domestically. Such purchases are subject to two limitations: the limit of resources generated by the export sector (reflected in the balance of payments, which includes not only trade but also service relations); and the limitations of monopoly on patents which leads monopolistic firms to prefer to transfer their machines in the form of capital rather than as commodities for sale. It is necessary to analyze these relations of dependence if we are to understand the fundamental structural limits they place on the development of these economies.

1. Industrial development is dependent on an export sector for the foreign currency to buy the inputs utilized by the industrial sector. The first consequence of this dependence is the need to preserve the traditional export sector, which limits economically the development of the internal market by the conservation of backward relations of production and signifies, politically, the maintenance of power by traditional decadent oligarchies. In the countries where these sectors are controlled by foreign capital, it signifies the remittance abroad of high profits, and political dependence on those interests. Only in rare instances does foreign capital not control at least the marketing of these products. In response to these limitations, dependent countries in the 1930s and 1940s developed a policy of exchange restrictions and taxes on the national and foreign export sector; today they tend toward the gradual nationalization of production and toward the imposition of certain timid limitations on foreign control of the marketing of exported products. Furthermore, they seek, still somewhat timidly, to

7. Paul Baran, *Political Economy of Growth* (Monthly Review Press, 1967).

obtain better terms for the sale of their products. In recent decades, they have created mechanisms for international price agreements, and today UNCTAD and ECLA press to obtain more favorable tariff conditions for these products on the part of the hegemonic centers. It is important to point out that the industrial development of these countries is dependent on the situation of the export sector, the continued existence of which they are obliged to accept.

2. Industrial development is, then, strongly conditioned by fluctuations in the balance of payments. This leads toward deficit due to the relations of dependence themselves. The causes of the deficit are three:

(a) Trade relations take place in a highly monopolized international market, which tends to lower the price of raw materials and to raise the prices of industrial products, particularly inputs. In the second place, there is a tendency in modern technology to replace various primary products with synthetic raw materials. Consequently the balance of trade in these countries tends to be less favorable (even though they show a general surplus). The overall Latin American balance of trade from 1946 to 1968 shows a surplus for each of those years. The same thing happens in almost every underdeveloped country. However, the losses due to deterioration of the terms of trade (on the basis of data from ECLA and the International Monetary Fund), including Cuba, were $26,383 million for the 1951-66 period, taking 1950 prices as a base. If Cuba and Venezuela are excluded, the total is $15,925 million.

(b) For the reasons already given, foreign capital retains control over the most dynamic sectors of the economy and repatriates a high volume of profit; consequently, capital accounts are highly unfavorable to dependent countries. The data show that the amount of capital leaving the country is much greater than the amount entering; this produces an enslaving deficit in capital accounts. To this must be added the deficit in certain services which are virtually under total foreign control—such as freight transport, royalty payments, technical aid, etc. Consequently, an important deficit is produced in the total balance of payments; thus limiting the possibility of importation of inputs for industrialization.

(c) The result is that "foreign financing" becomes necessary, in two forms: to cover the existing deficit, and to "finance" development by means of loans for the stimulation of investments and to "supply" an internal economic surplus which was decapitalized to a large extent by the remittance of part of the surplus generated domestically and sent abroad as profits.

Foreign capital and foreign "aid" thus fill up the holes that they themselves created. The real value of this aid, however, is doubtful. If overcharges resulting from the restrictive terms of the aid are subtracted from the total amount of the grants, the average net flow, according to calculations of the Inter-American Economic and Social Council, is approximately 54 percent of the gross flow [8].

If we take account of certain further facts—that a high proportion of aid is paid in local currencies, that Latin American countries make contributions to international financial institutions, and that credits are often "tied"—we find a "real component of foreign aid" of 42.2 percent on a very favorable hypothesis and of 38.3 percent on a more realistic one[9]. The gravity of the situation becomes even clearer if we consider that these credits are used in

---

8. Consejo Interamericano Economico Social (CIES) O.A.S., Interamerican Economic and Social Council, External Financing for Development in L.A. *El Financiamiento Externo para el Desarrollo de America Latina* (Pan-American Union, Washington, 1969).

9. Ibid., II-33.

large part to finance North American investments, to subsidize foreign imports which compete with national products, to introduce technology not adapted to the needs of underdeveloped countries, and to invest in low-priority sectors of the national economies. The hard truth is that the underdeveloped countries have to pay for all of the "aid" they receive. This situation is generating an enormous protest movement by Latin American governments seeking at least partial relief from such negative relations.

3. Finally, industrial development is strongly conditioned by the technological monopoly exercised by imperialist centers. We have seen that the underdeveloped countries depend on the importation of machinery and raw materials for the development of industries. However, these goods are not freely available in the international market; they are patented and usually belong to the big companies. The big companies do not sell machinery and processed raw materials as simple merchandise: they demand either the payment of royalties, etc., for their utilization or, in most cases, they convert these goods into capital and introduce them in the form of their own investments. This is how machinery which is replaced in the hegemonic centers by more advanced technology is sent to dependent countries as capital for the installation of affiliates. Let us pause and examine these relations, in order to understand their oppressive and exploitative character.

The dependent countries do not have sufficient foreign currency, for the reasons given. Local businessmen have financing difficulties, and they must pay for the utilization of certain patented techniques. These factors oblige the national bourgeois governments to facilitate the entry of foreign capital in order to supply the restricted national market, which is strongly protected by high tariffs in order to promote industrialization. Thus, foreign capital enters with all the advantages: in many cases, it is given exemption from exchange controls for the importation of machinery; financing of sites for installation of industries is provided; government financing agencies facilitate industrialization; loans are available from foreign and domestic banks, which prefer such clients; foreign aid often subsidizes such investments and finances complementary public investments; after installation, high profits obtained in such favorable circumstances can be invested freely. Thus it is not surprising that the data of the U.S. Department of Commerce reveal that the percentage of capital brought in from abroad by these companies is but a part of the total amount of invested capital. These data show that in the period from 1946 to 1967 the new entries of capital into Latin America for direct investment amounted to $5,415 million, while the sum of reinvested profits was $4,424 million. On the other hand, the transfers of profits from Latin America to the United States amounted to $14,775 million. If we estimate total profits as approximately equal to transfers plus reinvestments we have the sum of $18,983 million. In spite of enormous transfers of profits to the United States, the book value of the United State's direct investment in Latin America went from $3,045 million in 1946 to $10,213 million in 1967. From these data it is clear that: (1) Of the new investments made by U.S. companies in Latin America for the period 1946-67, 55 percent corresponds to new entries of capital and 45 percent to reinvestment of profits; in recent years, the trend is more marked, with reinvestments between 1960 and 1966 representing more than 60 percent of new investments. (2) Remittances remained at about 10 percent of book value throughout the period. (3) The ratio of remitted capital to new flow is around 2.7 for the period 1946-67; that is, for each dollar that enters $2.70 leaves. In the 1960's this ratio roughly doubled, and in some years was considerably higher.

The *Survey of Current Business* data on sources and uses of funds for direct North American investment in Latin America in the period 1957-64 show that, of the total sources of direct investment in Latin America, only 11.8 percent came from the United States. The remainder is, in large part, the result of the activities of North American firms in Latin America (46.4 percent net income, 27.7 percent under the heading of depreciation), and from "sources located abroad" (14.1 percent). It is significant that the funds obtained abroad that are external to the companies are greater than the funds originating in the United States.

5. EFFECTS ON THE PRODUCTIVE STRUCTURE

It is easy to grasp, even if only superficially, the effects that this dependent structure has on the productive system itself in these countries and the role of this structure in determining a specified type of development, characterized by its dependent nature.

The productive system in the underdeveloped countries is essentially determined by these international relations. In the first place, the need to conserve the agrarian or mining export structure generates a combination between more advanced economic centers that extract surplus value from the more backward sectors, and also between internal "metropolitan" centers and internal interdependent "colonial" centers[10]. The unequal and combined character of capitalist development at the international level is reproduced internally in an acute form. In the second place the industrial and technological structure responds more closely to the interests of the multinational corporations than to internal developmental needs (conceived of not only in terms of the overall interests of the population, but also from the point of view of the interests of a national capitalist development). In the third place, the same technological and economic-financial concentration of the hegemonic economies is transferred without substantial alteration to very different economies and societies, giving rise to a highly unequal productive structure, a high concentration of incomes, underutilization of installed capacity, intensive exploitation of existing markets concentrated in large cities, etc.

The accumulation of capital in such circumstances assumes its own characteristics. In the first place, it is characterized by profound differences among domestic wage-levels, in the context of a local cheap labor market, combined with a capital intensive technology. The result, from the point of view of relative surplus value, is a high rate of exploitation of labor power. (On measurements of forms of exploitation, see.[11])

This exploitation is further aggravated by the high prices of industrial products enforced by protectionism, exemptions and subsidies given by the national governments, and "aid" from hegemonic centers. Furthermore, since dependent accumulation is necessarily tied into the international economy, it is profoundly conditioned by the unequal and combined character of international capitalist economic relations, by the technological and financial control of the imperialist centers by the realities of the balance of payments, by the economic policies of the state, etc. The role of the state in the growth of national and foreign capital merits a much fuller analysis than can be made here.

Using the analysis offered here as a point of departure, it is possible to understand the limits that this productive system imposes on the growth of the internal markets of these countries. The survival of traditional relations in the countryside is a serious limitation on the

---

10. Andre G. Frank, *Development and Underdevelopment in Latin America* (Monthly Review Press, 1968).

11. Pablo Gonzalez Casanova, *Sociologia de la explotación*, Siglo XXI (Mexico, 1969).

size of the market, since industrialization does not offer hopeful prospects. The productive structure created by dependent industrialization limits the growth of the internal market.

First, it subjects the labor force to highly exploitative relations which limit its purchasing power. Second, in adopting a technology of intensive capital use, it creates very few jobs in comparison with population growth, and limits the generation of new sources of income. These two limitations affect the growth of the consumer goods market. Third, the remittance abroad of profits carries away part of the economic surplus generated within the country. In all these ways limits are put on the possible creation of basic national industries which could provide a market for the capital goods this surplus would make possible if it were not remitted abroad.

From this cursory analysis we see that the alleged backwardness of these economies is not due to a lack of integration with capitalism but that, on the contrary, the most powerful obstacles to their full development come from the way in which they are joined to this international system and its laws of development.

5. SOME CONCLUSIONS: DEPENDENT REPRODUCTION

In order to understand the system of dependent reproduction and the socioeconomic institutions created by it, we must see it as part of a system of world economic relations based on monopolistic control of large-scale capital, on control of certain economic and financial centers over others, on a monopoly of a complex technology that leads to unequal and combined development at a national and international level. Attempts to analyze backwardness as a failure to assimilate more advanced models of production or to modernize are nothing more than ideology disguised as science. The same is true of the attempts to analyze this international economy in terms of relations among elements in free competition, such as the theory of comparative costs which seeks to justify the inequalities of the world economic system and to conceal the relations of exploitation on which it is based.[12]

In reality we can understand what is happening in the underdeveloped countries only when we see that they develop within the framework of a process of dependent production and reproduction. This system is a dependent one because it reproduces a productive system whose development is limited by those world relations which necessarily lead to the development of only certain economic sectors, to trade under unequal conditions,[13] to domestic competition with international capital under unequal conditions, to the imposition of relations of superexploitation of the domestic labor force with a view to dividing the economic surplus thus generated between internal and external forces of domination.[14]

In reproducing such a productive system and such international relations, the development of dependent capitalism reproduces the factors that prevent it from reaching a nationally and internationally advantageous situation; and it thus reproduces backwardness, misery, and social marginalization within its borders. The development that it produces benefits very narrow sectors, encounters unyielding domestic obstacles to its continued economic growth (with respect to both internal and foreign markets), and leads to the progressive accumulation of balance-of-payments deficits, which in turn generate more dependence and more superexploitation.

---

12. Cristian Palloix, *Problémes de la Croissance en Economie Ouverte* (Maspero, Paris, 1969).

13. A. Emmanuel, *L'Echange Inégal* (Maspero, Paris, 1969).

14. Paul Baran, *Political Economy of Growth* (Monthly Review Press, 1967).

The political measures proposed by the developmentalists of ECLA, UNCTAD, BID, etc., do not appear to permit destruction of these terrible chains imposed by dependent development. We have examined the alternative forms of development presented for Latin America and the dependent countries under such conditions elsewhere.[15] Everything now indicates that what can be expected is a long process of sharp political and military confrontations and of profound social radicalization which will lead these countries to a dilemma: governments of force which open the way to fascism, or popular revolutionary governments, which open the way to socialism. Intermediate solutions have proved to be in, in such a contradictory reality, empty and utopian.

15. Theotonio Dos Santos, *La dependencia económica y las alternativas de cambio en América Latina*, Ponencia al IX Congreso Latinoamericano de Sociologia (Mexico, Nov., 1969).

Chapter Four

Sub-Systemic Lens

Introduction to Sub-systemic Lens

"The Sub-systemic Lens"

How can we explain what states do? For instance, why was the Cold War such a remarkable "long peace" between the superpowers? Why did the United States, serving as hegemonic leader of the West, provide a security umbrella, anchor the world market economy on the dollar as the key currency, dispense aid and issue commercial loans, open its markets to international commerce, and lead in the creation and maintenance of the liberal Bretton Woods economic regime? As we have seen, various perspectives in the ***Security*** and ***IPE*** Lenses explain such questions by focusing on *systemic* variables: for example, the balance of power, security, the distribution of wealth, trade and growth strategies, and the dynamic international roles of technology and capital.

However, ***Security*** and ***IPE*** omit important causal factors within states themselves. Their systemic level variables may constrain, but cannot eliminate choice. Focusing on structural relations among states, the Security Lens views states as "black boxes." What happens within them is seen as far less important than what happens between them. This view masks the fact that state behavior reflects *beliefs* and *political systems*, as well as innumerable small decisions, based on many diverse goals, across a complex policy structure of actors and institutions. What, for example, was the significance of individual personalities for the outcome of the Cold War? What if Stalin had died in 1945 and Roosevelt lived for a decade after World War II? What is the significance of ideology, political culture, political systems, and intragovernmental politics? Similarly, IPE theories omit important factors that explain why states do what they do. These ideologies and theories recognize that states value economic as well as security goals, and that increasingly important linkages connect domestic and foreign policies. However, the IPE lens is less comprehensive on issues such as beliefs and leadership; it also masks how states make ***choices*** about wealth, power, and values.

The **Sub-systemic** lens suggests that international relations is best understood as the consequence of ***choice***. This lens deflects the systemic focus of the first two lenses and peers into the "black box" of how states make and implement choices in international relations. Peering through this lens provides a potent supplement to explanations developed with the systemic approaches of ***Security*** and ***IPE***.

In order to understand ***"Why do states do what they do?"*** and ***"What causes conflict and cooperation among states?"*** we must open the "black box" and discard the deterministic assumption of the systemic approach. States act differently in the international environment not just because of the search for power, or even the relationship between wealth and power. In many cases, states act the way they do because they *choose* to act in certain ways. This conceptual lens suggests that beliefs and political systems affect state behavior. Further, this lens argues that states are not the only actors affecting outcomes in the international system.

Beliefs held by both elite decision-makers and the general public act as prisms—distorting reality, restricting options, differentiating distinctiveness, and often legitimizing specific policies. Strong beliefs—whether they are religious, ideological, nationalistic, or philosophical—force international actors to interpret people, countries, and events in different ways. Beliefs can be powerful incentives for behavior. Why, against all odds, did the Melians oppose the Spartans? Why, given the carnage and destruction "Over There," did President Wilson commit the United States to "the war to end all wars"? Why, in spite of both economic and political upheavals, did communism remain such a powerful ideology for over 70 years in the Soviet Union? Are democratic societies really more peaceful than authoritarian or totalitarian societies? Will democracies fight each other? Are authoritarian regimes more likely to act aggressively in the international system? Why, even with awareness of the "lessons" of fanatical nationalism learned prior to and during World War II, do we now see neo-Nazi fanatics and "ethnic cleansing" reappearing in the 1990's? To some degree, the answer lies in the power of beliefs—especially nationalism—and how they affect choice in the international system.

Specific types of *political systems* and the types of foreign policy-making processes that they produce (i.e., unitary or pluralistic) also often make "why states do what they do" a matter of choice. The *way* decisions are made can make a difference. Are foreign policy decisions really a matter of rational choice? Or an organizational output? Or a political resultant? Who *really* decides? Systemic structures and markets do not make and execute policy. People do. Institutions and organizations do. Policy-making structures and processes do. Even if the "black boxes" in the international system attempt to act rationally, the political decision-making process, individual beliefs and perceptions, and group dynamics can affect why states do what they do.

States and markets are fundamentally important actors in international relations. We learn valuable insights into how and why states respond to the international environment by examining states and markets. People and institutions within the state and on behalf of the state formulate and execute state policies. These sub-systemic actors shape policy in response to the international environment. In this process, people and institutions filter their perceptions of the international environment (and its implications for states and markets) through beliefs and types of political systems. By using this lens, one recognizes the importance of a host of sub-systemic interests: societal, cultural, institutional, organizational, constituent, and personal. In the ***Security*** and ***IPE*** lenses, the international environment significantly influences state policies. Often these influences are direct, as in the case of wars, capital flows, and tourism. More often, however, these influences are filtered and manipulated politically by sub-systemic actors and policy-making processes.

Thus, the ***Sub-systemic*** lens adds significantly to our ability to understand and explain what states do by illuminating the roles, interests, and processes of these actors. How? Keep in mind that the theme of this book is *intellectual pluralism.* International relations are too complex, dynamic, and diverse to be understood solely through descriptions or to be "captured" by any single theoretical approach. Therefore, we place a premium on using different conceptual lenses to guide our explanations. Since these lenses are distinct from one another, the explanations they produce act as cross-checks on how we explain what we want to know, as well as supplements to help us discover what we don't know.

Hence, we turn to the sub-systemic lens to help us fill in the voids in our explanations of international relations. Anchored to the preeminently political nature of state *choice*, the sub-systemic lens keys on two major questions:

> If policy and policy making are inherently political, to what degree are policy and policy making rational, coherent, and consistent? What are the implications of this "rationality quotient" for the effectiveness of policy, and for the legitimacy of the policy process?

In keeping with our theme of *intellectual pluralism,* this lens includes a number of variables and models for explaining state behavior. These variables and models differ in terms of premises about the first question above; namely, the degree of rationality and coherence in policy making. Why are these different perspectives important? How does each perspective guide explanation? What is the role of rationality in foreign policy making? These questions provide the context for the readings that follow. Some readings illuminate the challenges and dilemmas for the United States, as a pluralistic superpower, in crafting its foreign policy. Insights offered by these readings are potent for understanding how other states and international actors behave. Other works in this lens were written to provide tools for analyzing the internal processes of all states.

Ideally, foreign policy making does it all—the policy process is discrete as well as accountable, effective as well as legitimate. Ideally, foreign policy achieves all—specific policies are rational and wise as well as politically attuned to both domestic and foreign sensitivities. However, history continues to record the gap between these ideals and actual foreign policy achievements. We should be neither distraught nor discouraged by the persistence of this gap if we appreciate that the path to understanding the cause of the gap lies in developing our habits of intellectual pluralism. Armed with the sub-systemic models presented in this section, we will be better able to develop our faculties for understanding the "essence of decision."

Suggestions for Further Reading

Allison, Graham and Philip Zelikow *Essence of Decision*. New York: Addison Wesley Longman, 1999.

Beiner, Ronald, ed. *Theorizing Nationalism.* Albany, NY: State University of New York Press, 1999.

Brown, Seyom, *The Faces of Power: Constancy and Change in U.S. Foreign Policy from Truman to Johnson*. New York: Colombia University Press, 1968.

Connor, Walker. "Nation-Building or Nation-Destroying." In Fred A. Sonderman, David S. McLellan, and William S. Olson, Eds. *The Theory and Practice of International Relations*. Englewood Cliffs, NJ: Prentice Hall, 1979.

De Rivera, Joseph. *The Psychological Dimension of Foreign Policy*. Columbus, Ohio: Merrill, 1968.

Eller, Jack David. *From Culture to Ethnicity to Conflict: An Anthropological Perspective On International Ethnic Conflict.* Ann Arbor, MI: University of Michigan Press, 1999.

Fukuyama, Francis. "The End of History?" *National Interest*, No. 16 (Summer 1989): 3-18.

George, Alexander. *Presidential Decisionmaking in Foreign Policy*. Boulder, CO: Westview, 1980.

Halperin, Morton H. *Bureaucratic Politics and Foreign Policy*. Washington, D.C.: The Brookings Institution, 1974.

Henkin, Louis, et. al. *Right Versus Might: International Law and the Use of Force*. New York: Council on Foreign Relations Press, 1991.

Hoffman, Stanley. *Janus and Minerva: Essays in the Theory and Practice of International Politics*. Boulder, CO: Westview Press, 1987.

Holsti, Ole R. "Crisis Decision-Making." In Phillip E.Tetlock, et al, eds. *Behavior, Society and Nuclear War*. New York: Oxford Univerity Press, 1989.

Huntington, Samuel P., "The Clash of Civilizations?" *Foreign Affairs* 72 (Summer 1993): 22-49.

Janis, Irving. *Groupthink.* Boston: Houghton Mifflin Company, 1972.
Jervis, Robert, "Hypotheses on Misperception." *World Politics* 20 (1968): 454-478.
Jervis, Robert. *Perception and Misperception in International Politics.* Princeton: Princeton University Press, 1976.
Krasner, Stephen D. "Are Bureaucracies Important? (Or Allison in Wonderland)". *Foreign Policy* No. 7 (Summer 1972):159-179.
Lebow, Richard Ned. *Between Peace and War.* Baltimore: Johns Hopkins University Press, 1981.
Levy, Jack S. and Michael N. Barnett, "Alliance Formation, Domestic Political Economy and Third World Security." *Jerusalem Journal of International Relations* 14 (December 1992): 19-40.
Moynihan, Daniel Patrick. *Pandemonium: Ethnicity in International Politics.* New York: Oxford University Press, 1993.
Posen, Barry R. *The Sources of Military Doctrine.* Ithaca, NY: Cornell University Press, 1984.
Rosenau, James N., ed. *Domestic Sources of Foreign Policy.* New York: Free Press, 1967.
Smith, Anthony, D. *Nationalism and Modernism: A Critical Survey of Recent Theories of Nations and Nationalism.* London: Routledge, 1998.
Snyder, Jack. *Myths of Empire: Domestic Politics and International Ambition.* Ithaca, NY: Cornell University Press, 1991.
Vincent, R.J. *Human Rights and International Relations.* New York: Cambridge University Press, 1986.
Welch, David A. "The Organizational Process and Bureaucratic Politics Paradigms: Retrospect and Prospect." *International Security* 17, 2 (Fall 1992): 112-146.
Werner, Suzanne and Douglas Lemke, "Opposites Do Not Attract: The Impact of Domestic Institutions, Power and Prior Commitments on Alignment Choices." *International Studies Quarterly* 41 (September 1997): 529-546.
Zeev, Maoz. *National Choices and International Processes.* New York: Cambridge University Press, 1990.

Regime Model

Roy C Macridis and Steven L. Burg
Political Regimes: A General Framework

Introduction to the Regime Model

The central assumption of the sub-systemic level of analysis is that domestic or internal factors help us understand *why states do what they do* in the international environment. Roy Macridis and Steven Burg provide an important foundation for this perspective by exploring the concept of political regime, which encompasses the primary political processes and structures within the state. The authors define political regime as the "particular combination of institutions, rules, and procedures" that help determine the nature and effectiveness of governance within a state.[1]

Macridis and Burg remind us that the study of domestic politics is concerned primarily with power and how it is exercised. Power, of course, is also at the center of the study of international relations. The critical difference is that politics within the state is fundamentally about the hierarchical organization of power, while international politics operates in a context of "anarchy" or the dispersion of power. Nevertheless, profound differences mark regimes in terms of the type of governance (democratic or authoritarian) and in the amount of authority and power enjoyed by the regime. In order to understand these differences, Macridis and Burg discuss four interactive processes that characterize all political regimes: the organization of command; the organization of consent; the configuration of interests; and the organization of rights.

The particular character of these processes allows us to distinguish among political regimes: whether a regime is democratic or authoritarian and whether it enjoys sufficient power and authority to ensure political stability. For example, the "organization of command" refers to the central institutions of the state and to the elites that control them. Most regimes have similar structures—such as executive, legislative, and bureaucratic organs—to perform the functions of the state.The constraints and qualifications on the power of the elites who control these institutions is an obvious determinant of democratic governance. Since many theorists maintain that democracies rarely, if ever, fight each other, understanding the regime "model" is a valuable tool for evaluating this argument.

Equally important, the regime model allows us to conceptualize the process of regime change, which in recent decades has involved efforts at democratization in authoritarian governments as diverse as Hungary and Taiwan. These transitions are important in part because they may affect the prospects for conflict and for cooperation among states. A number of political scientists argue that although established democracies tend to have peaceful foreign policies, democratizing states are fundamentally unstable and prone to aggressive behavior. Once again, an evaluation of this argument requires the study of regimes that have not yet established strong patterns of governance.

The "Third Wave" transitions of the past three decades compel us to study anew the enduring question of the sources of political instability.[2] A linked issue, also raised by the "Third Wave," concerns the effects of political instability on the international behavior of

1. Macridis and Burg, p. 10.

2. For a comparative and authoritative examination of global democratization over the past three decades,
see Samuel Huntington, *The Third Wave* (Norman, Oklahoma: University of Oklahoma Press), 1991.

states. In their exploration of the first question, Macridis and Burg suggest that the legitimacy and effectiveness of a regime requires the cohesion of governing elites and their belief in their "right to rule." Cracks in this consensus may undermine the stability of both democratic (the American Civil War) and authoritarian regimes (post-Franco authoritarian Spain).

The quintessential example is the Soviet Union under Mikhail Gorbachev. Gorbachev's reforms were, in essence, an attempt to reduce the power and privileges of certain groups of the Soviet power elite. The resistance of these groups influenced the reformers to expand political reform in their search for allies in society, unleashing a "democratizing" process that further divided the ruling elite and profoundly unsettled the Soviet state. Similarly, Gorbachev's extensive concessions to the Western powers during this period were due in large part to his attempt to gain *external* allies in his faltering struggle for reform *and* political stability at home. In other words, Gorbachev's attempt to reform the Soviet regime and stay in power had a decisive impact on content of his foreign policy.

The experience of the Soviet Union also suggests caution in assuming that a state's foreign policy is governed by a rational assessment of threats and opportunities in the international environment. Gorbachev allowed political reform in East-Central Europe to proceed because he wanted to curry favor with the West. But he also deeply believed that these countries would remain closely tied to the Soviet Union because of their prevailing interests *and* values. It would seem that Gorbachev's miscalculation was heavily influenced by the nature of the Soviet regime, whose highly authoritarian character prevented even its leadership from effectively gauging public opinion in its "external" empire.

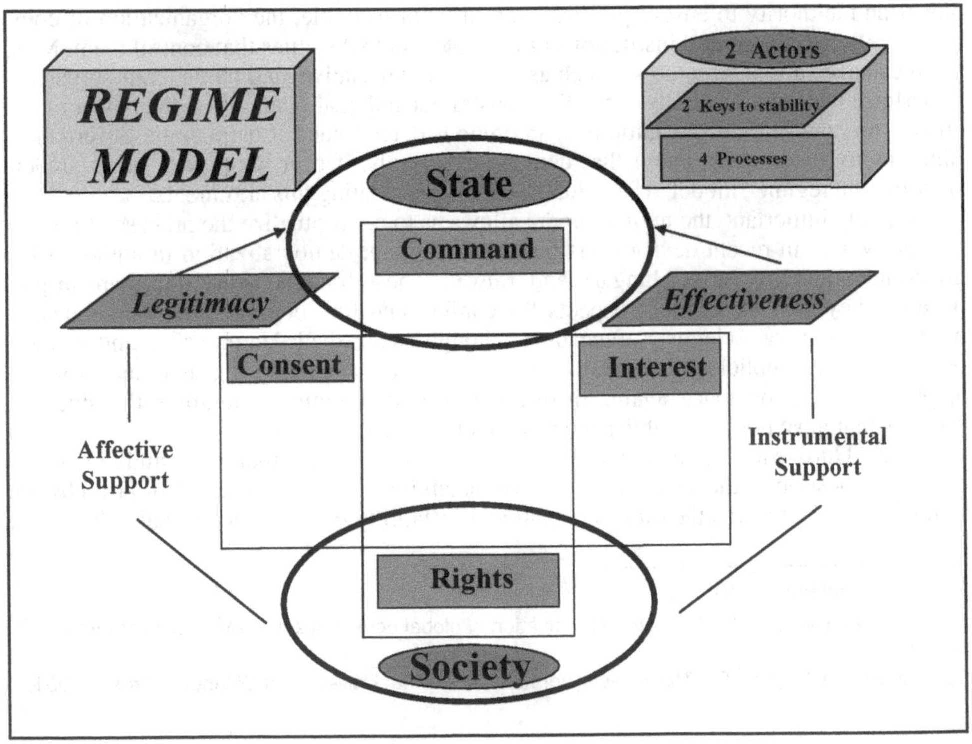

Political Regimes: A General Framework

Roy C. Macridis and Steven L. Burg

INTRODUCTION

To establish a general framework of comparative analysis, let us begin at the abstract level of system theory. A political system consists of *functions* and *structures*. *Functions* refers to the things that have to be done. Structures refers to the institutions, the mechanisms, the arrangements and the procedures through which these things are done. System theory suggests the major functions of a political system and their interrelationships and interdependence, but only in general terms. These are:

1. Generate commonly shared goals. To do so, a political system must provide for socialization; i.e., for the common acceptance by the population of the goals and the institutions through which these goals are to be realized. This concept underlines the importance of commonly shared ideas or the existence of a prevailing ideology.
2. Provide mechanisms for decision making, including both decision-making institutions and agreed-upon rules of procedure.
3. Provide for the ways and means whereby decision makers are selected, together with the rules for their succession.
4. Establish mechanisms for the articulation and aggregation of those interests that must be taken into account in the determination of policy.
5. Maintain order by defining agreed-upon rules of political behavior, and providing for effective means of enforcing them.
6. Be capable of self-preservation.[1]

All political regimes attempt to perform these functions through the institutions they establish. Different types of political regimes differ in the particular ways and means by which these functions are structured and patterned into institutions and procedures, and in the way such institutions and procedures relate to one another.

There are four major interacting processes that characterize all political systems. It is the differences among these that we will use to distinguish political regimes. They are:

1. The organization of command—in essence the state and its agencies—what we often refer to as "the government"
2. The organization of consent
3. The configuration of interests
4. The organization of rights

[1] For a discussion of the structural-functional approach that has mesmerized teachers and students for the last thirty years, see David Apter, *Introduction to Political Analysis* (Boston: Little, Brown, 1982), unit VI, pp. 377-451; also Gabriel Almond and G. Brigham Powell, Jr., Comparative Politics: A Developmental Approach (Boston: Little, Brown, 1981).

THE ORGANIZATION OF COMMAND

The Role of the State

Politics and the study of political regimes are concerned primarily with power and its exercise. Command, imperium (what the Greeks called "kyrion"), souverain, and sovereignty are the terms we most frequently come across to denote the existence of political power within a given territory. As a noted British author wrote more than a half century ago, "The state consists of a relatively small number of persons who issue and execute orders which affect a larger number in whom they are themselves included; it is of the essence of its character that, within its allotted territory, all citizens are legally bound by those orders."[2] In the language of system theory, the state makes "authoritative decisions"; that is, decisions expected to be obeyed and enforced.

The state differs from all other associations in a great number of ways: First of all, it is all-inclusive. Some of us may be members of a Catholic or Unitarian church; some of us may belong to a trade union or the American Medical Association or the Chamber of Commerce; others are proud members of the Elks or the Lions; but all of us are in the state.

Second, the purposes of the Elks, the Lions, the Catholics, the Unitarians, or the American Medical Association are special purposes, usually narrow in scope. The purposes of the state, however, are far more encompassing than those of all other associations combined. The state rules on matters such as defense, order, and social justice. Harry Eckstein waxes enthusiastic, very much in the spirit of Aristotle, when he writes that in the last analysis the state represents the principle of justice: "It is the only awesome power we have"![3]

Third, individuals can move from one association to another or withdraw from all or any of them. But it is extremely difficult to move out of the state into which you are born, even if that state places no legal restrictions on emigration.

Fourth, you can disobey the rules and regulations of an association, and nobody will bother you except your friends or your conscience. You are free to comply or not. But you do not have the same freedom when it comes to the tax collector, the judge, or the traffic light. The state possesses what no other association has: the right to use force to secure compliance. It sanctions its decisions with force and enjoys a monopoly over the use of force in the territory it controls.

Finally, while the state can use force, it also must rely on emotional supports and loyalty. The modern state, except in some extreme and usually short-lived cases, requires widespread consent and popular support in order to have its decisions obeyed without resort to coercion. The implicit ability to employ force is usually enough to insure against the few who refuse to comply. As long as the majority of its citizens comply, the state can function with a minimum of force. But, if the majority do not comply, then the state cannot survive for long.

---

2. Harold Laski, *The Grammar of Politics* (London: George Allen and Unwin, 1925), p. 295.

3. Harry Eckstein, "On the Science of the State," *Daedalus* (Fall 1979), 18; also Eric Nordlinger, *On the Autonomy of the Democratic State* (Cambridge, Mass.: Harvard University Press, 1981). According to Nordlinger, however, there is nothing awesome in the state. It is but another actor that manipulates the political forces. It is not the embodiment of justice.

Major Organs of Command

Despite the many differences, the formal organs—but not, of course, the actual political practices—most commonly associated with the command structure appear to be similar in virtually all political regimes: an executive body at the top, and administrative or bureaucratic agencies through which it carries out policy subordinate to it; a legislative body to make laws; and a judiciary to apply and settle disputes about the law. In almost all regimes, there is a functional division of judicial, legislative, and executive power, and separate institutions correspond to these functions. Another similarity is that their relationships are arranged by a constitution: A written (but occasionally unwritten) set of rules that sets forth the limits of power, the manner in which power will be used, and the responsibilities and freedoms of the citizens. Actual practices and especially the relative power and autonomy of these elements of command vary greatly among different regimes. Even within a single state, changes in these relationships over time may produce a change in regime.

Governing Elites

In studying the command structure and the institutions and agencies operating within it, we do not limit ourselves to those persons officially elected or appointed. In most political regimes the decision-makers— generally the officials who hold responsible positions (they issue and execute orders)—are part of what may loosely be called the governing elite. All discussions about elites begin with the pithy statement of the Italian sociologist Gaetano Mosca: There is "a class that rules and a class that is ruled." This division is a universal phenomenon. The ruling class is "always the less numerous, performs all political functions, monopolizes power and enjoys the advantages that power brings."[4] The "other" class, the ruled, consists of the great majority of people.

To many people, this statement is unduly cynical. It is difficult to reconcile it with democracy, where the majority are supposed to govern and where egalitarianism is the dominant concept. Nonetheless, if we study the organization of contemporary societies, we find that they are all stratified by status, power, and wealth: the few are at the top and the many are at the base. Also, there are oligarchic tendencies present in all organizations. The few invariably assume positions of authority and command, whether in business organizations, educational institutions, trade unions, political parties, or fraternal associations. In all organizations and especially in political ones, including the political party and the state, there is what another author called, in a famous phrase, an "iron law of oligarchy."[5]

A group of people with the power to make others conform to its preferences and to prevent others from following preferences contrary to its own is an elite. An elite can act directly, by occupying the decision-making organs and shaping policy and policy outcomes. In this case it assumes the status of a political elite. But it can also exercise its power indirectly, by influencing the political leaders who make policy. In the past, powerful industrialists were reputed to have operated behind the scenes of government, and it has been said that they pulled the strings: J. P. Morgan or the Rockefellers, for instance, or the "two hundred families" that ruled France, or Krupp, the German industrial magnate who exclaimed gleefully in 1932 "we have hired Herr Hitler." Today, in many democra-

4. Gaetano Mosca, *The Ruling Class* (New York: McGraw-Hill, 1939).

5. Robert Michels, *Political Parties: A Sociological Study of the Oligarchical Tendencies of Modern Democracy* (London: Collier Books, 1962).

cies, big corporations and multinationals are often alleged to be exercising the same influence. There are also other elites to be reckoned with: the high clergy, university presidents, the military, managerial groups, labor union leaders, owners and directors of the media, leaders of mass organizations and, of course, the wealthy. In liberal democratic regimes there are many competing elites. In authoritarian regimes, the more dominant role of the state and of those who control it reduces the power and influence of all others. Milovan Djilas, the Yugoslav communist leader who broke with the party and became a leading critic of communism, spoke of the political, administrative, and managerial leaders of the totalitarian Soviet Union, united in the Communist party of the Soviet Union, as a "new class": a new oligarchy who ruled over the many, so that communist regimes were also divided between the "powerful" and the "powerless."[6]

Elites propagate ideas that allow them to maintain as well as legitimize their position. For an elite to maintain its position, it helps to have a common ideology. Differences, cracks, and splits in the ideology invariably suggest lack of cohesiveness. They herald a crisis. The existence of a coherent, agreed-upon ideology is prima facie evidence of unity and potentially great power in relation to society. Where it cannot be found, we may infer that the elite is divided, in conflict, or in the process of rapid internal transformation. The ideology held by ruling elites with regard to socioeconomic modernization is particularly critical in assessing its survival or not.

The monopoly of power exercised by an elite is determined by the degree to which decision making is reserved to state organs or by how much participation in the authoritative decision-making process is extended to individuals and groups outside the elite. The scope of participation outside the elite, in turn, reflects the degree to which constraints or limitations have been imposed on the elite.

Constraints often appear in the form of guarantees for the governed that limit elite power and qualify the monopoly of power. Such constraints and qualifications have developed throughout the world in the last two centuries. These guarantees consist not only of things that the elite cannot do but also of what the governed can do and what sanctions the people can impose upon the elites. We will pay particular attention to the institutionalized procedures through which members of the elite can be sanctioned.

If the existence of an elite is a universal phenomenon, its power relative to the rest of society and the guarantees available to the governed to protect them against the elite become crucial variables in any comparative survey. But the arguments that some regimes are elitist and others are democratic, that in some the people govern while in others it is the bosses who rule, miss the point. The point is that there are elites in all regimes. But regimes differ, often fundamentally, in how inequality is perceived, how it is maintained, what privileges are bestowed on some, and what deprivations others suffer. In sum, if there are elites every where, some are more powerful than others, and some regimes are more elitist than others. Likewise, while the many are ruled everywhere, in some regimes they are a little more powerful than in others.

Thus, the study of the elite will almost always provide us with insight into perhaps the most important characteristic of the command structure: the distribution and limits of power. Just how much influence elites have over the authoritative decision-making process in any given regime is generally reflected in the organization of consent, the configuration

---

6. Milovan Djilas, *The New Class* (New York: Praeger, 1957).

of interests, and the organization of rights; in short, in the relationship between state and society.

As we examine various types of regimes, we will try to identify the decision-making elite: officials in government and the most powerful groups in society operating within or behind the government. We will try to find out what distinguishes the elite of one regime from that of another, and what institutional devices different elites use to organize their powers.

THE ORGANIZATION OF CONSENT

A medieval French writer wrote that oxen are bound by their horns and people by their words and wills. The structure of command is fundamentally a matter of fashioning relationships that will allow some to command with the expectation of being obeyed. It is more a matter of values, myths, symbols, and habits than force.

A political regime needs supports in order to maintain itself and to survive over a given period of time. Supports consist of the positive orientations and attitudes of the citizenry with regard to their political regime. They may be addressed, wholly or in part, to the community of people—the "nation"—encompassed by the state; to the particular political regime within the state; to a particular government in power; or to a given policy or policies or policy outcomes. Supports are usually broken into two major types: affective (or diffuse) and instrumental (or specific).

Affective and Instrumental Supports[7]

Affective supports are the diffuse or generalized attachments the population has for the political community and, perhaps, the regime. Those who sing the national anthem during their morning shower obviously have a deep affective orientation for their country and its political regime. The opposite of this is found in those who dream and plot to destroy it. It takes many years to develop such deep emotional attachments, usually as the result of socialization in childhood and continuing socializing forces in adulthood. Once established, such feelings can become crystallized or hardened in political attitudes and behavior and create a firm foundation for the continuing survival of the regime.

In contrast to affective supports, instrumental supports are very specific. They are generated primarily by utilitarian considerations. They relate to the satisfaction of personal interests and to the realization of personal goals and demands. In short, they are the product of a regime's own performance. A regime that has maintained order, provided important services, kept the people out of war or did not lose one, preserved individual security and rights, and allocated resources evenly and generously will be accepted and respected and supported by most. The people give support in return for what they are getting. It is a quid pro quo arrangement. It is a case of "I'll do something for my country if my country does enough for me." In other words, acceptance of the regime is conditional. Instrumental support, therefore, is more subject to rapid erosion than affective support and is a less powerful basis for the survival of a regime.

---

7. We are following an argument closely associated with the work of David Easton. See in particular his articles, "An Approach to the Analysis of Political Systems," *World Politics* 9 (April 1957), pp. 383-400; and "A Reassessment of the Concept of Political Support," *British Journal of Political Science* 5, 1975, pp. 435-457. See also the discussion of political support in Steven L. Burg and Michael L. Berbaum, "Community, Integration, and Stability in Multinational Yugoslavia," *American Political Science Review* 83, 2 (June 1989), pp. 535-554.

When both affective and instrumental supports go hand in hand, the extent and intensity of consent to and acceptance of the regime is likely to be very wide and deep. The opposite is equally true: If the regime is not valued and does not provide adequate services, its legitimacy is very uncertain. More intriguing are the cases where there is tension between affective and instrumental supports.

When a regime performs well but is not valued (i.e., when affective support is low but instrumental support is strong) there may be a gradual increase in popular acceptance until the regime becomes legitimized. Prosperity and well-being may satisfy all but the most deeply opposed. Such continuing opposition tends to arise out of two types of sources: deeply felt attractions for another type of regime, as among democratic dissenters in authoritarian regimes and radical revolutionaries in democratic ones, and the nationalism of ethnic, linguistic, or racial minorities. The latter, in fact, is quite common in multiethnic states and represents a powerful force for political change. In virtually all other cases, instrumental support generated by positive regime performance can, with the help of ongoing socialization, be converted into affective support. This, in fact, explains the survival of many nondemocratic regimes.

While regimes based on instrumental support may be vulnerable to the effects of declining performance, those that enjoy deep affective supports are less so. Take the 1929 depression in the United States. Can such a failure impair affective supports? How fast? We frankly cannot answer this in the abstract. It all depends on how deep and time-honored the affective or diffuse supports have been and on how serious and lasting the crisis facing a regime is. In societies where legitimacy is not deep and a regime has shown only marginal performance, a crisis, such as war or an economic depression, may unhinge the regime. Conversely, in societies where both legitimacy and performance (in other words, both affective and instrumental supports) have been strong for a long time, nonperformance and the resulting waning of instrumental supports may not affect legitimacy even if the problem continues for a fairly long time. In 1929 and throughout the economic depression, few Americans turned against their government or the Constitution. However, in Germany, in 1933, three years after an equally severe economic depression, the Germans had toppled their democratic constitution. The American political regime had a thick cushion of legitimacy and managed to withstand the crisis; not so the German democratic constitution—it was replaced by the Nazi dictatorship. Some regimes can afford mistakes and even prolonged periods of nonperformance; in others, the cushion of legitimacy is but thin ice on which they skate at their own peril.

Even for political regimes that have enjoyed legitimacy for a long time there is a point of crisis. The combination of conflict over domestic civil rights and widespread resistance to the growing war in Vietnam (1960-1973) gave rise to the first serious political crisis in the United States since the Civil War; many people turned not only against their government but against the political institutions—against the political regime and the Constitution. In the case of a regime whose affective support is tenuous, a sharp decline in performance may erode instrumental support enough to bring on crisis. The onset of mass demonstrations and ethnic violence in the Soviet Union under Mikhail Gorbachev, the outbreak of political unrest in Yugoslavia in the post-Tito era, and the series of dramatic regime changes in Eastern Europe in 1989 and 1990 for example, seem to be attributable, at least in part, to such conditions.

When people accept the regime they live in even though they do not agree with some specific policy decisions, we call the regime consensual, or "legitimate." It is based on shared wills and shared values between those who make decisions or "authoritatively allocate values" in the command structures and the population at large. The people consent rather than obey, and those who make decisions need exercise only their authority, not their power.

There are four processes associated with the organization of consent:

1. Socialization
2. Representation
3. Participation
4. Mobilization

(1) *Socialization* comprises the various processes through which loyalties and attachments to a political regime and its institutions are developed. It plays a crucial role in the development of support. The family, the school, and various associations propagate values consistent with the goals and the institutions of the given regime.[8] An ideology is often propagated as a means to rationalize the existing political regime. By the time most children become adults, they have been imbued with the prevailing ideology and are ready to give their support. Habit is equally important: the sheer imitation of the elders; the doing of things the way they are done by others; the tendency to follow peer groups or to act in accord with neighbors and friends or other reference groups; all these factors shape and crystallize orientations and loyalties vis-à-vis the political regime. Specifically how different regimes socialize the young and the citizens, or how they fail to do so, is a matter we will examine when we discuss individual cases. The socialization process in general, however, is necessary for the maintenance of any political regime, regardless of the specific methods used.

(2) *Representation*, at least in theory, puts elected representatives in charge of the command structure. In democratic regimes, representative assemblies speak for the whole and are beholden to the whole. In obeying, therefore, the citizenry simply obeys decisions made by delegates they themselves have chosen. In nondemocratic regimes, the popular legitimacy or authority of such institutions is limited.

(3) *Participation* provides an active communication and interaction between the citizenry and those in command positions. In democratic regimes, the citizenry organizes and agitates and talks about everything from trash collections to a nuclear freeze. Associations promote various points of view on domestic and foreign policy questions. And through a political party or even without one, people exert all sorts of efforts (and often expenditures) to ensure that those who reach a position of command are those they want elected. Even in nondemocratic regimes, participation—even if restricted—is an important foundation of political order. Of all the agencies that provide for such participation, in democratic and nondemocratic regimes alike, the political party is considered to be the most important one.

(4) *Mobilization* is often used to denote the awakening of political involvement of people who had remained disenfranchised or alienated. For instance, nationalism and national independence movements mobilized the masses in Europe in the nineteenth century and throughout the Third World after World War II. It brought them into politics. But

8. Kenneth Langton, *Political Socialization* (New York: Oxford University Press, 1969); Richard E. Dawson and Kenneth Prewitt, *Political Socialization* (Boston: Little, Brown, 1969).

the word can also be used, and we use it in this sense, to denote intensive participation: a great commitment and sustained activity, a deep involvement.

Such participation may arise spontaneously, out of personal interest, or it may be encouraged by political activists seeking to enhance support for their cause. Thus, one might say that organized groups, such as those that support and oppose abortion in the United States, mobilize the population into political action. They spur citizens to intensive political activity. The issues raised by the war in Vietnam spontaneously mobilized many millions of Americans into political action, as did legislation prepared by the French socialist government that appeared to interfere with the autonomy of Catholic schools. Gorbachev's calls for *glasnost* (openness), *demokratizatsiia* (democratization), and *perestroika* (economic restructuring) have led to an explosion of spontaneous popular political activity in the Soviet Union. In the Soviet and other communist systems, the Communist party led efforts to mobilize the population into controlled activities that supported these regimes. The downfall of communism in Eastern Europe was brought about by the sudden increase in mass political activity, organized from below, which followed the onset of glasnost and which could not be contained by existing institutions. When we use the term "mobilization," we refer to such intensive participation, whether spontaneous and initiated from below or initiated and orchestrated from above.

THE CONFIGURATION OF INTERESTS

Within a political regime various actors, both groups and individuals, seek to articulate their various interests. They have certain expectations, they make certain demands, and they seek the realization of their needs and desires. The term *interests* should be defined in the broadest possible sense: material interests; family interests; professional interests; religious convictions; and heartfelt values such as honor, patriotism, rights, and humanitarian considerations.

Interests speak through organizations, usually associations and groups. Groups are generally identified and defined in terms of some shared objective traits such as tribal membership, occupation, age, religion, or ethnic identity. Associations are formally constituted and organized by individuals in order to protect their common interests: the American Association of Retired Persons, the NAACP, the NAM, the AMA, and the AFL-CIO are a few examples.[9] Such associations may be formed voluntarily, as in democratic regimes, or they may be established by the state itself, as in some nondemocratic regimes. Political parties are associations that bring many interests together into a general purposive activity. The party expresses these interests, reconciles those that conflict, and synthesizes them in support of common policy goals. In democratic regimes, the formal party platform embodies the goals to be pursued by the party leader if that party should assume control of the command structure. In nondemocratic regimes, parties also devise such programs and attempt to implement them.

The configuration of interests in any regime is greatly affected by the levels of economic and social modernization. Economic development—the change from simple agricultural societies to more complex industrial ones, and especially the shift from low to

9. For interest group analysis, especially with reference to American politics, one should consult the pioneering works of Pendleton Herring, especially his *Group Representation Before Congress* (1929; rpt. New York: Russell & Russell, 1967). See also Arthur F. Bentley, *The Process of Government* (New Brunswick, N.J.: Transaction Books, 1983) and David Truman, *The Governmental Process* (New York: Alfred A. Knopf, 1947).

high technologies—produces new groups that expand the basic social categories associated with early industrialization. The division between working class and peasantry is supplemented by the rise of intellectual strata, technical and scientific specialists, administrative and bureaucratic functionaries, and many other specialized groups. This dual process of structural differentiation and functional specialization arising out of the modernization process increases the number of groups and interests with which individuals become identified and, therefore, increases the number of potential bases for their political mobilization.[10]

Modernization produces increased material wealth for the population. Improving standards of living produce the expectation of further improvements. This "revolution of rising expectations" increases the level of popular demands placed on regimes to continue to produce material benefits. Where the distribution of wealth is uneven, inequality itself produces demands for greater equality.

The social foundation of this process is the spread of education; at first, simple literacy, but at later stages of modernization, specialized higher education. With increasing education come new values and increasing demands upon the political order from the population; demands for greater personal freedom, greater political liberty, increased material prosperity, and a more egalitarian society. Such established mechanisms of social control as churches, trade unions, and schools lose their effectiveness, and the regime is compelled to create new bases for its legitimacy. If it is to do so, a regime must deal with the most central issue in political development: the institutionalization of popular participation. Political parties represent the most widespread agencies not only for *mobilizing* participation, but for *institutionalizing* it, as well.[11]

THE ORGANIZATION OF RIGHTS

Individual rights have traditionally been defined as individual claims *against* the state. Originally they were the claims against absolutist monarchies: freedom to think, to worship, to form associations, to be immune from arrests, to have the right to a fair trial, to be presumed innocent until found guilty. However, since World War II, claims *for* services—especially claims for health services, welfare arrangements, education, and employment—have also come to be regarded as rights. In this case, people expect these services to be provided by the government. They feel that they are entitled to them. The first are, strictly speaking, referred to as *individual rights* or civil rights; the second, inasmuch as they involve groups and the provision of material and economic services for them, are referred to as *social rights*. Finally, there are also *political rights:* to vote, run for office, or organize political associations and political parties. Political regimes vary in their relative emphasis on individual rights, social rights, and political rights. Some emphasize all three; others, one or two. But few regimes fail to pay attention to any. The particular protections they provide and the values that are attached to them are a matter for empirical study of particular political regimes.

---

10. For a summary of the political challenges inherent in the modernization process, see Leonard Binder, "The Crises of Political Development" in Leonard Binder et al., *Crises and Sequences in Political Development* (Princeton, N.).: Princeton University Press, 1971), pp.

11. For an extensive treatment of the institutionalization of participation, see Samuel P. Huntington, *Political Order in Changing Societies* (New Haven, Conn.: Yale University Press, 1968).

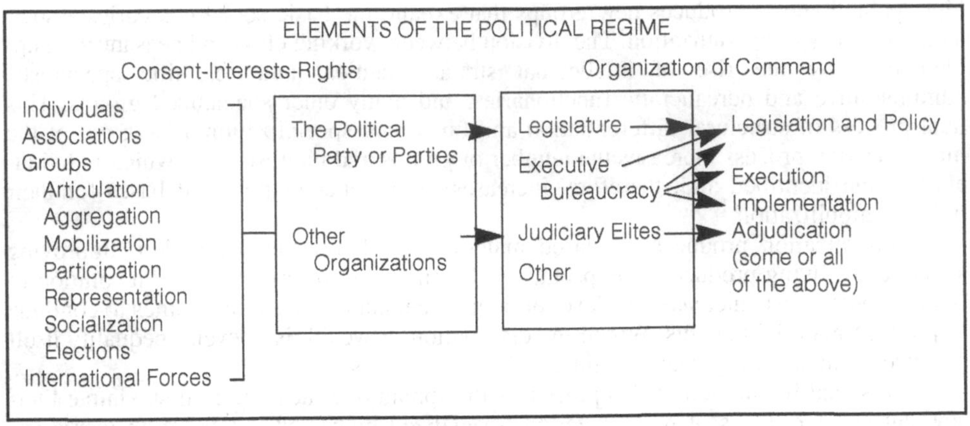

Figure 1.

POLITICAL REGIMES: TWO MAJOR MODELS

In all political regimes there is constant flux in the relationship between command, consent, interests, and rights. We have sketched out the elements of a political regime in Figure 1.1. There is a constant interaction and tension between the various groupings and associations and the command structure. Relationships among the executive, the administration, the legislature, and the judiciary also shift and change. In democratic regimes, "presidential government" and "congressional government" may alternate over time. In one period "the party is king"; in another, "the party is over." Legislative supremacy may give place to cabinet supremacy; political leaders may be replaced by so-called experts or "technocrats." In nondemocratic regimes, an autocrat may give way to collective leadership, or political parties may grow in importance as popular support wanes. In every regime, political institutions gain or lose autonomy in their relationships with social, economic, or other organizations. The role of the army, the party, the state, the trade unions, the clergy, and other institutions may change. In democratic regimes, the influence over decision makers exerted by political associations and groupings—lobbies, single-issue associations, political action committees, and others—waxes and wanes, depending on the issues involved, the amount of popular support they can mobilize, and even the personal convictions of the decision makers themselves. Even in nondemocratic regimes there may be a wide variation in the range of participation by groups, associations, and institutions, in the level of popular support and consent, and even in the organization of rights.

All we can do, therefore, is identify the predominant institutional patterns and relationships that distinguish major regime "types." In a changing world, particular attention must be paid to the boundaries between types: How much change must take place before one type of regime is transformed into another? We shall do so in terms of the four basic categories we set forth above: the organization of *command,* the organization of *consent,* the configuration of *interests,* and the organization of *rights.*

Democratic vs. Authoritarian

In this book we focus on two major types of political regimes: democratic and authoritarian. They correspond to major descriptive generalizations based on the criteria set forth, i.e., the different ways in which command, consent, interests, and rights are organized. In doing so, we shall be defining the relationship between the state and society in each.

Our descriptive generalizations reach out to identify only general characteristics, not detailed profiles. As we will see, there are significant variations from one democratic regime to another, and there are a great variety of authoritarian regimes. One type of authoritarian regime will be given separate and more detailed, treatment: the totalitarian regime. Although the totalitarian regimes seem to be approaching extinction rapidly, the differences between them and other authoritarian regimes are especially important. For the amelioration of totalitarianism would appear to be a prerequisite for the eventual democratization of such regimes.

The Democratic Model

In democratic theory (and, to varying degrees, in democratic regimes) there is a sharp distinction made between state and society. The basic assumption is that in society individuals are free, rational, independent entities, born with inalienable rights to life, liberty, and property. Individuals seek fulfillment in religious, artistic, economic, and many other forms of expression, and the state permits the existence of outlets for achieving these aspirations. Relations among individuals and the associations they form are based on equality: there is no subordination of one to another. Since associations and groups are freely formed and remain free and independent of each other, they denote a pluralistic pattern, allowing a great variety of forms of expression. Morality and the "good life" are what individuals decide they are; people pursue their own interests. They are each armed with a little pocket calculator, so to speak, figuring out what is pleasurable and good (in the most material but also in the loftiest sense of those words) and what is painful or bad, pursuing the one and avoiding the other without any outside interference.

According to this liberal democratic model, the state—the command structure—has one single narrow function: to preserve order. It has the right to use force but only to prevent violence and to provide us the opportunity to "do our thing." The state has no overriding ethical purpose. It cannot decide what is true or false, moral or immoral. Individuals, as members of the society, consent to form a state when they agree to set up a constitution that spells out the organization of the state, the limits of its power, and the rights to be preserved. After they have set up a constitution that defines the organization of individual rights and sets limits to state action, they return to their pursuits in society with the knowledge and the guarantee that they will be able to live in peace and tranquility.

This democratic model stacks the cards on the side of the individuals and the associations they voluntarily form, which represent the creative forces of progress and change. The state is their creature, dependent upon society for its existence and limited by the established rules. Thus, while society is *independent* of the state, the state is *dependent* upon society. The individual is sacred; the state is a necessary evil, like an insurance policy we take against the many hazards that confront us.

Despite many profound and radical social and economic changes that have accounted for drastic reconsiderations of this model, it still remains the true one for most liberal and democratic regimes. Institutional arrangements continue to safeguard individual rights and the pluralism of groups and interests. The political "rules of the game" distinguish sharply between what belongs to the state (and comes under the purview of its activities) and what belongs to individuals, including their free and spontaneous world of social life. Democracy from liberalism to socialism has continued to emphasize (despite growing interdependencies between the state and society and the growing scope of state action, especially in the economy, the *separateness* between the state and society.

A democracy limits the power of its decision-makers. First of all, the command structure is ordered in such a way that the decision-makers cannot make arbitrary decisions; they are bound by an established legal order. The element of separateness that we just mentioned ensures that the political power given to the decision-makers will be a *limited* power. Second, those who occupy the command structure are held responsible for their decisions. They can tax and they can drop an atom bomb, but they will be held *accountable* for what they do. Periodic and free elections, among many other mechanisms, institutionalize this accountability.

The Authoritarian Model

Authoritarianism and the various forms of authoritarian regimes continue to be an expression of the oldest and, some would say, the most corrupt aspect of political life: rule by force. In fact, authoritarianism is a catch-all name for political regimes that we are all more or less familiar with: autocracy, tyranny, satrapy, dictatorship, absolutism, bonapartism, despotism, military rule, junta, oligarchy, "political bossism," theocracy, and even outright gangsterism. They all provide for command arrangements that concentrate power and force in the hands of one or a few leaders who rule without much regard for the organization of consent, with little or no regard for the organization of interests, and needless to say, without respect for individual rights.

Table 1. Authoritarian and Democratic Regimes

	Authoritarian	Democratic
1. Limitation on command structure	Little to none	Many
2. Effective responsibility	None	Considerable to great
3. Organization of command structure:		
State	Yes	State and state agencies
Bureaucracy/military	Yes	Subordinate
Individual leader	Yes	Collective/elections
Police, force, intimidation	Yes	Subordinate
4. "Penetration" (inclusiveness) of society by political organs*	Complete to selective	Limited
5. Mobilization for supports*	Induced/variable	Spontaneous
6. Official ideology*	Varies in strength and mobilization	Weak
7. Parties*	Single or none	Many
8. Individual rights (protection)	Virtually none	Yes

*It is primarily with regard to penetration of the society, mobilization of supports (through the single party) and the official ideology that distinctions have been made between authoritarian and totalitarian regimes. The essence of totalitarianism lies precisely in the full penetration and mobilization of the society in the name of an official ideology disseminated and imposed through the single party; many authoritarian regimes—especially dynastic and military regimes—fail to do so.

Thus, the authoritarian model advances a diametrically different view of the relationship between the state and society (individuals, groups, and associations) than the democratic one. The command structure—and all the means through which it is organized and through which it manifests itself—is controlled by a political elite, to the exclusion of all others. In its most extreme form, the state dominates society. It constrains initiative, it defines what is true and what is false, it establishes official organizations to control all social activities: economic, cultural, religious, even familial. In some instances this control is exercised directly, in others it is exercised through a single political party. Table 1.1 summarizes the differences between authoritarian and democratic regimes.

In this way, authoritarian regimes manipulate and determine the organization of interest, the organization of consent, and the organization of rights. In its most extreme form, the authoritarian regimes makes individuals, groups, and associations "march in step" for the attainment of a prearranged purpose. In some authoritarian regimes (which we identify as totalitarian), there is a high level of *social mobilization* aimed at creating popular support. But in most authoritarian regimes there is no attempt to mobilize the population. In fact, the authoritarian leader and his supporters attempt to prevent the populace from becoming too active; they seek to protect and perpetuate the status quo. They are satisfied to rule a passive and obedient populace over which they hold the instruments of force: the army, the secret police, the tax collector and, not infrequently, the economy.

Bibliography

Almond, Gabriel, and Sidney Verba. *The Civic Culture.* Princeton, N.J.: Princeton University Press, 1963.

Almond, Gabriel, and G. Bingham Powell. *Comparative Politics: System, Process and Policy.* Boston: Little, Brown, 1981.

Apter, David. *Introduction to Political Analysis.* Cambridge, Mass.: Winthrop/ Boston: Little, Brown, 1982.

Bill, James A., and Robert L. Hardgrave, Jr. *Comparative Politics: The Quest for Theory.* Lanham, Md.: University Press of America, 1982.

Blondel, Jean. *World Leaders: Heads of Government in the Postwar Period.* Beverly Hills, Calif.: Sage Publications, 1980.

___________. *Comparative Political Institutions.* New York: Praeger, 1973.

Davis, Morton R., and Vaughan A. Lewis. *Model of Political System.* New York: Praeger, 1971.

Easton, David. *A Framework for Political Analysis.* Chicago: University of Chicago Press, 1979.

Eckstein, Harry, and David Apter. *Comparative Politics: A Reader.* Glencoe, Ill.: The Free Press, 1963.

Finer, Samuel H. *Comparative Government.* London: Penguin Books, 1970.

Friedrich, Carl J. *Man and His Government: An Empirical Theory of Politics.* New York: McGraw-Hill, 1963.

Holt, Robert T., and John E. Turner. *The Methodology of Comparative Research.* New York: The Free Press, 1970.

Macridis, Roy, and Bernard Brown (eds.). *Comparative Politics: Notes and Readings.* 7th ed. Belmont, Calif.: Brooks/Cole Publishing Co., Wadsworth Inc., 1990.

Mahler, Gregory S. *Comparative Politics: An Institutional and Cross-National Approach.* Cambridge, Mass.: Shenkman Publishers, 1983.

Michels, Robert. *Political Parties: A Sociological Study of Oligarchical Tendencies in Modern Democracies.* (Originally published in German in 1911); rpt. London: Macmillan, 1962.

Mosca, Gaetano. *The Ruling Class.* Trans. by Hannah Kahn. Westport, Conn.: Greenwood Press, 1980.

Putnam, Robert D. *The Comparative Study of Political Elites.* Englewood Cliffs, N.J.: Prentice-Hall, 1976.

Taylor, C. C., and O. A. Jodich. *World Handbook of Politics and Social Indicators.* New Haven, Conn.: Yale University Press, 1983.

Tilly, Charles (ed.). *The Formation of Nation States in Western Europe.* Princeton, N.J.: Princeton University Press, 1975.

Omnibalancing

Steven R. David

Explaining Third World Alignment

Introduction to Omnibalancing

The theory of omnibalancing serves as a theoretical bridge between the international relations and comparative politics fields. It addresses the state's internal threat as an independent variable, as well as the external threat, to better understand state alignment behavior, the dependent variable. Specifically, the theory looks at weaker states, whose legitimacy is inextricably linked to their security in the context of the international system. This is exciting academically, but it also serves a useful purpose for practitioners.

The changing world and its resultant ambiguities requires sophisticated foreign policy and sophisticated implementers of that policy. For example, military officers serving on the ground must understand the political context of their missions, that is, to understand what futurists Alvin and Heidi Toffler refer to as the "knowledge terrain." It's not good enough to know just key terrain. The military must understand the political, cultural, economic, and social contexts of a region and/or state before deployment in order to successfully implement policy. Our military leaders and policy makers must know their allies, neutrals, and enemies, alike.[1] How else does a state identify an adversary's center of gravity? Conversely, how does a state recognize its allies and its own centers of gravity?

In recent years, the international community's focus and concern has emphasized intra-state conflict. This type of conflict is not new, but there are new norms and expectations of these states-in-the-making, which has made the international community reevaluate such conflicts. However, state-making is not an easy task. It requires the state to successfully control the means of violence and coercion within a specific territory. There's competition for power as well as resources, and ethnic conflict is one manifestation of this state-making process. Quite often, these states have very weak state institutions, and they cannot properly provide for the people. Consequently, the people look elsewhere and that sometimes means that they look to their ethnic group. Unfortunately, weak states tend to have porous boundaries, so intra-state problems can easily escalate to regional and, perhaps, global problems. Finally, the international community expects states-in-the-making to abide by international norms concerning human rights. This tension has made the international community rethink concepts such as sovereignty and criteria for intervention, as highlighted in the debates surrounding NATO's use of force in the former Yugoslavia.[2]

Theoretically, the current ambiguities of the international system require students of international security to truly engage in intellectual pluralism and rethink their theoretical premises and research approaches. Specifically, scholars and practitioners must modify

---

1. The idea of knowledge and key terrain is found in Heidi and Alvin Toffler, *War and Anti-War: Survival at the Dawn of the 21st Century* (Boston, Little Brown and Company, 1993). 158. USMA recognizes the importance for officers to understand their allies, neutrals, and enemies, on a cultural level, in "Educating Army Leaders for the 21st Century," USMA Academic Board and Office of the Dean Staff, USMA, West Point, 1998: 28.

2. A great deal has been written on issues of state making and the implications of weak state institutions. Specifically, for state-making, see Mohammed Ayoob, *The Third World Security Predicament* (Boulder: Lynne Rienner Publishers, 1995), 22-23. His explanation of current state-making in the context of international norms is found in Ibid., 85, and Ayoob discusses this in more detail in his chapter four. The discussion of weak state institutions is found broadly in the institutionalist literature, specifically in Naomi Chazan, "Ethnicity in Economic Crisis: Development Strategies and Patterns of Ethnicity in Africa," in *Ethnicity, Politics, and Development,* eds. Dennis L. Thompson and Dov Ronen (Boulder: Lynne Rienner Publishers, 1986), 137-158.

some of the assumptions of realism which underline Stephen M. Walt's theory on state alignment and reassess the Cold War's focus on the systems level approach. Systems-level theory and NeoRealism, in particular, failed to predict the change in the international system, i.e., the change from the Cold War to post-Cold War eras. While there is a need to rethink how best to explain state behavior now, the basic tenets of realism, which have formed the basis of some of the Cold War era theories, are still valid. States are still operating in an international system, albeit a different one; therefore, the effects of the international system on state behavior, in the current context of the post-Cold War era, are still important. However, scholars cannot ignore the effects of the numerous examples of regime instability on the international system. The republics of the former Soviet Union, the former Yugoslavia, Somalia, and Rwanda are only a few examples of regime instability at work today. This instability not only incites regime failure, but it also greatly influences the international system. Consequently, scholars must simultaneously analyze the effects of regime instability on the international system, as well as the international system on the regime.[3]

Omnibalancing facilitates the understanding of weak state behavior because leaders of weak states have internal security threats, which they must consider. It calls for the assessment of external and internal threats, with respect to the leader's political survival, not the state's survival. David offers some departures from systems theory. The significant departure from realism is that leaders of weak states may view external threats as less dangerous than internal threats. Domestic threats directly affect these leaders' right or ability to rule; therefore, these leaders are addressing their self- interests, not necessarily their states' interests.[4]

David limits his test to Third World–superpower alignments, which necessarily limits him to the Cold War era. However, he offers a theory and concepts which scholars and practitioners may apply to the current world situation, especially as policy makers are exploring new ways to prevent conflict and build peace. Additionally, David's focus is on weak states, and it appears that currently, the international community shares that focus. It is imperative that scholars and practitioners work together so that they may better understand the causal factors for state behavior and craft appropriate policy.

---

3. There have been numerous critiques on the Realist perspective and specifically on Steven M. Walt, *The Origins of Alliances* (Ithaca: Cornell University Press, 1987), to include Paul Schroeder, "Historical Reality vs NeoRealist Theory, *International Security,* 19, no. 1: 108-148 and Randall L. Schweller, "Bandwagoning for Profit: Bringing the Revisionist State Back In," *International Security,* 19, no. 1 (September 1994): 72-107.

4. Steven R. David, *Choosing Sides: Alignment and Realignment in the Third World* (Baltimore: The Johns Hopkins University Press, 1991), xi and 6. See also Barry Buzan, *People, States and Fear: An Agenda for International Security Studies in the Post-Cold War Era* (Boulder: Lynne Rienner Publishers, 1991) for an in-depth view of the nature of weak states.

Explaining Third World Alignment

Steven R. David

Most of the earth's people and states are part of the Third World. Yet Third World foreign policy, especially why Third World states align as they do, is not well understood. Balance of power, the most widely used theory in international relations, is particularly inadequate as an explanation of Third World alignments because it does not take into account the distinctive characteristics of the Third World. The need for a theory that considers those characteristics is critical because understanding the Third World is and will remain central to understanding the course of international politics.

The theory of "omnibalancing" meets this need. It draws upon some of the key assumptions of balance of power while also correcting those elements of the theory that make it inapplicable to the Third World. Omnibalancing agrees with the central assumption of balance of power—that threats will be resisted. But it departs from balance of power in explaining Third World alignment decisions as a result of the Third World leadership's need to counter *all* threats. Thus, whereas balance of power focuses on the state's need to counter threats from other states, omnibalancing considers internal and external threats to the leadership, and, as a result, it fundamentally alters our understanding of why Third World leaders align as they do and also provides insights that explain a wide range of Third World behavior.

The argument is presented in four parts. First, the theories of balance of power and omnibalancing are reviewed, with special emphasis on the Points of agreement and disagreement. Second, the characteristics that distinguish the Third World from the rest of the world and why these characteristics support the applicability of omnibalancing over balance of power are considered. Third, two specific cases are examined. These illustrate how omnibalancing explains and predicts Third World alignments in ways that balance of power (as well as other theories) do not. Finally, there is a discussion of the centrality of an understanding of the Third World, including Third World alignment, to the study of international politics.

BALANCE OF POWER

Alignment occurs when a state brings its policies into close cooperation with another state in order to achieve mutual security goals.[1] Balance of power theory argues that states align to protect themselves against the power of or threats from other states.[2] The key concern of states is to align in such a way as to prevent (by balancing against) any other state or group of states from achieving preponderance. States behave this way because they recognize that the emergence of a hegemonic power will ultimately threaten their own survival.

---

1. For a comprehensive discussion of what connotes alignment, see George T. Duncan and Randolph M. Siverson, "Flexibility of Alliance Partner Choice in a Multipolar System," *International Studies Quarterly* 26 (December 1982), 511-38, at 518.

2. In my use of the term balance of power, I include the efforts of statesmen to counter both power and threats. For more on this point, see Stephen M. Walt, *The Origins of Alliances* (Ithaca, N.Y.: Cornell University Press, 1987), 5, 21-26: and Inis L. Claude, Jr., *Power and International Relations* (New York: Random House, 1962), 64-65.

Steven R. David, "Explaining Third World Alignment," *World Politics* 43 (January 1991), 233-56. Reprinted with permission of Johns Hopkins University Press, Baltimore, MD.

Balance of power theory emphasizes that the determinants of alignment come overwhelmingly from the structure of the international system, particularly the actual and potential *external* threats that states face.[3] Accordingly, the internal characteristics of the states are usually not considered relevant in influencing alignments.[4]

This view is reinforced by the recurring formation of balances made up of states that have little more than a threat in common. The alliance of democratic France with tsarist Russia against Germany prior to World War I illustrates this.[5] The apparent irrelevance of internal factors is reinforced by the fact that states with similar political systems that might otherwise be expected to maintain an alignment do not in the absence of a common external threat.[6] An example of this phenomenon is the failure of the Soviet Union and the People's Republic of China to remain aligned despite their common allegiance to communism.

Although they base their work on the experience of states outside the Third World, many balance of power theorists argue that their theory holds for the states of the Third World as well.[7] One can expect the balance of power theory to prevail, it is argued, whenever states seeking to survive and expand their power interact in an anarchic order[8] Since there is nothing in the nature of Third World states or in the international system they inhabit that would contradict these requirements, balance of power politics should apply equally to them.

OMNIBALANCING

Although the balance of power theory contains important insights, it does not adequately explain Third World alignment and realignment. Instead, the most powerful determinant of Third World alignment behavior is the rational calculation of Third World leaders as to which outside power is most likely to do what is necessary to keep them in power. This is so because of the unstable, dangerous, and often fatal nature of the international and *domestic* political environment that characterizes the Third World. This deceptively simple observation changes our understanding of why Third World

---

3. Kenneth Waltz and, to a lesser extent. Hans Morgenthau, base their balance of power theory on the capabilities of states. (generally speaking, the greater the capability of a state: the greater the threat it poses to other states; see Waltz, *Theory of International Politics* (Reading, Mass.: Addison-Wesley, 1979), esp. chap. 6; and Hans Morgenthau and Kenneth Thompson, *Politics among Nations,* 6th ed. (New York: Knopf. 1985), esp. chap. 11. George Liska also emphasizes the role of external threat. calling it the "primary source of alliances"; see *Nations in Alliance: The Limits of Interdependence* (Baltimore, Md.: Johns Hopkins University Press, 1962), 13.

4. Ole R. Holsti, P. Terrence Hopmann. and John 1). Sullivan, *Unity and Disintegration in International Alliances: Comparative Studies (New* York: John Wiley, 1973), 5. Based on an exhaustive survey of the literature, the authors concluded that most balance of power writings argue this.

5. Kenneth Waltz, "Theory of International Relations," in Fred I. Greenstein and Nelson W. Polsby, eds., *Handbook of Political Science: International Politics* (Reading, Mass: Addison Wesley. 1975), 8:43

6. The notion is widespread that alliance cohesion weakens when there is no external threat. See, for example, Arnold Wolfers, *Discord and Collaboration* (Baltimore, Md.: Johns Hopkins University Press, 1962), 29; and Kenneth E. Boulding, *Conflict and Defense: A General Theory* (New York: Harper and Row, 1962), 162.

7. This is a major argument made by Stephen Walt, who asserts that his theory is supported by the experiences of states in the Middle East. He does. however, modify balance of power theory to focus on threats (instead of power) from other states. See Walt (fn. 2), 13-14.

8. Waltz (fn. 3), 121; and Morgenthau and Thompson (fn. 3), 228.

leaders align and realign, and it explains those decisions better than does balance of power. The uniquely dangerous context in which Third World politics takes place also explains why theories derived from the eighteenth- and nineteenth-century European experience (such as balance of power) are inadequate in explaining the alignment decisions of Third World leaders.

The essence of balance of power theory is correct: leaders of Third World states as well as leaders of other states align in ways that help them better resist the threats they face. But conditions in the Third World require, in addition, a theory of alignment that applies primarily to the Third World. To that end, three separate and distinct repairs of balance of power theory are offered. First, rather than just balance against threats or power, leaders of states will appease—that is, align with—secondary adversaries so that they can focus their resources on prime adversaries. Other states may be less threatening than the secondary threat, but it may be that they cannot be harnessed for the alignment either because they do not care about the dispute or because they are unable to resolve it. So the threatened leadership has no choice: it must align with one threat to address the other. The Soviet Union's alignment with the United States and Great Britain against Nazi Germany during World War It is an example of this type of behavior.

As with the leaders of great powers, Third World leaders, too, seek to appease secondary threats in order to counter those that are more pressing. But in the Third World, this often means appeasing other states (which often pose less pressing threats) in order to counter the more immediate and dangerous domestic threats. They seek to split the alignment against them and focus their energies on their most dangerous (domestic) opponents. To do this they appease the international allies of their domestic opponents. This superficially appears to be "bandwagoning," that is, a case of a state accommodating a threatening adversary in the hope of appeasing it or sharing in the spoils.[9] But it is better classified as balancing; the accommodation, made to conserve strength for the battle against the prime threat, is part of a general policy of resistance.

Finally, since the dominant goal of Third World leaders is to stay in power, they will sometimes protect themselves at the expense of the interests of the state. This form of balancing behavior—not covered by balance of power theory—must be addressed if the alignment decisions are to be understood.

Omnibalancing, the theory that emerges from these observations, applies largely to the Third World. It incorporates the need of leaders to appease secondary adversaries, as well as to balance against both internal and external threats in order to survive in power. This theory rests on the assumptions that leaders are weak and illegitimate and that the stakes for domestic politics are very high—conditions that are much more common in the Third World than elsewhere. It assumes that the most powerful determinant of alignment is the drive of Third World leaders to ensure their political and physical survival.

Although omnibalancing is framed in opposition to balance of power, it also shares much of the latter's realist underpinnings. In accordance with realism, omnibalancing argues that international politics focuses on power, interests, and rationality.[10] Omnibalancing accepts the realist view that the world is characterized by international anarchy,

---

9. The first mention I have been able to find of "bandwagoning" in the sense used here is in Arnold Wolfers, *Discord and Collaboration: Essays in International Politics* (Baltimore, Md.: Johns Hopkins University Press, 1982), 15. See also Walt (fn. 2), 19-21.

10. See Morgenthau and Thompson (fn. 3), chaps. 1, 3, for a concise description of realism.

that interests are bound to conflict, and that the use of force is always an option for heads of state. Omnibalancing furthermore accepts the realist argument that there are clear hierarchies of issues, with survival being the most important. In addition, omnibalancing rests on the fundamental realist assumption that "politics, like society in general, is governed by objective laws that have their roots in human nature," namely, in this instance, the desire of Third World leaders to survive.[11]

Omnibalancing also acknowledges the central lesson of realism, that international politics can best be understood by asking an observer to imagine how she or he would rationally behave under given conditions.[12] A decision is elucidated, therefore, by showing how it was reasonable in light of the leader's objectives.[13] As Hans Morgenthau explains:

> In other words, we put ourselves in the position of a statesman who must meet a certain problem of foreign policy under certain circumstances, and we ask ourselves what the rational alternatives are from which a statesman may choose who must meet this problem under these circumstances (presuming always that he acts in a rational manner), and which of these rational alternatives this particular statesman, acting under these circumstances, is likely to choose.[14]

Despite the overall realist approach, omnibalancing departs in fundamental ways from the understanding of realism put forth by scholars such as Morgenthau and Waltz.[15] The essence of the difference is that omnibalancing asserts that realism must be broadened to examine internal threats in addition to focusing on external threats and capabilities (that is, structural arguments), and that the leader of the state rather than the state itself should be used as the level of analysis. As such, omnibalancing challenges the core assumptions of Morgenthau and Waltz, that states are unitary actors pursuing the national interest. If omnibalancing is correct, then alignment decisions of Third World leaders cannot be understood without reference to the role of internal threats to their leadership.

This approach changes the way we go about explaining alignment decisions. Balance of power assumes that the decision maker asks, "How does this policy affect the power of the state?"[16] Omnibalancing assumes instead that the decision maker asks, "How does this policy affect the probability of my remaining in power?" And whereas balance of power assumes the state's leaders ask, "Which outside power is most likely protect my state from the threats posed by other states?" omnibalancing assumes the decision maker asks, "Which outside power is most likely to protect me from the internal and external threats

---

11. Ibid., 4,

12. This lesson comes from the two central works of realism, Morgenthau's *Politics among Nations (fn. 3)* and Thucydides' *History of the Peloponnesian War* (New York: Penguin, 1985). See also Robert O. Keohane, "Theory of World Politics: Structural Realism and Beyond," in Keohane, ed., *Neorealism and Its Critics* (New York: Columbia University Press, 1986), 163, or elaboration of this point.

13. This is in conformity with Graham Allison's Model 1: see Allison, *The Essence of Decisions: Explaining the Cuban Missile Crisis* (Boston: Little Brown, 1971), 5

14. Morgenthau and Thompson (fn 3). 5

15. See, for example, Morgenthau (fn. g), esp. chaps. 1, 3, as well as Waltz (fn. 3). Although differences exist between the two interpretations, they are treated together in that they both accept the view of realism that envisions a world of international anarchy in which the principal actors are states that seek to expand and survive.

16. Morgenthau and Thompson (fn 3). 14.

(as well as combinations of both) that I face." Just as the questions differ, so do the responses.

By taking internal threats into account, omnibalancing is less parsimonious than is balance of power in explaining Third World alignment and realignment. The loss in simplicity is more than compensated, however, by the increased explanatory and predictive power of the theory. Demonstrating this requires showing that one can generalize about the Third World and that these generalizations support the view that broader conception of balance of power is needed in order to explain why Third World leaders make the alignment decisions they do.

GENERALIZING ABOUT THE THIRD WORLD

Despite the vast differences among the states considered as belonging the Third World, there are also fundamental similarities that justify considering them together.[17] These similarities have created a situation which internal threats (with or without external backing) are far more likely to challenge a Third World leader's hold on power than are threats from other states. Only a handful of Third World leaders (for example, Uganda's Idi Amin, Cambodia's Pol Pot, Panama's Manuel Noriega) have fallen to outside invasions. Hundreds of Third World leaders, however, have been overthrown by their internal enemies. In fact, more Third World states have experienced either a forceful overthrow of the government (from within) or a nearly successful attempt. Since 1945 wars within states have outnumbered wars between states, a gap that is especially pronounced in the Third World.[18] Coups d'Ètat alone have accounted for nearly two hundred regime changes in the Third World, making it the most common form of coercive regime change and perhaps the most common form of regime change in general in the Third World.[19] Third World leaders understandably have to pay special attention to retaining their hold on power, especially in the face of domestic challenges.

The reasons for the prevalence of internal threats in the Third World stem from the characteristics of most Third World states.[20] Unlike countries outside the Third World that evolved over centuries, the great majority of Third World states had been colonies out of

17. This study considers the Third World as including all countries except the United States, the Soviet Union, Canada, Japan, Australia, New Zealand, South Africa, the European states, and the People's Republic of China. For an especially good description of the differences between Third World states, see Benjamin Cohen, *The Question of Imperialism: The Political Economy of Dominance and Dependence* (New York: Basic Books, 1973). 145-52

18. J. David Singer and Melvin Small. *Resort to Arms: International and Civil Wars, 1816-1980* (Beverly Hills, Calif: Sage, 1982), 92-95, 98-99, 229-32. For additional treatment of this point, see John Lewis Gaddis, *The Long Peace: Inquiries into the History of the Cold War* (New York: Oxford University Press, 1987), 224.

19. From 1945 to mid-1985 there were at least 183 successful coups and 174 unsuccessful coup attempts in the Third World. See Steven R. David, *Third World Coups d'Ètat and International Security* (Baltimore, MD: Johns Hopkins University Press, 1987), 1-2. These numbers are just conservative estimates; the actual number of coups and coup attempts may be much higher. For a comprehensive examination of estimates of numbers of coups, see Milton Leitenberg, "Appendix 2: World-Wide Military Coups since 1945: A Short Note on Data Collections," in Asbjorn Eide and Marek Thee, eds., *Problems of Contemporary Militarism* (London: Croom Helm, 1980), 378-85.

20. For an excellent discussion of why internal threats are so common in the Third World, see Mohammed Ayoob, "Security in the Third World: the Worm about to Turn?" *International Affairs* 60 (Winter 1983-84) 41-52.

which foreign powers created states where none had existed. Although the degree to which the newly formed boundaries coincide with the boundaries of indigenous societies varies in the Third World (for example, it is high in Southeast Asia and low in Africa), in all cases a formal division replaced what had been a flexible demarcation. Because of the arbitrariness of their borders, therefore, many Third World states began and remain more as an artificial construct than a coherent unit.[21]

The artificiality of thc Third World state has created a situation in which subnational groups owe allegiance to and act on behalf of interests other than the national interest. Instead of identifying with the state, individuals identify with ethnic, religious. or regional groupings This type of narrowly defined interest perpetuates itself by preventing the formation of a national consciousness With anticolonial nationalism dissipating in the wake of decolonizations, identification with the group over the state is getting stronger with time.[22] Rather than transcending the differences among these different groups, the state is often simply the representative of a group that holds power in the capital. In such a situation, the leadership becomes just one other contender in a struggle for power that knows few constraints.[23]

Legitimacy is likely to be weaker for Third World leaders than for leaders elsewhere. Many regimes in the Third World are narrowly based, came to power through force, and use suppression to remain in power. Because they lack legitimacy, they face continual threats to their rule.[24] Threats are also likely to emerge because Third World leaders control much more wealth and power than do the other groups in the society. Gaining control of the state is therefore the only means by which the ambitious can meet their needs. Hence, the state is especially vulnerable because many different groups and individuals seek to control it. At the same time, those in power will mightily resist attempts to replace them because they do not want to relinquish their only opportunity to acquire and keep wealth and influence.[25] Equally important, since the consequence of loss of power in the Third World is often loss of life, Third World leaders are understandably more aggressive than other leaders in their efforts to maintain their positions.

Most Third World states are governed by authoritarian rule, which exacerbates and focuses the conflicts that do arise. Despite the rise of nationalism, meaningful political participation by the population at large in most Third World countries remains the exception. Decisions, especially in foreign policy, are usually made by a single individual or at most by a narrow elite. Although this elite does not have total flexibility in making policy, it typically needs to be far less responsive to national or institutional concerns than leaders elsewhere need to be. Public opinion in Third World states often carries little influence,

---

21. Robert H. Jackson and Carl G. Rosberg, "Why Africa's Weak States Persist: The Empirical and the Juridical in Statehood," *World Politics* 35 (October 1982), 1-24; Mutiah Alagappa, *The National Security of Developing States: Lessons from Thailand* (Dover, Mass.: Auburn House, 1987), 4-6; Christopher Clapham, *Third World Politics* (Madison: University of Wisconsin Press, 1985), 8.

22. Caroline Thomas, In Search of Security (Boulder, Colo.: Rienner, 1987), 2.

23. For an excellent discussion of the role of subnational groups in Third World states (i this case, West Africa), see I. William Zartman, *International Relations in the New Africa* (Englewood Cliffs, N.J.: Prentice-Hall, 1966), 47-48.

24. Alagappa (fn. 21), 9. The problems of weak legitimacy are as common to the "old" Third World states of Latin America as they are to the newer states of Africa and Southeast Asia.

25. Clapham (fn. 21), 39-43.

and bureaucracies play only a minor role in foreign policy.[26] Moreover, due to the effects of colonialism and cultural factors, rulers see themselves and are seen as an alien imposition on the society.[27]

An interrelationship between internal and external threats also characterizes the Third World. Third World leaders and insurgents commonly seek outside support to advance their interests. Their requests for help either to threaten or to protect a state's leadership are often granted by outside states.[28] Internal threats, so prevalent in the Third World, are an ideal vehicle for advancing the interests of outside states. Since the leadership of Third World states is often determined by the outcome of internal threats, other countries with an interest in the Third World state may seek to determine that outcome. Moreover, the military weakness of most Third World states enhances their willingness to back or help suppress internal threats against their neighbors. Most Third World states simply lack the weapons and the logistical capability for direct, protracted conflict beyond their borders. Although wars between states do occur, and although troops may at times be sent far afield (as in the case of Cuba), these actions are relatively rare. At the same time, the experience of Third World states that have employed external attacks, for example, Egypt and Syria versus Israel in 1967 and 1973; the Iran-Iraq War of 1980~88) confirms the prohibitive price and risks incurred by states that mount wars against formidable adversaries. Providing aid to or against insurgent groups, on the one hand, or backing or suppressing coups, on the other hand, is a relatively inexpensive and effective means of asserting one's power.[29]

Finally, one can categorize Third World states according to their self-identification. A country that considers itself to be a Third World country is likely to have a set of attitudes and goals that will be defined by its Third Worldness." This is not a tautology. Third World states overwhelmingly supported the huge price increases in OPEC oil despite the devastating economic impact on them. Third World solidarity has also been displayed in the Non-aligned Movement and the Law of the Sea Conference. One can speak of a Third World, therefore, because member states do and because they act in some ways at least because of that self-identification.[30]

These generalizations about the Third World are not intended to suggest that all Third World countries share these characteristics equally Different states manifest different

---

26. Joel S. Migdal, "Internal Structure and External Behaviour: Explaining Foreign Policies of Third World States," *International Relations* 4 (May 1974), 519-20.

27. Clapham (fn. 21), 19.

28. On foreign involvement in internal conflicts, see James Rosenau, ed., *International Aspects of Civil Strife* (Princeton: Princeton University Press, 1964); Asti Suhrke and Lela N. Garner, eds., *Ethnic Conflict in International Relations* (New York: Praeger, 1977); and Herbert K. Tillema, "Foreign Overt Intervention in the Nuclear *Age," Journal of Peace Research* 26 (1989), 179-85.

29. Even threats such as coups d'Ètat, which are thought of as strictly internal, frequently have a foreign dimension. From 1945 to mid-1985 foreign involvement played a significant role in the support of at least twenty-four successful and unsuccessful coup attempts and in efforts to suppress fourteen coups in the Third World. Foreign involvement was thus involved in slightly over 10% of the total of all coups and coup attempts. See David (fn. 19), 2.

30. According to Stephen Krasner, Third World states behave alike in global negotiations, not out of a common desire for economic development, but rather out of a common need for regime security. This view supports the contentions that one can generalize about the Third World and that concerns over survival assume central importance in Third World decision making. See Krasner, "Third World Vulnerabilities and Global Negotiations," *Review of International Studies* 9 (October 1983), 235-51

strengths and weaknesses. Nor do these generalizations apply only to the Third World. As clearly demonstrated by the toppling of Eastern European governments in 1989, states outside of the Third World also suffer from such problems as lack of consensus and weak legitimacy. What justifies considering the Third World as an analytic category is that whatever combination of factor may exist in a particular Third World state, the cumulative impact o those factors makes most Third World leaders more vulnerable to overthrow—particularly from internal threats—than leaders elsewhere Thus, while the leaders of all states must be concerned about threats, in the Third World such concerns assume an urgency and priority that is rarely matched elsewhere.

WHY THE NATURE OF THE THIRD WORLD SUPPORTS THE THEORY OF OMNIBALANCING

The characteristics of Third World states demonstrate why structural theories of alignment such as balance of power are inapplicable to the Third World. At the heart of balance of power theory is the distinction between the anarchy of the international system and the order of domestic politics. Adherents emphasize that international politics has no central government with the power and authority to resolve conflicts. The absence of a strong consensus in international politics, moreover, exacerbates the ensuing struggle for power. In such an environment, balancing plays a central role in ensuring the survival of states against the aggressive designs of other states. Within states, however, balance of power advocates argue that conflicts take place in an "integrated society, kept together by a strong consensus and the normally unchallengeable power of a central government."[31] Balance of power theory acknowledges that internal balancing takes place as groups combine (or balance) to advance their interests. Because the central government ensures that the survival of losers in domestic struggles is not threatened, however, supporters of balance of power assert that balancing is of much less importance in domestic politics than it is in international politics.[32]

The problem with this distinction is that central governments in the Third World often lack the power to resolve disputes within their borders.

Thus, there is often no "strong consensus" or "integrated society" to inhibit conflict, and the Third World reproduces rather than provides a haven from the anarchy of international politics. Instead of sharply differentiating what occurs on the international scene from what occurs within states, it is more accurate to consider Third World domestic politics as a microcosm of international politics. As a result, balancing to ensure survival is as critical for groups within states as it is between states.[33]

Balance of power theory focuses on the state as the principal level of analysis; that is, for most of its adherents, the state, and not the individual ruler, is the main actor in international politics.[34] They view the state as a fully formed unit with clearly defined borders capable of operating autonomously because they perceive domestic politics as "hierarchi-

---

31. Morgenthau and Thompson (fn. 3), 190.

32. See ibid., 189-92, for a concise description on why internal balancing is supposedly fundamentally different from balancing between states.

33. For an intriguing argument that order is more common between Third World (in this case, African) states than within them, see Jackson and Rosberg (fn. 21).

34. For an argument of why states should be considered the main actors in international politics, see Waltz (fn. 3). 93-95; and see also Keohane (fn. 12), 160.

cally ordered"; that is, the central government can command the obedience of different groups under its authority and thereby control what goes on within its borders. According to the theory, this justifies a focus on the behavior of the state.[35]

These assumptions, however, are of little relevance to Third World states, with their arbitrary borders encompassing many groups that often successfully resist domination from the top. It is the leadership of the state and not the state itself that is the proper unit of analysis for understanding Third World foreign policy, particularly alignment. When we refer to Egypt or Ethiopia becoming pro-American or pro-Soviet, we are really referring to the orientation of a narrow authoritarian elite. The distinction is fundamental, because the interests of this elite need not be synonymous with the interests of the state. Understanding why leaders make the alignment decisions they do requires an understanding of what is in the best interests of the leaders and not of what is in the best interests of the state. This is especially true when the survival of the leadership is at stake. Very few Third World leaders need to worry about losing their country—the mortality rate of even Third World states is very low. It is reasonable to assume, however, that Third World leaders do worry about the much more common, but (from their perspective) equally consequential prospect of being removed from power. It follows that when a leadership is confronted with a choice between aligning so as to benefit the state but endangering its hold on power or aligning in such a way that harms the state but preserves its power, it will choose the latter.

Balance of power theory assumes that states will seek to expand their power as much as they can to provide a "margin of safety" to ensure their survival.[36] In the Third World, however, the prevalence of threats against leaders places a premium, not on expanding power per se, but surviving. In this respect, politics in the Third World supports some the observations of neorealism, in particular, that elites have their own interests, the most important of which is to stay in power. Neorealism also recognizes that efforts to maximize power produce resistance it will ultimately jeopardize one's security. Consequently, leaders prefer align with states that ensure their hold on power rather than with states that may increase their power, but at the risk of endangering their survival. Conditions in the Third World, however, call into question neorealism's emphasis on countering threats from other states as the prime determinant of alignment.[37]

Balance of power theory is flawed in its application to the Third World because it ignores internal threats; that is, it overlooks the most likely source of challenge to the leadership of Third World states. Balance of power theory therefore also cannot accurately assess the strength of external threats because such threats usually depend for their effectiveness on internal conditions that are susceptible to outside manipulation. In 1971, for example, the Pakistani leadership believed it had counter a secessionist threat from the East Bengalis in order to remain power. This meant confronting India, which supported the secessionist movement. India alone posed a considerable but manageable external threat to Pakistan. What made the Indian threat unmanageable and led to the decisive Pakistani defeat in the 1971 Indo-Pakistani War was Indian power *combined* with the massive internal threat mounted by the East Bengalis.[38] Even where there is a pressing external

35. Waltz (fn 3) 81.

36. Morgenthau and Thompson (fn. 3), 227-28.

37. For a thorough examination of neorealism, see Keohane, ed., *Neorealism and Its Critics* (fn. 12); see also Robert O. Keohane, "Alliances, Threats, and the Uses of Neorealism" *International Security* 13 (Summer 1988), 169-76, at 173.

threat, therefore, a Third World leader's estimation of the need for outside support to counterbalance the threat often depends on internal factors that can affect the magnitude of the external threat.

In sum, in seeking to explain Third World alignment, the overall nature of the Third World supports omnibalancing while making the applicability of balance of power highly suspect. For those cases in which the principal threats to the leadership are from other states, balance of power theory indeed applies. But it is only prudent to consider the impact of domestic challenges before assuming that external threats alone have determined an alignment, because in what appears to be the vast majority of Third World cases, internal threats play a major role. Omnibalancing therefore needs to be invoked. Omnibalancing also respects the complexity and multifaceted nature of the threats confronting Third World leaders; it recognizes that they typically face many threats from many sources and that lesser challenges must be appeased in order to resist the principal ones. Omnibalancing is thus not misled into concluding that bandwagoning to threatening states necessarily means that the leadership chose not to balance against the most pressing threats it faced.

CASES OF OMNIBALANCING: MENGISTU AND SADAT

The superiority of omnibalancing for explaining Third World alignment can be seen in the decisions of Ethiopia's Mengistu Haile Mariam to align with the Soviet Union and of Egypt's Anwar Sadat to align with the United States. These examples. of course, do not confirm the overall applicability of omnibalancing to the Third World (only an in-depth analysis of all Third World alignment decisions could do that). Nevertheless, they are particularly valuable in showing how conditions that are prevalent in the Third World prevent balance of power theory from explaining or predicting the alignments of leaders in key Third World countries. Moreover, these cases illustrate how alternative explanations of alignment, such as bandwagoning and ideology, also fail to match the ability of omnibalancing to explain the alignment decisions of these leaders.

By the standards of balance of power, the military officers (subsequently labeled the Derg) who overthrew Haile Selassie in 1974 should have made every effort to maintain Ethiopia's alignment with the United States.[39] For the twenty years prior to the Derg's takeover, the United States had been the principal supporter of Ethiopia, providing it with the largest amount of military and economic assistance sent to a sub-Saharan African country. Moreover, despite the radical rhetoric of the Derg, especially that of its emerging leader, Mengistu Haile Mariam, the United States emphasized its intention to support the new government. To that end, American assistance to Mengistu's regime dramatically

---

38. Ayoob (fn. 20), 43. On the background of the 1971 Indo-Pakistani War (including Indian support of the East Bengalis), see Robert Jackson, *South Asian Crisis: India, Pakistan, and Bangladesh: A Political and Historical Analysis of the 1971 War* (New York: Praeger, 1974 and Pran Chopra, *India's Second Liberation* (Cambridge: MIT Press, 1974). On the need the Pakistani leadership to prevent the secession of East Pakistan in order to survive power, see Jackson, 26-27.

39. For background on why Mengistu aligned with the Soviet Union, see Marina Ottaway, *Soviet and American Influence in the Horn of Africa* (New York: Praeger, 1983); David A. Korn, *Ethiopia. the United States, and the Soviet Union* ((Carbondale: Southern Illinois University Press, 1986); Colin Legum and Bill Lee. *The Horn of Africa in Continuing Crisis* (New York: Africana, 1979); and Paul 23. Henze. *Russians and the Horn: (Opportunism and the Long View,* European-American Institute for Security Research, The EAI Papers, No. 5 (Marina del Ray, Calif.: European American Institute, 1983).

increased, from levels provided Haile Selassie. Fully one-third of all military equipment delivered to Ethiopia by the United States arrived in the two year after the Derg took power. American economic aid to Ethiopia both bilaterally and through multilateral institutions also showed marked in creases.[40]

Any doubts about Mengistu's maintaining his alignment with the United States ought to have (by balance of power logic) been erased by the Soviet backing of Ethiopia's chief adversary, Somalia. 03ecause of Soviet support, Somalia, which maintained irredentist aims against Ethiopia, had been transformed into one of the most powerful countries in sub-Saharan Africa. Beginning in 1962 and dramatically escalating after the Derg took power in Ethiopia, Moscow provided huge amounts of military equipment and hundreds of advisers to the Somali armed forces. America's increased assistance to the Mengistu government proved essential in maintaining a rough parity between the Ethiopian and Somali forces and deterring additional Soviet involvement. It would appear that Mengistu would do all that he could to keep American support to enable him to continue to resist (or balance against) his Soviet-backed adversary.

And yet the Derg under Mengistu chose not to intensity its alignment with the United States but instead attempted to realign with the Soviet Union—the backer of Ethiopia's primary external threat. From the time that Haile Selassie was overthrown, Mengistu and his colleagues on the Derg pressed the Soviet Union to replace the United States as Ethiopia's principal supporter. While still dependent on the United States for security assistance, Mengistu transformed Ethiopia along Marxist-Leninist lines and followed the Soviet lead in foreign policy. After three years the USSR finally acceded to Mengistu's requests: in 1977 the Soviet Union became Ethiopia's primary military supplier, and in 1978 a formal treaty of friendship and cooperation with the Soviet Union replaced the mutual defense treaty Ethiopia had concluded with the United States.

Why did this take place, in violation of balance of power theory? Mengistu's ideological leanings may have made him more comfortable with the Soviet Union, but there is no evidence that it played an important role in his alignment. The Ethiopian leader never manifested pro-Communist sympathies before seizing power, did not hesitate to purge orthodox Communist groups ruthlessly, and bitterly resisted the establishment of a Marxist-Leninist vanguard party. Thus, none of Mengistu's major decisions can be explained as a consequence of ideology.[41] Bandwagoning may appear to have been a factor, with

---

40. Korn (fn. 39), 8, 13; Bereket Habte Selassie, *Conflict and Intervention in the Horn of Africa* (New York: Monthly Review Press, 1980), 138; U.S. Arms Control and Disarmament Agency, *World Military Expenditures and Arms Transfers,* 1968-1977 (Washington, D.C.: (G.P.O., 1979), 157; Agency for International Development. U.S. *Overseas Loans and Grants and Assistance from International Organizations* (Washington, D.C.; G.P.O., 1979), 101.

41. There is a widespread consensus among analysts across the ideological spectrum that Mengistu and the Derg were not driven by ideological factors but, rather, acted simply to survive in power. See, for example, Marina Ottaway and David Ottawav, *Ethiopia. Empire in Revolution* (New York: Africana, 1978). 149; Korn (fn. 39), 111; Fred Halliday and Maxine Molyneux, *The Ethiopian Revolution* (London: Unwin, 1981), 99; Paul B. Henze, "Beyond the Ethiopian Famine: Anatomy of a Revolution II," *Encounter* (London) (July 1986), 15-27 at 19; and Michael Chege, "The Revolution Betrayed: Ethiopia, 1974-1979" *Journal of Modern African Studies* 17 (September 1979), 359-80. Mengistu's recent retreat from Marxism-Leninism (which not so coincidentally coincides with reduced Soviet support) and his reestablishment of military ties to Israel further support the view that ideological factors do not dominate his decision making.

Mengistu seeking to appease Soviet aggression. But Mengistu at no point attempted to appease or align with his principal threat, Somalia, as bandwagoning would predict.

Only omnibalancing explains Mengistu's decision to align with the Soviet Union, by recognizing that the United States, contrary to balance of power assessments, was actually not providing adequate military support to the Ethiopian leadership. It supplied enough help for Ethiopia to deal with the external threat posed by Somalia, but it did not provide enough assistance for Ethiopia to deal with the myriad of internal threats as well. Foremost among these threats was the rebellion in the Ethiopian province of Eritrea, which involved far more Ethiopian troops than were stationed even along the Somali front.[42] Mengistu recognized that he could not survive in power without satisfactorily coping with the Eritrean revolt. Accordingly, gaining outside assistance to suppress the rebellion played a major role in his turn to the Soviet Union. The assumption of balance of power that the need to resist internal threats, such as the one posed by Eritrea, is irrelevant in determining alignment is clearly wrong in the case of Mengistu.[43]

Omnibalancing also recognizes that Mengistu's alignment to the Soviet Union was not bandwagoning but actually a form of balancing behavior not included in balance of power theory. By turning to the Soviet Union, Mengistu was not seeking to appease the principal threats arrayed against him (Ethiopia was far too unimportant to justify direct Soviet action). Rather, he was trying to resist them by appeasing the secondary threat posed by the Soviet Union. As the major supporter of Somalia and an indirect backer of the Eritrean rebellion, the Soviet Union clearly *contributed* to the threats that were most likely to topple Mengistu. But by backing the Somalis and the Eritreans, the USSR was also in the best position to undermine the threats they presented simply by withholding assistance and getting its allies to do the same. Balance of power may be correct that states will not normally appease threats be cause of fear of placing one's survival in the hands of an adversary. But, as demonstrated by Mengistu, leaders will appease secondary threats in order to defeat more pressing ones.

Anwar Sadat's alignment with the United States following the 1973 October War is another clear example of the limitations of balance of power theory.[44] After assuming power following Nasser's death in 1970, Sadat enhanced Egypt's alignment with the Soviet Union. A treaty of friendship and cooperation was concluded, and Moscow provided Egypt with record levels of military assistance. Soviet support reached a peak during the 1973 October War with Israel, enabling Sadat to achieve a smashing political victory. Nevertheless, after the war Sadat decided to forsake his alignment with Moscow and turn to the United States—the backer of his chief external threat—for support.

As in the case of Mengistu, neither ideology nor bandwagoning explains Sadat's alignment with the United States. Ideological explanations for Sadat's realignment decision—that he underwent a fundamental change in his world view—are not very convincing. At the very least, that Sadat could profess being comfortable with the Soviet Union

---

42. Some useful works on Eritrea include Hagai Erlich, *The Struggle over Eritrea 1962-1978* (Stanford, Calif.: Hoover Institution, 1983); G. H. K. Trevaskis, *Eritrea: A Colony in Transition* (London: Oxford University Press, 1960); and Richard Sherman, *Eritrea: The Unfinished Revolution* (New York: Praeger, 1980). See also John Markakis, *National and Class Conflict in the Horn of Africa* (London: Cambridge University Press, l987), 104-45.

43. Many analysts make the point that Mengistu could not survive without a satisfactory settlement of the Eritrean conflict. See, for example, Legum and Lee (fn. 39), 39, Suzanne Kasikas, *The Arc of Socialist Revolutions* (Cambridge, Mass.: Schenkman, 1982), 142; and Selassie (fn. 40). 37. 71.

and then the United States demonstrates an ideological commitment too weak to dictate the choice of alignment partners. Similarly, bandwagoning was not in evidence, as Sadat made no effort to appease or align with Israel.

Only omnibalancing's emphasis on internal threats explains Sadat's decision to align with the United States. Omnibalancing recognizes that Israel, the primary external threat faced by Egypt, did not directly threaten Sadat's hold on power. Since the end of the War of Attrition in 1970 (in which Israeli and Egyptian forces exchanged fire across the Suez Canal), Israel had had no offensive designs against Sadat's Egypt. The Israeli threat stemmed not from Israel itself but from the effect of the continuing Israeli occupation of Egyptian land (a result of the 1967 war) an various Egyptian groups. The Egyptian military, workers, intellectuals, and students had grown increasingly impatient with the continuing stalemate and sought to force the Egyptian leader to regain the territories from Israel. For Sadat to deal with the threats from the Egyptian groups, he had to force Israel to return the lands it had seized. The Soviet Union, however, fearing a confrontation with the United States and believing that Egypt would lose any war with Israel, would not provide Sadat with the capability to end the Israeli occupation. Moscow's unwillingness to do what was necessary to extricate Sadat from the continuing stalemate exacerbated the domestic threats he confronted and eventually led him to dissolve the Egyptian-Soviet alignment.[45]

Sadat subsequently aligned with the United States out of a recognition that that was the best means of balancing against his principal, domestic threats. The United States, by virtue of its support for Israel, was the only great power willing and able to force an end to the Israeli occupation of the Sinai. Thus, the reasons for Sadat's alignment with the United States only become clear when assessed in light of the domestic threats he faced and the impact of the Israeli occupation on those threats.

Both cases clearly show how omnibalancing offers the necessary correctives to balance of power to explain Third World alignments. Mengistu and Sadat both appeased an international threat (posed by the Soviet Union and the United States, respectively) in order to defeat a more pressing domestic challenge. The notion that Third World leaders appease (or bandwagon with) an external threat in order to balance against a domestic threat is not as contradictory as it may appear. As Robert Jervis argues, politics in a complex environment results in unintended consequences. Instead of attempting to achieve a

44. Some good background treatments of Anwar Sadat's Egypt, including his decision to reject his alignment with the Soviet Union and turn to the United States, include Anwar el Sadat, *In Search of Identity: An Autobiography* (New York: Harper and Row, 1978); Raymond William Baker, *Egypt's Uncertain Revolution under Nasser and Sadat* (Cambridge: Harvard University Press, 1978); Raymond A. Hinnebusch. Jr., *Egyptian Politics under Sadat* (Cambridge: Cambridge University Press, 1985); A. I. Dawaisha, *Egypt in the Arab World: Thc Elements of Foreign Policy* (New York: Macmillan, 1976); Mohammed Heikal, *Thc Sphinx and the Commissar: The Rise and Fall of Soviet Influence in the Arab World* (London: Collins, 1978); Shimon Shamir, "Egypt's Reorientation towards the U.S.: Factors and Conditions of Decision Making," in Haim Shaked and Itamar Rabinovich, eds., *The Middle East and thc United States: Perceptions and Policies* (New Brunswick, N.J.: Transaction, 1980); Mark Cooper, *The Transformation of Egypt* (Baltimore, Md.: Johns Hopkins University Press, 1982); Alvin Z. Rubinstein, *Red Star on the Nile: The Soviet-Egyptian Influence Relationship since the June War* (Princeton: Princeton University Press, 1977); and Robert O. Freedman, *Soviet Policy toward the Middle East Since 1970* (New York: Praeger, 1975).

45. Extensive accounts of the internal threats besetting Sadat can be found in Baker (fn. 44); Hinnebusch (fn. 44); and Cooper (fn. 44).

goal by heading straight for it, one is often better off adopting an indirect approach or even one that heads in the opposite direction.[46] As seen by Mengistu and Sadat—Third World leaders confronting a great number of threats from many different sources—a simple balance of power approach would not have maximized the chances of survival. Instead, a Third World leadership often stands the best chance of defeating the threats it confronts by adopting a policy that is indirect and seemingly opposed to what it wishes to achieve.

The examples of Mengistu and Sadat also show how focusing on the interests of the leadership elite better explains alignment than does focusing on the interests of the state as a whole. It is unclear whether Mengistu's alignment with the Soviet Union or Sadat's alignment with the United States benefited their respective countries. Ethiopia, in particular, suffered as a result of its alignment with the Soviet Union.[47] But if the alignments did not benefit Ethiopia or possibly even Egypt, they unquestionably benefited the leaders of those counties by enhancing their hold on power. In comparison with other leaders, those in the Third World tend to face more threats and pay a higher price for failure; presumably, then, the concern for political survival that characterized Mengistu's and Sadat's alignment decisions exists throughout the Third World.

The two cases furthermore call into question the contention that Third World leaders will align with the outside state that provides them with the most benefits. Both leaders rejected patrons who gave them record assistance for others whose level of support could not be guaranteed. Mengistu had little reason to believe that Soviet economic assistance would ever approach the quantity and quality of that provided by the United States, and Sadat could not reply on a United States beholden to Israel to match the amount of weaponry supplied to Egypt by the Soviet Union. Both leaders did have reason to believe, however, that realigning would place them in a better position to defeat the principal threats confronting them. In deciding to change patrons, therefore, they behaved more consistently with omnibalancing's emphasis on aligning to resist threats rather than on aligning with the better provider.

Finally, both cases demonstrate how focusing exclusively on external threats—and ignoring internal threats—can fail to explain or predict Third World alignments. Internal threats, either alone or backed by outside states, played a central role in the alignments of Ethiopia and Egypt.

Such threats continue to determine Third World alignments today. In Latin America, for example, requests for American security assistance have come from the leaders of Colombia and Bolivia (which face threats from well-armed drug dealers). In the Middle East domestic pressure from Palestinians has contributed to the decision on the part of Jordan's King Hussein to align his state more closely with Iraq, and in Southeast Asia, Cambodia's ultimate alignment will be determined by that country's civil war. The determinative role of internal threats in Third World alignments should not be surprising given the prevalence of such threats. What is surprising is the belief that balance of power can be applied generally to explain Third World alignment, despite its neglect of the kind of threats that are most likely to confront the leaders of the Third World.

---

46. Jervis, "Systems Theories and Diplomatic History," in Paul Gordon Lauren, ed., *Diplomacy: New Approaches in History, Theory and Policy* (New York: Free Press, 1979), 218.

47. For how aligning with the USSR exacerbated Ethiopia's problems, see Paul B. Henze, "Communism and Ethiopia," *Problems of Communism* 30 (May-June 1981). 55-74.

THE DEFENSE OF BALANCE OF POWER

Supporters of balance of power have responded to the prevalence of internal threats in the Third World generally and to their impact on specific countries by maintaining that it does not invalidate the balance of power theory. Some adherents of the theory, such as Waltz, recognize that violence and the use of force to deal with it occur as often (or more so) within states as between states. For Waltz, this means that neither the occurrence of violence nor the use of force per se can be used as a standard by which to distinguish domestic from international politics. Instead, he argues, the distinction is marked by government's monopoly on the *legitimate* use of force to deal with violence. Citizens, therefore, need not worry about protecting themselves; they can appeal to the government for assistance. In international politics, by contrast, states can only rely on themselves for defense. Thus, international politics is a system of self-help, whereas domestic politics is not.[48]

In a consideration of Third World alignment, however, this largely cogent analysis is problematic. First, the notion of a legitimate government protecting its citizens from private acts of violence often does not apply: for large groups of people in the Third World the government is neither legitimate nor a protector. Whether one is a southern Sudanese seeking autonomy in Nimeiri's Sudan, or an Eritrean seeking independence in Mengistu's Ethiopia, or an individual seeking just to survive in Pol Pot's Cambodia, the government is less of a guardian against threats than it is the chief threat. Second, Waltz's observations are largely irrelevant in terms of the alignment decisions of Third World leaders. Eve if it is granted that a government has a monopoly on the legitimate us of force, its leadership must still act to guard itself from all threats, including "illegitimate" ones and those that originate within their own countries. A Third World leadership struggling to survive bases in alignment decisions on how best to protect itself from the threats it face not on abstract considerations of whether the threat is "legitimate" or whether its source is domestic or international.

It has also been argued that it does not matter whether the assumptions of balance of power are true as long as the theory based on those assumptions accurately predicts what occurs. Assumptions are seen a simplifications of the truth, their role being not to describe what actually happens but to enable theories to be constructed. According to Walt; "We can freely admit, then, that states are in fact not unitary, purposive actors." As such, the fact that Third World states do not conform to the ideal assumed by balance of power theory is irrelevant. So long as balance of power theory accurately predicts the behavior of Third World states the thinking continues, it remains a valuable theory for the Third World.[49]

As this analysis has shown, however, it has not yet been demonstrate that Third World states do in fact conduct themselves in a manner predicted by the balance of power theory. Moreover, even if balance of power theory accurately predicts the behavior of most Third World states, it is worth knowing whether it is right for the wrong reason' Especially where theory is used to guide policy (as balance of power does), it is critical to know which policies are likely to produce which outcomes. Basing one's policies on overall outcomes might prove catastrophic in a specific, vital case.

---

48. Waltz (fn. 3), 103-4

49. Waltz (fn 5), 37-38.

Most important, the pursuit of knowledge is worthy in its own right. If assumptions do not conform to reality, regardless of the value of the theories they underlie, they should be revised. This is especially the case when those assumptions grew out of the study of states the present nature and historical experiences of which are vastly different from what one finds in the Third World. At the very least, refining our assumption in light of Third World realities holds out the prospect of an improved theory. This is particularly important for theories such as balance of power, whose explanatory and predictive value leaves much room for improvement.

Finally, some have argued that although many states in the Third World do not follow the dictates of balance of power when aligning, that does not detract from the value of the balance of power theory. As Waltz argues (in the context of defending the primacy of states over transnational actors), "So long as the major states are the major actors, the structure of international politics is defined in terms of them."[50] Since the major states are not Third World states, their behavior is apparently not efficient to invalidate theories of international politics. Moreover, those states that are driven by internal threats (and thus do not follow balance power dictates) are likely to be weak, in which case they will not affect the global balance of power anyway.[51]

Why then concern ourselves with these exceptions? First, it matters little that international politics may be defined by the major states if this definition does not help in the understanding of why Third World leads make the alignment decisions they do. Second, any theory of international relations that is of questionable applicability for most of the world's states and people requires refinement. Finally, as discussed below, understanding the Third World is central to the understanding of me of the fundamental issues in international relations.

THE SIGNIFICANCE OF THE THIRD WORLD

The importance of the Third World is most clearly seen when considering questions of war and peace. Understanding why states go to war has traditionally been at the heart of the study of international relations. Since World War II wars between and within non-Third World states have virtually ceased to exist. Many reasons are offered to explain this unprecedented phenomenon, including fear of nuclear war, economic entanglement, desire to avoid another World War II, and a growing acceptance of Western liberal democracy.[52] The disagreements about why war has ended outside the Third World should not, however, obscure the recognition that conflict continues unabated in the Third World. Such conflict persists in threatening both Third World and non–Third World states. Because war has

---

50. Waltz (fn. 3), 94.

51. Walt makes this point in connection with bandwagoning; see Walt (fn. 2), 179.

52. On the possible reasons for the absence of war among states outside the Third World, see Michael W. Doyle, "Kant, Liberal Legacies, and Foreign Affairs," *Philosophy and Public Affairs* 12 (Summer-Fall 1983), 205-35, 323-53; idem, "Liberalism and World Politics," *American Political Science Review* 80 (December 1986), 1151-69; Bruce Russett, "The Politics of an Alternative Security System: Toward a More Democratic and Therefore More Peaceful World" in Burns Weston, ed., *Alternatives to Nuclear Deterrence* (Boulder, Colo.: Westview Press, 1989); Gaddis (fn. 18), esp. chap. 8; John Mueller, "The Essential Irrelevance of Nuclear Weapons: Stability in the Postwar World," *International Security* 13 (Fall 1988), 55-79; and Francis Fukuyama, "The End of History," *National Interest* 16 (Summer 1989), 3-18.

become a virtual Third World monopoly, it is impossible to understand the causes and possible solutions of international conflict without understanding the Third World.

Present trends point to the increasing importance of the Third World in matters of international security. The proliferation of weapons and weapons-related technology has dramatically enhanced the strength of many Third World states. Approximately a dozen Third World countries have chemical or biological weapons, and roughly the same number maintain ballistic missiles.[53] Several Third World countries have or are very close to having nuclear weapons. Even without exotic weapons, Third World militaries have become formidable institutions. Many Third World countries (for example, Iraq, India, and Vietnam) have military forces larger and better equipped than those of most European countries. A dozen deploy a thousand or more battle tanks. In most cases; the increasing strength of Third World armies has not been accompanied by a commensurate increase in stability.

Ironically, the apparent lessened interest of the Soviet Union in the Third World, if continued, will enhance the Third World's role in issues of international security. A Soviet departure from the Third World would not end the threats to global security posed by Third World states. On the contrary, for some threats (for example, nuclear proliferation, regional conflict), a Soviet withdrawal could eliminate an important constraint. Most important, were the Soviets to abandon their efforts to expand their influence throughout the world, the Third World would be left as the principal threat to international stability. At the very least, therefore, the *relative* importance of the Third World to international security concerns would increase in the wake of overall Soviet retrenchment.

Many of the issues that are likely to dominate international relations for the foreseeable future have a critical Third World component. Economically, the exploding growth of the newly industrialized countries of East Asia and the steady development of major Third World powers such as India and Brazil will make them powerful forces in determining the shape and direction of the international economy.[54] And as the world's dependence on petroleum increases in the coming years, the importance of the Persian Gulf will be enhanced.[55] The Third World also plays a major role in the global environment. There is increasing evidence that the burning of tropical forests contributes to the greenhouse effect, whereby the climate of the earth is substantially warmed. Dealing with this problem will require the cooperation of the Third World states in which the forests are located. In addition, problems such as overpopulation and drug trafficking are increasingly dependent on the Third World for resolution. Far from being marginal actors, the Third World is central to the course of international relations, and it will become even more so.

---

53. For a list of Third World countries with chemical arms, see *Newsweek* September 1988; for lists of Third World countries with ballistic missiles, see W. Seth Carus, "Missiles in the Middle East: A New Threat to Stability," Washington Institute for Near East Policy, *Policy Focus 6* (June 1988), 1-9; and Aaron Karp, "Ballistic Missiles in the Third World," *International Security* 9 (Winter 1984-85), 166-95. On nuclear proliferation, see Leonard S. Spector, with Jacqueline R. Smith, *Nuclear Ambitions* (Boulder, Colo.: Westview Press, 1990).

54. For more on the growing economic power of the Third World, see U.S. Department of Defense, *Sources of Change in the Future Security Environment* (Washington, D.C.: G.P.O. 1988). 4

55. United States Department of Energy, *Energy Security: A Report to thc President of thc United States* (Washington, D.C.: G.P.O. 1987).

OMNIBALANCING AND THE THIRD WORLD

Omnibalancing's explanation of why Third World leaders align as they do addresses the implications of the increasing importance of the Third World in two critical ways. First, understanding why Third World leaders make the alignment decisions they do enables other states to influence those decisions in order to encourage favorable alignments. Omnibalancing's emphasis on the need to meet the security concerns of Third World leaders in order to secure an alignment with them suggests approaches (for example, a greater emphasis on dealing with internal threats) that differ from those deriving from the focus of balance of power on protecting states from other states. If omnibalancing provides a better guide or policy than does balance of power, states that follow its precepts are more likely to secure the alignments they seek. And states that secure alignments with Third World leaders, at the very least, insulate themselves from the growing power and threats those leaders can pose.

The emphasis on the overriding need of Third World leaders to act in ways that will ensure their hold on power also has implications for a broad range of Third World behavior that goes beyond decisions on alignment. As seen in the cases of Egypt and Ethiopia, powerful forces are at work when Third World leaders take the risky and problematic step of breaking an alignment with one great power in order to align with another. This suggests that other decisions relating to both foreign and domestic policy should also be examined in terms of the Third World leader's drive to remain in power. Insights into questions concerning when Third World leaders will go to war or how to enlist their cooperation in solving global problems could well be gained by focusing on the need of Third World leaders to ensure their survival in the face of both external and internal threats.[56]

The Third World is and will continue to be central to the study of international relations. For both theoretical and pragmatic reasons, understanding Third World foreign policies, including why Third World states align as they do, is essential for the broader understanding of world politics. In seeking such an understanding, it makes little sense to rely on a theory derived from a different historical experience that fails to address the reality of the Third World. That reality is dominated by the efforts of Third World leaders to do what they can, including seeking outside support, to survive in power. Ignorance of this simple truth prevents an understanding of the politics that determines the destiny of most of the world.

Of the many who offered advice, I would like to thank especially Aaron Friedberg and Stephen Van Evera for their detailed comments and suggestion

---

56. For example, Richard Ned Lebow cites the political vulnerability of a leader as one of the key factors that can induce a policy of brinkmanship; Lebow, *Between Peace and War: The Nature of International Crises* (Baltimore, Md.: Johns Hopkins University Press, 1981) 69-79.

Nationalism

General

Donald L. Horowitz
A Harvest of Hostility

Nationalism and War

Michael E. Brown
The Causes of Internal Conflict: An Overview

Introduction to Nationalism

"Insanity in individuals is rare—but in groups, parties, *nations*, and epochs, it is the rule."[1]

—*Friedrich Nietzsche*

"The breakup of Yugoslavia is a classic example of nationalism from the top down--a *manipulated nationalism* in a region where peace has historically prevailed more than war and in which a quarter of the population were in mixed marriages"[2]

—*Warren Zimmermann, the last Ambassador to Yugoslavia*

During the twentieth century, nationalism has been one of the most widespread and irresolvable catalysts of conflict. Two major world wars in the first half-century testify to the causal links between nationalism and war. During the Cold War, although strategists and scholars may have played down the significance of nationalism in the face of the East-West ideological struggle, nationalism continued to fuel over 30 struggles world-wide. What's more, partly as a result of the Soviet system's collapse, the first decade of the post-Cold War era has also been marked by devastating ethnic conflicts along the southern rim of the former Soviet Union, in the Balkans, and around the Great Lakes region of Africa. The purpose of this section is to examine the fundamental and immediate reasons for nationalism and conflict.[3]

Nationalism lies in the sub-systemic lens because it looks inside the 'black box' to detect how nationalist ideology can drive trans- and sub-state actors toward conflict. Before describing the three articles in this section, it is first necessary to clarify some basic terms. A *nation* is a group of people who see themselves as a nation. In other words, a nation is more about attitudinal boundaries than genealogical or geographic boundaries. To be sure, many nations are characterized by common histories, common cultures, common territories, common languages, and common ancestries. However, it is the recognition of the idea of shared membership in the nation, not the shared characteristics, that are essential to the notion of ethnic nationhood.[4]

Nationalism as an ideology is a relatively new phenomenon, the advent of which most historians associate with the American and French Revolutions in the last part of the eighteenth century. Prior to the French Revolution, the nation as a cultural unit and the state as a political unit were not connected. The state was simply a territorial and legal entity. However, in October 1789, the king of France became the king of the French, thereby coupling the nation and the state into one single conception. This event helped move this idea of nation-statehood—a historic and legal concept—toward the ideology of nationalism. As

---

1. Freidrich Nietzsche, quoted in *The Harper Book of Quotations*, 3d ed., ed. Robert I. Fitzhenry (New York, NY: HarperPerennial, 1993), 117.

2. Warren Zimmermann, "The Last Ambassador," *Foreign Affairs* 74 (March/April 1995): 12. Mr. Zimmermann was Ambassador to Yugoslavia from 1989 to 1992.

3. John Hutchinson and Anthony D. Smith, eds., *Nationalism* (Oxford: Oxford University Press, 1994), 11; and see Trent N. Thomas, "Global Assessment for Current and Future Trends in Ethnic and Religious Conflict" in *Ethnic Conflict and Regional Instability*, eds. Robert L. Pfaltzgraff and Richard H. Shultz, Jr. (Carlisle, PA: Strategic Studies Institute, 1994), 34, 36.

4. Ernest Gellner, *Nations and Nationalism* (Ithaca, NY: Cornell Univeristy Press, 1983), 7.

an ideology, *nationalism* postulates that the cultural (nation) and the political (state) unit should be congruent in a universal system of nation-states.[5] Moreover, after 1792 when Napoleon began exporting French nationalistic ideals throughout Europe, he provoked strong reactions in England, Spain, Germany, Poland, and Russia. This backlash intensified and spread the idea of civic nationalism across Europe.[6]

However, the era of royalist reaction from 1815 to 1848 precipitated a greater emphasis on the ethnic character of nationalism, in contrast to the civic versions of nationalism that had emerged earlier in the United States and France. It is important to distinguish between *civic* and *ethnic* nationalism since ethnic nationalism and its concomitant consequences—intrastate conflicts—has been more problematic in the post-Cold War period. *Civic nationalism* generally bodes well for cooperation inside states whereas an increase in *ethnic nationalist* sentiment generally augurs some form of tumult or conflict inside and across states. Jack Snyder maintains that *civic nationalism* is normally manifest in well-institutionalized democracies whereas *ethnic nationalism* usually emerges when state institutions have collapsed. *Civic nationalism* guarantees equal and universal citizenship rights within a supporting framework of laws. When *civic nationalism* predominates, loyalty to the state outweighs loyalty to any ethnic group. However, *ethnic nationalism* appears as the default option when state institutions fail to provide for ethnic groups' basic economic, cultural, political, and physical security needs. When *ethnic nationalism* prevails, loyalty to the ethnic group outweighs loyalty to the state. Snyder argues that an intensification of ethnic-nationalist sentiment will probably contribute to an increase in conflict with other groups.[7]

The aforementioned discussion begs another question—how, when, and why does ethnic nationalism emerge and intensify? Consequently, this section relies on three articles to help answer these questions succinctly and cogently. In "The Ethnic Sources of Nationalism," Anthony D. Smith looks at the historical and cultural processes which shape the collective level of ethnic or national identity. Simply stated, Smith helps explain how and when an ethnic nation forms. Donald Horowitz's "A Harvest of Hostilities" offers another perspective on the concepts of ethnicity and ethnic nationalism. Horowitz examines the international implications of secessionist and irredentist movements. He also identifies the practical and legal problems that stem from two irreconcilable international principles: state sovereignty and self-determination.

Finally, in "The Causes of Internal Conflict," Michael E. Brown reviews, critiques, and synthesizes some scholarly explanations for ethno-nationalism, arriving at a theoretical framework that points to the causal relationships between nationalism and conflict. Given the assumption that an increase in nationalism will increase the likelihood of conflict, Brown identifies the underlying and proximate causes of ethnic conflict. Moreover, for the proximate causes, he explains two sets of independent variables (external and internal to the state) that cause increases in the intensity of ethnic nationalism (the dependent variable), and consequently, also contribute to the outbreak of conflict. Together, these three articles very concisely help us understand some of the central questions concerning nationalism and conflict inside and across state borders.[8]

5. Alfred Cobban, "The Rise of the Nation-State System" in *Nationalism*, 249.

6. Hutchinson and Smith, 7.

7. Jack Snyder, "Nationalism and the Crisis of the Post-Soviet State," *Survival* 35 (Spring 1993): 12, 19; and Hutchinson and Smith, 7.

Movements and groups energized by the ideas of ethnic nationalism play no small part in catalyzing conflict in the current international environment. A survey of the places where U.S. forces have deployed for combat or peace operations over the last decade reveals the salience of ethnic nationalism. Northern Iraq, Macedonia, Rwanda, Bosnia, and Kosovo are among the locations where U.S. forces have deployed in response to ethnically triggered conflicts.

Many of the areas US forces deploy are rife with ethnic conflict: 1996 Bosnia-Herzegovina to stop genocide of Croatians & Bosniaks by Serbs; 1999 Kosovo to stop ethnic cleansing by Serbs against Kosovar Albanians; 203 Iraq with Sunni, Shia and Kurds. By first understanding why these ethnic groups are fighting, policy-makers can develop policies to address and hopefully solve those problems.

---

[8] Anthony D. Smith, "The Ethnic Sources of Nationalism," *Survival* 35 (Spring 1993); Donald L. Horowitz, "A Harvest of Hostility: Ethnic Conflict and Self-Determination after the Cold War," *Defense Intelligence Journal* 1 (1992): 137-63; and Michael E. Brown, "The Causes of Internal Conflict: An Overview" in *Nationalism and Ethnic Conflict*, eds. Michael E. Brown, Owen R. Cote, Sean M. Lynn-Jones, and Steven E. Miller (Cambridge, MA: MIT Press, 1997).

A Harvest of Hostility: Ethnic Conflict and Self-Determination After the Cold War

Donald L. Horowitz

Severe ethnic conflict around the world often comes as a shock to Americans. Of course, they are no longer surprised by racial conflict, if that term is limited to Black-White conflict, but inhabitants of the New World have some difficulty imagining why Protestants and Catholics in Northern Ireland or Serbs and Croats, Armenians and Azeris, Sinhalese and Tamils, Sikhs and Hindus, Hausa and Ibo, Zulu and Xhosa, Malays and Chinese might engage in conflict that sometimes produces rather serious violence and increasingly jeopardizes the cohesion of states.

The insularity of the United States is not merely spatial; it is also temporal. We are separate not merely by virtue of two oceans, but by virtue of two centuries. True, our own past has had a fair share of similar conflict. Ethno-religious divisions were among the most salient cleavages of late colonial America, often determinative of Loyalist or Revolutionary political positions during the independence struggle.[1] The nineteenth century witnessed a great deal of ethnic conflict between so-called natives and immigrants. In 1844, an ugly anti-Irish riot erupted in Philadelphia, and in 1855 a good many people were killed in anti-German violence in Louisville. Only after the Civil War did Black-White cleavages begin to supplant others. From that time on, lynching of Black victims in the South, then anti-Black riots in the North, and finally Black riots in many parts of the country eclipsed other types of ethnic violence.[2] Even through this period, however, other cleavages had some salience, as the successful movement to restrict immigration from Southern and Eastern Europe and events such as the Zoot Suit (anti-Mexican) riots and the anti-Japanese campaign, both of these in California, attest.

Nevertheless, we are what we have become, and what we have become, so far as Whites are concerned, is a remarkably congenial society by world standards. Admittedly, of course, world standards are low. Yet, a recent study finds that, despite quite different starting points, the major White ethnic groups in the United States have achieved decidedly similar levels of educational attainment, occupational status, and income;[3] and several studies document the growth of an overarching "White" or "just American" ethnic category.[4] Some of this White amalgamation is no doubt the product of the surpassing importance of the Black-White cleavage, but some of it also is traceable to the central myth that America constitutes a community of ideas and not of blood, that America is a haven for the persecuted of all nations

1. Janet Merrill Alger, "The Impact of Ethnicity and Religion on Social Development in Revolutionary America," in Wendell Bell and Walter E. Freeman, editors, *Ethnicity and Nation-Building* (Beverly Hills: Sage, 1974), pp. 327-339.

2. See Donald L. Horowitz, "Racial Violence in the United States," in Nathan Glazer and Ken Young, editors, *Ethnic Pluralism and Public Policy: Achieving Equality in the United* States and Britain (London: Heinemann, 1983), pp. 187-211.

3. Stanley Lieberson, "Socioeconomic Attainment," in Donald I. Horowitz and Gerard Noiriel, editors, *Immigrants in Two Democracies: French and American Experience* (New York: NYU Press, 1992), pp. 301-330.

who migrate in search of freedom. On this basis, it is not surprising that groups such as Mexican-Americans frequently express unfashionably patriotic, sometimes even assimilative, sentiments in sample surveys or that intermarriage among Japanese-Americans has run at rates in excess of 50 percent since the late 1960s.[5]

These are not the behavioral indicators of a severely divided society, and although some other societies, notably France, have somewhat comparable histories of absorbing immigrants,[6] still the American achievement in overcoming nativism[7] is qualitatively different—and that, in some measure, disqualifies us for understanding much of what is going on in the world. For while Americans may have a keen sense of the history of slavery and its aftermath, their notion of community is, in precept and often in practice, more open than what prevails elsewhere, even in the West.[8]

On these grounds, then, perhaps it is best to begin with a fairly basic explanation of what ethnic loyalties entail in a severely divided society, then proceed to a treatment of political patterns in such societies—especially territorially based claims that have international security implications—and continue with some consideration of the gaps in our knowledge of the techniques that might ameliorate ethnic conflict. At the conclusion of this essay, I shall make some remarks about the recent upsurge in movements for self-determination and the growing importance of the international law of self-determination in the post-Cold War period. This, I shall suggest, is an unfortunate conjunction, because the international law on this subject is not well attuned to the nuances of ethnic conflict and is therefore too hospitable to secessionist claims at the expense of those the secessionists would dominate.

THE NATURE OF ETHNIC LOYALTIES

When Americans lament the decline of the family, they are referring to the nuclear family. In much of the rest of the world, however, the extended family rather than the nuclear family is the norm. Ethnic affiliations resemble and build on family affiliations in several different ways.[9]

First of all, both share the birth principle of membership: most people are born into the same ethnic group in which they will die, just as most people are born into the same family in which they will die. Notice, however, that I said "most people" in both cases. We admit people to membership in families by adoption as if by birth, and other forms of fic-

---

4. Richard Alba, *Ethic Identity, The Transformation of White America* (New Haven: Yale University Press, 1990); Mary C. Waters, *Ethnic Options: Choosing Identities in America* (Berkeley: University of California Press, 1990); Herbert Gans, "Symbolic Ethnicity: The Future of Ethnic Groups and Cultures in America," *Ethnic and Racial Studies,* Vol. 2, no. 1 (January 1979), pp. 1- 19.

5. See Donald L. Horowitz, "Conflict and Accommodation: Mexican-Americans in the Cosmopolis," in Walker Connor, editor, *Mexican-Americans in Comparative Perspective* (Washington, DC: Urban Institute, 1985), pp. 84-85; Akemi Kikimura, *Through Harsh Winters: The Life of a Japanese Immigrant Woman* (Novati, California: Chandler & Sharp, 1981), p. 134.

6. See Gérard Noiriel, *Le creuset français* (Paris: Seuil, 1988).

7. On the strong history of nativism in America, see John Higham, *Strangers in the Land* (New York: Atheneum, 1968).

8. I have made this argument in some detail in "Immigration and Group Relations in France and America," in Horowitz and Noiriel, *Immigrants in Two Democracies,* pp. 10 13.

9. In this and succeeding sections, I am drawing on Donald L. Horowitz, *Ethnic Groups in Conflict* (Berkeley: University of California Press, 1985).

tive kinship are also well known. Similarly, people are sometimes admitted to membership in an ethnic group by comparable processes of "passing" (that is, concealing birth identity, sometimes with and sometimes without the knowledge and acquiescence of members of the receiving group), or conversion (where the basis of group identity is religious), or language change (where the basis of group identity is linguistic), or adoption of the cultural markers of the recipient group, sometimes accompanied by intermarriage. Groups vary in the degree to which their boundaries are porous, and groups change over time in their willingness to admit strangers to group membership. The Sikhs, who formerly received many Hindus into their ranks, receive fewer today. Their boundaries have hardened.

Groups in severe conflict frequently experience a decline in rates of intermarriage. By contrast, many groups that have avoided severe conflict maintain quite porous boundaries. This is the case in much of Latin America, where Indians can often become Ladinos without much difficulty. But whether the boundaries of a group are porous or not, there is generally some birth notion to ethnic group membership, some core conception that the group is the way it is by virtue of innate, natural characteristics, albeit characteristics frequently augmented by a unique and recognizable inventory of cultural traits, features said to be typical of group members.

The ethnic group, then, is an ascriptive group. On the continuum of affiliations, between birth at one end and choice at the other—between the family and the social club—the ethnic group is clearly at the birth end, despite individual exceptions

An ethnic group shares a notion of common origin recruitment mainly by birth, and a sense of distinctiveness This deliberately elastic conception is inclusive enough to embrace groups differentiated by language, color, religion, and even regional origin; It can cover *tribes, nationalities, races,* and *castes.* Despite American notions that color and physical appearance make for qualitatively different "racial" affiliations—I call this the figment of the pigment—the fact is that people whose gene pools are more or less identical are easily able to identify themselves by ascriptive affiliations where those affiliations come to have some importance. It does not take more than a few seconds for people in Northern Ireland to sort each other out by group identity, and deadly mobs in one country after another have devised ghoulishly reliable methods of ascertaining ethnic identity in their effort to accomplish simultaneously two goals: to kill members of a target group and to avoid killing members of one's own group or of a third group. If they cannot rely on visual cues to Identity, they find others.

If ethnic membership is ascriptively based, it follows that ethnic membership is continuous with family membership: one is simultaneously born into both affiliations. Indeed, the ethnic group is a very greatly extended family. This helps group members to think in terms of family resemblances, of traits held in common, and to utilize, almost reflexively, concepts of mutual obligation and hostility to outsiders that often characterize family life. Ethnic ties are layered on family ties, and there need be no consciousness among participants that such a process is taking place. Family duty and family sentiment can easily be transferred to the wider field, where it becomes ethnic duty and ethnic sentiment, at least for insiders. For outsiders, it may become something far more insidious. What insiders may think of as helping a relative or someone like a relative—an innocuous bit of nepotism—may be experienced by outsiders as ethnic discrimination.

If family ties are strong there is a sounder basis on which to build ethnic ties. In much of the world many tasks outside the home are performed by family groups, including extended family groups. If it seems natural to call on family ties, it is more likely to seem natural to call on ethnic ties. In unfamiliar situations, far from home, ethnicity is often called upon to fill in for the family, to perform family-like functions of mutual assistance in finding jobs, housing, and the like.[10] In such cases, ethnic affiliations have considerable force, and often lead to ethnic conflict.

COMPARISON AND CONFLICT

Now add to this mix one further ingredient and it is possible to see just how such ties produce not merely ethnic loyalty but ethnic conflict. Add the element of cleavage and comparison. There is a strong tendency for populations to divide up even without a cultural or ideological basis for differentiation. Once groups form, group loyalty quickly takes hold. In interactions between groups, favoritism toward in-groups and discrimination against out-groups are exhibited. Experimental evidence suggests that groups seek a favorable comparative evaluation, an authoritative judgment of their relative worth, even if achieving such an evaluation actually entails costs in the attainment of absolute values.[11] Groups aim to distinguish themselves from others on some positively evaluated dimension.

For a variety of historical reasons, ethnic groups are often juxtaposed along backward-advanced dimensions. Some groups, usually underrepresented in education and in the modern, urban sector of the economy, are regarded (and regard themselves) as weak, ill-adapted to competition, ignorant, indolent, inefficient, and lacking in initiative; while others are seen to be diligent, intelligent, aggressive, motivated, and achievement-oriented. This is an obvious axis along which to categorize and to dichotomize; and, with the spread of Western norms of achievement around the world, such dimensions of human behavior have become increasingly important in the last century or so.

Given the strong desire for a favorable evaluation of group worth, the invidious distribution of group worth, along with the accompanying stereotypes, is an extremely irritating feature of intergroup relations, the more so as the evaluations tend to be shared across group lines. To be backward in the modern world is to be stigmatized, and so-called backward groups virtually everywhere are in what they themselves describe as a race to "catch up" with others in the same environment. Often that task involves emulating the behavior of those others, behavior that in-group members learned in childhood is not especially enviable but that their elites now tell them is necessary to competitive success.

To convert such intergroup comparisons into political conflict it is only necessary to place the competitively-evaluated groups within the confines of the modern state. Groups seeking a favorable evaluation of group worth and wishing the evaluation to be authoritative will enlist the state in making the evaluation. Collective social recognition is everywhere conferred by political affirmation. So, for example, in recurrent disputes over whose language will have official status, one language is said to be more suitable to modern science, law, economic planning, and government administration than another. The message is not lost on those whose language is disparaged, and they tend to seek, all the more vigorously, its official recognition. If Bengalis call Assamese "a donkey's language," as in one tense demonstration they did, what have they said about the Assamese? If Malaysian Chinese contend that the courts cannot function in Malay, what have they said about the

10. See *ibid.*, pp. 77-81.

11. See, *e.g.*, Henri Tajfel, *Human Groups and Social Categories* (Cambridge: Cambridge University Press, 1981).

Malays? If Mauritanian Kewri argue that Arabic is not up to the standards of French for purposes of government administration, what have they said about the limitations of the Moors, who are more proficient in Arabic than in French? In all of these countries, the official language question has been violent and vexing, largely because of its crucial symbolic significance for intergroup evaluations, and in all of them claims have been made to make the disparaged language official.

Official action does not merely confirm group status but can help to change it. If the Malay language is not yet up to standard and needs help, so do the Malays—and so do countless other groups similarly situated. With official status go language institutes to do lexicological work, spelling standardization, textbook translation, and, inevitably, purification of vocabulary so that the influence of ethnic strangers is reduced. Similar claims for collective improvement are made more directly, in the form of demands for preferential policies to bring so-called backward groups into the modern sector of the economy and into advanced education. These, too, are justified by the need to catch up in order to compete. Such preferences, says a proponent in Andhra Pradesh, India, are "medicine," which "cannot be withdrawn if a patient continues to be sick."[12] The advantages said to be possessed by those who are not sick and not in need of preferences are characterological: ambition, diligence, intelligence, aggressiveness.

Preferences also are justified on another ground, also based on a dichotomy that distinguishes between groups in conflict. That ground has to do with attachment to the country. Most often it is framed in terms of indigenousness versus alienage, but sometimes it takes the form of a special religious or other relation to the soil that the proponents of such policies possess and that drives their claim to have greater legitimacy in the state than their competitors have. The same notions of legitimacy underpin various policy demands. If Assam is for the Assamese, and Bengalis are mere sojourners, then Assamese should be the sole official language, the Assamese should have preferences in jobs and school places, and the character of the state should generally reflect Assamese wishes. Conversely, of course, groups excluded from full political participation, or even citizenship, on such grounds make claims for full equality, based on universally applicable principles. And so the particular confronts the universal, the struggle for group worth overlays a struggle for group legitimacy in the state, and the most fundamental questions—whose state is this? who should feel at home here? who is worthy?—are implicated in the most mundane decisions of ethnic politics.

All of this takes place on top of, or interwoven with, the usual claims, demands, and tensions of politics. For example, in such societies, politics is, as elsewhere, a way of enhancing one's material well-being. Consequently, a decision about an official language, with all of its implications for group legitimacy in the state and for group comparative evaluations, also implicates the usual ambitions of people to make a living. If a certain language becomes official, then civil servants will have to demonstrate their proficiency in it. The more rigorous the examinations, the more likely it is that ethnic strangers cannot pass them, and the more likely their promotions will be delayed or their careers will be ended. This prospect is not lost on their competitors whose native tongue has become official and who would like to use the newly-imposed competitive disability of their ostensible career colleagues to advance their own careers. As a result, people whose educational background may have been suffused with

12. Quoted in Myron Weiner, *Sons of the Soil: Migration and Ethnic Conflict in India* (Princeton: Princeton University Press, 1978), p. 250.

universal values (and whose culture is most similar to that of their competitors) nevertheless become avid practitioners of exclusionary ethnic politics.

Ethnic politics, then, is about inclusion and exclusion and about the terms on which inclusion might take place. Typically, ethnic politics is carried out through a medium that seems rather strange to American eyes, the ethnically based political party. It is well known that in the United States some ethnic groups give their support disproportionately to one political party or another. The historical bases of such tendencies relate to the early political socialization of immigrant groups in the United States (under the auspices of which party did it take place?) or the position of the parties on some crucial ethnic issue, sometimes relating to politics in the country of origin. This is familiar, and it is not unique to the United States. But the United States does not have ethnically based parties—that is, parties that derive their support virtually entirely from one or another of the ethnic groups (or clusters of groups) in conflict.

The same could not be said of Nigeria right after independence, for there one party represented Northerners, another Yaruba, and another Ibo; or of Sri Lanka, which had two main parties representing Sinhalese and two representing Tamils; or of scores of other divided societies. Now superimpose parliamentary elections on such a divided society, with a similarly divided party system, and it quickly becomes apparent that majority rule takes on a new and ominous meaning. In ethnically divided societies, majority rule often comes to mean ethnic majority rule; a meaning very far from the original intent, which contemplated fluid and shifting majorities based on electoral choice. With ethnic parties and majority rule, if a Sinhalese party controls parliament, it does so to the exclusion of Tamil parties and the people they represent.

The history of post-independence Sri Lanka (and many other countries) reflects exactly this situation. At first, the Indian Tamils (who migrated to Sri Lanka in the late nineteenth and early twentieth centuries) were stripped of their citizenship and advised to "return" to India. Then Sinhala was made the sole official language, and Ceylon Tamils (who had arrived, on average, 1,000 years earlier) were discriminated against in the civil service, and elsewhere. Later, Buddhism, professed exclusively by the Sinhalese, was made the official state religion, the presence of the Tamil minority was ignored altogether in a new constitution, and Tamils were increasingly excluded from higher educational institutions in which they, as an "advanced group, had formed a disproportionately prominent share. Can anyone wonder why many Tamils, who were at first deeply committed to one Sri Lanka, eventually turned to a strategy of territorial separatism?

Note that the Sri Lankan tale, which, as I have said, has many points in common with such tales elsewhere, is compounded of several parts: intergroup competition along "backward-advanced" lines, struggles for group priority based on claims of the Sinhalese (and of Buddhism) to a special relation to the land, the resulting exclusionary policies relating to the symbols of the state and group access to opportunities, and all of this carried on within the framework of an ethnically based party system, in which the ruling party had no electoral reason to accommodate those it did not represent. Majority rule here has nothing to do with the shifting sands of political choice; it reflects instead the solid rock of birth.

It takes no special perspicacity to see what has gone wrong here. No doubt, the fundamental bases of group juxtapositions into "backward" and "advanced," and even the differential claims to priority in the land, as well as the ordinary ambitions of aspiring civil servants, teachers, and professionals, are not readily alterable. But if ethnically based parties are a major means of converting exclusionary claims into official policy, essentially a means of creating groups of citizens rejected by and alienated from the polity, can nothing be done about this gave institutional deficiency? Even in the face of intergroup conflict, is there not a way to engineer a politics of compromise in lieu of a politics of domination?

My answer to this problem, which I shall discuss in more detail later, is that something can be done. Here all that needs to be said is that those states that tried to do something about this early on, mainly in Africa, by outlawing ethnically based parties, failed to solve the problem. They did not abolish ethnic sentiments and aspirations, and neither did they even abolish ethnic parties (which found it easy to find figurehead members of other groups to serve as office-bearers and candidates). In the end, confronted with ethnic opposition, such regimes simply abolished the opposition altogether and became single-party states, driving ethnic discontent underground and precluding any electoral accountability or public debate on ethnic policy. The decline of democracy in many Asian and African states went hand-in-hand with the suppression of ethnically based opposition. The same may yet be true in Eastern Europe and the former Soviet Union. So the most direct methods of dealing with the coincidence of ethnic group and party are at best ineffective and at worst draconian. There are better and more democratic ways to solve the problem of ethnic parties or at least to mitigate it. No policy problem of severely divided societies is more urgent.

SECESSIONS AND IRREDENTAS: ETHNICITY AND TERRITORY

To pick up the story of conflict, rather than to jump ahead to its amelioration, perhaps it is best to turn now to those forms of ethnic conflict that have territorial manifestations: secessionist movements and irredentist movements. For present purposes, secessionist movements are undertaken by ethnic groups that wish to withdraw themselves and their territory from what I shall call an undivided state. Irredentist movements are undertaken by states that wish to retrieve ethnically kindred people and their territory across an international boundary, joining it to the retrieving state.

Now it will be seen at once that secession is a group-led movement, whereas irredentism, although group-initiated, requires the action of a neighboring state. It is no accident that there have been few irredentas but many secessionist movements in the post-World War II period. Because irredentism requires state action, it is subject to all the circumspection, all the inhibitions, that prevent states, most of the time, from taking rash, aggressive actions across international borders. Irredentas can be deterred by displays of force, and they can be requited, or at least sidetracked, by concessions; concessions that may have to do with the condition of the group that is to be retrieved or with some unrelated matter of interstate relations. By the same token, putative irredentist states may not be—most likely are not—ethnically homogeneous. Consequently, to pursue an irredenta that will, if successful, change ethnic balances in the retrieving state is a dangerous course for internal ethnic politics, whether or not it is dangerous internationally. Moreover, the group to be retrieved may not wish to be retrieved. The retrieving state may be poorer or more authoritarian or in some other way less desirable than the undivided state; or the group to be retrieved may be apprehensive about its future position in the retrieving state. Finally—and crucially important—politicians in the group sought to be retrieved may anticipate that their own position will not necessarily improve if their region is merely transferred from one large state to another: either way, they are small fish in a big pond.

For all of these reasons and others, in relation to the many groups that straddle international borders, there are few active irredentas.[13] To say that there are relatively few irredentas does not mean there are none. The Armenian seizure of Nagorno-Karabakh, across the Azeri border, is one very active case. The periodic resurgence of Pakistan's claim to Kashmir, Somalia's claim to the Ogaden in Ethiopia, Albania's potential claim to Kosovo in Serbia, and Hungary's potential claims to parts of Slovakia and Romania are all examples of irredentas that may be on a back burner but are simmering slowly.

Nevertheless, in all of these cases there are substantial restraints on irredentism. In Kashmir, the outcome of greatly increased Pakistani aid to Kashmiri Muslims is very likely to be secession rather than merger in Pakistan; and a second withdrawal from the Pakistani embrace (the first having been accomplished by Bangladesh) may signal an end to Pakistan's claim to be the successor to all the compact Muslim territories of British India. For ethnically divided—and discontented—Pakistan, this would be devastating and potentially disintegrating. The effects would quickly be felt in Sindh and Baluchistan. Likewise, the Somalis in the Ogaden belong to the Darood group. To incorporate them in Somalia would unbalance a Somalia already in the midst of group warfare. Precisely the same would be true for Albania, balanced as it is between Ghegs and Tosks, but sharply unbalanced if Kosovo were to accede to Albania. Hungary no doubt sees in the post-Soviet East European order a chance to regain what was lost after World War I, and it has been at best ambiguous about its continuing support for the post-World War I treaties that legitimize its present borders. Nevertheless, Hungary must be chastened by the prospect of absorbing numerous hostile Transylvanian Romanians along with Hungarians in Transylvania, as Romania may be chastened in its irredentism by the prospect of absorbing many Ukrainians and Ruthenians in North Bukovina or Russians in Moldova. It is one thing to proclaim solidarity across borders and another to get serious and use force to alter them.

Secession, however, is a completely different story. It is a less calculative decision. Most secessions, in fact, are begun by members of groups stigmatized as "backward."[14] Quickly convinced that they are unable to compete in the undivided state without the sort of help that state authorities are unwilling to furnish, often in effect colonized by civil servants and administrators from other regions, and subject to uncongenial policies on language and other important symbolic issues, such groups are apt to seek independence. More often than not, they do so heedless of the economic costs. If the region is economically backward, as the Southern Sudan, the Southern Philippines, the former East Pakistan, and the hill country of Burma all are relative to the remainder of the undivided state, secession very likely means a loss of subsidies from the center. One reason people living in such regions nonetheless choose secession is that their political and ethnic goals outweigh the economic benefits that come with the undivided state. Another reason is that the interests of their elites—political and economic interests—lie with independence. For rather than be a minority political leader in a heterogeneous larger society, independence makes it possible to be at the center of things. Rather than be a very junior civil servant, if other groups have longer traditions of education and have produced many more senior civil servants, independence makes it possible to jump the queue—in fact, to push the queue aside altogether.

---

13. For fuller treatment of these issues, see Donald L. Horowitz, "Irredentas and Secessions: Adjacent Phenomena, Neglected Connections," in Naomi Chazan, editor, *Irredentism and International Politics* (Boulder: Lynne Rienner, 1991), pp. 9-22; Horowitz, *Ethnic Groups in Conflict,* pp. 28 1-288.

14. Donald L. Horowitz, "Patterns of Ethnic Separatism," *Comparative Studies in Society and History,* Vol, 23, no. 2 (April 1981), pp. 165- 195.

Perhaps more puzzling is the degree to which secessionists persist, despite the many obstacles to success. For nearly a half century after World War II, only one state was created by a secessionist movement that had to resort to force of arms—Bangladesh—and Bangladesh was able to secure independence because of the fortuitous intervention of the Indian army.[15] I say fortuitous, because the conditions that led to the Indian intervention at a decisive level of force were idiosyncratic. India had an irresistible chance to weaken permanently its long-term enemy, Pakistan. Bengalis in India were clamoring loudly for help for their cousins across the border; and a realistic but very unattractive alternative to establishing Bangladesh quickly was the growth of a Bengali irredentist movement that would either attach Bangladesh to India, greatly upsetting Indian ethnic and religious balances, or detach West Bengal from India to create a new, larger pan-Bengali state. Intervention seemed to New Delhi far preferable to letting any of these things happen. The fear of irredentism probably abetted secession.

The idiosyncratic character of the Indian intervention is attested to by the fact that in scores of other cases secessionist movements have received military aid across borders in quantities or in duration insufficient to make good their exit from the undivided state by force. Many states will meddle in the affairs of their neighbors for some gain or other; but, once the gain is theirs or once the decide the costs in retaliation are too high, they often withdraw, as the Iranian government suddenly withdrew its support for the Iraqi Kurds in the mid-1970s when the Iraqis settled an unrelated claim with Iran. Fickleness is the norm in support for secessionists.

STATE PROLIFERATION AND THE INTERNATIONAL SYSTEM

Three recent events have changed the prospects of success for secessionist movements in ways that augur the growth of more such serious movements. If so, such a trend will have enormous internal and international implications around the world.

The first event was the victory of the Eritrean secessionists in Ethiopia, in concert with other insurgent movements. Of course, this movement took decades to reach a successful conclusion, and it only did so because several movements simultaneously attacked the Ethiopian state. Nevertheless, this was an unprecedented secessionist victory, with serious implications for other African states. The Eritrean victory occurred, moreover, at roughly the same time as ethnically repressive regimes were being driven from office in Liberia and Somalia. In both cases, the result for the moment is a territorial stalemate within the confines of the former states, but at least one of the Somali movements has aspirations to secessionist statehood.[16] All of this must combine to make African boundaries seem more uncertain than they have been since decolonization.

The second event was the disintegration of the Soviet Union, more or less by consent, or at least more or less peacefully. In its sake, a new wave of subsecessions is already in the making in Moldova, in Ukraine, in Tajikistan,[17] in Georgia, and in Kazakhstan, among others. So consensual separatism may provide a fillip for the next generation of forcible attempts to separate.

---

15. Singapore's separation from Malaysia in 1965, although often referred to as secession, was in fact a case of expulsion.

16. On the disintegration of Somalia, see Said S. Samatar, *Somalia: A Nation in Turmoil* (London: Minority Rights Group, 1991).

17. For a useful description, see *Far Eastern Economic Review*, May 21, 1992, pp. 15-16.

The third event was the successful creation of independent Slovenia, Croatia, and Bosnia, followed swiftly by international recognition. There has been a sharp change in the willingness of the international community, or at least the Western states in that community, to recognize the claims of secessionists to statehood. No doubt, some of the change is attributable to the fact that, with the demise of the Soviet Union, the issue was first faced in connection with the Baltic states, which appeared to have by far the strongest claims to independence. But, whatever the reason, the implications of this change have not been faced.

Put these three events together, and they add up to a revised structure of incentives. Groups that were resigned to living together with others no longer need to feel quite so resigned. The ability of secessionists for the first time in memory quickly to defeat central governments; the shift in the international community from favoring undivided states to favoring secession as an exercise in "self-determination" —which, often, gives the presence of vulnerable minorities within secessionist regions, it is not; and the willingness of the Soviets finally to accede to what virtually no other state had within recent memory been willing to accede to, namely, its decomposition into an array of secessionist successor-states: all of this must give enormous encouragement to putative secessionists, who have previously shown, in any case, that they do not need strong prospects of success in order to begin fighting.

One wonders, for example, how long it will take for an ethnically differentiated militia in Afghanistan, if it should find itself on the losing side in a struggle for control of the center, to turn the battle into a war of secession. Afghanistan is an obvious candidate for disintegration, but there are many others.

The prospect is, then, for an increase in the number of states in the international system. The creation of new states by secession may also internationalize a number of ethnic conflicts that are now domestic. At the time of the Biafra and Bangladesh wars of nearly a quarter century ago, most of the major powers sided with central governments against most secessionists. There was a vague fear of widespread disintegration and instability if secessionist regions made good their separation. Some analysts, on the other hand, thought this fear was misplaced and argued for greater tolerance for secession, which they thought might bring more good than harm.[18] They assumed that secession would generally produce more homogeneous states rather than merely smaller but still sharply divided states. In fact, neither secessionist regions nor the rump states they leave behind are homogeneous. More than this, secession places an international boundary between former domestic ethnic antagonists, potentially transforming their conflicts into international warfare and making violence more likely by placing kindred minorities beyond the reach of their cousins, where their plight produces sympathy and urgency. That, after all, is what happened as the Soviet Union and Yugoslavia disintegrated. Large numbers of Russians and Serbs suddenly found themselves separated from Russia and Serbia by new international boundaries. The Russian forces fighting in Moldova and the Serbs fighting in Croatia and Bosnia are a sign of the new internationalization of ethnic conflict.

Ironically, one consequence is that secession can actually create irredentism. If secessionist groups consummate their independence and take minorities with them, kindred

---

18. See Nathaniel H. Leff, "Bengal, Biafra and the Bignese Bias," *Foreign Policy,* no. 3 (Summer 1971), pp. 129-139. Others thought separation might be the least bad of a number of attractive alternatives for ethnically divided states. See Samuel Huntington, *Civil Violence and the Process of Development* (London: International Institute for Strategic Studies, Adelphi Paper No. 83, 1971), p. 14.

groups across the border may seek to undo the creation of the boundary and retrieve those located on the wrong side of it. The fears of the Biafra-Bangladesh period may not have been articulated with precision, but they were not altogether misplaced.

Yet there will be a structural bias against irredentism in international law. As I shall suggest in a moment, legal norms in effect favoring secession have been growing. On the other hand, irredentism involves a breach in the prohibition on the acquisition of territory by force. So a revitalized international law will not be evenhanded with respect to secessions and irredentas.

Along with the increase in the number of states, there is also a prospect for an asymmetry between classes of states. Alongside the many smaller states that emerge—the Bosnias, the Lithuanias, the Eritreas, perhaps the Kashmirs, Slovakias, and Quebecs—there will remain a number of strong, centrally governed, undivided, and indivisible states, among them Japan, China, the United States, and the major powers of Western Europe. How this asymmetry will affect the relations between big powers and small powers, and how the proliferation of new states along ethnic lines will affect ethnic relations within the large centrally governed states are among the most important international relations and domestic ethnic politics questions of the fin de siècle period.

THE QUEST FOR AMELIORATION

We have already seen enough to know that unrestrained ethnic conflict is a troubling force in human affairs. Often it produces zero-sum outcomes: one group is included in the polity, in power, and in the perquisites of power, and another is excluded. Often it produces great spasms of violence, in the form of ethnic riots, replete with massive killing, grotesque tortures and mutilations, and very large numbers of refugees. Often, too, it produces warfare: civil and secessionist warfare, occasionally dangerous international warfare. Even when its outcomes seem tranquil and supportive of self-determination, some groups get to determine their own future and also get to determine the future of others in the same new unit. Rare is the territorial unit that is so homogeneous that self-determination really does mean liberation for all within the unit. As the American Founding Fathers recognized, localized tyrannies are hardly preferable to larger ones. In a significant way, national self-determination is the problem and not the solution, for Sinhalese self-determination has come at the expense of the Tamils, Georgian self-determination may come at the expense of the Ossetians, and down the line Eritrean Muslim self-determination may come at the expense of Eritrean Christians. There is much to be said for deemphasizing national self-determination and substituting concepts of mutual accommodation. I shall say more about this later.

Be that as it may, it is certainly clear that ethnic conflict needs regulation and restraint, in the interest of international security and in the interest of domestic tranquility all around the world. When it comes to the strategies and techniques of conflict control, it is not the case that we know nothing but we certainly are far behind where we ought to be at this stage of our understanding of ethnicity.

Consider first the question of military politics and ethnic conflict. In ethnically divided societies, membership in the officer corps is ethnically skewed. Either groups that have disproportionate representation in educational institutions are disproportionately represented in the officer corps (if that corps is composed of products of a service academy, functioning as an institution of higher education), or else groups disproportionately at the low end of the educational scale are heavily represented in the officer corps (if commissioning takes place from the ranks). Either way, there is skewing. Now how is the civilian regime composed? That is a function of how demography and ethnic parties break out. Where the civilian regime and the officer corps are composed of the same ethnic groups or clusters of ethnic groups, the chances for the persistence of the civilian regime increase. Where, however, the civilian regime consists of members of one group or cluster and the officer corps consists of members of an opposed group or cluster, the chances for military involvement in civilian ethnic politics increase dramatically.

Post-independence coups in Nigeria, Sierra Leone, Congo (Brazzaville), Togo, and a good many other states can be traced to civil-military ethnic dissonance of this sort. The main effects of the coup are two. First, the coup simply—and completely—replaces incumbents of one group or cluster with incumbents of another, opposed group or cluster. Second, and longer term, since military rulers do not need to worry about elections, and indeed since elections previously brought the "wrong" people to power, military rulers tend not to resort to elections. This means, in turn, that they need not worry about mustering the support of a majority of voters or even of a majority of the ethnic groups. The result is that the officers who came to power and shared a common overarching ethnic identity (call them "Northerners") vis-à-vis a differentiated regime ("Southerners") quickly fall out among themselves. A process of ethnic attrition may begin within the military regime. Typically, it ends, as it did with Idi Amin's regime in Uganda, with a small ethnic minority clique in control and ruling the rest of the country by brute force. Around the world, there are many minority regimes, many of them military, that have proved to be durable and brutal.

What do we know about ways to prevent such a sequence from occurring? Quite a lot but not enough. We know that civilian regimes have tried many devices, most of them involving tinkering with the ethnic composition of the regular army or creating countervailing, ethnically differentiated, paramilitary forces outside the regular army. We also know, however, that, at least as often as such measures have deterred coups, they have provoked the very coups they sought to avert. If newly democratized regimes are to have a good chance of survival in divided societies, we—and they—need to know much more about coup-proofing than we now know.

We also need to know more about some of the key pressure points of ethnic conflict—the events that seem to accelerate it, to put it on a qualitatively more dangerous plane. Ethnic violence—specifically, riots—is one of these pressure points, for it gives a great boost to the proponents of exclusionary politics and of civil and secessionist warfare. There are a number of studies in progress on how to end civil wars. There are fewer microlevel studies of the slide *toward* civil war and the points at which (and the methods by which) it might be arrested.[19]

To be sure, if we knew how to govern severely divided societies in more democratic and accommodating ways to begin with, we might worry less about such issues. Ethnically based military coups would presumably be less frequent, and so would ethnic violence, not to mention ethnic warfare on a grand scale. Here, again, there are some things we know, but there are others we do not, and, worst of all, there are some false leads that have proved altogether too attractive.

I have already adverted to one thing we know: exclusionary politics is greatly facilitated by ethnically based party systems, which are very common in severely divided societies, wherever parties have an opportunity to organize freely. This is not surprising, for

---

19. *Cf.* Coral Bell, *The Conventions of Crisis* (London: Oxford University Press, 1971).

parties tend to follow the main cleavages in a society. That is why it is fruitless, as well as undemocratic, to forbid such organization.

Nevertheless, democratic constitutional engineers, concerned about the prospect of ethnic conflict, do not need to sit supine while parties form on an ethnic basis. They can build in incentives for interethnic cooperation and coalition even among ethnically differentiated parties. There are several ways to do this, using both territorial and electoral incentives. In a federal system, for example, the number of states is not a given, and, as the Nigerians and Indians have both shown, some divisions of territory are more conducive than others are to interethnic cooperation and moderation. Likewise, neither the Anglo-American plurality electoral system nor the Continental proportional representation system is a given: there are many equally democratic ways of counting votes, and some of them are decidedly more likely to foster interethnic accommodation than others.[20] In short, structures that provide *incentives* for accommodation are far more likely to produce it than are rules that simply impose constraints and prohibitions.

Such an approach, however, is sometimes less attractive to policymakers than are more detailed approaches that seem more certain in their prescriptions but in the end will be less effective in their results. One such formulaic approach, which has appealed to a good many scholars, is called "consociational democracy."

Drawing on the successful smaller democracies in the divided societies of Western Europe—most notably the Netherlands and Switzerland—consociationalists arrived at a set of institutional recommendations. There needs to be, they argued, a "grand coalition" of all the parties representing all the groups, consensus decision-making in the executive, mutual group vetoes on important items, a proportional representation electoral system, ethnic proportionality in major governmental institutions, and a large measure of cultural autonomy for each group.[21] Now here is a developed formula into which policymakers might sink their teeth and around which academics might—and did—organize their research.

Unfortunately, however, the consociational paradigm cannot be made to do service in severely divided societies. It postulates some conditions that cannot be realized in such societies. By an act of statesmanship, political leaders are told, they must spontaneously recognize that they are living in dangerous conditions and must therefore agree on consociational rules of power-sharing,[22] the rules listed above. All of those rules, of course, relate to the very things each group wants for itself and is unwilling to give others. This is statesmanship unsupported by tangible rewards. As Northern Irish statesmen, among others, have discovered, it is the sort of statesmanship that is conducive to political suicide, as the concessions that such statesmen make on these matters produce steady erosions of support.[23]

---

20. For such examples, see Donald L. Horowitz, "Electoral Systems for a Divided Society," chapter 5 of Horowitz, A *Democratic South Africa? Constitutional Engineering in a Divided Society* (Berkeley: University of California Press, 1991), pp. 163-203.

21. For the most elaborate statement, see Arend Lijphart, *Democracy in Plural Societies* (New Haven: Yale University Press, 1977). There are, however, other variants that differ in detail.

22. See Arend Lijphart, *Power Sharing in South Africa* (Berkeley: University of California Institute of International Studies, 1985), p. 107.

23. See Richard Rose, *Northern Ireland: Time of Choice* (Washington, DC: American Enterprise Institute, 1976), pp. 27-31.

These reciprocal concessions are to be supported by an electoral system (list-system proportional representation) that does everything possible to deprive any party of incentives to make electoral appeals across ethnic group lines—the very appeals that might make intergroup concessions electorally rewarding. Constraints without rewards for adhering to the constraints are not durable.

Moreover, even if it were possible to put together a grand coalition of all parties representing all ethnic groups, this coalition would break apart as soon as concessions were made. For electoral opportunities would then be abundantly available for politicians to accuse the conciliators of selling out the interests of the group they represent. The sellout argument is the very stuff of party competition in a divided society when conciliation begins. It is no accident that of the divided countries in the developing world that have been identified as practicing consociational democracy, none actually had a grand coalition. The sine qua non of the consociational formula turns out to be structurally impossible.

What, then, is the problem? At bottom, the model is based on lessons that reverse cause and effect. A good case can be made that those Western European democracies using consociational practices are able to maintain them because their conflicts have moderated over the centuries and decades; they are nothing like the severe conflicts of Asia, Africa, Eastern Europe, and the former Soviet Union. In short, moderate conflict permits consociational democracy; consociational democracy does not produce moderate conflict.

This is not surprising when one considers the absence of a mechanism, a motive force that might drive politicians to use and be faithful to consociational rules if they were adopted. The behavior of Archbishop Makarios of Cyprus is typical of the way politicians in severely divided societies are likely to treat consociational devices. At the earliest opportunity, Makarios abolished them.

I have dwelt on consociational devices, because, whatever else may be said of consociational theory, it is well-developed and clearly stated: It is a paradigm. What this field urgently needs are equally well-developed, equally clearly stated alternatives—alternatives that are more likely to produce accommodative effects in fact. My own view is that the road to such a theory must pass through the terrain of political incentives. No one should think, however, that a better theory will make ethnic problems disappear. Rather—and this is the virtue of a theory that balances incentives to accommodation against incentives to conflict—there will be a constant struggle between the tendency of aspirations to be exclusive and the reasons that can be built in on the other hand to moderate that exclusiveness.

Still less should anyone think about abolishing ethnic affiliations, as Marxists, for example, used to dream of displacing them with class affiliations. What I have said at the outset of this article ought to suffice to explain that ethnic affiliations are important, and they are functional: they serve purposes. They are not about to wither away. Even as we move to limit the more virulent effects of ethnic conflict, we should not make the mistake of thinking that ethnic affiliations themselves are dispensable, that one can hope to live in anything like a nonethnic world, a world without ascriptive divisions.

ETHNICITY, SELF-DETERMINATION, AND INTERNATIONAL LAW

What we need, as we work toward policies and institutions of conflict reduction, is a simultaneous reconceptualization of national self-determination, a doctrine that has far too long been viewed in excessively rosy terms. In the ethnically plural world in which we live, national self-determination, with all the appurtenances of sovereignty, can frequently be achieved only at the cost of enormous harm to others in the same environment.

Self-determination, after all, gives us states that are supposed to belong to particular peoples. Romania is thought to belong to the Romanians, Fiji to the Fijians. The problem is that other peoples also live within the bounds of such states. Robert Hayden, writing of the new states of what used to be Yugoslavia, notes that they are based on a constitutional structure that gives sovereignty to one people and deprives all the others of any future in the territory, thereby driving them to their own secessions in turn.[24] The chilling logic of these developments is that Croatia is for the Croats alone—as its constitution indeed declares—and Serbs in Croatia are subject to "negative action." The same happens, in reverse, in Serbia.

Unfortunately, just as students of ethnicity may come to doubt the utility and moral force of national self-determination, international lawyers and diplomats have embraced the concept with growing and uncritical enthusiasm. Self-determination is thought of as a legal right.

Furthermore, the particular configuration of evolving international law norms seems unsuited to the amelioration of ethnic conflict. Four pieces of doctrine are being frozen into an unfortunate template of rights and prohibitions.[25] First, "peoples" are supposed to be entitled to self-determination. Second, self-determination is increasingly thought to include the possibility of secession. Third, "ethnic groups are merely to enjoy minority rights. If a majority in a region has seceded, those minority rights are to be exercised within the boundaries of the secessionist state. Fourth, great respect will be given to preexisting regional territorial boundaries, at least if they demarcated states in a federation like Yugoslavia, even if that means encapsulating a minority within a secessionist state, just as the secessionists were previously encapsulated in the undivided state. All of this rules out a realignment of the minority in the secessionist state with its kin across the boundary; and, as I said earlier, as these rules are loaded against irredentism, they create the conditions that make irredentism more tempting.

In concrete terms, international law accords the Croats in Croatia and the Croats and Muslims in Bosnia self-determination, in the form of independent statehood, but relegates the large Serbian minority in both to mere minority rights, precluding their own secession and their accession to Serbia.[26] One frontier, between Croatia and Serbia, is proclaimed to be alterable, but below that level frontiers are said to be firm. The evolving international law thus values simultaneously self-determination and the sanctity of frontiers principles necessarily in collision. Naturally, peculiar results follow from mixing conflicting principles of social organization: birth and territorial proximity. So, some people get to determine the future of others, just as others did before, but now within smaller units.

On several counts, international law seems out of step with the emerging body of knowledge about ethnicity. It is exceedingly difficult to imagine what differences might separate "peoples" from ethnic groups. Even if a *people* comprises all who live in a terri-

---

24. Robert Hayden, "Constitutional Nationalism in Yugoslavia, 1990-91," paper presented at the annual meeting of the American Anthropological Association, Chicago, November 23, 991.

25. For a useful doctrinal summary, see Ruth Lapidoth, "Sovereignty in Transition," *Journal of International Affairs,* Vol. 45, no. 2 (Winter 1992), p. 2-23.

26. See "Conference pour la paix en Yougoslavie," Avis de la Commission d'arbitrage, nos. 1-3, 29 Novembre 1991 and 11 Janvier 1992, in *Revue Générale de Droit Internationale Publique,* Vol. 92, no. 1 (1992), pp. 264-269. The commission did suggest that the Serbian minority might opt for Serbian nationality. *Ibid.*, p. 267. I am grateful to Benedict Kingsbury for calling these materials to my attention.

tory, irrespective of ethnicity, the effective meaning will be that majorities can claim the right to determine the future of minorities. Moreover, it is fanciful to think that a satisfying resolution of contending group claims can be achieved by legitimating secession without further border rectification—a fact that ought to lead to second thoughts about the initial secession. In most cases, secession results in subordinating the interests of minorities within the secessionist region. The hasty and frequent declaration of such legal rights, moreover, will make the demystification of national self-determination a long and arduous process, for that doctrine is now as firm as it has been in a very long time.

The matter is compounded by the coincidence of two phenomena arising from the end of the Cold War: the increasing incidence of overt ethnic conflict around the world and the increasing efficacy of an insufficiently refined international law. Both of these were made possible by a break in the logjam created by the confrontation of two superpowers. If the doctrines of international law were attuned more closely to patterns of ethnic conflict behavior, the growing invocation of such norms might contribute to the regulation of ethnic conflict. As things stand, however, an international community that supports secessions uncritically—and often with some degree of enthusiasm—stands to make things worse. It is not surprising that the Serbian government in Belgrade accepted defeat at the hands of more or less homogeneous Slovenia but fought in heterogeneous Croatia and Bosnia-Herzegovina. All three cases, however, were regarded by the international community as entailing the right to self-determination, even though it was impossible to foresee the extent to which longstanding Serbian minorities in the latter two would be affected adversely if those states were to achieve independence.[27] Or, more accurately, it was possible to foresee their future, and that future was grim.[28] Majorities in Croatia and Bosnia simply appropriated the right to determine everyone's future. This created an opening for proponents of a Greater Serbia and for the forces that wanted to purge territories inhabited by Serbs of the other people who lived alongside them. In Bosnia, Croats also sought military control of Croat-majority areas, eventually setting up a self-governing Croat enclave.[29] As the Serbs feared minority status in Croatia and Bosnia, the Croats felt equally insecure in a Muslim-dominated Bosnia. Now, as the international community increasingly gains the power to intervene in ethnic warfare, one wishes that the gap between social processes and the a priori declaration of rights were narrower.

East Europeans have long been aware that the term "nation-state" does not actually describe the states in their region but rather legitimizes the status of one group that purports to be the group at the core of the alleged nation. The conflict-producing characteristics of such notions are again being noted in Eastern Europe.[30] The lesson is generalizable worldwide.

---

27. See F. Stephen Larrabee, "Ethnic Conflict in the Balkans," paper presented at the Defense Intelligence College conference on "Ethnic Conflict: Challenge to U.S. Security?" June 23-24, 1992. None of this implies, of course, that the rump Yugoslav regime behaved appropriately in the conflict that followed.

28. Hayden, "Constitutional Nationalism in Yugoslavia," documents, for example, the actions taken by the new Croatian regime to give the state an exclusively Croat character and to purity it of Serbian political and cultural influence.

29. See Henry R. Huttenbach, "The Emerging Ugly Secret: The Serbian-Croatian Collusion to Partition Bosnia Hercegovina," in Association for the Study of Nationalities (USSR and Eastern Europe), *Analysis of Current Events,* Vol. 3, nos. 8-9 (July 1992), pp. 5-7.

This is a field in which ideas matter, as is illustrated, for example, by the sharp contrast between French and German conceptions of who is French or German, who belongs in the polity, and who is entitled to citizenship and on what terms.[31] Germany, influenced by Romantic ideas of blood-based nationalism and *Volksgeist,* confers citizenship largely on the basis of *jus sanguinis* (family origin), making it difficult for foreigners to become German, legally and socially. France, with its republican and Jacobin ideals, depends much less on birth and has a history of incorporating foreign immigrants into the polity. The United States, with its immigrant ideology and Citizenship based on *jus soli* (birthplace), carries the whole matter a large step further.[32] So there are varying conceptions of the self in self-determination, and the current emphasis on national, in the sense of ethnic, self-determination (which also has roots in Romantic conceptions of state formation) is hardly the only one possible.

Self-determination is a magnificently resonant term, even in the United States, where it conjures up notions of popular sovereignty. The problem is that Americans typically do not understand the highly variable, and in many cases extraordinarily restrictive, blood-based foundation of the "nation" to determine itself.

We have already seen the impact of ideas—and the need to recast them more clearly—in the case of the concept of "majority rule," which easily lends itself to ethnic majority rule. The same goes for self-determination. The international community has been insufficiently attentive to the ethnic impact of national self-determination, and seeds sown after World War I are again beginning to produce a bumper harvest of hostility. Alongside the practical work of conflict reduction, there needs to be some serious intellectual work that scales down the maximal claims of self-determination or, better still, provides a new, alternative formulation altogether. This would be abstract theorizing with, ultimately, a most impressive practical payoff.

---

30. See Nicolae Gheorghe, "Roma-Gypsy Ethnicity in Eastern Europe," *Social Research, Vol.* 58, no. 4 (Winter 1991), pp. 830-844, at p. 843; compare Solomon F. Bloom, "The Peoples of My Home Town: Before Nationalism Crushed Rumania's Design for Living," *Commentary,* April 1947, pp. 329-335.

31. See Rogers Brubaker, *Citizenship and Nationhood in France and Germany* (Cambridge: Harvard University Press, 1992).

32. For the comparative spectrum, see Donald L. Horowitz, "Europe and America: A Comparative Analysis of 'Ethnicity,'" in *Revue Européene des Migrations Internationales,* Vol. 5, no. 1 (2eme trimestre 1989), pp. 47-59.

The Causes of Internal Conflict: An Overview

Michael E. Brown

Many policymakers and journalists believe that the causes of internal conflicts are simple and straightforward.[1] The driving forces behind these violent conflicts, it is said, are the "ancient hatreds" that many ethnic and religious groups have for each other. In Eastern Europe, the former Soviet Union, and elsewhere, these deep-seated animosities were held in check for years by authoritarian rule. The collapse of authoritarian rule, it is argued, has taken the "lid" off these ancient rivalries, allowing long-suppressed grievances to come to the surface and escalate into armed conflict. U.S. President George Bush, for example, maintained that the war in Bosnia between Serbs, Croats, and Muslims grew out of "age-old animosities."[2] His successor, Bill Clinton, argued that the end of the Cold War "lifted the lid from a cauldron of long-simmering hatreds. Now, the entire global terrain is bloody with such conflicts."[3] Writing about the Balkans, the American political commentator Richard Cohen declared that "Bosnia is a formidable, scary place of high mountains, brutish people, and tribal grievances rooted in history and myth born of boozy nights by the fire. It's the place where World War I began and where the wars of Europe persist, an ember of hate still glowing for reasons that defy reason itself."[4]

Serious scholars reject this explanation of internal conflict.[5] This simple but widely held view cannot explain why violent conflicts have broken out in some places, but not others, and it cannot explain why some disputes are more violent and harder to resolve than others. It is undeniably true that Serbs, Croats, and Bosnian Muslims have many historical grievances against each other, and that these grievances have played a role in the Balkan conflicts that have raged since 1991. But it is also true that other groups—Czechs and Slovaks, Ukrainians and Russians, French-speaking and English-speaking Canadians, the Flemish and the Walloons—have historical grievances of various kinds that have *not* led to violent conflict in the 1990s. This single-factor explanation, in short, cannot account for significant variation in the incidence and intensity of internal and ethnic conflict.

1. This chapter is based on Michael E. Brown, "Introduction" and "The Causes and Regional Dimensions of Internal Conflict," in Brown, ed., *The International Dimensions of Internal Conflict* (Cambridge, Mass.: MIT Press, 1996), pp. 1-31, 571-401.

2. Bush is quoted in Jack Snyder, "Nationalism and the Crisis of the Post-Soviet State," in Michael E. Brown, ed., *Ethnic Conflict and International Security* (Princeton, N.J.: Princeton University Press, 1993), pp. 79-101 at p. 79.

3. Clinton is quoted in Ann Devroy, "President Cautions Congress on 'Simplistic Ideas' in Foreign Policy," *Washington Post* May 26, 1994.

4. Richard Cohen, "Send in the Troops," *Washington Post* November 28, 1995.

5. See, for example, Snyder, "Nationalism and the Crisis of the Post-Soviet State"; Barry Posen "The Security Dilemma and Ethnic Conflict," in Brown, *Ethnic Conflict and International Security* pp. 103-124; Susanne Hoeber Rudolph and Lloyd I Rudolph, "Modern Hate," *New Republic* March 22, 1993, pp. 24-29.

In this chapter, I will provide an overview of the scholarly literature on the causes of internal conflict, developing four main arguments along the way. First, the literature on internal conflict has focused on the underlying factors or permissive conditions that make some places and some situations more predisposed to violence than others. Four sets of factors have been singled out in this regard: structural factors; political factors; economic/social factors; and cultural/perceptual factors. Second, the scholarly literature is weak when it comes to analyzing the catalytic factors or proximate causes of internal conflicts. I contend that internal conflicts can be triggered in four different ways: by internal, mass-level factors (bad domestic problems); by external, mass-level factors (bad neighborhoods); by external, elite-level factors (bad neighbors); and by internal, elite-level factors (bad leaders). Third, the scholarly literature pays insufficient attention to the role played by domestic elites in transforming potentially violent situations into deadly confrontations. Many internal conflicts are triggered by the actions of domestic elites, and these actions therefore merit special attention. Here, too, we need to distinguish between different kinds of conflicts: ideological conflicts, criminal assaults on state sovereignty, and raw power struggles. Fourth and more generally, it is important to recognize that there are many different types of internal conflict, each caused by different things. The challenge for scholars is to identify these different types of conflicts and the different sets of factors that bring them about. The search for a single factor or set of factors that explains everything is comparable to the search for the Holy Grail—noble, but futile.

The first section of this chapter will analyze the scholarly literature on the underlying causes of internal conflict. The second section will examine the proximate causes of internal conflict and develop a framework for analyzing different sets of proximate causes. The third section will focus on the roles played by domestic elites in different types of internal conflicts. I conclude with some observations about the policy implications of this analysis, and with some thoughts on the implications of this analysis for the study of internal conflict.

THE UNDERLYING CAUSES OF INTERNAL CONFLICT

The scholarly literature on internal conflict has tended to focus on the underlying factors or permissive conditions that make some places and some situations more prone to violence than others. More specifically, scholars have identified four main clusters of factors that make some places more predisposed to violence than others: structural factors; political factors; economic/social factors; and cultural/perceptual factors. (See Table 1.)

Structural Factors

Three main structural factors have drawn scholarly attention: weak states; intra-state security concerns; and ethnic geography. Weak state structures are the starting point for many analyses of internal conflict.[6] Some states are born weak. Many of the states that were carved out of colonial empires in Africa and Southeast Asia, for example, were artificial constructs. They lacked political legitimacy, politically sensible borders, and political institutions capable of exercising meaningful control over the territory placed under their nominal supervision. The same can be said of many of the states created out of the rubble of the Soviet Union and Yugoslavia. The vast majority

---

6. See I. William Zartman, "Introduction: Posing the Problem of State Collapse," in Zartman, ed., *Collapsed States The Disintegration and Restoration of Legitimate Authority* (Boulder, Colo.: Lynne Rienner Publishers, 1995), pp. 1-11; Gerald B. Helman and Steven R. Ratner, "Saving Failed States," *Foreign Policy* No. 89 (Winter 1992-93), pp. 3 20.

Table 1: Underlying Causes of Internal Conflict

Structural Factors	*Economic/Social Factors*
Weak states	Economic problems
Intra-state security concerns	Discriminatory economic systems
Ethnic geography	Economic development and modernization
Political Factors	*Cultural/Perceptual Factors*
Discriminatory political institutions	Patterns of cultural discrimination
Exclusionary national ideologies	Problematic group histories
Inter-group politics	
Elite politics	

of these new entities came into existence with only the most rudimentary political institutions in place.

In many parts of the world, Africa perhaps most notably, states have become weaker over time. In some cases, external developments such as reductions in foreign aid from major powers and international financial institutions and drops in commodity prices played key roles in bringing about institutional decline. In others, states have been weakened by internal problems such as endemic corruption, administrative incompetence, and an inability to promote economic development. Many countries have suffered from several of these problems.

When state structures weaken, violent conflict often follows. Power struggles between and among politicians and would-be leaders intensify. Regional leaders become increasingly independent and, should they consolidate control over military assets, become virtual warlords. Ethnic groups which had been oppressed by the center are more able to assert themselves politically, perhaps in the form of developing more administrative autonomy or their own states. Ethnic groups which had been protected by the center or which had exercised power through the state find themselves more vulnerable. Criminal organizations become more powerful and pervasive, as we have seen in the Caucasus, Afghanistan, and elsewhere. Borders are controlled less effectively. Crossborder movements of militia, arms, drugs, smuggled goods, refugees, and migrants therefore increase. Massive humanitarian problems, such as famines and epidemics, can develop. Widespread human rights violations often take place. The state in question might ultimately fragment or simply cease to exist as a political entity.

When states are weak, individual groups within these states feel compelled to provide for their own defense; they have to worry about whether other groups pose security threats. This is the second structural factor that has drawn attention in the scholarly literature.[7] If the state in question is very weak or if it is expected to become weaker with time, the incentives for groups to make independent military preparations grow. The problem is that, in taking steps to defend themselves, groups often threaten the security of others. This can lead neighboring groups to take steps that will diminish the security of the first group: this is the security dilemma. These problems are

7. See Posen, "The Security Dilemma and Ethnic Conflict." See also Milton J. Esman, *Ethnic Politics* (Ithaca, N.Y.: Cornell University Press, 1994), pp. 244-245.

especially acute when empires or multiethnic states collapse and ethnic groups suddenly have to provide for their own security. One group's rush to deploy defensive forces will appear threatening to other groups. Moreover, the kinds of forces most commonly deployed—militia and infantry equipped with light arms—have inherent offensive capabilities even if they are mobilized for defensive purposes; this inevitably intensifies the security concerns of neighboring groups.

The third structural factor that has received attention is ethnic geography.[8] More specifically, states with ethnic minorities are more prone to conflict than others, and certain kinds of ethnic demographics are more problematic than others. Some states are ethnically homogeneous, and therefore face few problems on this score. However, of the more than 180 states in existence today, fewer than 20 are ethnically homogeneous in the sense that ethnic minorities account for less than 5 percent of the population.[9] Some of these states, such as Japan and Sweden, have had a uniform ethnic composition for some time. Others—contemporary Poland, Hungary, the Czech Republic—have few minorities today because of the population transfers and the genocide that took place during World War II, and the way borders were drawn after the war. One of the reasons why Poland, Hungary, and the Czech Republic are relatively stable today is their lack of contentious minorities. It is important to note, however, that ethnic homogeneity is no guarantee of internal harmony: Somalia is the most ethnically homogeneous state in sub-Saharan Africa, yet it has been riven by clan warfare and a competition for power between and among local warlords.

In some states with ethnic minorities, ethnic groups are intermingled; in others, minorities tend to live in separate provinces or regions of the country. Countries with different kinds of ethnic geography are likely to experience different kinds of internal problems.[10] Countries with highly intermingled populations are less likely to face secessionist demands because ethnic groups are not distributed in ways that lend themselves to partition. However, if secessionist demands develop in countries with inter-mingled populations, ethnic groups will seek to establish control over specific tracts of territory. Direct attacks on civilians, intense guerilla warfare, ethnic cleansing, and genocide may result. Countries with groups distributed along regional lines are more likely to face secessionist demands, but warfare, if it develops, will generally be more conventional in character.[11]

Most states, particularly those carved out of former empires, have complex ethnic demographics and face serious ethnic problems of one kind or another. In Africa, for example, arbitrary borders have divided some ethnic groups and left them in two or more countries. Most African countries contain large numbers of ethnic groups, some of which are historic enemies." Many of the states of the former Soviet Union inherited borders that were deliberately designed to maximize ethnic complications and

---

8. See Stephen Van Evera, "Hypotheses on Nationalism and War; Posen, "The Security Dilemma and Ethnic Conflict."

9. See David Welsh, "Domestic Politics and Ethnic Conflict," in Brown, *Ethnic Conflict and International Security* pp. 43-60 at p. 45.

10. See Alicia Levine, 'Political Accommodation and the Prevention of Secessionist Violence," in Brown, *International Dimensions of Internal Conflict*, chap. 9.

11. See Stephen John Stedman, "Conflict and Conciliation in Sub-Saharan Africa," in Brown, *The International Dimensions of Internal Conflict*, chap. 7.

cripple the political effectiveness of local leaders with respect to what used to be the center.[12]

Political Factors

Four main political factors have attracted attention in the scholarly literature on internal conflict: discriminatory political institutions; exclusionary national ideologies; inter-group politics; and elite politics.

First, many argue that the prospects for conflict in a country depend to a significant degree on the type and fairness of its political system. Closed, authoritarian systems are likely to generate considerable resentment over time, especially if the interests of some ethnic groups are served while others are trampled. Even in more democratic settings, resentment can build if some groups are inadequately represented in government, the courts, the military, the police, political parties, and other state and political institutions. The legitimacy of the system as a whole can, over time, fall into question. Internal conflict is especially likely if oppression and violence are commonly employed by the state or if a political transition is under way. The latter can take many forms, including democratization, which can be destabilizing in the short run even if it promises stability in the long run.[13]

Second, it is said that much depends on the nature of the prevailing national ideology in the country in question. In some places, nationalism and citizenship are based on ethnic distinctions, rather than the idea that everyone who lives in a country is entitled to the same rights and privileges. Although the existence of civic conceptions of nationalism is no guarantee of stability—civic nationalism prevails in Indonesia—conflict is more likely when ethnic conceptions of nationalism predominate. Under what conditions are these two conceptions of nationalism likely to emerge? According to Jack Snyder, civic nationalism normally appears in well institutionalized democracies. Ethnic nationalism, in contrast, appears spontaneously when an institutional vacuum occurs. By its nature, nationalism based on equal and universal citizenship rights within a territory depends on a supporting framework of laws to guarantee those rights, as well as effective institutions to allow citizens to give voice to their views. Ethnic nationalism, in contrast, depends not on institutions, but on culture. Therefore, ethnic nationalism is the default option: it predominates when institutions collapse, when existing institutions are not fulfilling people's basic needs, and when satisfactory alternative structures are not readily available.[14]

It is not surprising, therefore, that there are strong currents of ethnic nationalism in parts of the Balkans, East-Central Europe, and the former Soviet Union, where state structures and political institutions have diminished capacities, and in those parts of the developing world where state structures and political institutions are weak.

12. See Matthew Evangelista, "Historical Legacies and the Politics of Intervention in the Former Soviet Union," in Brown, *The International Dimensions of Internal Conflict*, chap. 3.

13. See, for example, Ted Robert Gurr and Barbara Harff, *Ethnic Conflict and World Politics* (Boulder, Colo.: Westview Press, 1994), chap. 5; Aralid Lijphart, *Democracy in Plural Societies* (New Haven, Conn.: Yale University Press, 1977); Edward D. Mansfield and Jack Snyder, "Democratization and the Danger of War," *International Security* Vol. 20, No. 1 (Summer 1995), pp. 5-38.

14. Snyder, "Nationalism and the Crisis of the Post-Soviet State," p. 86. See also William Pfaff, "Revive Secular Citizenship Above 'Ethnic' Nationality," *International Herald Tribune*, July 20, 1993.

It is important to keep in mind that exclusionary national ideologies do not have to be based on ethnicity. Religious fundamentalists committed to establishing theocratic states divide societies into two groups: those who subscribe to a theologically derived political, economic, and social order; and those who do not.

Third, many scholars argue that the prospects for violence in a country depend to a significant degree on the dynamics of domestic, inter-group politics.[15] The prospects for violence are great, it is said, if groups—whether they are based on political, ideological, religious, or ethnic affinities—have ambitious objectives, strong senses of identity, and confrontational strategies. Conflict is especially likely if objectives are incompatible, groups are strong and determined, action is feasible, success is possible, and if inter-group comparisons lead to competition, anxiety, and fears of being dominated. The emergence of new groups and changes in the inter-group balance of power can be particularly destabilizing.

Fourth, some scholars have emphasized elite politics and, more specifically, the tactics employed by desperate and opportunistic politicians in times of political and economic turmoil. According to this line of thinking, ethnic conflict is often provoked by elites in times of political and economic turmoil in order to fend off domestic challengers. Ethnic bashing and scapegoating are tools of the trade, and the mass media are employed in partisan and propagandistic ways that further aggravate inter-ethnic tensions. The actions of Slobodan Milosevic in Serbia and Franjo Tudjman in Croatia stand out as cases in point.[16]

Economic/Social Factors

Three broad economic and social factors have been identified as potential sources of internal conflict: economic problems; discriminatory economic systems; and the trials and tribulations of economic development and modernization.

First, most countries experience economic problems of one kind or another sooner or later, and these problems can contribute to intra-state tensions. In the industrialized world, problems can emerge even if a country's economy is growing—if it is not growing as fast as it once was, or fast enough to keep pace with societal demands. In Eastern Europe, the former Soviet Union, parts of Africa, and elsewhere, transitions from centrally-planned to market-based economic systems have created a host of economic problems, ranging from historically high levels of unemployment to rampant inflation. Many countries in what we would like to think of as the developing world seem to be in a semi-permanent state of economic shambles. Others are in an economic free-fall. Unemployment, inflation, and

---

15. See Joseph Rothschild, *Ethnopolitics: A Conceptual Framework* (New York: Columbia University Press, 1981); Donald L. Horowitz, *Ethnic Groups in Conflict* (Berkeley: University of California Press, 1985); Charles Tilly, *From Mobilization to Revolution* (Reading, Mass.: Addison-Wesley, 1978); Charles Tilly, "Does Modernization Breed Revolution?" *Comparative Politics*, Vol. 5, No. 3 (April 1973), pp. 425-447; Lewis Coser, *The Functions of Social Conflict* (Glencoe, IL.: Free Press, 1956); Gurr and Harff, *Ethnic Conflict and World Politics*; Van Evera, "Hypotheses on Nationalism and War." For an overview, see Saul Newman, "Does Modernization Breed Ethnic Conflict?" *World Politics*, Vol. 43, No. 3 (April 1991), pp. 451-478; Jack A. Goldstone, "Theories of Revolution: The Third Generation," *World Politics*, Vol. 32, No. 3 (April 1980), pp. 425-453.

16. See V.P. Gagnon, Jr., "Ethnic Nationalism and International Conflict: The Case of Serbia," in this volume; Human Rights Watch, *Playing the "Communal Card": Communal Violence and Human Rights* (New York: Human Rights Watch, 1995); Warren Zimmermann, "The Last Ambassador: A Memoir of the Collapse of Yugoslavia," *Foreign Affairs*, Vol. 74, No. 2 (March-April 1995), pp. 2-20.

resource competitions, especially for land, contribute to societal frustrations and tensions, and can provide the breeding ground for conflict. Economic reforms do not always help and can contribute to the problem in the short term, especially if economic shocks are severe and state subsidies for staples, services, and social welfare are cut. In short, economic slowdowns, stagnation, deterioration, and collapse can be deeply destabilizing.[17]

Second, discriminatory economic systems, whether they discriminate on a class basis or an ethnic basis, can generate feelings of resentment and levels of frustration prone to the generation of violence.[18] Unequal economic opportunities, unequal access to resources such as land and capital, and vast differences in standards of living are all signs of economic systems that disadvantaged members of society will see as unfair and perhaps illegitimate. This has certainly been the case in Sri Lanka, for example, where Tamils have been discriminated against in recent decades by the Sinhalese majority. Economic development is not necessarily the solution. Indeed, it can aggravate the situation: economic growth always benefits some individuals, groups, and regions more than others, and those who are on top to begin with are likely to be in a better position to take advantage of new economic opportunities than the downtrodden. Even if a country's overall economic picture is improving, growing inequities and gaps can aggravate intra-state tensions.

Third, many scholars have pointed to economic development and modernization as taproots of instability and internal conflict.[19] The process of economic development, the advent of industrialization, and the introduction of new technologies, it is said, bring about a wide variety of profound social changes: migration and urbanization disrupt existing family and social systems and undermine traditional political institutions; better education, higher literacy rates, and improved access to growing mass media raise awareness of where different people stand in society. At a minimum, this places strains on existing social and political systems.[20] It also raises economic and political expectations, and can lead to mounting frustration when these expectations are not met. This

---

17. For a general discussion and several case studies, see S.W.R. de A. Samarasinghe and Reed Coughlan, eds., *Economic Dimensions of Ethnic Conflict* (London: Pinter Publishers, 1991). For a detailed discussion of the economic roots of the wars in the former Yugoslavia, see Susan L. Woodward, *Balkan Tragedy: Chaos and Dissolution After the Cold War* (Washington: The Brookings Institution, 1995), especially chap. 3. For a discussion of the economic sources of turmoil in South Asia, see Sandy Gordon, "Resources and Instability in South Asia," *Survival*, Vol 35, No. 2 (Summer 1993), pp. 66-87.

18. For an overview of Marx on this question, see James B. Rule, *Theories of Civil Violence* (Berkeley: University of California Press, 1988), chapter 2; A.S. Cohan, *Theories of Revolution* (New York: Wiley, 1975), chaps. 4-5. For a discussion of how this applies to the developing world in particular, see Gordon, "Resources and Instability in South Asia."

19. See Samuel P Huntington, *Political Order in Changing Societies* (New Haven, Conn.: Yale University Press, 1968); Samuel P. Huntington, "Civil Violence and the Process of Development," in *Civil Violence and the International System*, Adelphi Paper No #3 (London: International Institute for Strategic Studies, 1971), pp. 1-15; Ted Robert Gurr, *Why Men Rebel* (Princeton, N.J.: Princeton University Press, 1970); Walker Conner, "Nation-Building or Nation-Destroying?" *World Politics*, Vol. 24, No. 3 (April 1972), pp. 319-355; Walker Conner, her *Ethnonationalism: The Quest for Understanding* (Princeton, N.J.: Princeton University Press, 1994). For an overview of this literature, see Newman, "Does Modernization Breed Ethnic Conflict?" For critiques of this approach, see Rod Aya, "Theories of Revolution Reconsidered: Contrasting Models of Collective Violence," *Theory and Society*, Vol. 8, No. 1 (July 1979), pp. 1-38; Tilly, "Does Modernization Breed Revolution?"

20. See Chalmers Johnson, Revolutionary Change (Boston: Little, Brown, 1966); Mark Hagopian, *The Phenomenon of Revolution* (New York: Dodd, Mead, 1974). For an overview, see Cohan, *Theories of Revolution* chap. 6; Goldstone, "Theories of Revolution," pp. 425-434.

can be particularly problematic in the political realm, because demands for political participation usually outpace the ability of the system to respond. According to Samuel Huntington, "The result is instability and disorder. The primary problem . . . is the lag in the development of political institutions behind social and economic change."[21]

Cultural/Perceptual Factors

Two cultural and perceptual factors have been identified in the scholarly literature as sources of internal conflict. The first is cultural discrimination against minorities. Problems include inequitable educational opportunities, legal and political constraints on the use and teaching of minority languages, and constraints on religious freedom. In extreme cases, draconian efforts to assimilate minority populations combined with programs to bring large numbers of other ethnic groups into minority areas constitute a form of cultural genocide. Aggressive forms of these policies were implemented by Josef Stalin in the Soviet Union in the 1930s and 1940s, particularly in the Caucasus. Similar policies have been pursued by China in Elbet since the 1950s. Somewhat less vicious forms of assimilationist policies have been pursued in Bulgaria with respect to ethnic Turks, in Slovakia with respect to ethnic Hungarians, and in Thailand with respect to members of northern and western hill tribes, for example.[22]

The second factor that falls under this broad heading has to do with group histories and group perceptions of themselves and others.[23] It is certainly true that many groups have legitimate grievances against others for crimes of one kind or another committed at some point in the distant or recent past. Some "ancient hatreds" have legitimate historical bases. However, it is also true that groups tend to whitewash and glorify their own histories, and they often demonize their neighbors, rivals, and adversaries. Explaining away the Hutu slaughter of 800,000-1,000,000 Tutsi in Rwanda in 1994, one Hutu who had been training for the priesthood insisted, "It wasn't genocide. It was self-defense."[24] Stories that are passed down from generation to generation by word of mouth become part of a group's lore. They often become distorted and exaggerated with time, and are treated as received wisdom by group members.

These ethnic mythologies are particularly problematic if rival groups have mirror images of each other, which is often the case. Serbs, for example, see themselves as heroic defenders of Europe and Croats as fascist, genocidal thugs. Croats see themselves as valiant victims of Serbian Hegemonic aggression. When two groups in close proximity have mutually exclusive, incendiary perceptions of each other, the slightest provoca-

---

21. Huntington, *Political Order in Changing Societies*, p 5.

22. Many argue that formal, minority rights safeguards are the solution See, For example, Jonathan Eyal, "Eastern Europe: What Ahout the Minorities?" *World Today*, Vol. 45, No. 12 (December 1989), pp. 205-208; Wiktor Osiatynski, "Needed Now: Bills of Rights," *Time*, December 24, 1990 L. Michael Hager, "To Get More Peace, Try More Justice," *International Herald Tribune*, July 30, 1992, Stephen S. Rosenfeld, "Serbs Are the Problem, Minority Rights the Solution," *International Herald Tribune*, September 26 27, 1992.

23. See Van Evera, "Hypotheses on Nationalism and War"; Posen, "The Security Dilemma and Ethnic Conflict," p. 107; Snyder, "Nationalism and the Crisis of the Post-Soviet State," pp. 92-93; Donald Rothchild and Alexander J. Groth, "Pathological Dimensions of Domestic and International Ethnicity," *Political Science Quarterly*, Vol. 110, No I (Spring 1995), pp. 69-82.

24. This Hutu apologist is quoted in "You're Saying We Did It?" Economist, June 3, 1995, p. 38 25. Rule, *Theories of Civil Violence*, p. 265.

tion on either side confirms deeply held beliefs and provides the justification for a retaliatory response. Under conditions such as these, conflict is hard to avoid and even harder to limit once started.

THE PROXIMATE CAUSES OF INTERNAL CONFLICT

The existing literature on internal conflict does a commendable job of surveying the underlying factors or permissive conditions that make some situations particularly prone to violence, but it is weak when it comes to identifying the catalytic factors—the triggers or proximate causes—of internal conflicts. As James Rule put it in his review of the literature on civil violence, "We know a lot of things that are true about civil violence, but we do not know when they are going to be true."[25] The result is that we know a lot less about the causes of internal conflict than one would guess from looking at the size of the literature on the subject.

However, the existing literature gives us a running start at developing a framework for analyzing the proximate causes of internal conflict because it provides us with a well-rounded set of factors that predispose some places to violence. If we assume that each of these twelve underlying factors can play a more catalytic role if rapid changes take place in the area in question, then we also have a list of twelve possible proximate causes of internal conflict.

In brief, states are especially prone to violence if state structures are collapsing due to external developments (such as sharp reductions in international financial assistance, sharp declines in commodity prices), internal problems (new, incompetent leaders or rampant corruption), or some combination of the above. Under these circumstances, states are increasingly unable to cope with societal demands.[26] When state structures weaken or when new states are created out of the rubble of a larger entity, groups have a heightened sense of potential security problems. They are more likely to take measures to protect themselves which, in turn, are more likely to generate fears in other groups. In situations such as these, security dilemmas are especially intense and arms races are especially likely. Changing military balances—or fears about possible adverse developments—make arms racing and conflict escalation difficult to control.[27] Demographic changes brought about by birth rate differentials, migration, urbanization, or sudden influxes of refugees can aggravate ethnic problems and further complicate the picture by changing the domestic balance of power.

Political transitions brought about by the collapse of authoritarian rule, democratization, or political reforms also make states particularly prone to violence.[28] The emergence and rise of exclusionary national ideologies, such as ethnic nationalism and religious fundamentalism, can be destabilizing as well. The emergence of dehumanizing ideologies, which literally deny the humanity of other ethnic groups, is particularly dangerous because it is often the precursor to genocidal slaughter.[29] The rise of new groups or changes in the intergroup balance of power can intensify inter-group competition and anx-

25. Rule, *Theories of Civil Violence*, p. 265.

26. See Zartman, "Introduction: Posing the Problem of State Collapse," pp. 1-11.

27. See Posen, "The Security Dilemma and Ethnic Conflict."

28. See Mansfield and Snyder, "Democratization and the Danger of War," pp. 5-38.

29. On ethnic nationalism, see Snyder, "Nationalism and the Crisis of the Post-Soviet State." On dehumanizing ideologies, see Helen Fein, "Explanations of Genocide," *Current Sociology*, Vol. 38, No 1 (Spring 1990), pp. 32-50; Leo Kuper, *Genocide: Its Political Use in the Twentieth Century* (New Haven, Conn.: Yale University Press, 1981), chap 3.

ieties, making political systems more volatile.[30] The emergence of power struggles between and among elites can be particularly problematic, because desperate and opportunistic politicians are particularly prone to employing divisive ethnic and nationalistic appeals.

Potentially catalytic economic and social problems include mounting economic problems, intensifying resource competitions, growing economic inequities and gaps, and fast-paced development and modernization processes.[31] Industrialized countries, countries attempting to make the transition from centrally-planned to market-driven systems, and developing countries gener ally have to contend with different kinds of problems, but they are all susceptible to economically and socially induced turmoil.

Finally, states are especially prone to violence if discrimination against minorities intensifies, or if politicians begin to blame some ethnic groups for whatever political and economic problems their country may be experiencing. Ethnic bashing and scapegoating are often precursors to violence.

Creating lists of possible underlying and proximate causes of internal conflict is a useful starting point for analyzing these issues, but it does not take us far enough. For starters, this list of twelve possible proximate causes does not distinguish sharply between elite-level and mass-level factors. It is incomplete, moreover, because it does not take into account the catalytic role that neighboring states and developments in neighboring states can play in triggering violence.

I argue that internal conflicts can be categorized according to: (1) whether they are triggered by elite-level or mass-level factors;[32] and (2) whether they are triggered by internal or external developments. There are, therefore, four main types of internal conflicts, and they can be depicted in a two-by-two matrix. (See Table 2.) Put another way, internal conflicts can, in theory, be triggered by any one of four sets of proximate causes.

First, conflicts can be triggered by internal, mass-level phenomena, such as rapid economic development and modernization or patterns of political and economic discrimination. To put it more prosaically, they can be caused by "bad domestic problems." The conflicts in Punjab and Sri Lanka are examples, the former being galvanized by rapid modernization and migration and the latter by long-standing patterns of political, economic, and cultural discrimination.[33]

Another example is the conflict over Nagorno-Karabakh, which was triggered by problematic ethnic geography and patterns of discrimination highlighted by the breakup of the Soviet Union.

The proximate causes of a second set of conflicts are mass-level but external in character: swarms of refugees or fighters crashing across borders, bringing turmoil and

30. See Rothschild, *Ethnopolitics*; Tilly, *From Mobilization to Revolution*; Horowitz, *Ethnic Groups in Conflict*; Gurr and Harff, *Ethnic Conflict and World Politics*; Van Evera, "Hypotheses on Nationalism and War."

31. See, for example, Gordon, "Resources and Instability in South Asia."

32. The utility of the distinction between elite-level and mass-level factors has been noted by others. See Renée de Nevers, *The Soviet Union and Eastern Europe: The End of an Era,* Adelphi Paper No. 249 (London International Institute for Strategic Studies, 1990), pp. 27-29: Stuart J. Kaufman, "An 'International' Theory of Inter-Ethnic War," *Review of International Studies*, Vol. 22, No. 2 (April 1996), pp. 149-171.

33. See Sumit Ganguly, "Internal Conflict in South and Southwest Asia," in Brown, *The International Dimensions of Internal Conflict*, chap. 4.

Table 2: The Proximate Causes of Internal Conflict

	Internally-driven	Externally-driven
Elite-triggered	Bad Leaders	Bad Neighbors
Mass-triggered	Bad Domestic Problems	Bad Neighborhoods

violence with them, or radicalized politics sweeping throughout regions. These are conflicts caused by the "contagion," "diffusion," and "spill-over" effects to which many policymakers, analysts, and scholars give much credence.[34] One could say that such conflicts are caused by "bad neighborhoods." The expulsion of radical Palestinians from Jordan in 1970 led many militants to resettle in Lebanon, where Muslim-Christian tensions were already mounting. This, one could argue, was the spark that ignited the civil war in Lebanon in 1975.

The proximate causes of a third set of conflicts are external but elite-level in character: they are the results of discrete, deliberate decisions by governments to trigger conflicts in nearby states for political, economic, or ideological purposes of their own. This only works, one must note, when the permissive conditions for conflict already exist in the target country; outsiders are generally unable to foment trouble in stable, just societies. Such conflicts, one could say, are caused by "bad neighbors." Examples include the Soviet Union's meddling in and subsequent 1979 invasion of Afghanistan, which has yet to emerge from chaos, and Russian meddling in Georgia and Moldova in the 1990s.[35] Another example is Rhodesia's establishment of RENAMO in 1976 to undermine the new government in Mozambique.[36]

The proximate causes of the fourth and final type of internal conflict are internal and elite-level in character. Variations include: power struggles involving civilian (Georgia) or military (Nigeria) leaders; ideological contests over how a country's political, economic, social, and religious affairs should be organized (Algeria, Peru); and criminal assaults on the state (Colombia). To put it in simple terms, conflicts such as these are triggered and driven by "bad leaders."

THE IMPORTANCE OF DOMESTIC ELITES

The scholarly literature on the causes of internal conflict is strong in its examination of structural, political, economic, social, and cultural forces that operate at a mass level—indeed, it clearly favors mass-level explanations of the causes of internal conflict—but it is weak in its understanding of the roles played by elites and leaders in insti-

34. See, for example, John A. Vascluez, "Factors Related to the Contagion and Diffusion of International Violence," in Manus I. Midlarsky, ed., *The Internationalization of Communal Strife* (London: Routledge, 1992), pp. 149-172; Ted Robert Gurr, *Minorities at Risk: A Global View of Ethnopolitical Conflicts* (Washington: U.5. Institute of Peace Press, 1993), pp. 132-135. For an excellent overview of this literature, see Stuart Hill and Donald Rothchild, "The Contagion of Political Conflict in Africa and the World," *Journal of Conflict Resolution*, Vol. 30, No. 4 (December 1986), pp. 716-735.

35. On Afghanistan, see Ganguty, "Internal Conflict in South and Southwest Asia." On Moldova and Georgia, see Evangelista, "Historical Legacies and the Politics of Intervention in the Former Soviet Union."

36. I thank Stephen Stedman for this observation.

gating violence. The latter has received comparatively little attention. The result is "no-fault" history that leaves out the pernicious effects of influential individuals, which is an important set of factors in the overall equation.

Although mass-level factors are clearly important underlying conditions that make some places more predisposed to violence than others, and although neighboring states routinely meddle in the internal affairs of others, the decisions and actions of domestic elites often determine whether political disputes veer toward war or peace. Leaving elite decisions and actions out of the equation, as many social scientists do, is analytically misguided. It also has important policy implications: under-appreciating the import of elite decisions and actions hinders conflict prevention efforts and fails to place blame where blame is due.

The proximate causes of many internal conflicts are the decisions and actions of domestic elites, but these conflicts are not all driven by the same domestic forces. There are three main variations: ideological struggles, which are driven by the ideological convictions of various individuals; criminal assaults on state sovereignty, which are driven primarily by the economic motivations of drug traffickers; and power struggles between and among competing elites, which are driven by personal, political motivations. Admittedly, these compartments are not water-tight.[37] It is nonetheless important to make these distinctions, however rough they might be: there are several, distinct motivational forces at work here—several identifiable proximate causes of internal violence. It is important to have an appreciation of the multifaceted nature of the problem, particularly if one is interested in enhancing international efforts to prevent, manage, and resolve internal conflicts.

Ideological Conflicts

First, some internally-driven, elite-triggered conflicts are ideological struggles over the organization of political, economic, and social affairs in a country. Some ideological struggles are defined in economic or class terms; others are fundamentalist religious crusades guided by theological frameworks. Ideological struggles over how political, economic, and social affairs should be organized have not gone away with the end of the Cold War, but they have tended to take on new forms. Class-based movements with Marxist agendas have faded from the scene in many parts of the world, including Southeast Asia, the Middle East, Africa, and Latin America, although some rebels in Colombia and Peru have remained largely true to form. Some rebel movements, have mutated and taken on the political agendas of indigenous peoples and ethnic minorities. In many places—Afghanistan, Algeria, Egypt, India, Iran, Sudan—conflicts have formed around new secularist-fundamentalist fault lines. These ethnic and fundamentalist movements draw on many of the same sources that impelled class-based movements in the Cold War era—patterns of political, economic, and cultural discrimination, and widespread dissatisfaction with the pace and equitability of economic development—but they are channeled in different directions. In other words, many of the underlying causes of these conflicts are the same, but their proximate causes have changed.

---

37. Some conflicts have mutated over time and have more than one distinguishing characteristic. Most power struggles are characterized by those involved in politically convenient ethnic or ideological terms. Many of these conflicts have powerful ethnic dimensions. These problems make analysis difficult, but not impossible.

Criminal Assaults on State Sovereignty

Second, some internally-driven, elite-triggered conflicts are in effect criminal assaults on state sovereignty. In several countries in Asia and Latin America, in particular, drug cartels have accumulated enough power to challenge state control over large tracts of territory. This is certainly true, for example, in Afghanistan, Brazil, Burma, Mexico, Tajikistan, and Venezuela. In Colombia, most notably, state sovereignty has been directly challenged by drug barons and their criminal organizations.[38] This problem shows no sign of abating. A related problem is that, with the end of the Cold War and reductions in financial support from Moscow and Washington, many ethnic groups and political movements turned to drug trafficking to finance their activities. This is true, for example, of various groups in Colombia and Peru.[39] In addition to its other pernicious effects, drug trafficking complicates the nature of the conflicts in question and therefore makes conflict management and resolution more difficult.

Power Struggles

Third, some conflicts are in essence power struggles between and among competing elites. Of the three types of internally-driven, elite-triggered conflicts outlined here, raw power struggles are clearly the most common. Some are sustained government campaigns to repress ethnic minorities and democratic activists. This would seem to be a fair characterization of the conflicts in Burma, Cambodia, Guatemala, Indonesia, Iraq, and Turkey, for example. Government repression is a prominent feature of other conflicts as well, but power struggles are particularly intense and the "ethnic card" is played very aggressively. Examples abound: Angola, Bosnia, Burundi, Croatia, Kenya, Liberia, the Philippines, Russia/Chechnya, Rwanda, Somalia, and Tajikistan.

One type of power struggle is particularly prominent and particularly pernicious: it accounts for the slaughter in the former Yugoslavia and Rwanda, and has played a role in the conflicts in Azerbaijan, Burundi, Cameroon, Chechnya, Georgia, India, Kenya, Nigeria, Romania, Sri Lanka, Sudan, Togo, Zaire, and elsewhere.[40] The starting point is a lack of elite legitimacy, which sooner or later leads to elite vulnerability. Vulnerabilities can be brought about by weakening state structures, political transitions, pressures for political reform, and economic problems. Those who are in power are determined to fend off emerging political challengers and anxious to shift blame for whatever economic and political setbacks their countries may be experiencing. In cases where ideological justifications for staying in power have been overtaken by events, they need to devise new formulas for legitimizing their rule. Entrenched politicians and aspiring leaders alike have powerful incentives to play the "ethnic card," embracing ethnic identities and proclaiming themselves the champions of ethnic groups.[41]

This produces a shift in the terms of public discourse from civic nationalism to ethnic nationalism and to increasingly virulent forms of ethnic nationalism. Ethnic minorities are often singled out and blamed for the country's problems: ethnic scape-

38. For a detailed discussion of drug-related problems in Latin America, see Marc Chernick, "Peacemaking and Violence in Latin America," in Brown, Tila *International Dimensions of Internal Conflict*, chap. 8.

39. Ibid.

40. See Human Rights Watch, *Playing the "Communal Card."* See also Stedman, "Conflict and Conciliation in Sub-Saharan Africa."

41. See Human Rights Watch, *Playing the "Communal Card."*

goating and ethnic bashing become the order of the day. When power struggles are fierce, politicians portray other ethnic groups in threatening terms, and inflate these threats to bolster group solidarity and their own political positions; perceived threats are extremely powerful unifying devices.[42] When leaders have control over the national media, these kinds of campaigns are particularly effective: a relentless drumbeat of ethnic propaganda can distort political discourse quickly and dramatically. Political campaigns such as these undermine stability and push countries towards violence by dividing and radicalizing groups along ethnic fault lines. In the former Yugoslavia, Serbian leader Slobodan Milosevic and Croatian leader Franjo Tudjman rose to power by polarizing their societies even though Serbs and Croats had coexisted peacefully for decades.

Why Do Followers Follow?

It is easy to understand why desperate and opportunistic politicians in the midst of power struggles would resort to nationalist and ethnic appeals. For many politicians, tearing their countries apart and causing thousands of people to be killed are small prices to pay for staying in or getting power. The more interesting question is: why do followers follow?[43] Given that politicians all over the world employ ethnic appeals of one kind or another, why do these appeals resonate in some places but not others? Why do large numbers of people follow the ethnic flag in some places at some times, but not others?

Two factors are particularly important in this regard: the existence of antagonistic group histories; and mounting economic problems. If groups have bad histories of each other and especially if they see themselves as victims of other, aggressive communities, ethnic bashing and inflated threats seem plausible. If economic problems such as unemployment and inflation are mounting and resource competitions are intensifying, ethnic scapegoating is more likely to resonate and more people are likely to accept a radical change in a country's political course, including armed confrontation. In short, the emergence of elite competitions might be the proximate causes of conflicts in places such as the former Yugoslavia and Rwanda, but hostilities escalate only because of the existence of other underlying problems or permissive conditions—problematic group histories and economic problems.

It appears that all three factors—intensifying elite competitions, problematic group histories, and economic problems—must be present for this kind of conflict to explode. Russians and Ukrainians, for example, have had to contend with collapsing economies and standards of living, and many Ukrainians do not have benign historical images of Russians. However, Ukrainian politicians have by and large refrained from making the kinds of nationalistic appeals that have caused trouble elsewhere. They undoubtedly recognize that provoking a Russian-Ukrainian confrontation would not bode well for Ukraine or for their own positions as leaders of an independent state. Some Russian politicians have been far less responsible in this regard, but their nationalistic appeals have not yet taken over the Russian national debate. Whether or not nationalistic and pseudo-nationalistic politicians remain confined to the margins

42. See Esman, *Ethnic Politics*, p. 244.

43. See Horowitz, *Ethnic Groups in Conflict*, p. 140.

of the Russian political debate is certainly one of the keys to its future and to the stability of a large part of the world.

A few parts of the world have experienced economic turmoil and power struggles, but have been blessed with homogeneous populations and few internal ethnic problems. Finland, for example, has experienced a sharp economic decline since the late 1980s, but has not experienced inter-ethnic strife because minorities are few and small and because inter-group relations are relatively harmonious. Similarly, Poland has gone through a complete political and economic transformation since 1989, but it has few minorities and few inter-group problems: nationalistic appeals have no audience. Poland's hotly contested 1995 presidential election was consequently fought along ideological lines.

Other parts of the world have deeply troubled ethnic histories and leaders who have not hesitated to do whatever was necessary to get and keep power, but they have been spared massive bloodlettings because of their comparatively rosy economic pictures. For example, Malaysia and Thailand experienced considerable turmoil during the Cold War but are quite stable today because of the economic boom that has swept most of the region. Indonesia has had to contend with simmering conflicts in East Elmor, Irian Jaya, and Aceh, but these conflicts have not escalated dramatically, nor has the country as a whole splintered into dozens or hundreds of ethnic fragments as it might have.[44] Much of this can be traced to a track record of sustained economic growth, which gives groups, even relatively disadvantaged groups, incentives to avoid conflict and destruction of a system that is bringing more and more economic benefits to more and more people.

One can also point to East-Central Europe, which has experienced more than its share of turmoil in the past and which is not blessed with leaders steeped in the principles of Jeffersonian democracy, but which has nonetheless avoided the carnage that has consumed the former Yugoslavia a few hundred miles to the south. East-Central Europe has been comparatively peaceful, even though every country in the region has been going through a political transition of the most profound sort; elites have been jockeying for position ever since 1989. If one had to point to one reason for East-Central Europe's stability, one would point to its comparatively good economic performance and prospects. The fact that the states of this region have a good chance of joining the European Union at some point in the not-too-distant future gives people powerful incentives to ignore nationalistic appeals and not rock the boat. This point is driven home with even greater force when one looks at differences within the region: nationalistic appeals have been less successful in Hungary, which has an ethnic diaspora but one of the region's strongest economies and one of the region's best chances of joining the European Union quickly, than in Romania, which has struggled economically.

Economic developments have also marked important turning points in the Middle East and Africa. The Middle East experienced considerable domestic turmoil in the 1950s and 1960s, when weak states were unable to meet societal demands, but less instability in some places in the 1970s and 1980s, when high oil prices and high levels of foreign aid from the United States and the Soviet Union gave governments more largesse to spread around. Potential opposition forces were pacified and, in essence,

44. See Trevor Findlay, "Turning the Corner in Southeast Asia," in Brown, *The International Dimensions of Internal Conflict*, chap. 5.

bought off. The fact that oil prices and foreign assistance levels have declined sharply in the 1990s does not bode well for the region's future.[45]

Much of sub-Saharan Africa has experienced similar problems for similar reasons. Many governments in West, Central, and East Africa were able to hold their heads above water in the 1970s and 1980s, even though they were riddled with ethnic problems and run by corrupt, incompetent leaders, because they received substantial amounts of financial support from two external sources: the superpowers and Western Europe; and international financial institutions such as the International Monetary Fund (IMF) and the World Bank. In the late 1980s, however, two things happened: the Cold War ended, and international financial institutions changed their ways of thinking about how financial assistance would be handed out. Direct aid from Washington and Moscow dried up, and most aid from Western Europe was redirected to Central and Eastern Europe. In addition, international financial institutions threatened to withhold aid unless governments overhauled their corrupt political systems and ineffective economic systems. This placed many leaders in Africa between a rock and a hard place: if they overhauled their patronage systems they would lose the support of their domestic constituencies and subsequently lose power; if they told the IMF and the World Bank that they would not implement political and economic reforms, they would not get financial assistance from abroad, their governments and economies would collapse, and they would lose power anyway. Many leaders in West, Central, and East Africa failed to resolve this dilemma, and consequently threw their countries into turmoil in the late 1980s and early 1990s.[46] Nigeria, which had substantial oil reserves, suffered similar financial setbacks when oil prices dropped and its government mismanaged the country's oil income. Although parts of Africa, particularly southern Africa, have stabilized since the end of the Cold War, much of the continent has moved in the other direction.

This points to how precarious Russia's position is. Russia is a country with a deeply xenophobic world view; it is comprised of dozens of ethnic groups, many of whom have spent centuries despising each other; with the break-up of the Soviet Union, many Russians now live as minorities in other, contiguous states; and the Russian economy has been in a free-fall since the mid-1980s. The fact that rabid nationalistic appeals have not yet taken over Russia's political debate is a minor miracle, attributable in large part to Boris Yeltsin's reluctance to go down this path and his willingness to use force to squelch his opposition. However, there are good reasons for fearing that more formidable nationalists will enter the picture, leaders not burdened with Vladimir Zhirinovsky's self-defeating tendencies. Given Russia's continuing economic crisis and its deeply troubled ethnic picture, the emergence of powerful nationalistic politicians could be the spark that ignites a highly combustible mixture. The key to defusing this situation—and a lever over which outside powers have at least some control—is turning Russia's economy around.

---

45. See Rachel Bronson, "Cycles of Conflict in the Middle East and North Africa," in Brown, *The International Dimensions of Internal Conflict,* chap. 6.

46. See Stedman, "Conflict and Conciliation in Sub-Saharan Africa."

Decision-Making Models

Graham T. Allison
Conceptual Models and the Cuban Missile Crisis

Alexander L. George
Adapting to Constraints on Rational Decisionmaking

Robert Putnam
Diplomacy and Domestic Politics: The Logic of Two-Level Games

Introduction to Decision-Making Models

Understanding the complex challenges inherent to developing solutions to current policy dilemmas such as how to fight the ongoing global war on terrorism (GWOT), how to facilitate productive negotiations toward a peaceful resolution to the seemingly endless Israeli-Palestinian conflict, or how to stop nuclear weapons proliferation programs like the one characterized by the Kim Jong Il regime in North Korea demands that policy makers look beyond the systemic "billiard ball" theories previously introduced to facilitate a better understanding of why actors in the international arena do what they do by focusing on the domestic pressures, influences and constraints that compel states to adopt a particular course of action. Toward that end, the readings in this section address why different states make the choices they make.

While systemic theories effectively address why states react in the international system of states (in response to other states), they often fall short in helping us understand why states make the specific choices they make. For example, Kenneth Waltz's theory of Structural Realism is a classic example of a "billiard ball" theory which makes the simplifying assumption that all states facing a similar stimulus will react the same way regardless of whether a pole in a bipolar world is a democracy or a dictatorship or if the Democrats or Republicans hold the White House. In contrast, Allison and other sub-systemic theorists (such as Alexander George, Robert Jervis, and others) assert that different states in the same situation will make different choices, based on domestic factors unique to their state.

In the following chapter, readers are introduced to Graham T. Allison, Alexander L. George, and Robert D. Putnam who help us understand challenges inherent in domestic-level decision making. First, Graham Allison introduces two alternative frameworks focusing on organizational and political influences on policy-makers' (or states') decision making processes. Alexander George addresses the stressful challenges faced by policy makers inherent to dealing with competing values and interests imbedded in a single issue in the absence of adequate information. And, Robert Putnam uses the logic of two-level games to explain the complex interrelation between domestic politics and international negotiations.

When Graham T. Allison published *Essence of Decision: Explaining the Cuban missile Crisis*[1] in 1971 he methodically looked "inside the black box" of the state to determine why states do what they do. Allison himself states that an aim of *Essence of Decision* is to "explore the influence of unrecognized assumptions upon our thinking about events like the missile crisis."[2] After first identifying "the basic frame of reference used by most

---

1. Graham Allison was a young assistant professor at Harvard University when he wrote *Essence of Decision.* The book flowed from discussions among a group of professors at Harvard who began meeting in the spring of 1966 to "discuss the impact of 'bureaucracy' on 'policy'—the gap between the intentions of the actors and the results of governmental action." The group included a number of academics who had previously served in the United States government (and many more who would in the future, including Allison himself). The book is thus a product of thinking about how government works—and fails to work—by a group of people who had themselves toiled inside bureaucracies.

2. Graham T. Allison, *Essence of Decision: Explaining the Cuban Missile Crisis,* (New York: HarperCollins, 1971), v.

people when thinking about foreign affairs," Allison outlines two alternative frameworks, each of which "highlights, magnifies, and reveals" some aspects of why a particular decision was made while neglecting others.[3] In an extraordinary example of intellectual pluralism, Allison illustrates the applicability of all three models against the case of the Cuban Missile Crisis. Each conceptual lens or model explains the actions of the Soviet Union or the United States differently to illustrate that the use of all three models will facilitate a closer approximation of the truth than what can be discovered through the use of one model by itself.[4]

It is important to remember that Allison's three lenses are not theories in the sense that they explain, predict, or prescribe state behavior; instead, they are guides for studying the foreign policy of states, each highlighting different factors that influenced the eventual decision that was made. The dependent variable Allison examines is thus the characterization of the foreign policy decision made by the state (i.e., addressing why states do *what* they do.) The independent variable is the factor (or actor) within the state which influenced that decision (organizations or bureaucratic players). And finally, the causality variable illustrates *how* the influencing factor within the state affected the decision made by the state.

It is difficult to overstate the importance of Allison's work for the field of international relations. His three Models have become a part of the vocabulary of the discipline; "Model II behavior" (Organizational Process Model) is a shorthand way of describing any institution which functions according to its traditions and history. An entire sub-discipline which examines the impact of personal experiences on foreign policy decision-making has evolved from Allison's Model III[5] (Bureaucratic Politics Model), while Model I (Rational Actor Model) remains the single most often used tool for thinking about foreign policy decision-making. These models have also contributed to the more practical side of foreign policy, as a number of academics focus on recognizing and reducing the impact of constraints on rational decision-making.

In *Adapting to Constraints on Rational Decisionmaking,* Alexander George further explores the personal aspect of the decision making process by addressing the incredibly stressful challenges inherent in dealing with competing values and interests imbedded in a single issue in the absence of adequate information. George argues that decision makers, in an effort to lower the stress related to multiple, competing values, will either develop complex strategies to satisfy all values, prioritize values to minimize the affects of not satisfying all of them, or simply attempt to avoid the value conflicts altogether. George also argues that decision makers devise methods to minimize the psychological tension associated with stressful decisions absent perfect information through calculated or defensive procrastination, self-imposed deadlines, the use of decision assisting aids, or "bolstering"—to increase the attractiveness of a preferred course of action over another while emphasizing the unattractiveness of a less preferred course of action.

---

3. Ibid.

4. The excerpts you read are from an article Allison published in *The American Political Science Review* in September 1969, during the preparation but before the publication of *Essence of Decision*. It presents a condensed and very rich summation of the three models; then it applies each model to the United States' decision to blockade Cuba during the Cuban Missile Crisis.

5. See especially Richard E. Neustadt and Ernest R. May, *Thinking in Time: The Uses of History for Decisionmakers*, (New York: The Free Press, 1986).

Like Allison, George demonstrates that the environment in which and by which decisions are made can lead to the adoption of a less-than-optimal course of action. George concludes by demonstrating how some of the most stressful decision making situations occur while dealing with international crisis, often resulting in the simultaneous tendency for decision makers from all sides of an issue to underestimate their own capabilities while overestimating the abilities of other involved actors—imposing more judgment-impairing stress on all who are involved in the decision making process.

As Alexander George concludes his essay discussing the challenges of international crisis management, Robert Putnam analyzes international negotiations as part of a two-level game in *Diplomacy and Domestic Politics: The Logic of Two-level Games*. Putnam describes the complex interrelation between international negotiations and domestic politics as a two stage process consisting of bargaining between negotiators at the international level toward a tentative agreement (Level-I), and separate discussions within each negotiator's group of constituents regarding ratification of the agreement (level-II). Since the actors at Level-II may represent bureaucratic agencies, interest groups, or social classes, chances of ratification without amendment can be challenging—often reopening Level-I negotiations.

Putnam characterizes a tentative Level-I agreement that would likely gain necessary support at Level-II for ratification as a "win-set" illustrating that larger win-sets facilitate a higher likelihood of Level-I agreement. Simply stated, the larger the win-sets between Level-I negotiators, the greater the chances are that they "overlap" one another. However, the size of a win-set is determined by a number of factors including the distribution of preferences and coalitions and the political institutions at Level-II, along with the strategies—often resulting from personal interests—of Level-I negotiators.

Like Allison's organizational process or bureaucratic politics models or George's constraints on rational decision making, Putnam's two-level game addresses the myriad ways in which states' policies are often products of complex and unique variables—often resulting in courses of action that are less than optimal—helping us answer the central question of why states do what they do.

Conceptual Models and the Cuban Missile Crisis

Graham T. Allison

The Cuban missile crisis is a seminal event. For thirteen days of October 1962, there was a higher probability that more human lives would end suddenly than ever before in history. Had the worst occurred, the death of 100 million Americans, over 100 million Russians, and millions of Europeans as well would make previous natural calamities and inhumanities appear insignificant. Given the probability of disaster—which President Kennedy estimated as "between 1 out of 3 and even"—our escape seems awesome. . . .

. . . This study proceeds from the premise that marked improvement in our understanding of such events depends critically on more self-consciousness about what observers bring to the analysis. What each analyst sees and judges to be important is a function not only of the evidence about what happened but also of the "conceptual lenses" through which he looks at the evidence. The principal purpose of this essay is to explore some of the fundamental assumptions and categories employed by analysts in thinking about problems of government behavior, especially in foreign and military affairs.

The general argument can be summarized in three propositions:

1. Analysts think about problems of foreign and military policy in terms of largely implicit conceptual models that have significant consequences for the content of their thought. . . .

2. Most analysts explain (and predict) the behavior of national governments in terms of various forms of one basic conceptual model, here entitled the Rational Policy Model (Model I). . . .

3. Two "alternative" conceptual models, here labeled an Organizational Process Model (Model II) and a Bureaucratic Politics Model (Model III) provide a base for improved explanation and prediction. . . .

MODEL I: A RATIONAL POLICY

. . . How do analysts attempt to explain the Soviet emplacement of missiles in Cuba? The most widely cited explanation of this occurrence has been produced by two RAND Sovietologists, Arnold Horelick and Myron Rush. They conclude that "the introduction of strategic missiles into Cuba was motivated chiefly by the Soviet leaders' desire to overcome. . . the existing large margin of U.S. strategic superiority." How do they reach this conclusion? In Sherlock Holmes style, they seize several salient characteristics of this action and use these features as criteria against which to test alternative hypotheses about Soviet objectives. For example, the size of the Soviet deployment, and the simultaneous emplacement of more expensive, more visible intermediate range missiles as well as medium range missiles, it is argued, exclude an explanation of the action in terms of Cuban defense—since that objective could have been secured with a much smaller number of medium range missiles alone. Their explanation presents an argument for one objective that permits interpretation of the details of Soviet behavior as a value-maximizing choice.

How do analysts account for the coming of the First World War? According to Hans Morgenthau, "the first World War had its origin exclusively in the fear of a disturbance of the European balance of power." In the period preceding World War I, the Triple Alliance precariously balanced the Triple Entente. If either power combination could gain a decisive advantage in the Balkans, it would achieve a decisive advantage in the balance of power. "It was this fear," Morgenthau asserts, "that motivated Austria in July 1914 to settle its accounts with Serbia once and for all, and that induced Germany to support Austria unconditionally. It was the same fear that brought Russia to the support of Serbia, and France to the support of Russia." How is Morgenthau able to resolve this problem so confidently? By imposing on the data a "rational outline."

The value of this method, according to Morgenthau, is that "it provides for rational discipline in action and creates astounding continuity in foreign policy which makes American, British, or Russian foreign policy appear as an intelligent, rational continuum. . . regardless of the different motives, preferences, and intellectual and moral qualities of successive statesmen.". . .

What is striking about these examples from the literature of foreign policy and international relations are the similarities among analysts of various styles when they are called upon to produce explanations. Each assumes that what must be explained is an action, i.e., the realization of some purpose or intention. Each assumes that the actor is the national government. Each assumes that the action is chosen as a calculated response to a strategic problem. For each, explanation consists of showing what goal the government was pursuing in committing the act and how this action was a reasonable choice, given the nation's objectives. This set of assumptions characterizes the rational policy model. . . .

Most contemporary analysts (as well as laymen) proceed predominantly— albeit most often implicitly—in terms of this model when attempting to explain happenings in foreign affairs. Indeed, that occurrences in foreign affairs are the *acts* of *nations* seems so fundamental to thinking about such problems that this underlying model has rarely been recognized: to explain an occurrence in foreign policy simply means to show how the government could have rationally chosen that action. . . .

Rational Policy Paradigm

Basic Unit of Analysis: Policy as National Choice

Happenings in foreign affairs are conceived as actions chosen by the nation or national government. Governments select the action that will maximize strategic goals and objectives. These "solutions" to strategic problems are the fundamental categories in terms of which the analyst perceives what is to be explained. . . .

Dominant Inference Pattern

This paradigm leads analysts to rely on the following pattern of inference: if a nation performed a particular action, that nation must have had ends towards which the action constituted an optimal means. The rational policy model's explanatory power stems from this inference pattern. Puzzlement is relieved by revealing the purposive pattern within which the occurrence can be located as a value-maximizing means.

General Propositions

The disgrace of political science is the infrequency with which propositions of any generality are formulated and tested. "Paradigmatic analysis" argues for explicitness about the terms in which analysis proceeds, and seriousness about the logic of explanation. Simply to illustrate the kind of propositions on which analysts who employ this model rely, the formulation includes several.

The basic assumption of value-maximizing behavior produces propositions central to most explanations. The general principle can be formulated as follows: the likelihood of any particular action results from a combination of the nation's (1) relevant values and objectives, (2) perceived alternative courses of action, (3) estimates of various sets of consequences (which will follow from each alternative), and (4) net valuation of each set of consequences. This yields two propositions.

A. An increase in the cost of an alternative, i.e., a reduction in the value of the set of consequences which will follow from that action, or a reduction in the probability of attaining fixed consequences, reduces the likelihood of that alternative being chosen.

B. A decrease in the costs of an alternative, i.e., an increase in the value of the set of consequences which will follow from that alternative, or an increase in the probability of attaining fixed consequences, increases the likelihood of that action being chosen. . . .

The U.S. Blockade of Cuba: A First Cut

The U.S. response to the Soviet Union's emplacement of missiles in Cuba must be understood in strategic terms as simple value-maximizing escalation. American nuclear superiority could be counted on to paralyze Soviet nuclear power; Soviet transgression of the nuclear threshold in response to an American use of lower levels of violence would be wildly irrational since it would mean virtual destruction of the Soviet Communist system and Russian nation. American local superiority was overwhelming: it could be initiated at a low level while threatening with high credibility an ascending sequence of steps short of the nuclear threshold. All that was required was for the United States to bring to bear its strategic and local superiority in such a way that American determination to see the missiles removed would be demonstrated, while at the same time allowing Moscow time and room to retreat without humiliation. The naval blockade—euphemistically named a "quarantine" in order to circumvent the niceties of international law—did just that.

The U.S. government's selection of the blockade followed this logic. Apprised of the presence of Soviet missiles in Cuba, the President assembled an Executive Committee (ExCom) of the National Security Council and directed them to "set aside all other tasks to make a prompt and intense survey of the dangers and all possible courses of action." This group functioned as "fifteen individuals on our own, representing the President and not different departments." As one of the participants recalls, "The remarkable aspect of those meetings was a sense of complete equality." Most of the time during the week that followed was spent canvassing all the possible tracks and weighing the arguments for and against each. Six major categories of action were considered.

1. Do nothing. U.S. vulnerability to Soviet missiles was no new thing. Since the U.S. already lived under the gun of missiles based in Russia, a Soviet capability to strike from Cuba too made little real difference. The real danger stemmed from the possibility of U.S. over-reaction. The U.S. should announce the Soviet action in a calm, casual manner thereby deflating whatever political capital Khrushchev hoped to make of the missiles.

This argument fails on two counts. First, it grossly underestimates the military importance of the Soviet resolve. Not only would the Soviet Union's missile capability be doubled and the U.S. early warning system outflanked. The Soviet Union would have an opportunity to reverse the strategic balance by further installations, and indeed, in the longer run, to invest in cheaper, shorter-range rather than more expensive longer-range missiles. Second, the political importance of this move was undeniable. The Soviet Union's act challenged the American President's most solemn warning. If the U.S. failed to respond, no American commitment would be credible.

2. Diplomatic pressures. Several forms were considered: an appeal to the U.N. or O.A.S. for an inspection team, a secret approach to Khrushchev, and a direct approach to Khrushchev, perhaps at a summit meeting. The United States would demand that the missiles be removed, but the final settlement might include neutralization of Cuba, U.S. withdrawal from Guantanamo base, and withdrawal of U.S. Jupiter missiles from Turkey or Italy.

Each form of the diplomatic approach had its own drawbacks. To arraign the Soviet Union before the U.N. Security Council held little promise since the Russians could veto any proposed action. While the diplomats argued, the missiles would be operational. To send a secret emissary to Khrushchev demanding that the missiles be withdrawn would be to pose untenable alternatives. On the one hand, this would invite Khrushchev to seize the diplomatic initiative, perhaps committing himself to strategic retaliation in response to an attack on Cuba. On the other hand, this would tender an ultimatum that no great power could accept. To confront Khrushchev at a summit would guarantee demands for U.S. concessions, and the analogy between U.S. missiles in Turkey and Russian missiles in Cuba could not be erased.

But why not trade U.S. Jupiters in Turkey and Italy, which the President had previously ordered withdrawn, for the missiles in Cuba? The U.S. had chosen to withdraw these missiles in order to replace them with superior, less vulnerable Mediterranean Polaris submarines. But the middle of the crisis was no time for concessions. The offer of such a deal might suggest to the Soviets that the West would yield and thus tempt them to demand more. It would certainly confirm European suspicions about American willingness to sacrifice European interests when the chips were down. Finally, the basic issue should be kept clear. As the President stated in reply to Bertrand Russell, "I think your attention might well be directed to the burglars rather than to those who have caught the burglars."

3. A secret approach to Castro. The crisis provided an opportunity to separate Cuba and Soviet Communism by offering Castro the alternatives, "split or fall." But Soviet troops transported, constructed, guarded, and controlled the missiles. Their removal would thus depend on a Soviet decision.

4. Invasion. The United States could take this occasion not only to remove the missiles but also to rid itself of Castro. A Navy exercise had long been scheduled in which Marines, ferried from Florida in naval vessels, would liberate the imaginary island of Vieques. Why not simply shift the point of disembarkment? (The Pentagon's foresight in planning this operation would be an appropriate antidote to the CIA's Bay of Pigs!)

Preparations were made for an invasion, but as a last resort. American troops would be forced to confront 20,000 Soviets in the first Cold War case of direct contact between the troops of the super powers. Such brinksmanship courted nuclear disaster, practically guaranteeing an equivalent Soviet move against Berlin.

5. Surgical air strike. The missile sites should be removed by a clean, swift conventional attack. This was the effective counter-action which the attempted deception deserved. A surgical strike would remove the missiles and thus eliminate both the danger that the missiles might become operational and the fear that the Soviets would discover the American discovery and act first.

The initial attractiveness of this alternative was dulled by several difficulties. First, could the strike really be "surgical"? The Air Force could not guarantee destruction of all the missiles. Some might be fired during the attack; some might not have been identified. In order to assure destruction of Soviet and Cuban means of retaliating, what was required was not a surgical but rather a massive attack—of at least 500 sorties. Second, a surprise air attack would of course kill Russians at the missile sites. Pressures on the Soviet Union to retaliate would be so strong that an attack on Berlin or Turkey was highly probable. Third, the key problem with this program was that of advance warning. Could the President of the United States, with his memory of Pearl Harbor and his vision of future U.S. responsibility, order a "Pearl Harbor in reverse"? For 175 years, unannounced Sunday morning attacks had been an anathema to our tradition.

6. Blockade. Indirect military action in the form of a blockade became more attractive as the ExCom dissected the other alternatives. An embargo on military shipments to Cuba enforced by a naval blockade was not without flaws, however. Could the U.S. blockade Cuba without inviting Soviet reprisal in Berlin? The likely solution to joint blockades would be the lifting of both blockades, restoring the new *status quo,* and allowing the Soviets additional time to complete the missiles. Second, the possible consequences of the blockade resembled the drawbacks which disqualified the air strike. If Soviet ships did not stop, the United States would be forced to fire the first shot, inviting retaliation. Third, a blockade would deny the traditional freedom of the seas demanded by several of our close allies and might be held illegal, in violation of the U.N. Charter and international law, unless the United States could obtain a two-thirds vote in the O.A.S. Finally, how could a blockade be related to the problem, namely, some 75 missiles on the island of Cuba, approaching operational readiness daily? A blockade offered the Soviets a spectrum of delaying tactics with which to buy time to complete the missile installations. Was a *fait accompli* not required?

In spite of these enormous difficulties the blockade had comparative advantages: (1) It was a middle course between inaction and attack, aggressive enough to communicate firmness of intention, but nevertheless not so precipitous as a strike. (2) It placed on Khrushchev the burden of choice concerning the next step. He could avoid a direct military clash by keeping his ships away. His was the last clear chance. (3) No possible military confrontation could be more acceptable to the U.S. than a naval engagement in the Caribbean. (4) This move permitted the U.S., by flexing its conventional muscle, to exploit the threat of subsequent non-nuclear steps in each of which the U.S. would have significant superiority.

Particular arguments about advantages and disadvantages were powerful. The explanation of the American choice of the blockade lies in a more general principle, however. As President Kennedy stated in drawing the moral of the crisis:

> Above all, while defending our own vital interests, nuclear powers must avert those confrontations which bring an adversary to a choice of either a humiliating retreat or a nuclear war. To adopt that kind of course in the nuclear age would be evidence only of the bankruptcy of our policy—of a collective death wish for the world.

The blockade was the United States' only real option.

MODEL II: ORGANIZATIONAL PROCESS

For some purposes, governmental behavior can be usefully summarized as action chosen by a unitary, rational decisionmaker: centrally controlled, completely informed, and value maximizing. But this simplification must not be allowed to conceal the fact that a "government" consists of a conglomerate of semi-feudal, loosely allied organizations, each with a substantial life of its own. Government leaders do sit formally, and to some extent in fact, on top of this conglomerate. But governments perceive problems through organizational sensors. Governments define alternatives and estimate consequences as organizations process information. Governments act as these organizations enact routines. Government behavior can therefore be understood according to a second conceptual model, less as deliberate choices of leaders and more as *outputs* of large organizations functioning according to standard patterns of behavior.

To be responsive to a broad spectrum of problems, governments consist of large organizations among which primary responsibility for particular areas is divided. Each organization attends to a special set of problems and acts in quasi-independence on these problems. But few important problems fall exclusively within the domain of a single organization. Thus government behavior relevant to any important problem reflects the independent output of several organizations, partially coordinated by government leaders. Government leaders can substantially disturb, but not substantially control, the behavior of these organizations.

To perform complex routines, the behavior of large numbers of individuals must be coordinated. Coordination requires standard operating procedures: rules according to which things are done. Assured capability for reliable performance of action that depends upon the behavior of hundreds of persons requires established "programs." Indeed, if the eleven members of a football team are to perform adequately on any particular down, each player must not "do what he thinks needs to be done" or "do what the quarterback tells him to do." Rather, each player must perform the maneuvers specified by a previously established play which the quarterback has simply called in this situation.

At any given time, a government consists of *existing* organizations, each with a *fixed* set of standard operating procedures and programs. The behavior of these organizations—and consequently of the government—relevant to an issue in any particular instance is, therefore, determined primarily by routines established in these organizations prior to that instance. But organizations do change. Learning occurs gradually, over time. Dramatic organizational change occurs in response to major crises. Both learning and change are influenced by existing organizational capabilities.

Borrowed from studies of organizations, these loosely formulated propositions amount simply to *tendencies*. Each must be hedged by modifiers like "other things being equal" and "under certain conditions." In particular instances, tendencies hold—more or less. In specific situations, the relevant question is: more or less? But this is as it should be. For, on the one hand, "organizations" are no more homogeneous a class than "solids." When scientists tried to generalize about "solids," they achieved similar results. Solids tend to expand when heated, but some do and some don't. More adequate categorization of the various elements now lumped under the rubric "organizations" is thus required. On the other hand, the behavior of particular organizations seems considerably more complex than the behavior of solids. Additional information about a particular organization is required for further specification of the tendency statements. In spite of these two caveats, the characterization of government action as organizational output differs distinctly from Model I. Attempts to understand problems of foreign affairs in terms of this frame of reference should produce quite different explanations.

Organizational Process Paradigm

Basic Unit of Analysis: Policy as Organizational Output

The happenings of international politics are, in three critical senses, outputs of organizational processes. First, the actual occurrences are organizational outputs. . . .

Government leaders can trim the edges of this output and exercise some choice in combining outputs. But the mass of behavior is determined by previously established procedures. Second, existing organizational routines for employing present physical capabilities constitute the effective options open to government leaders confronted with any problem. The fact that fixed programs (equipment, men, and routines which exist at the particular time) exhaust the range of buttons that leaders can push is not always perceived by these leaders. But in every case it is critical for an understanding of what is actually done. Third, organizational outputs structure the situation within the narrow constraints of which leaders must contribute their "decision" concerning an issue. Outputs raise the problem, provide the information, and make the initial moves that color the face of the issue that is turned to the leaders. As Theodore Sorensen has observed: "Presidents rarely, if ever, make decisions— particularly in foreign affairs—in the sense of writing their conclusions on a clean slate. . . . The basic decisions, which confine their choices, have all too often been previously made." If one understands the structure of the situation and the face of the issue—which are determined by the organizational outputs—the formal choice of the leaders is frequently anti-climactic. . . .

General Propositions

A number of general propositions have been stated above. In order to illustrate clearly the type of proposition employed by Model II analysts, this section formulates several more precisely.

A. *Organizational Action.* Activity according to SOPs and programs does not constitute far-sighted, flexible adaptation to "the issue" (as it is conceived by the analyst). Detail and nuance of actions by organizations are determined predominantly by organizational routines, not government leaders' directions.

1. SOPs constitute routines for dealing with *standard* situations. Routines allow large numbers of ordinary individuals to deal with numerous instances, day after day, without considerable thought, by responding to basic stimuli. But this regularized capability for adequate performance is purchased at the price of standardization. If the SOPs are appropriate, average performance, i.e., performance averaged over the range of cases, is better than it would be if each instance were approached individually (given fixed talent, timing, and resource constraints). But specific instances, particularly critical instances that typically do not have "standard" characteristics, are often handled sluggishly or inappropriately.

2. A program, i.e., a complex action chosen from a short list of programs in a repertoire, is rarely tailored to the specific situation in which it is executed. Rather, the program is (at best) the most appropriate of the programs in a previously developed repertoire.

3. Since repertoires are developed by parochial organizations for standard scenarios defined by that organization, programs available for dealing with a particular situation are often ill-suited.

B. *Limited Flexibility and Incremental Change.* Major lines of organizational action are straight, i.e., behavior at one time is marginally different from that behavior at $t-1$. Simple-minded predictions work best: Behavior at $t+1$ will be marginally different from behavior at the present time.

1. Organizational budgets change incrementally—both with respect to totals and with respect to intra-organizational splits. Though organizations could divide the money available each year by carving up the pie anew (in the light of changes in objectives or environment), in practice, organizations take last year's budget as a base and adjust incrementally. Predictions that require large budgetary shifts in a single year between organizations or between units within an organization should be hedged.

2. Once undertaken, an organizational investment is not dropped at the point where "objective" costs outweigh benefits. Organizational stakes in adopted projects carry them quite beyond the loss point.

C. *Administrative Feasibility.* Adequate explanation, analysis, and prediction must include administrative feasibility as a major dimension. A considerable gap separates what leaders choose (or might rationally have chosen) and what organizations implement.

1. Organizations are blunt instruments. Projects that require several organizations to act with high degrees of precision and coordination are not likely to succeed.

2. Projects that demand that existing organizational units depart from their accustomed functions and perform previously unprogrammed tasks are rarely accomplished in their designed form.

3. Government leaders can expect that each organization will do its "part" in terms of what the organization knows how to do.

4. Government leaders can expect incomplete and distorted information from each organization concerning its part of the problem.

5. Where an assigned piece of a problem is contrary to the existing goals of an organization, resistance to implementation of that piece will be encountered. . . .

The U.S. Blockade of Cuba: A Second Cut

Organizational Intelligence. At 7:00 P.M. on October 22, 1962, President Kennedy disclosed the American discovery of the presence of Soviet strategic missiles in Cuba, declared a "strict quarantine on all offensive military equipment under shipment to Cuba," and demanded that "Chairman Khrushchev halt and eliminate this clandestine, reckless, and provocative threat to world peace." This decision was reached at the pinnacle of the U.S. Government after a critical week of deliberation. What initiated that precious week were photographs of Soviet missile sites in Cuba taken on October 14. These pictures might not have been taken until a week later. In that case, the President speculated, "I don't think probably we would have chosen as prudently as we finally did." U.S. leaders might have received this information three weeks earlier—if a U-2 had flown over San Cristobal in the last week of September. What determined the context in which American leaders came to choose the blockade was the discovery of missiles on October 14.

There has been considerable debate over alleged American "intelligence failures" in the Cuban missile crisis. But what both critics and defenders have neglected is the fact that the discovery took place on October 14, rather than three weeks earlier or a week later, as a consequence of the established routines and procedures of the organizations which constitute the U.S. intelligence community. These organizations were neither more nor less successful than they had been the previous month or were to be in the months to follow.

The notorious "September estimate," approved by the United States Intelligence Board (USIB) on September 19, concluded that the Soviet Union would not introduce offensive missiles into Cuba. No U-2 flight was directed over the western end of Cuba (after September 5) before October 4. No U-2 flew over the western end of Cuba until the flight that discovered the Soviet missiles on October 14. Can these "failures" be accounted for in organizational terms?

On September 19 when USIB met to consider the question of Cuba, the "system" contained the following information: (1) shipping intelligence had noted the arrival in Cuba of two large-hatch Soviet lumber ships, which were riding high in the water; (2) refugee reports of countless sightings of missiles, but also a report that Castro's private pilot, after a night of drinking in Havana, had boasted: "We will fight to the death and perhaps we can win because we have everything, including atomic weapons"; (3) a sighting by a CIA agent of the rear profile of a strategic missile; (4) U-2 photos produced by flights of August 29, September 5 and 17 showing the construction of a number of SAM sites and other defensive missiles. Not all of this information was on the desk of the estimators, however. Shipping intelligence experts note the fact that large-hatch ships were riding high in the water and spelled out the inference: the ships must be carrying "space consuming" cargo. These facts were carefully included in the catalogue of intelligence concerning shipping. For experts sensitive to the Soviets' shortage of ships, however, these facts carried no special signal. The refugee report of Castro's private pilot's remark had been received at Opa Locka, Florida, along with vast reams of inaccurate reports generated by the refugee community. This report and a thousand others had to be checked and compared before being sent to Washington. The two weeks required for initial processing could have been shortened by a large increase in resources, but the yield of this source was already quite marginal. The CIA agent's sighting of the rear profile of a strategic missile had occurred on September 12; transmission time from agent sighting to arrival in Washington typically took 9 to 12 days. Shortening this transmission time would impose severe cost in terms of danger to subagents, agents, and communication networks.

On the information available, the intelligence chiefs who predicted that the Soviet Union would not introduce offensive missiles into Cuba made a reasonable and defensible judgment. Moreover, in the light of the fact that these organizations were gathering intelligence not only about Cuba but about potential occurrences in all parts of the worlds, the informational base available to the estimators involved nothing out of the ordinary. Nor, from an organizational perspective, is there anything startling about the gradual accumulation of evidence that led to the formulation of the hypothesis that the Soviets were installing missiles in Cuba and the decision on October 4 to direct a special flight over western Cuba.

The ten-day delay between that decision and the flight is another organizational story. At the October 4 meeting, the Defense Department took the opportunity to raise an issue important to its concerns. Given the increased danger that a U-2 would be downed, it would be better if the pilot were an officer in uniform rather than a CIA agent. Thus the Air Force should assume responsibility for U-2 flights over Cuba. To the contrary, the CIA argued that this was an intelligence operation and thus within the CIA's jurisdiction. Moreover, CIA U-2's had been modified in certain ways which gave them advantages over Air Force U-2 s in averting Soviet SAM's. Five days passed while the State Department pressed for less risky alternatives such as drones and the Air Force (in Department of Defense guise) and CIA engaged in territorial disputes. On October 9 a flight plan over San Cristobal was approved by COMOR, but to the CIA's dismay, Air Force pilots rather than CIA agents would take charge of the mission. At this point details become sketchy, but several members of the intelligence community have speculated that an Air Force pilot in an Air Force U-2 attempted a high altitude overflight on October 9 that "flamed out," i.e., lost power, and thus had to descend in order to restart its engine. A second round between Air Force and CIA followed, as a result of which Air Force pilots were trained to fly CIA U-2's. A successful overflight took place on October 14.

This ten-day delay constitutes some form of "failure." In the face of well-founded suspicions concerning offensive Soviet missiles in Cuba that posed a critical threat to the United States' most vital interest, squabbling between organizations whose job it is to produce this information seems entirely inappropriate. But for each of these organizations, the question involved the issue: "*Whose* job was it to be?" Moreover, the issue was not simply, which organization would control U-2 flights over Cuba, but rather the broader issue of ownership of U-2 intelligence activities—a very long standing territorial dispute. Thus though this delay was in one sense a "failure," it was also a nearly inevitable consequence of two facts: many jobs do not fall neatly into precisely defined organizational jurisdictions; and vigorous organizations are imperialistic.

Organizational Options. Deliberations of leaders in ExCom meetings produced broad outlines of alternatives. Details of these alternatives and blueprints for their implementation had to be specified by the organizations that would perform these tasks. These organizational outputs answered the question: What, specifically, *could* be done?

Discussion in the ExCom quickly narrowed the live options to two: an air strike and a blockade. The choice of the blockade instead of the air strike turned on two points: (1) the argument from morality and tradition that the United States could not perpetrate a "Pearl Harbor in reverse"; (2) the belief that a "surgical" air strike was impossible. Whether the United States *might* strike first was a question not of capability but of morality. Whether the United States *could* perform the surgical strike was a factual question concerning capabilities. The majority of the members of the ExCom, including the President, initially preferred the air strike. What effectively foreclosed this option, however, was the fact that the air strike they wanted could not be chosen with high confidence of success. After having tentatively chosen the course of prudence—given that the surgical air strike was not an option— Kennedy reconsidered. On Sunday morning, October 21, he called the Air Force experts to a special meeting in his living quarters where he probed once more for the option of a "*surgical*" air strike. General Walter C. Sweeny, Commander of Tactical Air Forces, asserted again that the Air Force could guarantee no higher than ninety percent effectiveness in a surgical air strike. That "fact" was false.

The air strike alternative provides a classic case of military estimates. One of the alternatives outlined by the ExCom was named "air strike." Specification of the details of this alternative was delegated to the Air Force. Starting from an existing plan for massive U.S. military action against Cuba (prepared for contingencies like a response to a Soviet Berlin grab), Air Force estimators produced an attack to guarantee success. This plan called for extensive bombardment of all missile sites, storage depots, airports, and, in deference to the Navy, the artillery batteries opposite the naval base at Guantanamo. Members of the ExCom repeatedly expressed bewilderment at military estimates of the number of sorties required, likely casualties, and collateral damage. But the "surgical" air strike that the political leaders had in mind was never carefully examined during the first week of the crisis. Rather, this option was simply excluded on the grounds that since the Soviet MRBM's in Cuba were classified "mobile" in U.S. manuals, extensive bombing was required. During the second week of the crisis, careful examination revealed that the missiles were mobile, in the sense that small houses are mobile: that is, they could be moved and reassembled in 6 days. After the missiles were reclassified "movable" and detailed plans for surgical air strikes specified, this action was added to the list of live options for the end of the second week.

Organizational Implementation. Ex-Com members separated several types of blockade: offensive weapons only, all armaments, and all strategic goods including POL (petroleum, oil, and lubricants). But the *"details"* of the operation were left to the Navy. Before the President announced the blockade on Monday evening, the first stage of the Navy's blueprint was in motion, and a problem loomed on the horizon. The Navy had a detailed plan for the blockade. The President had several less precise but equally determined notions concerning what should be done, when, and how. For the Navy the issue was one of effective implementation of the Navy's blockade—without the meddling and interference of political leaders. For the President, the problem was to pace and manage events in such a way that the Soviet leaders would have time to see, think, and blink.

A careful reading of available sources uncovers an instructive incident. On Tuesday the British Ambassador, Ormsby-Gore, after having attended a briefing on the details of the blockade, suggested to the President that the plan for intercepting Soviet ships far out of reach of Cuban jets did not facilitate Khrushchev's hard decision. Why not make the interception much closer to Cuba and thus give the Russian leader more time? According to the public account and the recollection of a number of individuals involved, Kennedy "agreed immediately," called McNamara, and over emotional Navy protest, issued the appropriate instructions." As Sorensen records,"in a sharp clash with the Navy, he made certain his will prevailed." The Navy's plan for the blockade was thus changed by drawing the blockade much closer to Cuba.

A serious organizational orientation makes one suspicious of this account. More careful examination of the available evidence confirms these suspicions, though alternative accounts must be somewhat speculative. According to the public chronology, a quarantine drawn close to Cuba became effective on Wednesday morning, the first Soviet ship was contacted on Thursday morning, and the first boarding of a ship occurred on Friday. According to the statement by the Department of Defense, boarding of the *Marcula* by a party from the *John R. Pierce* "took place at 7:50 *A.M.*, E.D.T., 180 miles northeast of Nassau." The *Marcula* had been trailed since about 10:30 the previous evening. Simple calculations suggest that the *Pierce* must have been stationed along the Navy's original arc which extended 500 miles out to sea from Cape Magsi, Cuba's eastern most tip. The blockade line was *not* moved as the President ordered, and the accounts report. What happened is not entirely clear. One can be certain, however, that Soviet ships passed through the line along which American destroyers had posted themselves before the official "first contact" with the Soviet ship. On October 26 a Soviet tanker arrived in Havana and was honored by a dockside rally for "running the blockade." Photographs of this vessel show the name *Vinnitsa* on the side of the vessel in Cyrillic letters. But according to the official U.S. position, the first tanker to pass through the blockade was the *Bucharest,* which was hailed by the Navy on the morning of October 25. Again simple mathematical calculation excludes the possibility that the *Bucharest* and *Vinnitsa* were the same ship. It seems probable that the Navy's resistance to the President's order that the blockade be drawn in closer to Cuba forced him to allow one or several Soviet ships to pass through the blockade after it was officially operative.

This attempt to leash the Navy's blockade had a price. On Wednesday morning, October 24, what the President had been awaiting occurred. The 18 dry cargo ships heading towards the quarantine stopped dead in the water. This was the occasion of Dean Rusk's remark, "We are eyeball to eyeball and I think the other fellow just blinked." But the Navy had another interpretation. The ships had simply stopped to pick up Soviet submarine escorts. The President became quite concerned lest the Navy—already riled because of Presidential meddling in its affairs—blunder into an incident. Sensing the President's fears, McNamara became suspicious of the Navy's procedures and routines for making the first interception. Calling on the Chief of Naval Operations in the Navy's inner sanctum, the Navy Flag Plot, McNamara put his questions harshly. Who would make the first interception? Were Russian speaking officers on board? How would submarines be dealt with? At one point McNamara asked Anderson what he would do if a Soviet ship's captain refused to answer questions about his cargo. Picking up the Manual of Navy Regulations the Navy man waved it in McNamara's face and shouted, "It's all in there." To which McNamara replied, "I don't give a damn what John Paul Jones would have done; I want to know what you are going to do, now." The encounter ended on Anderson's remark: "Now, Mr. Secretary, if you and your Deputy will go back to your office the Navy will run the blockade."

MODEL III: BUREAUCRATIC POLITICS

The leaders who sit on top of organizations are not a monolithic group. Rather, each is, in his own right, a player in a central, competitive game. The name of the game is bureaucratic politics: bargaining along regularized channels among players positioned hierarchically within the government. Government behavior can thus be understood according to a third conceptual model not as organizational outputs, but as outcomes of bargaining games. In contrast with Model I, the bureaucratic politics model sees no unitary actor but rather many actors as players, who focus not on a single strategic issue but on many diverse intra-national problems as well, in terms of no consistent set of strategic objectives but rather according to various conceptions of national, organizational, and personal goals, making government decisions not by rational choice but by the pulling and hauling that is politics.

The apparatus of each national government constitutes a complex arena for the intra-national game. Political leaders at the top of this apparatus plus the men who occupy positions on top of the critical organizations form the circle of central players. Ascendancy to this circle assures some independent standing. The necessary decentralization of decisions required for action on the broad range of foreign policy problems guarantees that each player has considerable discretion. Thus power is shared.

Men share power. Men differ concerning what must be done. The differences matter. This milieu necessitates that policy be resolved by politics. What the nation does is sometimes the result of the triumph of one group over others. More often, however, different groups pulling in different directions yield a resultant distinct from what anyone intended. What moves the chess pieces is not simply the reasons which support a course of action, nor the routines of organizations which enact an alternative, but the power and skill of proponents and opponents of the action in question.

This characterization captures the thrust of the bureaucratic politics orientation. If problems of foreign policy arose as discreet issues, and decisions were determined one game at a time, this account would suffice. But most "issues," e.g., Vietnam or the proliferation of nuclear weapons, emerge piecemeal, over time, one lump in one context, a second in another. Hundreds of issues compete for players' attention every day. Each player is forced to fix upon his issues for that day, fight them on their own terms, and rush on to the next. Thus the character of emerging issues and the pace at which the game is played converge to yield government "decisions" and "actions" as collages. Choices by one player, outcomes of minor games, outcomes of central games, and "foul-ups"—these pieces, when stuck to the same canvas, constitute government behavior relevant to an issue.

The concept of national security policy as political outcome contradicts both public imagery and academic orthodoxy. Issues vital to national security, it is said, are too important to be settled by political games. They must be "above" politics. To accuse someone of "playing politics with national security" is a most serious charge. What public convention demands, the academic penchant for intellectual elegance reinforces. Internal politics is messy; moreover, according to prevailing doctrine, politicking lacks intellectual content. As such, it constitutes gossip for journalists rather than a subject for serious investigation. Occasional memoirs, anecdotes in historical accounts, and several detailed case studies to the contrary, most of the literature of foreign policy avoids bureaucratic politics. The gap between academic literature and the experience of participants in government is nowhere wider than at this point.

Bureaucratic Politics Paradigm

. . . Individuals become players in the national security policy game by occupying a critical position in an administration. For example, in the U.S. government the players include "Chiefs": the President, Secretaries of State, Defense, and Treasury, Director of the CIA, Joint Chiefs of Staff, and, since 1961, the Special Assistant for National Security Affairs; "Staffers": the immediate staff of each Chief; "Indians": the political appointees and permanent government officials within each of the departments and agencies; and *"Ad Hoc* Players": actors in the wider government game (especially "Congressional Influentials"), members of the press, spokesmen for important interest groups (especially the "bipartisan foreign policy establishment" in and out of Congress), and surrogates for each of these groups. Other members of the Congress, press, interest groups, and public form concentric circles around the central arena—circles which demarcate the permissive limits within which the game is played.

Positions define what players both may and must do. The advantages and handicaps with which each player can enter and play in various games stems from his position. So does a cluster of obligations for the performance of certain tasks. The two sides of this coin are illustrated by the position of the modern Secretary of State. First, in form and usually in fact, he is the primary repository of political judgment on the political-military issues that are the stuff of contemporary foreign policy; consequently, he is a senior personal advisor to the President. Second, he is the colleague of the President's other senior advisers on the problems of foreign policy, the Secretaries of Defense and Treasury, and the Special Assistant for National Security Affairs. Third, he is the ranking U.S. diplomat for serious negotiation. Fourth, he serves as an Administration voice to Congress, the country, and the world. Finally, he is "Mr. State Department" or "Mr. Foreign Office," "leader of officials, spokesman for their causes, guardian of their interests, judge of their disputes, superintendent of their work, master of their careers." But he is not first one, and then the other. All of these obligations are his simultaneously. His performance in one affects his credit and power in the others. The perspective stemming from the daily work which he must oversee—the cable traffic by which his department maintains relations with other foreign offices—conflicts with the President's requirement that he serve as a generalist and coordinator of contrasting perspectives. The necessity that he be close to the President restricts the extent to which, and the force with which, he can front for his department. When he defers to the Secretary of Defense rather than fighting for his department's position—as he often must—he strains the loyalty of his officialdom. The Secretary's resolution of these conflicts depends not only upon the position, but also upon the player who occupies the position.

For players are also people. Men's metabolisms differ. The core of the bureaucratic politics mix is personality. How each man manages to stand the heat in his kitchen, each player's basic operating style, and the complementarity or contradiction among personalities and styles in the inner circles are irreducible pieces of the policy blend. Moreover, each person comes to his position with baggage in tow, including sensitivities to certain issues, commitments to various programs, and personal standing and debts with groups in the society. . . .

. . . "Solutions" to strategic problems are not derived by detached analysts focusing coolly on *the* problem. Instead, deadlines and events raise issues in games, and demand decisions of busy players in contexts that influence the face the issue wears. The problems for the players are both narrower and broader than *the* strategic problem. For each player focuses not on the total strategic problem but rather on the decision that must be made now. But each decision has critical consequences not only for the strategic problem but for each player's organizational, reputational, and personal stakes. Thus the gap between the problems the player was solving and the problem upon which the analyst focuses is often very wide.

. . . Bargaining games do not proceed randomly. Action-channels, i.e., regularized ways of producing action concerning types of issues, structure the game by pre-selecting the major players, determining their points of entrance into the game, and distributing particular advantages and disadvantages for each game. Most critically, channels determine "who's got the action," that is, which department's Indians actually do whatever is chosen. Weapon procurement decisions are made within the annual budgeting process; embassies' demands for action cables are answered according to routines of consultation and clearance from State to Defense and White House; requests for instructions from military groups (concerning assistance all the time, concerning operations during war) are composed by the military in consultation with the Office of the Secretary of Defense, State, and White House; crisis responses are debated among White House, State, Defense, CIA, and Ad Hoc players; major political speeches, especially by the President but also by other Chiefs, are cleared through established channels.

. . . Government decisions are made and government actions emerge neither as the calculated choice of a unified group, nor as a formal summary of leaders' preferences. Rather the context of shared power but separate judgments concerning important choices, determines that politics is the mechanism of choice. Note the *environment* in which the game is played: inordinate uncertainty about what must be done, the necessity that something be done, and crucial consequences of whatever is done. These features force responsible men to become active players. The *pace of the game*—hundreds of issues, numerous games, and multiple channels—compels players to fight to "get others' attention," to make them "see the facts," to assure that they "take the time to think seriously about the broader issue." The *structure of the game*— power shared by individuals with separate responsibilities—validates each player's feeling that "others don't see my problem," and "others must be persuaded to look at the issue from a less parochial perspective." The *rules of the game*—he who hesitates loses his chance to play at that point, and he who is uncertain about his recommendation is overpowered by others who are sure—pressures players to come down on one side of a 51-49 issue and play. The *rewards of the game*—effectiveness, i.e., impact on outcomes, as the immediate measure of performance—encourages hard play. Thus, most players come to fight to "make the government do what is right." The strategies and tactics employed are quite similar to those formalized by theorists of international relations.

. . . Important government decisions or actions emerge as collages composed of individual acts, outcomes of minor and major games, and foul-ups. Outcomes which could never have been chosen by an actor and would never have emerged from bargaining in a single game over the issue are fabricated piece by piece. Understanding of the outcome requires that it be disaggregated.

. . . If a nation performed an action, that action was the *outcome* of bargaining among individuals and groups within the government. That outcome included *results* achieved by groups committed to a decision or action, *resultants* which emerged from bargaining among groups with quite different positions and *foul-ups*. Model III's explanatory power is achieved by revealing the pulling and hauling of various players, with different perceptions and priorities, focusing on separate problems, which yielded the outcomes that constitute the action in question.

General Propositions

1. Action and Intention. Action does not presuppose intention. The sum of behavior of representatives of a government relevant to an issue was rarely intended by any individual or group. Rather separate individuals with different intentions contributed pieces which compose an outcome distinct from what anyone would have chosen.

2. Where you stand depends on where you sit. Horizontally, the diverse demands upon each player shape his priorities, perceptions, and issues. For large classes of issues, e.g., budgets and procurement decisions, the stance of a particular player can be predicted with high reliability from information concerning his seat. In the notorious B-36 controversy, no one was surprised by Admiral Radford's testimony that "the B-36 under any theory of war, is a bad gamble with national security," as opposed to Air Force Secretary Symington's claim that "a B-36 with an A-bomb can destroy distant objectives which might require ground armies years to take."

3. Chiefs and Indians. The aphorism "where you stand depends on where you sit" has vertical as well as horizontal application. Vertically, the demands upon the President, Chiefs, Staffers, and Indians are quite distinct.

The foreign policy issues with which the President can deal are limited primarily by his crowded schedule: the necessity of dealing first with what comes next. His problem is to probe the special face worn by issues that come to his attention, to preserve his leeway until time has clarified the uncertainties, and to assess the relevant risks.

Foreign policy Chiefs deal most often with the hottest issue *de jour,* though they can get the attention of the President and other members of the government for other issues which they judge important. What they cannot guarantee is that "the President will pay the price" or that "the others will get on board." They must build a coalition of the relevant powers that be. They must "give the President confidence" in the right course of action.

Most problems are framed, alternatives specified, and proposals pushed, however, by Indians. Indians fight with Indians of other departments; for example, struggles between International Security Affairs of the Department of Defense and Political-Military of the State Department are a microcosm of the action at higher levels. But the Indian's major problem is how to get the *attention* of Chiefs, how to get an issue decided, how to get the government "to do what is right."

In policy making then, the issue looking *down* is options: how to preserve my leeway until time clarifies uncertainties. The issue looking *sideways* is commitment: how to get others committed to my coalition. The issue looking *upwards* is confidence; how to give the boss confidence in doing what must be done. To paraphrase one of [Richard E.] Neustadt's assertions which can be applied down the length of the ladder, the essence of a responsible official's task is to induce others to see that what needs to be done is what their own appraisal of their own responsibilities requires them to do in their own interests.

Specific Propositions

. . . The probability of nuclear attack depends primarily on the probability of attack emerging as an outcome of the bureaucratic politics of the attacking government. First, which players can decide to launch an attack? Whether the effective power over action is controlled by an individual, a minor game, or the central game is critical. Second, though Model I's confidence in nuclear deterrence stems from an assertion that, in the end, governments will not commit suicide, Model III recalls historical precedents. Admiral Yamamoto, who designed the Japanese attack on Pearl Harbor, estimated accurately: "In the first six months to a year of war against the U.S. and England I will run wild, and I will show you an uninterrupted succession of victories; I must also tell you that, should the war be prolonged for two or three years, I have no confidence in our ultimate victory." But Japan attacked. Thus, three questions might be considered. One: Could any member of the government solve his problem by attack? What patterns of bargaining could yield attack as an outcome? The major difference between a stable balance of terror and a questionable balance may simply be that in the first case most members of the government appreciate fully the consequences of attack and are thus on guard against the emergence of this outcome. Two: what stream of outcomes might lead to an attack? At what point in that stream is the potential attacker's politics? If members of the U.S. government had been sensitive to the stream of decisions from which the Japanese attack on Pearl Harbor emerged, they would have been aware of a considerable probability of that attack. Three: how might miscalculation and confusion generate foul-ups that yield attack as an outcome? For example, in a crisis or after the beginning of conventional war, what happens to the information available to, and the effective power of members of the central game.

The U.S. Blockade of Cuba: A Third Cut

The Politics of Discovery. A series of overlapping bargaining games determined both the *date* of the discovery of the Soviet missiles and the *impact* of this discovery on the Administration. An explanation of the politics of the discovery is consequently a considerable piece of the explanation of the U.S. blockade.

Cuba was the Kennedy Administration's "political Achilles' heel." The months preceding the crisis were also months before the Congressional elections, and the Republican Senatorial and Congressional Campaign Committee had announced that Cuba would be "the dominant issue of the 1962 campaign." What the administration billed as a "more positive and indirect approach of isolating Castro from developing, democratic Latin America," Senators Keating, Goldwater, Capehart, Thurmond, and others attacked as a "do-nothing" policy. In statements on the floor of the House and Senate, campaign speeches across the country, and interviews and articles carried by national news media, Cuba—particularly the Soviet program of increased arms aid—served as a stick for stirring the domestic political scene.

These attacks drew blood. Prudence demanded a vigorous reaction. The President decided to meet the issue head-on. The Administration mounted a forceful campaign of denial designed to discredit critics' claims. The President himself manned the front line of this offensive, though almost all Administration officials participated. In his news conference on August 19, President Kennedy attacked as "irresponsible" calls for an invasion of Cuba, stressing rather "the totality of our obligations" and promising to "watch what happens in Cuba with the closest attention." On September 4, he issued a strong statement denying any provocative Soviet action in Cuba. On September 13 he lashed out at "loose talk" calling for an invasion of Cuba. The day before the flight of the U-2 which discovered the missiles, he campaigned in Capehart's Indiana against those "self-appointed generals and admirals who want to send someone else's sons to war."

On Sunday, October 14, just as a U-2 was taking the first pictures of Soviet missiles, McGeorge Bundy was asserting:

> *I know* that there is no present evidence, and I think that there is no present likelihood that the Cuban government and the Soviet government would, in combination, attempt to install a major offensive capability.

In this campaign to puncture the critics' charges, the Administration discovered that the public needed positive slogans. Thus, Kennedy fell into a tenuous semantic distinction between "offensive" and "defensive" weapons. This distinction originated in his September 4 statement that there was no evidence of "offensive ground to ground missiles" and warned "were it to be otherwise, the gravest issues would arise." His September 13 statement turned on this distinction between "defensive" and "offensive" weapons and announced a firm commitment to action if the Soviet Union attempted to introduce the latter into Cuba. Congressional committees elicited from administration officials testimony which read this distinction and the President's commitment into the *Congressional Record.*

What the President wanted to hear, the CIA was most hesitant to say plainly. On August 22 John McCone met privately with the President and voiced suspicions that the Soviets were preparing to introduce offensive missiles into Cuba. Kennedy heard this as what it was: the suspicion of a hawk. McCone left Washington for a month's honeymoon on the Riviera. Fretting at Cap Ferrat, he bombarded his deputy, General Marshall

Carter, with telegrams, but Carter, knowing that McCone had informed the President of his suspicions and received a cold reception, was reluctant to distribute these telegrams outside the CIA. On September 9 a U-2 "on loan" to the Chinese Nationalists was downed over mainland China. The Committee on Overhead Reconnaissance (COMOR) convened on September 10 with a sense of urgency. Loss of another U-2 might incite world opinion to demand cancellation of U-2 flights. The President's campaign against those who asserted that the Soviets were acting provocatively in Cuba had begun. To risk downing a U-2 over Cuba was to risk chopping off the limb on which the President was sitting. That meeting decided to shy away from the western end of Cuba (where SAMs were becoming operational) and modify the flight pattern of the U-2s in order to reduce the probability that a U-2 would be lost. USIB's unanimous approval of the September estimate reflects similar sensitivities. On September 13 the President had asserted that there were no Soviet offensive missiles in Cuba and committed his Administration to act if offensive missiles were discovered. Before Congressional committees, Administration officials were denying that there was any evidence whatever of offensive missiles in Cuba. The implications of a National Intelligence estimate which concluded that the Soviets were introducing offensive missiles into Cuba were not lost on the men who constituted America's highest intelligence assembly.

The October 4 COMOR decision to direct a flight over the western end of Cuba in effect "overturned" the September estimate, but without officially raising that issue. The decision represented McCone's victory for which he had lobbied with the President before the September 10 decision, in telegrams before the September 19 estimate, and in person after his return to Washington. Though the politics of the intelligence community is closely guarded, several pieces of the story can be told. By September 27, Colonel Wright and others in DIA [Defense Intelligence Agency] believed that the Soviet Union was placing missiles in the San Cristobal area. This area was marked suspicious by the CIA on September 29 and certified top priority on October 3. By October 4 McCone had the evidence required to raise the issue officially. The members of COMOR heard McCone's argument, but were reluctant to make the hard decision he demanded. The significant probability that a U-2 would be downed made overflight of western Cuba a matter of real concern.

The Politics of Issues. The U-2 photographs presented incontrovertible evidence of Soviet offensive missiles in Cuba. This revelation fell upon politicized players in a complex context. As one high official recalled, Khrushchev had caught us "with our pants down." What each of the central participants saw, and what each did to cover both his own and the Administration's nakedness, created the spectrum of issues and answers.

At approximately 9:00 A.M., Tuesday morning, October 16, McGeorge Bundy went to the President's living quarters with the message: "Mr. President, there is now hard photographic evidence that the Russians have offensive missiles in Cuba." Much has been made of Kennedy's "expression of surprise," but "surprise" fails to capture the character of his initial reaction. Rather, it was one of startled anger, most adequately covered by the exclamation, "He can't do that to *me!*" In terms of the President's attention and priorities at that moment, Khrushchev had chosen the most unhelpful act of all. Kennedy had staked his full Presidential authority on the assertion that the Soviets would not place offensive weapons in Cuba. Moreover, Khrushchev had assured the President through the most direct and personal channels that he was aware of the President's domestic political problem and that nothing would be done to exacerbate this problem. The Chairman had *lied* to the President. Kennedy's initial reaction entailed action. The missiles must be removed. The alternatives of "doing nothing" or "taking a diplomatic approach" could not have been less relevant to *his* problem.

These two tracks—doing nothing and taking a diplomatic approach— were the solutions advocated by two of his principal advisors. For Secretary of Defense McNamara, the missiles raised the spectre of nuclear war. He first framed the issue as a straightforward strategic problem. To understand the issue, one had to grasp two obvious but difficult points. First, the missiles represented an inevitable occurrence: narrowing of the missile gap. It simply happened sooner rather than later. Second, the United States could accept this occurrence since its consequences were minor: "seven-to-one missile 'superiority,' one-to-one missile 'equality,' one-to-seven missile 'inferiority'—the three postures are identical."McNamara's statement of this argument at the first meeting of the ExCom was summed up in the phrase, "a missile is a missile." "It makes no great difference," he maintained, "whether you are killed by a missile from the Soviet Union or Cuba." The implication was clear. The United States should not initiate a crisis with the Soviet Union, risking a significant probability of nuclear war over an occurrence which had such small strategic implications.

The perceptions of McGeorge Bundy, the President's Assistant for National Security Affairs, are the most difficult of all to reconstruct. There is no question that he initially argued for a diplomatic track. But was Bundy laboring under his acknowledged burden of responsibility in Cuba I? Or was he playing the role of devil's advocate in order to make the President probe his own initial reaction and consider other options?

The President's brother, Robert Kennedy, saw most clearly the political wall against which Khrushchev had backed the President. But he, like McNamara, saw the prospect of nuclear doom. Was Khrushchev going to force the President to an insane act? At the first meeting of the ExCom, he scribbled a note, "Now I know how Tojo felt when he was planning Pearl Harbor." From the outset he searched for an alternative that would prevent the air strike.

The initial reaction of Theodore Sorensen, the President's Special Counsel and "alter ego," fell somewhere between that of the President and his brother. Like the President, Sorensen felt the poignancy of betrayal. If the President had been the architect of the policy which the missiles punctured, Sorensen was the draftsman. Khrushchev's deceitful move demanded a strong counter-move. But like Robert Kennedy, Sorensen feared lest the shock and disgrace lead to disaster.

To the Joint Chiefs of Staff the issue was clear. *Now* was the time to do the job for which they had prepared contingency plans. Cuba I had been badly done; Cuba II would not be. The missiles provided the *occasion* to deal with the issue: cleansing the Western Hemisphere of Castro's Communism. As the President recalled on the day the crisis ended, "An invasion would have been a mistake—a wrong use of our power. But the military are mad. They wanted to do this. It's lucky for us that we have McNamara over there."

McCone's perceptions flowed from his confirmed prediction. As the Cassandra of the incident, he argued forcefully that the Soviets had installed the missiles in a daring political probe which the United States must meet with force. The time for an air strike was now.

The Politics of Choice. The process by which the blockade emerged is a story of the most subtle and intricate probing, pulling, and hauling; leading, guiding, and spurring. Reconstruction of this process can only be tentative. Initially the President and most of his advisers wanted the clean, surgical air strike. On the first day of the crisis, when informing Stevenson of the missiles, the President mentioned only two alternatives: "I suppose the alternatives are to go in by air and wipe them out, or to take other steps to render them inoperable." At the end of the week a sizeable minority still favored an air strike. As Robert Kennedy recalled: "The fourteen people involved were very significant. . . . If six of them had been President of the U.S., I think that the world might have been blown up." What prevented the air strike was a fortuitous coincidence of a number of factors—the absence of any one of which might have permitted that option to prevail.

First, McNamara's vision of holocaust set him firmly against the air strike. His initial attempt to frame the issue in strategic terms struck Kennedy as particularly inappropriate. Once McNamara realized that the name of the game was a strong response, however, he and his deputy Gilpatric chose the blockade as a fallback. When the Secretary of Defense—whose department had the action, whose reputation in the Cabinet was unequaled, in whom the President demonstrated full confidence—marshalled the arguments for the blockade and refused to be moved, the blockade became a formidable alternative.

Second, Robert Kennedy—the President's closest confidant—was unwilling to see his brother become a "Tojo." His arguments against the air strike on moral grounds struck a chord in the President. Moreover, once his brother had stated these arguments so forcefully, the President could not have chosen his initially preferred course without, in effect, agreeing to become what RFK had condemned.

The President learned of the missiles on Tuesday morning. On Wednesday morning, in order to mask our discovery from the Russians, the President flew to Connecticut to keep a campaign commitment, leaving RFK as the unofficial chairman of the group. By the time the President returned on Wednesday evening, a critical third piece had been added to the picture. McNamara had presented his argument for the blockade. Robert Kennedy and Sorensen had joined McNamara. A powerful coalition of the advisers in whom the President had the greatest confidence, and with whom his style was most compatible, had emerged.

Fourth, the coalition that had formed behind the President's initial preference gave him reason to pause. *Who* supported the air strike—the Chiefs, McCone, Rusk, Nitze, and Acheson—as much as *how* they supported it, counted. Fifth, a piece of inaccurate information, which no one probed, permitted the blockade advocates to fuel (potential) uncertainties in the President's mind. When the President returned to Washington Wednesday evening, RFK and Sorensen met him at the airport. Sorensen gave the President a four-page memorandum outlining the areas of agreement and disagreement. The strongest argument was that the air strike simply could not be surgical. After a day of prodding and questioning, the Air Force had asserted that it could not guarantee the success of a surgical air strike limited to the missiles alone.

Thursday evening, the President convened the ExCom at the White House. He declared his tentative choice of the blockade and directed that preparations be made to put it into effect by Monday morning. Though he raised a question about the possibility of a surgical air strike subsequently, he seems to have accepted the experts' opinion that this was no live option. (Acceptance of this estimate suggests that he may have learned the lesson of the Bay of Pigs—"Never rely on experts"—less well than he supposed.)

But this information was incorrect. That no one probed this estimate during the first week of the crisis poses an interesting question for further investigation.

A coalition, including the President, thus emerged from the President's initial decision that something had to be done; McNamara, Robert Kennedy, and Sorensen's resistance to the air strike; incompatibility between the President and the air strike advocates; and an inaccurate piece of information.

CONCLUSION

This essay had obviously bitten off more than it has chewed. For further developments and synthesis of these arguments the reader is referred to the larger study. In spite of the limits of space, however, it would be inappropriate to stop without spelling out several implications of the argument and addressing the question of relations among the models and extensions of them to activity beyond explanation.

At a minimum, the intended implications of the argument presented here are four. First, formulation of alternative frames of reference and demonstration that different analysts, relying predominantly on different models, produce quite different explanations should encourage the analyst's selfconsciousness about the nets he employs. The effect of these "spectacles" in sensitizing him to particular aspects of what is going on—framing the puzzle in one way rather than another, encouraging him to examine the problem in terms of certain categories rather than others, directing him to particular kinds of evidence, and relieving puzzlement by one procedure rather than another— must be recognized and explored.

Second, the argument implies a position on the problem of "the state of the art." While accepting the commonplace characterization of the present condition of foreign policy analysis—personalistic, non-cumulative, and sometimes insightful—this essay rejects both the counsel of despair's justification of this condition as a consequence of the character of the enterprise, and the "new frontiersmen's" demand for *a priori* theorizing on the frontiers and *ad hoc* appropriation of "new techniques." What is required as a first step is noncasual examination of the present product: inspection of existing explanations, articulation of the conceptual models employed in producing them, formulation of the propositions relied upon, specification of the logic of the various intellectual enterprises, and reflection on the questions being asked. Though it is difficult to overemphasize the need for more systematic processing of more data, these preliminary matters of formulating questions with clarity and sensitivity to categories and assumptions so that fruitful acquisition of large quantities of data is possible are still a major hurdle in considering most important problems.

The Paradigm	Model I	Model II	Model III
	National Government [Black Box] Goals (objective function) Options Consequences Choice	National Government [Leaders; A B C D E F G] Organizations (A-G) Goals SOP's and programs	National Government [A B / z r / C y D E y / n t z / x y r F / p r] Players in positions (A-F) Goals, interests, stakes, and stands (r-z) Power Action-channels
Basic unit of analysis	Governmental action as choice	Governmental action as organizational output	Governmental action as political resultant
Organizing concepts	National actor The problem Static selection Action as rational choice Goals and objectives Options Consequences Choice	Organizational actors (constellation of which is the government) Factored problems and fractioned power Parochial priorities and perceptions Action as organizational output Goals: contraints defining acceptable performance Sequential attention to goals Standard operating procedures Programs and repertoires Organizational learning and change Central coordination and control Decisions of government leaders	Players in positions Parochial priorities and perceptions Goals and interests Stakes and stands Deadlines and faces of issues Power Action-channels Rules of the game Action as political resultant
Dominant inference pattern	Governmental action = choice with regard to objectives	Governmental action (in short run) = output largely determined by present SOPs and programs Governmental action (in longer run) = output importantly affected by organizational goals, SOPs, etc.	Governmental action = resultant of bargaining
General propositions	Substitution effect	Organizational implementation Organizational options Limited flexibility and incremental change Long-range planning Goals and tradeoffs Imperialism Options and organization Administrative feasibility Directed change	Political resultants Action and intention Problems and solutions Where you stand depends on where you sit Chiefs and indians The 51-49 principle Inter- and intra-national relations Misperception, misexpectation, miscommunication, and reticence Styles of play

Adapting to Constraints on Rational Decisionmaking

Alexander L. George

Much of foreign policymaking consists of efforts to calculate the utility of alternative courses of action.[1] Rational calculation of this kind requires (1) *information* about the situation; (2) *substantive knowledge* of cause-and-effect relationships that is relevant for assessing the expected consequences of alternative courses of action; and (3) a way of applying the *values* and interests engaged by the problem at hand in order to judge which course of action is "best" and/or least costly and which, therefore, should be chosen.

These three requirements are imperfectly met by the way in which most foreign policy issues present themselves. As a result, the policymaker must proceed under the handicap of severe constraints on the possibility of meeting these requirements of rational decisionmaking. These constraints are often referred to as the problems of a "value-complexity" and "uncertainty."

Considerable psychological stress—in the form of anxiety, fear, shame, or guilt—can be evoked in a decisionmaker who struggles to cope with these two types of constraints on his ability to work out a good solution to the policy problem that confronts him. It is a central thesis . . . that a policymaker often experiences decisional conflicts in attempting to deal with the value complexity and uncertainty imbedded in a problem and that the resulting psychological stress, depending on how the decisionmaker copes with it, can impair adaptive responses to policy issues.[2]

The policymaker can deal with the psychological stress of decision-making in either of two ways: (1) by utilizing *analytical* modes of coping with value-complexity and uncertainty or (2) by resorting to *defensive* modes of coping with the malaise they engender. This chapter discusses these different modes of coping with value-complexity and uncertainty and calls attention to their implications for the quality of information processing and appraisal. . . .

VALUE-COMPLEXITY AND UNCERTAINTY: SOME DEFINITIONS

A brief statement of what is meant by "value-complexity" and by "uncertainty" is useful at the outset. *"Value-complexity" refers to the presence of multiple, competing values and interests that are imbedded in a single issue.* When this is the case, it is difficult, if not impossible, for the decisionmaker to formulate a single yardstick that encompasses and aggregates all of the competing values and interests. Lacking a single criterion of util-

---

1. In preparing this chapter, I have drawn on my earlier discussion of some of these problems in A. L. George, "Adaptation to Stress in Political Decision Making," in George V. Coelho, David A. Hamburg, and John E. Adams, eds., *Coping and Adaptation* (New York: Basic Books, 1974).

2. A similar postulate underlies the "conflict theory" developed by Janis and Mann. The desire to avoid the stress of decisional conflicts, they emphasize, is a more general motivation than the consistency-striving postulated in early cognitive dissonance theory. Janis and Mann note, further, that neo-dissonance theory has moved in the direction of this more general motivational concept (I.L. Janis and L. Mann, *Decision Making: A Psychological Analysis of Conflict, Choice, and Commitment* [New York: Free Press, 1977], pp. 17, 420).

Reprinted from *Presidential Decisionmaking in Foreign Policy: The Effective Use of Information and Advice* by Alexander L. George, 1980 by permission of Westview Press, Boulder, Colorado. Portions of the text and some footnotes have been omitted.

ity, the decisionmaker may experience great difficulty judging which course of action is "best" on an overall basis. He is confronted instead by a value-tradeoff problem which can be extremely difficult and painful to deal with. In order to do so he may attempt to order his value priorities and decide which of the competing values and interests to pursue in the given situation at the expense of the other values and interests that are also at stake. Value tradeoff decisions of this kind are often extremely stressful for the decisionmaker. Neither the analytical nor the defensive modes of coping with value-complexity adopted by the decisionmaker may be conducive to sound policy even though they may be successful in relieving or reducing the malaise he experiences. . . .

Finally, we take note of the fact that the effect of value-complexity on decisionmaking can be considerably accentuated by what has been referred to as "value extension,"[3] i.e., the all too familiar tendency of policy issues to arouse a variety of motives and interests that are extraneous to values associated with even a very broad conception of the national interest. "Thus, foreign-policy issues and the circumstances in which they arise may arouse the policymaker's personal motives and values, his political interests, or those of the administration or political party to which he belongs. This is not surprising since the way in which a policymaker deals with a particular foreign-policy problem can indeed have important consequences for his personal well-being and political fortunes: thus, it can:

- satisfy or frustrate personal values held by the policymaker;
- provide an outlet for expressing his deep-seated motives and impulses;
- obtain approval or disapproval from those who are significant figures in his life;
- enhance or damage his self-esteem;
- advance or set back his career prospects;
- strengthen or weaken his bureaucratic resources.

At times the policymaker's personal stakes in a foreign-policy issue may lead him in the same direction as his objective conception of where the national interest lies. But often, whether he is aware of his personal motives and interests or attempts to repress such awareness, they add to the problem of value-complexity and exacerbate his value conflicts. As a result, the dilemma of choice the decisionmaker experiences can become accentuated, and the value trade-off problem he faces in trying to decide what to do may become even more difficult. Finally, the decisionmaker may be willing or unwilling, able or unable, to prevent his personal motives and interests from affecting his perception of the policy problem and his judgment in dealing with it.

"Uncertainty," as the term is used here, refers to the lack of adequate information about the situation at hand and/or the inadequacy of available general knowledge needed for assessing the expected outcomes of different courses of action. Uncertainty complicates the task of making good assessments of the problem facing the decisionmaker and the additional task of deciding how to deal with it. In the face of uncertainty the decisionmaker has difficulty in making reliable cost-benefit appraisals of the alternative courses of action under consideration. He is faced with the necessity of choosing from among the options without a firm basis for confidence in his judgment. Uncertainty of this kind adds to the stress of decision-

---

3. The concept of "value extension" is taken from the valuable discussion of constraints on rational decisionmaking in John D. Steinbruner, *The Cybernetic Theory of Decision* (Princeton, N.J.: Princeton University Press, i974), p. 145.

making. This is an important consideration to keep in mind when focusing upon emotional and psychological factors that can affect decisionmaking. Some of the ways available to individuals and organizations for coping with stress induced by uncertainty can seriously degrade the quality and effectiveness of the decisions that emerge.

Together, the presence of value-complexity and uncertainty impose severe limits on the possibility of raising policymaking to the level of rationality associated with models of "pure" rationality in decision theory.[4] Very often, both value-complexity and uncertainty are present in a problem which the policymaker is trying to decide. For purposes of analysis and presentation, however, we shall deal with them separately in this chapter.

DEALING WITH VALUE-COMPLEXITY

There are, as decision theorists have emphasized, analytical ways of dealing with value-complexity in choice situations in order to strive for as "efficient" and acceptable a solution to such problems as possible. We shall not review this technical literature here, nor attempt to judge how germane it is for different types of foreign-policy problems. Such analytical techniques may be relevant in principle but, for various reasons, difficult to apply in practice in the settings in which foreign-policy decisions are made.

Precisely because it is so difficult to employ objective analysis to deal with value-complexity, the top executive is expected by others in the policymaking group to reconcile competing values and interests by going through an "internal debate." The hope is that a subjective ordering and aggregation of the competing values by the executive will enable him to offer a satisfactory solution to what would otherwise be left to be settled entirely via conflict and bargaining among the actors within the policymaking system. To the extent that the top executive accepts and discharges this unique task of leadership, he may be able to make a decisive contribution to lessening the social-political tensions and costs associated with making policy in a highly pluralistic political system. As Dean Pruitt has noted, the executive is in a better position to deal with value conflict than a small group or an organization because his own intrapersonal tensions are "more easily resolved, since [he] can better subordinate one value to another".[5]

Internal debate and subjective aggregation of competing values and interests do not always work. The top executive may search for but be unable to find a course of action that promises to safeguard all of the multiple stakes aroused for him by that issue. Faced with this dilemma, he may attempt to deal with it strategically as, for example, by assigning higher priority to achieving some of the values and interests at stake and by utilizing available information and analytical skills as best he can for this purpose. But even a strategic approach for dealing with difficult value trade-offs may not be wholly successful and may result in the decisionmaker experiencing considerable frustration, anxiety, self-doubts, etc. To cope with the ensuing emotional stress, he may react defensively in ways that may further prejudice the possibilities for a more satisfactory response to the policy problem. In

---

4. For useful discussions of these cognitive limits on rational choice and some of their implications in the arena of political decisionmaking, *see*, for example, James G. March and Herbert A. Simon, *Organizations* (New York: Wiley, 1958); and Charles E. Lindblom, "The Science of 'Muddling Through'," *Public Administration Quarterly* 29 (Spring 1959):79–88. An incisive discussion of these issues is provided in Chapter 2, The Analytic Paradigm," in Steinbruner, *Cybernetic Theory.*

5. Dean Pruitt, *Problem Solving in the Department of State,* Monograph Series in World Affairs, no. 2 (Denver: University of Denver, 1965), p. 62; *see also* John McDonald, "How the Man at the Top Avoids Crises," *Fortune* 81 (1970): 121–22, 152–55.

sum, the decisionmaker may deal with value-complexity analytically and strategically; or he may resort to defensive psychological modes of coping with the emotional stress of being faced by difficult value trade-off problems. It is also possible that his response will include elements of both analytical-strategic and defensive modes of coping.

It is useful to distinguish three different ways in which a policymaker may attempt to deal with the malaise associated with value-complexity. First, he may *resolve* the value conflict, at least in his own mind, by devising a course of action that constitutes either a genuinely creative analytical solution to the problem or a spurious and illusory resolution of it that may also be psychologically comforting even though analytically defective. A second way is to *accept* the value conflict as unavoidable and to face up to the need to make the difficult trade-off choice as part of one's role requirements as a decisionmaker. This, too, can be psychologically comforting; but whether the decisionmaker is correct in perceiving the value conflict as unavoidable and whether he deals adequately with the trade-off is another matter. Finally, the decisionmaker may seek to *avoid* a value conflict by denying its existence or playing down its importance. This strictly defensive mode of coping may succeed in reducing or banishing psychological stress, but it may do so only at the cost of markedly impairing information processing and appraisal. Let us examine these three models of dealing with value-complexity more closely.

Value-Conflict Resolution

This way of dealing with value-complexity takes the form of attempting to satisfy, to some extent at least, all of the competing values and interests of which one is aware. This is usually a formidable task, if not an impossible one. But, if the policymaker is successful in doing so, the rewards are considerable; not only does he achieve a high-quality decision, he derives inner psychological satisfaction from doing so and may also expect political benefits from satisfying many different constituencies. Particularly in a democracy or in a pluralistic policymaking system the executive is under strong temptation and indeed often under strong political pressure to try to reconcile conflicting values imbedded in an issue he must decide. In these circumstances, the inventive executive may indeed come up with a creative, novel option that genuinely resolves the apparent value conflict, demonstrating thereby that the values in question were really congruent. More often, the best that can be done is the lesser, but still significant achievement of reconciling the value conflict through some kind of compromise. The weaker solution of value compromise may result in a policy that sacrifices the quality of the decision for greater acceptability.

The resolution of value conflict may be attained in one of two ways: (1) by inventing a single policy that yields some satisfaction for each of the multiple interests and values at stake; or (2) by staging or scheduling satisfaction for these values/ interests via a series of separate actions or policies over a longer period of time. In the latter case, the policymaker realizes that the value trade-off problem cannot be avoided entirely. His initial action is designed to promote only some of the competing values/interests; he may try to promote the remaining values/interests damaged or neglected by his initial policy by additional actions shortly thereafter. This type of "scheduling" may prove to be beneficial or damaging to foreign policy objectives, depending on circumstances and the perspicacity of the policymaker. Inept "scheduling," of course, may produce a policy that is incoherent and inconsistent.

We have to recognize that, however effective in relieving the policymaker's psychological stress, efforts to resolve value conflicts may in fact be unrealistic, spurious, and illusory. Some value conflicts simply cannot be resolved. Efforts to do so may actually impede the search for effective policies, resulting in highly questionable compromises of all or most of the values imbedded in the issue. A decisionmaker who impulsively or rigidly strives to resolve or reconcile value conflicts shirks thereby his responsibility to determine value priorities and to make reasoned trade-off choices. Thus, while value-conflict resolution, is the best strategy when it is possible and skillfully done, it is often not feasible, and other strategies for dealing with the problem posed by conflicting values are then preferable.

Value-Conflict Acceptance

In this way of dealing with a complex mix of values the decisionmaker faces up to the fact that a difficult choice among them must be made. It is important, however, that he should not determine value priorities prematurely; rather, he should maintain unimpaired receptivity to information that illuminates the full range of values imbedded in the issue. Only then should he proceed to make a reasoned, conscientious determination of value priorities in order to resolve the trade-off problem that confronts him.

To do so requires the policymaker to accept the fact that he has to put aside or give lesser weight to some salient values and interests in order to advance those judged to be of greater importance or, at least, those with the greatest chance of being realized in the situation at hand. Ideally, he does so without engaging in a fruitless effort to achieve a genuine, full resolution of the value conflict or resorting to defensive psychological mechanisms of denying or minimizing the conflict. . . .

By identifying with the role of executive and viewing oneself as being a role player, the individual may find it possible to make difficult decisions with greater detachment and also with greater sensitivity to priorities among competing interests and values. At the same time, being a good role player may enable the individual to experience less stress and less personal damage when he is obliged to make a decision that sacrifices some interests. For then he may see these losses as an unavoidable consequence of fulfilling his role requirements, which oblige him to make the best possible decision that focuses on the most important of the various stakes at issue. Finally, by fulfilling difficult role requirements of this kind, as Truman did, the individual may in fact derive personal satisfaction—if not also the respect and praise of others—that bolsters and protects his self-esteem.

But, as with the first mode of dealing with the analytical difficulty and psychological stress of value-complexity which has already been discussed, this second mode, too, may be performed ineptly so far as its impact on foreign policy is concerned. Critical in this respect is whether the decisionmaker is correct in perceiving a value conflict as being unavoidable. As a matter of fact, he may arrive at this conclusion prematurely without adequate information or analysis of the policy problem. Being a good role player, insofar as concerns fulfilling the requirement to make difficult decisions when necessary, does not guarantee good judgment. . . .

Value-Conflict Avoidance

To avoid or minimize the psychological malaise created for him by perception of important value conflicts an individual may resort to the tactics of ignoring or playing down some of the competing values and interests that are imbedded in the decisional problem. Defensive maneuvers of this kind have received considerable attention in psychological studies of decisional stress. A variety of psychological devices are available to any individual for reducing his perception of a value conflict that would otherwise create severe stress. These mechanisms are described in various psychological theories of balance, consistency, dissonance, and conflict. The two which seem of greatest importance here are "cognitive restructuring" and "devaluation."

In the first of these, cognitive restructuring, the individual finds a way of turning aside incoming information that calls attention to or heightens a value conflict. Thus, he may ignore, discount, deny, forget, or unintentionally misinterpret information about some of the competing values. In "devaluation," on the other hand, the individual downgrades one of the values or interests that he or others close to him hold. Doing so minimizes the value conflict he would otherwise experience and makes it more manageable, psychologically and analytically. Devaluation may lead the individual to reduce or abandon his identification with significant others who are going to be damaged as a result of his ignoring their interests or values. The decisionmaker may cut out of his consultations those holding the devalued values, or refuse to credit the information they put before him, or even denigrate them before others.

Avoiding value conflicts in these two ways is more likely to impede information processing than other mechanisms that may also be utilized for the same purpose.[6]

Thus, cognitive restructuring and devaluation are likely to distort the decisionmaker's perception of the full range of values imbedded in the issue and hamper appraisal of options that best deal with the multiplicity of values and interests at stake.

Cognitive restructuring exemplifies a more general tendency displayed by individuals and organizations to see what they expect to see and to assimilate incoming information to preexisting images, beliefs, hypotheses, and theories. . . .

Choices are indeed easier when there is no need to consider value trade-offs. Avoidance of value complexity is particularly likely. . . when a decisionmaker initially considers only one or two of the values involved in the problem at hand and comes to favor a particular policy for dealing with it because it seems appropriate for safeguarding or enhancing those particular values. Later, when he becomes aware that other important values and interests are also imbedded in the problem, he may proceed to bolster his premature adherence to a favored policy option by finding questionable or ill-considered arguments for believing that the same action will also somehow safeguard, or at least not seriously damage, the other values and interests. As a result, the process of information "search" and "appraisal" is inhibited and cut short before the decisionmaker has examined the range of values at stake more fully and weighed the evidence of a conflict among them more carefully.

Psychological avoidance of hard choices may be detected also in instances when foreign-policymakers fail to recognize that the set of goals they are pursuing are in fact likely to be inconsistent with one another. Thus, for example, as World War II drew to an end American policymakers were disposed to agree that the Soviet Union's security requirements made it necessary for her to have friendly regimes on its borders in Eastern Europe; but, at the same time, American leaders also strongly embraced the idea of free elections in Eastern Europe. President Roosevelt appears to have avoided a clear recognition of the likely incompatibility of these two goals—and hence a dilemma for U.S. policy—by embracing the optimistic but highly questionable expectation, which he stated at the Yalta

6. For example, after having made a decision that ignores or gives insufficient weight to some values, the policymaker may attempt to convince those damaged by his action that it was the right or necessary thing to do, or to demonstrate that he is a worthwhile person who is still identified with their interests and welfare, or to resort to acts of expiation or asceticism in order to relieve the self-disapproval or guilt that he experiences as a result of having acted contrary to their interests and values (*see* Janis and Mann, *Decision Making,* pp. 144–47).

Conference, that free elections in Eastern Europe would result in governments "thoroughly friendly to the Soviet [Union] for years to come." Roosevelt's unwillingness to contemplate that Eastern European governments formed via free elections might be hostile to the Soviet Union made it possible for U.S. foreign policy to embrace what were in fact mutually incompatible objectives, thus laying the groundwork for further exacerbation of Soviet-American relations later on.[7]

As this case illustrates, the failure of policymakers to perceive an admittedly difficult value trade-off spawns unrealistic policies that can prove damaging to the realization of either of the conflicting objectives. It is well to recognize that excessive consistency-striving is often abetted, as in the case just cited, by the *political* constraints under which policymakers operate. To face up to the necessity for choice can sometimes entail severe political costs, whichever way the value trade-offs resolved. Perception of value conflicts can be blurred, moreover, when—as is often the case when policymakers attempt to assess the "national interest"—the values in question are vague or ill-defined. Perception of value trade-offs can be muted also when the impact of the policy chosen upon the values in question will not be felt immediately and when the longer-term consequences of the policy cannot be reliably predicted.

DEALING WITH UNCERTAINTY

When the information and knowledge needed for making an important decision are inadequate, this, too, can create emotional stress for the executive.[8] Thus, in a pioneering essay on political decisionmaking many years ago, three political scientists called attention to the need to look for the "devices" employed by decisionmakers to minimize "the psychological tensions which accompany decisionmaking under circumstances of uncertainty and lack of complete information." Continuing, they asked: "How do decisionmakers learn to live with the possibility of 'unacceptable error'? And what effects do the devices used to cope with uncertainty have on their deliberations?"[9] We shall list and discuss briefly a number of well-known ways in which individuals deal with uncertainty in making decisions. Some of these devices serve to minimize psychological tension for the decisionmaker without necessarily helping him to deal effectively with the situation.

Calculated Procrastination

It is understandable that in the face of stress induced by uncertainty executives often find it difficult to act. Indeed, some leaders go so far as to conclude that the best strategy of

7. This example is taken from Jervis, *Perception and Misperception* (Princeton: Princeton University Press,1977) p.140. Of course, we cannot be certain of the psychological explanation advanced here for Roosevelt's policy. It is possible that Roosevelt was well aware that the Eastern European governments might prove to be hostile to the USSR but accepted that possibility as a calculated risk.

8. A particularly vivid example of the stress produced for an executive by his inability to cope with decisional complexity is provided by President Warren G. Harding. On one occasion, Harding unburdened himself to a friend: "John, I can't make a damn thing out of this tax problem. I listen to one side and they seem right, and then God! I talk to the other side and they seem just as right, and there I am where I started. I know somewhere there is a book that would give me the truth, but hell, I couldn't read the book. I know somewhere there is an economist who knows the truth, but I don't know where to find him and haven't the sense to know him and trust him when I did find him. God, what a job!" (Quoted by Richard Fenno, *The President's Cabinet* [Cambridge, Mass: Harvard University Press, 1959], pp. 40–41).

9. R.C. Snyder, H.W. Bruck, and B. Sapin, *Foreign Policy Decisionmaking* (New York: Free Press, 1962), p. 167.

leadership is to do as little as possible, hoping that the problems that seem to require their attention will go away or find some other solution.

Of the many executives in political life or in other sectors of society who have adopted this philosophy as a strategy for dealing with decisional uncertainty, it will suffice to take note of Calvin Coolidge's well-known principle of "calculated inactivity." As one political scientist has put it, Coolidge's strategy in the presidency "was to 'sit down and keep still' in the face of problems rather than to confront them, to remain silent until an issue is reduced to its lowest terms, until it boils down to something like a moral issue. 'If you see ten troubles coming down the road, you can be sure that nine will run down into the ditch before they reach you and you have to battle with only one.'"[10]

The philosophy of "calculated procrastination" may be surprisingly effective under some circumstances, but it carries with it the risk that the executive will be confronted by acute crises more often than would otherwise have been the case had he taken action on a timely basis to deal with emerging problems.

Defensive Procrastination

While some executives adopt the general *strategy* of "calculated procrastination" to deal with uncertainty in a variety of situations, many more executives will resort to the *tactic* of procrastination only on occasion.[11] It is useful in this connection to distinguish between "rational (or calculated) procrastination" and "defensive procrastination." When the relative merits of alternative courses of action for dealing with a particular problem are clouded by uncertainty, it may be quite rational to postpone making a decision if (a) there is no time pressure to do so, or (b) there is reason to hope that more information and a better appraisal of the problem and of the options may be available later on; or (c) there is reason to believe that the situation itself may improve.

"Defensive procrastination" occurs, on the other hand, when a person seizes upon the fact that there is no immediate necessity for a decision to escape from the decisional conflict that the uncertainty has created by putting the problem out of his mind and turning his attention to other matters. (Delegating the problem to an assistant or to a committee, in effect for "burial," can facilitate defensive procrastination.) A person who engages in "defensive procrastination" displays lack of interest in the issue thereafter, with the consequence that he foregoes further information search, appraisal, and contingency planning. In contrast, the person who engages in "rational procrastination" sees to it that active search, appraisal, and contingency planning continue.

In brief, whereas the defensive procrastinator "leaves the field" in order to escape the unpleasantness of uncertainty, the rational procrastinator *uses* the time the lack of a deadline offers, taking steps to reduce the uncertainty that plagues the decision he will have to make.

Examples of both kinds of procrastination can be found in the conduct of foreign policy. In the management of conflict relations with other states, decisionmaking is often geared to externally imposed time pressure, by deadlines implicit in rapidly developing situations or deliberately created by other actors in the international arena. Viewed from this standpoint, international crises may have a necessary and useful catalytic function in forcing foreign-

---

10. Fenno, *President's Cabinet,* pp. 40–41.

11. The discussion of "defensive procrastination" here and the "discussion of hypervigilance," "defensive avoidance," and "bolstering" draw in part on the work of Irving L. Janis. *See* particularly Janis and Mann, *Decision Making.*

policymakers to come to grips with and to decide difficult issues on which they would rather procrastinate. A similar function may be performed, of course, by a variety of other events—for example, congressional budget hearings, summit meetings, press conferences, etc. . . .

Dealing with Uncertainty Under Time Pressure

We have noted that in the face of uncertainty imbedded in complex issues executives often find it difficult to act. How *does* a leader overcome such inhibitions? There are, after all, many situations in which the policymaker has to decide what to do even when the relative merits of alternative options are by no means clear and when he perceives serious risks in any course of action. Self-imposed deadlines and time pressures facilitate choice in such situations, but they do not by themselves make it easier for the decisionmaker to cope with the malaise of having to make an important decision in a matter that is laden with uncertainty.[12] What, we may ask, does forced choice under these circumstances do to the quality of search and appraisal?

Social psychologists who have studied decisionmaking under circumstances of this kind have noted two different ways in which information processing and appraisal can be impaired. One type of impairment results from "hypervigilance"; the other from "defensive avoidance." The first refers to a panic like state of mind that is accompanied by a marked loss of cognitive efficiency. The second refers to psychological devices used to escape from current worrying about a decision by not exposing oneself to cues that evoke awareness of a decisional conflict or dilemma that is fraught with potential losses. While hypervigilance is relatively rare, defensive avoidance is a highly pervasive tendency that is encountered in many different types of decisions, whether in business, family affairs, or in politics.[13]

We have already discussed one type of defensive avoidance, namely, "defensive procrastination." Another manifestation of defensive avoidance is what is sometimes called "bolstering," a phenomenon that occupies a prominent role in the theory of cognitive dissonance and in related social psychological theories.[14]

"Bolstering"

"Bolstering" refers to the psychological tendency under certain conditions of decisional stress to increase the attractiveness of a preferred (or chosen) option and doing the opposite for options which one is inclined to reject (or has rejected). Thus, the expected gains from the preferred alternative are magnified and its expected costs/risks are minimized. Similarly, the expected gains from rejected alternatives are downgraded; their expected costs/risks are magnified.

It is important to note that bolstering makes the decisionmaker's task of choosing what to do easier; it reduces the malaise of making a decision that is clouded by uncer-

---

12. The importance of deadlines and the functions they serve has been stressed in the work of a number of specialists on organizational decisionmaking. For a summary of research findings, *see* Lennart A. Arvedson, *Deadlines and Organizational Behavior* (Ph.D. diss., Stanford University, July 1974).

13. As Janis notes (in a personal communication), defensive avoidance is probably rare when different persons at different levels of an organization work independently on a policy problem, insofar as this increases the likelihood that flimsy rationalizations entertained by any one person or group will be ehallenged by others. The absence of such conditions, on the other hand, is likely to increase the incidence of defensive avoidance. For a fuller discussion, *see* Janis and Mann, *Decision Making.*

14. Janis and Mann also discuss a third type of defensive avoidance—the familiar practice of "buck-passing" *(Decision Making,* pp. 58, 312–14).

tainty. [15] It does so by *"spreading the alternatives,"* i.e., making one option seem more attractive than the alternative options. Thus, bolstering is accompanied by *distorted information-processing and appraisal.*

Bolstering can occur before a decision is made as well as, perhaps more often, afterwards. [16] Predecisional bolstering occurs when the decisionmaker believes that a firm deadline for decision is approaching and when he believes that he will not obtain additional relevant information of much consequence. He will then move towards closure by selecting what he regards as the least objectionable alternative and then consolidate his choice by reinterpreting the uncertainties to make it appear more attractive than it has seemed to be earlier.

It should be noted that the decisionmaker's belief that there is little time left to make the decision and his belief that no additional useful information can be expected may both be in error. In order to cut short the stress and malaise of decisional dilemma he may rush his decision, thereby foregoing the possibility of using the remaining time to obtain still additional information and advice. In other words, anxiety and stress may push the decisionmaker towards premature closure, cutting off search and appraisal in the interest of resolving his decisional dilemma via bolstering. Supportive bolstering by sycophantic (or equally troubled) subordinates can aggravate this danger.[17]

It has to be recognized, of course, that bolstering can be of positive value to the decisionmaker if it is preceded by search and appraisal that is as thorough as circumstances permit. Then a last-minute bolstering—one that does not cut short search and appraisal—can help the decisionmaker to avoid suffering gnawing self-doubts that can further drain his time and energy. Of course, if carried too far in this respect, last-minute bolstering may render the decisionmaker less capable of monitoring the consequences of his decision and less inclined to reconsider his policy on the basis of evidence that is not working.

A variety of rationalizations and other psychological devices may be utilized by the decisionmaker who resorts to bolstering in order to achieve the comforting feeling that the action he is taking is likely to lead to a successful outcome. An *incomplete* list includes the following:

1. He may convert the genuine uncertainty that exists as to the likelihood of different outcomes into spuriously calculated risks to which he assigns probabilities.
2. He may distort the estimate of the probability of future events, exaggerating the likelihood that his action will lead to a favorable outcome and minimizing the likelihood of an unfavorable outcome.
3. He may exaggerate in his own mind possibilities open to him for reversing his decision, should it turn out badly, or for limiting or correcting whatever undesirable effects it may have.
4. He may reevaluate some of the negative consequences his decision may entail by attributing certain long-range benefits to them.

---

15. Bolstering also occurs when the decisionmaker resorts to consistency-striving devices to avoid value trade-off problems; the present discussion focuses on its use in dealing with uncertainty, as defined here.

16. This is still something of a controversial issue among social psychologists, with some of those associated with cognitive dissonance theory holding that bolstering or dissonance reduction occurs only *after* a decision is made. However, Janis and Mann present evidence that under certain conditions bolstering occurs *before* a decision is made.

17. I am indebted for the last point to Lincoln Bloomfield (personal communication).

5. He may engage in wishful thinking as to the likelihood that the risks of his policy will materialize, if at all, only in the long-run whereas its benefits will emerge more quickly.
6. He may attempt to convince himself that if his policy fails, its failure will at least not be highly and widely visible or that he will not in any case be held personally responsible for its failure.
7. He may believe that even if his policy fails in the end, it will have done enough good to have been worthwhile.[18]

The Use of Aids to Decision and Simple Decision Rules

In addition to "bolstering," which *provides psychological* assistance for enabling the policymaker to come to a decision, there are a variety of *cognitive aids* that enable him to cope with the intellectual problem of deciding what to do in the face of uncertainty.[19]

Most individuals have learned to diagnose new situations even when the available information is ambiguous or incomplete. And most individuals have also acquired ways of choosing among alternative courses of action even when limitations of knowledge and information exclude the possibility of assessing the expected outcomes by applying a comprehensive, rigorous, analytic model. Let us review quickly some of the major decision rules and strategies employed to cope with decisional uncertainty.

The Use of a "Satisficing" Rather than an "Optimizing" Decision Rule. Because the search for a course of action that will yield the highest possible payoff is often impractical, most people settle for a course of action that is "good enough," one that offers a sufficient rather than a maximum payoff.[20] Not only does the use of "satisficing" as a decision rule fit the severe limitations of man's capacity to process information—and, only to a lesser extent, that of organizations as well—it is also an appropriate way of adjusting to the fact that to apply an "optimizing" decision rule requires enormous quantities of information and analytical resources such as are often simply not available or could be obtained only at great cost.

A distinction needs to be made between the most limited application of the "satisficing" criterion, in which the decisionmaker selects the first option coming to his attention that offers some degree of improvement over the present state of affairs, and "satisficing" after a more persistent search for an option that does better than the others that have been considered.

The Strategy of "Incrementalism." Incrementalism converts the "satisficing" decision rule for dealing with uncertainty for any single decision problem into a strategy covering a whole sequence of decisions aimed at improving the present state of affairs gradually by

---

18. This seventh type of rationalization is suggested by Jervis, *Perception and Misperception, p.* 135. who gives as an example the argument of the type made by McGeorge Bundy in February 1965 for the bombing of North Vietnam.

19. The following discussion draws upon and elaborates the ideas presented earlier in George, "Adaptation to Stress."

20. This simple (and widely used) distinction between seeking a satisfactory (i.e., sufficient and good enough) as against an optimal outcome was made by Herbert A. Simon, "A Behavioral Model of Rational Choice," *Ouarterly Journal of Economics* 69 (February 1955). *See also* James G. March and Herbert A. Simon, *Organizations* (New York: Wiley, 1958), pp.140–41; and Richard M. Cyert and James G. March, *A Behavioral Theory of the Firm* (Englewood Cliffs, N.J.: Prentice-Hall, 1964).

means of small steps.[21] The incremental approach recommends itself to leaders when they find it difficult to obtain agreement on longer-range objectives and when the knowledge and information needed to devise more comprehensive plans to achieve them is in any case lacking. Under these circumstances, a decisionmaker employing the incremental strategy will consider a narrow range of policy alternatives that differ only slightly from existing policies and aim at securing marginal rather than dramatic improvements. The strategy relies on feedback as part of a "remedial," "serial," "exploratory" attack on the problem at issue—hence, the description of incrementalist strategy as "the art of muddling through."

While the incrementalist approach may recommend itself to the policymaker as a way of hedging against uncertainty and as a conservative strategy that avoids the risks of seeking more far-reaching changes, it nonetheless entails risks of its own that are not always recognized. The marginal improvements sought may be proven illusory or grossly insufficient. Incrementalism may degenerate into a costly series of trial-and-error actions that fail to secure a cumulative improvement in the situation. Reliance upon incrementalism may encourage policies that attack symptoms and offer marginal relief rather than deal with root causes. There is, in brief, no guarantee that the decisionmaker will somehow muddle through successfully. And, by focusing on securing marginal improvements in the near future, the policymaker may fail to see opportunities for larger gains by means of strategies geared to longer-range objectives. Further, particularly in foreign policy but also in domestic policy, incrementalism can be dangerously myopic insofar as the actions taken to achieve short-term gains, as in U.S. policy in Vietnam, may turn out to be steps on a slippery slope to highly unfavorable outcomes. . . .

The Strategy of Sequential Decisionmaking. This strategy attempts to bring incremental decisionmaking into a framework of sophisticated policy planning, thereby giving policymakers an opportunity to avoid or minimize the worst consequences of sloppy, myopic incrementalism.[22] It does so in two ways: (I) by breaking up a big policy decision into a series of smaller-step decisions over time and (2) by attempting to deal with different uncertainties at optimal points in the sequence of interrelated decisions.

In developing an appropriate decision strategy for dealing with a complex policy problem, it is important for the policymaker to determine what has to be decided now and what can be left for decision later. Making the component decisions seriatim in this way often enables the policymaker to develop options that did not exist at the outset and to obtain better inputs from his analysts and experts for some aspects of the evolving policy later on.

This strategy attempts to turn to account the fact that the informational and analytical requirements differ for different parts of an evolving policy. By breaking up a big decision into smaller component decisions, the strategy uses the available time to improve the qual-

---

21. Charles E. Lindblom is perhaps the foremost expositor and exponent of incremental decisionmaking. *See* "The Science of 'Muddling Through'," which appeared originally in *Public Administration Review* 29 (1959):79–88 and has been widely reprinted. For a fuller development of his views, in which he doubted that incrementalism was an appropriate strategy in foreign policy, *see* C.E. Lindblom and D. Braybrooke, *A Strategy of Decision* (New York: Free Press, 1963), and C.E. Lindblom, *The Policy-making Process* (Englewood Cliffs, N.J.: Prentice-Hall, 1968). For an important reformulation of incrementalism, *see* Steinbruner, *Cybernetic Paradigm,* Chapter 3.

22. This section draws upon A.L. George, "Problem-oriented Forecasting," in Nazli Choucri and Thomas W. Robinson, eds., *Forecasting in International Relations* (San Francisco: W. H . Freeman & Co., 1978), pp. 329–36.

ity of some of the analytical inputs needed for later component decisions. For the policymaker to deal intelligently with uncertainties imbedded in the problem, it is useful, as systems analysts have emphasized, to distinguish among the various types of uncertainty. In addition to statistical uncertainty, there are technological and economic uncertainties as well as uncertainties with regard to human behavior and future environments. Stratagems for dealing with one type of uncertainty are not appropriate for coping with other types of uncertainty.[23]

One should not ignore the possible risks and costs of attempting to create a variety of options and to retain as much policy flexibility as possible. The policymaker who employs this decision strategy may find that the options he has created for planning purposes often create or attract support from influential actors in the policymaking system and the public, thereby achieving a momentum that may force the policymaker's hand.[24] But while the practice of "flexible options" may have been oversold or misapplied on occasion in the past, the strategy of sequential decisionmaking with which it is associated nonetheless constitutes a more sophisticated variant of the strategy of incrementalism in that it attempts to find a way of coping with and avoiding the worst consequences of "muddling through."

"Consensus Politics." The policymaker may decide what to do on the basis of what enough people want and will support rather than attempt to master the cognitive complexity of the problem by means of analysis. In the search for an effective decision there is often a potential trade-off between the substantive "quality" of a decision and its "acceptability" to those whose support the decisionmaker feels he would like to have or, indeed, must have. When the search for a "quality" option is handicapped by the difficulty of calculating expected outcomes, the policymaker may fall back on the decision rule of "consensus." In effect, then, the decisionmaker bypasses the thorny trade-off dilemma between "quality" and "acceptability" by making the criterion of "acceptability" a substitute for that of "quality."

Use of Historical Analogies. Many thoughtful observers have remarked about the universal human tendency to force the present into constructs of the past. Thus, "history does not repeat itself in the real world but it does repeat itself in the 'reality world' of the mind. . . ."[25]

Our purpose here is not to call attention once more to the lessons of an earlier historical case or of misapplying the correct lessons of that case to a new situation which differs from it in important respects. Rather, attention is drawn to the fact that policymakers often cope with the difficulty of comprehending and dealing with new situations by resorting to historical analogies. Thus, an earlier historical case that had made a particularly strong impression on the policymaker becomes an aid to diagnosing the present situation and for deciding what is the best or

---

23. *See,* for example, the discussion of uncertainties in Edward Quade and Wayne Boucher, eds., *Systems Analysis and Policy Planning* (New York: American Elsevier Co., 1968), pp. 39–40, 312, 355–57, 371–72, 384–85. *See also* Edward Quade, ed., *Analysis for Military Decisions* (Santa Monica: The Rand Corporation, 1964), pp. 136, 170–72, 228ff., 232, 235.

24. The emphasis of this strategy on creating options and maintaining policy flexibility encounters other criticisms as well, among them that there are often hidden costs to avoiding clear-cut and timely policy commitments. *See,* for example, Thomas L. Hughes, "Relativity in Foreign Policy," *Foreign Affairs,* July 1967.

25. Davis Bobrow, "The Chinese Communist Conflict System," *Orbis 9 (Winter* 1966):931. *See also* Jervis, *Perception and Misperception,* chapter 6.

necessary way with which to respond to it. Very often it is relatively recent history events that the statesman personally experienced earlier in his life or which he experienced vicariously through contact with significant figures in his intellectual development—that provides the models or analogies to which the decisionmaker turns most readily. Very often, too, it is the "remembered history" of his generation on which he draws. Thus, as World War II began to draw to a close and Franklin Roosevelt addressed himself to the peace that would follow, he was influenced particularly by a desire to avoid the mistakes Woodrow Wilson had made at the end of World War I. As for Harry Truman, when the Korean War unexpectedly broke out in late June of 1950, he quickly oriented himself by viewing it in terms of its presumed parallel with the events of the 1930s, when the democracies had failed to act in the face of totalitarian aggression against Manchuria, Ethiopia, and Austria, thus encouraging the totalitarian powers to go further until World War II broke out. . . .[26]

Ideology and General Principles as Guides to Action. Other sources of relatively simple decision rules for coping with decisional complexity and the uncertainties that hamper calculation of outcomes are to be found in the ideological beliefs and moral principles of the policymaker. They provide a generalized, deductive belief system which, applied to a particular situation, can help the decisionmaker to cut through its complexity to illuminate whether, when, and how he should respond to it.

Thus, for example, Cordell Hull, secretary of state under Franklin D. Roosevelt, had memorized as a youth a set of maxims from Jefferson and Gladstone. "As I faced the stupendous problems to be dealt with abroad," Hull wrote of his first month in office, "it gave me some relief and greater confidence to feel that I was strongly grounded on the fundamental propositions that should govern relations among nations. I proceeded to assemble and classify these principles, all of which the President, too, believed in strongly, and to make practical application of them at appropriate times."[27]

Hull's principles no doubt served to simplify and structure the problem of action he faced repeatedly as secretary of state. Whether they also enabled him to exercise consistently good judgment in foreign policy is another matter. Arthur Schlesinger, Jr., for one, wrote critically of the use to which Hull put his "principles": "often. . . they served as a means of avoiding problems until he could find an aspect reducible to his set of principles, or of disguising, even from himself, some of his less creditable impulses. . . . Hull's moral world was bounded, in other words, not by the facts or by original moral convictions, but by the copy-book maxims into which he absorbed both the facts and his emotions."[28]

Beliefs About Correct Strategy and Tactics. The problem of action in the face of uncertainty is eased for the decisionmaker by fundamental beliefs he holds about (a) the nature of international politics and conflict; (b) the extent to which historical developments can be shaped by intelligent or misguided action; and (c) axioms regarding correct

---

26. For a useful discussion, *see* Ernest R. May, *Lessons of the Past: The Uses and Misuses of History in American Foreign Policy* (New York: Oxford University Press, 1972), p. 161.

27. Cordell Hull, *Memoirs* (New York: Macmillan, 1948), vol. 1, p. 173.

28. Arthur Schlesinger, "The Roosevelt Era: Stimson and Hull," *The Nation* (June 5, 1948). As Schlesinger's essay indicates, historians often employ cognitive psychology to interpret the behavior of historical actors. Available historical materials contain considerable data relevant for such analysis, but they are seldom studied systematically and with a more explicit theoretical framework.

strategy and tactics for dealing with friendly and unfriendly actors in domestic and world political arenas. Most political actors have developed relatively stable views on many of these matters. These beliefs are part of the "cognitive map" which enables them to process information and engage in appraisals of alternative courses of action.

The term "operational code" has been employed in referring to beliefs of this kind held by a particular statesman or policy elite. But the term is somewhat a misnomer insofar as it implies or permits the inference that a leader's "operational code" consists of a set of recipes or rules for action that he applies mechanically in his decisionmaking. Rather, beliefs of this kind serve as a prism or filter that influences the actor's perception and diagnosis of political situations and that provides norms and standards to guide and channel his choices of action in specific situations. The function of an operational code belief system in decisionmaking, then, is to provide the actor with "diagnostic propensities" and "choice propensities." Neither his diagnosis of situations nor his choice of action for dealing with them is rigidly prescribed and determined by these beliefs. Rather, their function is to *simplify* and *channel* the task of processing information, inventing and appraising options, and choosing the action that seems best in the circumstances. Stated in another way, these beliefs serve to adapt the actor's effort to engage in optimal informational processing and in rational calculation to the complexity and uncertainty that are characteristic of so much political decisionmaking. . . .

Each of the seven cognitive aids to decisionmaking that have now been discussed can enable the policymaker to cope in some way with the intellectual problem he faces when the decision he must make is clouded with uncertainty. The substantive quality of the decision is, of course, another matter. Leaving aside a direct answer to this question, let us consider instead the implications of the policymaker's use of these cognitive aids and simple decision rules for his ability to benefit from the contribution that close advisers and the organizational information-processing system can make to his search for an effective decision.

The first thing to be noted is the danger that the executive will resort *prematurely* to one of his favored cognitive aids or simple decision rules—for example, a historical analogy or a maxim of correct strategy, a "satisficing" or a "consensus" decision rule—or *rely too heavily* on it in making his decision. The result may well be to cut himself off from the possibility of benefiting from a broader or in-depth analysis of the problem that advisers or the organizational information-processing system can provide. Cognitive aids and decision rules may be indispensable, but they carry the risk of serving as filters that screen, channel, or block the executive's receptivity to information and advice from others. The cognitive aid or decision rule an executive leans on in order to reach a decision can easily serve to define in a narrow way his informational needs in that situation. He will tend to pay less attention or give less weight to available information and advice that is not directly relevant and usable with respect to the cognitive aid or decision rule he utilizes in order to cut through the intellectual complexity and "confusion" surrounding the problem at hand. This has important implications for the design and management of advisory relationships and organizational information-processing systems.

INTERNATIONAL CRISES AS A SOURCE OF STRESS

Diplomatic confrontations and military crises can be extremely stressful for policymakers and, depending on how policymakers cope with the emotions aroused, can impair information processing and performance of the cognitive tasks associated with policymaking.[29]

Let us consider first the characteristics of crises and confrontations that can generate high levels of stress:

First, stress is generated by the fact that an international crisis typically entails *a strong threat to major values and interests* that top officials are responsible for safeguarding.

A second source of stress is present when, as is so often the case, the crisis comes as a *surprise* to policymakers—that is, with little warning. Even crises that have been anticipated to some extent can have quite a shock effect insofar as they present novel features that were not foreseen.

A third source of stress stems from the fact that crises often require *quick decisions*. Short response time is typical of many international crises, and it imposes an additional psychological burden on decisionmakers.

Finally, a fourth source of stress is the cumulative *emotional and physical fatigue* that an international crisis often imposes on top policymakers and their staffs. In a crisis, minutes seem like hours, hours like days, days like weeks. The demands on one's energies and emotions are intense; at the same time, opportunities for rest and recuperation are limited. Robert Kennedy's memoir of the Cuban missile crisis makes it clear that tensions during some days reached an almost unbearable intensity: "that kind of [crisis-induced] pressure does strange things to a human being, even to brilliant, self-confident, mature, experienced men. For some it brings out characteristics and strengths that perhaps even they never knew they had, and for others the pressure is too overwhelming.[30] Theodore Sorensen, also a participant in the policymaking group during the missile crisis, reports that he saw firsthand, "during the long days and nights of the Cuban crisis, how brutally physical and mental fatigue can numb the good sense as well as the senses of normally articulate men."[31]

What, then, can be said about the effects of crisis-induced stress on performance of policymaking tasks? Only a brief summary of laboratory and field studies will be presented here. It is true that *mild* levels of stress often facilitate and may actually improve

---

29. Pioneering research of a systematic kind on the stress-inducing effects of international crises on decisionmaking has been done by Charles F. Hermann in *Crises in Foreign Policy: A Simulation Analysis* (Indianapolis: Bobbs-Merrill, 1969) and in a later book which he edited: *International Crises: Insights from Pehavioral Research* (New York: Free Press, 1972). Important pioneering work on the effects of stress on policymakers during the events leading to World War I was undertaken by Robert North and his associates at Stanford University; the fullest account is Ole R. Holsti, *Crisis, Escalation, War* (Montreal and London: McGill-Queen's University Press, 1972).

An important synthesis of the effects of crisis-induced stress on foreign-policy decisionmaking, together with suggestions for monitoring and dealing with these effects, was presented by Margaret G. Hermann and Charles F. Hermann, "Maintaining the Quality of Decision-making in Foreign Policy Crises: A Proposal," in A. L. George et al., *Towards A More Soundly Based Foreign Policy: Making Better Use of Information, vol.* 2, Appendices, Commission on the Organization of the Government for the Conduct of Foreign Policy, June 1975 (Washington, D.C.: U.S. Government Printing Office, 1976). A broader summary of research findings of the effects of stress from a variety of sources, including crises, was presented by Ole R. Holsti and Alexander L. George, "The Effects of Stress on the Performance of Foreign Policy-makers," in Cornelius P. Cotter, ed., *Political Science Annual* vol. 6, 197S (Indianapolis: Bobbs-Merrill, 1976), pp. 255–319.

30. Robert F. Kennedy, *Thirteen Days* (New York: W.W. Norton & Co., 1969), p. 22.

31. Theodore C. Sorensen, *Decision-Making in the White House* (New York: Columbia University Press, 1964), p. 76.

performance, especially if the responses required by the situational task are relatively uncomplicated. But as stress increases to higher levels, performance worsens. This general relationship between stress and performance—often referred to as an "inverted U" curve—is well supported by research findings for a variety of tasks and conditions. At some point, every individual reaches a "threshold" or crossover point at which increased stress no longer improves performance but leads to a more or less rapid decline in performance. However, the point at which the "threshold" is reached varies for different individuals so that, fortunately, one would expect some members of a decisionmaking group to be functioning effectively even though the performance of others has sharply deteriorated. Moreover, the threshold for any given individual varies depending on the nature of the task and the setting in which he or she is experiencing the stress.

While stress affects the performance of a variety of tasks, we are interested here in its effects on the types of complex cognitive tasks associated with foreign-policy decisionmaking. The following is a brief summary of major types of effects that have been noted.

1. *Impaired attention and perception:* (a) important aspects of the crisis situation may escape scrutiny; (b) conflicting values may be overlooked; (c) the range of perceived alternatives is likely to narrow but not necessarily to the best alternatives; and (d) "search" for relevant information and options tends to be dominated by past experience, with a tendency to fall back on familiar solutions that have worked in the past whether or not they are appropriate to the present situation.
2. *Increased cognitive rigidity:* (a) impaired ability to improvise and reduced creativity; (b) reduced receptivity to information that challenges existing beliefs; (c) increased stereotypic thinking; and (d) reduced tolerance for ambiguity, which results in a tendency to cut off information search and evaluation and make decisions prematurely.
3. *Shortened and narrowed perspective:* (a) less attention to longer-range consequences of options; (b) less attention to side effects of options.
4. *Shifting the burden to the opponent:* the belief that one's own options are quite limited and that only the other side has it within its power to prevent an impending disaster.

Many other events and situations that arise in the conduct of foreign policy share some of the same characteristics of threat, surprise, and short response time associated with international crises and, hence, can have similar effects on performance. This is the case, for example, when decisionmakers must meet deadlines on important matters. It is also the case at times when decisionmakers experience role conflicts and role overload. The effects of situationally aroused stress upon performance, therefore, are not confined to international crises. The fundamental constraints of value complexity and uncertainty that are imbedded in so many foreign-policy problems are themselves capable of generating psychological stress in policymakers that can impair their judgment.

Diplomacy and Domestic Politics: The Logic of Two-level Games

Robert D. Putnam

INTRODUCTION: THE ENTANGLEMENTS OF DOMESTIC AND INTERNATIONAL POLITICS

Domestic politics and international relations are often somehow entangled, but our theories have not yet sorted out the puzzling tangle. It is fruitless to debate whether domestic politics really determine international relations, or the reverse. The answer to that question is clearly "Both, sometimes." The more interesting questions are "When?" and "How?" This article offers a theoretical approach to this issue, but I begin with a story that illustrates the puzzle.

One illuminating example of how diplomacy and domestic politics can become entangled culminated at the Bonn summit conference of 1978.[1] In the mid-1970s, a coordinated program of global reflation, led by the "locomotive" economies of the United States, Germany, and Japan, had been proposed to foster Western recovery from the first oil shock.[2] This proposal had received a powerful boost from the incoming Carter administration and was warmly supported by the weaker countries, as well as the Organization for Economic Co-operation and Development (OECD) and many private economists, who argued that it would overcome international payments imbalances and speed growth all around. On the other hand, the Germans and the Japanese protested that prudent and successful economic managers should not be asked to bail out spendthrifts. Meanwhile, Jimmy Carter's ambitious National Energy Program remained deadlocked in Congress, while Helmut Schmidt led a chorus of complaints about the Americans' uncontrolled appetite for imported oil and their apparent unconcern about the falling dollar. All sides conceded that the world economy was in serious trouble, but it was not clear which was more to blame, tight-fisted German and Japanese fiscal policies or slack-jawed U.S. energy and monetary policies.

At the Bonn summit, however, a comprehensive package deal was approved, the clearest case yet of a summit that left all participants happier than when they arrived. Helmut Schmidt agreed to additional fiscal stimulus, amounting to 1 percent of GNP, Jimmy Carter committed himself to decontrol domestic oil prices by the end of 1980, and Takeo Fukuda pledged new efforts to reach a 7 percent growth rate. Secondary elements

[1] The following account is drawn from Robert D. Putnam and C. Randall Henning, "The Bonn Summit of 1978: How Does International Economic Policy Coordination Actually Work?" *Brookings Discussion Papers in International Economics, no. 53* (Washington, D.C.: Brookings Institution, October 1986), and Robert D. Putnam and Nicholas Bayne, *Hanging Together: Cooperation and Conflict in the the Seven-Power Summits,* rev. ed. (Cambridge, Mass.: Harvard University Press, 1987), pp. 62-94.

[2] Among interdependent economies, most economists believe, policies can often be more effective if they are internationally coordinated. For relevant citations, see Putnam and Bayne, *Hanging Together,* p. 24.

ROBERT D. PUTNAM is the Peter and Isabel Malkin Professor of Public Policy at Harvard University. He has served on the staff of the National Security Council.

International Organization, Volume 42, Number 3 (Summer 1988), pp. 427-460.

in the Bonn accord included French and British acquiescence in the Tokyo Round trade negotiations; Japanese undertakings to foster import growth and restrain exports; and a generic American promise to fight inflation. All in all, the Bonn summit produced a balanced agreement of unparalleled breadth and specificity. More remarkably, virtually all parts of the package were actually implemented.

Most observers at the time welcomed the policies agreed to at Bonn, although in retrospect there has been much debate about the economic wisdom of this package deal. However, my concern here is not whether the deal was wise economically, but how it became possible politically. My research suggests, first, that the key governments at Bonn adopted policies different from those that they would have pursued in the absence of international negotiations, but second, that agreement was possible only because a powerful minority within each government actually favored on domestic grounds the policy being demanded internationally.

Within Germany, a political process catalyzed by foreign pressures was surreptitiously orchestrated by expansionists inside the Schmidt government. Contrary to the public mythology, the Bonn deal was not forced on a reluctant or "altruistic" Germany. In fact, officials in the Chancellor's Office and the Economics Ministry. as well as in the Social Democratic party and the trade unions, had argued privately in early 1978 that further stimulus was domestically desirable, particularly in view of the approaching 1980 elections. However, they had little hope of overcoming the opposition of the Finance Ministry, the Free Democratic party (part of the government coalition), and the business and banking community, especially the leadership of the Bundesbank. Publicly, Helmut Schmidt posed as reluctant to the end. Only his closest advisors suspected the truth: that the chancellor "let himself be pushed" into a policy that he privately favored, but would have found costly and perhaps impossible to enact without the summit's package deal.

Analogously, in Japan a coalition of business interests, the Ministry of Trade and Industry (MITI), the Economic Planning Agency, and some expansion-minded politicians within the Liberal Democratic Party pushed for additional domestic stimulus, using U.S. pressure as one of their prime arguments against the stubborn resistance of the Ministry of Finance (MOF). Without internal divisions in Tokyo, it is unlikely that the foreign demands would have been met, but without the external pressure, it is even more unlikely that the expansionists could have overridden the powerful MOF. "Seventy percent foreign pressure, 30 percent internal politics," was the disgruntled judgment of one MOF insider. "Fifty-fifty," guessed an official from MITI.[3]

In the American case, too, internal politicking reinforced, and was reinforced by, the international pressure. During the summit preparations American negotiators occasionally invited their foreign counterparts to put more pressure on the Americans to reduce oil imports. Key economic officials within the administration favored a tougher energy policy, but they were opposed by the president's closest political aides, even after the summit. Moreover, congressional opponents continued to stymie oil price decontrol, as they had under both Nixon and Ford. Finally, in April 1979, the president decided on gradual administrative decontrol, bringing U.S. prices up to world levels by October 1981. His domestic advisors thus won a postponement of this politically costly move until after the 1980 presidential election, but in the end, virtually every one of the pledges made at

---

3. For a comprehensive account of the Japanese story, see I. M. Destler and Hisao Mitsuyu, "Locomotives on Different Tracks: Macroeconomic Diplomacy, 1977-1979," in I. M. Destler and Hideo Sato, eds., *Coping With U.S.-Japanese Economic Conflicts* (Lexington, Mass.: Heath, 1982).

Bonn was fulfilled. Both proponents and opponents of decontrol agree that the summit commitment was at the center of the administration's heated intramural debate during the winter of 1978-79 and instrumental in the final decision.[4]

In short, the Bonn accord represented genuine international policy coordination. Significant policy changes were pledged and implemented by the key participants. Moreover—although this counterfactual claim is necessarily harder to establish—those policy changes would very probably not have been pursued (certainly not the same scale and within the same time frame) in the absence of the international agreement. Within each country, one faction supported the policy shift being demanded of its country internationally, but that faction was initially outnumbered. Thus international pressure was a necessary condition for these policy shifts. On the other hand, without domestic resonance international forces would not have sufficed to produce the accord no matter how balanced and intellectually persuasive the overall package. In the end, each leader believed that what he was doing was in his nation's interest—and probably in his own political interest, too, even though not all his aides agreed.[5] Yet without the summit accord he probably would not (or could not) have changed policies so easily. In that sense, the Bonn deal successfully meshed domestic and international pressures.

Neither a purely domestic nor a purely international analysis could account for this episode. Interpretations cast in terms either of domestic causes and international effects ("Second Image"[6]) or of international causes and domestic effects ("Second Image Reversed"[7]) would represent merely "partial equilibrium" analyses and would miss an important part of the story, namely, how the domestic politics of several countries became entangled via an international negotiation. The events of 1978 illustrate that we must aim instead for "general equilibrium" theories that account simultaneously for the interaction of domestic and international factors. This article suggests a conceptual framework for understanding how diplomacy and domestic politics interact.

DOMESTIC-INTERNATIONAL ENTANGLEMENTS: THE STATE OF THE ART

Much of the existing literature on relations between domestic and international affairs consists either of ad hoc lists of countless "domestic influences" on foreign policy or of generic observations that national and international affairs are somehow "linked."[8] James Rosenau was one of the first scholars to call attention to this area, but his elaborate taxonomy of "linkage politics" generated little cumulative research, except for a flurry of work correlating domestic and international "conflict behavior."[9]

---

4. For an excellent account of U.S. energy policy during this period, see G. John Ikenberry, "Market Solutions for Stale Problems: The International and Domestic Politics of American Oil Decontrol," *International Organization* 42 (Winter 1988).

5. It is not clear whether Jimmy Carter fully understood the domestic implications of his Bonn pledge at the time. See Putnam and Henning. The Bonn Summit," and Ikenberry, "Market Solutions for State Problems."

6. Kenneth N. Waltz, *Man, the State, and War: A Theoretical Analysis* (New York: Columbia University Press, 1959).

7. Peter Gourevitch, "The Second Image Reversed: The International Sources of Domestic Politics," *International Organization* 32 (Autumn 1978), pp. 881-911.

8. I am indebted to Stephan Haggard for enlightening discussions about domestic influences on international relations.

A second stream of relevant theorizing began with the work by Karl Deutsch and Ernst Haas on regional integration.[10] Haas, in particular, emphasized the impact of parties and interest groups on the process of European integration, and his notion of "spillover" recognized the feedback between domestic and international developments. However, the central dependent variable in this work was the hypothesized evolution of new supranational institutions, rather than specific policy developments, and when European integration stalled, so did this literature. The intellectual heirs of this tradition, such as Joseph Nye and Robert Keohane, emphasized interdependence and transnationalism, but the role of domestic factors slipped more and more out of focus, particularly as the concept of international regimes came to dominate the sub-field.[11]

The "bureaucratic politics" school of foreign policy analysis initiated another promising attack on the problem of domestic-international interaction. As Graham Allison noted, "Applied to relations between nations, the bureaucratic politics model directs attention to intra-national games, the overlap of which constitutes international relations."[12] Nevertheless, the nature of this "overlap" remained unclarified, and the theoretical contribution of this literature did not evolve much beyond the principle that bureaucratic interests matter in foreign policymaking.

More recently, the most sophisticated work on the domestic determinants of foreign policy has focused on "structural" factors, particularly "state strength." The landmark works of Peter Katzenstein and Stephen Krasner, for example, showed the importance of domestic factors in foreign economic policy. Katzenstein captured the essence of the problem: "The main purpose of all strategies of foreign economic policy is to make domestic policies compatible with the international political economy."[13] Both authors stressed the crucial point that central decision-makers ("the state") must be concerned simultaneously with domestic and international pressures.

More debatable, however, is their identification of "state strength" as the key variable of interest. Given the difficulties of measuring "state strength," this approach courts tautology,[14] and efforts to locate individual countries on this ambiguous continuum have proved problematic.[15] "State strength," if reinterpreted as merely the opposite of governmental fragmentation, is no doubt of some interest in the comparative study of foreign

9. James Rosenau. "Toward the Study of National-International Linkages," in his *Linkage Politics: Essays on the Convergence of National and International Systems* (New York: Free Press. 1969), as well as his "Theorizing Across Systems: I, Politics Revisited," in Jonathan Wilkenfeld, ed. *Conflict Behavior and Linkage Politics* (New York: David McKay, 1973), especially p. 49.

10. Karl W. Deutsch et al., *Political Community in the North Atlantic Area: International Organization in the Light of Historical Experience* (Princeton: Princeton University Press, 1957) and Ernst B. Haas, *The Uniting of Europe: Political, Social, and Economic Forces, 1950-1957* (Stanford, Calif.: Stanford University Press, 1958).

11. Robert O. Keohane and Joseph S. Nye, *Power and Interdependence* (Boston: Little, Brown, 1977). On the regime literature, including its neglect of domestic factors, see Stephan Haggard and Beth Simmons. "Theories of International Regimes," *International Organization*,41 (Summer 1987). pp. 491-517.

12. Graham T. Allison, *Essence of Decision: Explaining the Cuban Missile Crisis* (Boston: Little, Brown. 1971). p. 149.

13. Peter J. Katzenstein, ed., *Between Power and Plenty: Foreign Economic Policies of Advanced Industrial States* (Madison: University of Wisconsin Press, 1978). p. 4. See also Katzenstein, "International Relations and Domestic Structures: Foreign Economic Policies of Advanced Industrial States," *International Organization* 30 (Winter 1976), pp. 1-45; Stephen D. Krasner, "United States Commercial and Monetary Policy: Unravelling the Paradox of External Strength and Internal Weakness," in Katzenstein, *Between Power and Plenty,* pp. 51-87; and Krasner. *Defending the National Interest: Raw Materials, Investments, and U.S. Foreign Policy* (Princeton: Princeton University Press, 1978).

policy. However, Gourevitch is quite correct to complain that "the strong state–weak-state argument suggests that . . . the identity of the governing coalition does not matter. This is a very apolitical argument."[16] Moreover, because "state structures" (as conceived in this literature) vary little from issue to issue or from year to year, such explanations are ill-suited for explaining differences across issues or across time (unless "time" is measured in decades or centuries). A more adequate account of the domestic determinants of foreign policy and international relations must stress *politics:* parties, social classes, interest groups (both economic and noneconomic), legislators, and even public opinion and elections, not simply executive officials and institutional arrangements.[17]

Some work in the "state-centric" genre represents a unitary-actor model run amok. "The central proposition of this paper," notes one recent study, "is that the state derives its interests from and advocates policies consistent with the international system at all times and under all circumstances."[18] In fact, on nearly all important issues "central decision-makers" disagree about what the national interest and the international context demand. Even if we arbitrarily exclude the legislature from "the state" (as much of this literature does), it is wrong to assume that the executive is unified in its views. Certainly this was true in *none* of the states involved in the 1978 negotiations. What was "the" position of the German or Japanese state on macroeconomic policy in 1978, or of the American state on energy policy? If the term "state" is to be used to mean "central decision-makers," we should treat it as a plural noun: not "the state, it . . ." but "the state, they . . ." Central executives have a special role in mediating domestic and international pressures precisely because they are directly exposed to both spheres, not because they are united on all issues nor because they are insulated from domestic politics.

Thus, the state-centric literature is an uncertain foundation for theorizing about how domestic and international politics interact. More interesting are recent works about the impact of the international economy on domestic politics and domestic economic policy, such as those by Alt, Evans, Gourevitch, and Katzenstein.[19] These case studies, representing diverse methodological approaches, display a theoretical sophistication on the international-to-domestic causal connection far greater than is characteristic of comparable studies on the domestic-to-international half of the loop. Nevertheless, these works do not purport to account for instances of reciprocal causation, nor do they examine cases in which the domestic politics of several countries became entangled internationally.

---

14. For example, see Krasner, "United States Commercial and Money Policy," p. 55: "The central analytic characteristic that determines the ability of a state to overcome domestic resistance is its strength in relation to its own society."

15. Helen Milner, "Resisting the Protectionist Temptation: Industry and the Making of Trade Policy in France and the United States during the 1970s," *International Organization* 41 (Autumn 1987), pp. 639-65.

16. Gourevitch, "The Second Image Reversed," p. 903.

17. In their more descriptive work, "state-centric" scholars are often sensitive to the impact of social and political conflicts, such as those between industry and finance, labor and business, and export-oriented versus import-competing sectors. See Katzenstein, *Between Power and Plenty,* pp. 333-36, for example.

18. David A. Lake. "The State as Conduit: The International Sources of National Political Action," presented at the 1984 annual meeting of the American Political Science Association, p. 13.

19. James E. Alt, "Crude Politics: Oil and the Political Economy of Unemployment in Britain and Norway, 1970-1985," *British Journal of Political Science* 17 (April 1987), pp. 149-99; Peter B. Evans, *Dependent Development: The Alliance of Multinational State and Local Capital in Brazil* (Princeton: Princeton University Press, 1979); Peter Gourevitch, *Politics in Hard Times: Comparative Responses to International Economic Crises* (Ithaca, N.Y.: Cornell University Press, 1986); Peter I. Katzenstein, *Small States in World Markets: Industrial Policy in Europe* (Ithaca, N.Y.: Cornell University Press, 1985).

In short, we need to move beyond the mere observation that domestic factors influence international affairs and vice versa, and beyond simple catalogs of instances of such influence, to seek theories that integrate both spheres, accounting for the areas of entanglement between them.

TWO-LEVEL GAMES: A METAPHOR FOR DOMESTIC-INTERNATIONAL INTERACTIONS

Over two decades ago Richard E. Walton and Robert B. McKersie offered a "behavioral theory" of social negotiations that is strikingly applicable to international conflict and cooperation.[20] They pointed out, as all experienced negotiators know, that the unitary-actor assumption is often radically misleading. As Robert Strauss said of the Tokyo Round trade negotiations: "During my tenure as Special Trade Representative, I spent as much time negotiating with domestic constituents (both industry and labor) and members of the U.S. Congress as I did negotiating with our foreign trading partners."[21]

The politics of many international negotiations can usefully be conceived as a two-level game. At the national level, domestic groups pursue their interests by pressuring the government to adopt favorable policies, and politicians seek power by constructing coalitions among those groups. At the international level, national governments seek to maximize their own ability to satisfy domestic pressures, while minimizing the adverse consequences of foreign developments. Neither of the two games can be ignored by central decision-makers, so long as their countries remain interdependent, yet sovereign.

Each national political leader appears at both game boards. Across the international table sit his foreign counterparts, and at his elbows sit diplomats and other international advisors. Around the domestic table behind him sit party and parliamentary figures, spokespersons for domestic agencies, representatives of key interest groups, and the leader's own political advisors. The unusual complexity of this two-level game is that moves that are rational for a player at one board (such as raising energy prices, conceding territory, or limiting auto imports)) may be impolitic for that same player at the other board. Nevertheless, there are powerful incentives for consistency between the two games. Players (and kibitzers) will tolerate some differences in rhetoric between the two games, but in the end either energy prices rise or they don't.

The political complexities for the players in this two-level game are staggering. Any key player at the international table who is dissatisfied with the outcome may upset the game board, and conversely, any leader who fails to satisfy his fellow players at the domestic table risks being evicted from his seat. On occasion, however, clever players will spot a move on one board that will trigger realignments on other boards, enabling them to achieve otherwise unattainable objectives. This "two-table" metaphor captures the dynamics of the 1978 negotiations better than any model based on unitary national actors.

Other scholars have noted the multiple-game nature of international relations. Like Walton and McKersie, Daniel Druckman has observed that a negotiator "attempts to build

---

20. Richard E. Walton and Robert B. McKersie, *A Behavioral Theory of Labor Negotiations: An Analysis of a Social Interaction System* (New York: McGraw-Hill, 1965).

21. Robert S. Strauss, "Foreword," in Joan E. Twiggs, *The Tokyo Round of Multilateral Trade Negotiations: A Case Study in Building Domestic Support for Diplomacy* (Washington, D.C.: Georgetown University Institute for the Study of Diplomacy, 1987), p. vii. Former Secretary of Labor John Dunlop is said to have remarked that "bilateral negotiations usually require three agreements—one across the table and one on each side of the table," as cited in Howard Raiffa, *The Art and Science of Negotiation* (Cambridge, Mass.: Harvard University Press, 1982), p. 166.

a package that will be acceptable both to the other side and to his bureaucracy." However, Druckman models the domestic and international processes separately and concludes that "the interaction between the processes . . . remains a topic for investigation."[22] Robert Axelrod has proposed a "Gamma paradigm," in which the U.S. president pursues policies vis-à-vis the Soviet Union with an eye towards maximizing his popularity at home. However, this model disregards domestic cleavages, and it postulates that one of the international actors—the Soviet leadership—cares only about international gains and faces no domestic constraint while the other—the U.S. president—cares only about domestic gains, except insofar as his public evaluates the international competition.[23] Probably the most interesting empirically based theorizing about the connection between domestic and international bargaining is that of Glenn Snyder and Paul Diesing. Though working in the neo-realist tradition with its conventional assumption of unitary actors, they found that, in fully half of the crises they studied, top decision-makers were *not* unified. They concluded that prediction of international outcomes is significantly improved by understanding internal bargaining, especially with respect to minimally acceptable compromises.[24]

Metaphors are not theories, but I am comforted by Max Black's observation that "perhaps every science must start with metaphor and end with algebra; and perhaps without the metaphor there would never have been any algebra."[25] Formal analysis of any game requires well-defined rules, choices, payoffs, players, and information, and even then, many simple two person, mixed-motive games have no determinate solution. Deriving analytic solutions for two-level games will be a difficult challenge. In what follows I hope to motivate further work on that problem.

TOWARDS A THEORY OF RATIFICATION: THE IMPORTANCE OF "WIN-SETS"

Consider the following stylized scenario that might apply to any two-level game. Negotiators representing two organizations meet to reach an agreement between them, subject to the constraint that any tentative agreement must be ratified by their respective organizations. The negotiators might be heads of government representing nations, for example, or labor and management representatives, or party leaders in a multiparty coalition, or a finance minister negotiating with an IMF team, or leaders of a House-Senate conference committee, or ethnic-group leaders in a consociational democracy. For the moment, we shall presume that each side is represented by a single leader or "chief negotiator," and that this individual has no independent policy preferences, but seeks simply to achieve an agreement that will be attractive to his constituents.[26]

---

22. Daniel Druckman, "Boundary Role Conflict: Negotiation as Dual Responsiveness." in I. William Zartman, ed. *The Negotiation Progress: Theories and Applications* (Beverly Hills: Sage, 1978), pp. 100-101, 109. For a review of the social-psychological literature on bargainers as representatives, see Dean C. Pruitt, *Negotiation Behavior* (New York: Academic Press, 1981). pp. 41-43.

23. Robert Axelrod, "The Gamma Paradigm for Studying the Domestic Influence on Foreign Policy," prepared for delivery at the 1987 Annual Meeting of the International Studies Association.

24. Glenn H. Snyder and Paul Diesing, *Conflict Among Nations: Bargaining Decision Making and System Structure in International Crises* (Princeton: Princeton University Press, 1977), pp. 510-25.

25. Max Black, *Models and Metaphors* (Ithaca, N.Y.: Cornell University Press, 1962), p. 242, as cited in Duncan Snidal, "The Game Theory of International Politics," *World Politics* 38 (October 1985), p. 36n.

26. To avoid unnecessary complexity, my argument throughout is phrased in terms of a single chief negotiator, although in many cases some of his responsibilities may be delegated to aides. Later in this article I relax the assumption that the negotiator has no independent preferences.

It is convenient analytically to decompose the process into two stages:

1. bargaining between the negotiators, leading to a tentative agreement; call that Level I.
2. separate discussions within each group of constituents about whether to ratify the agreement; call that Level II.

This sequential decomposition into a negotiation phase and a ratification phase is useful for purposes of exposition, although it is not descriptively accurate. In practice, expectational effects will be quite important. There are likely to be prior consultations and bargaining at Level II to hammer out an initial position for the Level I negotiations. Conversely, the need for Level II ratification is certain to affect the Level I bargaining. In fact, expectations of rejection at Level II may abort negotiations at Level I without any formal action at Level II. For example, even though both the American and Iranian governments seem to have favored an arms-for-hostages deal, negotiations collapsed as soon as they became public and thus liable to de facto "ratification." In many negotiations, the two-level process may be iterative, as the negotiators try out possible agreements and probe their constituents' views. In more complicated cases, as we shall see later, the constituents' views may themselves evolve in the course of the negotiations. Nevertheless, the requirement that any Level I agreement must, in the end, be ratified at Level II imposes a crucial theoretical link between the two levels.

"Ratification" may entail a formal voting procedure at Level II, such as the constitutionally required two-thirds vote of the U.S. Senate for ratifying treaties, but I use the term generically to refer to any decision-process at Level II that is required to endorse or implement a Level I agreement, whether formally or informally. It is sometimes convenient to think of ratification as a parliamentary function, but that is not essential. The actors at Level II may represent bureaucratic agencies, interest groups, social classes, or even "public opinion." For example, if labor unions in a debtor country withhold necessary cooperation from an austerity program that the government has negotiated with the IMF, Level II ratification of the agreement may be said to have failed; ex ante expectations about that prospect will surely influence the Level I negotiations between the government and the IMF.

Domestic ratification of international agreements might seem peculiar to democracies. As the German Finance Minister recently observed, "The limit of expanded cooperation lies in the fact that we are democracies, and we need to secure electoral majorities at home."[27] However, ratification need not be "democratic" in any normal sense. For example, in 1930 the Meiji Constitution was interpreted as giving a special role to the Japanese military in the ratification of the London Naval Treaty;[28] and during the ratification of any agreement between Catholics and Protestants in Northern Ireland, presumably the IRA would throw its power onto the scales. We need only stipulate that, for purposes

---

27. Gerhardt Stoltenberg, *Wall Street Journal Europe*, 2 October 1986, as cited in C. Randall Henning, *Macroeconomic Diplomacy in the 1980s: Domestic Politics and International Conflict Among the United States, Japan, and Europe*, Atlantic Paper No. 65 (New York: Croom Helm, for the Atlantic Institute for International Affairs, 1987), p. 1.

28. Ito Takashi, "Conflicts and Coalition in Japan, 1930: Political Groups and the London Naval Disarmament Conference," in Sven Groennings et al., eds, *The Study of Coalition Behavior* (New York: Holt, Rinehart, & Winston, 1970); Kobayashi Tatsuo, "The London Naval Treaty, 1930," in James W. Morley, ed., *Japan Erupts: The London Naval Conference and the Manchurian Incident, 1928-1932* (New York: Columbia University Press, 1984), pp. 11-117. 1 am indebted to William Jarosz for this example.

of counting "votes" in the ratification process, different forms of political power can be reduced to some common denominator.

The only formal constraint on the ratification process is that since the identical agreement must be ratified by both sides, a preliminary Level I agreement cannot be amended at Level II without reopening the Level I negotiations. In other words, final ratification must be simply "voted" up or down; any modification to the Level I agreement counts as a rejection, unless that modification is approved by all other parties to the agreement.[29] Congresswoman Lynn Martin captured the logic of ratification when explaining her support for the 1986 tax reform bill as it emerged from the conference committee: "As worried as I am about what this bill does, I am even more worried about the current code. The choice today is not between this bill and a perfect bill; the choice is between this bill and the death of tax reform."[30]

Given this set of arrangements, we may define the "win-set" for a given Level II constituency as the set of all possible Level I agreements that would "win"—that is, gain the necessary majority among the constituents—when simply voted up or down.[31] For two quite different reasons, the contours of the Level II win-sets are very important for understanding Level I agreements.

First, **larger win-sets make Level I agreement more likely,** *ceteris paribus.*[32] By definition, any successful agreement must fall within the Level II win-sets of each of the parties to the accord. Thus, agreement is possible only if those win-sets overlap, and the larger each win-set, the more likely they are to overlap. Conversely, the smaller the win-sets, the greater the risk that the negotiations will break down. For example, during the prolonged prewar Anglo-Argentine negotiations over the Falklands/Malvinas, several tentative agreements were rejected in one capital or the other for domestic political reasons; when it became clear that the initial British and Argentine win-sets did not overlap at all, war became virtually inevitable.[33]

A brief, but important digression: The possibility of failed ratification suggests that game theoretical analyses should distinguish between *voluntary* and *involuntary defection.* Voluntary defection refers to reneging by a rational egoist in the absence of enforceable contracts—the much-analyzed problem posed, for example, in the prisoner's dilemma and other dilemmas of collective action. Involuntary defection instead reflects the behavior of an agent who is unable to deliver on a promise because of failed ratifica-

---

29. This stipulation is, in fact, characteristic of most real-world ratification procedures, such as House and Senate action on conference committee reports, although it is somewhat violated by the occasional practice of appending "reservations" to the ratification of treaties.

30. *New York Times,* 26 September 1986.

31. For the conception of win-set, see Kenneth A. Shepsle and Barry R. Weingast, "The Institutional Foundations of Committee Power," *American Political Science Review* 81 (March 1987), pp. 85-104. 1 am indebted to Professor Shepsle for much help on this topic.

32. To avoid tedium, I do not repeat the "other things being equal" proviso in each of the propositions that follow. Under some circumstances an expanded win-set might actually make practicable some outcome that could trigger a dilemma of collective action. See Vincent P. Crawford, "A Theory of Disagreement in Bargaining." *Econometrica* 50 (May 1982), pp. 607-37.

33. The Sunday Times Insight Team. *The Falklands War (*London: Sphere. 1982); Max Hastings and Simon Jenkins. *The Battle for the Falklands* (New York: Norton, 1984); Alejandro Dabat and Luis Lorenzano, *Argentina: The Malvinas and the End of Military Rule (*London: Verso, 1984). I am indebted to Louise Richardson for these citations.

tion. Even though these two types of behavior may be difficult to disentangle in some instances, the underlying logic is quite different.

The prospects for international cooperation in an anarchic, "self-help" world are often said to be poor because "unfortunately, policy makers generally have an incentive to cheat."[34] However, as Axelrod, Keohane, and others have pointed out, the temptation to defect can be dramatically reduced among players who expect to meet again.[35] If policymakers in an anarchic world were in fact constantly tempted to cheat, certain features of the 1978 story would be very anomalous. For example, even though the Bonn agreement was negotiated with exquisite care, it contained no provisions for temporal balance, sequencing, or partial conditionality that might have protected the parties from unexpected defection. Moreover, the Germans and the Japanese irretrievably enacted their parts of the bargain more than six months before the president's action on oil price decontrol and nearly two years before that decision was implemented. Once they had done so, the temptation to the president to renege should have been overpowering, but in fact virtually no one on either side of the decontrol debate within the administration dismissed the Bonn pledge as irrelevant. In short, the Bonn "promise" had political weight, because reneging would have had high political and diplomatic costs.

On the other hand, in any two-level game, the credibility of an official commitment may be low, even if the reputational costs of reneging are high, for the negotiator may be unable to guarantee ratification. The failure of Congress to ratify abolition of the "American Selling Price" as previously agreed during the Kennedy Round trade negotiations is one classic instance; another is the inability of Japanese Prime Minister Sato to deliver on a promise made to President Nixon during the "Textile Wrangle."[36] A key obstacle to Western economic coordination in 1985-87 was the Germans' fear that the Reagan administration would be politically unable to carry out any commitment it might make to cut the U.S. budget deficit, no matter how well-intentioned the president.

Unlike concerns about voluntary defection, concern about "deliver-ability" was a prominent element in the Bonn negotiations. In the post-summit press conference, President Carter stressed that "each of us has been careful not to promise more than he can deliver." A major issue throughout the negotiations was Carter's own ability to deliver on his energy commitments. The Americans worked hard to convince the others, first, that the president was under severe domestic political constraints on energy issues, which limited what he could promise, but second, that he could deliver what he was prepared to promise. The negotiators in 1978 seemed to follow this presumption about one another: "He will do what he has promised, so long as what he has promised is clear and within his power."

Involuntary defection, and the fear of it, can be just as fatal to prospects for cooperation as voluntary defection. Moreover, in some cases, it may be difficult, both for the other side and for outside analysts, to distinguish voluntary and involuntary defection, particularly since a strategic negotiator might seek to misrepresent a voluntary defection

---

34. Matthew E. Canzoneri and Jo Anna Gray, "Two Essays on Monetary Policy in an Interdependent World," International Finance Discussion Paper 219 (Board of Governors of the Federal Reserve System, February 1983).

35. Robert Axelrod, *The Evolution of Cooperation* (New York: Basic Books, 1984); Robert O. Keohane, *After Hegemony: Cooperation and Discord in the World Political Economy* (Princeton: Princeton University Press, 1984), esp. p. 116; and the special issue of *World Politics* "Cooperation Under Anarchy," Kenneth A. Oye, ed., vol. 38 (October 1985).

36. I. M. Destler, Haruhiro Fukui, and Hideo Sato, *The Textile Wrangle: Conflict in Japanese-American Relations, 1969-1971* (Ithaca, N.Y.: Cornell University Press, 1979), pp. 121-57.

as involuntary. Such behavior is itself presumably subject to some reputational constraints, although it is an important empirical question how far reputations generalize from collectivities to negotiators and vice versa. Credibility (and thus the ability to strike deals) at Level I is enhanced by a negotiator's (demonstrated) ability to "deliver" at Level II; this was a major strength of Robert Strauss in the Tokyo Round negotiations.[37]

Involuntary defection can only be understood within the framework of a two-level game. Thus, to return to the issue of win-sets, the smaller the win-sets, the greater the risk of involuntary defection, and hence the more applicable the literature about dilemmas of collective action.[38]

The second reason why win-set size is important is that **the relative size of the respective Level II win-sets will affect the distribution of the joint gains from the international bargain.** The larger the perceived win-set of a negotiator, the more he can be "pushed around" by the other Level I negotiators. Conversely, a small domestic win-set can be a bargaining advantage: "I'd like to accept your proposal, but I could never get it accepted at home." Lamenting the domestic constraints under which one must operate is (in the words of one experienced British diplomat) "the natural thing to say at the beginning of a tough negotiation."[39]

This general principle was, of course, first noted by Thomas Schelling nearly thirty years ago:

> The power of a negotiator often rests on a manifest inability to make concessions and meet demands. . . . When the United States Government negotiates with other governments . . . if the executive branch negotiates under legislative authority, with its position constrained by law, . . . then the executive branch has a firm position that is visible to its negotiating partners. . . . [Of course, strategies such as this] run the risk of establishing an immovable position that goes beyond the ability of the other to concede, and thereby provoke the likelihood of stalemate or breakdown.[40]

Writing from a strategist's point of view, Schelling stressed ways in which win-sets may be manipulated, but even when the win-set itself is beyond the negotiator's control, he may exploit its leverage. A Third World leader whose domestic position is relatively weak (Argentina's Alfonsin?) should be able to drive a better bargain with his international creditors, other things being equal, than one whose domestic standing is more solid (Mexico's de la Madrid?).[41] The difficulties of winning congressional ratification are often exploited by American negotiators. During the negotiation of the Panama Canal

---

37. Gilbert R. Winham, "Robert Strauss, the MTN, and the Control of Faction," *Journal of World Trade Law* 14 (September-October 1980), pp. 377-97, and his *International Trade and the Tokyo Round* (Princeton: Princeton University Press, 1986).

38. This discussion implicitly assumes uncertainty about the contours of the win-sets on the part of the Level I negotiators, for if the win-sets were known with certainty, the negotiators would never propose for ratification an agreement that would be rejected.

39. Geoffrey W. Harrison, in John C. Campbell, ed., *Successful Negotiation: Trieste 1954* (Princeton: Princeton University Press, 1976), p. 62.

40. Thomas C. Schelling, *The Strategy of Conflict* (Cambridge, Mass.: Harvard University Press, 1960), pp. 19-28.

41. I am grateful to Lara Putnam for this example. For supporting evidence, see Robert R. Kaufman, "Democratic and Authoritarian Responses to the Debt Issue: Argentina, Brazil, Mexico," *International Organization* 39 (Summer 1985), pp. 473-503.

Treaty, for example, "the Secretary of State warned the Panamanians several times . . . that the new treaty would have to be acceptable to at least sixty-seven senators," and "Carter, in a personal letter to Torrijos, warned that further concessions by the United States would seriously threaten chances for Senate ratification."[42] Precisely to forestall such tactics, opponents may demand that a negotiator ensure himself "negotiating room" at Level II before opening the Level I negotiations.

The "sweet-and-sour" implications of win-set size are summarized in Figure 1, representing a simple zero-sum game between X and Y. XM and YM represent the maximum outcomes for X and Y, respectively, while X1 and Y1 represent the minimal outcomes that could be ratified. At this stage any agreement in the range between X1 and Y1 could be ratified by both parties. If the win-set of Y were contracted to, say, Y2 (perhaps by requiring a larger majority for ratification), outcomes between Y1 and Y2 would no longer be feasible, and the range of feasible agreements would thus be truncated in Y's favor. However, if Y, emboldened by this success, were to reduce its win-set still further to Y3 (perhaps by requiring unanimity for ratification), the negotiators would suddenly find themselves deadlocked, for the win-sets no longer overlap at all.[43]

Figure 1. Effects of reducing win-set size

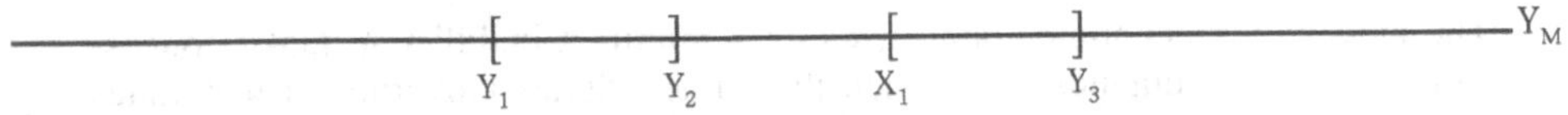

---

42. W. Mark Habeeb and I. William Zartman, *The Panama Canal Negotiations* (Washington, D.C.: John Hopkins foreign Policy Institute, 1986), pp. 40, 42.

43. Several investigators in other fields have recently proposed models of linked games akin to this "two-level" game. Kenneth A. Shepsle and his colleagues have used the notion of "interconnected games" to analyze, for example, the strategy of a legislator simultaneously embedded in two games, one in the legislative arena and the other in the electoral arena. In this model, a given action is simultaneously a move in two different games, and one player maximizes the sum of his payoffs from the two games. See Arthur Denzau, William Riker, and Kenneth Shepsle, "Farquharson and Fenno: Sophisticated Voting and Home Style," *American Political Science Review* 79 (December 1985), pp. 1117-34; and Kenneth Shepsle, "Cooperation and Institutional Arrangements," unpublished manuscript, February 1986. This approach is similar to models recently developed by economists working in the "rational expectations" genre. In these models, a government contends simultaneously against other governments and against domestic trade unions over monetary policy. See, for example, Kenneth Rogoff, "Can International Monetary Policy Cooperation be Counterproductive," *Journal of International Economics* 18 (May 1985), pp. 199-217, and Roland Vaubel, "A Public Choice Approach to International Organization," *Public Choice 51* (1986), pp. 39-57. George Tsebelis ("Nested Games: The Cohesion of French Coalitions," *British Journal of Political Science* 18 [April 1988], pp. 145-70) has developed a theory of "nested games," in which two alliances play a competitive game to determine total payoffs, while the individual players within each alliance contend over their shares. Fritz Sharpf ("A Game-Theoretical Interpretation of Inflation and Unemployment in Western Europe," *Journal of Public Policy* 7 [1988], pp. 227-257) interprets macroeconomic policy as the joint outcome of two simultaneous games; in one, the government plays against the unions, while in the other, it responds to the anticipated reactions of the electorate. James E. Alt and Barry Eichengreen ("Parallel and Overlapping Games: Theory and an Application to the European Gas Trade," unpublished manuscript, November 1987) offer a broader typology of linked games, distinguishing between "parallel" games, in which "the same opponents play against one another at the same time in more than one arena," and "overlapping" games, which arise "when a particular player is engaged at the same time in games against distinct opponents, and when the strategy pursued in one game limits the strategies available in the other." Detailed comparison of these various linked-game models is a task for the future.

DETERMINANTS OF THE WIN-SET

It is important to understand what circumstances affect win-set size. Three sets of factors are especially important:

- Level II preferences and coalitions
- Level II institutions
- Level I negotiators' strategies

Let us consider each in turn.

1. The size of the win-set depends on the distribution of power preferences and possible coalitions among Level II constituents.

Any testable two-level theory of international negotiation must be rooted in a theory of domestic politics, that is, a theory about the power and preferences of the major actors at Level II. This is not the occasion for even a cursory evaluation of the relevant alternatives, except to note that the two level conceptual framework could in principle be married lo such diverse perspectives as Marxism, interest group pluralism, bureaucratic politics, and neo-corporatism. For example, arms negotiations might be interpreted in terms of a bureaucratic politics model of Level II politicking, while class analysis or neo-corporatism might be appropriate for analyzing international macroeconomic coordination.

Abstracting from the details of Level II politics, however, it is possible to sketch certain principles that govern the size of the win-sets. For example, the lower the cost of "no-agreement" to constituents, the smaller the winset.[44] Recall that ratification pits the proposed agreement, *not* against an array of other (possibly attractive) alternatives, but only against "no-agreement."[45] No-agreement often represents the status quo, although in some cases no-agreement may in fact lead to a worsening situation; that might be a reasonable description of the failed ratification of the Versailles Treaty.

Some constituents may face low costs from agreement and others high costs, and the former will be more skeptical of Level I agreements than the latter. Members of two-wage-earner families should be readier to strike, for example, than sole breadwinners, and small-town barbers should be more isolationist than international bankers. In this sense, some constituents may offer either generic opposition to, or generic support for, Level I agreements, more or less independently of the specific content of the agreement, although naturally other constituents' decisions about ratification will be closely conditioned on the specifics. The size of the win-set (and thus the negotiating room of the Level I negotiator) depends on the relative size of the "isolationist" forces (who oppose international cooperation in general) and the "internationalists" (who offer "all-purpose" support). All-purpose support for international agreements is probably greater in smaller, more dependent countries with more open economies, as compared to more self-sufficient countries, like the United States, for most of whose citizens the costs of no-agreement are generally lower. *Ceteris paribus,* more self-sufficient states with smaller win-

---

44. Thomas Romer and Howard Rosenthal. "Political Resource Allocation, Controlled Agendas. and the Status Quo," *Public Choice* 33 (no. 4, 1978), pp. 27-44.

45. In more formal treatments, the no-agreement outcome is called the "reversion point." A given constituent's evaluation of no-agreement corresponds to what Raiffa terms a seller's "walk-away price," that is, the price below which he would prefer "no-deal." (Raiffa, *Art and Science of Negotiation.*) No-agreement is equivalent to what Snyder and Diesing term "breakdown," or the expected cost of war. (Snyder and Diesing, *Conflict Among Nations.)*

sets should make fewer international agreements and drive harder bargains in those that they do make.

In some cases, evaluation of no-agreement may be the *only* significant disagreement among the Level II constituents, because their interests are relatively homogeneous. For example, if oil imports are to be limited by an agreement among the consuming nations—the sort of accord sought at the Tokyo summit of 1979, for example—then presumably every constituent would prefer to maximize his nation's share of the available supply, although some constituents may be more reluctant than others to push too hard, for fear of losing the agreement entirely. Similarly, in most wage negotiations, the interests of constituents (either workers or shareholders) are relatively homogeneous, and the most significant cleavage within the Level II constituencies is likely to be between "hawks" and "doves," depending on their willingness to risk a strike. (Walton and McKersie refer to these as "boundary" conflicts, in which the negotiator is caught between his constituency and the external organization.) Other international examples in which domestic interests are relatively homogeneous except for the evaluation of no-agreement might include the SALT talks, the Panama Canal Treaty negotiations, and the Arab-Israeli conflict. A negotiator is unlikely to face criticism at home that a proposed agreement reduces the opponents' arms too much, offers too little compensation for foreign concessions, or contains too few security guarantees for the other side, although in each case opinions may differ on how much to risk a negotiating deadlock in order to achieve these objectives.

The distinctive nature of such "homogeneous" issues is thrown into sharp relief by contrasting them to cases in which constituents' preferences are more heterogeneous, so that any Level I agreement bears unevenly on them. Thus, an internationally coordinated reflation may encounter domestic opposition *both* from those who think it goes too far (bankers, for example) *and* from those who think it does not go far enough (unions, for example). In 1919, some Americans opposed the Versailles Treaty because it was too harsh on the defeated powers and others because it was too lenient.[46] Such patterns are even more common, as we shall shortly see, where the negotiation involves multiple issues, such as an arms agreement that involves tradeoffs between seaborne and airborne weapons, or a labor agreement that involves tradeoffs between take-home pay and pensions. (Walton and McKersie term these "factional" conflicts, because the negotiator is caught between contending factions within his own organization.)

The problems facing Level I negotiators dealing with a *homogenous* (or "boundary") conflict are quite different from those facing negotiators dealing with a *heterogeneous* (or "factional") conflict. In the former case, the more the negotiator can win at Level I—the higher his national oil allocation, the deeper the cuts in Soviet throw-weight, the lower the rent he promises for the Canal, and so on—the better his odds of winning ratification. In such cases, the negotiator may use the implicit threat from his own hawks to maximize his gains (or minimize his losses) at Level I, as Carter and Vance did in dealing with the Panamanians. Glancing over his shoulder at Level II, the negotiator's main problem in a homogeneous conflict is to manage the discrepancy between his constituents' expectations and the negotiable outcome. Neither negotiator is likely to find much sympathy for the enemy's demands among his own constituents, nor much support for his constituents' positions in the enemy camp. The effect of domestic division, embodied in hard-line opposition from hawks, is to raise the risk of involuntary defection and thus to impede

46. Thomas A. Bailey, *Woodrow Wilson and the Great Betrayal* (New York: Macmillan, 1945), pp. 16-37.

agreement at Level I. The common belief that domestic politics is inimical to international cooperation no doubt derives from such cases.

The task of a negotiator grappling instead with a heterogeneous conflict is more complicated, but potentially more interesting. Seeking to maximize the chances of ratification, he cannot follow a simple "the more, the better" rule of thumb; imposing more severe reparations on the Germans in 1919 would have gained some votes at Level II but lost others, as would hastening the decontrol of domestic oil prices in 1978. In some cases, these lines of cleavage within the Level II constituencies will cut across the Level I division, and the Level I negotiator may find silent allies at his opponent's domestic table. German labor unions might welcome foreign pressure on their own government to adopt a more expansive fiscal policy, and Italian bankers might welcome international demands for a more austere Italian monetary policy. Thus transnational alignments may emerge, tacit or explicit, in which domestic interests pressure their respective governments to adopt mutually supportive policies. This is, of course, my interpretation of the 1978 Bonn summit accord.

In such cases, domestic divisions may actually improve the prospects for international cooperation. For example, consider two different distributions of constituents' preferences as between three alternatives: A, B, and no agreement. If 45 percent of the constituents rank these A > no-agreement > B, 45 percent rank them B > no-agreement > A, and 10 percent rank them B > A > no-agreement, then both A and B are in the win-set, even though B would win in a simple Level-II-only game. On the other hand, if 90 percent rank the alternatives A > no-agreement > B, while 10 percent still rank them B > A > no-agreement, then only A is in the win-set. In this sense, a government that is internally divided is more likely to be able to strike a deal internationally than one that is firmly committed to a single policy.[47] Conversely, to impose binding ex ante instructions on the negotiators in such a case might exclude some Level I outcomes that would, in fact, be ratifiable in both nations.[48]

Thus far we have implicitly assumed that all eligible constituents will participate in the ratification process. In fact, however, participation rates vary across groups and across issues, and this variation often has implications for the size of the winset. For example, when the costs and/or benefits of a proposed agreement are relatively concentrated, it is reasonable to expect that those constituents whose interests are most affected will exert special influence on the ratification process.[49] One reason why Level II games are more important for trade negotiations than in monetary matters is that the "abstention rate" is higher on international monetary issues than on trade issues.[50]

47. Raiffa notes that "the more diffuse the positions are within each side, the easier it might be to achieve external agreement." (Raiffa, *Art and Science of Negotiation*, p. 12.) For the conventional view, by contrast, that domestic unity is generally a precondition for international agreement, see Michael Artis and Sylvia Ostry, *International Economic Policy Coordination* Chatham House Papers: 30 (London: Routledge & Kegan Paul, 1986), pp. 75-76.

48. "Meaningful consultation with other nations becomes very difficult when the internal process of decision-making already has some of the characteristics of compacts between quasi-sovereign entities. There is an increasing reluctance to hazard a hard-won domestic consensus in an international forum." Henry A. Kissinger, "Domestic Structure and Foreign Policy," in James N. Rosenau, ed., *International Politics and Foreign Policy* (New York: Free Press, 1969), p. 266.

49. See James Q. Wilson, *Political Organization* (New York: Basic Books, 1975) on how the politics of an issue are affected by whether the costs and the benefits are concentrated or diffuse.

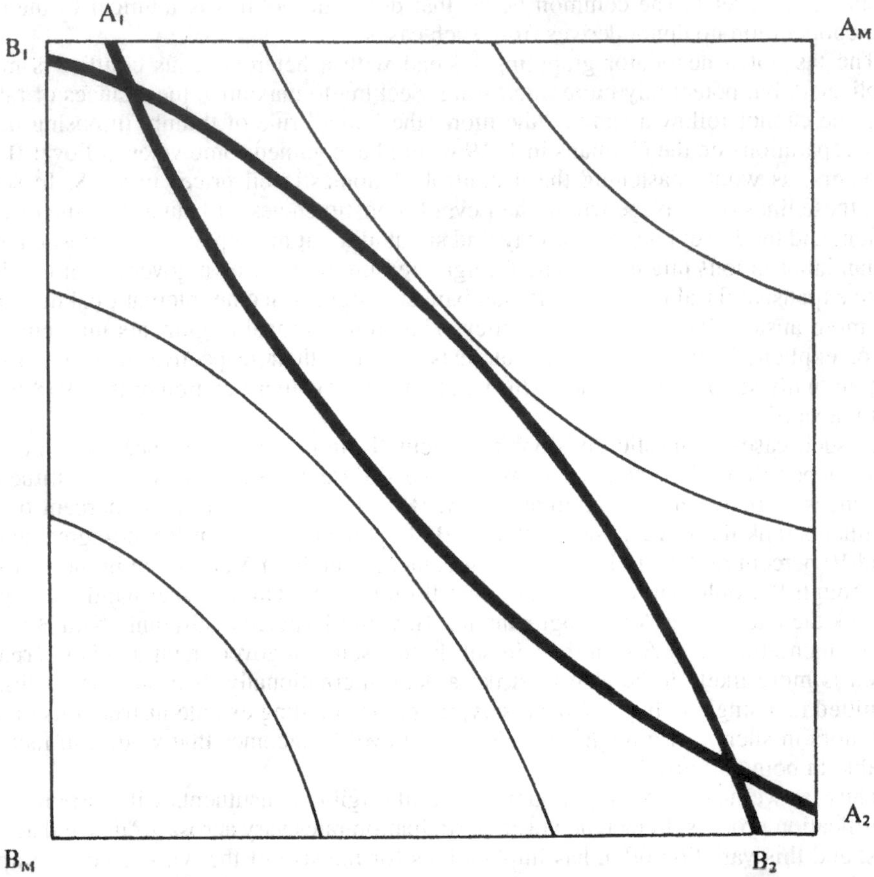

The composition of the active Level II constituency (and hence the character of the win-set) also varies with the politicization of the issue. Politicization often activates groups who are less worried about the costs of no-agreement, thus reducing the effective win-set. For example, politicization of the Panama Canal issue seems to have reduced the negotiating flexibility on both sides of the diplomatic table.[51] This is one reason why most professional diplomats emphasize the value of secrecy to successful negotiations. However, Woodrow Wilson's transcontinental tour in 1919 reflected the opposite calculation, namely, that by expanding the active constituency he could ensure ratification of the Versailles Treaty, although in the end this strategy proved fruitless.[52]

50. Another factor fostering abstention is the greater complexity and opacity of monetary issues, as Gilbert R. Winham ("Complexity in International Negotiation," in Daniel Druckman, ed., *Negotiations: A Social-Psychological Perspective* [Beverly Hills: Sage, 1977], p. 363) observes, "complexity can strengthen the hand of a negotiator vis-à-vis the organization he represents ."

51. Habeeb and Zartman, *Panama Canal Negotiations.*

52. Bailey, *Wilson and the Great Betrayal.*

Another important restriction of our discussion thus far has been the assumption that the negotiations involve only one issue. Relaxing this assumption has powerful consequences for the play at both levels.[53] Various groups at Level II are likely to have quite different preferences on the several issues involved in a multi-issue negotiation. As a general rule, the group with the greatest interest in a specific issue is also likely to hold the most extreme position on that issue. In the Law of the Sea negotiations, for example, the Defense Department felt most strongly about sea-lanes, the Department of the Interior about sea-bed mining rights, and so on.[54] If each group is allowed to fix the Level I negotiating position for "its" issue, the resulting package is almost sure to be "non-negotiable" (that is, non-ratifiable in opposing capitals).[55]

Thus, the chief negotiator is faced with tradeoffs across different issues: how much to yield on mining rights in order to get sea-lane protection, how much to yield on citrus exports to get a better deal on beef, and so on. The implication of these tradeoffs for the respective win-sets can be analyzed in terms of iso-vote or "political indifference" curves. This technique is analogous to conventional indifference curve analysis, except that the operational measure is vote loss, not utility loss. Figure 2 provides an illustrative Edgeworth box analysis.[56] The most-preferred outcome for A (the outcome which wins unanimous approval from both the beef industry and the citrus industry) is the upper right-hand corner (AM). and each curve concave to point AM represents the locus of all possible tradeoffs between the interests of ranchers and farmers, such that the net vote in favor of ratification at A's Level II is constant. The bold contour A1-A2 represents the minimal vote necessary for ratification by A, and the wedge-shaped area northeast of A1-A2 represents A's win-set. Similarly, B1B2 represents the outcomes that are minimally ratifiable by B, and the lens-shaped area between A1-A2 and B1-B2 represents the set of feasible agreements. Although additional subtleties (such as the nature of the "contract curve") might be extracted from this sort of analysis, the central point is simple: the possibility of package deals opens up a rich array of strategic alternatives for negotiators in a two-level game.

One kind of issue linkage is absolutely crucial to understanding how domestic and international politics can become entangled.[57] Suppose that a majority of constituents at Level II oppose a given policy (say, oil price decontrol), but that some members of that majority would be willing to switch their vote on that issue in return for more jobs (say, in export industries). If bargaining is limited to Level II, that tradeoff is not technically feasible, but if the chief negotiator can broker an international deal that delivers more jobs (say, via faster growth abroad), he can, in effect, overturn the initial outcome at the domestic table. Such a transnational issue linkage was a crucial element in the 1978 Bonn accord.

---

53. I am grateful to Ernst B. Haas and Robert O. Keohane for helpful advice on this point.

54. Ann L. Hollick, U.S. *Foreign Policy and the Law of the Sea* (Princeton: Princeton University Press, 1981), especially pp. 208-37, and James K. Sebenius, *Negotiating the Law of the Sea* (Cambridge, Mass.: Harvard University Press, 1984), especially pp. 74-78.

55. Raiffa, Art *and Science of Negotiation,* p. 175.

56. I am indebted to Lisa Martin and Kenneth Shepsle for suggesting this approach, although they are not responsible for my application of it. Note that this construction assumes that each issue, taken individually, is a "homogeneous" type, not a "heterogeneous" type. Constructing iso-vote curves for heterogeneous-type issues is more complicated.

57. I am grateful to Henry Brady for clarifying this point for me.

Note that this strategy works not by changing the preferences of any domestic constituents, but rather by creating a policy option (such as faster export growth) that was previously beyond domestic control. Hence, I refer to this type of issue linkage at Level I that alters the feasible outcomes at Level II as *synergistic linkage.* For example, "in the Tokyo Round . . . nations used negotiation to achieve internal reform in situations where constituency pressures would otherwise prevent action without the pressure (and tradeoff benefits) that an external partner could provide."[58] Economic interdependence multiplies the opportunities for altering domestic coalitions (and thus policy outcomes) by expanding the set of feasible alternatives in this way—in effect, creating political entanglements across national boundaries. Thus, we should expect synergistic linkage (which is, by definition, explicable only in terms of two-level analysis) to become more frequent as interdependence grows.

2. The size of the win-set depends on the Level II political institutions.

Ratification procedures clearly affect the size of the win-set. For example, if a two-thirds vote is required for ratification, the win-set will almost certainly be smaller than if only a simple majority is required. As one experienced observer has written: "Under the Constitution, thirty-four of the one hundred senators can block ratification of any treaty. This is an unhappy and unique feature of our democracy. Because of the effective veto power of a small group, many worthy agreements have been rejected, and many treaties are never considered for ratification."[59] As noted earlier, the U.S. separation of powers imposes a tighter constraint on the American win-set than is true in many other countries. This increases the bargaining power of American negotiators, but it also reduces the scope for international cooperation. It raises the odds for involuntary defection and makes potential partners warier about dealing with the Americans.

The Trade Expansion Act of 1974 modified U.S. ratification procedures in an effort to reduce the likelihood of congressional tampering with the final deal and hence to reassure America's negotiating partners. After the American Selling Price fiasco, it was widely recognized that piecemeal congressional ratification of any new agreement would inhibit international negotiation. Hence, the 1974 Act guaranteed a straight up-or-down vote in Congress. However, to satisfy congressional sensitivities, an elaborate system of private-sector committees was established to improve communication between the Level I negotiators and their Level II constituents, in effect co-opting the interest groups by exposing them directly to the implications of their demands.[60] Precisely this tactic is described in the labor-management case by Walton and McKersie: "Instead of taking responsibility for directly persuading the principals [Level II constituents] to reduce their expectations, [the Level I negotiator] structures the situation so that they (or their more immediate representatives) will persuade themselves."[61]

Not all significant ratification practices are formalized; for example, the Japanese propensity for seeking the broadest possible domestic consensus before acting constricts

58. Gilbert R. Winham, "The Relevance of Clausewitz to a Theory of International Negotiation," prepared for delivery at the 1987 annual meeting of the American Political Science Association.

59. Jimmy Carter, *Keeping Faith: Memoirs of a President* (New York: Bantam Books, 1982), p. 225.

60. Winham (see note 37); Twiggs, *The Tokyo Round.*

61. Walton and McKersie, *Behavioral Theory of Labor Organizations* p. 321.

the Japanese win-set, as contrasted with majoritarian political cultures. Other domestic political practices, too, can affect the size of the win-set. Strong discipline within the governing party, for example, increases the win-set by widening the range of agreements for which the Level I negotiator can expect to receive backing. For example, in the 1986 House-Senate conference committee on tax reform, the final bill was closer to the Senate version, despite (or rather, *because of*) Congressman Rostenkowski's greater control of his delegation, which increased the House winset. Conversely, a weakening of party discipline across the major Western nations would, *ceteris paribus*, reduce the scope for international cooperation.

The recent discussion of "state strength" and "state autonomy" is relevant here. The greater the autonomy of central decision-makers from their Level II constituents, the larger their win-set and thus the greater the likelihood of achieving international agreement. For example, central bank insulation from domestic political pressures in effect increases the win-set and thus the odds for international monetary cooperation; recent proposals for an enhanced role for central bankers in international policy coordination rest on this point.[62] However, two-level analysis also implies that, *ceteris paribus*, the stronger a state is in terms of autonomy from domestic pressures, the weaker its relative bargaining position internationally. For example, diplomats representing an entrenched dictatorship are less able than representatives of a democracy to claim credibly that domestic pressures preclude some disadvantageous deal.[63] This is yet another facet of the disconcerting ambiguity of the notion of "state strength."

For simplicity of exposition, my argument is phrased throughout in terms of only two levels. However, many institutional arrangements require several levels of ratification, thus multiplying the complexity (but perhaps also the importance) of win-set analysis. Consider, for example, negotiations between the United States and the European Community over agricultural trade. According to the Treaty of Rome, modifications of the Common Agricultural Policy require unanimous ratification by the Council of Ministers, representing each of the member states. In turn, each of those governments must, in effect, win ratification for its decision within its own national arena, and in coalition governments, that process might also require ratification within each of the parties. Similarly, on the American side, ratification would (informally, at least) necessitate support from most, if not all, of the major agricultural organizations, and within those organizations, further ratification by key interests and regions might be required. At each stage, cleavage patterns, issue linkages, ratification procedures, side-payments, negotiator strategies, and so on would need to be considered. At some point in this analytic regress the complexity of further decomposition would outweigh the advantages, but the example illustrates the need for careful thought about the logic of multiple-level games.

3. The size of the win-set depends on the strategies of the Level I negotiators.

Each Level I negotiator has an unequivocal interest in maximizing the other side's win-set, but with respect to his own win-set, his motives are mixed. The larger his win-set, the more easily he can conclude an agreement, but also the weaker his bargaining position vis-à-vis the other negotiator. This fact often poses a tactical dilemma. For

62. Artis and Ostry, *International Economic Policy Coordination.* Of course, whether this is desirable in terms of democratic values is quite another matter.

63. Schelling, *Strategy of Conflict* p. 28.

example, one effective way to demonstrate commitment to a given position in Level I bargaining is to rally support from one's constituents (for example, holding a strike vote, talking about a "missile gap," or denouncing "unfair trading practices" abroad). On the other hand, such tactics may have irreversible effects on constituents' attitudes, hampering subsequent ratification of a compromise agreement.[64] Conversely, preliminary consultations at home, aimed at "softening up" one's constituents in anticipation of a ratification struggle, can undercut a negotiator's ability to project an implacable image abroad.

Nevertheless, disregarding these dilemmas for the moment and assuming that a negotiator wishes to expand his win-set in order to encourage ratification of an agreement, he may exploit both conventional side-payments and generic "good will." The use of side-payments to attract marginal supporters is, of course, quite familiar in game theory, as well as in practical politics. For example, the Carter White House offered many inducements (such as public works projects) to help persuade wavering Senators to ratify the Panama Canal Treaty.[65] In a two-level game the side-payments may come from unrelated domestic sources, as in this case, or they may be received as part of the international negotiation.

The role of side-payments in international negotiations is well known. However, the two-level approach emphasizes that the value of an international side-payment should be calculated in terms of its marginal contribution to the likelihood of ratification, rather than in terms of its overall value to the recipient nation. What counts at Level II is not total national costs and benefits, but their *incidence relative to existing coalitions and proto-coalitions.* An across-the-board trade concession (or still worse, a concession on a product of interest to a committed free trade congressman) is less effective than a concession (even one of lesser intrinsic value) that tips the balance with a swing voter. Conversely, trade retaliation should be targeted, neither at free-traders nor at confirmed protectionists, but at the uncommitted.

An experienced negotiator familiar with the respective domestic tables should be able to maximize the cost-effectiveness (to him and his constituents) of the concessions that he must make to ensure ratification abroad, as well as the cost effectiveness of his own demands and threats, by targeting his initiatives with an eye to their Level II incidence, both at home and abroad. In this endeavor Level I negotiators are often in collusion, since each has an interest in helping the other to get the final deal ratified. In effect, they are moving jointly towards points of tangency between their respective political indifference curves. The empirical frequency of such targeting in trade negotiations and trade wars, as well as in other international negotiations, would be a crucial test of the relative merits of conventional unitary-actor analysis and the two-level approach proposed here.[66]

In addition to the use of specific side-payments, a chief negotiator whose political standing at home is high can more easily win ratification of his foreign initiatives. Although generic good will cannot guarantee ratification, as Woodrow Wilson discovered, it is useful in expanding the win-set and thus fostering Level I agreement, for it constitutes a kind of "all-purpose glue" for his supporting coalition. Walton and McKersie cite members of the United Auto Workers who, speaking of their revered leader, Walter

64. Walton and McKersie, *Behavioral Theory of Labor Organizations*, p. 345.

65. Carter, *Keeping Faith*, p. 172. See also Raiffa, *Art and Science of Negotiation*, p. 183.

Reuther, said, "I don't understand or agree with this profit-sharing idea, but if the Red Head wants it, I will go along."[67] The Yugoslav negotiator in the Trieste dispute later discounted the difficulty of persuading irredentist Slovenes to accept the agreement, since "the government [i.e., Tito] can always influence public opinion if it wants to."[68]

Note that each Level I negotiator has a strong interest in the popularity of his opposite number, since Party A's popularity increases the size of his win-set, and thus increases both the odds of success and the relative bargaining leverage of Party B. Thus, negotiators should normally be expected to try to reinforce one another's standing with their respective constituents.

Partly for this reason and partly because of media attention, participation on the world stage normally gives a head of government a special advantage vis-à-vis his or her domestic opposition. Thus, although international policy coordination is hampered by high transaction costs, heads of government may also reap what we might term "transaction benefits." Indeed, the recent evolution of Western summitry, which has placed greater emphasis on publicity than on substance, seems designed to appropriate these "transaction benefits" without actually seeking the sort of agreements that might entail transaction costs.[69]

Higher status negotiators are likely to dispose of more side-payments and more "good will" at home, and hence foreigners prefer to negotiate with a head of government than with a lower official. In purely distributive terms, a nation might have a bargaining advantage if its chief negotiator were a mere clerk. Diplomats are acting rationally, not merely symbolically, when they refuse to negotiate with a counterpart of inferior rank. America's negotiating partners have reason for concern whenever the American president is domestically weakened.

UNCERTAINTY AND BARGAINING TACTICS

Level I negotiators are often badly misinformed about Level II politics, particularly on the opposing side. In 1978, the Bonn negotiators were usually wrong in their assessments of domestic politics abroad; for example, most American officials did not appreciate the complex domestic game that Chancellor Schmidt was playing over the issue of German reflation. Similarly, Snyder and Diesing report that "decision makers in our cases

---

66. The strategic significance of targeting at Level II is illustrated in John Conybeare, "Trade Wars: A Comparative Study of Anglo-Hanse, Franco-Italian, and Hawley-Smoot Conflicts," *World Politics* 38 (October 1985), p. 157: Retaliation in the Anglo-Hanse trade wars did not have the intended deterrent *effect, because it was not (and perhaps could not have been) targeted at the crucial members* of the opposing Level II coalition. Compare Snyder and Diesing, *Conflict Among Nations,* p. 552: "If one faces a coercive opponent, but the opponent's majority coalition includes a few wavering members inclined to compromise, a compromise proposal that suits their views may cause their defection and the formation of a different majority coalition. Or if the opponent's strategy is accommodative, based on a tenuous soft-line coalition. one knows that care is required in implementing one's own coercive strategy to avoid the opposite kind of shift in the other state."

67. Walton and McKersie, *Behavioral Theory of Labor Negotiations,* p. 319.

68. Vladimir Velebit, in Campbell, *Trieste 1954,* p. 97. As noted earlier, our discussion here assumes that the Level I negotiator wishes to reach a ratifiable agreement; in cases (alluded to later) when the negotiator's own preferences are more hard-line than his constituents, his domestic popularity might allow him to resist Level I agreements.

69. Transaction benefits may be enhanced if a substantive agreement is reached, although sometimes leaders can benefit domestically by loudly rejecting a proffered international deal.

only occasionally attempted such assessments, and when they tried they did pretty miserably. . . . Governments generally do not do well in analyzing each other's internal politics in crises [and, I would add, in normal times], and indeed it is inherently difficult."[70] Relaxing the assumption of perfect information to allow for uncertainty has many implications for our understanding of two-level games. Let me illustrate a few of these implications.

Uncertainty about the size of a win-set can be both a bargaining device and a stumbling block in two-level negotiation. In purely distributive Level I bargaining, negotiators have an incentive to understate their own win-sets. Since each negotiator is likely to know more about his own Level II than his opponent does, the claim has some plausibility. This is akin to a tactic that Snyder and Diesing describe, when negotiators seek to exploit divisions within their own government by saying, in effect, "You'd better make a deal with me, because the alternative to me is even worse."[71]

On the other hand, uncertainty about the opponent's win-set increases one's concern about the risk of involuntary defection. Deals can only be struck if each negotiator is convinced that the proposed deal lies within his opposite number's winset and thus will be ratified. Uncertainty about party A's ratification lowers the expected value of the agreement to party B, and thus party B will demand more generous side-payments from party A than would be needed under conditions of certainty. In fact, party B has an incentive to feign doubt about party A's ability to deliver, precisely in order to extract a more generous offer.[72]

Thus, a utility-maximizing negotiator must seek to convince his opposite number that his own win-set is "kinky," that is, that the proposed deal is certain to be ratified, but that a deal slightly more favorable to the opponent is unlikely to be ratified. For example, on the energy issue in 1978, by sending Senator Byrd on a personal mission to Bonn before the summit and then by discussing his political problems in a lengthy tête-à-tête with the chancellor, Carter sought successfully to convince Schmidt that immediate decontrol was politically impossible, but that decontrol by 1981 was politically doable. Kinky win-sets may be more credible if they pivot on what Schelling calls a "prominent" solution, such as a 50-50 split, for such outcomes may be distinctly more "saleable" at home. Another relevant tactic is for the negotiator actually to submit a trial agreement for ratification, in order to demonstrate that it is not in his win-set.

Uncertainty about the contours of the respective "political indifference curves" thus has strategic uses. On the other hand, when the negotiators are seeking novel packages that might improve both sides' positions, misrepresentation of one's winset can be counterproductive. Creative solutions that expand the scope for joint gain and improve the odds of ratification are likely to require fairly accurate information about constituents' preferences and points of special neuralgia. The analysis of two-level games offers many illustrations of Zartman's observation that all negotiation involves "the controlled exchange of partial information."[73]

---

70. Snyder and Diesing, *Conflict Among Nations*, pp. 516, 522-23. Analogous misperceptions in Anglo-American diplomacy are the focus of Richard E. Neustadt, *Alliance Politics* (New York: Columbia University Press, 1970).

71. Synder and Diesing, *Conflict Among Nations*, p. 517.

72. I am grateful to Robert O. Keohane for pointing out the impact of uncertainty on the expected value of proposals.

RESTRUCTURING AND REVERBERATION

Formally speaking, game-theoretic analysis requires that the structure of issues and payoffs be specified in advance. In reality, however, much of what happens in any bargaining situation involves attempts by the players to restructure the game and to alter one another's perceptions of the costs of no-agreement and the benefits of proposed agreements. Such tactics are more difficult in two-level games than in conventional negotiations, because it is harder to reach constituents on the other side with persuasive messages. Nevertheless, governments do seek to expand one another's win-sets. Much ambassadorial activity—wooing opinion leaders, establishing contact with opposition parties, offering foreign aid to a friendly, but unstable government, and so on—has precisely this function. When Japanese officials visit Capitol Hill, or British diplomats lobby Irish-American leaders, they are seeking to relax domestic constraints that might otherwise prevent the administration from cooperating with their governments.

Another illuminating example of actions by a negotiator at the opposing Level II to improve the odds of ratification occurred during the 1977 negotiations between the International Monetary Fund and the Italian government. Initial IMF demands for austerity triggered strong opposition from the unions and left-wing parties. Although the IMF's bargaining position at Level I appeared strong, the Fund's negotiator sought to achieve a broader consensus within Italy in support of an agreement, in order to forestall involuntary defection. Accordingly, after direct consultations with the unions and leftist leaders, the IMF restructured its proposal to focus on long-term investment and economic recovery (incidentally, an interesting example of targeting), without backing off from its short-term demands. Ironically, the initial Communist support for this revised agreement subsequently collapsed because of conflicts between moderate and doctrinaire factions within the party, illustrating the importance of multilevel analysis.[74]

In some instances, perhaps even unintentionally. international pressures "reverberate" within domestic politics, tipping the domestic balance and thus influencing the international negotiations. Exactly this kind of reverberation characterized the 1978 summit negotiations. Dieter Hiss, the German sherpa and one of those who believed that a stimulus program was in Germany's own interest, later wrote that summits change national policy only insofar as they mobilize and/or change public opinion and the attitude of political groups. . . . Often that is enough, if the balance of opinion is shifted, providing a bare majority for the previously stymied actions of a strong minority. . . . No country vio-

---

73. I. William Zartman, *The 50% Solution* (Garden City, N.J.: Anchor Books, 1976), p. 14. The present analysis assumes that constituents are myopic about the other side's Level II, an assumption that is not unrealistic empirically. However, a fully informed constituent would consider the preferences of key players on the other side, for if the current proposal lies well within the other side's win-set, then it would be rational for the constituent to vote against it, hoping for a second-round proposal that was more favorable to him and still ratifiable abroad; this might be a reasonable interpretation of Senator Lodge's position in 1919 *(Bailey, Wilson and the Great Betrayal)*. Consideration of such strategic voting at Level II is beyond the scope of this article.

74. John R. Hillman, "The Mutual Influence of Italian Domestic Politics and the International Monetary Fund," The Fletcher Forum 4 (Winter 1980). pp. 1-22. Luigi Spaventa, "Two Letters of Intent: External Crises and Stabilization Policy, Italy, 1973-77," in John Williamson. ed., *IMF Conditionality* (Washington. D.C.: Institute for International Economics. i983), pp. 441-73, argues that the unions and the Communists actually favored the austerity measures, but found the IMF demands helpful in dealing with their own internal Level II constituents.

lates its own interests, but certainly the definition of its interests can change through a summit with its possible tradeoffs and give-and-take.[75]

From the point of view of orthodox social-choice theory, reverberation is problematic, for it implies a certain interconnectedness among the utility functions of independent actors, albeit across different levels of the game. Two rationales may be offered to explain reverberation among utility-maximizing egoists. First, in a complex, interdependent, but often unfriendly world, offending foreigners may be costly in the long run. "To get along, go along" may be a rational maxim. This rationale is likely to be more common the more dependent (or interdependent) a nation, and it is likely to be more persuasive to Level II actors who are more exposed internationally, such as multinational corporations and international banks.

A second rationale takes into account cognitive factors and uncertainty. It would be a mistake for political scientists to mimic most economists' disregard for the suasive element in negotiations.[76] Given the pervasive uncertainty that surrounds many international issues, messages from abroad can change minds, move the undecided, and hearten those in the domestic minority. As one reluctant German latecomer to the "locomotive" cause in 1978 explained his conversion, "In the end, even the Bank for International Settlements [the cautious Basle organization of central bankers] supported the idea of coordinated relation." Similarly, an enthusiastic advocate of the program welcomed the international pressure as providing a useful "tailwind" in German domestic politics.

Suasive reverberation is more likely among countries with close relations and is probably more frequent in economic than in political-military negotiations. Communiques from the Western summits are often cited by participants to domestic audiences as a way of legitimizing their policies. After one such statement by Chancellor Schmidt, one of his aides privately characterized the argument as "not intellectually valid, but politically useful." Conversely, it is widely believed by summit participants that a declaration contrary to a government's current policy could be used profitably by its opponents. Recent congressional proposals to ensure greater domestic publicity for international commentary on national economic policies (including hitherto confidential IMF recommendations) turn on the idea that reverberation might increase international cooperation.[77]

Reverberation as discussed thus far implies that international pressure expands the domestic win-set and facilitates agreement. However, reverberation can also be negative, in the sense that foreign pressure may create a domestic backlash. Negative reverberation is probably less common empirically than positive reverberation, simply because foreigners are likely to forgo public pressure if it is recognized to be counter-productive. Cognitive balance theory suggests that international pressure is more likely to reverberate negatively if its source is generally viewed by domestic audiences as an adversary rather than an ally.

---

75. Dieter Hiss, "Weltwirtschaftsgipfel: Betrachtungen eines Insiders [World Economic Summit: Observations of an Insider]," in Joachim Frohn and Reiner Staeglin, eds., *Ernpirische Wirtschaftsforschung* (Berlin: Duncker and Humblot, 1980), pp. 286-87.

76. On cognitive and communications explanations of international cooperation, see, for example, Ernst B. Haas, "Why Collaborate? Issue-Linkage and International Regimes," *World Politics* 32 (April 1980), pp 357-405; Richard N. Cooper, "International Cooperation in Public Health as a Prologue to Macroeconomic Cooperation," Brookings Discussion Papers in International Economics 44 (Washington, D.C.: Brookings Institution, 1986); and *Zartman, 50% Solution,* especially Part 4.

77. Henning, *Macroeconomic Diplomacy in the 1980s,* pp. 62-63.

Nevertheless, predicting the precise effect of foreign pressure is admittedly difficult, although empirically, reverberation seems to occur frequently in two-level games.

The phenomenon of reverberation (along with synergistic issue linkage of the sort described earlier) precludes one attractive short-cut to modeling two-level games. If national preferences were exogenous from the point of view of international relations, then the domestic political game could be molded separately, and the "outputs" from that game could be used as the "inputs" to the international game.[78] The division of labor between comparative politics and international relations could continue, though a few curious observers might wish to keep track of the play on both tables. But if international pressures reverberate within domestic politics, or if issues can be linked synergistically, then domestic outcomes are not exogenous, and the two levels cannot be modeled independently.

THE ROLE OF THE CHIEF NEGOTIATOR

In the stylized model of two-level negotiations outlined here, the chief negotiator is the only formal link between Level I and Level II. Thus far, I have assumed that the chief negotiator has no independent policy views, but acts merely as an honest broker, or rather as an agent on behalf of his constituents. That assumption powerfully simplifies the analysis of two-level games. However, as principal-agent theory reminds us, this assumption is unrealistic.[79] Empirically, the preferences of the chief negotiator may well diverge from those of his constituents. Two-level negotiations are costly and risky for the chief negotiator, and they often interfere with his other priorities, so it is reasonable to ask what is in it for him.

The motives of the chief negotiator include:

1. Enhancing his standing in the Level II game by increasing his political resources or by minimizing potential losses. For example, a head of government may seek the popularity that he expects to accrue to him if he concludes a successful international agreement, or he may anticipate that the results of the agreement (for example, faster growth or lower defense spending) will be politically rewarding.
2. Shifting the balance of power at Level II in favor of domestic policies that he prefers for exogenous reasons. International negotiations sometimes enable government leaders to do what they privately wish to do, but are powerless to do domestically. Beyond the now-familiar 1978 case, this pattern characterizes many stabilization programs that are (misleadingly) said to be "imposed" by the IMF. For example, in the 1974 and 1977 negotiations between Italy and the IMF,

78. This is the approach used to analyze the Anglo-Chinese negotiations over Hong Kong in Bruce Bueno de Mesquita, David Newman, and Alvin Rabushka, *Forecasting Political Events: The Future of Hong Kong* (New Haven: Yale University Press, 1985).

79. For overviews of this literature, see Terry M. Moe, "The New Economics of Organization," *American Journal of Political Science* 28 (November 1984), pp. 739-77; John W. Pratt and Richard J. Zeckhauser, eds., *Principals and Agents: The Structure of Business* (Boston, Mass.: Harvard Business School Press, 1985); and Barry M. Mitnick, "The Theory of Agency and Organizational Analysis," prepared for delivery at the 1986 annual meeting of the American Political Science Association. This literature is only indirectly relevant to our concerns here, for it has not yet adequately addressed the problems posed by multiple principals (or constituents, in our terms). For one highly formal approach to the problem of multiple principals, see R. Douglas Bernheim and Michael D. Whinston, "Common Agency," *Econometrica* 54 (July 1986), pp. 923-42.

domestic conservative forces exploited IMF pressure to facilitate policy moves that were otherwise infeasible internally.[80]

3. To pursue his own conception of the national interest in the international context. This seems the best explanation of Jimmy Carter's prodigious efforts on behalf of the Panama Canal Treaty, as well as of Woodrow Wilson's ultimately fatal commitment to the Versailles Treaty.

It is reasonable to presume, at least in the international case of two-level bargaining, that the chief negotiator will normally give primacy to his domestic calculus, if a choice must be made, not least because his own incumbency often depends on his standing at Level II. Hence, he is more likely to present an international agreement for ratification, the less of his own political capital he expects to have to invest to win approval, and the greater the likely political returns from a ratified agreement.

This expanded conception of the role of the chief negotiator implies that he has, in effect, a veto over possible agreements. Even if a proposed deal lies within his Level II win-set, that deal is unlikely to be struck if he opposes it.[81] Since this proviso applies on both sides of the Level I table, the actual international bargaining set may be narrower—perhaps much narrower—than the overlap between the Level II win-sets. Empirically, this additional constraint is often crucial to the outcome of two-level games. One momentous example is the fate of the Versailles Treaty. The best evidence suggests, first, that perhaps 80 percent of the American public *and* of the Senate in 1919 favored ratification of the treaty, if certain reservations were attached, and second, that those reservations were acceptable to the other key signatories, especially Britain and France. In effect, it was Wilson himself who vetoed this otherwise ratifiable package, telling the dismayed French Ambassador, "I shall consent to nothing."[82]

Yet another constraint on successful two-level negotiation derives from the leader's existing domestic coalition. Any political entrepreneur has a fixed investment in a particular pattern of policy positions and a particular supporting coalition. If a proposed international deal threatens that investment, or if ratification would require him to construct a different coalition, the chief negotiator will be reluctant to endorse it, even if (judged abstractly) it could be ratified. Politicians may be willing to risk a few of their normal supporters in the cause of ratifying an international agreement, but the greater the potential loss, the greater their reluctance.

In effect, the fixed costs of coalition-building thus imply this constraint on the win-set: How great a realignment of prevailing coalitions at Level II would be required to ratify a particular proposal? For example, a trade deal may expand export opportunities for Silicon Valley, but harm Aliquippa. This is fine for a chief negotiator (for example, Reagan?) who can easily add Northern California yuppies to his support coalition and who has no hope of winning Aliquippa steelworkers anyhow. But a different chief negotiator with a different support coalition (for example, Mondale?) might find it costly or even impossible to convert the gains from the same agreement into politically usable

80. Hillman, "Mutual Influence," and Spaventa, "Two Letters of Intent."

81. This power of the chief negotiator is analogous to what Shepsle and Weingast term the "penultimate" or "ex post veto" power of the members of a Senate House conference committee. (Shepsle and Weingast, "Institutional Foundations of Committee Power."

82. Bailey, *Wilson and the Great Betrayal.* quotation at p. 15.

form. Similarly, in the 1978 "neutron bomb" negotiations between Bonn and Washington, "asking the United States to deploy [these weapons] in West Germany might have been possible for a Christian Democratic Government: for a Social Democratic government, it was nearly impossible."[83] Under such circumstances, simple "median-voter" models of domestic influences on foreign policy may be quite misleading.

Relaxing the assumption that the chief negotiator is merely an honest broker, negotiating on behalf of his constituents, opens the possibility that the constituents may be more eager for an agreement (or more worried about "no-agreement") than he is. Empirical instances are not hard to find: in early 1987, European publics were readier to accept Gorbachev's "double-zero" arms control proposal than European leaders, just as in the early 1970s the American public (or at least the politically active public) was more eager for a negotiated end to the Vietnam War than was the Nixon administration. As a rule, the negotiator retains a veto over any proposed agreement in such cases. However, if the negotiator's own domestic standing (or indeed, his incumbency) would be threatened if he were to reject an agreement that falls within his Level II win-set, and if this is known to all parties, then the other side at Level I gains considerable leverage. Domestic U.S. discontent about the Vietnam War clearly affected the agreement reached at the Paris talks.[84] Conversely, if the constituents are (believed to be) hard-line, then a leader's domestic weakness becomes a diplomatic asset. In 1977, for example, the Americans calculated that "a delay in negotiating a treaty . . . endangered [Panamanian President Omar] Torrijos' position; and Panama without Torrijos most likely would have been an impossible negotiating partner."[85] Similarly, in the 1954 Trieste negotiations, the weak Italian government claimed that "'Unless something is done in our favor in Trieste, we can lose the election.' That card was played two or three times [reported the British negotiator later], and it almost always took a trick."[86]

My emphasis on the special responsibility of central executives is a point of affinity between the two-level game model and the "state-centric" literature, even though the underlying logic is different. In this "Janus" model of domestic-international interactions, transnational politics are less prominent than in some theories of interdependence.[87] However, to disregard "cross-table" alliances at Level II is a considerable simplification, and it is more misleading, the lower the political visibility of the issue, and the more frequent the negotiations between the governments involved.[88] Empirically, for example, two-level games in the European Community are influenced by many direct ties among Level II participants, such as national agricultural spokesmen. In some cases, the same multinational actor may actually appear at more than one Level II table. In negotiations

83. Robert A. Strong and Marshal Zeringue, "The Neutron Bomb and the Atlantic Alliance," presented at the 1986 annual meeting of the American Political Science Association, p. 9.

84. I. William Zartman, "Reality, Image, and Detail: The Paris Negotiations, 1969-1973," in Zartman, *50% Solution*. pp. 372-98.

85. Zbigniew Brzezinski, *Power and Principle* (New York: Farrar, Straus and Giroux, 1983), p. 136, as quoted in Habeeb and Zartman, *Panama Canal Negotiations*, pp. 39-40.

86. Harrison in Campbell, *Trieste 1954*, p. 67.

87. Samuel P. Huntington, "Transnational Organizations in World Politics," *World Politics* 25 (April 1973), pp. 333-68; Keohane and Nye, *Power and Interdependence;* Neustadt, *Alliance Politics*.

88. Barbara Crane, "Policy Coordination by Major Western Powers in Bargaining with the Third World: Debt Relief and the Common Fund," *International Organization* 38 (Summer 1984), pp. 399-428.

over mining concessions in some less-developed countries, for example, the same multinational corporation may be consulted privately by both the home and host governments. In subsequent work on the two-level model, the strategic implications of direct communication between Level II players should be explored.

CONCLUSION

The most portentous development in the fields of comparative politics and international relations in recent years is the dawning recognition among practitioners in each field of the need to take into account entanglements between the two. Empirical illustrations of reciprocal influence between domestic and international affairs abound. What we need now are concepts and theories that will help us organize and extend our empirical observations. Analysis in terms of two-level games offers a promising response to this challenge. Unlike state-centric theories the two-level approach recognizes the inevitability of domestic conflict about what the national interest requires. Unlike the "Second Image" or the "Second Image Reversed" the two-level approach recognizes that central decision-makers strive to reconcile domestic and international imperatives simultaneously. As we have seen, statesmen in this predicament trace distinctive strategic opportunities and strategic dilemmas. This theoretical approach highlights several significant features of the links between diplomacy and domestic politics including:

- the important distinction between voluntary and involuntary defection from international agreements;
- the contrast between issues on which domestic interests are homogeneous simply pitting hawks against doves and issues on which domestic interests are more heterogeneous so that domestic cleavage may actually foster international cooperation;
- the possibility of synergistic issue linkage in which strategic moves at one game-table facilitate unexpected coalitions at the second table;
- the paradoxical fact that institutional arrangements which strengthen decision-makers at home may weaken their international bargaining position and vice versa;
- the importance of targeting international threats offers and side-payments with an eye towards their domestic incidence at home and abroad;
- the strategic uses of uncertainty about domestic politics, and the special utility of kinky win-sets;
- the potential reverberation of international pressures within the domestic arena;
- the divergences of interest between a national leader and those on whose behalf he is negotiating, and in particular the international implications of his fixed investments in domestic politics

Two-level games seem a ubiquitous feature of social life from Western economic summitry to diplomacy in the Balkans and from coalition politics in Sri Lanka to legislative maneuvering on Capitol Hill. Far-ranging empirical research is needed now to test and deepen our understanding of how such games are played.

Chapter Five

Grinding New Lenses

Introduction to Shattering Lenses

The central argument of most of this text is that an observer can gain a more complete understanding of international relations by viewing events through alternative lenses. This approach reflects the *positivist* approach to the social sciences. Positivism assumes that it is possible to make "descriptive or explanatory *inferences* on the basis of empirical information about the world."[1] In other words, knowledge about the social world is both objective and obtainable. Knowledge of the social world is objective if there are fixed truths and clear causal connections between social phenomena. Knowledge of the social world is attainable if those truths can be discovered through scientific inquiry. Implicit in this approach is the assumption that the observer is detached from the event being observed. Positivism asserts that different observers, provided they use proper scientific procedures, can reach the same conclusions about social phenomena.

However, many scholars, broadly described as "critical theorists," question these assumptions. Critical theorists argue that world politics is "socially constructed." Some critical theorists argue that objective knowledge about the social world is unattainable. These theorists trace their intellectual heritage to Fredrich Nietzsche, who argued that "there are no facts; only interpretations." These theorists reject the very idea of applying the scientific method to international politics. Other critical theorists argue that while material facts regarding international politics do indeed exist, these facts "acquire meaning for human action only through the structure of shared knowledge in which they are embedded."[2] In other words, the identities and values of observers affect the meanings that those observers attach to particular events. For example, in strictly material terms, 500 British nuclear weapons are every bit as dangerous to the United States as 500 North Korean nuclear weapons. However, the United States views Great Britain as an ally and North Korea as an adversary. That view cannot be justified in strictly material terms; it can only explained by the presence or absence of shared understandings among these societies.[3]

Critical theorists do not subscribe to a single theory, but instead represent a broad philosophical tradition. While critical theorists tend to agree that world politics is socially constructed, they differ on the fundamental basis of that construction. The articles presented in this section of the text represent several, but by no means all, of the important strands of critical theory. The "constructivist" approach is represented by Alexander Wendt's *Constructing International Politics*. The feminist approach is represented by J. Ann Tickner's *Toward a Nongendered Perspective on Global Security*. The neo-Marxist approach is represented by Robert W. Cox' *Social Forces, States and World Orders*.

In *Constructing International Politics*, Alexander Wendt provides an alternative viewpoint of state behavior in anarchy. Wendt is responding to structural realism's claim that the anarchic environment of international politics promotes security competition among states.[4] Wendt claims that security competition is not an inevitable response to anarchy.

---

1. Gary King, Robert O. Keohane, Sidney Verba, *Designing Social Inquiry* (Princeton, N.J.: Princeton University Press, 1994): 7.

2. Alexander Wendt, Constructing International Politics, *International Security* 20, no. 1: 73.

3. Ibid.

Instead, security competition is a set of social practices chosen by states, and is not the only choice available to states wishing to ensure their survival in anarchy.

In *Toward a Nongendered Perspective on Global Security,* J. Ann. Tickner argues that the discourse about international security issues has been shaped by men. Women, who have traditionally been limited to the periphery of such discourse, have a different and equally valid perspective on security issues. More importantly, the synthesis of these two gender-based perspectives may yield a more complete understanding of world politics than can either perspective taken in isolation.

In *Social Forces, States and World Orders: Beyond International Relations Theory,* Robert W. Cox questions the validity of neo-realist theory. Like Wendt, Cox recognizes that neo-realism has become the dominant mode of discourse in the study of international politics. Unlike Wendt, Cox questions the validity of neorealism's assumption that states are and must be the dominant actors in international politics. A neo-Marxist, Cox argues that the existing state system reflects and reinforces a particular kind of property relationships. If those relationships were to change, international politics would change as well.

There is no doubt that the diversity of these approaches—constructivism, feminism, neo-Marxism—is considerable. Nonetheless, critical theorists share a common commitment to question the concepts that the positivist approach takes as given. The role of discourse, gender, and the state itself are all called into question. In doing so, critical theorists cast doubt on our ability to observe the social world objectively through carefully constructed lenses.

Suggestions for Further Reading

Cox, Robert W. *Neorealism and Its Critics*. New York: Columbia University Press, 1986.

Hoffman, Stanley. "The Politics and Ethics of Military Intervention." *Survival* 37, no.1 (1995-1996.)

Hopf, Ted. "The Promise of Constructivism in International Relations." *International Security* 23, no. 1 (Summer 1998.)

Keohane, Robert. "International Relations Theory: Contributions of a Feminist Standpoint. " *Millenium: Journal of International Studies* 18, no. 2 (1989.)

Murphy, Craig N. "Seeing Women, Recognizing Gender, Recasting International Relations." *International Organization* 50, no. 3 (Summer 1996.)

Runyan, Anne Sisson and V. Spike Peterson. "The Radical Future of Realism: Feminist Subversion of IR Theory." *Alternatives* 16 (1991.)

Varyen, Tarja. "Ethnic Communality and Conflict Resolution." *Cooperation and Conflict* 33, no.1 (March 1998.)

Wendt, Alexander. "Anarchy is What You Make of It: The Social Construction of International Politics." *International Organization* 46, no.2 (Spring 1992.)

---

4. Specifically, Wendt is replying to John J. Mearsheimers The False Promise of International Institutions, *International Security* 19, No. 3 (Winter 1994/95). Mearsheimer argues that in anarchy, states are uncertain about and fearful of the offensive power wielded by other states, and that each state therefore has powerful incentives to maximize its relative power position in order to survive.

Constructivism

Alexander Wendt

Constructing International Politics

Constructing International Politics

Alexander Wendt

John J. Mearsheimer's "The False Promise of International Institutions"[1] is welcome particularly in two respects. First, it is the most systematic attempt to date by a neorealist to address critical international relations (IR) theory.[2] Second, it reminds neoliberals and critical theorists, normally locked in their own tug-of-war, that they have a common, non-realist interest in the institutional bases of international life.[3] "False Promise" is likely, therefore, to spur productive discussions on all sides.

Unfortunately, it will be hard for most critical theorists to take seriously a discussion of their research program so full of conflations, half-truths, and misunderstandings. However, to some extent misunderstanding is inevitable when anthropologists from one culture first explore another. A dialogue between these two cultures is overdue, and "False Promise" is a good beginning.

Critical IR "theory," however, is not a single theory. It is a family of theories that includes postmodernists (Ashley, Walker), constructivists (Adler, Kratochwil, Ruggie, and now Katzenstein), neo-Marxists (Cox, Gill), feminists (Peterson, Sylvester), and others. What unites them is a concern with how world politics is "socially constructed,"[4] which involves two basic claims: that the fundamental structures of international politics are social rather than strictly material (a claim that opposes materialism), and that these structures shape actors' identities and interests, rather than just their behavior (a claim that opposes rationalism). However, having these two claims in common no more makes critical theory a single theory than does the fact that neorealism and neoliberalism both use game theory makes them a single theory. Some critical theorists are statists and some are not; some believe in science and some do not; some are optimists and some pessimists; some stress process and some structure.[5] Thus, in my reply I speak only for myself as a "constructivist," hoping that other critical theorists may agree with much of what I say. I address four issues: assumptions, objective knowledge, explaining war and peace, and policymakers' responsibilities.

---

1. John J. Mearsheimer, "The False Promise of International Institutions," *International Security,* Vol. 19. No. 3 (Winter 1994/95). Subsequent references appear in parentheses in the text.

2. Other efforts include Robert Gilpin, "The Richness of the Tradition of Political Realism," *International Organization,* Vol. 38, No. 2 (Spring 1984), pp. 287-304, and Markus Fischer, "Feudal Europe, 800-1300," *International Organization,* Vol. 46, No. 2 (Spring 1992), pp. 427-466.

3. On neoliberalism and critical theory, see Robert Keohane, "International Institutions: Two approaches," *International Studies Quarterly,* Vol. 32, No. 4 (December 1988), pp. 379-396, and Wendt, "Collective Identity Formation and the International State," *American Political Science Review,* Vol. 88, No. 2 (June 1994), pp. 384-396. Mearsheimer treats collective security as a third form of institutionalism, but this is unwarranted. Collective security is an approach to international order, arguable on either neoliberal or critical grounds, not a form of institutional analysis.

4. This makes them all "constructivist" in a broad sense, but as the critical literature has evolved, this term has become applied to one particular school.

5. These are far more than differences of "emphasis," as suggested by Mearsheimer's disclaimer, note 127.

"Constructing International Politics" by Alexander Wendt, *International Security,* Vol 20, No. 1 (Summer, 1995), pp. 71-81.

ASSUMPTIONS

I share all five of Mearsheimer's "realist" assumptions (p. 10): that international politics is anarchic, and that states have offensive capabilities, cannot be 100 percent certain about others' intentions, wish to survive, and are rational. We even share two more: a commitment to states as units of analysis, and to the importance of systemic or "third image" theorizing.

The last bears emphasis, for in juxtaposing "structure" to "discourse" and in emphasizing the role of individuals in "critical theory" (p. 40), Mearsheimer obscures the fact that constructivists are structuralists. Indeed, one of our main objections to neorealism is that it is not structural enough: that adopting the individualistic metaphors of micro-economics restricts the effects of structures to state behavior, ignoring how they might also constitute state identities and interests.[6] Constructivists think that state interests are in important part constructed by systemic structures, not exogenous to them; this leads to a sociological rather than micro-economic structuralism.

Where neorealist and constructivist structuralisms really differ, however, is in their assumptions about what structure is made of. Neorealists think it is made only of a distribution of material capabilities, whereas constructivists think it is also made of social relationships. Social structures have three elements: shared knowledge, material resources, and practices.[7]

First, social structures are defined, in part, by shared understandings, expectations, or knowledge. These constitute the actors in a situation and the nature of their relationships, whether cooperative or conflictual. A *security dilemma*, for example, is a social structure composed of intersubjective understandings in which states are so distrustful that they make worst-case assumptions about each others' intentions, and as a result define their interests in self-help terms. A *security community* is a different social structure, one composed of shared knowledge in which states trust one another to resolve disputes without war.[8] This dependence of social structure on ideas is the sense in which constructivism has an idealist (or "idea-ist") view of structure. What makes these ideas (and thus structure) "social," however, is their intersubjective quality. In other words, sociality (in contrast to "materiality," in the sense of brute physical capabilities) is about shared knowledge.

Second, social structures include material resources like gold and tanks. In contrast to neorealists' desocialized view of such capabilities, constructivists argue that material resources only acquire meaning for human action through the structure of shared knowl-

---

6. "Constitute" is an important term in critical theory, with a special meaning that is not captured by related terms like "comprise," consist of," or "cause." To say that "X [for example, a social structure] constitutes Y [for example, an agent]," is to say that the properties of those agents are made possible by, and would not exist in the absence of, the structure by which they are "constituted." A constitutive relationship establishes a conceptually necessary or logical connection between X and Y, in contrast to the contingent connection between independently existing entities that is established by causal relationships.

The identity-behavior distinction is partly captured by Robert Powell's distinction between preferences over outcomes and preferences over strategies; Robert Powell, "Anarchy in International Relations Theory," *International Organization*, Vol. 48, No. 2 (Spring 1994), pp. 313-344. The main exception to the mainstream neglect of structural effects on state identity is Kenneth Waltz's argument that anarchy produces "like units"; Kenneth Waltz, *Theory of International Politics* (Reading, Mass.: Addison-Wesley, 1979), pp. 74-77. Constructivists think there are more possibilities than this; see Alexander Wendt, "Anarchy is What States Make of It: The Social Construction of Power Politics," *International Organization*, Vol. 46, No. 2 (Spring 1992), pp. 391-425.

7. What follows could also serve as a rough definition of "discourse."

8. See Karl Deutsch, et al., *Political Community and the North Atlantic Area* (Princeton: Princeton University Press, 1957).

edge in which they are embedded.[9] For example, 500 British nuclear weapons are less threatening to the United States than 5 North Korean nuclear weapons, because the British are friends of the United States and the North Koreans are not, and amity or enmity is a function of shared understandings. As students of world politics, neorealists would probably not disagree, but as theorists the example poses a big problem, since it completely eludes their materialist definition of structure. Material capabilities as such explain nothing; their effects presuppose structures of shared knowledge, which vary and which are not reducible to capabilities. Constructivism is therefore compatible with changes in material power affecting social relations (cf. Mearsheimer, p. 43), as long as those effects can be shown to presuppose still deeper social relations.

Third, social structures exist, not in actors' heads nor in material capabilities, but in practices. Social structure exists only in process. The Cold War was a structure of shared knowledge that governed great power relations for forty years, but once they stopped acting on this basis, it was "over."

In sum, social structures are real and objective, not "just talk." But this objectivity depends on shared knowledge, and in that sense social life is "ideas all the way down" (until you get to biology and natural resources). Thus, to ask "when do ideas, as opposed to power and interest, matter?" is to ask the wrong question. Ideas always matter, since power and interest do not have effects apart from the shared knowledge that constitutes them as such.[10] The real question, as Mearsheimer notes (p. 42), is why does one social structure exist, like self-help (in which power and self-interest determine behavior), rather than another, like collective security (in which they do not).

The explanatory as opposed to normative character of this question bears emphasis. Constructivists have a normative interest in promoting social change, but they pursue this by trying to explain how seemingly natural social structures, like self-help or the Cold War, are effects of practice (this is the "critical" side of critical theory). This makes me wonder about Mearsheimer's repeated references (I count fourteen) to critical theorists' "goals," "aims," and "hopes" to make peace and love prevail on Earth. Even if we all had such hopes (which I doubt), and even if these were ethically wrong (though Mearsheimer seems to endorse them; p. 40), they are beside the point in evaluating critical theories of world politics. If critical theories fail, this will be because they do not explain how the world works, not because of their values. Emphasizing the latter recalls the old realist tactic of portraying opponents as utopians more concerned with how the world ought to be than how it is. Critical theorists have normative commitments, just as neorealists do, but we are also simply trying to explain the world.

OBJECTIVITY

Mearsheimer suggests that critical theorists do not believe that there is an objective world out there about which we can have knowledge (pp. 41ff). This is not the case. There are two issues here, ontological and epistemological.

The ontological issue is whether social structures have an objective existence, which I addressed above. Social structures are collective phenomena that confront individuals as

---

9. For a good general discussion of this point, see Douglas Porpora, "Cultural Rules and Material Relations," *Sociological Theory,* Vol. 11, No. 2 (July 1993), pp. 212-229.

10. On the social content of interests, see Roy D'Andrade and Claudia Strauss, eds., *Human Motives and Cultural Models* (Cambridge: Cambridge University Press, 1992).

externally existing social facts. The Cold War was just as real for me as it was for Mearsheimer.

The epistemological issue is whether we can have objective knowledge of these structures. Here Mearsheimer ignores a key distinction between modern and postmodern critical theorists. The latter are indeed skeptical about the possibility of objective knowledge, although in their empirical work even they attend to evidence and inference. Constructivists, however, are modernists who fully endorse the scientific project of falsifying theories against evidence. In an article cited by Mearsheimer, I advocated a scientific-realist approach to social inquiry, which takes a very pro-science line.[11] And despite his claims, there is now a substantial body of constructivist empirical work that embodies a wholly conventional epistemology.[12]

Mearsheimer is right, however, that critical theorists do not think we can make a clean distinction between subject and object. Then again, almost all philosophers of science today reject such a naive epistemology. All observation is *theory-laden* in the sense that what we see is mediated by our existing theories, and to that extent knowledge is inherently problematic. But this does not mean that observation, let alone reality, is *theory-determined.* The world is still out there constraining our beliefs, and may punish us for incorrect ones. Montezuma had a theory that the Spanish were gods, but it was wrong, with disastrous consequences. We do not have unmediated access to the world, but this does not preclude understanding how it works.

EXPLAINING WAR AND PEACE

Mearsheimer frames the debate between realists and critical theorists as one between a theory of war and a theory of peace. This is a fundamental mistake. Social construction talk is like game theory talk: analytically neutral between conflict and cooperation.[13] Critical theory does not predict peace.[14] War no more disproves critical theory than peace disproves realism. The confusion stems from conflating description and explanation.

The descriptive issue is the extent to which states engage in practices of *realpolitik* (warfare, balancing, relative-gains seeking) versus accepting the rule of law and institutional constraints on their autonomy. States sometimes do engage in power politics, but this hardly describes all of the past 1300 years, and even less today, when most states fol-

---

11. See Alexander Wendt, "The Agent-Structure Problem in International Relations Theory," *International Organization,* Vol. 41, No. 3 (Summer 1987), pp. 339-370; and, for fuller discussion, Ian Shapiro and Alexander Wendt, "The Difference that Realism Makes," *Politics and Society,* Vol. 20, No. 2, June 1992), pp. 197-223.

12. See, among others, Michael Barnett, "Institutions, Roles, and Disorder," *International Studies Quarterly,* Vol. 37, No. 3 (September 1993), pp. 271-296; David Lumsdaine, *Moral Vision in International Politics* (Princeton: Princeton University Press, 1993); Samuel Barkin and Bruce Cronin, "The State and the Nation," *International Organization,* Vol. 48, No. 1 (Winter 1994), pp. 107-130; Rey Koslowski and Friedrich Kratochwil, "Understanding Change in International Politics," *International Organization,* Vol. 48, No. 2 (Spring 1994), pp. 215-248; Thomas Biersteker and Cynthia Weber, eds., *State Sovereignty as Social Construct* (Cambridge: Cambridge University Press, forthcoming); and Peter Katzenstein, ed., *Constructing National Security* (working title), forthcoming.

13. On the social basis of conflict, see Georg Simmel, *Conflict and the Web of Group Affiliations* (Glencoe, IL: Free Press, 1955). This is also why I prefer to avoid the term "institutionalism," since it associates sociality with peace and cooperation.

14. Fischer's suggestion that critical theory predicts cooperation in feudal Europe is based on a failure to understand the full implications of this point; see Fischer, "Feudal Europe, 800-1300."

low most international law most of the time,[15] and when war and security dilemmas are the exception rather than the rule, Great Powers no longer tend to conquer small ones, and free trade is expanding rather than contracting.[16] The relative frequency of *realpolitik*, however, has nothing to do with "realism." Realism should be seen as an explanation of *realpolitik*, not a description of it. Conflating the two makes it impossible to tell how well the one explains the other, and leads to the tautology that war makes realism true. Realism does not have a monopoly on the ugly and brutal side of international life. Even if we agree on a *realpolitik* description, we can reject a realist explanation.

The exploratory issue is *why* states engage in war or peace. Mearsheimer's portrayal of constructivist "causal logic" on this issue is about 30 percent right. The logic has two elements, structure and agency. On the one hand, constructivist theorizing tries to show how the social structure of a system makes actions possible by constituting actors with certain identities and interests, and material capabilities with certain meanings. Missing from Mearsheimer's account is the constructivist emphasis on how agency and interaction produce and reproduce structures of shared knowledge over time. Since it is not possible here to discuss the various dynamics through which this process takes place,[17] let me illustrate instead. And since Mearsheimer does not offer a neorealist explanation for inter-state cooperation, conceding that terrain to institutionalists, let me focus on the "hard case" of why states sometimes get into security dilemmas and war, that is, why they sometimes engage in *realpolitik* behavior.

In "Anarchy is What States Make of It" I argued that such behavior is a self-fulfilling prophecy,[18] and that this is due to both agency and social structure. Thus, on the agency side, what states do to each other affects the social structure in which they are embedded, by a logic of reciprocity. If they militarize, others will be threatened and arm themselves, creating security dilemmas in terms of which they will define egoistic identities and interests. But if they engage in policies of reassurance, as the Soviets did in the late 1980s, this will have a different effect on the structure of shared knowledge, moving it toward a security community. The depth of interdependence is a factor here, as is the role of revisionist states, whose actions are likely to be especially threatening. However, on the structural side, the ability of revisionist states to create a war of all against all depends on the structure of shared knowledge into which they enter. If past interactions have created a structure in which status quo states are divided or naive, revisionists will prosper and the system will tend toward a Hobbesian world in which power and self-interest rule. In contrast, if past interactions have created a structure in which status quo states trust and identify with each other, predators are more likely to face collective security responses like the Gulf War.[19] *History matters.* Security dilemmas are not acts of God: they are effects of

---

15. See Louis Henkink, *How Nations Behave* (New York: Council on Foreign Relations, 1979), p. 47.

16. On the inadequacy of "realist" descriptions of international politics, see Paul Schroeder, "Historical Reality vs. Neo-realist Theory," *International Security*, Vol. 19, No. 1 (Summer 1994), pp. 108-148.

17. For a start, see Alexander Wendt, "Collective Identity Formation," and Emanuel Adler, "Cognitive Evolution, in Emanuel Adler and Beverly Crawford, eds., *Progress in Postwar International Relations* (New York: Columbia University Press, 1991), pp. 43-88. The best introduction to processes of social construction remains Peter Berger and Thomas Luckman, *The Social construction of Reality* (New York: Anchor Books, 1966).

18. 18. A similar argument is developed in John Vasquez, *The War Puzzle* (Cambridge: Cambridge University Press, 1993).

practice. This does not mean that once created they can necessarily be escaped (they are, after all, "dilemmas"), but it puts the causal locus in the right place.

Contrast this explanation of power politics with the "poverty of neorealism."[20] Mearsheimer thinks it significant that in anarchy, states cannot be 100 percent certain that others will not attack. Yet even in domestic society, I can-not be certain that I will be safe walking to class. There are no guarantees in life, domestic or international, but the fact that in anarchy war is possible does not mean "it may at any moment occur."[21] Indeed, it may be quite unlikely, as it is in most interactions today. Possibility is not probability. Anarchy as such is not a structural cause of anything. What matters is its social structure, which varies across anarchies. An anarchy of friends differs from one of enemies, one of self-help from one of collective security, and these are all constituted by structures of shared knowledge. Mearsheimer does not provide an argument for why this is wrong; he simply asserts that it is.

Other realist explanations for power politics fare somewhat better. Although neorealists want to eschew arguments from human nature, even they would agree that to the extent human-beings-in-groups are prone to fear and competition, it may predispose them to war.[22] However, this factor faces countervailing dynamics of interdependence and collective identity formation, which sometimes overcome it. The distribution of material capabilities also matters, especially if offense is dominant, and military build-ups will of course concern other states. Again, however, the meaning of power depends on the underlying structure of shared knowledge. A British build-up will be less threatening to the United States than a North Korean one, and build-ups are less likely to occur in a security community than in a security dilemma.

In order to get from anarchy and material forces to power politics and war, therefore, neorealists have been forced to make additional, *ad hoc* assumptions about the social structure of the international system. We see this in Mearsheimer's interest in "hyper-nationalism," Stephen Walt's emphasis on ideology in the "balance of threat," Randall Schweller's focus on the status quo-revisionist distinction and, as I argued in my "Anarchy" piece, in Waltz's assumption that anarchies are self-help systems.[23] Incorporating these assumptions generates more explanatory power, but how? In these cases the crucial causal work is done by social, not material, factors. This is the core of a constructivist view of structure, not a neorealist one.

The problem becomes even more acute when neorealists try to explain the relative absence of inter-state war in today's world. If anarchy is so determining, why are there not more Bosnias? Why are weak states not getting killed off left and right? It stretches credu-

---

19. On the role of collective identity in facilitating collective security, see Wendt, "Collective Identity Formation."

20. Richard Ashley, "The Poverty of Neorealism," *International Organization,* Vol. 38, No. 2 (Spring 1984), pp. 225-286.

21. Kenneth Waltz, *Man, the State, and War* (New York: Columbia University Press, 1959), p. 232.

22. For a good argument to this effect, see Jonathan Mercer, "Anarchy and Identity," *International Organization,* Vol. 49, No. 2 (Spring 1995).

23. John J. Mearsheimer, "Back to the Future," *International Security,* Vol. 15, No. I (Summer 1990), pp. 5-56; Stephen Walt, *The Origins of Alliances* (Ithaca: Cornell University Press, 1987); Randall Schweller, "Tripolarity and the Second World War," *International Studies Quarterly,* Vol. 37, No. 1 (March 1993), pp. 73 103; and Wendt, "Anarchy is What States Make of It."

lity to think that the peace between Norway and Sweden, or the United States and Canada, or Nigeria and Benin are all due to material balancing. Mearsheimer says cooperation is possible when core interests are not threatened (p. 25), and that "some states are especially friendly for historical or ideological reasons" (p. 31). But this totally begs the question of why in an ostensibly "realist" world states do not find their interests continually threatened by others, and the question of how they might become friends. Perhaps Mearsheimer would say that most states today are status quo and sovereign.[24] But again this begs the question. What is sovereignty if not an institution of mutual recognition and non-intervention? And is not being "status quo" related to the internalization of this institution in state interests? David Strang has argued that those states recognized as sovereign have better survival prospects in anarchy than those that are not.[25] Far from challenging this argument, Mearsheimer presupposes it.

Neorealists' growing reliance on social factors to do their explanatory work suggests that if ever there were a candidate for a degenerating research program in IR theory, this is it.[26] The progressive response (in the Lakatosian sense) would be to return to realism's materialist roots by showing that the background understandings that give capabilities meaning are caused by still deeper material conditions, or that capabilities have intrinsic meaning that cannot be ignored. To show that the material base determines international superstructure, in other words, realists should be purging their theory of social content, not adding it as they are doing.[27] And anti-realists, in turn, should be trying to show how the causal powers of material facts presuppose social content, not trying to show that institutions explain additional variance beyond that explained by the distribution of power and interest, as if the latter were a privileged pre-social baseline.

RESPONSIBILITY

An important virtue of "False Promise" is that it links neorealism and its rivals to the ethical responsibilities of foreign policymakers. These responsibilities depend in part on how much it is possible to change the structure of shared knowledge within anarchy. If such change is impossible, then Mearsheimer is right that it would be irresponsible for those charged with national security to pursue it. On the other hand, if it is possible, then it would be irresponsible to pursue policies that perpetuate destructive old orders, especially if we care about the well-being of future generations.

To say that structures are socially constructed is no guarantee that they can be changed.[28] Sometimes social structures so constrain action that transformative strategies are impossible. This goes back to the collective nature of social structures; structural change depends on changing a system of expectations that may be mutually reinforcing. A

24. Mearsheimer and Waltz both assume sovereignty, without acknowledging its institutional character; see Mearsheimer, "False Promise," p. 11, and Waltz, *Theory of International Politics*, pp. 95-96.

25. David Strang, "Anomaly and Commonplace in European Political Expansion," *International Organization*, Vol. 45, No. 2 (Spring 1991), pp. 143 162.

26. "Degenerating" problem shifts are adjustments to a theory that are ad hoc, while "progressive" shifts are those that have a principled basis in its hard core assumptions. See Imre Lakatos, "Falsification and the Methodology of Scientific Research Programmes," in Lakatos and Alan Musgrave, eds., *Criticism and the Growth of Knowledge* (Cambridge: Cambridge University Press, 1970), pp. 91-196.

27. The significance of Dan Deudney's work lies partly in his appreciation of this point; see Dan Deudney, "Dividing Realism: Structural Realism versus Security Materialism on Nuclear Security and Proliferation," *Security Studies*. Vol. 1, Nos. 2 and 3 (1993), pp. 7-37.

key issue in determining policymakers' responsibilities, therefore, is how much "slack" a social structure contains. Neorealists think there is little slack in the system, and thus states that deviate from power politics will get punished or killed by the "logic" of anarchy. Institutionalists think such dangers have been greatly reduced by institutions such as sovereignty and the democratic peace, and that there is therefore more possibility for peaceful change.

The example of Gorbachev is instructive in this respect, since the Cold War was a highly conflictual social structure. I agree with Mearsheimer (p. 46) that Soviet nuclear forces gave Gorbachev a margin of safety for his policies. Yet someone else in his place might have found a more aggressive solution to a decline in power. What is so important about the Gorbachev regime is that it had the courage to see how the Soviets' own practices sustained the Cold War, and to undertake a reassessment of Western intentions. This is exactly what a constructivist would do, but not a neorealist, who would eschew attention to such social factors as naive and as mere superstructure. Indeed, what is so striking about neorealism is its total neglect of the explanatory role of state practice.[29] It does not seem to matter what states do: Brezhnev, Gorbachev, Zhirinovsky, what difference does it make? The logic of anarchy will always bring us back to square one. This is a disturbing attitude if *realpolitik* causes the very conditions to which it is a response; to the extent that realism counsels *realpolitik*, therefore, it is part of the problem. Mearsheimer says critical theorists are "intolerant" of realists for this reason (p. 42). The ironies of this suggestion aside, what matters is getting policymakers to accept responsibility for solving conflicts rather than simply managing or exploiting them. If neorealism can move us in that direction, then it should, but as I see it, neorealist ethics come down to "*sauve qui peut.*"

To analyze the social construction of international politics is to analyze how processes of interaction produce and reproduce the social structures—cooperative or conflictual—that shape actors' identities and interests and the significance of their material contexts. It is opposed to two rivals: the materialist view, of which neorealism is one expression, that material forces *per se* determine international life, and the rational choice-theoretic view that interaction does not change identities and interests. Mearsheimer's essay is an important opening to the comparative evaluation of these hypotheses. But neorealists will contribute nothing further to the debate so long as they think that constructivists are subversive utopians who do not believe in a real world and who expect peace in our time.

For their exceptionally detailed and helpful comments I am grateful to Mike Barnett, Mlada Bukovansky, Bud Duvall, Peter Katzenstein, Mark Laffey, David Lumsdaine, Sylvia Maxfield, Nina Tannenwald, Jutta Weldes, and the members of the Yale IR Reading Group.

---

28. Hence, contra Mearsheimer, there is nothing problematic about the fact that critical theorists do not make predictions about the future. What happens in the future depends on what actors do with the structures they have made in the past.

29. 29. This is not true of classical realists; for a sympathetic discussion of the latter from a critical standpoint, see Richard Ashley, "Political Realism and Human Interests," *International Studies Quarterly*, Vol. 25, No. 2 (June 1981), pp. 204-237.

Feminist Theory

J. Ann Tickner

Toward a Nongendered Perspective on Global Security

Toward a Nongendered Perspective on Global Security

J. Ann Tickner

> If you dream about an egalitarian and just society it cannot be created by men alone You cannot ignore 50% of the population.
>
> —*Shekhar Pathah*[1]

> It's terribly important, maybe even to the future of the world, for women to take part in making the decisions that shape our destiny.
>
> —*Jeane Kirkpatrick*[2]

> The woman most in need of liberation is the woman within every man.
>
> —*William Sloane Coffin*[3]

I have argued that traditional notions of national security are becoming dysfunctional. The heavy emphasis on militarily defined security, common to the foreign policy practices of contemporary states and to the historical traditions from which these practices draw their inspiration, does not ensure, and sometimes may even decrease, the security of individuals, as well as that of their natural environments. Many forms of insecurity in the contemporary world affect the lives of individuals, including ethnic conflict, poverty, family violence; and environmental degradation; all these types of insecurity can be linked to the international system, yet their elimination has not been part of the way in which states have traditionally defined their national security goals.

I have also called attention to the extent to which these various forms of military, economic, and ecological insecurity are connected with unequal gender relations. The relationship between protectors and protected depends on gender inequalities; a militarized version of security privileges masculine characteristics and elevates men to the status of first class citizens by virtue of their role as providers of security. An analysis of economic insecurities suggests similar patterns of gender inequality in the world economy, patterns that result in a larger share of the world's wealth and the benefits of economic development accruing to men. The traditional association of women with nature, which places both in a subordinate position to men, reflects and provides support for the instrumental and exploitative attitude toward nature characteristic of the modern era, an attitude that contributes to current ecological insecurities.

This analysis has also suggested that attempts to alleviate these military, economic, and ecological insecurities cannot be completely successful until the hierarchical social relations, including gender relations, intrinsic to each of these domains are recognized and substantially altered. In other words, the achievement of peace, economic justice, and eco-

1. Pathah epigraph quoted in Dankelman and Davidson, *Women and Environment in the Third World*, p. 171.

2. Kirkpatrick epigraph quoted in Crapol, *Women and American Foreign Policy*, p. 153

3. Coffin epigraph quoted in Reardon, *Sexism and the War System*, p. 51.

logical sustainability is inseparable from overcoming social relations of domination and subordination; genuine security requires not only the absence of war but also the elimination of unjust social relations, including unequal gender relations.[4]

If the world is insecure because of these multiple insecurities, then international relations, the discipline that analyzes international insecurity and prescribes measures for its alleviation, must be reformulated. The reconceptualization of security in multidimensional and multilevel terms is beginning to occur on the fringes of the discipline; a more comprehensive notion of security is being used by peace researchers, critics of conventional international relations theory, environmentalists, and even some policy makers. But while all these contemporary revisionists have helped to move the definition of security beyond its exclusively national security focus toward additional concerns for the security of the individual and the natural environment, they have rarely included gender as a category of analysis; nor have they acknowledged similar, earlier reformulations of security constructed by women.

Including previously hidden gender inequalities in the analysis of global insecurity allows us to see how so many of the insecurities affecting us all, women and men alike, are gendered in their historical origins, their conventional definitions, and their contemporary manifestations. Using gender as a category of analysis reveals the masculinist assumptions of both traditional and revisionist theories of international politics and economics. It also allows us to see the extent to which unequal gender relationships are a form of domination that contributes to many of the dimensions of the contemporary insecurities analyzed by various new thinkers. Feminists deny the separability of gendered insecurities from those describable in military, economic, and ecological terms; such problems cannot be fully resolved without also overcoming the domination and exploitation of women that takes place in each of these domains.

Such a conception of security is based on the assumption that social justice, including gender justice, is necessary for an enduring peace. While acknowledging that unequal social relations are not the only sources of insecurity, feminists believe that contemporary insecurities are doubly engendered. Beyond the view that all social institutions, including those of world politics, are made by human beings and are therefore changeable, they recognize that comprehensive security requires the removal of gender-linked insecurities. Revealing these gender inequalities allows us to see how their elimination would open up new possibilities for the alleviation of the various domains of global insecurity that I have described. Overcoming gender inequalities is necessary, not only for the security of women but also for the realization of a type of security that does not rely on characteristics associated with the hegemonic masculinity that has produced a kind of security that can be a threat to men's security also. Men are themselves insecure partly because of the exclusionary, gendered way their own security has been defined.

This will draw together some of the ways in which the integration of these gendered perspectives on international security can contribute to reformulating the discipline of international relations. However, the ultimate goal of such a reformulation must not be to replace the masculinist perspective on international relations that presently obtains with a feminist perspective. The integration of feminist perspectives into the discipline is but a necessary first step toward transcending gender as a category of analysis. The possibility

---

4. For a postmodern analysis that denies the claim that various forms of oppression are necessarily connected, see Laclau and Mouffe, *Hegemony and Socialist Strategy*.

of moving beyond these gendered perspectives would depend on redefining the discipline of international relations in such a way that women's experiences were included in its subject matter on an equal basis with men's. Such a transcendence can come about, however, only when oppressive gender hierarchies are eliminated.

WHAT DO GENDERED PERSPECTIVES ON GLOBAL SECURITY TELL US ABOUT THE DISCIPLINE OF INTERNATIONAL RELATIONS?

The gendered perspectives on security I have presented point to the conclusion that the discipline of international relations, as it is presently constructed, is defined in terms of everything that is not female. While classical realism has constructed its analysis out of the behavior and experiences of men, neorealism's commitment to a positivist methodology that attempts to impose standards of scientific inquiry used in the natural sciences, has resulted in an extreme depersonalization of the field that only serves to hide its masculinist underpinnings. My analyses of "political" and "economic" man, and the state as an international political and economic actor, all suggest that, beneath its claim to objectivity, realism has constructed an approach that builds on assumptions and explanations based on behaviors associated with masculinity. While many forms of masculinity and femininity exist that vary across class, race, culture, and history, international relations theories, and the world they analyze, privilege values associated with a socially constructed hegemonic masculinity. This hegemonic masculinity consists of a set of characteristics that, while they are drawn from certain behaviors of Western males, do not necessarily fit the behavior of all men, Western men included.

Political and economic man, abstractions crucial to the assumptions upon which both realist international relations and liberal political economy have been built, have been constructed out of masculine characteristics—such as autonomy, power, independence, and an instrumental notion of rationality—highly valued in the world of international politics. Realist and economic nationalist explanations of the political and economic behavior of states, as well as prescriptions for their success in the international system, are presented in similar terms. State of nature myths, at the heart of realist assumptions about the international system, which emphasize the dangers of and need to control wild and dangerous spaces, parallel Enlightenment science's attitude toward nature. This view of nature has been an important aspect of the ideological underpinnings of an expansionary Eurocentric state system and a capitalist world economy, as well as of Western projects of political and economic development.

The individual, the state, and the international system, the levels of analysis favored by realists for explaining international conflict, are not merely discrete levels of analysis around which artificial boundaries can be drawn; they are mutually reinforcing constructs, each based on behaviors associated with hegemonic masculinity. While various approaches to international relations critical of realist thinking have questioned the adequacy of these assumptions and explanations of contemporary realities, they have not done so on the basis of gender. Marxist analyses of the world economy are also constructed out of the historical experiences of men in the public world of production. Revealing the masculinist underpinnings of both these types of discourse suggests that realism, as well as the approaches of many of its critics, has constructed worldviews based on the behavior of only half of humanity.

Bringing to light this association between an idealized manhood and international relations reveals the possibility of constructing alternative perspectives divorced from historical associations with masculinity. However, if the worlds of international statecraft and strategic and foreign policy-making are worlds whose key protagonists are mostly men, one could claim that the discipline that describes them is a representation of reality at least with respect to its gender biases. The privileging of concepts such as power and autonomy and the emphasis on war and conflict do conform to patterns of behavior of many states in the international system. However, the feminist perspectives on national security, international political economy, and ecology that I have presented, which are based on different assumptions, demonstrate that there are equally plausible alternative ways of conceptualizing security and prescribing for its realization. They also draw our attention to examining the world from perspectives not of elite decision-makers but of those who are outside positions of power yet can present an equally plausible representation of reality.

While the traditional national security approach is based on the assumption that security demands autonomy and separation, in the highly interdependent world facing the multidimensional threats that I have described, autonomy may no longer be possible or desirable. Feminist approaches offer us new tools with which to question this exclusionary way of thinking. Drawing on experiences more typical of women, feminist theories start with the assumption that striving for attachment and community is as much a part of human nature as is the desire for independence. Conventional international relations thinking, which has prioritized "high politics," or issues relating to international conflict, draws our attention away from other activities in the international system, activities that are closer to behaviors traditionally associated with the feminine. Although it has been devalued in the way in which we usually think about international relations, building community is also an aspect of the political and economic behavior of states in the international system. Assuming the need for interdependence as one part of human behavior allows us to see community building not as an aberration but as another dimension of international behavior. Regional integration schemes, such as the European Community, suggest that we may be moving toward modes of international organization that demand different models of analysis, models not based on an exclusionary definition of national sovereignty.

Realist models of international relations have been built on assumptions of rigid boundary distinctions between outside and inside, anarchy and order, and foreign and domestic. The outside is portrayed in terms of dangerous spaces where violence is unsanctioned. This threat of violence must be guarded against and controlled if security on the inside is to be achieved. Feminist perspectives point to the inadequacy of these boundary distinctions for understanding the roots of conflict and suggest other possible ways of thinking about national security. By emphasizing the interrelationship of violence at all levels of society—as well as its relation to family violence, which also takes place in spaces that are usually beyond the sanction of the law—these feminist perspectives can help us to rethink such boundary distinctions.

Threats of nuclear annihilation and environmental degradation and the interdependence of states in their economic relations all suggest that statist approaches to national security are becoming dysfunctional. We can no longer afford to think in terms of the hierarchical boundary distinctions fostered by the exclusionary we/they attitude of the modern state system. Technologies of modern warfare have broken down boundaries between protectors and protected. Interventionist practices of great powers in the conflicts of weaker states, as well as ethnic strife caused by the lack of coincidence between state boundaries and the various nationalities living within these internationally sanctioned borders, blur distinctions between domestic and international violence. If this feminist analysis has suggested that true security can be achieved only with the elimination of rigid hierarchical gender distinctions, the same conclusion could apply to the hierarchical distinctions through which we have been socialized into thinking about the international system.

Models of economic development and prescriptions for maximizing world welfare have not taken into account women's particular needs or the roles that women play in the world economy. Since women have not been at the center of political and economic decision making, approaches that draw on women's experiences can give us perspectives on security based on standpoints of those outside traditional structures of power. For example, feminist critiques of Marxism emphasize the need to recognize the contribution that women make to production and reproduction in their household roles and in the subsistence economy. They also point to the fact that the exploitation of women's unpaid or underpaid labor has been crucial for the expansion of the capitalist world economy.

Since women are disproportionately located on the peripheries of the international system and at the bottom of the economic scale, feminist perspectives on security prioritize issues associated with the achievement of justice, issues that are frequently ignored in conventional theories of international politics, which have been preoccupied with questions relating to order. While one of the most important goals of feminism is to overcome women's marginalization from institutions of power, women's prominent role in social movements and in new forms of economic production provides examples of new ways of thinking about democratic decentralization, a restructuring of society that offers important alternative models for the achievement of a more comprehensive form of security.

Because women have been peripheral to the institutions of the state and transnational capital, feminist perspectives on international relations must take a critical stance with respect to these institutions, questioning whether they are able to cope with global security problems such as militarism, poverty, and the natural environment. Building a model of political economy that starts at the bottom and takes into account individuals and the local satisfaction of their basic needs envisages a state that is more self-reliant with respect to the international system and more able to live within its own resource limits; such a state would be less militaristic and could therefore give priority to social issues rather than military considerations.[5] Such a model would depend on an extended definition of security that goes beyond a nationalist, militarist focus and begins to speak to the economic and ecological security needs of individuals and states alike.

Concern for the natural environment is an issue that has made a relatively new appearance on the agenda of international politics; yet the rate at which new threats to ecological security are appearing suggests that it is an issue that will demand increasing attention from scholars of international relations in the future. As efforts to manage problems of environmental degradation fail to keep pace with newly discovered threats, ecologists point to more fundamental problems of humans' exploitative attitude toward nature. Ecofeminists have taken an important additional step by making explicit the interrelationship between the historical foundations of modern science's exploitative attitude toward nature, the birth of the modern state and the capitalist world economy, and the separation of gender roles that resulted in the delegitimation of the feminine in public life. Beginning in seventeenth-century Europe, the dichotomization of gender roles has served as an important part of the foundation upon which modern theories of international politics and economics, as well as modern attitudes toward nature, have been constructed. Linking

5. For the development of such a model see Tickner, *Self-Reliance Versus Power Politics*, ch. 8.

these changing worldviews to the international behavior of modern states and the expansion of the global economy offers us important new ways to think about the interrelationship of political, economic, and ecological insecurities. It also allows us to explain the international behavior of states, not as realists have portrayed it in terms of timeless practices that can be expected to repeat themselves indefinitely into the future, but as behavior constructed out of the value system of the modern West. This historical construction allows us to envisage possibilities for transcending the present system in ways that could offer more secure futures.

IS A BETTER FUTURE FEMALE?

If characteristics associated with hegemonic masculinity are not serving to increase security in our contemporary world, do more secure futures depend on the substitution of values or characteristics more typically associated with femininity? Certain contemporary feminists have celebrated gender difference and hypothesized a special female world superior to and separate from the world of men. In her book entitled *Is The Future Female?,* Lynne Segal claims that this type of thinking is dangerous and divisive and unlikely to achieve the major goal of feminism, which should be to work for the equality of women.[6] Segal argues that women, whose many gendered identities are constructed in terms of race, class, culture, and historical circumstances, cannot be characterized in these essentialist categories. Contemporary characterizations of women in terms similar to the Victorian ideal of the "good woman" serve only to make men more powerful. The celebration of female virtues supports the view of males as protectors and reinforces the separation between public and private spheres, relegating women to the latter. It also diverts attention from the agenda of working toward women's political, economic, and social equality, an agenda necessary for the achievement of genuine security.

Characteristics that have typically been associated with femininity must therefore be seen not in essentialist terms but as characteristics that women have developed in response to their socialization and their historical roles in society. The association of women with moral virtues such as caring comes not from women's innate moral superiority but from women's activities in the private sphere where these values are accepted in theory, if not always in practice. Since they are linked to women and the private sphere, however, these feminine characteristics have been devalued in the public realm, particularly in the world of international politics. The question then becomes how to revalue them in public life in ways that can contribute to the creation of a more just and secure world. Taking care not to elevate these feminine characteristics to a position of superiority, we can regard them as an inspiration that can contribute to our thinking about ways to build better futures. Even if the better future is not female, a human future that rejects the rigid separation of public and private sphere values and the social distinctions between women and men requires that the good qualities of both are equally honored and made available to all.

In the modern West, women's activities have typically been associated with a devalued world of reproduction and maintenance, while men's have been tied to what have been considered the more elevated tasks of creating history and meaning. Yet all these activities are equally important for human well-being. History and the construction of meaning help us to achieve the kind of security that comes from an understanding of who we are as individuals and as citizens, while reproduction and maintenance are necessary for our survival.

---

6. Segal, *Is the Future Female?,* introduction.

In the discourse of international politics, however, our national identities as citizens have been tied to the heroic deeds of warrior-patriots and our various states' successful participation in international wars. This militarized version of national identity has also depended on a devaluation of the identities of those outside the boundaries of the state. Additionally, it has all but eliminated the experiences of women from our collective national memories. A less militarized version of national identity, which would serve us better in the contemporary world where advances in technology are making wars as dangerous for winners as for losers, must be constructed out of the equally valued experiences of both women and men. To foster a more peaceful world, this identity must also rest on a better understanding and appreciation of the histories of other cultures and societies.

The multidimensional nature of contemporary insecurities also highlights the importance of placing greater public value on reproduction and maintenance. In a world where nuclear war could destroy the earth and most of its inhabitants, we can no longer afford to celebrate the potential death of hundreds of thousands of our enemies; the preservation of life, not its destruction, must be valued. The elimination of structural violence demands a restructuring of the global economy so that individuals' basic material needs take priority over the desire for profit. An endangered natural environment points to the need to think in terms of the reproduction rather than the exploitation of nature. This ethic of caring for the planet and its inhabitants has been devalued by linking to the private realm associated with the activities of women; yet caring and responsibility are necessary aspects of all dimensions of life, public and private. They will be valued in the public realm only when men participate equally in the private realm in tasks associated with maintenance and responsibility for child rearing. If we are to move toward a more secure future, what we value in the public realm, including the realm of international politics, should not be so rigidly separated from the values we espouse in the home.

Rewards for men and women for behaviors associated with caring for life in both the public and private spheres should be an important aspect of any redefinition of the meaning of patriotism. Replacing warrior-patriots with citizen-defenders provides us with models that are more conducive to women's equal participation in international politics. Such a reorientation of patriotism involves what Jean Elshtain calls undermining the strategic voice, the language of national security experts. Elshtain claims that this discourse is the preserve of trained experts and is not available to most citizens, male or female, for the ordinary tasks of everyday life.[7] Yet it is a language that we are taught to respect in matters of international politics and one that has widespread support; to question its authority is considered unpatriotic.

Looking toward possible alternative futures, R. W. Connell believes that the hegemony of authoritative masculinity is being disrupted in Western societies. He claims that this disruption allows us to envisage alternative models of human behavior that are not constructed out of characteristics that depend on gender inequality.[8] Since the behavior of states is partly constituted out of the behaviors of their citizens, we might also begin to consider alternative models of state behavior not constructed out of characteristics associated with hegemonic masculinity. Such models could provide us with a less militarized version of national identity as well as with a greater appreciation of the identity of others outside our own state.

---

7. Elshtain, *Women and War,* p. 245.

8. Connell, *Gender and Power,* ch. 13.

In international politics, one model of human behavior that denies gender inequality could be built around the idea of mediator rather than warrior. Hypothesizing new models of masculinity, Mark Gerzon portrays "the Mediator," whom he describes as one no longer enamored with violence. Gerzon constructs the mediator out of an interview with William Ury of the Harvard Negotiation Project. Mediators need patience, empathy, and sensitivity, qualities that Ury recognized as those usually described as feminine.[9] Another such model is used by social psychologist Herbert Kelman in his problem-solving workshops that bring together parties in conflict for purposes of mediation. The goal of these workshops is for each side to try to understand, and see as legitimate, the other's perspective in other words, to attempt to break down barriers that rigidly separate parties in international conflicts. An important part of this process is building trust. Striving to understand the other's point of view and building trust are not processes that have been valued in the traditional practices of statecraft; they are, however, processes that depend on breaking down political and social hierarchies, including gender hierarchies.[10]

While states' behavior in the international system can often be described in terms similar to characteristics associated with hegemonic masculinity, states do vary across time and space, with respect both to their attitude toward security enhancement and to their attitude toward women, yet rarely have these attitudes been examined together. In an unusual cross cultural study, which examines the role of values in the choices that states make in selecting development paths, Geert Hofstede uses gender as one of his categories of analysis. In all the societies examined in the study, women were perceived as caring for people and the quality of life. In societies that Hofstede labeled masculine, men tended to see their roles as maximally different from those of women. In societies labeled as feminine, considerable overlap in gender roles was evident; men were less assertive and more oriented toward caring. Hofstede's findings suggest that Scandinavian countries scored high on characteristics he labeled as feminine. In policy terms this has translated into sympathy for the weak at home and support for foreign aid programs abroad. According to Hofstede, both national and international disputes tend to get solved peacefully in such societies.[11]

Although the Scandinavian countries are not widely perceived as significant actors in the international system, their policymakers have often taken leading roles in working for peace and the natural environment, and their foreign aid programs rank among the highest in terms of per capita contributions. These countries also rank high in terms of public policies that serve the interests of women. In an interview with the *New York Times* (May 22, 1991), Gro Brundtland, the prime minister of Norway and the leading author of the Report of the World Commission on Environment and Development, claimed that in Norway, where women hold half the cabinet positions, a much stronger emphasis has been placed on child care, education, and family life than in other states. According to Hofstede, the Scandinavian example suggests that states with less militaristic foreign policies and a greater commitment to economic and ecological security may also rely on less gendered models of national identity.

---

9. Gerzon, *A Choice of Heroes*, p. 248.

10. Kelman, "Interactive Problem Solving A Social-Psychological Approach to Conflict Resolution," in Klassen, ed., *Dialogue Toward Inter-Faith Understanding.*

11. Hofstede, "The Role of Cultural Values in Economic Development," in Arvedson, Lönnroth, and Rydén, eds., *Economics and Values*, pp. 122-135. Hofstede claims that both the United States and the former Soviet Union have strongly masculine value systems.

WHAT IS TO BE DONE? BEYOND A GENDERED PERSPECTIVE ON INTERNATIONAL RELATIONS

In most of the contemporary world men do not need to give up their gender identity in order to practice foreign policy; however, the same cannot be said for women. Until we reach a point where values associated with femininity are more universally valued in public life, women will continue to try to give up being feminine when they enter the world of international politics, for those who are the most successful are those who can best deny their femininity.

Given the generally masculine nature of international politics, how could such a change in values be effected? Underscoring the masculinist orientation in the discipline of international relations does nothing to change the masculinist underpinnings of states' behavior in the international system. In the world of statecraft, no fundamental change in the hierarchy of the sexes is likely to take place until women occupy half, or nearly half, the positions at all levels of foreign and military policy-making. No change in the hierarchy of gender will occur until mediators and care givers are as valued as presidents as citizen-warriors currently are. This will not come about until we have a new vision of international relations and until we live in a world in which gender hierarchies no longer contribute to women's oppression. To the very limited extent they have been visible in the world of international politics, women have generally been perceived as victims or problems; only when women's problems or victimization are seen as being the result of unequal, unjust, or exploitative gender relations can women participate equally with men as agents in the provision of global security.

When women have been politically effective, it has generally been at the local level. Increasingly, women around the world are taking leadership roles in small-scale development projects such as cooperative production and projects designed to save the natural environment. Women are also playing important roles in social movements associated with peace and the environment. While these decentralized democratic projects are vital for women to achieve a sense of empowerment and are important building blocks for a more secure future, they will remain marginal as long as they are seen as women's projects and occur far from centers of power. Hence it is vitally important that women be equally represented, not just in social movements and in local politics but at all levels of policy-making. If foreign policy-making within states has been a difficult area for women to enter, leadership positions in international organizations have been equally inaccessible.

While women must have access to what have traditionally been seen as centers of power where men predominate, it is equally important for women and men to work together at the local level. Victories in local struggles are important for the achievement of the kind of multidimensional, multilevel security I have proposed. The feminist perspectives presented in this book suggest that issues of global security are interconnected with, and partly constituted by, local issues; therefore the achievement of comprehensive security depends on action by women and men at all levels of society. Such action is only possible when rigid gender hierarchies are challenged.

To begin to construct this more secure world requires fundamental changes in the discipline that describes and analyzes world politics. The focus of this book has been on how the discipline of international relations would be changed by the introduction of gender as a category of analysis. To begin to think about how gender might be introduced into the discipline and to recapitulate and extend the arguments made in this book, I shall conclude by drawing on the work of feminist scholar Peggy McIntosh, who outlines five phases of curriculum change necessary for introducing gender into scholarly disciplines. While she uses history as an example, her analysis could equally well apply to the discipline of international relations.[12]

The first phase is what McIntosh describes as a womanless world; this type of analysis describes only the activities of those holding high positions of power, usually in dominant states. It is a mode of analysis that has the effect of reinforcing the existing system. My analysis of traditional approaches to the discipline suggests that this is where most of our conventional teaching about international relations has been situated. Phase two, which also has the effect of reinforcing the existing system, notes the absence of women and adds a famous few to the curriculum. While these additions provide role models for women, they do nothing to change the discipline in ways that acknowledge that anything can be learned from women's experiences; rather, they suggest that women can be recognized by the discipline only if they become like men in the public world.[13] In phase three, the absence of women is seen as a problem as we begin to understand the politics implicit in a curriculum constructed without the inclusion of women's experiences; in this phase, women are typically seen as victims. Moving to phase four involves seeing women as valid human beings whose various life experiences have shaped the world in which we live, even though their contributions involve tasks that are often unacknowledged. The final phase of McIntosh's curriculum development brings us to the point where the subject matter of the discipline genuinely includes the experiences of all individuals regardless of race, culture, class, and gender.

Were it to be realized, such a "re-vision" would have a profound impact on the discipline of international relations, which is noteworthy for its exclusionary perspective both with respect to women as well as to non-Western cultures. As this analysis has suggested, a discipline that includes us all would require a radical redrawing of the boundaries of its subject matter. The absence of women from the study of international relations has been so complete that the masculine orientation of the discipline goes unnoticed by most scholars and students. Yet constructing explanations for their absence is only a first step in realizing a nongendered perspective on international relations. For such a perspective to be achieved, it is necessary to go beyond an investigation of the reasons for women's absence from the subject matter of the discipline by demonstrating the many ways in which women's life experiences have an impact on and are affected by the world of international politics, even if they have been largely invisible. Only through analysis that recognizes gender differences but does not take them as fixed or inevitable can we move toward the creation of a nongendered discipline that includes us all.

---

12. McIntosh, "Interactive Phases of Curricular Re-Vision"

13. An example of this attitude can be found in a recent international relations undergraduate textbook that contains a picture of former British prime minister Margaret Thatcher riding in a tank during a NATO exercise. The author notes that since two of Thatcher's most important achievements were the war against Argentina in 1982 and the doubling of the number of British troops facing Iraq in 1990, women cannot be expected to change the way in which we conduct international politics. Rourke, *International Politics on the World Stage,* p. 86.

Post-Modernism

Robert Cox

Social Forces, States, and World Orders: Beyond International Relations Theory

Social Forces, States and World Orders: Beyond International Relations Theory

Robert W. Cox

Academic conventions divide up the seamless web of the real social world into separate spheres, each with its own theorizing; this is a necessary and practical way of gaining understanding. Contemplation of undivided totality may lead to profound abstractions or mystical revelations, hut practical knowledge (that which can be put to work through action) is always partial or fragmentary in origin. Whether the parts remain as limited, separated objects of knowledge, or become the basis for constructing a structured and dynamic view of larger wholes, is a major question of method and purpose. Either way, the starting point is some initial subdivision of reality, usually dictated by convention.

It is wise to bear in mind that such a conventional cutting up of reality is at best just a convenience of the mind. The segments which result, however, derive indirectly from reality insofar as they are the result of practices, that is to say, the responses of consciousness to the pressures of reality. Subdivisions of social knowledge thus may roughly correspond to the ways in which human affairs are organized in particular times and places. They may, accordingly, appear to he increasingly arbitrary when practices change.

International relations is a case in point. It is an area of study concerned with the interrelationships among states in an epoch in which states, and most commonly nation-states, are the principal aggregations of political power. It is concerned with the outcomes of war and peace and thus has obvious practical importance. Changing practice has, however, generated confusion as to the nature of the actors involved (different kinds of state, and non-state entities), extended the range of stakes (low as well as high politics), introduced a greater diversity of goals pursued, and produced a greater complexity in the modes of interaction and the institutions within which action takes place.

One old intellectual convention which contributed to the definition of international relations is the distinction between state and civil society. This distinction made practical sense in the eighteenth and early nineteenth centuries when it corresponded to two more or less distinct spheres of human activity or practice: to an emergent society of individuals based on contract and market relations which replaced a status-based society, on the one hand, and a state with functions limited to maintaining internal peace, external defense and the requisite conditions for markets, on the other. Traditional international relations theory maintains the distinctness of the two spheres, with foreign policy appearing as the pure expression of state interests. Today, however, state and civil society are so interpenetrated that the concepts have become almost purely analytical (referring to difficult-to-define aspects of a complex reality) and are only very vaguely and imprecisely indicative of distinct spheres of activity.

One recent trend in theory has undermined the conceptual unity of the state by perceiving it as the arena of competing bureaucratic entities, while another has reduced the relative importance of the state by introducing a range of private transnational activity and transgovernmental networks of relationships among fragments of state bureaucracies. The state, which remained as the focus of international relations thinking, was still a singular concept: a state was a state was a state. There has been little attempt within the bounds of international relations theory to consider the state/society complex as the basis entity of international relations. As a consequence, the prospect that there exist a plurality of forms of state, expressing different configurations of state/society complexes, remains very largely unexplored, at least in connection with the study of international relations.

The Marxist revival of interest in the state might have been expected to help fill this gap by broadening and diversifying the notion of state and, in particular, by amplifying its social dimensions. Some of the foremost products of this revival, however, either have been of an entirely abstract character, defining the state as a "region" of a singularly conceived capitalist mode of production (Althusser, Poulantzas), or else have shifted attention away from the state and class conflict toward a motivational crisis in culture and ideology (Habermas). Neither goes very far toward exploring the actual or historical differences among forms of state, or considering the implications of the differences for international behavior.

Some historians, both Marxist and non-Marxist, quite independently of theorizing about either international relations or the state, have contributed in a practical way toward filling the gap. E. H. Carr and Eric Hobsbawm have both been sensitive to the continuities between social forces, the changing nature of the state and global relationships. In France, Fernand Braudel (1979) has portrayed these interrelationships in the sixteenth and seventeenth centuries on a vast canvas of the whole world. Inspired by Braudel's work a group led by Immanuel Wallerstein (1974 and 1979) has proposed a theory of world systems defined essentially in terms of social relations: the exploitative exchange relations between a developed core and an underdeveloped periphery, to which correspond different forms of labor control, for example, free labor in the core areas, coerced labor in the peripheries, with intermediate forms in what are called semi-peripheries. Though it offers the most radical alternative to conventional international relations theory, the world systems approach has been criticized on two main grounds: first, for its tendency to undervalue the state by considering the state as merely derivative from its position in the world system (strong states in the core, weak states in the periphery); second, for its alleged, though unintended, system-maintenance bias. Like structural-functional sociology, the approach is better at accounting for forces that maintain or restore a system's equilibrium than identifying contradictions which can lead to a system's transformation.[1]

The above comments are not, however, the central focus of this essay but warnings prior to the following attempt to sketch a method for understanding global power relations: look at the problem of world order in the whole, but beware of reifying a world system.[2] Beware of underrating state power, but in addition give proper attention to social forces and processes and see how they relate to the development of states and world orders. Above all, do not base theory on theory but rather on changing practice and empirical-historical study, which are a proving ground for concepts and hypotheses.

ON PERSPECTIVES AND PURPOSES

Theory is always *for* someone and *for* some purpose. All theories have a perspective. Perspectives derive from a position in time and space, specifically social and political time

---

1. Among critics of the world systems approach, note especially Skocpol (1977 and 1979) and Brenner (1977).

and space. The world is seen from a standpoint definable in terms of nation or social class, of dominance or subordination, of rising or declining power, of a sense of immobility or of present crisis, of past experience, and of hopes and expectations for the future. Of course, sophisticated theory is never just the expression of a perspective. The more sophisticated a theory is, the more it reflects upon and transcends its own perspective; but the initial perspective is always contained within a theory and is relevant to its explication. There is, accordingly, no such thing as theory in itself, divorced from a standpoint in time and space. When any theory so represents itself, it is the more important to examine it as ideology, and to lay bare its concealed perspective.

To each such perspective the enveloping world raises a number of issues; the pressures of social reality present themselves to consciousness as problems. A primary task of theory is to become clearly aware of these problems, to enable the mind to come to grips with the reality it confronts. Thus, as reality changes, old concepts have to be adjusted or rejected and new concepts forged in an Initial dialogue between the theorist and the particular world he tries to comprehend. This initial dialogue concerns the *problematic* proper to a particular perspective. Social and political theory is history-bound at its origin, since it is always traceable to a historically conditioned awareness of certain problems and issues, a problematic, while at the same time it attempts to transcend the particularity of its historical origins in order to place them within the framework of some general propositions or laws.

Beginning with its problematic, theory can serve two distinct purposes One is a simple, direct response: to be a guide to help solve the problems posed within the terms of the particular perspective which was the point of departure. The other is more reflective upon the process of theorizing itself to become clearly aware of the perspective which gives rise to theorizing, and its relation to other perspectives (to achieve a perspective on perspectives); and to open up the possibility of choosing a different valid perspective from which the problematic becomes one of creating an alternative world. Each of these purposes gives rise to a different kind of theory.

The first purpose gives rise to *problem-solving* theory: It takes the world as it finds it, with the prevailing social and power relationships and the institutions into which they are organized, as the given framework for action. The general aim of problem-solving is to make these relationships and institutions work smoothly by dealing effectively with particular sources of trouble. Since the general pattern of institutions and relationships is not called into question, particular problems can be considered in relation to the specialized areas of activity in which they arise. Problem-solving theories are thus fragmented among a multiplicity of spheres or aspects of action, each of which assumes a certain stability in the other spheres (which enables them in practice to be ignored) when confronting a problem arising within its own The strength of the problem-solving approach lies in its ability

2. I use the term "world order" in preference to interstate system: as it is relevant to all historical periods (and not only those in which states have been the component entities, and in preference to "world system" as it is more indicative of a structure having only a certain duration in time and avoiding the equilibrium connotations of system. "World" designates the relevant totality, geographically limited by the range of probable interactions (some past "worlds" being limited to the Mediterranean, to Europe, to China, etc.). "Order" is used in the sense of the way things usually happen (not the absence of turbulence); thus disorder is included in the concept of order. An interstate system is one historical form of world order. The term is used in the plural to indicate that particular patterns of power relationships which have endured in time can be contrasted in terms of their principal characteristics as distinctive world orders.

to fix limits or parameters to a problem area and to reduce the statement of a particular problem to a limited number of variables which are amenable to relatively close and precise examination. The *ceteris paribus* assumption, upon which such theorizing is based, makes it possible to arrive at statements of laws or regularities which appear to have general validity but which imply, of course, the institutional and relational parameters assumed in the problem-solving approach.

The second purpose leads to *critical theory.* It is critical in the sense that it stands apart from the prevailing order of the world and asks how that order came about. Critical theory, unlike problem-solving theory, does not take institutions and social and power relations for granted but calls them into question by concerning itself with their origins and how and whether they might be in the process of changing. It is directed toward an appraisal of the very framework for action, or problematic which problem-solving theory accepts as its parameters. Critical theory is directed to the social and political complex as a whole rather than to the separate parts. As a matter of practice, critical theory, like problem-solving theory, takes as its starting point some aspect or particular sphere of human activity. But whereas the problem-solving approach leads to further analytical subdivision and limitation of the issue to be dealt with, the critical approach leads toward the construction of a larger picture of the whole of which the initially contemplated part is just one component, and seeks to understand the processes of change in which both parts and whole are involved.

Critical theory is theory of history in the sense of being concerned not just with the past but with a continuing process of historical change. Problem-solving theory is nonhistorical or ahistorical, since it, in effect, posits a continuing present (the permanence of the institutions and power relations which constitute its parameters). The strength of the one is the weakness of the other. Because it deals with a changing reality, critical theory must continually adjust its concepts to the changing object it seeks to understand and explain.[3] These concepts and the accompanying methods of inquiry seem to lack the precision that can be achieved by problem-solving theory, which posits a fixed order as its point of reference. This relative strength of problem-solving theory, however, rests upon a false premise, since the social and political order is not fixed but (at least in a long-range perspective) is changing. Moreover, the assumption of fixity is not merely a convenience of method, but also an ideological bias. Problem-solving theories can be represented, in the broader perspective of critical theory, as serving particular national, sectional, or class interests, which are comfortable within the given order. Indeed, the purpose served by problem-solving theory is conservative, since it aims to solve the problems arising in various parts of a complex whole in order to smooth the functioning of the whole. This aim rather belies the frequent claim of problem-solving theory to be value-free. It is methodologically value-free insofar as it treats the variables it considers as objects (as the chemist treats molecules or the physicist forces and motion); but it is value-bound by virtue of the fact that it implicitly accepts the prevailing order as its own framework. Critical theory contains problem-solving theories within itself, but contains them in the form of identifiable ideologies, thereby pointing to their conservative consequences, not to their usefulness as guides to action Problem-solving theory stakes its claims on its greater precision

---

3. E. P Thompson (1978:231-242) argues that historical concepts must often "display extreme elasticity and allow for great irregularity"

and, to the extent that it recognizes critical theory at all, challenges the possibility of achieving any scientific knowledge of historical processes.

Critical theory is, of course, not unconcerned with the problems of the real world. Its aims are just as practical as those of problem-solving theory, but it approaches practice from a perspective which transcends that of the existing order, which problem-solving theory takes as its starting point. Critical theory allows for a normative choice in favor of a social and political order different from the prevailing order, but it limits the range of choice to alternative orders which are feasible transformations of the existing world. A principal objective of critical theory, therefore, is to clarify this range of possible alternatives. Critical theory thus contains an element of utopianism in the sense that it can represent a coherent picture of an alternative order, but its utopianism is constrained by its comprehension of historical processes. It must reject improbable alternatives just as it rejects the permanency of the existing order. In this way critical theory can be a guide *to* strategic action for bringing about an alternative order, whereas problem-solving theory is a guide to tactical actions which, intended or unintended, sustain the existing order.

The perspectives of different historical periods favor one or the other kind of theory. periods of apparent stability or fixity in power relations favor the problem-solving approach. The Cold War was one such period. In international relations, it fostered a concentration upon the problems of how to manage an apparently enduring relationship between two superpowers. However, a condition of uncertainty in power relations beckons to critical theory as people seek to understand the opportunities and risks of change. Thus the events of the 1970s generated a sense of greater fluidity in power relationships, of a many-faceted crisis, crossing the threshold of uncertainty and opening the opportunity for a new development of critical theory directed to the problems of world order. To reason about possible future world orders now, however, requires a broadening of our inquiry beyond conventional international relations, so as to encompass basic processes at work in the development of social forces and forms of state, and in the structure of global political economy. Such, at least, is the central argument of this essay.

REALISM, MARXISM, AND AN APPROACH TO A CRITICAL THEORY OF WORLD ORDER

Currents of theory which include works of sophistication usually share some of the features of both problem-solving and critical theory but tend to emphasize one approach over the other. Two currents which have had something important to say about interstate relations and world orders—realism and Marxism—are considered here as a preliminary to an attempted development of the critical approach.

The realist theory of international relations had its origin in a historical mode of thought. Friedrich Meinecke (1957), in his study on *raison d'état,* traced it to the political theory of Machiavelli and the diplomacy of Renaissance Italian city-states quite distinct from the general norms propagated by the ideologically dominant institution of medieval society, the Christian church. In perceiving the doctrines and principles underlying the conduct of states as a reaction to specific historical circumstances, Meinecke's interpretation of *raison d'état* is a contribution to critical theory. Other scholars associated with the realist tradition, such as E. H. Carr and Ludwig Dehio, have continued this historical mode of thought, delineating the particular configurations of forces which fixed the framework of international behavior in different periods and trying to understand institutions, theories and events within their historical contexts.

Since the Second World War, some American scholars, notably Hans Morgenthau and Kenneth Waltz, have transformed realism into a form of problem-solving theory. Though individuals of considerable historical learning, they have tended to adopt the fixed ahistorical view of the framework for action characteristic of problem-solving theory, rather than standing back from this framework, in the manner of E. H. Carr, and treating it as historically conditioned and thus susceptible to change. It is no accident that this tendency in theory coincided with the Cold War, which imposed the category of bipolarity upon international relations, and an overriding concern for the defense of American power as a bulwark of the maintenance of order.

The generalized form of the framework for action postulated by this new American realism (which we shall henceforth call neorealism, which is the ideological form abstracted from the real historical framework imposed by the Cold War) is characterized by three levels, each of which can be understood in terms of what classical philosophers would call substances or essences, that is, fundamental and unchanging substrata of changing and accidental manifestations or phenomena. These basic realities were conceived as: (1) the nature of man, understood in terms of Augustinian original sin or the Hobbesian "perpetual and restless desire for power after power that ceaseth only in death" (Hobbes 16: part 1, ch. xi); (2) the nature of states, which differ in their domestic constitutions and in their capabilities for mobilizing strength, but are similar in their fixation with a particular concept of national interest (a Leibnizian monad) as a guide to their actions; and (3) the nature of the state system, which places rational constraints upon the unbridled pursuit of rival national interests through the mechanism of the balance of power.

Having arrived at this view of underlying substances, history becomes for neorealists a quarry providing materials with which to illustrate variations on always recurrent themes. The mode of thought ceases to be historical even though the materials used are derived from history. Moreover, this mode of reasoning dictates that, with respect to essentials, the future will always be like the past.[4]

In addition, this core of neorealist theory has extended itself into such areas as game theory, in which the notion of substance at the level of human nature is presented as a rationality assumed to be common to the competing actors who appraise the stakes at issue, the alternative strategies, and the respective payoffs in a similar manner. This idea of a common rationality reinforces the nonhistorical mode of thinking. Other modes of thought are to be castigated as inapt; and there is no attempt to understand them in their own terms (which makes it difficult to account for the irruption into international affairs of a phenomenon like Islamic integralism for instance).

The "common rationality" of neorealism arises from its polemic with liberal internationalism. For neorealism, this rationality is the one appropriate response to a postulated anarchic state system. Morality is effective only to the extent that it is enforced by physical power. This has given neorealism the appearance of being a non-normative theory. It is "value-free" in its exclusion of moral goals (wherein it sees the weakness of liberal internationalism) and in its reduction of problems to their physical power relations. This non-normative quality is, however, only superficial. There is a latent normative element which

---

4. Kenneth Waltz (1980) asked the question "will the future be like the past?" which he answered affirmatively—not only was the same pattern of relationships likely to prevail but it would be for the good of all that this should be so. It should be noted that the future contemplated by Waltz was the next decade or so.

derives from the assumptions of neorealist theory: security within the postulated interstate system depends upon each of the major actors understanding this system in the same way, that is to say, upon each of them adopting neorealist rationality as a guide to action. Neorealist theory derives from its foundations the prediction that the actors, from their experiences within the system, will tend to think in this way; but the theory also performs a proselytizing function as the advocate of this form of rationality. To the neorealist theorist, this proselytizing function (wherein lies the normative role of neorealism) is particularly urgent in states which have attained power in excess of that required to balance rivals, since such states may be tempted to discard the rationality of neorealism and try to impose their own moral sense of order, particularly if, as in the case of the United States, cultural tradition has encouraged more optimistic and moralistic views of the nature of man, the state and world order.[5]

The debate between neorealist and liberal internationalists reproduces, with up to date materials, the seventeenth-century challenge presented by the civil philosophy of Hobbes to the natural-law theory of Grotius. Each of the arguments is grounded in different views of the essences of man, the state and the interstate system. An alternative which offered the possibility of getting beyond this opposition of mutually exclusive concepts was pointed out by the eighteenth-century Neapolitan Giambattista Vico, for whom the nature of man and of human institutions (among which must be included the state and the interstate system) should not be thought of in terms of unchanging substances but rather as a continuing creation of new forms. In the duality of continuity and change, where neorealism stresses continuity, the Vichian perspective stresses change; as Vico wrote (1744/1970: para. 349), ". . . this world of nations has certainly been made by men, and its guise must therefore be found within the modifications of our own human mind."

This should not be taken as a statement of radical idealism, (that is, that the world is a creation of mind). For Vico, everchanging forms of mind were shaped by the complex of social relations in the genesis of which class struggle played the principal role, as it later did for Marx. Mind is, however, the thread connecting the present with the past, a means of access to a knowledge of these changing modes of social reality Human nature (the modifications of mind) and human institutions are identical with human history; they are to be understood in genetic and not in essentialist terms (as in neorealism) or in teleological terms (as in functionalism). One cannot, in this Vichian perspective, properly abstract man and the state from history so as to define their substances or essences *as prior to* history, history being but the record of interactions of manifestations of these substances. A proper study of human affairs should be able to reveal both the coherence of minds and institutions characteristic of different ages, and the process whereby one such coherent pattern—which we can call a historical structure—succeeds another. Vico's project, which we would now call social science, was to arrive at a "mental dictionary" or set of common concepts, with which one is able to comprehend the process of "ideal eternal history" or what is most gen-

5. A recent example of this argument is Stephen Krasner (1978) The normative intent of the new realism is most apparent as a polemic response to liberal moralism This was also the case for E H. Carr (1946), who offered a "scientific" mode of thinking about international relations in opposition to the "utopianism" of the supporters of the League of Nations in Britain. Dean Acheson and George Kennan, in laying the foundations of U.S. Cold War policy, acknowledged their debt to Reinhold Niebuhr, whose revival of a pessimistic Augustinian view of human nature challenged the optimistic Lockean view native to American culture. Krasner's chosen target is "Lockean liberalism" which he sees as having undermined the rational defense of U.S. national interests.

eral and common in the sequence of changes undergone by human nature and institutions (paras. 35, 145, 161, 349). The error which Vico criticized as the "conceit of scholars,' who will have it that "what they know is as old as the world,' consists in taking a form of thought derived from a particular phase of history (and thus from a particular structure of social relations) and assuming it to be universally valid [para. 127]. This is an error of neorealism and more generally, the flawed foundation of all problem-solving theory. It does not, of course, negate the practical utility of neorealism and problem-solving theories within their ideological limits. The Vichian approach, by contrast, is that of critical theory.

How does Marxism relate to this method or approach to a theory of world order? In the first place, it is impossible, without grave risk of confusion, to consider Marxism as a single current of thought. For our purposes, it is necessary to distinguish two divergent Marxist currents, analogous to the bifurcation between the old realism and the new. There is a Marxism which reasons historically and seeks to explain, as well as to promote, changes in social relations; there is also a Marxism, designed as a framework for the analysis of the capitalist state and society, which turns its back on historical knowledge in favor of a more static and abstract conceptualization of the mode of production. The first we may call by the name under which it recognizes itself: historical materialism. It is evident in the historical works of Marx, in those of present-day Marxist historians such as Eric Hobsbawm, and in the thought of Gramsci. It has also influenced some who would not be considered (or consider themselves) Marxist in any strict sense, such as many of the French historians associated with the *Annales*. The second is represented by the so-called structural Marxism of Althusser and Poulantzas ("so-called" in order to distinguish their use of "structure" from the concept of historical structure in this essay) and most commonly takes the form of an exegesis of *Capital* and other sacred texts. Structural Marxism shares some of the features of the neorealist problem-solving approach such as its ahistorical, essentialist epistemology, though not its precision in handling data nor, since it has remained very largely a study in abstractions, its practical applicability to concrete problems. To this extent it does not concern us here. Historical materialism is, however, a foremost source of critical theory and it corrects neorealism in four important respects.

The first concerns dialectic, a term which, like Marxism, has been appropriated to express a variety of not always compatible meanings, so its usage requires some definition. It is used here at two levels: the level of logic and the level of real history. At the level of logic, it means a dialogue seeking truth through the explorations of contradictions.[6] One aspect of this is the continual confrontation of concepts with the reality they are supposed to represent and their adjustment to this reality as it continually changes. Another aspect, which is part of the method of adjusting concepts, is the knowledge that each assertion concerning reality contains implicitly its opposite and that both assertion and opposite are not mutually exclusive but share some measure of the truth sought, a truth, moreover, that is always in motion, never to be encapsulated in some definitive form. At the level of real history, dialectic is the potential for alternative forms of development arising from the confrontation of opposed social forces in any concrete historical situation.

Both realism and historical materialism direct attention to conflict. Neorealism sees conflict as inherent in the human condition, a constant factor flowing directly from the

---

6. See, for instance, R. G Collingwood's (1942) distinction between dialectical and eristical reasoning Collingwood takes dialectic back to its Greek origins and spares us the assertions of theological Marxism concerning "Diamat"

power-seeking essence of human nature and taking the political form of a continual reshuffling of power among the players in a zero-sum game, which is always played according to its own innate rules. Historical materialism sees in conflict the process of a continual remaking of human nature and the creation of new patterns of social relations which change the rules of the game and out of which—if historical materialism remains true to its own logic and method—new forms of conflict may be expected ultimately to arise. In other words, neorealism sees conflict as a recurrent consequence of a continuing structure, whereas historical materialism sees conflict as a possible cause of structural change.

Second, by its focus on imperialism, historical materialism adds a vertical dimension of power to the horizontal dimension of rivalry among the most powerful states, which draws the almost exclusive attention of neorealism. This dimension is the dominance and subordination of metropole over hinterland, center over periphery, in a world political economy.

Third, historical materialism enlarges the realist perspective through its concern with the relationship between the state and civil society. Marxists, like non-Marxists, are divided between those who see the state as the mere expression of the particular interests in civil society and those who see the state as an autonomous force expressing some kind of general interest. This, for Marxists, would be the general interest of capitalism as distinct from the particular interests of capitalists. Gramsci (1971:158-168) contrasted historical materialism, which recognizes the efficacy of ethical and cultural sources of political action (though always relating them with the economic sphere), with what he called historical economism or the reduction of everything to technological and material interests. Neorealist theory in the United States has returned to the state/civil society relationship, though it has treated civil society as a constraint upon the state and a limitation imposed by particular interests upon *raison d'état,* which is conceived of, and defined as, independent of civil society.[7] The sense of a reciprocal relationship between structure (economic relations) and superstructure (the ethico-political sphere) in Gramsci's thinking contains the potential for considering state/society complexes as the constituent entities of a world order and for exploring the particular historical forms taken by these complexes.[8]

Fourth, historical materialism focuses upon the production process as a critical element in the explanation of the particular historical form taken by a state/society complex. The production of goods and services, which creates both the wealth of a society and the basis for a state's ability to mobilize power behind its foreign policy, takes place through a power relationship between those who control and those who execute the tasks of production. Political conflict and the action of the state either maintain, or bring about changes in, these power relations of production. Historical materialism examines the connections between power in production, power in the state, and power in international relations. Neorealism has, by contrast, virtually ignored the production process. This is the point on

7. As in Krasner (1978b) and Katzenstein (1978) The United States is represented by these authors as a state which is weak in relation to the strength of civil society (or more particularly of interests in civil society), whereas other states—e.g., Japan or France—are stronger in relation to their societies. Civil society is thus seen in the U.S. case as limiting the effectiveness of the state.

8. Gramsci saw ideas, politics, and economics as reciprocally related, convertible into each other and bound together in a *blocco storico.* "Historical materialism" he wrote, "is in a certain sense a reform and development of Hegelianism. It is philosophy freed from unilateral ideological elements, the full consciousness of the contradictions of philosophy" (1975:471, my rough translation).

which the problem-solving bias of neorealism is most clearly to be distinguished from the critical approach of historical materialism. Neorealism implicitly takes the production process and the power relations inherent in it as a given element of the national interest, and therefore as part of its parameters. Historical materialism is sensitive to the dialectical possibilities of change in the sphere of production which could affect the other spheres, such as those of the state and world order.

This discussion has distinguished two kinds of theorizing as a preliminary to proposing a critical approach to a theory of world order. Some of the basic premises for such a critical theory can now be restated:

(1) An awareness that action is never absolutely free but takes place within a framework for action which constitutes its problematic Critical theory would start with this framework, which means starting with historical inquiry or an appreciation of the human experience that gives rise to the need for theory;[9]

(2) A realization that not only action but also theory is shaped by the problematic Critical theory is conscious of its own relativity but through this consciousness can achieve a broader time-perspective and become less relative than problem-solving theory. It knows that the task of theorizing can never be finished in an enclosed system but must continually be begun anew;

(3) The framework for action changes over time and a principal goal of critical theory is to understand these changes;

(4) This framework has the form of a historical structure, a particular combination of thought patterns, material conditions and human institutions which has a certain coherence among its elements These structures do not determine people's actions in any mechanical sense but constitute the context of habits, pressures, expectations and constraints within which action takes place;

(5) The framework or structure within which action takes place is to be viewed, not from the top in terms of the requisites for its equilibrium or reproduction (which would quickly lead back to problem-solving), but rather from the bottom or from outside in terms of the conflicts which arise within it and open the possibility of its transformation [10]

FRAMEWORKS FOR ACTION: HISTORICAL STRUCTURES

As its most abstract, the notion of a framework for action or historical structure is a picture of a particular configuration of forces. This configuration does not determine actions in any direct, mechanical way but imposes pressures and constraints. Individuals and groups may move with the pressures or resist and oppose them, but they cannot

9. The notion of a framework for action recalls what Machiavelli (1531/1970:105-106) called *necessità*, a sense that the conditions of existence require action to create or sustain a form of social order. *Necessità* engenders both the possibility of a new order and all the risks inherent in changing the existing order. "Few men ever welcome new laws setting up a new order in the state unless necessity makes it clear to them that there is a need for such laws; and since such a necessity cannot arise without danger, the state may easily be ruined before the new order has been brought to completion"

10. In this regard, Stanley Hoffmann (l977) has written: "Born and raised in America, the discipline of international relations is, so to speak, too close to the fire. It needs triple distance: it should move away from the contemporary world toward the past; from the perspective of a superpower (and a highly conservative one), toward that of the weak and the revolutionary—away from the impossible quest for stability; from the glide into policy science, back to the steep ascent toward the peaks which the questions raised by traditional political philosophy represent (p. 59).

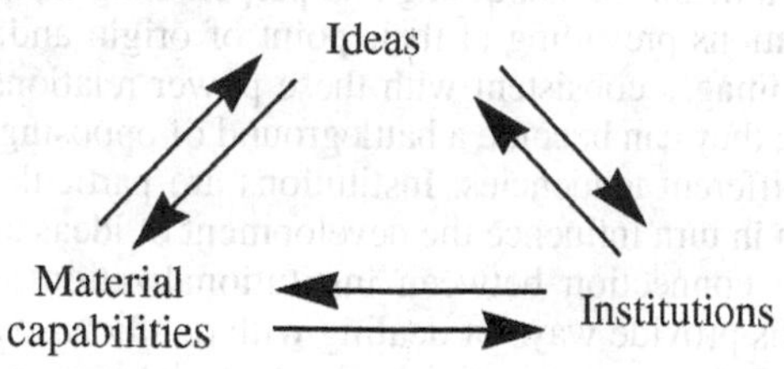

Figure 1.

ignore them. To the extent that they do successfully resist a prevailing historical structure, they buttress their actions with an alternative, emerging configuration of forces, a rival structure.

Three categories of forces (expressed as potentials) interact in a structure: material capabilities, ideas and institutions (see fig. 1). No one way determinism need be assumed among these three; the relationships can be assumed to be reciprocal. The question of which way the lines of force run is always a historical question to be answered by a study of the particular case.

Material capabilities are productive and destructive potentials. In their dynamic form these exist as technological and organizational capabilities, and in their accumulated forms as natural resources which technology can transform, stocks of equipment (for example, industries and armaments), and the wealth which can command these.

Ideas are broadly of two kinds. One kind consists of intersubjective meanings, or those shared notions of the nature of social relations which tend to perpetuate habits and expectations of behavior (Taylor 1965). Examples of intersubjective meanings in contemporary world politics are the notions that people are organized and commanded by states which have authority over defined territories; that states relate to one another through diplomatic agents; that certain rules apply for the protection of diplomatic agents as being in the common interest of all states; and that certain kinds of behavior are to be expected when conflict arises between states, such as negotiation, confrontation, or war. These notions, though durable over long periods of time, are historically conditioned. The realities of world politics have not always been represented in precisely this way and may not be in the future. It is possible to trace the origins of such ideas and also to detect signs of a weakening of some of them.[11]

The other kind of ideas relevant to a historical structure are collective images of social order held by different groups of people. These are differing views as to both the nature and the legitimacy of prevailing power relations, the meanings of justice and public good, and so forth. Whereas intersubjective meanings are broadly common throughout a particular historical structure and constitute the common ground of social discourse (including conflict), collective images may be several and opposed.[12] The clash of rival collective images provides evidence of the potential for alternative paths of development and raises questions as to the possible material and institutional basis for the emergence of an alternative structure.

---

[11] Taylor (1965) points out that expectations with regard to negotiating behavior are culturally differentiated in the present world. Garrett Mattingly (1955) studied the origin of the ideas outlined in this paragraph which are implicit in the modern state system.

Institutionalization is a means of stabilizing and perpetuating a particular order. Institutions reflect the power relations prevailing at their point of origin and tend, at least initially, to encourage collective images consistent with these power relations. Eventually, institutions take on their own life; they can become a battleground of opposing tendencies, or rival institutions may reflect different tendencies. Institutions are particular amalgams of ideas and material power which in turn influence the development of ideas and material capabilities.

There is a close connection between institutionalization and what Gramsci called hegemony. Institutions provide ways of dealing with conflicts so as to minimize the use of force. There is an enforcement potential in the material power relations underlying any structure, in that the strong can clobber the weak if they think it necessary. But force will not have to be used in order to ensure the dominance of the strong to the extent that the weak accept the prevailing power relations as legitimate. This the weak may do if the strong see their mission as hegemonic and not merely dominant or dictatorial, that is, if they are willing to make concessions that will secure the weak's acquiescence in their leadership and if they can express this leadership in terms of universal or general interests, rather than just as serving their own particular interests.[13] Institutions may become the anchor for such a hegemonic strategy since they lend themselves both to the representations of diverse interests and to the universalization of policy.

It is convenient to be able to distinguish between hegemonic and nonhegemonic structures, that is to say between those in which the power basis of the structure tends to recede into the background of consciousness, and those in which the management of power relations is always in the forefront. Hegemony cannot, however, be reduced to an institutional dimension. One must beware of allowing a focus upon institutions to obscure either changes in the relationship of material forces, or the emergence of ideological challenge to an erstwhile prevailing order. Institutions may be out of phase with these other aspects of reality and their efficacy as a means of regulating conflict (and thus their hegemonic function) thereby undermined. They may be an expression of hegemony but cannot be taken as identical to hegemony.

The method of historical structures is one of representing what can be called limited totalities. The historical structure does not represent the whole world but rather a particular

12. Collective images are not aggregations of fragmented opinions of individuals such as are compiled through surveys; they are coherent mental types expressive of the world views of specific groups such as may be reconstructed through the work of historians and sociologists—e.g., Max Weber's reconstructions of forms of religious consciousness.

13. Gramsci's principal application of the concept of hegemony was to the relations among social classes—e.g., in explaining the inability of the Italian industrial bourgeoisie to establish its hegemony after the unification of Italy and in examining the prospects of the Italian industrial workers establishing their class hegemony over peasantry and petty bourgeoisie so as to create a new *blocco storico* (historic bloc), a term which in Gramsci's work corresponds roughly to the notion of historic structure in this essay. The term "hegemony" in Gramsci's work is linked to debates in the international Communist movement concerning revolutionary strategy and in this connection its application is specifically to classes. The form of the concept, however, draws upon his reading of Machiavelli and is not restricted to class relations; it has a broader potential applicability Gramsci's adjustment of Machiavellian ideas to the realities of the world he knew as an exercise in dialectic in the sense defined above. It is an appropriate continuation of his method to perceive the applicability of the concept to world order structures as suggested here. For Gramsci, as for Machiavelli, the general question involved in hegemony is the nature of power, and power is a centaur, part man, part beast, a combination of force and consent. See Machiavelli (1513/1977:149-150) and Gramsci (1971:169-170).

sphere of human activity in its historically located totality. The *ceteris paribus* problem, which falsifies problem-solving theory by leading to an assumption of total stasis, is avoided by juxtaposing and connecting historical structures in related spheres of action. Dialectic is introduced, first, by deriving the definition of a particular structure, not from some abstract model of a social system or mode of production, but from a study of the historical situation to which it relates, and second, by looking for the emergence of rival structures expressing alternative possibilities of development. The three sets of forces indicated in figure 8.1 are a heuristic device, not categories with a predetermined hierarchy of relationships. Historical structures are contrast models: like ideal types they provide, in a logically coherent form, a simplified representation of a complex reality and an expression of tendencies, limited in their applicability in time and space, rather than fully realized developments.

For the purpose of the present discussion, the method of historical structures is applied to the three levels, or spheres of activity: (1) organization of production, more particularly with regard to the *social forces* engendered by the production process; (2) *forms of state* as derived from a study of state/society complexes; and (3) *world orders,* that is, the particular configurations of forces which successively define the problematic of war or peace for the ensemble of states. Each of these levels can be studied as a succession of dominant and emergent rival structures.

The three levels are interrelated. Changes in the organization of production generate new social forces which, in turn, bring about changes in the structure of states; and the generalization of changes in the structure of states alters the problematic of world order. For instance, as H. H. Carr (1945) argued, the incorporation of the industrial workers (a new social force) as participants within western states from the late nineteenth century, accentuated the movement of these states toward economic nationalism and imperialism (a new form of state), which brought about a fragmentation of the world economy and a more conflictual phase of international relations (the new structure of world order).

The relationship among the three levels is not, however, simply unilinear. Transnational social forces have influenced states through the world structure, as evidenced by the effect of expansive nineteenth-century capitalism, *les bourgeois conquérants* (Morazé 1957), upon the development of state structures in both core and periphery. Particular structures of world order exert influence over the forms which states take: Stalinism was, at least in part, a response to a sense of threat to the existence of the Soviet state from a hostile world order; the military-industrial complex in core countries, justifies its influence today by pointing to the conflictual condition of world order; and the prevalence of repressive militarism in periphery countries can be explained by the external support of imperialism as well as by a particular conjunction of internal forces. Forms of state also affect the development of social forces through the kinds of domination they exert, for example, by advancing one class interest and thwarting others.[14]

Considered separately, social forces, forms of state, and world orders can be represented in a preliminary approximation as particular configurations of material capabilities, ideas and institutions (as indicated in figure 1). Considered in relation to each other, and thus moving toward a fuller representation of historical process, each will he seen as containing, as well as bearing the impact of, the others (as in figure 2)[15]

14. A recent discussion of the reciprocal character of these relations is in Gourevitch (l978).

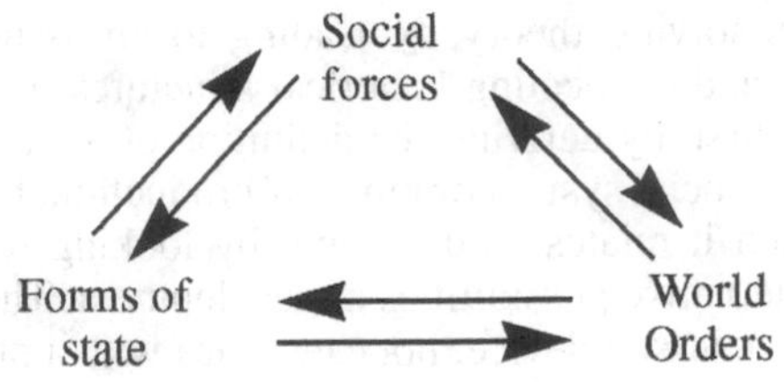

Figure 2. *Hegemony and World Orders*

How are these reciprocal relationships to be read in the present historical conjuncture? Which of the several relationships will tell us the most? A sense of the historicity of concepts suggests that the critical relationships may not he the same in successive historical periods, even within the post-Westphalian era for which the term "state system" has particular meaning. The approach to a critical theory of world order, adumbrated here, takes the form of an interconnected series of historical hypotheses.

Neo-realism puts the accent on states reduced to their dimension of material force and similarly reduces the structure of world order to the balance of power as a configuration of material forces. Neorealism, which generally dismisses social forces as irrelevant, is not much concerned with differentiating forms of state (except insofar as "strong societies" in liberal democratic polities may hamper the use of force by the state or advance particular interests over the national interest), and tends to place a low value on the normative and institutional aspects of world order.

One effort to broaden the realist perspective to include variations in the authority of international norms and institutions is the theory of "hegemonic stability" which, as stated by Robert Keohane (1980), "holds that hegemonic structures of power, dominated by a single country, are most conducive to the development of strong international regimes, whose rules are relatively precise and well-obeyed."[16] The classic illustrations of the theory discussed by Keohane are thc *pax Britannica* of the mid-nineteenth century and the *pax Americana* of the years following the Second World War. The theory appears to be confirmed by the decline in observance of the norms of the nineteenth-century order which accompanied Britain's relative decline in state power from the late-nineteenth century Exponents of the theory see a similar decline, since the early 1970s, in the observance of norms of the postwar order, relating it to a relative decline in U.S. power. Robert Keohane has tested the theory in particular issue areas (energy, money and trade) on the grounds that power is not a fungible asset, hut has to be differentiated according to the contexts in which a state tried to be influential. He finds that, particularly in the areas of trade and money, changes in U.S. power are insufficient to explain the changes that have occurred

15. I have been engaged with Jeffrey Harrod in a study of production relations on a world scale which begins with an examination of distinctive patterns of power relations in the production process as separate historical structures and which then leads to a consideration of different forms of state and global political economy. Bringing in these last two levels is necessary to an understanding of the existence of the different patterns of production relations and the hierarchy of relationships among them. One could equally well adopt forms of state or world orders at the point of departure and ultimately be required to bring the other levels in to explain the historical process.

and need to be supplemented by the introduction of domestic political, economic and cultural factors.

An alternative approach might start by redefining what it is that is to be explained, namely, the relative stability of successive world orders. This can be done by equating stability with a concept of hegemony that is based on a coherent conjunction or fit between a configuration of material power, the prevalent collective image of world order (including certain norms) and a set of institutions which administer the order with a certain semblance of universality (that is, not just as the overt instruments of a particular state's dominance). In this formulation, state power ceases to be the sole explanatory factor and becomes part of what is to be explained. This rephrasing of the question addresses a major difficulty in the neorealist version signalled by Keohane and others, namely, how to explain the failure of the United States to establish a stable world order in the interwar period despite its preponderance of power If the dominance of a single state coincides with a stable order on some occasions but not on others, then there may be some merit in looking more closely at what is meant by stability and more broadly at what may be its sufficient conditions. Dominance by a powerful state may be a necessary but not a sufficient condition of hegemony.

The two periods of the *pax Britannica* and the *pax Americana* also satisfy the reformulated definition of hegemony. In the mid-nineteenth century, Britain's world supremacy was founded on its sea power, which remained free from challenge by a continental state as a result of Britain's ability to play the role of balancer in a relatively fluid balance of power in Europe. The norms of liberal economics (free trade, the gold standard, free movement of capital and persons) gained widespread acceptance with the spread of British prestige, providing a universalistic ideology which represented these norms as the basis of a harmony of interests. While there were no formal international institutions, the ideological separation of economics from politics meant that the City could appear as administrator and regulator according to these universal rules, with British sea power remaining in the background as potential enforcer.

The historical structure was transformed in its three dimensions during the period running from the last quarter of the nineteenth century through the Second World War. During this period British power declined relatively, losing its undisputed supremacy at sea, first with the German challenge and then with the rise of U.S. power; economic liberalism foundered with the rise of protectionism, the new imperialisms and ultimately the end of

---

16. Keohane cites as others who have contributed to this theory Charles Kindleberger, Robert Gilpin, and Stephen Krasner. "Hegemony" is used by Keohane here in the limited sense of dominance by a state. This meaning is to be distinguished from its meaning in this article, which is derived from Gramsci—i.e., hegemony as a structure of dominance, leaving open the question of whether the dominant power is a state or a group of states or some combination of state and private power, which is sustained by broadly based consent through acceptance of an ideology and of institutions consistent with this structure. Thus a hegemonic structure of world order is one in which power takes a primarily consensual form, as distinguished from a nonhegemonic order in which there are manifestly rival powers and no power has been able to establish the legitimacy of its dominance. There can be dominance without hegemony; hegemony is one possible form dominance may take. Institutionalized hegemony, as used in this essay, corresponds to what Keohane calls a "strong international regime" His theory can be restated in our terms as: dominance by a powerful state is most conducive to the development of hegemony. In this present text, the term "hegemony" is reserved for a consensual order and "dominance" refers only to a preponderance of material power. Keohane's discussion of hegemony is developed in his later work (1984) but without affecting the distinction made here.

the gold standard; and the belated and abortive attempt at international institutionalization through the League of Nations, unsustained either by a dominant power or a widely accepted ideology, collapsed in a world increasingly organized into rival power blocs.

The power configuration of the *pax Americana* was more rigid than that of the earlier hegemony, taking the form of alliances (all hinging on U.S. power) created in order to contain the Soviet Union. The stabilization of this power configuration created the conditions for the unfolding of a global economy in which the United States played a role similar to that of Britain and mid-nineteenth century. The United States rarely needed to intervene directly in support of specific national economic interests; by maintaining the rules of an international economic order according to the revised liberalism of Bretton Woods, the strength of U.S. corporations engaged in the pursuit of profits was sufficient to ensure continuing national power. The *pax Americana* produced a greater number of formal international institutions than the earlier hegemony. The nineteenth-century separation of politics and economics had been blurred by the experience of the Great Depression and the rise of Keynesian doctrines. Since states now had a legitimate and necessary overt role in national economic management, it became necessary both to multi-lateralize the administrative management of the international economy and to give it an intergovernmental quality.

The notion of hegemony as a fit between power, ideas and institutions makes it possible to deal with some of the problems in the theory of state dominance as the necessary condition for a stable international order; it allows for lags and leads in hegemony. For example, so appealing was the nostalgia for the nineteenth-century hegemony that the ideological dimension of the *pax Britannica* flourished long after the power configuration that supported it had vanished. Sustained, and ultimatelv futile efforts were made to revive a liberal world economy along with the gold standard in the interwar period. Even in the postwar period, British policy continued to give precedence to balance of payments problems over national industrial development and employment considerations.[17] A "lead" case is that of the United States, where the growth indicators of material power during the interwar period were insufficient predictors of a new hegemony. It was necessary that U.S. leaders should come to see themselves in ideological terms as the necessary guarantors of a new world order. The Roosevelt era made this transition, including both the conscious rejection of the old hegemony (e.g., by torpedoing the world economic conference in 1933 and abandoning the gold standard) and the gradual incorporation of New-Deal principles into the ideological basis of the new world order. There followed U.S. initiative to create the institutions to administer this order.[18] Neomercantilists in the United States now warn against a danger of repeating the British error, urging U.S. policymakers not to continue to operate according to doctrines appropriate to the *pax Americana* when the United States can no longer afford to act as guarantor for a universalist world order. Their persuasive efforts underline the point that in these matters ideology is a determining sphere of action which has to be understood in its connections with material power relations.

---

17. Two classic studies relevant particularly to the interwar period are Karl Polanyi (1957b) and E. H. Carr (1946). Stephen Blank (1978) comments on postwar British economic policy; as does Stephen Krasner (1976). Also see R. Harrod (1951).

18. The international implications of the New Deal are dealt with in several passages in Arthur M. Schlesinger, Jr. (1960: vol. 2). Charles Maier (1978) discusses the relationship between the New Deal and the postwar ideology of world order. Richard Gardner (1956) shows the link between New Deal ideas and the institutions of world economy set up after World War II in the Bretton Woods negotiations.

SOCIAL FORCES, HEGEMONY AND IMPERIALISM

Represented as a fit between material power, ideology and institutions, hegemony may seem to lend itself to a cyclical theory of history; the three dimensions fitting together in certain times and places and coming apart in others. This is reminiscent of earlier notions of *virtù* or of the *weltgeist* migrating from people to people. The analogy merely points to something which remains unexplained. What is missing is some theory as to how and why the fit comes about and comes apart. It is my contention that the explanation may be sought in the realm of social forces shaped by production relations.

Social forces are not to be thought of as existing exclusively within states. Particular social forces may overflow state boundaries, and world structures can be described in terms of social forces just as they can be described as configurations of state power. The world can be represented as a pattern of interacting social forces in which states play an intermediate though autonomous role between the global structure of social forces and local configurations of social forces within particular countries This may be called a political economy perspective of the world power is seen as *emerging* from social processes rather than taken as given in the form of accumulated material capabilities, that is as the result of these processes (Paraphrasing Marx, one could describe the latter, neorealist view as the "fetishism of power.")[19] In reaching for a political economy perspective, we move from identifying the structural characteristics of world orders as configurations of material capabilities, ideas and institutions (fig. 1.) to explaining their origins, growth and demise in terms of the interrelationships of the three levels of structures (fig. 2).

It is, of course, no great discovery to find that, viewed in the political economy perspective, the *pax Britannica* was based both on the ascendancy of manufacturing capitalism in the international exchange economy, of which Britain was the center, and on the social and ideological power, in Britain and other parts of northwest Europe, of the c lass which drew its wealth from manufacturing. The new bourgeoisie did not need to control states directly; its social power became the premise of state politics.[20]

The demise of this hegemonic order can also be explained by the development of social forces. Capitalism mobilized an industrial labor force in the most advanced countries, and from the last quarter of the nineteenth century industrial workers had an impact on the structure of the state in these countries. The incorporation of the industrial workers, the new social force called into existence by manufacturing capitalism, into the nation involved an extension in the range of state action in the form of economic intervention and social policy. This in turn brought the factor of domestic welfare (i.e., the social minimum required to maintain the allegiance of the workers) into the realm of foreign policy. The claims of welfare competed with the exigencies of liberal internationalism within the management of states; as the former gained ground, protectionism, the new imperialism and ultimately the end of the gold standard marked the long decline

19. The basic point I am making here is suggested by a passage from Gramsci (1971:176-177; 1975:1562) which reads: "Do international relations precede or follow (logically) fundamental social relations? There can be no doubt but that they follow. Any organic innovation in the social structure, through its technical-military expressions, modifies organically absolute and relative relations in the international field too." Gramsci used the term "organic" to refer to relatively long-term and permanent changes, as opposed to "conjunctural."

20. E. J. Hobsbawm (l977: l5) writes: "The men who officially presided over the affairs of the victorious bourgeois order in its moment of triumph were a deeply reactionary country nobleman from Prussia, an imitation emperor in France and a succession of aristocratic landowners in Britain."

of liberal internationalism.[21] The liberal form of state was slowly replaced by the welfare nationalist form of state.

The spread of industrialization, and the mobilization of social classes it brought about, not only changed the nature of states but also altered the international configuration of state power as new rivals overtook Britain's lead. Protectionism, as the means of building economic power comparable to Britain's, was for these new industrial countries more convincing than the liberal theory of comparative advantage. The new imperialisms of the major industrial powers were a projection abroad of the welfare nationalist consensus among social forces sought or achieved within the nations. As both the material predominance of the British economy and the appeal of the hegemonic ideology weakened, the hegemonic world order of the mid-nineteenth century gave place to a non-hegemonic configuration of rival power blocs.

Imperialism is a rather loose concept which in practice has to be newly defined with reference to each historical period. There is little point in looking for any "essence" of imperialism beyond the forms which dominance and subordination take in different successive world order structures. The actual form, whether activated by states, by social forces (e.g., the managements of multinational corporations), or some combination of both, and whether domination is primarily political or economic, is to be determined by historical analysis, and not by deductive reasoning.

The expansive capitalism of the mid-nineteenth century brought most of the world into the exchange relations of an international economy centered in London. The liberal imperialism of this phase was largely indifferent as to whether or not peripheral countries were formally independent or under the political-administrative control of a colonial power, provided that the rules of the international economy were observed.[22] Canada and Argentina, for example, had similar positions in real terms, though one had colonial and the other independent status. In the phase of liberal imperialism, local authorities, who were often precapitalist in their relationship to the production process (e.g., traditional agrarian-based rulers), kept their countries in the commercial system. During the second phase, that of the so-called new imperialism following the 1870s, direct state control began to supplant the less formal patterns of the commercial period. Capitalist production relations under this political aegis penetrated the periphery more thoroughly, notably in the extraction of raw materials and the building of the infrastructure (roads, railways, ports, and commercial and governmental administrations) required to link the colonies more closely with the metropole.

Capitalist production relations generated new social forces in the periphery. Outsiders came to play important roles in the local society, some as agents of the colonial administration and of big capital from the metropole, others in smaller businesses, filling the interstices between big capital and traditional local production (for example, the Chinese in southeast Asia, the Indians in east Africa, or the Lebanese in West Africa). A local workforce often numerically small and materially better off than the majority of the population, was drawn into capitalist production This politically strategic group was opposed to capital on wage and labor issues but aligned with it as regards the development of the capitalist

---

21. Among analysts who concur in this are Karl Polanyi (1957b); Gunnar Myrdal (1960j; and Geoffrey Barraclough (1968).

22. George Lichtheim (l97l) has proposed a periodization of imperialisms, and I have taken the term "liberal imperialism" from him.

production sector. An indigenous petty bourgeoisie also grew up, occupying the subordinate positions in colonial administration and metropole-based enterprises, as well as in local small business. A local state apparatus emerged under colonial tutelage, encouraging the new production relations by methods ranging from the introduction of compulsory labor or a head tax as a means of generating a labor force, to reproducing in the colonial context, some of the institutions and procedures of the industrial relations of the metropole.

The existence in the colonial territory of these new social forces, labor and the petty bourgeoisie, which could agree on a nationalist political program, together with the introduction by the colonial administration of the elements of a modern state apparatus (control of which could he the aim of this program) laid the basis for the anticolonial revolt which swept the colonial world after the Second World War. This movement reacted against administrative control from the metropole, but not continued involvement in capitalist production and exchange relations. The anti-imperialist label on the forces which replaced the structures created by the second phase or new imperialism obscured their role in ushering in vet a third phase of imperialism.

James Petras (1980), in his use of the concept of an imperial state system, has posed a number of questions concerning the structural characteristics of states in the present world order. The dominant imperial state and subordinate collaborator states differ in structure and have complementary functions in the imperial system; they are not just more and less powerful units of the same kind, as might be represented in a simple neorealist model. A striking feature in his framework is that the imperial state he analyzes is not the whole U.S. government; it is "those executive bodies within the 'government' which are charged with promoting and protecting the expansion of capital across state boundaries." The imperial system is at once more than and less than the state. It is more than the state in that it is a transnational structure with a dominant core and dependent periphery. This part of the U.S. government is at the system's core, together (and here we may presume to enlarge upon Petras' indications) with interstate institutions such as the IMF and the World Bank symbiotically related to expansive capital, and with collaborator governments (or at any rate parts of them linked to the system in the system's periphery. It is less than the state in the sense that non-imperial, or even anti-imperial, forces may be present in other parts of both core and periphery states. The unity of the state, posited by neorealism, is fragmented in this image, and the struggle for and against the imperial system may go on within the state structures at both core and periphery as well as among social forces ranged in support and opposition to the system. The state is thus a necessary but insufficient category to account for the imperial system. The imperial system itself becomes the starting point of inquiry.

The imperial system is a world order structure drawing support from a particular configuration of social forces, national and transnational, and of core and periphery states. One must beware of slipping into the language of reification when speaking of structures; they are constraints on action, not actors. The imperial system includes some formal and less formal organizations at the system level through which pressures on states can be exerted without these system-level organizations actually usurping state power. The behavior of particular states or of organized economic and social interests, however, finds its meaning in the larger totality of the imperial system. Actions are shaped either directly by pressures projected through the system or indirectly by the subjective awareness on the part of actors of the constraints imposed by the system. Thus one cannot hope to understand the imperial system by identifying imperialism with actors, be they states or multinationals; these are both dominant elements in the system, but the system as a structure is more than their sum. Furthermore, one must beware of ignoring the principle of dialectic by overemphasizing the power and coherence of a structure, even a very dominant one. Where a structure is manifestly dominant, critical theory leads one to look for a counter-structure, even a latent one, by seeking out its possible bases of support and elements of cohesion.

At this point, it is preferable to revert to the earlier terminology which referred to hegemonic and nonhegemonic world order structures. To introduce the term "imperial" with reference to the *pax Americana* risks both obscuring the important difference between hegemonic and nonhegemonic world orders and confusing structurally different kinds of imperialism (e.g., liberal imperialism, the new or colonial imperialism, and the imperial system just outlined). The contention here is that the *pax Americana* was hegemonic: it commanded a wide measure of consent among states outside the Soviet sphere and was able to provide sufficient benefits to the associated and subordinate elements in order to maintain their acquiescence. Of course, consent wore thin as one approached the periphery where the element of force was always apparent, and it was in the periphery that the challenge to the imperial system first became manifest.

It was suggested above how the particular fit between power, ideology, and institutions constituting the *pax Americana* came into being. Since the practical issue at the present is whether or not the *pax Americana* has irretrievably come apart and if so what may replace it, two specific questions deserving attention are: (1) what are the mechanisms for maintaining hegemony in this particular historical structure? and (2) what social forces and/or forms of state have been generated within it which could oppose and ultimately bring about a transformation of the structure?

THE INTERNATIONALIZATION OF THE STATE

A partial answer to the first question concerns the internationalization of the state. The basic principles of the *pax Americana* were similar to those of the *pax Britannica*—relatively free movement of goods, capital and technology and a reasonable degree of predictability in exchange rates. Cordell Hull's conviction that an open trading world was a necessary condition of peace could be taken as its ideological text, supplemented by confidence in economic growth and ever-rising productivity as the basis for moderating and controlling conflict. The postwar hegemony was, however, more fully institutionalized than the *pax Britannica* and the main function of its institutions was to reconcile domestic social pressures with the requirements of a world economy. The International Monetary Fund was set up to provide loans to countries with balance of payments deficits in order to provide time in which they could make adjustments, and to avoid the sharp deflationary consequences of an automatic gold standard. The World Bank was to be a vehicle for longer term financial assistance. Economically weak countries were to be given assistance by the system itself, either directly through the system's institutions or by other states after the system's institutions had certified their conformity to the system's norms. These institutions incorporated mechanisms to supervise the application of the system's norms and to make financial assistance effectively conditional upon reasonable evidence of intent to live up to the norms.

This machinery of surveillance was, in the case of the western allies and subsequently of all industrialized capitalist countries, supplemented by elaborate machinery for the harmonization of national policies. Such procedures began with the mutual criticism of reconstruction plans in western European countries (the U.S. condition for Marshall aid funds), continued with the development of annual review procedure in NATO (which dealt with defense and defense support programs), and became an acquired habit of mutual consultation and mutual review of national policies (through the OECD and other agencies).

The notion of international obligation moved beyond a few basic commitments, such as observance of the most favored nation principle or maintenance of an agreed exchange rate, to a general recognition that measures of national economic policy affect other countries and that such consequences should be taken into account before national policies are adopted. Conversely, other countries should be sufficiently understanding of one country's difficulties to acquiesce in short-term exceptions. Adjustments are thus perceived as responding to the needs of the system as a whole and not to the will of dominant countries. External pressures upon national policies were accordingly internationalized.

Of course, such an internationalized policy process presupposed a power structure, one in which central agencies of the U.S. government were in a dominant position. But it was not necessarily an entirely hierarchical power structure with lines of force running exclusively from the top down, nor was it one in which the units of interaction were whole nation-states. It was a power structure seeking to maintain consensus through bargaining and one in which the bargaining units were fragments of states. The power behind the negotiation was tacitly taken into account by the parties.

The practice of policy harmonization became such a powerful habit that when the basic norms of international economic behavior no longer seemed valid, as became the case during the 1970s, procedures for mutual adjustment of national economic policies were, if anything, reinforced. In the absence of clear norms, the need for mutual adjustment appeared the greater.[23]

State structures appropriate to this process of policy harmonization can be contrasted with those of the welfare nationalist state of the preceding period. Welfare nationalism took the form of economic planning at the national level and the attempt to control external economic impacts upon the national economy. To make national planning effective, corporative structures grew up in most industrially advanced countries for the purpose of bringing industry, and also organized labor, into consultation with the government in the

23. Max Beloff (1961) was perhaps the first to point to the mechanisms whereby participation in international organizations altered the internal policymaking practices of states. R. W. Cox and H. K. Jacobson et al. (1972) represented the political systems of international organizations as including segments of states. R. O. Keohane and J. S. Nye (1974) pointed to the processes whereby coalitions are formed among segments of the apparatuses of different states and the ways in which international institutions facilitate such coalitions. These various works, while they point to the existence of mechanisms for policy coordination among states and for penetration of external influences within states, do not discuss the implications of these mechanisms for the structure of power within states. It is this structural aspect I wish to designate by the term "internationalization of the state." Christian Palloix (1975:82) refers to "l'internationalisation de l'appareil de l'État national, de certains lieux de cet appareil d'État" by which he designates those segments of national states which serve as policy supports for the internationalization of production. He thus raises the question of structural changes in the state, though he does not enlarge upon the point. Keohane and Nye (1977) linked the transgovernmental mechanism to the concept of "interdependence" I find this concept tends to obscure the power relationships involved in structural changes in both state and world order and prefer not to use it for that reason. Gourevitch (1978) does retain the concept of interdependence while insisting that it be linked with power struggles among social forces within states.

formulation and implementation of policy. National and industrial corporative structures can raise protectionist or restrictive obstacles to the adjustments required for adaptation of national economies to the world economy in a hegemonic system. Corporatism at the national level was a response to the conditions of the interwar period; it became institutionally consolidated in western Europe just as the world structure was changing into something for which national corporatism was ill-suited.

The internationalization of the state gives precedence to certain state agencies—notably ministries of finance and prime ministers' offices— which are key points in the adjustment of domestic to international economic policy. Ministries of industries, labor ministries, planning offices, which had been built up in the context of national corporatism, tended to be subordinated to the central organs of internationalized public policy. As national economies became more integrated in the world economy, it was the larger and more technologically advanced enterprises that adapted best to the new opportunities. A new axis of influence linked international policy networks with the key central agencies of government and with big business. This new informal corporative structure overshadowed the older more formalized national corporatism and reflected the dominance of the sector oriented to the world economy over the more nationally oriented sector of a country's economy.[24]

The internationalization of the state is not, of course, limited to advanced capitalist core countries. It would not be difficult to make a catalogue of recent cases in peripheral countries where institutions of the world economy, usually as a condition for debt renewal, have dictated, policies which could only be sustained by a coalition of conservative forces. Turkey, Peru, and Portugal are among those recently affected. As for Zaire, a conference

---

24. There is, of course, a whole literature implicit in the argument of this paragraph. Some sketchy references may be useful. Andrew Shonfield (1965) illustrated the development of corporative-type structures of the kind I associate with the welfare-nationalist state. The shift from industry-level corporatism to an enterprise-based corporatism led by the big public and private corporations has been noted in some industrial relations works, particularly those concerned with the emergence of a "new working class" e.g., Serge Mallet (l963), but the industrial relations literature has generally not linked what I have elsewhere called enterprise corporatism to the broader framework suggested here (R. W. Cox 1977). Erhard Friedberg (1974:94-108) discusses the subordination of the old corporatism to the new. The shift in terminology from planning to industrial policy is relate to the internationalizing of state and economy. Industrial policy has become a matter of interest to global economic policymakers (see William Diebold 1980, and John Pinder, Takashi Hosomi and William Diebold, for the Trilateral Commission, 1979). If planning evokes the specter of economic nationalism, industrial policy, as the Trilateral Commission study points out, can be looked upon with favor from a world economy perspective as a necessary aspect of policy harmonization: "We have argued that industrial policies are needed to deal with structural problems in the modern economies. Thus, international action should not aim to dismantle these policies. The pressure should, rather, be toward positive and adaptive industrial policies, whether on the part of single countries or groups of countries combined. Far from being protectionist, industrial policy can help them to remove a cause of protectionism, by making the process of adjustment less painful" (p. 50). It may be objected that the argument and references presented here are more valid for Europe than for the United States, and that, indeed, the very concept of corporatism is alien to U.S. ideology To this it can be replied that since the principal levers of the world economy are in the United States, the U.S. economy adjusts less than those of European countries and peripheral countries, and the institutionalization of adjustment mechanisms is accordingly less developed. Structural analyses of the U. S. economy have, however, pointed to a distinction between a corporate internationally oriented sector and a medium and small business nationally oriented sector, and to the different segments of the state and different policy orientations associated with each. Cf. John Kenneth Galbraith (l974) and James O'Connor (1973). Historians point to the elements of corporatism in the New Deal, e.g., Schlesinger (1960).

of creditors laid down the condition that officials of the IMF be placed within the key ministries of the state to oversee the fulfillment of the conditions of debt renewal.[25]

THE INTERNATIONALIZATION OF PRODUCTION

The internationalization of the state is associated with the expansion of international production. This signifies the integration of production processes on a transnational scale, with different phases of a single process being carried out in different countries. International production currently plays the formative role in relation to the structure of states and world order that national manufacturing and commercial capital played In the mid-nineteenth century.

International production expands through direct investment, whereas the rentier imperialism, of which Hobson and Lenin wrote, primarily took the form of portfolio investment. With portfolio investment, control over the productive resources financed by the transaction passed with ownership to the borrower. With direct investment, control is inherent in the production process itself and remains with the originator of the investment. The essential feature of direct investment is possession, not of money, but of knowledge—in the form of technology and especially in the capacity to continue to develop new technology. The financial arrangements for direct investment may vary greatly, but all are subordinated to this crucial factor of technical control. The arrangements may take the form of wholly owned subsidiaries, joint ventures with local capital sometimes put up by the state in host countries, management contracts with state-owned enterprises, or compensation agreements with socialist enterprises whereby, in return for the provision of technology, these enterprises become suppliers of elements to a globally organized production process planned and controlled by the source of the technology. Formal ownership is less important than the manner in which various elements are integrated into the production system.

Direct investment seems to suggest the dominance of industrial capital over finance capital. The big multinational corporations which expand by direct investment are, to some degree, self-financing and to the extent that they are not they seem capable of mobilizing money capital in a number of ways, such as through local capital markets (where their credit is better than that of national entrepreneurs), through the Euro-currency markets, through infusions of capital from other multinationals linked to technology and production agreements, through state subsidies, and so forth. And yet, particularly since the 1970s, finance capital seems to be returning to prominence through the operations of the multinational banks, not only in the old form of rentier imperialism administering loans to peripheral states, but also as a network of control and private planning for the world economy of international production. This network assesses and collectivizes investment risks and allocates investment opportunities among the participants in the expansion of international production, that is, it performs the function of Lenin's collective capitalist in the conditions of late-twentieth-century production relations.

INTERNATIONAL PRODUCTION AND CLASS STRUCTURE

International production is mobilizing social forces, and it is through these forces that its major political consequences vis-à-vis the nature of states and future world orders may

25. The Zaire case recalls the arrangements imposed by western powers on the Ottoman Empire and Egypt in the late nineteenth century, effectively attaching certain revenues for the service of foreign debt. See Herbert Feis (1961:332-342, 384-397)

be anticipated. Hitherto, social classes have been found to exist within nationally defined social formations, despite rhetorical appeals to the international solidarity of workers. Now, as a consequence of international production, it becomes increasingly pertinent to think in terms of a global class structure alongside or superimposed upon national class structures.

At the apex of an emerging global class structure is the transnational managerial class. Having its own ideology, strategy and institutions of collective action, it is a class both in itself and for itself. Its focal points of organization, the Trilateral Commission, World Bank, IMF and OECD, develop both a framework of thought and guidelines for policies. From these points, class action penetrates countries through the process of internationalization of the state. The members of this transnational class are not limited to those who carry out functions at the global level, such as executives of multinational corporations or as senior officials of international agencies, but include those who manage the internationally oriented sectors within countries, the finance ministry officials, local managers of enterprises linked into international production systems, and so on.[26]

National capitalists are to be distinguished from the transnational class. The natural reflex of national capital faced with the challenge of international production is protectionism. It is torn between the desire to use the state as a bulwark of an independent national economy and the opportunity of filling niches left by international production in a subordinate symbiotic relationship with the latter.

Industrial workers have been doubly fragmented. One line of cleavage is between established and nonestablished labor. Established workers are those who have attained a status of relative security and stability in their jobs and have some prospects of career advancement. Generally they are relatively skilled, work for larger enterprises, and have effective trade unions. Nonestablished workers, by contrast, have insecure employment, have no prospect of career advancement, are relatively less skilled, and confront great obstacles in developing effective trade unions. Frequently, the nonestablished are disproportionately drawn from lower-status ethnic minorities, immigrants and women. The institutions of working class action have privileged established workers. Only when the ideology of class solidarity remains powerful, which usually means only in conditions of high ideological polarization and social and political conflict, do organizations controlled by established workers (unions and political parties) attempt to rally and act for nonestablished workers as well.

---

26. The evidence for the existence of a transnational managerial class lies in actual forms of organization, the elaboration of ideology, financial supports, and the behavior of individuals. Other structures stand as rival tendencies—e.g., national capital and its interests sustained by a whole other structure of loyalties, agencies, etc. Individuals or firms and state agencies may in some phases of their activity be caught up now in one, now in another, tendency. Thus the membership of the class may be continually shifting though the structure remains. It is sometimes argued that this is merely a case of U.S. capitalists giving themselves a hegemonic aura, an argument that by implication makes of imperialism a purely national phenomenon. There is no doubting the U.S. origin of the values carried and propagated by this class, but neither is there any doubt that many non-U.S. citizens and agencies also participate in it nor that its world view is global and distinguishable from the purely national capitalisms which exist alongside it. Through the transnational managerial class American culture, or a certain American business culture, has become globally hegemonic. Of course, should neomercantilist tendencies come to prevail in international economic relations, this transnational class structure would wither

The second line of cleavage among industrial workers is brought about by the division between national and international capital (i.e., that engaged in international production). The established workers in the sector of international production are potential allies of international capital. This is not to say that those workers have no conflict with international capital, only that international capital has the resources to resolve these conflicts and to isolate them from conflicts involving other labor groups by creating an enterprise corporatism in which both parties perceive their interest as lying in the continuing expansion of international production.

Established workers in the sector of national capital are more susceptible to the appeal of protectionism and national (rather than enterprise) corporatism in which the defense of national capital, of jobs and of the workers' acquired status in industrial relations institutions, are perceived to be interconnected [27]

Nonestablished labor has become of particular importance in the expansion of international production Production systems are being designed so as to make use of an increasing proportion of semi-skilled (and therefore frequently nonestablished) in relation to skilled (and established) labor.[28] This tendency in production organization makes it possible for the center to decentralize the actual physical production of goods to peripheral locations in which an abundant supply of relatively cheap nonestablished labor is to be found, and to retain control of the process and of the research and development upon which its future depends.

As a nonestablished workforce is mobilized in Third-World countries by International production, governments in these countries have very frequently sought to preempt the possibility of this new social force developing its own class-conscious organizations by imposing upon it structures of state corporatism in the form of unions set up and controlled by the government or the dominant political party. This also gives total governments, through their control over local labor, additional leverage with international capital regarding the terms of direct investment. If industrial workers in Third-World countries have thus sometimes been reduced to political and social quiescence, state corporatism may prove to be a stage delaying, but in the long run not eliminating, a more articulate self-consciousness [29]

Even if industry were to move rapidly into the Third World and local governments were, by and large, able to keep control over their industrial workforces, most of the populations of these countries may see no improvement, but probably a deterioration, in their conditions New industrial jobs lag far behind increases in the labor force, while changes in agriculture (dispossess many in the rural population. No matter how fast International production spreads, a very large part of the world's population in the poorest areas remains

27. Some industries appear as ambiguously astride the two tendencies—e.g., the automobile industry. During a period of economic expansion, the international aspect of this industry dominated in the United States, and the United Auto Workers union took the lead in creating world councils for the major international auto firms with a view to inaugurating multinational bargaining. As the industry was hit by recession, protectionism came to the fore.

28. See Cox (1978). This tendency can be seen as the continuation of a long-term direction of production organization of which Taylorism was an early stage, in which control over the work process is progressively wrested from workers and separated out from the actual performance of tasks so as to be concentrated with management. See Harry Braverman (1974).

29. Recent news from Brazil indicates restiveness on the part of Sao Paulo workers whose unions have been subjected to a state corporatist structure since the time of President Vargas.

marginal to the world economy, having no employment or incomes or the purchasing power derived from it. A major problem for international capital in its aspiration for hegemony is how to neutralize the effect of this marginalization of perhaps one-third of the world's population so as to prevent its poverty from fueling revolt.[30]

SOCIAL FORCES, STATE STRUCTURES, AND FUTURE WORLD ORDER PROSPECTS

It would, of course, be logically inadmissible, as well as imprudent, to base predictions of future world order upon the foregoing considerations. Their utility is rather in drawing attention to factors which could incline an emerging world order in one direction or another. The social forces generated by changing production processes are the starting point for thinking about possible futures. These forces may combine in different configurations, and as an exercise one could consider the hypothetical configurations most likely to lead to three different outcomes as to the future of the state system. The focus on these three outcomes is not, of course, to imply that no other outcomes or configurations of social forces are possible.

First, is the prospect for a new hegemony being based upon the global structure of social power generated by the internationalizing of production. This would require a consolidation of two presently powerful and related tendencies: the continuing dominance of international over national capital within the major countries, and the continuing internationalization of the state. Implicit in such an outcome is a continuance of monetarism as the orthodoxy of economic policy, emphasizing the stabilization of the world economy (anti-inflationary policies and stable exchange rates) over the fulfillment of domestic sociopolitical demands (the reduction of unemployment and the maintenance of real-wage levels).

The interstate power configuration which could maintain such a world order, provided its member states conformed to this model, is a coalition centering upon the United States, the Federal Republic of Germany, and Japan, with the support of other OECI) states, the co-optation of a few of the more industrialized Third-World countries, such as Brazil, and of leading conservative OECD countries, and the possibility of revived détente allowing for a greater linkage of the Soviet sphere into the world economy of international production. The new international division of labor, brought about through the progressive decentralization of manufacturing into the Third World by international capital, would satisfy demands for industrialization from those countries. Social conflict in the core countries would be combated through enterprise corporatism, though many would be left unprotected by this method, particularly the nonestablished workers. In the peripheral countries, social conflict would he contained through a combination of state corporatism and repression.

The social forces opposed to this configuration have been noted above. National capital, those sections of established labor linked to national capital, newly mobilized nonestablished workers in the Third World, and social marginals in the poor countries are all in some way or another potentially opposed to international capital, and to the state and

---

30. The World Bank promotes rural development and birth control. The concept of "self-reliance," once a slogan of anti-imperialism meaning "decoupling" from the imperial system, has been co-opted by the imperial system to mean self-help among populations becoming marginalized—a do-it-yourself welfare program.

world order structures most congenial to international capital. These forces do not, however, have any natural cohesion, and might be dealt with separately, or neutralized, by an effective hegemony. If they did come together under particular circumstances in a particular country, precipitating a change of regime, then that country might be dealt with in isolation through the world structure. In other words, where hegemony failed within a particular country, it could reassert itself through the world structure.

A second possible outcome is a nonhegemonic world structure of conflicting power centers. Perhaps the most likely way for this to evolve would be through the ascendancy in several core countries of neomercantilist coalitions which linked national capital and established labor, and were determined to opt out of arrangements designed to promote international capital and to organize their own power and welfare on a national or sphere-of-influence basis. The continuing pursuit of monetarist policies may be the single most likely cause of neomercantilist reaction. Legitimated as anti-inflationary, monetarist policies have been perceived as hindering national capital (because of high interest rates), generating unemployment (through planned recession), and adversely affecting relatively deprived social groups and regions dependent upon government services and transfer payments (because of budget-balancing cuts in state expenditures). An opposing coalition would attack monetarism for subordinating national welfare to external forces, and for showing an illusory faith in the markets (which are perceived to be manipulated by corporate-administered pricing). The likely structural form of neomercantilism within core states would be industry-level and national-level corporatism, bringing national capital and organized labor into a relationship with the government for the purpose of making and implementing of state policy. Peripheral states would have much the same structure as in the first outcome, but would be more closely linked to one or another of the core-country economies.

A third and more remotely possible outcome would be the development of a counter-hegemony based on a Third-World coalition against core-country dominance and aiming toward the autonomous development of peripheral countries and the termination of the core-periphery relationship. A counter-hegemony would consist of a coherent view of an alternative world order, backed by a concentration of power sufficient to maintain a challenge to core countries. While this outcome is foreshadowed by the demand for a New International Economic Order, the prevailing consensus behind this demand lacks a sufficiently clear view of an alternative world political economy to constitute counter-hegemony. The prospects of counter-hegemony lies very largely in the future development of state structures in the Third World.

The controlling social force in these countries is, typically, what has been called a "state class,"[31] a combination of party, bureaucratic and military personnel and union leaders, mostly petty-bourgeois in origin, which controls the state apparatus and through it attempts to gain greater control over the productive apparatus in the country. The state class can he understood as a local response to the forces generated by the internationalizing of production, and an attempt to gain some local control over these forces. The orientation of the state class is indeterminate. It can be either conservative or radical. It may either bargain for a better deal within the world economy of international production, or it may seek to overcome the unequal internal development generated by international capital.

---

31. I have borrowed the term from Hartmut Elsenhans (n.d.)

State classes of the first orientation are susceptible to incorporation into a new hegemonic world economy, and to the maintenance of state corporatist structures as the domestic counterpart to international capital. The second orientation could provide the backing for counter-hegemony. However, a state class is only likely to maintain the second and more radical orientation if it is supported from below in the form of a genuine populism (and not just a populism manipulated by political leaders). One may speculate that this could come about through the unfolding social consequences of international production, such as the mobilization of a new nonestablished labor force coupled with the marginalization of an increasing part of the urban population. The radical alternative could be the form of response to international capital in Third-World countries, just as neomercantilism could be the response in richer countries. Each projects a particular state structure and vision of world order.

POSTSCRIPT 1985

Robert Keohane's proposal to include my article published in *Millennium* in the summer of 1981 in this collection of readings is a challenge to define my position in relation to the other texts selected. These other texts are all part of a single debate stimulated by recent works by Waltz and Gilpin. My article stems from a different—and very largely idiosyncratic—intellectual process. It does, however, touch upon themes that emerged in this debate, making of me a Monsieur Jourdain, writing prose without having been aware of the fact.

I have deliberately refrained from revising my text and have made only some strictly stylistic and editorial changes to the 1981 version so as to adapt it to the present volume. Once placed before the public, a text is entitled to respect for its own integrity. It has a lift of its own, rich or poor. The author too is entitled to assume a certain independence of the text. My own views (as I hope those of most authors) have evolved since 1981. Accordingly, I prefer to try to make the link with the other readings through this postscript.

In the range of their different arguments, I find myself in agreement and in disagreement with aspects of each of the other authors' texts. I am, however, left with the general impression that this is a specifically American debate even though it is couched in terms of international or world systems. Stanley Hoffmann (1977) put it that international relations is an *American* social science. This is not (on my part any more than on Hoffmann's) to suggest that American thought is cast in a single mold. (I protest in advance my innocence of Robert Gilpin's strictures against lumping together authors whose views differ in important respects.) What is common, it seems to me, is (1) the perspective of the United States as the preponderant of the two major powers in the system and consequently the sharing of a certain measure of responsibility for U.S. policy, and (2) the organization of argument around certain obligatory themes of debates, notably those of power versus morality and of science versus tradition. The first of these is, to employ Waltz's language, a systemic conditioning of American thought. The second derives more from an explicitly American cultural process. One aspect of this process was the intellectual conversion of U.S. policymakers to the use of the accumulated physical power of the United States for the performance of a world system-creating and system-maintaining role. Important influences in this conversion were European-formed thinkers like Reinhold Niebuhr and Hans Morgenthau who introduced a more pessimistic and power-oriented view of mankind into an American milieu conditioned by eighteenth-century optimism and nineteenth-century belief in progress. Another aspect was the need to legitimate this newfound realism in "scientific" terms. The second aspect can be read as the revenge of eighteenth-century natural-law thinking for the loss of innocence implicit in the first. Richard Ashley has well recounted the socializing process through which successive cohorts of American (and by assimilation Canadian) graduate students have been brought into this stream of thinking.

At this point, following Gilpin's example, an autobiographical reference is in order: The reader should know that this author did not experience the abovementioned process of intellectual formation. His introduction to international political processes came through practice as an "empathetic neutral" (Cox and Jacobson 1977) in his role of international official in one of the less salient spheres of policy. His only formal academic training was in the study of history. Accordingly, he never shared a sense of responsibility for nor aspired to influence U.S. policy or that of any other country, though he has been well aware that his destiny, like that of the rest of mankind, is profoundly shaped by what he cannot influence. These circumstances have inclined him toward an initial acceptance of the realist position. The political world is at the outset a *given* world. Men make history, as Marx wrote, but not in conditions of their own choosing. To have any influence over events, or at the very least to forestall the worst eventualities, it is necessary to begin with an understanding of the conditions not chosen by oneself in which action is possible.

The intellectual influences that contributed to the formation of this idiosyncratic view share with realism a common source in Machiavelli. They diverge in having followed a historicist current, through Giambattista Vico to Georges Sorel and, above all, Antonio Gramsci. These thinkers were not concerned primarily with international relations; they addressed the problem of knowledge about society and social transformations. Historians provided the more specific light on international structures—to some extent the twentieth-century British Marxist historians, and more particularly Fernand Braudel and the French *Annales* school. Intellectual points of contact with influences upon other contributors to this volume include E. H. Carr (especially with Gilpin), Friedrich Meinecke, Ludwig Dehio, and Karl Polanyi (especially with Ruggie). So much for autobiography: the point is that the itinerary to the *Millennium* article did not pass through neorealism; it contemplates neorealism from the destination reached.

To change the world, we have to begin with an understanding of the world as it is, which means the structures of reality that surround us. "Understanding" is the key word here. The issues in the confrontation of approaches are linked to different modes of knowledge: positivism and historicism. Since these two terms have been used in contradictory ways in different texts included in this book, I reiterate my own usage here.

By "positivism" I mean the effort to conceive social science on the; model of physics (or more particularly, physics as it was known in the eighteenth and nineteenth centuries before it had assimilated the principles of relativity and uncertainty). This involves positing a separation of subject and object. The data of politics are externally perceived events brought about by the interaction of actors in a field. The field itself being an arrangement of actors, has certain properties of its own which can be called "systemic" The concept of "cause" is applicable within such a framework of forces. Powerful actors are "causes" of change in the behavior of less powerful ones, and the structure of that system "causes" certain forms of behavior on the part of actors.

I use "historicism" to mean a quite different approach to knowledge about society which was well defined by Giambattista Vico (1774/1970) and has continued as a distinctive tradition to the present. In this approach, human institutions are made by people—not by the individual gestures of "actors" but by collective responses to a collectively perceived problematic that produce certain practices. Institutions and practices are therefore to be understood through the changing mental processes of I their makers. There is, in this perspective, an identity of subject and object. The objective realities that this approach encompasses—the state, social classes, the conflict groups that Robert Gilpin (following Ralf Dahrendorf) refers to and their practices—are constituted by intersubjective ideas. As Gilpin says, none of these realities exist in the same way that individuals exist, but individuals act *as though* these other realities exist, and by so acting they reproduce them. Social and political institutions are thus seen as collective responses to the physical material context (natural nature) in which human aggregates find themselves. They in turn form part of the social material framework (artificial nature or the network of social relations) in which historical action takes place. Historicism thus understood is the same as historical materialism. The method of historical materialism—or, in Robert Keohane's term, its research program—is to find the connections between the mental schema through which people conceive action and the material world which constrains both what people can do and how they can think about doing it.

The two approaches—positivist and historicist—yield quite different versions of the task of science. There can be no dispute about Kenneth Waltz's adherence to the positivist approach and he lays out clearly the tasks of a positivist science: to find laws (which are regularities in human activity stateable in the form of "if A, then B"); and to develop theories which explain why observable laws hold within specific spheres of activity. Laws and theories advance knowledge beyond what would otherwise be "mere description," i.e., the cataloguing of externally observed events.[32]

Insofar as this approach aspires to a general science of society, it cannot discriminate between times and places. All human activity is its province (though this activity is arbitrarily divided among a priori categories of activity of which international relations is one), all of it treated as raw material for the finding of laws and the development of theories. I believe this to be the root of the major defect in Waltz.'s approach pointed to by his critics (see especially Keohane and Ruggie): the inability of his theory to account for or to explain structural transformation. A general (read: universally applicable) science of society can allow for variations in technologies and in the relative capabilities of actors, but not in either the basic nature of the actors (power-seeking) or in their mode of interaction (power-balancing). The universality of these basic attributes of the social system comes to be perceived as standing outside of and prior to history. History becomes but a mine of data illustrating the permutations and combinations that are possible within an essentially unchanging human story. Despite his wide historical learning, Waltz's work is fundamen-

32. The term "description" as used in positivist discourse (often preceded by "mere") is meaningless in historicist discourse. Description, for the historicist, is inseparable from interpretation or understanding—i.e., the appraisal of a unique fact through the medium of an explanatory hypothesis. The task of theory is to develop such hypotheses and the concepts of limited historical applicability in which they are expressed—i.e., concepts like mercantilism, capitalism, fascism, etc. The difference between "description" (positivist) and "understanding" (historicist) is reflected in the words used to denote the object of study: datum (positivist) versus fact (historicist). The distinction is less self-evident in English than in Latin languages, where the corresponding words are past participles of the verbs "to give" and "to make" Positivism deals with externally perceived givens; historicism with events or institutions that are "made"—i.e., that have to be understood through the subjectivity of the makers as well as in terms of the objective consequences that flow from their existence.

tally ahistorical. The elegance he achieves in the clarity of his theoretical statement comes at the price of an unconvincing mode of historical understanding.

The historicist approach to social science does not envisage any general or universally valid laws which can be explained by the development of appropriate generally applicable theories. For historicism, both human nature and the structures of human interaction change, if only very slowly. History is the process of their changing. One cannot therefore speak of "laws" in any generally valid sense transcending historical eras, nor of structures as outside of or prior to history.[33] Regularities in human activities may indeed be observed within particular eras, and thus the positivist approach can be fruitful within defined historical limits, though not with the universal pretensions it aspires to. The research program of historicism is to reveal the historical structures characteristic of particular eras within which such regularities prevail. Even more important, this research program is to explain transformations from one structure to another. If elegance is what Robert Keohane writes of as "sparc, logically tight" theory (p. 197), then the historicist approach does not lead to elegance. It may, however, lead to better appraisal of historically specific conjunctures. One person's elegance is another's oversimplification.

In choosing between the two approaches, much depends upon one's idea of what theory is for. I have suggested two broad purposes corresponding to the two approaches: a problem-solving purpose, i.e., tacitly assuming the permanency of existing structures, which is served by the positivist approach; and a critical purpose envisaging the possibilities of structural transformation which is served by the historicist approach. The usefulness of all theory, whether problem-solving or critical, is in its applicability to particular situations. Rut whereas problem-solving theory assimilates particular situations to general rules, providing a kind of programmed method for dealing with them, critical theory seeks out the developmental potential within the particular.

Developmental potential signifies a possible change of structure. It can be grasped by understanding the contradictions and sources of conflict within existing structures; and this task may be aided by an understanding of how structural transformations have come about in the past.[34] Thus the determination of breaking points between successive structures—those points at which transformations take place—becomes a major problem of method. John Ruggie raised this issue in pointing to the structural disjuncture between the medieval and modern world system, and to the inability of Waltz's structural realism to even consider let alone explain this transformation. The case is extremely important, since it contrasts two worlds constituted by quite distinct intersubjectivities. The entities as well as the modes of relations among them are of different orders.

---

33. Nor can one speak of "cause" in historicist discourse, except in a most trivial sense. The "cause" of a murder is the contraction of the murderer's finger on a trigger which detonates a charge in a cartridge, sending a bullet into the vital parts of the victim. Explanation is the purpose of historicist inquiry. It is much more complex, requiring an assembling of individual motivations and social structures to be connected by explanatory hypotheses.

34. This does not imply the presumption that the future will be like the past. But there can be tin the historicist approach) no complete separation between past and and future. The practical utility of knowledge about the past is in the development of explanatory hypotheses about change. Fernand Braudel (I958) employed the metaphor of a ship for such hypotheses. The hypothesis sails well in certain waters under a range of conditions; it remains becalmed or it founders in others. The task of theory is to explore the limits of validity of particular hypotheses and to devise new hypotheses to explain those cases in which they fail.

This case of transformation can be contrasted to the frequent invocations of Thucydides in neorealist literature in support of the contention that a balance-of-power system is the universal condition. What these invocations do establish is that there have been other periods in history where structures analogous to the balance of power of the modern states system have appeared. They do not consider that there have likewise been otherwise-constituted historical structures of which the medieval order of European Christendom was one. The instinct of structural realism may be to reduce the medieval order to its power model; but if so that would be to reject an opportunity for scientific exploration.

Ruggie suspects—and I share his suspicions—that the transformation from the medieval to the modern order cannot be understood solely in terms of a general international-systems theory (indeed, one could point out that the very term "international," derived from modern practice, is inapposite to the medieval world) but probably has also to be explained in terms of changing state structures and changing modes of production. This joins the substantive point of my argument: I have tried to sketch out a research program that would examine the linkage between changes in production, in forms of state and in world orders.

The relevancy of such a research program is strictly practical. It flows from the question whether the present age is one of those historical breaking points between world-order structures, whether the present world situation contains the development potential of a different world order. If this were to be the case, what then would be the range of future structural possibilities? What social and political forces would have to be mobilized in order to bring about one or another of feasible outcomes? The practical use of political theory should be to help answer such questions. That they are present in the minds of the contributors to this volume is clear—for instance in Keohane's primary concern to discover the means of bringing about peaceful change, and Gilpin's with the problems of change under conditions of declining hegemony: Neither of these authors sees clearly how structural realism can be a guide to the answers. My suggestion is that the approach of historical structures would be more apposite.

For Fernand Braudel (1958), a historical structure is the *longue durée,* the enduring practices evolved by people for dealing with the recurrent necessities of social and political life and which come by them to be regarded as fixed attributes of human nature and social intercourse. But, particularly with regard to the world system, how long is the *longue durée?* Ruggie pointed to the breaking point between medieval and modern world orders, but have there been other breaking points since then? What is the proper periodization of world orders? I am inclined to answer that yes, there have been further breaking points, and to suggest a succession of mercantilist, liberal (*pax Britannica*), neoimperialist, and neoliberal (*pax Americana*) orders. At the same time, I would not want to give the impression that this was in some manner the uncovering of an ontological substratum of world history, that these successive world orders were real entities fixed in order of time within some immutable world-historic plan. This periodizing is an intellectual construct pertinent to the present and useful for the purpose of understanding how changes in economic and political practices and in the relations of social groups contribute to the genesis of new world orders. The approach is not reductionist in the sense of making one single factor or set of factors the explanation of all changes. It is grounded in the notion of reciprocal relationships among basic forces shaping social and political practice.[35]

Ruggie made another point in suggesting that Waltz's exclusive stress on power capabilities precludes consideration of other significant factors differentiating international systems, in particular the presence or absence of hegemony. Indeed, in neorealist discourse the term "hegemony" is reduced to the single dimension of dominance, i.e., a physical capabilities relationship among states. The Gramscian meaning of hegemony which I have used (see also Cox 1983), and which is important in distinguishing the *pax Britannica* and *pax Americana* from the other world orders of the sequence suggested above, joins an ideological and intersubjective element to the brute power relationship. In a hegemonic order, the dominant power makes certain concessions or compromises to secure the acquiescence of lesser powers to an order that can be expressed in terms of a general interest. It is important in appraising a hegemonic order, to know both (a) that it functions mainly by consent in accordance with universalist principles, and (b) that it rests upon a certain structure of power and serves to maintain that structure. The consensual element distinguishes hegemonic from nonhegemonic world orders. It also tends to mystify the power relations upon which the order ultimately rests.

The hegemonic concept has analytical applicability at the national as well as the international level (indeed, Gramsci developed it for application at the national level). I would differ from Gilpin when he (and Stephen Krasner 1978a, in line with him) suggests that it is possible to distinguish a national interest from the welter of particular interests, if they mean that such a general will exists as some form of objective reality. I can accept their proposition if national interest is understood in a hegemonic sense, i.e., as the way in which the dominant groups in the state have been able—through concessions to the claims of subordinate groups— to evolve a broadly accepted mode of thinking about general or national interests. Unfortunately, (Gilpin (and Krasner) end their inquiry with the identification of national interests. When the concept of hegemony is introduced, it becomes necessary to ask what is the form of power that underlies the state and produces this particular understanding of national interest, this particular *raison d'état*—or in Gramscian terms, what is the configuration of the historic bloc?

Finally, there is the troublesome question of the ideological nature of thought—troublesome insofar as the imputation of ideology may appear to be insulting to the positivist who draws a line between his science and another's ideology. I should make it clear that I do not draw such a line; I accept that my own thought is grounded in a particular perspective; and I mean no offense in pointing to what appears to be a similar grounding in other people's thought. Science, for me, is a matter of rigor in the development of concepts and in the appraisal of evidence. There is an inevitable ideological element in science which lies in the choice of subject and the purposes to which analysis is put. The troublesome part comes when some scientific enterprise claims to transcend history and to propound some universally valid form of knowledge Positivism, by its pretensions to escape from history, runs the greater risk of falling into the trap of unconscious ideology.

There arc two opposed concepts of history, each of which is intellectually grounded in the separation of subject and object. One is a methodological separation wherein events are conceived as an infinite series of objectified data. This approach seeks universal laws of behavior. Structural realism, as noted, is one of its manifestations. The other sees the

---

35. Waltz writes of reductionism and reification in a curious way in saying that systems are reified by political scientists when they reduce them to their interacting parts (p 61). In my reading of his work, Waltz comes close to the opposite of this position, reifying the international system by treating it not as an intellectual construct but as a "cause," and deriving the behavior of its parts, i.e., states, from the system itself; thus international relations is reduced to the workings of a reified system.

subjectivity of historical action as determined by an objectified historical process. It seeks to discover the "laws of motion" of history. Both of these concepts of history lend themselves readily to ideology: the one becoming an ideology reifying the status quo; the other an ideology underpinning revolution by revealing the certainty of a particular future. Both remove the element of uncertainty inherent in the historicist expectation of dialectical development arising out of the contradictions of existing forces—a conception in which, as argued above, subject and object are united.

Neorealism, both in its Waltzian structuralist form and in its game-theoretic interactionist form, appear ideologically to be a science at the service of big-power management of the international system. There is an unmistakably Panglossian quality to a theory published in the late 1970s which concludes that a bipolar system is the best of all possible worlds. The historical moment has left its indelible mark upon this purportedly universalist science.

To the American social science of international relations, Marxism is the great "other" the ideology supportive of the rival superpower. It is also that most readily associated with the alternative mode of separation of subject and object. In the works of this American social science, Marxism is politely recognized but usually reduced to a few simple propositions which do not impinge upon its own discourse. If there is any dialogue between the American science of international relations and Marxism, it is a *dialogue de sourds.* Gilpin was justified in protesting the richness and diversity of realist thought, but it is at least as justifiable to point to the diversity of Marxist thought. It cuts across all the epistemological distinctions discussed above. There is a structuralist Marxism which, as Richard Ashley has indicated, has analogies to structural realism, not in the use to which theory is put but in its conception of the nature of knowledge. There is a determinist tradition (perhaps less evident at present) which purports to reveal the laws of motion of history. And there is a historicist Marxism that rejects the notion of objective laws of history and focuses upon class struggle as the heuristic model for the understanding of structural change. It is obviously in the last of these Marxist currents that this writer feels most comfortable. Were it not for the contradictory diversity of Marxist thought, he would be glad to acknowledge himself (in a parody of Reaganite rhetoric) as your friendly neighborhood Marxist-Leninist subversive. But as things stand in the complex world of Marxism, he prefers to be identified simply as a historical materialist.

Chapter Six

Putting It All Together

Introduction

Conclusion:
The Shape of the Future: A Globalized World

At the end of a semester spent learning a number of theories which help us to understand "Why states do what they do" and "What causes conflict and cooperation among states", most students, moving into their own futures, need help in assimilating all of the theories into a coherent worldview. The final readings assist in that effort. Donald M. Snow's "National Security in a World of Tiers"[1] presents a framework within which all of the theories we have studied to date can be fitted together to help make sense of the rapidly changing world in which we live. James N. Rosenau's "The Complexities and Contradictions of Globalization" presents an alternative view of the present and makes different predictions about the future.[2]

Donald Snow is a Professor of Political Science at the University of Alabama who has also taught at the U.S. Army War College, the U.S. Naval War College, and the U.S. Air Command and Staff College. He is in many ways a structural realist. Like Waltz, he believes that the structure of the international system matters and that the number of pole states in the system affects much of what happens in the world. Snow looks at the world in the wake of the collapse of the Soviet Union and finds just one superpower, forming what Ken Waltz would call a unipolar world. Snow argues that the United States has shaped much of the world in its own image through its economic hegemony and regime formation, helping to create what he calls the "First Tier" of economically advanced liberal democracies. Michael Doyle, one of the primary authors of Democratic Peace Theory, refers to this same group of states as a "Zone of Peace" within which war is essentially inconceivable. Francis Fukayama has gone so far as to describe the triumph of liberal capitalist democracy as "The End of History", arguing that this system has proven so successful that there is simply no imaginable alternative to it.[3]

However, the First Tier comprises only about one-seventh of the world's population. The rest of the globe—ruled by governments which are either not fully democratic, do not have industrialized capitalist economies, or both—does not enjoy the same freedom from concerns about warfare among states or inside their own states. Instead, traditional balance of power politics, mercantilism, and instrumental nationalism continue all too often to make life "Nasty, brutish, and short." The crucial state-behavior level independent variable for Snow is whether a state resides in the First or Second Tier; its position in one of those

1. The essay is edited and excerpted from Donald M. Snow, National Security: Defense Policy for a New International Order, 3rd Edition (New York: St. Martins Press, 1995). See also Snows The Shape of the Future: The Post-Cold War World (New York: M.E. Sharpe, 1995).

2. This article was originally published in *Current History,* November 1997, pp. 360-364. For other perspectives on globalization, see Thomas L. Friedman, *The Lexus and the Olive Tree: Explaining Globalization* (New York: Farrar Straus & Giroux, 1999), and Daniel Yergin and Joseph Stanislaw, *The Commanding Heights: The Battle Between Government and the Marketplace That Is Remaking the Modern World* (New York: Simon and Schuster, 1998).

3. Francis Fukayama, *The End of History and the Last Man* (New York: The Free Press, 1992).

two categories will have profound implications for which international relations theories can best be used to describe, predict, and explain the actions of the state.

With regard to our second question—how international relations reflect cooperation and conflict—the primary problem of international relations for the foreseeable future is how the states of the First Tier will deal with those that languish in the Second Tier. Under what circumstances will the industrialized democracies of the world intervene in conflicts among Second Tier states—or within them? Will the people of the First Tier support intervention in conflicts on the periphery when the vital interests of their states are not affected? Will they demand such intervention when through the miracle of cable television they see and hear horrible atrocities inflicted upon innocent people? Will they demand military intervention, humanitarian assistance, or nationbuilding to lessen the danger of terrorism striking them at home as it did on 9/11?

These are vitally important questions, and ones we hope that this course will help you to answer. To get you started, we have provided a provocative look into the future as our final reading. James N. Rosenau is a Professor of International Affairs at George Washington University. He has thought deeply about the intersection between international relations and global economics. Rosenau, like Snow, believes that the world has changed dramatically at the end of the twentieth century, and like Snow, he believes that the countries that are economically developed and democratic will act differently than will countries that are not. While Snow focuses on the number of great powers in the system, however, Rosenau looks at the relations among all of the states in the system. He argues that the post-Cold War world may be more accurately described as the globalizing world—a world in which national borders no longer serve as barriers to the free flow of transactions of goods, services, and most importantly, ideas.[4]

Rosenau discusses a tension which exists in the modern world between the forces which are increasingly driving commerce and ideas across national borders, pushing the world toward globalization, and those forces of localization which lead individuals to narrow their horizons and limit their interests. Both of these processes are occurring all over the world all of the time, often simultaneously in the same country or village; Rosenau describes the simultaneous fragmenting forces of localization and the integrating forces of globalization as "fragmegration". Rosenau explicitly presents a hypothesis about the future course of this struggle that is testable and that, if correct, has profound implications for the future of the international system. Because of information technology and global markets, he suggests, the world is increasingly being shaped into the image of the United States.

This fact is not universally popular with those who would prefer to maintain their local traditions and customs, and many individuals and nations will attempt to resist it by holding onto what has traditionally mattered to them in their own localities. Because of the changes now being wrought by these forces, including the increasing power of individuals and small groups, those who resist the globalization of the world can present a real threat to the entire system, as repeatedly demonstrated by Al Qaeda and associated groups in the last few years. It will be your task to protect American interests against these individuals

---

4. One of the more important originators of those ideas, and beneficiaries of the new global system, is recognized in another book on the phenomenon of globalization. See Walter LaFeber, *Michael Jordan and the New Global Capitalism* (New York: W.W. Norton, 1999)

and small groups, as well as against the traditional state-on-state threats that have long represented one of the central features of international relations.

We examine "Why states do what they do" and "What causes conflict and cooperation among states" in order to accomplish four primary tasks: to *describe* and *explain* the world as it is, and to *predict* the future direction of world events. To the extent that we are able to understand the forces that drive history, we may even be able to *prescribe* directions for U.S. policy in the world to make that future more favorable for ourselves and for our children. You are the future leaders in this increasingly complex and fast-moving world, one in which the collapse of Asian currency markets or ancient nationalisms stirred up by tyrannical or ideological leaders may be the cause of conflicts which affect U.S. interests. Many authors believe that change will happen even faster over the next twenty or thirty years than it has in the fifteen years since the fall of the Berlin Wall—no end to history here! Snow provides one framework with which to explain the changing world to your soldiers. Rosenau describes some of the forces that are rapidly reshaping that world, and which may make it necessary for America to put soldiers in harm's way. We hope that both of these articles, taken together with the theories you have learned in this book, will help you to understand the world in which you will be charged with representing the interests of the United States.

World of Tiers

Donald M. Snow
National Security in a World of Tiers

National Security in a World of Tiers

Donald M. Snow

TIERS AND THE SECURITY EQUATION: A FIRST BRUSH

It is now reasonably clear what the general nature of the international system that is succeeding the Cold War system will be. We lack general agreement on the terminology with which to describe the new arrangements. For lack of a better set of terms, I will refer to it as a "world of tiers."

The basic idea is simple: as the post-Cold War world evolves, the international system is clearly divided into two distinct groups (or tiers) of states. The first tier, composed basically of the membership of the Organization of Economic Cooperation and Development (OECD), represents the most prosperous countries in the world. The second tier, representing the rest of humankind (about six-sevenths of the world's population, according to Max Singer and the late Aaron Wildavksy), is composed of those countries materially and politically less prosperous and content.

This division suggests that the system consists of two separate components, each with a different set of governing rules and dynamics such that no single set of descriptions can encompass them both. Rather, each has its own distinct set of relationships and problems. The national security equation, in turn, will largely be the result of where the two tiers intersect.

The First Tier

The defining characteristic of the countries of the first tier is their political and economic similarity: all have democratic political systems (although the form of democracy is not uniform) and they all share a commitment to market-driven capitalist economics. Moreover, they are all part of the interlocking global international economy in which the distinctly national basis of economic activity is decreasingly possible.

These countries thus have much more in common than they have that divides them. The central relationship among them is probably most dramatically symbolized by the ongoing concert of summit meetings between their leaders, such as the Group of Seven (G-7) biannual meetings. Certainly they are not in accord on all matters. They disagree, for instance, on the terms of trade among themselves and on the amount and pace of assistance that should be given to rehabilitate Russia and other parts of the former Soviet Union.

Their disagreements are, however, marginal, not central. The leadership has progressed into the third industrial revolution that has globalized economic activity; their economic differences can hardly deteriorate except beyond the peripheries of the central relationship. Cultural differences may create a different view on democratic politics (say American versus Japanese variants), but the core common commitment remains the same among the most consequential members of the international system.

This commonality leads to a striking, if intuitively obvious, national security consequence: *it is essentially impossible to think of war among any of the members of the first tier.* Singer and Wildavsky, indeed, refer to the first tier as the "zone of peace." This means that among the most technologically advanced countries—those with the prospects of raising the most sophisticated and formidable threats—there is basically no national security problem.

Why is this so? For one thing, it has become an accepted tenet that modern political democracies do not go to war with one another: free people do not willingly choose to attack other free people. At the same time, there is little reason for any of the countries of the first tier to fight; the economic and political ideological differences that marked the Cold War have simply disappeared.

Because the countries of the first tier comprise the heart of the international system, this also means the absence of conflicts that could basically threaten the viability of the system as a whole, as did the confrontation between the United States-led North Atlantic Treaty Organization coalition and the Soviet-led Warsaw Pact. Rather than being divided, the first tier stands together. Our principal disagreements arise over how to deal with the problems of the second tier and with instances where the problems of the second tier offer the prospects of disruption within the general tranquillity of the first tier.

The Second Tier

The basic tranquillity and unity of the first tier stands in stark contrast to the roughly six-sevenths of the world's population that comprises the second tier. Roughly speaking, the second tier is made up of most of what used to be called the Third World—the developing countries of Africa, Asia, and Latin America—and the majority of the former Second (or communist/socialist) World, although the status of some formerly communist countries is in question. For instance, it is possible that several of the formerly communist Eastern and Central European countries such as Poland or Hungary will join the first tier, while countries such as Albania or Bulgaria will almost certainly join the second tier.

The most obvious characteristic of the second tier is its diversity. What distinguishes the second tier from the First is that its countries lack either or both a commitment to, or attainment of, political democracy or advanced market capitalism, defined as entrance into the high technology revolution. Those countries that most closely resemble the first tier approximate it on one dimension or the other. The so-called Four Tigers of East Asia (Republic of Korea, Hong Kong, Taiwan, and Singapore) have economies that look much akin to those of the first tier, but they have not evolved the politically democratic forms of the first tier. In the former Second World, a number of states (Poland and the Baltic states, for example) have made political progress, but still lag behind economically.

second tier states differ from one another on both the political and economic dimensions. There are very wealthy second tier states—the oil-rich states of the Middle East come to mind—that have highly undemocratic political systems, and there are extremely poor countries such as Bangladesh and Mali. Similarly, India is the world's largest democracy, but various forms of despotism are the rule in many areas.

Although there are exceptions, the second tier is marked by instability and the potential or actuality of violence that is quite absent in the first tier. Some of this instability is a concomitant of the developmental process itself, as economic and political forces adjust to modernization. At the same time, what Samuel Huntington has called democracy's "third wave" has spawned a form of revived, exclusionary nationalism that is tearing apart nation-states and is forcing a redrawing of political maps in many places.

The instability and violence has both internal and international roots. Domestically, the post-Cold War world has watched in increasing horror a surge of national self-assertion by ethnic and national groups within states seeking power at the expense of other groups. Primordial nationalism—an attachment to ethnic and other roots not overcome by socialization into a broader national identity—has torn the fabric of states as diverse as Yugoslavia, Iraq, a number of the successor states of the Soviet Union (such as Armenia, Azerbaijan, and Georgia), and much of Africa (Somalia, Sudan, Mozambique, Rwanda, and Angola, for example).

The worst of these conflicts involve countries divided on religious and/or ethnic grounds, where attempts to suppress differences in the past have failed and where the hints of freedom have been expressed not in a desire for inclusionary democracy but in a mean and spiteful exclusionary self-determination that pits neighbors against one another in frenzies of hatred and violence with incredible passion. The communal bloodletting in Bosnia is the most visible instance of this for most Americans; it is, unfortunately, by no means rare. . . .

International violence may also increase in the second tier. Regional conflicts—disagreements between neighboring countries in geographic regions—have long festered in places such as the Asian subcontinent and Southeast Asia. During the Cold War, a certain control was imposed by the superpowers, which generally supported opposite sides (the Soviets aiding India, the United States helping Pakistan, for instance) in regional conflicts. Motivated by a desire to avoid being drawn physically into shooting conflicts with escalatory potential, the superpowers sought to contain those conflicts within reasonable bounds that did not risk direct confrontation.

As the Soviet Union dissolved and its successor Russia retreated from this competition, so too did the United States; consequently, many of the constraints have disappeared as well. As we shall see in Chapter 8, these conflicts are now enlivened by the introduction of weapons of mass destruction—notably nuclear, biological, or chemical (NBC) munitions—and ballistic missile means of delivery that potentially raise notably the stakes and deadliness of already volatile situations.

Three of the world's largest and most important states, China, India, and the former Soviet Union, reside in the second tier, and each has some or all of these problems. China continues its economic miracle as one of the world's most vibrant economies, but within a system of political repressiveness that the New York Times called "market Leninism" in 1993. China's future raises questions of inevitable demands for political liberalization and the possibility of political breakup at the peripheries—for instance, in Tibet.

India, the world's second most populous country after China, faces severe challenges. Internally, the possibility of secessionary demands that could break apart the Indian state are clear and compelling. These are especially evident in the northern states such as Kashmir, but they could occur also in the south (the Tamil region, for instance) as well. India is also locked in a long international conflict with Pakistan that is made more tense by the mutual possession—or near possession—of nuclear weapons.

The breakup of the former Soviet Union has also unleashed violence and instability with two bases. First, Soviet policy consciously encouraged the migration of national groups across the boundaries of the internal republics (states) that are now independent nation-states. Most notably, over 25 million ethnic Russians live outside Russia and are potentially subject to repression that Russia is unlikely to ignore.

Second, Stalinist policy drew arbitrary boundaries between the republics that now manifest themselves in international violence. The most obvious case in point is the Armenian-Azerbaijani conflict over the Armenian enclave of Nagorno-Karabakh within Azerbaijan and the Azeri enclave of Nakichevan within Armenia. These conflicts are especially lively in those parts of the former Soviet Union where Islam and Christianity collide—a general source of problems in those parts of the world where it occurs.

First Tier–Second Tier Intersection and the National Security Problem

Violence and instability in the second tier is not a new phenomenon; both internal and international wars were waged regularly throughout the Cold War period. Three factors, however, have raised second tier conflict to a position on the national security agenda that it formerly did not occupy.

The first and most obvious factor is that second tier violence is the *major, even sole,* source of violence in the system. If one is to see where the general tranquillity is being upset, it is in the second tier. Second, the mechanisms that used to serve to moderate that violence have largely disappeared. The superpowers have reduced their commitments in most second tier areas, and most of the regions lack regional organizations that can readily restore or enforce the peace.

Third, and possibly most importantly, second tier violence is much more public than it used to be, courtesy of global television outlets such as Cable News Network (CNN) and the Independent Television Network (ITN). Violence and its accompanying atrocities and gore are an everyday part of television news, impossible to ignore. The visual images that television produces are far more evocative than written accounts of violence: it is one thing to read that 100 civilians were killed in fighting somewhere; it is quite another to see the maimed bodies, live and in color.

Television may, in an indirect and largely unintended way, be setting the national security agenda. People see an atrocity and are horrified by it. The result is clamor for redress, the "do something syndrome." Would the United States have come to the aid of the Iraqi Kurds huddled on Turkish mountainsides had CNN not publicized their suffering? Would there have been such a public outpouring had televised pictures not shown us Somali starvation? Would we have been so embarrassed by our apparent impotence had the siege of Sarajevo not been a nightly reality? Slaughter of innocents and acts of barbarity are nothing new; unrelenting coverage of them is.

Because of the general peace in the first tier, the way we think about national security changes. We no longer need to devote considerable resources to preventing a general war that could threaten to destroy the system, as we once did. The violence and instability to be dealt with now is at the periphery of the central system defined as the first tier. The traditional military base of national security now lies at the intersection of the First and second tiers.

What should be our attitude toward violence in the second tier? To begin answering that question requires confronting two realities about the pattern. First, it is difficult—maybe impossible—to think of any conflict in the second tier that has the escalatory potential to engulf the entire system in general war—that is, World War III or its equivalent. Probably the worst case that one can conjure is a general war on the Asian subcontinent between India and Pakistan that escalated to nuclear exchange. Such a prospect would be gruesome and awful, and the literal fallout would pose a health hazard for those downwind. Such a war would *not,* however, necessarily draw in the major countries, except possibly as mediaries to end the violence. Although it can only be viewed as a hypothesis, there is no conflict that can occur in the second tier that would compel first tier (including American) involvement. We can, quite literally, ignore such conflicts and, by any objective manner, be hardly worse off.

This leads to the second reality: *with the possible exception of areas where there are large amounts of petroleum, first tier (including American) important interests are nowhere threatened by second tier military conflict.* The traditional use of military force has been grounded in so-called vital interests, conditions a state would not willingly tolerate and which it would use armed force to prevent. A European continent forcibly communized represented a vital threat to the United States; a militantly anti-American, nuclear-armed Mexico would also.

With the exception of the Persian Gulf, from which the oil necessary to satisfy first tier petroleum addiction comes, there are no equivalents in the second tier. When one combines this realization with the assertion that none of these conflicts threatens the central system, the calculation of national security also must change.

First, the changed conditions mean that, at least for the foreseeable future, the United States will employ armed forces *where it chooses to do so, not where it has to fight.* A realpolitik analysis will not send us to war in any but the most unforeseen situations. Unforeseen things do, of course, happen, and one must be prepared for uncertainty. Who would have thought in early 1990, for example, that we would mount a huge military expedition against Iraq? The offshoot of the "optional use of force" is not that we do not need force, but that the calculation of when we may use it is different.

This leads to a second conditioning observation: the way we view national security will be increasingly nontraditional. Responses to events in places such as Iraq and Somalia suggested to many (most notably, United Nations Secretary-General Boutros Boutros-Ghali) a new category of occasions to use force. Called "humanitarian vital interests," this category calls for employing force—probably under U.N. auspices—in situations where the atrocious behavior of states against their own people or other states violates basic humanitarian standards. This idea had broad currency as the vestiges of the Cold War dissipated; the souring of the most glowing application of the principle in Somalia has cooled the ardor. The idea is unlikely to go away, however. Other nontraditional roles will also likely emerge. One way in which second tier states can affect the first tier is through the promotion of terrorism or the production of narcotics. These kinds of acts do not threaten the first tier, but they are annoyances with which we may decide to deal. At the same time, it has become fashionable to think of so-called transnational issues such as environmental degradation and the population explosion in something like national security terms.

NATIONAL SECURITY IN A WORLD OF TIERS

In structural terms, the major difference between the Cold War system and that of the present is the disappearance of the old Second World and the adversarial relationship between the First and Second Worlds that was its principal dynamic and the driver of the national security system. Indeed, one reason to redesignate the system into two tiers is to remove the ordinal gap created by having to go directly from the first to the third worlds. That the notion of ordinality and, thus, implicit rank remains is an unavoidable limitation of language; zones of peace and turmoil, despite the absence of overt ordinality, still retain the core value (peace is better than turmoil).

The disappearance of the Second World has more impact on the national security structure than on any other aspect of the dynamics of the international system. The reason, simply enough, is that the East-West confrontation, while both political and military in nature, was basically a military competition; if one side or the other fell perilously vulnerable on the military dimension, nothing else was of great consequence.

It is because of this centrality that thinking about national security is more affected in the new order than thinking about other issues such as economic development or the environment. Lifting the veil of East-West confrontation allows clarification of other issues; development, for instance, can now be argued on its own merits, shorn of Marxist-market or anticommunist-communist political arguments. Lifting the Cold War veil from the national security structure leaves a decidedly intellectually naked emperor; there is very little intellectual structure left.

How does the end of the Cold War affect the remaining structures? It can be argued that it simply clarifies relations that were blurred by the Cold War obsession. The countries of the first tier, for instance, have been growing more alike for well over a decade. Now that the Cold War has disappeared, we simply have the time to concentrate on the implications of that similarity. The dynamics of the second tier also are different from what they were during the Cold War, but only to the extent that existing differences are no longer caught up in the chess game between East and West. There was conflict and instability within and among second tier states then, and there still is now. The perspective through which we view those problems is different, however, and we have yet to come entirely to grips with what that new perspective means in national security terms.

National Security in the First Tier

The relations among the states of the first tier remain in a state of basic tranquillity. The key word here is *remain.* The national security problem of opposing Soviet communism and its expansion was part of the glue that bound together the countries that composed the first tier; the transformation of Japan and Germany into market democracies was largely motivated in terms of geopolitics, for instance. However, as time has passed and the countries of the first tier have become more economically and politically similar, their common bonds have come to transcend the military competition. We no longer need the negative glue of common opposition to remain in harmony.

Some argue that this is too optimistic an assessment, that the collapse of the common enemy will allow us to turn upon one another and to invigorate old differences suppressed in the name of a united front before the enemy. Thus, for instance, Japan no longer needs the United States to form a shield against Soviet expansionism in the Far East, and it can now act more independently—specifically, in terms of the economic competition between the two. Similarly, the European members of NATO no longer need American protection from the Red Army; differences about questions such as terms of trade can now become more prominent, driving wedges between first tier states.

All of this may indeed, be true, but the central point is that the countries of the first tier have become so much more alike that disputes among them are disagreements between friends that may cause occasional acrimony but do not threaten the basic friendship. Japan and the United States, for instance, have too much involvement in one another's economies for either to take action that would threaten the other, and the same is largely true of Europe and the United States. To project "the coming war with Japan" (the title of a sensational book about likely trade wars) is to miss the point.

The standard rejoinder to this kind of optimism is to go back to the period leading to World War I, when it was widely argued that the economies of Europe were so interdependent that general war was impossible. That analogy, however, is flawed: the governments of that time were not uniformly democratic, and the narrower horizons of people then allowed a demonization of other peoples that is quite unlikely today. To suggest that the popularly elected government of Japan could make the case to its citizens to go to war with the "demon Americans, the white hordes" (or vice versa) is absolutely fanciful.

The countries of the first tier share four basic characteristics with overwhelming national security implications. First, there is a general structure of peace among them that is likely to endure. Second, there is general agreement among them about the kind of overall international system and national security environment they prefer. Third, their economic superiority to the second tier nations extends to military might; the first tier has the bulk of the political, economic, and military power in the international system. Fourth, the natural leader of the first tier is the United States, and the rest of the first tier will turn to it for leadership whenever such leadership is forthcoming (which it will not necessarily always be).

In a sense, none of these characteristics is new; only the environment in which they are pursued is different. The countries of the first tier have been at peace with one another since 1945; they have generally preferred a peaceful world and have looked to American leadership. The only thing different is that Soviet power made the superiority of Western military power arguable during the Cold War.

The general peace, to repeat, has two basic elements. The first is the existence of the shared values of political democracy and the capitalist, market economics among first tier members. The second is economic interdependence among the members. Each of these characteristics reinforces the general pacificity among them. Political democracies do not engage in physical violence with one another, because free people do not choose to initiate war, especially with other peoples who share their basic political values. Interdependence adds to this general predilection in two ways. It promotes greater interchange among the economic elite, who get to know one another and thus become impervious to appeals based in their differences. It also makes war more difficult because of mutual dependence on one another for production.

The result is to create a condition within the first tier roughly analogous to that in eighteenth century Europe, where the elites of the major countries shared a common ideology and freely circulated among the capitals of Europe that effectively comprised the international system. The series of economic summits (G-7) in which the major economic powers engage likewise provides an ongoing forum for interchange. The successful conclusion of the Uruguay Round of GATT shows that problems can be overcome through patience and compromise, and the emergence of truly international corporations—especially the so-called stateless corporations— provides a circulation of economic elites similar to that in the eighteenth century.

The bottom line is that there are no significant national security problems among members of the first tier. Time, effort, and resources do not need to be devoted to military preparations to deter or defend against military attacks from other first tier states. Since these states, by virtue of their superior technological bases, possess the greatest military power, the result is a situation where there are no military threats that threaten the integrity of the international order which the first tier dominates.

This simple difference is the greatest contrast between the current order and the Cold War system. That system was necessarily obsessed with avoiding a nuclear confrontation between the major protagonists, and there is simply no analogous problem in the current environment.

This revelation does not mean that the millenium is upon us. The eighteenth century analogy may be instructive: it was the emergence of diverse political ideologies spawned by the American and French Revolutions that reintroduced divergent political ideology to the European continent and divided states along political lines worth fighting over. It is not apparent what parallel division might create the same effect in the contemporary world, but it would be foolhardy not to admit the possibility.

The second shared characteristic of first tier nations is their general preference for an orderly, peaceful world. Expanding the pacific nature of First World relations to the second tier via expansion of the ring of market democracies is a shared preference, even if it is recognized that such a process will be difficult and, in some cases, impossible. It is, nonetheless, a preference both because a peaceful world would be one where first tier states would not be drawn into second tier conflict and where the climate for expanding the global economy more broadly would be enhanced.

There is nothing Pollyannish in this preference, and the first tier is under no illusions about the prospects. Faced with very certain breaches in worldwide tranquillity, this preference suggests that collective efforts to enforce the peace are preferred to unilateral efforts. This tendency arises both from the recognition that there are more disturbances of the peace than any one, or handful, of states, can deal with, and their general agreement on the world they prefer.

There will, nevertheless, remain special circumstances in which individual first tier states will feel the need to act individually in pursuit of their particular interests. A general breakdown in the Philippines, for instance, would evoke a particularly strong American response. The Russians, although not admitted members of the first tier, have already demonstrated in Georgia that they will take a strong hand in unrest in the former Soviet Union, and former colonial rulers will be more prone to act where they once held power and authority.

The third characteristic of the first tier is their preponderance of military power. The source of this strength is not numbers: only about one-seventh of the people on earth, according to Singer and Wildawsky, live in the zone of peace. Rather, the source of preponderance lies in technological superiority that allows smaller but more sophisticated military forces to overwhelm and defeat much larger but less sophisticated forces. This advantage holds even when second tier forces possess some of the advanced weaponry associated with the first tier because of differences in training and competence.

This advantage is reinforced because most of the first tier militaries have practice in coordinating the application of military force as members of NATO. While NATO is an organization with a questionable future due to the disappearance of its enemy, it has allowed the militaries of the major powers to learn how to deal with one another in detailed ways. This coordination, for example, contributed to the ability of the British and French to interact with the United States in Operation Desert Storm (despite the fact that France is not technically a member of the military command of NATO).

This military advantage is not without limitations. There have been, and will continue to be, situations where there will not be consensus that even a coordinated effort will bring about a favorable outcome. Bosnia is the obvious example. As well, the major self-limitation for all first tier states will be public opinion, which generally opposes the application of military force except in very measured ways or where overwhelming interests are clearly involved—neither of which characteristics are clearly present in most second tier conflicts.

Fourth and finally, there is general, if in some cases grudgingly admitted, agreement that the United State must provide the significant leadership in first tier security matters. This is so partially because of its status as the remaining superpower, which includes the fact that it is the only country that still retains global military reach. It also reflects the fact that the Americans retain more military punch than other first tier states.

The American leadership role is bounded. The rest of the first tier may look to the United States to lead, but it increasingly does so through the United Nations. The United States is in a push-and-shove match with the United Nations about the relations between the world body and its most powerful member. The issue is basically about leadership: is the U.N. the vehicle for carrying out first tier wishes, or does the U.N. set the agenda? President Clinton's September 1993 entreaty that the U.N. must learn to say no in some cases of possible actions before the United States says yes defines that relationship. The ongoing debate about the creation of a permanent U.N. force creates a continuing debate. Resolution of this critical question of leadership is made more difficult because the United States has yet to articulate a coherent set of policies and strategies for dealing with second tier unrest.

National Security in the Second Tier

The tranquillity within the first tier is clearly not matched in the second tier, the locus of almost all of the world's instability and unrest. Much of the violence in the second tier can be traced back to the pattern of decolonization that began after World War II. States unprepared by their colonial masters for political independence inherited situations of great poverty, imperfect political boundaries, and a host of other conditions that would have made stable governance difficult for the best prepared. For those lacking the skills and experience of self-rule, the task was overwhelming. The last spate of decolonization is currently at work in the successor states of the Soviet Union and, sadly enough, the same pattern is emerging.

It oversimplifies matters to talk of a single second tier. Rather, we can identify four characteristics that make up the national security problem of the second tier, noting its differential application in specific regions. The first characteristic is, indeed, that very lack of uniformity: some parts of the second tier are more unstable than others. Next, the second tier lacks a set of common values that would enable it to approach the first tier in any monolithic sense. Third, the splintered nature of the second tier leads to a preference to view military matters in terms of collective defense rather than collective security, which has great import for the United Nations. Finally, the military capabilities of the second tier limit the kind and extent of goals that can be pursued by military means.

The pattern of instability in various regions of the second tier is depicted by conflict type in Table 1. As the table shows, the potential for internal conflict resides in all regions, although it is most prevalent in specific subregions. Sub-Saharan Africa, notably central Africa, has shown the most internal violence, and places such as Zaire are almost certain to experience this form of violence in the future. Latin American internal violence is mostly found in Central America and the poorest regions of the Caribbean such as Haiti. There is potential for internal unrest in Iraq and the most

Table 1. Instability in the Second Tier

Form	Africa	Latin America	Middle East	Asia	Second World
Internal	X	X	X	X	X
Regional			X	X	X

politically backward of the oil-rich states such as Saudi Arabia. South and Southeast Asia have simmering internal problems, and the Balkans and the southern successor states to the Soviet Union show considerable violence potential. Major regional conflicts are concentrated in the Persian Gulf, South and Southeast Asia, and in Korea.

One striking note is that the potential for violence is least pronounced in those parts of the second tier that are closest to joining the first tier. In the past decade or so, large-scale democratization has occurred in South America that, while still in its infancy, has nonetheless stabilized politics on the continent. Regional conflict between the two major South American states, Brazil and Argentina, seems considerably more unlikely than it did 10 years ago. The Pacific Rim countries, with the exception of divided Korea, has likewise achieved considerable tranquillity.

This diversity is also manifested in the absence of common bonds between and among second tier regions. There is a common cry and appeal for developmental assistance from the first tier, but it is largely drowned out by particularism and attempts to gain special status. There is some commonality on aspirations to attainment of first tier status, but on specific attributes of first tier characteristics such as human rights, there is less than accord, as was clearly manifest in the 1993 U.N. Conference on Human Rights and Development. At that conference, mostly authoritarian second tier regimes tried, without success, to argue that the meaning of human rights was cultural rather than universal, largely a way to cover up what are human rights abuses by western standards. The inability to articulate common values and thereby present a united front compromises any leverage the second tier has with the First.

The third characteristic is that the second tier will likely look increasingly toward individual, rather than collective, solutions to their problems. The collective security, multilateral approach to problem solving evolving in the first tier will likely be unmatched in the second tier, for the simple reason that collective efforts will be organized *against* second tier states, including possible intervention in internal conflicts that entails violation of the state sovereignty of select second tier states. Since there will be far fewer cases where individual first tier states will act unilaterally in second tier conflicts, the best strategy for noninterference is to avoid the principle of collective action. . . . This preference will make second tier interaction with the United Nations more adversarial than it has been in the past.

Fourth and finally, the absence of advanced military capability will limit the kinds of military involvement of second tier states. While those states possessing NBC capabilities are a partial exception, this has three direct consequences. The first is that internal wars are likely to continue to be fought in the manner of low-intensity conflicts, for the simple reason that insurgents will have little alternative and that governments will be militarily incapable of anything but counterinsurgency. The second is that regional conflicts will also be self-limited in terms of ambition by the absence of physical capacity for greater ambition. The possible exceptions to this rule are South Asia (India and Pakistan) and the Persian Gulf (Iran and Iraq).

NATIONAL SECURITY AT THE INTERSECTION OF THE TIERS

For the countries of the first tier generally, and for the United States specifically, the implications of this analysis for national security are clear. Shorn of the old Cold War rivalry, the national security problem now moves to the intersection between the First and second tiers (including parts of the old Second World that became part of the second tier). The reason is equally clear: the occasions for employing military force are in the second tier, not the First.

Once again, there is nothing terribly new about this scenario. Since World War II, the United States has been involved in a series of military activities which, with the exception of the Berlin Airlift of 1948, have been in areas that are part of the second tier: Korea, Quemoy and Matsu (islands off the Chinese coast that are part of Taiwan), the Dominican Republic, Vietnam, Lebanon, Grenada, Iran, Panama, and Iraq, to name the most prominent.

The common thread in all but the most recent of these involvements was the Cold War confrontation. Communist North Korea invaded anticommunist South Korea, Communist China threatened the Republic of China, communists were purportedly posed to take over the Dominican Republic and later Grenada, and the Republic of Vietnam was menaced by the communist North Vietnamese.

The Cold War provided criteria to guide possible involvement that are absent in the wake of communism's effective disappearance. Instead, we can begin to think about where we will likely become involved by asking a series of four questions, the answers to which we will then try to convert into possible priorities in the final section of this chapter. The first question is: What is the nature of the first tier-second tier relationship? Do we care what happens in large parts of the second tier? The second has to do with connecting interests and threats: How do we resolve the interest-threat mismatch? The third is a matter of first tier/American role in the second tier: How much do we wish to impose? Finally, there is the question of self-limitation: How much involvement will democratic publics allow?

The kind of relationship the first tier has to the Second is likely to depend on situation-specific circumstances. The question, in essence, is what—if any—basis for involvement in the second tier exists in the absence of a Cold War motivation. For former colonial powers, the answer may be residual interests in former colonies: economic investments or colonial settler populations that need protection in the event of hostilities, for instance. Geographic proximity may also provide motivation in some cases.

These kinds of motivations will not activate American concern except in limited ways: the United States might feel the need for involvement should the New People's Army be on the verge of taking over power in the Philippines, and it has historically shown an interest in quelling anti-American unrest in Central America and in protecting American access to vital petroleum reserves, as in the Persian Gulf.

But what of involvement where those criteria are not met? It is difficult to imagine any overwhelming sense of kindredness or traditional American interest that would involve the United States in internal violence and atrocity on the African continent. As noted, we have ignored very brutal, atrocious wars in places like Angola, Mozambique, Burundi, Rwanda, and the Sudan within the last few years; the same is true of the Asian subcontinent. At the same time, the United States became involved in the longest war in its history in Vietnam, where no discernible American interests existed, and it threw its military might into the fray in Somalia. The answer to the question, "Do we care?" appears to be, "Sometimes."

The second question returns the discussion to the matter of national interests and the interest-threat mismatch. In traditional terms, the situation can be restated: the threats in the new environment are not particularly interesting, and American interests are not particularly threatened by the pattern of second tier instability and violence. A traditional analysis would suggest that the United States would hardly ever involve itself physically in the violent affairs of most of the second tier.

There are two polar responses to the mismatch. One is simply to acknowledge it, argue that the mismatch is irreconcilable, and conclude that the United States has little business getting involved in internal wars and regional conflicts where demonstrable American vital interests are not affected adversely by worst outcomes. This position is the classic realist argument. Had it been applied, for instance, to Somalia, the United States would have stayed home; the only demonstrable American interests in the Horn of Africa are access to the Suez Canal and as a staging area to move into the Persian Gulf. The level of those interests is questionable, and it is unclear how any outcome in Somalia would affect those interests adversely.

The other polar response is to realign interests to match the threat. The mechanism for doing so is to expand those situations deemed of national vital interest. The specific instrument is the adoption of humanitarian vital interests to justify intervention in the internal affairs of states that act atrociously toward their populations. The accompanying precept of this expansion of interest is to adopt the notion of universal sovereignty, thereby making it both an interest and an obligation to aid the beleaguered. This has become the position of the idealists; their agency of choice to carry out the mission is the United Nations. Accepting this rationale provides the justification for involvement in Somalia and future analogous situations.

This debate about interests turns the traditional realist-idealist debate on its head. In the Cold War, realists were more likely to advocate the use of American force out of geopolitical necessity: countering communist expansion was the definition of vitality of interest. Idealists, on the other hand, generally counseled the husbanding of force, preferring nonmilitary solutions and downplaying the vital importance of unfavorable worst case outcomes. The debate over what to do about the Sandinistas in Nicaragua during the early 1980s captures this traditional debate nicely: the possibility of a hostile Marxist regime in Central America aroused realists to call for action to overthrow the Sandinistas, while idealists argued that vital interests were not involved and that force was thus not justified.

In the post-Cold War system, positions on the use of force are nearly reversed. The realist analysis suggests a very limited role for American force in the world, because traditional vital interests are generally unaffected by second tier violence. The idealist position embraces the expansion of what constitutes a vital interest and thus concludes that the use of American force is justified in nontraditional situations. Thus, idealists favor a more expanded use of force than do realists.

The third question has to do with the kind of role that the United States and other first tier states will acquire in dealing with second tier problems. Recognizing that there are more candidate situations for involvement—particularly if involvement in internal wars is part of the list—than there are available resources, the question has two parts.

The first part is the extent of involvement. Is the first tier to intervene only in select cases and for the limited objectives of peacekeeping as outlined by Boutros-Ghali? Or is the purpose to impose an order wherever violence and atrocity occur, and to act as a collective hegemon over the second tier? The latter is clearly a much more involved, expensive, and demanding task and leads to the second part of the question: Who will do the work? If either goal is to be pursued, American leadership will have to be evident, but it is also clear that the United States cannot physically lead in all instances for reasons of resources and will. That being the case, what mechanisms will exist for choosing those who will lead specific missions? Assuming that something like the lead country concept would be in place, who will choose the leader?

This topic leads to the fourth question, which is about the extent to which first tier publics will support military actions in the second tier. The concern arises because the chief military limitation on democratic states of the first tier is public support. This is nothing new: Carl von Clausewitz articulated the "holy trinity" of linkage between the government, the army, and the people over a century and a half ago: If any element in the trinity fails to support the use of military force, it will likely fail.

This problem is not only American, because the first tier countries that possess the military might to intervene into the second tier are all democracies. A corollary to the proposition that democracies do not initiate wars against other democracies is that democracies do not accept casualties—body bags coming home—unless there is some compelling justification that will often be difficult to make and sustain, especially if involvement becomes lengthy. The afterglow of Vietnam makes Americans particularly sensitive to this charge; depending on the eventual outcome, Somalia may provide a parallel caution for the future.

THE FOGGY FUTURE

Predicting the future is always much more treacherous than describing the past because, as I pointed out in an earlier book, *The Shape of the Future,* the past has happened and the future has not. The future always entails occurrences that we are unable to predict—factors unforeseen and, in some cases, unforeseeable. The problem is particularly acute when the change in conditions is fundamental and the search for analogies proves difficult, as is clearly the case today.

The American national security apparatus is in the midst of a crisis about its future role and mission. Its predicament approaches the state of a dilemma. The professional community is, on the whole, conservative and realist in its orientation. It does not view lightly the idea of putting young American lives at risk unless there is some demonstrable threat to American interests. The dilemma is that the apparatus also faces severe reductions in resources that can only be staunched by embracing uses of force that contradict its own basic realist precepts. The strained attempt of the professional officer corps to find a way to embrace support for the United Nations—an institution it has reflexively rejected for decades—captures the agony involved.

The early post-Cold War experience does not provide much guidance as to where and when the United States should use force in the future. The contrast between systemic reaction in Somalia and inaction in Bosnia provides little positive direction; if anything, images of the residents of Sarajevo suffering a second snowy winter under siege bred cynicism about the system's reactions.

Table 2. Involvement Factors

What We Know:
1. Level of atrocity
2. Amount of publicity
3. Recognition factor
What We Are Asked to Do:
4. Burden sharing/leadership
5. Time commitment
Prospects Of Success:
6. Interests involved
7. Efficacy of force
8. Cost
9. End game

With this conceptual uncertainty in mind, the best we can do is to suggest some guidelines for the United States in choosing when and where to apply force in the second tier. To this end, nine influences will be identified and presented, in no particular order of importance, on the assumption that some will be more important than others. The first three address the question of our level of awareness of situations. The next two concern what the United States is being asked to undertake. The last four influences reflect National Security Advisor Anthony Lake's four rules on using force and suggest the likelihood of success. For clarity's sake, the factors are summarized in Table 2.

The first factor is the level of atrocity and horror of a given situation. As a general rule, the greater the horror and atrocity involved, the more likely some form of international action will be contemplated. In the two post–Cold War situations in which the United States became involved, Operation Provide Comfort for the Kurds and Operation Restore Hope in Somalia, the term "genocide" was prominently mentioned. Kurdish fears (warranted or not) of genocidal attacks by Iraqi forces caused them to flee; genocidal levels of death predicted in Somalia from starvation similarly partly motivated intervention. By contrast, in Bosnia, there have been occasional accusations of genocide in isolated occasions, but all three principal parties have been accused of the practice at one time or another.

Genocide represents a level of atrocity that could reasonable activate international efforts, including an American component, especially if such acts were committed by a country signatory to the U.N. Convention on Genocide (which includes most countries). Operationalizing genocide, however, is never easy in individual cases, and it leaves open the question of what actions short of genocide should create international intervention.

A second and corollary factor is the level of publicity received by instances of second-tier violence. This factor suggests the strong role of global television, which has the option of publicizing instances of great suffering and atrocity or ignoring them. In some cases, global television has been effectively prevented from covering the gory details of ethnic and other violence, as in the Sudan. There is also, as mentioned earlier, the possibility that the viewing public will eventually become desensitized to carnage, to the point that television pictures will not activate the "do something syndrome." In addition, the effect of moderate levels of coverage, as in Burundi in 1993 or in Azerbaijan and Armenia, on world opinion is still an open question.

A third factor, influenced by the first two, is the average American's low degree of recognition of distant places and the people involved. The well-chronicled American lack of interest and knowledge about foreign affairs is specially great in matters dealing with the countries of the second tier, and it will be hard to gain widespread public support for sending forces to places and/or over issues of which the average citizen has never heard. Stimulating sufficient public interest—especially where threats are not particularly compelling—will require a good deal of citizen education, a process in which the global media will play a major role.

The next two factors on the list deal with what the American people, through their armed forces, are being asked to do in specific situations. Who will authorize and participate in the actions? The United States has shown willingness to act unilaterally where its interests are clearly engaged or where it simply feels that it must. We would, for instance, have conducted Operation Desert Storm on our own had others not volunteered, and the same was true of early efforts in Somalia.

Burden sharing, however, will be a hallmark of American willingness in the future, especially if the roster of actions expands. Spreading the lead country role widely will be necessary for the American people, who instinctively shrink from being designated the world's "globocop." Moreover, it remains to be seen how long the "honeymoon" between American military forces and the United Nations will last. If the U.N. bureaucracy insists on an aggressive, inclusive presence wherever violence breaks out—that is, if it fails to learn to say no, in President Clinton's terms—that relationship will likely sour. At the same time, the active campaign to attach American forces directly to U.N. control will create an anti-U.N. backlash.

The fifth factor is the duration of the operations. It is virtually an axiom in democratic societies that they tolerate best military actions that are quick, decisive, and generally as bloodless as possible. Lengthy involvements are tolerated only when the aims are so overwhelmingly important as to justify greater sacrifice, an idea elaborated in Snow and Drew, *From Lexington to Desert Storm.* Second-tier actions will hardly ever meet this criterion. Recent evidence of this truism is found in Somalia: the first time in was short, decisive, bloodless, and overwhelmingly popular. When the Americans returned for an apparently open-ended stay, the public debate quickly turned to a congressional–White House debate on setting a time limit to get the troops out and forced their withdrawal.

The last four factors, borrowed with acknowledgment from Lake, address the likelihood of achieving goals to which the American people can subscribe. Item six raises the question of what American interests are involved. This is important both as a guiding criterion and as the basis for rationalizing action to the American people. The statement of what American interests are engaged in some unfavorable outcome are, in effect, a statement of why the country is asking some Americans to sacrifice, up to and including their lives.

This will, in my view, be a principal bone of contention that will end up limiting American participation in the second tier. Those favoring broad involvement argue that the forces are, after all, well-paid professionals who volunteered to be placed in harm's way: they go wherever they are sent. Those hastening caution retort that those professionals are also the sons and daughters of voters who will take out their displeasure on officials who put their children in physical danger for less than truly vital reasons. The interventionist argument is better cocktail party talk than good politics.

The seventh item turns on whether the insertion of American forces can actually do any good. Despite the high combat effectiveness of American forces, the answer is not always obvious. A number of the potential roles will be in peace imposition, and it is not at all clear that military force can solve those situations. Inaction in the primary contemporary situation where peace imposition might have been contemplated, Bosnia, suggests recognition of the possibility that applying American force might not be efficacious in all circumstances.

The eighth factor is cost and its acceptability. If potential engagements are short and decisive, cost is less likely to be a problem. But if commitments become extensive and individual involvements are extended, then cost—including the sacrifices entailed in other areas—will have to become part of the calculation.

Finally, there is the necessity of finding a way to end commitment—the endgame. The United Nations record is not encouraging here: peacekeeping missions develop a life of their own and, in places such as Cyprus, become solutions of their own. The United States, upon returning to Somalia, was faced with the question of how to know when its purpose had been accomplished and it was time to go home. Setting and implementing an arbitrary date for withdrawal answered the second part of that question, but not the first. Involvements are likely to be inversely attractive to their open-endedness.

All these issues are in a state of flux, forcing us to think about national security in very different ways than we did only a few years ago. The future is foggy because it is so unlike the recent past and because we have been unable to find satisfactory parallels in history to guide us.

The very real difference between the contemporary setting and the Cold War is defined by the kinds of questions that are swirling in the public policy debate about national security, some of which have been represented in this essay. If someone had proposed as little as six or seven years ago that the primary national security questions we would face today would deal with how the first tier would engage with the second tier, the response would have been a blank stare of noncomprehension. But that is, indeed, the nature of defense policy for the new international order.

Globalization

James N. Rosenau
The Complexities and Contradictions of Globalization

The Complexities and Contradictions of Globalization

James N. Rosenau

Globalization, we are told, is what every business should be pursuing, and what every nation should welcome. But what, exactly, is it? James Rosenau offers a nuanced understanding of a process that is much more real, and transforming, than the language of the marketplace expresses.

The mall at Singapore's airport has a food court with 15 food outlets, all but one of which offering menus that cater to local tastes; the lone standout, McDonald's, is also the only one crowded with customers. In New York City, experts in *feng shui,* an ancient Chinese craft aimed at harmonizing the placement of man-made structures in nature, are sought after by real estate developers in order to attract a growing influx of Asian buyers who would not be interested in purchasing buildings unless their structures were properly harmonized.

Most people confronted with these examples would probably not be surprised by them. They might even view them as commonplace features of day-to-day life late in the twentieth century, instances in which local practices have spread to new and distant sites. In the first case the spread is from West to East and in the second it is from East to West, but both share a process in which practices spread and become established in profoundly different cultures. And what immediately comes to mind when contemplating this process? The answer can be summed up in on word: globalization, a label that is presently in vogue to account for peoples, activities, norms, ideas, goods, services, and currencies that are decreasingly confined to a particular geographic space and its local and established practices.

Indeed, some might contend that "globalization" is the latest buzzword to which observers resort when things seem different and they cannot otherwise readily account for them. That is why, it is reasoned, a great variety of activities are labeled as globalization, with the result that no widely accepted formulation of the concept has evolved. Different observers use it to describe different phenomena, and often there is little overlap among the various usages. Even worse, the elusiveness of the concept of globalization is seen as underlying the use of a variety of other, similar terms—world society, interdependence, centralizing tendencies, world system, globalism, universalism, internationalization, globality—that come into play when efforts are made to grasp why public affairs today seem significantly different from those of the past.

Such reasoning is misleading. The proliferation of diverse and loose definitions of globalization as well as the readiness to use a variety of seemingly comparable labels are not so much a reflection of evasive confusion as they are an stage in a profound ontological shift, a restless search for new ways of understanding unfamiliar phenomena. The lack of precise formulations may suggest the presence of buzzwords for the inexplicable, but a more convincing interpretation is that such words are voiced in so many different contexts because of a shared sense that the human condition is presently undergoing profound transformations in all of its aspects.

Reprinted with permission from James Rosenau, "The Complexities and Contradictions of Globalization," *Current History,* November 1997, pp. 360-364.

WHAT IS GLOBALIZATION?

Let us first make clear where globalization fits among the many buzzwords that indicate something new in world affairs that is moving important activities and concerns beyond the national seats of power that have long served as the foundations of economic, political, and social life. While all the buzzwords seem to cluster around the same dimension of the present human condition, useful distinctions can be drawn among them. Most notably, if it is presumed that the prime characteristic of this dimension is change—a transformation of practices and norms—then the term "globalization" seems appropriate to denote the "something" that is changing humankind's preoccupation with territoriality and the traditional arrangements of the state system. It is a term that directly implies change, and thus differentiates the phenomenon as a process rather than as a prevailing condition or a desirable end state.

Conceived as an underlying process, in other words, globalization is not the same as globalism, which points to aspirations for a state of affairs where values are shared by or pertinent to all the world's more than 5 billion people, their environment, and their role as citizens, consumers, or producers with an interest in collective action to solve common problems. And it can also be distinguished from universalism, which refers to those values that embrace all of humanity (such as the values that science or religion draws on), at any time or place. Nor is it coterminous with complex interdependence, which signifies structures that link people and communities in various parts of the world.

Although related to these other concepts, the idea of globalization developed here is narrower in scope. It refers neither to values nor to structures, but to sequences that unfold either in the mind or in behavior, to processes that evolve as people and organizations go about their daily tasks and seek to realize their particular goals. What distinguishes globalizing processes is that they are not hindered or prevented by territorial or jurisdictional barriers. As indicated by the two examples presented at the outset, such processes can readily spread in many directions across national boundaries, and are capable of reaching into any community anywhere in the world. They consist of all those forces that impel individuals, groups, and institutions to engage in similar forms of behavior or to participate in more encompassing and coherent processes, organizations, or systems.

Contrariwise, localization derives from all those pressures that lead individuals, groups, and institutions to narrow their horizons, participate in dissimilar forms of behavior, and withdraw to less encompassing processes, organizations, or systems. In other words, any technological, psychological, social, economic, or political developments that foster the expansion of interests and practices beyond established boundaries are both sources and expressions of the processes of globalization, just as any developments in these realms that limit or reduce interests are both sources and expressions of localizing processes.

Note that the processes of globalization are conceived as only *capable* of being worldwide in scale. In fact, the activities of no group, government, society, or company have never been planetary in magnitude, and few cascading sequences actually encircle and encompass the entire globe. Televised events such as civil wars and famines in Africa or protests against governments in Eastern Europe may sustain a spread that is worldwide in scope, but such a scope is not viewed as a prerequisite of globalizing dynamics. As long as it has the potential of an unlimited spread that can readily transgress national jurisdictions, any interaction sequence is considered to reflect the operation of globalization.

Obviously, the differences between globalizing and localizing forces give rise to contrary conceptions of territoriality. Globalization is rendering boundaries and identity with the land less salient while localization, being driven by pressures to narrow and withdraw, is highlighting borders and intensifying the deep attachments to land that can dominate emotion and reasoning.

In short, globalization is boundary-broadening and localization is boundary-heightening. The former allows people, goods, information, norms, practices, and institutions to move about oblivious to despite boundaries. The boundary-heightening processes of localization are designed to inhibit or prevent the movement of people, goods, information, norms, practices, and institutions. Efforts along this line, however, can be only partially successful. Community and state boundaries can be heightened to a considerable extent, but they cannot be rendered impervious. Authoritarian governments try to make them so, but their policies are bound to be undermined in a shrinking world with increasingly interdependent economies and communications technologies that are not easily monitored. Thus it is hardly surprising that some of the world's most durable tensions flow from the fact that no geographic borders can be made so airtight to prevent the infiltration of ideas and goods. Stated more emphatically, some globalizing dynamics are bound, at least in the long run, to prevail.

The boundary-expanding dynamics of globalization have become highly salient precisely because recent decades have witnessed a mushrooming of the facilities, interests, and markets through which a potential for worldwide spread can be realized. Likewise, the boundary-contracting dynamics of localization have also become increasingly significant, not least because some people and cultures feel threatened by the incursions of globalization. Their jobs, their icons, their belief systems, and their communities seem at risk as the boundaries that have sealed them off from the outside world in the past no longer assure protection. And there is, of course, a basis of truth in these fears. Globalization does intrude; its processes do shift jobs elsewhere; its norms do undermine traditional mores. Responses to these threats can vary considerably. At one extreme are adaptations that accept the boundary-broadening processes and make the best of them by integrating them into local customs and practices. At the other extreme are responses intended to ward off the globalizing processes by resort to ideological purities, closed borders, and economic isolation.

THE DYNAMICS OF FRAGMEGRATION

The core of world affairs today thus consists of tensions between the dynamics of globalization and localization. Moreover, the two sets of dynamics are causally linked, almost as if every increment of globalization gives rise to an increment of localization, and vice versa. To account for these tensions I have long used the term "fragmegration," an awkward and perhaps even grating label that has the virtue of capturing the pervasive interactions between the fragmenting forces of localization and the integrative forces of globalization. One can readily observe the unfolding of fragmegrative dynamics in the struggle of the European Union to cope with proposals for monetary unification or in the electoral campaigns and successes of Jean-Marie Le Pen in France, Patrick Buchanan in the United States, and Pauline Hanson in Australia—to mention only three examples.

It is important to keep in mind that fragmegration is not a single dynamic. Both globalization and localization are clusters of forces that, as they interact in different ways and through different channels, contribute to more encompassing processes in the case of globalization and to less encompassing processes in the case of localization. These various dynamics, moreover, operate in all realms of human activity, from the cultural and social to the economic and political.

In the political realm, globalizing dynamics underlie any developments that facilitate the expansion of authority, policies, and interests beyond existing socially constructed territorial boundaries, whereas the politics of localization involves any trends in which the scope of authority and policies undergoes contraction and reverts to concerns, issues, groups, and institutions that are less extensive than the prevailing socially constructed territorial boundaries. In the economic realm, globalization encompasses the expansion of production, trade, and investments beyond their prior locales, while localizing dynamics are at work when the activities of producers and consumers are constricted to narrower boundaries. In the social and cultural realms, globalization operates to extend ideas, norms, and practices beyond the settings in which they originated, while localization highlights or compresses the original settings and thereby inhibits the inroad of new ideas, norms, and practices.

It must be stressed that the dynamics unfolding in all these realms are long-term processes. They involve fundamental human needs and thus span all of human history. Globalizing dynamics derive from peoples' need to enlarge the scope of their self-created orders so as to increase the goods, services, and ideas available for their well-being. The agricultural revolution, followed by the industrial and postindustrial transformations, are among the major sources that have sustained globalization. Yet even as these forces have been operating, so have contrary tendencies toward contraction been continuously at work. Localizing dynamics derive from people's need for the psychic comforts of close-at-hand, reliable support—for the family and neighborhood, for local cultural practices, for a sense of "us" that is distinguished from "them." Put differently, globalizing dynamics have long fostered large-scale order, whereas localizing dynamics have long created pressure for small-scale order. Fragmegration, in short, has always been an integral part of the human condition.

GLOBALIZATION'S EVENTUAL PREDOMINANCE

Notwithstanding the complexities inherent in the emergent structures of world affairs, observers have not hesitated to anticipate what lies beyond fragmegration as global history unfolds. All agree that while the contest between globalizing and localizing dynamics is bound to be marked by fluctuating surges in both directions, the underlying tendency is for the former to prevail over the latter. Eventually, that is, the dynamics of globalization are expected to serve as the bases around which the course of events is organized.

Consensus along these lines breaks down, however, over whether the predominance of globalization is likely to have desirable or noxious consequences. Those who welcome globalizing processes stress the power of economic variables. In this view the globalization of national economies through the diffusion of technology and consumer products, the rapid transfer of financial resources, and the efforts of transnational companies to extend their market shares is seen as so forceful and durable as to withstand and eventually surmount any and all pressures toward fragmentation. This line acknowledges that the diffusion that sustains the processes of globalization is a centuries-old dynamic, but the difference is that the present era has achieved a level of economic development in which it is possible for innovations occurring in any sector of any country's economy to be instantaneously transferred to and adapted in any other country or sector. As a consequence, when this process of diffusion collides with cultural or political protectionism, it is culture and protectionism that wind up in the shop for repairs. Innovation accelerates. Productivity increases. Standards of living improve. There are setbacks, of course. The newspaper headlines are full of them. But we believe that the time required to override these setbacks has shortened dramatically in the developed world. Indeed, recent experience suggests that, in most cases, economic factors prevail in less than a generation.

Thus understood, globalization—the spread of economic innovations around the world and the political and cultural adjustments that accompany this diffusion—cannot be stopped . . . As history teaches, the political organizations and ideologies that yield superior economic performance survive, flourish, and replace those that are less productive.

While it is surely the case that robust economic incentives sustain and quicken the processes of globalization, this line of theorizing nevertheless suffers from not allowing for its own negation. The theory offers no alternative interpretations as to how the interaction of economic, political, and social dynamics will play out. One cannot demonstrate the falsity—if falsity it is—of the theory because any contrary evidence is seen merely as "setbacks," as expectable but temporary deviations from the predicted course. The day may come, of course, when event so perfectly conform to the predicted patterns of globalization that one is inclined to conclude that the theory has been affirmed. But in the absence of alternative scenarios, the theory offers little guidance as to how to interpret intervening events, especially those that highlight the tendencies toward fragmentation. Viewed in this way, it is less a theory and more an article of faith to which one can cling.

Other observers are much less sanguine about the future development of fragmegration. They highlight a litany of noxious consequences that they see as following from the eventual predominance of globalization: "its economism; its economic reductionism; its technological determinism; its political cynicism, defeatism, and immobilism; its de-socialization of the subject and resocialization of risk; its teleological subtext of inexorable global 'logic' driven exclusively by capital accumulation and the market; and its ritual exclusion of factors, causes, or goals other than capital accumulation and the market from the priority of values to be pursued by social action."

Still another approach, allowing for either desirable or noxious outcomes, has been developed by Michael Zurn. He identifies a mismatch between the rapid extension of boundary-crossing activities and the scope of effective governance. Consequently, states are undergoing what is labeled "uneven denationalization;" a primary process in which "the rise of international governance is still remarkable, but not accompanied by mechanisms for... democratic control; people, in addition, become alienated from the remote political process… The democratic state in the Western world is confronted with a situation in which it is undermined by the process of globalization and overarched by the rise of international institutions."

While readily acknowledging the difficulties of anticipating where the process of uneven denationalization is driving the world, Zurn is able to derive two scenarios that may unfold: "Whereas the pessimistic scenario points to instances of fragmentation and emphasizes the disruption caused by the transition, the optimistic scenario predicts, at least in the long run, the triumph of centralization." The latter scenario rests on the presumption that the increased interdependence of societies will propel them to develop ever more effective democratic controls over the very complex arrangements on which international institutions must be founded.

UNEVEN FRAGMEGRATION

My own approach to theorizing about the fragmegrative process builds on these other perspectives and a key presumption of my own—that there is no inherent contradiction between localizing and globalizing tendencies—to develop an overall hypothesis that anticipates fragmegrative outcomes and that allows for its own negation: *the more pervasive globalizing tendencies become, the less resistant localizing reactions will be to further globalization.* In other words, globalization and localization will coexist, but the former will continue to set the context for the latter. Since the degree of coexistence will vary from situation to situation (depending on the salience of the global economy and the extent to which ethnic and other noneconomic factors actively contribute to localization), I refer, borrowing from Zurn, to the processes depicted by the hypothesis as *uneven fragmegration.* The hypothesis allows for continuing pockets of antagonism between globalizing and localizing tendencies even as increasingly (but unevenly) the two accommodate each other. It does not deny the pessimistic scenario wherein fragmentation disrupts globalizing tendencies; rather it treats fragmentation as more and more confined to particular situations that may eventually be led by the opportunities and requirements of greater interdependence to conform to globalization.

For globalizing and localizing tendencies to accommodate each other, individuals have to come to appreciate that they can achieve psychic comfort in collectivities through multiple memberships and multiple loyalties, that they can advance both local and global values without either detracting from the other. The hypothesis of uneven fragmegration anticipates a growing appreciation along these lines because the contrary premise, that psychic comfort can only be realized by having a highest loyalty, is becoming increasingly antiquated. To be sure, people have long been accustomed to presuming that, in order to derive the psychic comfort they need through collective identities, they had to have a hierarchy of loyalties and that, consequently, they had to have a highest loyalty that could only be attached to a single collectivity. Such reasoning, however, is a legacy of the state system, of centuries of crises that made people feel they had to place nation-state loyalties above all others. It is a logic that long served to reinforce the predominance of the state as the "natural" unit of political organization and that probably reached new heights during the intense years of the cold war.

But if it is the case, as the foregoing analysis stresses, that conceptions of territoriality are in flux and that the failure of states to solve pressing problems has led to a decline in their capabilities and a loss of legitimacy, it follows that the notion that people must have a "highest loyalty" will also decline and give way to the development of multiple loyalties and an understanding that local, national, and transnational affiliations need not be mutually exclusive. For the reality is that human affairs are organized at all these levels for good reasons; people have needs that can only be filled by close-at-hand organizations and other needs that are best served by distant entities at the national or transnational level.

In addition, not only is an appreciation of the reality that allows for multiple loyalties and memberships likely to grow as the effectiveness of states and the salience of national loyalties diminish, but it also seems likely to widen as the benefits of the global economy expand and people become increasingly aware of the extent to which their well-being is dependent on events and trends elsewhere in the world. At the same time, the distant economic processes serving their needs are impersonal and hardly capable of advancing the need to share with others in a collective affiliation. This need was long served by the nation-state, but with fragmegrative dynamics having undermined the national level as a source of psychic comfort and with transnational entities seeming too distant to provide the psychic benefits of affiliation, the satisfactions to be gained through more close-at-hand affiliations are likely to seem ever more attractive.

THE STAKES

It seems clear that fragmegration has become an enduring feature of global life; it is also evident that globalization is not merely a buzzword, that it encompasses pervasive complexities and contradictions that have the potential both to enlarge and to degrade our humanity. In order to ensure that the enlargement is more prevalent than the degradation, it is important that people and their institutions become accustomed to the multiple dimensions and nuances as our world undergoes profound and enduring transformations. To deny the complexities and contradictions in order to cling to a singular conception of what globalization involves is to risk the many dangers that accompany oversimplification.

Terrorism

Bruce Hoffman

Defining Terrorism

Defining Terrorism

Bruce Hoffman

What is terrorism? Few words have so insidiously worked their way into our everyday vocabulary. Like 'Internet'—another grossly over-used term that has similarly become an indispensable part of the argot of the late twentieth century—most people have a vague idea or impression of what terrorism is, but lack a more precise, concrete and truly explanatory definition of the word. This imprecision has been abetted partly by the modern media, whose efforts to communicate an often complex and convoluted message in the briefest amount of air-time or print space possible have led to the promiscuous labelling of a range of violent acts as 'terrorism'. Pick up a newspaper or turn on the television and—even within the same broadcast or on the same page—one can find such disparate acts as the bombing of a building, the assassination of a head of state, the massacre of civilians by a military unit, the poisoning of produce on supermarket shelves or the deliberate contamination of over-the-counter medication in a chemist's shop all described as incidents of terrorism. Indeed, virtually any especially abhorrent act of violence that is perceived as directed against society—whether it involves the activities of anti-government dissidents or governments themselves, organized crime syndicates or common criminals, rioting mobs or persons engaged in militant protest, individual psychotics or lone extortionists—is often labelled 'terrorism'.

Dictionary definitions are of little help. The pre-eminent authority on the English language, the much-venerated *Oxford English Dictionary [OED]*, is disappointingly unobliging when it comes to providing edification on this subject, its interpretation at once too literal and too historical to be of much contemporary use:

> **Terrorism:** A system of terror. 1. Government by intimidation as directed and carried out by the party in power in France during the revolution of 1789–94; the system of 'Terror'. 2. *gen.* A policy intended to strike with terror those against whom it is adopted; the employment of methods of intimidation; the fact of terrorizing or condition of being terrorized.

These definitions are wholly unsatisfying. Rather than learning what terrorism is, one instead finds, in the first instance, a somewhat potted historical—and, in respect of the modern accepted usage of the term, a uselessly anachronistic—description. The second definition offered is only slightly more helpful. While accurately communicating the fear-inducing quality of terrorism, the definition is still so broad as to apply to almost any action that scares ('terrorizes') us. Though an integral part of 'terrorism', this definition is still insufficient for the purpose of accurately defining the phenomenon that is today called 'terrorism'.

A slightly more satisfying elucidation may be found in the *OED*'s definition of the perpetrator of the act than in its efforts to come to grips with the act itself. In this respect, a 'terrorist' is defined thus:

> 1. As a political term: a. Applied to the Jacobins and their agents and partisans in the French Revolution, esp. to those connected with the Revolutionary tribunals during the 'Reign of Terror'. b. Any one who attempts to further his views by a system of coercive intimidation; *spec.* applied to members of one of the extreme revolutionary societies in Russia.

This is appreciably more helpful. First, it immediately introduces the reader to the notion of terrorism as a *political* concept. As will be seen, this key characteristic of terrorism is absolutely paramount to understanding its aims, motivations and purposes and critical in distinguishing it from other types of violence.

Terrorism, in the most widely accepted contemporary usage of the term, is fundamentally and inherently political. It is also ineluctably about power: the pursuit of power, the acquisition of power, and the use of power to achieve political change. Terrorism is thus violence—or, equally important, the threat of violence—used and directed in pursuit of, or in service of, a political aim. With this vital point clearly illuminated, one can appreciate the significance of the additional definition of 'terrorist' provided by the *OED*: 'Any one who attempts to further his views by a system of coercive intimidation'. This definition underscores clearly the other fundamental characteristic of terrorism: that it is a planned, calculated, and indeed systematic act.

Given this relatively straightforward elucidation, why, then, is terrorism so difficult to define? The most compelling reason perhaps is because the meaning of the term has changed so frequently over the past two hundred years.

THE CHANGING MEANING OF TERRORISM

The word 'terrorism' was first popularized during the French Revolution. In contrast to its contemporary usage, at that time terrorism had a decidedly *positive* connotation. The system or *régime de la terreur* of 1793–4—from which the English word came—was adopted as a means to establish order during the transient anarchical period of turmoil and upheaval that followed the uprisings of 1789, as it has followed in the wake of many other revolutions. Hence, unlike terrorism as it is commonly understood today, to mean a *revolutionary* or anti-government activity undertaken by non-state or subnational entities, the *régime de la terreur* was an instrument of governance wielded by the recently established revolutionary *state*. It was designed to consolidate the new government's power by intimidating counter-revolutionaries, subversives and all other dissidents whom the new regime regarded as 'enemies of the people'. The Committee of General Security and the Revolutionary Tribunal ('People's Court' in the modern vernacular) were thus accorded wide powers of arrest and judgement, publicly putting to death by guillotine persons convicted of treasonous (i.e. reactionary) crimes. In this manner, a powerful lesson was conveyed to any and all who might oppose the revolution or grow nostalgic for the *ancien régime*.

Ironically, perhaps, the terrorism in its original context was also closely associated with the ideals of virtue and democracy. The revolutionary leader Maximilien Robespierre firmly believed that virtue was the mainspring of a popular government at peace, but that during the time of revolution must be allied with terror in order for democracy to triumph. He appealed famously to 'virtue, without which terror is evil; terror, without which virtue is helpless', and proclaimed; 'Terror is nothing but justice, prompt, severe and inflexible; it is therefore an emanation of virtue.'

Despite this divergence from its subsequent meaning, the French Revolution's 'terrorism' still shared at least two key characteristics in common with its modern-day variant. First, the *régime de la terreur* was neither random nor indiscriminate, as terrorism is often portrayed today, but was organized, deliberate and systematic. Second, its goal and its very justification—like that of contemporary terrorism—was the creation of a 'new and better society' in place of a fundamentally corrupt and undemocratic political system. Indeed, Robespierre's vague and utopian exegeses of the revolution's central goals are remarkably similar in tone and content to the equally turgid, millenarian manifestos issued by many contemporary revolutionary—primarily left-wing, Marxist-oriented—terrorist organizations. For example, in 1794 Robespierre declared, in language eerily presaging the communiqués issued by groups such as Germany's Red Army Faction and Italy's Red Brigades nearly two centuries later:

> We want an order of things . . . in which the arts are an adornment to the liberty that ennobles them, and commerce the source of wealth for the public and not of monstrous opulence for a few families . . . In our country we desire morality instead of selfishness, honesty and not mere 'honor', principle and not mere custom, duty and not mere propriety, the sway of reason rather than the tyranny of fashion, a scorn for vice and not a contempt for the unfortunate . . .

Like many other revolutions, the French Revolution eventually began to consume itself. On 8 Thermidor, year two of the new calendar adopted by the revolutionaries (26 July 1794), Robespierre announced to the National Convention that he had in his possession a new list of traitors. Fearing that their own names might be on that list, extremists joined forces with moderates to repudiate both Robespierre and his *régime de la terreur.* Robespierre and his closest followers themselves met the same fate that had befallen some 40,000 others: execution by guillotine. The Terror was at an end; thereafter terrorism became a term associated with the abuse of office and power—with overt 'criminal' implications. Within a year of Robespierre's demise, the word had been popularized in English by Edmund Burke who, in his famous polemic against the French Revolution, described the 'Thousands of those Hell hounds called Terrorists . . . let loose on the people'.

One of the French Revolution's more enduring repercussions was the impetus it gave to anti-monarchial sentiment elsewhere in Europe. Popular subservience to rulers who derived their authority from God through 'divine right of rule', not from their subjects, was increasingly questioned by a politically awakened continent. The advent of nationalism, and with its notions of statehood and citizenship based on the common identity of a people rather than the lineage of a royal family, were resulting in the unification and creation of new nation-states such as Germany and Italy. Meanwhile, the massive socio-economic changes engendered by the industrial revolution were creating new 'universalist' ideologies (such as communism/Marxism), born of the alienation and exploitative conditions of nineteenth-century capitalism. From this milieu a new era of terrorism emerged, in which the concept had gained many of the familiar revolutionary, anti-state connotations of today. Its chief progenitor was arguably the Italian republican extremist, Carlo Pisacane, who had forsaken his birthright as duke of San Giovanni only to perish in 1857 during an ill-fated revolt against Bourbon rule. A passionate advocate of federalism and mutualism, Pisacane is remembered less on this account than for the theory of 'propaganda by deed', which he is credited with defining—an idea that has exerted a compelling influence on rebels and terrorists alike ever since. 'The propaganda of the idea is a chimera,' Pisacane wrote. 'Ideas result from deeds, not the latter from the former, and the people will not be free when they are educated, but educated when they are free.' Violence, he argued, was necessary not only to draw attention to, or generate publicity for, a cause, but to inform, educate and ultimately rally the masses behind the revolution. The didactic purpose of violence, Pisacane argued, could never be effectively replaced by pamphlets, wall posters or assemblies.

Perhaps the first organization to put into practice Pisacane's dictum was the Narodnaya Volya, or People's Will (sometimes translated as People's Freedom), a small group of

Russian constitutionalists that had been founded in 1878 to challenge tsarist rule. For the Narodnaya Volya, the apathy and alienation of the Russian masses afforded few alternatives to the resort to daring and dramatic acts of violence designed to attract attention to the group and its cause. However, unlike the many late twentieth-century terrorist organizations who have cited the principle of 'propaganda by deed' to justify the wanton targeting of civilians in order to assure them publicity through the shock and horror produced by wholesale bloodshed, the Narodnaya Volya displayed an almost quixotic attitude to the violence they wrought. To them, 'propaganda by deed' meant the selective targeting of specific individuals whom the group considered the embodiment of the autocratic, oppressive state. Hence their victims—the tsar, leading members of the royal family, senior government officials—were deliberately chosen for their 'symbolic' value as the dynastic heads and subservient agents of a corrupt and tyrannical regime. An intrinsic element in the group's collective beliefs was that 'not one drop of superfluous blood' should be shed in pursuit of aims, however noble or utilitarian they might be. Even having selected their targets with great care and the utmost deliberation, group members still harboured profound regrets about taking the life of a fellow human being. Their unswerving adherence to this principle is perhaps best illustrated by the failed attempt on the life of the Grand Duke Serge Alexandrovich made by a successor organization to the Narodnaya Volya in 1905. As the royal carriage came into view, the terrorist tasked with the assassination saw that the duke was unexpectedly accompanied by his children and therefore aborted his mission rather than risk harming the intended victim's family (the duke was killed in a subsequent attack). By comparison, the mid-air explosion caused by a terrorist bomb on Pan Am flight 103 over Lockerbie, Scotland, December 1988 indiscriminately claimed the lives of all 259 persons on board—innocent men, women and children alike—plus eleven inhabitants of the village where the plane crashed.

Ironically, the Narodnaya Volya's most dramatic accomplishment also led directly to its demise. On 1 March 1881 the group assassinated Tsar Alexander II. The failure of eight previous plots had led the conspirators to take extraordinary measures to ensure the success of this attempt. Four volunteers were given four bombs each and deployed along the alternative routes followed by the tsar's cortege. As two of the bomber-assassins stood in wait on the same street, the sleighs carrying the tsar and his Cossack escort approached the first terrorist, who hurled his bomb at the passing sleigh, missing it by inches. The whole entourage came to a halt as soldiers seized the hapless culprit and the tsar descended from his sleigh to check on a bystander wounded by the explosion. 'Thank God, I am safe,' the tsar reportedly declared—just as the second bomber emerged from the crowd and detonated his weapon, killing both himself and his target. The full weight of the tsarist state now fell on the heads of the Narodnaya Volya. Acting on information provided by the arrested member, the secret police swept down on the group's safe houses and hide-outs, rounding up most of the plotters, who were quickly tried, convicted and hanged. Further information from this group led to subsequent arrests, so that within a year of the assassination only one member of the original executive committee was still at large. She too was finally apprehended in 1883, at which point the first generation of Narodnaya Volya terrorists ceased to exist, although various successor organizations subsequently emerged to carry on the struggle.

At the time, the repercussions of the tsar's assassination could not have been known or appreciated by either the condemned or their comrades languishing in prison or exiled to Siberia. But in addition to precipitating the beginning of the end of tsarist rule, the group also deeply influenced individual revolutionaries and subversive organizations elsewhere. To the nascent anarchist movement, the 'propaganda by deed' strategy championed by the Narodnaya Volya provided a model to be emulated. Within four months of the tsar's murder, a group of radicals in London convened an 'anarchist conference' which publicly applauded the assassination and extolled tyrannicide as a means to achieve revolutionary change. In hopes of encouraging and coordinating worldwide anarchist activities, the conferees decided to establish an 'Anarchist International' (or 'Black International'). Although this idea, like most of their ambitious plans, came to nought, the publicity generated by even a putative 'Anarchist International' was sufficient to create a myth of global revolutionary pretensions and thereby stimulate fears and suspicions disproportionate to its actual impact or political achievements. Disparate and uncoordinated though the anarchists' violence was, the movement's emphasis on individual action or operations carried out by small cells of like-minded radicals made detection and prevention by the police particularly difficult, thus further heightening public fears. For example, following the assassination of US President William McKinley in 1901 (by a young Hungarian refugee, Leon Czolgocz, who, while not a regular member of any anarchist organization, was nonetheless influenced by the philosophy), Congress swiftly enacted legislation barring known anarchists or anyone 'who disbelieves in or is opposed to all organized government' from entering the United States. However, while anarchists were responsible for an impressive string of assassinations of heads of state and a number of particularly notorious bombings from about 1878 until the second decade of the twentieth century, in the final analysis, other than stimulating often exaggerated fears, anarchism made little tangible impact on either the domestic or the international politics of the countries affected. It does, however, offer an interesting historical footnote: much as the 'information revolution' of the late twentieth century is alleged to have made the means and methods of bomb-making and other types of terrorist activity more readily available via the Internet, on CD-ROM, and through ordinary libraries and bookstores, one of anarchism's flourishing 'cottage industries' more than a century earlier was the widespread distribution of similar 'how-to' or DIY-type manuals and publications of violence and mayhem.

On the eve of the First World War, terrorism still retained its revolutionary connotations. By this time, growing unrest and irredentist ferment had already welled up within the decaying Ottoman and Habsburg Empires. In the 1880s and 1890s, for example, militant Armenian nationalist movements in eastern Turkey pursued a terrorist strategy against continued Ottoman rule of a kind that would later be adopted by most of the post–Second World War ethno-nationalist/separatist movements. The Armenians' objective was simultaneously to strike a blow against the despotic 'alien' regime through repeated attacks on its colonial administration and security forces, in order to rally indigenous support, as well as to attract international attention, sympathy and support. Around the same time, the Inner Macedonian Revolutionary Organization (IMRO) was active in the region overlapping present-day Greece, Bulgaria and Serbia. Although the Macedonians did not go on to suffer the catastrophic fate that befell the Armenians during the First World War (when an estimated one million persons perished in what is considered to be the first officially implemented genocide of the twentieth century), IMRO never came close to achieving its aim of an independent Macedonia and thereafter degenerated into a mostly criminal organization of hired thugs and political assassins.

The events immediately preceding the First World War in Bosnia are of course more familiar because of their subsequent cataclysmic impact on world affairs. There, similar groups of disaffected nationalists—Bosnian Serb intellectuals, university students and even schoolchildren, collectively known as Mlada Bosnia, or Young Bosnians—arose against continued Habsburg suzerainty. While it is perhaps easy to dismiss the movement, as some historians have, as comprised of 'frustrated, poor, dreary and maladjusted' adolescents— much as many contemporary observers similarly denigrate modern-day terrorists as mindless, obsessive and maladjusted—it was a member of Young Bosnia, Gavrilo Princip, who is widely credited with having set in motion the chain of events that began on 28 June 1914, when he assassinated the Habsburg Archduke Franz Ferdinand in Sarajevo, and culminated in the First World War. Whatever its superficially juvenile characteristics, the group was nonetheless passionately dedicated to the attainment of a federal South Slav political entity—united Slovenes, Croats and Serbs—and resolutely committed to assassination as the vehicle with which to achieve that aim. In this respect, the Young Bosnians perhaps had more in common with the radical republicanism of Giuseppe Mazzini, one of the most ardent exponents of Italian unification in the nineteenth century, than with groups such as the Narodnaya Volya—despite a shared conviction in the efficacy of tyrannicide. An even more significant difference, however, was the degree of involvement in, and external support provided to, Young Bosnian activities by various shadowy Serbian nationalist groups. Principal among these was the pan-Serb secret society, the Narodna Obrana ('The People's Defence' or 'National Defence').

The Narodna Obrana had been established in 1908 originally to promote Serb cultural and national activities. It subsequently assumed a more subversive orientation as the movement became increasingly involved with anti-Austrian activities—including terrorism—mostly in neighbouring Bosnia and Hercegovina. Although the Narodna Obrana's exclusionist pan-Serbian aims clashed with the Young Bosnians' less parochial South Slav ideals, its leadership was quite happy to manipulate and exploit the Bosnians' emotive nationalism and youthful zeal for their own purposes. To this end, the Narodna Obrana actively recruited, trained and armed young Bosnians and Hercegovinians from movements such as the Young Bosnians who were then deployed in various seditious activities against the Habsburgs. As early as four years before the archduke's assassination, a Hercegovinian youth, trained by a Serb army officer with close ties to the Narodna Obrana, had attempted to kill the governor of Bosnia. But, while the Narodna Obrana included among its members senior Serbian government officials, it was not an explicitly government-controlled or directly state-supported entity. Whatever hazy government links it maintained were further and deliberately obscured when a radical faction left the Narodna Obrana in 1911 and established the Ujedinjenje ili Smrt, 'The Union of Death' or 'Death or Unification'—more popularly known as the Crna Ruka, or the 'Black Hand'. This more militant and appreciably more clandestine splinter has been described by one historian as combining

> the more unattractive features of the anarchist cells of earlier years—which had been responsible for quite a number of assassinations in Europe and whose methods had a good deal of influence via the writings of Russian anarchists upon Serbian youth—and of the [American] Ku Klux Klan. There were gory rituals and oaths of loyalty, there were murders of backsliding members, there was identification of members by number, there were distributions of guns and bombs. And there was a steady traffic between Bosnia and Serbia.

This group, which continued to maintain close links with its parent body, was largely composed of serving Serbian military officers. It was led by Lieutenant-Colonel Dragutin Dmitrievich (known by his pseudonym, Apis), himself the chief of the Intelligence

Department of the Serbian general staff. With this key additional advantage of direct access to military armaments, intelligence and training facilities, the Black Hand effectively took charge of all Serb-backed clandestine operations in Bosnia.

Although there were obviously close links between the Serbian military, the Black Hand and the Young Bosnians, it would be a mistake to regard the relationship as one of direct control, much less outright manipulation. Clearly, the Serbian government was well aware of the Black Hand's objectives and the violent means the group employed in pursuit of them; indeed, the Serbian Crown Prince Alexander was one of the group's benefactors. But this does not mean that the Serbian government was necessarily as committed to war with Austria as the Black Hand's leaders were, or that it was prepared to countenance the group's more extreme plans for fomenting cross-border, anti-Habsburg terrorism. There is some evidence to suggest that the Black Hand may have been trying to force Austria's hand against Serbia and thereby plunge both countries into war by actively abetting the Young Bosnians' plot to assassinate the archduke. Indeed, according to one revisionist account of the events leading up to the murder, even though the pistol used by Princip had been supplied by the Black Hand from a Serb military armoury in Kragujevac, and even though Princip had been trained by the Black Hand in Serbia before being smuggled back across the border for the assassination, at the eleventh hour Dmitrievich had apparently bowed to intense government pressure and tried to stop the assassination. According to this version, Princip and his fellow conspirators would hear nothing of it and stubbornly went ahead with their plans. Contrary to popular assumption, therefore, the archduke's assassination may not have been specifically ordered or even directly sanctioned by the Serbian government. However, the obscure links between high government officials and their senior military commanders and ostensibly independent, transnational terrorist movements, and the tangled web of intrigue, plots, clandestine arms provision and training, intelligence agents and cross-border sanctuary these relationships inevitably involved, provide a pertinent historical parallel to the contemporary phenomenon known as 'state-sponsored' terrorism (that is, the active and often clandestine support, encouragement and assistance provided by a foreign government to a terrorist group), which is discussed below.

By the 1930s, the meaning of 'terrorism' had changed again. It was now used less to refer to revolutionary movements and violence directed against governments and their leaders, and more to describe the practices of mass repression employed by totalitarian states and their dictatorial leaders against their own citizens. Thus the term regained its former connotations of abuse of power by governments, and was applied specifically to the authoritarian regimes that had come to power in Fascist Italy, Nazi Germany and Stalinist Russia. In Germany respectively, the accession to office of Hitler and Mussolini had depended in large measure on the 'street'—the mobilization and deployment of gangs of brown- or black-shirted thugs to harass and intimidate political opponents and root out other scapegoats for public vilification and further victimization. 'Terror? Never,' Mussolini insisted, demurely dismissing such intimidation as 'simply . . . social hygiene, taking those individuals out of circulation like a doctor would take out a bacillus'. The most sinister dimension of this form of 'terror' was that it became an intrinsic component of Fascist and Nazi governance, executed at the behest of, and in complete subservience to, the ruling political party of the land—which had arrogated to itself complete, total control of the country and its people. A system of government-sanctioned fear and coercion was thus created whereby political brawls, street fights and widespread persecution of Jews, communists and other declared 'enemies of the state' became the means through which complete and submissive compliance was ensured. The totality of party control over, and perversion of, government was perhaps most clearly evinced by a speech given by Hermann Goering, the newly appointed Prussian minister of the interior, in 1933. 'Fellow Germans,' he declared,

> My measures will not be crippled by any judicial thinking. My measures will not be crippled by any bureaucracy. Here I don't have to worry about Justice; my mission is only to destroy and exterminate, nothing more. This struggle will be a struggle against chaos, and such a struggle I shall not conduct with the power of the police. A bourgeois State might have done that. Certainly, I shall use the power of the State and the police to the utmost, my dear Communists, so don't draw any false conclusions; but the struggle to the death, in which my fist will grasp your necks, I shall lead with those there— the Brown Shirts.

The 'Great Terror' that Stalin was shortly to unleash in Russia both resembled and differed from that of the Nazis. On the one hand, drawing inspiration from Hitler's ruthless elimination of his own political opponents, the Russian dictator similarly transformed the political party he led into a servile instrument responsive directly to his personal will, and the state's police and security apparatus into slavish organs of coercion, enforcement and repression. But conditions in the Soviet Union of the 1930s bore little resemblance to the turbulent political, social and economic upheaval afflicting Germany and Italy during that decade and the previous one. On the other hand, therefore, unlike either the Nazis or the Fascists, who had emerged from the political free-for-alls in their own countries to seize power and then had to struggle to consolidate their rule and retain their unchallenged authority, the Russian Communist Party had by the mid-1930s been firmly entrenched in power for more than a decade. Stalin's purges, in contrast to those of the French Revolution, and even to Russia's own recent experience, were not 'launched in time of crisis, or revolution and war . . . [but] in the coldest of cold blood, when Russia had at last reached a comparatively calm and even moderately prosperous condition'. Thus the political purges ordered by Stalin became, in the words of one of his biographers, a 'conspiracy to seize total power by terrorist action', resulting in the death, exile, imprisonment or forcible impressment of millions.

Certainly, similar forms of state-imposed or state-directed violence and terror against a government's own citizens continue today. The use of so-called 'death squads' (often off- duty or plain-clothes security or police officers) in conjunction with blatant intimidation of political opponents, human rights and aid workers, student groups, labour organizers, journalists and others has been a prominent feature of the right-wing military dictatorships that took power in Argentina, Chile and Greece during the 1970s and even of elected governments in El Salvador, Guatemala, Colombia and Peru since the mid-1980s. But these state- sanctioned or explicitly ordered acts of *internal* political violence directed mostly against domestic populations—that is, rule by violence and intimidation by those *already* in power against their own citizenry—are generally termed 'terror' in order to distinguish that phenomenon from 'terrorism', which is understood to be violence committed by non-state entities.

Following the Second World War, in another swing of the pendulum of meaning, 'terrorism' regained the revolutionary connotations with which is it most commonly associated today. At that time, the term was used primarily in reference to the violent revolts then being prosecuted by the various indigenous nationalist/anti-colonialist groups that emerged in Asia, Africa and the Middle East during the late 1940s and 1950s to oppose continued European rule. Countries as diverse as Israel, Kenya, Cyprus and Algeria, for example, owe their independence at least in part to nationalist political movements that employed terrorism against colonial powers. It was also during this period that the 'politically correct' appellation of 'freedom fighters' came into fashion as a result of the political legitimacy that the international community (whose sympathy and support was actively courted by many of these movements) accorded to struggles for national liberation and self- determination. Many newly independent Third World countries and communist bloc states in particular adopted this vernacular, arguing that anyone or any movement that fought against 'colonial' oppression and/or Western domination should not be described as 'terrorists', but were properly deemed to be 'freedom fighters'. This position was perhaps most famously explained by the Palestine Liberation Organization (PLO) chairman Yassir Arafat, when he addressed the United Nations General Assembly in November 1974. 'The difference between the revolutionary and the terrorist,' Arafat stated, 'lies in the reason for which each fights. For whoever stands by a just cause and fights for the freedom and liberation of his land from the invaders, the settlers and the colonialists, cannot possibly be called terrorist. . . .'

During the late 1960s and 1970s, terrorism continued to be viewed within a revolutionary context. However, this usage now expanded to include nationalist and ethnic separatists groups outside a colonial or neo-colonial framework as well as radical, entirely ideologically motivated organizations. Disenfranchised or exiled nationalist minorities—such as the PLO, the Quebecois separatist group FLQ (Front de Libération du Québec), the Basque ETA (Euskadi ta Askatasuna, or Freedom for the Basque Homeland) and even a hitherto unknown South Moluccan irredentist group seeking independence from Indonesia—adopted terrorism as a means to draw attention to themselves and their respective causes, in many instances with the specific aim, like their anti-colonial predecessors, of attracting international sympathy and support. Around the same time, various left- wing political extremists—drawn mostly from the radical student organizations and Marxist/Leninist/Maoist movements in Western Europe, Latin America and the United States—began to form terrorist groups opposing American intervention in Vietnam and what they claimed were the irredeemable social and economic inequalities of the modern capitalist liberal-democratic state.

Although the revolutionary cum ethno-nationalist/separatist and ideological exemplars continue to shape our most basic understanding of the term, in recent years 'terrorism' has been used to denote broader, less distinct phenomena. In the early 1980s, for example, terrorism came to be regarded as a calculated means to destabilize the West as part of a vast global conspiracy. Books like *The Terror Network* by Claire Sterling propagated the notion to a receptive American presidential administration and similarly susceptible governments elsewhere that the seemingly isolated terrorist incidents perpetrated by disparate groups scattered across the globe were in fact linked elements of a massive clandestine plot, orchestrated by the Kremlin and implemented by its Warsaw Pact client states, to destroy the Free World. By the middle of the decade, however, a series of suicide bombings directed mostly against American diplomatic and military targets in the Middle East was focusing attention on the rising threat of state-sponsored terrorism. Consequently, this phenomenon—whereby various renegade foreign governments such as the regimes in Iran, Iraq, Libya and Syria became actively involved in sponsoring or commissioning terrorist acts— replaced communist conspiracy theories as the main context within which terrorism was viewed. Terrorism thus became associated with a type of covert or surrogate warfare whereby weaker states could confront larger, more powerful rivals without the risk of retribution.

In the early 1990s the meaning and usage of the term 'terrorism' were further blurred by the emergence of two new buzzwords: 'narco-terrorism' and the so-called 'gray area phenomenon'. The former term revived the Moscow-orchestrated terrorism conspiracy theories of previous years while introducing the critical new dimension of narcotics trafficking. Thus 'narco-terrorism' was defined by one of the concept's foremost propagators as the 'use of drug trafficking to advance the objectives of certain governments and terrorist organizations'—identified as the 'Marxist-Leninst regimes' of the Soviet Union, Cuba, Bulgaria and Nicaragua, among others. The emphasis of 'narco-terrorism' as the latest manifestation of the communist plot to undermine Western society, however, had the unfortunate effect of diverting official attention away from a bona fide emerging trend. To a greater extent than ever in the past, entirely criminal (that is, violent, *economically* motivated) organizations were now forging strategic alliances with terrorist and guerrilla organizations or themselves employing violence for specifically political ends. The growing power of the Colombian cocaine cartels, their close ties with left-wing terrorist groups in Colombia and Peru, and their repeated attempts to subvert Colombia's electoral process and undermine successive governments constitute perhaps the best-known example of this continuing trend.

Those who drew attention to this 'gray area phenomenon' were concerned less with grand conspiracies than with highlighting the increasingly fluid and variable nature of subnational conflict in the post–Cold War era. Accordingly, in the 1990s terrorism began to be subsumed by some analysts within the 'gray area phenomenon'. Thus the latter term came to be used to denote 'threats to the stability of nation states by non-state actors and non-governmental processes and organizations'; to describe violence affecting 'immense regions or urban areas where control has shifted from legitimate governments to new half-political, half-criminal powers'; or simply to group together in one category the range of conflicts across the world that no longer conformed to traditionally accepted notions of war as fighting between the armed forces of two or more established states, but instead involved irregular forces as one or more of the combatants. Terrorism had shifted its meaning again from an individual phenomenon of subnational violence to one of several elements, or part of a wider pattern, of non-state conflict.

WHY IS TERRORISM SO DIFFICULT TO DEFINE?

Not surprisingly, as the meaning and usage of the word have changed over time to accommodate the political vernacular and discourse of each successive era, terrorism has proved increasingly elusive in the face of attempts to construct one consistent definition. At one time, the terrorists themselves were far more cooperative in this endeavour than they are today. The early practitioners didn't mince their words or hide behind the semantic camouflage of more anodyne labels such as 'freedom fighter' or 'urban guerrilla'. The nineteenth- century anarchists, for example, unabashedly proclaimed themselves to be terrorists and frankly proclaimed their tactics to be terrorism. The members of Narodnaya Volya similarly displayed no qualms in using these same words to describe themselves and their deeds. However, such frankness did not last. The Jewish terrorist group of the 1940s known as Lehi (the Hebrew acronym for Lohamei Herut Yisrael, the Freedom Fighters for Israel, more popularly known simply as the Stern Gang after their founder and first leader, Abraham Stern) is thought to be one of the last terrorist groups actually to describe itself publicly as such. It is significant, however, that even Lehi, while it may have been far more candid than its latter-day counterparts, chose as the name of the organization not 'Terrorist Fighters for Israel', but the far less pejorative 'Freedom Fighters for Israel'. Similarly, although more than twenty years later the Brazilian revolutionary Carlos Marighela displayed few compunctions about openly advocating the use of 'terrorist' tactics, he still insisted on depicting himself and his disciples as 'urban guerrillas' rather than 'urban terrorists'. Indeed, it is clear from Marighela's writings that he was well aware of the word's undesirable connotations, and strove to displace them with positive resonances. 'The words "aggressor" and "terrorist"', Marighela wrote in his famous *Handbook of Urban Guerrilla War* (also known as the 'Mini-Manual'), 'no longer mean what they did. Instead of arousing fear or censure, they are a call to action. To be called an aggressor or a terrorist in Brazil is now an honour to any citizen, for it means that he is fighting, with a gun in his hand, against the monstrosity of the present dictatorship and the suffering it causes.'

This trend towards ever more convoluted semantic obfuscations to side-step terrorism's pejorative overtones, has, if anything, become more entrenched in recent decades. Terrorist organizations almost without exception now regularly select names for themselves that consciously eschew the word 'terrorism' in any of its forms. Instead these groups actively seek to evoke images of:

- freedom and liberation (e.g. the National Liberation Front, the Popular Front for the Liberation of Palestine, Freedom for the Basque Homeland, etc.);
- armies or other military organizational structures (e.g. the National Military Organization, the Popular Liberation Army, the Fifth Battalion of the Liberation Army, etc.);
- actual self-defence movements (e.g. the Afrikaner Resistance Movement, the Shankhill Defence Association, the Organization for the Defence of the Free People, the Jewish Defense Organization, etc.);
- righteous vengeance (the Organization for the Oppressed on Earth, the Justice Commandos of the Armenian Genocide, the Palestinian Revenge Organization, etc.);

—or else deliberately choose names that are decidedly neutral and therefore bereft of all but the most innocuous suggestions or associations (e.g. the Shining Path, Front Line, al- Dawa ('The Call'), Alfaro Lives—Damn It!, Kach ('Thus'), al-Gamat al-Islamiya ('The Islamic Organization'), the Lantero Youth Movement, etc.).

What all these examples suggest is that terrorists clearly do not see or regard themselves as others do. 'Above all I am a family man,' the arch-terrorist Carlos, 'The Jackal', described himself to a French newspaper following his capture in 1994. Cast perpetually on the defensive and forced to take up arms to protect themselves and their real or imagined constituents only, terrorists perceive themselves as reluctant warriors, driven by desperation—and lacking any viable alternative—to violence against a repressive state, a predatory rival ethnic or nationalist group, or an unresponsive international order. This perceived characteristic of self-denial also distinguishes the terrorist from other types of political extremists as well as from persons similarly involved in illegal, violent avocations. A communist or a revolutionary, for example, would likely readily accept and admit that he is in fact a communist or a revolutionary. Indeed, many would doubtless take particular pride in claiming either of those appellations for themselves. Similarly, even a person engaged in illegal, wholly disreputable or entirely selfish violence activities, such as robbing banks or carrying out contract killings, would probably admit to being a bank robber or a murderer for hire. The terrorist, by contrast, will *never* acknowledge that he is a terrorist and moreover will go to great lengths to evade and obscure any such inference or connection. Terry Anderson, the American journalist who was held hostage for almost seven years by the Lebanese terrorist organization Hezbollah, relates a telling conversation he had with one of his guards. The guard had objected to a newspaper article that referred to Hezbollah as terrorists. 'We are not terrorists,' he indignantly stated, 'we are fighters.' Anderson replied, 'Hajj, you are a terrorist, look it up in the dictionary. You are a terrorist, you may not like the word and if you do not like the word, do not do it.' The terrorist will always argue that it is society or the government or the socio-economic 'system' and its laws that are the *real* 'terrorists', and moreover that if it were not for this oppression, he would not have felt the need to defend either himself or the population he claims to represent. Another revealing example of this process of obfuscation-projection may be found in the book *Invisible Armies*, written by Sheikh Muhammad Hussein Fadlallah, the spiritual leader of the Lebanese terrorist group responsible for Anderson's kidnapping. 'We don't see ourselves as terrorists,' Fadlallah explains, 'because we don't believe in terrorism. We don't see resisting the occupier as a terrorist action. We see ourselves as *mujihadeen* [holy warriors] who fight a Holy War for the people.'

On one point, at least, everyone agrees: terrorism is a pejorative term. It is a word with intrinsically negative connotations that is generally applied to one's enemies and opponents, or to those with whom one disagrees and would otherwise prefer to ignore. 'What is called terrorism', Brian Jenkins has written, 'thus seems to depend on one's point of view. Use of the term implies a moral judgement; and if one party can successfully attach the label *terrorist* to its opponent, then it has indirectly persuaded others to adopt its moral viewpoint.' Hence the decision to call someone or label some organization 'terrorist' becomes almost unavoidably subjective, depending largely on whether one sympathizes with or opposes the person/group/cause concerned. If one identifies with the victim of the violence, for example, then the act is terrorism. If, however, one identifies with the perpetrator, the violent act is regarded in a more sympathetic, if not positive (or, at the worst, an ambivalent) light; and it is not terrorism.

The implications of this associational logic were perhaps most clearly demonstrated in the exchanges between Western and non-Western member states of the United Nations following the 1972 Munich Olympics massacre, in which eleven Israeli athletes were killed. The debate began with the proposal by the then UN Secretary-General, Kurt Waldheim, that the UN should not remain a 'mute spectator' to the acts of terrorist violence then occurring throughout the world but should take practical steps that might prevent further bloodshed. While a majority of the UN member states supported the Secretary-General, a disputatious minority—including many Arab states and various African and Asian countries—derailed the discussion, arguing (much as Arafat would do two years later in his own address to the General Assembly) that 'people who struggle to liberate themselves from foreign oppression and exploitation have the right to use all methods at their disposal, including force'.

The Third World delegates justified their position with two arguments. First, they claimed that all bona fide liberation movements are invariably decried as 'terrorists' by the regimes against which their struggles for freedom are directed. The Nazis, for example, labelled as terrorists the resistance groups opposing Germany's occupation of their lands, Moulaye el-Hassen, the Mauritanian ambassador, pointed out, just as 'all liberation movements are described as terrorists by those who have reduced them to slavery'. Therefore, by condemning 'terrorism' the UN was endorsing the power of the strong over the weak and of the established entity over its non-established challenger—in effect, acting as the defender of the status quo. According to Chen Chu, the deputy representative of the People's Republic of China, the UN thus was proposing to deprive 'opposed nations and peoples' of the only effective weapon they had with which to oppose 'imperialism, colonialism, neo- colonialism, racism and Israeli Zionism'. Second, the Third World delegates argued forcefully that it is not the violence itself that is germane, but its 'underlying causes': that is, the 'misery, frustration, grievance and despair' that produce the violent acts. As the Mauritanian representative again explained, the term 'terrorist' could 'hardly be held to apply to persons who were denied the most elementary human rights, dignity, freedom and independence, and whose countries objected to foreign occupation'. When the issue was again raised the following year, Syria objected on the grounds that 'the international community is under legal and moral obligation to promote the struggle for liberation and to resist any attempt to depict this struggle as synonymous with terrorism and illegitimate violence'. The resultant definitional paralysis subsequently throttled UN efforts to make any substantive progress on international cooperation against terrorism beyond very specific agreements on individual aspects of the problem (concerning, for example, diplomats and civil aviation).

The opposite approach, where identification with the victim determines the classification of a violent act as terrorism, is evident in the conclusions of a parliamentary working group of NATO (an organization comprised of long-established, status quo Western states). The final report of the 1989 North Atlantic Assembly's Subcommittee on Terrorism states: 'Murder, kidnapping, arson and other felonious acts constitute criminal behavior, but many non-Western nations have proved reluctant to condemn as terrorist acts what they consider to be struggles of natural liberation.' In this reasoning, the defining characteristic of terrorism is the act of violence itself, not the motivations or justification for or reasons behind it. This approach has long been espoused by analysts such as Jenkins who argue that terrorism should be defined 'by the nature of the act, not by the identity of the perpetrators or the nature of their cause'. But this is not an entirely satisfactory solution either, since it fails to differentiate clearly between violence perpetrated by states and by non-state entities, such as terrorists. Accordingly, it plays into the hands of terrorists and their apologists who would argue that there is no difference between the 'low-tech' terrorist pipe-bomb placed in the rubbish bin at a crowded market that wantonly and indiscriminately kills or maims everyone within a radius measured in tens of feet and the 'high-tech' precision-guided ordnance dropped by air force fighter-bombers from a height of 20,000 feet or more that achieves the same wanton and indiscriminate effects on the crowded marketplace far below. This rationale thus equates the random violence inflicted on enemy population centres by military forces—such as the Luftwaffe's raids on Warsaw and Coventry, the Allied firebombings of Dresden and Tokyo, and the atomic bombs dropped by the United States on Hiroshima and Nagasaki during the Second World War, and indeed the countervalue strategy of the post-war superpowers' strategic nuclear policy, which deliberately targeted the enemy's civilian population—with the violence committed by substate entities labelled 'terrorists', since both involve the infliction of death and injury on noncombatants. Indeed, this was precisely the point made during the above-mentioned UN debates by the Cuban representative, who argued that 'the methods of combat used by national liberation movements could not be declared illegal while the policy of terrorism unleashed against certain peoples [by the armed forces of established states] was declared legitimate'.

It is a familiar argument. Terrorists, as we have seen, deliberately cloak themselves in the terminology of military jargon. They consciously portray themselves as bona fide (freedom) fighters, if not soldiers, who—though they wear no identifying uniform or insignia—are entitled to treatment as prisoners of war (POWs) if captured and therefore should not be prosecuted as common criminals in ordinary courts of law. Terrorists further argue that, because of their numerical inferiority, far more limited firepower and paucity of resources compared with an established nation-state's massive defence and national security apparatus, they have no choice but to operate clandestinely, emerging from the shadows to carry out dramatic (in other words, bloody and destructive) acts of hit-and-run violence in order to attract attention to, and ensure publicity for, themselves and their cause. The bomb-in-the-rubbish-bin, in their view, is merely a circumstantially imposed 'poor man's air force': the only means with which the terrorist can challenge—and get the attention of—the more powerful state. 'How else can we bring pressure to bear on the world?' one of Arafat's political aides once enquired. 'The deaths are regrettable, but they are a fact of war in which innocents have become involved. They are no more innocent than the Palestinian women and children killed by the Israelis and we are ready to carry the war all over the world.'

But rationalizations such as these ignore the fact that, even while national armed forces have been responsible for far more death and destruction than terrorists might ever aspire to bring about, there nonetheless is a fundamental qualitative difference between the two types of violence. Even in war there are rules and accepted norms of behaviour that prohibit the use of certain types of weapons (for example, hollow-point or 'dum-dum' bullets, CS 'tear' gas, chemical and biological warfare agents), proscribe various tactics and outlaw attacks on specific categories of targets. Accordingly, in theory, if not always in practice, the rules of war—as observed from the early seventeenth century when they were first proposed by the Dutch jurist Hugo Grotius and subsequently codified in the famous Geneva and Hague Conventions on Warfare of the 1860s, 1899, 1907 and 1949—not only grant civilian non-combatants immunity from attack, but also

- prohibit taking civilians as hostages;
- impose regulations governing the treatment of captured or surrendered soldiers (POWs);
- outlaw reprisals against either civilians or POWs;
- recognize neutral territory and the rights of citizens of neutral states; and
- uphold the inviolability of diplomats and other accredited representatives.

Even the most cursory review of terrorist tactics and targets over the past quarter-century reveals that terrorists have violated all these rules. They not infrequently have

- taken hostage civilians, whom in some instances they have then brutally executed (e.g. the former Italian prime minister Aldo Moro and the German industrialist Hans Martin Schleyer, who were respectively taken captive and later murdered by the Red Brigades and the Red Army Faction);
- similarly abused and murdered kidnapped military officers—even when they were serving on UN-sponsored peacekeeping or truce supervisory missions (e.g. the American Marine Lieutenant-Colonel William Higgins, the commander of a UN truce monitoring detachment, who was abducted by Lebanese Shi'a terrorists in 1989 and subsequently hanged);
- undertaken reprisals against wholly innocent civilians, often in countries far removed from the terrorists' ostensible 'theatre of operation', thus disdaining any concept of neutral states or the rights of citizens of neutral countries (e.g. the brutal

1986 machine-gun and hand-grenade attack on Turkish Jewish worshippers at an Istanbul synagogue carried out by the Palestinian Abu Nidal Organization in retaliation for a recent Israeli raid on a guerrilla base in southern Lebanon); and

- repeatedly attacked embassies and other diplomatic installations (e.g. the bombings of the US embassies in Beirut and Kuwait City in 1983 and 1984, and the mass hostage-taking at the Japanese ambassador's residence in Lima, Peru, in 1996–7), as well as deliberately targeting diplomats and other accredited representatives (e.g. the British ambassador to Uruguay, Sir Geoffrey Jackson, who was kidnapped by leftist terrorists in that country in 1971, and the fifty-two American diplomats taken hostage at the Tehran legation in 1979).

Admittedly, the armed forces of established states have also been guilty of violating some of the same rules of war. However, when these transgressions do occur—when civilians are deliberately and wantonly attacked on war or taken hostage and killed by military forces—the term 'war crime' is used to describe such acts and, imperfect and flawed as both international and national judicial remedies may be, steps nonetheless are often taken to hold the perpetrators accountable for these crimes. By comparison, one of the fundamental *raisons d'être* of international terrorism is a refusal to be bound by such rules of warfare and codes of conduct. International terrorism disdains any concept of delimited areas of combat or demarcated battlefields, much less respect of neutral territory. Accordingly, terrorists have repeatedly taken their often parochial struggles to other, sometimes geographically distant, third party countries and there deliberately enmeshed persons completely unconnected with the terrorists' cause or grievances in violent incidents designed to generate attention and publicity.

The reporting of terrorism by the news media, which have been drawn into the semantic debates that divided the UN in the 1970s and continue to influence all discourse on terrorism, has further contributed to the obfuscation of the terrorist/'freedom fighter' debate, enshrining imprecision and implication as the lingua franca of political violence in the name of objectivity and neutrality. In striving to avoid appearing either partisan or judgemental, the American media, for example, resorted to describing terrorists—often in the same report—as variously guerrillas, gunmen, raiders, commandos and even soldiers. A random sample of American newspaper reports of Palestinian terrorist activities between June and December 1973, found in the terrorism archives and database maintained at the University of St. Andrews in Scotland, provided striking illustrations of this practice. Out of eight headlines of articles describing the same incident, six used the word 'guerrillas' and only two 'terrorists' to describe the perpetrators. An interesting pattern was also observed whereby those accounts that immediately followed a particularly horrific or tragic incident—that is, involving the death and injury of innocent persons (in this instance, the attack on a Pan Am airliner at Rome airport, in which thirty-two passengers were killed)— tended to describe the perpetrators as 'terrorists' and their act as 'terrorism' (albeit in one case only in the headline, before reverting to the more neutral terminology of 'commando', 'militants', and 'guerrilla attack' in the text) more frequently than did reports of less serious or non-lethal incidents. One *New York Times* leading article, however, was far less restrained than the stories describing the actual incident, describing it as 'bloody' and 'mindless' and using the words 'terrorists' and 'terrorism' interchangeably with 'guerrillas' and 'extremists'. Only six months previously, however, the same newspaper had run a story about another terrorist attack that completely eschewed the terms 'terrorism' and 'terrorist', preferring 'guerrillas' and 'resistance' (as in 'resistance movement') instead. The *Christian Science Monitor*'s reports of the Rome Pan Am attack similarly avoided 'terrorist' and 'terrorism' in favour of 'guerrillas' and 'extremists'; an Associated Press story in the next day's *Los Angeles Times* also stuck with 'guerrillas', while the two *Washington Post* articles on the same incident opted for the terms 'commandos' and 'guerrillas'.

This slavish devotion in terminological neutrality, which David Rapoport first observed over twenty years ago, is still in evidence today. A recent article appearing in the *International Herald Tribune* (a Paris-based newspaper published in conjunction with the *New York Times* and *Washington Post*) reported an incident in Algeria where thirty persons had been killed by perpetrators who were variously described as 'terrorists' in the article's headline, less judgementally as 'extremists' in the lead paragraph and as the still more ambiguous 'Islamic fundamentalists' in the article's third paragraph. In a country that since 1992 has been afflicted with an unrelenting wave of terrorist violence and bloodshed that has claimed the lives of an estimated 75,000 persons, one might think that the distinctions between 'terrorists', mere 'extremists' and ordinary 'fundamentalists' would be clearer. Equally interesting was the article that appeared on the opposite side of the same page of the newspaper that described the 'decades of sporadic *guerrilla* [my emphasis] warfare by the IRA' in Northern Ireland. Yet fifty years ago the same newspaper apparently had fewer qualms about using the word 'terrorists' to describe the two young Jewish men in pre- independence Israel who, while awaiting execution after having been convicted of attacking British military targets, committed suicide. Other press accounts of the same period in *The Times* of London and the *Palestine Post* similarly had no difficulties, for example, in describing the 1946 bombing by Jewish terrorists of the British military headquarters and government secretariat located in Jerusalem's King David Hotel as a 'terrorist' act perpetrated by 'terrorists'. Similarly, in perhaps the most specific application of the term, the communist terrorists against whom the British fought in Malaya throughout the late 1940s and 1950s were routinely referred to as 'CTs'—for 'Communist terrorists'. As Rapoport warned in the 1970s, 'In attempting to correct the abuse of language for political purposes our journalists may succeed in making language altogether worthless.'

The cumulative effect of this proclivity towards equivocation is that today there is no one widely accepted or agreed definition for terrorism. Different departments or agencies of even the same government will themselves often have very different definitions for terrorism. The US State Department, for example, uses the definition of terrorism contained in Title 22 of the United States Code, Section 2656f(d):

> premeditated, politically motivated violence perpetrated against noncombatant targets by subnational groups or clandestine agents, usually intended to influence an audience,

while the US Federal Bureau of Investigation (FBI) defines terrorism as

> the unlawful use of force or violence against persons or property to intimidate or coerce a Government, the civilian population, or any segment thereof, in furtherance of political or social objectives,

and the US Department of Defense defines it as

> the unlawful use of—or threatened use of—force or violence against individuals or property to coerce or intimidate governments or societies, often to achieve political, religious, or ideological objectives.

Not surprisingly, each of the above definitions reflects the priorities and particular interests of the specific agency involved. The State Department's emphasis is on the premeditated and planned or calculated nature of terrorism in contrast to more spontaneous acts of political violence. Its definition is also the only one of the three to emphasize both the ineluctably political nature of terrorism and the perpetrators' fundamental 'subnational' characteristic. The State Department definition, however, is conspicuously deficient in failing to consider the psychological dimension of terrorism. Terrorism is as much about the threat of violence as the violent act itself and, accordingly, is deliberately conceived to have far- reaching psychological repercussions beyond the actual target of the act among a wider, watching, 'target' audience. As Jenkins succinctly observed two decades ago, 'Terrorism is theatre.'

Given the FBI's mission of investigating and solving crimes—both political (e.g. terrorism) and other—it is not surprising that its definition focuses on different elements. Unlike the State Department, this definition does address the psychological dimensions of the terrorist act described above, laying stress on terrorism's intimidatory and coercive aspects. The FBI definition also identifies a much broader category of terrorist targets than only 'noncombatants', specifying not only governments and their citizens, but also inanimate objects, such as private and public property. The FBI definition further recognizes social alongside political objectives as fundamental terrorist aims—though it offers no clearer elucidation of either.

The Department of Defense definition of terrorism is arguably the most complete of the three. It highlights the terrorist threat as much as the actual act of violence and focuses on terrorism's targeting of whole societies as well as governments. The Defense Department definition further cites the religious and ideological aims of terrorism alongside its fundamental political objectives—but curiously omits the social dimension found in the FBI's definition.

It is not only individual agencies within the same governmental apparatus that cannot agree on a single definition of terrorism. Experts and other long-established scholars in the field are equally incapable of reaching a consensus. In the first edition of his magisterial survey, *Political Terrorism: A Research Guide*, Alex Schmid devoted more than a hundred pages to examining more than a hundred different definitions of terrorism in an effort to discover a broadly acceptable, reasonably comprehensive explication of the word. Four years and a second edition later, Schmid was no closer to the goal of his quest, conceding in the first sentence of the revised volume that the 'search for an adequate definition is still on'. Walter Laqueur despaired of defining terrorism in both editions of his monumental work on the subject, maintaining that it is neither possible to do so nor worthwhile to make the attempt. 'Ten years of debates on typologies and definitions', he responded to a survey of definitions conducted by Schmid, 'have not enhanced our knowledge of the subject to a significant degree.' Laqueur's contention is supported by the twenty-two different word categories occurring in the 109 different definitions that Schmid identified in his survey (see Table 1).

At the end of this exhaustive exercise, Schmid asks 'whether the above list contains all the elements necessary for a good definition. The answer', he suggests, 'is probably "no".' If it is impossible to define terrorism, as Laqueur argues, and fruitless to attempt to cobble together a truly comprehensive definition, as Schmid admits, are we to conclude that terrorism is impervious to precise, much less accurate definition? Not entirely. If we cannot define terrorism, then we can at least usefully distinguish it from other types of violence and identify the characteristics that make terrorism the distinct phenomenon of political violence that it is.

Table 1.1 *Frequencies of Definitional Elements in 109 Definitions of 'Terrorism'*

	Element	Frequency (%)
1	Violence, force	83.5
2	Political	65
3	Fear, terror emphasized	51
4	Threat	47
5	(Psychological) effects and (anticipated) reactions	41.5
6	Victimtarget differentiation	37.5
7	Purposive, planned, systematic, organized action	32
8	Method of combat, strategy, tactic	30.5
9	Extranormality, in breach of accepted rules, without humanitarian constraints	30
10	Coercion, extortion, induction of compliance	28
11	Publicity aspect	21.5
12	Arbitrariness; impersonal, random character; indiscrimination	21
13	Civilians, noncombatants, neutrals, outsiders as victims	17.5
14	Intimidation	17
15	Innocence of victims emphasized	15.5
16	Group, movement, organization as perpetrator	14
17	Symbolic aspect, demonstration to others	13.5
18	Incalculability, unpredictability, unexpectedness of occurrence of violence	9
19	Clandestine, covert nature	9
20	Repetitiveness; serial or campaign character of violence	7
21	Criminal	6
22	Demands made on third parties	4

Source: Alex P. Schmid, Albert J. Jongman et al., *Political Terrorism: A New Guide to Actors, Authors, Con cepts, Data Bases, Theories, and Literature*. New Brunswick, Transaction Books, 1988, pp. 5-6.

DISTINCTIONS AS A PATH TO DEFINITION

Guerrilla warfare is a good place to start. Terrorism is often confused or equated with, or treated as synonymous with, guerrilla warfare. This is not entirely surprising, since guerrillas often employ the same tactics (assassination, kidnapping, bombings of public gathering-places, hostage-taking, etc.) for the same purposes (to intimidate or coerce, thereby affecting behaviour through the arousal of fear) as terrorists. In addition, both terrorists and guerrillas wear neither uniform nor identifying insignia and thus are often indistinguishable from noncombatants. However, despite the inclination to lump both terrorists and guerrillas into the same catch-all category of 'irregulars', there are nonetheless fundamental differences between the two. 'Guerrilla', for example, in its most widely accepted usage, is taken to refer to a numerically larger group of armed individuals, who operate as a military unit, attack enemy military forces, and seize and hold territory (even if only ephemerally during daylight hours), while also exercising some form of sovereignty or control over a defined geographical area and its population. Terrorists, however, do not function in the open as armed units, generally do not attempt to seize or hold territory, deliberately avoid engaging enemy military forces in combat and rarely exercise any direct control or sovereignty either over territory or population.

It is also useful to distinguish terrorists from ordinary criminals. Like terrorists, criminals use violence as a means to attaining a specific end. However, while the violent act itself may be similar—kidnapping, shooting, arson, for example—the purpose or motivation clearly is not. Whether the criminal employs violence as a means to obtain money, to acquire material goods, or to kill or injure a specific victim for pay, he is acting primarily for selfish, personal motivations (usually material gain). Moreover, unlike terrorism, the ordinary criminals' violent act is not designed or intended to have consequences or create psychological repercussions beyond the act itself. The criminal may of course use some short-term act of violence to 'terrorize' his victim, such as waving a gun in the face of a bank clerk during a robbery in order to ensure the clerk's expeditious compliance. In these instances, however, the bank robber is conveying no 'message' (political or otherwise) through his act of violence beyond facilitating the rapid handing over of his 'loot'. The criminal's act therefore is not meant to have any effect reaching beyond either the incident itself or the immediate victim. Further, the violence is neither conceived nor intended to convey any message to anyone other than the bank clerk himself, whose rapid cooperation is the robber's only objective. Perhaps most fundamentally, the criminal is not concerned with influencing or affecting public opinion: he simply wants to abscond with his money or accomplish his mercenary task in the quickest and easiest way possible so that he may reap his reward and enjoy the fruits of his labours. By contrast, the fundamental aim of the terrorist's violence is ultimately to change 'the system'—about which the ordinary criminal, of course, couldn't care less.

The terrorist is also very different from the lunatic assassin, who may use identical tactics (e.g. shooting, bombing) and perhaps even seeks the same objective (e.g. the death of a political figure). However, while the tactics and targets of terrorists and lone assassins are often identical, their purpose is not. Whereas the terrorist's goal is again ineluctably *political* (to change or fundamentally alter a political system through his violent act), the lunatic assassin's goal is more often intrinsically idiosyncratic, completely egocentric and deeply personal. John Hinckley, who tried to kill President Reagan in 1981 to impress the actress Jodie Foster, is a case in point. He acted not from political motivation or ideological conviction but to fulfil some profound personal quest (killing the president to impress his screen idol). Such entirely *apolitical* motivations can in no way be compared to the rationalizations used by the Narodnaya Volya to justify its campaign of tyrannicide against the tsar and his minions, nor even to the Irish Republican Army's efforts to assassinate Prime Minister Margaret Thatcher or her successor, John Major, in hopes of dramatically changing British policy towards Northern Ireland. Further, just as one person cannot credibly claim to be a political party, so a lone individual cannot be considered to constitute a terrorist group. In this respect, even though Sirhan Sirhan's assassination of presidential candidate and US Senator Robert Kennedy in 1968 had a political motive (to protest against US support for Israel), it is debatable whether the murder should be defined as a terrorist act since Sirhan belongs to no organized political group and acted entirely on his own, out of deep personal frustration and a profound animus that few others shared. To qualify as terrorism, violence must be perpetrated by some organizational entity with at least some conspiratorial structure and identifiable chain of command beyond a single individual acting on his or her own.

Finally, the point should be emphasized that, unlike the ordinary criminal or the lunatic assassin, the terrorist is not pursuing purely egocentric goals—he is not driven by the wish to line his own pocket or satisfy some personal need or grievance. The terrorist is fundamentally an *altruist*: he believes that he is serving a 'good' cause designed to achieve a greater good for a wider constituency—whether real or imagined—which the terrorist and his organization purport to represent. The criminal, by comparison, serves no cause at all, just his own personal aggrandizement and material satiation. Indeed, a 'terrorist without a cause (at least in his own mind)', Konrad Kellen has argued, 'is not a terrorist'. Yet the possession or identification of a cause is not a sufficient criterion for labelling someone a terrorist. In this key respect, the difference between terrorists and political extremists is clear. Many persons, of course, harbour all sorts of radical and extreme beliefs and opinions, and many of them belong to radical or even illegal or proscribed political organizations. However, if they do not use violence in the pursuance of their beliefs, they cannot be considered terrorists. The terrorist is fundamentally a *violent intellectual*, prepared to use and indeed committed to using force in the attainment of his goals.

By distinguishing terrorists from other types of criminals and terrorism from other forms of crime, we come to appreciate that terrorism is

- ineluctably political in aims and motives;
- violent—or, equally important, threatens violence;
- designed to have far-reaching psychological repercussions beyond the immediate victim or target;
- conducted by an organization with an identifiable chain of command or conspiratorial cell structure (whose members wear no uniform or identifying insignia); and
- perpetrated by a subnational group or non-state entity.

We may therefore now attempt to define terrorism as the deliberate creation and exploitation of fear through violence or the threat of violence in the pursuit of political change. All terrorist acts involve violence or the threat of violence. Terrorism is specifically designed to have far-reaching psychological effects beyond the immediate victim(s) or object of the terrorist attack. It is meant to instil fear within, and thereby intimidate, a wider 'target audience' that might include a rival ethnic or religious group, an entire country, a national government or political party, or public opinion in general. Terrorism is designed to create power where there is none or to consolidate power where there is very little. Through the publicity generated by their violence, terrorists seek to obtain the leverage, influence and power they otherwise lack to effect political change on either a local or an international scale.

> ***Bruce Hoffman*** *is an authoritative analyst of terrorism and a recipient of the U.S. Intelligence Community Seal Medallion, the highest level of commendation given to a non-government employee. He is currently the director of the Washington, D.C., office of the RAND Corporation, where he heads the terrorism research unit, and he regularly advises both governments and businesses throughout the world. This reading is a chapter from his book Inside Terrorism.*

Glossary[1]

Absolute Gains Acquisition that is independent of any standard; not relative or comparative; in examining inter-state relationships, idealists think in absolute gains terms

Affective Supports The diffuse or generalized attachments the population has for the political community; usually the result of socialization and are therefore lasting

Alliance (DOD) An alliance is the result of formal agreements (i.e., treaties) between two or more nations for broad, long-term objectives which further the common interests of the members.

Anarchy A system without a government or ruling authority to be the arbiter of disputes. Therefore, states struggle for *power* with one another, must look out for their own interests, and cannot appeal to some higher authority.

Arms Control (DOD) A concept that connotes: (a) any plan, arrangement, or process, resting upon explicit or implicit international agreement, governing any aspect of the following: the numbers, types, and performance characteristics of weapon systems (including the command and control, logistics support arrangements, and any related intelligence-gathering mechanism); and the numerical strength, organization, equipment, deployment, or employment of the Armed Forces retained by the parties (it encompasses disarmament); and (b) on some occasions, those measures taken for the purpose of reducing instability in the military environment.

Arms Races An image of two states competing against the other by increasing military capabilities.

Autarky Political self-rule; complete independence, particularly economic self-sufficiency, in which through government controls a nation's economy (or a group of nations) is isolated from the rest of the world. During the Cold War the Soviet bloc practiced economic autarchy, trading only within itself.

Authoritarianism A governmental or political system in which individual freedom is completely subordinate to the power and authority of the state, centered either in one person or a small group that is not constitutionally accountable to the people.

Balance of Power A concept describing an equilibrium among states and, according to *realists*, a self-regulatory mechanism maintaining *stability* in the international system. Disagreement exists about whether this equilibrating or balancing phenomena occurs (1) as the result of explicit state policy or (2) as an inherent characteristic of international politics.

Balancing A normal pattern of state behavior where, if several major powers are competing with one another, they will group together in order to prevent any one power or group from becoming dominant. According to the DOD, a "balance" is a "concept as applied to an arms control measure that connotes: (a) adjustments of armed forces and armaments in such a manner that one state does not obtain military advantage over other states agreeing to the measure; and (b) internal adjustments by one state of its forces in such manner as to enable it to cope with all aspects of remaining threats to its security in a post arms control agreement era."

Bandwagoning The action states take when confronted by a significant external threat in which they align with the state that is the source of danger. *Bandwagoning* is opposite of *Balancing*.

Basic Needs Strategy This long-term development strategy for developing nations focuses on investments in a country's population - education, shelter, health care, and nutrition—in order to raise the standard of living of the poorest parts of the population.

Beliefs *Beliefs* act as prisms—distorting reality, restricting options, differentiating distinctiveness, and often legitimizing specific policies. *Beliefs* often frame *choice*.

---

[1] All definitions identified as from the Department of Defense (DOD) are drawn from Joint Publication 1-02, "DOD Dictionary of Military and Associated Terms." This is available on the WWW at http://www.dtic.mil/doctrine/jel/doddict/.

Bipolarity The condition of having two major powers (or poles) in the international system. This condition was most recently reflected in the *structure* of the international system during the height of the *Cold War.*

Bourgeoisie Another term for "capitalists," referring to the ruling class in a capitalist society.

Bretton Woods Named for the Bretton Woods, New Hampshire location where the post-World War II economic talks were first convened in 1944. The term refers to the post-WWII monetary and finance system used by the Western states. It featured the re-establishment of an international fixed exchange rate monetary regime and the establishment of an International Bank for Reconstruction and Development (IBRD) and an *International Monetary Fund (IMF).*

Capitalism An economic theory featuring the principles of *laissez-faire* (or free) enterprise. Capitalist economic theory espouses the distribution of scarce economic resources across a society by a market (or profit-incentive) system where prices for resources are set by supply-and-demand and private owners seek to maximize profits. Domestically, *Capitalism* calls for individual ownership and an absence of government restraints on economic activity. Internationally, *Capitalism* espouses the free movement of labor and goods across state borders and an international division of labor with national production specialization.

Causality A condition where the variation in one aspect of international politics directly produces the change in another aspect of international relations. *Causality* is more difficult to prove than statements claiming that two events are merely associated.

Civil Society Refers to a society in which associations in movements, political parties, and other groups allow people peacefully to transcend their traditional kinship and blood ties. *Civil society* has three components: *membership* in associations and movements; *civility* or the willingness to tolerate the disparate political views and memberships of fellow citizens; and *citizenship*, or a sense of responsibility to the society. In most stable democratic countries *civil society* is the crucial buffer between the raw power of government and the individual citizen.

Classical Realism A perspective on international relations that focuses on the state as a *unitary* and rational actor and on the actions and interactions of states.

Coalition (DOD) An ad hoc arrangement between two or more nations for common action.

Cognitive Dissonance A means of resolving the mental stress caused by the incongruence of behavior and belief.

Cold War Historically, "the" Cold War was a struggle between the U.S. and Western Europe against the Soviet Union and its Eastern European allies. It involved confrontation but no actual "hot" warfare. The Cold War began in the 1940s when the U.S. believed it was imperative to check Soviet Expansionist designs on Western Europe. It reached its height during the 1950s and 1960s, when the threat of nuclear annihilation hung over the world, particularly during the Cuban missile crisis in 1962. The Cold War made itself felt all over the globe; it was as if the entire world was divided into two units, East and West. No small regional Third World conflict was insignificant. The U.S. backed any regime that was anti-communist; while the Soviets tried to expand their influence anywhere they could, from Cuba and Central America to the Middle East and Africa. The Cold War eased slightly during the 1970s as a result of the U.S.-Soviet policy of dètente. It finally began to wind down in the late 1980s. In 1985, Mikhail Gorbachev had come to power in the Soviet Union and had begun his policies of glasnost (openness) and perestroika (restructuring). The Soviet Union and the U.S. agreed to wide-ranging arms control measures. Then when communism crumbled in Eastern Europe in 1989, without resistance from Moscow, U.S.-Soviet relations warmed dramatically. By 1990, the Cold War was virtually over.

More generally, according to the DOD, a "cold war" is a "state of international tension wherein political, economic, technological, sociological, psychological, paramilitary, and military measures short of overt armed conflict involving regular military forces are employed to achieve national objectives."

Collective Defense A concept similar to collective security in that aggression against one of the member state is considered aggression against all and should be defeated by the collective action of all.

The distinction, however, is that the collective defense organization's focus is external (i.e., the aggressor is not a member of the organization as is the case for a collective security organizaiton).

Collective Goods These goods, in their ideal form, possess the properties of indivisibility, *nonexcludability*, and *jointness of supply*. No one can deny another the use of these goods and no matter how much one consumes, the amount available to others is not diminished. *Collective goods* also are called "public" goods.

Collective Security The original concept behind the League of Nations that is based on a collective international consensus that aggression against one state is aggression against all and should be defeated by the collective action of all. "Collective Security arrangements, as opposed to "collective defense arrangements" are internally focused (i.e., member states agree to oppose any member state which attacks another member state).

Common Market A stage of economic integration where members enjoy the free trade of factors of production, goods, and services. It is based on the liberal assumption that trade is not a *zero-sum* game and that all members will be better off in the long run.

Communism The political system under which the economy, including capital, property, major industries, and public services, is controlled and directed by the state, and in that sense is "communal." Communism also involves a social structure that restricts individual freedom of expression. Modern communism is based on Marxism, as interpreted by the Russian revolutionary leader Vladimir Ilyitch Lenin (1870-1924).

Comparative Advantage A doctrine introduced by Ricardo in 1817 that argues that one country can always produce any specific good with a lower opportunity cost than another country because of differences in natural resources, climate, technology, labor, or capital. Therefore, each nation should specialize in and export goods in which it has a *comparative advantage* and import goods in which it does not.

Compellence One of the four functions of the use of force (or *strategies of influence*). It involves influencing others *to stop* doing something that they are currently doing or *to do* something that they are currently not doing (i.e., use of the atomic bomb versus Japan to *compel* surrender or the 1990 Iraqi invasion of Kuwait to *compel* Kuwait to raise oil prices).

Complex Interdependence Mutual dependence or situations characterized by reciprocal effects among countries or actors. It is *complex* because interdependence is characterized by multiple channels of connection, communication and influence between societies and because no one set of issues (such as security issues) dominates the policy agenda of states.

Constructivism An approach to studying international relations that emphasizes the impact of ideas; the interests and identities of states are highly malleable products of historical processes; discourse in society shapes beliefs and interests and establishes norms for behavior; identity and interests can be dependent variables as well as independent variables.

Cooperation The condition of a relative lack of conflict in the international system when the politics actually followed by one government are regarded by other actors as facilitating realization of their own objectives. It often results from active coordination between states over specific policy issues.

Counterforce Nuclear targeting doctrine where one or both sides could eliminate or drastically reduce the other side's retaliatory capacity by directing the first strike at the opponent's nuclear striking forces rather than at cities.

Countervalue Targeting cities and economic infrastructure instead of military targets.

Critical Theory A body of theory that stands apart from the prevailing order of the world and asks how that order came to be; institutions and relationships are not taken for granted but rather, their origins are questioned and how they are changing is important; directed at the social and political realm as a whole, rather than at separate parts; feminism, post-modernism and some constructivism are all works of critical theory

Deduction The logical process of reasoning by inference from the general to the specific, where the conclusion follows necessarily from the stated *premises*.

Defense One of the four functions of the use of force (or *strategies of influence*). *Defense* is the use of military force by a sovereign state to defeat an attack and to minimize damage to oneself if attacked. *Defense* is accomplished by the use of military force against the military forces of the attacker rather than the attacker's population.

Democracy Government by the people; the rule of the majority. There is no precise definition of democracy on which all could agree. Even communist countries tend to call themselves democratic, and the mere fact that a government is elected by a majority of the popular vote does not of itself guarantee a democracy. A broad definition might include the following points (based on Thomas R. Dye and L. Harmon Ziegler's book *The Irony of Democracy*): Participation by the mass of people in the decisions that shape their lives; government by majority rule, with recognition of the rights of minorities; freedom of speech, press, and assembly; freedom to form opposition political parties and to run for office; commitment to individual dignity and to equal opportunities for people to develop their full potential.

Democratic Dilemma This dilemma of foreign policy-making in a democracy centers on the tension between governmental checks and balances versus the concentration of presidential power.

Democratization The introduction of democratically elected representational institutions and limited government, accompanied by individual rights and political participation, into formerly closed political societies. *Democratization* often follows abrupt political events, such as a war or acute economic crises, that undermine formerly authoritarian systems.

Dependence The condition of *Third World* countries whereby their economic growth and political development are controlled by wealthier economies.

Dependent Variable The concept or event that is explained or accounted for by a *hypothesis* or *theory* (i.e. the *frequency* or *severity of war*).

Deterrence One of the four functions of the use of force (or *strategies of influence*). Dissuading an adversary from taking a course of action by posing the prospect of risk and cost outweighing any prospective gain. Timing and initiative is left to the opponent. According to the DOD, deterrence is "the prevention from action by fear of the consequences. Deterrence is a state of mind brought about by the existence of a credible threat of unacceptable counteraction."

Dialectic The recurring process of a thesis (the present) clashing with an antithesis (the opposite of the present condition) until the two produce a compromise synthesis, which becomes the future.

Diplomacy The conduct of official state to state relations. Customary norms and procedures developed over time for state to state interactions.

Discord A condition of conflict or lack of cooperation in the international system that may or may not lead to the outbreak of actual war.

Distribution of Capabilities Part of the *neo-realist* definition of *structure*, the *distribution of capabilities of states* determines a state's relative power and, hence, the ability to affect other states' behavior.

Domestic Growth Phase The first phase of the *Product Cycle*. The *domestic growth phase* entails development of an industry within a state. This phase ends when the home market reaches saturation.

Economic Liberalism One of the three core ideologies of *liberalism* (others are moral and political), *economic liberalism* holds that individuals must be free to shape their situation through various contractual relations conducted in an open market. *Economic liberalism*, as espoused by Adam Smith in his seminal treatise *The Wealth of Nations*, is centered on the belief that unfettered channels of economic activity—both markets and trade—are the best instruments for growth of individual and national wealth because *absolute* gains are maximized.

Ethnic Category A population characterized as a distinct cultural (usually, linguistic) group by outsiders (often scholars, missionaries, travelers, and traders), but possessing little or no sense of common ethnicity. There are many *ethnic categories* in the world.

Ethnic Cleansing Expulsion from one's homeland or, in the extreme form, a "final solution" genocide.

Ethnic Nationalism An *ideology* which conceives of the nation as based on a community with a vernacular (folk) culture and a common genealogy (however fictive). Different from civic and territorial conceptions of a nation which go beyond a common culture to include common laws and territorial citizenship.

Ethnic Purification A movement advocating the return to a particular, vernacular culture or homogenous society, based on a belief in the sanctity of that culture and the need to preserve it in an unadulterated form. Nonmembers cannot be incorporated, only expelled.

Ethnicity A source of identification among human beings based on a belief in a common history, culture, blood kinship, territorial claim, and desire for autonomy as an international group.

Ethnie (Ethnic Community) A named human population with a belief of common ancestry, shared memories and cultural elements, a link with an historic territory or homeland, and a measure of solidarity.

European Community (EC) *EC*, or *Common Market*, was established by six West European countries in the Treaty of Rome in 1957. Its purpose was to create a unified economic entity in Europe. Today, the *European Economic Community (EEC)*, now 14 countries, is attempting to lead the *Community* into a political, economic, and possibly even military union (*European Union*) by 1999.

Export-Led Industrialization (ELI) Development strategy, generally premised on the *liberal* economic notions of *comparative advantage* and the gains from international trade, advocating expansion of domestic manufacturing production and exportation overseas.

First World This term, originating during the *Cold War*, refers to the advanced industrialized countries, primarily in the West.

Foreign Export Phase The fourth phase of the *Product Cycle*. As manufacture of a product increases overseas and decreases in the original home market, the product will begin to be exported from foreign countries to the original market. This situation causes the further decline of manufacture in the original market.

Foreign Investment Phase The third phase of the *Product Cycle*. As the domestic market for a particular product reaches the saturation point, manufacture of the good will shift to overseas producers. Producers in the original market will peak and begin to decline.

Fourteen Points Enunciated by Woodrow Wilson in an address to Congress on 8 January, 1918 as a declaration of U. S. war aims and as a basis for a negotiated peace. The *Fourteen Points* included such aims as, among others, free trade, freedom of navigation, universal self-determination and the creation of an international organization to safeguard international peace and stability.

Fourth World This term, originating during the *Cold War*, refers to some extremely poor and nondeveloped countries such as Bangladesh, Cambodia, Haiti, Somalia, or Uganda. In the post-Cold War era, these countries usually are referred to as *Nondeveloped* countries.

Fragmegration A label that accounts for the tensions between the integrative forces of globalization and fragmenting forces of localization occurring in the world today

Free Trade International exchange of goods without government regulation, such as tariffs, quotas, exchange controls, subsidies to domestic producers, etc. The principles of free trade hold that a country which is efficient at producing a given product will profit from exporting it to countries which are less efficient at producing it. In return, such a country can use the wealth it gains for exports to buy goods and services that are being more efficiently produced elsewhere. When each country focuses on what it does best, market forces of supply and demand organize distribution for maximum economic growth, and consumers benefit from lover prices. In 1995 the General Agreement on Tariffs and Trade (GATT) marked a new leap towards worldwide free trade. Tariffs will be cut by an average of 40 percent in the 124 participating countries.

Game Theory An analytical approach that uses games as tools for understanding socio-political behavior (e.g. *Prisoner's Dilemma* and *Stag Hunt*). For example, games can be used to test hypotheses that attempt to illustrate how people can become trapped by self-defeating acts.

General Agreement on Tariffs and Trade (GATT) The regime that governs the expansion of free trade through multilateral negotiations to lower tariffs progressively. Originally intended as a temporary treaty in the aftermath of World War II until the Havana Charter was implemented, its main goal is to maximize world trade by reducing trade barriers, eliminating tariffs, and prohibiting quantitative restrictions and other non-tariff barriers.

General Assembly One of the six principal organs of the *United Nations*, this body functions as the general conference with one vote per member state. The *General Assembly* debates global problems that a majority wish to consider. It sponsors seven main committees that work on issues from global economics to agriculture to human rights.

Globalism Points to aspirations for a state of affairs where values are shared by all the world's more than 5 billion people, their environment and their role as citizens, consumers or producers with an interest in collective action to solve common problems

Globalization All the forces which impel individuals, groups and institutions to engage in similar forms of behavior or to participate in more encompassing and coherent processes, organizations or systems; not hindered or prevented by territorial or jurisdictional boundaries

Hegemon A state with the preponderance of material resources, military capability, and political power. Hegemonic powers must also have control over sources of capital, control over markets, and competitive advantage in the production of highly valued goods.

Historicism Human institutions are made by people, through *collective* responses to collectively perceived problems; institutions and practices are to be understood through the changing mental processes of their makers.

Hobbesian A condition characterized by *anarchic* politics (or the absence of a sovereign or central authority). This term is derived from the influence of Thomas Hobbes, a 17th century English political philosopher, who claimed that security rests more on *power* and the *balance of power* than on law, norms, or other rules.

Hypotheses Propositions usually relating two or more variables but subject to *empirical* or factual test. Usually these propositions are put in an *"If . . (x) . . then . . (y) . ."* format.

Idealism An *ideology* that contends a permanent world peace can be achieved through establishing a "good" and globalized political institution, through education, and through "fair" and "just" implementation of international law. Its advocates believe in an "ideal" vision of peaceful world order.

Ideology A belief system, set of ideas, or set of values that often offers explanations and predictions of international or social relations.

Imperialism The policy that aims at building and maintaining an empire, in which many states and peoples, spread over a wide geographical area, are controlled by one dominant state.

Import Substitution Industrialization (ISI) Development strategy, premised on *neo-mercantilist* or neo-Marxist notions of the value of protectionist trade barriers, advocating expansion of domestic industry by limiting imports of competing manufactured goods.

Incremental Approach A policy-making technique in which the decision-maker serially employs alternatives only marginally different than existing policy, notes the feedback from the marginal change, and then makes another decision.

Independent Variable Non-interrelated quantitative or qualitative factors that help to explain or predict specified outcomes (*dependent variables*) in a *hypothesis* or *theory.*

Induction The logical process of reasoning by inference from specific observations to general principles.

Influence The ability to affect another actor's behavior.

Instrumental Supports Supports for a regime based on the satisfaction of specific needs and desires; a results of the regime's performance; supports given in return for what is received

Integration The joining of separate states or other political units under a common authority. *Integration* can be viewed as either a process or as an outcome that encourages *cooperation* among states operating in the *anarchic system.*

Intellectual Pluralism The deliberate use of multiple, competing "lenses" and theories to examine ideas and facts in order to explain why things happen.

Inter-Governmental Organization (IGO) International actors composed of more than one state (i.e., the United Nations).

Intercontinental Ballistic Missiles (ICBMs) Delivery vehicles for nuclear or thermonuclear weapons. According to the DOD, "A ballistic missile with a range capability from about 3,000 to 8,000 nautical miles."

Interest A valued object or desired state of affairs, which Morgenthau defines in terms of *power.* The pursuit of *power* is the driving force that guides states through the landscape of international politics.

International Bank for Reconstruction and Development (IBRD) Also named the *World Bank*, this specialized agency of the United Nations was established by the 1944 *Bretton Woods* Agreement. The *IBRD* was chartered to provide money for reconstruction of states devastated in World War II and to promote economic development in underdeveloped lands. Headquartered in Washington D.C., this *Inter-Governmental Organization* now has over 150 nation-state members and provides loans to member governments and to some private development projects. The *World Bank* focuses its loans on long-term infrastructure and development projects for *Lesser Developed Countries* and newly emerging democracies.

International Court of Justice (ICJ) The principal judicial organ of the United Nations, sometimes known simply as the World Court. Its jurisdiction covers cases that are submitted to it by U.N. members; it gives advisory opinions and renders judgments. The Court has 15 judges, elected by the General Assembly and the Security Council, for 9-year terms. It sits in The Hague, Netherlands.

International Law Rules, principles and conventions that govern the relations between states. International law has been built up piecemeal through agreements, tribunals, international conferences, long-established customs. There is no international law-making body, as such, and national governments themselves decide whether they will adhere to the principles and conventions of international law. The Statute of the International Court states the basis on which international law rests, and on which it adjudicates in cases brought before it: "(a) international conventions, whether general or particular, establishing rules expressly recognized by the contesting states; (b) international custom, as evidence of a general practice accepted as law; (c) the general principles of law recognized by civilized nations."

International Monetary Fund (IMF) Originally a 30-member *Inter-Governmental Organization (IGO)* created in 1944, it comprised part of the *Bretton Woods* international financial system charged with supervising currency exchange rates and balance of payments adjustments. It was the institutional center of a new international monetary regime to facilitate liberal trade and payments after World War II.

International Political Economy (IPE) The reciprocal and dynamic interaction of economics and politics in international relations between the pursuit of *power* and the pursuit of *wealth*. *IPE* can be thought of as a set of policy issues (i.e. economic growth, trade, finance, development, debt, collective goods), as the conceptual nexus between international politics and economics, and as a set of alternative *ideologies* about this conceptual nexus.

International Relations The total of political, economic, cultural, social, and other interactions between the players (*nations*, *states*, *IGOs*, *NGOs*, *MNCs*, etc.) in the international system.

Irredentism One of the four patterns of ethnic conflict most threatening to regional stability. One state's attempt to claim or reincorporate contiguous territory occupied by ethnic kinsmen (Russians in Kazakhastan, Somalis in Ethiopia, or Tajiks in Afghanistan, for example).Caused by territorial boundaries which for a host of reasons have been imprecisely drawn.

Keynesianism The economic theories of John Maynard Keynes (1883-1946), and his followers. The Englishman Keynes's best known work was the General Theory of Employment, Interest and Money, published in 1936 at the height of the Great Depression. Keynes shifted the attention of economists from microeconomics to macroeconomics. Much of his book is on the causes of unemployment. Keynes stated that the economy had no self-balancing equilibrium that resulted in full employment, as classical economics insisted. On the contrary, it could be in equilibrium at less than full employment (the first time this theory had been proposed). Keynes believed it was therefore the job of government to stimulate spending through deficit financing to ensure full employment. Keynes's theory was vastly influential. Since then governments have tended to accept a responsibility to provide full employment—although they have not always been successful in doing so.

League of Nations An international organization established by the Treaty of Versailles after World War I. The goal of the League was to foster international peace and stability through arbitration and collective security and to assist in economic, social and legal cooperation among states.

Legitimacy A situation where an act is viewed as "right" and "best", thereby mandating support and obedience by others.

Lesser Developed Countries (LDCs) Countries that are, in comparison to the developed countries, poor economically and usually unstable politically.

Liberal Imperialism This concept is the antithesis of Schumpeter's *liberal pacifism.* It suggests that republics are the ideal polity for imperialist expansion because their values of liberty, common good, and public glory create strong and aggressive states.

Liberal Internationalism A strand of thought in international politics, traced to Kant, that relates *liberalism* and democracy to a "perpetual peace". Republican governments (democracies) united in a federation can achieve peace provided all share a universal respect for human rights and freedom.

Liberal Pacifism The belief associated with Schumpeter (1919) and others that the interactions between *capitalism* and democracy foster *peace* and are antithetical to *imperialism.* Only special interests groups profit from war, and no democracy would bear the high costs of *imperialism* to benefit only a minority interest.

Liberalism In the nineteenth century in Europe, the great age of liberalism, the term stood for freedom from church and state authority and the reduction of the power of royalty and aristocracy, free enterprise economics, and the free development of the individual. Liberalism advocated freedom of the press, religious toleration, self-determination for nations. It was liberalism that established parliamentary democracy. The Founding Fathers might be termed liberals. In the twentieth century, liberal parties were caught in between conservatives and socialists and their influence declined. Today, liberalism stands for something rather different than it did in the nineteenth century (more government rather than less government).

Linkages The tying together of issues, ideas, or policies from multiple areas or subjects, especially in international negotiations.

Machiavellian A condition characterized by the amoral behavior of diplomats who, regardless of means, aim to achieve state objectives based on self-interest. This condition is derived from the influence of Niccolo Machiavelli, a 16th century Florentine political philosopher, who claimed that the ends of the state (security and survival) justified whatever means necessary to achieve them.

Macro-Economic Policy The branch of economics that examines the workings and problems of the economy as a whole - economic growth, inflation, unemployment, and economic fluctuations

Market-Friendly Development Belief of some developing countries (notably the "Asian Tigers" and generally the *Newly Industrializing Countries*) that market forces must be recognized when drawing up development strategies. *"Market friendly" development* may allow for a limited role for the state in the national economy; even where the state is involved, however, it recognizes the importance of the market in allocating resources and setting prices. *Market-friendly development* must include respect for property rights, transparent economic and financial regulations, and a strong but even-handed enforcement structure.

Marxism The domestic based theory developed by Karl Marx and Friedrich Engels, which became the official doctrine of communism. According to Marxism, the key to how society operated was economics; all other aspects of society, such as politics and religion, were conditioned by the economic system. Under capitalism, society was divided into two classes: the capitalists who owned the means of production and distribution, and the workers, or proletariat, whose labor was exploited by the ruling class. Marx saw history as a dialectical process in which two opposing forces (thesis and antithesis) generate a third, synthesizing force. According to this view, capitalism would eventually break down because of its own contradictions and this would lead to the proletarian revolution and the establishment of the classless society.

Mercantilism An ideology of *international political economy* which holds that all economic activity is best accomplished in conjunction with the goals and objectives of the state. Individual wealth and prosperity is only significant to the extent that it contributes to state power and wealth. In *classical mercantilism,* wealth and power are closely related. Political and military power are said to determine the economic prosperity of the state; therefore, *mercantilist* states compete over the division of economic resources in the international arena and also protect their own wealth by inflated currency values and the protection of domestic industries through high tariffs, quotas and other trade barriers. States are concerned with *relative gains* versus *absolute gains* and seek to accumulate specie through positive trade balances to have wealth for armies.

Model An intellectual construct representing reality that organizes our thinking and guides our research. A *model* codifies a set of assumptions and concepts that helps us sort and analyze data, identify relationships, and explain relationships. Although not a *theory* in the sense of deductively-developed and empirically-tested social science, this explicit conceptual guide serves as a framework for studying a state's foreign policy from a variety of perspectives.

Morality Conception of ethical behavior. Moral arguments may move and constrain people, and hence may affect state behavior. Although some *realists* suggest that morality is mere propaganda, states may (and often do) act because of moral *choice*.

Multinational Corporation (MNC) A business enterprise with headquarters in one country but with production facilities in more than one country (i.e. General Motors).

Multinational Operations (DOD) A collective term to describe military actions conducted by forces of two or more nations, typically organized within the structure of a coalition or alliance.

Multipolarity The condition of having more than two major powers (or poles) in the international system. The structure of the international system prior to World War I.

Nation A large group of people bound together by common tradition and culture and usually language. Sometimes used synonymously with state, but this can be misleading, since one state may contain many nations. For example, Great Britain is a state, but contains the English, Scottish, Welsh, and part of the Irish nations. Iraq is a state, but contains three distinct nations: the non-Arab Kurds, the Shi'ite Muslims in the south and the Sunnu Muslims who hold power in Baghdad. And single nations may be scattered across many states, as was the case with the Jewish nation which existed in many states before the creation of the state of Israel in 1948, and is now the case with the Kurds.

Nation-State Usually used to describe the modern state, but strictly speaking applies only when the whole population of a state feels itself to belong to the same nation. This is certainly more the case now than it was in the nineteenth century and earlier, when large empires, such as Austria-Hungary, were states but contained many nations. But many states today still contain many nations (partly because of the arbitrary way that the borders of states were redrawn after both World Wars, and by the colonial powers as they withdrew from Asia and Africa), and with the rise of nationalism that has followed the fall of communism, this has been one of the main reasons for instability in states such as the Soviet Union and Yugoslavia.

National Objectives (DOD) The aims, derived from national goals and interests, toward which a national policy or strategy is directed and efforts and resources of the nation are applied.

National Policy (DOD) A broad course of action or statements of guidance adopted by the government at the national level in pursuit of national objectives.

National Power Capabilities of states that determine their ability to control or influence outcomes or the actions of others. Elements of *national power* include geography, natural resources, industrial capacity, military preparedness, population, national character, national morale, the quality of *diplomacy*, and the quality of government.

National Security (DOD) A collective term encompassing both national defense and foreign relations of the United States. Specifically, the condition provided by: a. a military or defense advantage over any foreign nation or group of nations, or b. a favorable foreign relations position, or c. a defense posture capable of successfully resisting hostile or destructive action from within or without, overt or covert.

National Security Strategy (DOD) The art and science of developing, applying, and coordinating the instruments of national power (diplomatic, economic, military, and informational) to achieve objectives that contribute to national security. Also called national strategy or grand strategy.

Nationalism Cohesion within a group due to the group's unique characteristics, which may include common language, race, ethnicity, history, etc.

New International Economic Order (NIEO) A major campaign (fought mainly in the UN General Assembly and the UN Conference on Trade and Development) initiated by a group of seventy-seven (G-77) *lesser developed countries (LDCs)* to implement a program of collective international action designed to revolutionize the existing world economy, to lessen the dependence of poor countries, and to emplace a new economic system more favorable to the interests of the poor countries. Group 77 (G-77) now consists of 120 states. Three demands were made initially: 1) changes in the terms of trade to favor the producers of primary commodities; 2) promotion of industrialization in the Third World; 3) increased transfers of development aid from wealthy countries combined with debt relief for Third World countries.

New Protectionism A self-centered, nationalist perspective that economic activities are and should be subordinate to the goal of state building and internal state interests. It consists of the increased use of Non-Tariff Barriers (NTBs), Orderly Market Arrangements (OMAs), and Voluntary Export Restraints (VERs).

Newly Industrializing Countries (NICs) A classification that describes former *Lesser Developed Countries (LDCs)* that have developed successfully and now compete in the international economic system reasonably well. The most commonly cited examples include the "Four Dragons of Asia": South Korea, Singapore, Hong Kong, and Taiwan.

Non-Governmental Organization (NGO) International organizations composed of private international actors (i.e. the International Red Cross).

Normative A guide to behavior based on the assumption that there is a "right" action, obligation, or standard.

Non-aligned Movement An organization of over 100 different countries whose members do not belong to any military alliance (such as NATO or the Warsaw Pact). The movement was founded by Prime Minister Nehru of India, and Presidents Tito of Yugoslavia, and Nasser of Egypt as a vehicle for non-aligned countries to come together to solve problems without benefit of military alliance. Its members represent the full spectrum of political systems from democratic to one-party communist forms of government including countries such as India, Pakistan, Singapore, Malaysia, Indonesia, Cuba, Egypt, most African and some Latin American countries. A summit is held every 3 years with the host country providing a chairman for the 3-year period until the next summit meeting. The Coordinating Bureau of Foreign Ministers meets more often. The headquarters is the host country.

North Atlantic Treaty Organization (NATO) A military alliance signed in 1949 by 16 countries including: Iceland, Norway, Denmark, Spain, Portugal, Greece, Turkey, Italy, Belgium, Netherlands, France, United Kingdom, Germany, Luxembourg, United States, and Canada. The purpose of NATO is the joint defense of all of its members and the peaceful coexistence with all nations; it regards an attack upon any one member as an attack upon all members. NATO organizes joint defense plans, and military training and exercises. The North Atlantic Council (NAC) is the principal organization of NATO which has permanent representatives from the 16 member countries; it has several committees such as the Defense Planning Committee (DPC) which meet on a regular basis. Headquarters is in Brussels, Belgium. In January, 1994, NATO agreed to accept new members. The most likely candidates are former members of the Warsaw Pact-Poland, Hungary, the Czech Republic, and Slovakia.

Omnibalancing The concept that Third World alignment decisions are made as a result of the need to counter all threats, internal and external

Operationalize To establish a methodology or test to measure *independent* and *dependent* variables.

Ordering Principle A defining characteristic of the system's *structure* that describes the arrangement of the units of the system.

Organization of African Unity (OAU) A regional, inter-governmental organization established in 1963 to end colonialism, develop unity, foster economic development and provide security for African states. Membership now includes the 51 states of Africa (excluding the Republic of South Africa). Its organization consists of an Assembly of Heads of State, which meets annually at *OAU* Headquarters in Addis Ababa, Ethiopia; and a loosely knit group of Liberation

Movements, including the African National Congress (South Africa) and the South-West African People's Organization—SWAPO (Namibia).

Organization of American States (OAS) A regional, inter-governmental organization established in 1948 to determine political, defense, economic and social policies for the Inter-American system. From an original membership of 21 American states, the *OAS* had grown to 35 member nations from North, Central and South America (34 "active" members; Cuba was suspended in 1962). The most prominent of six activities and sub-organizations is the Inter-American Conference, meeting every five years to consider issues of importance to the member states.

Organization for Economic Cooperation and Development (OECD) An international, inter-governmental organization with 24 member countries; promotes policies designed to achieve the rapid economic growth, employment, and standard of living in member countries, encourages sound economic expansion of world trade on a multilateral, nondiscriminatory basis in accordance with international obligations. Holds annual ministerial meeting every May in Paris, France where its headquarters is located.

Organization of Command

Organization of Petroleum Exporting Countries (OPEC) A functionally-oriented, inter-governmental organization (21 oil-exporting African, Asian, and South American countries) established by treaty in 1961. *OPEC* attempts to act like a cartel to regulate production limits for oil among its members and to establish agreed-upon oil prices in the world market place.

Pax Americana A period of time in the 20th century in which relative world peace rested on alliances formed through US leadership to contain the Soviet Union; from the assurance of security came an unfolding of the global economy where again the US provided leadership

Pax Britannica A period of time in the mid-nineteenth century in which British seapower and its flexibility in using it to balance European powers, resulted in a relative peace; the norms of liberal economics spread with British prestige, providing a universal ideology which represented those norms as the basis of harmony of interest

Periphery In Dependency theory, the *Periphery* is the group of the poorest countries (*LDCs* or the *Third World*) that is dependent on the hegemonic *Center* for its economic growth. As the states in this category attempt to develop their economies, a significant degree of uneven development occurs within each state.

Political Economy The reciprocal and dynamic interaction of economics and politics. *Political Economy* can be thought of as a set of policy issues (i.e. economic growth, trade and finance) generated by the interaction of the state and the market, as the embodiment of politics and economics in the modern world, and as the conceptual nexus between politics and economics.

Political Realism An approach that assumes people by nature are aggressive, and that statecraft should be devoted to the acquisition of power in order for the state to survive in a hostile environment.

Political Systems The organizing principles upon which governments are based. Political systems (e.g., democratic or authoritarian) and the types of foreign policy-making processes they produce often make "why states do what they do" a matter of choice. Three models highlight competing interpretations of these processes: the rational actor model, the organizational process model, and the bureaucratic politics model.

Positive Law A view of international law that holds that international law is created by people and that the obligation to follow law is based on self-interest, utility, and consent. Law is what states agree to and is based on the behavior of states.

Post-Modernism Objectivity is impossible to achieve and therefore one cannot approach the study of international relations scientifically; text and narrative history play a crucial role in shaping the world

Power Control over the minds and actions of other actors in order to maintain the distribution of power that exists at a particular moment. More generally, the ability to control resources, to control the behavior of other actors, to control events, to control the outcomes of interaction—even to control the structure of the interaction itself. It also describes the ability of one state to achieve its aims despite the efforts of competing states. *Power* can take many forms, such as military, economic, or political influence.

Pre-emptive Strike An attack conducted as a defensive measure when a state believes that another *state's* attack on it is imminent. A *pre-emptive* strike allows a state to seize the initiative and gain the advantage of surprise. According to the DOD it is "an attack initiated on the basis of incontrovertible evidence that an enemy attack is imminent."

Preferential Trade Trade concessions designed to benefit selected countries by lowering or eliminating tariffs on their exports. Examples of preferential trade agreements include *common markets* and *free-trade areas*, such as the *North American Free Trade Area (NAFTA).*

Premise A proposition upon which an argument or *theory* is based or from which a conclusion is drawn.

Prestige Reputation for *power.* The purpose of *prestige* is to impress other nations with the *power* one's nation actually possesses, or with the *power* it believes, or wants the other nation to believe, it possesses. Morgenthau identifies two instrumentalities that serve this purpose: diplomatic ceremonies and the display of military force.

Price Stabilization Policy goal of promoting steady global economic growth by reducing or eliminating fluctuation of prices, particularly the prices of primary commodities exported by *Lesser Developed Countries (LDCs).*

Post-Modernism

Prisoner's Dilemma A situation created by an incentive structure marked by distrust of others that forces a state to act on self-interest rather than group interests (even if those group interests are more beneficial).

Privatization Process of reducing or eliminating state participation or ownership in major sectors of a national economy. *Privatization* can include sales of all or portions of major industries, and usually takes place as part of a wider economic reform policy. In many cases *privatization* has provided fiscally strapped governments with large and badly needed—albeit temporary—infusions of cash.

Probability Statement A general expression of a cause and effect relationship which is a valid expectation for a class of phenomenon most of the time. This expectation is established as likely through the observation of patterns and the testing of cases. In the social sciences, *theories* are sets of these statements and explanations of why these behavior patterns occur.

Proletariat In Marxist terminology, this term refers to the ruled class (or the working class) in a *capitalist* society.

Propositions Testable statements in which the subjects or causal relationships are affirmed or denied. Sometimes called *hypotheses*, these statements are the basis for confirming or denying expected behaviors or proposed explanations in specific cases.

Radicalism An umbrella *ideology* of international relations which denies the legitimacy of established norms, laws and procedures of international politics and international economics. *Radicalism* views the basic tenets of international law, capitalism, and order in the state system to be inherently unjust (especially economic) and to be permanently resistant to any evolutionary, non-violent alteration. *Radicalism*, therefore, espouses the revolutionary, violent overthrow of the international system of economics and politics as the most efficient and most moral means toward establishing a just world order.

Realism A *systemic* lens of *international relations* that focuses on the state as a *unitary* and rational actor and suggests that states expand their power in order to secure their interests in an anarchic world. Originating from *classical realism*, a modern version of this perspective is *structural* (or *neo-*) *realism.*

Realpolitik A *realist* notion that emphasizes the importance of *self-help* and *power* in *international relations* (also known as "power politics"). German term now used in English that means politics based on strictly practical rather than theoretical or idealistic notions, and practiced with a hard or cynical edge, without any sentimental illusions. Realpolitik is power politics; the practitioner of realpolitik pursues the interests of his own group or country ruthlessly; he expects the other side to the same.

Regime A set of implicit or explicit *principles, norms, rules*, and *decision-making procedures* around which actors' expectations converge in a given area of *international relations*—thereby regularizing behavior and creating patterns of expectations concerning the behavior of all actors.

Relative Gains Acquisition which has its significance only in comparison to something else; not absolute of independent; realists value this concept in examining inter-state relations

Satisficing Searching for an acceptable choice, one that is good enough to meet a minimal set of requirements. Instead of reviewing all possible alternatives, the "satisficer" usually will pick the first alternative that meets the minimal set of requirements.

Second World Originating during the *Cold War*, this term refers to the formerly *Communist* countries that were headed by the USSR. Also referred to as the *East* by some *International Political Economy* theorists.

Security Community A social structure in which states share knowledge and trust each other to resolve disputes without war

Security Council One of the six principal organs of the *United Nations (UN)*, this body is assigned primary responsibility by the UN Charter for maintaining peace and security in the world. Consisting of five permanent members with veto power (Britain, China, France, the US and Russia) and ten elected members serving two-year terms, the Council is empowered to enforce pacific settlements on international disputes; or, when determining that an act of aggression or a deliberate threat to the peace has occurred, it may call uponteral issues of how to deal with members of reduced stature (i.e., Great Britain and France).

Security Dilemma A pervasive phenomenon wherein the means by which one state prepares to defend itself are perceived by another state as threatening—as offensive rather than defensive.

Self Reliance This development strategy involves removing one's country from the capitalist world economy to escape *dependence*, to remove foreign penetration, and to achieve *autarky*. It implies shifting economic ties away from *Center* (Core) countries, *Multinational Corporations (MNCs)*, and Western aid-giving agencies such as the *International Monetary Fund (IMF)*.

Self-Determination The doctrine that a group of people who consider themselves separate and distinct from others has the right to determine for themselves the state in which they live and the form of government it will have. *Self-determination* usually involves a process, based on *ethnic nationalism*, by which an *ethnic community* demands external and internal *sovereignty* over a given territory. Such a claim derives from a cultural-historical interpretation of the territory as an ethnic homeland. It is the vehicle by which national groups seek to insure their identity by institutionalizing *sovereign* states. *Self-determination* not only demands sovereignty, but is the moral doctrine which justifies it—applying not only to aspirants to statehood, but also to those who already have states. Woodrow Wilson (and his famous *Fourteen Points* detailing his 1918 peace aims) is the name most closely associated with national *self-determination*.

Self-Help A characteristic of the *anarchic* international system whereby states must act out of self-interest, must look out for their own security, and should not assume the help of other states.

Sensitivity How quickly changes in one country bring about changes in another, and how great the effects are. In addition to *vulnerability*, it is one measure of the degree of interdependence between states.

Socialism According to Karl Marx, a "historical stage" of human civilization and an *ideology* that emphasizes socialized production and socialized property rights. It is also a domestic political system in which the means of production, distribution and exchange are mostly owned by the state, and used, at least in theory, on behalf of the people. The idea behind socialism is that the capitalist system is intrinsically unfair, because it concentrates wealth in a few hands and does nothing to safeguard the overall welfare of the majority. Under socialism, the state redistributes the wealth of society in a more equitable way, with the ideal of social justice replacing the profit motive.

Socialization The process by which the population comes to accept the goals of the political system and the institutions by which the goals are to be realized

Sovereignty The attribute of a state that refers to its right to exercise complete jurisdiction over its own territory.

Specificity of Function Part of the *neo-realist* definition of *structure, specification of function* reflects the tasks that units of a system face. Units are categorized in terms of similar functions or in reference to a division of labor.

Stag Hunt Similar to the *prisoner's dilemma,* but the payoff/incentive structure is different. In Rousseau's *Stag Hunt,* if all hunters cooperate, they will kill the stag and all will eat well. But if one hunter defects to chase a rabbit—which all like less than the stag—none of the others will get anything. Thus all hunters have the same preference order, and there is a solution that gives each his first choice. Unless each hunter thinks that the others will cooperate, though, each hunter will tend to defect (chase the rabbit).

Standard Operating Procedures (SOPs) and Routines. Methodical and predictable procedures or rules. Organizations often adopt these procedures in order to standardize behavior. According to the DOD and NATO, an SOP is a set of instructions covering those features of operations which lend themselves to a definite or standardized procedure without loss of effectiveness. The procedure is applicable unless ordered otherwise.

State A legal abstraction with institutions to control a territorial area and the people who reside in that territory.

Status Quo The existing state of affairs, at any given time, as in "people opposed to the proposed changes fought to maintain the status quo."

Structural Adjustment A development prescription mandating that developing countries cut government spending to balance budgets, eliminate trade barriers and social subsidies, encourage exports, tighten monetary policies, devalue currency and dismantle barriers to foreign investment.

Structure The positional arrangement of a system's units determined by the *ordering principle,* by the specification of functions of differentiated units, and by the distribution of capabilities across units.

Subsystemic Lens A *subsystemic* lens (or perspective) of international relations that deflects the *systemic* focus of *Security* and *International Political Economy* and peers into the "black box" of how the state makes and implements choices in *international relations.* This lens consists of beliefs, political systems, and decision-making models and suggests that *international relations* is best understood as the consequence of *choice.*

Sub-systemic-Level Approach A conceptual approach that looks inside the "black box" of nations to determine how and why states behave and how decisions are made.

Supranational Organizations above nation-states, such as international organizations.

Swaggering One of the four functions of the use of force (or *Strategies of Influence*). It is part of a residual category—the deployment of military power for purposes other than defense, deterrence, or compellence. It involves the use of force for objectives that are diffuse, ill-defined, and problematic.

Systemic-Level Approach Political analysis of the influences on foreign policy that are external and that originate outside the state's boundaries.

Theory A set of interconnected statements that comprise sentences introducing terms that refer to the basic concepts, sentences that relate the basic concepts to each other, and sentences that relate some statements to a set of possible observations. The primary purposes of using theory or conducting scientific investigation are description, explanation, and prediction.

Third World This term, originating during the *Cold War,* refers to the *Lesser Developed Countries (LDCs)* in Africa, Asia, and Latin America.

Underdevelopment A condition of political, economic, social, and industrial weakness most prevalent in the lesser developed countries (LDCs) as compared to conditions in the leading industrialized states.

Unitary Player The assumption, prevalent in the *Rational Actor Model* and in both the *Realism* and *International Political Economy* lenses, that states tend to act as a coherent whole.

United Nations (UN) An international, inter-governmental organization created in 1945 in the wake of World War II to establish a "rule of law" in the international community by outlawing aggressive war, providing for a peaceful settlement of international disputes, regulating armaments, governing special trust territories, and encouraging cooperation among nations. The UN Charter—a 111 article document signed and ratified by the initial 51 *UN* member states—was intended to function like the Constitution of the United States in setting-up the six major organs and the broad principles and procedures to be followed by the *UN*. Currently (1998) consists of 185 member countries.

Value Complexity The presence of multiple, competing values and interests that are imbedded in a single issue. One example of this concept is the Cuban Missile Crisis in which the United States did not wish to begin a war with the Soviet Union. However, the US was not willing to accede to the provocative Soviet decision to install nuclear missiles in Cuba.

Variable A quantitative or qualitative characteristic of an object or class of objects used to develop *causal* relationships in the development of *hypotheses* and *theories*.

Vulnerability A measurement of the costs incurred by a state to cope with externally induced changes caused by a disruption in the flow of goods across borders or the levels of transactions between governments and societies. *Vulnerability*, along with *sensitivity*, is a measure of the degree of interdependence. According to the DOD, vulnerability is the following: 1. The susceptibility of a nation or military force to any action by any means through which its war potential or combat effectiveness may be reduced or its will to fight diminished. 2. The characteristics of a system which cause it to suffer a definite degradation (incapability to perform the designated mission) as a result of having been subjected to a certain level of effects in an unnatural (manmade) hostile environment.

War Hostilities between states or within a state or territory undertaken by means of armed force. *War* is said to exist, in the legal sense, when two or more states officially declare that a condition of hostilities exists between them. The level of hostilities may range from *total war* (seeking the unconditional surrender or the total destruction of the enemy and using all the military weaponry at a state's disposal) to *limited war* (where both the means and the objectives are reduced in scope).

War Powers Act (1973) Congressional act to limit the war-making power of the president by requiring congressional authorization for any American troop commitment lasting sixty days. An additional thirty days may be approved without a declaration of war if Congress agrees that the safety of the forces involved requires it. After ninety days Congress can, by passing a concurrent resolution, require the withdrawal of American forces. The president can not override the resolution by veto.

Warsaw Pact Also referred to as the Warsaw Treaty Organization (WTO), this regional military group (created pursuant to the Treaty of Friendship, Cooperation, and Mutual Assistance concluded in 1955 in Warsaw) included the formerly communist eastern European states of Bulgaria, Czechoslovakia, East Germany, Hungary, Poland, and the Soviet Union. Albania, Romania, and Yugoslavia were partial or political, rather than full military participants.

Wealth A measure of scarce resources or total assets that has several connotations to include (1) anything (land, capital, labor) that can generate further income; (2) the annual produce of land and labor of a society; or (3) the means of want satisfaction (the stock of resources).

World Bank *See* International Bank for Reconstruction and Development (IBRD)

World Government A global political entity that ensures world peace and security through a supreme authority established over the state system.

World View This concept generally refers to the lens or theoretical perspective that one believes best illuminates the interactions of actors in the international system. In addition, it is one of three specific elements (see also *Character* and *Style*) analysts use to examine whether a president will be a successful leader. Analysts describe a president's *world view* in terms of the president's perception of what the great issues of the time are and what forces shape them.

Zero-Sum A belief that the elements of power and wealth are finite entities in international relations. Consequently, a gain by one state is a loss by another.

Index

E

F

MAP 1: Europe (1999)

MAP 2: Middle East (1999)

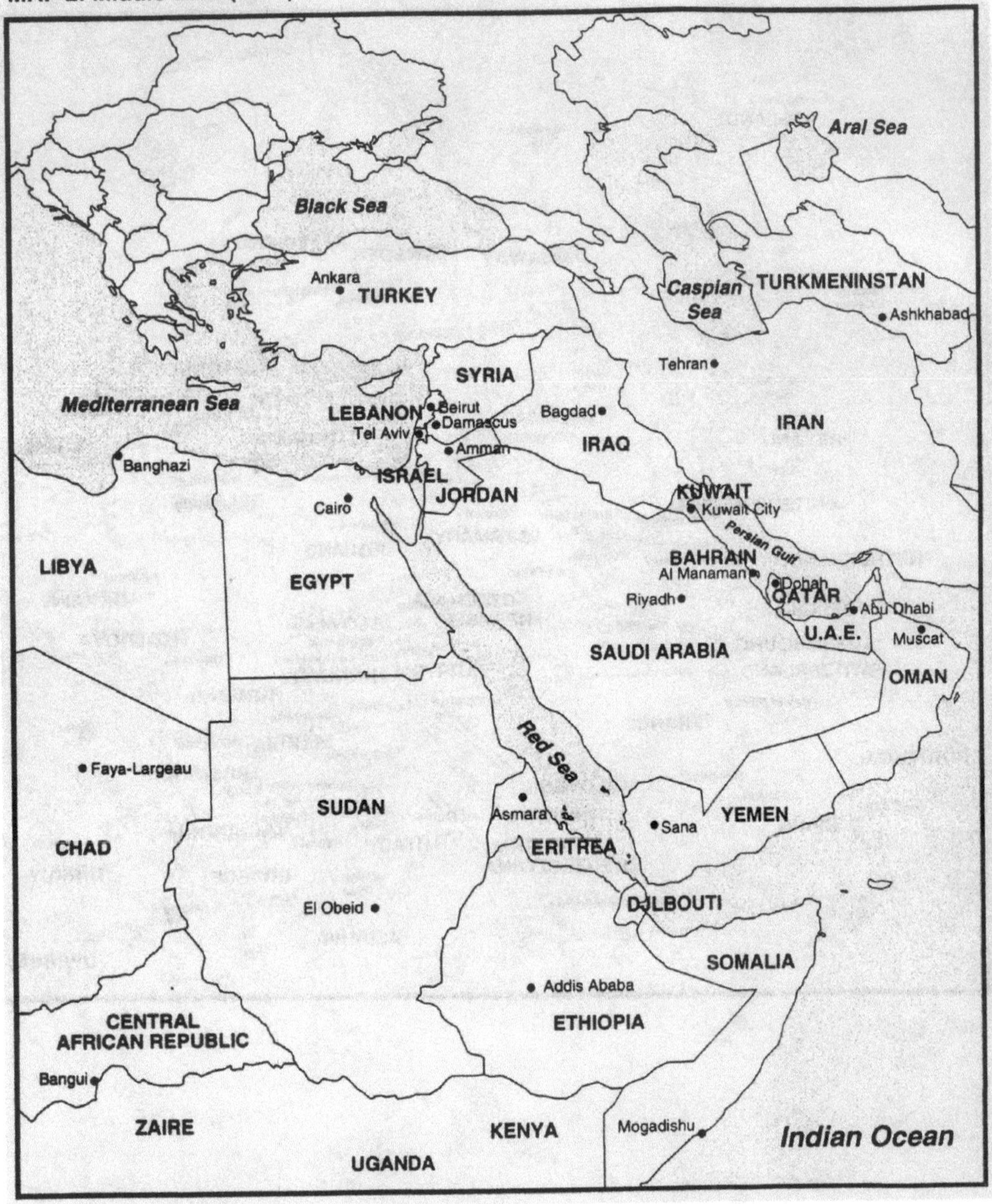

MAP 3: East Asia (1999)

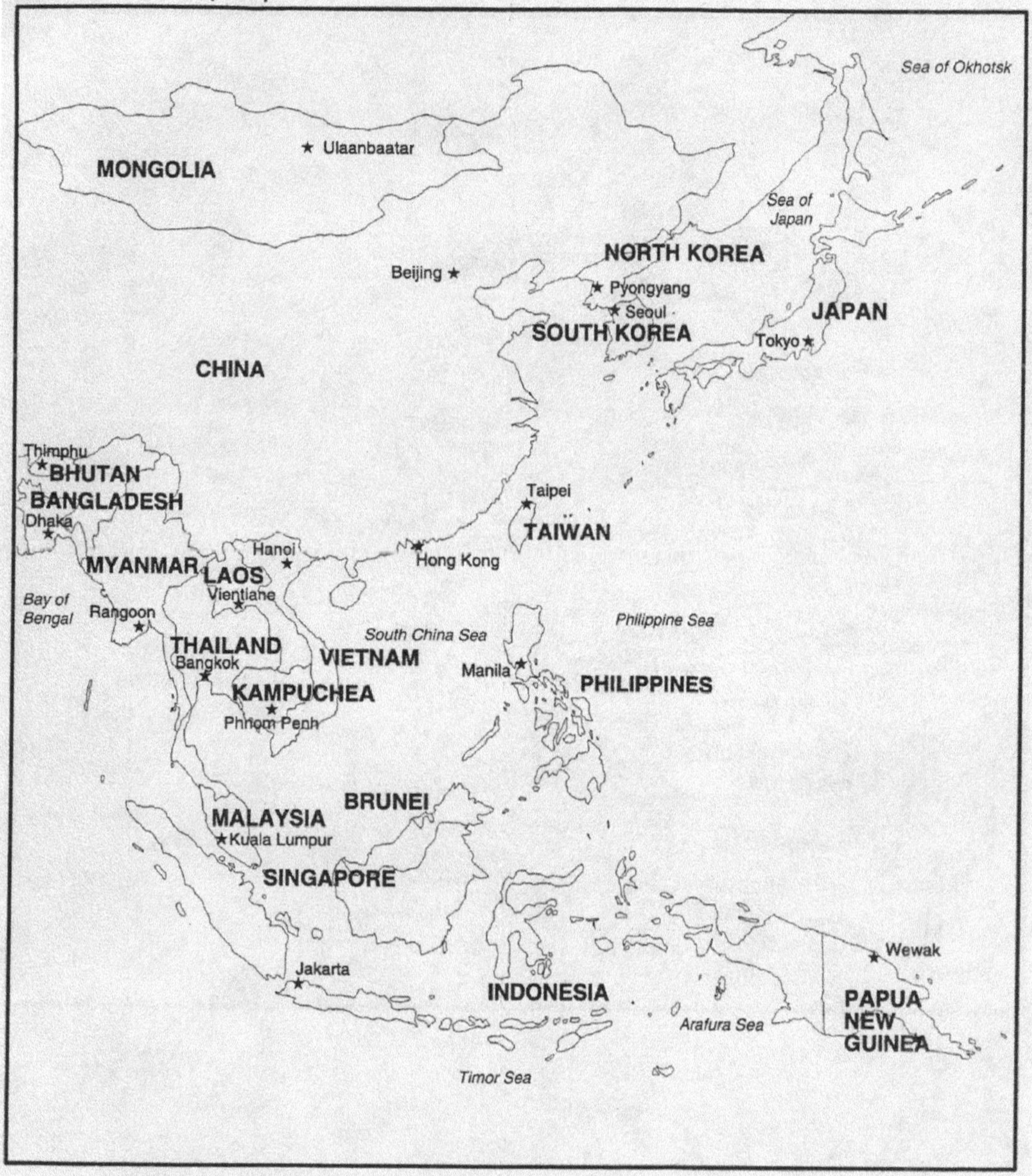

Sea of Okhotsk
Ulaanbaatar
MONGOLIA
Sea of Japan
NORTH KOREA
Beijing
Pyongyang
Seoul
JAPAN
SOUTH KOREA
Tokyo
CHINA
Thimphu
BHUTAN
BANGLADESH
Dhaka
Taipei
TAIWAN
Hanoi
Hong Kong
MYANMAR
LAOS
Vientiane
Bay of Bengal
Rangoon
South China Sea
Philippine Sea
THAILAND
VIETNAM
Bangkok
Manila
PHILIPPINES
KAMPUCHEA
Phnom Penh
BRUNEI
MALAYSIA
Kuala Lumpur
SINGAPORE
Wewak
Jakarta
INDONESIA
PAPUA NEW GUINEA
Arafura Sea
Timor Sea